About Pearson

Pearson is the world's learning company, with presence across 70 countries worldwide. Our unique insights and world-class expertise comes from a long history of working closely with renowned teachers, authors and thought leaders, as a result of which, we have emerged as the preferred choice for millions of teachers and learners across the world.

We believe learning opens up opportunities, creates fulfilling careers and hence better lives. We hence collaborate with the best of minds to deliver you class-leading products, spread across the Higher Education and K12 spectrum.

Superior learning experience and improved outcomes are at the heart of everything we do. This product is the result of one such effort.

Your feedback plays a critical role in the evolution of our products and you can contact us at reachus@ pearson.com. We look forward to it.

D1509827

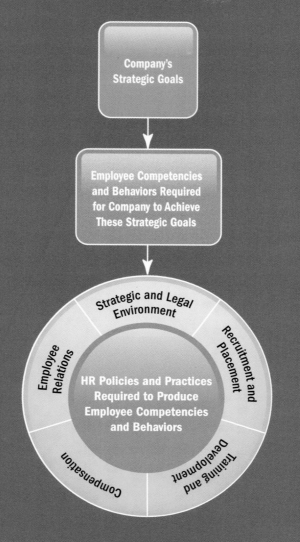

Company's
Strategic Goals

Employee Competencies
and Behaviors Required
for Company to Achieve
These Strategic Goals

Strategic and Legal
Environment

Recruitment and
Placement

HR Policies and Practices
Required to Produce
Employee Competencies
and Behaviors

Training and
Development

Compensation

Employee
Relations

WHERE WE ARE NOW

The framework above introduces each
chapter and makes the following point:
That the firm's HR policies and practices
should produce the employee skills and
behaviors the company needs to achieve
its strategic aims.

Human Resource Management

Fifteenth Edition

GARY DESSLER
Florida International University

BIJU VARKKEY
Indian Institute of Management Ahmedabad

 Pearson

Authorized adaptation from the United States edition, entitled *Human Resource Management, Fifteenth Edition*, ISBN 9780134235455, by Dessler, Gary, published by Pearson Education, Inc, Copyright © 2017.

Indian Subcontinent Adaptation
Copyright © 2018 Pearson India Education Services Pvt. Ltd

ISBN 978-93-528-6265-8

First Impression

This edition is manufactured in India and is authorized for sale only in India, Bangladesh, Bhutan, Pakistan, Nepal, Sri Lanka and the Maldives. Circulation of this edition outside of these territories is UNAUTHORIZED.

Published by Pearson India Education Services Pvt. Ltd, CIN: U72200TN2005PTC057128.

Head Office: 15th Floor, Tower-B, World Trade Tower, Plot No. 1, Block-C, Sector-16, Noida 201 301, Uttar Pradesh, India.
Registered Office: 4th Floor, Software Block, Elnet Software City, TS-140, Block 2 & 9, Rajiv Gandhi Salai, Taramani, Chennai 600 113, Tamil Nadu, India.
Fax: 080-30461003, Phone: 080-30461060
Website: in.pearson.com; Email: companysecretary.india@pearson.com

Compositor: Cameo Corporate Services, Coimbatore.
Printed in India by Thomson Press India Ltd.

FOR CLAUDIA

BRIEF CONTENTS

CONTENTS

APPENDICES

PREFACE

Human Resource Management, 15th edition, provides students in human resource management courses and practicing managers with a full and practical introduction to modern human resource management concepts and techniques in a highly readable form. With employers increasingly shifting HR tasks to managers and employees, I feel even more strongly than I did when I wrote the first edition that all managers—not just HR managers—need a strong foundation in human resource management concepts and techniques to do their jobs. You will therefore find an emphasis here on practical material you need to perform your day-to-day management responsibilities, even if you never spend one day as a human resource manager.

Things are changing fast in human resource management, and as this book makes clear we are today on the cusp of what is really the New Human Resource Management. For example, Accenture estimates that social media tools like LinkedIn will soon produce up to 80% of new recruits.[1] Cloud computing and intuitive user interfaces let managers monitor goal attainment and give real-time performance feedback continuously and interactively, rather than once or twice per year.[2] Mobile applications enable HR capabilities ranging from employee location monitoring to checking digital identities at time clocks. Websites like Knack and True Office help employers add gaming features to training, performance appraisal, and recruiting. Data mining and talent analytics revolutionized how employers such as Google and Xerox identify competencies and recruit and select job candidates.[3]

As we'll see with real examples throughout this book, tools like these are doing more than changing how employers recruit, select, appraise, train, and pay employees—they're also changing who "does" HR. In the New Human Resource Management, digital devices and social media are shifting more HR tasks from central human resource departments to employees and line managers: For instance, easily finding and vetting capable candidates through social media already let many line managers bypass HR to find their own recruits.[4] Changes like these give the line managers more human resource management responsibilities. And they mean that many human resource managers can refocus their efforts *from* day-to-day activities like interviewing candidates *to* broader, strategic efforts, such as formulating plans for boosting employee performance and engagement.

CHANGES AND NEW FEATURES

You'll therefore find six important changes for this edition:

- **New *Trends Shaping HR* Features**

Many employers are living the future of HR management today. To bring this New Human Resource Management to life, just about every chapter has one or more **Trends Shaping HR** features, each focusing on Digital and Social

---

[1] Accenture, "Top Trends That Will Reshape the Future of HR: The Future of HR," www.accenture.com/us-en/insight-future-of-hr.aspx, accessed March 6, 2015.

[2] https://go.oracle.com/LP=3174?elqCampaignId=6310&src1=ad:pas:go:dg:tal&src2=wwmk1405 4343mpp012&SC=sckw=WWMK14054343MPP012, accessed April 4, 2015.

[3] Josh Bersin, "Big Data in Human Resources: Talent Analytics (People Analytics) Comes of Age," www.forbes.com/sites/joshbersin/2013/02/17/bigdata-in-human-resources-talent-analytics-comes-of-age/, accessed March 29, 2015.

[4] Accenture, "Top Trends That Will Reshape the Future of HR."

Media, Customized Talent Management, Science in Talent Management, or The Extended Workforce. Here are some examples from the book:

TRENDS SHAPING HR: *DIGITAL AND SOCIAL MEDIA*

In designing and developing its training program, the employer will have to decide how the program will be delivered. Increasingly, this is occurring via "the cloud." Basically, **the cloud** refers to placing software programs and services on vendors' remote servers, from which they can then deliver these programs and services seamlessly to employees' digital devices. For example, you may use Microsoft Office 365, which resides on

TRENDS SHAPING HR: *CUSTOMIZED TALENT MANAGEMENT THROUGH DIFFERENTIAL DEVELOPMENT ASSIGNMENTS*

In today's competitive environment, the usual HR practice of allocating development opportunities and other scarce resources across the board or based solely on performance makes less sense. It often makes more sense to focus more of the employer's resources on the "mission-critical employees" who the employer deems most crucial to the its future growth.

We'll look closer at how employers do this in the following chapter, but several examples follow:

TRENDS SHAPING HR: *SCIENCE IN TALENT MANAGEMENT*

Data analytics permits making decisions based on a measurable and objective review of the situation. Managers have a name for this. *Evidence-based human resource management* means using data, facts, analytics, scientific rigor, critical evaluation, and critically evaluated research/case studies to support human resource management proposals, decisions, practices, and conclusions.[51]

You may sense that being evidence based is similar to being scientific, and if so, you are correct. A recent *Harvard Business Review* article even argues that managers must become more scientific and "think like scientists" when making business decisions.[52]

But how can managers think like scientists? Objectivity, experimentation, and pre-

- **New *The Strategic Context* Features**

As employers devolve more HR tasks to supervisors and employees and use performance management systems to link employees' actions to the company's goals, supervisors and employees need a "line of sight" that shows them how their HR actions impact the company's goals. I've therefore added to this edition **The Strategic Context** features. Integrated with chapter-opening scenarios, these features show how actual managers adjusted their HR actions to produce the employee competencies and skills that were needed to achieve the company's strategic aims.

In addition, a **Fully Integrated Strategy Case and Strategy Maps** again provide the most comprehensive treatment of strategic human resource management in any HR survey text:

✓ Chapter 1 introduces and Chapter 3 presents the concepts and techniques of human resource strategy.

✓ Each chapter starting with Chapter 3 contains a continuing "Hotel Paris" case, written to help make strategic human resource management come alive for readers. The continuing case shows how this hotel company's HR director uses that chapter's human resource management concepts and techniques to create HR policies and practices that produce the employee skills and behaviors the Hotel Paris needs to improve its service and thereby achieve its strategic goals.

✓ An overall strategy map for the Hotel Paris on the book's Page xxxviii helps readers understand and follow the strategic implications of the hotel's HR decisions.

✓ "Eiffel Tower" callouts in each chapter draw students' attention to the Hotel Paris case.

- **New *Employee Engagement Guide for Managers* Features**

Employee engagement refers to being psychologically involved in, connected to, and committed to getting one's jobs done. Trends including intensifying global competition and more millennials in the workforce make employee engagement crucial today (a fact recognized by the new Employee Engagement section in the Society for Human Resource Management's certification exams).

Recent surveys show that about 70% of employees are disengaged at work. I use new *Employee Engagement Guide for Managers* sections in Chapters 3–17 to show how managers use human resource activities to improve employee engagement. For example, Chapter 3's guide shows how Kia Motors (UK) improved employee engagement and Chapter 14's guide shows how "Great Companies to Work For" like Google and SAS develop the positive employee relations that help foster employee engagement.

- **New *SHRM* Coverage**

Starting in 2015,the Society for Human Resource Management (SHRM) began offering its own competency and knowledge-based testing and certifications for SHRM Certified Professionals and SHRM Senior Certified Professionals, based on its own certification exams.[5] The new SHRM exams put new emphases on Employee Engagement and on Employee Relations, two topics that this new 15th edition covers more comprehensively than does any other survey book with which I'm familiar (with the exception of my *Fundamentals of Human Resource Management, 4th edition*, Pearson 2015).

I've also summarized separately the SHRM and the HR Certification Institute's (HRCI's) knowledge bases in Appendices A and B of this book, (pages 583–600). One covers SHRM's functional knowledge areas (such as employee relations). The other covers HRCI's seven main knowledge areas (such as Strategic Business Management and Workforce Planning and Employment). The latter also lists about 91 specific HRCI "Knowledge of" subject areas within these seven main topic areas with which those taking the test should be familiar. You'll also find throughout this book special Knowledge Base icons starting in Chapter 2 to denote coverage of SHRM and/or HRCI knowledge topics.

- **Revised Chapter 10 (Managing Careers) and Chapter 14 (Building Positive Employee Relations)**

With the new Employee Engagement Guide for Managers features in most chapters, I revised Chapter 10 (Managing Careers and Retention, formerly Managing Employee Retention, Engagement, and Careers) to focus more on career management practices and employee retention techniques. With SHRM's new emphasis on employee relations, I also revised Chapter 14 (formerly Ethics, Employee Relations, and Fair Treatment at Work) to more comprehensively address (unique to this book) how real companies build employee relations.

- **New: Sustainability and HRM**

In a world where sea levels are rising, glaciers are crumbling, and increasing numbers of people view financial inequity as outrageous, more and more people say that businesses can't just measure "performance" in terms of maximizing profits. This 15th edition contains all-new material on sustainability and on the roles of HR management in implementing companies' sustainability efforts.

FEATURES CONTINUED FROM 14TH EDITION

Given the very positive response to the 14th edition and to the continuing challenges that world economies still face, I continued the 14th edition's emphasis on improving performance, productivity, and profitability in this 15th edition, and kept several features:

Improving Performance: features again demonstrate real-world human resource management tools and practices that managers actually use to improve performance.

---

[5] www.shrm.org/certification/pages/default.aspx#sthash.JRZQeAWR.dpuf, accessed September 8, 2015.

> ▶ **IMPROVING PERFORMANCE:** *HR as a Profit Center*
>
> **Boosting Customer Service**
>
> A bank installed special software that made it easier for its customer service representatives to handle customers' inquiries. However, the bank did not otherwise change the service reps' jobs in any way. Here, the new software system did help the service reps handle more calls. But otherwise, this bank saw no big performance gains.[23]
> A second bank installed the same software. But, seeking to capitalize on how the new software freed up customer reps' time, this bank also had its human resource team upgrade the customer service repre-

Improving Performance: HR as a Profit Center: contains actual examples of how human resource management practices add value by reducing costs or boosting revenues.

Improving Performance: HR Tools for Line Managers and Small Businesses: explains that many line managers and entrepreneurs are "on their own" when it comes to human resource management, and describes work sampling tests and other straightforward HR tools that line managers and entrepreneurs can create and safely use to improve performance.

> ▶ **IMPROVING PERFORMANCE:** *HR Tools for Line Managers and Small Businesses*
>
> **How to Conduct an Effective Interview**
>
> You may not have the time or inclination to create a structured situational interview. However, there is still much you can do to make your interviews systematic and productive.
>
> **Step 1:** First, know the job. Do not start the interview unless you understand the job's duties and what human skills you're looking for. Study the job description.
>
> **Step 2:** Structure the interview. Any structuring is better than none. If pressed for time, you can still do several things to ask more consistent and job-relevant questions, without developing a full-blown structured interview.[78] For example:[79]
> • Base questions on *actual job duties*. This will minimize irrelevant questions.
> • Use *job knowledge, situational, or behavioral questions*. Questions that simply ask for opinions and attitudes, goals and aspirations, and self-descriptions and self-evaluations allow candidates to present themselves in an overly favorable manner or avoid revealing

> ▶ **IMPROVING PERFORMANCE:** *HR Practices around the Globe*
>
> **Career Development at Medtronic[39]**
>
> Medtronic is a global medical technology company with more than 85,000 employees around the world. The company offers a wide range of career planning and development support tools aimed at helping employees understand their occupational strengths and weaknesses and reach their potential. These tools include customized development plans, self-assessment and feedback tools, mentoring programs, compre-

Improving Performance: HR Practices Around the Globe: shows how actual companies around the globe use HR practices to improve their teams' and companies' performance, while illustrating the challenges managers face in managing internationally.

 Improving Performance Through HRIS: are embedded features that demonstrate how managers use human resource technology to improve performance.

And as in the 14th edition:

 Know Your Employment Law sections within each chapter discuss the practical implications of the employment laws that apply to that chapter's topics, such as the laws relating to recruitment (Chapter 5), selection (Chapter 6), training (Chapter 8), and safety (Chapter 16).

 Diversity Counts features provide practical insights for managing a diverse workforce, for instance, regarding gender bias in selection decisions, bias in performance appraisal, and "hidden" gender bias in some bonus plans (Chapter 12).

Treatment of Global HR and Small Business HR Management

While this 15th edition again has two chapters devoted to Global HR and to Small Business HR, you will also find in this new 15th edition *Managing HR Around the Globe* boxed features throughout the book, and, similarly, *HR Tools for Line Managers and Small Businesses* boxed features throughout the book.

INSTRUCTOR RESOURCES

At the Instructor Resource Center (http://www.pearsoned.co.in/GaryDessler/), instructors can easily register to gain access to a variety of instructor resources available with this text in downloadable format. If assistance is needed, our dedicated technical support team is ready to help with the media supplements that accompany this text. Visit http://247.pearsoned.com for answers to frequently asked questions and toll-free user support phone numbers.

The following supplements are available with this text:

- Instructor's Resource Manual
- Test Bank
- TestGen® Computerized Test Bank
- PowerPoint Presentation

ACKNOWLEDGMENTS

Everyone involved in creating this book is proud of what we've achieved. *Human Resource Management* is one of the top-selling books in this market, and, as you read this, students and managers around the world are using versions translated into about a dozen languages, including Thai, French, Spanish, Indonesian, Russian, and Chinese.

Although I am responsible for *Human Resource Management*, I want to thank several people for their assistance. They include, first, the faculty who carefully reviewed the 14th edition, and who made many useful and insightful suggestions:

John Durboraw, *Columbia College*
Lisa Nieman, *Wesleyan University*
Brooke Sorrells, *Virginia College*
Craig Tunwell, *Troy University*

I am very grateful to Gordon Schmidt (Indiana University/Purdue University Fort Wayne) and Angela Boston (University of Texas) for their hard work on updating and improving the supplements for the 15th edition, and to the MyLabs team of Project Manager Toni Ackley, Gordon Schmidt (Indiana University/Purdue University Fort Wayne), Susan C. Schanne (Eastern Michigan University), and Leslie Carnes, SPHR (Ivy Tech Community College).

At Pearson, thank you for the support and dedicated assistance of all involved. I particularly appreciate the insights, suggestions, and personal involvement of Editor-in-Chief Stephanie Wall and Senior Acquisitions Editor Kris Ellis-Levy. Thank you again to my outstanding production team, with whom I've worked for many years: Jeff Holcomb, Project Management Team Lead, and Kelly Warsak, my irreplaceable Project Manager. Thanks to Lenny Ann Kucenski, Field Marketing Manager, and the Pearson sales staff, without whose efforts this book would languish on the shelf, and to Sarah Holle, Program Manager, and Lauren Russell, Editorial Assistant. I want to thank everyone at Pearson International for successfully managing *Human Resource Management's* internationalization. Development editor Kerri Tomasso was extraordinarily helpful, and thank you to Margaret McConnell at Integra.

At home, I want to thank my wife, Claudia, for her support during the many hours I spent working on this edition. My son, Derek, always a source of enormous pride, was very helpful. Lisa, Samantha, and Taylor are always in my thoughts. My parents were always a great source of support and encouragement and would have been very proud to see this book.

Gary Dessler,
Florida International University

Many people have wholeheartedly supported and contributed to the 15th edition of this book. Working with Gary Dessler for the past many years has been a privilege, and I am humbled by the opportunity. I am thankful for the constant support and encouragement provided by my family, colleagues, organizational leaders and members of the HR fraternity with whom I interact with and learn, research staff and students of different program and institutions, and the team at Pearson India. This book will remain incomplete if I fail to record my gratitude to them, and acknowledge their contribution.

First of all, IIM Ahmedabad (IIMA) has provided me with the platform, freedom, and resources to pursue academic and professional interests, including working in areas of professional impact. Former Director of IIMA,

Ashish Nanda, who was a good friend, always supported and encouraged me to start working in the new area of Professional Services. My colleagues in the HRM area of IIMA – Sunil, Manjari, Rajesh, Promila, and Miguel – have used this book for teaching, and they have always been strong pillars of support. The student community of IIMA continuously inspire faculty members to think differently and be continuously challenged. Interactions with them have helped in conceptualizing the revision plan and approaching the book from the learner's perspective. Support from colleagues and friends like Abraham Koshy, Sunil Sharma, Chetan Soman, Dhiman Bhadra, Meenakshi Sharma, Vaibhavi, Kirti Sharada, Joshy Jacob, Saral Mukerjee, Dheeraj Sharma, and Sebastian Morris is also acknowledged. Lakshmi, my office secretary, deserves special mention for her dedication to work, and also my associates – Lutufi, Rasika Soman, Ashini, Bhumi, and Khushi – for the direct and indirect help in completion of this book.

Special acknowledgement to my teachers in NIBM Pune, Jacob and Aruna Mankidy and Rajagiri College's faculty – Sebastian Mampilly, James T. Thomas, and (Late) Philip Koshy – from whom I learned HRM. I have also benefited from the knowledge and support of academics, professionals, and mentors like Besanat Raj, Aruna Besant Raj, Pritam Singh, Satish Kalra, Rajen Gupta, T. V. Rao, Anamika Sinha, Prashant Nair, Rupasree Baral, Mathew Manimala, Sibi Jose, Emmanuel David, and Manoj Varghese. As a member of the global Wage Indicator project and leader of PayCheck India, I had the opportunity to interact with a group of wonderful people as well as trade unions and collectives from different countries.

An extremely interesting part of working in IIMA is that it allows to be associated closely with practice and create external impact. I have been benefited from the board-level positions that I hold and the peers in the board from whom I continue to learn. In addition, there are government committee work, research projects, executive education and problem-solving consulting assignments that have helped me in learning about organizations, management, and people, and some of the insights have definitely been reflected in the revised edition.

I have been fortunate to have a great team at Pearson India in Varun Goenka and Amrita Marik, who patiently waited and gently reminded me about deadlines. Without them, this edition would not have seen light.

Shoshan, my wife, and our son, Aman Oommen, my mother, mother in law, brothers and their family – all of them have been great source of inspiration and comfort.

And a last word – Thank you God for all the blessings, strength, and opportunities.

Biju Varkkey,
Indian Institute of Management Ahmedabad

Human Resource Management

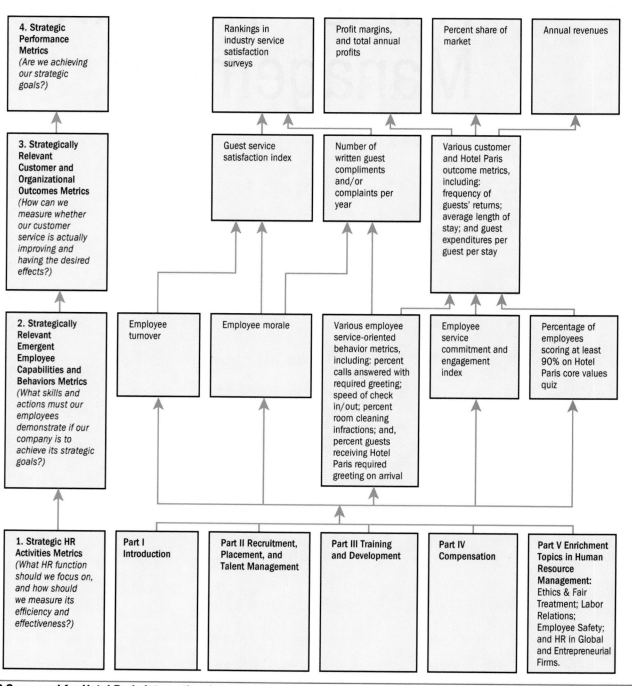

4. Strategic Performance Metrics
(Are we achieving our strategic goals?)

Rankings in industry service satisfaction surveys

Profit margins, and total annual profits

Percent share of market

Annual revenues

3. Strategically Relevant Customer and Organizational Outcomes Metrics
(How can we measure whether our customer service is actually improving and having the desired effects?)

Guest service satisfaction index

Number of written guest compliments and/or complaints per year

Various customer and Hotel Paris outcome metrics, including: frequency of guests' returns; average length of stay; and guest expenditures per guest per stay

2. Strategically Relevant Emergent Employee Capabilities and Behaviors Metrics
(What skills and actions must our employees demonstrate if our company is to achieve its strategic goals?)

Employee turnover

Employee morale

Various employee service-oriented behavior metrics, including: percent calls answered with required greeting; speed of check in/out; percent room cleaning infractions; and, percent guests receiving Hotel Paris required greeting on arrival

Employee service commitment and engagement index

Percentage of employees scoring at least 90% on Hotel Paris core values quiz

1. Strategic HR Activities Metrics
(What HR function should we focus on, and how should we measure its efficiency and effectiveness?)

Part I Introduction

Part II Recruitment, Placement, and Talent Management

Part III Training and Development

Part IV Compensation

Part V Enrichment Topics in Human Resource Management: Ethics & Fair Treatment; Labor Relations; Employee Safety; and HR in Global and Entrepreneurial Firms.

HR Scorecard for Hotel Paris International

Note: An abbreviated example showing selected HR practices and outcomes aimed at implementing the competitive strategy, "To use superior guest services to differentiate the Hotel Paris properties and thus increase the length of stays and the return rate of guests, and thus boost revenues and profitability and help the firm expand geographically.

1

Introduction to Human Resource Management

LEARNING OBJECTIVES

1-1 Explain what human resource management is and how it relates to the management process.

1-2 Briefly discuss and illustrate each of the important trends influencing human resource management.

1-3 Briefly describe "distributed HR" and other important aspects of human management today.

1-4 List at least four important human resource manager competencies.

1-5 Outline the plan of this book.

For many people websites like Guru (www.guru.com) and Elance (www.elance.com) symbolize much of what's new in human resource management. Millions of freelancers from graphic designers to translators, accountants, and lawyers register on these sites. Employers then use Guru and Elance to find, screen, hire, and pay the talent they need, in more than 180 countries.[1]

WHERE ARE WE NOW ...

The purpose of this chapter is to explain what human resource management is, and why it's important to all managers. We'll see that human resource management activities such as hiring, training, appraising, compensating, and developing employees are part of every manager's job. And we'll see that human resource management is also a separate function, usually with its own human resource or "HR" manager. The main topics we'll cover here include what is human resource management, the trends shaping human resource management, human resource management today, the new human resource manager, and the plan of this book. The framework above (which introduces each chapter) makes this point: That the firm's HR policies and practices should produce the employee skills and behaviors the company needs to achieve its strategic aims.

What is Human Resource Management?

organization

A group consisting of people with formally assigned roles who work together to achieve the organization's goals.

manager

Someone who is responsible for accomplishing the organization's goals, and who does so by managing the efforts of the organization's people.

managing

To perform five basic functions: planning, organizing, staffing, leading, and controlling.

management process

The five basic functions of planning, organizing, staffing, leading, and controlling.

human resource management (HRM)

The process of acquiring, training, appraising, and compensating employees, and of attending to their labor relations, health and safety, and fairness concerns.

To understand what human resource management is, it's useful to start with what managers do. Elance is an *organization*. An **organization** consists of people (in this case, people like Elance's own in-house sales managers and Web designers) with formally assigned roles who work together to achieve the organization's goals. A **manager** is someone who is responsible for accomplishing the organization's goals, and who does so by managing the efforts of the organization's people.

Most writers agree that **managing** involves performing five basic functions: planning, organizing, staffing, leading, and controlling. In total, these functions represent the **management process**. Some of the specific activities involved in each function include:

- *Planning.* Establishing goals and standards; developing rules and procedures; developing plans and forecasts
- *Organizing.* Giving each subordinate a specific task; establishing departments; delegating authority to subordinates; establishing channels of authority and communication; coordinating the work of subordinates
- *Staffing.* Determining what type of people should be hired; recruiting prospective employees; selecting employees; setting performance standards; compensating employees; evaluating performance; counseling employees; training and developing employees
- *Leading.* Getting others to get the job done; maintaining morale; motivating subordinates
- *Controlling.* Setting standards such as sales quotas, quality standards, or production levels; checking to see how actual performance compares with these standards; taking corrective action as needed

In this book, we will focus on one of these functions—the staffing, personnel management, or *human resource management* function. **Human resource management (HRM)** is the process of acquiring, training, appraising, and compensating employees, and of attending to their labor relations, health and safety, and fairness concerns. The topics we'll discuss should therefore provide you with the concepts and techniques every manager needs to perform the "people" or personnel aspects of management. These include:

- *Conducting job analyses* (determining the nature of each employee's job).
- *Planning human resource needs* and *recruiting* job candidates.
- *Selecting* job candidates.
- *Orienting and training* new employees.
- *Managing wages and salaries* (compensating employees).
- *Providing incentives and benefits.*
- *Appraising performance.*
- *Communicating* (interviewing, counseling, disciplining).
- *Training employees*, and *developing managers.*
- *Building employee relations and engagement.*

And what a manager should know about:

- Labor law and statutory compliances.
- Employee health and safety.
- Handling grievances and labor relations.

Why Is Human Resource Management Important to All Managers?

The concepts and techniques in this book are important to all managers for several reasons. In the Indian context as well, human resource management is important to all managers because organizations, nowadays, give much more importance to people than earlier.

AVOID PERSONNEL MISTAKES First, having a command of this knowledge will help you avoid the *personnel mistakes you don't want to make* while managing. For example, you don't want

- To have your employees not doing their best.
- To hire the wrong person for the job.
- To experience high turnover.
- To have your company in court due to your discriminatory actions and non-compliance.
- To have your company cited for unsafe practices.
- To let a lack of training undermine your department's effectiveness.
- To commit any unfair labor practices.

Carefully studying this book can help you avoid mistakes like these.

IMPROVING PROFITS AND PERFORMANCE More important, it can *help ensure that you get results—through people.*[2] Remember that you could do everything else right as a manager—lay brilliant plans, draw clear organization charts, set up modern assembly lines, and use sophisticated accounting controls—but still fail, for instance, by hiring the wrong people or by not motivating subordinates. On the other hand, many managers—from generals to presidents to supervisors—have been successful even without adequate plans, organizations, or controls. They were successful because they had the knack for hiring the right people for the right jobs and then motivating, appraising, and developing them. Remember as you read this book that *getting results* is the bottom line of managing and that, as a manager, you will have to get these results through people. This fact hasn't changed from the dawn of management. As one company president summed it up:

> For many years it has been said that capital is the bottleneck for a developing industry. I don't think this any longer holds true. I think it's the workforce and the company's inability to recruit and maintain a good workforce that does constitute the bottleneck for production. I don't know of any major project backed by good ideas, vigor, and enthusiasm that has been stopped by a shortage of cash. I do know of industries whose growth has been partly stopped or hampered because they can't maintain an efficient and enthusiastic labor force, and I think this will hold true even more in the future.[3]

Because of global competition, technological advances, and economic turmoil, that statement has never been truer than it is today. Human resource management methods like those in this book can help any line manager/supervisor (or HR manager) boost his or her team's and company's levels of engagement, profits and performance. Here are two examples we'll meet in this book:

> *NTPC Limited* is India's largest state-owned power generation company. It is considered as a good employer with innovative HRM practices. The company places employees before Plant Load Factor (or PLF, the ratio between actual power generation and maximum possible for a power plant), which indicates the importance given to human resource management. Along with keeping in mind the growth and profitability of the firm, NTPC also respects the personal growth and well being of its employees and their families by providing excellent facilities such as residential townships, social clubs, education facilities, hospitals, childcare benefits, and post-retirement medical benefits. In order to provide an opportunity for employees to enhance their skills and qualifications through further education, NTPC also has linkages with top-ranked educational institutions and colleges such as IIT Delhi, BITS Pilani, MDI Gurgaon, and Indian Institute of Managements (IIMs) to make available various courses for their employees.

> *A call center* in the US averaged 18.6 vacancies per year (about a 60% turnover rate). The researchers estimated the cost of a call-center operator leaving at about $21,500. They estimated total annual cost of agent turnover for the call center at $400,853. Cutting that rate in half would save this firm about $200,000 per year.

YOU MAY SPEND SOME TIME AS AN HR MANAGER   Here is another reason to study this book: *you might spend time as a human resource manager*. The 2015 India CHRO Survey showed that only 60% of Indian chief human resource officers (CHROs) had only HR related experience, indicating the possibility of businesses appointing HR leaders with experience in other functions.[4] Thus, Pearson Corporation (which publishes this book) promoted the head of one of its publishing divisions to chief human resource executive at its corporate headquarters. The HR Head of Indian pharmaceutical company, Zydus Cadilla, had experience in others functions like supply chain and manufacturing. Why? Some think these people may be better equipped to integrate the firm's human resource activities (such as pay policies) with the company's strategic needs (such as by tying executives' incentives to corporate goals).[5] Appointing non-HR people can also be good for the manager. For example, one CEO served a three-year stint as chief human resource officer on the way to becoming CEO. The first CEO said the experience he got was invaluable in learning how to develop leaders and in understanding the human side of transforming a company.[6] Arundhati Bhattacharya, who was the Chairperson of State Bank of India, had earlier served a tenure in the human resources management department of the bank.

However, most top human resource executives do have prior human resource experience. In the US, about 80% of those in one survey worked their way up within HR. About 17% had the HR Certification Institute's Senior Professional in Human Resources (SPHR) designation, and 13% were certified Professional in Human Resources (PHR). In India, the National Institute of Personnel Management (NIPM) conducts a master's course in HR and National Human Resource Development Network (NHRD) offers various courses in HRM. Most of the HR managers in the country have qualifications in management, social work, or law. Apart from the IIMs, XLRI, TISS, XISS, Rajagiri College, and MDI Gurugram are some of the other institutes offering postgraduate level HR programs.

HR FOR SMALL BUSINESSES   And here is one other reason to study this book: you *may well end up as your own human resource manager*. More than half the people working in the United States work for small firms. Small businesses as a group also account for most of the 600,000 or so new businesses created every year. India is also home to a large number of small and medium enterprises (SMEs), estimated to be 3.3 million, and provides employment to more than 18 million people. Small businesses are viewed by the government as a sector with huge potential for job creation. Statistically speaking, therefore, most people graduating from college in the next few years will either work for small businesses or create new small businesses of their own.[7] Small firms generally don't have the critical mass required for a full-time human resource manager (let alone an HR department).[8] The owner and his or her other managers (and perhaps assistant or spouse) handle tasks such as signing employees on. Gaining a command of the techniques in this book should help you to manage a small firm's human resources more effectively. We'll address human resource management for small businesses in later chapters.

Line and Staff Aspects of Human Resource Management

All managers have always been, in a sense, human resource managers, because they all get involved in recruiting, interviewing, selecting, and training their employees. Yet most firms also have a human resource department with its own top manager. How do the duties of this human resource manager and department relate to the human resource duties of sales and production and other managers? Answering this requires a short definition of line versus staff authority. **Authority** is the right to make decisions, to direct the work of others, and to give orders. Managers usually distinguish between line authority and staff authority.

In organizations, **line authority** traditionally gives managers the right to *issue orders* to other managers or employees. Line authority therefore creates a superior (order giver)–subordinate (order receiver) relationship. When the vice president of sales tells her sales director to "get the sales presentation ready by Tuesday," she is exercising her line authority. **Staff authority** gives a manager the right to *advise* other managers or employees. It creates an advisory relationship. When the human

authority
The right to make decisions, direct others' work, and give orders.

line authority
Traditionally gives managers the right to *issue orders* to other managers or employees.

staff authority
Gives a manager the right to *advise* other managers or employees

line manager
A manager who is authorized to
direct the work of subordinates and
is responsible for accomplishing the
organization's tasks.

staff manager
A manager who assists and advises
line managers.

resource manager suggests that the plant manager use a particular selection test, he or she is exercising staff authority.

On the organization chart, managers with line authority are **line managers**. Those with staff (advisory) authority are **staff managers**. In popular usage, people tend to associate line managers with managing departments (like sales or production) that are crucial for the company's survival. Staff managers generally run departments that are advisory or supportive, like purchasing and human resource management. Human resource managers are usually staff managers. They assist and advise line managers in areas like recruiting, hiring, and compensation.

Line Managers' Human Resource Management Responsibilities

However, line managers do have many human resource duties. This is because the direct handling of people has always been part of every line manager's duties, from president down to first-line supervisors. One major company outlines its line supervisors' responsibilities for effective human resource management under these general headings:

1. Placing the right person in the right job
2. Starting new employees in the organization (induction or orientation)
3. Training employees for jobs that are new to them
4. Improving the job performance of each person
5. Gaining creative cooperation and developing smooth working relationships
6. Interpreting the company's policies and procedures
7. Controlling labor costs
8. Developing the abilities of each person
9. Creating and maintaining departmental morale
10. Protecting employees' health and physical conditions

And we'll see in this chapter that, if anything, digital tools like *LinkedIn hiring* and cloud computing are actually expanding many line managers' HR responsibilities.

The Human Resource Department

In small organizations, line managers may carry out all these personnel duties unassisted. But as the organization grows, line managers usually need the assistance, specialized knowledge, and advice of a separate human resource staff. In larger firms, the *human resource department* provides such specialized assistance. In Indian family businesses and SMEs, most of the times, it is observed that the entrepreneur himself or the family members act as a human resource manager. However, as the business expands, a professional human resource manager from outside is hired.[9] Figure 1-1 shows human resource management jobs in one organization. Typical positions include compensation and benefits manager, employment and recruiting supervisor, training specialist, and employee relations executive. To suit the growing organizational and employee demands, new HR roles have been created. As a result, in Indian organizations, new HR roles such as Chief Happiness Officer, Diversity Officer, Talent Management Specialist, and HR Analytics Officer are now available. Examples of job duties include:

- *Recruiters:* Maintain contacts within the community and perhaps travel extensively to search for qualified job applicants.
- *Diversity officer or SC/SC cell (in PSU/government):* Investigate and resolve grievances, examine organizational practices for potential violations, and compile and submit compliance reports.
- *Job analysts:* Collect and examine detailed information about job duties to prepare job descriptions.
- *Compensation managers:* Develop compensation plans and handle the employee benefits program.
- *Training or Learning and Development specialists:* Plan, organize, and direct training/learning activities.
- *Labor (Employment/Industrial) relations specialists:* Advise management on all aspects of union–management relations.

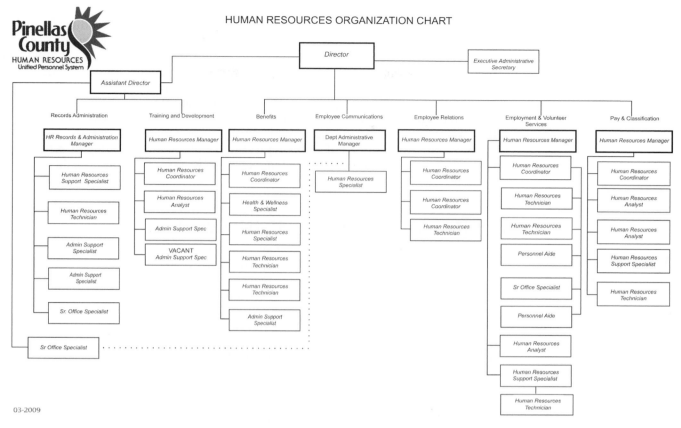

FIGURE 1-1 **Human Resource Department Organization Chart Showing Typical HR Job Titles**

Source: "Human Resource Development Organization Chart Showing Typical HR Job Titles," www.co.pinellas.fl.us/persnl/pdf/orgchart.pdf. Courtesy of Pinellas County Human Resources. Reprinted with permission.

- *Employee welfare officer:* Takes care of employee welfare, as prescribed by the law (The Factories Act, 1948).
- *Happiness officer:* Responsible for helping organizations to improve employee engagement levels by helping them to achieve happiness, both personally and professionally.
- *Talent management specialist:* Responsible for hiring and managing high performing and committed employees, and helping organizations retain them.
- *HR analytics officer:* Analyze trends using big data and analytical tool and provide insights for people management related decision-making.

NEW APPROACHES TO ORGANIZING HR   However, what HR departments do and how they do it are changing. Because of this, many employers are taking a new look at how they organize their human resource functions.[10] For example, one survey found that 44% of the large firms surveyed planned to change how they organize and deliver HR services.[11] Most plan to use technology to institute more "*shared services*" (or "*transactional*") arrangements.[12] The Amara Raja Group, Hyderabad, has set up an in-house shared services center to provide support to all group entities. Husys Consulting Limited, an HR function outsourcing company, provides such support to many SME clients. These establish centralized HR units whose employees are shared by all the companies' departments to assist the departments' line managers in human resource matters. These shared services HR teams generally offer their services through intranets or centralized call centers; they aim to provide managers and employees with specialized support in day-to-day HR activities (such as discipline problems). You may also find specialized *corporate HR teams* within a company. These assist top management in top-level issues such as developing the personnel aspects of the company's long-term strategic plan. *Embedded HR teams* have HR generalists (also known as "relationship managers" or "HR business partners") assigned to functional departments like sales and production. They provide the selection and other assistance the departments need. *Centers of expertise* are basically specialized HR consulting firms within the company. For example, one center might provide specialized advice in areas such as organizational change to all the company's various units. The HR function of Amara Raja Group is organized along the above mentioned pattern. The HRM software helps to simplify the work of HR managers and employees. The firm, ZingHR, has developed a cloud-based HRM software called 'Hire to Retire' that helps in managing human resources from the day an employee thinks of applying to the company until the day of retirement. To cater to the current and future demands, ZingHR has been mobile enabled, and it is available in app format.

The Trends Shaping Human Resource Management

Working cooperatively with line managers, human resource managers have long helped employers hire and fire employees, administer benefits, and conduct appraisals. However, trends are occurring in the environment of human resource management that are changing how employers get their human resource management tasks done. These trends include workforce trends, trends in how people work, technological trends, and globalization and economic trends.

Workforce Demographics and Diversity Trends

Despite the recession and job losses, trends in workforce demographic are making hiring good employees more of a challenge around the world. India has not been immune to these effects. Acute skill shortage has been identified as the main hurdle in achieving the demographic dividend from its young, growing population. The Indian government has made skill development a top priority in its agenda of economic growth. Most of the growing sectors in India face acute skill shortage. The country's growing hospitality sector is expected to require more than 2,00,000 trained people annually, while the annual supply is less than 10% of the required number. Core sectors like power and petroleum are also facing the skill supply crunch. The working group on power for the Eleventh Five-Year Plan has estimated the immediate shortage of power talent as 33%. The growth experienced in other sectors of the economy, including financial services, manufacturing, retail, etc., has created huge demand for skill labor. The Indian fish processing industry's experience, which is a large foreign exchange earner, is interesting. In recent years, the processing companies are experiencing difficulty to attract workers, mostly females. The traditional workers prefer other employment avenues like retail sector. Skilled labor shortage has also prompted the construction industry to source specialized talent from abroad (e.g., carpenters from South Korea).

Other firms are shifting to nontraditional workers. Nontraditional workers are those who hold multiple jobs, or who are "temporary" or part-time workers, or those working in alternative arrangements (such as a mother–daughter team sharing one clerical job). Others serve as "independent contractors" for specific projects.

Some employers find millennials or "generation Y" employees (those born roughly between 1982 and 2004) a challenge to deal with, and this isn't just an American phenomenon. For example, the *New York Times* recently reported that because China's one-child rule led many parents to pamper their children. India's millennial and young workforce entering the job market is as an asset, though finding employment opportunities for them is a challenge. China's senior army officers are having problems getting millennial-aged volunteers and conscripts to shape up.[13]

On the other hand, millennials also bring a vast array of skills. They've grown up with social media and are expert at collaborating online. And, having grown up with Apple and Google, they're comfortable with innovation.

Trends in How People Work

At the same time, work has shifted from manufacturing jobs to service jobs in North America and Western Europe. In India too, the contribution of services sector has outgrown the agricultural sector. Today over two-thirds of the U.S. workforce is employed in producing and delivering services, not products. By 2020, service-providing industries are expected to account for 131 million out of 150 million (87%) of wage and salary jobs overall. With advancements in technology and the growing need for work-life balance, the way people work in India has been changing continuously. Unlike the traditional jobs where people went to work in the office, options like working-from-home and alternate places are becoming a possibility. Freelancing is a growing trend in India just like the western countries. Truelancer is one such online platform where large number of Indians have registered for seeking opportunities. According to this portal, though it hires freelance workers across the globe, India has a freelance population of 15 million, which is growing day by day; in comparison, there are about 53 million freelancers in the US. The estimated worth of India's freelancing market is US$ 1 billion against the global US$ 2–3 billion.[14]

ON-DEMAND WORKERS   Anyone who has registered on Uber or Ola already knows something about on-demand workers.[15] At last count, they was signing up almost 40,000 new independent contractor drivers per month, a rate that was doubling every few months.

Today, in more and more companies like Uber, Ola, Elance, and Airbnb, employees aren't employees at all, but are freelancers and independent contractors who work when they can on what they want to work on, when the company needs them.[16] So, for example, Airbnb can run in essence a vast lodging company with only a fraction of the "regular" employees one like Hilton Worldwide would need (because the lodgings are owned and managed by the homeowners themselves). Other sites tapping on-demand workers include Amazon's Mechanical Turk, Elance-oDesk, TaskRabbit, and Handybook (which lets users tap Handy's thousands of freelance cleaners and furniture assemblers when they need jobs done).[17] The head of Elance-oDesk, which places millions of short-term professionals via its site, says those on its site are viewed as "mobile, independent bundles of skills."[18]

The fact that employers increasingly rely on such Uber-like "extended workforces" has implications for HR. For example, companies that rely on freelancers, consultants, and other such nontraditional employees will need to create personnel policies on matters like compensation for these "nonemployees," and become more expert as talent brokers in matching specific workers with specific tasks that need to be done.

On-demand models like Elance's and Uber's have detractors. Some people who work for on-demand services say the sometimes menial jobs can make them feel somewhat disrespected. One critic says such work is unpredictable and insecure. An article in the *New York Times* said this: "The larger worry about on-demand jobs is not about benefits, but about a lack of agency—a future in which computers, rather than humans, determine what you do, when and for how much."[19] Some drivers recently sued to become regular (rather than freelance independent contractor) employees. Strikes and unionization of Uber and Ola drivers have taken place in a handful of Indian cities as well.[20]

HUMAN CAPITAL   One big consequence of such demographic and workforce trends is employers' growing emphasis on their workers' knowledge, education, training, skills, and expertise—in other words on their "human capital."

Service jobs like consultant and lawyer always emphasized education and knowledge. And today's proliferation of IT-related businesses like Google and Facebook of course demands high levels of human capital. The big change is that even "traditional" manufacturing jobs like assembler are increasingly high-tech. Similarly bank tellers, retail clerks, bill collectors, process specialists in business process outsourcing (BPO) firms, and package deliverers today need a level of technological sophistication they wouldn't have needed a few years ago. So in our increasingly knowledge-based economy, "… the acquisition and development of superior human capital appears essential to firms' profitability and success."[21]

For managers, the challenge here is that they have to manage such workers differently. For example, empowering workers to make more decisions presumes you've selected, trained, and rewarded them to make more decisions themselves. Employers therefore need new human resource management practices to select, train, and engage these employees.[22] The accompanying HR as a Profit Center illustrates how employers took advantage of their human capital.

▶ IMPROVING PERFORMANCE: *HR as a Profit Center*

Boosting Customer Service

A bank installed special software that made it easier for its customer service representatives to handle customers' inquiries. However, the bank did not otherwise change the service reps' jobs in any way. Here, the new software system did help the service reps handle more calls. But otherwise, this bank saw no big performance gains.[23]

A second bank installed the same software. But, seeking to capitalize on how the new software freed up customer reps' time, this bank also had its human resource team upgrade the customer service representatives' jobs. This bank taught them how to sell more of the bank's services, gave them more authority to make decisions, and raised their wages. Here, the new computer system dramatically improved product sales and profitability, thanks to the newly trained and empowered customer service reps. Value-added human resource practices like these improve employee performance and company profitability.[24] ■

Based on "Human Resources Wharton," www.knowledge.wharton.upe.edu; Anthea Zacharatos et al., "High-Performance Work Systems and Occupational Safety," *Journal of Applied Psychology*, 90, no. 1, 2005, pp. 77–93. See also Jennifer Schramm, "Effective HR Practices Drive Profit," *HR Magazine*, November 2012, p. 88.

Employee Engagement at the Bank of Baroda

Bank of Baroda (BoB), a leading Indian public sector bank with international presence, considers its employees as the primary drivers of business performance. In 2015–16, after the business performance dipped, BoB initiated a transformation exercise throughout the organization. The aim was to create a more agile and capable organization, equipped with more effective control systems and digital technology. The transformation was aimed to make BoB future ready and competitive.

While process innovation and technology infusion could help the bank, success of the transformation exercise in the banking industry depended heavily on high levels of employee engagement. BoB had 52,000 employees across the globe and engaging all of them was necessary. In terms of age composition, majority of the employees were young, and a higher number of women had joined the ranks.

At first, the Human Resource (HR) department, with the support from an external consultant, conducted an Employee Engagement Survey (ESS) in February 2016. The aim of this survey was to understand the engagement levels of employees, particularly their perceptions, beliefs, views, etc. so that the HR department could tailor various HR activities or initiatives to address the gaps and to improve the employee engagement levels. More than 85% of the staff members (officers and clerks) participated in this survey. The engagement scores were around 55%, as against the industry average of 65% (approx.). Hence, it was felt that an immediate focus was required on reducing the proportion of 'Actively Disengaged' employees. Other key findings of the survey were around inadequate leadership connect, inadequate role clarity and guidance, work tasks, rewards and recognition programs, etc. The findings were shared with the Board, top management, and all employees including Officers' Association and Unions. The HR department charted different action programs to improve the overall engagement levels of employees. The initiatives had the support of BoB's Board of Directors and top management.

To improve engagement levels, BoB launched Baroda Anubhuti Program. It was officially inaugurated on the bank's foundation day, i.e., 20 July 2016. This initiative has been designed to augment the overall employee experience while working in BoB. After the launch of this program, several other initiatives were also designed and introduced. The aim of these initiatives was to foster the spirit of positive attitude, recognition measures, and team bonding leading to improved business outcomes and to reach out to all employees. At present, five initiatives are operating under the Baroda Anubhuti Program, which are:

1. **Employee of the Month**
   - Identified in every branch, every month
   - Special badge and rolling trophy awarded

2. **Spot Recognition Prizes**
   - Capture 'WOW' moments in branch offices and rewarding them.

3. Zero (Fun) Hour

- Organize at least one occasion every month, for activities that infuse fun and entertainment.

4. Compulsory Community Service or Social Service Activity By Employees

- Mandatory community outreach activity once in six months
- The activity has to be a collective effort, i.e., all employees and families should also join.
- Separate budget allocation for each branch

5. Anubhuti Workshops at Bank Branches

- Brainstorming workshops of staff members on how to improve work climate, employee involvement, customer experience, and business performance
- To be facilitated by HR professionals who would travel to locations.

Besides this, a specified *Employee Experience Manager* in each regional office has been identified, who is responsible for driving engagement initiatives. With this executive's support, a few more initiatives like sports clubs of employees, organizing league-type competitions, encouraging fitness and wellness among employees, dramatics and debate clubs, and community outreach activities were introduced. Unlike the traditional approach of one program for the entire bank, each region had the flexibility to customize these initiatives, without losing sight of the big picture. Now, BoB plans to conduct the engagement survey again in 2017, and it hopes that with the initiatives taken, the engagement levels have improved and positively impacted business results. ■

Globalization Trends

Globalization refers to companies extending their sales, ownership, and/or manufacturing to new markets abroad. Thus Toyota builds Camrys in Kentucky, while Apple assembles iPhones in China. Free trade areas—agreements that reduce tariffs and barriers among trading partners—further encourage international trade. The North American Free Trade Agreement (NAFTA) and the European Union (EU) are examples.

Globalization has boomed for the past 50 or so years. Evolving economic and political philosophies drove this boom. Governments dropped cross-border taxes or tariffs, formed economic free trade areas, and took other steps to encourage the free flow of trade among countries. The fundamental economic rationale was that by doing so, all countries would gain, and indeed, economies around the world did grow quickly until recently.

At the same time, globalization vastly increased international competition. More globalization meant more competition, and more competition meant more pressure to be "world class"—to lower costs, to make employees more productive, and to do things better and less expensively.

As multinational companies jockey for position, many transfer operations abroad, not just to seek cheaper labor but to tap into new markets. For example, Toyota has thousands of sales employees based in America, while GE has over 10,000 employees in France. The search for greater efficiencies prompts some employers to *offshore* (export jobs to lower-cost locations abroad, as when Dell offshored some call-center jobs to India). Some employers offshore even highly skilled jobs such as lawyer.[25] Managing the "people" aspects of globalization is a big task for any company that expands abroad—and for its HR managers. However, Globalisation also has its backlashes. Indian IT companies which benefited from liberal policies that supported movement of people are likely to face problems in the coming years because of the changes that the US and other governments have introduced to the praactive of giving work visas. H1B visa is a visa category where the US firms are allowed to hire temporary foreign workers with specialized skills for executing certain projects. It was very common for Indian companies to send their employees to the US on temporary basis, and such employees are believed to displace Americans from their jobs.[26]

Technology Trends

However, it may be technology that most characterizes the trends shaping human resource management today.[27] For example, the consulting firm Accenture estimates that social media connections via tools like LinkedIn will soon produce as many as 80% of new recruits—often letting line managers bypass the human resource management unit.[28]

Five main types of digital technologies are driving this transfer of functionality from HR professionals to automation. Employers increasingly use *social media* tools such as Twitter, Facebook, and LinkedIn (rather than, say, as many employment agencies) to recruit new employees. Employers use new *mobile applications*, for instance, to monitor employee location and to provide digital photos at the facility clock-in location to identify workers. The feedback, fun, and objectives inherent in *gaming* support many new training applications, and websites such as Knack, Gild, and True Office enable employers to inject gaming features into training, performance appraisal, and recruiting. *Cloud computing* and more intuitive user interfaces enable employers to monitor and report on things like a team's goal attainment and to provide real-time evaluative feedback. Finally, *data analytics* basically means using statistical techniques, algorithms, and problem-solving to identify relationships among data for the purpose of solving particular problems (such as what are the ideal candidate's traits, or how can I tell in advance which of my best employees is likely to quit?). When applied to human resource management, data analytics is called *talent analytics.*

As one example, talent analytics is revolutionizing how employers look for job candidates. For example, one employer reportedly operated for many years on the assumption that what mattered was the school the candidate attended, the grades they had, and their references. A retrospective talent analytics study showed that these traits didn't matter at all. What mattered were things like: their résumés were grammatically correct, they didn't quit school until obtaining some degree, they were successful in prior jobs, and they were able to succeed with vague instructions.[29]

Technological change is also affecting the nature of jobs.[30] When someone thinks of "tech jobs," jobs at Apple and Google come to mind, but technology affects all sorts of jobs. Technology is, therefore, changing the way the entire employee life cycle is managed. Companies are using technologies, such as, artificial intelligence (AI), machine learning, and robotics to manage their human resources.

Indian HR software firm, ZingHR offers cloud-based HCM (Human Capital Management) solution software that takes care of various HR functions in digital mode. It is now working on an upgraded version of the software, which incorporates machine learning and AI tools. The software performs functions such as e-recruiting, digital hiring and on-boarding, payroll processing, and performance management digitally. The upgraded software will be capable of picking up trends and patterns which can be used for faster and better decision-making.

Today's New Human Resource Management

A Brief History of Personnel/Human Resource Management

LEARNING OBJECTIVE 1-3
Briefly describe "distributed HR" and other important aspects of human management today.

"Personnel management" is not new.[31] Ancient armies and organized efforts always required attracting, selecting, training, and motivating workers. But personnel tasks like these were mostly just part of every manager's job, something that lasted in most countries until the late 1800s. At that time, labor problems began arising in many of the post–industrial revolution's new factories. Soon employers were setting up "welfare offices" and "welfare secretaries" to manage activities like factory washrooms, and "safety bureaus" to oversee plant safety. By 1900, employers set up the first "hiring offices," training programs, and factory schools. Personnel management had begun.

In these early firms, personnel managers took over hiring and firing from supervisors, ran the payroll departments, and administered benefits plans. As expertise in testing emerged, personnel departments played a greater role in employee selection and training.[32] New union laws in the 1930s added "Helping the employer deal with unions" to personnel's tasks. New equal employment laws in the 1960s made employers more reliant on personnel management to avoid discrimination claims.[33]

By the 1970s globalization made gaining a competitive edge through engaged employees—and therefore personnel management—increasingly important. Today economic and demographic trends (recall the diminishing workforce participation rate and aging population, for instance) make finding, hiring, and motivating employees more challenging, while more high tech and service jobs means employers must excel at managing employees' knowledge, skills, and expertise (human capital) through aptly renamed human resource management departments. Furthermore, as we've seen, technological trends including mobile and social media are changing how employers recruit, select, train, appraise, and motivate employees.[34] In a sense, a new human resource management is emerging. We'll look at this next.

Distributed HR and the New Human Resource Management

Perhaps most importantly, more and more human resource management tasks are now being redistributed *from* a central HR department *to* the company's employees and line managers, thanks to digital technologies like mobile phones and social media.[35] Many Indian companies use popular collaborative tools like Yammer for employees to interact with each other. Tools like Skype (for one-to-one and group meetings), Google Docs, and Dropbox are used extensively, particularly by SMEs and freelancers. WhatsApp is popular among Indian project and sales teams, for communication and information sharing. Similarly, hiring managers in some companies bypass human resource management to find candidates directly via LinkedIn. At Google, when someone applies for a job, his or her information goes into a system that matches the recruit with current Google employees based on interests and experiences. In a process Google calls "crowdsourcing," Google employees then get a big say in who Google hires.

Some experts say that if current trends continue, many aspects of HR and talent management will become "fully embedded in how work gets done throughout an organization [distributed], thereby becoming an everyday part of doing business."[36] So, somewhat ironically, we seem to be shifting in some respects back toward the time before the first personnel departments when line managers did more of the personnel tasks. As an example, Hilton Worldwide is placing more HR activities in the hands of employees, while redirecting the savings thus attained to building up the more strategic aspects of what its human resource managers do.[37] In the following chapters, we'll use Trends Shaping HR features like the accompanying one to present more examples.

TRENDS SHAPING HR: *DIGITAL AND SOCIAL MEDIA*

Digital and social media tools and the new human resource management.
Digital and social media tools are changing how people look for jobs, and how companies recruit, retain, pay, and train employees. In doing so, they've transformed the practice of human resource management, and created, in a sense, a new human resource management. Here are some examples.

Career sites now make the inner workings of employers more transparent than they've ever been.[38] Sites such as Glassdoor, CareerBliss, CareerLeak, and JobBite let their members share insights into hundreds of thousands of employers, including specific company-by-company commentaries, salary reports, and CEO approval ratings. According to one report, 48% of job seekers surveyed said they've used Glassdoor during their job search, including checking before applying for employment at a company.[39] Among other things, such transparency prompted sensible human resource (and other) managers to redouble their efforts to ensure that their internal processes (such as promotion decisions, pay allocations, and performance appraisals) are fair, and that their recruitment processes are civil—for instance, by responding to rejected job candidates and providing them with some closure.

Recruitment is one of the most familiar ways that digital and social media revolutionized human resource management. For example, as we'll see in Chapter 5,

Photosindia.com/Getty Images

Like many employers, Hilton Worldwide is "distributing HR"—placing more HR activities in the hands of employees.

managers use LinkedIn to find passive employment candidates (those not actively looking for jobs), and to check out active candidates. Another site, Gild, lets managers find skilled software engineers by searching the Web for open source code, and then evaluating the code's programmers in part by scanning technology forums to assess the programmers' reputations.

Talent analytics algorithms help managers improve employee retention. They do this, for example by identifying the factors (such as experience, career advancement, performance reviews, compensation, and even a surge in activity on social media sites) that flag high-potential employees who are more likely to leave.

To improve training, talent analytics tools synthesize information from learning management systems (such as training courses taken) and customer management systems (such as each salesperson's sales performance) to identify which training courses have the biggest impact, and why.

Rather than just matching mentors and protégés informally, new, eHarmony-type tools let managers match them also based on personality.

And with about 70% of all openings now available online, new analytical tools scrutinize online job ads and identify hiring trends by industry and occupation, and real-time competitive pay and benefits information. For the past two to three years, the digital recruiting trend has been on the rise. Social media sites such as Facebook, LinkedIn, and Twitter are very popular in India, and companies are using these sites to recruit candidates.

Many Indian companies like HCL Technologies and various startups are conducting recruitment drives exclusively through social media platforms. L'Oréal India also has a Facebook page called L'Oréal Careers. The Tata Group has a unique way of recruiting women who could not get back to their careers because of breaks. The group has created a Facebook group called Tata SCIP (Second Careers. Inspiring Possibilities), where Tata Group recruiters connect with women who have taken break and are Facebook users. Digital media and social media help to find the passionate and committed women employees for the Tata Group companies, who otherwise may be out of the traditional hiring systems radar. ■

FIGURE 1-2 What Trends Mean for Human Resource Management

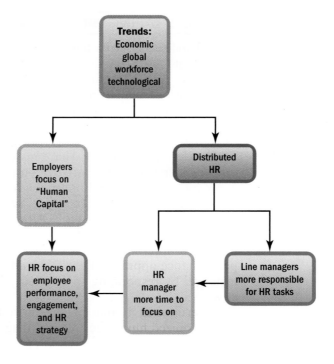

A Quick Summary

We can summarize important trends to this point as follows:

- One big consequence of globalized competition, economic and demographic trends, and the shift to high-tech and service jobs is the growing emphasis by employers on getting the best from their "human capital," in other words, from their workers' knowledge, education, training, skills, and expertise.
- This requires, among other things, using human resource methods to improve employee performance and engagement.
- Thanks to digital devices and social media, employers are shifting (distributing) more HR tasks from central human resource departments to employees and line managers.
- This gives many line managers more human resource management responsibilities.
- And this means that many human resource managers can refocus their efforts *from* day-to-day activities like interviewing candidates *to* broader efforts, such as formulating strategies for boosting employee performance and engagement. Figure 1-2 illustrates this.

We'll look next at human resource management's roles in strategy, performance, and employee engagement next.

HR and Strategy

strategic human resource management
Formulating and executing human resource policies and practices that produce the employee competencies and behaviors the company needs to achieve its strategic aims.

First, today's human resource managers are focusing more on longer term, strategic "big picture" issues. We'll see in Chapter 3 (Strategy) that **strategic human resource management** means formulating and executing human resource policies and practices that produce the employee competencies and behaviors the company needs to achieve its strategic aims. We illustrate this throughout this book with Strategic Context features such as the accompanying one.

IMPROVING PERFORMANCE: *The Strategic Context*

Building L.L.Bean

Strategic human resource management means formulating and executing human resource policies and practices that produce the employee competencies and behaviors the company needs to achieve its strategic aims.

L.L.Bean illustrates how companies do this. The heart of L.L.Bean's strategy has always been offering great outdoor equipment with outstanding service and expert advice. As its company history said, "L.L.Bean, Inc., quickly established itself as a trusted source for reliable outdoor equipment and expert advice. The small company grew. Customers spread the word of L.L.Bean's quality and service."[40]

To provide such service, L.L.Bean needs special people as employees, ones whose love of the outdoors helps them deal knowledgably and supportively with the company's customers. To paraphrase its Website, L.L.Bean is looking for a special type of employee, one (like its customers) who loves the outdoors, and the company therefore treats its employees just as well as it famously treat its customers.[41]

L.L.Bean's HR policies and practices attract and develop just such employees. For one thing, the company knows just who to recruit for. It wants sociable, friendly, experienced, outdoors-oriented applicants and employees.[42] To attract and cultivate these sorts of employee competencies and behaviors, the company uses multiple interviews to screen out applicants who might not fit in. And L.L.Bean offers an outdoors-oriented work environment and competitive pay and benefits. It was a *Fortune* "100 Best Companies to Work For" employer in 2015.

To help encourage great employee service, L.L.Bean also provides a supportive environment. For example, when its Web sales recently for the first time exceeded phone sales, L.L.Bean closed four local call centers, but arranged for the 220 employees to work from their homes. And instead of sending jobs abroad, the company keeps its jobs close to the town where Leon Leonwood Bean started his company almost 100 years ago.[43] L.L.Bean's managers built the firm's strategy and success around courteous, expert service. They know that having the right employees is the key to its success, and that it takes the right blend of human resource practices to attract and nurture such employees. ∎

Source: Based on "Our Story", L.L.Bean, pp. 1-19, from www.llbean.com/customerService/aboutLLBean/images/110408_About-LLB.pdf; www.llbean.com/; Michael Arndt, "L.L.Bean Follows Its Shoppers to the Web," *Business Week*, March 1, 2010. http://www.llbean.com/llb/shop/515428.

As in the Strategic Context feature, today's employers want their HR managers to put in place practices that will produce the employee behaviors that help the company achieve its strategic aims. We use a model opening each chapter to illustrate this idea, but in brief the model follows this three-step sequence: Set the firm's strategic aims → Pinpoint the employee behaviors and skills we need to achieve these strategic aims → Decide what HR policies and practices will enable us to produce these necessary employee behaviors and skills.

HR and Performance

Employers also expect their human resource manager/"people experts" to spearhead employee performance-improvement efforts. Here they can apply three levers. The first is the *HR department lever*. The HR manager ensures that the human resource management function is delivering services efficiently. For example, this might include outsourcing certain activities such as benefits management, and using technology to deliver its services more cost-effectively.

The second is the *employee costs lever*. For example, the human resource manager takes a prominent role in advising top management about the company's staffing levels, and in setting and controlling the firm's compensation, incentives, and benefits policies.

The third is the *strategic results lever*. Here the HR manager puts in place the policies and practices that produce the employee competencies and skills the company needs to achieve its strategic goals. That's what was done at L.L.Bean, for instance.

HR AND PERFORMANCE MEASUREMENT   Improving performance requires measuring what you are doing. Human resource managers use performance measures (or "metrics") to validate claims like these. For example, median HR expenses as a percentage of companies' total operating costs average just under 1%.[44] A good performance management system considers employee performance and rewards fairly, and is transparent. Technology offers features such as systematic approach and transparency, which enable fairness. For instance, ZingHR is a Mumbai-based human resource solution firm that has developed a performance management software to support appraisals. It has developed an e-performance management software with 360 Degree PMS, where performance reviews not only focus on the outcomes to rate the employees but also help the managers understand about the volatility in the market environment as well as the current economic and technological conditions, and rate performance accordingly. The PMS software offers flexibility to the HR managers to design complex HR processes in a simple manner. It helps the employees to understand how their performance is being evaluated and gives clarity on what level of performance is expected from them.[45] We'll address this in Chapter 3.

HR AND EVIDENCE-BASED MANAGEMENT   Basing decisions on such evidence is the heart of *evidence-based human resource management*. This is the use of data, facts, analytics, scientific rigor, critical evaluation, and critically evaluated research/case studies to support human resource management proposals, decisions, practices, and conclusions.[46] Put simply, evidence-based human resource management means using the best-available evidence in making decisions about the human resource management practices you are focusing on.[47] The evidence may come from *actual measurements* (such as, how did the trainees like this program?). It may come from *existing data* (such as, what happened to company profits after we installed this training program?). Or, it may come from published *research studies* (such as, what does the research literature conclude about the best way to ensure that trainees remember what they learn?).

Sometimes, companies translate their findings into what management gurus call *high-performance work systems,* "sets of human resource management practices that together produce superior employee performance."[48] For example, at GE's assembly plant in the US's Durham, North Carolina, highly trained self-directed teams produce high-precision aircraft parts. We'll also discuss how they do this in Chapter 3.

HR AND ADDING VALUE   The bottom line is that today's employers want their human resource managers to *add value* by boosting profits and performance. Professors Dave

Ulrich and Wayne Brockbank describe this as the "HR Value Proposition."[49] They say human resource programs (such as benefits plans) are just a means to an end. The HR manager's ultimate aim must be to add value. *Adding value* means helping the firm and its employees improve in a measurable way as a result of the human resource manager's actions. We'll see in this book how human resource practices do this. For example, we'll use, in each chapter, HR as a Profit Center features like the one on page 10 to illustrate this.

HR and Performance and Sustainability

In a world where sea levels are rising, glaciers are crumbling, and people increasingly view financial inequity as offensive, more and more people say that businesses can't just measure "performance" in terms of maximizing profits. They argue that companies' efforts should be "sustainable," by which they mean judged not just on profits, but on their environmental and social performance as well.[50] As one example, PepsiCo has a goal to deliver "Performance with Purpose"—in other words, to deliver financial performance while also achieving human sustainability, environmental sustainability, and talent sustainability. PepsiCo wants to achieve business and financial success while leaving a positive imprint on society (click www.pepsico.com, then click *What We Believe*, and then *Performance with Purpose*). In one survey, about 80% of large surveyed companies report their sustainability performance.[51] We'll see that sustainability trends have important consequences for human resource management.

HR and Employee Engagement

employment engagement
The extent to which an organization's employees are psychologically involved in, connected to, and committed to getting their jobs done.

Employee engagement refers to being psychologically involved in, connected to, and committed to getting one's jobs done. Engaged employees "experience a high level of connectivity with their work tasks," and therefore work hard to accomplish their task-related goals.[52]

Employee engagement is important because it drives performance. For example (as we will discuss in Chapter 3), based on one Gallup survey, business units with the highest levels of employee engagement have an 83% chance of performing above the company median; those with the lowest employee engagement have only a 17% chance.[53] A survey by consultants Watson Wyatt Worldwide concluded that companies with highly engaged employees have 26% higher revenue per employee.[54]

The problem for employers is that, depending on the study, only about 21–30% of today's employees nationally are engaged.[55] In one survey, about 30% were engaged, 50% were not engaged, and 20% were actively disengaged (anti-management).[56]

We will see in this book that managers improve employee engagement by taking concrete steps to do so. For example, a few years ago, Kia Motors (UK) turned its performance around, in part by boosting employee engagement.[57] As we will discuss more fully in Chapter 3, it did this with new HR programs. Similarly, Bank of Baroda focused on improving employee engagement to support the business transformation exercise. These included new *leadership development* programs, new *employee recognition* programs, improved *internal communications* programs, a new *employee development* program, and by modifying its *compensation and other policies*. We use special Employee Engagement Guide for Managers sections in most chapters to show how managers use human resource activities such as recruiting and selection to improve employee engagement.

The New Human Resource Manager

LEARNING OBJECTIVE 1-4
List at least four important human resource manager competencies.

It's more complicated being a human resource manager today.[58] Tasks like formulating strategic plans and making data-based decisions require new competencies and skills. HR managers can't just be good at traditional personnel tasks like hiring and training. Instead, they must "speak the CFO's language" by defending human resource plans in measurable terms (such as return on investment).[59] To create strategic plans, the human resource manager must understand strategic planning, marketing, production, and finance.[60] As companies merge and expand abroad, they must be able to formulate and implement large-scale organizational changes, drive employee engagement, and redesign organizational structures and work processes. None of this is easy.

When asked, "Why do you want to be an HR manager?" many people basically say, "Because I'm a people person." Being sociable is certainly important, but it takes much more. What does it take to be a human resource manager today? Recently, the Society for Human Resource Management (SHRM) in the US introduced a new "competency model" (called the SHRM Body of Competency and Knowledge™); it itemizes the competencies, skills, and knowledge and expertise human resource managers need. Here are the behaviors or competencies (with definitions) SHRM says today's HR manager should be able to exhibit:

- *Leadership & Navigation* The ability to direct and contribute to initiatives and processes within the organization.
- *Ethical Practice* The ability to integrate core values, integrity, and accountability throughout all organizational and business practices.
- *Business Acumen* The ability to understand and apply information with which to contribute to the Organization's strategic plan.
- *Relationship Management* The ability to manage interactions to provide service and to support the organization.
- *Consultation* The ability to provide guidance to organizational stakeholders.
- *Critical Evaluation* The ability to interpret information with which to make business decisions and recommendations.
- *Global & Cultural Effectiveness* The ability to value and consider the perspectives and backgrounds of all parties.
- *Communication* The ability to effectively exchange information with stakeholders.

SHRM also says human resource managers must have command of the basic knowledge in the functional areas of HR, such as employee relations. The basic knowledge of principles, practices, and functions they need here should cover:

- Functional Area #1: Talent Acquisition & Retention
- Functional Area #2: Employee Engagement
- Functional Area #3: Learning & Development
- Functional Area #4: Total Rewards
- Functional Area #5: Structure of the HR Function
- Functional Area #6: Organizational Effectiveness & Development
- Functional Area #7: Workforce Management
- Functional Area #8: Employee Relations
- Functional Area #9: Technology & Data
- Functional Area #10: HR in the Global Context
- Functional Area #11: Diversity & Inclusion
- Functional Area #12: Risk Management
- Functional Area #13: Corporate Social Responsibility
- Functional Area #14: U.S. Employment Law & Regulations
- Functional Area #15: Business & HR Strategy

HR and the Manager's Skills

The aim of this book is to help every manager develop the skills he or she needs to carry out the human resource management–related aspects of his or her job, such as recruiting, selecting, training, appraising, and incentivizing employees, and providing them with a safe and fulfilling work environment.[61] Special HR Tools for Line Managers and Small Businesses features provide small business owners/managers in particular with techniques to better manage their small businesses. Know Your Employment Law features highlight the practical information all managers need to make better HR-related decisions that work. Employee Engagement Guide for Managers features show how managers improve employee engagement.

HR managers can't just be good at traditional personnel tasks like hiring and training, but must "speak the CFO's language" by defending human resource plans in measurable terms.

Dmitriy Shironosov/Alamy

HR and Ethics

Regrettably, news reports today are filled with stories of otherwise competent managers who have run amok. Many Indian organizations have been accused and found guilty of encouraging unethical practices like employment of child labor or denying rights of workers. In 2015, an Indian diamond company (which otherwise has good HR policies) was in the news for denying a management graduate job because of his religion.[62] Behaviors like these risk torpedoing even otherwise competent managers and employers. **Ethics** means *the standards someone uses to decide what his or her conduct should be.* We will see that many serious workplace ethical issues—workplace safety and employee privacy, for instance—are human resource management related.[63]

ethics
The principles of conduct governing an individual or a group; specifically, the standards you use to decide what your conduct should be.

HR Manager Certification

Many human resource managers use qualifications and certifications in HRM, labor laws, etc., to demonstrate their mastery of contemporary human resource management knowledge and competencies.

Unlike in the US, where professional association like the SHRM certifies the HR professional, the practice does not exist in India. Under the law, specific educational qualification from university or technical institution is prescribed for Welfare Officer (in factories, plantations, etc.), Occupational Health Officer, and Safety Officer. Most HR professionals have educational background in social work, management, psychology, or law. Apart from the IIMs, XLRI, MDI, TISS, Rajagiri Kochi, Symbiosis, and many state university departments offer postgraduate level qualification in HRM.

Professional bodies like National Institute of Personnel Management (NIPM), National HRD Network (NHRDN), and Indian Society for Training & Development (ISTD) organize various courses and workshops to keep HR professionals constantly updated about the changing knowledge and skills required to succeed in organizations. SHRM India (an arm of the SHRM USA) has also started offering its certifications in the country, with course content adapted to the Indian context.

HR and the Manager's Human Resource Philosophy

Technical expertise is important, but at the end of the day, people's actions are always based in part on the basic assumptions they make, and this is especially true in regard to human resource management. The basic assumptions you make about people—Can they be trusted? Do they dislike work? Why do they act as they do? How should they be treated?—together comprise your philosophy of human resource management. And every personnel decision you make—the people you hire, the training you provide, your leadership style, and the like—reflects (for better or worse) this basic philosophy. The Tata group, which is a model employer in India, has a distinct HR philosophy. (Details will be discussed in Annexture I of this chapter.)

How do you go about developing such a philosophy? To some extent, it's preordained. There's no doubt that you will bring to your job an initial philosophy based on your experiences, education, values, assumptions, and background. But your philosophy doesn't have to be set in stone. It should evolve as you accumulate knowledge and experiences. For example, after a worker uprising in China at the Hon Hai-owned Foxconn plant that assembles Apple iPhones, the personnel philosophy at the plant softened in response to the workers' (and Apple's) discontent.[64] In any case, no manager should manage others without first understanding the personnel philosophy that is driving his or her actions.

One of the things molding your own philosophy is that of your organization's top management. While it may or may not be stated, it is usually communicated by the managers' actions and permeates every level and department in the organization. For example, here is part of the personnel philosophy of the founder of the Polaroid Corp., stated many years ago:

> To give everyone working for the company a personal opportunity within the company for full exercise of his talents—to express his opinions, to share in the progress of the company as far as his capacity permits, and to earn enough money so that the need for earning more will not always be the first thing on his mind. The opportunity, in short, to make his work here a fully rewarding and important part of his or her life.[65]

Current "best companies to work for" lists include many organizations with similar philosophies. For example, the CEO of software giant SAS has said,

> We've worked hard to create a corporate culture that is based on trust between our employees and the company . . . a culture that rewards innovation, encourages employees to try new things and yet doesn't penalize them for taking chances, and a culture that cares about employees' personal and professional growth.[66]

Similarly, when Google founders Larry Page and Sergey Brin began building Google, they set out to make it a great place to work. Google doesn't just offer abundant benefits and stock options.[67] Google's team of social scientists run experiments, for instance, to determine successful middle managers' skills.[68] The aim is to keep "Googlers" happy (and Google successful and growing). We'll look closer at how managers maintain positive employee relations in Chapters 3 and 13.

The Plan of This Book

The Basic Themes and Features

LEARNING OBJECTIVE 1-5
Outline the plan of this book.

In this book, we'll use four themes and features to highlight particularly important issues, and to provide continuity from chapter to chapter.

Practical Tools For Every Manager

First, human resource management is the *responsibility of every manager*—not just those in human resources. Throughout every page in this book, you'll therefore find an emphasis on practical material that you as a manager will need to perform your day-to-day management responsibilities, even if you never spend one day as an HR manager.

Second, managers use human resource management techniques to *improve performance, productivity, and profitability.* To highlight this, you will find special boxed features titled:

> ***Improving Performance: HR Tools for Line Managers and Small Businesses.***
> These features highlight actual tools and practices any manager can use to improve performance at work.

Improving Performance: HR as a Profit Center. We've seen that employers need human resource management practices that add value. To illustrate this throughout the book, most chapters contains an illustrative Improving Performance: HR as a Profit Center feature. These show actual examples of how human resource management practices add measurable value—by reducing costs or boosting revenues.

Improving Performance: HR Practices Around the Globe. These features highlight how actual companies around the globe use effective HR practices to improve their teams' and companies' performance.

Improving Performance Through HRIS. These features highlight how managers use human resource technology to improve performance.

Diversity Counts. These features provide insights and guidelines for managing a diverse workforce.

Third, the book emphasizes how digital and high-tech trends are shaping human resource management. You'll therefore find *Trends* features such as **Trends Shaping HR: Digital and Social Media** in most chapters.

Fourth, particularly with today's "distributed HR", every line and staff manager should understand how the employer's human resource management policies and practices produce the employee skills and performance the company needs *to achieve its strategic aims*. Special chapter-opener scenarios and *Improving Performance: The Strategic Context* features illustrate this in most chapters. And use the Hotel Paris continuing case starting in Chapter 3 to apply that idea.

Chapter Contents Overview

Following is a brief overview of the chapters and their content.

Part 1: Introduction

Chapter 1: Introduction to Human Resource Management. The manager's human resource management jobs; crucial global and competitive trends; how managers use technology and modern HR measurement systems to create high-performance work systems.

Chapter 2: Employment Law in India and the US. What you should know about equal opportunity laws; how these laws affect activities such as interviewing, selecting employees, and evaluating performance; *Know Your Employment Law* features highlight important laws in each chapter.

Chapter 3: Human Resource Management Strategy and Analysis. What is strategic planning; strategic human resource management; building high-performance HR practices; tools for evidence-based HR; employee engagement at Kia Motors.

Part 2: Recruitment, Placement, and Talent Management

Chapter 4: Job Analysis and the Talent Management Process. How to analyze a job; how to determine the human resource requirements of the job, as well as its specific duties; and what is talent management.

Chapter 5: Personnel Planning and Recruiting. Human resource planning; determining what sorts of people need to be hired; recruiting them.

Chapter 6: Employee Testing and Selection. Techniques you can use to ensure that you're hiring the right people.

Chapter 7: Interviewing Candidates. How to interview candidates effectively.

Part 3: Training and Development

Chapter 8: Training and Developing Employees. Providing the training and development to ensure that your employees have the knowledge and skills needed to accomplish their tasks.

Chapter 9: Performance Management and Appraisal. Techniques you can use for appraising employee performance.

Chapter 10: Managing Careers and Retention. Causes of and solutions for employee turnover, and how to help employees manage their careers.

Part 4: Compensation

Chapter 11: Establishing Strategic Pay Plans. How to develop equitable pay plans for your employees.

Chapter 12: Pay for Performance and Financial Incentives. Pay-for-performance plans such as financial incentives, merit pay, and incentives that help tie performance to pay.

Chapter 13: Benefits and Services. Providing benefits that make it clear the firm views its employees as long-term investments and is concerned with their welfare.

Part 5: Enrichment Topics in Human Resource Management

Chapter 14: Building Positive Employee Relations. Developing employee relations programs and employee involvement strategies; ensuring ethical and fair treatment through discipline and grievance processes

Chapter 15: Labor Relations and Collective Bargaining. How to deal with unions, including the union organizing campaign; negotiating and agreeing upon a collective bargaining agreement between unions and management; and managing the agreement via the grievance process.

Chapter 16: Safety, Health, and Risk Management. How to make the workplace safe, including the causes of accidents; laws governing your responsibilities for employee safety and health; risk management methods.

Chapter 17: Managing Global Human Resources. Special topics in managing the HR side of multinational operations.

Chapter 18: Managing Human Resources in Small and Entrepreneurial Firms. Special topics for managing human resources in smaller firms.

The Topics Are Interrelated

In practice, do not think of each of this book's topics as being unrelated to the others. Each topic interacts with and affects the others, and all should align with the employer's strategic plan. For example, hiring people who don't have the potential to learn the job will doom their performance, regardless of how much training they get. Similarly, we will see throughout this book that each human resource management function, from job analysis to recruiting, selecting, training, and rewarding employees, should aim to produce the employee behaviors and competencies that the company needs to achieve its strategic goals.

Chapter Review

Chapter Section Summaries

1-1. All managers should be able to answer, **What is human resource management, and why is it important?** Doing so helps managers avoid problems like hiring the wrong person for the job. And more important, it can help ensure that managers get results through people. Line managers' human resource duties include placing the right person on the job, and orienting and training new employees.

1-2. **The trends shaping human resource management** are influencing what human resource managers do and how they do it. Globalization means more competition, and more competition means more pressure to lower costs and to make employees more productive and quality conscious. Technology is requiring more employees to be technologically well informed and pressuring employers to improve their human resource processes by applying new distributive technological tools. There is more emphasis on "knowledge work" and therefore on building "human capital," the knowledge, education, training, skills, and expertise of a firm's employees. Workforce and demographic changes mean that the workforce is becoming older and more diverse.

1-3. New digital technologies such as mobile and social media will make **human resource management today** more distributed. Traditionally, personnel/HR managers focused on administrative issues such as running the payroll department.

Today, employers expect their human resource management teams to focus more on big-picture issues, including instituting human resource policies and practices that support the companies' strategic objectives, and to foster high performance through engaged employees.

1-4. To do so, **the human resource managers** need **new competencies.** They should be able to apply evidence-based human resource management, which means the use of data, facts, analytics, scientific rigor, critical evaluation, and critically evaluated research/case studies to support human resource management proposals, decisions, practices, and conclusions.

1-5. In understanding the overall **plan of this book,** keep several important themes in mind: that human resource management is the responsibility of every manager, that the workforce is increasingly diverse, that employers and their human resource managers face the need to manage in challenging economic times, and that human resource managers must be able to defend their plans and contributions in measurable terms— to use evidence-based management—to show they've added value.

Discussion Questions

1-1. Explain what HR management is and how it relates to the management process.

1-2. Give examples of how HR management concepts and techniques can be of use to all managers.

1-3. Illustrate the HR management responsibilities of line and staff managers.

1-4. Compare the authority of line and staff managers. Give examples of each.

Individual and Group Activities

1-5. Working individually or in groups, develop outlines showing how trends like workforce diversity, technological innovation, globalization, and changes in the nature of work have affected the college or university you are attending now. Present in class.

1-6. Working individually or in groups, contact the HR manager of a local PSU bank. Ask the HR manager how he or she is working as a strategic partner to manage human resources, given the bank's strategic goals and objectives. Back in class, discuss the responses of the different HR managers.

1-7. Working individually or in groups, interview an HR manager. Based on that interview, write a short presentation regarding HR's role today in building competitive organizations.

1-8. Working individually or in groups, bring several business publications such as *Business Today* the *Economic Times* and *Business Standard* to class, or access them in class via the Web. Based on their contents, compile a list titled "What HR Managers and Departments Do Today."

1-9. Based on your personal experiences, list 10 examples showing how you used (or could have used) human resource management techniques at work or school.

1-10. Laurie Siegel, former senior vice president of human resources for Tyco International, took over her job just after numerous charges forced the company's previous board of directors and top executives to leave the firm. Hired by new CEO Edward Breen, Siegel had to tackle numerous difficult problems starting the moment she assumed office. For example, she had to help hire a new management team. She had to do something about what the outside world viewed as a culture of questionable ethics at her company. And she had to do something about the company's top-management compensation plan, which many felt contributed to the allegations by some that some former company officers had used the company as a sort of private ATM.

Siegel came to Tyco after a very impressive career. For example, she had been head of executive compensation at Allied Signal, and was a graduate of the Harvard Business School. But, as strong as her background was, she obviously had her work cut out for her when she took the senior vice president of HR position at Tyco.

Working individually or in groups, conduct an Internet search and/or library research to answer the following questions: What human resource management–related steps did Siegel take to help get Tyco back on the right track? Do you think

she took the appropriate steps? Why or why not? What, if anything, do you suggest she do now?

1-11. Appendices A and B at the end of this book (pages 583–600) list the knowledge someone studying for the HRCI (Appendix A) or SHRM (Appendix B) certification exam needs to have in each area of human resource management (such as in Strategic Management, and Workforce Planning). In groups of several students, do four things: (1) review Appendix A and/or B; (2) identify the material in this chapter that relates to the Appendix A and/or B required knowledge lists; (3) write four multiple-choice exam questions on this material that you believe would be suitable for inclusion in the HRCI exam and/or the SHRM exam; and, (4) if time permits, have someone from your team post your team's questions in front of the class, so that students in all teams can answer the exam questions created by the other teams.

Experiential Exercise

HR and "The Profit"

Purpose: The purpose of this exercise is to provide practice in identifying and applying the basic concepts of human resource management by illustrating how managers use these techniques in their day-to-day jobs.

Required Understanding: Be thoroughly familiar with the material in this chapter, and with at least one or two episodes of CNBC's *The Profit* with Marcus Lemonis www.tv.com/shows/the-profit/watch/. (Access a library of past episodes at URLs such as www.cnbc.com/live-tv/the-profit)

How to Set Up the Exercise/Instructions:
- Divide the class into teams of several students.
- Read this: As you may know by watching billionaire Marcus Lemonis as he works with actual small businesses in which he's taken an ownership share, human resource management often plays an important role in what he and the business owners and managers need to do to be successful. For example, at Grafton Furniture, a lack of clarity about who does what (a lack of up-to-date job descriptions) leads to inadequate supervision of some ongoing

orders and to lower profit margins. Questions also arise at Grafton about, for instance, the effectiveness of the training that some managers (including the owner's son) have received.
- Watch several of these shows (or reruns of the shows), and then meet with your team and answer the following questions:

1-12. What specific HR functions (recruiting, interviewing, training, and so on) can you identify Mr. Lemonis addressing on this show? Make sure to give specific examples based on the show.

1-13. What specific HR functions can you identify as being problematical in this company? Again, please give specific answers.

1-14. In terms of HR functions (such as recruiting, selection, interviewing, compensating, appraising, and so on) what exactly would you recommend doing to improve this company's performance?

1-15. Present your team's conclusions to the class.

Application Case

Jack Nelson's Problem

As a new member of the board of directors for a local bank, Jack Nelson was being introduced to all the employees in the home office. When he was introduced to Ruth Johnson, he was curious about her work and asked her what the machine she was using did. Johnson replied that she really did not know what the machine was called or what it did. She explained that she had only been working there for 2 months. However, she did know precisely how to operate the machine. According to her supervisor, she was an excellent employee.

At one of the branch offices, the supervisor in charge spoke to Nelson confidentially, telling him that "something was wrong," but she didn't know what. For one thing, she explained, employee turnover was too high, and no sooner had one employee been put on the job than another one resigned. With customers to see and loans to be made, she continued, she had little time to work with the new employees as they came and went.

All branch supervisors hired their own employees without communication with the home office or other branches. When an opening developed, the supervisor tried to find a suitable employee to replace the worker who had quit.

After touring the 22 branches and finding similar problems in many of them, Nelson wondered what the home office should do or what action he should take. The banking firm generally was regarded as being a well-run institution that had grown from 27 to 191 employees during the past 8 years. The more he thought about the matter, the more puzzled Nelson became. He couldn't quite put his finger on the problem, and he didn't know whether to report his findings to the president.

Questions

1-16. What do you think is causing some of the problems in the bank's home office and branches?

1-17. Do you think setting up an HR unit in the main office would help?

1-18. What specific functions should an HR unit carry out? What HR functions would then be carried out by supervisors and other line managers? What role should the Internet play in the new HR organization?

Source: From Supervision in Action: The Art of Managing Others, 4th edition, Pearson Education, Inc., Upper Saddle River, New Jersey.

Continuing Case

Carter Cleaning Company

Introduction

A main theme of this book is that human resource management activities like recruiting, selecting, training, and rewarding employees are not just the job of a central HR group but rather a job in which every manager must engage. Perhaps nowhere is this more apparent than in the typical small service business. Here the owner/manager usually has no HR staff to rely on. However, the success of his or her enterprise (not to mention his or her family's peace of mind) often depends largely on the effectiveness through which workers are recruited, hired, trained, evaluated, and rewarded. Therefore, to help illustrate and emphasize the front-line manager's HR role, throughout this book we will use a continuing case based on an actual small business in the southeastern United States. Each chapter's segment of the case will illustrate how the case's main player—owner/manager Jennifer Carter—confronts and solves personnel problems each day at work by applying the concepts and techniques of that particular chapter. Here is background information that you will need to answer questions that arise in subsequent chapters. (We also present a second, unrelated "application case" case incident in each chapter.)

Carter Cleaning Centers

Jennifer Carter graduated from State University in June 2008 and, after considering several job offers, decided to do what she always planned to do—go into business with her father, Jack Carter.

Jack Carter opened his first laundromat in 1998 and his second in 2001. The main attraction of these coin laundry businesses for him was that they were capital- rather than labor-intensive. Thus, once the

investment in machinery was made, the stores could be run with just one unskilled attendant and none of the labor problems one normally expects from being in the retail service business.

The attractiveness of operating with virtually no skilled labor notwithstanding, Jack had decided by 2004 to expand the services in each of his stores to include the dry cleaning and pressing of clothes. He embarked, in other words, on a strategy of "related diversification" by adding new services that were related to and consistent with his existing coin laundry activities. He added these for several reasons. He wanted to better utilize the unused space in the rather large stores he currently had under lease. Furthermore, he was, as he put it, "tired of sending out the dry cleaning and pressing work that came in from our coin laundry clients to a dry cleaner 5 miles away, who then took most of what should have been our profits." To reflect the new, expanded line of services, he renamed each of his two stores Carter Cleaning Centers and was sufficiently satisfied with their performance to open four more of the same type of stores over the next 5 years. Each store had its own on-site manager and, on average, about seven employees and annual revenues of about $500,000. It was this six-store chain that Jennifer joined after graduating.

Her understanding with her father was that she would serve as a troubleshooter/consultant to the elder Carter with the aim of both learning the business and bringing to it modern management concepts and techniques for solving the business's problems and facilitating its growth.

Questions

1-19. Make a list of five specific HR problems you think Carter Cleaning will have to grapple with.

1-20. What would you do first if you were Jennifer?

Key Terms

Endnotes

1. www.elance.com/p/lpg/freelancing/?rid=1TN5N&utm_source=bing&utm_medium=cpc&utm_campaign=c-bBrand-Exact&utm_term=elance%20odesk&ad={creative}&bmt=e&adpos={adposition}, accessed May 12, 2015. Note that the owner of Elance and its related company oDesk recently rebranded itself as Upwork, www.upwork.com, accessed May 12, 2015.

2. See, for example, Seongmin Ryu and Sunghoon Kim, "First-Line Managers' Involvement and HR Effectiveness: The Case of South Korea," *Human Resource Management* 52, no. 6 (November–December 2013), pp. 947–966.

3. Fred K. Foulkes, "The Expanding Role of the Personnel Function," *Harvard Business Review,* March–April 1975. See also www.bls.gov/oco/ocos021.htm, accessed October 3, 2011.

4. State of the CHRO 2015, www.peoplematters.in, [Navigation--Home--Strategy--Leadership--Article], as accessed on 08 August 2017 at 4pm IST.

5. Steve Bates, "No Experience Necessary? Many Companies Are Putting Non-HR Executives in Charge of HR with Mixed Results," *HR Magazine* 46, no. 11 (November 2001), pp. 34–41. See also Adrienne Fox, "Do Assignments Outside HR Pay Off?" *HR Magazine,* November 2011, p. 32.

6. "Why Chief Human Resources Officers Make Great CEOs," *Harvard Business Review,* December 2014, p. 31.

7. See "Small Business: A Report of the President" (1998), www.SBA.gov/ADV/stats, accessed March 9, 2006; and www.census.gov/econ/smallbus.html, accessed May 13, 2015.

8. Susan Mayson and Rowena Barrett, "The 'Science' and 'Practice' of HR in Small Firms," *Human Resource Management Review* 16 (2006), pp. 447–455.

9. Price Water Coopers (PWC), https://www.pwc.in, PwC India Family Business Survey 2016, (c) 2016-2017 PWC, [Navigation--PWC India---Private and Entrepreneurial Services].

10. Some firms have recently worked on eliminating their traditional human resource departments, with generally mixed results. See, for example, Todd Henneman, "Is HR at Its Breaking Point?" *Workforce Management,* March 22, 2013, pp. 29–33.

11. See Dave Ulrich, "The New HR Organization," *Workforce Management,* December 10, 2007, pp. 40–44, and Dave Ulrich, "The 21st-Century HR Organization," *Human Resource Management* 47, no. 4 (Winter 2008), pp. 829–850.

12. "Technology to Play Role in Updating HR Delivery Services, Report Finds," *Bloomberg BNA Bulletin to Management,* September 4, 2012, p. 281. See also Meg McSherry Breslin, "Strategic Move? Report Examines Future of HR," *Workforce Management,* November 2012, p. 14.

13. Jane Perlez, "Coddled Recruits Are Hindering China's Army," *New York Times,* February 18, 2015, p. 85.

14. Khetarpal, Sonal, 'The Rise of the Freelancer', Business Today, 24 April 2016, www.business-today.in, [Navigation--Home---Magazine--Story], as accessed on 08 August 2017 at 4pm IST

15. Farhad Manjoo, "Uber's Business Model Could Change Your Work," *New York Times,* January 29, 2015, pp. B1, B8.

16. Accenture, "Top Trends That Will Reshape the Future of HR," www.accenture.com/us-en/Pages/insight-future-of-HR.aspx, accessed March 6, 2015.

17. Lauren Weber and Rachel Silverman, "On-Demand Workers: 'We Are Not Robots,'" *Wall Street Journal,* January 28, 2015, pp. B1, B7.

18. Erica Fry, "Start Up: You," *Fortune* 171, no. 1 (January 1, 2015), pp. 84–87.

19. Manjoo, "Uber's Business Model Could Change Your Work," p. B8.

20. Tyagi, Chhavi, 'Ola, Uber drivers to strike again on Tuesday', 17 April 2017, http://economictimes.indiatimes.com, [Navigation---Home--RISE--

Startups--Article], as accessed on 08 August 2017 at 8pm IST

21. Russell Crook et al., "Does Human Capital Matter? A Meta-Analysis of the Relationship Between Human Capital and Firm Performance," *Journal of Applied Psychology* 96, no. 3 (2011), pp. 443–456.

22. Peter Drucker, "The Coming of the New Organization," *Harvard Business Review,* January–February 1988, p. 47. See also James Guthrie et al., "Correlates and Consequences of High Involvement Work Practices: The Role of Competitive Strategy," *International Journal of Human Resource Management,* February 2002, pp. 183–197.

23. "Human Resources Wharton," www.knowledge.wharton.upe.edu, accessed January 8, 2006.

24. See, for example, Anthea Zacharatos et al., "High-Performance Work Systems and Occupational Safety," *Journal of Applied Psychology* 90, no. 1 (2005), pp. 77–93. See also Jennifer Schramm, "Effective HR Practices Drive Profit," *HR Magazine,* November 2012, p. 88.

25. "Study Predicts 4.1 Million Service Jobs Offshored by 2008," *BNA Bulletin to Management,* August 2, 2005, p. 247; and Patrick Thibodeau, "Offshoring Shrinks Number of IT Jobs, Study Says," *Computerworld,* March 21, 2012, www.computerworld.com/s/article/9225376/Offshoring_shrinks_number_of_IT_jobs_study_says_, accessed October 5, 2012.

26. Due to rising costs abroad and customer pushback, many firms today are bringing jobs back. See, for example, "Here, There and Everywhere," *The Economist,* January 19, 2013, pp. 1–20.

27. Anthony Abbatiello, "The Digital Override," *Workforce,* May 2014, pp. 36–39.

28. Accenture, "Top Trends That Will Reshape the Future of HR."

29. Josh Bersin, "Big Data in Human Resources: Talent Analytics (People Analytics) Comes of Age," www.forbes.com/sites/joshbersin/2013/02/17/bigdata-in-human-resources-talent-analytics-comes-of-age, accessed March 29, 2015.

30. See "A Third Industrial Revolution," *The Economist,* April 21, 2012, pp. 1–20; and Jeffrey Immelt, "The CEO of General Electric on Sparking an American Manufacturing Renewal," *Harvard Business Review,* March 2012, pp. 43–46.

31. This is based on Bruce Kaufman, "The Historical Development of American HRM Broadly Viewed," *Human Resource Management Review* 24 (2014), pp. 196–218. See also D. Ulrich and J. H. Dulebohn, "Are We There Yet? What's Next for HR?" *Human Resource Management Review* 25, no. 2 (June 2015), pp. 188–204; and D. J. Cohen, "HR Past, Present and Future: A Call for Consistent Practices and a Focus on Competencies," *Human Resource Management Review* 25, no. 2 (June 2015), pp. 205–215.

32. For a book describing the history of human resource management, see, for example, SHRM, *A History of Human Resources,* www.shrmstore.shrm.org/a-history-of-human-resources.html, accessed October 4, 2012.

33. "Human Capital Critical to Success," *Management Review,* November 1998, p. 9. See also "HR 2018: Top Predictions," *Workforce Management* 87, no. 20 (December 15, 2008), pp. 20–21; and Edward Lawler III, "Celebrating 50 Years: HR: Time for a Reset?" *Human Resource Management* 50, no. 2 (March–April 2011), pp. 171–173.

34. See, for example, D. L. Stone, D. I. Deadrick, J. M. Lukaszewski, and R. Johnson, "The Influence of Technology on the Future of Human Resource Management," *Human Resource Management Review* 25, no. 2 (June 2015), pp. 216–231.

35. Abbatiello, "The Digital Override."

36. Tim Good, Catherine Farley, Himanshu Tambe, and Susan Cantrell, "Trends Reshaping the Future of HR: Digital Radically Disrupts HR," Accenture 2015.

37. Ibid. Some companies today think they're better off without

an HR department, but the results are decidedly mixed. Lauren Weber and Rachel Feintzeig, "Is It a Dream or a Drag? Companies Without HR," *Wall Street Journal,* April 9, 2014, pp. 81, B7.

38. This is based on "The Future of Business: Human Resources, How HR Leaders Are Reinventing Their Roles in Transforming Business," *The Economist Intelligence Unit,* 2014.

39. Ibid.

40. www.llbean.com/customerService/aboutLLBean/images/110408_About-LLB.pdf, accessed June 1, 2011; www.llbean.com/llb/shop/515428, accessed May 14, 2015.

41. http://llbeancareers.com/culture.htm, accessed February 28, 2010; www.llbean.com/llb/shop/515428, accessed May 14, 2015.

42. http://llbeancareers.com/culture.htm, accessed February 28, 2010; www.llbean.com/llb/shop/515428, accessed May 14, 2015.

43. Michael Arndt, "L.L.Bean Follows Its Shoppers to the Web," *Business Week,* March 1, 2010.

44. Chris Brewster et al., "What Determines the Size of the HR Function? A Cross National Analysis," *Human Resource Management* 45, no. 1 (Spring 2006), pp. 3–21.

45. www.zinghr.com, (Navigation--Product--Performance Management & Appraisal), as accessed on 14 August 2017 at 2pm IST

46. See, for example, www.personneltoday.com/blogs/hcglobal-human-capital-management/2009/02/theres-no-such-thing-as-eviden.html, accessed April 18, 2009.

47. The evidence-based movement began in medicine. In 1996, in an editorial published by the *British Medical Journal,* David Sackett, MD, defined *evidence-based medicine* as "use of the best-available evidence in making decisions about patient care" and urged his colleagues to adopt its tenets. "Evidence-Based Training™: Turning Research into Results for Pharmaceutical Sales Training," an AXIOM White Paper © 2006 AXIOM Professional Health Learning LLC. All rights reserved.

48. "Super-Human Resources Practices Result in Better Overall Performance, Report Says," *BNA Bulletin to Management,* August 26, 2004, pp. 273–274. See also Wendy Boswell, "Aligning Employees with the Organization's Strategic Objectives: Out of Line of Sight, Out of Mind," *International Journal of Human Resource Management* 17, no. 9 (September 2006), pp. 1014–1041. A study found that some employers took a lower-cost approach to human

resource practices, with mixed results. See Soo Min Toh et al., "Human Resource Configurations: Investigating Fit with the Organizational Context," *Journal of Applied Psychology* 93, no. 4 (2008), pp. 864–882.

49. Susan Wells, "From HR to the Top," *HR Magazine,* June 2003, p. 49. See also "HR Will Have More Opportunities to Demonstrate Value in 2012," *Bloomberg BNA Bulletin to Management,* January 17, 2012, p. 22.

50. Sully Taylor, Joyce Osland, and Caroline Egri, "Guest Editors' Introduction: Introduction to HRM's Role in Sustainability: Systems, Strategies, and Practices," *Human Resource Management* 51, no. 6 (November–December 2012), p. 789.

51. Cathy Dubois and David Dubois, "Strategic HRM as Social Design for Environmental Sustainability Organization," *Human Resource Management* 51, no. 6 (November–December 2012), p. 799.

52. Michael Christian, Adela Garza, and Jerel Slaughter, "Work Engagement: A Quantitative Review and Test of Its Relations with Task and Contextual Performance," *Personnel Psychology* 60, no. 4 (2011), pp. 89–136.

53. Adrienne Fox, "Raising Engagement," *HR Magazine,* May 2010, pp. 35–40.

54. Except as noted, this is based on Kathryn Tyler, "Prepare for Impact," *HR Magazine* 56, no. 3, (March 2011), pp. 53–56.

55. www.gallup.com/strategicconsulting/163007/state-american-workplace.aspx; Bruce Louis Rich et al., "Job Engagement: Antecedents and Effects on Job Performance," *Academy of Management Journal* 53, no. 3 (2010), pp. 617–635; "Special Report: Employee Engagement—Losing Lifeblood," *Workforce Management,* July 2011, pp. 24–27.

56. "Five Ways to Improve Employee Engagement Now," *Gallup Business Journal.* Gallup.com, accessed April 7, 2014.

57. Ibid.

58. Richard Vosburgh, "The Evolution of HR: Developing HR as an Internal Consulting Organization," *Human Resource Planning* 30, no. 3 (September 2007), pp. 11–24; and the RBL Group, "2012 Human Resource Competency Study," www.rbl.net/index.php/hrcs/index/overview, accessed October 4, 2012.

59. Dave Ulrich and Wayne Brockbank, *The HR Value Proposition.* Boston: Harvard Business School Publishing, 2005.

60. See, for example, "Employers Seek HR Executives with Global Experience, SOX Knowledge, Business Sense," *BNA Bulletin*

to Management, September 19, 2006, pp. 297–298; and Robert Rodriguez, "HR's New Breed," *HR Magazine,* January 2006, pp. 67–71.

61. HR-related questions that line managers have to address include: What are our talent needs? How should we meet our talent needs? How can we do a better job of hiring? How can we develop internal talent? And, How can we manage our employees' career paths? (These are quoted from Peter Cappelli, "HR for Neophytes," *Harvard Business Review,* October 2013, pp. 25–27.)

62. Anahita Mukherji & Partha Sinha | TNN | May 22, 2015, 03.20 AM IST, 'Mumbai diamond export firm refuses Muslim MBA job', The Times of India, http://timesofindia.indiatimes.com, [Navigation--News Home--India--Article], as accessed on 14 August 2017 at 6pm IST.

63. Kevin Wooten, "Ethical Dilemmas in Human Resource Management," *Human Resource Management Review* 11 (2001), p. 161. See also Ann Pomeroy, "The Ethics Squeeze," *HR Magazine* 51, no. 3 (March 2006), pp. 48–55.

64. See, for example, "When the Jobs Inspector Calls," *The Economist,* March 31, 2012, p. 73; and Paul Mozur, "Foxconn Workers: Keep Our Overtime," *Wall Street Journal,* December 18, 2012, pp. B1–B2.

65. Fred Foulkes and Henry Morgan, "Organizing and Staffing the Personnel Function," *Harvard Business Review,* May–June 1977.

66. "Working at SAS: An Ideal Environment for New Ideas," SAS website, April 20, 2012. Copyright © 2011 by SAS Institute, Inc. Reprinted with permission. All rights reserved.

67. Manjoo, "Uber's Business Model Could Change Your Work."

68. Ibid.

69. Accenture "The High Performance Workforce Study 2007: India" 2007, available at http://www.accenture.com/Global/Consulting/Change_Mgmt/R_and_I/IndiaWorkforceStudy2007.htm,

70. Aneeta Madhok "Similar Challenges" from "CEO Survey 2006" cited by, Robert J Grossman "Hr's Rising Star in India" available at http://www.shrm.org/india/07_risingstar.asp

71. Accessed on September 9, 2017 at https://www.peoplematters.in/article/leadership/state-chro-2015-ceos-perspectives-11432?utm_source=peoplematters&utm_medium=interstitial&utm_campaign=learnings-of-the-day.

72. Azmi T F and Mashtaq S (2015), Role of line managers

in HRM in India: Empirical evidence from India, International Journal of Human Resource Management, Volume 26, Issue 5. Published online 21 July 2014, pp 613-637.

73. Srimannarayana M (2012) Line and HR conflict: Some empirical insights, Indian Journal of Industrial Relations, Vol 47, No 4 April, pp 700 – 716.

74. C S Venkita Ratnam and B K Srivastava, "Personnel Management and Industrial Relations", (Tata McGraw Hill, New Delhi 1991) pp

75. Baldev Sharma, "Managerial Unionism – Issues in perspective' Sriram Center for Industrial Relations and Human Resources (1993)

76. Jerome Joseph, "Strategic Industrial Relations Management" (Global Business Press, New Delhi) pp 304

77. Udai Pareek and T Venkiteshwara Rao "Designing and Managing HR systems" (Oxford and IBH Publishing) p 4

78. T. Venkiteshwara Rao, "The HRD Missionary" (Oxford & IBH Publishing). 1990 pp

79. Arun Monappa and M.A Joshi, "The Personnel Function – A Managerial Perspective" in Personnel Management by. N.K.Singh and G K Suri. (Eds) (Vikas Publishing House Pvt Ltd.,1992). Pp 124 - 136

80. K B Akhilesh and Sekar "Personnel Profession in India: Select Results of a National Survey" in HRM 2000 Indian Perspectives in Akhilesh. K.B & Nagaraj. D. R (Eds), (Wiley Eastern Limited, New Delhi.)

81. Rao, T.V. & Abraham, E (1988) "Research in Human Resources Development: Present Trends and Future Directions" in Readings in Human Resources Development by Rao. T.V.(Ed), Oxford & IBH Publishing Company Pvt. Ltd., New Delhi. pp 51

82. V R S Cowlagi, "The National Renewal Fund: Promise, Prospects and Performance: Vikalpa, October – December 1994.

83. Chalam K S, National Renewal Fund and Welfare of Working Classes, Economic and Political Weekly, Issue No 49, December 07, 1996.

84. Sunil Maheshwari and Vikas Kulkarni, "Implementation of VRS in India," Vikalpa, April – June 2003.

85. Varkkey, Biju and Kumar, Randhir "Keeping the Sparkle on: Workforce retention in the Indian diamond CPDs during recessions" International Journal of Organisational Analysis, April 2014 p 454-470.

86. Varkkey Biju and Rupa Korde (2013), Gender pay gap in the formal sector in India 2006 - 2013 : Preliminary Evidences from Paycheck India data, Wageindicator Data Report Series, No 3: September 2013.

87. http://www.businesstoday.in/magazine/management/career/hr-practices-social-media-for-attendance-recruitment-hiring/story/221107.html

88. Accessed on September 9, 2017 at http://www.businesstoday.in/union-budget-2017-18/news/budget-2017-finance-minister-revives-labour-law-reforms/story/245541.html.

89. Accessed on September 9, 2017 at http://www.livemint.com/Politics/SZEpN8UBTtYOE5QUbQKkkM/Change-law-for-allowing-women-to-work-night-shifts-states-t.html.

90. Chabdrashekar CP and Ghosh Jayanti (2014), The Absurd Clamour for Labour Market Reforms", The Indian Worker (INTUC Publication), November 1-15, 2015, p 11.

91. Joseph Jerome (2014) "Quo Vadis: Industrial Relations Dispute Resolution" Indian Journal of Industrial Relations, Vol 50, No 1, July 2014.

92. Mona Khare, Employment, Employability and Higher Education in India: The Missing links, Higher Education for Future, (2014), Sage Publishing.

93. Accessed on September 9, 2017 at http://www.dnaindia.com/india/report-only-34-of-graduates-are-employable-survey-1933055.

94. Accessed on September 9, 2017 at Indian Skills Report 2017, available athttps://wheebox.com/static/wheebox_pdf/india-skills-report-2017.pdf.

95. Aspiring Minds: National Employability Report – Engineers 2016 available at http://www.aspiringminds.com/sites/default/files/National%20Employability%20Report%20-%20Engineers%20Annual%20Report%202016.pdf.

96. Accessed on September 28, 2017 at http://www.npiu.nic.in/PDF/Mentoring%20and%20Audting/B-Employbility%20and%20Skill%20set%20of%20newly%20graduated%20engineers%20in%20India.pdf and http://www.aspiringminds.com/sites/default/files/National%20Employability%20Report%20-%20Engineers%20Annual%20Report%202016.pdf.

97. Peoplestrong BITS Pilani, L&D Trends Study 2016; accessed on 9 September 2017 at https://www.peoplematters.in/download/training-development/learning-development-trends-study-2016-setting-the-building-blocks-14374.

98. http://indiatoday.intoday.in/story/employment-scenario-job-crunch-jobless-growth-economy/1/647573.html

99. http://www.livemint.com/Industry/4CXsLIIZXf8uVQLs6uFQvK/Top-7-IT-firms-including-Infosys-Wipro-to-lay-off-at-least.html

100. Rajesh K. Chandwani, Biju Varkkey, (2015) "APML drives a culture of ownership and innovation: Open-door policy makes employees feel part of the organization, Human Resource Management International Dijest, Vol 23, 2015.

Appendix A for Chapter 1

Evolution and Challenges of HRM in India

The HR function in Indian organizations continue to face new challenges. While the population has crossed one billion and the country is economically progressing, organizations in the formal sector continue to face serious challenges in people management. The high economic growth and the consequent demand for employable people to help achieve and sustain this growth has made the HR function sit up and think. While the importance of human resource management (HRM) is undisputedly recognized, the ability of HR function to cope up with the demands of a high performing organization has been questioned. The High Performance Workforce Study 2007, conducted by the consulting firm Accenture, notes that Indian organizations have traditionally ignored considering people as a source of distinct competitive advantage and they find people management as the second important challenge faced by their chief executive officers (CEOs).[69] Another study among Indian CEOs identified the following people management challenges before the top executives, which reads like a list for any western country's CEO.[70]

1. Creating a high-performance culture
2. Retaining talent
3. Recruiting
4. Moving from patriarchic, hierarchical management to a more team-based, informal organizational culture
5. Linking training with performance
6. Compensating knowledge workers
7. Building interpersonal relationships or managing conflict
8. Going global

In 2015, another study on Indian CEOs' expectations from their chief human resource officers (CHROs) was conducted. The study found that the CEOs expected their CHROs to contribute to organization's future, partner in business progression, and strategically partner with the CEO in executing his/her or organizational plans.[71] All the studies indicate that the CEOs concern on people issues, which points to the criticality placed by top leadership on HRM in organizations in India. All the reports have also identified that the Indian CEOs doubted the ability of a large section of HR functionaries to be the strategic business partner. These reports cited the failure of organizational leadership to encourage HR to move from the traditional roles as a backroom support function, fire-fighting, and handling crisis to the frontline and align with business as the reason for this situation.

As Indian organizations are realizing the need for professional HRM, there is growing demand for trained HR professionals. Business schools and other institutions, including law universities, have been offering specialized courses to train HR professionals. In a few organizations, line managers are shifted to handle HR responsibilities and career HR professionals have also been successfully shifting to other roles like marketing and operations, with a few of them assuming CEO roles later. A study conducted in the Indian context, which examined the relationship between the HRM role performed by line managers in top Indian companies and the effectiveness of HRM, showed mixed support.[72] Another study, which collected information from 210 line managers, indicated that there are points of conflict between the HR and line managers in India. Promotion decisions, salary, employee transfers, managing attrition, and handling employee grievances are highest in the list of conflict areas between the HR function and line managers.[73] Realizing the importance of building HR capabilities among line managers and potential leaders, organizations have been building relevant capabilities by organizing structured training programs (HR ones for non-HR personnel), stressing the importance of people management, holding HRM activities for early career/first time managers, or providing relevant exposure to HRM activities.

Evolution of HRM in India

References about personnel management systems and practices can be found in the ancient Indian text *Arthasastra,* which includes the job description of a supervisor and performance-linked pay for goldsmiths. Traditional India was famous for craftsmanship, and the society itself was organized according to occupations. The high in quality and unique Indian goods, made by traditional craftsmen, were shipped to Europe and other continents, as early as 17th century. Even before that, India had trade relations with the Arab countries and South East Asia. Employer–employee relationship during that era might have been guided by master–servant relationship.

Formal industrial organizations emerged in the country only after 1850. Merchants, particularly from Europe, developed trade and established factories in India. Cotton and jute mills were the initial industries followed by others, such as, steel, leather, and coal. The British rulers institutionalized systems for running the government, which included formal personnel management systems for recruitment and postings of government servants.

In the industrial sector, conditions of labor and work during the early years can best be described as poor. Enquiry commissions set up by the government, and committees studied the situation of workers and their recommendations led to the formation of labor and social security legislations. In line with this thought, the Royal Commission on Labor (1929-1931) was set up to examine the situation, and it recommended appointment of labor officers and other changes, including emphasizing the need to collect data for use in policy making and decisions. The changes suggested led to bringing in a degree of standardization, which became the early moves to introduce personnel management in Indian organizations. Formation of trade unions, with close link with political leaders like Mahatma Gandhi (Textile Labor Association in Ahmedabad, founded in 1920) also influenced the way industrial workers were managed.

At the same time, there were progressive employers who on their own cared about the well being of their employees. For example, Tata Steel had introduced a series of welfare measures for its workers, much before it became mandatory by law. (See Table 1-1).

After India gained independence in 1947, considerable improvements happened in the personnel management approach of organizations. The post-independence period encouraged mixed economy as the Indian growth model. Industrial organizations were broadly classified as public sector (including the administrative arm of the government) and the private sector. Public sector organizations were the largest employers and received huge investments. The Constitution of India had the objective of achieving socialistic society and various constitutional provisions supported giving protection to the working class. Numerous legislations were introduced to protect workers, and specific officials were appointed to take care of worker interests, notably the office of the Welfare Officer in large factories and plantations.

Along with industrialization, the trade union movement also grew in India. The rapid growth of trade unions also catalyzed the development of personnel systems in the organizations that employed them. Workers became more aware about their rights, and it became increasingly difficult to exploit them. Thus, in the 1970's & 80's typical personnel function in an organization included: (a) Personnel & Administration (b) Industrial Relations, and (c) Labor welfare.[74] The prescribed and assumed role was "crisis driven" or "issue driven". High level of union activism, protection, and employee behaviors like absenteeism also led to situations of over staffing, and the decision frameworks took a legal turn, with focus to be on the right side of law.

The same period also saw a rise of managerial unionism, mainly in the public sector enterprises where supervisors and managers without formal union rights joined to form associations that acted as pressure groups.[75] Managerial unions were able to exert influence in the public sector and called for attention to managing the non-worker staff also. Managerial union gained prominence in sectors like the public-sector banking and insurance, and, at a point, it was accused of greatly influencing decision-making.

Though not widespread, industry also was open to adopting tools and techniques that could help improve efficiency and productivity. In 1961, with full co-operation from trade unions, the Indian Aluminum Company Limited conducted a plant-wide work study at its Alupuram, Kerala plant, which led to defining work output, staffing patterns, and productivity-linked incentive scheme.[76] The establishment of management training institutes and business schools like ASCI Hyderabad, XLRI, and IIMs helped the industry to imbibe modern management principles and thoughts.

TABLE 1-1: Labor Welfare Measures in Tata Steel

Welfare Measures	Tata Introduced	Enforced By Law	Legal Measures
Eight hour Working Day	1912	1948	Factories Act
Free Medical Aid	1915	1948	Employee's State Insurance Act
Establishment of Welfare Department	1917	1948	Factories Act
Schooling facilities for children	1917		
Formation of Works Committee for handling complaints, service conditions and grievances	1919	1947	Industrial Dispute's Act
Leave with pay	1920	1948	Factories Act
Workers Provident Fund Scheme	1920	1952	Employee's Provident Fund Act
Workmen's Accident Compensation Scheme	1920	1924	Workmen's Compensation Act
Technical Institute for Training of Apprentices, Craftsmen & Engineering graduates	1921	1961	Apprentice's Act
Maternity Benefit	1928	1946	Bihar Maternity Benefit Act
Profit Sharing Bonus	1934	1965	Bonus Act
Retiring Gratuity	1937	1972	Payment of Gratuity Act
Ex-gratia Payment for road accident while coming to or returning from duty	1979		
Social Audit	1980		First in India
Pension Scheme	1989		
Social Responsibility as a Key Business Process	1988		

Source: Mirza S Saiyadian, Modernisation of Mind at Tata Steel" *Indian Journal of Industrial Relations*, 2001 p 375.

It could be very well summarized that up to mid 1980s, HRM function in Indian organizations grew through various phases, under the influence of these factors: (i) philanthropic viewpoint about doing good for workers (ii) legislations (iii) government policies (iv) trade unions (v) influenced by emerging trends/concepts in management, and (vi) changes in the economy. By then most organizations, business as well as nonbusiness had established separate departments to handle the personnel function, with senior level managers heading it.

Shift to Human Resource Development Orientation

Professors Udai Pareek and T. V. Rao were among the pioneers who not only introduced the human resource development (HRD) concept in India, but also assisted many organizations in designing development-oriented human resource (HR) systems. They have discussed the paradigm shift from traditional personnel function to HR system, as summarized in Table 1-2.[77]

The 1980s saw such large-scale introduction of the developmental concept in Indian organizations. By then, it was recognized that systematic attention to human resources was the only way to increase organizational effectiveness.[78] This awareness created stage for direct involvement of top managers and line mangers in the HRM process.

However, there were questions about the real impact created by HRD. A study of HR professionals concluded that the HR (personnel) function was considered to be in the lower order of hierarchy in terms of importance, i.e., not at par with other functions.[79] Another survey-based study conducted in the latter half of 1980s, observed that the major hurdle for the HR professionals in their effective performance, was the lack of top management support and lack of adequate and meaningful research inputs to the profession.[80] At the same time, the survey noticed the change in role and status of the HR profession within organizations. Another study conducted in 1984 found that 30% of the 54 companies studied had separate HRD departments and other 38% had a separate HRD function as a part of the personnel department.[81]

Towards Total Human Resource Management

Opening up of the Indian economy after the dream budget in 1992, saw Indian firms facing direct competition from multinational companies (MNCs) entering the country. The government started discussions about strategic disinvestments of public sector undertakings (PSUs) and introducing competition in sectors like banking and insurance as well as allowing foreign direct investments in many sectors. While the trade unions resisted the move, they found that their support base was diminishing. As part of the structural reforms, the government resorted to reorganization, privatization, and even sale of PSUs. In February 1992, it established a social security system for displaced workers through the National Renewal Fund (NRF), which was eventually wound up.[82] The objectives of NRF included retraining or skill development, employment opportunity creation, and job-loss compensation for affected workers; however, a review of its performance shows a dismal picture because organizations reportedly did not focus on skill development or job creation.[83] Liberalization also prompted Indian firms to consider voluntary retirement schemes (VRS) to rationalize the workforce, as the existing legal provisions (Industrial Disputes Act, 1947) made downsizing difficult. A study about post-liberalization VRS schemes indicated that Indian organizations have not really benefited from introducing it.[84]

At the same time, the liberalization of economy created demand for talent in the emerging sectors, and the traditional organizations (both in the public and private sectors) became talent sources. Workforce attrition became an important topic of discussion in the Indian HR literature. The highly competitive higher education system consisting of network of IITs, NITs (National Institute of Technology), IIMs, state government, and private institutions had already created a focused pool of professionals for the new wave to ride on. At the same time,

TABLE 1.2: Comparison between Personnel and HR Systems

Personnel Function	Human Resources System
Independent	Sub-system of larger system
Several Functions	Organic whole
Coping Role	Proactive role
Responsible for personnel department	Shared responsibility with line managers
Achieve efficiency	Shared values and reduce human wastage
Maintenance function	Developmental
Motivation by salary	Motivation by challenges

Adapted from: Udai Pareek and T. V. Rao, *Designing and Managing Human Resource Systems*, (Oxford & IBH 1992) pp. 4.

a section of managerial employees viewed the opening up of the economy as an opportunity to experiment with new experiences and also to improve their earnings.

Another significant event that happened was the development of the Information Technology sector, riding on the Y2K wave. Indian organizations such as Infosys, Wipro, TCS, and Patni Computers positioned themselves as cost-effective and reliable suppliers of human resources to international companies with legacy systems, so that they can tide over the crisis. Their strength was the ability to mobilize a vast pool of technically-trained people and deploy at client location, with development support from India. Massive staffing requirements saw recruitment evolving as very specialized function, separate from, but closely interlinked with the other HRM functions. As demand exceeded supply of technical talent, compensation levels also rose right at the entry point. India witnessed the arrival of the "knowledge worker"-- who is well skilled, individualistic, and ambitious about career. Attrition, till then a restricted phenomenon, became common place and it placed the next set of demands on the HR function.

The demonstrated success of Y2K allowed Indian companies to get sustained business from abroad. This entailed continuing with the massive sourcing exercises and also making sure that internally organizations remained stable. It was also necessary that employees distributed across geographic locations are connected with the organization. Information technology supported solution, particularly ERP based Human Resource Information Systems (HRIS) like SAPHR, People Soft HR, Oracle, or Ramco became handy. Innovative HR practices adopted by the IT industry, including the much discussed Dating Allowance of NIIT, employee stock ownership plans (ESOPs), etc., workplaces resembling college campus more than the traditional factory floor became the new face of HRM. At least in the more evolved sectors, increased emphasis was given to work-life balance practices (including flexible working hours, work-from-home option, employee support services, etc.) and initiatives towards health and wellness at work place. Soon, similar practices were adopted by traditional manufacturing and service firms, which realized that the new, younger Indian workforce demanded better and different treatment.

Post 2000, competitive pressures and budget cuts were forcing many global organizations, including governments, to cut operating costs. India was gaining recognition as a cost- effective location for outsourcing work, particularly for those involving application of information technology. China had already gained similar status for manufacturing. This gave rise to the ITES (Information Technology Enabled Services) or BPO (Business Process Outsourcing) firms, where global organizations could transfer their internal processes to be executed in India. The advantages India had were its English speaking, university educated population and relatively lesser operating cost. While the IT industry concentrated on the technically educated talent, the ITES focused on the large number of non-technical students from Indian universities. However, this resulted in massive displacement of jobs aboard leading to opposition from international trade unions and political parties so much that it became highly discussed points during elections in the US and European nations. The growth also created new jobs and career opportunities in large numbers, mostly for providing support services, such as transport, food, security, and staff services, and saw the entry of firms, including MNCs, in these sector leading to their formalization, which had traditionally remained informal.

In a globalized world, Indian firms could not remain immune for long from the effects of global business cycles. Many sectors faced the need for hiring talent in huge numbers to meet business requirements as well as for discharging employees when the demand fell. In the case of workers and unionized employees in the formal sector, the existing legislation framework placed restrictions in introducing required flexibility at workplaces. Many firms resorted to employing contractual and casual labor in large numbers, thus reducing the scope for creating better quality jobs in the process. This move, on some occasions, went out of control, leading to labor unrest. Meanwhile, there were also instances where some employers in the impacted sectors, like diamond cutting and polishing, retained the trained and skilled employees even during the downturn, while attempting other means of cost control. Such firms could capitalize on the opportunities given by the upturn that followed.[85] At the same time, at least in some sectors such as the ITES and retail that had recruited in large numbers many years before, a lot of employees are facing end-of-road careers because of competency, qualification gaps, introduction of automation tools, and artificial intelligence (AI). The same influence has impacted the manufacturing sector in the form of process automation and robotic applications. Studies have also indicated the existence of high levels of gender pay gap,[86] and problems in integrating more persons with disabilities and of different orientations in the workplaces. At the same time, positive HRM initiatives could be seen in terms of attracting more women to workplace, and employment to members of LGBT community. To cope with the new requirements of organizations and employees, more Indian organizations are adopting flexible work practices (work-from-home or co-working arrangements) and employment contracts (freelances, part-timers, etc.)

The Age of Digital HR

With the growing complexity of organizational processes and the increasing size as well as spread of organizations, it has become a challenge for the HR functionaries to handle all HRM activities including recruitment, training and development, performance management, payroll management, and so on. Already publically available websites, such as www.paycheck.in

and Glassdoor, allow employees and organizations to reach out on matters related to compensation, working conditions, etc. Advancements in technology, modern job roles, efficiency demands, and the practice of using data for decisions have prompted the HR function to go digital. Advanced technologies such as machine learning, geo-fencing and tagging, AI, and robotics are being used to make the management of HR function simple, as well as efficient, both for organizational managers and employees. Zing HR is one such firm that provides modern digital HR platform to Indian companies.

Responding to the social media savvy employees, many organizations have started to use social media tools for improving internal HRM systems. Most social media applications are in the areas of hiring, employee engagement, communication, and employee learning.[87] Social media analytics is also being used to understand the workforce trends, and craft appropriate strategies.

'Make in India' and the HR Challenge

Election of a new government in 2014, had led to revitalizing the sentiments about economic environment and revival of manufacturing sector as an agenda through the Make in India campaign. Through this, the central government wanted to promote India as the global manufacturing destination and invite global investment. To achieve the same, the government planned to optimally utilize the young Indian population by investing in skill development. India was also positioning to become skill supplier to rest of the world. The previous government had already initiated investments in skill development by establishing the National Skill Development Corporation (NSDC), with industry and private participation. The current government, for the first time, created an independent ministry for skill development and entrepreneurship, with the mandate to consolidate the efforts in this area. The national target is to skill 500 million people by 2022.

Another government initiative was to reform the existing labor legislation and administration framework, which was one of the long pending demands from the industry. The challenge was to ensure that labor reforms are not restricted to allowing the freedom to hire and fire alone, but facilitate the Indian industry to become globally competitive. At the same time, welfare of workers had to be taken care of as well. Some of the major reforms introduced during 2014—17 are: a) allotment of Labor identification numbers to 6 lakh forms and facilitating e-filing of compliance; b) reforming the labor inspection process to include random inspection and transparency; c) promoting apprentice training; d) allowing portability of Provident Fund Scheme through Universal Identification Number (UID); e) enhancing maternity benefits; and e) enhancing the salary limit for bonus, social security, etc.

The Union Budget of 2017 reiterated government's commitment to "a conducive labor environment wherein labor rights are protected and harmonious labor relations lead to higher productivity." It declared the government's intention to reform labor legislation framework, by proposing to divide the existing legislation into four codes on: (i) wages; (ii) industrial relations; (iii) social security and welfare; and (iv) safety and working conditions.[88] With the central government actively pushing reforms, a few state governments have also eased some of the restrictions, like employment of women in night shifts (Maharashtra and Karnataka, for example), while placing controls for safety and security.[89]

Though many of the reform moves and proposals have won support of the industry, trade unions remain skeptical about the changes. Trade unions cite that according to the Annual Survey of Industries 2011-12, worker wages or emoluments in factories are approximately 4.5% of input costs, and hence the point that labor rigidity is the cause for Indian industry being uncompetitive is an unsubstantiated claim.[90] Experts also argue that while introducing reforms in labor legislation and administration, which should encourage speedy resolution of disputes, care should be taken not to sacrifice the basic tenants of workplace democracy.[91]

The year 2016 will remain known for the bold economic initiative of demonetizing high value currencies and substituting it with new denominations. Though this led to temporary hardship and disruptions, particularly in sectors such as the small and medium enterprises and construction sectors that employed large numbers of daily wage workers who were paid in cash, the positives included increased penetration of digitization and formalization of workforce. Following this move, in its Union Budget of 2017, the Indian government had envisaged to give priority to job generation and creation of skilled workforce in the economy. To take the nation to the future and encourage entrepreneurship or self-employment, initiatives like Start-Up India and Digital India were introduced.

To achieve its aims, the government plans to educate and skill the emerging workforce, particularly the vulnerable and poorer sections of the economy and give thrust to the local economy by creating jobs in the rural areas. The allocation of funds for job creation and skill development was enhanced from ₹14,870 crore in FY'17 to ₹17,273 crore in FY'18 (an approximately 16% increase).

The Indian government's ambitious program of enhancing the skills of a large number of Indians, was addressing a challenge to HRM. While India had an established system of training workforce for industry requirements, effectiveness and quality of such training were always questioned. Large numbers of technically-trained personnel were found unemployable, according to many studies and surveys.[92] A CII supported survey in 2013 placed the percentage share of employables among Indian graduates at 34%[93], which improved to 40% in 2016.[94] Meanwhile, another survey indicated that only

7% of Indian engineering graduates are employable.[95] The study also pointed out that aspirations and salary expectations of the new workforce are rising, but employability has not improved. Such a situation of mismatch places the HR function in a difficult spot.

The government expects the industry to collaborate in the exercise of skilling India, and expect firms to use the opportunity to hire necessary talent. Studies have shown that some of the limitations with existing employability-oriented systems are: being ineffective and having outdated curriculum[96]; poor training delivery and trainers; poor soft skill development; and lack of accreditation and standardization. The government is working to put in place the National Accreditation Standards and improve the quality of vocational training as well as higher education. In the meantime, Indian organizations have also adopted different approaches including setting up captive skill development institutions, linking and sharing resources with educational institutions, helping institutions improve standards through better institute-academia interactions, etc. to ensure that they have access to skilled workforce.

In addition to technical skill upgradation, supervisory skill improvement, management capability building, and leadership development are also challenges before Indian organizations. In response to the requirements, nowadays, learning and development (L&D) function (earlier HRD or training function) has assumed significance in companies. The trend is clearly visible from the number of firms partnering with institutions like IIMA for customized programs. A survey conducted in 2016 indicated that the L&D function is currently viewed as growth partner, with mandate to move beyond traditional performance improvement and equip the workforce to face future skills requirements.[97] To ensure that learning becomes accessible to all, Indian firms are also embracing digital technology including Interactive Online Learning Methodology (IOLM), game-based learning, mobile learning (M-learning).

At the same time, developments in the Indian economy and global economy affects Indian organizations as well. The IT or outsourcing industry, a leading employer and home to progressive HRM practices, faces challenges from competition, cost escalation, and restrictions in major markets like the US and Europe. Statistics point that the country's economy is experiencing jobless growth, which may not be a good news for India's young workforce. This sluggishness in economy is attributed to weak industrial growth, low productivity, widespread drought that impacted agriculture sector, cost rationalization, automation, and the impact of general global slowdown.[98] In the first half of 2017, the news about layoffs in the IT sector and expected slowdown in job creation had sent shock waves. In-addition, automation and introduction of AI based tools have reduced demand for employees, particularly those with obsolete skills. Though the IT industry leaders have termed the job losses as routine and performance linked, it has seen government intervention in the matter,[99] and the call for unionization in the Indian IT sector has become stronger.

It's a fact that, many Indian firms have joined the league of organizations, where HRM has evolved to a stage where it can rightfully claim a position in the decision-making hierarchy of organizations. In such firms, HR professionals and line managers are aware of the importance of HRM in gaining competitive advantage. Traditional firms such as RPG and Bajaj Auto and MNCs of Indian origin such as the Tata Group and Aditya Birla Group have been focusing on developing leadership talent from within, and have stated investing in employees from pipeline building perspective, rather than short-term focus.

At the same time, it should be recognized that there are Indian firms where HRM is still at the primitive state, as also the large section of unorganized workforce in India, which still awaits for its share of the fruits of economic development. HRM practices in the SME sector firms have still to evolve on professional line. Many other firms continue to function with the traditional mindset of 'employees as extended family member'[100] and HRM practices are, thus, shaped by faith and/or community values. Though India is committed to providing decent work conditions, it still remains a dream for many. The legal protection enjoying Indian workforce and the firms that employ progressive HRM practices cover only 7% to 8% of the total workforce, while a large segment remains within the unorganized sector. Further debates about extension of reservation in jobs for the economically and socially weaker sections of society and extension of labor-law protection to the unorganized sector workforce are yet to be concluded. In future, Indian HRM's emerging challenge will be to move beyond the confines of formal workplaces to become more inclusive in its approach, so that the large population base can become driver of economic growth.

2

Employment Laws in India and the US

LEARNING OBJECTIVES

2-1 Explain the importance of and list the basic features of Title VII of the 1964 Civil Rights Act and at least five other equal employment laws.

2-2 Describe post-1990 employment laws including the Disabilities Law and how to avoid accusations of sexual harassment at work.

2-3 Illustrate two defenses you can use in the event of discriminatory practice allegations, and cite specific discriminatory personnel management practices in recruitment, selection, promotion, transfer, layoffs, and benefits.

2-4 List the steps in the enforcement process.

2-5 Discuss why diversity management is important and how to install a diversity management program.

A university recently fired its career services director after years of good evaluations. This happened about a year after his new boss gave him his first poor evaluation while peppering him with questions like "when are you going to retire?" The dismissed employee soon sued for age discrimination.[1] We will see how to avoid such problems.

WHERE ARE WE NOW . . .

Every HR action you take as a manager, from interviewing applicants to training, appraising, and rewarding them, has equal employment implications. Therefore, the purpose of this chapter is to provide you with the knowledge to deal more effectively with equal employment questions on the job.

Labor Legislation in India

Legislations (or laws) related to workforce management, employment, and trade unions are termed as labor or employment laws, and they fall within the broad category of industrial laws. Good labor laws protect the rights of workers and employers, thus helping to build a strong and fair society. They are considered as indicators of any modern nation. Labor laws or employment legislations came into existence due to employees' demands for better working conditions, recognition of their right to form collectives (trade unions), and, at the same time, to meet the demand from employers to ensure that excessive exertion of organized power of workers is contained and they (employers) have the flexibility to run the enterprise profitably by keeping operating costs low.

Labor law in India has been influenced by the British law and political economy. It's said, since getting Indian workers to work in British establishments was difficult, laws for hiring and keeping them were made. Primarily, the aim was to protect their businesses. The colonial rulers had enacted multiple legislations to protect their business interests and also on considerations of modern political and social thinking in their home country. The Trade Disputes Act, 1929, was one of the earliest such laws affecting employment and employment relations in India. After gaining independence in 1947, the new Indian government amended many of these labor legislations and introduced new ones to meet the new requirements and political reality. The Constitution of India, which is the source for all legislations in the country, has set the basic framework for Indian labor laws. (Constitutional provisions related with labor are discussed later in this section.)

The post-liberalization economic growth of India and the resultant increase in efforts to attract international investments into the country have invited attention to the limitations and possibilities existing in Indian labor legislation framework. The general perception is that Indian labor laws are inflexible and out of tune with the requirements of economic growth. It is argued, particularly by employers, that if the rigidities of labor legislations are taken away, India can experience higher economic growth. As one of the managers of the Tata Group, which is considered to be a employee-friendly company with many firsts in terms of labor-friendly policies, has said, "Indian labor laws were intended to be friendly to employers, but they have ended up becoming anti-employment."[2]

The other side of this argument, as proposed by labor collectives, is that relaxation in labor laws will increase labor insecurity. Also, it will be subject to the whims and fancies of employers. Because of these differences, labor law reforms continue to be one of the contentious reform-related issues before the country. Today, according to a report, generation of employment and policies to make work decent are major challenges in India.[3] Though there have been efforts from the Indian government to reform labor legislations, critics point out that it can be, at best, termed as stuck in the middle.[4] Currently, the efforts to reform labor laws have gained momentum, which we will discuss later in the chapter.

Recent Developments Related to Labor Reforms in India

With regards to labor law reforms in India, the year 2014 can be considered a landmark because a string of reforms were brought about to amend different legislations and also to improve various processes.

LABOR LEGISLATION AND THE CONSTITUTION OF INDIA   The Constitution of India, rooted in the principles of democracy, socialism, and secularism, has articulated the basic principles that form the cornerstone of Indian labor-legislation framework. The specific provisions concerned with labor and work are found in the sections pertaining to Fundamental Rights and the Directive Principles of State Policy. Labor laws have been listed in List III or Concurrent List of the Seventh Schedule of the Constitution of India. The following entries are significant from the labor or human resource management (HRM) perspective:

Entry No. 22: Trade unions, industrial as well as labor disputes

Entry No. 23: Social security and social insurance

Entry No. 24: Welfare of labor

Entry No. 36: Factories

Having listed labor in the Concurrent List, the Constitution also distributes the powers to handle labor-related legislations between central and state legislatures. In practice, most labor laws are enacted by the central government, and the state governments have adopted them with modifications. Hence, there is uniformity in most acts across the country.

Matters related to labor appear in Part III of the Constitution (i.e., Fundamental Rights). The following fundamental rights, which, according to a Supreme Court judgement, is a pattern of guarantees on the basic structure of human rights and impose negative obligations on the State not to encroach upon individual liberty in its various dimensions[5]:

- Article 14 refers to equality before law (applicable to any person, company, or association); Article 15 to prohibition of discrimination on grounds of religion, race, caste, sex, or place of birth; Article 16 to equality of opportunity in matters of public employment; and Article 17 to abolition of untouchability.
- The right related to freedom of speech and association is covered by Article 19 which provides protection of certain rights regarding freedom of speech, to assemble peacefully, to form associations or unions, etc.
- The right against exploitation is allocated under Article 21, including the right to life; Article 23 prohibits traffic of human beings and forced labor; and Article 24 prohibits employment of children in factories, etc.
- Under Article 32, the right to enforce the fundamental rights (or remedy in case of violation of fundamental rights) through courts are given. This article is considered very important, as it protects the citizens and other bodies against any form of violation.

Similarly, the Directive Principles of the State Policy are covered by the following directives (Part IV of the Constitution):

- The Directive Principles of State Policy are a set of expectations established by the Constitution, before the State. Both legislature and executive are responsible to achieve the same. It is very clear that between Fundamental Rights and Directive Principles, the former is superior and the building block of good governance. And as stated in Article 37, the Directive Principles cannot be enforced through the court of law. Hence, the best way to describe the existence of Directive Principles is that they establish a "positive obligation" before the State (while Fundamental Rights create negative obligation, or that the State should not do something or allow something to happen.)
- Under Article 38, the State is to secure a social order for the promotion of welfare of the people; and Article 41 covers the right to work, to education, and to public assistance in certain cases;
- Article 42 mentions provision for just and humane conditions of work and maternity relief; Article 43 makes provision for providing a living wage, etc., for workers, while Article 43A covers the participation of workers in management of industries.

Some other articles that cover basic state policies are:

- Article 45 provides for free and compulsory education for children.
- Article 46 covers promotion of educational and economic interests of Scheduled Castes, Scheduled Tribes, and other weaker sections.
- Article 47 states that it is the duty of the State to raise the level of nutrition and the standard of living and improve public health.

ARTICLES AFFECTING GOVERNMENT EMPLOYMENT   The government and its associated agencies are the largest formal sector employers in India. A government job, by its nature, cannot always be strictly classified along the type of work done as in case of private organizations that are covered by other labor legislations. The Indian constitution has laid down separate provisions related to government employees, for both central and state governments. Article 309 refers to recruitment and conditions of service of people employed by the government. Article 310 specifies the tenure of persons holding office, and Article 311 refers to dismissal, removal, and demotion of government employees.

LABOR JURISDICTION FOR CENTRAL AND STATE GOVERNMENTS   Article 246 and the Seventh Schedule of the Constitution of India specify the distribution of powers (legislative) between the central and state governments. Labor is placed in the Concurrent List [The Seventh Schedule divides responsibilities into three groups: the Union (Central), the State, and the Concurrent], where both the central and state governments are competent to enact legislations. Even then, some matters will be reserved for the central government to enact legislation.

FEATURES OF LABOR LEGISLATION IN INDIA   One main point of critique about Indian labor laws is the proliferation in the number of legislations that are operational in this sphere. Each legislation has been enacted to serve a specific objective. Court judgments, i.e., of the high courts of different states and the Supreme Court of India, have lead to clarifications, revisions, and reinterpretations from time to time. The objective of each legislation is specified in the legislations, under the heading "Prefatory Note—Statement of Objectives and Reasons." The legislations have been classified according to the objective of the respective act.

REFORMING INDIAN LABOR LAWS: FOUR LABOR CODES   There are more than 150 labor-related laws in India (including central and state), which has turned labor law compliance a nightmare for industries and workers. Many laws have unique definitions for employers, workers (workmen in some acts), wages, etc., which result in different and, sometimes, contradictory interpretations and subsequent legal issues. Hence, compliance was a challenge due to multiplicity of laws; for example, there were 19 laws dealing with working conditions and industrial relations alone. (This was cited as a reason for poor labor management and administrative inefficiency in the country.)

Though discussions about reforming Indian labor laws have been taking place for many years, there was no concrete action taken by previous governments. Some states, on their own accord, had made modifications, but the overall umbrella structure remained the same. The present government started the initiative of reforming the country's labor laws by codification and amalgamation of 44 major central laws into four labor codes. The topic was mentioned in the Budget Speech of 2017, which has given hope of consolidation. The codes were:

1. Labor Code on Wages
2. Labor Code on Industrial Relations
3. Labor Code on Social Security and Welfare
4. Labor Code on Safety and Working Conditions.

Another initiative taken was to simplify the compliance reporting process. Instead of industry furnishing multiple returns, separately under each act, a single annual return was introduced. The return can be filed online, which has been welcomed by the industry. The government also enhanced coverage and applicability of the acts, by: (a) enhancing compensation to workmen (in case of accidents) and (b) increasing the coverage limits, in terms of the wages earned for the payment of bonus and social security. The government is also planning to increase the quantum of gratuity payment to workers.

While the reforms would help in improving administrative efficiencies and compliance, the major concern was continued protection of rights of workers. The proposed reforms are expected to be implemented in the coming years. In the next section, we will discuss the major features of present laws.

Laws Related to Industrial Relationships

Maintaining smooth relation between management and labor has been one of the main objectives of Indian industrial relations. Laws falling under this domain are mainly "regulative" in nature. They specify the dos and don'ts.

The **Trade Unions Act, 1926**, is an important piece of law, which gives legal identity to collectives. It was passed before Independence to provide legal protection to employee collectives and to regulate them. Under the act, trade unions have to be registered with the appropriate government-appointed Registrar of Trade Unions. The Trade Unions Act, 1926, allowed freedom for any seven employees to apply to register a trade union, but a later amendment (2001) specified minimum membership as 10% of unionizable employees or 100, whichever is less. The act does not make recognition of trade union as representative of workers by the employers as compulsory. It permits registration of the union, and it gives protection to registered trade unions from certain civil and criminal actions. The act does not specify any criterion or method for recognition of trade union by the employer as the representative of employees. Various state governments (e.g., Maharashtra) have enacted separate legislations to deal with recognition.

The **Industrial Employment (Standing Orders) Act, 1946,** is regulatory in nature, and is applicable to industrial establishments under the jurisdiction of central and state governments. By formally defining conditions of employment, this act serves to reduce conflict, and it also becomes a communication mechanism between the management and labor.

As per this legislation, industrial establishments have to frame standing orders and apply for their certifications as well. A designated officer will provide certification, after inviting objections from workmen or trade unions and considering the objections. In the absence of certified standing orders, the model standing orders provided in the act will automatically apply, except in Gujarat and Maharashtra.

The primary tone of the **Industrial Disputes (ID) Act of 1947** is regulatory, as it puts restrictions on the direct actions that can be taken by both parties involved in an industrial dispute. Different conflict resolution forums have been proposed, including works committee (Section 3), conciliation officers (Section 4), boards of conciliation (Section 5), courts of inquiry (Section 6) and labor courts (Section 7), tribunals (Section 7A), and the national tribunal (Section 7B). This act also allows the government to intervene in the interest of maintaining industrial peace. Since it came to force, the legislation has been amended many times.

In the context of demand for labor reforms, the suitability of the different provisions of this act has been questioned from the perspective of increasing employment, productivity, and flexibility. The debate on the ID Act starts with the definition of "industry" itself, which got widened by the Supreme Court in the landmark *Bangalore Water Supply and Sewage Board vs. Rajappa (1978)* case.

The ID Act also requires organizations to give a notice of change (Section 9 A)—an advance notice of 21 days—for any change at the workplace affecting the workers. However, Section 9B allows the government to exempt firms from Section 9A in terms of public interest. Section 10 of the ID Act gives the government power to refer industrial disputes to boards, courts, or tribunals for arriving at a settlement.

The act also places restrictions on employees in public utilities going on strike (Section 22, 23, and 24) without appropriate notice (6 weeks and 14 days before giving the notice), or when any conciliation effort is operational. It also has provisions (these are discussed in Chapter 5) for firms employing more than 50 workmen (Section 25A) regarding layoffs, payment of layoff compensation (Section 25C), retrenchment of workmen after giving sufficient notice (Section 25F), and for closure of undertakings (Section 25 FFA).

Laws Related to Wages

The **Payment of Wages Act of 1936** has the objective of ensuring payment of wages to certain groups of employees, at regular intervals, and without any unauthorized deductions. The act also provides relief to the group of employees in case of nonpayment of wages on time (Section 5) or if unauthorized deductions are made (Section 7).

The objective of the **Minimum Wages Act of 1948** is to ensure that a minimum rate of wages is paid to all those who are engaged in wage employment. The state and union governments are empowered to declare minimum wages (Section 3) for employment categories given in Schedule I and II of the act. It also specifies the structure of minimum wage (Section 4) and the procedure for fixing and revising minimum wages at regular intervals (Section 5). Under the legislation, nonpayment of minimum wages is an offence.

With more than 1,500 minimum wages (MW) declared by the central and state governments, India has one of the most complicated MW systems. PayCheck India (www.paycheck.in) maintains an updated database of MW of all the states and central sphere.

Please note that the wage related legislations will soon be replaced with a Wage Code, which will comprise the Minimum Wages Act of 1948, Payment of Wages Act of 1936, Payment of Bonus Act of 1965, and Equal Remuneration Act of 1976.

Laws Related to Working Hours and Conditions of Services and Employment

The **Factories Act of 1948** is one of the most important legislations covering the manufacturing sector. The act provides safeguards for workers to protect their health, provides for safety at the workplace when dealing with machinery, improves the physical conditions at the workplace, and provides welfare amenities.

The act also restricts the hours of work, provides for overtime and spread of working hours (Sections 51, 54, 55, and 56), employment of young persons (Sections 69, 70, 71, 72, and 73), and places restriction on employment of women during the night hours (Section 66).

Factories are approved, licensed, and registered under the Factories Act (Section 6), and authorities are appointed by the government [Chief Inspector of Factories and Inspectors (Sections 8 and 9)]. Certifying Surgeons (Section 10) ensure implementation of the act. This legislation also provides for the appointment of welfare officers in factories employing more than 500 workers (Section 49) and safety officers if more than 1000 workers are employed (Section 40B), with appropriate qualifications.

While the factory workers are protected and given some rights under the act (Section 111A), there are obligations placed to abide by the rules set in their interests of health, safety, and welfare (Section 111); violating workers are liable to be punished.

The **Shops and Commercial Establishments Act of 1961** has seen enactments from most of the states in India. In fact, various state legislations existed even before the central act came into force in 1961. With the growth of IT and ITES sector, this act has become significant; because of the nature of work, IT and ITES firms are covered by this law. The act deals with important work-related aspects like restrictions on working hours, period of work, extra wages for overtime, and earned and sick leave. It also prohibits employment of children, underage people, and women during night hours, and lays down the procedure for dismissal, discharge, and termination of employment. In the interest of encouraging IT/ITES firms to function more effectively, many states have made suitable amendments in the state acts, particularly to allow employment of women during night hours and even permit 24-hour operation.

Laws Related to Equality and Empowerment of Women

The **Maternity Benefit Act of 1961,** a social-welfare oriented law aimed at empowering women, provides security (both employment and financial) for women employees working in certain establishments (except those dismissed for gross misconduct only, as the act prohibits discharge or dismissal during the period of pregnancy) for defined periods before and after childbirth.

Section 5 of the act makes it the right of women to avail maternity benefits including pay and leave, and employers liable to provide the same. Some states have added provisions that provide for additional benefits such as free medical aid, maternity bonus, provision of crèches, and additional rest intervals.

The act also provides for cash and non-cash benefits, including a maximum period of leave of twelve weeks, divided equally between pre-birth and post-birth periods. Non-cash benefits include a reduced workload (Section 4.3), a medical bonus if the employer does not provide pre- and post-natal support (Section 8), and two nursing breaks every working day till the child attains fifteen months (Section 11).

The **Equal Remuneration Act, 1976,** has its basis in Article 39 of the Constitution of India. The act directs the state to ensure "equal pay for equal work for men and women." It stipulates that there should be no discrimination between genders in the matters of remuneration for the same type of work (Section 4) and in recruitment and, subsequently, in promotions, training, or transfers (Section 5), unless the law explicitly prohibits employment of women. This legislation assumes significance in the context of wide wage gap existing between genders in India. (This act will be part of the newly proposed Wage Code.)

Laws Related to Social Security

The **Employees' Compensation Act of 1923** (previously Workmen's Compensation Act, 1923) is the earliest social security legislation in India. It was enacted to make the employer liable to pay compensation to employees who are affected by personal injury arising out of accidents. Compensation is payable for death, partial disablement [Section 2 (1) (g)] and total disablement [Section 2 (1) (l)].

The claim for compensation arises if the event is "out of" and "in the course of" employment, even though not necessarily taken place in the formal place of work. The expression "out of" the course of employment refers to the causal connection between accident and employment, while "in the course of" refers to the time of accident.[6] If only one condition is fulfilled, the claim for compensation is not admissible.

The **Employees State Insurance Act of 1948** has been enacted with the objective of securing financial relief in cases of sickness, maternity, disablement, and for providing medical benefits to employees of factories and establishments and their dependents. The Act is also applicable to non-seasonal factories using power and employing 10 or more employees, and non-power using factories and certain other establishments employing 20 or more employees. Employees and employers make contribution to the scheme and various benefits are given to eligible employees like:

- Sickness Benefit — in cash (Section 46 (1) (a))
- Maternity Benefit — in cash (Section 46(1) (b))
- Disablement Benefit — in cash (Section 46 (1) (c))
- Dependents' Benefit — in cash. (Section 46 (1) (d))
- Funeral Expenses — in cash. (Section 46 (1) (f))
- Medical Benefit —as service and kind. (Section 46 (1) (e))

The **Employees' Provident Funds and Miscellaneous Provisions Act, 1952,** is a social security legislation for employees working in factories and other establishments. A dedicated Provident Fund has been created with contribution from employers and employees. The objective is to provide monetary assistance to employees and their families, when they are in distress, unable to meet family and social obligations, and to protect them in old age, disablement, early death (of the employee), and in some other contingencies.

Gratuity is an additional financial benefit given to employees of organizations irrespective of salary or status, when their services end because of superannuation, retirement, resignation, death, or disablement. This provision has been created by Section 4 of the Payment of Gratuity Act of 1972. This legislation provides for gratuity payment to all employees at the prescribed rates (currently 15 days for every year of service).

Five years of continuous service (as defined in Section 2A) is required for an employee to be eligible (except in case of death or disablement) to receive gratuity. The maximum amount receivable as gratuity is ₹10,00,000 (now proposed to be ₹20,00,000) and the amount is exempt from income tax. However, under Section 4(5) of the law, employers can enter into an agreement with employees and pay higher amount, though the difference is taxable in the hands of the receiver.

Applicability of Labor Laws to the IT and ITES Sector

One of the questions asked in the HR circles is regarding the applicability of labor laws to the IT and ITES (BPO) sector. The common perception is that this sector is outside the purview of labor legislations.

From the nature of work performed, it can be said that the Shops and Commercial Establishments Act (1961) covers the IT/ITES companies. The act deals with working hours, overtime rate, spreadovers, employment of women and young persons at night, etc. Many states have come with state-specific acts that are more suited to the requirements of the state. However, many states have granted exemptions for IT companies from many critical aspects of labor legislations. (For example, they have been exempted from Apprentices Act and Industrial Employment (Standing Orders) Act of 1946. They also have the flexibility in opening and closing times, employment of women in night shifts, weekly offs, etc. While these exemptions may have provided the required flexibility related to employee management, some writers argue that the freedom may be misused by a section.[7])

For example, in January 2014, the Karnataka government exempted IT/ITES firms in the state from the Industrial Employment (Standing Orders) Act for a further period of five years. Some months before this notification, the earlier exemption was over, and firms had to draft their standing orders and get it certified from the labor department. The latest exemption was granted with specific conditions including: a) setting up of a committee for handling sexual harassment complaints in accordance with the relevant act, b) formulating an internal committee for handling employee grievances, and c) the relevant authorities (jurisdictional Deputy Labor Commissioner and Commissioner of Labor, Karnataka State) have to be informed about cases of disciplinary, dismissals, termination, etc.[8] Following this notification, in one of the much publicized cases, the Labor Department after hearing a case filed by a terminated employee of the Indian office of an US-based software company (non-managerial employee who had received good hike in compensation and congratulatory letters for performance) decided that the termination was unfair and ordered the company to compensate.[9]

ITES or BPO employees fall easily within the definition of "workmen" under the Industrial Disputes Act, unless they are in the managerial cadre. In the interest of facilitating this sector, many state governments have declared IT/ITES companies as "public utility services," where restrictions on strikes and lockouts exist (Section 22 of the ID Act of 1947). Similarly, exemptions from application of labor law are a common feature of SEZs (special economic zones).

The given relaxations do not mean that the IT/ITES industry is outside the purview of all labor legislations that provide a protective cover to the employees. Many exemptions are for a specific period of time or specific locations (like SEZs) and cannot be considered as permanent. Many governments have also allowed self-certification instead of inspections, and the firms are expected to abide by the law of the land.

Equal Opportunity Laws Enacted in the US (1964–1991)

Hardly a day goes by without equal opportunity lawsuits at work.[10] One survey of corporate counsels found that such lawsuits were their biggest litigation fears.[11] Performing day-to-day supervisory tasks like hiring employees without understanding these laws is fraught with peril.

Actually, laws barring discrimination in the United States are nothing new. The Fifth Amendment to the U.S. Constitution (ratified in 1791) states that "no person shall be deprived of life, liberty, or property, without due process of the law." The Thirteenth Amendment (1865) outlawed slavery, and courts have held that it bars racial discrimination. The Civil Rights Act of 1866 gives all persons the same right to make and enforce contracts and to benefit from U.S. laws.[12] But as a practical matter, Congress and presidents avoided dramatic action on implementing equal employment until the early 1960s. At that point, civil unrest among minorities and women and changing traditions prompted them to act. Congress passed a multitude of new civil rights laws.

LEARNING OBJECTIVE 2-1

Explain the importance of and list the basic features of Title VII of the 1964 Civil Rights Act and at least five other equal employment laws.

Title VII of the 1964 Civil Rights Act
The section of the act that says an employer cannot discriminate on the basis of race, color, religion, sex, or national origin with respect to employment.

Equal Employment Opportunity Commission (EEOC)
The commission, created by Title VII, empowered to investigate job discrimination complaints and sue on behalf of complainants.

affirmative action
Steps that are taken for the purpose of eliminating the present effects of past discrimination.

Office of Federal Contract Compliance Programs (OFCCP)
This office is responsible for implementing the executive orders and ensuring compliance of federal contractors.

LEARNING OBJECTIVE 2-2
Describe post-1990 employment laws including the Americans with Disabilities Act and how to avoid accusations of sexual harassment at work.

Civil Rights Act of 1991 (CRA 1991)
The act that places the burden of proof back on employers and permits compensatory and punitive damages.

Title VII of the 1964 Civil Rights Act

Title VII of the 1964 Civil Rights Act was one of the first of these laws. As amended by the 1972 Equal Employment Opportunity Act, Title VII states that an employer cannot discriminate based on race, color, religion, sex, or national origin. Specifically, it states that it shall be an unlawful employment practice for an employer:

1. To fail or refuse to hire or to discharge an individual or otherwise to discriminate against any individual with respect to his or her compensation, terms, conditions, or privileges of employment, because of such individual's race, color, religion, sex, or national origin.
2. To limit, segregate, or classify employees or applicants for employment in any way that would deprive or tend to deprive any individual of employment opportunities or otherwise adversely affect his or her status as an employee, because of such individual's race, color, religion, sex, or national origin.

Title VII bars discrimination on the part of most employers, including all public or private employers of 15 or more persons and most labor unions. It also covers all private and public educational institutions, the federal government, and state and local governments. It bars public and private employment agencies from failing or refusing to refer for employment any individual because of race, color, religion, sex, or national origin.

Title VII established the **Equal Employment Opportunity Commission (EEOC)** to administer and enforce the Civil Rights Act at work. It consists of five members appointed by the president with the advice and consent of the Senate. Each member serves a 5-year term. In popular usage, the EEOC also includes the thousands of staff the EEOC has around the United States. They receive and investigate job discrimination complaints from aggrieved individuals. When the EEOC finds reasonable cause that the charges are justified, it attempts (through conciliation) to reach an agreement.[13] If this fails, it can go to court. The EEOC may file discrimination charges on behalf of aggrieved individuals, or the individuals may file on behalf of themselves.[14] We'll discuss the EEOC procedure later in this chapter.

Executive Orders

Various U.S. presidents signed executive orders expanding equal employment in federal agencies. For example, the Johnson administration (1963–1969) issued Executive Orders 11246 and 11375. These required that government contractors with contracts of more than $50,000 and 50 or more employees take **affirmative action** to ensure employment opportunities for those who may have suffered past discrimination. They also established the **Office of Federal Contract Compliance Programs (OFCCP)**. It implements the orders and ensures compliance.[15]

The Laws Enacted from 1991 to the Present

The Civil Rights Act of 1991

Several subsequent Supreme Court rulings in the 1980s limited the protection of women and minority groups under equal employment laws. For example, they raised the plaintiff's burden of proving that the employer's acts were in fact discriminatory. This prompted Congress to pass a new Civil Rights Act. President George H. W. Bush signed the **Civil Rights Act of 1991 (CRA 1991)** into law in November 1991. The effect of CRA 1991 was to roll back equal employment law to where it stood before the 1980s decisions, and to place more responsibility on employers.

BURDEN OF PROOF First, CRA 1991 addressed the issue of *burden of proof.* Burden of proof—what the plaintiff must show to establish possible illegal discrimination, and what the employer must show to defend its actions—plays a central role in equal employment cases.[16] Today, in brief, once an aggrieved applicant or employee demonstrates that an employment practice (such as "must lift 100 pounds") has an adverse impact on a particular group, then the burden of proof shifts to the employer, who must show that the challenged practice is job related.[17] For example, the employer has to show that lifting 100 pounds is required for performing the job in question, and that the business could not run efficiently without the requirement—that it is a business necessity.[18]

MONEY DAMAGES   Before CRA 1991, victims of *intentional* discrimination (which lawyers call *disparate treatment*) who had not suffered financial loss and who sued under Title VII could not then sue for compensatory or punitive damages. All they could expect was to have their jobs reinstated (or to get a particular job). They were also eligible for back pay, attorneys' fees, and court costs.

CRA 1991 makes it easier to sue for *money damages* in such cases. It provides that an employee who is claiming intentional discrimination can ask for (1) compensatory damages and (2) punitive damages, if he or she can show the employer engaged in discrimination "with malice or reckless indifference to the federally protected rights of an aggrieved individual."[19]

<table>
<tr><td>

"mixed-motive" case

A discrimination allegation case in which the employer argues that the employment action taken was motivated not by discrimination, but by some nondiscriminatory reason such as ineffective performance.

</td><td>

MIXED MOTIVES   Some employers in **"mixed-motive" cases** had taken the position that even though their actions were discriminatory, other factors like the employee's dubious behavior made the job action acceptable. Under CRA 1991, an employer cannot avoid liability by proving it would have taken the same action—such as terminating someone—even without the discriminatory motive.[20] *If there is any such motive, the practice may be unlawful.*[21]

</td></tr>
</table>

The Americans with Disabilities Act

Americans with Disabilities Act (ADA)

The act requiring employers to make reasonable accommodations for disabled employees; it prohibits discrimination against disabled persons.

The **Americans with Disabilities Act (ADA)** of 1990 prohibits employment discrimination against qualified disabled individuals.[22] It prohibits employers with 15 or more workers from discriminating against qualified individuals with disabilities, with regard to applications, hiring, discharge, compensation, advancement, training, or other terms, conditions, or privileges of employment.[23] It also says employers must make "reasonable accommodations" for physical or mental limitations unless doing so imposes an "undue hardship" on the business.

The ADA does not list specific disabilities. Instead, EEOC guidelines say someone is disabled when he or she has a physical or mental impairment that "substantially limits" one or more major life activity. Initially, impairments included any physiological disorder or condition, cosmetic disfigurement, or anatomical loss affecting one or more of several body systems, or any mental or psychological disorder, but the list is growing.[24] The act specifies conditions that it does *not* regard as disabilities, including homosexuality, compulsive gambling, pyromania, and certain disorders resulting from the current illegal use of drugs.[25]

Mental disabilities account for the greatest number of ADA claims.[26] Under EEOC ADA guidelines, "mental impairment" includes "any mental or psychological disorder, such as…emotional or mental illness." Examples include major depression, anxiety disorders, and personality disorders. The ADA also protects employees with intellectual disabilities, including those with IQs below 70–75.[27] The guidelines say employers should be alert to the possibility that traits normally regarded as undesirable (such as chronic lateness, hostility, or poor judgment) may reflect mental impairments. Reasonable accommodation might then include providing barriers between work spaces.

<table>
<tr><td>

qualified individuals

Under ADA, those who can carry out the essential functions of the job.

</td><td>

QUALIFIED INDIVIDUAL   Just being disabled doesn't qualify someone for a job, of course. Instead, the act prohibits discrimination against **qualified individuals**— those who, with (or without) a reasonable accommodation, can carry out the *essential functions* of the job. The individual must have the requisite skills, educational background, and experience. A job function is essential when, for instance, it is the reason the position exists, or it is so highly specialized that the employer hires the person for his or her expertise or ability to perform that particular function. For example, when an Iowa County highway worker had an on-the-job seizure, his driver's license was suspended and the court ruled he had no ADA claim because he couldn't perform the essential functions of the job.[28]

</td></tr>
</table>

FIGURE 2-1 **Examples of How to Provide Reasonable Accommodation**

- Employees with *mobility or vision impairments* may benefit from voice-recognition software.
- Word-prediction software suggests words based on context with just one or two letters typed.
- Real-time translation captioning enables employees to participate in meetings.
- Vibrating text pagers notify employees when messages arrive.
- Arizona created a disability-friendly website to help link prospective employees and others to various agencies.

REASONABLE ACCOMMODATION   If the individual can't perform the job as currently structured, the employer must make a "reasonable accommodation" unless doing so would present an "undue hardship."[29] Reasonable accommodation might include redesigning the job, modifying work schedules, or modifying or acquiring equipment or other devices; widening door openings or permitting telecommuting are examples.[30] For example, about 70% of working-age blind adults are unemployed or underemployed. Existing technologies such as screen-reading programs might enable most to work successfully.[31]

Attorneys, employers, and the courts continue to work through what "reasonable accommodation" means.[32] In one classic case, a Walmart door greeter with a bad back asked if she could sit on a stool while on duty. The store said no. The federal district court agreed door greeters must act in an "aggressively hospitable manner," which can't be done from a stool.[33] Standing was an essential job function. You can use technology and common sense to make reasonable accommodation (see Figure 2-1).

THE ADA AMENDMENTS ACT OF 2008 (ADAAA)   Employers traditionally prevailed in almost all—96%—federal circuit court ADA decisions.[34] One case typifies what plaintiffs faced. An assembly worker sued Toyota, arguing that carpal tunnel syndrome prevented her from doing her job.[35] The U.S. Supreme Court ruled that the ADA covers carpal tunnel syndrome only if her impairments affect not just her job performance, but also her daily living activities. The employee admitted that she could perform personal chores such as washing her face and fixing breakfast. The Court said the disability must be central to the employee's daily living (not just to his or her job).[36]

However, the ADA Amendments Act of 2008 (ADAAA) has made it easier for employees to show that their disabilities are influencing one of their "major life activities," such as reading and thinking.[37] For example, sensitivity to perfume might be considered a disability.[38] Employers must therefore redouble their efforts to ensure they're complying with the ADA.[39]

Many employers simply take a progressive approach. Common employer concerns about people with disabilities (for instance, that they are less productive and have more accidents) are generally baseless.[40] For example, Walgreens tries to fill at least one-third of the jobs at its large distribution centers with people with disabilities.[41]

Figure 2-2 summarizes some important ADA guidelines for managers and employers.

FIGURE 2-2 **ADA Guidelines for Managers and Employers**

- *Do not* deny a job to a disabled individual if the person is qualified and able to perform the essential job functions.
- *Make* a reasonable accommodation unless doing so would result in undue hardship.
- *Know* what you can ask applicants. In general, you may *not* make preemployment inquiries about a person's disability before making an offer. However, you *may* ask questions about the person's ability to perform essential job functions.
- *Itemize* essential job functions on the job descriptions. In virtually any ADA legal action, a central question will be, what are the essential functions of the job?
- *Do not* allow misconduct or erratic performance (including absences and tardiness), even if that behavior is linked to the disability.

In Summary: Religious and Other Types of Discrimination[42]

The EEOC enforces laws prohibiting discrimination based on age, disability, equal pay/compensation, genetic information, national origin, pregnancy, race/color, religion, retaliation, sex, and sexual harassment. The EEOC has also held that discrimination against an individual because that person is transgender is discrimination because of sex and therefore covered under Title VII. The Commission has also found that sexual orientation claims by lesbian, gay, and bisexual individuals alleging sex stereotyping have a sex discrimination claim under Title VII.

Religious discrimination involves treating someone unfavorably because of his or her religious beliefs. The law protects not only people who belong to traditional, organized religions, such as Buddhism, Christianity, Hinduism, Islam, and Judaism, but also others who have sincerely held religious, ethical, or moral beliefs. Unless it would be an undue hardship on the employer, an employer must reasonably accommodate an employee's religious beliefs or practices. This applies to schedule changes or leave for religious observances, as well as to such things as religious dress or grooming practices. These might include, for example, wearing particular head coverings or other religious dress (such as a Jewish yarmulke or a Muslim headscarf), or wearing certain hairstyles or facial hair (such as Rastafarian dreadlocks or Sikh uncut hair and beard). Religious discrimination claims are increasing. In one case truck drivers claimed that requiring them to deliver alcoholic drinks violated their religious faith.[43]

John Lee/First Light/AGE Fotostock

Technology enables employers to accommodate disabled employees.

Sexual Harassment Law in India

For a long time, India did not have a formal law that dealt with sexual harassment in workplaces. In 1997, taking cognizance of the gang rape of a social worker, the Supreme Court of India, on the basis of a petition filed by NGOs (non-governmental organizations) and social activists, had given guidelines and norms to handle cases of sexual harassment of women in workplaces [*Vishaka and other vs States of Rajasthan and others,* (1997) in 6 SCC 241)]

The Vishaka judgement is considered as a landmark because it enabled talks of protection and safety of female workers in India, and many organizations initiated steps to implement the same. The National Commission for Women (NCW) developed drafts of a proposed law, and the "Protection of Women against Sexual Harassment at Workplace Bill" was introduced in 2007. After a series of amendments, the act came into force in 2013.

The Sexual Harassment of Women at Workplace (Prevention, Prohibition and Redressal) Act, 2013, is a legislation aimed to provide protection against sexual harassment of women at workplace and for the prevention and redress of complaints of sexual harassment. The law is anchored in the Constitution of India, because any act of sexual harassment leads to violation of the fundamental rights of a citizen— the Right for Equality under Articles 14 and 15; the Right to Live and Dignity (Article 21); and the Right to Engage in a Profession (Article 19).

The law covers a wide variety of enterprises, including government, private sector, trusts, NGOs, educational institutions, sports venues, and competitions. In case, the work requires women employees to travel, harassment in the location and even in company provided transportation have been covered. The act also applies to the unorganized sector workplaces and non-traditional forms of work (like telecommuting). The law has defined sexual harassment to include the following behaviors [Section 2 (n)]:

• Physical contact or advances
• A demand or request for sexual favors

- Making sexually colored remarks
- Showing pornography
- Any other unwelcome physical, verbal or non-verbal conduct of sexual nature

In addition, if the following conditions exist, the act or behavior can be deemed as sexual harassment under Section 3 (2).

1. Implied or explicit promise of preferential treatment in employment
2. Implied or explicit threat of detrimental treatment in employment
3. Implied or explicit threat about her present or future employment status
4. Interferes with work or creates an intimidating/hostile/offensive work environment
5. Humiliating treatment likely to affect her health and safety

The most important part of the law is the prescribed redress mechanism (Section 4). All organizations have to constitute an internal complaint handling arrangement (internal complaints committee or ICC). The committee should be headed by a senior woman employee (Presiding Officer) and half of the members of this committee should be women. Participation of representatives from external agencies (like NGOs) is also mandated.

In case, offices of the firm are distributed in different locations, ICC has to be formed for each location. For government and other workers, a Local Complaints Committee has to be constituted at all districts, to handle cases. This is applicable in cases of firms without an internal committee, or if the complaint is against the employer (Section 6). In case of non-availability of senior women to be part of committee, representatives of other organizations are allowed to be part of this group.

On receipt of the complaint (within three months of the incident or in case of series of incidents three months from the last incident), the internal or local committee has to initiate an enquiry. In case of complaints from domestic workers, the matter has to be reported to the police [Section 11 (1)]. The procedure for enquiry and subsequent action will be according to the service rules of the company. In case the complaint is found not to be true, then the committee can report that no action needs to be taken [Section 13(2)]. However, if the complaint has been made with malicious intent, and the intent has been proved, action can be taken against the complainant according to service rules [Section 14 (1)]. Similar action is prescribed against false witnesses in a case.

The internal committee has powers of a civil court for trying the cases [Section 11 (3)] and has to complete the enquiry within 90 days. The committee also has powers to work out a conciliation agreement if the aggrieved party requests, without involvement of any money.

After enquiry, the committee can recommend a compensation to be paid. Under Section 16, the identity of complainant and witnesses have to be protected, and even the committee members who act against the provision can be punished (Section 17).

The employer's duty under the act has also been specified. They are bound to set up the complaints committee, organize awareness about the program, hold training programs, and build capacity of ICC members to handle the issues. In case of failure of employer to comply with the Act, they can be fined, and in extreme cases, it can lead to cancellation or non-renewal of the licence to operate.

In addition to protection under the act, working women also has support from other legislations like the Indian Penal Code and the Information Technology Act. In the event of facing an act of sexual harassment, an FIR (First Information Report) can be filed with the police.

Sexual Harassment Law in the US

Under Title VII, **sexual harassment** generally refers to harassment on the basis of sex when such conduct has the purpose or effect of substantially interfering with a person's work performance or creating an intimidating, hostile, or offensive work environment.

sexual harassment
Harassment on the basis of sex that has the purpose or effect of substantially interfering with a person's work performance or creating an intimidating, hostile, or offensive work environment.

In one recent year, the EEOC received 11,717 sexual harassment charges, about 15% of which were filed by men.[44] (The U.S. Supreme Court held, in *Oncale v. Sundowner Offshore Services Inc.,* that same-sex sexual harassment is also actionable under Title VII.[45]) One study found "women experienced more sexual harassment than men, minorities experienced more ethnic harassment than whites, and minority women experience more harassment overall than majority men, minority men, and majority women."[46]

Under EEOC guidelines, employers have an affirmative duty to maintain workplaces free of sexual harassment and intimidation. CRA 1991 permits victims of intentional discrimination, including sexual harassment, to have jury trials and to collect compensatory damages for pain and suffering and punitive damages, where the employer acted with "malice or reckless indifference" to the person's rights.[47] The **Federal Violence Against Women Act of 1994** further provides that a person "who commits a crime of violence motivated by gender and thus deprives another" of her rights shall be liable to the party injured.

Federal Violence Against Women Act of 1994
The act that provides that a person who commits a crime of violence motivated by gender shall be liable to the party injured.

WHAT IS SEXUAL HARASSMENT? EEOC guidelines define *sexual harassment* as unwelcome sexual advances, requests for sexual favors, and other verbal or physical conduct of a sexual nature that takes place under any of the following conditions:

1. Submission to such conduct is made either explicitly or implicitly a term or condition of an individual's employment.
2. Submission to or rejection of such conduct by an individual is used as the basis for employment decisions affecting such individual.
3. Such conduct has the purpose or effect of unreasonably interfering with an individual's work performance or creating an intimidating, hostile, or offensive work environment.

PROVING SEXUAL HARASSMENT   There are three main ways someone can prove sexual harassment:

1. *Quid Pro Quo.* The most direct is to prove that rejecting a supervisor's advances adversely affected what the EEOC calls a "tangible employment action," such as hiring, firing, promotion, demotion, and/or work assignment. In one case, the employee showed that continued job success and advancement were dependent on her agreeing to the sexual demands of her supervisors. "Sexual harassment" generally requires that the behavior be pervasive or severe. Thus, in one case, the court ruled that although the supervisor had touched the employee's shoulder twice as he drove her back from work and also mentioned that she "owed him" for hiring her, she did not have a trial-able sexual harassment claim.[48]
2. *Hostile Environment Created by Supervisors.* The harassment need not have tangible consequences such as demotion. For example, one court found that a male supervisor's behavior had substantially affected a female employee's emotional and psychological ability to the point that she felt she had to quit her job. Therefore, even though the supervisor made no direct threats or promises in exchange for sexual advances, his advances interfered with the woman's performance and created an offensive work environment. That was sufficient to prove sexual harassment. Courts generally do not interpret as sexual harassment sexual relationships that arise during the course of employment but that do not have a substantial effect on that employment.[49] The U.S. Supreme Court also held that sexual harassment law doesn't cover ordinary "intersexual flirtation." In his ruling, Justice Antonin Scalia said courts must carefully distinguish between "simple teasing" and truly abusive behavior.[50]
3. *Hostile Environment Created by Coworkers or Nonemployees.* Coworkers or nonemployees can trigger such suits. One U.S. court held that a mandatory sexually provocative uniform led to lewd comments by customers. When the employee refused to wear the uniform, she was fired. The employer couldn't show there was a job-related necessity for the uniform, and only female employees

wore it. The court ruled that the employer, in effect, was responsible for the sexually harassing behavior. Such abhorrent client behavior is more likely when the clients are in positions of power, and when they think no one will penalize them.[51] Employers are also liable for the sexually harassing acts of nonsupervisory employees if the employer knew or should have known of the conduct.

WHEN IS THE ENVIRONMENT "HOSTILE"? Hostile environment sexual harassment generally means the intimidation, insults, and ridicule were sufficiently severe to alter the employee's working conditions. Courts look at several things. These include whether the discriminatory conduct is *frequent or severe*; whether it is *physically threatening* or humiliating, or a mere offensive utterance; and whether it unreasonably *interferes* with an employee's work performance.[52] Courts also consider whether the employee subjectively *perceives* the work environment as being abusive. For example, did he or she welcome the conduct or immediately complain?[53]

Implications for Employers and Managers   These decisions suggest an employer can defend itself against sexual harassment liability by showing two things:

- First, it must show "that the employer exercised reasonable care to *prevent* and *correct promptly* any sexually harassing behavior."[54]
- Second, it must demonstrate that the plaintiff "unreasonably *failed to take advantage* of any preventive or corrective opportunities provided by the employer." The employee's failure to use formal reporting systems would satisfy the second component.[55]

Prudent employer steps therefore include:[56]

- Constitute an internal complaints committee (ICC) as per the provisions of the act. Take all complaints about harassment seriously.
- Issue a strong policy statement condemning such behavior. Describe the prohibited conduct, assure protection against retaliation, describe a confidential complaint process, and provide impartial investigation and corrective action.
- Take steps to prevent sexual harassment from occurring. For example, communicate to employees that the employer will not tolerate sexual harassment, and take immediate action when someone complains.
- Establish a management response system that includes an immediate reaction and investigation.
- Train supervisors and managers to increase their awareness of the issues, and discipline managers and employees involved in sexual harassment.
- Involve trade unions and other representatives in communication and awareness building activities.

WHEN THE LAW ISN'T ENOUGH   Unfortunately, two practical considerations often outdo the legal requirements. First, "Women perceive a broader range of socio-sexual behaviors (touching, for instance) as harassing."[57] In one study, about 58% of employees reported experiencing potentially harassment-type behaviors at work. Overall, about 25% found it flattering and about half viewed it as benign. But on closer examination, about four times as many men as women found the behavior flattering or benign.[58] Sexual harassment training and policies can reduce this problem.[59] A second problem is that employees often won't complain.

WHAT THE EMPLOYEE CAN DO   First, complain. Remember that courts generally look to whether *the harassed employee used the employer's reporting procedures to file a complaint promptly.* If the employer has an effectively communicated complaint procedure, use it and then cooperate in the investigation.[60] In that context, steps an employee can take include:

1. File a verbal contemporaneous complaint with the harasser and the harasser's boss, stating that the unwanted overtures should cease because the conduct is unwelcome.
2. If the unwelcome conduct does not cease, file verbal and written reports regarding the unwelcome conduct and unsuccessful efforts to get it to stop with the harasser's manager and/or the human resource director.
3. If the letters and appeals to the employer do not suffice, contact the authorities to file the necessary claim. In very serious cases, the employee can also consult a lawyer about suing the harasser.

TRENDS SHAPING HR: *DIGITAL AND SOCIAL MEDIA*

For employers, social media brings both benefits and reasons for caution. For one thing, some employees will use Facebook and other accounts to harass and bully coworkers (as with disparaging comments). Here, employers must distinguish between illegal online harassment (that applying to race, religion, national origin, age, sex/gender, genetic information, and disability discrimination) and common personality conflicts. However, at a minimum, employers should have a zero-tolerance policy on bullying.[61]

On the positive side, we'll see that social media has been a boon for staffing, for instance for finding candidates on LinkedIn or for checking out current applicants on Facebook. However, viewing an applicant's social media profile can be problematic, as it may reveal information on things like religion, race, and sexual orientation.[62] Some states forbid employers from requiring or even requesting employees' or applicants' passwords. It's therefore sensible to put in place policies restricting who can check out candidates online and how they can do it. And supervisors should think twice about doing such checking themselves. ∎

LEARNING OBJECTIVE 2-3

Illustrate two defenses you can use in the event of discriminatory practice allegations, and cite specific discriminatory personnel management practices in recruitment, selection, promotion, transfer, layoffs, and benefits.

Defenses Against Discrimination Allegations in the US

To understand how employers defend themselves against employment discrimination claims, we should first briefly review some basic legal terminology.

Discrimination law distinguishes between disparate *treatment* and disparate *impact. Disparate treatment* means intentional discrimination. Disparate treatment "exists where an employer treats an individual differently because that individual is a member of a particular race, religion, gender, or ethnic group."[63] A rule that says "we don't hire drivers over 60 years of age" exemplifies this.

Disparate impact means that "an employer engages in an employment practice or policy that has a greater adverse impact (effect) on the members of a protected group under Title VII than on other employees, regardless of intent."[64] A rule that says "employees must have college degrees to do this particular job" exemplifies this (because more white males than some minorities earn college degrees).

Disparate impact claims do not require proof of discriminatory intent. Instead, the plaintiff must show that the apparently neutral employment practice (such as requiring a college degree) creates an adverse impact—a significant disparity— between the proportion of (say) minorities in the available labor pool and the proportion you hire. Thus, disparate impact allegations require showing that the act produced an adverse impact. If it has, then the employer will probably have to defend itself (for instance, by arguing that there is a business necessity for the practice). Adverse impact "refers to the total employment process that results in a significantly higher percentage of a protected group in the candidate population being rejected for employment, placement, or promotion."[65] Then the burden of proof shifts to the employer.

adverse impact
The overall impact of employer practices that result in significantly higher percentages of members of minorities and other protected groups being rejected for employment, placement, or promotion.

The Central Role of Adverse Impact

Showing that one of the employer's employment practices or policies has an **adverse impact** therefore plays a central role in discriminatory practice allegations.[66] Under Title VII and CRA 1991, a person who believes that (1) he or she was a victim of unintentional discrimination because of an employer's practices need only (2) establish a *prima facie* case of discrimination. This means showing, for instance, that the employer's selection procedures (like requiring a college degree for the job) did have an adverse impact on the protected minority group.

So, for example, if a minority applicant feels he or she was a victim of discrimination, the person need only show that the employer's selection process resulted in an adverse impact on his or her group. (For example, if 80% of the white applicants passed the test, but only 20% of the black applicants passed, a black applicant has a *prima facie* case proving adverse impact.) Then the burden of proof shifts to the employer. It becomes the employer's task to prove that its test (or application blank or the like) is a valid predictor of performance on the job (and that it applied its selection process fairly and equitably to both minorities and nonminorities).

In practice, an applicant or employee can use one of the following five methods to show that one of an employer's procedures (such as a selection test) has an adverse impact on a protected group.

disparate rejection rates
A test for adverse impact in which it can be demonstrated that there is a discrepancy between rates of rejection of members of a protected group and of others.

DISPARATE REJECTION RATES   The **disparate rejection rate** method compares the rejection rates for a minority group and another group (usually the remaining U.S. nonminority applicants).[67]

Federal agencies use a **"4/5ths rule"** to assess disparate rejection rates: "A selection rate for any racial, ethnic, or sex group which is less than four-fifths or 80% of the rate for the group with the highest rate will generally be regarded as evidence of adverse impact, while a greater than four-fifths rate will generally not be regarded as evidence of adverse impact." For example, suppose the employer hires 60% of male applicants but only 30% of female applicants. Four-fifths of the 60% male hiring rate would be 48%. Because the female hiring rate of 30% is less than 48%, adverse impact exists as far as these federal agencies are concerned.[68]

4/5ths rule
Federal agency rule that a minority selection rate less than 80% (4/5ths) of that for the group with the highest rate is evidence of adverse impact.

THE STANDARD DEVIATION RULE   Similarly, the courts have used the *standard deviation rule* to confirm adverse impact. (The standard deviation is a statistical measure of variability. It is a measure of the dispersion of a set of data from its mean. Suppose we calculate the average height of students in your management class. In simplest terms, the standard deviation helps to describe, among other things, how wide a range there is in height between the shortest and tallest students and the class's average student height.) In selection, the standard deviation rule holds that, as a rule of thumb, the difference between the numbers of minority candidates we *would have expected* to hire and whom *we actually hired* should be less than two standard deviations.

Consider this example. Suppose 300 applicants apply for 20 openings; 80 of the applicants are women, and the other 220 are men. We use our screening processes and hire 2 females and 18 males. Did our selection process have an adverse impact? To answer this, we can compute the standard deviation:

$$SD = \sqrt{\frac{(\text{Number of minority applicants})}{(\text{Number of total applicants})} \times \frac{(\text{Number of non-minority applicants})}{(\text{Number of total applicants})} \times (\text{Number of applicants selected})}$$

In our case:

$$SD = \sqrt{\left(\frac{80}{300} \times \frac{220}{300} \times 20\right)} = \sqrt{(0.2667 \times 0.7333 \times 20)}$$

$$= \sqrt{3.911} = SD = 1.977$$

In our example, women are 26% (80/300) of the applicant pool. We should therefore *expect* to hire 26% of the 20 people hired, or about 5 women. We *actually* hired 2 women. The difference between the numbers of women we would expect to hire and whom we actually hired is 5 − 2 = 3. We can use the standard deviation rule to gauge if there is adverse (disparate) impact. In our example, the standard deviation is 1.977. Again, the standard deviation rule holds that as a rule of thumb, the difference between the numbers of minority candidates we would have expected to hire and whom we actually hired should be less than two standard deviations. Two times 1.9777 is about 4. Since the difference between the number of women we would have expected to hire (5) and actually hired (2) is 3, the results suggest that our screening did not have adverse impact on women. (Put another way, in this case, hiring just 2 rather than 5 is not a highly improbable result.)[69]

restricted policy
Another test for adverse impact, involving demonstration that an employer's hiring practices exclude a protected group, whether intentionally or not.

RESTRICTED POLICY   The **restricted policy** approach means demonstrating that the employer's policy intentionally or unintentionally excluded members of a protected group. Here the problem is usually obvious—such as policies against hiring guards less than 6 feet tall. Evidence of restricted policies such as these is enough to prove adverse impact and to expose an employer to litigation.

POPULATION COMPARISONS   This approach compares (1) the percentage of minority/protected group and white workers in the organization with (2) the percentage of the corresponding group in the labor market.

"Labor market," of course, varies with the job. For some jobs, such as secretary, it makes sense to compare the percentage of minority employees with the percentage of minorities in the surrounding community, since they will come from that community. But determining whether an employer has enough black engineers might involve determining the number available nationwide, not in the surrounding community.

Employers use *workforce analysis* to analyze the data regarding the firm's use of protected versus nonprotected employees in various job classifications. The process of comparing the percentage of minority employees in a job (or jobs) at the company with the number of similarly trained minority employees available in the relevant labor market is *utilization analysis*.

MCDONNELL-DOUGLAS TEST IN USA   Lawyers in disparate impact cases use the previous approaches (such as population comparisons) to test whether an employer's policies or actions have the effect of unintentionally screening out disproportionate numbers of women or minorities. Lawyers use the McDonnell-Douglas test for showing (intentional) disparate treatment, rather than (unintentional) disparate impact.

This test grew out of a case at the former McDonnell-Douglas Corporation. The applicant was qualified, but the employer rejected the person and continued seeking applicants. Did this show that the hiring company intentionally discriminated against the female or minority candidate?

Diversity Management

LEARNING OBJECTIVE 2-5
Discuss why diversity management is important and how to install a diversity management program.

diversity
The variety or multiplicity of demographic features that characterize a company's workforce, particularly in terms of race, sex, culture, national origin, handicap, age, and religion.

White males no longer dominate the labor force. Women and minorities will account for most labor force growth in the near future.[70] Employers today therefore often strive for diversity not just because the law says they must but due to self-interest.[71] **Diversity** means being diverse or varied and at work means having a workforce composed of two or more groups of employees with various racial, ethnic, gender, cultural, national origin, handicap, age, and religious backgrounds.[72] We introduce diversity and diversity management here, and then address them in features throughout the book.

Potential Threats to Diversity

Workforce diversity produces both benefits and problems for employers. Unmanaged, it can produce behavioral barriers that reduce cooperation. Potential problems include:

- **Stereotyping**. Here someone ascribes specific behavioral traits to individuals based on their apparent membership in a group.[73] For example, "older people can't work hard." *Prejudice* is a bias toward prejudging someone based on that person's traits, as in "we won't hire him because he's old." Some people's biases are subconscious. To check, try asking questions like, "Do I typically hire the same type of person?" and "To whom do I generally assign the best projects?"[74]
- **Discrimination** is prejudice in action. It means taking specific actions toward or against the person based on the person's group.[75] Of course, it's generally illegal to discriminate at work based on someone's age, race, gender, disability, or national origin. But in practice, discrimination may be subtle. For example, many argue that a "glass ceiling," enforced by an "old boys' network" (friendships built in places like exclusive clubs), hinders women from reaching top management.
- **Tokenism** means a company appoints a small group of women or minorities to high-profile positions, rather than more aggressively seeking full representation for that group.[76]
- **Ethnocentrism** is the tendency to view members of other social groups less favorably than one's own. Thus, in one international study, managers attributed the performance of some less to their abilities and more to help they received from others. The same managers attributed the performance of other employees not belonging to specific groups to their own abilities.[77]
- Discrimination against women goes beyond glass ceilings. Working women also confront **gender-role stereotypes**, the tendency to associate women with certain (frequently nonmanagerial) jobs.

On the other hand, diversity can be an engine of performance, as the following feature shows.

▶ IMPROVING PERFORMANCE: *HR as a Profit Center*

Diversity can actually drive higher profits. In one study, researchers examined the diversity climate in 654 stores of a large U.S. retail chain. They defined *diversity climate* as the extent to which employees in the stores said the firm promotes equal opportunity and inclusion. They found the highest sales growth in stores with the highest pro-diversity climate, and the lowest in stores where subordinates and managers reported less hospitable diversity climates.[78] Another study found racial discrimination to be related negatively to employee commitment, although organizational efforts to support diversity reduced such negative effects.[79]

More than 50 of the largest U.S. companies, including GE, Microsoft, and Walmart, recently filed briefs with the U.S. Supreme Court arguing that affirmative action produces increased sales and profits. Thus, when Merck needed halal certification for one of its medicines, it turned to its Muslim employees. They helped Merck bring the product to market faster and helped ensure its acceptance among Muslims.[80] ■

Managing Diversity

The key to deriving such benefits is properly managing diversity's potential problems. **Managing diversity** means maximizing diversity's potential benefits while minimizing the potential problems—such as prejudice—that can undermine cooperation. In practice, diversity management involves both compulsory and voluntary actions. However, compulsory actions can't guarantee cooperation. Managing diversity therefore usually relies on taking voluntary steps to encourage employees to work together productively.[81]

Typically, this starts at the top. The employer institutes a *diversity management program*. A main aim is to make employees more sensitive to and better able to adapt to individual cultural differences.

Here one writer advocates a four-step "AGEM" diversity training process: Approach, Goals, Executive commitment, and Mandatory attendance. First, determine if diversity training is the solution or if some other approach is more advisable. If training is the solution, then set measurable program goals, for instance, having training participants evaluate their units' diversity efforts. Next, make sure a high-visibility executive commits to the program. Finally, make training mandatory.[82]

To expand on this, five sets of voluntary organizational activities often constitute such company-wide diversity management programs:[83]

Provide strong leadership. Companies with exemplary reputations in managing diversity typically have CEOs who champion the cause of diversity. Leadership here means, for instance, becoming a role model for the behaviors required for the change. One study concluded that top managers who excelled at creating inclusive organizations were also those who were personally passionate about encouraging inclusion and diversity.[84]

Assess the situation. One study found that the most common tools for assessing a company's diversity include equal employment hiring and retention metrics, employee attitude surveys, management and employee evaluations, and focus groups.

Provide diversity training and education. The most common starting point for a diversity management effort is usually some type of employee education program.

Change culture and management systems. Combine education programs with other concrete steps aimed at changing the organization's culture and management systems. For example, change the performance appraisal procedure to appraise supervisors based partly on their success in reducing intergroup conflicts.

Evaluate the diversity management program. For example, do employee attitude surveys now indicate any improvement in employees' attitudes toward diversity?

McDonald's Corp. doesn't call its diversity program a "program" at all—because it says diversity management should be an ongoing effort. At McDonald's, employee attendance at the company's Intercultural Learning Lab facilitates dialogue and communication among employees.[85]

One expert helps turn high-potential special group employees into senior leaders; he says employers tend to make four mistakes when cultivating minorities for higher positions. Rather than centralizing diversity management, *they distribute diversity tasks* among various recruiting teams, while limiting their diversity departments primarily to retention and inclusiveness; the solution here is more central direction. They *focus on "inputs"* such as mentoring programs, rather than on outcomes such as the number of diversity candidates who gained promotions; goal setting is one solution. They focus on *"fixing the culture,"* which is typically a multiyear process; cultural change should be just one element of the process. Finally, they often *staff* their diversity departments with new minority employees; the solution is to rotate high-performance minority or nonminority line executives into diversity roles.[86]

The following HR as a Profit Center feature provides another example of diversity management's benefits.

▶ IMPROVING PERFORMANCE: *HR as a Profit Center*

Workforce diversity makes strategic sense. With strong top-management support, IBM created several minority task forces focusing on groups such as women and Native Americans. One effect of these teams has been internal: In the 10 or so years since forming them, IBM has boosted the number of U.S.-born ethnic minority executives by almost 2 ½ times.[87]

However, the firm's diversity program also aided IBM's strategy of expanding its markets and business results. For example, one task force decided to focus on expanding IBM's market among multicultural and women-owned businesses. It did this in part by providing "much-needed sales and service support to small and midsize businesses, a niche well populated with minority and female buyers."[88] As a direct result, this IBM market grew from $10 million to more than $300 million in revenue in just 3 years. ■

Implementing the Affirmative Action Program

Equal employment opportunity aims to ensure that anyone, regardless of race, color, disability, sex, religion, national origin, or age, has an equal opportunity based on his or her qualifications. *Affirmative action* means taking actions (in recruitment, hiring, promotions, and compensation) to eliminate the current effects of past discrimination.

EMPLOYEE RESISTANCE   Avoiding employee resistance to affirmative action programs is important. Here, studies suggest that current employees need to believe the program is fair. *Transparent selection procedures* (making it clear what selection tools and standards the company uses) help in this regard. *Communication* is also crucial. Show that the program doesn't involve preferential selection standards. Provide details on the qualifications of all new hires (both minority and nonminority). *Justifications* for the program should emphasize redressing past discrimination and the practical value of diversity, not underrepresentation.[89]

PROGRAM EVALUATION   How can one tell if the diversity initiatives are effective? Some commonsense questions can be asked:

- Are there women and minorities reporting directly to senior managers?
- Do women and minorities have a fair share of the jobs that are the traditional stepping-stones to successful careers in the company?
- Do women and minorities have equal access to international assignments?
- Is the employer taking steps that ensure that female and minority candidates will be in the company's career development pipeline?
- Are turnover rates for female and minority managers the same or lower than those for white males?
- Do employees report that they perceive positive behavior changes as a result of the diversity efforts?[90]

Reverse Discrimination

reverse discrimination
Claim that due to affirmative action quota systems, white males are discriminated against.

Reverse discrimination means discriminating against *non*minority applicants and employees. Many court cases addressed these issues, but until recently, few consistent answers emerged.

The bottom line seems to be that employers should emphasize the external recruitment and internal development of better-qualified minority and female employees, "while basing employment decisions on legitimate criteria."[91]

Chapter Review

Chapter Section Summaries

2-1. Employment-related laws (labor laws) existed in Indian before Independence. All the laws have their basis in the Indian Constitution. India has more than 150 laws related to labor, which has led to administrative inefficiency. Currently, the government is proposing consolidation of laws into four codes. In the US, several of the most important **equal employment opportunity laws became law in the period from 1964 to 1991.**

- Of these, Title VII of the 1964 Civil Rights Act was pivotal, and states that an employer cannot discriminate based on race, color, religion, sex, or national origin. This act established the Equal Employment Opportunity Commission, and covers most employees.
- Under the Equal Pay Act of 1963 (amended in 1972), it is unlawful to discriminate in pay on

the basis of sex when jobs involve equal work, skills, effort, and responsibility and are performed under similar working conditions.
- The Age Discrimination in Employment Act of 1967 made it unlawful to discriminate against employees or applicants who are between 40 and 65 years of age.

2-2. Equal employment law continues to evolve, with important **new legislation being enacted since 1990–1991**.

- Although in India, the Sexual Harassment of Women at Workplace (Prevention, Prohibition and Redressal) Act of 2013 or POSH Act and in the US, Title VII made sexual harassment at work illegal. The Federal Violence Against Women Act of 1994 provided women in the US with another way to seek relief for (violent) sexual harassment. Basically, sexual harassment refers to unwelcome sexual advances, requests for sexual favors, and other verbal or physical conduct of a sexual nature that takes place, for instance, when such conduct is made either explicitly or implicitly a term or condition of an individual's employment. Three main ways to prove sexual harassment include *quid pro quo*, hostile environment created by supervisors, and hostile environment created by coworkers who are not employees.

2-3. With an increasingly diverse workforce, **diversity management** is a key managerial skill. Managing diversity means maximizing diversity's potential benefits while minimizing the potential barriers. In one typical approach, the steps include providing strong leadership, assessing the situation, providing diversity training and education, changing the culture and management systems, and evaluating the diversity management program's results. Affirmative action generally means taking actions to eliminate the present effects of past discrimination. Many employers still pursue voluntary, good-faith effort strategies in identifying and eliminating the obstacles to hiring and promoting women and minorities, while some employers are under court-mandated requirement to do so.

Discussion Questions

2-1. What important precedents were set by the *Griggs v. Duke Power Company* case? The *Albemarle v. Moody* case?

2-2. Explain the four labor codes proposed in India.

2-3. What is sexual harassment? How can an employee prove sexual harassment?

2-4. What is the difference between disparate treatment and disparate impact?

Individual and Group Activities

2-5. Working individually or in groups, respond to these three scenarios based on what you learned in this chapter. Under what conditions (if any) do you think the following constitute sexual harassment? (a) A female manager fires a male employee because he refuses her requests for sexual favors. (b) A male manager refers to female employees as "sweetie" or "baby." (c) A female employee overhears two male employees exchanging sexually oriented jokes.

2-6. Working individually or in groups, discuss how you would set up an affirmative action program.

2-7. Working individually or in groups, write a one-page paper titled "What the Manager Should Know About Labor Laws for Effective Management?"

2-8. Explain the difference between affirmative action and equal employment opportunity.

2-9. Assume you are the manager in a small restaurant; you are responsible for hiring employees, supervising them, and recommending them for promotion. Working individually or in groups, compile a list of potentially discriminatory management practices you should avoid.

2-10. Appendices A and B at the end of this book (pages 583–600) list the knowledge someone studying for the HRCI (Appendix A) or SHRM (Appendix B) certification exam needs to have in each area of human resource management (such as in Strategic Management, and Workforce Planning). In groups of several students, do four things: (1) review Appendix A and/or B; (2) identify the material in this chapter that relates to the Appendix A and/or B required knowledge lists; (3) write four multiple-choice exam questions on this material that you believe would be suitable for inclusion in the HRCI exam and/or the SHRM exam; and, (4) if time permits, have someone from your team post your team's questions in front of the class, so that students in all teams can answer the exam questions created by the other teams.

Experiential Exercise

"While in Transit"

On February 21, 2008, the Supreme Court of India dismissed an appeal by the former Managing Director (MD) of HP GlobalSoft, the BPO arm of Hewlett Packard headquartered in Bengaluru. The appeal was made against an order of the High Court of Karnataka that held the MD responsible for violating provisions of the labor law.

The relevant law pertained to Section 25 of the Karnataka Shops and Commercial Establishments Act of 1961, which prohibited employment of women and young persons during night shifts. But an amendment to the above Act in 2002 allowed the state government to exempt IT and ITES companies, subject to certain conditions. One of the conditions was that the employers were responsible for the transport and safety of women employees who were scheduled to work in night shifts. When a woman employee of HP GlobalSoft was murdered by the driver of the vehicle under contract to the company, the MD was charged for

failing to provide security, as mandated by the law. Though the final verdict has not come in yet, if held liable by the court, the MD faces a maximum fine of ₹1,000 under Section 30 (1) of the Act.

Purpose: The purpose of this exercise is to provide practice in analyzing and applying knowledge of legislation to a real problem.

Required Understanding: Be thoroughly familiar with the material presented in this chapter.

How to Set Up the Exercise/Instructions:
- Divide the class into groups.
- Each group should develop answers to the following questions:
  2-12. Based on what you read in this chapter, on what legal basis could the employer be held responsible?

Application Case

An Accusation of Sexual Harassment in Pro Sports

The jury in a sexual harassment suit brought by a former high-ranking New York Knicks basketball team executive awarded her more than $11 million in punitive damages. Officials of Madison Square Garden (which owns the Knicks) said they would appeal the verdict. However, even if they were to win on appeal (which one University of Richmond Law School professor said was unlikely), the case still exposed the organization and its managers to a great deal of unfavorable publicity.

The federal suit pitted Anucha Browne Sanders, the Knicks' senior vice president of marketing and business operations (and former Northwestern University basketball star), against the team's owner, Madison Square Garden, and its president, Isiah Thomas. The suit charged them with sex discrimination and retaliation. Ms. Browne Sanders accused Mr. Thomas of verbally abusing and sexually harassing her over a 2-year period. She said the Garden fired her about a month after she complained to top management about the harassment. At the trial, the Garden cited numerous explanations for the dismissal, saying she had "failed to fulfill professional responsibilities." At a news conference, Browne Sanders said that Thomas "refused to stop his demeaning and repulsive behavior and the Garden refused to intercede." Mr. Thomas vigorously insisted he was innocent. According to one report of the trial, her claims of harassment and verbal abuse had little corroboration from witnesses, but neither did the Garden's claims that her performance had been subpar. After the jury decision came in, Browne Sanders's lawyers said, "This [decision] confirms what we've

been saying all along, that [Browne Sanders] was sexually abused and fired for complaining about it." The Garden's statement said, in part, "We look forward to presenting our arguments to an appeals court and believe they will agree that no sexual harassment took place."

Questions

2-16. Do you think Ms. Browne Sanders had the basis for a sexual harassment suit? Why?

2-17. From what you know of this case, do you think the jury arrived at the correct decision? If not, why not? If so, why?

2-18. Based on the few facts that you have, what steps could Garden management have taken to protect itself from liability in this matter?

2-19. Aside from the appeal, what would you do now if you were the Garden's top management?

2-20. "The allegations against Madison Square Garden in this case raise ethical questions with regard to the employer's actions." Explain whether you agree or disagree with this statement, and why.

Sources: "Jury Awards $11.6 Million to Former Executive of Pro Based on "Jury Awards $11.6 Million to Former Executive of Pro Basketball Team in Harassment Case," BNA Bulletin to Management, October 9, 2007, p. 323; Richard Sandomir, "Jury Finds Knicks and Coach Harassed a Former Executive," *New York Times*, www.nytimes.com/2007/10/03/sports/basketball/03garden.html?em&ex 1191556800&en 41d47437f805290d&ei5087%0A accessed November 30, 2007. and "Thomas Defiant in Face of Harassment Claims," espn.com accessed November 30, 2007.

Continuing Case

Carter Cleaning Company

A Question of Discrimination

One of the first problems Jennifer faced at her father's Carter Cleaning Centers concerned the inadequacies of the firm's current HR management practices and procedures.

One problem that particularly concerned her was the lack of attention to equal employment matters. Each store manager independently handled virtually all hiring; the managers had received no training regarding such fundamental matters as the types of questions they should not ask of job applicants. It was therefore not unusual for female applicants to be asked questions such as "Who's going to take care of your children while you are at work?" and for minority applicants to be asked questions about arrest records and credit histories. Nonminority applicants—three store managers were white males and three were white females—were not asked these questions, as Jennifer discerned from her interviews with the managers. Based on discussions with her father, Jennifer deduced two reasons for the laid-back attitude toward equal employment: (1) her father's lack of insight about the legal requirements and (2) the fact that, as Jack Carter put it, "Virtually all our workers are women or minority members anyway, so no one can come in here and accuse us of being discriminatory, can they?"

Jennifer decided to mull that question over, but before she could, she was faced with two serious equal rights problems. Two women in one store privately confided to her that their manager was making unwelcome sexual advances toward them. One claimed he had threatened to fire her unless she "socialized" with him after hours. And during a fact-finding trip to another store, an older gentleman—he was 73 years old—complained of the fact that although he had almost 50 years of experience, he was paid less than people half his age in the same job. Jennifer's review of the stores resulted in the following questions.

Questions

2-21. Is it true, as Jack Carter claims, that "virtually all our workers are women or minority members anyway, so no one can come in here and accuse us of being discriminatory"?

2-22. How should Jennifer and her company address the sexual harassment charges and problems?

2-23. How should she and her company address the possible problems of age discrimination?

2-24. Given the fact that each of its stores has only a handful of employees, is her company covered by equal rights legislation?

2-25. And finally, aside from the specific problems, what other personnel management matters (application forms, training, and so on) have to be reviewed given the need to bring them into compliance with equal rights laws?

Key Terms

Title VII of the 1964 Civil Rights Act, 44
Equal Employment Opportunity Commission (EEOC), 44
affirmative action, 44
Office of Federal Contract Compliance Programs (OFCCP), 44

Civil Rights Act of 1991 (CRA 1991), 44
"mixed-motive" case, 45
Americans with Disabilities Act (ADA), 45

qualified individuals, 45
sexual harassment, 48

Federal Violence Against Women Act of 1994, 49
adverse impact, 52
disparate rejection rates, 52
4/5ths rule, 52
restricted policy, 53
diversity, 53
stereotyping, 54

discrimination, 54
tokenism, 54
ethnocentrism, 54
gender-role stereotypes, 54
managing diversity, 54
reverse discrimination, 56

Endnotes

1. Michael Winerip, "Pushed Out of a Job Early," *New York Times,* December 7, 2013, pp. B1, B2.
2. T. Damu, "It's Time to Liberalize Labour Legislation", 2002; available at www.tata.com.
3. The Hans India , Understanding Labour reforms and soociated issues; 2017, September 21, www.thehansindia.com
4. C. S. Venkata Ratnam, "Labour Reforms Stuck in the Middle" *Business Manager,* September 2007, pp. 6-14.
5. Menaka Gandhi V/S Union of India, SC, All India Review,

1978, SC 597, quoted in Radhi PK (2011) Labour and Industrial Law, PHI, p 2.
6. P. N. Sinha, Indu Bala Sinha, and Seema Priyadarshini Shekar, *Industrial Relations, Trade Unions and Labour Legislation* (New Delhi:Pearson Education, 2004), p. 430.
7. Surendra Pratap (2011) Challenges in Organising BPO Workers, accessed at http://www.amrc.org.hk/node/1088 on Novermber 15, 2014
8. The official notification dated January 25, 2014 can be accessed at http://www.

bangaloreitbt.in/docs/2014/Labour-Notification-dated-25th-jan-2014.pdf accessed on Noverber 15, 2014
9. Suchit Kidiyoor (2014) http://timesofindia.indiatimes.com/city/bengaluru/Pay-techie-₹-12-5-lakh-for-sacking-her-Karnataka-labour-department-orders-US-based-firm/articleshow/45034667.cms, November 4, 2015 accessed on November 14, 2014.
10. For example, see http://eeoc.gov/eeoc/newsroom/index.cfm. As another example, in a recent conciliation agreement

between FedEx Corp. and the Department of Labor's Office of Federal Contract Compliance Programs, FedEx agreed to pay $3 million and amend its practices to settle charges that it discriminated against thousands of applicants. "FedEx to Pay $3 Million, Amend Practices to Settle OFCCP Charges of Bias in Hiring," *Bloomberg BNA Bulletin to Management,* March 27, 2012, p. 97.
11. Betsy Morris, "How Corporate America Is Betraying Women," *Fortune,* January 10, 2005, pp. 64–70.

12. Based on or quoted from International Association of Official Human Rights Agencies, *Principles of Employment Discrimination Law* (Washington, DC.). See also Bruce Feldacker, *Labor Guide to Labor Law* (Upper Saddle River, NJ: Prentice Hall, 2000); "EEOC Attorneys Highlight How Employers Can Better Their Nondiscrimination Practices," *BNA Bulletin to Management*, July 20, 2008, p. 233; and www.eeoc.gov, accessed August 4, 2013. Plaintiffs still bring equal employment claims under the Civil Rights Act of 1866. For example, in 2008 the U.S. Supreme Court held that the act prohibits retaliation against someone who complains of discrimination against others when contract rights (in this case, an employment agreement) are at stake. Charles Louderback, "U.S. Supreme Court Decisions Expand Employees' Ability to Bring Retaliation Claims," *Compensation & Benefits Review*, September/October 2008, p. 52. Employment discrimination law is a changing field, and the appropriateness of the rules, guidelines, and conclusions in this chapter may also be affected by factors unique to the employer's operation. They should be reviewed by the employer's attorney before implementation.

13. For a recent conciliation agreement, see "FedEx to Pay $3 Million, Amend Practices to Settle OFCCP Charges of Bias in Hiring," *Bloomberg BNA Bulletin to Management*, March 27, 2012, p. 97.

14. Individuals may file under the Equal Employment Act of 1972.

15. "The Employer Should Validate Hiring Tests to Withstand EEOC Scrutiny, Officials Advise," *BNA Bulletin to Management*, April 1, 2008, p. 107. President Obama's administration recently directed more funds and staffing to the OFCCP. "Restructured, Beefed Up OFCCP May Shift Policy Emphasis, Attorney Says," *BNA Bulletin to Management*, August 18, 2009, p. 257.

16. Bruce Feldacker, *Labor Guide to Labor Law* (Upper Saddle River, NJ: Prentice Hall, 2000), p. 513.

17. "The Eleventh Circuit Explains Disparate Impact, Disparate Treatment," *BNA Fair Employment Practices*, August 17, 2000, p. 102. See also Kenneth York, "Disparate Results in Adverse Impact Tests: The 4/5ths Rule and the Chi Square Test," *Public Personnel Management* 31, no. 2 (Summer 2002), pp. 253–262; and "Burden of Proof Under the Employment Non-Discrimination Act," www.civilrights.org/ lgbt/enda/burden-of-proof.html, accessed August 8, 2011.

18. We'll see that the process of filing a discrimination charge goes something like this: The plaintiff (say, a rejected applicant) demonstrates that an employment practice (such as a test) has a disparate (or "adverse") impact on a particular group. *Disparate impact* means that an employer engages in an employment practice or policy that has a greater adverse impact (effect) on the members of a protected group under Title VII than on other employees, regardless of intent. (Requiring a college degree for a job would have an adverse impact on some minority groups, for instance.) Disparate impact claims do *not* require proof of discriminatory intent. Instead, the plaintiff's burden is to show two things. First, he or she must show that a significant disparity exists between the proportion of (say) women in the available labor pool and the proportion hired. Second, he or she must show that an apparently neutral employment practice, such as word-of-mouth advertising or a requirement that the jobholder "be able to lift 100 pounds," is causing the disparity. Then, once the plaintiff fulfills his or her burden of showing such disparate impact, the *employer* has the heavier burden of proving that the challenged practice is job related. For example, the employer has to show that lifting 100 pounds is actually required for effectively performing the position in question, and that the business could not run efficiently without the requirement—that it is a business necessity.

19. Commerce Clearing House, "House and Senate Pass Civil Rights Compromise by Wide Margin," *Ideas and Trends in Personnel*, November 13, 1991, p. 179.

20. Mark Kobata, "The Civil Rights Act of 1991," *Personnel Journal*, March 1992, p. 48.

21. Again, though, if the "employer shows that it would have taken the same action even absent the discriminatory motive, the complaining employee will not be entitled to reinstatement, back pay, or damages"; www. eeoc.gov/policy/docs/caregiving. html#mixed, accessed September 24, 2011.

22. Elliot H. Shaller and Dean Rosen, "A Guide to the EEOC's Final Regulations on the Americans with Disabilities Act," *Employee Relations Law Journal* 17, no. 3 (Winter 1991–1992), pp. 405–430; and www.eeoc. gov/ada, accessed November 20, 2007.

23. "ADA: Simple Common Sense Principles," *BNA Fair Employment Practices*, June 4, 1992, p. 63; and www.eeoc.gov/ facts/ada17.html, accessed September 24, 2011.

24. Shaller and Rosen, "A Guide to the EEOC's Final Regulations," p. 408. Other specific examples include "epilepsy, diabetes, cancer, HIV infection, and bipolar disorder"; www1.eeoc.gov//laws/ regulations/adaaa_fact_sheet, accessed October 3, 2011.

25. Shaller and Rosen, "A Guide to the EEOC's Final Regulations," p. 409. Thus, one court recently held that a worker currently engaging in illegal use of drugs was "not a qualified individual with a disability" under the ADA. "Drug Addict Lacks ADA Protection, Quarter Firms," *BNA Bulletin to Management*, April 26, 2011, p. 133.

26. James McDonald Jr., "The Americans with Difficult Personalities Act," *Employee Relations Law Journal* 25, no. 4 (Spring 2000), pp. 93–107; and Betsy Bates, "Mental Health Problems Predominate in ADA Claims," *Clinical Psychiatry News*, May 2003, http://findar- ticles.com/p/articles/mi_hb4345/ is_5_31/ai_n29006702, accessed September 24, 2011. For a detailed discussion of dealing with this issue, see www.eeoc.gov/ facts/intellectual_disabilities. html, accessed September 2, 2011.

27. "EEOC Guidance on Dealing with Intellectual Disabilities," *Workforce Management*, March 2005, p. 16.

28. "Driver Fired After Seizure on Job Lacks ADA Claim," *BNA Bulletin to Management*, January 4, 2011, p. 6.

29. www.ada.gov/reg3a. html#Anchor-Appendix-52467, accessed January 23, 2009.

30. See "EEOC Guidance on Telecommuting as ADA Accommodation Discussed," *Bloomberg BNA Bulletin to Management*, October 16, 2012, p. 335.

31. Martha Frase, "An Underestimated Talent Pool," *HR Magazine*, April 2009, pp. 55–58; and Nicole LaPorte, "Hiring the Blind, While Making a Green Statement," *New York Times*, March 25, 2012, p. b3.

32. M. P. McQueen, "Workplace Disabilities Are on the Rise," *Wall Street Journal*, May 1, 2007, p. A1.

33. "No Sitting for Store Greeter," *BNA Fair Employment Practices*, December 14, 1995, p. 150. For more recent illustrative cases, see Tillinghast Licht, "Reasonable Accommodation and the ADA-Courts Draw the Line," at http://library.findlaw. com/2004/Sep/19/133574.html, accessed September 6, 2011.

34. For example, a U.S. circuit court recently found that a depressed former kidney dialysis technician could not claim ADA discrimination after the employer fired him for attendance problems. The court said he could not meet the essential job function of predictably coming to work. "Depressed Worker Lacks ADA Claim, Court Decides," *BNA Bulletin to Management*, December 18, 2007, p. 406. See also www.eeoc.gov/press/5- 10-01-b.html, accessed January 8, 2008.

35. *Toyota Motor Manufacturing of Kentucky, Inc. v. Williams*. 534 U.S. 184 (2002).

36. "Supreme Court Says Manual Task Limitation Needs Both Daily Living, Workplace Impact," *BNA Fair Employment Practices*, January 17, 2002, p. 8.

37. "EEOC Issued Its Final Regulations for ADA Amendments Act," *Workforce Management*, June 2011, p. 12.

38. "Rise in ADA Cases Calls for Focus on Accommodations, Job Descriptions," *Bloomberg BNA Bulletin to Management*, September 25, 2012, p. 310.

39. Lawrence Postol, "ADAAA Will Result in Renewed Emphasis on Reasonable Accommodations," *Society for Human Resource Management Legal Report*, January 2009, pp. 1–3.

40. Mark Lengnick-Hall et al., "Overlooked and Underutilized: People with Disabilities Are an Untapped Human Resource," *Human Resource Management* 47, no. 2 (Summer 2008), pp. 255–273.

41. Susan Wells, "Counting on Workers with Disabilities," *HR Magazine*, April 2008, p. 45.

42. Quoted or paraphrased from www.eeoc.gov/laws/types/index .cfm; www.eeoc.gov/laws/ types/religion.cfm; www.eeoc .gov/eeoc/internal_eeo/index .cfm; and www.eeoc.gov/ federal/otherprotections.cfm, all accessed May 9, 2013.

43. Melanie Trottman, "Religious Discrimination Claims on the Rise," *Wall Street Journal,* October 28, 2013, p. B1.

44. www.eeoc.gov/types/sexual_ha- rassment.html, accessed April 24, 2009; and www.eeoc.gov/ eeoc/statistics/enforcement/sex- ual_harassment.cfm, accessed October 3, 2011.

45. Richard Wiener et al., "The Fit and Implementation of Sexual Harassment Law to Workplace Evaluations," *Journal of Applied Psychology* 87, no. 4 (2002), pp. 747–764. Recently, for instance, a U.S. Court of Appeals told a male Walmart employee that he could proceed with his claim that a female supervisor had sexually harassed him. "Man's Harassment Claims Advanced," *BNA Bulletin to Management*, September 6, 2011, p. 285.

46. Jennifer Berdahl and Celia Moore, "Workplace Harassment: Double Jeopardy for Minority Women," *Journal of Applied Psychology* 91, no. 2 (2006), pp. 426–436.

47. Larry Drake and Rachel Moskowitz, "Your Rights in the Workplace," *Occupational Outlook Quarterly* (Summer 1997), pp. 19–29.

48. "EEOC: "Boss's Shoulder Touching Not Sexual Harassment," *Bloomberg BNA Bulletin to Management,* February 11, 2014, p. 45.

49. Patricia Linenberger and Timothy Keaveny, "Sexual Harassment: The Employer's Legal Obligations," *Personnel* 58 (November/December 1981), p. 64; and "Court Examines Workplace Flirtation," http://hr.blr.com/HR-news/Discrimination/Sexual-Harassment/Court-Examines-Workplace-Flirtation, accessed October 2, 2011.

50. Edward Felsenthal, "Justice's Ruling Further Defines Sexual Harassment," *Wall Street Journal,* March 5, 1998, p. B5.

51. Hilary Gettman and Michele Gelfand, "When the Customer Shouldn't Be King: Antecedents and Consequences of Sexual Harassment by Clients and Customers," *Journal of Applied Psychology* 92, no. 3 (2007), pp. 757–770.

52. See the discussion in "Examining Unwelcome Conduct in a Sexual Harassment Claim," *BNA Fair Employment Practices,* October 19, 1995, p. 124. See also Michael Zugelder et al., "An Affirmative Defense to Sexual Harassment by Managers and Supervisors: Analyzing Employer Liability and Protecting Employee Rights in the U.S.," *Employee Responsibilities and Rights* 18, no. 2 (2006), pp. 111–122.

53. Ibid.; "Examining Unwelcome Conduct in a Sexual Harassment Claim," p. 124.

54. For example, a server/bartender filed a sexual harassment claim against Chili's Bar & Grill. She claimed that her former boyfriend, also a restaurant employee, had harassed her. The court ruled that the restaurant's prompt response warranted ruling in favor of it. "Ex-Boyfriend Harassed, but Employer Acted Promptly," *BNA Bulletin to Management,* January 8, 2008, p. 14.

55. See Mindy D. Bergman et al., "The (Un)reasonableness of Reporting: Antecedents and Consequences of Reporting Sexual Harassment," *Journal of Applied Psychology* 87, no. 2 (2002), pp. 230–242. See also www.eeoc.gov/policy/docs/harassment-facts.html, accessed October 2, 2011.

56. Adapted from *Sexual Harassment Manual for Managers and Supervisors* (Riverwood, IL: CCH Incorporated, a Wolters-Kluwer Company, 1991); www.eeoc.gov/types/sexual_harassment.html, accessed May 6, 2007; and www.eeoc.gov/policy/docs/harassment-facts.html, accessed October 2, 2011.

57. Maria Rotundo et al., "A Meta-Analytic Review of Gender Differences in Perceptions of Sexual Harassment," *Journal of Applied Psychology* 86, no. 5 (2001), pp. 914–922. See also Nathan Bowling and Terry Beehr, "Workplace Harassment from the Victim's Perspective: A Theoretical Model and Meta Analysis," *Journal of Applied Psychology* 91, no. 5 (2006), pp. 998–1012.

58. Jennifer Berdahl and Karl Aquino, "Sexual Behavior at Work: Fun or Folly?" *Journal of Applied Psychology* 94, no. 1 (2009), pp. 34–47.

59. Jathan Janov, "Sexual Harassment and the Three Big Surprises," *HR Magazine* 46, no. 11 (November 2001), p. 123ff. California mandates sexual harassment prevention training for supervisors: See "California Clarifies Training Law; Employers Take Note," *BNA Bulletin to Management,* November 20, 2007, p. 375.

60. Mary Rowe, "Dealing with Sexual Harassment," *Harvard Business Review,* May–June 1981, p. 43; the quoted material goes on to say that "the employer still bears the burden of proving that the employee's failure was unreasonable. If the employee had a justifiable fear of retaliation, his or her failure to utilize the complaint process may not be unreasonable" and is quoted from www.uiowa.edu/~eod/policies/sexual-harassment-guide/employer-liablity.htm, accessed October 3, 2011.

61. "Employers Should Address Inappropriate Behavior on Social Sites," *Bloomberg BNA,* February 19, 2013, p. 62.

62. "Be Careful with Social Media When Vetting Potential Workers," *Bloomberg BNA Bulletin to Management,* June 25, 2013, p. 206.

63. John Moran, *Employment Law* (Upper Saddle River, NJ: Prentice Hall, 1997), p. 166.

64. "The Eleventh Circuit Explains Disparate Impact, Disparate Treatment," p. 102.

65. John Klinefelter and James Thompkins, "Adverse Impact in Employment Selection," *Public Personnel Management,* May/June 1976, pp. 199–204; and www.eeoc.gov/policy/docs/factemployment_procedures.html, accessed October 2, 2011.

66. Moran, *Employment Law,* p. 168.

67. Employers use several types of statistics in addressing adverse impact. (For a discussion, see Robert Gatewood and Hubert Feild, *Human Resource Selection* [Fort Worth, TX: The Dryden Press, 1994], pp. 40–42, and Jean Phillips and Stanley Gulley, *Strategic Staffing* [Upper Saddle River, NJ: Pearson, 2012], pp. 68–69.) For example, *stock statistics* might compare *at a single point in time* (1) the percentage of female engineers the company has, as a percentage of its total number of engineers, with (2) the number of trained female engineers in the labor force as a percentage of the total number of trained engineers in the labor force. Here, the question of relevant labor market is important. For example, the relevant labor market if you're hiring unskilled assemblers might be the local labor market within, say, 20 miles from your plant, whereas the relevant labor market for highly skilled engineers might well be national and possibly international. *Flow statistics* measure proportions of employees, in particular, groups at two points in time: before selection and after selection takes place. For example, when comparing the percentage of minority applicants who applied with the percentage hired, the employer is using flow statistics. An employer's company-wide minority hiring statistics may be defensible company-wide but not departmentally. The employer therefore may employ *concentration statistics* to drill down and determine the concentration of minorities versus nonminorities in particular job categories.

68. One study found that using the 4/5ths rule often resulted in false-positive ratings of adverse impact, and that incorporating tests of statistical significance could improve the accuracy of applying the 4/5ths rule. See Philip Roth, Philip Bobko, and Fred Switzer, "Modeling the Behavior of the 4/5ths Rule for Determining Adverse Impact: Reasons for Caution," *Journal of Applied Psychology* 91, no. 3 (2006), pp. 507–522.

69. The results must be realistic. In this example, hiring 2 out of 5 women suggests there is no adverse impact. But suppose we had hired only 1 woman. Then the difference between those we would be expected to hire (5) and whom we actually hired (1) would rise to 4. Hiring just one less woman might then trigger adverse impact issues, because twice the standard deviation is also about 4. However, realistically, it probably would not trigger such concerns, because with such small numbers, one

person makes such a difference. The point is that tools like the 4/5ths rule and the standard deviation rule are only rules of thumb. They do not themselves determine if the employer's screening process is discriminatory. This fact may work both for and against the employer. As the Uniform Guidelines (www.uniformguidelines.com/qandaprint.html) put it, "Regardless of the amount of difference in selection rates, unlawful discrimination may be present, and may be demonstrated through appropriate evidence...."

70. See, for example, "Diversity Is Used as Business Advantage by Three Fourths of Companies, Survey Says," *BNA Bulletin to Management,* November 7, 2006, p. 355; and Claire Armstrong et al., "The Impact of Diversity and Equality Management on Firm Performance: Beyond High Performance Work Systems," *Human Resource Management* 49, no. 6 (November–December 2010), pp. 977–998.

71. Brian O'Leary and Bart Weathington, "Beyond the Business Case for Diversity in Organizations," *Employee Responsibilities and Rights* 18, no. 4 (December 2006), pp. 283–292.

72. See, for example, Michael Carrell and Everett Mann, "Defining Work-Force Diversity in Public Sector Organizations," *Public Personnel Management* 24, no. 1 (Spring 1995), pp. 99–111; Richard Koonce, "Redefining Diversity," *Training and Development Journal,* December 2001, pp. 22–33; and Kathryn Canas and Harris Sondak, *Opportunities and Challenges of Workplace Diversity* (Upper Saddle River, NJ: Pearson, 2008), pp. 3–27. Others list race and ethnicity diversity, gender diversity, age diversity, disability diversity, sexual diversity, and cultural and national origin diversity as examples. Lynn Shore et al., "Diversity in Organizations: Where Are We Now and Where Are We Going?" *Human Resource Management Review* 19 (2009), pp. 117–133.

73. Taylor Cox Jr., *Cultural Diversity in Organizations* (San Francisco, CA: Berrett Kohler Publishers, Inc., 1993), p. 88; also see Stefanie Johnson et al., "The Strong, Sensitive Type: Effects of Gender Stereotypes and Leadership Prototypes on the Evaluation of Male and Female Leaders," *Organizational Behavior and Human Decision Processes* 106, no. 1 (May 2008), pp. 39–60.

74. "Outsmarting Our Brains: Overcoming Hidden Biases to Harness Diversity's True Potential,"

CHAPTER 2

Ernst & Young LLP, 2013; and Dana Wilkie, "Bringing Bias into the Light," *HR magazine,* December 2014, pp. 32–27.

75. Cox, *Cultural Diversity in Organizations,* p. 64.

76. Cox, *Cultural Diversity in Organizations,* pp. 179–80.

77. J. H. Greenhaus and S. Parasuraman, "Job Performance Attributions and Career Advancement Prospects: An Examination of Gender and Race Affects," *Organizational Behavior and Human Decision Processes* 55 (July 1993), pp. 273–298. Much research here focuses on how ethnocentrism prompts consumers to avoid certain products based on their country of origin. See, for example, T. S. Chan et al., "How Consumer Ethnocentrism and Animosity Impair the Economic Recovery of Emerging Markets," *Journal of Global Marketing* 23, no. 3 (July/August 2010), pp. 208–225.

78. Patrick McKay et al., "A Tale of Two Climates: Diversity Climate from Subordinates' and Managers' Perspectives and Their Role in Store Unit Sales Performance," *Personnel Psychology* 62 (2009), pp. 767–791.

79. Maria del Carmen Triana, Maria Fernandez Garcia, and Adrian Colella, "Managing Diversity: How Organizational Efforts to Support Diversity Moderate the Effects of Perceived Racial Discrimination on Affective Commitment," *Personnel Psychology* 63 (2010), pp. 817–843.

80. "Selling the Supremes on Diversity," *Bloomberg Businessweek,* October 20–October 28, 2012, p. 38.

81. As another example, leaders who facilitated high levels of power sharing within their groups helped to reduce the frequently observed positive relationship between increased diversity and increased turnover. But leaders who were inclusive of only a select few followers "may actually exacerbate the relationship between diversity and turnover" (p. 1422). Lisa Nishii and David Mayer, "Do Inclusive Leaders Help to Reduce Turnover in Diverse Groups? The Moderating Role of Leader—Member Exchange in the Diversity to Turnover Relationship," *Journal of Applied Psychology* 94, no. 6 (2009), pp. 1412–1426.

82. Faye Cocchiara et al., "A Gem for Increasing the Effectiveness of Diversity Training," *Human Resource Management* 49, no. 6 (November–December 2010), pp. 1089–1106.

83. For diversity management steps, see Cox, *Cultural Diversity in Organizations,* p. 236. See also Patricia Digh, "Creating a New Balance Sheet: The Need for Better Diversity Metrics," *Mosaics,* Society for Human Resource Management, September/October 1999, p. 1; and Richard Bucher, *Diversity Consciousness* (Upper Saddle River, NJ: Pearson Prentice Hall, 2004), pp. 109–137.

84. Boris Groysberg and Katherine Connolly, "Great Leaders Who Make the Mix Work," *Harvard Business Review,* September 2013, pp. 68–76.

85. Susan Hauser, "The Clone Danger," *Workforce Management,* April 2013, p. 40.

86. John Rice, "Why Make Diversity So Hard to Achieve?" *Harvard Business Review,* June 2012, p. 40.

87. David Thomas, "Diversity as Strategy," *Harvard Business Review,* September 2004, pp. 98–104; see also J. T. Childs Jr., "Managing Global Diversity at IBM: A Global HR Topic That Has Arrived," *Human Resource Management* 44, no. 1 (Spring 2005), pp. 73–77.

88. Ibid., p. 99.

89. David Harrison et al., "Understanding Attitudes Toward Affirmative Action Programs in Employment: Summary and Meta-Analysis of 35 Years of Research," *Journal of Applied Psychology* 91, no. 5 (2006), pp. 1013–1036.

90. Bill Leonard, "Ways to Tell If a Diversity Program Is Measuring Up," *HR Magazine,* July 2002, p. 21; and Ye Yang Zheng and Brenda White, "The Evaluation of a Diversity Program at an Academic Library," *Library Philosophy and Practice,* 2007, http://unllib.unl.edu/LPP/yang.pdf, accessed October 2, 2011.

91. Ibid., p. 560.

CHAPTER 2

3

Human Resource Management Strategy and Analysis

LEARNING OBJECTIVES

3-1 Explain with examples each of the seven steps in the strategic management process.

3-2 List with examples the main types of strategies.

3-3 Define *strategic human resource management* and give an example of strategic human resource management in practice.

3-4 Give at least five examples of HR metrics.

3-5 Give five examples of what employers can do to have high-performance systems.

3-6 Describe how you would execute a program to improve employee engagement.

When the Ritz-Carlton Company took over managing the Portman Hotel in Shanghai, China, the hotel already had a good reputation among business travelers. However, many luxury hotels were opening there. To stay competitive, the Portman's new managers decided to reposition the hotel with a new strategy, one that emphasized outstanding customer service. But they knew that improving the service would require new employee behaviors, and therefore new selection, training, and pay policies and practices. We will see what they did.

WHERE ARE WE NOW ...

The next part of this book, Part 2, turns to the nuts and bolts of human resource management, including activities like analyzing jobs and recruiting and selecting employees. Ideally, activities like these should produce the employee behaviors and competencies the firm needs to achieve its strategic goals. Therefore, the main purpose of the present chapter is to explain how managers formulate human resource strategies for their companies. We'll address the strategic management process, types of strategies, strategic human resource management, HR metrics and benchmarking, high-performance work systems, and employee engagement. We'll turn in the following chapter to how to analyze jobs and recruit employees.

The Strategic Management Process

Employers can't intelligently design their human resource policies and practices without understanding the role these policies and practices are to play in achieving their companies' strategic goals. In this chapter, we look at how managers design strategic and human resource plans, and how they evaluate the results of their plans. We start with an overview of the basic management planning process.

The Management Planning Process

The basic management planning process consists of five steps: setting objectives, making basic planning forecasts, reviewing alternative courses of action, evaluating which options are best, and then choosing and implementing your plan. A *plan* shows the course of action for getting from where you are to the goal. *Planning* is always "goal-directed" (such as, "double sales revenue to ₹16 million in fiscal year 2017").

In companies, it is traditional to view the goals from the top of the firm down to front-line employees as a chain or *hierarchy of goals*. Figure 3-1 illustrates this. At the top, the president sets long-term or "strategic" goals (such as "double sales revenue to ₹16 million in fiscal year 2017"). His or her vice presidents then set goals for their units that flow from, and make sense in terms of accomplishing, the president's goal (see Figure 3-1). Then their own subordinates set goals, and so on down the chain.[1]

Policies and procedures provide day-to-day guidance employees need to do their jobs in a manner that is consistent with the company's plans and goals. Policies set broad guidelines delineating how employees should act. For example, "It is the policy of this company to comply with all laws, regulations, and principles of ethical conduct." *Procedures* spell out what to do if a specific situation arises. For example,

> Any employee who believes this policy has been violated must report this belief to the employee's immediate supervisor. If that is not practical, the employee should file a written report with the Director of Human Resources. There is to be no retaliation in any form.[2]

Employers write their own policies and procedures, or adapt ones from existing sources (or both). For example, most employers have employee manuals listing the company's human resource policies and procedures. A Google search would produce many vendors of such policies and procedures.[3] They offer prepackaged HR policies manuals covering appraisal, compensation, equal employment compliance, and other policies and procedures.

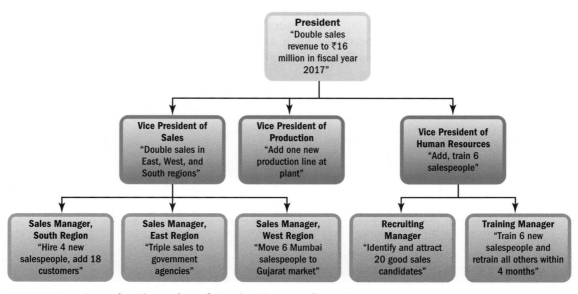

FIGURE 3-1 **Sample Hierarchy of Goals Diagram for a Company**

strategic plan
The company's plan for how it will match its internal strengths and weaknesses with external opportunities and threats in order to maintain a competitive advantage.

strategy
A course of action the company can pursue to achieve its strategic aims.

strategic management
The process of identifying and executing the organization's strategic plan by matching the company's capabilities with the demands of its environment.

What Is Strategic Planning?

As noted, the company's hierarchy or chain of goals flows from top management's overall strategic plan for the company. A **strategic plan** is the company's overall plan for how it will match its internal strengths and weaknesses with its external opportunities and threats in order to maintain a competitive position. The strategic planner asks, "Where are we now as a business, and where do we want to be?" He or she then formulates a strategic plan to help guide the company to the desired destination.[4] When Yahoo! tries to figure out whether to sell its search business to concentrate on offering more content, or when Apple branches out into selling watches, they are engaged in strategic planning.

Strategic plans are similar to but not the same as *business models*. Those investing in a business will ask top management, "What's your business model?" A business model "is a company's method for making money in the current business environment." It pinpoints whom the company serves, what products or services it provides, what differentiates it, its competitive advantage, how it provides its product or service, and, most importantly, how it makes money.[5] For example, Google doesn't make money by requiring people to pay for searches; it makes money by offering targeted paid advertisements based on what you're searching for.

A **strategy** is a course of action. Both PepsiCo and Coca-Cola face the same basic problem—people are drinking fewer sugared drinks. However, they each chose different strategies to deal with this. PepsiCo *diversified* by selling more food items like chips. Coca-Cola *concentrated* on sweet beverages, and on boosting advertising to (hopefully) boost Coke sales. Indigo Airlines makes money by offering cheaper and no-frills-attached air travel to customers by removing full-service airline benefits like free meals on board or entertainment. On the other hand, Vistara, the full-service airline, offers three-class configuration and choice of meals.

Finally, **strategic management** is the process of identifying and executing the organization's strategic plan by matching the company's capabilities (strengths and weaknesses) with the demands of its environment (its competitors, customers, and suppliers, for instance).

The Strategic Management Process

Figure 3-2 summarizes the strategic management process. Its seven steps include (1) ask, "What business are we in now?" (2) evaluate the firm's internal and external strengths, weaknesses, opportunities, and threats, (3) formulate a new business direction, (4) decide on strategic goals, and (5) choose specific strategies or courses of action. Steps (6) and (7) are to implement and then evaluate the strategic plan.

The strategic management process begins (step 1) by asking, "What business are we in?" Here the manager defines the company's current business. Specifically, "What products do we sell, where do we sell them, and how do our products or services differ from our competitors'?" For example, the Coca-Cola Company sells mostly sweetened beverages such as Coke and Sprite, while PepsiCo sells drinks but also foods such as Quaker Oats and Frito chips.

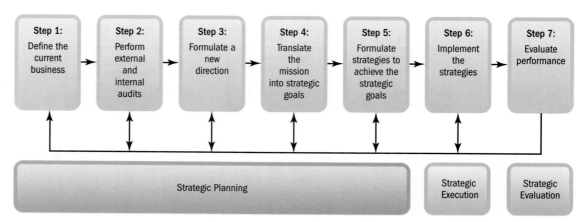

FIGURE 3-2 **The Strategic Management Process**

The second step is to ask, "*Are we in the right business* given our strengths and weaknesses and the challenges that we face?" To answer this, managers "audit" or study both the firm's environment and the firm's internal strengths and weaknesses. The *environmental scan worksheet* in Figure 3-3 is a guide for compiling information about the company's environment. As you can see, this includes the economic, competitive, and political trends that may affect the company. The *SWOT chart* in Figure 3-4 is widely used. Managers use it to compile and organize the company strengths, weaknesses, opportunities, and threats. This audit may also include analyzing the so-called PEST factors. These include Political factors such as government regulations and employment laws; Economic factors including unemployment and economic growth; Social factors such as changing demographics and health consciousness trends; and Technological factors such as use of social media and digitalization and of self-driving vehicles. In any case, the manager's aim is to create a strategic plan that makes sense in terms of the company's strengths, weaknesses, opportunities, and threats.

FIGURE 3-3 Worksheet for Environmental Scanning

Economic Trends
(such as recession, inflation, employment, monetary policies)

_____
_____
_____
_____

Competitive and Market Trends
(such as market/customer trends, entry/exit of competitors, new products from competitors)

_____
_____
_____
_____

Political Trends
(such as legislation and regulation/deregulation)

_____
_____
_____
_____

Technological Trends
(such as introduction of new production/distribution technologies, rate of product obsolescence, trends in availability of supplies and raw materials)

_____
_____
_____
_____

Social Trends
(such as demographic trends, mobility, education, evolving values)

_____
_____
_____
_____

Geographic Trends
(such as opening/closing of new markets, factors affecting current plant/office facilities location decisions)

_____
_____
_____
_____

FIGURE 3-4 **SWOT Matrix, with Generic Examples**

Potential Strengths

- Market leadership
- Strong research and development
- High-quality products
- Cost advantages
- Patents

Potential Opportunities

- New overseas markets
- Failing trade barriers
- Competitors failing
- Diversification
- Economy rebounding

Potential Weaknesses

- Large inventories
- Excess capacity for market
- Management turnover
- Weak market image
- Lack of management depth

Potential Threats

- Market saturation
- Threat of takeover
- Low-cost foreign competition
- Slower market growth
- Growing government regulation

vision statement
A general statement of the firm's intended direction; it shows, in broad terms, "what we want to become."

mission statement
Summarizes the answer to the question, "What business are we in?"

corporate-level strategy
Type of strategy that identifies the portfolio of businesses that, in total, comprise the company and the ways in which these businesses relate to each other.

LEARNING OBJECTIVE 3-2
List with examples the main types of strategies.

Next, based on this analysis (in other words, on the environmental scan, SWOT, and PEST analyses), the task in step 3 will be to decide *what should our new business be*, in terms of what we sell, where we will sell it, and how our products or services differ from competitors' products and services? Some managers express the essence of their new business with a *vision statement*. A **vision statement** is a general statement of the firm's intended direction; it shows, in broad terms, "what we want to become."[6] PepsiCo's vision is "Performance with Purpose." CEO Indra Nooyi says her company's executives choose which businesses to be in based on Performance with Purpose's focus on human sustainability, environmental sustainability, and talent sustainability.[7] For example, that vision prompted PepsiCo to add the healthy Quaker Oats and Gatorade to its lineup of products.

Whereas the vision statement describes in broad terms what the business should be, the company's **mission statement** summarizes what the company's main tasks are today. Several years ago, Ford adopted what was for several years a powerful Ford mission statement—making "Quality Job One."

In any case, the manager's next step (step 4) is to translate the desired new direction into *strategic goals*. At Ford, for example, what exactly did making "Quality Job One" mean for each department in terms of how they would boost quality? The answer was laid out in goals such as "no more than 1 initial defect per 10,000 cars."

Next, (step 5) the manager *chooses strategies*—courses of action—that will enable the company to achieve its strategic goals. For example, how should Ford pursue its goal of no more than 1 initial defect per 10,000 cars? Perhaps open two new high-tech plants, and put in place new, rigorous employee selection, training, and performance-appraisal procedures.

Step 6, *strategy execution,* means translating the strategies into action. This means actually hiring (or firing) people, building (or closing) plants, and adding (or eliminating) products and product lines.

Finally, in step 7, the manager *evaluates* the results of his or her planning and execution. Things don't always turn out as planned. All managers should periodically assess the progress of their strategic decisions.

Types of Strategies

In practice, managers engage in three types or levels of strategic planning, *corporate-level* strategic planning, *business unit* (or *competitive*) strategic planning, and *functional* (or *departmental*) strategic planning (see Figure 3-5, page 69).

Corporate Strategy

For any business, the corporate strategy answers the question, "What businesses will we be in?" Specifically, the **corporate-level strategy** identifies the portfolio of businesses that, in total, comprise the company and how these businesses relate to each other. For example,

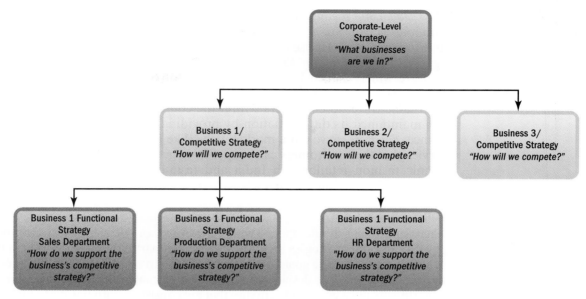

FIGURE 3-5 **Type of Strategy at Each Company Level**

with a *concentration* (single-business) corporate strategy, the company offers one product or product line, usually in one market. WD-40 Company is one example. With one spray lubricant its product scope is narrow. A *diversification* corporate strategy means the firm will expand by adding new product lines. PepsiCo is diversified. Thus, PepsiCo added Frito-Lay chips and Quaker Oats to its drinks businesses. Here product scope is wider. Similarly, milk cooperative company, Gujarat Cooperative Milk Marketing Federation Limited (GCMMF), which is the producer of popular Amul branded products, has diversified its product range. Amul has added various new products to its portfolio. Today, GCMMF sells products including milk, the famous Amul butter, chocolates, sweets, milk-based drinks, cheese, and other foods like pizza and bread. A *vertical integration* strategy means the firm expands by, perhaps, producing its own raw materials, or selling its products directly. Thus, Apple opened its own Apple stores around the world and GCMMF started Amul Parlors across India. With a *consolidation* strategy, the company reduces its size. With *geographic expansion*, the company grows by entering new territorial markets, for instance, by taking the business abroad.

Competitive Strategy

On what basis will each of our businesses compete? Within a company like PepsiCo, each business unit (such as Pepsi and Frito-Lay) needs a *business-level competitive strategy.* A **competitive strategy** identifies how to build and strengthen the business unit's long-term competitive position in the marketplace.[8] It shows, for instance, how Domino's would compete with Pizza Hut or how Big Bazaar would compete with Reliance Retail.

Managers build their competitive strategies around their businesses' competitive advantages. **Competitive advantage** means any factors that allow a company to differentiate its product or service from those of its competitors to increase market share. Coca-Cola has a "secret formula" that shows how to create its famous beverage. However, competitive advantages needn't be tangible. For example, here is how a former vice president of human resources at the Toyota Motor Manufacturing facility in Georgetown, Kentucky, described the importance of human capital as a competitive advantage:

> People are behind our success. Machines don't have new ideas, solve problems, or grasp opportunities. Only people who are involved in thinking can make a difference . . . Every auto plant in the United States has basically the same machinery. But how people are utilized and involved varies widely from one company to another. The workforce gives any company its true competitive edge.[9]

Managers typically adopt one or more of three standard competitive strategies—cost leadership, differentiation, or focus—to achieve competitive advantage.

competitive strategy
A strategy that identifies how to build and strengthen the business's long-term competitive position in the marketplace.

competitive advantage
Any factors that allow an organization to differentiate its product or service from those of its competitors to increase market share.

Cost leadership means becoming the low-cost leader in an industry. Walmart is an example. Maruti Suzuki Automobiles, which produces Alto and M800 series of cars, and Indian Coffee House (ICH) chain of restaurants are examples of low-cost strategy. With d*ifferentiation,* the firm seeks to be unique in its industry along dimensions that are widely valued by buyers.[10] Thus, Volvo stresses the safety of its cars, and Papa John's stresses fresh ingredients. In India, low-cost airline Indigo, which offers affordable travel to customers within the country and to international destinations, has maintained its differentiation by providing superior service and on-time performance. *Focusers* carve out a market niche (like Bugatti cars). They offer a product or service that their customers cannot get from generalist competitors (such as Toyota). Ethnic fashion retailer Fab India and restaurant chain Soda Bottle Openerwala focus on selling ethnic Indian fashion and serving authentic Parsi cuisine, respectively.

Functional Strategy

functional strategy
A strategy that identifies the broad activities that each department will pursue in order to help the business accomplish its competitive goals.

Each department should operate within the framework of its business's competitive strategy. **Functional strategies** identify what each department must do to help the business accomplish its strategic goals. Thus, for, say, P&G to make its Oil of Olay products a top-tier brand, its product development, production, marketing, sales, and human resource departments must engage in activities that are consistent with this unit's high-quality mission. Inferior products, cheap packaging, or sloppy salespeople would not do.

Managers' Roles in Strategic Planning

Devising the company's overall strategic plan is top management's responsibility. However, few top executives formulate strategic plans without lower-level managers' input. No one knows more about the firm's competitive pressures, product and industry trends, and employee capabilities than do the company's department managers.

For example, the human resource manager is in a good position to supply "competitive intelligence"—information on competitors. Details regarding competitors' incentive plans, employee opinion surveys about customer complaints, and information about pending legislation such as labor laws are examples. Human resource managers should also be the masters of information about their own firms' employees' strengths and weaknesses.

In practice, devising the firm's overall strategic plan involves frequent discussions among and between top and lower-level managers. The top managers then use this information to hammer out their strategic plan.

EXAMPLE: IMPROVING MERGERS AND ACQUISITIONS   Mergers and acquisitions (M&A) are among the most important strategic decisions companies make. When mergers and acquisitions fail, it's often not due to financial issues but to personnel-related ones, such as employee resistance.[11] Prudent top managers therefore tap their human resource managers' input early in the merger process.

Critical human resource M&A tasks include choosing top management, communicating changes to employees, merging the firms' cultures, and retaining key talent.[12] Aon Hewitt India and other consultancies provide merger-related human resource management services. For instance, they help firms undergoing M&A related corporate transition to assess and structure their leadership teams, evaluate the effectiveness of organization and workforce, gauge compliance issues, and help make the overall move of the firm efficient as well as effective.[13]

Strategic Human Resource Management

LEARNING OBJECTIVE 3-3
Define *strategic human resource management* and give an example of strategic human resource management in practice.

The company's top managers choose overall corporate strategies, and then choose competitive strategies for each of the company's businesses. Then departmental managers within each of these businesses formulate functional strategies for their departments. Their aim should be to have functional strategies that will support the competitive strategy and the company-wide strategic aims. The marketing department would have marketing strategies. The production department would have production strategies. The human resource management ("HR") department would have *human resource management strategies.*

HR in Practice at the Hotel Paris Starting as a single hotel in a Paris suburb in 1990, the Hotel Paris is now a chain of nine hotels, with two in France, one each in London and Rome, and others in New York, Miami, Washington, Chicago, and Los Angeles. To see how managers use strategic human resource management to improve performance, see the Hotel Paris Case on pages 88–90 and answer the questions.

What Is Strategic Human Resource Management?

strategic human resource management
Formulating and executing human resource policies and practices that produce the employee competencies and behaviors the company needs to achieve its strategic aims.

Every company's human resource management policies and activities should make sense in terms of the firm's strategic aims. For example, a luxury hotel like the Taj Mahal Palace Hotel in Mumbai or ITC Grand Chola in Chennai, will have different employee selection, training, and pay policies than the Ginger Hotels. Similarly, the HR policies of Maruti Suzuki and Nexa showrooms are different, though both sell products manufactured by the same company, Maruti Suzuki India Limited (MSIL). **Strategic human resource management** means formulating and executing human resource policies and practices that produce the employee competencies and behaviors the company needs to achieve its strategic aims. The following Strategic Context feature illustrates.

▶ IMPROVING PERFORMANCE: *The Strategic Context*

Recruitment at HDFC Bank in India

HDFC Bank (estd. 1994) is a leading financial institution in India. As on June 2017, it has more than 4,700 branches across the country. Its business philosophy is based on four core values: operational excellence, customer focus, product leadership, and people. The bank is considered as an organization with progressive HR policies, while it leads on digital technology front, including introduction of India's first humanoid robot in its branches.

HDFC Bank selectively recruits talent from business schools, while keeping away from top tier schools like the Indian Institute of Managements (IIMs). IIM graduates with professional experience are recruited directly for lateral positions. Hiring is taken seriously with extensive reference checking. For senior-level leaders, the bank has entered into an agreement with Indian Institute of Management Ahmedabad (IIMA) for leadership training.

The bank's management protects its cultural uniqueness, and these factors have made it a preferred employer. Emphasis is given to employee participation in decision-making and celebration of success. At present, the bank is focusing on digitization and efficiency improvement, and aligning its processes accordingly and altering the HR architecture, including redeploying people and not hiring against positions that were vacant because of regular attrition.[14] ■

The basic idea of strategic human resource management is this: In formulating human resource management policies and activities, the manager should aim to formulate policies that produce the employee skills and behaviors that the company needs to achieve its strategic goals.

Figure 3-6 outlines this idea. First, the manager formulates *strategic plans* and goals. Next, he or she asks, "What *employee skills and behaviors* will we need to achieve these plans and goals?" And finally, he or she asks, "Specifically what recruitment, selection, training, and other *HR policies and practices* should we put in place so as to produce the required employee skills and behaviors?" Managers often refer to their specific HR policies and practices as *human resource strategies*.[15] The accompanying HR as a Profit Center feature presents another strategic human resource management example.

▶ IMPROVING PERFORMANCE: *HR As a Profit Center*

The Zappos "WOW" Way

When your strategy involves selling shoes and clothes online to people who can't try them on, you need employees who are energized and enjoy what they're doing—Zappos wants employees to deliver "WOW" through service.[16] That's why Zappos' founders knew they needed special methods for hiring, developing, and retaining employees, and that's just what they created. As their website says, "This ain't your mama's HR! Recruiting, benefits, and employee relations keep this cruise ship afloat with fun, inventive ways of getting employees motivated and educated about the Zappos Family of companies, their benefits, and the other fun stuff going on around here!"[17]

While they may not appeal to everyone, these "fun, inventive techniques" include interviewing job applicants in what looks like the set of a talk show, asking employees to submit their own designs for Steve Madden shoes, and (during Zappos' annual "Bald & Blue Day") having some employees volunteer to shave their heads or dye their hair blue.[18] And, by the way, if you're not happy working at Zappos, the company will pay you to leave—it wants no one there who doesn't truly want to be there.

Again, that may not be for everyone, but it works for Zappos. It knows that selling online successfully requires energized employees who really enjoy what they're doing. Management uses these special HR practices to cultivate the energized and fun environment that Zappos needs to execute its strategy, and judging from Zappos' success they seem to be working. ■

FIGURE 3-6 **The HR Strategy Model**

Note: This figure opens each chapter of this book and says this: The company's HR policies and practices should produce the employee competencies and behaviors that the company needs to achieve its strategic goals.

strategy map
A strategic planning tool that shows the "big picture" of how each department's performance contributes to achieving the company's overall strategic goals.

Sustainability and Strategic Human Resource Management

Today's emphasis on *sustainability* has important consequences for human resource management. *Strategic human resource management* means having human resource policies and practices that produce the employee skills and behaviors that are necessary to achieve the company's strategic goals, and these include sustainability goals.

For example, PepsiCo wants to deliver "Performance with Purpose." This means achieving financial performance while also achieving human sustainability, environmental sustainability, and talent sustainability.[19] PepsiCo's human resource managers can help the company achieve these goals.[20] For example, they can use its *workforce planning* processes to help determine how many and what sorts of environmental sustainability ("green") jobs the company will need to recruit for. They can work with top management to institute *flexible work arrangements* that help sustain the environment by reducing commuting. They can change its employee *orientation* process to include more emphasis on socializing new employees into PepsiCo's sustainability goals. They can modify its *performance appraisal* systems to measure which managers and employees are successful in reaching their individual sustainability goals. They can use *incentive systems* that motivate employees to achieve PepsiCo's sustainability goals.[21] The bottom line is that HR policies and practices can support a firm's sustainability strategy and goals.

Strategic Human Resource Management Tools

Managers use several tools to translate the company's strategic goals into human resource management policies and practices. These tools include the strategy map, the HR scorecard, and the digital dashboard.

STRATEGY MAP The **strategy map** summarizes how each department's performance contributes to achieving the company's overall strategic goals. It helps the manager and each employee visualize and understand the role his or her department plays in achieving the company's strategic plan. Management gurus sometimes say that the map clarifies employees' "line of sight." It does this by visually linking their efforts with the company's ultimate goals.[22]

Figure 3-7 presents a strategy-map example for Southwest Airlines. The top-level target is to achieve its profitability, costs, and revenue goals. Then the strategy map shows the chain of activities that help Southwest Airlines achieve these goals. Like Walmart, Big Bazaar Retail, Indigo Airlines, and Ginger Hotels, Southwest has a low-cost-leader strategy. So, for example, to boost revenues and profitability Southwest must fly fewer planes (to keep costs down), maintain low prices, and maintain on-time flights. In turn (further down the strategy map), on-time flights and low prices require fast turnaround. This, in turn, requires motivated ground and flight crews. The resulting strategy map helps each department understand what it needs to do to support Southwest's low-cost strategy.[23]

FIGURE 3-7 **Strategy Map for Southwest Airlines**

Source: Based on TeamCHRYSALIS.com, accessed July 2006; http://mcknightkaney.com/Strategy_Maps_Primer.html; www.strategymap.com.au/home/StrategyMapOverview.html.

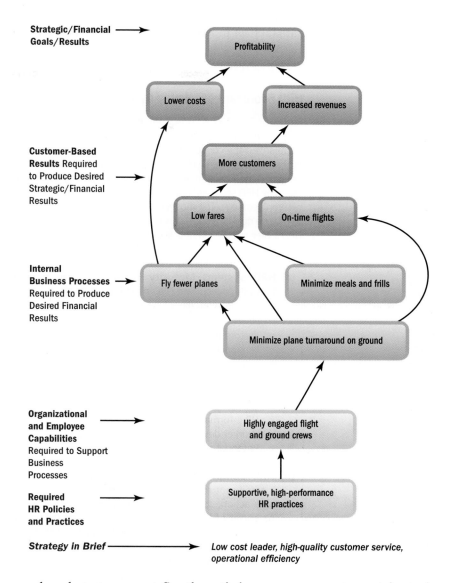

For example, what steps must Southwest's human resource team take to boost the motivation and dedication of its ground crews? A similar strategy map can be drawn for Indian low-cost airline, Indigo, and the full-service airline, Vistara. We will find that the strategy map will be different in both the cases.

HR scorecard

A process for assigning financial and nonfinancial goals or metrics to the human resource management–related chain of activities required for achieving the company's strategic aims and for monitoring results.

THE HR SCORECARD   Many employers quantify and computerize the strategy map's activities. The HR scorecard helps them to do so. The **HR scorecard** is not a scorecard. It refers to a process for assigning financial and nonfinancial goals or metrics to the human resource management–related strategy-map chain of activities required for achieving the company's strategic aims.[24] (Metrics for Southwest and Indigo or Vistara might include airplane turnaround time, percent of on-time flights, and ground crew productivity.) The idea is to take the strategy map and to quantify it.

Managers use special scorecard software to facilitate this. The computerized scorecard process helps the manager quantify the relationships between (1) the HR activities (amount of testing, training, and so forth), (2) the resulting employee behaviors (customer service, for instance), and (3) the resulting firm-wide strategic outcomes and performance (such as customer satisfaction and profitability).[25] The HR scorecard derives from the "balanced scorecard" planning approach, which aims to balance hard data such as financial measures with soft data such as customer satisfaction in assessing a company's performance.

▶ IMPROVING PERFORMANCE: HR SCORECARD

HRD Scorecard developed by TVRLS, India.

Professor T. V. Rao, a consultant and formerly an IIM Ahmedabad faculty member, introduced the concept of Human Resource Development or HRD scorecard in India. T V Rao Learning Systems (www.TVRLS.com) popularized the concept by organizing training programs and communication exercises to that effect. The author used the term HRD to signify the people-development orientation of organizations, a concept pioneered in India by him and Professor Udai Pareek, based on their work done in L&T Limited in 1974.

The HRD scorecard is an indicator of the level of HR maturity of an organization and its alignment with organization's strategy. The model is based on the assumption that competent and motivated employees are needed to provide quality products and services at competitive rates and ways that enhance customer satisfaction. In the HRD scorecard, the maturity level of HRD in a firm is measured on four dimensions on a ten-point scale (where 10 represents the highest maturity level, 5 represents a moderate maturity level, and 1 represents the least level of maturity). The four indicators, as described below, are used to arrive at a comprehensive score for HRD maturity.

(a) **HRD Systems Maturity Score:** Employee competencies and commitment can be developed through appropriate HRD mechanisms (tools and systems). In a HRD mature organization, there will be well-developed HRD systems (as listed below).
- Human resource planning and recruitment
- Performance Management Systems
- Feedback and coaching mechanisms
- Training
- Career development and succession planning
- Job-rotation
- OD Interventions
- HR Information Systems (HRIS)
- Worker development methods and systems
- Potential appraisal and development
- Other subsystems (if any)

(b) **HRD Competence Score:** HRD competencies of the HR department and the line managers play a significant role in implementing the systems and processes in ways that could ensure employee satisfaction, competence building, and customer satisfaction. For this section of scorecard, the competencies of the staff from different groups (HR department, Top Management, Line Managers and Supervisors, Trade Union Leaders, and Blue/White Collar employees) are measured. Each group is assessed on the following dimensions:
- The level of HRD skills possessed.
- Attitude and support towards learning and their own development.
- Extent to which they facilitate learning among others in the corporation and those who work with them.
- Their attitude and support to HRD function and systems.

(c) **The HRD Culture:** This measures values and processes created by the HRD tools. Employees and their styles also play a crucial role in building sustainable competencies in the organization. These efforts need to be measured and monitored. It is possible for some organizations to have minimal of formal HR systems and yet have a high level of HR competencies and HR culture. Specialized questionnaires have been developed for measuring the of HRD culture of such organizations.

(d) **Business Linkage Score:** HRD systems, competencies, and culture must be aligned with the business goals of the corporation. This score indicates the extent to which HRD efforts (tools, processes, culture, etc.) are driven to achieve business goals or goals of the organization. The business linkage goals include:
- Business excellence, including profitability, and other outcomes the organization is expected to achieve
- Internal operational efficiencies
- Internal customer satisfaction
- External customer satisfaction
- Employee motivation and commitment
- Cost effectiveness and cost consciousness among employees.
- Quality orientation
- Technology adoption

The above four indices are the four pillars of HRD maturity of any organization. All the four dimensions are scored using a ten point rating system provided on the next page.

A* Highest Score and Highest Maturity Level
A   Very High Maturity level
B* High Maturity Level
B   Moderately High Maturity Level
C* Moderate Maturity Level
C   Moderately low Maturity level
D* Low Maturity Level
D   Very low Maturity level
F   Not at all present
U   Ungraded

Trained assessors carry out the process of measurement (see Figure 3.8). Some multi-unit or locational companies have developed a pool of internal assessors who peer rate different units or locations. A comprehensive score is also prepared for the company. ∎

FIGURE 3.8 A Sample HRD Score Card

Source: Adapted from www. hrdaudit.org/hrdscorecard.htm and www.tvrls.com, accessed on 15 February 2010.

Name of the Organization		XYZ		
HRD systems Maturity Grade	HRD Competence Score	HRD Culture Grade	Business Linkage Grade	Overall HRD Maturity rating
F	D*	C	D*	FD*CD*

digital dashboard

Presents the manager with desktop graphs and charts, and so a computerized picture of where the company stands on all those metrics from the HR scorecard process.

DIGITAL DASHBOARDS   The saying "a picture is worth a thousand words" explains the purpose of the digital dashboard. A **digital dashboard** presents the manager with desktop graphs and charts, showing a computerized picture of how the company is doing on all the metrics from the HR scorecard process. As in the accompanying illustration, a top airline manager's dashboard might display real-time trends for various strategy-map activities, such as fast turnarounds and on-time flights. This enables the manager to take corrective action. For example, if ground crews are turning planes around slower today, financial results tomorrow may decline unless the manager takes action.

Figure 3-9 summarizes the three strategic planning tools.

A digital dashboard presents the manager with desktop graphs and charts, showing a computerized picture of how the company is doing on all the metrics from the HR scorecard process.

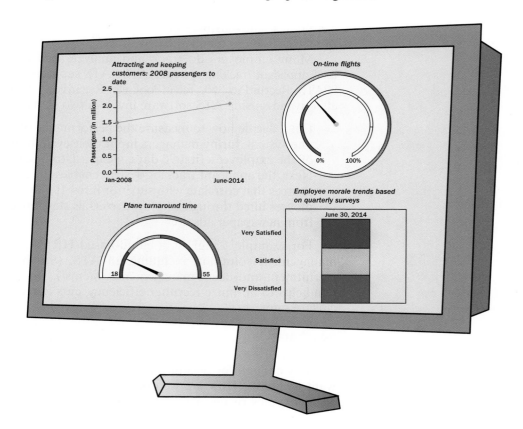

Strategy Map	HR Scorecard	Digital Dashboard
Graphical tool that summarizes the chain of activities that contribute to a company's success, and so shows employees the "big picture" of how their performance contributes to achieving the company's overall strategic goals.	A process for assigning financial and nonfinancial goals or metrics to the human resource management–related chain of activities required for achieving the company's strategic aims and for monitoring results.	Presents the manager with desktop graphs and charts, so he or she gets a picture of where the company has been and where it's going, in terms of each activity in the strategy map.

FIGURE 3-9 **Three Important Strategic HR Tools**

HR Metrics, Benchmarking, and Data Analytics

We've seen that strategic human resource management means formulating HR policies and practices that produce the employee competencies and behaviors the company needs to achieve its strategic goals. Being able to measure results is essential to this process. For example, it would have been futile for the HDFC Bank's managers to set "better customer service" as a goal if they couldn't measure customer service.[26] Relevant measures might include, for instance, hours of training per employee, productivity per employee, and (via customer surveys) customer satisfaction.

LEARNING OBJECTIVE 3-4
Give at least five examples of HR metrics.

human resource metrics
The quantitative gauge of a human resource management activity, such as employee turnover, hours of training per employee, or qualified applicants per position.

Human resource managers use many such measures (or "**human resource metrics**"). For example, there is (on average) one human resource employee per 100 company employees for firms with 100–249 employees. The HR employee-to-employee ratio drops to about 0.79 for firms with 1,000–2,499 employees and to 0.72 for firms with more than 7,500 employees.[27] Figure 3-10 illustrates other human resource management metrics. They include employee tenure, cost per hire, and annual overall turnover rate.[28]

Improving Performance Through HRIS: Tracking Applicant Metrics for Improved Talent Management

As an example of using metrics, many employers spend thousands of dollars (or more) recruiting employees without measuring which hiring source produces the best candidates. The sensible solution is to assess recruitment effectiveness using measures or metrics such as quality of new hires.[29]

Many employers do track and analyze such data with the help of computerized applicant tracking systems (ATS). ATS suppliers include Resumefox, Talent Recruit, 99ATS, RecruitPro 360, TalentPool, etc. Regardless of the vendor, analyzing recruitment effectiveness using ATS software involves two steps:

- First, decide how to measure the performance of new hires. For example, with one system, hiring managers input their evaluations of each new hire at the end of the employee's first 90 days, using a 1-to-5 scale.[30]
- Next, the applicant tracking system enables the employer to track the recruitment sources that correlate with superior hires. It may show, for instance, that new employees hired through employee referrals stay longer and work better than those from newspaper ads do.

For example, ZingHR, a cloud-based HRMS, provides recruitment and talent management solutions, including an ATS. (See https://www.zinghr.com/products/recruitment-and-talent-management-systems/). According to the company, its system helps to optimize recruiter efficiency, cuts costs, and ensures better fit as well as closure rates. ∎

Benchmarking

Just measuring how one is doing (for instance, in terms of employee productivity) is rarely enough for deciding what (if anything) to change. Instead, most managers want to know "How are we doing?" *in relation to something*. For example, are our accident rates rising or falling? Similarly, the manager may want to *benchmark* the

Organizational Data

- Revenue
- Revenue per FTE
- Net Income Before Taxes
- Net Income Before Taxes per FTE
- Positions Included Within the Organization's Succession Plan

HR Department Data

- Total HR Staff
- HR-to-Employee Ratio
- Percentage of HR Staff in Supervisory Roles
- Percentage of HR Staff in Professional/Technical Roles
- Percentage of HR Staff in Administrative Support Roles
- Reporting Structure for the Head of HR
- Types of HR Positions Organizations Expect to Hire in 2011

HR Expense Data

- HR Expenses
- HR Expense to Operating Expense Ratio
- HR Expense to FTE Ratio

Compensation Data

- Annual Salary Increase
- Salaries as a Percentage of Operating Expense
- Target Bonus for Non-Executives
- Target Bonus for Executives

Tuition/Education Data

- Maximum Reimbursement Allowed for Tuition/Education Expenses per Year
- Percentage of Employees Participating in Tuition/Education Reimbursement Programs

Employment Data

- Number of Positions Filled
- Time-to-Fill
- Cost-Per-Hire
- Employee Tenure
- Annual Overall Turnover Rate
- Annual Voluntary Turnover Rate
- Annual Involuntary Turnover Rate

Expectations for Revenue and Organizational Hiring

- Percentage of Organizations Expecting Changes in Revenue in 2011 Compared to 2010
- Percentage of Organizations Expecting Changes in Hiring in 2011 Compared to 2010

Metrics for More Profitable Organizations

- Total HR Staff
- HR-to-Employee Ratio
- HR Expenses
- HR Expense to Operating Expense Ratio
- HR Expense to FTE Ratio
- Annual Salary Increase
- Target Bonus for Non-Executives
- Target Bonus for Executives
- Maximum Reimbursement Allowed for Tuition/Education Expenses per year
- Percentage of Employees Participating in Tuition/Education Reimbursement Programs
- Time-to-Fill
- Cost-Per-Hire
- Annual Overall Turnover Rate

FIGURE 3-10 **Metrics for the SHRM® 2011–2012 Customized Human Capital Benchmarking Report**

Source: Reprinted with permission from the Society for Human Resource Management. All rights reserved.

results—compare high-performing companies' results to your own, to understand what makes them better.[31]

In the US, the Society for Human Resource Management's (SHRM's) benchmarking service enables employers to compare their own HR metrics with those of other companies. The employer can request comparable (benchmark) figures not just by industry, but by employer size, company revenue, and geographic region. (See http://shrm.org/research/benchmarks/.) Such a comparison system is yet to be freely available in India. Recently, the Department of Public Enterprises under the government of India initiated plans to create a database of best HRM practices in the central public sector undertakings (PSUs).

Figure 3-11 illustrates one of the SHRM's many sets of comparable benchmark measures. It shows how much employers are spending for tuition reimbursement programs.

Strategy and Strategy-Based Metrics

Benchmarking provides one perspective on how your company's human resource management system is performing.[32] It shows how your human resource management system's performance compares to the competition. However, it may *not* reveal the extent to which your firm's HR practices are supporting its strategic goals. For example, if the strategy calls for doubling profits by improving customer service, to what extent are our new training practices helping to improve customer service?

FIGURE 3-11 **SHRM Customized Human Capital Benchmarking Report**

Source: "HR Expense Data," from *SHRM Customized Human Capital Benchmarking Report.* Reprinted with permission from the Society for Human Resource Management. All rights reserved. www.shrm.org/Research/benchmarks/Documents/sample_humnba_capital_report.pdf.

Tuition/Education Data					
	n	25th Percentile	Median	75th Percentile	Average
Maximum reimbursement allowed for tuition/education expenses per year	32	$1,000	$5,000	$7,500	$6,000
Percentage of employees participating in tuition/education reimbursement programs	32	1.0%	3.0%	5.0%	4.0%

strategy-based metrics
Metrics that specifically focus on measuring the activities that contribute to achieving a company's strategic aims.

HR audit
An analysis by which an organization measures where it currently stands and determines what it has to accomplish to improve its HR functions.

Managers use *strategy-based metrics* to answer such questions. **Strategy-based metrics** measure the activities that contribute to achieving a company's strategic aims.[33] Thus, for the Taj Hotels, the strategic HR metrics might include 100% employee testing, 80% guest returns, incentive pay as a percent of total salaries, and sales up 50%. If changes in HR practices such as increased training have their intended effects, then strategic metrics like guest returns should also rise.

What Are HR Audits?

Human resource managers often collect data on matters like employee turnover and safety via *human resource audits.* One practitioner calls an **HR audit** "an analysis by which an organization measures where it currently stands and determines what it has to accomplish to improve its HR function."[34] The HR audit generally involves using a checklist to review the company's human resource functions (recruiting, testing, training, and so on), as well as ensuring that the firm is adhering to regulations, laws, and company policies. The HR auditor may first review payroll data, focusing on what and when each employee was paid. He or she will then turn to whether the human resource records are in order (for instance, are medical records kept separate from résumés?). He or she will also review the employer's handbooks and policies, for instance, checking for disability accommodation policies, social media policies, and family and medical leave policies.[35] He or she may also want to benchmark the results to comparable companies'.

HR audits vary in scope. Typical areas audited include:[36]

1. Roles and headcount (including job descriptions, and employees categorized by executives/workmen/trainees and full- or part-time)
2. Compliance with central, state, and local employment-related legislation
3. Recruitment and selection (including use of selection tools, background checks, and so on)
4. Compensation (policies, incentives, survey procedures, and so on)
5. Employee relations (union agreements, performance management, disciplinary procedures, employee recognition)
6. Mandated benefits (Social Security, unemployment insurance, workers' compensation, and so on)
7. Group benefits (insurance, time off, flexible benefits, and so on)
8. Payroll management
9. Documentation and record keeping. For example, do our files include résumés and applications, offer letters, job descriptions, performance evaluations, benefit enrollment forms, payroll change notices, and documentation related to personnel actions such as employee handbook acknowledgments?[37]
10. Training and development (new employee orientation, development, technical and safety, career planning, and so on)
11. Employee communications (employee handbook, newsletter, recognition programs)
12. Termination and transition policies and practices

▶ IMPROVING PERFORMANCE: APPLICATION OF HR AUDIT METHODOLOGY

CII HR Excellence Model

Confederation of Indian Industry (CII) runs the annual HR Excellence Award, a program which extensively uses HR Audit as its methodology. The objective of this model is to help Indian organizations improve HRM processes and become globally competitive. Participating companies submit a detailed application document (self audit) according to the CII HR Excellence 6 Box Model criteria, with a total of 1000 points. The six criteria involved are:

- Leadership
- Human Resource Strategy
- Learning and Development
- People Wellbeing and Employee Engagement
- HRM Processes
- Business Results

The evaluation of each criterion is done based on the RADAR framework (Results, Achievement, Deployment, Assessment & Refinement), which point to not only the outcomes but the approach taken by the organization. Firms are assessed by trained peer assessors and participating organizations do not compete with each other. Based on the scores, four categories of awards are given:

- Role Model Organization
- Leadership in HR Excellence
- Significant Achievement in HR Excellence
- Strong Commitment to HR Excellence

All participating firms are provided with a detailed Assessment Report, which enables them to improve their HRM framework through gap identification, root cause analysis, and action. Some of the companies that participated in the exercise are Amara Raja Batteries, Tata Steel, J K Cements, Tech Mahindra, Cadila Healthcare Limited, JSW Steel, VS Commercial Vehicles Limited, Aditya Birla Finance Limited, etc.

Source: Csuite (2010), "Where Excellence is a Way of Life," *People Matters*, accessed on August 22, 2017 at https://www.peoplematters.in/article/c-suite/where-excellence-is-a-way-of-life-1199 and retrieved on 22 August 2017 from https://www.mycii.in/image/eventimages/eventmainimages/E000034010_HR%20Excellence%20Award%202017.pdf. ■

TRENDS SHAPING HR: *DIGITAL AND SOCIAL MEDIA*

Data like monthly labor costs are interesting but relatively useless until converted to information. Information is data presented in a form that makes it useful for making decisions. For example knowing your cost per hire is interesting. However, presenting cost-per-hire data in a way that shows whether the cost is trending up or down provides information you can use to make decisions. Yet in one study, only 10% of respondents said they use such data to analyze their workplace practices' effectiveness.[38]

But this is changing. *Data analytics* means using statistical and mathematical analysis and algorithms to find relationships and make predictions. For example, when online bookstores use algorithms to predict which books you're most likely to buy based on things like what books you've already bought and similarities between you and other groups, they are using data analytics.[39] Data analytics relies on data mining. Data mining sifts through huge amounts of employee data to identify correlations that employers then use to improve their employee-selection and other practices. *Data mining* is "the set of activities used to find new, hidden, or unexpected patterns in data."[40]

Big data is basically data analytics on steroids. The basic idea (of scientifically analyzing data to find relationships and make predictions) is the same. However, with "big data" the volume, velocity, and variety of data that are analyzed are much greater. In terms of *volume*, for example, Walmart now collects about 2.5 petabytes of data—2.5 million gigabytes—*every hour* from its customer transactions.[41] Similarly, in terms of *velocity*, all these data are being created more or less instantaneously; that means companies can use them to more quickly to adapt in real time (for instance, to who's buying what products, and therefore how to adjust online promotions). Finally, big data capitalizes on the huge *variety* of data now available. For instance, data come not just from a bank's or supermarket's transactions but from customers' mobile phones, GPS, and social networks too.

TALENT ANALYTICS   Data analytics tools like these enable employers to analyze together employee data (like employee demographics, training, and performance ratings) from traditional sources such as employee records, as well as data from new sources (like company internal social media sites, GPS tracking, and e-mail activity).[42] Employers then use *talent analytics* (data analytics applied to HR issues) to answer questions that in the past they couldn't answer, or couldn't answer as well. For example, HR software ZingHR has an inbuilt Analytics Engine, which analyzes employee performance and other data. Computer dashboards then enable its clients to answer questions such as "Are there potential turnover trends we should further analyze to head off potential problems?"[43] "What factors drive our high-performing salespeople?" And, "what sorts of people are most likely to have accidents and submit claims?"

Talent analytics can produce striking profitability results. For example, Best Buy used talent analytics to discover that a 0.1% increase in employee engagement led to a more than $100,000 rise in a Best Buy store annual operating income.[44] A study in India by an analytics company shows that the trend of using talent analytics is catching up in the country, and MNCs are ahead in this than Indian companies. However, the budget allocated by 78% of the companies were less than ₹50 lakhs.[45] Employers use talent analytics to answer several types of talent management questions.

Human Capital Facts   For example, "What are the key indicators of my organization's overall health?"

Analytical HR   For example, "Which units, departments, or individuals need attention?"

Human Capital Investment Analysis   For example, "Which actions have the greatest impact on my business?" By monitoring employee satisfaction levels, Cisco was able to improve its employee retention rate from 65% to 85%, saving the company nearly $50 million in recruitment, selection, and training costs. A Google talent analytics team analyzed data on employee backgrounds, capabilities, and performance.[46] It identified factors (such as an employee feeling underutilized) likely to lead to the employee leaving—and thus helped it reduce turnover. Microsoft identified correlations among the schools and companies its employees arrived from and the employees' subsequent performance. This helped it improve its recruitment and selection practices.[47] By gathering thousands of observations across 100 variables about managers, Google identified what traits its best managers shared, including: good coach; empowers and does not micromanage; expresses interest in and concern for team members' success and personal well-being; productive and results-oriented; good communicator; helps with career development; has a clear vision and strategy for the team; and has key technical skills the team needs.[48] ConAgra Foods uses talent analytics to discover relationships among employee demographics, training, and performance and their relationships with various performance indicators[49] ∎

Digital tools like talent analytics disrupt how HR departments do things. They require HR managers to be more scientific and analytical. And, they often shift "who does HR" *from* the human resource department *to* other departments (such as finance), and sometimes to line managers like the heads of departments.

Digital tools like these also show great promise. In one study, 82% of high-performing organizations gave human resource management leaders such analytical workforce data, compared with 33% of low-performing ones.[50]

TRENDS SHAPING HR: *SCIENCE IN TALENT MANAGEMENT*

Data analytics permits making decisions based on a measurable and objective review of the situation. Managers have a name for this. *Evidence-based human resource management* means using data, facts, analytics, scientific rigor, critical evaluation, and critically evaluated research/case studies to support human resource management proposals, decisions, practices, and conclusions.[51]

You may sense that being evidence based is similar to being scientific, and if so, you are correct. A recent *Harvard Business Review* article even argues that managers must become more scientific and "think like scientists" when making business decisions.[52]

But how can managers think like scientists? Objectivity, experimentation, and prediction are the heart of science. In gathering evidence, scientists (or managers) first need to be *objective*, or there's no way to trust their conclusions. Recently, a medical school disciplined several professors. They had failed to reveal that they were on the payroll of the drug company that supplied the drugs, the results of which the doctors were studying. Who could trust their objectivity or conclusions?

Being scientific also requires *experimentation.* An experiment is a test one sets up in such a way as to ensure that he or she understands the reasons for the results obtained. For example, in their *Harvard Business Review* article, "A Step-by-Step Guide to Smart Business Experiments," the authors argue that if you want to judge a new incentive plan's impact on corporate profits, don't start by implementing the plan with all employees. Instead, implement it with an "experimental" group (which gets the incentive plan) *and* with a "control" group (a group that does *not* get the incentive plan). Doing so will help you gauge if any performance improvement stemmed from the incentive or from some other cause (such as a new company-wide training program).[53] And, it will enable you to *predict* how changing the incentive plan will affect performance.

For managers, the point of being "scientific" is to make better decisions by forcing you to gather the facts. "Is this sales incentive plan really boosting sales?" "We've spent ₹40,000 per employee in the past five years on our tuition-refund plan; what (if anything) did we get out of it?" What's the evidence?

Successful HR managers need to be scientific today. As an example, the chemical company BASF Corp. used talent analytics to analyze data on the relationship among stress, health, and productivity in its 15,000 U.S. headquarters staff. Based on that analysis, the company instituted health programs that it calculated would more than pay for themselves in increased productivity by reducing stress.[54]

HCL Technologies used talent analytics for improving its hiring process, and to ensure that the hired candidates are made billable resources early. It deployed an intelligent neural network base to analyze data of 5 million candidates using natural language analysis and semantics. The insights collected, according to the company, resulted in better quality hires.[55] Throughout this book we will show examples of how managers use evidence to make better human resource management decisions. For example: Which recruitment source produces our best candidates? Does it pay to use this testing program? And, does our safety program really lead to fewer accidents?

High-Performance Work Systems

LEARNING OBJECTIVE 3-5
Give five examples of what employers can do to have high-performance systems.

One reason to measure, benchmark, and scientifically analyze HR practices is to promote high-performance work practices. A **high-performance work system (HPWS)** is a set of human resource management policies and practices that together produce superior employee performance.

high-performance work system (HPWS)
A set of human resource management policies and practices that promote organizational effectiveness.

What exactly are these high-performance work practices? In one recent study, researchers collected data from 359 firms before, during, and after the 2007–2009 recession. They found that firms that used more effective staffing and training outperformed competitors before, during, and after the recession.[56]

Another study looked at 17 manufacturing plants, some of which adopted high-performance work system practices. The high-performance plants paid more (median wages of $16 per hour compared with $13 per hour for all plants), trained more, used more sophisticated recruitment and hiring practices (tests and validated interviews, for instance), and used more self-managing work teams.[57] Those with the high-performance HR practices performed significantly better than did those without such practices. Service companies (such as hotels) particularly gain from such high-performance work systems and practices.[58]

Studies like these show that high-performance work systems' policies and practices do differ from less productive ones (Table 3-1). For example, high-performing companies recruit more job candidates, use more selection tests, and spend many more hours training employees. Table 3-1 illustrates three things:

First, it shows examples of *human resource metrics* such as hours of training per employee, or qualified applicants per position. (In Table 3-1, the metric for "Number of qualified applicants per position" is 37 in the high-performing companies.) Managers use these to assess their companies' performance and to compare one firm with another.[59]

Second, it illustrates *what employers must do* to have high-performance systems. For example, high-performing companies have more than four times the number of qualified applicants per job than do low performers. They also hire based on validated selection tests, and extensively train employees.

Third, Table 3-1 shows that high-performance work practices usually *aspire to encourage employee involvement and self-management.* In other words, an aim of the high-performance recruiting, screening, training, and other human resources practices is to nurture an engaged, involved, informed, empowered, and self-motivated workforce.[60]

TABLE 3-1 Examples Selected from Several Studies of How Recruitment, Selection, Training, Appraisal, Pay, and Other Practices Differ in High-Performance and Low-Performance Companies

	Lower-Performance Companies' HR Practice Averages (e.g., company performance in terms of sales/employee, innovation, and employee retention)*	Higher-Performance Companies' HR Practice Averages (e.g., company performance in terms of sales/employee, innovation, and employee retention)*
Recruitment: Average number of qualified applicants per position	8	37
Selection: Average percentage of employees hired based on a validated *selection* test	4%	30%
Training: Average number of hours of *training* for new employees	35 hours	117 hours
Appraisal: Average percentage of employees receiving a regular *performance appraisal*	41%	95%
Pay Practices: Average percentage of the workforce eligible for *incentive pay*	28%	84%
Use of Teams: Average percentage of the workforce routinely working in all teams: semiautonomous, cross-functional, or project teams	11%	42%
Self-Directed Teams: Percent of companies with *semiautonomous or autonomous* work teams	9%	70%
Operational Information Sharing: Employees receive relevant operating performance information	62%	82%
Financial Information Sharing: Employees receive relevant financial performance information	43%	66%

*Findings rounded.

Based on "Comparison of HR Practices in High-Performance and Low-Performance Companies," by B. E. Becker, et al., from *The HR Scorecard: Linking People, Strategy and Performance* (Boston: Harvard Business School Press, 2001); Barry Macy, Gerard Farias, Jean-Francois Rosa, and Curt Moore, "Built to Change: High-Performance Work Systems and Self-Directed Work Teams—A longitudinal Field Study," *Research in Organizational Change and Development,* 16, pp. 339–418, 2007; James Gathrie, Wenchuan Liu, Patrick Flood, and Sarah MacCurtain, "High Performance Work Systems, Workforce Productivity, and Innovation: A Comparison of MNCs and Indigenous Firms," The Learning, Innovation and Knowledge (LINK) Research Centre Working Paper Series, WP 04-08, 2008.

Employee Engagement Guide for Managers: Employee Engagement and Performance

Employee engagement refers to being psychologically involved in, connected to, and committed to getting one's jobs done. Engaged employees "experience a high level of connectivity with their work tasks," and work hard to accomplish their task-related goals.[61]

Employee engagement is important because it drives performance and productivity. For example, based on a Gallup survey, business units with the highest levels of employee engagement have an 83% chance of performing above the company median; those with the lowest employee engagement have only a 17% chance.[62] According to one review of the evidence, employee engagement is correlated with employees' customer service productivity, and improvements in employee engagement were associated with significant increases in sales, product quality, productivity, safety incidents at work, retention and absenteeism, and revenue growth.[63] One consulting firm estimates that a 5% increase in employee engagement correlates to a 0.7% increase in operating margins.[64] Companies with highly engaged employees are also less likely to be unionized.[65] In India, Dale Carnegie along with NHRDN conducted a survey among chief HR officers and HR executives across the country in 2014, and it found that the engagement levels of employees are high because of their relationship with supervisor, pride in the organization, and their faith and trust in the senior management. According to the report, 61% of the respondents were willing to work extra without any additional incentives. The study also found that employees in the healthcare sector to be most engaged whereas to be the least in the education sector.

The Employee Engagement Problem

The problem is that, depending on the study, only about 21–30% of employees nationally are engaged.[66] Gallup distinguishes among engaged employees "who work with passion and feel a profound connection to their company," not-engaged employees who are essentially "checked out," and actively disengaged employees. The latter "act out their unhappiness" by undermining what their engaged coworkers are accomplishing.[67] Gallup found that about 30% of employees were engaged, 50% were not engaged, and 20% were actively disengaged.

What Can Managers Do to Improve Employee Engagement?

Managers improve employee engagement by taking concrete steps to do so. We'll look more closely at how they do this in a moment, but one important activity is *providing supportive supervision.* For example, a Gallup survey found that managers who focus their support and coaching on their employees' strengths can "practically eliminate active disengagement"; conversely, "bosses from hell" kill employee engagement.[68] Other steps managers can take to foster engagement include making sure employees (1) *understand* how their departments contribute to the company's success; (2) *see how their efforts contribute* to achieving the company's goals; (3) get a *sense of accomplishment* from working at the firm;[69] and (4) are highly *involved*—as when working in self-managing teams.[70] Employers should also *hold managers responsible* for employee engagement. A study of 82 Indian companies showed that two HR practices, namely, training and rewards have strong relationship with organizational performance.[71] In Godrej Consumer Products, senior leaders connected with younger managers through Learning Cafe, which allowed for joint problem solving and team building.[72] With a large number of women in its payroll, flexible timings and extended maternity leave were introduced as engagement initiatives.

Small finance bank, Ujjivan Financial Services (earlier a microfinance company), engages employees with employee stock ownership plans (ESOPs), developmental prospects, and social impact making opportunities. Each branch has a budget of ₹50,000, and employees join customers to identify opportunities for improvement in the local area. As a result, Ujjivan has found place in India's preferred workplace listing.[73]

How to Measure Employee Engagement

Surveys are generally used to measure employee engagement. Global firms like Gallup (www.gallup.com), and Towers Watson (go to www.towerswatson.com/en-US, then click Solutions, and then Surveys) offer comprehensive employee engagement survey services. Many Indian firms approach institutions like IIMA or XLRI to conduct employee engagement surveys among their employees. However, monitoring employee engagement needn't be complicated. With about 180,000 employees worldwide, the consulting firm Accenture uses a three-part "shorthand" method it calls "say, stay, and strive." First, Accenture assesses how positively the employee speaks about the company and recommends it to others. Second, it looks at who stays with the company, and why. Third, it looks at "strive." For instance, "do employees take an active role in the overall success of the organization by moving beyond just doing tasks to going above and beyond?"[74]

The Employee Engagement Guide for Managers sections in this and the following chapters will show how managers use human resource activities to improve employee engagement.

How Kia Motors (UK) Improved Performance with an HR Strategy Aimed at Boosting Employee Engagement

Kia Motors today is a successful automobile manufacturer employing tens of thousands of employees around the world, and one famous for its 10-year warranty and for the quality and value of its products. However, Kia was not always so successful. In July 1997, Kia was under bankruptcy protection and having difficulty servicing its $10.6 billion of debt.[75] In 1998, Hyundai Motorcar Company of Korea purchased 51% of Kia. That triggered a multiyear program aimed at improving Kia's operating performance. Today, Hyundai owns about one-third of Kia Motors, although Kia is still a close-knit part of Hyundai Motor Group.

THE CHALLENGES After several years of improving operating conditions under Hyundai Motor Group, Kia (as well as most auto manufacturers around the world) ran into strong headwinds as credit tightened and consumers cut spending around 2006. Looking at the situation in 2006–2007, Kia's chairman, writing in the company's annual report said,

> In today's automobile industry, competition is so severe that even the bold at heart, if well-informed, would be hesitant to confidently predict future victors in the car market. Japanese automobile companies are unrelenting in their measures against us, while latecomers, such as China, are speeding up to catch up with us as far as they can. Stagnation and the world economic growth, coupled with exchange-rate risks and other major threats, present unfavorable economic conditions for any global player.[76]

In the face of these challenges, the chairman went on to lay out what Kia's strategy for dealing with this intense global competition would be. As he said:

> We intend to base future growth on raising our competencies as a global maker in all areas including production, sales, marketing, branding, as well as before and after servicing. We will also concentrate on our global quality management we have driven so far. We will first strengthen our basic competitiveness in terms of production costs and final products. Second, we will exclude all the unnecessary elements from the management through advanced systems to groundwork the base of stable profit making. Third, we will efficiently invest in new future businesses with our specialized R&D and global production bases.[77]

Also in 2006–2007, Kia Motor's UK subsidiary (Kia UK), which employed about 2,500 people, faced particularly dire circumstances; these included rapidly falling sales, increased financial losses, and low levels of employee engagement. Employee turnover was 31%. The direct cost to the company from the 31% turnover alone was estimated at about 600,000 British pounds (about $1 million) in 2006 (due to higher than necessary recruitment, legal, and employee dismissal costs).[78]

THE NEW HUMAN RESOURCE MANAGEMENT STRATEGY   Gary Tomlinson, Kia UK's newly appointed head of HR, believed that Kia UK's low employee engagement was probably both a cause and an effect of the unit's poor performance. In fact, a survey of Kia UK employees had identified numerous personnel issues including possibly poor morale and communications. He knew Kia UK needed a new HR strategy to address this. He also knew that this strategy should support the parent company's strategy of basing "future growth on raising our competencies as a global maker in all areas including production, sales, marketing, branding, as well as before and after servicing."

Tomlinson (with the support of Kia UK's top management) wisely decided to develop, as he put it, "an employee engagement strategy to improve employee morale and address the high levels of employee turnover."[79] In brief, the idea was that, by (1) putting in place new HR policies and practices aimed at improving employee engagement, he could (2) change Kia UK employees' behavior (improve performance and reduce turnover, for instance) and thereby (3) support the parent company's stated strategy of "raising our competencies as a global maker in all areas." The following shows what he actually did to boost employee engagement.

HOW TO EXECUTE AN EMPLOYEE ENGAGEMENT STRATEGY   Actually executing Kia UK's employee engagement HR strategy involved six steps (and these provide a roadmap for any such endeavor). First, Kia UK set *measurable objectives* for the program. These objectives included improving by at least 10% survey feedback scores for line managers' behaviors in terms of communication, the quality of appraisal feedback they gave their direct reports, the recognition of work done, and the respect between manager and employee.[80] Other objectives included reducing employee turnover employment costs (e.g., recruitment costs) by at least 10% per year.

Second, Kia UK held an extensive *leadership development* program. For example, it sent all managers for training to improve their management skills. Kia then tested the new skills with "360-degree" assessment tools (having managers' bosses, peers, and subordinates rate the managers' new leadership skills).

Third, Kia UK instituted new *employee recognition programs*. These included, for instance, giving "Outstanding Awards" to selected employees quarterly, and "Kia thank you" cards for jobs well done.[81]

Fourth, Kia UK *improved internal communications*. For example, it instituted quarterly employee briefings and more extensive use of performance appraisals, and launched a new corporate intranet called Kia Vision (this provided key business information and other useful communiqués to all employees). Based on employee feedback, Kia UK also decided, as part of the enhanced communications, to institute an *employee forum*. This consisted of one representative from each department; the forum in effect empowered and involved employees by enabling them to express opinions, suggestions, and concerns about their jobs.

Fifth, Kia instituted a new *employee development program*. This involved using the company's appraisal process to identify employees' training needs. Kia then created training plans for each employee. It based these plans on Kia's needs and on the employee's stated career aspirations.

Sixth, Kia UK made a number of changes to its *compensation and other policies*. For instance, it eliminated bonuses and substituted fixed-rate percentage-based salary increases. It also rewrote the entire employee handbook and all HR policies and procedures "to ensure they were aligned with [Kia UK's new] cultural values."[82]

THE RESULTS   The results of the new employee engagement program were impressive. Employee surveys of employee engagement and of line managers' communications and other behaviors improved markedly; employee turnover fell from 31% in 2006 to 15% in 2007, to 5% in 2008, and to below 2% by the end of 2009. Recruitment and turnover costs fell by more than 400,000 British pounds within two years, a 71% reduction.[83]

Earlier we said that *strategic human resource management* means having the HR policies and practices that will produce the employee competencies and behaviors that the company needs to achieve its strategic goals. Kia UK's employee engagement program illustrates how one company actually did this.

Chapter Review

Chapter Section Summaries

3-1. All managers' personnel and other decisions should be consistent with the goals that cascade down from the firm's overall strategic plan. Those goals form a hierarchy, starting with the president's overall strategic goals (such as double sales revenue to $16 million) and filtering down to what each individual manager needs to do in order to support that overall company goal.

 The strategic planning process's seven steps include: (1) ask, "Where are we now as a business?" (2) evaluate the firm's internal and external strengths, weaknesses, opportunities, and threats, (3) formulate a new business direction, (4) decide on strategic goals, and (5) choose specific strategies or courses of action; steps (6) and (7) are to implement and then evaluate the strategic plan.

3-2. We distinguished among **three types of strategies:** corporate, business/competitive, and functional/department strategies.

3-3. Each function or department in the business needs its own functional strategy, and **strategic human resource management** means formulating and executing human resource policies and practices that produce the employee competencies and behaviors the company needs to achieve its strategic aims. Human resource strategies are the specific human resource management policies and practices managers use to support their strategic aims. Important and popular **strategic human resource management** tools include the strategy map, the HR scorecard, and digital dashboards.

3-4. The manager will want to gather and analyze data prior to making decisions. **Human resource metrics** (quantitative measures of some human resource management activities such as employee turnover) are critical in creating high-performance human resource policies and practices.

3-5. A **high-performance work system** is a set of human resource management policies and practices that together produce superior employee performance.

3-6. Employee engagement is important because it drives performance and productivity. For example, based on a Gallup survey, business units with the highest levels of employee engagement have an 83% chance of performing above the company median; those with the lowest employee engagement have only a 17% chance.

 Actually **executing Kia UK's employee engagement HR strategy** involved six steps. These were: set *measurable objectives* for the program; provide *leadership development,* for example, send all managers for training to improve their management skills; institute new *employee recognition programs,* for instance, giving "Outstanding Awards" to selected employees quarterly; institute a new *employee development program,* for instance, using the company's appraisal process to identify employees' training needs and to create training plans for each employee; and change the *compensation* and *other policies* to ensure they are aligned with the new cultural values.

Discussion Questions

3-1. Give an example of hierarchical planning in an organization.

3-2. What is the difference between a corporate strategy and a competitive strategy? Give one example of each.

3-3. Explain why strategic planning is important to all managers.

3-4. Explain with examples each of the eight steps in the strategic management process.

3-5. Explain with examples how human resources management can be instrumental in helping a company create a competitive advantage.

3-6. Outline how you would implement an employee engagement program.

Individual and Group Activities

3-7. With three or four other students, form a strategic management group for your college or university. Your assignment is to develop the outline of a strategic plan for the college or university. This should include such things as strategic goals; and corporate, competitive, and functional strategies. In preparing your plan, make sure to show the main strengths, weaknesses, opportunities, and threats the college faces, and which prompted you to develop your particular strategic plans.

3-8. Using the Internet or library resources, review the annual reports of five companies. Bring to class examples of how those companies say they are using their HR processes to help the company achieve its strategic goals.

3-9. Interview an HR manager and write a short report on "The Strategic Roles of the HR Manager at XYZ Company."

3-10. Using the Internet or library resources, bring to class and discuss at least two examples of how companies are using an HR scorecard or Audit to help create HR systems that support the company's strategic aims. Do all managers seem to mean the same thing when they refer to HR scorecards or Audit results?? If not, how do they differ?

3-11. In teams of several students, choose a company for which you will develop an outline of a strategic HR plan. What seem to be this company's main strategic aims? What is the firm's competitive strategy? What would the strategic map for this company look like? How would you summarize your recommended strategic HR policies for this company?

3-12. Appendices A and B at the end of this book (pages 583–600) list the knowledge someone studying for the HRCI (Appendix A) or SHRM (Appendix B) certification exam needs to have in each area of human resource management (such as in Strategic Management, and Workforce Planning). In groups of several students, do four things: (1) review Appendix A and/or B; (2) identify the material in this chapter that relates to the Appendix A and/or B required knowledge lists; (3) write four multiple-choice exam questions on this material that you believe would be suitable for inclusion in the HRCI exam and/or the SHRM exam; and, (4) if time permits, have someone from your team post your team's questions in front of the class, so that students in all teams can answer the exam questions created by the other teams.

Experiential Exercise

Developing an HR Strategy for CCD

Café Coffee Day (CCD) was an early entrant into the coffee chain business in India and played a critical role in establishing coffee culture in the country. The company aspires to become the best café chain that offers great experience at affordable prices. However, with the entry of global competitors like Starbucks and Costa Coffee, and evolution of a new tea culture, CCD is facing challenge. If appropriate strategies are not developed, sales per store can decline which would affect its growth and profitability. You need to help the CEO to formulate a new direction.

Purpose: The purpose of this exercise is to give you experience in developing an HR strategy, in this case, by developing one for CCD.

Required Understanding: You should be thoroughly familiar with the material in this chapter.

How to Set Up the Exercise/Instructions: Set up groups of three or four students for this exercise. You are probably already quite familiar with what it's like to have a cup of coffee or tea in a CCD, Starbucks, or any other coffee shop, but if not, spend some time in one prior to this exercise. You may also visit some of the tea lounges in your place. Meet in groups and develop an outline for an HR strategy for CCD. Assume that for a corporate strategy, CCD will remain primarily a national chain of coffee shops. Your outline should include four basic elements: a business/competitive strategy for CCD, the workforce requirements (in terms of employee competencies and behaviors) this strategy requires, specific HR policies and the activities necessary to produce these workforce requirements, and suggestions for metrics to measure the success of the HR strategy.

Application Case

Siemens Builds a Strategy-Oriented HR System

Siemens is a 150-year-old German company, but it's not the company it was even a few years ago. Until recently, Siemens focused on producing electrical products. Today the firm has diversified into software, engineering, and services. It is also global, with more than 400,000 employees working in 190 countries. In other words, Siemens became a world leader by pursuing a corporate strategy that emphasized diversifying into high-tech products and services, and doing so on a global basis.

With a corporate strategy like that, human resource management plays a big role at Siemens. Sophisticated engineering and services require more focus on employee selection, training, and compensation than in the average firm, and globalization requires delivering these services globally. Siemens sums up the basic themes of its HR strategy in several points. These include:

1. **A living company is a learning company.** The high-tech nature of Siemens' business means that employees must be able to learn on a continuing basis. Siemens uses its system of combined classroom and hands-on apprenticeship training around the world to help facilitate this. It also offers employees extensive continuing education and management development.
2. **Global teamwork is the key to developing and using all the potential of the firm's human resources.** Because it is so important for employees throughout Siemens to feel free to work

together and interact, employees have to understand the whole Siemens process not just bits and pieces. To support this, Siemens provides extensive training and development. It also ensures that all employees feel they're part of a strong, unifying corporate identity. For example, HR uses cross-border, cross-cultural experiences as prerequisites for career advances.

3. **A climate of mutual respect is the basis of all relationships—within the company and with society.** Siemens contends that the wealth of nationalities, cultures, languages, and outlooks represented by its employees is one of its most valuable assets. It therefore engages in numerous HR activities aimed at building openness, transparency, and fairness, and supporting diversity.

Questions

3-13. Based on the information in this case, provide examples for Siemens of at least four strategically required organizational outcomes, and four required workforce competencies and behaviors.
3-14. Identify at least four strategically relevant HR policies and activities that Siemens has instituted in order to help human resource management contribute to achieving Siemens' strategic goals.
3-15. Provide a brief illustrative outline of a strategy map for Siemens.

Continuing Case

Carter Cleaning Company

The High-Performance Work System

As a person who keeps up with the business press, Jennifer Carter is familiar with the benefits of programs such as total quality management and high-performance work systems.

Jack, her father, actually installed a total quality program of sorts at Carter, and it has been in place for about 5 years. This program takes the form of employee meetings. Jack holds employee meetings periodically, but particularly when there is a serious problem in a store—such as poor-quality work or machine breakdowns. When problems like these arise, instead of trying to diagnose them himself or with Jennifer, he contacts all the employees in that store and meets with them when the store closes. Hourly employees get extra pay for these meetings. The meetings have been useful in helping Jack to identify and rectify several problems. For example, in one store all the fine white blouses were coming out looking dingy. It turned out that the cleaner/spotter

had been ignoring the company rule that required cleaning ("boiling down") the perchloroethylene cleaning fluid before washing items like these. As a result, these fine white blouses were being washed in cleaning fluid that had residue from other, earlier washes.

Jennifer now wonders whether these employee meetings should be expanded to give the employees an even bigger role in managing the Carter stores' quality. "We can't be everywhere watching everything all the time," she said to her father. "Yes, but these people only earn about $8 to $15 per hour. Will they really want to act like mini-managers?" he replied.

Questions

3-16. Would you recommend that the Carters expand their quality program? If so, specifically what form should it take?
3-17. Assume the Carters want to institute a high-performance work system as a test program in one of their stores. Write a one-page outline summarizing important HR practices you think they should focus on.

Translating Strategy into HR Policies and Practices Case*,§

*The overall map on page xxxviii of this book outlines the relationships involved.

Improving Performance at the Hotel Paris

The Hotel Paris International

Starting as a single hotel in a Paris suburb in 1990, the Hotel Paris is now a chain of nine hotels, with two in France, one each in London

and Rome, and others in New York, Miami, Washington, Chicago, and Los Angeles. As a corporate strategy, the Hotel Paris's management and owners want to continue to expand geographically. They believe doing so will let them capitalize on their reputation for good service, by providing multicity alternatives for their satisfied guests. The problem

§Written by and copyright Gary Dessler, PhD.

is, their reputation for good service has been deteriorating. If they cannot improve service, it would be unwise for them to expand, since their guests might prefer other hotels after trying the Hotel Paris.

Several things are complicating their problem. Elected in 2012, French president Francois Hollande has found it hard to halt or even slow the country's economic decline. His attempts to impose incremental tax rates of 75% on wealthy citizens prompted many to contemplate leaving France. Furthermore, many tourists—faced with similar economic challenges elsewhere—are increasingly staying at short-term rental apartments in Paris, found on the Web, (often through sites such as airbnb.com) for a fraction of what a fine hotel stay might cost.

The Strategy

Top management, with input from the HR and other managers, and with the board of directors' approval, chooses a new competitive strategy and formulates new strategic goals. It decides: "The Hotel Paris International will use superior guest services to differentiate the Hotel Paris properties, and to thereby increase the length of stays and the return rate of guests, and thus boost revenues and profitability." All Hotel Paris managers—including the director of HR services—must now formulate strategies that support this competitive strategy.

The Strategically Required Organizational Outcomes

The Hotel Paris's basic strategy is to use superior guest services to expand geographically. For HR director Lisa Cruz, reviewing the hotel's activities makes it clear that achieving the hotel's strategic aims means achieving a number of required organizational outcomes. For example, Lisa and her management colleagues must take steps that produce fewer customer complaints and more written compliments, more frequent guest returns and longer stays, and higher guest expenditures per visit.

The Strategically Relevant Workforce Competencies and Behaviors

The question facing Lisa, then, is this: What competencies and behaviors must our hotel's employees exhibit, if we are to produce required organizational outcomes such as fewer customer complaints, more compliments, and more frequent guest returns? Thinking through this question helps Lisa come up with an answer. For example, the hotel's required employee competencies and behaviors would include, "high-quality front-desk customer service," "taking calls for reservations in a friendly manner," "greeting guests at the front door," and "processing guests' room service meals efficiently." All require motivated, high-morale employees.

The Strategically Relevant HR Policies and Activities

The HR manager's task now is to identify and specify the HR policies and activities that will enable the hotel to produce these crucial workforce competencies and behaviors. For example, "high-quality front-desk customer service" is one such required behavior. From this, the HR director identifies HR activities to produce such front-desk customer service efforts. For example, she decides to *institute practices to improve the disciplinary fairness and justice in the company*, with the aim of *improving employee morale*. Her assumption is that enhanced fairness will produce higher morale and that higher morale will produce improved front-desk service.

The Strategy Map

Next, Lisa, working with the hotel's chief financial officer (CFO), outlines a strategy map for the hotel. This outlines the cause-and-effect links among the HR activities, the workforce behaviors, and the organizational outcomes (the figure on this book's Page xxxviii shows the overall map).

This map and its linkages reflect certain assumptions on Lisa's part. For example, based on experience and discussions with the firm's other managers, she formulates the following *hypothesis* about how HR affects hotel performance: Improved grievance procedures cause improved morale, which leads to improved front-desk service, which leads to increased guest returns, which leads to improved financial performance. The HR director then chooses metrics to measure each of these factors. For example, she decides to measure "improved disciplinary procedures" in terms of how many grievances employees submit each month. She measures "improved morale" in terms of "scores on our hotel's semiannual attitude survey," and measures "high-quality front-desk customer service" in terms of "customer complaints per month."

She moves on to quantifying the cause-and-effect links among these measures. For example: "Can we show top management that there is a measurable, sequential link between improved disciplinary procedures, high morale, improved front-desk service, number of guest return visits, and hotel financial performance (revenues and profits)?" If she can show such links, she has a persuasive case that shows HR's measurable contribution to the hotel's bottom-line financial performance.

In practice, the HR manager may well just rely on a largely subjective but logical argument to make the case for such cause-and-effect linkages. But ideally, she will use statistical methods such as correlation analysis to determine if measurable links exist, and (if so) what their magnitudes are. In this way, she might find, for instance, that a 10% improvement in grievance rates is associated with an almost 20% improvement in morale. Similarly, a 20% improvement in morale is associated with a 30% reduction in customer front-desk complaints. Furthermore, a 30% reduction in complaints is associated with a 20% increase in guest return visits, and a 20% increase in return rate is associated with a 6% rise in hotel revenues. It would appear that a relatively small HR effort in reducing grievances might have a big effect on this hotel's bottom-line performance!

Several things complicate this measurement process. For example, it's risky to draw cause–effect conclusions from correlation measures like these (do fewer grievances lead to higher morale, or vice versa?). Furthermore, it's rare that a single factor (such as grievance rates) will have such effects alone, so we may want to measure the effects of several HR policies and activities on morale simultaneously.

As explained in this chapter, computerization could enable Lisa to build a more comprehensive HR scorecard process, one that might handle links among dozens of cause-and-effect metrics. (Several vendors supply such scorecard software.) If not, then she will rely more on the logic and common sense underlying the strategy map to make her case.

How We Will Use the Hotel Paris Case

A Hotel Paris case in each chapter will show how Lisa, the Hotel Paris's HR director, uses that chapter's concepts and techniques to: (1) create HR policies and practices that help the Hotel Paris (2) produce the employee competencies and behaviors the company needs (3) to produce the customer service the Hotel Paris requires to achieve its strategic goals.

For example, she will endeavor to improve workforce competencies and behaviors by instituting improved recruitment processes (Chapter 5), and measure improved recruitment in terms of "number of qualified applicants per position." Similarly, she will recommend to management that they change the company's pay policies, so that the "target percentile for total compensation is in the top 25%." She could argue, based on competitors' experience, that doing so will translate into improved customer service behavior, more satisfied customers, and improved hotel performance. In practice, all the human resource management functions we discuss in this book influence employee competencies and behaviors, and thereby organizational performance.

The summary map on page xxxviii of this book outlines the overall relationships involved for the Hotel Paris.

Questions

3-18. Draw a more simplified and abbreviated strategy map for the Hotel Paris. Specifically, summarize in your own words an example of the hierarchy of links among the hotel's *HR practices*, necessary *workforce competencies* and behaviors, and required *organizational outcomes*.

3-19. Using Table 3-1 and Figure 3-10, list at least 15 metrics the Hotel Paris could use to measure its HR practices.

Key Terms

strategic plan, 66
strategy, 66
strategic management, 66
vision statement, 68
mission statement, 68

corporate-level strategy, 68
competitive strategy, 69
competitive advantage, 69
functional strategy, 70

strategic human resource
  management, 71
strategy map, 72
HR scorecard, 73
digital dashboard, 75

human resource metric, 76
strategy-based metrics, 78
HR audit, 78
high-performance work system
  (HPWS), 81

Endnotes

1. For a good discussion of aligning goals, see, for example, Eric Krell, "Change Within," *HR Magazine,* August 2011, pp. 43–50.
2. James Jenks, *The Hiring, Firing (And Everything in Between) Personnel Forms Book* (Round Lake Publishing Co., 1994).
3. Such as http://store.bizmanualz.com/Human-Resources-Policies-and-Procedures-p/abr41m.htm.
4. For perspectives on strategic planning, see, for example, Donald Sull and Kathleen Eisenhardt, "Simple Rules for a Complex World," *Harvard Business Review,* September 2012, pp. 69–75; and Martin Reeves, Claire Love, and Philipp Tillmann, "Your Strategy Needs a Strategy," *Harvard Business Review,* September 2012, pp. 76–83.
5. Thomas Wheelen and J. David Hunger, *Strategic Management and Business Policy* (Upper Saddle River, NJ: Pearson Education, 2010), pp. 142–143.
6. See, for example, Fred David, *Strategic Management* (Upper Saddle River, NJ: Prentice Hall, 2007), p. 11.
7. Tony Bingham and Pat Galagan, "Doing Good While Doing Well," *Training & Development,* June 2008, p. 33. See also www.pepsico.com/Purpose/Our-Mission-and-Values, accessed July 31, 2014.
8. Paul Nutt, "Making Strategic Choices," *Journal of Management Studies,* January 2002, pp. 67–96.
9. Commerce Clearing House, "HR Role: Maximize the Competitive Advantage of People," *Ideas and Trends in Personnel,* August 5, 1992, p. 121.
10. Michael Porter, *Competitive Strategy* (New York: The Free Press, 1980), p. 14. See also Chris Zook and James Allen, "The Great Repeatable Business Model," *Harvard Business Review,* November 2011, pp. 107–112.
11. Andy Cook, "Make Sure You Get a Prenup," *European Venture Capital Journal,* December/January 2007, p. 76, www.accessmylibrary.com/coms2/summary_0286-29140938_ITM, accessed June 29, 2009.
12. www.towersPerrin.com, accessed December 4, 2007. See also Ingmar Bjorkman, "The HR Function in Large-Scale Mergers and Acquisitions: The Case of Nordea," *Personnel Review* 35, no. 6 (2006), pp. 654–671; Elina Antila and Anne Kakkonen, "Factors Affecting the Role of HR Managers in International Mergers and Acquisitions: A Multiple Case Study," *Personnel Review* 37, no. 3 (2008), pp. 280–299; Linda Tepedino and Muriel Watkins, "Be a Master of Mergers and Acquisitions," *HR Magazine,* June 2010, pp. 53–56; and Yaakov Weber and Yitzak Fried, "Guest Editor's Note: The Role of HR Practices in Managing Culture Clash During the Post Merger Integration Process," *Human Resource Management* 50, no. 5 (September–October 2011), p. 565.
13. This is paraphrased or quoted from "HR Services, Service Offerings: Mergers, Acquisitions and Restructuring," www.towersPerrin.com, accessed December 4, 2007.
14. Accessed on September 14, 2017, at http://www.business-standard.com/article/education/applying-for-a-private-bank-job-a-brief-on-the-private-banking-jobs-117052300728_1.html; accessed on September 14, 2017, at ww.hdfcbank.com/careers; and accessed on September 14, 2017, at http://indiatoday.intoday.in/story/hdfc-bank-staff-fiscal-year-2017-employee-strength/1/935311.html.
15. Brian Hults, "Integrate HR with Operating Strategy," *HR Magazine,* October 2011, pp. 54–56. One review of strategic human resource management research in the United States concluded that "strategic human resource management researchers as a group deserve a D to F grade." Bruce Couchman, "Strategic Human Resource Management Research in the United States: A Failing Grade After 30 Years?" *Academy of Management Perspectives,* May 2012, pp. 12–34.
16. Michael Hargis and Don Bradley III, "Strategic Human Resource Management in Small and Growing Firms: Aligning Valuable Resources," *Academy of Strategic Management Journal* 10, no. 2, July 2011, pp. 105–126; http://about.zappos.com/our-unique-culture/zappos-core-values, accessed March 16, 2015.
17. "Meet the Zappos Family: Human Resources" from Zappos website. Copyright © 1999–2012 by Zappos.com, Inc. http://about.zappos.com/meet-zappos-family/zapposcom-inc/human-resources. Reprinted with permission.
18. www.weknownext.com/workplace/delivering-hr-at-zappos-hr-magazine-june-2011, accessed August 23, 2012.
19. www.pepsico.com/Purpose/Performance-with-Purpose/Goals, accessed May 5, 2014.
20. For an excellent discussion of how human resource management practices can support sustainability goals, see Dubois and Dubois, op. cit., pp. 816–818.
21. www.pepsico.com/Purpose/Performance-with-Purpose/Goals, accessed May 5, 2014.
22. Paul Buller and Glenn McEvoy, "Strategy, Human Resource Management and Performance: Sharpening Line of Sight," *Human Resource Management Review* 22 (2012), pp. 43–56.
23. Managers can use the Active-Strategy Company's

ActiveStrategy Enterprise to create and automate their strategy maps, and to access them through an iPhone or similar devices. See www.activestrategy.com/solutions/strategy_mapping.aspx, accessed March 24, 2009.

24. When focusing on HR activities, managers call this an *HR scorecard*. When applying the same process broadly to all of the company's activities, including, for example, sales, production, and finance, managers call it the "balanced scorecard process."

25. The "balanced" in *balanced scorecard* refers to a balance of goals—financial and nonfinancial.

26. See, for example, "Using HR Performance Metrics to Optimize Operations and Profits," *PR Newswire*, February 27, 2008; and "How to 'Make Over' Your HR Metrics," *HR Focus* 84, no. 9 (September 2007), p. 3.

27. SHRM Human Capital Benchmarking Study: 2007 Executive Summary.

28. For additional information on HR metrics, see, for example, Karen M. Kroll, "Repurposing Metrics for HR: HR Professionals Are Looking Through a People-Focused Lens at the CFO's Metrics on Revenue and Income per FTE," *HR Magazine* 51, no. 7 (July 2006), pp. 64–69; and http://shrm.org/metrics/library_publishedover/measurementsystemsTOC.asp, accessed February 2, 2008.

29. Connie Winkler, "Quality Check: Better Metrics Improve HR's Ability to Measure—and Manage—the Quality of Hires," *HR Magazine* 52, no. 5 (May 2007), pp. 93–94, 96, 98.

30. Ibid.

31. See, for example, "Benchmarking for Functional HR Metrics," *HR Focus* 83, no. 11 (November 2006), p. 1; and John Sullivan, "The Last Word," *Workforce Management*, November 19, 2007, p. 42. SHRM makes various metrics calculators available at www.shrm.org/TemplatesTools/Samples/Metrics/Pages/GeneralHumanResources.aspx, accessed October 6, 2012.

32. See Brian Becker and Mark Huselid, "Measuring HR? Benchmarking Is Not the Answer!" *HR Magazine* 8, no. 12 (December 2003), www.charmed.org, accessed February 2, 2008.

33. Ibid.

34. Lin Grensing-Pophal, "HR Audits: Know the Market, Land Assignments," SHRM Consultants Forum, December 2004, www.shrm.org/-hrdisciplines/consultants/Articles/Pages/CMS_010705.aspx, accessed July 7, 2010.

35. "Best Practices for a Human Resources Compliance Audit,"

Bloomberg BNA Bulletin to Management, January 21, 2014, pp. 22–24.

36. Grensing-Pophal, "HR Audits: Know the Market"; and Bill Coy, "Introduction to the Human Resources Audit," La Piana Associates, Inc., www.lapiana.org/consulting, accessed May 1, 2008.

37. Dana R. Scott, "Conducting a Human Resources Audit," *New Hampshire Business Review,* August 2007. See also Eric Krell, "Auditing Your HR Department," *HR Magazine,* September 2011, pp. 101–103.

38. "Executive Workplace Analytics," www.aon.com/human-capital-consulting/hrbpo, accessed March 19, 2013.

39. Andrew McAfee and Erik Brynjolfsson, "Big Data: The Management Revolution," *Harvard Business Review,* October 1, 2012, https://hbr.org/2012/10/big-data-the-management-revolution/ar, accessed April 4, 2015.

40. George Marakas, *Decision Support Systems* (Upper Saddle River, NJ: Prentice Hall, 2003), p. 326.

41. Ibid.

42. Josh Bersin, "Big Data in Human Resources: Talent Analytics (People Analytics) Comes of Age," February 17, 2013, http://www.forbes.com/sites/joshbersin/2013/02/17/bigdata-in-human-resources-talent-analytics-comes-of-age/ accessed June 20, 2015.

43. Ibid., p. 54. See also Cliff Stevenson, "Five Ways High Performance Organizations Use HR Analytics," www.i4cp.com/print/trendwatchers/2012/12/12/five-ways-high- performance-organizations-use-hr-analytics, accessed July 14, 2013.

44. Thomas Davenport, Jeanne Harris, and Jeremy Shapiro, "Competing on Talent Analytics," *Harvard Business Review*, October 2010, pp. 52–58.

45. Krishnan, Arun, "Cos Should Spend More on Talent Analytics," 30 March 2017, 07.30am, DNA, www.dnaindia.com, (Navigation--Money--Column), as accessed on 08 August 2017 at 3pm IST.

46. Ed Frauenheim, "Keeping Score with Analytics Software," *Workforce Management* 86, no. 10 (May 21, 2007), pp. 25–33. See also Andrew McAfee and Eric Brynjolfsson, "Big Data: The Management Revolution," *Harvard Business Review*, October 2012, pp. 61–68.

47. Steven Baker, "Data Mining Moves to Human Resources," *Bloomberg Businessweek*, March 12, 2009, www.BusinessWeek.com/magazine/, accessed April 13, 2011.

48. Howard Risher, "Investing in Managers to Improve Performance," *Compensation & Benefits Review* 45, no. 6, 2013, pp. 324–328; D. Garvin, "How Google Sold Its Engineers on Management," *Harvard Business Review* 91, no. 2 (2013), pp. 74–82.

49. Dave Zielinski, "Get Analytical," *HR Magazine,* November 2014, pp. 61–62.

50. Cliff Stevenson, "Five Ways High Performance Organizations Use HR Analytics," www.i4cp.com/print/trendwatchers/2012/12/12/five-ways-high-performance-organizations-use-hr-analytics, accessed July 14, 2013.

51. See, for example, www.personneltoday.com/blogs/hcglobal-human-capital-management/2009/02/theres-no-such-thing-as-eviden.html, accessed October 2, 2012.

52. Eric Anderson and Duncan Simester, "A Step-by-Step Guide to Smart Business Experiments," *Harvard Business Review*, March 2011, pp. 98–105.

53. Ibid.

54. Bill Roberts, "How to Put Analytics on Your Side," *HR Magazine*, October 2009, pp. 43–46.

55. Namrata Singhi, "India Companies Use Analytics Tools to Spot Talent and Trouble Startups," *The Times of India*, 11 October 2016.

56. Youngsang Kim and Robert Ployhart, "The Effects of Staffing and Training on Firm Productivity and Profit Growth Before, During, and After the Great Recession," *Journal of Applied Psychology* 99, no. 3 (2014), p. 378.

57. www.bls.gov/opub/ted/2006/may/wk2/art01.htm, accessed April 18, 2009; and "Super Human Resources Practices Result in Better Overall Performance, Report Says," *BNA Bulletin to Management*, August 26, 2004, pp. 273–274. See also Wendy Boswell, "Aligning Employees with the Organization's Strategic Objectives: Out of Line of Sight, Out of Mind," *International Journal of Human Resource Management* 17, no. 9 (September 2006), pp. 1014–1041. A study found that some employers, which the researchers called *cost minimizers*, intentionally took a lower-cost approach to human resource practices, with mixed results. See Soo Min Toh et al., "Human Resource Configurations: Investigating Fit with the Organizational Context," *Journal of Applied Psychology* 93, no. 4 (2008), pp. 864–882.

58. Samuel Aryee et al., "Impact of High Performance Work Systems on Individual—and

Branch—Level Performance: Test of a Multilevel Model of Intermediate Linkages," *Journal of Applied Psychology* 97, no. 2 (2012), pp. 287–300. See also Achim Krausert, "HRM Systems for Knowledge Workers: Differences Among Top Managers, Middle Managers, and Professional Employees," *Human Resource Management* 53, no. 1 (January–February 2014), pp. 67–87.

59. See, for example, www.halogensoftware.com/blog/are-you-using-hr-analytics-and-metrics-effectively, accessed August 27, 2014.

60. See, for example, J. G. Messersmith, "Unlocking the Black Box: Exploring the Link Between High-Performance Work Systems and Performance," *Human Resource Management International Digest* 20, no. 3 (2012), pp. 1118–1132.

61. Michael Christian, Adela Garza, and Jerel Slaughter, "Work Engagement: A Quantitative Review and Test of Its Relations with Task and Contextual Performance," *Personnel Psychology* 60, no. 4 (2011), pp. 89–136.

62. Adrienne Fox, "Raising Engagement," *HR Magazine*, May 2010, pp. 35–40. See also www.gallup.com/strategicconsulting/163007/state-american-work place.aspx.

63. Kevin Kruse, "Why Employee Engagement? (These 28 Research Studies Prove the Benefits)," September 4, 2012, www.forbes.com.

64. Ibid.

65. "Employee Engagement and Labor Relations," *Gallup Business Journal*, www.businessjournal.gallup.com, accessed April 10, 2014.

66. www.gallup.com/strategic consulting/163007/state-american-workplace.aspx; Bruce Louis Rich et al., "Job Engagement: Antecedents and Effects on Job Performance," *Academy of Management Journal*, 53, no. 3 (2010), pp. 617–635; "Special Report: Employee Engagement—Losing Lifeblood," *Workforce Management*, July 2011, pp. 24–27.

67. "Five Ways to Improve Employee Engagement Now," *Gallup Business Journal*: www.businessjournal.gallup.com, accessed April 7, 2014.

68. www.gallup.com/strategic consulting/163007/state-american-workplace.aspx and http://www.gallup.com/services/178514/state-american-workplace.aspx accessed June 20, 2015.

69. Rich et al., "Job Engagement."

70. Alison Konrad, "Engaging Employees through High-Involvement Work Practices,"

CHAPTER 3

Ivey Business Journal, March/April 2006, p. 1.

71. Kuldeep Singh, "Impact of HR Practices on Perceived Firm Performance in India," *Asia Pacific Journal of Human Resources*, December 2004.

72. ET Bureau, "India's Best Companies to Work for 2017: The Complete List," *The Economic Times*, www.economictimes. indiatimes.com, (Navigation--ET Home--News--Company--

Corporate Trends), as accessed on 8 August 2017 at 2pm IST.

73. Dasgupta, Brinda, "India's best workplaces of 2016: Ujjivan's people are motivated by their job's nature," *The Economic Times*, http://economictimes. indiatimes.com, (Navigation--ET Home--News--Company--Corporate Trends), as accessed on 08 August 2017 at 2pm IST.

74. Paula Ketter, "What's the Big Deal About Employee

Engagement?" *Training & Development*, January 2008, pp. 47–48.

75. "Kia Motors in Big Trouble," *Business Career* 14, no. 8 (August 1997), pp. 12–13.

76. Kia Motors Corporation, 2006 annual report, page 6.

77. Ibid.

78. Gary Tomlinson, "Building a Culture of High Employee Engagement," *Strategic HR Review* 9, no. 3 (2010), pp. 25–31.

79. Ibid.

80. Ibid.

81. Ibid.

82. Ibid.

83. Ibid. Note that during these years economic activity in the UK was tumbling, which may account for at least some of the reduced turnover.

4

Job Analysis and the Talent Management Process

LEARNING OBJECTIVES

4-1 Define talent management and explain why it is important.

4-2 Discuss the process of job analysis, including why it is important.

4-3 Explain how to use at least three methods of collecting job analysis information, including interviews, questionnaires, and observation.

4-4 Explain how you would write a job description.

4-5 Explain how to write a job specification.

4-6 List some human traits and behaviors you would want an employee to bring to a job if employee engagement is important to doing the job well.

4-7 Explain competency-based job analysis, including what it means and how it's done in practice.

The technological advancements in the banking sector posed a challenge for the old players in the industry. Banks were adopting more customer-centric approach and embracing technological advancements that were defining the new-age banking norms. The public sector banks lagged in modernization because of the traditional and bureaucratic banking norms that were in force. Traditionally, working hours, modes of transaction, and other processes were rigidly defined and regulated. In the face of competition, public sector banks like the State Bank of India and Bank of Baroda had to hire new talent and keep an open mind about evolving norms as per the market requirements. How do you hire people whose job duties may change frequently? In this chapter, we will see what they did.

WHERE ARE WE NOW ...

Because managers should know what a job entails before deciding who to recruit and hire for it, human resource management really starts with deciding what the job entails. The main purpose of this chapter is to show you how to analyze jobs and write job descriptions. We discuss several techniques for analyzing jobs, and explain how to write job descriptions and job specifications. The main topics we address include the talent management process, the basics of job analysis, methods for collecting job analysis information, writing job descriptions, writing job specifications, employee engagement and job analysis, and using models and profiles in talent management. Then, in Chapter 5 (Personnel Planning and Recruiting), we'll turn to the methods managers use to actually find the employees they need.

The Talent Management Process

For many people, Chapters 4–13 represent the heart of the book, specifically recruitment, selection, training, appraisal, career planning, and compensation. Managers traditionally view these activities as a series of steps:

1. Decide what positions to fill, through job analysis, personnel planning, and forecasting.
2. Build a pool of job applicants, by recruiting internal or external candidates.
3. Obtain application forms and perhaps have initial screening interviews.
4. Use selection tools like tests, interviews, background checks, and physical exams to identify viable candidates.
5. Decide to whom to make an offer.
6. Orient, train, and develop employees so they have the competencies to do their jobs.
7. Appraise employees to assess how they're doing.
8. Compensate employees to maintain their motivation.

This stepwise view makes sense. For example, the employer needs job candidates before selecting whom to hire.

The problem with the stepwise view is twofold. First, the process usually isn't really stepwise. For example, managers do not just train employees (step 6 above) and then appraise how they're doing (step 7). Instead (to use our example), the appraisal may well also loop back to shape the employee's subsequent training. So, first, rather than view these eight HR activities as stepwise, it is best to view them holistically—because the steps interactively affect each other and work together. The second problem is that focusing just on each step may cause the manager to miss, as it were, the forest for the trees. It's not just each step but the *results you obtain* by applying them together that's important. So, second, it's important to remember that each and every step should be focused on achieving, in unison, some specific result (such as, say, improving customer service).

Recognizing all this, the trend today is to view these eight activities not stepwise but as part of a coordinated *talent management* effort.[1] We will define **talent management** as *the holistic, integrated and results and goal-oriented process of planning, recruiting, selecting, developing, managing, and compensating employees.*[2] What does this mean in practice? As an example, the manager who takes a talent management approach tends to take actions such as the following:

talent management
The goal-oriented and integrated process of planning, recruiting, developing, managing, and compensating employees.

1. He or she starts with the results and asks, "What recruiting, testing, training, or pay action should I take to produce the employee competencies we need *to achieve our company's goals?*"
2. He or she treats activities such as recruiting and training as interrelated. For example, the manager knows that having employees with the right skills depends as much on recruiting and training as on applicant testing.
3. Because talent management is holistic and integrated, he or she will probably use the same "profile" of required human skills, knowledge, and behaviors ("competencies") for formulating a job's recruitment plans as for making selection, training, appraisal, and compensation decisions for it.
4. He or she takes steps to actively coordinate/integrate talent management functions such as recruiting and training. For example, HR managers meet to make sure they are using the same skills profile to recruit as to select, train, and appraise for a particular job, or use talent management software like the following to do so.

Improving Performance Through HRIS: Talent Management Software

Because talent management is holistic and interdependent, many employers use talent management software systems to coordinate their talent-related activities. For example, Talent Management Solutions' (www.talentmanagement101.com) *Talent Management Suite* includes recruiting, employee performance management, a learning management system, and compensation management support. It "ensures that all levels of the organization are aligned—all working for the same goals."[3]

ZingHR is a talent management software developed for Indian companies. It includes e-recruiting, onboarding, performance management, and compliance management. It uses a cloud-based HCM software wherein job aspirants are provided with candidate portals where they could provide information even before they come for a face-to-face interview. This helps recruiting managers to invite only those candidates who are fit for job interview. Thus, this helps in lowering the processing time, thereby reducing costs.[4] ■

The Basics of Job Analysis

Talent management starts with understanding what jobs need to be filled, and the human traits and competencies employees need to do those jobs effectively.

What Is Job Analysis?

Organizations consist of positions that have to be staffed. The organization chart (see Figure 4-1) shows the title of each supervisor's position and, by means of connecting lines, who is accountable to whom, who has authority for each area, and who is expected to communicate with whom. **Job analysis** is the procedure through which you determine the duties of the company's positions and the characteristics of the people to hire for them.[5] Job analysis produces information for writing **job descriptions** (a list of what the job entails) and **job** (or "person") **specifications** (what kind of people to hire for the job). Virtually every personnel-related action—interviewing applicants, and training and appraising employees, for instance—requires knowing what the job entails and what human traits one needs to do the job well.[6]

The supervisor or human resources specialist normally collects one or more of the following types of information via the job analysis:

job analysis
The procedure for determining the duties and skill requirements of a job and the kind of person who should be hired for it.

job descriptions
A list of a job's duties, responsibilities, reporting relationships, working conditions, and supervisory responsibilities—one product of a job analysis.

job specifications
A list of a job's "human requirements," that is, the requisite education, skills, personality, and so on—another product of a job analysis.

- *Work activities.* Information about the job's actual work activities, such as cleaning, selling, teaching, or painting. This list may also include how, why, and when the worker performs each activity.
- *Human behaviors.* Information about human behaviors the job requires, like sensing, communicating, lifting weights, or walking long distances.
- *Machines, tools, equipment, and work aids.* Information regarding tools used, materials processed, knowledge dealt with or applied (such as finance or law), and services rendered (such as counseling or repairing).
- *Performance standards.* Information about the job's performance standards (in terms of quantity or quality levels for each job duty, for instance).

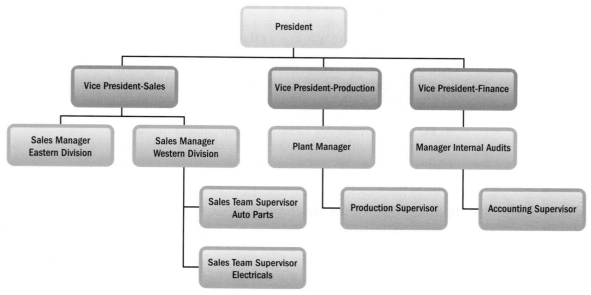

FIGURE 4-1 **Organization Chart**

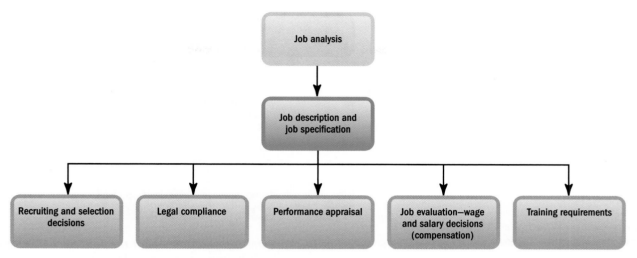

FIGURE 4-2 **Uses of Job Analysis Information**

- *Job context.*   Information about such matters as physical working conditions, work schedule, incentives, and, for instance, the number of people with whom the employee would normally interact.
- *Human requirements.*   Information such as knowledge or skills (education, training, work experience) and required personal attributes (aptitudes, personality, interests).

Uses of Job Analysis Information

As Figure 4-2 summarizes, job analysis is important because it supports just about all human resource management activities.

RECRUITMENT AND SELECTION   Information about what duties the job entails and what human characteristics are required to perform these duties helps managers decide what sort of people to recruit and hire.

COMPLIANCE AND EMPLOYMENT RELATIONS   In public sector undertaking (PSU) banks, job analysis was conducted, and after negotiation with unions, initiatives like one-window banking and core banking were introduced.

PERFORMANCE APPRAISAL   A performance appraisal compares each employee's actual performance with his or her duties and performance standards. Managers use job analysis to learn what these duties and standards are.

COMPENSATION   Compensation (such as salary and bonus) usually depends on the job's required skill and education level, safety hazards, degree of responsibility, and so on—all factors you assess through job analysis.

TRAINING   The job description lists the job's specific duties and requisite skills—thus pinpointing what training the job requires.

Conducting a Job Analysis

There are six steps in doing a job analysis of a job, as follows.

Step 1: Decide How You Will Use the Information   Some data collection techniques—like interviewing the employee—are good for writing job descriptions. Other techniques, like the position analysis questionnaire we describe later, provide numerical ratings for each job; these can be used to compare jobs for compensation purposes.

FIGURE 4-3 **Process Chart for Analyzing a Job's Workflow**

Source: Henderson, Richard I., Compensation Management in a Knowledge -Based World, 9th Ed., © 2003, p.137. Reprinted and Electronically reproduced by permission of Pearson Education, Inc., Upper Saddle River, New Jersey.

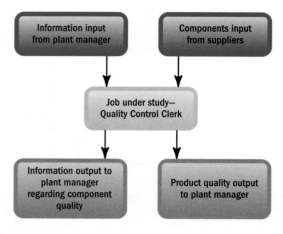

organization chart
A chart that shows the organization-wide distribution of work, with titles of each position and interconnecting lines that show who reports to and communicates with whom.

process chart
A workflow chart that shows the flow of inputs to and outputs from a particular job.

Step 2: Review Relevant Background Information About the Job, Such as Organization Charts and Process Charts[7] It is important to understand the job's context. For example, **organization charts** show the organizationwide division of work, and where the job fits in the overall organization. A **process chart** provides a detailed picture of the workflow. Thus, in the process chart in Figure 4-3, the quality control clerk should review components from suppliers, check components going to the plant managers, and give information regarding the components' quality to these managers. Finally, an existing job description may provide a starting point for revising the job description.

Workflow Analysis Reviewing the organization chart, process chart, and job description helps the manager identify what a job's duties and demands are now. However, it does *not* answer questions like "Does how this job relates to other jobs make sense?" or "Should this job even exist?" To answer such questions, the manager may conduct a *workflow analysis*. **Workflow analysis** is a detailed study of the flow of work from job to job in one identifiable work process (such as processing a mortgage application). In turn, this analysis may lead to changing or "reengineering" the job. The accompanying HR as a Profit Center feature illustrates workflow analysis.

In conducting a workflow analysis, the manager may use a *flow process chart*; this lists in order each step of the process. The manager may convert this step-by-step flow process chart into a diagrammatic process chart. This shows, with arrows and circles, each step in the process.

workflow analysis
A detailed study of the flow of work from job to job in a work process.

business process reengineering
Redesigning business processes, usually by combining steps, so that small multifunction process teams using information technology do the jobs formerly done by a sequence of departments.

Business Process Reengineering The workflow analysis at American Atlantic led to a *reengineering* of its claims processing operation. **Business process reengineering** means redesigning business processes, usually by combining steps, so that small multifunction teams, often using information technology, do the jobs formerly done by a sequence of departments. The basic reengineering approach is to

1. Identify a business process to be redesigned (such as processing an insurance claim)
2. Measure the performance of the existing processes
3. Identify opportunities to improve these processes
4. Redesign and implement a new way of doing the work
5. Assign ownership of sets of formerly separate tasks to an individual or a team who use new computerized systems to support the new arrangement

As at firms following this, reengineering usually requires redesigning individual jobs. For example, workers doing date stamping must now know how to use the new date-stamping machine.

job enlargement
Assigning workers additional same-level activities.

job rotation
Systematically moving workers from one job to another.

job enrichment
Redesigning jobs in a way that increases the opportunities for the worker to experience feelings of responsibility, achievement, growth, and recognition.

Job Redesign   Early economists enthusiastically described why specialized jobs were more efficient (as in, "practice makes perfect"). Today, most agree that specialized jobs can backfire, for instance by sapping morale. Experts typically suggest three ways to redesign specialized jobs to make them more challenging. **Job enlargement** means assigning workers additional same-level activities. Thus, the worker who previously only bolted the seat to the legs might attach the back too. **Job rotation** means systematically moving workers from one job to another. In Indian public sector banks, it's mandatory that branch level clerical employees are rotated between jobs every six month. Job rotation helps the employees develop new skills and attitudes. It also reduces work monotony. Thus, the bank is able to develop motivated and multi-skilled employees.

Psychologist Frederick Herzberg argued that the best way to motivate workers is through what he called job enrichment. **Job enrichment** means redesigning jobs in a way that increases the opportunities for the worker to experience feelings of responsibility, achievement, growth, and recognition—and therefore more motivation. It does this by *empowering* the worker—for instance, by giving the worker the skills and authority to inspect the work, instead of having supervisors do that. A simple example of enrichment is to allow a front-office receptionist to be responsible for activities like travel booking or basic customer relationship management. Empowerment, in this context, implies that the individual is made responsible for providing service as well as other dimensions like cost reduction and customer satisfaction. Herzberg said empowered employees would do their jobs well because they wanted to, and quality and productivity would rise. That philosophy, in one form or another, is the theoretical basis for the team-based self-managing jobs in many companies around the world today.

Step 3: Select Representative Positions   With a job to analyze, the manager then generally selects a sample of positions to focus on. For example, to analyze an assembler's job, it is usually unnecessary to analyze the jobs of all the firm's 200 assembly workers; instead a sample of 10 jobs will do.

Step 4: Actually Analyze the Job   In brief, the actual job analysis involves greeting each job holder; briefly explaining the job analysis process and the participants' roles in this process; spending about 15 minutes interviewing the employee to get agreement on a basic summary of the job; identifying the job's broad areas of responsibility, such as "calling on potential clients"; and then interactively identifying specific duties/tasks within each area using one of the methods we describe just below.[8]

Step 5: Verify the Job Analysis Information with the Worker Performing the Job and with His or Her Immediate Supervisor   This will help confirm that the information (for instance, on the job's duties) is factually correct and complete and help to gain their acceptance.

Step 6: Develop a Job Description and Job Specification   The *job description* lists the duties, activities, and responsibilities of the job, as well as its important features, such as working conditions. The *job specification* summarizes the personal qualities, traits, skills, and background required for getting the job done.

LEARNING OBJECTIVE 4-3
Explain how to use at least three methods of collecting job analysis information, including interviews, questionnaires, and observation.

Methods for Collecting Job Analysis Information

There are many ways (interviews, or questionnaires, for instance) to collect job information. The basic rule is to use those that best fit your purpose. Thus an interview might be best for creating a list of job duties. The more quantitative "position analysis questionnaire" method may be best for quantifying each job's worth for pay purposes. Before actually analyzing the job, keep several things in mind.

- Make the job analysis a *joint effort by a human resources manager, the worker, and the worker's supervisor.* The human resource manager might observe the worker doing the job, and have both the supervisor and worker fill out job questionnaires. Then he or she lists the job's duties and required human traits. The supervisor and worker then verify the HR manager's list of job duties.
- *Make sure the questions and the process are both clear* to the employees. (For example, some might not know what you mean when you ask about the job's "mental demands.")
- *Use several job analysis methods.* For example, a questionnaire might miss a task the worker performs just occasionally. Therefore it's prudent to follow up the questionnaire with a short interview.

The Interview

Job analysis interviews range from unstructured ("Tell me about your job") to highly structured ones containing hundreds of specific items to check off.

Managers may conduct individual interviews with each employee, group interviews with groups of employees who have the same job, and/or supervisor interviews with one or more supervisors who know the job. Use group interviews when a large number of employees are performing similar or identical work, since this can be a quick and inexpensive way to gather information. As a rule, the workers' immediate supervisor attends the group session; if not, you can interview the supervisor separately.

The interviewee should understand the reason for the interview. There's a tendency for workers to view such interviews, rightly or wrongly, as "efficiency evaluations." If so, interviewees may hesitate to describe their jobs accurately.

TYPICAL QUESTIONS   Typical interview questions include the following:

What is the job being performed?

Who all are members of your work group?

How long have you been doing this work?

What exactly are the major duties of your position?

What geographic and physical locations do/have you work in?

What are the education, experience, skill, and [where applicable] certification and training requirements?

In what shop-floor level activities do you participate?

What are the job's responsibilities and duties?

What are the basic accountabilities or performance standards that typify your work?

What are the environmental and working conditions involved?

What are the job's physical demands? The emotional and mental demands?

What are the health and safety conditions?

Are you exposed to any hazards or unusual working conditions?

STRUCTURED INTERVIEWS   Many managers use questionnaires to guide the interview. Figure 4-4 presents one example. It includes questions regarding matters like the general purpose of the job; supervisory responsibilities; job duties; and education, experience, and skills required.

Such structured lists are not just for interviews. Job analysts who collect information by personally observing the work or by using questionnaires—two methods explained later—can also use structured lists.[9]

PROS AND CONS   The interview's wide use reflects its advantages. It's a simple and quick way to collect information. Skilled interviewers can also unearth important activities that occur only occasionally, or informal contacts that aren't on the organization chart. The employee can also vent frustrations that might otherwise go unnoticed.

Distortion of information is the main problem.[10] Job analysis often precedes changing a job's pay rate. Employees therefore may legitimately view it as pay-related, and exaggerate some responsibilities while minimizing others. In one study, researchers listed possible job duties either as simple task statements ("record phone messages and other routine information") or as ability statements ("ability to record phone messages and other routine information"). Respondents were more likely to report the ability-based versions of the statements. There may be a tendency for people to inflate their job's importance when abilities are involved, to impress the perceptions of others.[11] Employees will even puff up their job titles to make their jobs seem more important.[12]

INTERVIEWING GUIDELINES   To get the best information possible:

- Establish rapport with the interviewee. Know the person's name, speak understandably, briefly review the interview's purpose, and explain how the person was chosen for the interview.
- Use a structured guide that lists questions and provides space for answers. This ensures you'll identify crucial questions ahead of time and that all interviewers (if more than one) cover all the required questions. (However, also ask, "Was there anything we didn't cover with our questions?")
- Make sure you don't overlook crucial but infrequently performed activities—like a nurse's occasional emergency room duties. Ask the worker to list his or her duties in order of importance and frequency of occurrence.
- After completing the interview, review the information with the worker's immediate supervisor and with the interviewee.

Questionnaires

Having employees fill out questionnaires to describe their job duties and responsibilities is another good way to obtain job analysis information.

Some questionnaires are structured checklists. Here each employee gets an inventory of perhaps hundreds of specific duties or tasks (such as "change and splice wire"). He or she must indicate if he or she performs each task and, if so, how much time is normally spent on each. At the other extreme, the questionnaire may simply ask, "describe the major duties of your job."

In practice, the best questionnaire often falls between these two extremes. As illustrated in Figure 4-4, a typical job analysis questionnaire might include several open-ended questions (such as "Give a brief description of the main function/purpose of your job?") as well as structured questions (concerning, for instance, education required).

All questionnaires have pros and cons. A questionnaire is a quick and efficient way to obtain information from a large number of employees; it's less costly than interviewing hundreds of workers, for instance. However, developing the questionnaire and testing it (perhaps by making sure the workers understand the questions) can be time-consuming. And as with interviews, employees may distort their answers.

Observation

Direct observation is especially useful when jobs consist mainly of observable physical activities—assembly-line worker and accounting clerk are examples. However, observation is usually not appropriate when the job entails a lot of mental activity (lawyer, design engineer). Nor is it useful if the employee only occasionally engages in important activities, such as a nurse who handles emergencies. *Reactivity*—the worker's changing what he or she normally does because you are watching—is another problem.

FIGURE 4-4 **Job Analysis Questionnaire for Developing Job Descriptions**
Source: Adapted from www.tsu.edu/PDFFiles/Human%20Resources/HR%20Forms/JAQ%20FORM_rev%20100809%20a.pdf; www.delaware personnel.com/class/forms/jaq/jaq.shtml; www.uh.edu/human-resources/forms/JAQ.doc; www.tnstate.edu/hr/documents/.../Job%20Analysis%20Questionnaire.doc (all accessed July 24, 2013).
*Copyright Gary Dessler, PhD

JOB ANALYSIS QUESTIONNAIRE*

PURPOSE AND INSTRUCTIONS

Because no one knows the job as well as the person doing it, we are asking you to complete this form. The purpose is to obtain current information on your job based on a review of job duties and responsibilities. We are not asking you about your job performance; only what your job requires you to do.

EMPLOYEE DATA (PLEASE PRINT):

Your Name: _____   Today's date _____

Employee ID: _____

Location/Department: _____

Your Job Title: _____   Job Code: _____

How long have you been in your current position: _____

Work Telephone Number: _____

Supervisor's Name: _____   Supervisor's Title: _____

SUMMARY OF DUTIES/RESPONSIBILITIES

Give a brief description of the main function/purpose of your job. This statement should be a brief summary of the responsibilities listed in the next section.

_____

_____

_____

Listing of Job Duties

What do you do on your job? Please list your job's specific duties/responsibilities in the space below. In doing so:

   Please list the most important duties/responsibilities first. Write a separate statement for each duty/responsibility.

   At the end of each statement please indicate the approximate percent of your workday (25%, 7%, etc.) you spend on that duty.

   Please place an asterisk (*) next to the duties that you consider to be absolutely essential to this job.

_____

_____

_____

_____

_____

(Add additional duties as necessary)

Are there duties you are now performing that are not now in your job description? If so please list them on back of this page.

(Continued)

FIGURE 4-4 *Continued*

Minimum Level of Education (or Equivalent Experience) This Job Requires

What is the minimum level of education necessary to perform your job? Select only one please:
1. Elementary education.
2. Some high school.
3. A high school pass or equivalent (SSLC).
4. A formal vocational training program (approximately one year), an apprenticeship, or some formal college education.
5. A diploma from polytechnic or equivalent.
6. A bachelor's degree (BA, BSc, B Tech) .
7. A Master's degree (MA, MS, MBA, MPA) .
8. A doctorate degree (Ph.D., Fellow title).
9. Are you required to be licensed or certified to perform your work?

[ ] Yes [ ] No List type _____

Required Training on Job

What is the level of on-the-job or classroom training someone requires to do your job? Please select one choice below:
1. No additional training required.
2. A day or two.
3. A week.
4. A month.
5. Several months.
6. One year.
7. Two years or more.

SUPERVISORY RESPONSIBILITIES

Do you supervise others as part of your job? If so please briefly describe the nature of your supervisory responsibilities.

PHYSICAL JOB DEMANDS

Please briefly describe this job's main physical demands. For example, does it involve Sitting? Walking? Standing? Lifting? Detailed repetitive motions? Climbing? Etc.

Working Conditions: Environmental and Safety Job Demands

Please list this job's working conditions, such as: air-conditioned office work; outdoor or indoor extreme heat or cold; wet; noise; job hazards; working in elevated conditions; etc.

EMPLOYEE COMMENTS

Is there any other information that would be important in understanding your job? If so, please give us your comments below.

SUPERVISOR'S REVIEW

Based on your understanding of the job as it currently exists, please review the employee's response and provide your own comments in the space below. **Please do not change the employee's responses.**

*Copyright Gary Dessler PhD

Managers often use direct observation and interviewing together. One approach is to observe the worker on the job during a complete work cycle. (The *cycle* is the time it takes to complete the job; it could be a minute for an assembly-line worker or an hour, a day, or longer for complex jobs.) Here you take notes of all the job activities. Then, ask the person to clarify open points and to explain what other activities he or she performs that you didn't observe.

Participant Diary/Logs

diary/log
Daily listings made by workers of every activity in which they engage along with the time each activity takes.

Another method is to ask workers to keep a **diary/log**; here for every activity engaged in, the employee records the activity (along with the time) in a log.

Some firms give employees pocket dictating machines and pagers. Then at random times during the day, they page the workers, who dictate what they are doing at that time.

Quantitative Job Analysis Techniques

Qualitative methods like interviews and questionnaires are not always suitable. For example, if your aim is to compare jobs for pay purposes, a mere listing of duties may not suffice. You may need to say that, in effect, "Job A is twice as challenging as Job B, and so is worth twice the pay." To do this, it helps to have quantitative ratings for each job. The position analysis questionnaire and the Department of Labor approach are quantitative methods for doing this.

position analysis questionnaire (PAQ)
A questionnaire used to collect quantifiable data concerning the duties and responsibilities of various jobs.

POSITION ANALYSIS QUESTIONNAIRE   The **position analysis questionnaire (PAQ)** is a very popular quantitative job analysis tool, consisting of a questionnaire containing 194 items.[13] The 194 items (such as "written materials") each represent a basic element that may play a role in the job. The items each belong to one of five PAQ basic activities: (1) Having Decision-Making/Communication/Social Responsibilities, (2) Performing Skilled Activities, (3) Being Physically Active, (4) Operating Vehicles/Equipment, and (5) Processing Information. The final PAQ "score" reflects the job's rating on each of these five activities. To get those scores, the job analyst decides if each of the 194 items (such as one on using "written materials") applies to the job and, if so, to what extent. For example, within the "Processing Information" activity section an item on the extent to which the job requires using "written materials" such as books and reports might get a rating of 4. Since the PAQ scale ranges from 1 to 5, a 4 suggests that written materials do play a significant role in this job. The analyst can use an online version of the PAQ (see www.paq.com) for each job he or she is analyzing.

One of the PAQ's strengths is in assigning jobs to job classes for pay purposes. With ratings for each job's decision-making, skilled activity, physical activity, vehicle/equipment operation, and information-processing characteristics, you can quantitatively compare jobs relative to one another,[14] and then classify jobs for pay purposes.[15]

U.S. DEPARTMENT OF LABOR (DOL) PROCEDURE   Experts at the U.S. Department of Labor did much of the early work developing job analysis.[16] They used their results to compile what was for many years the bible of job descriptions, the *Dictionary of Occupational Titles*. This mammoth book contained detailed information on virtually every job in America. Internet-based tools have largely replaced the *Dictionary*. However, the U.S. Department of Labor job analysis procedure remains a good example of how to quantitatively rate, classify, and compare jobs. As Table 4-1 shows, the DOL method uses a set of standard activities called *worker functions* to describe what a worker must do with respect to *data, people*, and *things*. With respect to data, for instance, the functions include synthesizing and copying. For people, they include mentoring and supervising. For things, basic functions include manipulating and handling.

Each worker function has an importance rating. Thus, "coordinating" is 1, whereas "copying" is 5. If you were analyzing the job of a receptionist/clerk, for example, you might label the job 5, 6, 7 to represent copying data, speaking/signaling people, and handling things. You might code a psychiatric aide in a hospital 1, 7, 5 in relation to data, people, and things. In practice, you would score each task that the worker performed as part of his or her job in terms of data, people, and things. Then you would use the highest combination (say 4, 6, 5) to rate the overall job, since this is the highest level that you would expect a successful job incumbent to attain. If you were selecting a worker for that 4, 6, 5 job, you'd expect him or her to be able to at least compute (4), speak/signal (6), and tend (5). If you were comparing jobs for pay purposes, a 4, 6, 5 job should rank higher (see Table 4-1) than a 6, 8, 6 job. The manager can then present a summary of the job along with its 3-digit rating on a form such as in Figure 4-5.[17]

Electronic Job Analysis Methods[18]

Employers increasingly rely on electronic or Web-based job analysis methods. For example, the manager or job analyst may use the Web to review existing information about a job. Then, rather than collecting information about a job through direct interviews or questionnaires, the analyst uses online systems to send job questionnaires to job experts (often job incumbents) in remote locations. The Web also facilitates sharing and discussing responses, for instance, via Skype or facilities available internally (many Indian companies have intranet, which can be used. Otherwise email and/or mobile connect facility is available in most companies. The job analyst may thereby convene job experts to discuss and finalize the knowledge, skills, abilities, and other characteristics required for doing the job and its tasks.[19]

Conducting the job analysis via the Internet is often an obvious choice.[20] Most simply, the human resource department can distribute standardized job analysis questionnaires to geographically disbursed employees via their company intranets, with instructions to complete the forms and return them by a particular date.

Of course, the instructions should be clear, and test the process first. Without a job analyst actually sitting there with the employee or supervisor, there's a chance that the employees won't cover important points or that misunderstandings will cloud the results.

TABLE 4-1 Basic US Department of Labor Worker Functions

	Data	People	Things
Basic Activities	0 Synthesizing	0 Mentoring	0 Setting up
	1 Coordinating	1 Negotiating	1 Precision working
	2 Analyzing	2 Instructing	2 Operating/controlling
	3 Compiling	3 Supervising	3 Driving/operating
	4 Computing	4 Diverting	4 Manipulating
	5 Copying	5 Persuading	5 Tending
	6 Comparing	6 Speaking/signaling	6 Feeding/offbearing
		7 Serving	7 Handling
		8 Taking instructions/helping	

Note: Determine employee's job "score" on data, people, and things by observing his or her job and determining, for each of the three categories, which of the basic functions illustrates the person's job. "0" is high; "6," "8," and "7" are lows in each column.

FIGURE 4-5 Sample Report Based on U.S. Department of Labor Job Analysis Technique

Job Analysis Schedule

1. Established Job Title _____ DOUGH MIXER _____

2. Ind. Assign _____ (bake prod.) _____

3. SIC Code(s) and Title(s) _____ 2051 Bread and other bakery products _____

4. JOB SUMMARY:

Operates mixing machine to mix ingredients for straight and sponge (yeast) doughs according to established formulas, directs other workers in fermentation of dough, and curls dough into pieces with hand cutter.

5. WORK PERFORMED RATINGS:

Worker Functions	D Data	P People	(T) Things
	5	6	2

Work Field _____ Cooking, Food Preparing _____

6. WORKER TRAITS RATING (to be filled in by analyst):

Training time required
Aptitudes
Temperaments
Interests
Physical demands
Environment conditions

The U.S. Navy used Internet-based job analysis.[21] To keep ambiguities to a minimum, it had the employees complete structured online job analysis forms step by step and duty by duty, as follows:

- First, the online form lists *a set of work activities* (such as "Getting Information" and "Monitor the Process")
- Next, the form directs employees to *select those work activities* that are important to their job.
- Then, the form asks them to *list actual duties* of their jobs that fit each of those selected work activities. For example, suppose an employee chose "Getting Information" as an important work activity. Now he or she would list next to "Getting Information" specific job duties, such as "watch for new orders from our vendors and bring them to the boss's attention."

Again, the main issue with online job analysis is to strip the process of ambiguities. The Navy's online method proved effective.[22]

Writing Job Descriptions

The most important product of job analysis is the job description. A job description is a written statement of what the worker actually does, how he or she does it, and what the job's working conditions are. You use this information to write a job specification; this lists the knowledge, abilities, and skills required to perform the job satisfactorily.[23]

LEARNING OBJECTIVE 4-4
Explain how you would write a job description.

HR in Practice at the Hotel Paris In reviewing the Hotel Paris's employment systems, the HR manager was concerned that virtually all the company's job descriptions were out of date, and that many jobs had no descriptions at all. She knew that without accurate job descriptions, all her improvement efforts would be in vain. To see how this was handled, see the case on pages 120–121 of this chapter.

Diversity Counts

Generally, it is assumed that job descriptions are written only for the jobs that are done in office settings and for business purposes. However, today in India, the trend in changing. People who are on the lookout for housemaids and domestic help also write job descriptions on various sites such as bookmybai.com and housemaidforyou.com. It is very important to write these descriptions so that there is no mismatch of expectations while looking out for a housemaid. With an increase in the number of Indian woman going out for work, the responsibility of cleaning and taking care of the house till the owner gets back falls on the housemaid. Thus, hiring a maid becomes the most important task in managing the household for the owner, and writing a job description gives an overview of the expectations from the maid, that is, what would her job entail, what will be she responsible for, how much will she be paid, what will be her work timings, etc.[24] ■

There is no standard format for writing a job description. However, most descriptions contain sections that cover:

1. Job identification
2. Job summary
3. Responsibilities and duties
4. Authority of incumbent
5. Standards of performance
6. Working conditions
7. Job specification

Figures 4-6 present two sample forms of job descriptions.

Job Identification

As in Figure 4-6, the job identification section (on top) contains several types of information.[25] The *job title* specifies the name of the job, such as supervisor of data processing operations, or inventory control clerk.

There may also be a space to indicate who approved the description and perhaps a space showing the location of the job in terms of its facility/division and department. This section might also include the immediate supervisor's title and information regarding salary and/or pay scale. There might also be space for the grade/level of the job, if there is such a category. For example, a firm may classify programmers as programmer II, programmer III, and so on.

Job Summary

The job summary should summarize the essence of the job, and include only its major functions or activities. Thus (in Figure 4-6), the telesales rep "… is responsible for selling college textbooks.…" For the job of mailroom supervisor, "the mailroom supervisor receives, sorts, and delivers all incoming mail properly, and he or she handles all outgoing mail including the accurate and timely posting of such mail."[26]

Some experts state unequivocally that "one item frequently found that should never be included in a job description is a 'cop-out clause' like 'other duties, as assigned,'"[27] since this leaves open the nature of the job. Finally, state in the summary that the employee is expected to carry out his or her duties efficiently, attentively, and conscientiously.

Relationships

There may be a "relationships" statement (not in Figure 4-6) that shows the job-holder's relationships with others inside and outside the organization. For a human resource manager, such a statement might say:[28]

JOB TITLE: Telesales Respresentative	JOB CODE: 100001
RECOMMENDED SALARY GRADE:	EXEMPT/NONEXEMPT STATUS:
JOB FAMILY: Sales	EEOC: Sales Workers
DIVISION: Higher Education	REPORTS TO: District Sales Manager
DEPARTMENT: In-House Sales	LOCATION: Mumbai
	DATE: April 2013

SUMMARY (Write a brief summary of job.)

The person in this position is responsible for selling college textbooks, software, and multimedia products to professors, via incoming and outgoing telephone calls, and to carry out selling strategies to meet sales goals in assigned territories of smaller colleges and universities. In addition, the individual in this position will be responsible for generating a designated amount of editorial leads and communicating to the publishing groups product feedback and market trends observed in the assigned territory.

SCOPE AND IMPACT OF JOB

Dollar responsibilities (budget and/or revenue)

The person in this position is responsible for generating approximately $2 million in revenue, for meeting operating expense budget of approximately $4000, and a sampling budget of approximately 10,000 units.

Supervisory responsibilities (direct and indirect)

None

Other

REQUIRED KNOWLEDGE AND EXPERIENCE (Knowledge and experience necessary to do job)

Related work experience

Prior sales or publishing experience preferred. One year of company experience in a customer service or marketing function with broad knowledge of company products and services is desirable.

Formal education or equivalent

Bachelor's degree with strong academic performance or work equivalent experience.

Skills

Must have strong organizational and persuasive skills. Must have excellent verbal and written communications skills and must be PC proficient.

Other

Limited travel required (approx 5%)

(Continued)

FIGURE 4-6 Sample Job Description, Pearson Education
Source: Reprinted and electronically reproduced by permission of Pearson Education, Inc., Upper Saddle River, New Jersey.

PRIMARY RESPONSIBILITIES (List in order of importance and list amount of time spent on task.)

Driving Sales (60%)
- Achieve quantitative sales goal for assigned territory of smaller colleges and universities.
- Determine sales priorities and strategies for territory and develop a plan for implementing those strategies.
- Conduct 15–20 professor interviews per day during the academic sales year that accomplishes those priorities.
- Conduct product presentations (including texts, software, and Web site); effectively articulate author's central vision of key titles; conduct sales interviews using the PSS model; conduct walk-through of books and technology.
- Employ telephone selling techniques and strategies.
- Sample products to appropriate faculty, making strategic use of assigned sampling budgets.
- Close class test adoptions for first edition products.
- Negotiate custom publishing and special packaging agreements within company guidelines.
- Initiate and conduct in-person faculty presentations and selling trips as appropriate to maximize sales with the strategic use of travel budget. Also use internal resources to support the territory sales goals.
- Plan and execute in-territory special selling events and book-fairs.
- Develop and implement in-territory promotional campaigns and targeted email campaigns.

Publishing (editorial/marketing) 25%
- Report, track, and sign editorial projects.
- Gather and communicate significant market feedback and information to publishing groups.

Territory Management 15%
- Track and report all pending and closed business in assigned database.
- Maintain records of customer sales interviews and adoption situations in assigned database.
- Manage operating budget strategically.
- Submit territory itineraries, sales plans, and sales forecasts as assigned.
- Provide superior customer service and maintain professional bookstore relations in assigned territory.

Decision-Making Responsibilities for This Position:
Determine the strategic use of assigned sampling budget to most effectively generate sales revenue to exceed sales goals.
Determine the priority of customer and account contacts to achieve maximum sales potential.
Determine where in-person presentations and special selling events would be most effective to generate the most sales.

Submitted By: Jim Smith, District Sales Manager	Date: April 10, 2013
Approval:	Date:
Human Resources:	Date:
Corporate Compensation:	Date:

FIGURE 4-6 *Continued*

Reports to: Vice president of employee relations.

Supervises: Human resource clerk, test administrator, industrial relations manager and one secretary.

Works with: All department managers and executive management.

Outside the company: Employment agencies, executive recruiting firms, union representatives, state and central government offices, and various vendors.[29]

Responsibilities and Duties

This is the heart of the job description. It should present a list of the job's significant responsibilities and duties. As in Figure 4-6, list each of the job's major duties separately, and describe it in a few sentences. In the figure, for instance, the job's duties include "achieve quantitative sales goal …" and "determine sales priorities.…" Typical duties for other jobs might include making accurate postings to accounts payable, maintaining favorable purchase price variances, and repairing production-line tools and equipment. This section may also define the jobholder's authority limits. For example, the jobholder might have authority to approve purchase requests up to ₹5,000, grant time off or leaves of absence, discipline department personnel, recommend salary increases, and interview and hire new employees.

Usually, the manager's basic question here is, "How do I determine what the job's duties are and should be?" The answer first is, from the *job analysis*; this should reveal what the employees on each job are doing now.

Second, you can review various sources of standardized job description information. In India, the National Classification of Occupation (NCO) plays a very important role in maintaining the standards of occupation, and it is used in the network of employment exchanges. The codes help in job search and job postings. Also, the classification is used in all census and sample surveys conducted in India. However, the system has not become popular in the private sector.[30]

The employer may also use other popular sources of job description information, such as www.jobdescription.com. Another simple solution is just to *Google* the job description you want, by seeing online what others are doing. Thus, someone writing job descriptions for jobs such as marketing manager would readily find relevant online descriptions as follows:

Go to http://hiring.monster.com. Then click Resource Center, then Recruiting and Hiring Advice, then Job descriptions, then Sample job descriptions. Then scroll down to Marketing and Sales Manager Sample Job Description.[31]

Go to www.careerplanner.com. Then click Job Descriptions, then scroll down to Marketing Manager Job Description.[32]

TRENDS SHAPING HR: *DIGITAL AND SOCIAL MEDIA*

Social media is helping to democratize HR, by enabling line managers to do things for which they formerly required HR managers, thus bypassing HR. For example, the hiring manager can easily unearth job titles and duties using social media like LinkedIn. Thus (to paraphrase what someone posted on LinkedIn): *I hope some of you IT recruiters out there can help me to better understand what I need to put into the job descriptions that I'm writing for the developers and system managers I'm recruiting for.* The first of many replies listed 12 tasks including: (1) Do technical skills match the desired job? (2) What technical problems were solved by the job seeker? and (3) Did job seeker know about Cloud Deployment?[33]

But some of the job titles you'll find on social media may be more creative than usable. For example, many Indian companies call employees Associates. Similarly, Pinterest is known to call its designers Pixel Pushers![34] ■

Writing clear job duties is an art. For a teacher, for example, one duty might be:[35]

Incorrect: Ensures that students learn 5th grade English with the aim of passing the required common exam.

Comment: What the teacher does is ambiguous, and the expected process and results of the teacher's actions aren't clear.

Correct: Studies past common English exams to understand what they typically involve, prepares yearly, weekly, and daily lesson plans, presents each day's lesson clearly with follow up questions to ensure learning, administers weekly tests to confirm learning, and counsel students with one on one in class lessons as necessary.

When job descriptions are written for the disabled, care has to be taken to ensure that they can perform essential functions of the job. The individual must have requisite skill, training, and experience for the job. Factors to consider are:

- Whether the position exists to perform that function,
- The number of other employees available to perform the function,
- The degree of expertise or skill required to perform the function.
- Whether employees in the position are actually required to perform the function.[36]
- What the degree of expertise or skill required to perform the function is.[37]

As an example, answering calls and directing visitors to the proper offices might be essential functions for a receptionist's job.

If the disabled individual can't perform the job as currently structured, the employer is required to make a "reasonable accommodation," unless doing so would present an "undue hardship." The Rights of People with Disabilities Act, 2016, which is the new Indian legislation for the disabled defines "reasonable accommodation" as "means necessary and appropriate modification and adjustments, without imposing a disproportionate or undue burden in a particular case, to ensure to persons with disabilities the enjoyment or exercise of rights equally with others..." [Section 2 (y)]. The new legislation views disability as an evolving and dynamic concept. Reasonable accommodation may include:

- acquiring or modifying equipment or devices (e.g., Microsign Industries, Bhavnagar, Gujarat builds custom machinery for the disabled),
- job redesign/restructuring,
- part-time or modified work schedules (giving an additional grace time for entry or exit),
- reassignment to a vacant position,
- adjusting or modifying examinations, training materials, or policies,
- providing readers and interpreters, and
- making the workplace readily accessible to and usable by people with disabilities. (by putting ramps, safety guards, warning lights, etc.)
- providing required support in places like restrooms, lunch halls, parking lots, etc. ■

Standard Occupational Classification (SOC)
Classifies all workers into one of 23 major groups of jobs that are subdivided into minor groups of jobs and detailed occupations.

Standards of Performance and Working Conditions

A "standards of performance" section lists the standards the company expects the employee to achieve for each of the job description's main duties and responsibilities. One way to set standards is to finish the statement, "I will be completely satisfied with your work when...." This sentence, if completed for each listed duty, should result in a usable set of performance standards. For example:

Duty: **Accurately Posting Accounts Payable**

1. Post all invoices received within the same working day.
2. Route all invoices to the proper department managers for approval no later than the day following receipt.
3. Commit an average of no more than three posting errors per month.

The job description may also list the job's working conditions, such as noise level, hazardous conditions, or heat.

▶ IMPROVING PERFORMANCE: *HR Tools for Line Managers and Small Businesses*

Using O*NET

Without their own job analysts or even HR managers, many small business owners face two hurdles when doing job analyses. First, most need a more streamlined approach than those provided by questionnaires like that in Figure 4-4. Second is the concern that, in writing their job descriptions, they'll overlook duties that subordinates should be assigned. What they need is an encyclopedia listing all the possible positions they might encounter, including a list of the duties normally assigned to these positions.

The small business owner has at least three options. The *Standard Occupational Classification*, mentioned earlier, provides detailed descriptions of thousands of jobs and their human requirements. Web sites like www.jobdescription.com provide customizable descriptions by title and industry. And the Department of Labor's O*NET is a third alternative. We'll focus here on how to write a job description using O*NET (http://online.onetcenter.org).[38] It is free to use.

O*NET

The U.S. Department of Labor's online occupational information network, called O*NET, enables anyone to see the most important characteristics of various occupations, as well as the experience, education, and knowledge required to do each job well. Both the Standard Occupational Classification and O*NET list the specific duties associated with numerous occupations. O*NET also lists skills, including *basic skills* such as reading and writing, *process skills* such as critical thinking, and *transferable skills* such as persuasion and negotiation.[39] An O*NET job listing also includes information on worker requirements (required knowledge, for instance), occupation requirements (such as compiling, coding, and categorizing data, for instance), and experience requirements (including education and job training). Employers and career planers also use O*NET to check the job's labor market characteristics, such as employment projections and earnings data.[40]

The steps in using O*NET to facilitate writing a job description follow.

Step 1. *Review your Plan.* Ideally, the jobs you need should flow from your departmental or company plans. Do you plan to enter or exit businesses? What do you expect your sales to be in the next few years? What departments will have to be expanded or reduced? What kinds of new positions will you need?

Step 2. *Develop an Organization Chart.* Start with the organization as it is now. Then produce a chart showing how you want it to look in a year or two. Microsoft Word includes an organization charting function.[41]

Step 3. *Use a Job Analysis Questionnaire.* Next, gather information about each job's duties. (You can use job analysis questionnaires, such as those shown in Figures 4-4 and 4-7).

FIGURE 4-7 **Simple Job Description Questionnaire**
Source: Copyright Gary Dessler, PhD.

Background Data for Job Description

Job Title _____   Department _____

Job Number _____   Written by _____

Today's Date _____   Applicable DOT Codes _____

I. Applicable DOT Definition(s):

II. Job Summary:
(List the more important or regularly performed tasks)

III. Reports To:

IV. Supervises: _____

V. Job Duties: _____
(Briefly describe, for each duty, what employee does and, if possible, how employee does it. Show in parentheses at end of each duty the approximate percentage of time devoted to duty.)

A. Daily Duties:

B. Periodic Duties:
(Indicate whether weekly, monthly, quarterly, etc.)

C. Duties Performed at Irregular Intervals:

Source: Reprinted by permission of O*NET OnLine.

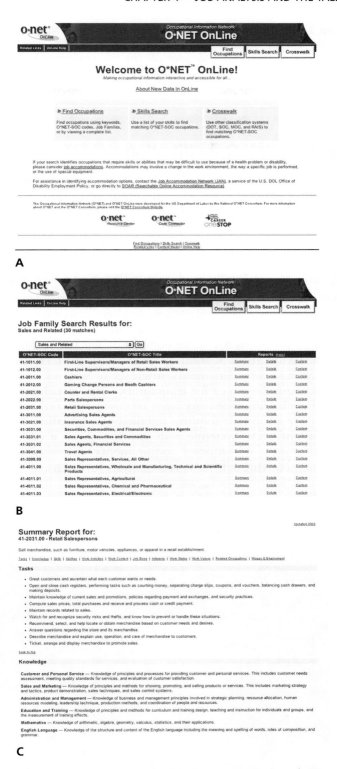

A

B

C

Step 4. *Obtain Job Duties from O*NET.* The list of job duties you uncovered through the job analysis in step 3 may or may not be complete. We'll therefore use O*NET to compile a more complete list. (Refer to the A, B, and C examples pictured just above.)

Start by going to http://online.onetcenter.org (A). Here, click on *Find Occupations*. Assume you want to create job descriptions for a retail salesperson. Key *Retail Sales* in the Keyword drop-down box. This brings you to the Occupations matching "retail sales" page (B).

Clicking on the *Retail Salespersons* summary produces the job summary and specific occupational duties for retail salespersons (C). For a small store, you might want to combine the duties of the "retail salesperson" with those of "first-line supervisors/managers of retail sales workers."

Step 5. *List the Job's Human Requirements from O*NET.*   Next, return to the summary for *Retail Salesperson* (C). Here, click, for example, Knowledge, Skills, and Abilities. Use this information to help develop a job specification for your job. Use this information for recruiting, selecting, and training your employees.

Step 6. *Finalize the Job Description.*   Finally, perhaps using Figure 4-7 as a guide, write an appropriate job summary for the job. Then use the information obtained previously in steps 4 and 5 to create a complete listing of the tasks, duties, and human requirements of each of the jobs you will need to fill. ∎

Writing Job Specifications

The job specification takes the job description and answers the question, "What human traits and experience are required to do this job effectively?" It shows what kind of person to recruit and for what qualities you should test that person. It may be a section of the job description, or a separate document. Often—as in Figure 4-6 on pages 108–109—it is part of the job description.[42]

Specifications for Trained versus Untrained Personnel

Writing job specifications for trained and experienced employees is relatively straightforward. Here job specifications tend to focus on factors such as length of previous service, quality of relevant training, and previous job performance.

The problems are more complex when you're filling jobs with untrained people (with the intention of training them on the job). Here you must specify qualities such as physical traits, personality, interests, or sensory skills that imply some potential for performing the job or for trainability. (This is a challenge in India, particularly when dealing with illiterate workforce, or migrant workforce in industries like construction. Thus, for a job that requires detailed manipulation in a circuit board assembly line, you might want someone who scores high on a test of finger dexterity. Employers identify the job's human requirements either through a subjective, judgmental approach or through statistical analysis (or both).

Filling jobs with untrained employees requires identifying the personal traits that predict performance.

Shutterstock.Prabhjit S. Kalsi

Specifications Based on Judgment

Most job specifications simply reflect the educated guesses of people like supervisors and human resource managers. The basic procedure here is to ask, "What does it take in terms of education, intelligence, training, and the like to do this job well?"

How does one make such "educated guesses"? You could simply review the job's duties, and deduce from those what human traits and skills the job requires. You can also choose human traits and skills from those listed in Web-based job descriptions like those at www.jobdescription.com. (For example, a typical job description there lists "Generates creative solutions" and "Manages difficult or emotional customer situations.")

In any case, use common sense. Don't ignore the behaviors that may apply to almost any job but that might not normally surface through a job analysis. Industriousness is an example. Who wants an employee who doesn't work hard? One researcher collected supervisor ratings and other information from 18,000 employees in 42 different hourly entry-level jobs.[43] Generic work behaviors that he found to be important to all jobs included thoroughness, attendance, unruliness [lack of], and scheduling flexibility (for instance, offers to stay late when store is busy). Another study, of over 7,000 executives, found that crucial top-leader behaviors included: takes initiative, practices self-development, displays high integrity, drives for results, and develops others.[44]

Job Specifications Based on Statistical Analysis

Basing job specifications on statistical analysis rather than only judgment is the more defensible approach, but it's also more difficult. The aim here is to determine statistically the relationship between (1) some *predictor* (human trait such as height, intelligence, or finger dexterity), and (2) some indicator or *criterion* of job effectiveness, such as performance as rated by the supervisor.

This procedure has five steps: (1) analyze the job and decide how to measure job performance; (2) select personal traits like finger dexterity that you believe should predict performance; (3) test candidates for these traits; (4) measure these candidates' subsequent job performance; and (5) statistically analyze the relationship between the human trait (finger dexterity) and job performance. Your aim is to determine whether the trait predicts performance.

Why is this more defensible than the judgmental approach? First, if the trait does not predict performance, why use it? Second, equal rights laws prohibit using traits that you can't prove distinguish between high and low job performers. But, in practice, most employers rely on judgmental approaches.

The Job-Requirements Matrix

job-requirements matrix
A more complete description of what the worker does and how and why he or she does it; it clarifies each task's purpose and each duty's required knowledge, skills, abilities, and other characteristics.

Although most employers use job descriptions and specifications to summarize their jobs' duties and responsibilities, the **job-requirements matrix** is also popular.[45] A typical matrix lists the following information, in five columns:

Column 1: Each of the job's four or five *main job duties* (such as Post Accounts Payable)

Column 2: The *task statements* for the main tasks associated with each main job duty

Column 3: The relative *importance* of each main job duty

Column 4: The *time spent* on each main job duty

Column 5: The *knowledge, skills, ability*, and *other* human characteristics (KSAO) related to each main job duty[46]

task statement
Written item that shows *what* the worker does on one particular job task; *how* the worker does it; the *knowledge, skills, and aptitudes required* to do it; and the *purpose of the task*.

The main step in creating a job-requirements matrix involves writing the *task statements*. Each **task statement** describes *what* the worker does on each of a main job duty's separate job tasks and *how* the worker does it.

Employee Engagement Guide for Managers

How does one identify candidates who have a high likelihood of becoming engaged employees? In terms of the job specification, the question is, "What desirable traits should someone possess to make it more likely that he or she will become an engaged employee?" The human resource consulting company Development Dimensions International conducted a study of 3,800 employees. It identified several personal characteristics that seemed to predict the likelihood someone would be engaged.[47] These traits included adaptability, passion for work, emotional maturity, positive disposition, self-advocacy, and achievement orientation.

A sensible suggestion is to seek out people who already have track records of being engaged employees. Since past behavior is often the best predictor of future behavior one suggestion is that if you want to hire people who are more likely to become engaged employees, "… look for examples of engagement in other areas of life."[48] For example, seek out candidates with a demonstrated commitment to serve others, such as nurses, veterans, and voluntary first responders.

Using Competencies Models

Many people still think of a "job" as a set of specific duties someone carries out for pay, but the concept of job is changing. Companies today are flattening their hierarchies, squeezing out managers, and leaving the remaining workers with more jobs to do. Changes like these tend to blur where one job starts and another ends. In situations like these, relying on a list of job duties that itemizes specific things you expect the worker to do is often impractical.[49]

Many employers are therefore using a newer job analysis approach. Instead of listing the job's duties, they are listing, in *competency models* (or profiles), the knowledge, skills, and experience someone needs to do the job. Such models or profiles (see Figure 4-8) list the competencies employees must be able to exhibit to get their jobs done.[50] In creating a competency model for HR managers, the Society for Human

FIGURE 4-8 HR Manager Competency Model

Source: The SHRM Body of Competency and Knowledge. ©2014, Society for Human Resource Management., Alexandria, VA. Used with permission. All rights reserved.

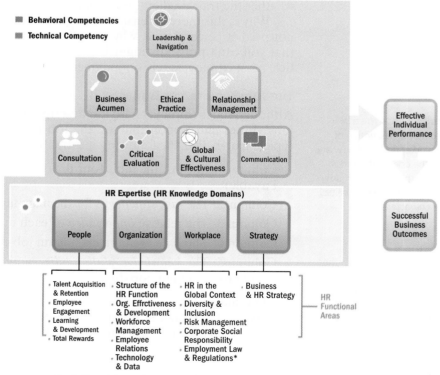

Resource Management describes a competency as a "cluster of highly interrelated attributes" (such as research design knowledge, critical thinking skills, and deductive reasoning abilities) that give rise to the behaviors (such as *critical evaluation)* someone would need to perform a given job (in this case, HR manager) effectively.[51]

The competency model or profile then becomes the guidepost for recruiting, selecting, training, evaluating, and developing employees for each job.[52] For instance, the manager *hires* new employees using tests that measure the profile's list of competencies, *trains* employees with courses that develop these competencies, and *appraises* performance by assessing the worker's competencies. The accompanying Strategic Context feature illustrates.

▶ IMPROVING PERFORMANCE: *The Strategic Context*

Daimler Alabama and the Government of India Examples

In planning its Alabama Mercedes-Benz factory, Germany-based Daimler's strategy was to design a high-tech factory.[53] The plant emphasizes *just-in-time* inventory methods, so inventories stay negligible due to the arrival "just in time" of parts. It also organizes employees into *work teams*, and emphasizes that all employees must dedicate themselves to *continuous improvement* (seeking continuously to find better ways to do things).

Such a production strategy requires certain employee competencies (skills and behaviors). For example, it requires multiskilled and flexible employees who are eager to work cooperatively in teams.

Competencies-based job analysis played an important role in this factory. Guidelines here regarding whom to hire and how to train them are based more on the competencies someone needs to do the job (such as "ability to work cooperatively on a team") than on lists of job duties. Because they don't have to follow detailed job descriptions showing what "my job" is, it's easier for employees to move from job to job within their teams. Not being pigeonholed also encourages workers to look beyond their own jobs to find ways to improve things. For instance, one team found a $0.23 plastic prong that worked better than the one for $2.50 the plant was using to keep car doors open during painting. Building its modern "continuous improvement" plant meant Daimler needed employees who thought for themselves. Organizing its jobs around worker competencies and using **competency-based job analysis** helped Daimler achieve its strategic aims here.

The government of India, with the objective of improving its effectiveness, initiated a project to introduce competency-based HRM process within its functioning. Under the 'Strengthening HRM of Civil Services' project, United Nations Development Program (UNDP) supported this initiative. The project identified 25 competencies, categorized into four groups: Ethos, Ethics, Equity, and Efficiency. The competency framework exercise would help the government in developing effective competency-based job descriptions. The generic framework suggested could be customized as per the needs of different government departments.[54] ■

competency-based job analysis
Describing the job in terms of measurable, observable, behavioral competencies (knowledge, skills, and/or behaviors) that an employee doing that job must exhibit to do the job well.

How to Write Competencies Statements

The process for identifying the job's required competencies is similar to traditional job analysis. For example, you might interview job incumbents and their supervisors and ask open-ended questions regarding job responsibilities and activities.

But instead of compiling lists of job duties, your aim is to finish the statement, "*In order to perform this job competently, the employee should be able to....*"

The ideal competency statement will include three elements.[55] One is the *name and a brief description* of the competency, such as "Project Management—creating accurate and effective project schedules." The second is a *description of the observable behaviors* that represent proficiency in the competency, such as "continuously manage project risks and dependencies by making timely decisions." Third are *proficiency levels.* For example (for project management from low to high):[56]

- *Proficiency Level 1. Identifies* project risks and dependencies and communicates routinely to stakeholders
- *Proficiency Level 2. Develops systems to monitor* risks and dependencies and report changes
- *Proficiency Level 3.* Anticipates changing conditions and impact to risks and dependencies and takes preventive action

FIGURE 4-9 Skills Matrix

Note: This is an example of a skills matrix for technical/engineering product development employees. The light blue boxes show the level required for each skill for these product development employees. An accompanying key would provide specific examples for each level of each skill, with difficulty increasing for each skill level starting at Level 1. For example, Level 1 for Technical Expertise/Skills might say "has or is in process of acquiring the basic knowledge necessary to do this type of job," while Level 6 might say, "Capable of conducting and supervising highly complex analytical tasks requiring advanced technical know-how and skills." *Source:* Copyright Gary Dessler PhD.

	Technical Expertise/Skills	Decision Making and Problem Solving Skills	Interpersonal Skills	Leadership Skills	Commercial Awareness Skills
Level 6	6	6	6	6	6
Level 5	5	5	5	5	5
Level 4	4	4	4	4	4
Level 3	3	3	3	3	3
Level 2	2	2	2	2	2
Level 1	1	1	1	1	1

BP EXAMPLE British Petroleum's (BP's) exploration division executives wanted to shift employees from a job duties–oriented "that's-not-my-job" attitude to one that motivated employees to obtain the skills required to accomplish broader responsibilities.[57]

Their solution was a skills matrix like that in Figure 4-9. They had skills matrices for each job or job family (such as drilling managers). As in Figure 4-9, each matrix listed (1) the types of skills required to do that job such as technical expertise, and (2) the minimum skill required for proficiency at each level. The figure's note shows how to actually use the matrix.

BP's skills matrix approach also supported its talent management efforts. Talent management efforts in this unit could now focus on recruiting, hiring, training, appraising, and rewarding employees based on the set of skills employees need to perform the job in question.

Chapter Review

Chapter Section Summaries

4-1. Employers today often view all the staff–train–reward activities as part of a single integrated *talent management* **process**. We defined talent management as *the holistic, integrated and results and goal-oriented process of planning, recruiting, selecting, developing, managing, and compensating employees.* When a manager takes a talent management perspective, he or she should keep in mind that the talent management tasks are parts of a single interrelated talent management process; make sure talent management decisions such as staffing and pay are goal-directed; use the same "profile" for formulating recruitment plans for a job as you do for making selection, training, appraisal, and payment decisions for it; and integrate/coordinate all the talent management functions.

4-2. All managers should be familiar with **the basics of job analysis**. Job analysis is the procedure through which you determine the duties of the department's positions and the characteristics of the people to hire for them. Job descriptions are a list of what the job entails, while job specifications identify what kind of people to hire for the job. The job analysis itself involves collecting information on matters such as work activities; required human behaviors; and machines, tools, and equipment used. Managers use job analysis information in recruitment and selection, compensation, training, and performance appraisal. The basic steps in job analysis include deciding on the use of the job analysis information, reviewing relevant background information including organization charts, analyzing the job, verifying the information, and developing job descriptions and job specifications.

4-3. There are various **methods for collecting job analysis information**. These include interviews, questionnaires, observation, participant diary/logs, and quantitative techniques such as position analysis questionnaires. Employers increasingly collect information from employees via the Internet.

4-4. Managers should know how to **write job descriptions**. While there is no standard format, most descriptions contain sections that cover job identification, a job summary, a listing of responsibilities and duties, the job incumbent's authority, and performance standards. The job description may also contain information regarding the job's working conditions, and the job specifications. Many employers use Internet sources such as www.jobdescription.com to facilitate writing job descriptions.

4-5. In **writing job specifications**, it's important to distinguish between specifications for trained versus untrained personnel. For trained employees, the process is relatively straightforward, because you're looking primarily for traits like experience. For untrained personnel, it's necessary to identify traits that might predict success on the job. Most job specifications come from the educated guesses of people like supervisors, and are based mostly on judgment. Some employers use statistical analyses to identify predictors or human traits that are related to success on the job.

4-6. Human traits and behaviors that may predict the job candidates' likelihood to be **engaged** and that the manager might therefore want to include in the job specification include adaptability, passion for work, emotional maturity, positive disposition, self-advocacy, achievement orientation, and a work history that includes a demonstrated commitment to serve others.

4-7. Employers are using **competencies models** and profiles in talent management. The aim is to create descriptions of what is required for exceptional performance in a given role or job, in terms of required competencies, personal attributes, knowledge, and experience. Each job's profile then becomes the anchor for creating recruitment, selection, training, and evaluation and development plans for each job. *Competency-based job analysis* means describing the job in terms of measurable, observable, behavioral competencies (such as specific skills) that an employee doing the job must exhibit to do the job well. With the job of, say, a team member possibly changing daily, one should identify the skills the employee may need to move among jobs.

Discussion Questions

4-1. Why, in summary, should managers think of staffing, training, appraising, and paying employees as a talent management process?

4-2. What items are typically included in the job description?

4-3. We discussed several methods for collecting job analysis data—questionnaires, the position analysis questionnaire, and so on. Compare and contrast these methods, explaining what each is useful for and listing the pros and cons of each.

4-4. Describe the types of information typically found in a job specification.

4-5. Explain how you would conduct a job analysis.

4-6. Do you think all companies can really do without detailed job descriptions? Why or why not?

4-7. Explain how you would create a job-requirements matrix for a job.

4-8. In a company with only 25 employees, is there less need for job descriptions? Why or why not?

Individual and Group Activities

4-9. Working individually or in groups, obtain copies of job descriptions for clerical positions at the college or university where you study, or the firm where you work. What types of information do they contain? Do they give you enough information to explain what the job involves and how to do it? How would you improve on the description?

4-10. Working individually or in groups, use information available on the AICTI and UGC websites to develop a job description for your local bank officer or manager. You can visit the branch to observe the work, and if possible, discuss with the job incumbent also. Based on that, use your judgment to develop a job specification. Compare your conclusions with those of other students or groups. Were there any significant differences? What do you think accounted for the differences?

4-11. Appendices A and B at the end of this book (pages 583–600) list the knowledge someone studying for the HRCI (Appendix A) or SHRM (Appendix B) certification exam needs to have in each area of human resource management (such as in Strategic Management, and Workforce Planning). In groups of several students, do four things: (1) review Appendix A and/or B; (2) identify the material in this chapter that relates to the Appendix A and/or Appendix B required knowledge lists; (3) write four multiple-choice exam questions on this material that you believe would be suitable for inclusion in the HRCI exam and/or the SHRM exam; and, (4) if time permits, have someone from your team post your team's questions in front of the class, so that students in all teams can answer the exam questions created by the other teams.

Experiential Exercise

The Instructor's Job Description

Purpose: The purpose of this exercise is to give you experience in developing a job description, by developing one for your instructor.

Required Understanding: You should understand the mechanics of job analysis and be thoroughly familiar with the job analysis questionnaires. (See Figures 4-4 and 4-7.)

How to Set Up the Exercise/Instructions: Set up groups of several students for this exercise. As in all exercises in this book, the groups should be separated and should not converse with each other. Half of the groups in the class will develop the job description using the job analysis questionnaire (Figure 4-4), and the other half of the groups will develop it using the job description questionnaire (Figure 4-7). Each student should review his or her questionnaire (as appropriate) before joining his or her group.

4-12. Each group should do a job analysis of the instructor's job: Half of the groups will use the Figure 4-4 job analysis questionnaire for this purpose, and half will use the Figure 4-7 job description questionnaire.

4-13. Based on this information, each group will develop its own job description and job specification for the instructor.

4-14. Next, each group should choose a partner group, one that developed the job description and job specification using the alternate method. (A group that used the job analysis questionnaire should be paired with a group that used the job description questionnaire.)

4-15. Finally, within each of these new combined groups, compare and critique each of the two sets of job descriptions and job specifications. Did each job analysis method provide different types of information? Which seems superior? Does one seem more advantageous for some types of jobs than others?

Application Case

The Flood

In October 2014, Cyclone Hudhud hit the coastal town of Vishakhapatnam and the Coastal Packing Company. The homes of many of its employees were devastated by this natural calamity. As a result many of them left the town for good. Coastal Packing found that it had to hire thirty completely new crews, ten for each shift. The problem was that the 'old timers' had known their jobs so well that no one ever bothered to draw job descriptions for them. When about thirty new employees began taking their places, there was a general confusion about what they should do and how they should do it. The cyclone quickly became old news to the firm's out-of-state customers, who wanted packing materials, not excuses. Karan Naidu, the firm's president, was at wits' end. He had about 30 new employees, 10 old-timers, and his original factory supervisor, Kumar. He decided to meet with Prof. Parathap Rao and Prof. Rani, who were consultants from the local university's business school. They immediately had the old timers fill up a job questionnaire that listed all their duties and developed a report.

Both Karan and Kumar thought that the old timers were exaggerating to make themselves look more important, while the old timers insisted that the lists faithfully reflected their duties. Meanwhile, the customers clamored for their orders.

Questions

4-16. Should the consultants ignore the old-timers' protests and write the job descriptions as they see fit? Why? Why not? How would you go about resolving the differences?

4-17. How would you have conducted the job analysis? What should Karan do now?

Continuing Case

Carter Cleaning Company

The Job Description

Based on her review of the stores, Jennifer concluded that one of the first matters she had to attend to involved developing job descriptions for her store managers.

As Jennifer tells it, her lessons regarding job descriptions in her basic management and HR management courses were insufficient to convince her of the pivotal role job descriptions actually play in the smooth functioning of an enterprise. Many times during her first few weeks on the job, Jennifer found herself asking one of her store managers why he was violating what she knew to be recommended company policies and procedures. Repeatedly, the answers were either "Because I didn't know it was my job" or "Because I didn't know that was the way we were supposed to do it." Jennifer knew that a job description, along with a set of standards and procedures that specified what was to be done and how to do it, would go a long way toward alleviating this problem.

In general, the store manager is responsible for directing all store activities in such a way that quality work is produced, customer relations and sales are maximized, and profitability is maintained through effective control of labor, supply, and energy costs. In accomplishing that general aim, a specific store manager's duties and responsibilities include quality control, store appearance and cleanliness, customer relations, bookkeeping and cash management, cost control and productivity, damage control, pricing, inventory control, spotting and cleaning, machine maintenance, purchasing, employee safety, hazardous waste removal, human resource administration, and pest control.

The questions that Jennifer had to address follow.

Questions

4-18. What should be the format and final form of the store manager's job description?

4-19. Is it practical to specify standards and procedures in the body of the job description, or should these be kept separate?

4-20. How should Jennifer go about collecting the information required for the standards, procedures, and job description?

4-21. What, in your opinion, should the store manager's job description look like and contain?

Translating Strategy into HR Policies and Practices Case*,§

Improving Performance at The Hotel Paris

The overall map on page xxxviii of this book outlines the relationships involved.

The New Job Descriptions

The Hotel Paris's competitive strategy is "To use superior guest service to differentiate the Hotel Paris properties, and to thereby increase the length of stay and return rate of guests, and thus boost revenues and profitability." HR manager Lisa Cruz must now formulate functional policies and activities that support this competitive strategy and boost performance by eliciting the required employee behaviors and competencies.

As an experienced human resource director, the Hotel Paris's Lisa Cruz knew that recruitment and selection processes invariably influenced employee competencies and behavior and, through them, the company's bottom line. Everything about the workforce—its collective skills, morale, experience, and motivation—depended on attracting and then selecting the right employees.

In reviewing the Hotel Paris's employment systems, she was therefore concerned that virtually all the company's job descriptions were out of date, and that many jobs had no descriptions at all. She knew that without accurate job descriptions, all her improvement efforts would be in vain. After all, if you don't know a job's duties, responsibilities, and human requirements, how can you decide whom to hire or how to train them? To create human resource policies and practices that would produce employee competencies and behaviors needed to achieve the hotel's strategic aims, Lisa's team first had to produce a set of usable job descriptions.

A brief analysis, conducted with her company's CFO, reinforced that observation. They chose departments across the hotel chain that did and did not have updated job descriptions. While they understood that many other factors might be influencing the results, they believed that the statistical relationships they observed did suggest that having job descriptions had a positive influence on various employee behaviors and competencies. Perhaps having the descriptions facilitated the employee selection process, or perhaps the departments with the descriptions just had better managers. In any case, Lisa received the go-ahead to design new job descriptions for the chain.

While the resulting job descriptions included numerous traditional duties and responsibilities, most also included several competencies unique to each job. For example, job descriptions for the front-desk clerks included competencies such as "able to check a guest in or out in five minutes or less." Most service employees' descriptions included the competency, "able to exhibit patience and guest supportiveness even when busy with other activities." Lisa knew that including these competencies would make it easier for her team to devise useful employee selection, training, and evaluation processes.

Questions

In teams or individually:

4-22. Based on the hotel's stated strategy and on what you learned here in Chapter 4 of Dessler Human Resource Management, list at least four more important employee behaviors important for the Hotel Paris's staff to exhibit.

4-23. If time permits, spend some time prior to class observing the front-desk clerk at a local hotel. In any case, create a job description for a Hotel Paris front-desk clerk.

Key Terms

talent management, 95
job analysis, 96
job description, 96
job specifications, 96
organization chart, 98

process chart, 98
workflow analysis, 98
business process
   reengineering, 98
job enlargement, 99

job rotation, 99
job enrichment, 99
diary/log, 104
position analysis questionnaire
   (PAQ), 104

job-requirements matrix, 115
task statement, 115
competency-based job
   analysis, 117

Endnotes

1. See, for example, Toni Hodges DeTuncq and Lynn Schmidt, "Examining Integrated Talent Management," *Training & Development*, September 2013, pp. 31–35.
2. www.talent_management101. com, accessed December 10, 2007; and www.astd.org/ Publications/Blogs/ASTD-B log/2009/05/How-DoYou-Define-Talent-Management, accessed June 16, 2014. See also Nikki Dries, "Talent Management, from Phenomenon to Theory: Introduction to the Special Issue," *Human Resource Management Review*, 23, 2013, pp. 267–271.
3. Ibid.
4. www.zinghr.com, (Navigation--Product-Performance Management & Appraisal), as accessed on 14 August 2017 at 2pm IST.
5. For a good discussion of job analysis, see James Clifford, "Job Analysis: Why Do It, and How Should It Be Done?" *Public Personnel Management* 23, no. 2 (Summer 1994), pp. 321–340; and "Job Analysis," www.paq.com/index. cfm?FuseAction=bulletins.job-analysis, accessed February 3, 2009.
6. One writer calls job analysis "the hub of virtually all human resource management activities necessary for the successful functioning organizations." See Parbudyal Singh, "Job Analysis for a Changing Workplace," *Human Resource Management Review* 18 (2008), p. 87.
7. Richard Henderson, *Compensation Management: Rewarding Performance* (Upper Saddle River, NJ: Prentice Hall, 1994), pp. 139–150. See also T. A. Stetz et al., "New Tricks for an Old Dog: Visualizing Job Analysis Results," *Public Personnel Management* 38, no. 1 (Spring 2009), pp. 91–100.
8. Darin Hartley, "Job Analysis at the Speed of Reality," *Training & Development*, September 2004, pp. 20–22.
9. See Henderson, *Compensation Management*, pp. 148–152.
10. Wayne Cascio, *Applied Psychology in Human Resource Management* (Upper Saddle River, NJ: Prentice Hall, 1998),

p. 142. Distortion of information is a potential problem with all self-report methods of gathering information. See, for example, http://apps.opm.gov/ ADT/ContentFiles/Assessment DecisionGuide071807.pdf, accessed October 1, 2011.
11. Frederick Morgeson et al., "Self Presentation Processes in Job Analysis: A Field Experiment Investigating Inflation in Abilities, Tasks, and Competencies," *Journal of Applied Psychology* 89, no. 4 (November 4, 2004), pp. 674–686; and Frederick Morgeson and Stephen Humphrey, "The Work Design Questionnaire (WDQ): Developing and Validating a Comprehensive Measure for Assessing Job Design and the Nature of Work," *Journal of Applied Psychology* 91, no. 6 (2006), pp. 1321–1339.
12. Arthur Martinez et al., "Job Title Inflation," *Human Resource Management Review* 18 (2008), pp. 19–27.
13. Note that the PAQ (and other quantitative techniques) can also be used for job evaluation, which is explained in Chapter 11.
14. We will see that job evaluation is the process through which jobs are compared to one another and their values determined for pay purposes. Some use the PAQ for job evaluation.
15. Jack Smith and Milton Hakel, "Convergence Among Data Sources, Response Bias, and Reliability and Validity of a Structured Job Analysis Questionnaire," *Personnel Psychology* 32 (Winter 1979), pp. 677–692. See also Frederick Morgeson and Stephen Humphrey, "The Work Design Questionnaire (WDQ): Developing and Validating a Comprehensive Measure for Assessing Job Design and the Nature of Work," *Journal of Applied Psychology* 91, no. 6 (2006), pp. 1321–1339; www.paq.com/index. cfm?FuseAction=bulletins.job-analysis, accessed February 3, 2009.
16. www.paq.com/index. cfm?FuseAction=bulletins.job-analysis, accessed February 3, 2009.

17. Another technique, *functional job analysis,* is similar to the DOL method. However, it rates the job not just on data, people, and things, but also on the extent to which performing the task requires four other things—specific instructions, reasoning and judgment, mathematical ability, and verbal and language facilities.
18. This is based on Dianna Stone et al., "Factors Affecting the Effectiveness and Acceptance of Electronic Selection Systems," *Human Resource Management Review* 23 (2013), pp. 53–54.
19. Ibid.
20. Roni Reiter-Palmon et al., "Development of an O*NET Web-Based Job Analysis and Its Implementation in the U.S. Navy: Lessons Learned," *Human Resource Management Review* 16 (2006), pp. 294–309.
21. Ibid., p. 295.
22. Digitizing the information also enables the employer to quantify, tag, and electronically store and access it more readily. Lauren McEntire et al., "Innovations in Job Analysis: Development and Application of Metrics to Analyze Job Data," *Human Resource Management Review* 16 (2006), pp. 310–323.
23. See, for example, Kathryn Tyler, "Job Worth Doing: Update Descriptions," *HR Magazine*, January 2013, pp. 47–49.
24. Jaiswal, Pooja Biraia, "Need House Help? There's an app 'maid' for you," March 14, 2016, *The Hindu*, www.hindu.com, (Navigation-Home-News-Cities-Mumbai Local), as accessed on 08 August 2017 at 4pm IST.
25. Regarding this discussion, see Henderson, *Compensation Management*, pp. 175–184. See also Louisa Wah, "The Alphabet Soup of Job Titles," *Management Review* 87, no. 6 (June 1, 1998), pp. 40–43.
26. For discussions of writing job descriptions, see James Evered, "How to Write a Good Job Description," *Supervisory Management*, April 1981, pp. 14–19; Roger J. Plachy, "Writing Job Descriptions That Get Results," *Personnel*, October 1987, pp. 56–58; and Jean Phillips and Stanley Gulley,

Strategic Staffing (Upper Saddle River, New Jersey: Pearson Education, 2012), pp. 89–95.
27. Evered, "How to Write a Good Job Description," p. 16.
28. Ibid.
29. Ibid.
30. Courtesy: National Career Service, www.ncs.gov.in, National Classification of Occupations - 2015, Vol-I, Govt. of India, (PDF link: https://www.ncs.gov. in/Documents/National%20 Classification%20of%20Occupations%20_Vol%20I-%202015.pdf)
31. http://hiring.monster.com/hr/ hr-best-practices/recruiting-hiring-advice/job-descriptions/ marketing-and-sales-manager-job-description-sample.aspx, accessed June 25, 2014.
32. http://job-descriptions.career planner.com/Marketing-Managers.cfm, accessed June 25, 2014.
33. www.linkedin.com/groups/ Best-job-descriptions-40949.S.201279941, accessed March 26, 2013.
34. Ashley Ross, "Job Titles Retailored to Fit," *New York Times*, September 1, 2013, p. 11.
35. http://academicaffairs.ucsd. edu/staffhr/classification/ task-statements.html, accessed March 27, 2013.
36. Deborah Kearney, *Reasonable Accommodations: Job Descriptions in the Age of ADA, OSHA, and Workers Comp* (New York: Van Nostrand Reinhold, 1994), p. 9. See also Paul Starkman, "The ADA's Essential Job Function Requirements: Just How Essential Does an Essential Job Function Have to Be?" *Employee Relations Law Journal* 26, no. 4 (Spring 2001), pp. 43–102; and Benjamin Wolkinson and Sarah Wolkinson, "The Pregnant Police Officer's Overtime Duties and Forced Leave Policies under Title VII, the ADA, and FMLA," *Employee Relations Law Journal* 36, no. 1 (Summer 2010), pp. 3–20.
37. Kearney, *Reasonable Accommodations*.
38. O*NET™ is a trademark of the U.S. Department of Labor, Employment, and Training Administration.
39. See, for example, Christelle Lapolice et al., "Linking

O*NET Descriptors to Occupational Literacy Requirements Using Job Component Validation," *Personnel Psychology* 61 (2008), pp. 405–441.

40. Mariani, "Replace with a Database."

41. Jorgen Sandberg, "Understanding Competence at Work," *Harvard Business Review*, March 2001, p. 28. Other organization chart software vendors include Nakisa, Aquire, and Human-Concepts. See "Advanced Org Charting," *Workforce Management*, May 19, 2008, p. 34.

42. Based on Ernest J. McCormick and Joseph Tiffin, *Industrial Psychology* (Upper Saddle River, NJ: Prentice Hall, 1974), pp. 56–61.

43. Steven Hunt, "Generic Work Behavior: An Investigation into the Dimensions of Entry-Level, Hourly Job Performance," *Personnel Psychology* 49 (1996), pp. 51–83.

44. "Are the Best People Being Promoted?" *Harvard Business Review*, September 2013, p. 89.

45. Jean Phillips and Stanley Gulley, *Strategic Staffing* (Upper Saddle River, NJ: Pearson Education, 2012), pp. 96–102.

46. Ibid., p. 102.

47. "Hiring engaged and self-motivated new employees is often the intangible ingredient that eludes managers in the selection process," www.HR.com, February 21, 2006, accessed January 21, 2014.

48. Paul Marciano, "How to Hire Engaged Employees," http://www.monster.com/about/b/how-to-hire-engaged-employees accessed June 20, 2015.

49. Jeffrey Shippmann et al., "The Practice of Competency Modeling," *Personnel Psychology* 53, no. 3 (2000), p. 703.

50. Michael Campion et al., "Doing Competencies Well: Best Practices in Competency Modeling," *Personnel Psychology* 64 (2011), pp. 225–262.

51. www.shrm.org/certification/Documents/SHRM-BoCK-FINAL4.pdf, p. 4, accessed March 20, 2015.

52. Richard S. Wellins et al., "Nine Best Practices for Effective Talent Management," DDI Development Dimensions International, Inc. www.ddiworld.com/DDIWorld/media/white-papers/ninebestpracticetalentmanagement_wp_ddi.pdf?extpdf, accessed August 20, 2011. For a discussion of competency modelling,

see Campion et al., "Doing Competencies Well."

53. Based on Lindsay Chappell, "Mercedes Factories Embrace a New Order," *Automotive News*, May 28, 2001. See also www.autoblog.com/2009/03/23/rumormillmercedes-benz-expected-to-expandalabama-plant, accessed March 25, 2009, http://mbusi.com, accessed August 20, 2009.

54. Accessed on 24 August 2017 at http://persmin.gov.in/otraining/Implementation%20Tool-kit.pdf.

55. This is adapted from Campion et al., "Doing Competencies Well."

56. Ibid.

57. See, for example, Carol Spicer, "Building a Competency Model," *HR Magazine,* April 2009, pp. 34–36.

5

Personnel Planning and Recruiting

LEARNING OBJECTIVES

5-1 Explain the main techniques used in employment planning and forecasting.

5-2 Explain and give examples for the need for effective recruiting.

5-3 Name and describe the main internal sources of candidates.

5-4 Discuss a workforce planning method you would use to improve employee engagement.

5-5 List and discuss the main outside sources of candidates.

5-6 Explain how to recruit a more diverse workforce.

5-7 Discuss practical guidelines for obtaining application information.

The Taj Mahal Palace Hotel in Mumbai is one of the top-ranked hotels in the world because of the extraordinary customer service that it provides to its guests. To do anything for guests and to put their interests at the forefront form the organizational culture of Taj, which is owned by the Tata Group. However, following this organizational culture for decades requires honest and committed employees. Using its unique recruitment system, Taj is successful in hiring the type of employees it wants, and we will study about it in detail in this chapter.[1]

WHERE ARE WE NOW …

In Chapter 4, we discussed job analysis and the methods managers use to create job descriptions, job specifications, and competency profiles or models. The purpose of this chapter is to improve your effectiveness in recruiting candidates. The topics we discuss include personnel planning and forecasting, using promotion from within to foster engagement, recruiting job candidates, and developing and using application forms. Then, in Chapter 6, we'll turn to the methods managers use to select the best employees from this applicant pool

Introduction

Job analysis identifies the duties and human requirements of each of the company's jobs. The next step is to decide which of these jobs you need to fill, and to recruit and select employees for them.

The recruiting and selecting process can be envisioned as a series of hurdles, as illustrated in Figure 5-1:

1. Decide what positions to fill, through *workforce/personnel planning and forecasting*.
2. Build a pool of candidates for these jobs, by *recruiting* internal or external candidates.
3. Have candidates complete *application forms* and perhaps undergo initial screening interviews.
4. Use *selection tools* like tests, background investigations, and physical exams to screen candidates.
5. Decide who to make an offer to, by having the supervisor and perhaps others *interview* the candidates.

This chapter focuses on personnel planning and on recruiting employees. Chapters 6 and 7 address tests, background checks, physical exams, and interviews.

Workforce Planning and Forecasting

LEARNING OBJECTIVE **5-1**
Explain the main techniques used in employment planning and forecasting.

workforce (or employment or personnel) planning
The process of deciding what positions the firm will have to fill, and how to fill them.

Workforce (or employment or personnel) planning is the process of deciding what positions the firm will have to fill, and how to fill them. Its aim is to identify and address the gaps between the employer's workforce today, and its projected workforce needs. Workforce planning should precede recruitment and selection. After all, if you don't know what your employment needs will be in the next few months or years, why are you hiring?

One international consulting firm's approach illustrates workforce planning.[2] Indian consulting firms also adopt similar approach. Many Indian companies conduct this exercise internally and, at least, in some cases, a simple rule of thumb or experience-based judgment is applied. The scientific method, as followed by this international consultant discussed here, has its merits. First, Towers Watson *reviews the client's business plan and workforce data* (for instance, on how sales influence staffing levels). This helps them better understand how projected business plan changes may influence the client's headcount and skills requirements. Second, they *identify what positions the firm will have to fill and potential workforce gaps,* by making workforce supply and demand projections; this helps them understand what new future positions they'll have to fill, and what current employees may be promotable into those positions. Third, they develop a *workforce strategic plan*; here they prioritize key workforce gaps (such as, what positions will have to be filled, and who do we have who can fill them?) and identify specific (training and other) plans for filling any gaps. Finally, they *implement* the changes (for instance, new recruiting and training programs),

FIGURE 5-1 **Steps in Recruitment and Selection Process**

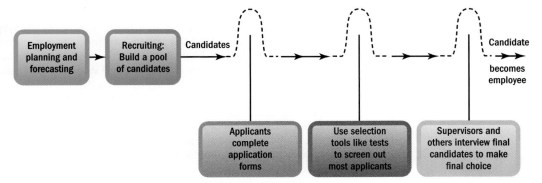

The recruitment and selection process is a series of hurdles aimed at selecting the best candidate for the job.

The dashboards, which are part of Towers Watson's workforce planning Internet software, help clients manage the workforce planning process.

Source: © Towers Watson 2012. Used with permission.

Workforce scan

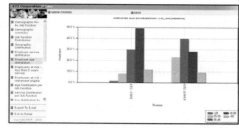

Dashboards

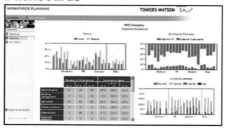

Workforce projection model

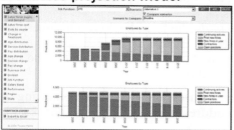

External labour scan

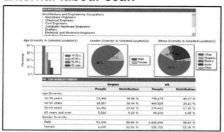

and use various metrics to monitor the process. According to the Indian Staffing Federation, there is a surge in the number of Indian companies that are approaching workforce planning very seriously. As a result, many IT and logistics firms have been using temporary staffing to meet short-term and seasonal talent shortage.[3] For the IT industry, multiple challenges of global business pressures and process automation ask for better workforce planning required to build a future ready organization.[4] Towers Watson clients can use its special "MAPS" software to facilitate the workforce planning process. MAPS contains dashboards (see the four exhibits above). The manager uses these, for instance, to monitor key recruitment metrics, and to conduct a detailed analysis of the current workforce and historical workforce trends.

Workforce planning embraces all future positions, from maintenance clerk to CEO. However, we'll see that most firms call the process of deciding how to fill executive jobs *succession planning.*[5]

Strategy and Workforce Planning

Workforce planning shouldn't occur in a vacuum. Instead, workforce/employment planning is best understood as an outgrowth of the firm's strategic and business planning. For example, plans to enter new businesses, to build new plants, or to reduce activities will all influence the number of and types of positions to be filled. At the same time, decisions regarding how to fill these positions will impact other HR plans, for instance, training and recruitment plans. The Strategic Context feature illustrates.

▶ IMPROVING PERFORMANCE: *The Strategic Context*

As noted earlier, the Taj Hotel's strategy is to be a world-class hotel chain which provides superior customer service and experience. To fulfill this strategy, the hotel requires committed and inspired employees who would walk an extra mile to delight its guests. In a world where employees are driven by money than anything else, how does Taj manage to get personnel who are highly committed and stand by the values of the organization? Taj's unique recruitment system makes this possible. It recruits from small and hinterland towns like Mangalore (not major towns like Mumbai or Delhi), and Tier B and Tier C business schools (not the A-ranked ones). Taj's recruitment principle is based on this belief that employees who live in the hinterland and small towns live by the culture of respecting elders and honesty rather than just earning money. Also, it believes that students from the Tier B and Tier C business schools look for a stable career and can adjust well with the customer-centric philosophy of Taj, which makes it easier to groom such employees. Therefore, Taj looks for personnel who have respect for elders and who exhibit cultural values such as honesty, integrity, and helpful nature. No wonder, recruiting employees who exhibit these values have made Taj successful in keeping its customers satisfied.[6]

Like any good plan, employment plans are built on forecasts—basic assumptions about the future. As at Taj Mahal Palace Hotel or a public-sector bank like the Bank of Baroda, which operates in a regulated but competitive and evolving environment, one basic employment planning decision will be whether to fill projected openings internally (with current employees) or externally (by bringing in new people). Therefore, you will usually need three sets of employment forecasts: one for personnel needs (demand), one for the supply of inside candidates, and one for the supply of outside candidates. With these, the manager can identify supply–demand gaps, and develop action plans to fill the projected gaps. We will start with forecasting personnel needs/demand.

Forecasting Personnel Needs (Labor Demand)

How many people with what skills will we need? Managers consider several factors.[7] For example, the public-sector-undertaking (PSU) banks are expected to face high levels of natural retirement in the coming years. Anticipating this, the Bank of Baroda intensified its entry-level recruitment initiative. The bank also approached the open market to recruit experienced employees.

A firm's future staffing needs reflect demand for its products or services, adjusted for changes the firm plans to make in its strategic goals and for changes in its turnover rate and productivity. Forecasting workforce demand therefore starts with estimating what the demand will be for your products or services. Short term, management should be concerned with daily, weekly, and seasonal forecasts.[8] For example, retailers track daily sales trends because they know, for instance, that Diwali or New Year produces a jump in business and a need for additional store staff. Seasonal forecasts are critical for retailers contemplating end-of-year holiday and festival sales, and for many firms such as landscaping and air-conditioning vendors. Indian e-commerce companies like Flipkart plan for such festivals in advance, and they ready additional employees for the festival rush and last mile delivery process.[9]

Longer term, managers will follow industry publications and economic forecasts closely, to try to get a sense for future demand. Such future predictions won't be precise, but should help you address the potential changes in demand.

The basic process for forecasting personnel needs is to forecast revenues first. Then estimate the size of the staff required to support this sales volume. However, managers must also consider other factors. These include projected turnover, decisions to upgrade (or downgrade) products or services, productivity changes, financial resources, and decisions to enter or leave businesses. The basic tools for projecting personnel needs include trend analysis, ratio analysis, and the scatter plot.

trend analysis
Study of a firm's past employment needs over a period of years to predict future needs.

TREND ANALYSIS **Trend analysis** means studying variations in the firm's employment levels over the past few years. For example, compute the number of employees at the end of each of the last 5 years in each subgroup (like sales, production, secretarial, and administrative) to identify trends.

Trend analysis can provide an initial rough estimate of future staffing needs. However, employment levels rarely depend just on the passage of time. Other factors (like productivity and retirements, for instance), and changing skill needs will influence impending workforce needs.

ratio analysis
A forecasting technique for determining future staff needs by using ratios between, for example, sales volume and number of employees needed.

RATIO ANALYSIS Another simple approach, **ratio analysis**, means making forecasts based on the historical ratio between (1) some causal factor (like sales volume) and (2) the number of employees required (such as number of salespeople). For example, suppose a salesperson traditionally generates ₹500,000 in sales. If the sales revenue to salespeople ratio remains the same, you would require six new salespeople next year (each of whom produces an extra ₹5,00,000) to produce a hoped-for extra ₹3 million in sales.

Like trend analysis, ratio analysis assumes that things like productivity remain about the same. If sales productivity were to rise or fall, the ratio of sales to salespeople would change.

scatter plot
A graphical method used to help identify the relationship between two variables.

THE SCATTER PLOT   A **scatter plot** shows graphically how two variables—such as sales and your firm's staffing levels—are related. If they are, then if you can forecast the business activity (like sales), you should also be able to estimate your personnel needs.

For example, suppose a 500-bed hospital expects to expand to 1,200 beds over the next 5 years. The human resource director wants to forecast how many registered nurses the hospital will need. The human resource director realizes she must determine the relationship between hospital size (in number of beds) and number of nurses required. She calls eight hospitals of various sizes and finds this:

Size of Hospital (Number of Beds)	Number of Registered Nurses
200	240
300	260
400	470
500	500
600	620
700	660
800	820
900	860

Figure 5-2's graph compares hospital size and number of nurses. If the two are related, then the points you plot (from the data above) will tend to fall on a straight line, as here. If you carefully draw in a line to minimize the distances between the line and each one of the plotted points, you will be able to estimate the number of nurses needed for each hospital size. Thus, for a 1,200-bed hospital, the human resource director would assume she needs about 1,210 nurses.

While simple, tools like scatter plots have drawbacks.[10]

1. Historical sales/personnel relationships assume that the firm's existing activities and skill needs will continue as is.
2. They tend to reward managers for adding employees, irrespective of the company's needs.
3. They tend to institutionalize existing ways of doing things, even in the face of change.

Computerized systems and Excel spreadsheets help managers translate estimates of projected productivity and sales levels into forecastable personnel requirements. *Computerized forecasts* enable managers to build more variables into their personnel projections.

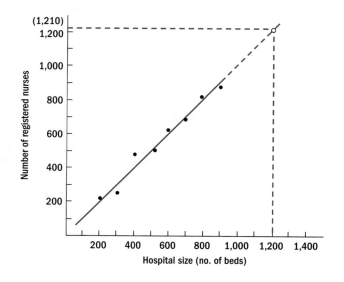

FIGURE 5-2 Determining the Relationship Between Hospital Size and Number of Nurses

Note: After fitting the line, you can project how many employees you'll need, given your projected volume.

Thus, at Chelan County Public Utility District in the US, the development manager built a statistical model encompassing such things as age, tenure, turnover rate, and time to train new employees.[11] This model helped quickly identify five occupational "hotspots" among 33 occupational groups at the company. This in turn prompted Chelan to focus more closely on creating plans to retain and hire, for instance, more systems operators.[12]

MANAGERIAL JUDGMENT   Few historical trends, ratios, or relationships will continue unchanged into the future. Judgment is thus needed to adjust the forecast. Important factors that may modify your initial forecast of personnel requirements include decisions to upgrade quality or enter into new markets; technological and administrative changes resulting in increased productivity; and financial resources available, for instance, a projected budget crunch.

Forecasting the Supply of Inside Candidates

The personnel demand forecast provides only half the staffing equation, by answering the question: "How many employees in what positions will we need?" Next, the manager must forecast the *supply* (availability) of inside and outside candidates.

Most firms start with possible inside candidates. The main task here is determining which current employees are qualified or trainable for the projected openings. Department managers or owners of smaller firms can use manual devices to track employee qualifications (or will simply know who can do what). For example, you can create your own *personnel skills inventory and development record form*.[13] For each current employee, list the person's skills, education, company-sponsored courses taken, career and development interests, languages, desired assignments, and other relevant experiences. Computerized versions of skills inventory systems are also available.[14]

Personnel replacement charts (Figure 5-3) are another option, particularly for the firm's top positions. They show the present performance and promotability for each position's potential replacement. As an alternative, with a **position replacement card** you create a card for each position, showing possible replacements as well as their present performance, promotion potential, and training.

personnel replacement charts
Company records showing present performance and promotability of inside candidates for the most important positions.

position replacement card
A card prepared for each position in a company to show possible replacement candidates and their qualifications.

FIGURE 5-3 Personnel or Management Replacement Chart Showing Development Needs of Potential Future Divisional Vice Presidents

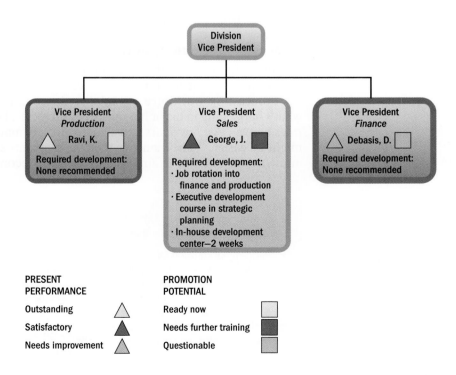

Larger firms obviously can't track the qualifications of hundreds or thousands of employees manually. They therefore computerize this information, using various packaged software systems such as Survey Analytics's Skills Inventory Software. Skills inventory systems enables employers to collect and compile employee skills information in real time via online employee surveys. Skills inventory programs help management anticipate staffing and skills shortages, and facilitate workforce planning, recruitment, and training.[15] They typically include items like *work experience codes, product knowledge*, the employee's *level of familiarity* with the employer's product lines or services, the person's *industry experience, formal education*, industry *experiences*, foreign *language* skills, *relocation* limitations, *career* interests, and *performance* appraisals.

The usual skills inventory process is for the employee, the supervisor, and human resource manager to enter information about the employee's background, experience, and skills via the system. Then, when a manager needs someone for a position, he or she uses key words to describe the position's specifications (for instance, in terms of education and skills). The computerized system then produces a list of qualified candidates. As the user of one such system said, "The [SumTotal] platform allows us to track and assess the talent pool and promote people within the company. … The succession module helps us to identify who the next senior managers could be and build development plans to help them achieve their potential. Online web sites like BabaJob (www.babajob.com) operates a digital platform that connects skilled and semiskilled individuals like drivers, maids, etc., seeking jobs with prospective employers, where the platform acts as the skill inventory. Similarly, the Blind People Association of India maintains skill inventory of differently-abled talent, which can be accessed by employers."[16]

The employer must secure all its employee data.[17] The U.S. Legislation gives employees legal rights regarding who has access to information about them.[18] Internet access makes it relatively easy for more people to access the firm's computerized files.[19] A few Indian firms dealing with employee data of overseas clients, were penalized for data leaks. Figure 5-4 summarizes some guidelines as practiced in the US for keeping employee data safe.

MARKOV ANALYSIS Employers also use a mathematical process known as *Markov analysis* (or "transition analysis") to forecast availability of internal job candidates. Markov analysis involves creating a matrix that shows the probabilities that employees in the chain of feeder positions for a key job (such as from junior engineer, to engineer, to senior engineer, to engineering supervisor, to director of engineering) will move from position to position and therefore be available to fill the key position.

Forecasting the Supply of Outside Candidates

If there won't be enough skilled inside candidates to fill the anticipated openings (or you want to go outside for another reason), you will turn to outside candidates.

Forecasting workforce availability depends first on the manager's own sense of what's happening in his or her industry and locale. For example, the U.S. unemployment rates above 7% a few years ago signaled to HR managers that finding good candidates might be easier.[20] The manager then supplements such observations with formal labor market analyses. For example, they look for economic and employment projections

FIGURE 5-4 Keeping Data Safe

Source: Reprinted with permission from HR Magazine, November 2005. © SHRM.

Since intruders can strike from outside an organization or from within, HR departments can help screen out potential identity thieves by following four basic rules:

- Perform background checks on anyone who is going to have access to personal information.
- If someone with access to personal information is out sick or on leave, don't hire a temporary employee to replace him or her. Instead, bring in a trusted worker from another department.
- Perform random background checks such as random drug tests. Just because someone passed 5 years ago doesn't mean their current situation is the same.
- Limit access to information such as SSNs, health information, and other sensitive data to HR managers who require it to do their jobs.

from the NITI Aayog (niti.gov.in), the Reserve Bank of India (rbi.org.in), and the Ministry of Labor, government of India.

Today's emphasis on technology means many applicants may lack basic skills such as math, communication, creativity, and teamwork.[21] Such needs, too, get factored into the employer's workforce and training plans.

Predictive Workforce Monitoring

Most employers review their workforce plans every year or so, but this isn't always sufficient For instance, having failed to do much formal workforce planning, Valero Energy almost lacked sufficient time to implement a plan to address replacing employees who would soon retire.

Workforce planning therefore often involves *paying continuous attention* to workforce planning issues. Managers call this *predictive workforce monitoring*. For example, Intel Corporation conducts semiannual "Organization Capability Assessments." The staffing department works with the firm's business heads twice a year to assess workforce needs—both immediate and up to 2 years in the future.[22] Boeing Corp. considers various factors when predicting talent gaps as part of its "workforce modeling" process. These include Boeing workforce characteristics such as age, retirement eligibility for employees with various skills, economic trends, anticipated increases or decreases in staffing levels, and internal transfers and promotions.[23] The accompanying HR as a Profit Center feature shows an example.

▶ IMPROVING PERFORMANCE: *HR as a Profit Center*

Predicting Labor Needs

Valero Energy created a "labor supply chain" for improving the efficiency of its workforce planning, recruiting, and hiring process. It includes an analytic tool that predicts Valero's labor needs based on past trends. And, it includes computer screen "dashboards" that show how components in the staffing chain, such as ads placed on job boards, are performing according to cost, speed, and quality. Before implementing the labor supply chain system, it took 41 pieces of paper to bring on board an employee and more than 120 days to fill a position; each hire cost about $12,000. The new system eliminated most of the paper forms needed to hire an employee, time to fill fell below 40 days, and cost per hire dropped to $2,300.[24] ■

Source: Based on Ed Frauenheim, "Valero Energy," Workforce Management, March 13, 2006.

Matching Projected Labor Supply and Labor Demand

Workforce planning should logically culminate in a workforce plan. This plan lays out the employer's projected workforce and skills gaps, as well as staffing plans for filling these gaps. For example, the plan should identify the positions to be filled; potential internal and external candidates or sources for these positions; the training and promotions moving people into the positions will entail; and the resources that implementing the plan will require, for instance, in recruiter fees, estimated training costs, relocation costs, and interview expenses.[25]

Succession Planning

succession planning
The ongoing process of systematically identifying, assessing, and developing organizational leadership to enhance performance.

Succession planning involves developing workforce plans for the company's top positions. **Succession planning** is the ongoing process of systematically identifying, assessing, and developing organizational leadership to enhance performance.[26] It entails three steps: identify key position needs, develop inside candidates, and assess and choose those who will fill the key positions.[27]

First, based on the company's strategic and business plans, top management and the human resource director identify what the company's future key position needs will be. Matters to address here include defining key positions and "high potentials," reviewing the company's current talent, and creating (based on the company's strategy) skills profiles for the key positions.[28]

After identifying future key positions, management turns to creating candidates for these jobs. "Creating" means identifying inside or outside candidates and providing them with the developmental experiences they require to be viable candidates. Employers develop high-potential employees through internal training and cross-functional experiences, job rotation, external training, and global/regional assignments.[29]

Finally, succession planning requires assessing these candidates and selecting those who will actually fill the key positions.[30]

EXAMPLE   At Dole Foods, the US-based marketer of fresh fruits and vegetables, the new president's strategy involved improving financial performance by reducing redundancies and centralizing certain activities, including succession planning.[31] Dole contracted with application system providers (ASPs) to handle things like payroll management.[32] For succession management, Dole chose software from Pilat NAI. The Pilat system keeps all the data on its own servers for a monthly fee. Dole's managers access the program via the Web using a password. They fill out online résumés for themselves, including career interests, and note special considerations such as geographic restrictions.

The managers also assess themselves on four competencies. Once the manager provides his or her input, the program notifies that manager's boss, who assesses his or her subordinate and indicates whether the person is promotable. This assessment and the online résumés then go automatically to the division head and the divisional HR director. Dole's senior vice president for human resources then uses the information to create career development plans for each manager, including seminars and other programs.[33]

LEARNING OBJECTIVE **5-2**

Explain and give examples for the need for effective recruiting.

employee recruiting
Finding and/or attracting applicants for the employer's open positions.

Why Effective Recruiting is Important

Assuming the company authorizes you to fill a position, the next step is to build up, through recruiting, an applicant pool. **Employee recruiting** means finding and/or attracting applicants for the employer's open positions.

Recruiting is important. If only two candidates apply for two openings, you may have little choice but to hire them. But if 10 or 20 applicants appear, you can use techniques like interviews and tests to screen out all but the best.

Even when unemployment rates are high, many employers have trouble finding qualified applicants. One survey found that about two-thirds of the manufacturing executives surveyed a few years ago faced a "moderate to severe shortage of skilled labor."[34] With manufacturing jobs increasingly high-tech, the available jobs require more math and science than most applicants possess.[35] A recent Lloyd's of London risk index listed "talent and skill shortages" as the number 2 risk facing businesses today ("loss of customers" was number 1).[36]

Of course, it's not just recruiting but effective recruiting that is important. Consider one study of recruiter effectiveness.[37] Subjects were 41 graduating college students who'd been on several job interviews. When asked after the initial job interview why they thought a particular company might be a good fit, 39 mentioned the nature of the job, but 23 said they'd been turned off by the recruiters. For example, some were dressed sloppily; others were "barely literate"; some were rude; and some made offensive comments. Also potentially undermining one's recruiting is the fact that some recruiting methods are superior to others, depending on the job, and that recruiting depends on nonrecruitment issues such as pay.[38] We've also seem that employment law prescribes what you can do.[39]

Even the employer's "brand" or reputation will impact recruiting success. Most obviously, it is futile to recruit if the employer's reputation is that it's an awful place to work.

How does the employer want others to see it as a place to work? The branding often focuses on what it's like to work at the company, including company values and the work

FIGURE 5-5 **Recruiting Yield Pyramid**

50	New hires
100	Offers made (2:1)
150	Candidates interviewed (3:2)
200	Candidates invited (4:3)
1,200	Leads generated (6:1)

environment.[40] GE, for instance, stresses innovation (hiring "bright, interesting people working together on new and exciting projects").[41] Mahindra Group emphasizes on providing talent with opportunities to "Rise", which is different from the conventional careers offered.[42] Similarly, the Indian Space Research Organization (ISRO) offers a challenge to aspirants by asking "Is sky the limit?"[43] Others stress being environmentally or socially responsible.[44]

The Recruiting Yield Pyramid

recruiting yield pyramid
The historical arithmetic relationships between recruitment leads and invitees, invitees and interviews, interviews and offers made, and offers made and offers accepted.

Filling a relative handful of positions might require recruiting dozens or hundreds of candidates. Managers therefore use a staffing or **recruiting yield pyramid**, as shown in Figure 5-5, to gauge the staffing issues it needs to address. In Figure 5-5, the company knows it needs 50 new entry-level accountants next year. From experience, the firm also knows the following:

- The ratio of offers made to actual new hires is 2 to 1.
- The ratio of candidates interviewed to offers made is 3 to 2.
- The ratio of candidates invited for interviews to candidates interviewed is about 4 to 3.
- Finally, the firm knows that of six leads that come in from all its recruiting sources, it typically invites only one applicant for an interview—a 6-to-1 ratio.

Therefore, the firm must generate about 1,200 leads to be able to invite in 200 viable candidates of which it interviews about 150, and so on.

KNOW YOUR EMPLOYMENT LAW

Recruiting Employees

As we explained in Chapter 2, numerous laws and court decisions restrict what employers can and cannot do when recruiting job applicants. In practice, "the key question in all recruitment procedures is whether the method limits qualified applicants from applying."[45] So, for example, gender-specific ads that call for "busboy" or "firemen" or a specific community (unless its a special recruitment drive which is legally allowed) would obviously raise red flags. Campus recruitment drives by the Indian public sector banks for probationary officer posts were questioned by the courts in 2015, as only a few institutions were patronized. At present, the government of India has prohibited PSUs from campus hiring because it violates the constitutional principle of equality.[46] Similarly, in the US courts will often question word-of-mouth recruiting, because workers tend to nominate candidates of the same nationality, race, and religion.[47]

Other laws are relevant. For example, it is illegal for employers to conspire not to hire each other's employees. Yet Apple and Google recently paid over $400 million to settle a claim alleging that they did just that.[48] ∎

THE SUPERVISOR'S ROLE Line and staff cooperation in recruitment is essential. The human resource manager charged with filling an open position is seldom very familiar with the job itself. So, for example, the recruiter will want to know from the supervisor what the job really entails and its job specifications, as well as informal things like the supervisor's leadership style and how the team gets along.

HR in Practice at the Hotel Paris As they reviewed the details of the Hotel Paris's current recruitment practices, Lisa Cruz and the firm's CFO became increasingly concerned. They found that the recruitment function was totally unmanaged. To see how they handled this, see the case on page 168 of this chapter.

LEARNING OBJECTIVE 5-3

Name and describe the main internal sources of candidates.

Internal Sources of Candidates

Recruiting typically brings to mind LinkedIn, employment agencies, and classified ads, but internal sources—in other words, current employees or "hiring from within"—are often the best sources of candidates.

Filling open positions with inside candidates has advantages. First, there is really no substitute for knowing a candidate's strengths and weaknesses, as you should after working with him or her for some time. Current employees may also be more committed to the company. Morale and engagement may rise if employees see promotions as rewards for loyalty and competence. And inside candidates should require less orientation and (perhaps) training than outsiders. Most Indian firms, particularly the PSUs, strictly followed the principle of filling positions from internally upto the very senior levels.

There are other advantages. External hires tend to come in at higher salaries than do those promoted internally, and some apparent "stars" hired from outside may turn out to have excelled more because of the company they came from than from their own skills.

One executive recruiter argues that internal candidates are always better than external ones unless the internal candidates simply can't pass muster. One study concluded that firms that hired their CEOs from inside rather than outside performed better. On the other hand, some firms—particularly those facing enormous challenges—such as IBM and Ford Motor Company—did extremely well by bringing in outside managers (respectively, Louis Gerstner and Alan Mullally). Two well-discussed cases in the Indian context about external hiring was that of the Tata Group and Infosys, where outsiders were recruited at the top level. In both cases, there were serious difference in opinion about the performance of the external recruits.[49]

Hiring from within can also backfire. Inbreeding is a potential drawback, if new perspectives are required. The process of posting openings and getting inside applicants can also be a waste of time, since often the department manager already knows whom he or she wants to hire. Rejected inside applicants may become discontented; telling them why you rejected them and what remedial actions they might take is crucial.

There are some practical rules to use in determining whether to go outside or promote from within. For example, if you need specific skills that aren't currently available in your company, or have to embark on a tough turnaround, or face a situation in which your current succession planning or skills inventory systems are inadequate, it may be best to look outside. On the other hand, if your company is thriving and you have effective succession planning and skills inventory systems, have the skills you need internally, and have a unique and strong company culture, then look within.[50]

Finding Internal Candidates

In a perfect world, the employer will adhere to formal internal-recruitment policies and procedures. These typically rely heavily on job posting and on the firm's skills inventories. **Job posting** means publicizing the open job to employees (usually by literally posting it on company intranets or bulletin boards). These postings list the job's attributes, like qualifications, supervisor, work schedule, and pay rate. Qualifications skills inventories also play a role. For example, they may reveal to the company's recruiters those employees

job posting

Publicizing an open job to employees (often by literally posting it on bulletin boards) and listing its attributes, like qualifications, supervisor, working schedule, and pay rate.

who have the right background for the open job. Ideally, the employer's system therefore matches the best inside candidate with the job. In practice, this doesn't always happen. For better or worse, internal politics and having the right connections may well lead to placements that seem (and indeed may be) unfair and suboptimal.

Rehiring someone who left your employ has pros and cons. Former employees are known quantities (more or less) and are already familiar with how you do things. On the other hand, employees who you let go may return with negative attitudes.[51] Inquire (before rehiring) about what they did during the layoff and how they feel about returning. After a probationary period, credit them with the years of service they had accumulated before they left.[52]

LEARNING OBJECTIVE 5-4

Discuss a workforce planning method you would use to improve employee engagement.

Employee Engagement Guide for Managers

Promotion from Within

Many employers encourage internal recruiting, on the reasonable assumption that doing so improves employee engagement. Thus, as IBM shifted from supplying mostly hardware to consulting, it assessed its skills gaps and instituted workforce plans to train current employees for new jobs; this assumedly fostered employee engagement. Similarly, International Paper appointed a single person "to provide support to all [business units], Staff Groups and Regions for Workforce Planning and Engagement."[53] Other employers, faced with strategic shifts, simply dismiss employees who don't "fit."

Internal recruitment and promotions from within are common in Indian family businesses and PSUs. It is common for an employee who started at the entry level to become the company head. A.M. Naik, who is the chairperson of engineering giant Larsen & Toubro Limited (L&T), and Arundati Bhattacharya, who was the chairperson of the State Bank of India (SBI), are two such examples. A.M. Naik started as a graduate engineer and worked his way up at L&T, and the former SBI chairperson joined the bank as a Probationary Officer. Both these organizations are known for investing in the development of their employees, and providing opportunity to work on unique roles, with a variety of challenges and exposure.

External recruitment is attempted only if internal talent is not available. However, in recent years, the trend is changing. Even PSU banks like Bank of Baroda and Canara Bank have hired CEOs from outside the public sector bank system. Recruitment from within contributes to higher level of employee engagement. We will discuss later (in Chapter 8 Careers), the effects of promotion from within, without effective performance appraisal and training.

A manager interested in fostering his or her employees' engagement can draw several useful guidelines from L&T's and SBI's promotion-from-within system: show a genuine interest in your employees' career aspirations; provide career-oriented appraisals; have a formal job-posting system; see that your employees have access to the training they need; and balance your desire to keep good employees with the benefits of helping them learn of and apply for other positions in your company.

Outside Sources of Candidates

Employers can't always get all the employees they need from their current staff, and sometimes they just don't want to. We look at the sources firms use to find outside candidates next.

LEARNING OBJECTIVE 5-5

List and discuss the main outside sources of candidates.

Informal Recruiting and the Hidden Job Market

Many (or most) job openings aren't publicized at all; jobs are created and become available when employers serendipitously encounter the right candidates. The author of *Unlock the Hidden Job Market* estimates that perhaps half of all positions are filled informally (without formal recruiting).[54] Similarly, one survey found that 28% of those surveyed found their most recent job through word of mouth. Nineteen percent used online job boards, 16% direct approaches from employers and employment services, 7% print ads, and only 1% social media sites (although 22% used sites like LinkedIn to *search* for jobs).[55]

Employee referrals is a good source for companies to recruit employees. The referral program taps on the network and goodwill of employees. Infosys recruits a major chunk of its employees through referrals. It has also used technology to make its employee referral system more systematic and efficient. An employee referral portal where all the details regarding requirements for prospective employees are given, so that, current employees can better match and refer for the positions. Since current employees know both the company and the prospective employee, a better match of skill, personality, and culture can be made. Many companies also reward existing employees for referring talent.[56]

Recruiting via the Internet

Most employers in India recruit through their websites or through online job portals like naukri.com, monster.com, timesjobs.com, etc.[57] Users may search for jobs by keyword, read job descriptions and salaries, save jobs to a list of favorites, and e-mail job links to anyone on their contact list. Employers increasingly use niche job boards such as jobsinsports.com and vetjobs.com.[58]

Online recruiting is getting more sophisticated. One example is the *virtual office tour*.[59] In China the local office of Accountants Deloitte Touche Tohmatsu Limited posted a virtual office tour on Weibo (similar to Twitter's messaging service). People visiting the site can virtually enter each of the company's offices in Asia, walking through meeting rooms and talking virtually with local employees, to get a feel of what working in that office is like. In India, Mahindra & Mahindra has posted employee testimonials on its career page, where employees discuss about work and work culture.

There are many other such online recruiting tools. For example, ResumePal (see www.jobfox.com) is an online standard universal job application. Job seekers submit it to participating employers, who can then use the standardized application's keywords to identify viable candidates more easily.[60] McDonald's Corp. posted a series of employee testimonials on social networking sites like Second Life to attract applicants.[61] Other employers simply screen through job boards' résumé listings.[62]

Monster helps employers integrate streaming video into their job postings.[63] The *dot-jobs* domain gives job seekers a one-click conduit for finding jobs at the employers who register at www.goto.jobs. For example, applicants seeking a job at Disneyland can go to www.Disneyland.jobs. HireVue "lets candidates create video interviews and send them to employers to review, share, and compare with other applicants."[64]

Virtual (fully online) job fairs are another option. Here online visitors see a similar setup to a regular job fair. They can listen to presentations, visit booths, leave résumés and business cards, participate in live chats, and get contact information from recruiters and even hiring managers.[65] Fairs last about 5 hours.

PROS AND CONS Online recruiting generates more responses quicker and for a longer time at less cost than just about any other method. And, because they are richer and more comprehensive in describing the jobs, web-based ads have a stronger effect on applicant attraction than do printed ads.[66] But, online recruiting has two potential problems.

First, older people and some groups are less likely to use the Internet, so online recruiting may inadvertently exclude more older applicants.[67]

The second problem is Internet overload: Employers end up deluged with résumés. Self-screening helps: A few firms like the HDFC Bank posts detailed job duties listings, so those not interested needn't apply. Another approach is to have job seekers complete a short online prescreening questionnaire, then use these to identify those who may proceed in the hiring process.[68]

Most employers also use applicant tracking systems, to which we now turn.

Improving Performance Through HRIS: Using Applicant Tracking

A deluge of applicants means that most employers now use applicant tracking software to screen applications.[69] **Applicant tracking systems (ATS)** are online systems that help employers attract, gather, screen, compile, and manage applicants.[70] They also provide

applicant tracking systems (ATS)

Online systems that help employers attract, gather, screen, compile, and manage applicants.

other services, including requisitions management (for monitoring the firm's open jobs), applicant data collection (for scanning applicants' data into the system), and reporting (to create various recruiting-related reports such as cost per hire and hire by source).[71] Most systems are from *application service providers* (ASPs). These basically redirect applicants from the employer's to the ASP's site. Thus, applicants who log on to take a test at the employer are actually taking the test at the ASP's site.[72] Major suppliers include Automatic Data Processing (ADP.com), HRSmart (hrsmart.com), SilkRoad Technology (silkroad.com), and Monster (monster.com).[73]

As one example, a bank uses its ATS to bump applicants who don't meet the basic job requirements; it then e-mails them suggesting they review the bank's site for more appropriate positions. This bank then uses either phone interviews or automated interview systems to whittle down the applicant pool to a few candidates. Then its recruiters interview those at headquarters and send them through the final selection process.[74] One Ohio-based nursing care facility company arranged to have the recruiting dashboard vendor jobs2Web integrate its dashboard with the employer's applicant tracking system. The recruiting manager now uses the dashboard to monitor recruitment data trends on things like which recruiting sources are doing the best job of attracting applications.[75] ■

TRENDS SHAPING HR: *SCIENCE IN TALENT MANAGEMENT*

Most employers use tools like job boards to produce large numbers of recruits, and then use ATS and screening systems to cut those numbers down. Google's "People Operations" (HR) group is more scientific. When their research showed that tools like job boards weren't cost-effective for them, they created their own in-house recruiting firm. This in-house team uses a proprietary candidate database called gHire. Google's recruiters continually expand and winnow this candidate list, by searching social networking and other sites, by searching who's working where, and by reaching out to prospective hires and maintaining dialogues with them, sometimes for years. These in-house recruiters produce hand-picked candidates and account for about half of Google's yearly hires.[76]

Google's career website is another big source of candidates. Applicants not only apply through it, but can share examples of their skills with Google employees, and through them discover what Google employment is like.

Google also actively solicits employee referrals. Because inside referrals turned out to be great candidates, Google analyzed how to boost employee referrals. It found that higher referral fees weren't the answer, (since Googlers loved recommending great candidates). Instead, Google streamlined the selection process, so more referrals got hired.

Google uses outside recruiters sparingly for special assignments, and dropped job boards several years ago.[77] ■

IMPROVING ONLINE RECRUITING EFFECTIVENESS The employer's online effort needs to be thought out. For example, one survey of Web-based recruiting uncovered these applicant objections: Job openings lacked relevant information (such as job descriptions); and, it was often difficult to format résumés and post them in the form required.[78]

Employers take several steps. Most place employment information one click away from their home pages.[79] Applicants can submit their résumés online at most *Fortune* 500 firms' websites. Fewer companies give job seekers the option of completing online applications, although that's what most applicants prefer.[80] Furthermore, the best Web ads don't just transfer newspaper ads to the Web. As one specialist put it, "Getting recruiters out of the 'shrunken want ad mentality' is a big problem." Figure 5-6 is an example of recycling a print ad to the Web. The ineffective Web ad has needless abbreviations, and doesn't say much about why the job seeker should want that job.[81]

Now look at the effective Web ad in Figure 5-6. It provides good reasons to work for this company. It starts with an attention-grabbing heading and uses the extra

FIGURE 5-6 Ineffective and Effective Web Ads

Ineffective Ad, Recycled from Magazine to the Web	Effective Web Ad (Space Not an Issue)
Process Engineer Pay: $65k–$85k/year Immediate Need in Florida for a Wastewater Treatment Process Engineer. Must have a min. 4–7 years Industrial Wastewater exp. Reply KimGD@ WatersCleanX.com	Do you want to help us make this a better world? We are one of the top wastewater treatment companies in the world, with installations from Miami to London to Beijing. We are growing fast and looking for an experienced process engineer to join our team. If you have at least 4–7 years' experience designing processes for wastewater treatment facilities and a dedication to make this a better world, we would like to hear from you. Pay range depending on experience is $65,000–$85,000. Please reply in confidence to KimGD@ WatersCleanX.com

space to provide more specific job information. Many employers include the entire job description.[82] Ideally, an ad also should provide a way (such as a checklist of the job's human requirements) for potential applicants to gauge if the job is a good fit.[83]

Finally, online recruiting requires caution for *applicants*. Many job boards don't check the legitimacy of the "recruiters" who place ads. Many applicants submit personal details, not realizing who is getting them.[84]

TRENDS SHAPING HR: *DIGITAL AND SOCIAL MEDIA*

Anyone seeking a job should probably sign up with LinkedIn. At present, India is the second largest user base for LinkedIn, after the US.[85] Accenture predicts that about 80% of new recruits will soon come through prospective employees' social media connections.[86]

Recruiters use social media recruiting in several ways. They dig through social websites and competitors' publications to find applicants who may not even be looking for jobs. They seek passive candidates (people not actively looking for jobs) by using social networking sites such as *LinkedIn Recruiter Lite* (a premium service) to browse members' résumés and to find such candidates.[87] Many firms use Twitter to announce job openings to job seekers who subscribe to their Twitter feeds.[88] Theladders.com's Pipeline™ networking tool lets recruiters maintain a dialogue with prospective job seekers even before they're interested in seeking a job. Others use Facebook's friend-finding search function, and Twitter, to learn more about prospective and actual candidates. TalentBin searches sites such as Pinterest to find qualified tech workers.[89] Many employers have social media strategies and career pages that establish an online presence highlighting the benefits of working for them.[90] At one diversity conference, consultants Hewitt Associates displayed posters asking attendees to text message *hewdiversity* to a specific 5-digit number. Each person texting then became part of Hewitt's "mobile recruiting network," periodically receiving text messages regarding Hewitt openings.[91]

LinkedIn Recruiter Lite not only lets employers post jobs on LinkedIn. The employer can also conduct its own LinkedIn search for talent, by using Recruiter Lite's search filters to search through LinkedIn's database to find the most relevant profiles (including names and profiles). Recruiters can then use LinkedIn's InMail to send short personalized messages to people they're interested in. And by joining relevant LinkedIn groups the recruiter can discover other LinkedIn group members who might be potential hires.[92] This not only helps them generate more relevant applicants, but provides a form of "crowdsourcing," by letting the recruiter mine the applicants' sites for feedback from the person's blog comments and his or her likes/dislikes. Recruiters also post job openings on professional associations and other social networks.[93]

Cloud-based applications such as Oracle Talent Acquisition Cloud enable employers to integrate recruiting with related activities including requisitions management, applicant tracking, and interview management. The Oracle Taleo Social Sourcing Cloud Service is integrated with social sites like LinkedIn, Twitter, and Facebook. It notifies the company's current employees about open positions, and then scans their social connections for referral suggestions that they may want to make to friends, or directly to the employer. With the My Staffing Pro applicant tracking system, applicants can apply on Facebook, share job openings, connect with managers, and log in with the social profile. Recruiters can post job openings on Twitter and Facebook, accept applications via Facebook, and more easily screen out the best applicants. ■

Advertising

While Web-based recruiting is replacing traditional help wanted ads, a glance at almost any paper will confirm that print ads are still popular. To use such help wanted ads successfully, employers should address two issues: the advertising medium and the ad's construction.

THE MEDIA The best medium—the local newspaper like *The Times of India, The Hindu,* and *The Economic Times* or magazines like *Business Today* and *Economic and Political Weekly (EPW),* for instance—depends on the positions for which you're recruiting. For example, the local newspaper is often a good source for local blue-collar help, clerical employees, and lower-level administrative employees. *The Economic Times* is suitable for senior level corporate positions and *EPW* for academic positions in economics or social sciences. On the other hand, if recruiting for workers with special skills, such as furniture finishers, you'd probably want to advertise in places with many furniture manufacturers, or if looking for tea processing experts, then Nilgris and Darjeeling area will be focused on. The point is to target your ads where they'll reach your prospective employees.

Help wanted ads in papers like *The Times of India* can be good sources of middle- or senior-management personnel. Most of these print outlets now include online ads with the purchase of print help wanted ads.

Technology lets companies be more creative.[94] For example, Electronic Arts (EA) uses its products to help solicit applicants. EA includes information about its internship program on the back of its video game manuals. Thanks to nontraditional techniques like these, EA has a database of more than 200,000 potential job candidates.

CONSTRUCTING (WRITING) THE AD Experienced advertisers use the guide AIDA (attention, interest, desire, action) to construct ads. First, you must attract attention to the ad, or readers may ignore it. Why does the ad in Figure 5-7 attract attention? The phrase "next key player" helps.

Next, develop interest in the job. For instance, "are you looking to make an impact?"

Create desire by spotlighting words such as *travel* or *challenge.* As an example, having a graduate school nearby may appeal to engineers and professional people.

Finally, the ad should prompt action with a statement like "call today."

Job applicants view ads with more specific job information as more attractive and more credible.[95] If the job has big drawbacks, consider a realistic ad.

Employment Agencies

There are three main types of employment agencies: (1) public agencies operated by federal, state, or local governments; (2) agencies associated with nonprofit organizations; and (3) privately owned agencies.

PUBLIC AND NONPROFIT AGENCIES Every state in India has a public, state-run employment service agency, or an employment exchange. The employment exchanges in India are run by the Director General of Employment and Training, Ministry of Labor, government of India. This directorate has a network of more than 900

FIGURE 5-7 **Help Wanted Ad That Draws Attention**
Source: "Help Wanted Ad That Draws Attention", in Giombetti Associates, Hampden, MA. Reprinted with permission.

Are You Our Next Key Player?

PLANT CONTROLLER   Northern New Jersey

Are you looking to make an impact? Can you be a strategic business partner and team player, versus a classic, "bean counter"? Our client, a growing **Northern New Jersey** manufacturer with two locations, needs a high-energy, self-initiating, technically competent Plant Controller. Your organizational skills and strong understanding of general, cost, and manufacturing accounting are a must. We are not looking for a delegator, this is a hands-on position. If you have a positive can-do attitude and have what it takes to drive our accounting function, read oh!

Responsibilities and Qualifications:
- Monthly closings, management reporting, product costing, and annual budget.
- Accurate inventory valuations, year-end physical inventory, and internal controls.
- 4-year Accounting degree, with 5–8 years experience in a manufacturing environment.
- Must be proficient in Microsoft Excel and have general computer skills and aptitude.
- Must be analytical and technically competent, with the leadership ability to influence people, situations, and circumstances.

If you have what it takes to be our next key player, tell us in your cover letter, *"Beyond the beans, what is the role of a Plant Controller?"* **Only cover** letters addressing that question will be considered. Please indicate your general salary requirements in your cover letter and email or fax your resume and cover letter to:

Ross Giombetti
Giombetti Associates
2 Allen Street, P.O. Box 720
Hampden, MA 01036
Email: Rossgiombetti@giombettiassoc.com
Fax: (413) 566-2009

employment exchanges. According to the Employment Exchanges (Compulsory Notification of Vacancies) Act of 1959, the public and private firms have to notify vacancies for specific jobs and fill these positions through employment exchanges. These exchanges also help candidates in searching jobs, pre-employment training as well as career guidance. Indian employers have mixed experiences with employment exchanges.

Some employers have mixed experiences with public agencies. For one thing, applicants for unemployment insurance are required to register and to make themselves available for job interviews. Some of these people are not interested in returning to work, so employers can end up with applicants who have little desire for immediate employment. And fairly or not, employers probably view some of these local agencies as lethargic in their efforts to fill area employers' jobs. In India, employment exchanges currently are going through a phase of technology infusion and modernization, and the Indian government plans to turn them into National Career Counseling Centers.[96]

Most (nonprofit) professional and technical societies, such as the Institute of Chartered Accountants of India (ICAI) have units that help members find jobs. The institution regularly organizes job fairs to help members, specifically for the newly qualified chartered accountants. Many special public agencies place people who are in special categories, such as those who are disabled. Currently, there are 50 state-run special employment exchanges in India (and 38 special cells) that focus on providing employment to the disabled. Separate exchanges are run for professionals, executives (the number was 14 in 2015), and university students.[97]

PRIVATE AGENCIES   Private employment agencies are important sources of clerical, white-collar, and managerial personnel. They charge fees (set by state law and posted in their offices) for each applicant they place. Most are "fee-paid" jobs, in which the employer pays the fee. Use one if:

1. Your firm doesn't have its own human resources department and feels it can't do a good job recruiting and screening.
2. You must fill a job quickly.
3. There is a perceived need to attract more minority or female applicants.
4. You want to reach currently employed individuals, who might feel more comfortable dealing with agencies than with competing companies.
5. You want to reduce the time you're devoting to recruiting.[98]

Yet using employment agencies requires avoiding the potential pitfalls. For example, the employment agency's screening may let poor applicants go directly to the supervisors responsible for hiring, who may in turn naively hire them. Conversely, improper screening at the agency could block potentially successful applicants.

To help avoid problems:

1. Give the agency an accurate and complete job description.
2. Make sure tests, application blanks, and interviews are part of the agency's selection process.
3. Periodically review equal employment data on candidates accepted or rejected by your firm, and by the agency.
4. Screen the agency. Check with other managers to find out which agencies have been the most effective at filling the sorts of positions you need filled. Review the Internet and classified ads to discover the agencies that handle the positions you seek to fill.
5. Supplement the agency's reference checking by checking at least the final candidate's references yourself.

Recruitment Process Outsourcers

Recruitment process outsourcers are special vendors that handle all or most of an employer's recruiting needs. They usually sign short-term contracts with the employer, and receive a monthly fee that varies with the amount of actual recruiting the employer needs done. This makes it easier for an employer to ramp up or ramp down its recruiting expenses, as compared with paying the relatively fixed costs of an in-house recruitment office.[99] Husys is an Indian company (Husys.in) that provides RPO (recruitment process outsourcing) services to small and medium enterprises (SMEs) in India. Large RPO providers with global presence (also operating in India) include Manpower Group Solutions, IBM, and Randstad Sourceright.[100]

Temporary Workers and Alternative Staffing

Employers increasingly supplement their permanent workforces by hiring contingent, contract, or temporary workers, often through temporary help employment agencies. Also known as *part-time* or *just-in-time workers*, the contingent workforce is big and growing. In the recent recession, about 26% of all jobs private-sector employers added were temporary positions, two to three times the comparable figures for the last two recessions. The contingent workforce isn't limited to clerical or maintenance staff. It includes thousands of engineering, science, and management support occupations, such as temporary chief financial officers, human resource managers, and chief executive officers.[101]

Employers use temps for many reasons. One is continuing weak economic confidence among employers. Another is the trend toward organizing around short-term projects. Temporary staffing companies help Indian corporates in finding temporary and seasonal workers. Many e-commerce firms use their services to meet peak season requirements. Team Lease Services Private Limited is one such company that helps Indian corporates to find temporary workers.[102] Flexibility is another concern, with more employers wanting to quickly reduce employment levels if the economic turnaround proves short-lived.[103] Other employers use temp agency–supplied workers to "try out" prospective employees.[104]

Employers have also long used "temps" to fill in for employees who were out sick or on vacation. Productivity in output per hour paid is higher, since temps are generally paid only when they're working—not for days off. However, temps often cost employers more per hour than comparable permanent workers, since the agency gets a fee.[105]

alternative staffing
The use of nontraditional recruitment sources.

Temporary employees are examples of **alternative staffing**—basically, the use of nontraditional recruitment sources. Other alternative staffing arrangements include "in-house temporary employees" (people employed directly by the company, but on an explicit short-term basis) and "contract technical employees" (highly skilled workers like engineers, who are supplied for long-term projects under contract from an outside technical services firm).

THE TEMP AGENCY   Employers can hire temp workers either through direct hires or through temporary staff agencies. Direct hiring involves simply hiring workers and placing them on the job. The employer usually pays these people directly, as it does all its employees, but classifies them separately, as casual, seasonal, or temporary employees, and often pays few if any benefits.[106] The other approach is to use a temp agency. Here the agency handles all the recruiting, screening, and payroll administration for the temps. Thus, Nike hired Kelly Services to manage Nike's temp needs. Hamara Angels is a temporary staffing agency based in Mumbai, specializing in providing household staff like guard, maid, nanny, etc. The company provides verified and trained candidates to customers (who are also screened) and ensures compliance with all relevant labor legislations in the country.[107]

When working with temporary agencies, understand their policies. For example, with temps, the time sheet is not just a verification of hours worked. Once the worker's supervisor signs it, it's usually an agreement to pay the agency's fees. What is the policy if the client wants to hire one of the agency's temps as a permanent employee? How does the agency plan to recruit employees? And finally, check their references.[108]

TEMP EMPLOYEES' CONCERNS   To make temporary relationships successful, those supervising temps should understand their concerns. In one survey, temporary workers said they were:

1. Treated by employers in a dehumanizing and ultimately discouraging way.
2. Insecure about their employment and pessimistic about the future.
3. Worried about their lack of insurance and pension benefits.
4. Misled about their job assignments and in particular about whether temporary assignments were likely to become full-time.
5. "Underemployed" (particularly those trying to return to the full-time labor market).[109]

KNOW YOUR EMPLOYMENT LAW

Contract Employees

There are various issues related to the employment of contract labor in India. Employers have to deal with legal formalities while dealing with contract labor. Chapter 2 gives a brief description of the relevant provisions of the Contract Labor (Regulation and Abolition) Act, 1970. There is possibility of lawsuits if firms do not follow the legal obligations. There are also social and public policy issues such as exploitation of the contract labors by the contractor and the obligation of the firm.[110] The fact that they actually work for another, temp-type company is no excuse. For purposes of most employment laws, with certain limited exceptions, employees of temporary staffing firms working in an employer's workplace will be considered to be employees both of the agency, and the employer has responsibility as the principal.[111] The employer's liability depends on the degree to which its supervisors control the temp and contract employee's activities. Therefore, the more the agency does the better. For example, have the agency handle training. Let it negotiate and set the pay rates and vacation/time-off policies.

Employers can take other steps to ensure that the contract employees are treated with dignity, and they deliver value. Require the agency to follow the employer's background checking process, and follow certain protocols like work timings, uniforms, etc. Carefully track how many temporary employees your company actually has. Screen and supervise temporary employees with care if they may have access to your intellectual property and computer systems.[112] For legal purposes, it's advised that don't treat temporary workers as "employees," for instance, in terms of business cards, employee handbooks, or employee ID badges.[113] ■

TRENDS SHAPING HR: *THE NEW EXTENDED WORKFORCE*

Many employers today build their staff wholly or in part around an extended workforce consisting, for instance, of freelance programmers, designers, or marketers. Freelancer community websites enable such employers to recruit the right freelance team based on the freelancer's reputation and work product. For example, Elance. com (see www.elance.com/) reports its members' skills assessments, and lists detailed project work experience, making it easier for prospective employers to decide who to hire. Similarly, the TopCoder.com (see www.topcoder.com/how-it-works/) programming community site enables employers to identify top programmers based on the reputations they earned within the community. New hiring sites like these may have a big impact on HR. Some employers may well use them to democratize HR, by letting their line managers recruit and hire new employees directly. ■

Offshoring and Outsourcing Jobs

Rather than bringing people in to do the company's jobs, outsourcing and offshoring send the jobs out. *Outsourcing* means having outside vendors supply services (such as benefits management, market research, or manufacturing) that the company's own employees previously did in-house. *Offshoring* means having outside vendors or employees *abroad* supply services that the company's own employees previously did in-house.

Employees, unions, legislators, and even many business owners feel that "shipping jobs out" (particularly overseas) is ill-advised. That notwithstanding, employers are sending jobs out, and not just blue-collar jobs. For example, GE's transportation division shifted some mid-level drafting jobs from Pennsylvania to India.[114] To take advantage of Chinese low-cost production environment, many Indian manufacturing companies have also shifted to China. However, as India became an attractive manufacturing destination, companies have again started shifting or preferring it to China. Foxconn and Apple are recent examples of this shift.[115]

The numbers of temporary and freelance workers are increasing all over the world.

Shutterstock.Dragon Images

Sending out jobs, particularly overseas, presents employers with special personnel challenges. One is the likelihood of cultural misunderstandings (such as between your home-based customers and the employees abroad). Others are security and information privacy concerns; the need to deal with foreign contract, liability, and legal systems issues; and the fact that the offshore employees need special training (for instance, in using pseudonyms like "Jim" without discomfort).

Rising wages in China and India, coupled with reputational and political issues and a desire to invest more in local communities, are prompting employers to bring jobs back. Several U.S. employers are shifting jobs back to America. [116]

Executive Recruiters

Executive recruiters (also known as *headhunters*) are special employment agencies employers retain to seek out top-management talent for their clients. The percentage of your firm's positions filled by these services might be small. However, these jobs include key executive and technical positions. For executive positions, headhunters may be your only source of candidates. The employer always pays the fees.

The challenging part of recruiting has always been finding potential candidates. Not surprisingly, Internet-based databases now dramatically speed up such searches. Executive recruiters are also creating specialized units aimed at specialized functions (such as sales) or industries (such as oil products).

Recruiters bring a lot to the table. They have many contacts and are relatively adept at finding qualified candidates who aren't actively looking to change jobs. They can keep your firm's name confidential, and can save top management's time by building an applicant pool. The recruiter's fee might actually turn out to be small when you compare it to the executive time saved.

The big issue is ensuring that the recruiter really understands your needs and then delivers properly vetted candidates. It is essential that the employer explain completely what sort of candidate is required. Some recruiters also may be more interested in persuading you to hire a candidate than in finding one who will really do the job. And one or two of the "final candidates" may actually just be fillers to make the recruiter's one "real" candidate look better.

WORKING WITH RECRUITERS   Retaining and working with executive recruiters require some caution. In choosing and working with one, guidelines include: [117]

1. Make sure the firm can conduct a thorough search. Under their ethics code, a recruiter can't approach the executive talent of a former client for a period of 2 years after completing a search for that client. Since former clients are off limits for 2 years, the recruiter must search from a constantly diminishing pool. [118]
2. Meet the individual who will actually handle your assignment.
3. Make sure to ask how much the search firm charges. Get the agreement in writing. [119]
4. Make sure the recruiter and you agree on what sort of individual to hire for the position.
5. Ask if the recruiter has vetted the final candidates. Do not be surprised if the answer is, "No, I just get candidates—we don't really screen them."
6. *Never* rely solely on any recruiter do all the reference checking. Let them check the candidates' references, but get notes of these references in writing from the recruiter (if possible). Recheck at least the final candidates' references yourself.
7. Consider using a recruiter who has a special expertise in your specific industry—he or she may have the best grasp of who's available.

INTERNAL RECRUITING   More employers are bringing management recruiting in-house. They still use executive recruiters such as Heidrick and Struggles to conduct top officer (CEO and president) and board member placements, and to conduct confidential searches.

But employers ranging from General Electric to Sears or Wipro and HCL now have their own internal executive recruiting offices doing most of their own management recruiting. They take support from recruitment consultants or RPOs, in specific areas. Time Warner reported saving millions of dollars per year using internal recruiting teams.[120]

With employers increasingly finding new ways of recruiting top management talent, executive search firms are diversifying. For example, the head of Korn/Ferry says his firm is increasingly being asked to investigate prospective candidates' backgrounds, and his firm is also expanding into areas such as employee development.[121] The accompanying HR Tools feature explains what small businesses can do.

▶ **IMPROVING PERFORMANCE:** *HR Tools for Line Managers and Small Businesses*

Recruiting 101

There comes a time in the life of most small businesses when it dawns on the owner that new blood is needed to take the company to the next level. Should the owner personally recruit this person?

While most large firms don't think twice about hiring executive search firms, small-firm owners will understandably hesitate before committing to a fee that could reach $60,000 or more for a $120,000 marketing manager.

However, engaging in a search like this is not like seeking supervisors or data entry clerks. Chances are, you won't find a top manager by placing ads. He or she is probably not reading the want ads. You'll end up with résumés of people who are, for one reason or another, out of work, unhappy with their work, or unsuited for your job. Many may be capable. But you will have to ferret out the gem by interviewing and assessing them.

You won't know where to place or how to write the ads; or where to search, who to contact, or how to screen out the laggards who may appear to be viable candidates. Even if you do, this process will be time-consuming and will divert your attention from other duties.

If you do decide to do the job yourself, consider retaining an industrial psychologist to spend 4 or 5 hours assessing the problem-solving ability, personality, interests, and energy level of the two or three candidates in which you are most interested. The input can provide a valuable perspective on the candidates.

Exercise special care when recruiting applicants from competing companies. Always check to see if applicants are bound by noncompete or nondisclosure agreements. And (especially when recruiting other firms' higher-level employees) perhaps check with an attorney before asking certain questions—regarding patents or potential antitrust issues, for instance.[122]

If you're a manager with an open position to fill in a *Fortune* 500 company, even you may find you have a dilemma. You may find that your local HR office will do little recruiting, other than, perhaps, placing an ad on CareerBuilder. On the other hand, your firm almost surely will not let you place your own help wanted ads. What to do? Use word of mouth to "advertise" your open position within and outside your company. And contact your colleagues in other firms to let them know you are recruiting. ■

Referrals and Walk-Ins

Employee referral campaigns are a very important recruiting option. Here the employer posts announcements of openings and requests for referrals on its website, bulletin boards, and/or wallboards. It often offers prizes or cash awards for referrals that lead to hiring.

Referral's big advantage is that it tends to generate "more applicants, more hires, and a higher yield ratio (hires/applicants)."[123] Current employees tend to provide accurate information about their referrals because they're putting their own reputations on the line. And the new employees may come with a more realistic picture of what the firm is like. A SHRM survey found that of 586 employer respondents, 69% said employee referral programs are more cost-effective than other recruiting practices and 80% specifically said they are more cost-effective than employment agencies. On average, referral programs cost around $400–$900 per hire in incentives and rewards.[124]

If morale is low, address that prior to asking for referrals. And if you don't hire someone's referral, explain to your employee/referrer why you did not hire his or her candidate. In addition, remember that relying on referrals might be discriminatory where a workforce is already homogeneous.

WALK-INS   Particularly for hourly workers, walk-ins—direct applications made at your office—are a big source of applicants. Sometimes, posting a "Help Wanted" sign outside the door may be the most cost-effective way of attracting good local applicants. It is common for Indian companies to organize walk-ins in different cities and small towns to attract talent. Treat walk-ins courteously, for both the employer's community reputation and the applicant's self-esteem. Many employers give every walk-in a brief interview, even if it is only to get information on the applicant "in case a position should be open in the future." Employers also typically receive unsolicited applications from professional and white-collar applicants. Good business practice requires answering all applicants' letters of inquiry promptly.

On-Demand Recruiting Services

on-demand recruiting services (ODRS)
Services that provide short-term specialized recruiting to support specific projects without the expense of retaining traditional search firms.

On-demand recruiting services (ODRS) are recruiters who are paid by the hour or project, instead of a percentage fee, to support a specific project. For example, when the human resource manager for a biotech firm had to hire several dozen people with scientific degrees and experience in pharmaceuticals, she used an ODRS firm. A traditional recruiting firm might charge 20% to 30% of each hire's salary. UrbanClap (www.urbanclap.com), a provider of home services like electricians, plumbers, yoga trainers, and drivers across many Indian cities, is an example of ORDS. UrbanClap identifies the home-service worker, registers them, and trains them so that customers are assured of quality and performance of the hired help. As on March 2017, UrbanClap had 65,000 registered service professionals, and it has served 1.5 million service users in the last two years.[125] It handled recruiting and prescreening, and left the client with a short list of qualified candidates.[126]

College Recruiting

college recruiting
Sending an employer's representatives to college campuses to prescreen applicants and create an applicant pool from the graduating class.

College recruiting—sending an employer's representatives to college campuses to prescreen applicants and create an applicant pool from the graduating class—is important. One study several years ago concluded, for instance, that new college graduates filled about 38% of all externally filled jobs requiring a college degree.[127]

One problem is that such recruiting is expensive. Schedules must be set well in advance, company brochures printed, interview records kept, and much time spent on campus. And recruiters are sometimes ineffective. Some are unprepared, show little interest in the candidate, and act superior. Many don't screen candidates effectively. Employers need to train recruiters in how to interview candidates, how to explain what the company has to offer, and how to put candidates at ease. The recruiter should be personable and have a record of attracting good candidates.[128]

The campus recruiter has two main goals. One is to determine if a candidate is worthy of further consideration. Usual traits to assess include communication skills, education, experience, and technical and interpersonal skills. The other aim is to make the employer attractive to candidates. A sincere and informal attitude, respect for the applicant, and prompt follow-up letters can help sell the employer to the interviewee.

Employers who build relationships with opinion leaders such as career counselors and professors have better recruiting results.[129] Building close ties with a college's career center provides recruiters with useful feedback regarding things like labor market conditions and the effectiveness of one's on- and offline recruiting ads.[130]

Employers generally invite good candidates for an on-site visit. The invitation should be warm but businesslike, and provide a choice of dates. Have a host meet the applicant, preferably at the airport or at his or her hotel. A package containing the applicant's schedule as well as other information—such as annual reports and employee benefits—should be waiting for the applicant at the hotel.

Plan the interviews and adhere to the schedule. Avoid interruptions; give the candidate the undivided attention of each person with whom he or she interviews. Have another recently hired graduate host the candidate's lunch. Make any offer as soon as possible, preferably at the time of the visit. Frequent follow-ups to "find out how the decision process is going" may help to tilt the applicant in your favor.

What else to do? A study of 96 graduating students provides some insights. Fifty-three percent said "on-site visit opportunities to meet with people in positions similar to those applied for, or with higher-ranking persons" had a positive effect. Fifty-one percent mentioned, "impressive hotel/dinner arrangements and having well-organized site arrangements." "Disorganized, unprepared interviewer behavior, or uninformed, useless answers" turned off 41%.[131]

POOLED CAMPUS HIRING Many Indian companies prefer to hire talent from different college campuses, however, time and cost constrains prevent them from doing so. Hence, they pool applicants from different colleges at one location for hiring. A few private employment agencies organize such events and invite both colleges and companies to participate. This approach often suits the recruitment requirements of the SMEs who find individual campus hiring costly.

INTERNSHIPS Internships can be win–win situations. For students, they can mean honing business skills, learning more about potential employers, and discovering one's career likes (and dislikes). And employers can use the interns to make useful contributions while evaluating them as possible full-time employees. A recent study found that about 60% of internships turned into job offers.[132]

Unfortunately, some internships turn into nightmares. Many interns, particularly in industries like fashion and media, report long unpaid days doing menial work. At present, internships have become a very valuable part of Indian students' life. Nowadays, interns are recruited either through online recruiting websites such as www.internshala.com or through college career/placement offices. The Reserve Bank of India (RBI) runs a structured internship program for students of economics and finance. Many B-Tech or BBA students receive paid internship opportunities from IIM faculty by directly approaching them. [133]

Telecommuters

Telecommuters do all or most of their work remotely, often from home, using information technology. For example, JetBlue Airways uses at-home agents to handle its reservation needs. These JetBlue employee "crewmembers" live in the Salt Lake City area and work out of their homes. They use JetBlue-supplied computers and technology, and receive JetBlue training.[134]

Military Personnel

Returning and discharged military personnel provide an excellent source of trained and disciplined recruits. Yet all too often they have trouble getting placed. The military also has programs to facilitate soldiers finding jobs. The office of Director General of Resettlement, under the Ministry of Defence, government of India (www.dgrindia.com) supports armed forces personnel to find jobs after they retire or are discharged. For assisting officers gain employment, the department has agreement with IIMs and other management institutes for a general management program.

Misconceptions about retired military personnel (for instance, that posttraumatic stress disorders influence job performance) are generally not valid.[135] The U.S. Army's Warrior Transition Command website (www.wtc.army.mil) discusses such misconceptions.

The accompanying Profit Center feature describes how one employer reduced recruiting costs.

▶ IMPROVING PERFORMANCE: *HR as a Profit Center*

Cutting Recruitment Costs

One problem raising recruiting costs is that more applicants is not always better. Realistically, the manager looking to hire five engineers probably won't be twice as selective with 20,000 applicants as with 10,000. Furthermore, the employer needs *qualified, hirable* applicants. An Internet ad may generate thousands of nonviable applicants. The employer's applicant tracking system should help compare recruiting sources, as we said, but many lack the tools to do so.[136]

GE Medical hires about 500 technical workers a year to design sophisticated medical devices such as CT scanners. It has cut its hiring costs by 17%, reduced time to fill the positions by 20% to 30%, and cut in half the percentage of new hires who don't work out.[137]

GE Medical's HR team accomplished this in part by applying its purchasing techniques to its dealings with recruiters. For example, it called a meeting and told 20 recruiters that it would work with only the 10 best. To measure "best," the company created measures inspired by manufacturing techniques, such as "percentage of résumés that result in interviews" and "percentage of interviews that lead to offers." Similarly, GE Medical discovered that current employees are very effective as references. For instance, GE Medical interviews just 1% of applicants whose résumés it receives, while 10% of employee referrals result in actual hires. So GE Medical took steps to double the number of employee referrals. It simplified the referral forms, eliminated bureaucratic submission procedures, and added a small reward like a Sears gift certificate for referring a qualified candidate. GE also upped the incentive—$2,000 if someone referred is hired, and $3,000 if he or she is a software engineer. ∎

Source: Based on Thomas Stewart, "In Search of Elusive Tech Workers," Fortune, February 16, 1998, pp. 171–172; and http://www.outsourcing-center.com/2006-10-ge-looks-to-recruitment-process-outsourcer-to-find-meat-and-potatoes-candidates-as-well-as-the-purple-squirrel-article-37479.html, accessed October 5, 2011. Gino Ruiz, "Special Report: Talent Acquisition," Workforce Management, July 23, 2007, p. 39.

Recruiting a More Diverse Workforce

LEARNING OBJECTIVE 5-6

Explain how to recruit a more diverse workforce.

We saw in Chapter 2 that recruiting a diverse workforce isn't just socially responsible. Given the rise in minority, older worker, and women candidates, it is a necessity. The recruiting tools we described to this point are certainly useful for minority and other applicants, too. However, diversity recruiting requires several special steps, to which we now turn.[138]

Recruiting Women

Given the progress women have made in getting and excelling in a wide range of professional, managerial, and military occupations, one might assume that employers need no special recruitment efforts to recruit women, but that's not necessarily the case. For example, women still face headwinds in certain male-dominated occupations such as engineering. Women also carry the heavier burden of child-rearing, fill proportionately fewer high-level managerial posts, and still earn only about 70% of what men earn for similar jobs. Many employers therefore focus particular efforts on recruiting qualified women.

The most effective strategy is top management driven.[139] Here the employer emphasizes the importance of recruiting women (as well as men), identifies gaps in the recruitment and retention of women, and puts in place a comprehensive plan to attract women applicants. The overall aim is to make it clear that the employer is the sort of place in which women want to work, and the details of any such plan needn't be complicated. For example, particularly for "nontraditional" jobs (like engineering) use the company website to highlight women now doing those jobs. Emphasize the effectiveness of the employer's mentoring program in moving women up. Offer real workplace flexibility; for example, not just flexible hours but the option of staying on a partner track even while working part-time. (For example, Yahoo! recently implemented a generous 8-week paid maternity/paternity leave policy.) Focus a portion of the recruiting effort on women's organizations, women's employment websites, and career fairs at women's colleges. Make sure benefits cover matters such as family planning and prenatal care. Maintain a zero-tolerance sexual harassment policy. Cummins India consciously increased the number of women in its workforce to 30% in 2016 from 7% in 2005. Women employees have also taken over roles like that of plant manager, which were traditionally held by men.[140]

Older Workers

When it comes to hiring older workers, employers don't have much choice.[141] The fastest-growing labor force segment is those from 45 to 64 years old. On the positive side, a survey in the US by AARP and SHRM concluded that older workers tend to have lower absenteeism rates, more reliability, and better work habits than younger

Not just single parents, but also their children may occasionally need some extra support.

shutterstock. Pranav Kukreja

workers.[142] State Bank of India hires retired bankers on contract for two or three years and uses their help in a few specialized areas. Similarly, private engineering colleges in many Indian states facing faculty shortage hire retired faculty from government colleges. Firms like Home Depot in the US capitalize on this by hiring older employees, who "serve as a powerful draw to baby boomer shoppers by mirroring their knowledge and perspective."[143]

It therefore makes sense for employers to encourage older workers to stay (or to come to work at the company). The big draw is probably to provide opportunities for flexible (and often shorter) work schedules.[144] At one company, workers over 65 can progressively shorten their work schedules; another company uses "mini shifts" to accommodate those interested in working less than full time. Other suggestions include the following: phased retirement that allows workers to ease out of the workforce; portable jobs for "snowbirds" who wish to live in warmer climates in the winter; part-time projects for retirees; and full benefits for part-timerss.[145]

As always in recruiting, projecting the right image is crucial. The most effective ads here emphasize schedule flexibility, and accentuate the firm's equal opportunity employment statement, not "giving retirees opportunities to transfer their knowledge" to the new work setting.[146]

 ### Diversity Counts

Older workers are good workers. A study focused on the validity of six common stereotypes about older workers: that they are less motivated, less willing to participate in training and career development, more resistant to change, less trusting, less healthy, and more vulnerable to work–family imbalance.[147] They actually found not a negative but a weakly positive relationship between age and motivation and job involvement (suggesting that as age goes up motivation actually rises). They did find a weak negative relationship between age and trainability. Age was weakly but positively related to willingness to change, and to being more trusting. Older workers were no more likely than younger ones to have psychological problems or day-to-day physical health problems, but were more likely to have heightened blood pressure and cholesterol. Older workers did not experience more work–family imbalance. So there was little support for the common age stereotypes.

Another category facing difficulty in India during recruitment is the LGBT community. Globally, companies like Bain & Company, Nike, Google, Microsoft, Unilever, etc. find a place to work for the members of LGBT community.[148] Explicit hiring of LGBT members is not adopted by Indian companies, but many firms are extending support to their LGBT employees and value them. However, organizations hesitate to hire them actively because the existing Indian legal framework is not supportive. To discuss concerns related to LGBT community at workplaces, a consortium of 30 companies including MNCs like IBM and Indian companies have been formed.[149] Kochi Metro Rail Limited (KMRL) took a progressive step to provide employment to 23 members from the transgender community (the plan was to hire 60) and deployed them in roles like ticket collection and housekeeping.[150]

What should employers do? First, raise employees', managers', and recruiters' consciousness about incorrect age stereotypes. And provide opportunities for more contacts with older people and for information flows between younger and older workers.[151] ■

Recruiting from Socially and Economically Backward Social Sections

The government of India has urged all companies to recruit from the economically and socially underprivileged sections of the society. By law, currently, mandatory reservations for jobs are applicable only for government or PSUs jobs. The government has issued detailed guidelines about the same, and the recruitment performance report is placed in the Indian Parliament. Extending job reservation to private sector is being discussed for many years. A few private sector companies have taken initiatives to hire, though they have no legal mandate to do so.

Tata Group is one such company which has a culture of inclusive development and has started the Tata Affirmative Action Programme (TAAP) where it is recruiting from the underprivileged sections of the society, and trains them on entrepreneurial skills as well as educates them further.[152]

The Disabled

The research is quite persuasive regarding the fact that in terms of virtually all work criteria, employees with disabilities are capable workers. In India, in order to protect the rights of the disabled, there exists the Persons with Disabilities Act, 1995. This law states that 3% of the jobs in the government and PSUs are reserved for the people with disabilities. In September 2014, the Supreme Court of India declared that this reservation is applicable for appointments and promotions in the government sector. Many private companies such as TCS and ITC have also taken steps to support the disabled. For instance, Microsign Products, which is a Gujarat-based plastic molding company, has successfully employed disabled people in different functions of the manufacturing process. Similarly, Safal Builders, a commercial property developer and management company, employs the disabled as elevator operators in the commercial complexes.[153]

<table>
<tr><td>

LEARNING OBJECTIVE 5-7

Discuss practical guidelines for obtaining application information.

application form
The form that provides information on education, prior work record, and skills.

</td></tr>
</table>

Developing and Using Application Forms

Purpose of Application Forms

With a pool of applicants, the prescreening process can begin. The **application form** is usually the first step in this process (some firms first require a brief, prescreening interview or online test).

A filled-in application provides four types of information. First, you can make judgments on *substantive matters*, such as whether the applicant has the education and experience to do the job. Second, you can draw conclusions about the applicant's *previous progress* and growth, especially important for management candidates. Third, you can draw tentative conclusions about the applicant's *stability* based on previous work record (although years of downsizing suggest the need for caution here). Fourth, you may be able to use the data in the application to *predict* which candidates will succeed on the job.

Application Guidelines

Ineffective use of the application can cost the employer dearly. Managers should keep several practical guidelines in mind. In the "Employment History" section, request detailed information on each prior employer, including the name of the supervisor and his or her e-mail address and telephone number; this is essential for reference checking. In signing the application, the applicant should certify that falsified statements may be cause for dismissal, that investigation of credit and employment and driving record is authorized, that a medical examination and drug screening tests may be required, and that employment is for no definite period.

Estimates of how many applicants exaggerate their qualifications range from 40% to 70%.[154] The most common problems concern education and job experience. A majority of graduating seniors reportedly believe that employers expect a degree of exaggeration on résumés. Much of this exaggeration occurs on résumés, but may occur on application forms too. Therefore, make sure applicants complete the form and sign a statement on it indicating that the information is true. The court will almost always support a discharge for falsifying information when applying for work.[155]

FIGURE 5-8 FBI Employment Application

Source: From FBI Preliminary Application for Honors Internship Program, Federal Bureau of Investigation.

FIELD OFFICE USE ONLY

HP

Div: Program:

FEDERAL BUREAU OF INVESTIGATION

Preliminary Application for
Honors Internship Program
(Please Type or Print in Ink)

Date: _____

I. PERSONAL HISTORY

Name in Full   (Last, First, Middle, Maiden)

List College(s) attended, Major, Degree (if applicable), Grade Point Average

Birth Date (Month, Day, Year)
Birth Place:

Social Security Number: (Optional)

Current Address

Home Phone

Street   Apt. No.

Work Phone

Area Code   Number

City   State   Zip Code

Area Code   Number

Are you: Licensed Driver ☐ Yes ☐ No   U. S. Citizen ☐ Yes ☐ No

Have you served on active duty in the Armed Forces of the United States? ☐ Yes ☐ No

Branch of military service and dates of active duty:

Type of Discharge

How did you learn or become interested in the FBI Honors Internship Program?

Do you have a foreign language background? ☐ Yes ☐ No   List proficiency for each language on reverse side.

Have you ever been arrested or charged with any violation including traffic, but excluding parking tickets? ☐ Yes ☐ No If so, list all such matters even if found not guilty, not formally charged, no court appearance, or matter settled by payment of fine or forfeiture of collateral. Include date, place, charge, disposition, details, and police agency on reverse side.

II. EMPLOYMENT HISTORY

Identify your most recent three years FULL-TIME work experience, after high school (excluding summer, part-time and temporary employment).

From	To	Description of Work	Name/Location of Employer

III. PERSONAL DECLARATIONS

Persons with a disability who require an accommodation to complete the application process are required to notify the FBI of their need for the accommodation.

Have you used marijuana during the last three years or more than 15 times? ☐ Yes ☐ No

Have you used any illegal drug(s) or combination of illegal drugs, other than marijuana, more than 5 times or during the last 10 years? ☐ Yes ☐ No

All Information provided by applicants concerning their drug history will be subject to verification by a preemployment polygraph examination.

Do you understand all prospective FBI employees will be required to submit to an urinalysis for drug abuse prior to employment? ☐ Yes ☐ No

I am aware that willfully withholding information or making false statements on this application constitutes a violation of Section 1001, Title 18, U.S. Code and if appointed, will be the basis for dismissal from the Federal Bureau of Investigation. I agree to these conditions and I hereby certify that all statements made by me on this application are true and complete, to the best of my knowledge.

_____
Signature of Applicant as usually written. (**Do Not Use Nickname**)

The Federal Bureau of Investigation is an equal opportunity employer.

Finally, doing a less-than-complete job of filling in the form may reflect poor work habits. Some applicants scribble "see résumé attached" on the application. This is not acceptable. You need the signed, completed form. Some firms no longer ask applicants for résumés at all, but instead request and then peruse Web presence links, such as Twitter or LinkedIn accounts.[156]

Most employers need several application forms. For technical and managerial personnel, the form may require detailed answers to questions about education and training. The form for hourly factory workers might focus on tools and equipment. Figure 5-8 illustrates one employment application.

Using Application Forms to Predict Job Performance

Some employers use analyses of application information ("biodata") to *predict* employee tenure and performance. In one study, the researchers found that applicants who had longer tenure with previous employers were less likely to quit, and also had higher performance within 6 months after hire.[157] Examples of predictive biodata items might include "quit a job without giving notice," "graduated from college," and "traveled considerably growing up."[158]

Choose biodata items with three things in mind. First, equal employment law limits the items you'll want to use (avoid age, race, or gender, for instance). And, noninvasive items are best. In one study, subjects perceived items such as "dollar sales achieved" and "grade point average in math" as not invasive. Items such as "birth order" and "frequent dates in high school" were more invasive. Finally, some applicants will fake biodata answers in an effort to impress the employer.[159]

Chapter Review

Chapter Section Summaries

5-1. Recruitment and selection start with **workforce planning and forecasting**. Workforce planning is the process of deciding what positions the firm will have to fill, and how to fill them. This often starts by forecasting personnel needs, perhaps using trend analysis, ratio analysis, scatter plots, or computerized software packages. Next forecast the supply of inside candidates. Here employers use manual systems and replacement charts, and computerized skills inventories. Forecasting the supply of outside candidates is important, particularly when unemployment is low and good candidates are more difficult to come by.

5-2. Managers need to understand why **effective recruiting is important**. Without enough candidates, employers cannot effectively screen the candidates or hire the best. Some employers use a recruiting yield pyramid to estimate how many applicants they need to generate in order to fill predicted job openings.

5-3. Filling open positions with **internal sources of candidates** has several advantages. You are familiar with their strengths and weaknesses, and they require less orientation. Finding internal candidates often utilizes job posting. For filling the company's projected top-level positions, succession planning—the ongoing process of systematically identifying, assessing, and developing organizational leadership to enhance performance—is the process of choice.

5-4. Workforce plans influence **employee engagement**. For example, plans to develop and retain employees and promote from within tend to foster engagement, while contrary policies may erode

it. Recognizing this, at some companies such as FedEx, internal recruiting and promotion from within both play central roles in employee engagement. The promotion-from-within policy includes helping employees identify and develop their promotion potential. It also requires a coordinated system for accessing career records and posting job openings, one that guarantees all eligible employees are informed of openings and considered for them.

5-5. Employers use a variety of **outside sources of candidates** when recruiting applicants. These include recruiting via the Internet, advertising and employment agencies (including public and nonprofit agencies, and private agencies), temporary agencies and other alternative staffing methods, executive recruiters, college recruiting, referrals and walk-ins, and military personnel.

5-6. Understanding how to **recruit a more diverse workforce** is important. Whether the target is the single parent, older workers, or minorities, the basic rule is to understand their special needs and to create a set of policies and practices that create a more hospitable environment in which they can work.

5-7. **Employers develop and use application forms** to collect essential background information about the applicant. The application should enable you to make judgments on substantial matters such as the person's education and to identify the person's job references and supervisors. Of course, it's important to make sure the application complies with equal employment laws, for instance, with respect to questions regarding physical handicaps.

Discussion Questions

5-1. Briefly outline the workforce planning process.
5-2. Briefly explain each step in the recruitment and selection process.
5-3. What are the four main types of information that application forms provide?

5-4. How, specifically, do equal employment laws apply to personnel recruiting activities?
5-5. What are the five main things you would do to recruit and retain a more diverse workforce?

Individual and Group Activities

5-6. Bring to class several classified and display ads from the Web or the Sunday help wanted ads. Analyze the effectiveness of these ads using the guidelines discussed in this chapter.
5-7. Working individually or in groups, develop a 5-year forecast of occupational market conditions for five occupations such as accountant, nurse, and engineer.
5-8. Working individually or in groups, visit the local office of your state employment agency (or check out its site online). Come back to class prepared to discuss the following questions: What types of jobs seem to be available through this agency, predominantly? To what extent do you think this particular agency would be a good source of professional, technical, and/or managerial applicants? What sorts of paperwork are applicants to the state agency required to complete before their applications are processed by the agency? What other services does the office provide? What other opinions did you form about the state agency?
5-9. Working individually or in groups, find at least five employment ads, either on the Internet or in a local newspaper, that suggest that the company is family friendly and should appeal to women,

minorities, older workers, and single parents. Discuss what the firm is doing to be family friendly.
5-10. Working individually or in groups, interview a manager between the ages of 25 and 35 at a local business who manages employees age 40 or older. Ask the manager to describe three or four of his or her most challenging experiences managing older employees.
5-11. Appendices A and B at the end of this book (pages 583–600) list the knowledge someone studying for the HRCI (Appendix A) or SHRM (Appendix B) certification exam needs to have in each area of human resource management (such as in Strategic Management, and Workforce Planning). In groups of several students, do four things: (1) review Appendix A and/or B; (2) identify the material in this chapter that relates to the Appendix A and/or B required knowledge lists; (3) write four multiple-choice exam questions on this material that you believe would be suitable for inclusion in the HRCI exam and/or the SHRM exam; and, (4) if time permits, have someone from your team post your team's questions in front of the class, so that students in all teams can answer the exam questions created by the other teams.

Experiential Exercise

The Nursing Shortage

As of August 2015, job losses in the IT/ITES and other sectors was still disappointingly high, and employers were still holding back on their hiring. However, while many people were unemployed, that was not the case with highly qualified technical and management professionals with Ph.D degrees and publications. Virtually every IIT and IIM was aggressively recruiting faculty. Many were turning to foreign-trained candidates, for instance, by recruiting faculty in the US and Europe. Experts expect faculty to be in very short supply for years to come and intake of students to increase during the same time.

Purpose: The purpose of this exercise is to give you experience in creating a recruitment program.

Required Understanding: You should be thoroughly familiar with the contents of this chapter, and with the

faculty recruitment program of an institute. (You may like to visit the faculty recruitment page of www.iitm.ac.in.)

How to Set Up the Exercise/Instructions:
Set up groups of four to five students for this exercise. The groups should work separately and should not converse with each other. Each group should address the following tasks:

5-12. Based on information available on the institute's website, create a hard-copy ad for the institution to place in *The Hindustan Times* (HT). Which (geographic) editions of the HT would you use, and why?
5-13. Analyze the current online ads. How would you improve on it?
5-14. Prepare in outline form a complete faculty recruiting program for this institute, including all recruiting sources your group would use.

CHAPTER 5

Application Case

Finding People Who Are Passionate About What They Do

Trilogy Enterprises Inc. of Austin, Texas, is a fast-growing software company, and provides software solutions to giant global firms for improving sales and performance. Many of its approaches to business practice are unusual, but in Trilogy's fast-changing and highly competitive environment, they seem to work.

There is no dress code and employees make their own hours, often very long. They tend to socialize together (the average age is 26), both in the office's well-stocked kitchen and on company-sponsored events and trips to places like local dance clubs and retreats in Las Vegas. Responsibility is heavy and comes early, with a "just do it now" attitude. New recruits get a few weeks of intensive training, described by participants as "more like boot camp than business school." Information is delivered as if with "a fire hose," and new employees are expected to commit their expertise and vitality to everything they do. Jeff Daniel, director of college recruiting, admits the intense and unconventional firm is not the employer for everybody.

The firm employs about 700 people. Trilogy's managers know the rapid growth they seek depends on having a staff of the best people they can find, quickly trained and given broad responsibility and freedom as soon as possible. CEO Joe Liemandt says, "At a software company, people are everything…. Of course, the leaders at every company say, 'People are everything.' But they don't act on it."

Trilogy makes finding the right people a company-wide mission. Recruiters actively scour college career fairs and computer science departments for talented overachievers with ambition and entrepreneurial instincts. Top managers conduct the first rounds of interviews. Employees take top recruits and their significant others out on the town when they fly into Austin for the standard, 3-day preliminary visit. A typical day might begin with grueling interviews but end with mountain biking.

One year, Trilogy reviewed 15,000 résumés, conducted 4,000 on-campus interviews, flew 850 prospects in for interviews, and hired 262 college graduates. The cost per hire was $13,000; Jeff Daniel believes it was worth every penny.

Questions

5-15. Identify some of the established recruiting techniques that apparently underlie Trilogy's unconventional approach to attracting talent.

5-16. What particular elements of Trilogy's culture most likely appeal to the kind of employees it seeks? How does it convey those elements to job prospects?

5-17. Would Trilogy be an appealing employer for you? Why? If not, what would it take for you to accept a job offer from Trilogy?

5-18. What suggestions would you make to Trilogy for improving its recruiting processes?

Sources: Chuck Salter, "Insanity, Inc.," *Fast Company*, January 1999, pp. 101–108; and www.trilogy.com/sections/careers/work, accessed August 24, 2007.

Continuing Case

Carter Cleaning Company

Getting Better Applicants

If you were to ask Jennifer and her father what the main problem was in running their firm, their answer would be quick and short: hiring good people. Originally begun as a string of coin-operated laundromats requiring virtually no skilled help, the chain grew to six stores, each heavily dependent on skilled managers, cleaner/spotters, and pressers. Employees generally have no more than a high school education, and the market for them is very competitive. Over a typical weekend, literally dozens of want ads for experienced pressers or cleaner/spotters can be found in area newspapers. All these people usually are paid around $15 per hour, and they change jobs frequently. Jennifer and her father thus face the continuing task of recruiting and hiring qualified workers out of a pool of individuals they feel are almost nomadic in their propensity to move from area to area and job to job. Turnover in their stores (as in the stores of many of their competitors) often approaches 400%. "Don't talk to

me about human resources planning and trend analysis," says Jennifer. "We're fighting an economic war, and I'm happy just to be able to round up enough live applicants to be able to keep my trenches fully manned."

In light of this problem, Jennifer's father asked her to answer the following questions:

Questions

5-19. First, how would you recommend we go about reducing the turnover in our stores?

5-20. Provide a detailed list of recommendations concerning how we should go about increasing our pool of acceptable job applicants so we no longer face the need to hire almost anyone who walks in the door. (Your recommendations regarding the latter should include completely worded online and hard-copy advertisements and recommendations regarding any other recruiting strategies you would suggest we use.)

Translating Strategy into HR Policies and Practices Case§

Improving Performance at the Hotel Paris

The New Recruitment Process

The Hotel Paris's competitive strategy is "to use superior guest service to differentiate the Hotel Paris properties, and to thereby increase the length of stay and return rate of guests, and thus boost revenues and profitability." HR manager Lisa Cruz must now formulate functional policies and activities that support this competitive strategy and boost performance, by eliciting the required employee behaviors and competencies.

As a longtime HR professional, Lisa Cruz was well aware of the importance of effective employee recruitment. If the Hotel Paris didn't get enough applicants, it could not be selective about who to hire. And, if it could not be selective about who to hire, it wasn't likely that the hotels would enjoy the customer-oriented employee behaviors that the company's strategy relied on. She was therefore disappointed to discover that the Hotel Paris was paying virtually no attention to the job of recruiting prospective employees. Individual hotel managers slapped together help wanted ads when they had positions to fill, and no one in the chain had any measurable idea of how many recruits these ads were producing or which recruiting approaches worked the best (or worked at all). Lisa knew that it was time to step back and get control of the Hotel Paris's recruitment function.

As they reviewed the details of the Hotel Paris's current recruitment practices, Lisa Cruz and the firm's CFO became increasingly concerned. What they found, basically, was that the recruitment function was totally unmanaged. The previous HR director had simply allowed the responsibility for recruiting to remain with each separate hotel, and the hotel managers, not being HR professionals, usually just took the path of least resistance when a job became available by placing help wanted ads in their local papers. There was no sense of direction from the Hotel Paris's headquarters regarding what sorts of applicants the company preferred, what media and alternative sources of recruits its managers should use, no online recruiting, and, of course, no measurement at all of effectiveness of the recruitment process. The company totally ignored recruitment-source metrics that other firms used effectively, such as number of qualified applicants per position, percentage of jobs filled from within, the offer-to-acceptance ratio, acceptance by recruiting source, turnover by recruiting source, and selection test results by recruiting source. This despite the fact, as the CFO put it, "that high performance companies consistently score much higher than low-

performing firms on HR practices such as number of qualified applicants per position, and percentage of jobs filled from within."

It was safe to say that achieving the Hotel Paris's strategic aims depended largely on the quality of the people that it attracted to, and then selected for, employment at the firm. "What we want are employees who will put our guests first, who will use initiative to see that our guests are satisfied, and who will work tirelessly to provide our guests with services that exceed their expectations," said the CFO. Lisa and the CFO both knew this process had to start with better recruiting. The CFO gave her the green light to design a new recruitment process.

Lisa and her team had the firm's IT department create a central recruiting link for the Hotel Paris's website, with geographical links that each local hotel could use to publicize its openings. The HR team created a series of standard ads the managers could use for each job title. These standard ads emphasized the company's service-oriented values, and basically said (without actually saying it) that if you were not people oriented you should not apply. They emphasized what it was like to work for the Hotel Paris, and the excellent benefits (which the HR team was about to get started on) the firm provided. It created a new intranet-based job posting system and encouraged employees to use it to apply for open positions. For several jobs, including housekeeping crew and front-desk clerk, applicants must now first pass a short prescreening test to apply. The HR team analyzed the performance (for instance, in terms of applicants/source and applicants hired/source) of the various local newspapers and recruiting firms the hotels had used in the past, and chose the best to be the approved recruiting sources in their local areas.

After 6 months with these and other recruitment function changes, the number of applicants was up on average 40%. Lisa and her team were now set to institute new screening procedures that would help them select the high-commitment, service-oriented, motivated employees they were looking for.

Questions

5-21. Given the hotel's required personnel skills, what recruiting sources would you have suggested it use, and why?

5-22. What would a Hotel Paris help wanted ad look like?

5-23. Based on what you know and on what you learned here in Chapter 5 of Dessler *Human Resource Management*, how would you suggest Hotel Paris measure the effectiveness of its recruiting efforts?

---

§Written by and copyright Gary Dessler, PhD.

Key Terms

Endnotes

1. Accessed on 14 August 2017 at www.hindustantimes.com/.../ how-taj...hr.../story-Ko3sRmSi-J5U36UKooMqnxL.htm.

2. This section is quoted or paraphrased from, "Workforce Planning: Translating the Business Plan into the People Plan," Towers Watson, www. towerswatson.com/en-GB/ Insights/IC-Types/Survey-Research-Results/2012/11/ workforce-planning-translating-the-business-plan-into-the-people-plan?page=0, accessed March 29, 2013.

3. Editorial Team (2012), Firms Adopt Temporary Staffing to Meet Margin Blues, *People Matters*, 10 Feb 2012.

4. Retrieved on 14 August 2017 from http://www.livemint.com/ Industry/jzfZ5tRfJdkEq6D-blNuggP/Crunch-time-for-IT-industry.html.

5. "Transforming Talent Management: Pursuing New Perspectives," 2013 Talent Management Conference & Exposition, Society for Human Resource Management, "Preparing for Tomorrow's Talent Gap: Five Strategies to Start Today" workshop, p. 4. See also "Succession Planning Orientation Guide," *Workforce,* February 2014, pp. 32–34.

6. Accessed on 18 September 2017 at http://www.hindustantimes. com/business/how-taj-hotel-s-hr-found-26-11-heroes/story-Ko3s-RmSiJ5U36UKooMqnxL.htm.

7. Jones Shannon, "Does HR Planning Improve Business Performance?" *Industrial Management,* January/February 2003, p. 20. See also Michelle Harrison et al., "Effective Succession Planning," *Training & Development,* October 2006, pp. 22–23.

8. Jean Phillips and Stanley Gully, *Strategic Staffing* (Upper Saddle River, NJ: Pearson Education, 2012), pp. 116–181.

9. Accessed on September 14, 2017, at http://indianon-lineseller.com/2016/03/ holidays-events-occasions-that-impact-ecommerce-sellers-in-india/)

10. Shannon, "Does HR Planning Improve Business Performance?" p. 16.

11. See, for example, Fay Hansen, "The Long View," *Workforce Management,* April 20, 2008, pp. 1, 14.

12. Bill Roberts, "Can They Keep Our Lights On?" *HR Magazine,* June 2010, pp. 62–68. For an example of a computerized personnel planning system, see www.kronos.com/

scheduling-software/scheduling. aspx, accessed October 2, 2011.

13. See, for example, www.shrm. org/TemplatesTools/hrqa/Pages/ Howcanaskillsinventorybeused for strategicHRplanning.aspx, accessed February 6, 2014.

14. http://skillsdbpro.com/SkillsDB-PROWeb.html; http://skillsdbpro. com/client-list/; and www.survey-analytics.com/skills-inventory. html, accessed June 22, 2015.

15. www.surveyanalytics.com/ skills-inventory-software.html, accessed June 1, 2011.

16. www.sumtotalsystems.com/data-sheets/sumt_succession_plan-ning.pdf, accessed June 1, 2011.

17. For a recent discussion see, for example, "Pitfalls Abound for Employers Lacking Electronic Information Retention Policies," *BNA Bulletin to Management,* January 1, 2008, pp. 1–2.

18. The legislation includes the Federal Privacy Act of 1974 (applies to federal workers), the New York Personal Privacy Act of 1985, HIPAA (regulates use of medical records), and the Americans with Disabilities Act.

19. Ibid. See also Bill Roberts, "Risky Business," *HR Magazine,* October 2006, pp. 69–72.

20. See, for example, Society for Human Resource Management, "HR's Insight into the Economy," *Workplace Visions* 4 (2008), p. 5.

21. www.astd.org/NR/rdonlyres/ CBAB6F0D-97FA-4B1F-920C-6EBAF98906D1/0/Bridgingth-eSkillsGap.pdf, accessed June 1, 2011.

22. "Next Generation Talent Management," www.hewittas-sociates.com/_MetaBasicC-MAssetCache_/Assets/Articles/ next_generation.pdf, accessed November 9, 2010.

23. "Boeing Soars Over Potential Talent Gaps with Its Workforce Planning Strategies," *Bloomberg BNA Bulletin to Management,* February 19, 2013, p. 57.

24. Ed Frauenheim, "Valero Energy," *Workforce Management,* March 13, 2006.

25. Phillips and Gully, *Strategic Staffing,* pp. 116–181.

26. See also Soonhee Kim, "Linking Employee Assessments to Succession Planning," *Public Personnel Management* 32, no. 4 (Winter 2003), pp. 533–547; Michael Laff, "Talent Management: From Hire to Retire," *Training & Development,* November 2006, pp. 42–48.

27. See, for example, David Day, "Developing Leadership Talent," SHRM Foundation, www.shrm. org/about/foundation/research/ Documents/Developing%20 Lead%20Talent-%20FINAL. pdf, accessed October 4, 2011.

28. Quoted in Susan Wells, "Who's Next," *HR Magazine,* November 2003, p. 43. See also Christee Atwood, "Implementing Your Succession Plan," *Training & Development,* November 2007, pp. 54–57; and Day, "Developing Leadership Talent."

29. See "Succession Management: Identifying and Developing Leaders," *BNA Bulletin to Management* 21, no. 12 (December 2003), p. 15; and Day, "Developing Leadership Talent."

30. Kim, "Linking Employee Assessments to Succession Planning."

31. Bill Roberts, "Matching Talent with Tasks," *HR Magazine,* November 2002, pp. 91–96.

32. www.sumtotalsystems.com/data-sheets/sumt_succession_plan-ning.pdf, accessed June 1, 2011.

33. Ibid., p. 34.

34. Susan Ladika, "Manufacturers Enroll in Recruiting 101," *Workforce Management,* May 2012.

35. David Ferris, "Ex-Factor for Factories Is Factoring in Recruiting," *Workforce Management,* December 2012, p. 8.

36. Susan Caminiti, "Leveraging Human Capital," Fortune.com/ edit sections, 2012, pp. 52–54.

37. Sara Rynes, Robert Bretz Jr., and Barry Gerhart, "The Importance of Recruitment and Job Choice: A Different Way of Looking," *Personnel Psychology* 44, no. 3 (September 1991), pp. 487–521.

38. Tom Porter, "Effective Techniques to Attract, Hire, and Retain 'Top Notch' Employees for Your Company," *San Diego Business Journal* 21, no. 13 (March 27, 2000), p. B36.

39. Jonathan Segal, "Land Executives, Not Lawsuits," *HR Magazine,* October 2006, pp. 123–130.

40. "Recruitment Marketing," www. recruiter.com/recruitment_mar-keting/, accessed May 1, 2012.

41. www.ge.com/careers/why_ ge.html, accessed May 1, 2012.

42. Retrieved on 16 August 2017 from http://www.mahindra.com/careers.

43. Retrieved on 16 August 2017 from http://www.isro.gov.in/careers.

44. Stanley Gully, Jean Phillips, William Castellano, Khongji Han, and Andrea Kim, "A Mediated Moderation Model of Recruiting Socially and Environmentally Responsible Job Applicants," *Personnel Psychology* 66 (2013), p. 966.

45. Kenneth Sovereign, *Personnel Law* (Upper Saddle River, NJ: Prentice Hall, 1999), pp. 47–49.

46. Ranjan, Amitav, "Centre to Stop Campus Hiring by PSUs, Banks; Says Selection Process Violated Constitution," April 15, 2017, 8.39am, *The Indian Express,* www.indianexpress.com, (Navigation--Home--India--

Article), as accessed on 08 August 2017 at 7pm IST.

47. Ibid., p. 48.

48. "Apple, Google Agree to Pay $415 Million in Settlement of Antitrust Hiring Charges," *Bloomberg BNA Bulletin to Management,* January 27, 2015, p. 27.

49. Todd Henneman, "The Insiders or the Outsiders?" *Workforce,* March 2014, pp. 29–31, 48.

50. Eric Krell, "Look Outside or Seek Within?" *HR Magazine,* January/February 2015, pp. 61–64.

51. "Hiring Works the Second Time Around," *BNA Bulletin to Management,* January 30, 1997, p. 40; and Issie Lapowsky, "How to Rehire Former Employees," *INC.,* May 18, 2010, www.inc. com/guides/2010/05/rehiring-former-employees.html, accessed October 3, 2011.

52. Ibid.

53. See www.linkedin.com/jobs2/ view/10696437, accessed June 22, 2015.

54. Lauren Weber and Leslie Kwoh, "Beware the Phantom Job Listing," *Wall Street Journal,* January 9, 2013, page B1.

55. "Many Workers Use Social Networking Sites in Job Hunt, Edit Own Content, Survey Finds," *BNA Bulletin to Management,* May 10, 2011, p. 147.

56. Khosla, Varun & Dasgupta, Brinda, "Hiring Via Employee Referrals on the Rise," *The Economic Times,* Aug 19, 2016, 01.46pm, www.economictimes. indiatimes.com, (Navigation--Jobs--Article), as accessed on 8 August 2017 at 4pm IST.

57. Tech.economictimes.indiatimes. com › ... › Hiring via employee referrals on the rise

58. Deborah Silver, "Niche Sites Gain Monster-Sized Following," *Workforce Management,* March 2011, pp. 10–11.

59. Except as noted, this *Online Recruiting* section is based on Lauren Weber, "Seeking Software Fix for Job-Search Game," *Wall Street Journal,* June 6, 2012, p. B8; and Juro Osawa and Paul Moser, "In China, Recruiting Gets Social," *Wall Street Journal,* August 2, 2012, p. B4.

60. "ResumePal: Recruiter's Friend?" *Workforce Management,* June 22, 2009, p. 28.

61. "Innovative HR Programs Cultivate Successful Employees," *Nation's Restaurant News* 41, no. 50 (December 17, 2007), p. 74.

62. J. De Avila, "Beyond Job Boards: Targeting the Source," *Wall Street Journal* (Eastern Edition), July 2, 2009, pp. D1, D5.

63. Gina Ruiz, "Firms Tapping Web Videos to Lure Jobseekers," *Workforce Management,* October 8, 2007, p. 12.

64. Sarah Fister Gale, "Social Media Transforms a Recruiting Source Software Industry," *Workforce Management,* workforce.com, June 2013, p. 26. See also Thomas Cottereau, "The Future of Live Video Interviews for Recruitment," *HR Magazine,* November 2014, pp. 48–50.

65. Elizabeth Agnvall, "Job Fairs Go Virtual," *HR Magazine,* July 2007, p. 85; Gary Stern, "Virtual Job Fairs Becoming More of a Reality," *Workforce Management,* February 2011, p. 11.

66. Matthias Baum and Rudiger Kabst, "The Effectiveness of Recruitment Advertisements and Recruitment Websites: Indirect and Interactive Effects on Applicant Attraction," *Human Resource Management* 53, no. 3 (May–June 2014), pp. 353–378.

67. "EEOC Issues Much Delayed Definition of 'Applicant,'" *HR Magazine,* April 2004, p. 29; Valerie Hoffman and Greg Davis, "OFCCP's Internet Applicant Definition Requires Overhaul of Recruitment and Hiring Policies," *Society for Human Resources Management Legal Report,* January/February 2006, p. 2.

68. This carries legal risks, particularly if the device disproportionately screens out minority or female applicants. Lisa Harpe, "Designing an Effective Employment Prescreening Program," *Employment Relations Today* 32, no. 3 (Fall 2005), pp. 43–51.

69. Lauren Weber, "Your Resume Versus Oblivion," *Wall Street Journal,* January 24, 2012, pp. B1, B6.

70. William Dickmeyer, "Applicant Tracking Reports Make Data Meaningful," *Workforce,* February 2001, pp. 65–67; and, as an example, www.icims.com/prelude/1101/3009?_vsrefdom=google_ppc&gclid=CPHki_nx1KsCF-cPt7QodmkjLDA, accessed October 4, 2011.

71. Paul Gilster, "Channel the Resume Flood with Applicant Tracking Systems," *Workforce,* January 2001, pp. 32–34; William Dickmeyer, "Applicant Tracking Reports Make Data Meaningful," *Workforce,* February 2001, pp. 65–67; and, as an example, www.icims.com/prelude/1101/3009?_vsrefdom=google_ppc&gclid=CPHki_nx1KsCF-cPt7QodmkjLDA, accessed October 4, 2011.

72. Note also that for EEO purposes, "Feds Want a Look at Online Job Sites," *HR Magazine,* November 2008, p. 12.

73. "E-Recruiting Software Providers," *Workforce Management,* June 22, 2009, p. 14.

74. Weber, "Your Resume Versus Oblivion."

75. Dave Zielinski, "Get to the Source," *HR Magazine,* November 2012, p. 68.

76. (Laszlo Bock, Work Rules! (New York: Twelve: 2015) 81, 82).

77. (Laszlo Bock, Work Rules! (New York: Twelve: 2015) 79 – 86)

78. Daniel Feldman and Brian Klaas, "Internet Job Hunting: A Field Study of Applicant Experiences with Online Recruiting," *Human Resource Management* 41, no. 2 (Summer 2002), pp. 175–192.

79. "Does Your Company's Website Click with Job Seekers?" *Workforce,* August 2000, p. 260.

80. "Study Says Career Web Sites Could Snare More Job Seekers," *BNA Bulletin to Management,* February 1, 2001, p. 36.

81. Sarah Gale, "Internet Recruiting: Better, Cheaper, Faster," *Workforce,* December 2001, p. 75.

82. "Help Wanted—and Found," *Fortune,* October 2, 2006, p. 40.

83. James Breaugh, "Employee Recruitment: Current Knowledge and Important Areas for Future Research," *Human Resource Management Review* 18 (2008), p. 114.

84. "Job Seekers' Privacy Has Been Eroded with Online Job Searchers, Report Says," *BNA Bulletin to Management,* November 20, 2003, p. 369.

85. Staff Reporter, *The Hindu,* 'India Ranks as Second-Largest Market for LinkedIn," Bengaluru, April 29, 2017, www.thehindu.com, (Navigation--Business--Industry--Article), as accessed on 08 August 2017 at 3pm IST.

86. Anthony Abbatiello, "The Digital Override," *Workforce,* May 2014, pp. 36–39; "Social Recruiting in 2012, the Ladders.com," Special Advertising Supplement to *Workforce Management,* 2012; and http://cdn.theladders.net/static/recruit-ladder/pdf/WP%20Social%20Recruiting %20in%202012.pdf, accessed July 2, 2014.

87. Aliah Wright, "Your Social Media Is Showing," *HR Magazine,* March 2012, p. 16.

88. Jennifer Arnold, "Twittering at Face Booking While They Were," *HR Magazine,* December 2009, p. 54.

89. Ibid.

90. *Bloomberg BNA Bulletin to Management,* "Certain Social Media Tools Are Helping HR Connect Swiftly with the Right Job Candidates," July 24, 2012, p. 233.

91. Jennifer Taylor Arnold, "Recruiting on the Run," February 2010, *HR Magazine,* pp. 65–67.

92. https://premium.linkedin.com/premiumhiring/features, accessed April 6, 2015.

93. Jim Lundy, "Research Note," *Aragon Research* 3 (January 31, 2014).

94. Eric Krell, "Recruiting Outlook: Creative HR for 2003," *Workforce,* December 2002, pp. 40–44.

95. Breaugh, "Employee Recruitment," p. 111.

96. Retrieved on 16 August 2017 from http://timesofindia.indiatimes.com/india/Employment-exchanges-to-turn-into-career-counseling-centres/articleshow/49339194.cms

97. PTI, "Employment Exchanges to Turn into Career Counseling Centres," *The Times of India,* Oct 13, 2015, 06.29pm, www.timesofindia.indiatimes.com, (Navigation--News--Home---India--Article), as accessed on 08 August 2017 at 8pm IST.

98. Ibid.

99. Robert Grossman, "How to Recruit a Recruitment Outsourcer," *HR Magazine,* July 2012, pp. 51–54; and Susan Ladika, "A Lot to Process," *Workforce Management,* July 2012, pp. 16–18. See also Max Mihelich, "RPO Is On the Go," *Workforce,* February 2014, pp. 44–47.

100. "Recruitment Process Outsourcing Providers," *Workforce Management,* February 2013, p. 20.

101. One "Wharton MBA and GE alum" manages short-term projects for major companies and served as interim CEO for one firm. See Jodi Greenstone Miller and Matt Miller, "The Best Executive and Professional Jobs May No Longer Be Full-Time Gigs," *Harvard Business Review,* May 2012, p. 51.

102. Retrieved on 16 August 2017 from www.teamlease.com/temporary-staffing

103. "As Hiring Falters, More Workers Are Temporary," *New York Times,* December 20, 2010, pp. A1, A4.

104. John Zappe, "Temp-to-Hire Is Becoming a Full-Time Practice at Firms," *Workforce Management,* June 2005, pp. 82–86.

105. Shari Cauldron, "Contingent Workforce Spurs HR Planning," *Personnel Journal,* July 1994, p. 60.

106. Robert Bohner Jr. and Elizabeth Salasko, "Beware the Legal Risks of Hiring Temps," *Workforce,* October 2002, pp. 50–57. See also Fay Hansen, "A Permanent Strategy for Temporary Hires," *Workforce Management,* February 26, 2007, p. 27; and Robert Grossman, "Strategic Temp–Tations," *HR Magazine,* March 2012, pp. 24–34.

107. Retrieved on 16 August 2017 from www.hamarangels.com.

108. This is based on or quoted from Nancy Howe, "Match Temp Services to Your Needs," *Personnel Journal,* March 1989, pp. 45–51. See also Stephen Miller, "Collaboration Is Key to Effective Outsourcing," *HR Magazine* 58 (2008), pp. 60–61; and, as an example, www.bbb.org/shreveport/accredited-business-directory/employment-contractors-temporary-help/plain-dealing-la, accessed September 23, 2011.

109. Daniel Feldman, Helen Doerpinghaus, and William Turnley, "Managing Temporary Workers: A Recurrent HRM Challenge," *Organizational Dynamics* 23, no. 2 (Fall 1994), p. 49. See also Kathryn Tyler, "Treat Contingent Workers with Care," *HR Magazine,* March 2008, p. 75; and www.employment.oregon.gov/EMPLOY/ES/BUS/index.shtml, accessed October 4, 2011.

110. Carolyn Hirschman, "Are Your Contractors Legal?" *HR Magazine,* March 2004, pp. 59–63. See also Dori Meinert, "Modern-Day Slavery," *HR Magazine,* May 2012, pp. 22–24.

111. Hirschman, "Are Your Contractors Legal?"

112. Margaret Steen, "More Employers Take on Temps, but Planning Is Paramount," *Workforce Management,* May 2011, p. 14.

113. Heather Jackson and Cary Donham, "Five Things to Know About Working with Staffing Firms," *Workforce Management,* October 2013, p. 47.

114. This section is based on Robyn Meredith, "Giant Sucking Sound," *Forbes,* 172, no. 6, September 29, 2003, p. 158; Jim McKay, "Inevitable Outsourcing, Offshoring Stirred Passions at Pittsburgh Summit," *Knight Ridder/Tribune Business News,* March 11, 2004; Peter Panepento, "General Electric Transportation to Outsource Drafting Jobs to India," *Knight Ridder/Tribune Business News,* May 5, 2004; Julie Harbin, "Recent Survey Charts Execs' Willingness to Outsource Jobs," *San Diego Business Journal* 25, no. 14 (April 5, 2004), pp. 8–10; and Ben W. Heineman Jr, "Why We Can All Stop Worrying About Offshoring and Outsourcing," *The Atlantic,* March 26, 2013, www.theatlantic.com/business/archive/2013/03/whywe-can-all-stop-worrying-about-offshoring-and-outsourcing/274388/, accessed August 20, 2014.

115. PTI, "China Must Worry About Jobs as Firms Move Production to India', *The Times of India,* Sep 26, 2016, 03.28pm, www.timesofindia.indiatimes.com, (Navigation--News--Home--World--China--Article), as accessed on 08 August 2017 at 6pm IST.

116. Ed Frauenheim, "Homeward Bound," *Workforce Management,* February 2013, pp. 26–31.

117. Michelle Martinez, "Working with an Outside Recruiter? Get It in Writing," *HR Magazine,* January 2001, pp. 98–105.

118. See, for example, Stephenie Overman, "Searching for the Top," *HR Magazine*, January 2008, p. 49.

119. Bill Leonard, "Recruiting from the Competition," *HR Magazine*, February 2001, pp. 78–86. See also G. Anders, "Secrets of the Talent Scouts," *New York Times* (Late New York Edition) (March 15, 2009), pp. 1, 7 (Sec. 3).

120. Carol Hymowitz and Jeff Green, "These Days, Anybody Can Headhunt," *Bloomberg Business Week*, January 27, 2013, pp. 19–20; Joann Lublin, "More Executive Recruiting Ships in House," *Wall Street Journal*, October 10, 2012, p. B8.

121. Lauren Weber, "Here's What Boards Want in Executives," *Wall Street Journal,* December 10, 2014, p. B5.

122. Based on John Wareham, *Secrets of a Corporate Headhunter* (New York: Playboy Press, 1981), pp. 213–225; Chip McCreary, "Get the Most Out of Search Firms," *Workforce*, August 1997, pp. S28–S30.

123. Breaugh, "Employee Recruitment," p. 109.

124. "Tell a Friend: Employee Referral Programs Earn High Marks for Low Recruiting Costs," *BNA Bulletin to Management*, June 28, 2001, p. 201.

125. Accessed on 18 September 2017 at http://www.livemint.com/Companies/ck6h9K-KDL9Aw1SCgzvMLRM/The-building-of-UrbanClap-one-ondemand-service-at-a-time.html.

126. Martha Frase-Blunt, "A Recruiting Spigot," *HR Magazine*, April 2003, pp. 71–79.

127. Sara Rynes, Marc Orlitzky, and Robert Bretz Jr., "Experienced Hiring Versus College Recruiting: Practices and Emerging Trends," *Personnel Psychology* 50 (1997), pp. 309–339. See also Lisa Munniksma, "Career Matchmakers: Partnering with Collegiate Career Centers Offers Recruiters Access to Rich Source of Applicants," *HR Magazine* 50, no. 2 (February 2005), p. 93.

128. See, for example, Breaugh, "Employee Recruitment," p. 111; "Recruiters Look to Be Big Man on Campus," *Workforce Management*, September 2010, p. 12.

129. Greet Van Hoye and Filip Lievens, "Tapping the Grapevine: A Closer Look at Word-of-Mouth as a Recruitment Source," *Journal of Applied Psychology* 94, no. 2 (2009), pp. 341–352.

130. Munniksma, "Career Matchmakers."

131. Wendy Boswell et al., "Individual Job Choice Decisions and the Impact of Job Attributes and Recruitment Practices: A Longitudinal Field Study," *Human Resource Management* 42, no. 1 (Spring 2003), pp. 23–37. See also Breaugh, "Employee Recruitment," p. 115.

132. Hao Zhao Oh and Robert Liden, "Internship: A Recruitment and Selected Perspective," *Journal of Applied Psychology* 96, no. 1 (2011), pp. 221–229.

133. Retrieved on 16 August 2017 from https://internshala.com.

134. Martha Frase-Blunt, "Call Centers Come Home," *HR Magazine*, January 2007, pp. 85–90.

135. See, for example, Stephanie Castellano, "The Value of Veterans," *Training & Development*, February 2013, p. 16.

136. Gino Ruiz, "Special Report: Talent Acquisition," *Workforce Management*, July 23, 2007, p. 39.

137. Thomas Stewart, "In Search of Elusive Tech Workers," *Fortune*, February 16, 1998, pp. 171–172; and www.outsourcing-center.com/2006-10-ge-looks-to-recruitment-process-outsourcer-to-find-meat-and-potatoes-candidates-as-well-as-the-purple-squirrel-article-37479.html, accessed October 5, 2011.

138. "Internship Programs Help These Recruiters Toward Qualified Students with Disabilities," *BNA Bulletin to Management,* July 17, 2003, p. 225.

139. www.recruitingtrends.com/recruiting-women/; http://online.wsj.com/article/SB10001424127887323764804578314450063914388.html; www.theresumator.com/blog/how-to-recruit-women-for-your-workforce/; http://blogs.kenan-flagler.unc.edu/2012/06/12/the-new-business-imperative-recruiting-and-retaining-women-in-the-workplace/. All accessed May 9, 2013.

140. Ganguly, Chawm, "Cummins Awarded the Top 10 Best Companies for Women in India," Dec 27, 2016, Core Sector Communique, www.corecommunique.com, (Navigation--Home--News--Article), as accessed on 08 August 2017 at 7pm IST

141. Sandra Block and Stephanie Armour, "Many Americans Retire Years Before They Want To," *USA Today*, July 26, 2006, http://usatoday.com, accessed December 23, 2007.

142. Phaedra Brotherton, "Tapping into an Older Workforce," *Mosaics* (Society for Human Resource Management, March/April 2000). See also Thomas Ng and Daniel Feldman, "The Relationship of Age to Ten Dimensions of Job Performance," *Journal of Applied Psychology* 90, no. 2 (2008), pp. 392–423.

143. Sue Shellenbarger, "Gray Is Good: Employers Make Efforts to Retain Older, Experienced Workers," *Wall Street Journal*, December 1, 2005.

144. Alison Wellner, "Tapping a Silver Mine," *HR Magazine*, March 2002, p. 29.

145. Sue Shellenbarger, "Gray Is Good." See also Robert Grossman, "Keep Pace with Older Workers," *HR Magazine*, May 2008, pp. 39–46.

146. Gary Adams and Barbara Rau, "Attracting Retirees to Apply: Desired Organizational Characteristics of Bridge Employment," Journal of Organizational Behavior 26, no. 6 (September 2005), pp. 649–660.

147. Thomas NG and Daniel Feldman, "Evaluating Six Common Stereotypes About Older Workers with Meta-analytical Data," Personnel Psychology 60, no. 6 (2012), pp. 821–858.

148. Retrieved on 16 August 2017 from http://www.businessinsider.in/The-25-Best-Companies-For-LGBT-Employees/article-show/31557433.cms

149. Retrieved on 16 August 2017 from http://economic-times.indiatimes.com/news/company/corporate-trends/companies-come-out-in-support-of-lgbt-community/article-show/58288344.cms

150. Retrieved on 16 August 2017 from http://english.

manoramaonline.com/news/kerala/2017/06/10/kochi-metro-life-women-transgender-employees-transforms.html.

151. Ibid.

152. Retrieved on 16 August 2017 from www.tatabex.com/assessment/taap-assessment

153. http://indianexpress.com/article/india/india-others/3-quota-must-for-disabled-in-all-govt-jobs-including-ias-supereme-court/accessed June 19,017

154. This paragraph is based on Jennifer L. Wood, James M. Schmidtke, and Diane L. Decker, "Lying on Job Applications: The Effects of Job Relevance, Commission, and Human Resource Management Experience," *Journal of Business and Psychology* 22 (2007), pp. 1–9.

155. Kenneth Sovereign, *Personnel Law* (Upper Saddle River, NJ: Pearson, 1999), p. 51, 132.

156. Rachel Emma Silverman, "No More Resumes, Say Some Firms," *Wall Street Journal*, January 24, 2012, p. B6.

157. Murray Barrick and Ryan Zimmerman, "Hiring for Retention and Performance," *Human Resource Management* 48, no. 2 (March/April 2009), pp 183–206.

158. James Breaugh, "The Use of Biodata for Employee Selection: Test Research and Future Directions," *Human Resource Management Review* 19 (2009), pp. 219–231. Utilizing biodata items presumes that the employer can show that the items predict performance. Biodata items such as "graduated from college" may have an adverse impact on minorities, but studies suggest that employers can avoid that problem through judicious choice of biodata items (p. 229).

159. Fred Mael, Mary Connerley, and Ray Morath, "None of Your Business: Parameters of Biodata Invasiveness," *Personnel Psychology* 49 (1996), pp. 613–650; and Kenneth Law et al., "Impression Management and Faking in Biodata Scores Among Chinese Job-Seekers," *Asia Pacific Journal of Management* 19, no. 4 (December 2002), pp. 541–556.

6

Employee Testing and Selection

LEARNING OBJECTIVES

6-1 Answer the question: Why is it important to test and select employees?

6-2 Explain what is meant by reliability and validity.

6-3 List and briefly describe the basic categories of selection tests, with examples.

6-4 Explain how to use two work simulations for selection.

6-5 Describe four ways to improve an employer's background checking process.

Employee turnover has become an expensive problem for all businesses. These costs are not only limited to the recruiting and training costs but also involve hidden costs. These hidden costs are in the form of a customer declaring not to visit a newly opened restaurant because of the dissatisfactory service provided by the restaurant. So, when some young founders in Ahmedabad opened a restaurant, they decided to minimize their recruiting costs. We will discuss this in detail in the chapter.

WHERE ARE WE NOW ...

Chapter 5 focused on how to build an applicant pool. The purpose of Chapter 6 is to explain how to use various tools to select the best candidate for the job. The main topics we'll cover include the selection process, basic testing techniques, types of tests, work samples and simulations, and making background and reference checks. In Chapter 7, we will turn to the techniques you can use to improve your skills at what is probably the most widely used screening tool, the selection interview.

Why Employee Selection is Important

After reviewing the applicants' résumés, the manager turns to selecting the best candidate for the job. This usually means reducing the applicant pool by using the screening tools we discuss in this and the following chapter: tests, assessment centers, interviews, and background and reference checks. The aim of employee selection is to achieve *person-job fit*. This means matching the knowledge, skills, abilities, and other competencies (KSACs) that are required for performing the job (based on job analysis) with the applicant's KSACs.

Of course, a candidate might be "right" for a job, but wrong for the organization.[1] For example, an experienced cabin crew member may perform well at Air India than Air Asia where the organizational values are different from the former. Therefore, while person-job fit is very important, person-organization fit (P-O) is important as well. P-O fit is necessary to ensure that the candidate fits well in the organizational culture and aligns with its values.

In any case, selecting the right employee is important for three main reasons. First, employees with the right skills will perform better for you and the company. Employees without these skills or who are abrasive or obstructionist won't perform effectively, and your own performance and the firm's will suffer. The time to screen out undesirables is before they are in the door.

Second, effective selection is important because it is costly to recruit and hire employees. One survey in the US found that the average cost of hiring an employee who doesn't work out is about $50,000.[2]

Third, it's important because inept hiring has legal consequences. For one thing, we saw in Chapter 2 that employment laws have to be followed. **Negligent hiring** is another such problem. It means hiring employees with criminal records or other problems who then use access to customers' homes (or similar opportunities) to commit crimes.[3] Following the rape of a woman customer who had hired an Uber cab, Uber India was accused of negligent hiring. This is because police investigation later found that the company had not done enough background check and the driver had criminal records.[4] In addition, it has been observed that hiring candidates with wrong credentials often leads to termination of employment for securing job with the help of wrong information. In one case in the US, *Ponticas v. K.M.S. Investments*, an apartment manager entered a woman's apartment and assaulted her.[5] The court found the apartment complex's owner negligent for not checking the manager's background properly.[6]

negligent hiring

Hiring workers with questionable backgrounds without proper safeguards.

The Basics of Testing and Selecting Employees

In this chapter, we'll discuss several popular selection tools, starting with tests. A *test* is basically a sample of a person's behavior. Any test or screening tool has two important characteristics, *reliability* and *validity*. We'll start with the former.

Reliability

Reliability is a selection tool's first requirement and refers to its consistency: "A reliable test is one that yields consistent scores when a person takes two alternate forms of the test or when he or she takes the same test on two or more different occasions."[7] If a person scores 90 on an intelligence test on a Monday and 130 when retested on Tuesday, you probably wouldn't have much faith in the test.

You can measure reliability in several ways. One is to administer a test to a group one day, re-administer the same test several days later to the same group, and then correlate the first set of scores with the second (called *test-retest reliability estimates*).[8] Or you could administer a test and then administer what experts believe to be an equivalent test later; this would be an *equivalent or alternate form estimate*. (The Scholastic Assessment Test [SAT] is one example.) Or, compare the test taker's answers to certain questions on the test with his or her answers to a separate set of questions on the same test aimed at measuring the same thing. This is an *internal*

reliability

The consistency of scores obtained by the same person when retested with the identical tests or with alternate forms of the same test.

FIGURE 6-1 **Test Score Correlation Examples**

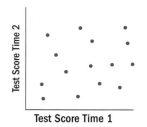

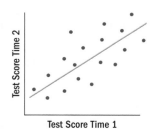

comparison estimate. For example, a psychologist includes 10 items on a test believing that they all measure interest in working outdoors, and then determines the degree to which responses to these 10 items vary together.

Many things cause a test to be unreliable. These include physical conditions (quiet one day, noisy the next), differences in the test taker (healthy one day, sick the next), and differences in test administration (courteous one day, curt the next). Or the questions may do a poor job of sampling the material; for example, test one focuses more on Chapters 1 and 3, while test two focuses more on Chapters 2 and 4.

Because measuring reliability generally involves comparing two measures that assess the same thing, it is typical to judge a test's reliability in terms of a *reliability coefficient*. This basically shows the degree to which the two measures (say, test score one day and test score the next day) are correlated.

Figure 6-1 illustrates correlation. In both the left and the right scatter plots, the psychologist compared each applicant's time 1 test score (on the *x*-axis) with his or her subsequent (time 2) test score (on the *y*-axis). On the left, the scatter plot points (each point showing one applicant's test score and subsequent test performance) are dispersed. There seems to be no correlation between test scores obtained at time 1 and at time 2. On the right, the psychologist tried a new test. Here the resulting points fall in a predictable pattern. This suggests that the applicants' test scores correlate closely with their previous scores.

Validity

test validity
The accuracy with which a test, interview, and so on, measures what it purports to measure or fulfills the function it was designed to fill.

Reliability, while indispensable, tells you only that the test is measuring something consistently. *Validity* tells you whether the test is measuring what you think it's supposed to be measuring.[9] **Test validity** answers the question "Does this test measure what it's supposed to measure?" Put another way, it refers to the correctness of the inferences that we can make based on the test.[10] For example, if Jane's scores on mechanical comprehension tests are higher than Jim's, can we be sure that Jane possesses more mechanical comprehension than Jim?[11] With employee selection tests, *validity* often refers to evidence that the test is job related—in other words, that performance on the test accurately predicts job performance. A selection test must be valid since, without proof of validity, there is no logical or legally permissible reason to use it to screen job applicants.

A test, as we said, is a sample of a person's behavior, but some tests are more clearly representative of the behavior being sampled than others. A swimming test clearly corresponds to a lifeguard's on-the-job behavior. On the other hand, there may be no apparent relationship between the test and the behavior. Thus, in Figure 6-2, the psychologist asks the person to interpret the picture, and then draws conclusions about the person's personality and behavior. Here it is more difficult to prove that the tests are measuring what they are said to measure, in this case, some trait of the person's personality—in other words, prove that they're valid.

criterion validity
A type of validity based on showing that scores on the test (predictors) are related to job performance (criterion).

There are several ways to demonstrate a test's validity.[12] **Criterion validity** involves demonstrating statistically a relationship between scores on a selection procedure and job performance of a sample of workers. For example, it means demonstrating that those who do well on the test also do well on the job, and that those who do poorly on the test do poorly on the job. The test has validity to the extent that the people with higher test scores perform better on the job. In psychological measurement, a *predictor* is the measurement (in this case, the test score) that you are trying to relate to a *criterion*, such as performance on the job. The term *criterion validity* reflects that terminology.

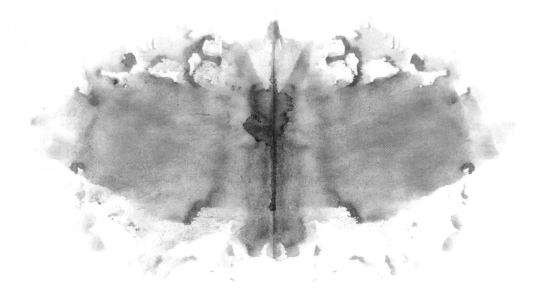

content validity

A test that is content valid is one that contains a fair sample of the tasks and skills actually needed for the job in question.

construct validity

A test that is construct valid is one that demonstrates that a selection procedure measures a construct and that construct is important for successful job performance.

Content validity is a demonstration that the content of a selection procedure is representative of important aspects of performance on the job. For example, employers may demonstrate the *content validity* of a test by showing that the test constitutes a fair sample of the job's content. The basic procedure here is to identify job tasks that are critical to performance, and then randomly select a sample of those tasks to test. In selecting students for dental school, one might give applicants chunks of chalk, and ask them to carve something like a tooth. If the content you choose for the test is a representative sample of the job, then the test is probably content valid. Clumsy dental students need not apply. Subject matter experts (SMEs, such as practicing dentists) help choose the tasks.

Construct validity means demonstrating that (1) a selection procedure measures a construct (an abstract idea such as morale or honesty) and (2) that the construct is important for successful job performance.

At best, invalid tests are a waste of time; at worst, they are discriminatory. Tests you buy "off the shelf" should include information on their validity.[13] But ideally, you should revalidate the tests for the job(s) at hand. In any case, tests rarely predict performance with 100% accuracy (or anywhere near it). Therefore, don't make tests your only selection tool; also use other tools like interviews and background checks.

TRENDS SHAPING HR: *Digital and Social Media*

Talent analytics is revolutionizing employee selection.[14] Its numbers-crunching data analysis tools including statistical techniques, algorithms, data mining, and problem-solving let employers search through their employee data to identify patterns and correlations that show what types of people succeed or fail. For example, department store chain Bon-Ton Stores Inc. had very high turnover among its cosmetics sales associates.

Bon-Ton chose 450 current cosmetics associates who filled out anonymous surveys aimed at identifying employee traits. By using talent analytics to analyze these and other data, the company identified cosmetics associates' traits that correlated with performance and tenure. Bon-Ton had assumed that the best associates were friendly and enthusiastic about cosmetics. However, the best were actually problem solvers. They take information about what the customer wants and needs, and solve the problem.[15] Talent analysis thereby helped Bon Ton formulate better selection criteria.

Talent analytics is gaining popularity in India as well. Leading IT firm, HCL Technologies, implemented talent analytics using intelligent neural network engine where database of 5 million applicants' information and employee records were analyzed.

The results helped improve quality of hiring because it provided insights about workforce characteristics. Using the information, recruiters could hire right candidates.[16] Companies like Stock Holding Corporation of India and Taj Hotels also utilize talent analytics to improve their hiring process.[17] ∎

Evidence-Based HR: How to Validate a Test

Employers often opt to demonstrate evidence of a test's validity using criterion validity. Here, in order for a selection test to be useful, you need evidence that scores on the test relate in a predictable way to performance on the job. Thus, other things being equal, students who score high on the graduate admissions tests also do better in graduate school. Applicants who score high on mechanical comprehension tests perform better as engineers. In other words, you validate the test before using it by ensuring that scores on the test are a good predictor of some *criterion* like job performance—thus demonstrating the test's *criterion validity*.[18]

An industrial psychologist usually conducts the validation study. The human resource department coordinates the effort. Strictly speaking, the supervisor's role is just to make sure that the job's human requirements and performance standards are clear to the psychologist. But in practice, anyone using tests (or test results) should know something about validation. Then you can better understand how to use tests and interpret their results. The validation process consists of five steps:

STEP 1: ANALYZE THE JOB The first step is to analyze the job and write job descriptions and job specifications. The aim here is to specify the human traits and skills you believe are required for job performance. For example, must an applicant be verbal, a good talker? These requirements become the *predictors,* the human traits and skills you believe predict success on the job. For an assembler's job, *predictors* might include manual dexterity and patience.[19]

In this first step, also define "success on the job," since it's this success for which you want predictors. The standards of success are *criteria*. You could use production-related criteria (quantity, quality, and so on), personnel data (absenteeism, length of service, and so on), or worker performance (reported by supervisors).

STEP 2: CHOOSE THE TESTS Once you know the predictors (such as manual dexterity) the next step is to decide how to test for them. Employers usually base this choice on experience, previous research, and "best guesses." They usually don't start with just one test. Instead, they choose several tests and combine them into a test battery. The test battery aims to measure an array of possible predictors, such as aggressiveness, extroversion, and numerical ability.

What tests are available and where do you get them? Ideally, use a professional, such as an industrial psychologist. However, many firms publish tests.[20] Some tests are available to virtually any purchaser, others only to qualified buyers (such as with degrees in psychology). Salahkaar Consultants, Institute of Banking Personnel Selection (IBPS) in Mumbai, and many other independent vendors offer numerous employment testing services to Indian firms. Many firms such as TCS and Infosys have also developed their internal tests. These tests should also be complemented

FIGURE 6-3 Examples of Web Sites Offering Information on Tests or Testing Programs

- www.hr-guide.com/data/G371.htm
  Provides general information and sources for all types of employment tests.
- www.wheelbox.com
  Provides validated tests for employment and nonemployment tests for career interests.
- www.ibps.in
  Provides information on placements and supports recruitment of banking personnel.
- www.kaplan.com
  Information from Kaplan test preparation on how various admissions tests work.
- www.husys.in
  Provides assessment and hiring solutions to SMEs in India.

with other tools like interviews. Figure 6-3 lists several Web sites that provide information about tests or testing programs.

However, do not let the widespread availability of tests blind you to this fact: You should use tests in a manner consistent with laws, and in a manner that is ethical and protects the test taker's privacy.

STEP 3: ADMINISTER THE TEST   Next, administer the selected test(s). One option is to administer the tests to employees currently on the job. You then compare their test scores with their current performance; this is *concurrent (at the same time) validation.* Its advantage is that data on performance are readily available. The disadvantage is that current employees may not be representative of new applicants (who, of course, are really the ones for whom you are interested in developing a screening test). Current employees have already had on-the-job training and screening by your existing selection techniques.

Predictive validation is the second and more dependable way to validate a test. Here you administer the test to applicants before you hire them, then hire these applicants using only existing selection techniques, not the results of the new tests. After they've been on the job for some time, measure their performance and compare it to their earlier test scores. You can then determine whether you could have used their performance on the new test to predict their subsequent job performance.

STEP 4: RELATE YOUR TEST SCORES AND CRITERIA   Here, ascertain if there is a significant relationship between test scores (the predictor) and performance (the criterion). The usual method is to determine the statistical relationship between (1) scores on the test and (2) job performance using correlation analysis, which shows the degree of statistical relationship.

If there is a correlation between test and job performance, you can develop an **expectancy chart**. This presents the relationship between test scores and job performance graphically. To do this, split the employees into, say, five groups according to test scores, with those scoring the highest fifth on the test, the second highest fifth, and so on. Then compute the percentage of high job performers in each of these five test score groups and present the data in an expectancy chart like that in Figure 6-4.

In this case, someone scoring in the top fifth of the test has a 97% chance of being a high performer, while one scoring in the lowest fifth has only a 29% chance of being a high performer.[21]

STEP 5: CROSS-VALIDATE AND REVALIDATE   Before using the test, you may want to check it by "cross-validating"—in other words, by again performing steps 3 and 4 on a new sample of employees. At a minimum, revalidate the test periodically.

expectancy chart
A graph showing the relationship between test scores and job performance for a group of people.

FIGURE 6-4 Expectancy Chart

Note: This expectancy chart shows the relation between scores made on the Minnesota Paper Form Board and rated success of junior draftspersons.

Example: Those who score between 37 and 44 have a 55% chance of being rated high performer and those scoring between 57 and 64 have a 97% chance.

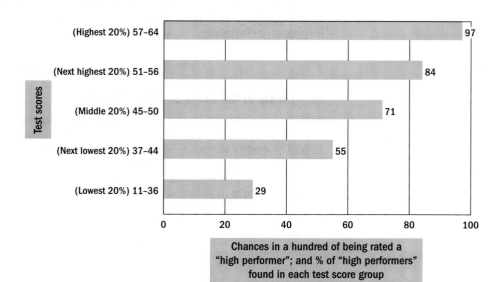

Chances in a hundred of being rated a "high performer"; and % of "high performers" found in each test score group

Some tests (such as the 16PF® Personality Profile) are professionally scored and interpreted. Thus Wonderlic, Inc., lets an employer administer the 16PF. The employer then faxes (or scans) the answer sheet to Wonderlic, which scores the candidate's profile and faxes (or scans) back the interpretive report. Psychologists easily score many psychological tests online or using interpretive Windows-based software. However, managers can easily score many tests, like the Wonderlic Personnel Test, themselves.

Bias

Most employers know they shouldn't use biased tests in the selection process.[22] For example, a particular IQ test may provide a valid measure of cognitive ability for middle-class whites but not for some minorities, if the score depends on familiarity with certain aspects of middle-class culture.[23] Until recently, many industrial psychologists believed they were adequately controlling test bias, but that issue is under review.[24] Employers should therefore redouble their efforts to ensure that the tests they're using aren't producing biased decisions.

Utility Analysis

Knowing that a test predicts performance isn't always of practical use. For example, if it is going to cost the employer ₹1,000 per applicant for the test, and hundreds of applicants must be tested, the cost of the test may exceed the benefits derived from hiring a few more capable employees.

Answering the question, "Does it pay to use the test?" requires *utility analysis*. Two selection experts say, "Using dollar and cents terms, [utility analysis] shows the degree to which use of a selection measure improves the quality of individuals selected over what would have happened if the measure had not been used."[25] The information required for utility analysis generally includes, for instance, the validity of the selection measure, a measure of job performance in dollars, applicants' average test scores, cost of testing an applicant, and the number of applicants tested and selected.

Prudent employers endeavor to streamline their selection processes, for instance to minimize how long it takes to fill a position. For example, with almost 60,000 job applicants per day, the U.S. federal government was taking about 122 days to fill a position. By reviewing each step in its hiring process, it reduced time to hire to about 105 days by, for instance, eliminating the applicant essay.[26] Similarly, Indian Railways adopted online testing for filling positions of Group 3 employees (which includes positions such as assistant stationmasters, goods guard, and junior accountant). They used the hiring tool to improve recruitment cycle performance. According to reports, around 92 lakh applicants had applied for 18,000 open positions in 2016.[27] The accompanying HR as a Profit Center feature shows how employers use tests to improve performance.

▶ IMPROVING PERFORMANCE: *HR as a Profit Center*

Using Tests to Cut Costs and Boost Profits

Financial services firm Key Bank knew it needed a better way to screen and select tellers and call-center employees.[28] The company calculated it cost about $10,000 to select and train an employee, but it was losing 13% of new tellers and call-center employees within the first 90 days. That turnover number dropped to 4% after Key Bank implemented a computerized *virtual job tryout candidate assessment screening tool*. "We calculated a $1.7 million cost savings in teller turnover in one year, simply by making better hiring decisions, reducing training costs and increasing quality of hires," said the firm's human resources director.

Outback Steakhouse has used preemployment tests almost from when the company started. The testing seems successful. While annual turnover rates for hourly employees may reach 200% in the restaurant industry, Outback's turnover ranges from 40% to 60%. Outback wants employees who are highly social, meticulous, sympathetic, and adaptable. They use a personality assessment test to screen out applicants who don't fit the Outback culture. This test is part of a three-step preemployment screening process. Applicants take the test, and managers then compare the candidates' results to the profile for Outback Steakhouse employees. Those who score low on certain traits (like compassion) don't move to the next step. Those who score high are interviewed by two managers, who ask behavioral questions such as "What would you do if a customer asked for a dish we don't have?"[29] ■

Source: Based on Dave Zielinski, "Effective Assessments," HR Magazine, January 2011, pp. 61–64.; Sarah Gale, "Three Companies Cut Turnover with Tests," Workforce, Spring 2002, pp. 66–69.

Validity Generalization

Many employers, particularly smaller ones, won't find it cost-effective to conduct validity studies for the selection tools they use. These employers must find tests and other screening tools that have been shown to be valid in other settings (companies), and then bring them in-house in the hopes that they'll be valid there, too.[30]

If the test is valid in one company, to what extent can we generalize those validity findings to our own company? *Validity generalization* "refers to the degree to which evidence of a measure's validity obtained in one situation can be generalized to another situation without further study."[31] Factors to consider include existing validation evidence regarding using the test for various specific purposes, the similarity of the subjects with those in your organization, and the similarity of the jobs.[32]

Under the Uniform Guidelines, validation of selection procedures is desirable, but "the Uniform Guidelines require users to produce evidence of validity only when adverse impact is shown to exist. If there is no adverse impact, there is no validation requirement under the Guidelines."[33]

Test Takers' Individual Rights and Test Security

Test takers have rights to privacy and feedback under the American Psychological Association's (APA) standard for educational and psychological tests; these guide psychologists but are *not* legally enforceable. Test takers have rights such as:

- To the confidentiality of test results.
- To informed consent regarding use of these results.
- To expect that only people qualified to interpret the scores will have access to them, or that sufficient information will accompany the scores to ensure their appropriate interpretation.
- To expect the test is fair. For example, no test taker should have prior access to the questions or answers.[34]

In India, the professional organization of clinical psychologists has proposed a code of conduct. This code prohibits purchase and use of psychological tests without certification. Clinical psychologists can only use assessment methods that are suitable to the competence and preference of language of an individual unless other language is suitable to the assessment issues. They must also communicate the uses and purposes of assessment techniques, and indicate 'limits of applicability' to clients.

If online testing is used, the code mandates that the computer adaptive testing should comprise a method of assessment which is valid and reliable, and administered after evaluating computer literacy of the person who takes the test.[35]

Fotosearch/AGE Fotostock

Many employers administer online employment tests to job candidates.

Diversity Counts: Gender Issues in Testing

Employers using selection tests should know that gender issues may distort results. Some parents and others socialize girls into traditionally female roles and boys into traditionally male roles. For example, they may encourage young boys but not girls to make things with tools, or young girls but not boys to take care of their siblings. Such encouragement may in turn translate into differences in how males and females answer items on and score on, say, tests of vocational interests. And these test score differences may in turn cause counselors and others to nudge men and women into what tend to be largely gender-segregated occupations, for instance, male engineers and female nurses.

The bottom line is that employers and others need to interpret the results of various tests (including of interests and aptitudes) with care. It may often be the case that such results say more about how the person was brought up and socialized than it does about the person's inherent ability to do some task. ■

How Do Employers Use Tests at Work?

About 41% of companies in one survey tested applicants for basic skills (defined as the ability to read instructions, write reports, and do arithmetic).[36] About 67% of the respondents required employees to take job skills tests, and 29% required some form of psychological measurement.[37] To see what such tests are like, try the short test in Figure 6-5.

Tests are not just for lower-level workers. In general, as work demands increase (in terms of skill requirements, training, and pay), employers tend to rely more on selection testing.[38] And, employers don't use tests just to find good employees, but also to screen out bad ones.[39] For good reason: In retail, employers apprehended about one out of every 28 workers for stealing.[40]

FIGURE 6-5 Sample Test

Source: Based on a sample selection test from the *New York Times.*

CHECK YES OR NO	YES	NO
1. You like a lot of excitement in your life.		
2. An employee who takes it easy at work is cheating on the employer.		
3. You are a cautious person.		
4. In the past three years you have found yourself in a shouting match at school or work.		
5. You like to drive fast just for fun.		

Analysis: According to John Kamp, an industrial psychologist, applicants who answered no, yes, yes, no, no to questions 1, 2, 3, 4, and 5 are statistically likely to be absent less often, to have fewer on-the-job injuries, and, if the job involves driving, to have fewer on-the-job driving accidents. Actual scores on the test are based on answers to 130 questions.

HR in Practice at the Hotel Paris As she considered what to do next to improve the employees' performance in a way that would support the Hotel Paris's strategy, Lisa Cruz, the Hotel Paris's HR director, knew that employee selection had to play a role. The Hotel Paris currently had an informal screening process in which local hotel managers obtained application forms, interviewed applicants, and checked their references. To see how she improved their system, see the case on page 189.

To see how she improved their system, see the case on page 189.

<table>
<tr><td>

LEARNING OBJECTIVE 6-3

List and briefly describe the basic categories of selection tests, with examples.

</td></tr>
</table>

Types of Tests

We can conveniently classify tests according to whether they measure cognitive (mental) abilities, motor and physical abilities, personality and interests, or achievement.[41] We'll look at each.

Tests of Cognitive Abilities

Cognitive tests include tests of general reasoning ability (intelligence) and tests of specific mental abilities like memory and inductive reasoning.

INTELLIGENCE TESTS Intelligence (IQ) tests are tests of general intellectual abilities. They measure not a single trait but rather a range of abilities, including memory, vocabulary, verbal fluency, and numerical ability. An adult's IQ score is a "derived" scored; it reflects the extent to which the person is above or below the "average" adult's intelligence score.

Intelligence is often measured with individually administered tests like the Stanford-Binet Test or the Wechsler Test. Employers can administer other IQ tests such as the Wonderlic individually or to groups of people.[42] In one illustrative study of firefighter trainees' performance over 23 years, the researchers found that a measure of general intellectual ability and a physical ability assessment were highly predictive of trainee performance.[43]

SPECIFIC COGNITIVE ABILITIES There are also measures of specific mental abilities, such as deductive reasoning, verbal comprehension, memory, and numerical ability.

Psychologists often call such tests *aptitude tests*, since they purport to measure aptitude for the job in question. Consider the Test of Mechanical Comprehension illustrated in Figure 6-6, which tests applicants' understanding of basic mechanical principles. This may reflect a person's aptitude for jobs—like that of machinist or engineer—that require mechanical comprehension. Other tests of mechanical aptitude include the Mechanical Reasoning Test and the SRA Test of Mechanical Aptitude. The revised Minnesota Paper Form Board Test consists of 64 two-dimensional diagrams cut into separate pieces. It provides insights into an applicant's mechanical spatial ability; you'd use it for screening applicants for jobs such as designers or engineers.

Tests of Motor and Physical Abilities

You might also want to measure motor abilities, such as finger dexterity, manual dexterity, and (if hiring pilots) reaction time. Thus, the Crawford Small Parts Dexterity

FIGURE 6-6 **Type of Question Applicant Might Expect on a Test of Mechanical Comprehension**

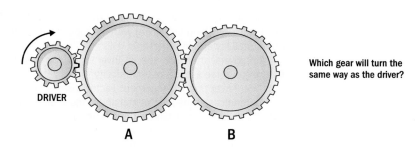

Test measures the speed and accuracy of simple judgment as well as the speed of finger, hand, and arm movements. Other tests include the Stromberg Dexterity Test and the Purdue Peg Board.

Tests of physical abilities may also be required. These include static strength (such as lifting weights), dynamic strength (pull-ups), body coordination (jumping rope), and stamina.[44] Applicants for the Indian Armed Forces or police must pass a physical test which includes running a specific distance within an allotted time.

Measuring Personality and Interests

A person's cognitive and physical abilities alone seldom explain his or her job performance. As one consultant put it, most people are hired based on qualifications, but are fired because of attitude, motivation, and temperament.[45]

Personality tests measure basic aspects of an applicant's personality, such as introversion, stability, and motivation. Industrial psychologists often focus on the "big five" personality dimensions: extraversion, emotional stability/neuroticism, agreeableness, conscientiousness, and openness to experience.[46]

> Neuroticism represents a tendency to exhibit poor emotional adjustment and experience negative effects, such as anxiety, insecurity, and hostility. Extraversion represents a tendency to be sociable, assertive, active, and to experience positive effects, such as energy and zeal. Openness to experience is the disposition to be imaginative, nonconforming, unconventional, and autonomous. Agreeableness is the tendency to be trusting, compliant, caring, and gentle. Conscientiousness is comprised of two related facets: achievement and dependability.[47]

Some personality tests are *projective*. The psychologist presents an ambiguous stimulus (like an inkblot or clouded picture) and the person reacts. The person supposedly projects into the ambiguous picture his or her attitudes, such as insecurity. Other projective techniques include Make a Picture Story (MAPS) and the Forer Structured Sentence Completion Test.

Other personality tests are *self-reported*: applicants fill them out. Thus, available online,[48] the Myers-Briggs test provides a personality type classification useful for decisions such as career selection and planning. Its DiSC Profile learning instrument enables the user to gain insight into his or her behavioral style.[49]

Personality test results do often correlate with job performance. For example "in personality research, conscientiousness has been the most consistent and universal predictor of job performance."[50] In another study, neuroticism was negatively related to motivation.[51] Extraversion correlates with success in sales and management jobs.[52] The responsibility, socialization, and self-control scales of the California Psychological Inventory predicted dysfunctional job behaviors among law enforcement officers.[53] Emotional stability, extroversion, and agreeableness predicted whether expatriates would leave their overseas assignments early.[54] The HR Practices feature presents an example.

▶ IMPROVING PERFORMANCE: *HR Practices Around the Globe*

Testing for Assignments Abroad

Living and working abroad require some special talents. Not everyone can easily adapt to having one's family far away, and to dealing with colleagues with different cultural values. Doing so requires high levels of adaptability and interpersonal skills.[55]

Employers often use special inventories such as the Global Competencies Inventory (GCI) here. It focuses on three aspects of adaptability.

- ✓ The Perception Management Factor assesses people's tendency to be rigid in their view of cultural differences, to be judgmental about those differences, and to deal with complexity and uncertainty.
- ✓ The Relationship Management Factor assesses a person's awareness of the impact he or she is having on others.
- ✓ The Self-Management Factor assesses one's mental and emotional health. ■

Source: Adapted from www.kozaigroup.com/-inventories.php, accessed March 3, 2008; and http:// ko-zaigroup .com/inventories/the-global competencies-inventory-gci/what is-the-gci/.

There are four caveats. *First,* projective personality tests are particularly hard to interpret. An expert must analyze the test taker's interpretations and infer from them his or her personality.

Second, personality tests can trigger legal challenges. For example, one court held that the Minnesota Multiphasic Personality Inventory (MMPI) is a medical test (because it can screen out applicants with psychological impairments), and so might violate the ADA.[56]

Third, a panel of distinguished industrial psychologists said using *self-report* personality tests in selection "should be reconsidered [due to low validity]."[57] Other experts call such concerns "unfounded."[58]

Fourth, people can and will fake responses to personality and integrity tests.[59] The bottom line: make sure the personality tests you use predict performance for the jobs you are testing for.

interest inventory
A personal development and selection device that compares the person's current interests with those of others now in various occupations so as to determine the preferred occupation for the individual.

INTEREST INVENTORIES **Interest inventories** compare one's interests with those of people in various occupations. Thus, the Strong-Campbell Interest Inventory provides a report comparing one's interests to those of people already in occupations like accounting or engineering. Someone taking the Self-Directed Search (SDS) (www.self-directed-search.com) uses it to identify likely high-fit occupations. The assumption is that someone will do better in occupations in which he or she is interested, and indeed such inventories can predict employee performance and turnover.[60] One study found that poor vocational fit correlated with counterproductive work behaviors, perhaps because poor fit frustrates the worker.[61]

Achievement Tests

Achievement tests measure what someone has learned. Most of the tests you take in school are achievement tests. They measure your "job knowledge" in areas like economics, marketing, or human resources. Achievement tests are also popular at work. For example, the Purdue Test for Machinists and Machine Operators tests the job knowledge of experienced machinists with questions like "What is meant by 'tolerance'"? Some achievement tests measure the applicant's abilities; a swimming test is one example.

Improving Performance Through HRIS: Computerization and Online Testing

Computerized and/or online testing is increasingly replacing paper-and-pencil tests. ZingHR, which is an HR software system, has the feature for online testing of candidates for recruitment. Candidates have to login to a portal and complete certain tests which are generally aptitude tests covering Mathematics and language abilities. This helps to reduce the pool of candidates for subsequent rounds. For the face-to-face interviews, the HR manager or recruiter of the firm using ZingHR software needs to call only those who have scored above the minimum expected standard. ZingHR also allows candidates to appear for tests through mobile phones. This helps companies reduce the costs to conduct face-to-face interview for every candidate. It also provides job applicants the flexibility to take the tests remotely.[62]

Computerized and online tests are increasingly sophisticated. For example, SHL (www.shl.com/us/) offers online adaptive personality tests. As a candidate answers each question, these tests adapt the next question to the test taker's answers to the previous question. This improves test validity and may reduce cheating (since each candidate basically gets a customized test).[63] Service firms like Unicru process and score online preemployment tests from employers' applicants. Most of the tests we describe are available in computerized form. ∎

COMPUTERIZED MULTIMEDIA CANDIDATE ASSESSMENT TOOLS Development Dimensions International developed a computerized multimedia skill test that Ford Motor Company uses for hiring assembly workers. "The company can test everything from how people tighten the bolt, to whether they followed a certain procedure correctly, to using a weight-sensitive mat on the floor that, when stepped on at the wrong time, will mark a candidate down in a safety category."[64]A report from Korn Ferry, an executive search and recruiting firm, on hiring practices in India showed that use of online tools, including multimedia-based assessment is high. DBS Bank's Asia Hub in Hyderabad uses multimedia-based tests and organizes hackathons to select technical talent. The online assessment tests are used to assess the programming skills and the hackathon tests for problem-solving skills as well as innovativeness of candidates.[65]

▶ **IMPROVING PERFORMANCE:** *The Strategic Context*

Crowdsourcing at Google

Google knows that to maintain its fast-growth strategy, it must keep innovating new services. To support that strategy, Google needs its employees engaged and collaborating with each other. Having employees thinking of themselves in isolated "silos" would inhibit the cross-pollination that Google's strategy depends on. In formulating its employee selection practices, Google therefore found a way to foster the employee engagement and collaboration its success depends on. Google uses "crowdsourcing" when it comes to making hiring decisions.[66]

Here's how it works.[67] When a prospective employee applies for a job, his or her information (such as school and previous employers) goes into Google's applicant tracking system (ATS). The ATS then matches the applicant's information with that of current Google employees. When it finds a match, it asks those Google employees to comment on the applicant's suitability for the position. This helps give Google recruiters a valuable insight into how the Google employees actually doing the work think the applicant will do at Google. And it supports Google's strategy, by fostering a sense of community and collaboration among Google employees, who see themselves working together to select new "Googlers." ∎

Source: Based on Wright, "At Google, It Takes a Village to Hire an Employee."

LEARNING OBJECTIVE **6-4**

Explain how to use two work simulations for selection.

Work Samples and Simulations

With **work samples**, you present examinees with situations representative of the job for which they're applying, and evaluate their responses.[68] Experts consider these (and *simulations,* like the assessment centers we also discuss in this section) to be tests. But they differ from most tests because they directly measure job performance.

work samples
Actual job tasks used in testing applicants' performance.

work sampling technique
A testing method based on measuring performance on actual basic job tasks.

Using Work Sampling for Employee Selection

The **work sampling technique** tries to predict job performance by requiring job candidates to perform one or more samples of the job's tasks. For example, work samples for a cashier may include operating a cash register and counting money.[69]

Work sampling has several advantages. It measures actual job tasks, so it's harder to fake answers. The work sample's content—the actual tasks the person must perform—is not as likely to be unfair to minorities (as might a personnel test that possibly emphasizes middle-class concepts and values).[70] Work sampling doesn't delve into the applicant's personality, so there's almost no chance of applicants viewing it as an invasion of privacy. Designed properly, work samples also exhibit better validity than do other tests designed to predict performance.

The basic procedure is to select a sample of several tasks crucial to performing the job, and then to test applicants on them.[71] An observer monitors performance on each task, and indicates on a checklist how well the applicant performs. For example, in creating a work sampling test for maintenance mechanics, experts first listed all possible job tasks (like "install pulleys and belts"). Four crucial tasks were installing pulleys and belts, disassembling and installing a gearbox, installing and aligning a motor, and pressing a bushing into a sprocket. Since mechanics could perform each task in a slightly different way, the experts gave different weights to different approaches.

FIGURE 6-7 Example of a Work Sampling Question

Note: This is one step in installing pulleys and belts.

Checks key before installing against:

—shaft   score 3
—pulley   score 2
—neither   score 1

Note: This is one step in installing pulleys and belts.

Figure 6-7 shows one of the steps required for the task *installing pulleys and belts*—"checks key before installing ..." Here the examinee might choose to check the key against (1) the shaft, (2) the pulley, or (3) neither. The right of the figure lists the weights (scores) reflecting the worth of each method. The applicant performs the task, and the observer checks off and scores the approach used.

Situational Judgment Tests

Situational judgment tests are personnel tests "designed to assess an applicant's judgment regarding a situation encountered in the workplace."[72] For example:

> You are a sales associate at Croma Retail in Coimbatore. The store sells electronic gadgets and smart electrical goods. Croma has competition from online firms like Flipkart and other neighborhood retailers. Customers who come to your store to check the prices of electronic goods end up buying them from an e-tailer like Amazon or Flipkart for a less price. As a sales associate, your responsibility is to provide exceptional customer service, demonstrate product knowledge, and maximize store sales. How would you respond to this situation?

1. Tell the customer to buy the phone on Flipkart.
2. Tell the customer to wait for 20 minutes while you are taking care of another customer.
3. Tell the customer to go to a retail store that is about 30 minutes away where they sell a similar handset at a lower price.
4. Explain the advantages of similar phones that you have and which will also fulfill the requirements of the buyer.
5. Request your supervisor to help you.

Management Assessment Centers

management assessment center
A simulation in which management candidates are asked to perform realistic tasks in hypothetical situations and are scored on their performance. It usually also involves testing and the use of management games.

A **management assessment center** is a 2- to 3-day simulation in which 10 to 12 candidates perform realistic management tasks (like making presentations) under the observation of experts who appraise each candidate's leadership potential. For example, The Cheesecake Factory created its Professional Assessment and Development Center to help select promotable managers. Candidates undergo 2 days of exercises, simulations, and classroom learning to see if they have the skills for key management positions.[73]

Typical simulated tasks include:

- *The in-basket.* The candidate gets reports, memos, notes of incoming phone calls, e-mails, and other materials collected in the actual or computerized in-basket of the simulated job he or she is about to start. The candidate must take appropriate action on each item. Trained evaluators review the candidate's efforts.
- *Leaderless group discussion.* Trainers give a leaderless group a discussion question and tell members to arrive at a group decision. They then evaluate each group member's interpersonal skills, acceptance by the group, leadership ability, and individual influence.

- *Management games.* Participants solve realistic problems as members of simulated companies competing in a marketplace.
- *Individual oral presentations.* Here trainers evaluate each participant's communication skills and persuasiveness.
- *Testing.* These may include tests of personality, mental ability, interests, and achievements.
- *The interview.* Most require an interview with a trainer to assess interests, past performance, and motivation.

Supervisor recommendations usually play a big role in choosing center participants. Line managers usually act as assessors and arrive at their ratings through consensus.[74] In India, Pearson has an assessment center known as Talent Lens Assessment Center. This assessment center uses three steps of assessment, feedback, and on-ground solutions to help the organization select and develop the right talent for the business. A variety of psychometric testing tools such as role play, in-basket exercise, management games, interviews, and presentations are used to select right candidates. Statistical analyses by various psychologists are used to analyze the results from the tests. These are then shared with the candidates and respective managers through individual reports, management diagnostic reports, and group feedback.[75] Defence Research and Development Organization (DRDO), the Indian scientific research organization for defense purposes, conducts regular assessment centers for hiring scientists. The Recruitment and Assessment Center (RAC) of DRDO is staffed with experts who are trained to conduct assessment centers.[76]

Assessment centers are expensive to develop, take longer than conventional tests, require managers acting as assessors, and often require psychologists. However, studies suggest they are worth it.[77]

Situational Testing and Video-Based Situational Testing

situational test
A test that requires examinees to respond to situations representative of the job.

Situational tests require examinees to respond to situations representative of the job. Work sampling (discussed earlier) and some assessment center tasks (such as in-baskets) fall in this category. So do video-based tests and miniature job training (described next), and the situational interviews we address in Chapter 7.[78] Some employers, such as Knack, use video games to determine candidates' creativity and ability to multitask.[79]

video-based simulation
A situational test in which examinees respond to video simulations of realistic job situations.

The **video-based simulation** presents the candidate with several online or computer video situations, each followed by one or more multiple-choice questions. For example, the scenario might depict an employee handling a situation on the job. At a critical moment, the scenario ends and the video asks the candidate to choose from several courses of action. For example:

(A manager is upset about the condition of the department and takes it out on one of the department's employees.)

MANAGER: Well, I'm glad you're here.

ASSOCIATE: Why?

MANAGER: I take a day off and come back to find the department in a mess. You should know better.

ASSOCIATE: But I didn't work late last night.

MANAGER: But there have been plenty of times before when you've left this department in a mess.

(The scenario stops here.)

If you were this associate, what would you do?

a. Let the other associates responsible for the mess know that you took the heat.
b. Straighten up the department, and try to reason with the manager later.
c. Suggest to the manager that he talk to the other associates who made the mess.
d. Take it up with the manager's boss.[80]

The Miniature Job Training and Evaluation Approach

miniature job training and evaluation
Training candidates to perform several of the job's tasks, and then evaluating the candidates' performance prior to hire.

Miniature job training and evaluation involves training candidates to perform several of the job's tasks, and then evaluating their performance prior to hire. The approach assumes that a person who demonstrates that he or she can learn and perform the sample of tasks will be able to learn and perform the job itself. Like work sampling, *miniature job training and evaluation* tests applicants with actual samples of the job, so it is inherently content relevant and valid.

For example, when Honda built an auto plant in Lincoln, Alabama, it had to hire thousands of new employees. Working with an Alabama industrial development training agency, Honda began running help wanted ads.

Honda and the Alabama agency first eliminated those applicants who lacked the education or experience, and then gave preference to applicants near the plant. About 340 applicants per 6-week session received special training at a new facility about 15 miles south of the plant. It included classroom instruction, watching videos of current Honda employees in action, and actually practicing particular jobs. Some candidates who watched the videos simply dropped out when they saw the work's pace and repetitiveness.

The training sessions serve two purposes. First, job candidates learn the actual skills they'll need to do the Honda jobs. Second, the training sessions provide an opportunity for special assessors from the Alabama state agency to scrutinize the trainees' work and to rate them. They then invite those who graduate to apply for jobs at the plants. Honda teams, consisting of employees from HR and departmental representatives, do the final screening. [81]

Realistic Job Previews

Sometimes, a dose of realism makes the best screening tool. For example, when Walmart began explicitly explaining and asking about work schedules and work preferences, turnover improved. [82] During faculty selection at IIM Ahmedabad and other B-schools, these institutes invite prospective candidates to visit their campus. In addition to giving a research seminar and interview, candidates directly engage with faculty members, representatives from the administration and, in some cases, with students. In general, applicants who receive realistic job previews are more likely to turn down job offers, but their employers are more likely to have less turnover. [83]

Choosing a Selection Method

The employer needs to consider several things before choosing to use a particular selection tool (or tools). These include the tool's reliability and validity, its return

Employers such as Honda first train and then have applicants perform several of the job tasks, and then evaluate the candidates before hiring them.

Bi Shanghong/Xinhua Press/Corbis

TABLE 6-1 **Evaluation of Selected Assessment Methods**

Assessment Method	Validity	Adverse Impact	Costs (Develop/Administer)
Cognitive ability tests	High	High (against minorities)	Low/low
Job knowledge test	High	High (against minorities)	Low/low
Personality tests	Low to moderate	Low	Low/low
Integrity tests	Moderate to high	Low	Low/low
Structured interviews	High	Low	High/high
Situational judgment tests	Moderate	Moderate (against minorities)	High/low
Work samples	High	Low	High/high
Assessment centers	Moderate to high	Low to moderate, depending on exercise	High/high
Physical ability tests	Moderate to high	High (against females and older workers)	High/high

Source: From Selection Assessment Methods, SHRM Foundation, 2005. Reprinted by permission from SHRM Foundation.

on investment (in terms of utility analysis), applicant reactions, usability, adverse impact, and the tool's *selection ratio* (does it screen out, as it should, a high percentage of applicants or admit virtually all?).[84] Table 6-1 summarizes the validity, potential adverse impact, and cost of several popular assessment methods. The HR Tools feature shows how line managers may devise their own tests.

▶ **IMPROVING PERFORMANCE:** *HR Tools for Line Managers and Small Businesses*

Employee Testing and Selection

One of the ironies of being a line manager in even the largest of companies is that, when it comes to screening employees, you're often on your own. Some large firms' HR departments may work with the hiring manager to design and administer the sorts of screening tools we discussed in this chapter. But the fact is that in many of these firms, the HR departments do little more than some preliminary prescreening (for instance, arithmetic tests for clerical applicants), and then follow up with background checks and drug and physical exams.

What should you do if you are, say, a marketing manager, and want to screen some of your job applicants more formally? It is possible to devise your own test battery, but caution is required. Purchasing and then using packaged intelligence tests or psychological tests or even tests of marketing ability could be problematical. Doing so may violate company policy, raise questions of validity, and even expose your employer to liability if problems arise.

A preferred approach is to devise and use screening tools, the face validity of which is obvious. The work sampling test we discussed is one example. It's not unreasonable, for instance, for the marketing manager to ask an advertising applicant to spend half an hour designing an ad, or to ask a marketing research applicant to quickly outline a marketing research program for a hypothetical product. Similarly, a production manager might reasonably ask an inventory control applicant to spend a few minutes using a standard inventory control model to solve an inventory problem.

For small business owners, some tests' ease of use makes them particularly good for small firms. One is the *Wonderlic Personnel Test*; it measures general mental ability in about 15 minutes. The tester reads the instructions, and then keeps time as the candidate works through the 50 short problems on two pages. The tester scores the test by totaling the number of correct answers. Comparing the person's score with the minimum scores recommended for various occupations shows whether the person achieved the minimally acceptable score for the type of job in question. The *Predictive Index* measures work-related personality traits on a two-sided sheet. For example, there is the "social interest" pattern for a person who is generally unselfish, congenial, and unassuming. This person would be a good personnel interviewer, for instance. A template makes scoring simple.

As many managers know, for some jobs past performance is a more useful predictor of performance than are formal selection tests. For example, one study of prospective NFL players concluded that collegiate performance was a significantly better predictor of NFL performance than were physical ability tests.[85] ■

Source: Based on Brian J. Hoffman, John W. Michel, and Kevin J. Williams, "On the Predictive Efficiency of Past Performance and Physical Ability: The Case of the National Football League," *Human Performance* 24, no. 2 (2011), pp. 158–172.

Background Investigations and Other Selection Methods

Testing is only part of an employer's selection process. Other tools may include background investigations and reference checks, preemployment information services, honesty testing, and substance abuse screening.

Why Perform Background Investigations and Reference Checks?

One major company was about to announce a new CEO until they discovered he had a wife and two children in one state as well as a wife and two children in another state.[86] More mundanely, the recruiter HireRight found that of the over 600,000 educational verifications they did in one recent 12-month period, 32% had discrepancies.[87]

One of the easiest ways to avoid hiring mistakes is to check the candidate's background thoroughly. Doing so is inexpensive and (if done right) useful. There's usually no reason why even supervisors in large companies can't check the references of someone they're about to hire, as long as they know the rules.

Most employers check and verify the job applicant's background information and references. In one survey of about 700 human resource managers, 87% said they conduct reference checks, 69% conduct background employment checks, 61% check employee criminal records, 56% check employees' driving records, and 35% sometimes or always check credit.[88] Commonly verified data include legal eligibility for employment (in compliance with immigration laws), dates of prior employment, military service (including discharge status), education, identification (including date of birth and address to confirm identity), county criminal records (current residence, last residence), motor vehicle record, credit, licensing verification, Social Security number, and reference checks.[89] Some employers check executive candidates' civil litigation records, with the candidate's prior approval.[90] Massachusetts and Hawaii prohibit private employers from asking about criminal records on initial written applications.[91]

There are two main reasons to check backgrounds—to verify the applicant's information (name and so forth) and to uncover damaging information.[92] Lying on one's application isn't unusual. A survey found that 23% of 7,000 executive résumés contained exaggerated or false information.[93]

Even relatively sophisticated companies fall prey to criminal employees, in part because they haven't conducted proper background checks. In Chicago, a pharmaceutical firm discovered it had hired gang members in mail delivery and computer repair. The crooks were stealing computer parts, and using the mail department to ship them to their own nearby computer store.[94]

How deeply you search depends on the position. For example, a credit check is more important for hiring an accountant than a groundskeeper. In any case, also periodically check the credit ratings of employees (like cashiers) who have easy access to company assets, and the driving records of employees who use company cars.

Yet most managers don't view references as very useful. Few employers will talk freely about former employees. For example, in one poll, the Society for Human Resource Management found that 98% of 433 responding members said their organizations would verify dates of employment for current or former employees. However, 68% said they wouldn't discuss work performance; 82% said they wouldn't discuss character or personality; and 87% said they wouldn't disclose a disciplinary action.[95]

Many supervisors don't want to damage a former employee's chances for a job; others might prefer giving an incompetent employee good reviews to get rid of him or her.

Another reason is legal. Employers providing references generally can't be successfully sued for defamation unless the employee can show "malice"—that is, ill will, culpable recklessness, or disregard of the employee's rights.[96] But many managers and companies understandably still don't want the grief. The following explains this.

How to Check a Candidate's Background

There are several things managers and employers can do to get better information.

Most employers at least try to verify an applicant's current (or former) position and salary with his or her current (or former) employer by phone (assuming you cleared doing so with the candidate). Others call the applicant's current and previous supervisors to try to discover more about the person's motivation, technical competence, and ability to work with others (although, again, many employers have policies against providing such information). Figure 6-8 shows one form for phone references. Many employers get background reports from commercial credit rating companies for information about credit standing, indebtedness, reputation, character, and lifestyle. (Others check social network sites, as we will see in a moment.)

Automated online reference checking can improve the results. With a system such as Pre-Hire 360 (www.skillsurvey.com/pre-hire-360), the hiring employer inputs the applicant's name and e-mail address. Then the person's preselected references rate the applicant's skills anonymously, using a survey. The system then compiles these references into a report for the employer.[97]

TRENDS SHAPING HR: *DIGITAL AND SOCIAL MEDIA*

Digital tools are changing the background-checking process. Employers are Googling applicants or checking Facebook and LinkedIn, and what they're finding isn't always pretty. One candidate described his interests on Facebook as smoking pot and shooting people. The student may have been kidding, but didn't get the job.[98] An article called "Funny, They Don't Look Like My References" notes that the new LinkedIn premium service "Reference Search" lets employers identify people in their own networks who worked for the same company when a job candidate did, and thus use them to get references on the candidate.[99] According to LinkedIn, you just select Reference Search, then enter a company name, candidate's name, and the timeframe, and click search. Employers are integrating such tools with software solutions such as Oracle/Taleo Verify to facilitate obtaining such information and then integrating it into the candidate's dashboard-accessible profile. Nowadays, many Indian employers are also viewing social media profiles of candidate. It's possible that some candidates were refused job offers after they were screened on social media. In India, however, the most common method used is that employers or HR managers use their personal networks and contacts to collect background information.

In any case, it's probably best to get the candidate's prior approval for social networking searches.[100] And do not use a pretext or fabricate an identity.[101] Maryland law restricts employer demands for applicant usernames and passwords.[102] Other states will undoubtedly follow.

The solution isn't necessarily to prohibit the legitimate use of social media–based information (unless perusing such information is illegal under the law, as in Maryland). Instead, follow intelligent social media staffing policies and procedures. For example, inform employees and prospective employees ahead of time regarding what information the employer plans to review. Assign one or two specially trained human resource professionals to search social media sites. And warn unauthorized employees (such as prospective supervisors) about accessing such information.[103] ∎

Using Preemployment Information Services

It is easy to have employment screening services check out applicants. Major global background checking providers include Automatic Data Processing Inc., First Advantage, HireRight, and Sterling Backcheck.[104] Quetzal is a Mumbai-based background verification company. It conducts advanced verification services like contact synchronizing, social mapping, and social reference checks.[105] They use databases to

FIGURE 6-8 Reference Checking Form

Source: Reprinted with permission of the Society for Human Resource Management (www.shrm.org), Alexandria, VA 22314.

(Verify that the applicant has provided permission before conducting reference checks.)

Candidate Name _____

Reference Name _____

Company Name _____

Dates of Employment
From: _____ To: _____

Position(s) Held _____

Salary History _____

Reason for Leaving _____

Explain the reason for your call and verify the above information with the supervisor (including the reason for leaving)
_____
_____

1. Please describe the type of work for which the candidate was responsible.
_____
_____

2. How would you describe the applicant's relationships with coworkers, subordinates (if applicable), and with superiors?
_____
_____

3. Did the candidate have a positive or negative work attitude? Please elaborate.
_____
_____

4. How would you describe the quantity and quality of output generated by the former employee?
_____
_____

5. What were his/her strengths on the job?
_____

6. What were his/her weaknesses on the job?
_____

7. What is your overall assessment of the candidate?
_____
_____

8. Would you recommend him/her for this position? Why or why not?
_____
_____

9. Would this individual be eligible for rehire? Why or why not?
_____
_____

Other comments?
_____
_____

access information about matters such as workers' compensation, credit histories, and conviction and driving records. For example, retail employers use First Advantage Corporation's Esteem Database to see if their job candidates have previously been involved in suspected retail thefts.[106] Another US-based firm advertises that for less than $50 it will do a criminal history report, motor vehicle/driver's record report, and (after the person is hired) a workers' compensation claims report history, plus confirm identity, name, and Social Security number. There are thousands of databases, including sex offender registries and criminal and educational histories. In India, collecting background data used to be a difficult task. To overcome this challenge, from July 1, 2017, the State Bank of India has made Aadhaar number mandatory for its recruitment applications. The purpose was to establish candidate's identity at all stages of hiring.[107]

There are three reasons to use caution with such services.[108] First, in countries like the US, EEO laws apply. For example, New Jersey recently became the 13th state to pass a "Ban the Box" law prohibiting prospective employees from questioning applicants about convictions until late in the hiring process.[109] So be careful not to use the product of an unreasonable investigation.

Second, in the US, various federal and state laws govern how employers acquire and use applicants' and employees' background information. Authorizing background reports while complying with these laws requires four steps (in the US legal context), as follows:

> *Step 1: Disclosure and authorization.* Before requesting reports, the employer must disclose to the applicant or employee that a report will be requested and that the employee/applicant may receive a copy. (Do this on the application form.)
>
> *Step 2: Certification.* The employer must certify to the reporting agency that the employer will comply with the federal and state legal requirements—for example, that the employer obtained written consent from the employee/applicant.
>
> *Step 3: Providing copies of reports.* Under the US federal law, the employer must provide copies of the report to the applicant or employee if adverse action (such as withdrawing a job offer) is contemplated. In India, while such information is not shared upfront, candidates may approach the employer requesting for information or, if applicable, file an RTI application requesting the same.[110]
>
> *Step 4: Notice after adverse action.* If the employer anticipates taking an adverse action, the employee/applicant must get an adverse action notice. This contains information such as the name of the consumer reporting agency. The employee/applicant then has various remedies under the laws.[111]

Third, the background information may be flawed. Many return "possible matches" for the wrong person (who happens to be a criminal).[112]

Making the Background Check More Valuable

There are steps one can take to improve the usefulness of the background information being sought. Specifically:

- Include on the application form a statement for applicants to sign explicitly authorizing a background and credit check, such as:

  > I hereby certify that the facts set forth in the above employment application are true and complete to the best of my knowledge. I understand that falsified statements or misrepresentation of information on this application or omission of any information sought may be cause for dismissal, if employed, or may lead to refusal to make an offer and/or to withdrawal of an offer. I also authorize investigation of credit, employment record, driving record, and, once a job offer is made or during employment, workers' compensation background if required.

- Telephone references tend to produce more candid assessments. Use a form, such as Figure 6-8. Remember that you can get relatively accurate information regarding dates of employment, eligibility for rehire, and job qualifications. It's more difficult to get other background information (such as reasons for leaving a previous job).[113]

- Persistence and attentiveness to possible red flags improve results. For example, if the former employer hesitates or seems to qualify his or her answer, don't go on to the next question. Try to unearth what the applicant did to make the former employer pause. If he says, "Samir Kumar requires some special care," say, "Special care?"
- Compare the application to the résumé; people tend to be more creative on their résumés than on their application forms, where they must certify the information.
- Try to ask open-ended questions (such as, "How much structure does the applicant need in his/her work?") to get the references to talk more about the candidate.[114] But in asking for information: Only ask for and obtain information that you're going to use; remember that using arrest information is highly problematical; use information that is specific and job related; and keep information confidential.
- Ask the references supplied by the applicant to suggest other references. You might ask each of the applicant's references, "Could you give me the name of another person who might be familiar with the applicant's performance?" Then you begin getting information from references that may be more objective, because they did not come directly from the applicant (or use LinkedIn's Reference Search service).

The Polygraph and Honesty Testing

The polygraph is a device that measures physiological changes like increased perspiration. The assumption is that such changes reflect changes in emotional state that accompany lying.

In India, the government conducts background checks for key appointments, using state machinery like the police and vigilance departments. This cannot be equated with polygraph testing.

In the US, local, state, and federal government employers (including the FBI) can use polygraphs for selection screening and other purposes, but state laws restrict many local and state governments. Private employers can use polygraph testing, but only under strictly limited circumstances.[115] These include firms with national defense or security contracts, nuclear power-related contracts with the Department of Energy, access to highly classified information, counterintelligence-related contracts with the FBI or Department of Justice, and private businesses (1) hiring private security personnel, (2) hiring persons with access to drugs, or (3) doing ongoing investigations involving economic loss or injury to an employer's business, such as a theft. In India, polygraphs testing, even for criminal investigations, can only be conducted by law enforcement authorities with the approval of courts and under strict guidelines passed by the Human Rights Commission. Hence, polygraph tests cannot be used for employee selection.[116]

WRITTEN HONESTY TESTS These are psychological tests designed to predict job applicants' proneness to dishonesty and other forms of counterproductivity.[117] Most measure attitudes regarding things like tolerance of others who steal and admission of theft-related activities. Tests include the Phase II profile. London House, Inc., and Stanton Corporation publish similar tests.[118]

Psychologists were initially skeptical about paper-and-pencil honesty tests, but studies support these tests' validity.[119] One study involved 111 employees hired by a convenience store chain to work at store or gas station counters.[120] The firm estimated that "shrinkage" equaled 3% of sales, and believed that internal theft accounted for much of this. Scores on an honesty test successfully predicted theft here (as measured by termination for theft). At Hospital Management Corp. in the US, an integrity test is the first step in the hiring process, and those who fail go no further. It instituted the test after determining that the test did weed out undesirable applicants. For example, after the test was used for several months, workers compensation claims dropped among new hires. Testing has not gained a foothold in India. Most firms depend on reference checking or use police verification/background checking for this purpose.[121]

Testing for Honesty: Practical Guidelines

With or without testing, there's a lot a manager can do to screen out dishonest applicants or employees. Specifically:

- Ask blunt questions.[122] Says one expert, there is nothing wrong with asking the applicant direct questions, such as, "Have you ever stolen anything from an employer?" "Have you recently held jobs other than those listed on your application?" "Is any information on your application misrepresented or falsified?"
- Listen, rather than talk. Thus liars may try to answer direct questions somewhat evasively. For example, ask them if they've ever used drugs, and they might say, "I don't take drugs."[123]
- Watch for telltale body signals.
- Do a credit check. Include a clause in your application giving you the right to conduct background checks, including credit checks and motor vehicle reports.
- Check all employment and personal references.
- Use written honesty tests and psychological tests.
- Establish a search-and-seizure policy and conduct searches. Give each applicant a copy of the policy and require each to return a signed copy. The policy should state, "All lockers, desks, and similar property remain the property of the company and may be inspected routinely."

Honesty testing requires caution. Having just taken and "failed" what is fairly obviously an "honesty test," the candidate may leave the premises feeling mistreated. Some "honesty" questions also pose invasion-of-privacy issues.

Graphology

Graphology is the use of handwriting analysis to determine the writer's basic personality traits. It thus has some resemblance to projective personality tests, although graphology's validity is highly suspect. The handwriting analyst studies an applicant's handwriting and signature to discover the person's needs, desires, and psychological makeup. In one typical example the graphologist notes that a writing sample has small handwriting, a vertical stance, and narrow letters (among other things) and so is indicative of someone with uptight tendencies.

Virtually all scientific studies suggest graphology is not valid, or that when graphologists do accurately size up candidates, it's because they are also privy to other background information. Yet some firms swear by it.[124] One 325-employee firm uses profiles based on handwriting samples to design follow-up interviews.[125] Most experts shun it. In India, many institutes are teaching or providing training in graphology courses, such as, the Graphology Institute World School of Handwriting in Mumbai and the International Institute of Graphology in Pune. However, its use in selection is yet to gain foothold because of the lack of scientific evidence as well as training.[126]

"Human Lie Detectors"

Some employers are using so-called "human lie detectors," experts who may (or may not) be able to identify lying just by watching candidates.[127] One Wall Street firm uses a former FBI agent. He sits in on interviews and watches for signs of candidate deceptiveness. Signs include pupils changing size (fear), irregular breathing (nervousness), crossing legs ("liars distance themselves from an untruth"), and quick verbal responses (scripted statements).

Physical Exams

Once the employer extends the person a job offer, a medical exam is often the next step in selection (although it may also occur after the new employee starts work).

There are several reasons for preemployment medical exams: to verify that the applicant meets the job's physical requirements, to discover any medical limitations you should consider in placement, and to establish a baseline for future workers' compensation claims. Exams can also reduce absenteeism and accidents and detect communicable diseases.

Substance Abuse Screening

Most employers in the US conduct drug screenings. The most common practice is to test candidates just before they're formally hired. Many also test current employees when there is reason to believe they've been using drugs—after a work accident, or with obvious behavioral symptoms such as chronic lateness. Some firms routinely administer drug tests on a random or periodic basis, while others require drug tests when they transfer or promote employees to new positions.[128] Most employers that conduct such tests use urine sampling. Numerous vendors provide workplace drug-testing services.[129]

Complying with Immigration Law

All nations have rules regarding employment of people with different nationalities. Employees hired in the United States must prove they are eligible to work here. The requirement to verify eligibility does not provide any basis to reject an applicant just because he or she is a foreigner, not a U.S. citizen, or an alien residing in the United States, as long as that person can prove his or her identity and employment eligibility. To comply with this law, employers should follow procedures outlined in the so-called I-9 Employment Eligibility Verification form.[130] More than 500,000 employers are using the federal government's voluntary electronic employment verification program, E-Verify.[131] Federal contractors must use it.[132] At present, the practice of hiring foreign nationals is under public criticism, which has prompted the U.S. government to introduce restrictions. Many Indian firms, particularly in the IT/ITES space, are affected by this move. Similarly, the Gulf Cooperation Council or GCC countries, which traditionally imported human resources, are also increasingly imposing such restrictions. Oman, the UAE, and Saudi Arabia, among others have introduced stricter norms that require employers to hire citizens.

Indian companies also employ foreign nationals (including people of Indian origin) in their Indian offices. According to the government of India's rules, only those who are highly skilled or professionally qualified can be offered work visa for a specific project. Their minimum emolument in India should be US$ 25,000 per annum. Only ethnic cooks, language teachers other than English, and translators are exempt from the wage limit. Those who do business in India are eligible for a business visa.[133]

Chapter Review

Chapter Section Summaries

6-1. Careful **employee selection is important** for several reasons. Your own performance always depends on your subordinates; it is costly to recruit and hire employees; and mismanaging the hiring process has various legal implications including equal employment, negligent hiring, and defamation.

6-2. Whether you are administering tests or making decisions based on test results, managers need to understand several **basic testing concepts**. Reliability refers to a test's consistency, while validity tells you whether the test is measuring what you think it's supposed to be measuring. Criterion validity means demonstrating that those who do well on the test also do well on the job while content validity means showing that the test constitutes a fair sample of the job's content. Validating a test involves analyzing the job, choosing the tests, administering the test, relating your test scores and criteria, and cross-validating and revalidating. Test takers have rights to privacy and feedback as well as to confidentiality.

6-3. Whether they are administered via paper and pencil, by computer, or online, we discussed several main **types of tests**. Tests of cognitive abilities measure things like reasoning ability and include intelligence tests and tests of specific cognitive abilities such as mechanical comprehension. There are also tests of motor and physical abilities, and measures of personality and interests. With respect to personality, psychologists often focus on the "big five" personality dimensions: extroversion, emotional stability/neuroticism, agreeableness, conscientiousness, and openness to experience. Achievement tests measure what someone has learned.

6-4. With **work samples and simulations**, you present examinees with situations representative of the jobs for which they are applying. One example is the management assessment center, a 2- to 3-day simulation in which 10 to 12 candidates perform realistic management tasks under the observation of experts who appraise each candidate's leadership potential. Video-based situational testing and the miniature job training and evaluation approach are two other examples.

6-5. Testing is only part of an employer's selection process; you also want to conduct **background investigations and other selection procedures**.

- The main point of doing a background check is to verify the applicant's information and to uncover potentially damaging information. However, care must be taken, particularly when giving a reference, that the employee not be defamed and that his or her privacy rights are maintained.
- Given former employers' reluctance to provide a comprehensive report, those checking references need to do several things. Make sure the applicant explicitly authorizes a background check, use a checklist or form for obtaining telephone references, and be persistent and attentive to potential red flags.
- Given the growing popularity of computerized employment background databases, many or most employers use preemployment information services to obtain background information.
- For many types of jobs, honesty testing is essential and paper-and-pencil tests have proven useful.
- Most employers also require that new hires, before actually coming on board, take physical exams. It's essential to comply with immigration law in case of foreigners.

Discussion Questions

6-1. What is the difference between reliability and validity?

6-2. Explain why you think a certified psychologist who is specifically trained in test construction should (or should not) be used by a small business that needs an employment test.

6-3. Why is it important to conduct preemployment background investigations? How would you do so?

6-4. Explain how you would get around the problem of former employers being unwilling to give bad references on their former employees.

6-5. How can employers protect themselves against negligent hiring claims?

Individual and Group Activities

6-6. Write a short essay discussing some of the ethical and legal considerations in testing.

6-7. Working individually or in groups, develop a list of specific selection techniques that you would suggest your dean use to hire the next HR professor at your school. Explain why you chose each selection technique.

6-8. Working individually or in groups, contact the publisher of a standardized test such as the Scholastic Assessment Test and obtain from it written information regarding the test's validity and reliability. Present a short report in class discussing what the test is supposed to measure and the degree to which you think the test does what it is supposed to do, based on the reported validity and reliability scores.

6-9. Appendices A and B at the end of this book (pages 583–600) list the knowledge someone studying for the HRCI (Appendix A) or SHRM (Appendix B) certification exam needs to have in each area of human resource management (such as in Strategic Management, and Workforce Planning). In groups of several students, do four things: (1) review Appendix A and/or B; (2) identify the material in this chapter that relates to the Appendix A and/or B required knowledge lists; (3) write four multiple-choice exam questions on this material that you believe would be suitable for inclusion in the HRCI exam and/or the SHRM exam; and, (4) if time permits, have someone from your team post your team's questions in front of the class, so that students in all teams can answer the exam questions created by the other teams.

Experiential Exercise

A Test for Airline Ticketing Assistant

Purpose: The purpose of this exercise is to give you practice in developing a test to measure *one specific ability* for the job of airline reservation clerk of a major airline. If time permits, you will be able to combine your tests into a test battery.

Required Understanding: You are working with a company that is getting into airline business. The first flight is expected on October 1, connecting four airports, namely, Bangalore, Kochi, Mumbai, and Lucknow. You should be fully acquainted with the procedure for developing a personnel test and should read the following description of an airline testing assistant's duties:

> Customers contact our airline's ticketing assistants to obtain flight schedules, process, and itinerates. The assistants look up the requested information on our airline's online flight schedule systems, which are updated continuously. They must speak clearly, deal courteously and expeditiously with the customer, and be able to find quickly alternative flight arrangements in order to provide the customer with the itinerary that he or she needs. Alternative flights and prices must be found quickly so that the customer is not kept waiting and our reservations operations group maintains its efficiency standards. There may be a dozen or

more alternative routes between the customer's starting point and destination.

You may assume that we will hire about one-third of the applicants as airline ticketing assistants. Therefore, your objective is to create a test that is useful in selecting a third of those available.

How to Set Up the Exercise/Instructions:

Divide the class into teams of five or six students. The ideal candidate will need to have a number of skills to perform this job well. Your job is to select a single skill and to develop a test to measure that skill. Please use only the materials available in the room. The test should permit quantitative scoring and may be an individual or a group test.

Please go to your assigned groups. As per our discussion of test development in this chapter, each group should make a list of the skills relevant to success in the airline reservation clerk's job. Each group should then rate the importance of these skills on a 5-point scale. Then, develop a test to measure what you believe to be the top-ranked skill. If time permits, the groups should combine the various tests from each group into a test battery. If possible, leave time for a group of students to take the test battery.

Application Case

The Insider

A federal jury convicted a stock trader who worked for a well-known investment firm, along with two alleged accomplices, of insider trading. According to the indictment, the trader got inside information about pending mergers from lawyers. The lawyers allegedly browsed around their law firm picking up information about corporate deals others in the firm were working on. The lawyers would then allegedly pass their information on to a friend, who in turn passed it on to the trader. Such "inside" information reportedly helped the trader (and his investment firm) earn millions of dollars. The trader would then allegedly thank the lawyers, for instance, with envelopes filled with cash.

Things like that are not supposed to happen. Federal and state laws prohibit them. And investment firms have their own compliance procedures to identify and head off shady trades. The problem is that controlling such behavior once the firm has someone working for it who may be prone to engage in inside trading isn't easy. "Better to avoid hiring such people in the first place," said one pundit.

Over lunch at Bouley restaurant in Manhattan's TriBeCa area, the heads of several investment firms were discussing the conviction, and what they could do to make sure something like that didn't occur in their firms. "It's not just compliance," said one. "We've got to keep out the bad apples." They ask you for your advice.

Questions

6-10. We want you to design an employee selection program for hiring stock traders. We already know what to look for as far as technical skills are concerned—accounting courses, economics, and so on. What we want is a program for screening out potential bad apples. To that end, please let us know the following: What screening test(s) would you suggest, and why? What questions should we add to our application form? Specifically how should we check candidates' backgrounds, and what questions should we ask previous employers and references?

6-11. What else (if anything) would you suggest?

Continuing Case

Carter Cleaning Company

Honesty Testing

Jennifer Carter, of the Carter Cleaning Centers, and her father have what the latter describes as an easy but hard job when it comes to screening job applicants. It is easy because for two important jobs—the people who actually do the pressing and those who do the cleaning/spotting—the applicants are easily screened with about 20 minutes of on-the-job testing. As with typists, Jennifer points out, "Applicants either know how to press clothes fast or how to use cleaning chemicals and machines, or they don't, and we find out very quickly by just trying them out on the job." On the other hand, applicant screening for the stores can also be frustratingly hard because of the nature of some of the other qualities that Jennifer would like to screen for. Two of the most critical problems facing her company are employee turnover and employee honesty. Jennifer and her father sorely need to implement practices that will reduce the rate of employee turnover. If there is a way to do this through employee testing and screening techniques, Jennifer would like to know about it because of the management time and money that are now being wasted by the never-ending need to recruit and hire new employees. Of even greater concern to Jennifer and her father is the need to institute new practices to screen out those employees who may be predisposed to steal from the company.

Employee theft is an enormous problem for the Carter Cleaning Centers, and not just cash. For example, the cleaner/spotter often opens the store without a manager present, to get the day's work started, and it is not unusual for that person to "run a route." Running a route means that an employee canvasses his or her neighborhood to pick up people's clothes for cleaning and then secretly cleans and presses them in the Carter store, using the company's supplies, gas, and power. It would also not be unusual for an unsupervised person (or his or her supervisor, for that matter) to accept a 1-hour rush order for cleaning or laundering, quickly clean and press the item, and return it to the customer for payment without making out a proper ticket for the item posting the sale. The money, of course, goes into the worker's pocket instead of into the cash register.

The more serious problem concerns the store manager and the counter workers who actually handle the cash. According to Jack Carter, "You would not believe the creativity employees use to get around the management controls we set up to cut down on employee theft." As one extreme example of this felonious creativity, Jack tells the following story: "To cut down on the amount of money my employees were stealing, I had a small sign painted and placed in front of all our cash registers. The sign said: YOUR ENTIRE ORDER FREE IF WE DON'T GIVE YOU A CASH REGISTER RECEIPT WHEN YOU PAY. CALL 552–0235. It was my intention with this sign to force all our cash-handling employees to give receipts so the cash register would record them for my accountants. After all, if all the cash that comes in is recorded in the cash register, then we should have a much better handle on stealing in our stores. Well, one of our managers found a way around this. I came into the store one night and noticed that the cash register this particular manager was using just didn't look right, although the sign was placed in front of it. It turned out that every afternoon at about 5:00 p.m. when the other employees left, this character would pull his own cash register out of a box that he hid underneath our supplies. Customers coming in would notice the sign and, of course, the fact that he was meticulous in ringing up every sale. But unknown to them, for about 5 months the sales that came in for about an hour every day went into his cash register, not mine. It took us that long to figure out where our cash for that store was going."

Here is what Jennifer would like you to answer:

Questions

6-12. What would be the advantages and disadvantages to Jennifer's company of routinely administering honesty tests to all its employees?

6-13. Specifically, what other screening techniques could the company use to screen out theft-prone and turnover-prone employees, and how exactly could these be used?

6-14. How should her company terminate employees caught stealing, and what kind of procedure should be set up for handling reference calls about these employees when they go to other companies looking for jobs?

Translating Strategy into HR Policies and Practices Case*,§

*The overall map on page xxxviii of this book outlines the relationships involved.

Improving Performance at The Hotel Paris

The New Employee Testing Program

The Hotel Paris's competitive strategy is "To use superior guest service to differentiate the Hotel Paris properties, and to thereby increase the length of stay and return rate of guests, and thus boost revenues and profitability." HR manager Lisa Cruz must now formulate functional policies and activities that support this competitive strategy and boost performance, by eliciting the required employee behaviors and competencies.

As she considered what to do next, Lisa Cruz, the Hotel Paris's HR director, knew that employee selection had to play a role. The Hotel Paris currently had an informal screening process in which local hotel managers obtained application forms, interviewed applicants, and checked their references. However, a pilot project using an employment test for service people at the Chicago hotel had produced startling results. Lisa found consistent, significant relationships between test performance and a range of employee competencies and behaviors such as speed of check-in/out, employee turnover, and percentage of calls answered with the required greeting. She knew that such employee capabilities and behaviors translated into the improved guest service performance the Hotel Paris needed to execute its strategy. She therefore had to decide what selection procedures would be best.

Lisa's team, working with an industrial psychologist, designs a test battery that they believe will produce the sorts of high-morale, patient, people-oriented employees they are looking for. It includes a preliminary, computerized test in which applicants for the positions of front-desk clerk, door person, assistant manager, and security guard must deal with an apparently irate guest; a work sample in which front-desk clerk candidates spend 10 minutes processing an incoming "guest"; a personality test aimed at weeding out applicants who lack emotional stability; the Wonderlic test of mental ability; and the Phase II Profile for assessing candidate honesty. Their subsequent validity analysis shows that scores on the test batteries predict scores on the hotel's employee capabilities and behavior metrics. A second analysis confirmed that, as the percentage of employees hired after testing rose, so too did the hotel's employee capabilities and behaviors scores, for instance (see the strategy map), in terms of speed of check-in/out, and the percent of guests receiving the Hotel Paris required greeting.

Lisa and the CFO also found other measurable improvements apparently resulting from the new testing process. For example, it took less time to fill an open position, and cost per hire diminished, so the HR department became more efficient. The new testing program thus did not only contribute to the hotel's performance by improving employee capabilities and behaviors. It also did so by directly improving profit margins and profits.

Questions

6-15. Provide a detailed example of a security guard work sample test.

6-16. Provide a detailed example of two personality test items you would suggest they use, and why you would suggest using them.

6-17. Based on what you read here in this Dessler *Human Resource Management* Chapter, what other tests would you suggest to Lisa, and why would you suggest them?

6-18. How would you suggest Lisa try to confirm that it is indeed the testing and not some other change that accounts for the improved performance.

§Written by and copyright Gary Dessler, PhD.

Key Terms

Endnotes

1. See, for example, Jean Phillips and Stanley Gully, *Strategic Staffing* (Upper Saddle River, NJ: Pearson Education, 2012), pp. 234–235.

2. "Regret That Bad Hire? It's an Expensive Global Problem," *Bloomberg BNA Bulletin to Management*, June 4, 2013, p. 179.

3. See, for example, Ann Marie Ryan and Marja Lasek, "Negligent Hiring and Defamation: Areas of Liability Related to Pre-Employment Inquiries," *Personnel Psychology* 44, no. 2 (Summer 1991), pp. 293–319. See also Jay Stuller, "Fatal Attraction," *Across the Board* 42, no. 6 (November–December 2005), pp. 18–23.

4. Accessed on September 4, 2017 at http://www.financialexpress.com/industry/uber-cabs-driver-allegedly-rapes-delhi-woman-company-reacts/16579/.

5. For example, Ryan Zimmerman, "Wal-Mart to Toughen Job Screening," *Wall Street Journal*, July 12, 2004, pp. B1–B8. See also Michael Tucker, "Show and Tell," *HR Magazine*, January 2012, pp. 51–52.

6. Negligent hiring highlights the need to think through what the job's human requirements really are. For example, "nonrapist" isn't likely to appear as a required knowledge, skill, or ability in a job analysis of an apartment manager, but in situations like this screening for such tendencies is obviously required. To avoid negligent hiring claims, "make a systematic effort to gain relevant information about the applicant, verify documentation, follow up on missing records or gaps in employment, and keep a detailed log of all attempts to obtain information, including the names and dates for phone calls or other requests." Fay Hansen, "Taking 'Reasonable' Action to Avoid Negligent Hiring Claims," *Workforce Management*, September 11, 2006, p. 31. Similarly, the Employers Liability Act of 1969 holds employers responsible for their employees' health and safety at work. Because personality traits may predict problems such as unsafe behaviors and bullying, this act makes careful employee selection even more advisable.

7. Kevin Murphy and Charles Davidshofer, *Psychological Testing: Principles and Applications* (Upper Saddle River, NJ: Prentice Hall, 2001), p. 73.

8. Ibid., pp. 116–119.

9. W. Bruce Walsh and Nancy Betz, *Tests and Assessment* (Upper Saddle River, NJ: Prentice Hall, 2001).

10. Murphy and Davidshofer, *Psychological Testing*, p. 74.

11. Ibid.

12. See James Ledvinka, *Federal Regulation of Personnel and Human Resource Management* (Boston: Kent, 1982), p. 113; and Murphy and Davidshofer, *Psychological Testing*, pp. 154–165.

13. www.siop.org/workplace/employment%20testing/information_to_consider_when_cre.aspx, accessed March 22, 2009.

14. Based on Joseph Walker, "Meet the New Boss: Big Data," *Wall Street Journal*, September 20, 2012, p. B1. Also see Josh Bersin, "Big Data in Human Resources: Talent Analytics (People Analytics) Comes of Age," www.forbes.com/sites/joshbersin/2013/02/17/bigdata-in-human-resources-talent-analytics-comes-of-age, accessed March 29, 2015.

15. Bill Roberts, "Hire Intelligence," *HR Magazine*, May 2011, p. 64.

16. Namrata Singh, 'India companies use analytics tools to spot talent and trouble', *The Times of India* - Startups (online), timesofindia.com, Oct 11, 2016, 09.39 AM IST, [Navigation: News Home » Startups » Trend Tracking] , as accessed on 04 September 2017 at 4pm IST.

17. Use psychometric tests to pick right candidates

18. The procedure you would use to demonstrate content validity differs from that used to demonstrate criterion validity (as described in steps 1 through 5). Content validity tends to emphasize judgment. Here, you first do a careful job analysis to identify the work behaviors required. Then combine several samples of those behaviors into a test. A typing and computer skills test for a clerk would be an example. The fact that the test is a comprehensive sample of actual, observable, on-the-job behaviors is what lends the test its content validity.

19. Murphy and Davidshofer, *Psychological Testing*, p. 73. See also Chad Van Iddekinge and Robert Ployhart, "Developments in the Criterion-Related Validation of Selection Procedures: A Critical Review and Recommendations for Practice," *Personnel Psychology* 60, no. 1 (2008), pp. 871–925.

20. Psychological Assessment Resources, Inc., in Odessa, Florida, is typical.

21. Experts sometimes have to develop separate expectancy charts and cutting points for minorities and nonminorities if the validation studies indicate that high performers from either group (minority or nonminority) score lower (or higher) on the test.

22. In employment testing, bias has a precise meaning. Specifically, "bias is said to exist when a test makes systematic errors in measurement or prediction." Murphy and Davidshofer, *Psychological Testing*, p. 303.

23. Ibid., p. 305.

24. Herman Aguinis, Steven Culpepper, and Charles Pierce, "Revival of Test Bias Research in Preemployment Testing," *Journal of Applied Psychology* 95, no. 4 (2010), p. 648.

25. Robert Gatewood and Hubert Feild, *Human Resource Selection* (Mason, OH: South-Western, Cengage Learning, 2008), p. 243.

26. Bill Leonard, "Wanted: Shorter Time to Hire," *HR Magazine*, November 2011, pp. 49–52.

27. Accessed on September 26, 2017, at http://www.huffingtonpost.in/2016/03/30/railways-is-conducting-wo_n_9570378.html.

28. This is based on Dave Zielinski, "Effective Assessments," *HR Magazine*, January 2011, pp. 61–64.

29. Sarah Gale, "Three Companies Cut Turnover with Tests," *Workforce*, Spring 2002, pp. 66–69.

30. The Uniform Guidelines say, "Employers should ensure that tests and selection procedures are not adopted casually by managers who know little about these processes … no test or selection procedure should be implemented without an understanding of its effectiveness and limitations for the organization, its appropriateness for a specific job, and whether it can be appropriately administered and scored."

31. Phillips and Gully, *Strategic Staffing*, p. 220.

32. Ibid., p. 220.

33. www.uniformguidelines.com/qandaprint.html, accessed July 19, 2013. Conversely, validating a test that suffers from adverse impact may not be enough. Under the Uniform Guidelines, the employer should also find an equally valid *but less adversely impacting* alternative.

34. A complete discussion of the APA's "Ethical Principles of Psychologists and Code of Conduct" is beyond this book's text's scope. But points it addresses include competence, integrity, respect for people's dignity, nondiscrimination, and sexual harassment. From "Ethical Principles of Psychologists and Code of Conduct," *American Psychologist* 47 (1992), pp. 1597–1611; and www.apa.org/ethics/code/index.aspx, accessed September 9, 2011.

35. Indian Association of clinical psychologists website

36. "One-Third of Job Applicants Flunked Basic Literacy and Math Tests Last Year, American Management Association Survey Finds," *American Management Association*, www.amanet.org/press/amanews/bjp2001.htm, accessed January 11, 2008.

37. Ibid. See also Alison Wolf and Andrew Jenkins, "Explaining Greater Test Use for Selection: The Role of HR Professionals in a World of Expanding Regulation," *Human Resource Management Journal* 16, no. 2 (2006), pp. 193–213.

38. Steffanie Wilk and Peter Capelli, "Understanding the Determinants of Employer Use of Selection Methods," *Personnel Psychology* 56 (2003), p. 117.

39. Kevin Hart, "Not Wanted: Thieves," *HR Magazine*, April 2008, p. 119.

40. Sarah Needleman, "Businesses Say Theft by Their Workers Is Up," *Wall Street Journal*, December 11, 2008, p. B8.

41. Except as noted, this is based on Laurence Siegel and Irving Lane, *Personnel and Organizational Psychology* (Burr Ridge, IL: McGraw-Hill, 1982), pp. 170–185. See also Cabot Jaffee, "Measurement of Human Potential," *Employment Relations Today* 17, no. 2 (Summer 2000), pp. 15–27; Maureen Patterson, "Overcoming the Hiring Crunch; Tests Deliver Informed Choices," *Employment Relations Today* 27, no. 3 (Fall 2000), pp. 77–88; Kathryn Tyler, "Put Applicants' Skills to the Test," *HR Magazine*, January 2000, p. 74; Murphy and Davidshofer, *Psychological Testing*, pp. 215–403; Elizabeth Schoenfelt and Leslie Pedigo, "A Review of Court Decisions on Cognitive Ability Testing, 1992–2004," *Review of Public Personnel Administration* 25, no. 3 (2005), pp. 271–287.

42. See, for example, Paul Agnello, Rachel Ryan, and Kenneth Yusko, "Implications of Modern Intelligence Research for Assessing Intelligence in the Workplace," *Human Resource Management Review* 25, no. 1 (2015), pp. 47–55; and C. A. Scherbaum and H. W. Goldstein, "Intelligence and the Modern World of Work," *Human Resource Management Review* 25, no. 1, March 2015, pp. 1–3.

43. Norman Henderson, "Predicting Long-Term Firefighter Performance from Cognitive and Physical Ability Measures,"

Personnel Psychology 60, no. 3 (2010), pp. 999–1039.

44. As an example, results of meta-analyses in one study indicated that isometric strength tests were valid predictors of both supervisory ratings of physical performance and performance on work simulations. See Barry R. Blakley, Miguel Quinones, Marnie Swerdlin Crawford, and I. Ann Jago, "The Validity of Isometric Strength Tests," *Personnel Psychology* 47 (1994), pp. 247–274; and www.military.com/military-fitness/marine-corps-fitness-requirements/marine-corps-fitness-test, accessed October 4, 2011.

45. William Wagner, "All Skill, No Finesse," *Workforce*, June 2000, pp. 108–116. See also, for example, James Diefendorff and Kajal Mehta, "The Relations of Motivational Traits with Workplace Deviance," *Journal of Applied Psychology* 92, no. 4 (2007), pp. 967–977.

46. See, for example, Joyce Hogan et al., "Personality Measurement, Faking, and Employee Selection," *Journal of Applied Psychology* 92, no. 5 (2007), pp. 1270–1285; Colin Gill and Gerard Hodgkinson, "Development and Validation of the Five Factor Model Questionnaire (FFMQ): An Adjectival-Based Personality Inventory for Use in Occupational Settings," *Personnel Psychology* 60 (2007), pp. 731–766; and Lisa Penney and Emily Witt, "A Review of Personality and Performance: Identifying Boundaries, Contingencies, and Future Research Directions," *Human Resource Management Review* 20, no. 1 (2011), pp. 297–310.

47. Timothy Judge et al., "Personality and Leadership: A Qualitative and Quantitative Review," *Journal of Applied Psychology* 87, no. 4 (2002), p. 765.

48. www.myersbriggsreports.com/?gcli =CK71m6rE-h6ACFVZS2godDEj gkw, accessed August 21, 2014.

49. Ibid.

50. L. A. Witt et al., "The Interactive Effects of Conscientiousness and Agreeableness on Job Performance," *Journal of Applied Psychology* 87, no. 1 (2002), pp. 164–169.

51. Timothy Judge and Remus Ilies, "Relationship of Personality to Performance Motivation: A Meta Analytic Review," *Journal of Applied Psychology* 87, no. 4 (2002), pp. 797–807.

52. Murray Barrick et al., "Personality and Job Performance: Test of the Immediate Effects of Motivation Among Sales Representatives," *Journal of Applied Psychology* 87, no. 1 (2002), p. 43.

53. Charles Sarchione et al., "Prediction of Dysfunctional Job Behaviors Among Law-Enforcement Officers," *Journal of Applied Psychology* 83, no. 6 (1998), pp. 904–912. See also W. A. Scroggins et al., "Psychological Testing in Personnel Selection, Part III: The Resurgence of Personality Testing," *Public Personnel Management* 38, no. 1 (Spring 2009), pp. 67–77.

54. Paula Caligiuri, "The Big Five Personality Characteristics as Predictors of Expatriate Desire to Terminate the Assignment and Supervisor Rated Performance," *Personnel Psychology* 53 (2000), pp. 67–68. For some other examples, see Ryan Zimmerman, "Understanding the Impact of Personality Traits on Individuals' Turnover Decisions: A Meta-Analytic Path Model," *Personnel Psychology* 60, no. 1 (2008), pp. 309–348.

55. Adapted from www.kozaigroup.com/-inventories.php, accessed March 3, 2008; and http://kozaigroup.com/inventories/the-global competencies-inventory-gci/what is-the-gci/, accessed August 21, 2014.

56. Diane Cadrain, "Reassess Personality Tests After Court Case," *HR Magazine* 50, no. 9 (September 2005), p. 30.

57. Frederick Morgeson et al., "Reconsidering the Use of Personality Tests in Personnel Selection Contexts," *Personnel Psychology* 60 (2007), p. 683; and Frederick Morgeson et al., "Are We Getting Fooled Again? Coming to Terms with Limitations in the Use of Personality Tests for Personnel Selection," *Personnel Psychology* 60 (2007), p. 1046.

58. Robert Tett and Neil Christiansen, "Personality Tests at the Crossroads: A Response to Morgeson, Campion, Dipboye, Hollenbeck, Murphy, and Schmitt," *Personnel Psychology* 60 (2007), p. 967. See also Deniz Ones et al., "In Support of Personality Assessment in Organizational Settings," *Personnel Psychology* 60 (2007), pp. 995–1027.

59. See also Edwin A. J. van Hoot and Marise Ph. Born, "Intentional Response Distortion on Personality Tests: Using Eye Tracking to Understand Response Processes When Thinking," *Journal of Applied Psychology* 97, no. 2 (2012), pp. 301–316.

60. Chad H. Van Iddeking et al., "Are You Interested? A Meta-Analysis of Relations Between Vocational Interests and Employee Performance and Turnover," *Journal of Applied Psychology* 96, no 6 (2011), pp. 1167–1194.

61. Dracos Iliescu et al., "Vocational Fit and Counterproductive Work Behaviors: A Self-Regulation Perspective," *Journal of Applied Psychology* 100, no. 1 (2015), pp. 21–39.

62. Accessed on September 4, 2017, at www.zinghr.com/.

63. Ed Frauenheim, "More Companies Go with Online Test to Fill in the Blanks," *Workforce Management*, May 2011, p. 12.

64. Except as noted, this is based on Dave Zielinski, "Effective Assessments," HR Magazine, January 2011, pp. 61–64.

65. HRK News Bureau New Delhi, Hack2Hire, "DBS Goes Digital to Recruit Local Talent for Technology Roles," HRKatha, February 2017.

66. Wright, "At Google, It Takes a Village to Hire an Employee."

67. Ibid.

68. Jeff Weekley and Casey Jones, "Video-Based Situational Testing," *Personnel Psychology* 50 (1997), p. 25.

69. Elaine Pulakos, *Selection Assessment Methods*, SHRM Foundation, 2005, p. 14.

70. However, studies suggest that blacks may be somewhat less likely to do well on work sample tests than are whites. See, for example, Philip Roth, Philip Bobko, and Lynn McFarland, "A Meta-Analysis of Work Sample Test Validity: Updating and Integrating Some Classic Literature," *Personnel Psychology* 58, no. 4 (Winter 2005), pp. 1009–1037; and Philip Roth et al., "Work Sample Tests in Personnel Selection: A Meta-Analysis of Black–White Differences in Overall and Exercise Scores," *Personnel Psychology* 60, no. 1 (2008), pp. 637–662.

71. Siegel and Lane, *Personnel and Organizational Psychology*, pp. 182–183.

72. Quoted from Deborah Whetzel and Michael McDaniel, "Situational Judgment Tests: An Overview of Current Research," *Human Resource Management Review* 19 (2009), pp. 188–202.

73. "Help Wanted—and Found," *Fortune*, October 2, 2006, p. 40. See also Brian Hoffman et al., "Exercises and Dimensions Are the Currency of Assessment Centers," *Personnel Psychology* 60, no. 4 (2011), pp. 351–395.

74. Annette Spychalski, Miguel Quinones, Barbara Gaugler, and Katja Pohley, "A Survey of Assessment Center Practices in Organizations in the United States," *Personnel Psychology* 50, no. 1 (Spring 1997), pp. 71–90. See also Winfred Arthur Jr. et al., "A Meta Analysis of the Criterion Related Validity of Assessment Center Data Dimensions," *Personnel Psychology* 56 (2003), pp. 124–154; and Brian Hoffman et al., "Exercises and Dimensions Are the Currency of Assessment Centers," *Personnel Psychology* 60, no. 4 (2011), pp. 351–395.

75. Accessed on September 4, 2017 at http://talentlens.in/assessment-centre/

76. Accessed on September 4, 2017 at www.rac.gov.in.

77. See, for example, John Meriac et al., "Further Evidence for the Validity of Assessment Center Dimensions: A Meta-Analysis of the Incremental Criterion-Related Validity of Dimension Ratings," *Journal of Applied Psychology* 93, no. 5 (2008), pp. 1042–1052.

78. Weekley and Jones, "Video-Based Situational Testing," p. 26.

79. Catherine Rampell, "Your Next Job Application Could Involve a Video Game," *New York Times*, January 25, 2014.

80. Ibid., p. 30.

81. Robert Grossman, "Made from Scratch," *HR Magazine*, April 2002, pp. 44–53.

82. Coleman Peterson, "Employee Retention, the Secrets Behind Wal-Mart's Successful Hiring Policies," *Human Resource Management* 44, no. 1 (Spring 2005), pp. 85–88. See also Murray Barrick and Ryan Zimmerman, "Reducing Voluntary, Avoidable Turnover Through Selection," *Journal of Applied Psychology* 90, no. 1 (2005), pp. 159–166.

83. James Breaugh, "Employee Recruitment: Current Knowledge and Important Areas for Future Research," *Human Resource Management Review* 18 (2008), pp. 106–107.

84. Phillips and Gully, *Strategic Staffing*, p. 223.

85. Brian J. Hoffman, John W. Michel, and Kevin J. Williams, "On the Predictive Efficiency of Past Performance and Physical Ability: The Case of the National Football League," *Human Performance* 24, no. 2 (2011), pp. 158–172.

86. Lara Walsh, "To Tell the Truth: Catching Tall Tales on Résumés," *Workforce*, December 2014, p. 10.

87. "Resume Fakery Is Rampant, Global; Employer Caution Needed, *Bloomberg BNA Bulletin to Management,* November 4, 2014, p. 351.

88. "Internet, E-Mail Monitoring Common at Most Workplaces," *BNA Bulletin to Management,* February 1, 2001, p. 34. See also "Are Your Background Checks Balanced? Experts Identify Concerns over Verifications," *BNA Bulletin to Management,* May 13, 2004, p. 153.

89. Merry Mayer, "Background Checks in Focus," *HR Magazine*, January 2002, pp. 59–62; and Carroll Lachnit, "Protecting People and Profits with Background Checks," *Workforce*, February 2002, p. 52.

90. Matthew Heller, "Special Report: Background Checking,"

Workforce Management, March 3, 2008, pp. 35–54.

91. Bill Roberts, "Close-up on Screening," *HR Magazine*, February 2011, pp. 23–29.

92. Seymour Adler, "Verifying a Job Candidate's Background: The State of Practice in a Vital Human Resources Activity," *Review of Business* 15, no. 2 (Winter 1993), p. 6.

93. Heller, "Special Report: Background Checking," p. 35.

94. This is based on Samuel Greengard, "Have Gangs Invaded Your Workplace?" *Personnel Journal*, February 1996, pp. 47–48.

95. Dori Meinert, "Seeing Behind the Mask," *HR Magazine* 56, no. 2 (February 2011), www.shrm.org/ Publications/hrmagazine/ EditorialContent/2011/0211/ Pages/0211meinert.aspx, accessed August 20, 2011.

96. Ibid., p. 55.

97. Michelle Goodman, "Reference Checks Go Tech," *Workforce Management*, May 2012, pp. 26–28.

98. Alan Finder, "When a Risqué Online Persona Undermines a Chance for a Job," *New York Times*, June 11, 2006, p. 1.

99. Natasha Singer, "Funny, They Don't Look Like My References," *New York Times,* November 9, 2014, p. 4.

100. Rita Zeidner, "How Deep Can You Probe?" *HR Magazine*, October 1, 2007, pp. 57–62.

101. "Web Searches on Applicants Are Potentially Perilous for Employers," *BNA Bulletin to Management*, October 14, 2008, p. 335.

102. "Maryland Is First State to Restrict Employer Demands for Employee, Applicant Passwords," *BNA Bulletin to Management*, May 8, 2012, p. 145.

103. "Practitioners Discuss Various Pitfalls of Using Social Media to Vet Job Applicants," www. bna.com/practitioners-discuss-various-n12884904116/, accessed July 4, 2014.

104. Max Mihelich, "More Background Noise," *Workforce*, September 2014, pp. 52–55.

105. Accessed on September 4, 2017 at https://in.linkedin.com/ company/quetzal-verify-pvt-ltd.

106. Stephanie Clifford and Jessica Silver-Greenberg, "Retailers Track Employee Thefts in Vast Databases," *New York Times*, April 4, 2013, pp. A1, A16.

107. "Aadhaar Number Mandatory for New SBI Recruits," Business Standard. June 3, 2017.

108. Jeffrey M. Hahn, "Pre-Employment Information Services: Employers Beware?" *Employee Relations Law Journal* 17, no. 1 (Summer 1991), pp. 45–69. See also "Pre-Employment Background Screenings Have Evolved, but So Have Liability Risks," *BNA Bulletin to Management*, November 1, 2005, p. 345.

109. "Employer Concerns About Liability Loom as Push for Ban the Box Policies Spread," *Bloomberg BNA Bulletin to Management,* August 19, 2014, pp. 257–258.

110. Under California law, applicants or employees must have the option of requesting a copy of the report regardless of action.

111. Teresa Butler Stivarius, "Background Checks: Steps to Basic Compliance in a Multistate Environment," *Society for Human Resource Management Legal Report*, March–April 2003, pp. 1–8.

112. See, for example, Dori Meinert, "Search and Verify," *HR Magazine*, December 2012, pp. 37–41.

113. See Paul Taylor et al., "Dimensionality and the Validity of a Structured Telephone Reference Check Procedure," *Personnel Psychology* 57 (2004), pp. 745–772, for a discussion of checking other work habits and traits.

114. "Getting Applicant Information Difficult but Still Necessary," *BNA Bulletin to Management*, February 5, 1999, p. 63. See also Robert Howie and Laurence Shapiro, "Pre-Employment Criminal Background Checks: Why Employers Should Look Before They Leap," *Employee Relations Law Journal*, Summer 2002, pp. 63–77.

115. After a tragedy in Manhattan several years ago, more parents began turning to private investigators and industrial psychologists to conduct checks, including polygraph tests, on prospective nannies. Gabrielle Birkner, "Nanny Interviews Get More Aggressive," *Wall Street Journal*, December 15–16, 2012, pp. A19, A21.

116. T. Murali Krishna, "Polygraph test (Lie detector) and Truth Serums," accessed on September 4, 2017 at http://www.scribd.com/ doc/262431196.

117. John Jones and William Terris, "Post-Polygraph Selection Techniques," *Recruitment Today*, May–June 1989, pp. 25–31.

118. Norma Fritz, "In Focus: Honest Answers—Post Polygraph," *Personnel*, April 1989, p. 8. See also Richard White Jr., "Ask Me No Questions, Tell Me No Lies: Examining the Uses and Misuses of the Polygraph," *Public Personnel Management* 30, no. 4 (Winter 2001), pp. 483–493.

119. A recent meta-analysis concluded that "relations between integrity tests and measures of job performance tend to be rather weak." Chad H. Van Iddeking et al., "The Criterion Related Validity of Integrity Tests: An Updated Meta-Analysis," *Journal of Applied Psychology* 97, no. 3 (2012), pp. 499–530, a point disputed by a panel of test publishers. William G. Harris et al., "Test Publishers' Perspective on 'An Updated Meta-Analysis': Comment on Van Iddeking, Ross, Raymark, and Odle-Dusseau (2012)," *Journal of Applied Psychology* 97, no. 3 (2012), pp. 531–536.

120. John Bernardin and Donna Cooke, "Validity of an Honesty Test in Predicting Theft Among Convenience Store Employees," *Academy of Management Journal* 36, no. 5 (1993), pp. 1097–1108.

121. Bill Roberts, "Your Cheating Heart," *HR Magazine*, June 2011, pp. 55–57.

122. These are based on "Divining Integrity Through Interviews," *BNA Bulletin to Management*, June 4, 1987, p. 184; and *Commerce Clearing House, Ideas and Trends*, December 29, 1998, pp. 222–223. See also Bridget A. Styers and Kenneth S. Shultz, "Perceived Reasonableness of Employment Testing Accommodations for Persons with Disabilities," *Public Personnel Management* 38, no. 3 (Fall 2009), pp. 71–91.

123. Ibid.

124. Bill Leonard, "Reading Employees," *HR Magazine*, April 1999, pp. 67–73.

125. Ibid.

126. WebIndia, Education & Career, career.webindia123.com, [Navigation: REGULAR COLLEGES OR EDUCATIONAL INSTITUTIONS –ARTS, SCIENCE AND COMMERCE---GRAPHOLOGY], as accessed on 04 September 2017 at 2pm IST.

127. This is based on Kyle Stock, "Wary Investors Turn to Lie Pros," *Wall Street Journal*, December 29, 2010, p. C3.

128. Scott MacDonald, Samantha Wells, and Richard Fry, "The Limitations of Drug Screening in the Workplace," *International Labor Review* 132, no. 1 (1993), p. 98. Not all agree that drug testing is worthwhile. See, for example, Veronica I. Luzzi et al., "Analytic Performance of Immunoassays for Drugs of Abuse Below Established Cutoff Values," *Clinical Chemistry* 50 (2004), pp. 717–722.

129. For example, www.questdiagnostics.com/home/companies/ employer/drug-screening/testing-reasons/pre-employment. html, accessed August 22, 2014.

130. For the form, see www.uscis. gov/files/form/i-9.pdf, accessed October 4, 2011.

131. "More Than 500,000 Employers Are Now Enrolled in E-Verify Program," *Bloomberg BNA Bulletin to Management,* January 28, 2014, p. 27.

132. "President Bush Signs Executive Order: Federal Contractors Must Use E-Verify," *BNA Bulletin to Management*, June 17, 2008, p. 193.

133. Accessed on September 4, 2017 at http://mha1.nic.in/pdfs/ ForeigD-work_visa_faq.pdf.

7

Interviewing Candidates

LEARNING OBJECTIVES

7-1 List and give examples of the main types of selection interviews.

7-2 List and explain the main errors that can undermine an interview's usefulness.

7-3 Define a structured situational interview and explain how to design and conduct effective selection interviews.

7-4 Discuss how to use employee selection methods to improve employee engagement.

7-5 List the main points to know about developing and extending the actual job offer.

Recruitment of customer service and tellers in banks is never an easy task. Although the job entails significant responsibility and dealing, especially with difficult customers, the positions are not highly paid. However, the turnover of these personnel is high. The head of recruiting for a private bank in India needed an interviewing system that could process large number of applicants quickly but effectively. In this chapter, we will see as to what the recruiters did.

WHERE ARE WE NOW ...

Chapter 6 discussed important tools managers use to select employees. Now we'll turn to one of these tools—the employment interview. The main topics we'll cover include types of interviews, things that undermine interviewing's usefulness, designing and conducting effective selection interviews, using a total selection process to improve employee engagement, and making the offer. In Chapter 8, we'll turn to training the new employee.

If the interview is just one of several selection tools, why devote a whole chapter to it? Because interviews are the most widely used selection procedure, and most people aren't nearly as good at interviewing as they think they are. [1]

Basic Types of Interviews

Managers use several interviews at work, such as performance appraisal interviews and exit interviews. A *selection interview* (the focus of this chapter) is a selection procedure designed to predict future job performance based on applicants' oral responses to oral inquiries.[2] Many techniques in this chapter also apply to appraisal and exit interviews. However, we'll postpone discussions of those two interviews until later chapters.

There are several ways to conduct selection interviews. For example, we can classify selection interviews according to

1. How *structured* they are
2. Their "content"—the *types of questions* they contain
3. How the firm *administers* the interviews (for instance, one-on-one or via a committee)

Each has pros and cons. We'll look at each.

LEARNING OBJECTIVE 7-1

List and give examples of the main types of selection interviews.

---

unstructured (or nondirective) interview

An unstructured conversational-style interview in which the interviewer pursues points of interest as they come up in response to questions.

structured (or directive) interview

An interview following a set sequence of questions.

Structured Versus Unstructured Interviews

First, most interviews vary in the degree to which the interviewer structures the interview process.[3] In **unstructured (or nondirective) interviews**, the manager follows no set format. A few questions might be specified in advance, but they're usually not, and there is seldom a formal guide for scoring "right" or "wrong" answers. Typical questions here might include, for instance, "Tell me about yourself," "Why do you think you'd do a good job here?" and "What would you say are your main strengths and weaknesses?" Some describe this type of interview as little more than a general conversation.[4]

At the other extreme, in **structured (or directive) interviews**, the employer lists questions ahead of time, and may even weight possible alternative answers for appropriateness.[5] McMurray's Patterned Interview was one early example. The interviewer followed a printed form to ask a series of questions, such as "How was the person's present job obtained?" Comments printed beneath the questions (such as "Has he/she shown self-reliance in getting his/her jobs?") then guide the interviewer in evaluating the answers. Some experts still restrict the term *structured interview* to interviews like these, which are based on carefully selected job-related questions with predetermined answers.

In practice, interview structure is a matter of degree. Sometimes the manager may just want to ensure he or she has a set list of questions to ask so as to avoid skipping any questions. Here, he or she might choose questions from a list like that in Figure 7-3 (page 215). The structured interview guide in Figure 7A-1 (pages 227–229) illustrates a more structured approach. As another example, a retail store in India can use the structured guide in Figure 7-1 to help screen retail sales officer candidates. It contains a formal candidate rating procedure, and also enables geographically dispersed interviewers to complete the form via the Web.[6]

Structured interviews are generally best.[7] In such interviews, all interviewers generally ask all applicants the same questions. Partly because of this, these interviews tend to be more consistent, reliable, and valid. Having a standardized list of questions can also help less talented interviewers conduct better interviews. Standardizing the interview also enhances job relatedness (we'll see that the questions chosen tend to provide insights into how the person will actually do the job), reduces overall subjectivity and thus the potential for bias, and may "enhance the ability to withstand legal challenge."[8] However, blindly following a structured format may not provide enough opportunity to pursue points of interest. The interviewer should always have an opportunity to ask follow-up questions and pursue points of interest as they develop. We'll see how to write a structured interview later in this chapter.

FIGURE 7-1 Retail Sales Officer Applicant Interview Form

Source: Developed by Biju Varkkey

SAMPLE INTERVIEW FORMAT IN XYZ CO.

Position: Sales Officer in Retail Store.

Application No:		Date		Time	
Name				Age	
Educational Qualifications					
Total Work Experience					

Note to interviewer: Add you observations in the space available in each box.

A.   Quality of prior work experience, applicable in Retail Sales environment **1 (Low) 2 (Poor) 3 (Average) 4 (Good) 5 (Excellent)**

B.   Knowledge of Sales related processes and IT applications. **1 (Low) 2 (Poor) 3 (Average) 4 (Good) 5 (Excellent)**

C.   Selling and Customer Service Skills. **1 (Low) 2 (Poor) 3 (Average) 4 (Good) 5 (Excellent)**

D.   Potential for Retail Sales Role (relative to comparable role holders in XYZ) **1 (Low) 2 (Poor) 3 (Average) 4 (Good) 5 (Excellent)**

E.   Leadership Potential **1 (Low) 2 (Poor) 3 (Average) 4 (Good) 5 (Excellent)**

Additional Remarks _____

_____

_____

Name of Panelist _____ Signature _____ Date _____

Interview Content (What Types of Questions to Ask)

situational interview
A series of job-related questions that focus on how the candidate would behave in a given situation.

behavioral interview
A series of job-related questions that focus on how the candidate reacted to actual situations in the past.

We can also classify interviews based on the "content" or the types of questions interviewers ask. Many interviewers ask relatively unfocused questions, such as "What do you want to be doing in 5 years?" Questions like these generally do not provide much insight into how the person will do on the job. That is why *situational, behavioral*, and *job-related* questions are best.

In a **situational interview**, you ask the candidate what his or her behavior *would be* in a given situation.[9] For example, ask a supervisory candidate how he or she would act in response to a subordinate coming to work late 3 days in a row.

Whereas situational interviews ask applicants to describe how they *would* react to a hypothetical situation today or tomorrow, **behavioral interviews** ask applicants to describe *how they reacted* to actual situations in the past.[10] *Situational* questions start with phrases such as, "Suppose you were faced with the following situation.... What would you do?" *Behavioral* questions start with phrases like, "Can you think of a time when.... What did you do?"[11] In one variant, Vanguard uses an interviewing technique it calls STAR. Vanguard managers ask interviewees about a particular situation (S) or task (T) they faced to uncover the actions (A) the candidates took, and the results (R) of their actions.[12] Behavioral interviews are increasingly used.[13]

When Citizen's Banking Corporation in Flint, Michigan, found that 31 of the 50 people in its call center quit in one year, the center's head switched to behavioral interviews. Many who left did so because they didn't enjoy irate questions from clients. So she no longer tries to predict how candidates will act based on asking them if they want to work with angry clients. Instead, she asks behavioral questions like, "Tell me about a time you were speaking with an irate person, and how you turned the situation around." This makes it harder to fool the interviewer; only four people left in the following year.[14]

Financial audit and advisory companies, such as, EY India and KPMG India, often conduct selection interview by giving a case study that includes a business scenario which provokes candidates to think out-of-the box and find business solutions to the case study problems.[15] Most other consulting firms (like Bain & Company) also use case interviews extensively in their selection process.

Technical interviews which focus on the subject understanding of a candidate is another distinct feature of many Indian companies, particularly the IT and technology firms. In such companies, the behavioral/cultural dimensions are separately assessed. However, a study of foreign and Indian companies operating in India showed that while interview as a selection tool is common across companies, multinational companies (MNCs) use technical interviews separately, more than others.[16]

job-related interview
A series of job-related questions that focus on relevant past job-related behaviors.

stress interview
An interview in which the applicant is made uncomfortable by a series of often rude questions. This technique helps identify hypersensitive applicants and those with low or high stress tolerance.

OTHER TYPES OF QUESTIONS In a **job-related interview**, the interviewer asks applicants questions about job-relevant past experiences. The questions here don't revolve around hypothetical or actual situations or scenarios. Instead, the interviewer asks questions such as, "Which courses did you like best in business school?" The aim is to draw conclusions about, say, the candidate's ability to handle the financial aspects of the job in question.

There are other, lesser-used types of questions. In a **stress interview**, the interviewer seeks to make the applicant uncomfortable with occasionally rude questions. The aim is supposedly to spot sensitive applicants and those with low (or high) stress tolerance. Thus, a candidate for a customer relations manager position who obligingly mentions having had four jobs in the past 2 years might be told that frequent job changes reflect irresponsible and immature behavior. If the applicant then responds with a reasonable explanation of why the job changes were necessary, the interviewer might pursue another topic. On the other hand, if the formerly tranquil applicant reacts explosively, the interviewer might deduce that the person has a low tolerance for stress.

The stress interview's invasive and ethically dubious nature demands that the interviewer be both skilled in its use and sure the job really requires handling stress. This is definitely not an approach for amateur interrogators or for those without the skills to keep the interview under control. Indian banking or financial companies like the HDFC conducts stress interviews, especially for the sales function, to see if the candidates can handle stress or pressure. Candidates are especially asked questions that would make them uncomfortable to see how they would respond to these questions.

Puzzle questions are popular. Recruiters see how candidates think under pressure. For example, an interviewer at Microsoft asked a tech service applicant this: "Mike and Todd have $21 between them. Mike has $20 more than Todd does. How much money has Mike, and how much money has Todd?"[17] (The answer is two paragraphs below.)

HR in Practice at the Hotel Paris As an experienced HR professional, Lisa knew that the company's new testing program would go only so far. To see how the Hotel Paris created a new interview process, see the case on page 223.

How Should We Conduct the Interview?

Employers also administer interviews in various ways: *one-on-one or by a panel of interviewers, sequentially or all at once, computerized or personally,* or *online.*

unstructured sequential interview
An interview in which each interviewer forms an independent opinion after asking different questions.

structured sequential interview
An interview in which the applicant is interviewed sequentially by several persons; each rates the applicant on a standard form.

panel interview
An interview in which a group of interviewers questions the applicant.

mass interview
A panel interviews several candidates simultaneously.

Most selection interviews are probably still *one-on-one* and *sequential*. In a one-on-one interview, two people meet alone, and one interviews the other by seeking oral responses to oral inquiries. Employers tend to schedule these interviews *sequentially*. In a *sequential (or serial) interview*, several persons interview the applicant, in sequence, one-on-one, and then make their hiring decision. In an **unstructured sequential interview**, each interviewer generally just asks questions as they come to mind. In a **structured sequential interview**, each interviewer rates the candidates on a standard evaluation form, using standardized questions. The hiring manager then reviews these ratings before deciding whom to hire.[18] (Answer: Mike had $20.50, Todd $0.50.)

A **panel interview**, also known as a board interview, is an interview conducted by a team of interviewers (usually two to three), who together question each candidate and then combine their ratings of each candidate's answers into a final panel score. This contrasts with the *one-on-one interview* (in which one interviewer meets one candidate) and a *serial interview* (where several interviewers assess a single candidate one-on-one, sequentially).[19]

The panel format enables interviewers to ask follow-up questions, much as reporters do in press conferences. This may elicit more meaningful responses than a series of one-on-one interviews. On the other hand, some candidates find panel interviews more stressful, so they may actually inhibit responses. (An even more stressful variant is the **mass interview** (also referred as group interviewing or discussion based interviewing.) Here a panel interviews several candidates simultaneously. The panel might pose a problem, and then watches to see which candidate takes the lead in formulating an answer.)

Whether panel interviews are more or less reliable and valid than sequential interviews depends on how the employer actually does the panel interview. For example, *structured* panel interviews in which members use scoring sheets with descriptive scoring examples for sample answers are more reliable and valid than those that don't. Training panel interviewers may boost interview reliability.[20]

For better or worse, some employers use "speed dating" interviewing. One sent e-mails to all applicants for an advertised position. Four hundred (of 800 applicants) showed up. Over several hours, applicants first mingled with employees, and then (in a so-called "speed dating area") had one-on-one contacts with employees for a few minutes. Based on this, the recruiting team chose 68 candidates for follow-up interviews.[21]

PHONE INTERVIEWS Employers also conduct interviews via phone. Somewhat counterintuitively, these can actually be more useful than face-to-face interviews for judging one's conscientiousness, intelligence, and interpersonal skills. Because they needn't worry about appearance or handshakes, each party can focus on answers. And perhaps candidates—somewhat surprised by an unplanned call from the recruiter—give more spontaneous answers.[22] In one study, interviewers tended to evaluate applicants more favorably in telephone versus face-to-face interviews, particularly where interviewees were less physically attractive. The applicants preferred the face-to-face interviews.[23]

COMPUTER-BASED JOB INTERVIEWS A *computerized selection interview* is one in which a job candidate's oral and/or keyed replies are obtained in response to computerized oral, visual, or written questions and/or situations. Most such interviews present a series of multiple-choice questions regarding background, experience, education, skills, knowledge, and work attitudes. Some confront candidates with realistic scenarios (such as irate customers) to which they must respond.[24]

WEB-BASED VIDEO INTERVIEWS With phone and tablet video functionalities and FaceTime™ and Skype™, Web-based "in-person" interview use is widespread; about 18% of candidates took such interviews in one recent year.[25] With the InterviewStream 360 Video Practice Interview System, college career centers and outplacement firms can have students or job seekers record interviews for their own development and for prospective employers.[26] InterviewStream, Inc., (www.InterviewStream.com) offers employer clients prerecorded and live video interview management systems for prescreening candidates and interviewing remote talent. Or, the client and candidate can use InterviewStream's live videoconference platform for a live interview.[27] Employers including Microsoft use the virtual community Second Life to conduct job interviews. Job seekers create avatars to represent themselves.[28]

For Hilton Worldwide, which recruits in 94 countries, distances often made in-person interviews impractical. Now, online video interviews make it easy for Hilton to do initial screening interviews.[29] Another firm's CEO conducts initial screening interviews via text-only chats or instant messaging because, he says, this reduces potential distractions like gender, ethnicity, and body language.[30]

An online video interview requires little special preparation for employers, but Career FAQs (www.careerfaqs.com.au) lists things that *interviewees* should keep in mind. It's often the obvious things people overlook (for more on how to take interviews, see Appendix 2 to this chapter, page 230):[31]

- *Look presentable.* It might seem silly sitting at home wearing a suit, but it could make a difference.
- *Clean up the room.* Do not let the interviewer see clutter.
- *Test first.* As Career FAQs says, "Five minutes before the video interview is not a good time to realize that your Internet is down…"
- *Do a dry run.* Record yourself before the interview to see how you're "coming across."
- *Relax.* The golden rule with such interviews is to treat them like face-to-face meetings. Smile, look confident and enthusiastic, make eye contact, and don't shout, but do speak clearly.

TRENDS SHAPING HR: *DIGITAL AND SOCIAL MEDIA*

Today the growing popularity of mobile-based (iPhone or iPad, for instance) interviews is disrupting how job interviewing is done. They enable the interviewee to "do" the interview at his or her leisure from wherever the person wants, and also allow even pre-screen interviews to occur directly between hiring managers and job applicants, rather than HR. ZingHR, a Mumbai-based company, provides a software application where interviews can be conducted by downloading an application on the mobile phone or a similar device. Candidates can participate in the interview at their convenience from wherever they wish to. Face-to-face interview, if required, happens at a later stage when the HR manager has reviewed all the answers given by the candidates and has further shortlisted the candidates who have to be invited for the face-to-face round.[32]

The HireVue system is another example.[33] As described at http://hirevue.com/mobile/, the free HireVue tool (available as an app for iPhone, iPad, and iPod) enables interviewees to take their HireVue Interviews

> anytime, anywhere when invited by a potential employer. You can complete your HireVue Digital Interview on your own time, when it works for you, anywhere you have an internet connection….

Candidates, at their convenience, record their responses to the employer's video and written questions. The recruiter then plays back the recorded information and rates the candidate. The employer can arrange for candidates to first respond to several such questions, and then arrange for a set time for a synchronous online interview. Another HireVue tool uses data analysis to examine what the vendor says is more than 15,000 digital interview attributes to predict which candidates are most likely to be top performers and identify which interviewers make the best hiring decisions.[34] The Improving Performance feature illustrates. ■

▶ **IMPROVING PERFORMANCE:** *The Strategic Context*

Urban Outfitters

Urban Outfitters, a fashion retail company with presence in North America and Europe, needs store employees who share its core values of community, pride, creativity, and Respect. The question is, how does it find and attract such applicants, while controlling hiring costs in the competitive retail industry? Because it receives so many applications, the company first used group interviews for selecting sales associates. Retail managers would interview six to eight candidates at once, in a group interview. Store managers didn't think this was a good fit for Urban Outfitter's culture, though.

Urban Outfitters switched to HireVue on-demand interviews in its 200 retail stores. The HireVue system enabled applicants to watch videos about Urban Outfitters and the job, and then to respond in writing and by video to Urban's interview questions and instructions, at their leisure, "on demand." The hiring managers then reviewed the recorded interviews, usually outside of peak business hours when the stores weren't as busy.

The new system reportedly has been a boon to Urban Outfitters. It reduced screening time by 80%, lets store managers process many more applicants, and is preferred by applicants, 90% of whom can do their interviews after hours. The HireVue system also supports Urban Outfitters' strategy. As it says,

> Moving to digital interviewing has transformed our hiring process into a true reflection of the Urban Outfitters culture. Our value in creativity and community and our nonconformist approach now begins with our candidate experience. No other initiative has impacted our hiring teams like digital recruiting has.[35] ■

Avoiding Errors That Can Undermine an Interview's Usefulness

Interviews hold an ironic place in the hiring process: Everyone uses them, but they're generally not particularly valid. The key is to do them properly. If you do, then the interview is generally a good predictor of performance and is comparable with many other selection techniques.[36] Keep three things in mind—use structured interviews, know what to ask, and avoid the common interviewing errors.

First, *structure the interview.*[37] Structured interviews (particularly structured interviews using situational questions) are more valid than unstructured interviews for predicting job performance. They are more valid partly because they are more reliable—for example, the same interviewer administers the interview more consistently from candidate to candidate.[38] Situational structured interviews yield a higher mean validity than do job-related (or behavioral) interviews, which in turn yield a higher mean validity than do "psychological" interviews (which focus more on motives and interests).[39]

Second, interviews are better at revealing some things than others, so know what to focus on. In one study, interviewers were able to size up the interviewee's extroversion and agreeableness. What they could *not* assess accurately were the traits that often matter most on jobs—like conscientiousness and emotional stability.[40] One implication seems to be, focus more on situational and job knowledge questions that help you assess how the candidate will actually respond to typical situations on that job.

Third, whether the interview is in person or online, effective employment interviewers understand and avoid the following common interview errors.

First Impressions (Snap Judgments)

Probably the most widespread error is that interviewers tend to jump to conclusions—make snap judgments—about candidates during the first few minutes of the interview (or even before the interview starts, based on test scores or résumé data). One researcher estimates that in 85% of the cases, interviewers had made up their minds before the interview even began, based on first impressions the interviewers gleaned from candidates' applications and personal appearance.[41] In one typical study, giving interviewers the candidates' test scores biased the ultimate assessment of the candidates. In another study, interviewers judged candidates who they were told formerly suffered from depression more negatively.[42]

First impressions are especially damaging when the prior information about the candidate is negative. In one study, interviewers who previously received unfavorable reference letters about applicants gave those applicants less credit for past successes and held them more personally responsible for past failures after the interview. And the interviewers' final decisions (to accept or reject those applicants) always reflected what they expected of the applicants based on the references, quite aside from the applicants' actual interview performance.[43]

Add to this two more interviewing facts. First, interviewers are more influenced by unfavorable than favorable information about the candidate. Second, their impressions are much more likely to change from favorable to unfavorable than from unfavorable to favorable. Indeed, many interviewers really search more for negative information, often without realizing it.

The bottom line is that most interviews are loaded against the applicant. One who starts well could easily end up with a low rating because unfavorable information tends to predominate. And for the interviewee who starts out poorly, it's almost impossible to overcome that first bad impression.[44] One psychologist interviewed CEOs of 80 top companies. She concluded that you "don't even get to open your mouth."[45] Instead, the interviewer will size up your posture, handshake, smile, and "captivating aura." It's difficult to overcome that first impression.

Not Clarifying What the Job Requires

Interviewers who don't have an accurate picture of what the job entails and what sort of candidate is best for it usually make their decisions based on incorrect impressions or stereotypes of what a good applicant is. They then erroneously match interviewees with their incorrect stereotypes. You should clarify what sorts of traits you're looking for, and why, before starting the interview.

One classic study involved 30 professional interviewers.[46] Half got just this brief job description: "the eight applicants here represented by their application blanks are applying for the position of secretary." The other 15 interviewers got much more explicit job information, including bilingual ability, for instance.

More job knowledge translated into better interviews. The 15 interviewers with more job information generally all agreed among themselves about each candidate's potential; those without it did not. The latter also didn't discriminate as well among applicants—they tended to give them all high ratings.

Candidate-Order (Contrast) Error and Pressure to Hire

Candidate-order (or contrast) error means that the order in which you see applicants affects how you rate them. In one study, managers had to evaluate a sample candidate who was "just average" after first evaluating several "unfavorable" candidates. They scored the average candidate more favorably than they might otherwise because, in contrast to the unfavorable candidates, the average one looked better than he actually was. This contrast effect can be huge: In some early studies, evaluators based only a small part of the applicant's rating on his or her actual potential.[47]

Pressure to hire accentuates this problem. Researchers told one group of managers to assume they were behind in their recruiting quota. They told a second group they were ahead. Those "behind" rated the same recruits more highly.[48]

Nonverbal Behavior and Impression Management

The applicant's nonverbal behavior (smiling, avoiding your gaze, and so on) can also have a surprisingly large impact on his or her rating. In one study, 52 human resource specialists watched videotaped job interviews in which *the applicants' verbal content was identical,* but their nonverbal behavior differed markedly. Researchers told applicants in one group to exhibit minimal eye contact, a low energy level, and low voice modulation. Those in a second group demonstrated the opposite behavior. Twenty-three of the 26 personnel specialists who saw the high-eye-contact, high-energy-level candidate would have invited him or her for a second interview. None who saw the low-eye-contact, low-energy-level candidate would have recommended a second interview.[49] So, it pays interviewees to "look alive."

candidate-order (or contrast) error

An error of judgment on the part of the interviewer due to interviewing one or more very good or very bad candidates just before the interview in question.

Nonverbal behaviors are probably so important because interviewers infer your personality from the way you act in the interview. In one study, 99 graduating college seniors completed questionnaires which included measures of personality, among other things. The students then reported their success in generating follow-up interviews and job offers. The interviewee's personality, particularly his or her level of extroversion, had a pronounced influence on whether he or she received follow-up interviews and job offers.[50] In turn, extroverted applicants seem particularly prone to self-promotion, and self-promotion is strongly related to the interviewer's perceptions of candidate–job fit.[51] Even structuring the interview doesn't seem to cancel out the effects of such nonverbal behavior.[52]

IMPRESSION MANAGEMENT   Clever candidates capitalize on that fact. One study found that some used ingratiation to persuade interviewers to like them. For instance, the candidates praised the interviewers or appeared to agree with their opinions, thus signaling they shared similar beliefs. Sensing that a perceived similarity in attitudes may influence how the interviewer rates them, some interviewees try to emphasize (or fabricate) such similarities.[53] Others make self-promoting comments about their accomplishments.[54] Self-promotion means promoting one's own skills and abilities to create the impression of competence.[55] Psychologists call using techniques like ingratiation and self-promotion "impression management." Self-promotion is an effective tactic, but faking or lying generally backfires.[56]

Effect of Personal Characteristics: Attractiveness, Gender and Race

Unfortunately, physical attributes also distort assessments.[57] For example, people usually ascribe more favorable traits and more successful life outcomes to attractive people.[58] Similarly, race can play a role, depending on how you conduct the interview. In one study, in the US, for example, the white members of a racially balanced interview panel rated white candidates higher, while the black interviewers rated black candidates higher. But in all cases, *structured* interviews produced less of a difference between minority and white interviewees than did unstructured ones.[59]

Interviewers' reactions to various stereotypes are complex. In one study in the US, the researchers dressed the "applicants" in either traditional Muslim attire (black scarf and full-length black robe) or simple two-piece black pantsuits. Both applicants got the same number of job offers. However, interactions were shorter and more interpersonally negative when applicants wore the black robe attire.[60] In India, though not openly stated, factors like community, language, and region can influence hiring decisions to some extent. Sometimes employers specifically ask for candidates with or without certain background.[61] Studies conducted in the Indian context have also indicated that discrimination is a reality in this region. A study in the context of hiring practices in India indicated that Dalit community members and candidates experience discrimination. In this study, researchers applied to advertised positions (from three English newspapers) with different surnames that give out social identity. Based on the responses received from the firms, they concluded that even at early stage of hiring, Dalits experience higher discrimination.[62] To avoid such discrimination and comparison with general population during interviews, the government of India has proposed safeguards for government and PSU job selection, by way of representation in panel, separate interviews, and making members aware of possible biases.[63]

In general, candidates evidencing various attributes and disabilities (such as child-care demands, HIV-positive status, or being wheelchair-bound) have less chance of obtaining a positive decision, even when they performed well in the structured interview.[64] The following expands on this.

Diversity Counts: Applicant Disability and the Employment Interview

Researchers in the US surveyed 40 disabled people from various occupations. The disabled people felt that interviewers tend to avoid directly addressing the disability, and therefore make their decisions without all the facts.[65]

What the disabled people prefer is a discussion that lets the employer address his or her concerns and reach a knowledgeable conclusion. Among the questions they said they would like interviewers to ask were these: Is there any kind of setting or special equipment that will facilitate the interview process for you? Is there any specific technology that you currently use or have used in previous jobs that assists the way you work? What other kind of support did you have in previous jobs? Is there anything that would benefit you? Discuss a barrier or obstacle, if any, that you have encountered in any of your previous jobs. How was that addressed? And, Do you anticipate any transportation or scheduling issues with the work schedule expected of this position?

In another study, the researchers manipulated the candidates' appearance, for instance "by placing scar-like marks on the cheeks of some of the applicants for some interviews, but not for others." Results revealed that managers who interviewed a facially stigmatized applicant (versus a non-stigmatized applicant) "rated the applicant lower [and] recalled less information about the interview" (in part, apparently, because staring at the "scars" distracted the interviewers).[66]

Welfare of the disabled population is an important activity pursued by the government of India. The Rights of Person with Disabilities Act of 2016, which defines disability as evolving and dynamic concept and lists 21 disabilities, is the law in India. Before its enactment, Persons With Disabilities (Equal Opportunities, Protection of Rights and Full Participation) Act of 1955 was the law for employing the disabled in India. As per the new law, disabled applicants are eligible for reservation in government jobs, which is not less than 4 percent.

The Indian government's Ministry of Social Justice and Empowerment is the nodal authority, and a separate department is responsible for managing the welfare of disabled in India, which functions as a part of the ministry.

To promote employment of disabled in India, the central government has launched an online portal, www.disabilityjobs.gov.in. Both job seekers and employers can avail benefits from this service. ■

▶ IMPROVING PERFORMANCE: *HR Practices Around the Globe*

Selection Practices Abroad

In choosing selection criteria abroad, the manager in a multinational subsidiary walks a thin line between using the parent company's selection process and adapting it to local cultural differences. One study focused on Bangladesh.[67] Traditional selection practices there are different from what one might expect in the United States. For example, "age is considered synonymous to wisdom." Therefore, job advertisements for mid- and senior-level positions often set a minimum age as a selection criteria. But managers of multinational subsidiaries there are slowly implementing their corporate headquarters' prescribed HRM practices. As a result, the multinationals are affecting local recruitment and selection practices. That said, a manager would still be wise to understand each country's unique cultural demands before holding an interview there. ■

Source: Based on Monowar Mahmood, "National Culture vs Corporate Culture: Employee Recruitment and Se-lection Practices of Multinationals in a Developing Country Context," Journal of International Management Studies 11, no.1, (Jan. 2011), p. 110. Published by International Academy of Business and Economics, From www.iabe.org/domains/iabe/journal.aspx?journalid.

Interviewer Behavior

Finally, the *interviewer's* behavior affects interviewee performance and rating.

For example, some interviewers inadvertently telegraph the expected answers,[68] as in: "This job involves a lot of stress. You can handle that, can't you?" Even subtle cues (like a smile or nod) can telegraph the desired answer.[69] Some interviewers talk so much that applicants have no time to answer questions. At the other extreme, some interviewers let the applicant dominate the interview, and so don't ask all their questions.[70] When interviewers have favorable pre-interview impressions of the applicant, they tend to act more positively toward that person (smiling more, for instance).[71] Other interviewers play interrogator, forgetting that it's uncivil to play "gotcha" by gleefully pouncing on inconsistencies. Some interviewers play amateur psychologist, unprofessionally probing for hidden meanings in what the applicant says. Others ask improper questions, forgetting that discriminatory questions "had a significant negative effect on participant's reactions to the interview and interviewer."[72] Other interviewers just can't conduct interviews.

In summary, interviewing errors to avoid include:

- First impressions (snap judgments)
- Not clarifying what the job involves and requires
- Candidate-order error and pressure to hire
- Nonverbal behavior and impression management
- The effects of interviewees' personal characteristics
- The interviewer's inadvertent behaviors

We'll address what *interviewees* can do to apply these findings and to excel in the interview in Appendix 2 to this chapter.

<table>
<tr><td>

LEARNING OBJECTIVE 7-3

Define a structured situational interview and give examples of situational questions, behavioral questions, and background questions that provide structure.

structured situational interview

A series of job-relevant questions with predetermined answers that interviewers ask of all applicants for the job.

</td>
<td>

How to Design and Conduct an Effective Interview

There's little doubt that the **structured situational interview**—a series of job-relevant questions with predetermined answers that interviewers ask of all applicants for the job—produces superior results.[73] The basic idea is to (1) write situational (what would you do), behavioral (what did you do), or job knowledge questions, *and* (2) have job experts (like those supervising the job) also write several answers for each of these questions, rating the answers from good to poor. The people who interview the applicants then use rating sheets anchored with these examples of good or bad answers to rate the interviewees' answers.[74]

Designing a Structured Situational Interview

The procedure is as follows.[75]

Step 1. Analyze the job. Write a job description with a list of job duties; required knowledge, skills, and abilities; and other worker qualifications.

Step 2. Rate the job's main duties. Rate each job duty, say from 1 to 5, based on how important it is to doing the job.

Step 3. Create interview questions. Create situational, behavioral, and job knowledge interview questions for each of the job duties, with more questions for the important duties.

The people who create the questions usually write them as critical incidents. For example, to probe for conscientiousness, the interviewer might ask this situational question:

Your spouse and two teenage children are sick in bed with colds. There are no relatives or friends available to look in on them. Your shift starts in 3 hours. What would you do?

Step 4. Create benchmark answers. Next, *for each question*, develop ideal (benchmark) answers for good (a 5 rating), marginal (a 3 rating), and poor (a 1 rating) answers. The structured interview guide (pages 227–229) presents an example. Three benchmark answers (from low to high) for the example question above might be, "I'd stay home—my spouse and family come first" (1); "I'd phone my supervisor and explain my situation" (3); and "Since they only have colds, I'd come to work" (5).

Step 5. Appoint the interview panel and conduct interviews. Employers generally conduct structured situational interviews using a panel, rather than one-on-one. The panel usually consists of three to six members, preferably the same ones who wrote the questions and answers. It may also

</td>
</tr>
</table>

include the job's supervisor and/or incumbent, and a human resources representative. The same panel interviews all candidates for the job.[76]

The panel members review the job description, questions, and benchmark answers before the interview. One panel member introduces the applicant, and asks all questions of all applicants in this and succeeding candidates' interviews (to ensure consistency). However, all panel members record and rate the applicant's answers on the rating sheet (as on pages 228–229). They do this by indicating where the candidate's answer to each question falls relative to the benchmark poor, marginal, or good answers. At the end of the interview, someone answers any questions the applicant has.[77]

Web-based programs help interviewers design and organize behaviorally based selection interviews. For example, SelectPro (www.selectpro.net) enables interviewers to create behavior-based selection interviews, custom interview guides, and automated online interviews. The HR Tools feature presents more guidance.

▶ IMPROVING PERFORMANCE: *HR Tools for Line Managers and Small Businesses*

How to Conduct an Effective Interview

You may not have the time or inclination to create a structured situational interview. However, there is still much you can do to make your interviews systematic and productive.

Step 1: **First, know the job.** Do not start the interview unless you understand the job's duties and what human skills you're looking for. Study the job description.

Step 2: **Structure the interview.** Any structuring is better than none. If pressed for time, you can still do several things to ask more consistent and job-relevant questions, without developing a full-blown structured interview.[78] For example:[79]

- Base questions on *actual job duties.* This will minimize irrelevant questions.
- Use *job knowledge, situational, or behavioral questions.* Questions that simply ask for opinions and attitudes, goals and aspirations, and self-descriptions and self-evaluations allow candidates to present themselves in an overly favorable manner or avoid revealing weaknesses.[80] Figure 7-2 illustrates structured questions.

FIGURE 7-2 Examples of Questions That Provide Interview Structure

Job Knowledge Questions
1. What steps would you follow in changing the fan belt on a Toyota Camry?
2. What factors would you consider in choosing a computer to use for work?

Experience Questions
3. What experience have you had actually repairing automobile engines?
4. What experience have you had creating marketing programs for consumer products?

Behavioral (Past Behavior) Questions
5. Tell me about a time when you had to deal with a particularly obnoxious person. What was the situation, and how did you handle it?
6. Tell me about a time when you were under a great deal of stress. What was the situation, and how did you handle it?

Situational (What Would You Do) Questions
7. Suppose your boss insisted that a presentation had to be finished by tonight, but your subordinate said she has to get home early to attend an online class, so she is unable to help you. What would you do?
8. The CEO just told you that he's planning on firing your boss, with whom you are very close, and replacing him with you. What would you do?

- *Use the same questions* with all candidates. This improves reliability. It also reduces bias by giving all candidates the same opportunity.
- For each question, if possible, *have several ideal answers* and a score for each. Then rate each candidate's answers against this scale.
- If possible, use an *interview form*. Interviews based on structured guides like the ones in Figure 7-1 (page 204) or Figure 7A-1, "structured interview guide" (pages 227–229), usually result in better interviews.[81] At the very least, list your questions before the interview.

Step 3: **Get organized.** Hold the interview in a private place to minimize interruptions (including text messages). Prior to the interview, review the candidate's application and résumé. Note any areas that are vague or that may indicate strengths or weaknesses.

Step 4: **Establish rapport.** The main reason for the interview is to find out about the applicant. Start by putting the person at ease. Greet the candidate and start the interview by asking a noncontroversial question, perhaps about the weather that day.

Step 5: **Ask questions.** Try to follow the situational, behavioral, and job knowledge questions you wrote out ahead of time. You'll find a sampling of other, supplementary questions (such as "Tell me a little about yourself?") in Figure 7-3.
As a rule,
Don't telegraph the desired answer.
Don't interrogate the applicant as if the person is on trial.
Don't monopolize the interview, nor let the applicant do so.
Do ask open-ended questions.
Do encourage the applicant to express thoughts fully.
Do draw out the applicant's opinions and feelings by repeating the person's last comment as a question (e.g., "You didn't like your last job?").
Do ask for examples.[82]
Do ask, "If I were to arrange for an interview with your boss, what would he or she say are your strengths, weaker points, and overall performance?"[83]

In its own selection process, Google emphasizes work samples and situational (and behavioral) interviews.[84] For specific questions, Google provides its interviewers with access to its "QDroid" system; this system e-mails each interviewer a list of specific questions to ask the candidate for the specific job. A common practice followed in India for senior positions, is the panel to agree on specific questions to be asked to each candidate. This helps in eliciting richer information.

Step 6: Take brief, unobtrusive notes during the interview. Doing so may help avoid making a snap decision early in the interview, and may also help jog your memory once the interview is complete. Jot down just the key points of what the interviewee says.[85]

Step 7: Close the interview. Leave time to answer any questions the candidate may have and, if appropriate, to advocate your firm to the candidate.
Try to end the interview on a positive note. Tell the applicant whether there is any interest and, if so, what the next step will be. Make rejections diplomatically—"Although your background is impressive, there are other candidates whose experience is closer to our requirements." Remember, as one recruiter says, "An interview experience should leave a lasting, positive impression of the company, whether the candidate receives and accepts an offer or not."[86] If the applicant is still under consideration but you can't reach a decision now, say so.

Step 8: Review the interview. Once the candidate leaves, review your interview notes, score the interview answers (if you used a guide), and make a decision. A few Indian firms have introduced the practice of contacting the candidates to collect feedback about their experiences, with the aim to improve the selection process.

In rejecting a candidate, one perennial question that remains is, should you provide an explanation or not? In one study, rejected candidates who received an explanation felt that the rejection process was fairer. Unfortunately, doing so may not be practical. Most employers say little, to avoid pushback and legal problems. Under the Indian Right to Information (RTI) rules, candidates can request for information about selection status. Hence, upon request, all firms make the list of selected candidates and the criterion used for selection public. Most Indian firms do not follow the practice of providing detailed observation report or individual feedback to candidates, even if they request for the same.[87] ■

Organization and Planning Skills *

1. Describe a specific situation which illustrates how you set objectives to reach a goal.
2. Tell me about a time when you had to choose between two or more important opportunities. How did you go about deciding which was most important to you?
3. Tell me how you normally schedule your time in order to accomplish your day-to-day tasks.
4. Describe a situation where you had a major role in organizing an important event. How did you do it?
5. Think about a lengthy term paper or report that you have written. Describe how you organized, researched, and wrote that report.
6. Give an example of how you organized notes and other materials in order to study for an important exam.
7. Describe a time when you reorganized something to be more efficient. How did you do it?
8. Think of a time when you made important plans that were fouled up. How did you react? What did you do?

Interaction and Leadership

1. Tell me about an event in your past which has greatly influenced the way you relate to people.
2. Give a specific example that best illustrates your ability to deal with an uncooperative person.
3. Some people have the ability to "roll with the punches." Describe a time when you demonstrated this skill.
4. Tell me when you had to work with someone who had a negative opinion of you. How did you overcome this?
5. Recall a time when you participated on a team. Tell me an important lesson you learned that is useful to you today.
6. Describe an instance when you reversed a negative situation at school, work, or home. How did you do it?
7. Describe a situation which best illustrates your leadership ability.
8. Think about someone whose leadership you admire. What qualities impress you?

Assertiveness and Motivation

1. Describe several work standards that you have set for yourself in past jobs. Why are these important to you?
2. Tell me a time when you have experienced a lack of motivation. What caused this? What did you do about it?
3. Describe a situation where you had to deal with someone whom you felt was dishonest. How did you handle it?
4. Describe a situation that made you extremely angry. How did you react?
5. Tell me about a time that best illustrates your ability to "stick things out" in a tough situation.
6. Describe a time when you motivated an unmotivated person to do something you wanted them to do.
7. Give me an example of a time when you were affected by organizational politics. How did you react?
8. Give me an example of when someone tried to take advantage of you. How did you react?

Decision Making and Problem Solving

1. Give an example that illustrates your ability to make a tough decision.
2. Tell me about a decision you made even though you did not have all the facts.
3. Describe a situation where you have had to "stand up" for a decision you made, even though it was unpopular.
4. Describe a situation where you changed your mind, even after you publicly committed to a decision.
5. Describe a situation that illustrates your ability to analyze and solve a problem.
6. Tell me about a time where you acted as a mediator to solve a problem between two other people.
7. Describe a problem that seemed almost overwhelming to you. How did you handle it?
8. Tell me about a time where you have used a creative or unique approach to solve a tough problem.

The following general questions will also help you prepare for employment interviews:

1. Tell me a little about yourself.
2. Why did you attend Indiana State University?
3. What led you to choose your major or career field?
4. What college subjects did you like best/least? What did you like/dislike about them?
5. What has been your greatest challenge in college?
6. Describe your most rewarding college experience.
7. Do you think that your grades are a good indication of your academic abilities?
8. If you could change a decision you made while at college, what would you change? Why?
9. What campus involvements did you choose? What did you gain/contribute?
10. What are your plans for continued or graduate study?
11. What interests you about this job? What challenges are you looking for in a position?
12. How have your educational and work experiences prepared you for this position?
13. What work experiences have been most valuable to you and why?
14. Why are you interested in our organization? In what way do you think you can contribute to our company?
15. How would you describe yourself?
16. What do you consider to be your greatest strengths? Weaknesses? Give examples.
17. If I asked the people who know you for one reason why I shouldn't hire you, what would they say?
18. What accomplishments have given you the most satisfaction? Why?
19. What are your long-range career objectives? How do you plan to achieve these?
20. How would you describe your ideal job?
21. What two or three things are most important to you in your job?
22. Do you have a geographical preference? Why?

FIGURE 7-3 **Suggested Supplementary Questions for Interviewing Applicants**

Source: "Suggested Supplementary Questions for Interviewing Applicants", from Indiana State University Career Center website. copyright © 2012 by Indiana.

Go into the interview with an accurate picture of the traits of an ideal candidate, know what you're going to ask, and be prepared to keep an open mind about the candidate.

Stephen Coburn. Shutterstock

Profiles and Employee Interviews

Employers using competency models or profiles (which list required skills, knowledge, behaviors, and other competencies) can use the profile for formulating job-related situational, behavioral, and knowledge interview questions. Table 7-1 summarizes illustrative skill, knowledge, trait, and experience profile items for chemical engineer candidates, with sample interview questions.

TABLE 7-1 Asking Profile-Oriented Interview Questions

Profile Component	Example	Sample Interview Question
Skill	Able to use computer drafting software	Tell me about a time you used CAD Pro computerized design software.
Knowledge	How extreme heat affects hydrochloric acid (HCl)	Suppose you have an application where HCl is heated to 400 degrees Fahrenheit at 2 atmospheres of pressure; what happens to the HCl?
Trait	Willing to travel abroad at least 4 months per year visiting facilities	Suppose you had a family meeting to attend next week and we informed you that you had to leave for a job abroad immediately. How would you handle that?
Experience	Designed pollution filter for acid-cleaning facility	Tell me about a time when you designed a pollution filter for an acid-cleaning facility. How did it work? What particular problems did you encounter?

LEARNING OBJECTIVE **7-4**
Discuss how to use employee selection methods to improve employee engagement.

Employee Engagement Guide for Managers

Building Engagement: A Total Selection Program

Many employers create a *total selection program* aimed at selecting candidates whose totality of attributes best fits the employer's total requirements. The program Toyota Motor uses to select employees for auto assembly team jobs illustrates this.

Toyota looks for several things in candidates. It wants employees with good interpersonal skills, due to the job's emphasis on teamwork. Toyota's emphasis on *kaizen*—on having the workers improve job processes through worker commitment to top quality—helps explain its emphasis on reasoning and problem-solving skills and on hiring intelligent, educated, and engaged workers.[88] Quality is a Toyota core value, and so Toyota looks for a history of quality commitment in those it hires. This helps explain why Toyota holds group interviews focusing on accomplishments. By asking candidates about what they are proudest of, Toyota gets a better insight into the person's values regarding quality and doing things right. Toyota is also looking for employees who have an eagerness to learn, and who are willing to try things Toyota's way or the team's way. Toyota's production system relies on consensus decision making, job rotation, and flexible career paths, and these also require open-minded, flexible team players, not dogmatists.

The Toyota Way

Toyota's hiring process aims to identify such assembler candidates. The process takes about 20 hours and six phases over several days:[89]

Step 1: an in-depth online application (20–30 minutes)

Step 2: a 2–5-hour computer-based assessment

Step 3: a 6–8-hour work simulation assessment

Step 4: a face-to-face interview

Step 5: a background check, drug screen, and medical check

Step 6: job offer

For example, in step 1, applicants complete an application form summarizing their experience and skills, and often view a video describing Toyota's work environment and selection system. This provides a realistic preview of the work and of the hiring process's extensiveness. Many applicants drop out here.

Step 2 aims to assess the applicant's technical knowledge and potential. Here applicants take tests that help identify problem-solving skills, learning potential, and occupational preferences. Skilled trade applicants (experienced mechanics, for instance) also take tool and die or general maintenance tests.

In step 3, applicants engage in simulated realistic production activities in Toyota's assessment center, under the observation of Toyota screening experts. The production (work sample) test assesses how well each candidate does on an actual assembler task. Also here, group discussion exercises help show how each applicant interacts with others in their group and solves problems.

In one simulation, candidates play the roles of the management and the workers of a firm that makes electrical circuits. During one scenario, the team must decide which circuit should be manufactured and how to effectively assign people, materials, and money to produce them. In another, participants role-play a team responsible for choosing new features for next year's car. Team members first individually rank 12 features based upon market appeal and then suggest one feature not included on the list. They must then come to a consensus on the best rank ordering. As one candidate who went through this process said, "There are three workstations in which you will be required to spend 2 hours at each one. You then have to get in a group and problem solve a special project with them for another hour or so. I left my house at 5 A.M. and did not return until 6:30 P.M.; it was a very long day."[90]

The time and effort applicants must invest in their Toyota visits are no accident. Toyota seeks engaged, flexible, quality-oriented team players, and those who lack these traits and values tend not to make it through the screening process. The rigorousness of the process tends to screen out those who are less engaged.

In summary, Toyota uses a total hiring process to identify and select engaged employees. While other firms do this in various ways, four common themes are apparent from Toyota's process. First, *value-based hiring* means it clarifies its own values before it embarks on an employee selection program. Whether based on excellence, kaizen/continuous improvement, integrity, or some other, value-based hiring begins with clarifying what your firm's values are and what you're looking for in employees.

Second, high-engagement firms such as Toyota commit the time and effort for an *exhaustive screening process*. Eight to ten hours of interviewing even for entry-level employees is not unusual, and firms like this will spend 20 hours or more with someone before deciding to hire. Many are rejected.

Third, the screening process doesn't just identify knowledge and technical skills. In addition, the candidate's *values and skills are matched* with the needs of the firm. Teamwork, kaizen, problem-solving, engagement, and flexibility are essential values at Toyota, so problem-solving skills, interpersonal skills, and engagement with the firm's commitment to quality are crucial human requirements.

Fourth, *self-selection* is an important screening practice here. In some firms this just means realistic previews. At others, practices such as long probationary periods in entry-level jobs help screen out those who don't fit. At Toyota, the screening process itself demands a sacrifice in terms of time and effort.

 TRENDS SHAPING HR: *SCIENCE IN TALENT MANAGEMENT*

As another example, Google takes a scientific, evidence-based approach to its selection (and other HR) practices.

In its hiring process, Google starts (as explained in Chapter 4) with strong candidates. Recall that where possible, its internal recruiting group proactively identifies candidates, rather than using job boards to attract unscreened résumés.

The main elements in Google's selection process include work samples, testing, and interviewing. Virtually all of Google's technical hires take work sample tests, such as actually writing algorithms. Work samples are combined with testing of cognitive ability (similar to IQ tests), and of conscientiousness. Early in its evolution Google was known for putting candidates through a dozen or more interviews. However Google's own analysis showed that after the first four interviews the amount of useful information it got was not large. It therefore now generally makes hiring decisions after the fourth interview.

The interview emphasizes situational and behavioral questions. For specific questions, Google provides (as noted) its interviewers with access to its QDroid system; this e-mails each interviewer specific questions to ask the candidate for the specific job. Google interviewers were once known for trick questions, but the emphasis today is on using validated questions (from the QDroid system). The questions aim to assess the candidate's cognitive ability, leadership (particularly willingness to lead projects), "Googleyness" (values such as fun-loving and conscientious), and role-related knowledge (such as in computer science). Who actually does the interviewing? Here Google believes in the "wisdom of crowds": the interviewing "crowd" includes not just the prospective boss but prospective subordinates and representatives of other unrelated departments. Google then averages all the interviewers' interview ratings on a candidate to get a score. Finally, the hiring committee reviews the file, as does a Google senior manager, and then the CEO before an offer is made.[91]

Google is continually analyzing and improving its selection process. For example, it periodically runs experiments using algorithms that identify common keywords so as to analyse résumés of successful Google employees in particular jobs. Google then looks for these keywords in applicants who it *rejected* over the past year, and reevaluates these rejected applicants for these keywords, hiring many of these former "rejects" as a result. Similarly, interviewers get printouts showing how effective they've been as interviewers in terms of candidates hired or not hired. The process is thus analytical, evidence-based, and scientific. ■

Developing and Extending the Job Offer

LEARNING OBJECTIVE 7-5

List the main points to know about developing and extending the actual job offer.

After all the interviews, background checks, and tests, the employer decides to whom to make an offer using one or more approaches. The *judgmental* approach subjectively weighs all the evidence about the candidate. The *statistical* approach quantifies all the evidence and perhaps uses a formula to predict job success. The *hybrid* approach combines statistical results with judgment. Statistical and hybrid are more defensible; judgmental is better than nothing.

The employer will base the actual offer on, for instance, the candidate's apparent attractiveness as a prospective employee, the level of the position, and pay rates for similar positions. Next the employer extends an actual job offer to the candidate verbally. Here, the employer's point person (who might be the person to whom the new employee will report, or the human resource director, for instance) discusses the offer's main parameters. These include, for instance, pay rates, benefits, and actual job duties. There may be some negotiations. Then, once agreement is reached, the employer will extend a written job offer to the candidate.

There are several issues to consider with the written offer. Perhaps most important, understand the difference between a job offer letter and a contract. In a job offer letter, the employer lists the offer's basic information. This typically starts with a welcome sentence. It then includes job-specific information (such as details on salary and pay), benefits information, paid leave information, and terms of employment (including, for instance, successful completion of job testing and physical exams). There should be a strong statement that the employment relationship will cease on giving and serving a notice period or paying a compensation (salary in lieu of this). This is necessary to protect the interests of both sides. In India, some firms insist on employees serving long notice periods (like pilots in the aviation sector and professionals in the IT sector), which was a point of discontent. There is then a closing statement. This again welcomes the employee, mentions who the employer's point person is if any questions arise, and instructs the candidate to sign the letter of offer if it is acceptable. It is prudent to have an attorney review the offer before extending it.[92]

For many positions (such as chief executive) a contract is in order. An employment contract may have a duration (such as 3 years). Therefore, the contract will also describe grounds for termination or resignation, and severance provisions. The contract will almost always also include terms regarding confidentiality, nondisclosure requirements, and covenants not to compete (although some job offer letters for positions such as engineer may include such provisions as well). See www.Shrm.org/template-tools/toolkits for more information.

Depending upon the position, the employment contract (and, occasionally, the offer letter) may include a relocation provision. This lays out what the employer is willing to pay the new employee to relocate, for instance, in terms of moving expenses. State law generally governs enforcement of individual employment contracts.

Chapter Review

Chapter Section Summaries

7-1. A selection interview is a selection procedure designed to predict future job performance based on applicants' oral responses to oral inquiries; we discussed several **basic types of interviews**. There are structured versus unstructured interviews. We also distinguished between interviews based on the types of questions and on how you administer the interview.

7-2. One reason selection interviews are often less useful than they should be is that managers make predictable **errors that undermine an interview's usefulness**. They jump to conclusions or make snap judgments based on preliminary information, they don't clarify what the job really requires, they succumb to candidate-order error and pressure to hire, and they let a variety of nonverbal behaviors and personal characteristics undermine the validity of the interview.

7-3. The manager should know how to **design and conduct an effective interview**. The structured situational interview is a series of job-related questions with predetermined answers that interviewers ask of all applicants for the job. Steps in creating a structured situational interview include analyzing the job, rating the job's main duties, creating interview questions, creating benchmark answers, and appointing the interview panel and conducting interviews.

7-4. High-engagement firms like Toyota use total hiring programs to select employees. Activities include clarifying the firm's values, committing the time and effort, matching the applicant's values with the firm's, having realistic previews, and encouraging self-selection.

7-5. After choosing which candidate to hire, the employer turns to **developing and extending the job offer**. Things to keep in mind here include understanding the difference between a job offer letter and a contract. A job offer letter lists the offer's basic information, including details on salary and pay, benefits information, paid leave information, and terms of employment. There should be a strong statement specifying that the employment relationship is "at will." In contrast to a letter of offer, it is not unusual for an employment contract to have a duration (such as 3 years).

Discussion Questions

7-1. There are several ways to conduct a selection interview. Explain and illustrate the basic ways in which you can classify selection interviews.

7-2. Briefly describe each of the following types of interviews: unstructured panel interviews, structured sequential interviews, job-related structured interviews.

7-3. For what sorts of jobs do you think unstructured interviews might be most appropriate? Why?

7-4. How would you explain the fact that structured interviews, regardless of content, are generally more valid than unstructured interviews for predicting job performance?

7-5. Briefly discuss what an interviewer can do to improve his or her interviewing performance.

7-6. What items should a letter of offer definitely contain?

7-7 What parallels do you see between the Toyota and Google total selection processes? What differences?

Individual and Group Activities

7-8. Prepare and give a short presentation titled "How to Be Effective as a Selection Interviewer."

7-9. Use the Internet to find employers who now do preliminary selection interviews via the Web. Do you think these interviews are useful? Why? How would you improve them?

7-10. In groups, discuss and compile examples of "the worst interview I ever had." What was it about these interviews that made them so bad? If time permits, discuss as a class.

7-11. In groups, prepare an interview (including a sequence of at least 20 questions) you'll use to interview candidates for the job of teaching a course in human resource management. Each group should present its interview questions in class.

7-12. Some firms swear by unorthodox interview methods. For example, Tech Planet, of Menlo Park, California, uses weekly lunches and "wacky follow-up sessions" as substitutes for first-round job interviews. During the informal meals, candidates are expected to mingle, and the Tech Planet employees they meet at the luncheons then review them. One Tech Planet employee asks candidates to ride a unicycle in her office to see if "they'll bond with the corporate culture or not." Toward the end of the screening process, the surviving group of interviewees has to solve brainteasers, and then openly evaluate their fellow candidates' strengths and weaknesses. What do you think of this screening process? What are its pros and cons? What changes, if any, would you recommend?[93]

7-13. Several years ago, Lockheed Martin Corp. sued the Boeing Corp. in Orlando, Florida, accusing it of using Lockheed's trade secrets to help win a multibillion-dollar government contract. Among other things, Lockheed Martin claimed that Boeing had obtained those trade secrets from a former Lockheed Martin employee who switched to Boeing.[94] But in describing methods companies use to commit corporate espionage, one writer says that hiring away the competitor's employees or hiring people to go through its dumpster are just the most obvious methods companies use to commit corporate espionage. As he says, "one of the more unusual scams—sometimes referred to as 'help wanted'—uses a person posing as a corporate headhunter who approaches an employee of the target company with a potentially lucrative job offer. During the interview, the employee is quizzed about his responsibilities, accomplishments, and current projects. The goal is to extract important details without the employee realizing there is no job."[95]

Assume you own a small high-tech company. What would you do (in terms of employee training, or a letter from you, for instance) to try to minimize the chance that one of your employees will fall into that kind of a trap? Also, compile a list of 10 questions that you think such a corporate spy might ask one of your employees.

7-14. Appendices A and B at the end of this book (pages 583–600) list the knowledge someone studying for the HRCI (Appendix A) or SHRM (Appendix B) certification exam needs to have in each area of human resource management (such as in Strategic Management, and Workforce Planning). In groups of several students, do four things: (1) review Appendix A and/or B; (2) identify the material in this chapter that relates to the Appendix A and/or B required knowledge lists; (3) write four multiple-choice exam questions on this material that you believe would be suitable for inclusion in the HRCI exam and/or the SHRM exam; and, (4) if time permits, have someone from your team post your team's questions in front of the class, so that students in all teams can answer the exam questions created by the other teams.

Experiential Exercise

The Most Important Person You'll Ever Hire

Purpose: The purpose of this exercise is to give you practice using some of the interview techniques you learned from this chapter.

Required Understanding: You should be familiar with the information presented in this chapter, and read this: For parents, children are precious. It's therefore interesting that parents who hire *"ayahs (caretakers)"* to take care of their children usually do little more than ask several interview questions and conduct what is often, at best, a perfunctory reference check. If both parents are working, it's necessary that the selected *ayah* is not only able to mind the child but also manage affairs of the house. Given the often questionable validity of interviews, and the (often) relative inexperience of the father or mother doing the interviewing, it's not surprising that many of these arrangements end in disappointment. You know from this chapter that it is difficult to conduct a valid interview unless you know exactly what you're looking for and, preferably, structure the interview. Most parents simply aren't trained to do this.

How to Set Up the Exercise/Instructions:

- Set up groups of five or six students. Two students will be the interviewees, while the other students in the group will serve as panel interviewers. The interviewees will develop an interviewer assessment form, and the panel interviewers will develop a structured situational interview for a "*ayah*."

   7-15. Instructions for the interviewees: The interviewees should leave the room for about 20 minutes. While out of the room, the interviewees should develop an "interviewer assessment form" based on the information presented in this chapter regarding factors that can undermine the usefulness of an interview. During the panel interview, the interviewees should assess the interviewers using the interviewer assessment form. After the panel interviewers have conducted the interview, the interviewees should leave the room to discuss their notes.

Did the interviewers exhibit any of the factors that can undermine the usefulness of an interview? If so, which ones? What suggestions would you (the interviewees) make to the interviewers on how to improve the usefulness of the interview?

   7-16. Instructions for the interviewers: While the interviewees are out of the room, the panel interviewers will have 20 minutes to develop a short structured situational interview form for a "*ayah*." The panel interview team will interview two candidates for the position. During the panel interview, each interviewer should be taking notes on a copy of the structured situational interview form. After the panel interview, the panel interviewers should discuss their notes. What were your first impressions of each interviewee? Were your impressions similar? Which candidate would you all select for the position and why?

Application Case

The Out-of-Control Interview

Maria Fernandez is a bright, popular, and well-informed mechanical engineer who graduated with an engineering degree from State University in June 2014. Anticipating that she could make into a nationally-ranked college, she took a break for one year after +2. Though she was able to be in the national rank list, she got branch of her choice only in the state university and choose that. During the last semester of engineering, she went out on many job interviews, most of which she thought were conducted courteously and were reasonably useful in giving both her and the prospective employer a good impression of where each of them stood on matters of importance to both of them. It was, therefore, with great anticipation that she looked forward to an interview with the one firm in which she most wanted to work: Apex Environmental. She had always had a strong interest in the environment and believed that the best use of her training and skills lay in working for a firm like Apex, where she thought she could have a successful career while making the world a better place.

The interview, however, was a disaster. Maria walked into a room where five men—the president of the company, two vice presidents, the marketing director, and another engineer—began throwing questions at her that she felt were aimed primarily at tripping her up rather than finding out what she could offer through her engineering skills. The questions ranged from being unnecessarily discourteous ("Why would you take a break after your +2 and take admission in a state university, if you're such an intelligent person?") to being irrelevant and sexist ("Do you have a boyfriend? Are you planning on getting married anytime soon?"). Then, after the interview, she met with two of the gentlemen individually (including the president), and the discussions focused on her technical expertise. She thought that these later discussions went fairly

well. Thereafter, a few candidates were made to wait in the lobby, and after two hours of wait, they were asked to leave. The receptionist informed them that the company will get back to them soon. However, given the apparent aimlessness and even mean-spiritedness of the panel interview, she was astonished when several days later the firm made her a job offer.

The offer forced her to consider several matters. From her point of view, the job itself was perfect. She liked what she would be doing, the industry, and the firm's location. And in fact, the president had been quite courteous in subsequent discussions. She was left wondering whether the panel interview had been intentionally tense to see how she'd stand up under pressure, and, if so, why they would do such a thing.

Questions

7-17. How would you explain the nature of the panel interview Maria had to endure? Specifically, do you think it reflected a well-thought-out interviewing strategy on the part of the firm or carelessness on the part of the firm's management? If it were carelessness, what would you do to improve the interview process at Apex Environmental?

7-18. Would you take the job offer if you were Maria? If you're not sure, what additional information would help you make your decision?

7-19. The job of applications engineer for which Maria was applying requires (a) excellent technical skills with respect to mechanical engineering, (b) a commitment to working in the area of pollution control, (c) the ability to deal well and confidently with customers who have engineering problems, (d) a willingness to travel worldwide, and (e) a very intelligent and well-balanced personality. List 10 questions you would ask when interviewing applicants for the job.

Continuing Case

Carter Cleaning Company

The Better Interview

Like virtually all the other HR-related activities at Carter Cleaning Centers, the company currently has no organized approach to interviewing job candidates. Store managers, who do almost all the hiring, have a few of their own favorite questions that they ask. But in the absence of any guidance from management, they all admit their interview performance leaves something to be desired. Similarly, Jack Carter himself is admittedly most comfortable dealing with what he calls the "nuts and bolts" machinery aspect of his business and has never felt particularly comfortable having to interview management or other job applicants. Jennifer is sure that this lack of formal interviewing practices, procedures, and training account for some of the employee turnover and theft problems. Therefore, she wants to do something to improve her company's performance in this important area.

Questions

7-20. In general, what can Jennifer do to improve her employee interviewing practices? Should she develop interview forms that list questions for management and nonmanagement jobs? If so, how should these look, and what questions should be included? Should she initiate a computer-based interview approach? If so, why and how?

7-21. Should she implement an interview training program for her managers, and if so, specifically what should be the content of such a training program? In other words, if she did decide to start training her management people to be better interviewers, what should she tell them and how should she tell it to them?

Translating Strategy into HR Policies and Practices Case*,§

The overall map on the page xxxviii of this book outlines the relationships involved.

Improving Performance at the Hotel Paris

The New Interviewing Program

The Hotel Paris's competitive strategy is "To use superior guest service to differentiate the Hotel Paris properties, and to thereby increase the length of stay and return rate of guests, and thus boost revenues and profitability." HR manager Lisa Cruz must now formulate functional policies and activities that support this competitive strategy, by eliciting the required employee behaviors and competencies.

As an experienced HR professional, Lisa knew that the company's new testing program would go only so far. She knew that, at best, employment tests accounted for perhaps 30% of employee performance. It was essential that she and her team design a package of interviews that her hotel managers could use to assess—on an interactive and personal basis—candidates for various positions. It was only in that way that the hotel could hire the sorts of employees whose competencies and behaviors would translate into the kinds of outcomes—such as improved guest services—that the hotel required to achieve its strategic goals.

Lisa received budgetary approval to design a new employee interview system. She and her team started by reviewing the job descriptions and job specifications for the positions of front-desk clerk, assistant manager, security guard, valet, door person, and housekeeper. Focusing on developing structured interviews for each position, the team set about devising interview questions. For example, for the front-desk clerk and assistant manager, they formulated several *behavioral questions*, including, "Tell me about a time when you had to deal with an irate person, and what you did," and "Tell me about a time when you had to deal with several conflicting demands at once, such as having to study for several final exams at the same time, while working. How did you handle the situation?" They also developed a number of *situational questions*, including "Suppose you have a very pushy incoming guest who insists on being checked in at once, while at the same time you're trying to process the check-out for another guest who must be at the airport in 10 minutes. How would you handle the situation?" For these and other positions, they also developed several *job knowledge* questions. For example, for security guard applicants, one question her team created was, "What are the local legal restrictions, if any, regarding using products like Mace if confronted by an unruly person on the hotel grounds?" The team combined the questions into structured interviews for each job, and turned to testing, fine-tuning, and finally using the new system.

Questions

7-22. For the jobs of security guard and valet, develop five additional situational, five behavioral, and five job knowledge questions, with descriptive good/average/poor answers.

7-23. Combine, (based on what you read in this Dessler, *Human Resource Management* chapter) your questions into a complete interview that you would give to someone who must interview candidates for these jobs.

---

§Written by and copyright Gary Dessler, PhD.

Key Terms

unstructured (or nondirective) interview, 195
structured (or directive) interview, 195
situational interview, 196

behavioral interview, 196
job-related interview, 197
stress interview, 197
unstructured sequential interview, 198

structured sequential interview, 198
panel interview, 198
mass interview, 198

candidate-order (or contrast) error, 201
structured situational interview, 204

Endnotes

1. Derek Chapman and David Zweig, "Developing a Nomological Network for Interview Structure: Antecedents and Consequences of the Structured Selection Interview," *Personnel Psychology* 58 (2005), pp. 673–702.

2. Michael McDaniel et al., "The Validity of Employment Interviews: A Comprehensive Review and Meta-Analysis," *Journal of Applied Psychology* 79, no. 4 (1994), p. 599. See also Laura Graves and Ronald Karren, "The Employee Selection Interview: A Fresh Look at an Old Problem," *Human Resource Management* 35, no. 2 (Summer 1996), pp. 163–180. For an argument against holding selection interviews, see D. Heath et al., "Hold the Interview," *Fast Company*, no. 136 (June 2009), pp. 51–52.

3. Therese Macan, "The Employment Interview: A Review of Current Studies and Directions for Future Research," *Human Resource Management Review* 19 (2009), pp. 203–218.

4. Duane Schultz and Sydney Schultz, *Psychology and Work Today* (Upper Saddle River, NJ: Prentice Hall, 1998), p. 830. A study found that interview structure "was best described by four dimensions: questioning consistency, evaluation standardization, question sophistication, and rapport building." Chapman and Zweig, "Developing a Nomological Network."

5. McDaniel et al., "The Validity of Employment Interviews," p. 602.

6. We'll see later in this chapter that there are other ways to "structure" selection interviews. Many of them have nothing to do with using structured guides like these.

7. See also Julia Levashina, Christopher Hartwell, Frederick Morageson, and Michael Campion, "The Structured Employment Interview: Narrative and Quantitative Review of the Research Literature," *Personnel Psychology* 67 (2014), pp. 241–293.

8. Laura Gollub Williamson et al., "Employment Interview on Trial: Linking Interview Structure with Litigation Outcomes," *Journal of Applied Psychology* 82, no. 6 (1996), p. 908. As an

example, the findings of one recent study "demonstrate the value of using highly structured interviews to minimize the potential influence of applicant demographic characteristics on selection decisions." Julie McCarthy, Chad Van Iddekinge, and Michael Campion, "Are Highly Structured Job Interviews Resistant to Demographic Similarity Effects?" *Personnel Psychology* 60, no. 3 (2010), pp. 325–359.

9. Williamson et al., "Employment Interview on Trial."

10. McDaniel et al., "The Validity of Employment Interviews," p. 602.

11. Paul Taylor and Bruce Small, "Asking Applicants What They Would Do Versus What They Did: A Meta-Analytic Comparison of Situational and Past Behavior Employment Interview Questions," *Journal of Occupational and Organizational Psychology* 75, no. 3 (September 2002), pp. 277–295.

12. Margery Weinstein, "You're Hired!" *Training* 48, no. 4, pp. 34–37; www.trainingmag.com/article/you%E2%80%99re-hired, accessed July 19, 2013.

13. Aparna Nancherla, "Anticipated Growth in Behavioral Interviewing," *Training & Development*, April 2008, p. 20.

14. Bill Stoneman, "Matching Personalities with Jobs Made Easier with Behavioral Interviews," *American Banker*, November 30, 2000, p. 8a.

15. Jaineel Aga, "Indian Consulting Interviews - My Experience With Ernst & Young," www.hyperink.com , [Navigation-Books » The Best Book on Getting Consulting Jobs In India » Indian Consulting Interviews - My Experience With Ernst & Young], as accessed on 31 August 2017 at 3pm IST.

16. Subash C Kundu, et al., "Recruitment and Selection Techniques Used in Corporate Sector: Comparative Study of Indian and Multinational Companies," Journal of Organization and Human Behavior, October 2015, pp. 40-50.

17. Martha Frase-Blunt, "Games Interviewers Play," *HR Magazine*, January 2001, pp. 104–114.

18. Kevin Murphy and Charles Davidshofer, *Psychological Testing* (Upper Saddle River,

NJ: Prentice Hall, 2001), pp. 430–431.

19. Marlene Dixon et al., "The Panel Interview: A Review of Empirical Research and Guidelines for Practice," *Public Personnel Management* 31, no. 3 (Fall 2002), pp. 397–429.

20. Ibid. See also M. Ronald Buckley, Katherine A. Jackson, and Mark C. Bolino, "The Influence of Relational Demography on Panel Interview Ratings: A Field Experiment," *Personnel Psychology* 60, no. 3 (Autumn 2007), pp. 627–646.

21. Emily Maltby, "To Find the Best Hires, Firms Become Creative," *Wall Street Journal*, November 17, 2009, p. B6.

22. "Phone Interviews Might Be the Most Telling, Study Finds," *BNA Bulletin to Management*, September 1998, p. 273; and Lisa M. Moynihan et al., "A Longitudinal Study of the Relationships Among Job Search Self-Efficacy, Job Interviews, and Employment Outcomes," *Journal of Business and Psychology* 18, no. 2 (Winter 2003), pp. 207–233. For phone interview job search suggestions, see, for example, Janet Wagner, "Can You Succeed in a Phone Interview?" *Strategic Finance* 91, no. 10 (April 2010), pp. 22, 61.

23. Susan Strauss et al., "The Effects of Videoconference, Telephone, and Face-to-Face Media on Interviewer and Applicant Judgments in Employment Interviews," *Journal of Management* 27, no. 3 (2001), pp. 363–381. If the employer records a video interview with the intention of sharing it with hiring managers who don't participate in the interview, it's advisable to first obtain the candidate's written permission. Matt Bolch, "Lights, Camera … Interview!" *HR Magazine*, March 2007, pp. 99–102.

24. Douglas Rodgers, "Computer-Aided Interviewing Overcomes First Impressions," *Personnel Journal*, April 1987, pp. 148–152; see also Linda Thornburg, "Computer-Assisted Interviewing Shortens Hiring Cycle," *HR Magazine*, February 1998, p. 73ff; and http://interviewstream.com/demorequest?gclid=COyxjOq d36sCFUbs7QodMziuOw, accessed August 22, 2014.

25. "LinkedIn Isn't Just for Hiring Anymore; Useful for Branding, Career Growth as Well," *Bloomberg BNA Bulletin to Management*, August 27, 2013, p. 275.

26. http://interviewstream.com/About, accessed August 22, 2014.

27. Job interviewing apps are also available through Apple's App Store. One is from *Martin's iPhone Apps*. For people seeking technical jobs, this app includes hundreds of potential interview questions, such as brain teasers and algorithms. www.martinreddy.net/iphone/interview, accessed August 21, 2014.

28. Anjali Athavaley, "A Job Interview You Don't Have to Show Up For," *Wall Street Journal*, June 20, 2007, http://online.wsj.com/article/SB118229876637841321.html, accessed April 8, 2011.

29. "Video Interviews Used to Connect with Candidates, Reduce Cost," *Bloomberg BNA Bulletin to Management,* March 11, 2014, p. 78.

30. Matt Mullenweg, "The CEO of Automattic on Holding 'Auditions' to Build a Strong Team," *Harvard Business Review*, April 2014, pp. 39–42.

31. These are quoted or adapted from www.careerfaqs.com.au/getthatjob_video_interview.asp, accessed March 2, 2009.

32. Retrieved on 31 August 2017 from https://www.zinghr.com/.

33. The following is largely quoted or abstracted directly from http://hirevue.com/mobile/, accessed June 25, 2015.

34. www.linkedin.com/company/hirevue, and https://www.linkedin.com/company/hirevue, accessed June 25, 2015.

35. http://learn.hirevue.com/urbanoutfitters-casestudy, accessed June 25, 2015.

36. For example, structured employment interviews using either situational questions or behavioral questions tend to yield high criterion-related validities (.63 versus .47). This is particularly so where the raters can use descriptively anchored rating scale answer sheets; these use short descriptors to illustrate good, average, or poor performance. Taylor and Small, "Asking Applicants What They Would Do Versus What They Did." See also McCarthy et al.,

"Are Highly Structured Job Interviews Resistant to Demographic Similarity Effects?" Some suggest using construct validity to validate employment interviews. Doing so involves showing which constructs (such as conscientiousness) explain interview ratings variations, explaining how these items may relate to job performance, and then testing the statistical relationships. Maria Ambani, Sorin Valcea, and M. Ronald Buckley, "The Relentless Pursuit of Construct Validity in the Design of Employment Interviews," *Human Resource Management Review* 24 (2014), pp. 160–175.

37. Williamson et al., "Employment Interview on Trial," p. 900.

38. Frank Schmidt and Ryan Zimmerman, "A Counterintuitive Hypothesis About Employment Interview Validity and Some Supporting Evidence," *Journal of Applied Psychology* 89, no. 3 (2004), pp. 553–561.

39. This validity discussion and these findings are based on McDaniel et al., "The Validity of Employment Interviews," pp. 607–610; the validities for situational, job-related, and psychological interviews were (.50), (.39), and (.29), respectively.

40. Murray Barrick et al., "Accuracy of Interviewer Judgments of Job Applicant Personality Traits," *Personnel Psychology* 53 (2000), pp. 925–951.

41. McDaniel et al., "The Validity of Employment Interviews," p. 608.

42. Anthony Dalessio and Todd Silverhart, "Combining Biodata Test and Interview Information: Predicting Decisions and Performance Criteria," *Personnel Psychology* 47 (1994), p. 313; and Nora Reilly et al., "Benchmarks Affect Perceptions of Prior Disability in a Structured Interview," *Journal of Business & Psychology* 20, no. 4 (Summer 2006), pp. 489–500.

43. S. W. Constantin, "An Investigation of Information Favorability in the Employment Interview," *Journal of Applied Psychology* 61 (1976), pp. 743–749. It should be noted that a number of the studies discussed in this chapter involve having interviewers evaluate interviews based on written transcripts (rather than face-to-face) and that a study suggests that this procedure may not be equivalent to having interviewers interview applicants directly. See Charles Gorman, William Glover, and Michael Doherty, "Can We Learn Anything About Interviewing Real People from 'Interviews' of Paper People? A Study of the External Validity Paradigm," *Organizational Behavior and Human Performance* 22, no. 2 (October 1978), pp. 165–192;

and Frederick P. Morgeson, Matthew H. Reider, Michael A. Campion, and Rebecca A. Bull, "Review of Research on Age Discrimination in the Employment Interview," *Journal of Business Psychology* 22 (2008), pp. 223–232.

44. David Tucker and Patricia Rowe, "Relationship Between Expectancy, Causal Attribution, and Final Hiring Decisions in the Employment Interview," *Journal of Applied Psychology* 64, no. 1 (February 1979), pp. 27–34. See also Robert Dipboye, Gail Fontenelle, and Kathleen Garner, "Effect of Previewing the Application on Interview Process and Outcomes," *Journal of Applied Psychology* 69, no. 1 (February 1984), pp. 118–128; and Reilly et al., "Benchmarks Affect Perceptions of Prior Disability in a Structured Interview."

45. Anita Chaudhuri, "Beat the Clock: Applying for Job? A New Study Shows That Interviewers Will Make Up Their Minds About You Within a Minute," *The Guardian*, June 14, 2000, pp. 2–6.

46. John Langdale and Joseph Weitz, "Estimating the Influence of Job Information on Interviewer Agreement," *Journal of Applied Psychology* 57 (1973), pp. 23–27.

47. R. E. Carlson, "Effect of Applicant Sample on Ratings of Valid Information in an Employment Setting," *Journal of Applied Psychology* 54 (1970), pp. 217–222.

48. R. E. Carlson, "Selection Interview Decisions: The Effect of Interviewer Experience, Relative Quota Situation, and Applicant Sample on Interview Decisions," *Personnel Psychology* 20 (1967), pp. 259–280.

49. See, for example, Scott T. Fleischmann, "The Messages of Body Language in Job Interviews," *Employee Relations* 18, no. 2 (Summer 1991), pp. 161–166; James Westphal and Ithai Stern, "Flattery Will Get You Everywhere (Especially If You're a Male Caucasian): How Ingratiation, Board Room Behavior, and a Demographic Minority Status Affect Additional Board Appointments at U.S. Companies," *Academy of Management Journal* 50, no. 2 (2007), pp. 267–288.

50. David Caldwell and Jerry Burger, "Personality Characteristics of Job Applicants and Success in Screening Interviews," *Personnel Psychology* 51 (1998), pp. 119–136.

51. Amy Kristof-Brown et al., "Applicant Impression Management: Dispositional Influences and Consequences for Recruiter Perceptions of Fit and Similarity," *Journal of Management* 28, no. 1 (2002), pp. 27–46. See

also Lynn McFarland et al., "Impression Management Use and Effectiveness Across Assessment Methods," *Journal of Management* 29, no. 5 (2003), pp. 641–661.

52. Timothy DeGroot and Janaki Gooty, "Can Nonverbal Cues Be Used to Make Meaningful Personality Attributions in Employment Interviews?" *Journal of Business Psychology* 24 (2009), p. 179.

53. Richard Posthuma, Frederick Morgeson, and Michael Campion, "Beyond Employment Interview Validity: A Comprehensive Narrative Review of Recent Research and Trends Over Time," *Personnel Psychology*, 2002, 55, pp. 1–87.

54. C. K. Stevens and A. L. Kristof, "Making the Right Impression: A Field Study of Applicant Impression Management During Interviews," *Journal of Applied Psychology* 80, pp. 587–606; Schultz and Schultz, *Psychology and Work Today*, p. 82. See also Jay Stuller, "Fatal Attraction," *Across the Board* 42, no. 6 (November/December 2005), pp. 18–23. See also Allen Huffcutt et al., "Understanding Applicant Behavior in Employment Interviews: A Theoretical Model of Interviewee Performance," *Human Resource Management Review* 20, no. 1 (2011), pp. 350–367.

55. Chad Higgins and Timothy Judge, "The Effect of Applicant Influence Tactics on Recruiter Perceptions of Fit and Hiring Recommendations: A Field Study," *Journal of Applied Psychology* 89, no. 4 (2004), pp. 622–632. Some researchers in this area question results like these. The problem is that much of the interviewing research uses students as raters and hypothetical jobs, so it's not clear that we can apply the findings to the real world. For example, see Frederick P. Morgeson, Matthew H. Reider, Michael A. Campion, and Rebecca A. Bull, "Review of Research on Age Discrimination in the Employment Interview," *Journal of Business Psychology* 22 (2008), pp. 223–232.

56. Brian Swider et al., "Managing and Creating an Image in the Interview: The Role of Interviewee Initial Impressions," *Journal of Applied Psychology* 96, no. 6 (2011), pp. 1275–1288.

57. See, for example, Madeline Heilmann and Lois Saruwatari, "When Beauty Is Beastly: The Effects of Appearance and Sex on Evaluations of Job Applicants for Managerial and Nonmanagerial Jobs," *Organizational Behavior and Human Performance* 23 (June 1979), pp. 360–372; and Cynthia Marlowe, Sandra Schneider, and Carnot

Nelson, "Gender and Attractiveness Biases in Hiring Decisions: Are More Experienced Managers Less Biased?" *Journal of Applied Psychology* 81, no. 1 (1996), pp. 11–21.

58. Marlowe et al., "Gender and Attractiveness Biases," p. 11.

59. Allen Huffcutt and Philip Roth, "Racial Group Differences in Employment Interview Evaluations," *Journal of Applied Psychology* 83, no. 2 (1998), pp. 179–189.

60. Eden King and Afra Ahmad, "An Experimental Field Study of Interpersonal Discrimination Toward Muslim Job Applicants," *Personnel Psychology* 63, no. 4 (2010), pp. 881–906.

61. Addrec Solutions: Building Capabilities for Growth, 9B14M124, 2015, as accessed on September 26, 2017 from https://www.iveycases.com/ProductView.aspx?id=66080.

62. Paul Attewell and Sukhadeo Thorat, 'The Legacy of Social Exclusion,' *Economic and Political Weekly*, Volume 42, Issue 41, October 2007.

63. Retrieved on 31 August 2017 from http://ncsc.nic.in/files/ncsc/new6/264.pdf (Chapter 4, page 144).

64. N. S. Miceli et al., "Potential Discrimination in Structured Employment Interviews," *Employee Responsibilities and Rights* 13, no. 1 (March 2001), pp. 15–38.

65. Andrea Rodriguez and Fran Prezant, "Better Interviews for People with Disabilities," *Workforce*, www.workforce.com, accessed November 14, 2003.

66. Juan Madera and Michele Hebl, "Discrimination Against Facially Stigmatized Applicants in Interviews: An Eye Tracking and Face-to-Face Investigation," *Journal of Applied Psychology* 97, no. 2, pp. 317–330.

67. Monowar Mahmood, "National Culture Versus Corporate Culture: Employee Recruitment and Selection Practices of Multinationals in a Developing Country Context," *Journal of International Management Studies* 11, no. 1 (Jan. 2011), p. 110. Published by International Academy of Business and Economics, www.iabe.org/domains/iabeX/journal.aspx?journalid=16, accessed July 19, 2013.

68. Arthur Pell, "Nine Interviewing Pitfalls," *Managers Magazine*, January 1994, p. 20.

69. Thomas Dougherty, Daniel Turban, and John Callender, "Confirming First Impressions in the Employment Interview: A Field Study of Interviewer Behavior," *Journal of Applied Psychology* 79, no. 5 (1994), p. 663.

70. See Pell, "Nine Interviewing Pitfalls," p. 29; Parth Sarathi, "Making Selection Interviews Effective," *Management and Labor Studies* 18, no. 1 (1993), pp. 5–7.

71. Posthuma, Morgeson, and Campion, "Beyond Employment Interview Validity," pp. 1–87.

72. Pell, "Nine Interviewing Pitfalls," p. 30; quote from Alan M. Saks and Julie M. McCarthy, "Effects of Discriminatory Interview Questions and Gender on Applicant Reactions," *Journal of Business and Psychology* 21, no. 2 (Winter 2006), p. 175.

73. This section is based on Elliot Pursell et al., "Structured Interviewing," *Personnel Journal* 59 (November 1980), pp. 907–912; and G. Latham et al., "The Situational Interview," *Journal of Applied Psychology* 65 (1980), pp. 422–427. See also Michael Campion, Elliott Pursell, and Barbara Brown, "Structured Interviewing: Raising the Psychometric Properties of the Employment Interview," *Personnel Psychology* 41 (1988), pp. 25–42; and Paul R. Bernthal, "Recruitment and Selection," www.ddi-world.com/DDIWorld/media/trend-research/recruitment-and-selection_ere_es_ddi.pdf?ext=.pdf, accessed October 10, 2011. For a recent approach, see K. G. Melchers et al., "Is More Structure Really Better? A Comparison of Frame-of-Reference Training and Descriptively Anchored Rating Scales to Improve Interviewers' Rating Quality," *Personnel Psychology* 64, no. 1 (2011), pp. 53–87.

74. Taylor and Small, "Asking Applicants What They Would Do Versus What They Did." Structured employment interviews using either situational questions or behavioral questions tend to yield high validities. However, structured interviews with situational question formats yield the higher ratings. This may be because interviewers get more consistent (reliable) responses with situational questions (which force all applicants to apply the same scenario) than they do with behavioral questions (which require each applicant to find applicable experiences). However, there is some evidence that for higher-level positions, situational question–based interviews are inferior to behavioral question–based ones, possibly because the situations are "just too simple to allow any real differentiation among candidates for higher level positions." Allen Huffcutt et al., "Comparison of Situational and Behavioral Description Interview Questions for Higher Level Positions," *Personnel Psychology* 54, no. 3 (2001), p. 619.

75. See Phillip Lowry, "The Structured Interview: An Alternative to the Assessment Center?" *Public Personnel Management* 23, no. 2 (Summer 1994), pp. 201–215. See also Todd Maurer and Jerry Solamon, "The Science and Practice of a Structured Employment Interview Coaching Program," *Personnel Psychology* 59, no. 2 (Summer 2006), pp. 433–456.

76. Pursell et al., "Structured Interviewing," p. 910.

77. From a speech by industrial psychologist Paul Green and contained in *BNA Bulletin to Management*, June 20, 1985, pp. 2–3. For additional practical guidance see, for example, www.state.gov/documents/organization/107843.pdf, accessed October 10, 2012.

78. Williamson et al., "Employment Interview on Trial," p. 901; Michael Campion, David Palmer, and James Campion, "A Review of Structure in the Selection Interview," *Personnel Psychology* 50 (1997), pp. 655–702. See also Maurer and Solamon, "The Science and Practice of a Structured Employment Interview."

79. Unless otherwise specified, the following are based on Williamson et al., "Employment Interview on Trial," pp. 901–902.

80. Campion, Palmer, and Campion, "A Review of Structure," p. 668.

81. Carlson, "Selection Interview Decisions."

82. Pamela Kaul, "Interviewing Is Your Business," *Association Management*, November 1992, p. 29. See also Nancy Woodward, "Asking for Salary Histories," *HR Magazine*, February 2000, pp. 109–112. Gathering information about specific interview dimensions such as social ability, responsibility, and independence (as is often done with structured interviews) can improve interview accuracy, at least for more complicated jobs. See also Andrea Poe, "Graduate Work: Behavioral Interviewing Can Tell You If an Applicant Just Out of College Has Traits Needed for the Job," *HR Magazine* 48, no. 10 (October 2003), pp. 95–96.

83. Edwin Walley, "Successful Interviewing Techniques," *The CPA Journal* 63 (September 1993), p. 70; and Randy Myers, "Interviewing Techniques: Tips from the Pros," *Journal of Accountancy* 202, no. 2 (August 2006), pp. 53–55.

84. Laszlo Bock, *Work Rules!* (New York: Twelve, 2015), pp. 93–94.

85. Catherine Middendorf and Therese Macan, "Note Taking in the Employment Interview: Effects on Recall and Judgment," *Journal of Applied Psychology* 87, no. 2 (2002), pp. 293–303.

86. Kristen Weirick, "The Perfect Interview," HR Magazine, April 1, 2008, p. 85.

87. Stephen Gilliland et al., "Improving Applicants' Reactions to Rejection Letters: An Application of Fairness Theory," *Personnel Psychology* 54 (2001), pp. 669–703.

88. See, for example, Gary Dessler, *Winning Commitment* (New York: McGraw-Hill, 1993).

89. "Toyota Looking for 1,500 Outstanding Mississippians from All Backgrounds," www.Mississippi.org/press-room/Toyota-looking-for-1500, accessed February 17, 2014.

90. "Toyota Hiring Process," www.indeed.com/forum/cmp/Toyota/Toyota-Hiring-Process/t31886, accessed August 22, 2014.

91. Bock, *Work Rules!*, pp. 87–127.

92. www.Shrm.org/template-tools/how-to-guides, accessed March 3, 2012.

93. Kris Maher, "New High-Tech Recruiting Tools: Unicycles, Yahtzee and Silly Putty," *Wall Street Journal*, June 6, 2000, p. B14; see also Paul McNamara, "Extreme Interview," *Network World*, June 25, 2001, p. 65.

94. Tim Barker, "Corporate Espionage Takes Center Stage with Boeing Revelation," *Knight Ridder/Tribune Business News*, June 15, 2003.

95. Ibid.

96. See, for example, the classic, excellent discussion of job hunting and interviewing in Richard Payne, *How to Get a Better Job Quickly* (New York: New American Library, 1979).

Appendix 1 for Chapter 7

Structured Interview Guide

STEP 1—Create a Structured Interview Guide

Instructions:
First, here in step 1, create a structured interview guide like this one (including a competency definition, a lead question, and benchmark examples and answers, for instance) *for each of the job's required competencies*:

Competency: Interpersonal Skills

De☒nition:
Shows understanding, courtesy, tact, empathy, concern; develops and maintains relationships; may deal with people who are dif☒cult, hostile, distressed; relates well to people from varied backgrounds and situations; is sensitive to individual differences.

Lead Questions:
Describe a situation in which you had to deal with people who were upset about a problem. What specific actions did you take? What was the outcome or result?

Benchmark Level	Level De☒nition	Level Examples
5	Establishes and maintains ongoing working relationships with management, other employees, internal or external stakeholders, or customers. Remains courteous when discussing information or eliciting highly sensitive or controversial information from people who are reluctant to give it. Effectively handles situations involving a high degree of tension or discomfort involving people who are demonstrating a high degree of hostility or distress.	Presents controversial ☒ndings tactfully to irate organization senior management of☒cials regarding shortcomings of a newly installed computer system, software programs, and associated equipment.
4		Mediates disputes concerning system design/ architecture, the nature and capacity of data management systems, system resources allocations, or other equally controversial/sensitive matters.
3	Cooperates and works well with management, other employees, or customers, on short-term assignments. Remains courteous when discussing information or eliciting moderately sensitive or controversial information from people who are hesitant to give it. Effectively handles situations involving a moderate degree of tension or discomfort involving people who are demonstrating a moderate degree of hostility or distress.	Courteously and tactfully delivers effective instruction to frustrated customers. Provides technical advice to customers and the public on various types of IT such as communication or security systems, data management procedures or analysis.
2		Familiarizes new employees with administrative procedures and of☒ce systems.
1	Cooperates and works well with management, other employees, or customers during brief interactions. Remains courteous when discussing information or eliciting non-sensitive or non-controversial information from people who are willing to give it. Effectively handles situations involving little or no tension, discomfort, hostility, or distress.	Responds courteously to customers' general inquiries. Greets and assists visitors attending a meeting within own organization.

FIGURE 7A-1 **Structured Interview Guide**

Source: From Conducting Effective Structured Interviews Resource Guide for Hiring Managers and Supervisors, 2005, United States Department of State Bureau of Human Resources.

STEP 2—INDIVIDUAL EVALUATION FORM

Instructions:
Next, in step 2, create a form for evaluating each job candidate on each of the job's competencies:

Candidate to be assessed: _____

Date of Interview:_____

Competency: Problem Solving

Definition:
Identifies problems; determines accuracy and relevance of information; uses sound judgment to generate and evaluate alternatives, and to make the recommendations.

Question:
Describe a situation in which you identified a problem and evaluated the alternatives to make a recommendation or decision. What was the problem and who was affected?

Probes:
How did you generate and evaluate your alternatives? What was the outcome?

Describe specific behaviors observed: (Use back of sheet, if necessary)

1–Low	2	3–Average	4	5–Outstanding
Uses logic to identify alternatives to solve routine problems. Reacts to and solves problems by gathering and applying information from standard materials or sources that provide a limited number of alternatives.		Uses logic to identify alternatives to solve moderately difficult problems. Identifies and solves problems by gathering and applying information from a variety of materials or sources that provide several alternatives.		Uses logic to identify alternatives to solve complex or sensitive problems. Anticipates problems and identifies and evaluates potential sources of information and generates alternatives to solve problems where standards do not exist.

Final Evaluation:	Printed Name:	Signature:

FIGURE 7A-1 *Continued*

STEP 3—PANEL CONSENSUS EVALUATION FORM

Instructions:
Finally, in step 3, create a panel consensus evaluation form like this one, which the members of the panel who interviewed the candidate will use to evaluate his or her interview performance.

Candidate: _____

Date:_____

Panel Consensus Evaluation Form

Instructions:
Translate each individual evaluation for each competency onto this form. If all of the individual competency evaluations are within one rating scale point, enter the average of the evaluations in the column labeled Group Evaluation. If more than one point separates any two raters, a consensus discussion must occur with each party justifying his/her evaluation. The lead interviewer or his/her designee should take notes on the consensus discussion in the space provided. Any changes in evaluation should be initialed and a final evaluation entered for each competency.

Competency	Final Individual Evaluations			Group Evaluation
	(1)	(2)	(3)	
Interpersonal Skills				
Self-Management				
Reasoning				
Decision Making				
Problem Solving				
Oral Communication				
Total Score				

Consensus Discussion Notes:

Signature Panel Member 1: _____

Signature Panel Member 2: _____

Signature Panel Member 3: _____

FIGURE 7A-1 *Continued*

CHAPTER 7

Appendix 2 for Chapter 7

Interview Guide for Interviewees

Before managers move into positions where they have to interview others, they usually must navigate some interviews themselves. It's therefore useful to apply some of what we discussed in this chapter to navigating one's own interviews.

Beyond trying to determine how you would perform the technical parts of the job, interviewers will try to discover what you are like as a person. In other words, how you get along with other people and your desire to work. They will look here at how you behave. For example, they will note whether you respond concisely, cooperate fully in answering questions, state personal opinions when relevant, and keep to the subject at hand; these are very important elements in influencing the interviewer's decision.

There are six things to do to get an extra edge in the interview.[96]

1. *Preparation is essential.* Before the interview, learn all you can about the employer, the job, and the people doing the recruiting. On the Web, using social media, or looking through business periodicals, find out what is happening in the employer's field. Try to unearth the employer's problems. Be ready to explain why you think you would be able to solve such problems, citing some of your *specific accomplishments* to make your case.

2. *Uncover the interviewer's real needs.* Spend as little time as possible briefly answering your interviewer's first questions and as much time as possible getting him or her to describe his or her needs. Determine what the person is expecting to accomplish, and the type of person he or she feels is needed. Use open-ended questions such as, "Could you tell me more about that?"

3. *Relate yourself to the interviewer's needs.* Once you know the type of person your interviewer is looking for and the sorts of problems he or she wants solved, you are in a good position to describe

your own accomplishments *in terms of the interviewer's needs.* Start by saying something like, "One of the problem areas you've said is important to you is similar to a problem I once faced." Then state the problem, describe your solution, and reveal the results.

4. *Think before answering.* Answering a question should be a three-step process: Pause—Think—Speak. *Pause* to make sure you understand what the interviewer is driving at, *think* about how to structure your answer, and then *speak.* In your answer, try to emphasize how hiring you will help the interviewer solve his or her problem.

5. *Remember that appearance and enthusiasm are important.* Appropriate clothing, good grooming, a firm handshake, and energy are important. Maintain eye contact. In addition, speak with enthusiasm, nod agreement, and remember to take a moment to frame your answer (pause, think, speak) so that you sound articulate and fluent.

6. *Make a good first impression.* Remember that in most cases interviewers make up their minds about the applicant early in the interview. A good first impression may turn to bad during the interview, but it's unlikely. Bad first impressions are almost impossible to overcome. Experts suggest paying attention to the following key interviewing considerations:

- Appropriate clothing
- Good grooming
- A firm handshake
- The appearance of controlled energy
- Pertinent humor and readiness to smile
- A genuine interest in the employer's operation and alert attention when the interviewer speaks
- Pride in past performance
- An understanding of the employer's needs and a desire to serve them

8

Training and Developing Employees

LEARNING OBJECTIVES

8-1 Summarize the purpose and process of employee orientation.

8-2 Give an example of how to design onboarding to improve employee engagement.

8-3 List and briefly explain each of the steps in the training process.

8-4 Explain how to use five training techniques.

8-5 List and briefly discuss four management development methods.

8-6 List and briefly discuss the importance of the steps in leading organizational change.

8-7 Explain why a controlled study may be superior for evaluating the training program's effects.

Mahindra Finance is a non banking financial company (NBFC), and it serves predominantly rural and semi-urban customers. With employee strength of more than 15,000 spread across India, providing Learning and Development (L&D) to a large group of field employees was a challenge. It was also observed that attrition was also high among them. Classroom-based training was time consuming and costly with limited reach. An internal study also indicated that most employees had access to mobile phones. In order to impart the required training to its staff, Mahindra Finance required coaching modules which were attractive and could be accessed anywhere.[1] We'll see what Mahindra Finance did to train its employees.

WHERE ARE WE NOW ...

Chapters 6 and 7 focused on the methods managers use to interview and select employees. Once employees are on board, the employer must train them. The purpose of this chapter is to increase your effectiveness in training employees. The main topics we'll cover include orienting employees, designing onboarding to improve employee engagement, the training process, analyzing training needs, implementing training and development programs, and evaluating the training effort. Then, in Chapter 9, we'll turn to appraising employees.

employee orientation
A procedure for providing new employees with basic background information about the firm.

Orienting and Onboarding New Employees

Carefully selecting employees doesn't guarantee they'll perform effectively. Even high-potential employees can't do their jobs if they don't know what to do or how to do it. Making sure your employees do know what to do and how to do it is the purpose of orientation and training. The human resources department usually designs the orientation and training programs, but the supervisor does most of the day-to-day orienting and training. Every manager therefore should know how to orient and train employees. We will start with orientation.

The Purposes of Employee Orientation/Onboarding

Employee orientation (or *onboarding*) provides new employees with the basic background information (such as computer passwords and company rules) they need to do their jobs; ideally it should also help them start becoming emotionally attached to and engaged in the firm.[2] The manager wants to accomplish four things when orienting new employees:

1. Make the new employee feel welcome and at home and part of the team.
2. Make sure the new employee has the basic information to function effectively, such as e-mail access, personnel policies and benefits, and expectations in terms of work behavior.
3. Help the new employee understand the organization in a broad sense (its past, present, culture, and strategies and vision of the future).
4. Start socializing the person into the firm's culture and ways of doing things.[3] Delhi Metro Rail Corporation Limited (DMRC) organizes an intensive orientation program for new recruits and trainee coach drivers to make them understand the organization's various roles and responsibilities. The in-house training institute is located in Shastri Park, New Delhi. During the induction program, the top leadership of DMRC regularly interacts with trainees to impress upon the unique culture and mission of the corporation.

The Orientation Process

The length of the orientation program depends on what you cover. Most take several hours. The human resource specialist (or, in smaller firms, the office manager) performs the first part of the orientation by explaining basic matters like working hours and benefits. Then the supervisor continues the orientation by explaining the department's organization, introducing the person to his or her new colleagues, familiarizing him or her with the workplace, and reducing first-day jitters. At a minimum, the orientation should provide information on matters such as employee benefits, personnel policies, safety measures and regulations, and a facilities tour;[4] new employees should receive (and sign for) print or Internet-based employee handbooks covering such matters. At the other extreme, the beauty company L'Oreal's onboarding program takes about 2 years. It includes special training and roundtable discussions, meetings with key insiders, on-the-job learning, individual mentoring, and special experiences such as site visits.[5] Indian mass footwear manufacturer, VKC Industries, has designed a six-month orientation program for the newly hired management trainees (MT). The MTs are exposed to the company culture and philosophy, the basics of footwear design and manufacturing, the management processes followed, and regulations. They are introduced to different supply chain partners. Under the mentorship of senior management, trainees work on variety of projects and visit different manufacturing locations and markets during this induction period. You'll find a variety of orientation checklists online.[6]

Supervisors should be vigilant. Follow up on and encourage new employees to engage in activities (such as taking breaks with colleagues) that will enable them to "learn the ropes." Especially for new employees with disabilities, integration and socialization are highly influenced by coworkers' and supervisors' behavior.[7]

THE EMPLOYEE HANDBOOK   The U.S. courts may find that the employee handbook's contents are legally binding commitments. Irrespective of this, it is necessary that new employees are given adequate information about terms and conditions of work. Even apparently sensible handbook policies (such as "the company will not retaliate against employees who raise concerns about important issues in the workplace") can backfire without the proper disclaimers because over time, the organization may have to change/modify/alter conditions of employment. The handbook should include a disclaimer stating "nothing in this handbook should be taken as creating a binding contract between employer and employees, and all employment is on an at will basis."[8] Say that statements of company policies, benefits, and regulations do not constitute the terms and conditions of an employment contract, either expressed or implied.

ORIENTATION TECHNOLOGY   Employers use technology to support orientation. For example, at the University of Cincinnati, new employees spend about 45 minutes online learning about their new employer's mission, organization, and policies and procedures. IBM uses virtual environments like Second Life to support orientation, particularly for employees abroad. The new employees choose virtual avatars, for instance, to learn how to enroll for benefits.[9] ION Geophysical uses an online onboarding portal solution called RedCarpet. It includes a streaming video welcome message, and photos and profiles of new colleagues.[10] With Workday's iPhone app, users can search their company's directory for names, images, and contact information; call or e-mail coworkers directly; and view physical addresses on Google Maps.[11] Some employers place scannable QR codes along the orientation tour's stops, to provide information about each department and its role.[12] Other companies "gamify" onboarding, for instance, by offering rewards and recognition for new hires' contributions.[13]

LEARNING OBJECTIVE 8-2

Give an example of how to design onboarding to improve employee engagement.

Employee Engagement Guide for Managers: Onboarding at Toyota

In many firms today, orientation goes well beyond providing basic information about things like work hours.[14] Onboarding at Toyota Motor Manufacturing USA illustrates this. While it does cover routine topics such as company benefits, its main aim is to engage Toyota's new employees in the firm's ideology of quality, teamwork, personal development, open communication, and mutual respect.[15] The initial program takes about 4 days:[16]

Day 1: The first day begins early and includes an overview of the program, a welcome to the company, and a discussion of the firm's organizational structure and human resource department by the firm's human resources vice president. He or she devotes about an hour and a half to discussing Toyota history and culture, and about 2 hours to employee benefits. Managers then spend several hours discussing Toyota's commitment to quality and teamwork.

Day 2: A typical second day focuses first on the importance of mutual respect, teamwork, and open communication at Toyota. The rest of the day covers topics such as safety, environmental affairs, and the Toyota production system.

Day 3: Given the importance of working in teams at Toyota, this day begins with 2 ½ to 3 hours devoted to communication training, such as "making requests and giving feedback." The rest of the day covers matters such as Toyota's problem-solving methods, quality assurance, hazard communications, and safety.

Day 4: Topics today include teamwork training and the Toyota suggestion system. This session also covers what work teams are responsible for and how to work together as a team. The afternoon session covers fire prevention and fire extinguisher training. By the end of day 4, new employees should be well on their way to being engaged in Toyota's ideology, in particular its mission of quality and its values of teamwork, continuous improvement, and problem-solving.[17]

Lately, Bank of Baroda (BoB) has started directly recruiting many officers at the senior management level, to meet its requirements in specialized areas of banking. Such officers go through a structured orientation program consisting of meetings or discussions with leaders, self learning, and interaction with different departments. The bottom line is that there's more to orienting employees than introducing them to new coworkers. Even without a program like Toyota's, use the onboarding opportunity to start instilling in the new employee the company values and traditions in which you expect the person to become engaged.

Overview of the Training Process

LEARNING OBJECTIVE 8-3

List and briefly explain each of the steps in the training process.

Directly after orientation, training should begin. **Training** means giving new or current employees the skills that they need to perform their jobs, such as showing new salespeople how to sell your product. Training might involve having the current job-holder explain the job to the new hire, or multi-week classroom or Internet classes. In one recent year, employers spent about $1,208 per employee on training.[18]

Training is important. If even high-potential employees don't know what to do and how to do it, they will improvise or do nothing useful at all. Furthermore, by one estimate, about three-fourths of 30-something-aged high achievers begin looking for new positions within a year of starting, often due to dissatisfaction with inadequate training.[19] Employers also increasingly capitalize on the fact that training fosters engagement. For instance, Coca Cola India has a development program called Catalyst which grooms senior-level managers to take up higher positions in the organization. This training program consists of on-the-job training as well as formal classroom training.[20]

Important though it is, training can't work miracles. To paraphrase Google's head of "People Operations" (HR), there are two ways to build a great workforce. One is to hire top performers (what he calls "90th percentile performers"), and the other is to hire average performers and then use training to try to make them 90th percentilers.[21] He found the former approach worked best for Google.

KNOW YOUR EMPLOYMENT LAW

Training and the Law

Managers should understand the legal implications of their training-related decisions. Various Indian legislations and regulators mandate that employees are adequately trained. For example, the Reserve Bank of India, which is the banking sector regulator, regularly intimates banks operating in the country to organize training programs for employees in areas like risk management, compliance, etc. Similarly, the Companies Act of 2013 also mandates that directors on the board of a firm, including independent directors, are trained in governance related topics.

negligent training
A situation where an employer fails to train adequately, and the employee subsequently harms a third party.

Inadequate training can also expose the employer to liability for **negligent training**. Among other things, the employer should confirm the applicant/employee's claims of skill and experience, provide adequate training (particularly where employees work with dangerous equipment), and evaluate the training to ensure that it is actually reducing risks.[22] ■

Aligning Strategy and Training

The employer's strategic plans should govern its training goals.[23] In essence, the task is to identify the employee behaviors the firm will need to execute its strategy, and then from that deduce what competencies (for instance, skills and knowledge) employees will need. Then, put in place training goals and programs to instill these competencies.[24] For example, with the health-care landscape in America changing fast, the Walgreens chain had to reformulate its strategy. It broadened its offerings, and today is the second-largest dispenser of flu shots in the United States. Its in-store health clinics provide medical care. It purchased drugstore.com.

Strategic changes like these affected the skills that Walgreens employees required, and therefore its training and other staffing policies. For example, Walgreens established Walgreens University. It offers more than 400 programs that Walgreens employees can take to build their skills (and even get college credit in pharmacy-related topics). For example, some programs develop assistant store manager skills, and Walgreens in-store health clinic nurse practitioners can take courses that expand their medical care expertise. Another example is Larsen and Toubro Limited (L&T) which created L&T Management Development Center to oversee all its training and development programs. Similarly, at Caterpillar University, the company executives set the university's policies and oversee the alignment of the corporation's learning needs with the enterprise's business strategy.[25] Training and development executives at Kelly Services Inc. meet periodically with the company's senior executives to "identify new priorities and relocate training dollars as needed, based on the strategic needs of the business".[26]

▶ **IMPROVING PERFORMANCE:** *The Strategic Context*

Unique Training Design of Mahindra Finance (MMFSL)

Mahindra and Mahindra Financial Services Limited (MMFSL) is a leading NBFC, which focuses on providing financing support in rural and semi-urban centers of India. MMFSL has more than 1,200 offices across the country, and it was awarded the Aon Hewitt Best Employer Award in 2017.[27]

Mahindra Finance has an employee strength of around 15,000 people, and a majority of them are stationed in the rural and semi-urban areas. The average age of MMFSL's employees is 25 years, and work required them to travel 100–150 kms each day, on two wheelers. The challenge before the firm was to provide employees with uniform and regular training inputs. Regular classroom-based training was not feasible due to the mobile nature of their work.

The top leadership and the HR department of MMFSL realized the need for a new approach. The HR team conducted a research and found that the young field force had distinct interests and learning styles. All of them were using smartphones, and they were fond of music, movies, and short audio /video clips. The employees were also emotionally connected to their two wheelers (motor bikes).

Thus, the company introduced a unique learning solution in the form of short audio clips, designed on the lines of popular TV series. The programs could be shared over WhatsApp and other social media platforms. The technique allowed employees to access the learning files at their convenience. Using this method, the company could reach 8,000 employees at once. The audio messages were supported by info-graphics and group discussions, using the technology platform.

After the success of the first module, MMFSL launched more programs in the same mode. ■

Source: Based on Shalini Sengupta "How Mahindra Finance Bear Attrition with Sopar Opera Style Learning," *People Matters,* July 18, 2017.

The ADDIE Five-Step Training Process
The employer should use a rational training process. The gold standard here is still the basic analysis-design-develop-implement-evaluate (ADDIE) training process model that training experts have used for years.[28] As an example, one training vendor describes its training process as follows:[29]

- *Analyze* the training need.
- *Design* the overall training program.
- *Develop* the course (actually assembling/creating the training materials).
- *Implement* training, by actually training the targeted employee group using methods such as on-the-job or online training.
- *Evaluate* the course's effectiveness.

We'll look at each step next.

Conducting the Training Needs Analysis

The training needs analysis may address the employer's *strategic/longer term* training needs and/or its *current* training needs.

STRATEGIC TRAINING NEEDS ANALYSIS Strategic goals (perhaps to enter new lines of business or to expand abroad) often mean the firm will have to fill new jobs. *Strategic training needs analysis* identifies the training employees will need to fill these future jobs. For example, when Cummins Generator Technologies India decided to build a new high technology green plant at Rangaon in Pune, the firm's top management knew that the plant's employees would need new skills to run the machines and work in the green environment. They worked closely with their HR team to formulate hiring policies which included recruiting employees from the nearby villages and conducting training programs to ensure that the firm would have the human resources required to populate the new plant.

CURRENT TRAINING NEEDS ANALYSIS Most training efforts aim to improve current performance—specifically training new employees, and those whose performance is deficient.

How you analyze current training needs depends on whether you're training new or current employees. The main task for *new* employees is to determine what the job entails and to break it down into subtasks, each of which you then teach to the new employee.

Analyzing *current* employees' training needs is more complex, because you must also ascertain whether training is the solution. For example, performance may be down due to poor motivation. Managers use *task analysis* to identify new employees' training needs, and *performance analysis* to identify current employees' training needs.

TASK ANALYSIS FOR ANALYZING NEW EMPLOYEES' TRAINING NEEDS Particularly with lower-level workers, it's customary to hire inexperienced personnel and train them. The aim here is to give these new employees the skills and knowledge they need to do the job. **Task analysis** is a detailed study of the job to determine what specific skills (like reading spreadsheets for a clerk) the job requires. For task analysis, job descriptions and job specifications are essential. They list the job's specific duties and skills, which are the basic reference points in determining the training required. Managers also uncover training needs by reviewing performance standards, performing the job, and questioning current jobholders and their supervisors.[30]

Some managers supplement the job description and specification with a *task analysis record form*. This form (see Table 8-1) consolidates information regarding required tasks and skills. As Table 8-1 illustrates, the form contains six columns of information, such as "Skills or knowledge required."

task analysis
A detailed study of a job to identify the specific skills required.

competency model
A graphic model that consolidates, usually in one diagram, a precise overview of the competencies (the knowledge, skills, and behaviors) someone would need to do a job well.

COMPETENCY PROFILES AND MODELS IN TRAINING AND DEVELOPMENT The **competency model** consolidates, usually in one diagram, a precise overview of the competencies someone would need to do the job well. Figure 4-10 (on page 116) was one example.

Many employers therefore design their training programs to foster these competencies. For example, the American Society for Training and Development (ASTD) built a competencies model for the job of training and development professional. It includes 10 core trainer competencies, including *being able to achieve performance improvement, instructional design,* and *training delivery.* Training a trainer would thus require, for instance, making sure he or she could, once training is complete, exhibit these skills and knowledge (competencies).[31] The Indian Society of Training and Development (ISTD) offers an 18-month diploma in Training and Development, which is recognized by the government of India (See http://www.istd.co.in/diploma). The course has eight theory papers and an internship that fulfills the competency requirements of training/HRD professionals. Employers are increasingly focusing on building work-related competencies or skills. For example, AT&T provides its employees with short "mini-degrees." These show readiness for specific jobs.[32]

With many competency-oriented training programs, trainees don't learn just by taking classes but through a mix of real-world exercises, teamwork, and online resources, under a learning coach; the aim is to show mastery of particular competencies.[33] For example, some college degrees in the US start with a list of competencies to be learned, criteria for assessing competencies mastery, and examples of the competencies (such as using a spreadsheet). Students then complete their projects and have their competencies evaluated.

performance analysis
Verifying that there is a performance deficiency and determining whether that deficiency should be corrected through training or through some other means (such as transferring the employee).

PERFORMANCE ANALYSIS: ANALYZING CURRENT EMPLOYEES' TRAINING NEEDS For underperforming current employees, you can't assume that training is the solution. In other words, is it lack of training, or something else? **Performance analysis** is the process of verifying that there is a performance deficiency and determining whether the employer should correct such deficiencies through training or some other means (like transferring the employee).

TABLE 8-1 Sample Task Analysis Record Form

	Task List	When and How Often Performed	Quantity and Quality of Performance	Conditions Under Which Performed	Skills or Knowledge Required	Where Best Learned
1.	Operate paper cutter	4 times per day		Noisy pressroom: distractions		
1.1	Start motor	4 times per day				On the job
1.2	Set cutting distance		± tolerance of 0.007 in.		Read gauge	On the job
1.3	Place paper on cutting table		Must be completely even to prevent uneven cut		Lift paper correctly	On the job
1.4	Push paper up to cutter				Must be even	On the job
1.5	Grasp safety release with left hand		100% of time, for safety		Essential for safety	On the job but practice first with no distractions
1.6	Grasp cutter release with right hand				Must keep both hands on releases	On the job but practice first with no distractions
1.7	Simultaneously pull safety release with left hand and cutter release with right hand				Must keep both hands on releases	On the job but practice first with no distractions
1.8	Wait for cutter to retract		100% of time, for safety		Must keep both hands on releases	On the job but practice first with no distractions
1.9	Retract paper				Wait until cutter retracts	On the job but practice first with no distractions
1.10	Shut off		100% of time, for safety			On the job but practice first with no distractions
2.	Operate printing press					
2.1	Start motor					

Note: Task analysis record form showing some of the tasks and subtasks performed by a printing press operator.

Performance analysis begins with comparing the person's actual performance to what it should be. Doing so helps to confirm that there is a performance deficiency, and (hopefully) helps the manager to identify its cause. Examples of performance deficiencies might be:

I expect each salesperson to make 10 new contracts per week, but John averages only six.

Other plants our size average no more than two serious accidents per month; we're averaging five.

Ways to identify how a current employee is doing include:

- Performance appraisals
- Job-related performance data (including productivity, absenteeism and tardiness, grievances, waste, late deliveries, product quality, downtime, repairs, equipment utilization, and customer complaints)
- Observations by supervisors or other specialists
- Interviews with the employee or his or her supervisor
- Tests of things like job knowledge, skills, and attendance
- Attitude surveys
- Individual employee daily diaries
- Assessment center results
- Special performance gap analytical software, such as from Saba Software, Inc.

CAN'T DO/WON'T DO Uncovering why performance is down is the heart of performance analysis. The aim here is to distinguish between can't-do and won't-do problems. First, determine whether it is a *can't-do* problem and, if so, its specific causes. For example: The employees don't know what to do or what your standards are; there are obstacles in the system such as lack of tools or supplies; there are no job aids (such as color-coded wires that show assemblers which wire goes where); you've hired people who haven't the skills to do the job; or training is inadequate.

Or, it might be a *won't-do* problem. Here employees could do a good job if they wanted to. One expert says, "Perhaps the biggest trap that trainers fall into is [developing] training for problems that training just won't fix."[34] Such situations are sometimes referred as attitudes, and change requires efforts more than training. For instance, the better solution might be to change the incentives or counseling.

Designing the Training Program

Armed with the needs analysis results, the manager next designs the training program. *Design* means planning the overall training program including training objectives, delivery methods, and program evaluation. Sub-steps include setting performance objectives, creating a detailed training outline (all training program steps from start to finish), choosing a program delivery method (such as lectures or Web), and verifying the overall program design with management. The design should include summaries of how you plan to set a training environment that motivates your trainees both to learn and to transfer what they learn to the job. It is also here that the manager reviews possible training program content (including workbooks, exercises, and activities), and estimates a budget for the training program.[35] If the program is to use technology, the manager should include a review of the technology he or she plans to use as part of the analysis.[36] We'll look more closely next at several specific design issues.

SETTING LEARNING OBJECTIVES[37] Training, development, learning, or (more generally) *instructional objectives* should specify in measurable terms what the trainee should be able to do after successfully completing the training program.[38] For example:

Most employers can build training programs like this one based on existing online and offline content offered by training content providers.

Shutterstock.Gundy Wongthai

The technical service representative will be able to adjust the color guidelines on this HP Officejet All-in-One printer copier within 10 minutes according to the device's specifications.

The learning objectives should first address the performance deficiencies that you identified via the needs analysis. Thus, if the sales team's sales are 40% too low, the objectives should focus on ensuring that the team members get the product knowledge, and attitudes they need to boost sales. But at the same time, the learning objectives must be practical, given the constraints.

One constraint is financial. The employer will generally want to see and approve a *training budget* for the program. Typical costs include the development costs (of having, say, a human resource specialist working on the program for a week or two), the direct and indirect (overhead) costs of the trainers' time, participant compensation (for the time they're actually being trained), and the cost of evaluating the program. There are algorithms for estimating training program costs, for instance, in terms of labor hours and direct costs.[39] The question, of course, isn't just "Can we afford this program?" but "Does it pay to spend this much, given the benefits we'll devise—will it improve performance, and if so by how much?" Therefore, prepare to defend the program on a benefits-versus-costs basis.

There are also other constraints to consider. For example, time constraints may require reducing three or four desirable learning objectives to one or two.

CREATING A MOTIVATIONAL LEARNING ENVIRONMENT   Municipalities running programs for traffic violators know there's often no better way to get someone's attention than to present a terrifying video accident. In other words, they know the best training starts not with a lecture but by making the material meaningful.

The same is true at work. Learning requires both ability and motivation, and the training program's design should accommodate both. In terms of *ability*, the learner–trainee needs (among other things) the required reading, writing, and mathematics skills. Trainees are rarely homogeneous, for instance, in terms of intellectual capacity. In setting the learning environment, the manager therefore should address several trainee-ability issues. For example, how will our program accommodate differences in trainee abilities? Do we need to provide remedial training?

Second, the learner must also be motivated. No manager should waste his or her time showing a disinterested employee how to do something (even if he or she has the requisite ability).

Many books exist on how to motivate employees, but several specific observations are pertinent here.[40] The training program's effects will be diminished if trainees return to their jobs to snide comments such as, "I hope you liked your little vacation" from colleagues. Therefore, the low-hanging fruit in motivating trainees is to make sure the trainee's peers and supervisor support the training effort. Ideally, particularly for larger programs, top management should visibly support the program. Beyond that, various motivation theories provide useful guidance. From behavior modification, we know that the training should provide opportunities for positive reinforcement. "Expectancy theory" shows us that the trainees need to know they have the ability to succeed in the program, and that the value to them of completing the program is high. Self-efficacy is crucial—trainees must believe they have the capacity to succeed. We can summarize such motivational points as follows.

MAKE THE LEARNING MEANINGFUL   Learners are more motivated to learn something that has meaning for them. Therefore:

1. At the start of training, provide a bird's-eye view of the material that you are going to present. For example, show why it's important, and provide an overview.[41]
2. Use familiar examples.
3. Organize the information so you can present it logically, in meaningful units.
4. Use terms and concepts that are already familiar to trainees.
5. Use visual aids.
6. Create a perceived training need in trainees' minds.[42] In one study, pilots who experienced pretraining accident-related events subsequently learned more from an accident-reduction training program than did those experiencing fewer such events.[43] Similarly, "before the training, managers need to sit down and talk with the trainee about why they are enrolled in the class, what they are expected to learn, and how they can use it on the job."[44]

MAKE SKILLS TRANSFER OBVIOUS AND EASY   Make it easy to transfer new skills and behaviors from the training site to the job site:

1. Maximize the similarity between the training situation and the work situation.
2. Provide adequate practice.
3. Label or identify each feature of the machine and/or step in the process.
4. Direct the trainees' attention to important aspects of the job. For example, if you're training a customer service rep to handle calls, explain the different types of calls he or she will encounter.[45]
5. Provide "heads-up" information. For example, supervisors often face stressful conditions. You can reduce the negative impact of such events by letting supervisory trainees know they might occur.[46]
6. Trainees learn best at their own pace. If possible, let them pace themselves.

REINFORCE THE LEARNING   Make sure the learner gets plenty of feedback. In particular:

1. Trainees learn best when the trainers immediately reinforce correct responses, perhaps with a quick "well done."
2. The learning curve goes down late in the day. Partial-day training is generally superior to full-day training.
3. Provide follow-up assignments at the close of training, so trainees are reinforced by having to apply back on the job what they've learned.[47]
4. Incentivize. Some companies, such as Hudson Trail Outfitters, an outdoor-gear retailer, offer trainees incentives of outdoor gear for completing each training program segment.[48]

ENSURE TRANSFER OF LEARNING TO THE JOB   Unfortunately, less than 35% of trainees seem to be transferring what they learned in training to their jobs a year after training. Improving on that sad statistic requires steps at each stage of training. *Prior to training*, get trainee and supervisor input in designing the program, institute a training attendance policy, and encourage employees to participate.

During training, provide trainees with training experiences and conditions (surroundings, equipment) that resemble the actual work environment. Goal-setting is important. In one study, some trainees set goals at the start of the program for the skills they were being taught. After training, they were rated more highly on these skills than were those who hadn't set goals.[49]

After training, reinforce what trainees learned, for instance, by appraising and rewarding employees for using new skills, and by making sure that they have the tools and materials they need to use their new skills.[50]

OTHER TRAINING DESIGN ISSUES Managers address several other issues during the training design stage. Most importantly, they review alternative training methodologies (lectures, Web-based, and so on) and choose likely methods for their program. They also decide how to organize the various training content components, choose how to evaluate the program, develop an overall summary plan for the program, and obtain management's approval to move ahead.

Developing the Program

Program development means actually assembling the program's training content and materials. It means choosing the specific content the program will present, as well as designing/choosing the specific instructional methods (lectures, cases, Web-based, and so on) you will use. Training equipment and materials include (for example) iPads, workbooks, lectures, PowerPoint slides, Web- and computer-based activities, course activities, trainer resources (manuals, for instance), and support materials.

Some employers create their own training content, but there's also a vast selection of online and offline content. IIM Ahmedabad Executive Education calendar (https://web.iima.ac.in/exed/) lists many courses for executives, including satellite-based courses. Similar management courses offered by reputed institutes like XLRI, MDI, TAPMI, MICA, etc., illustrate the many off-the-shelf training and development offerings that are available. It includes certificate programs on topics such as coaching, consulting skills, and presentation skills, as well as online workshops on hundreds of topics such as game design, survey design, and developing a mentoring program. (Trainers Warehouse and G.Neil are among thousands of suppliers.)[51] Turnkey training packages often include a trainer's guide, self-study book, video, and other content.

Once you design, approve, and develop the program, management can implement and then evaluate it. *Implement* means actually provide the training, using one or more of the instructional methods (such as lectures) that we discuss next. In general, there are several more practical steps a manager can take before, during, and after the training to improve participants' learning and engagement. *Before* the training, send announcements far in advance, provide directions, provide a point of contact, and make sure participants have pretraining materials. *During* training, make sure all participants have a point of contact in case they have questions or need guidance. *After* training, remember training does not end when the program ends. Instead, periodically ascertain that trainees are transferring their learning to the job.[52]

TRENDS SHAPING HR: *DIGITAL AND SOCIAL MEDIA*

the cloud
Refers to placing software programs and services on vendors' remote servers, from which they can then deliver these programs and services seamlessly to employees' digital devices

In designing and developing its training program, the employer will have to decide how the program will be delivered. Increasingly, this is occurring via "the cloud." Basically, **the cloud** refers to placing software programs and services on vendors' remote servers, from which they can then deliver these programs and services seamlessly to employees' digital devices. For example, you may use Microsoft Office 365, which resides on Microsoft's servers but which you use on your own (or employer's) computer devices. Similarly, when you start watching reruns of *Downton Abbey* on a TV, and then finish watching it on an iPad on the train home, you're using cloud-based services.

Cloud-based training is revolutionizing the training industry, by enabling employers to outsource much or all of their training activities. Because both the courses and the overall learning management system are hosted by the vendor, the employer need not concern itself with setting up or updating the programs on its own computers; the vendor manages the software for it. Furthermore the more advanced cloud-based learning systems let trainees access the training software and courses from wherever they are, using a variety of mobile devices. This not only improves convenience, but facilitates collaboration among employees when, for instance, they're working together on a training-based project. Cloud-based learning systems tend to be cost-effective, since the vendor handles upgrades and maintenance. The employer and vendor can store the on-the-cloud course modules and specific course content (such as PowerPoint slides, lectures, webinars, and photos); this makes it easier to build and modify e-learning courses. Typical cloud-based learning management system features include a course library, assessments and quizzes, reports and dashboards (for monitoring training performance), gamification elements (such as points and badges), messaging and notification systems, and a facility for scheduling and delivering both virtual and classroom training.[53] ■

Implementing the Training Program

HR in Practice at the Hotel Paris As Lisa and the CFO reviewed measures of the Hotel Paris's current training efforts, it was clear that some changes were in order. Most other service companies provided at least 40 hours of training per employee per year, while the Hotel Paris offered, on average, no more than 5 or 6. To see how they handled this, see the case on pages 259–260.

on-the-job training (OJT)
Training a person to learn a job while working on it.

On-the-Job Training

We'll see that much training today takes place online or uses other digital tools such as iPhones or iPads. However, much training is still in-person and interpersonal, as on-the-job training notably illustrates.

On-the-job training (OJT) means having a person learn a job by actually doing it. Every employee, from mailroom clerk to CEO, should get on-the-job training when he or she joins a firm. In many firms, OJT is the only training available.[54]

TYPES OF ON-THE-JOB TRAINING The most familiar on-the-job training is the *coaching or understudy method*. Here, an experienced worker or the trainee's supervisor trains the employee. This may involve simply observing the supervisor, or (preferably) having the supervisor or job expert show the new employee the ropes, step by step. On-the-job training is part of multifaceted training at Men's Wearhouse, which combines on-the-job training with comprehensive initiation programs and continuing-education seminars. Every manager is accountable for developing his or her subordinates.[55] *Job rotation*, in which an employee (usually a management trainee) moves from job to job at planned intervals, is another OJT technique. *Special assignments* similarly give lower-level executives firsthand experience in working on actual problems.

Do not take the on-the-job training effort for granted. Instead, plan out and structure the OJT experience. Train the trainers themselves (often the employees' supervisors), and provide training materials. They should know, for instance, how to motivate learners. Because low expectations may translate into poor trainee performance, supervisor/trainers should emphasize their high expectations.

Many firms use "peer training" for OJT.[56] For example, some adopt "peer to peer development." The employer selects several employees who spend several days per week over several months learning what the technology or change will entail, and then spread the new skills and values to their colleagues back on the job.[57] Others use employee teams to analyze jobs and prepare training materials.

They reportedly conduct task analyses more quickly and effectively than do training experts. Figure 8-1 presents steps to help ensure OJT success.[58]

Apprenticeship Training

Apprenticeship training is a process by which people become skilled workers, usually through a combination of formal learning and long-term on-the-job training, often under the tutelage of a master craftsperson. Indian steel producer, Tata Steel, has been running an award winning apprenticeship scheme for many years. Amara Raja Group has established the Amara Raja Skill Development Center where prospective candidates from the nearby locality are trained intensively for 6 months to 1 year, and they are later offered employment in the group's factories or other offices. When steelmaker Dofasco (now part of ArcelorMittal) discovered that many of its employees would be retiring within 5 to 10 years, it decided to revive its apprenticeship training. New recruits spend about 32 months in an internal apprenticeship training program, learning various jobs under the tutelage of experienced employees.[59]

The Apprentice Act of 1961 allows Indian companies, both public and private, to hire apprentices and provide them training. The act has been amended recently (i.e., in 2014) to make it more contemporary. Now, the Board of Apprenticeship Training (BOAT) is responsible for the implementation and promotion of this activity (http://www.apprenticeship.gov.in).

As skill development and employment generation are priority activities for the government of India, special efforts are made in this direction. The

FIGURE 8-1 Steps in On-the-Job Training

Step 1: Prepare the learner
1. Put the learner at ease.
2. Explain why he or she is being taught.
3. Create interest and find out what the learner already knows about the job.
4. Explain the whole job and relate it to some job the worker already knows.
5. Place the learner as close to the normal working position as possible.
6. Familiarize the worker with equipment, materials, tools, and trade terms.

Step 2: Present the operation
1. Explain quantity and quality requirements.
2. Go through the job at the normal work pace.
3. Go through the job at a slow pace several times, explaining each step. Between operations, explain the difficult parts, or those in which errors are likely to be made.
4. Again, go through the job at a slow pace several times; explain the key points.
5. Have the learner explain the steps as you go through the job at a slow pace.

Step 3: Do a tryout
1. Have the learner go through the job several times, slowly, explaining each step to you. Correct mistakes and, if necessary, do some of the complicated steps the first few times.
2. Run the job at the normal pace.
3. Have the learner do the job, gradually building up skill and speed.
4. Once the learner can do the job, let the work begin, but don't abandon him or her.

Step 4: Follow-up
1. Designate to whom the learner should go for help.
2. Gradually decrease supervision, checking work from time to time.
3. Correct faulty work patterns before they become a habit. Show why the method you suggest is superior.
4. Compliment good work.

FIGURE 8-2 **Some Popular Apprenticeships**

Source: The Board of Apprenticeship publishes a list of trades covered under the Apprentice Act, 1961. Accessed on 31 July 2017 at http://rdatkolkata.in/Trades%20under%20the%20Apprentices%20Act,%201961.pdf.

- Fitter
- Turner
- Carpenter
- Plumber
- Mason
- Machinist
- Lift Mechanic
- Cook
- Hotel Clerk
- Plastic Mould-Maker
- Footwear Maker

National Apprenticeship Training Scheme (NATS) has been established to help technically qualified candidates gain industry experience for one year. Trainees are paid by the industry, and the government reimburses a part of their expenses (http://mhrdnats.gov.in/about-us). The scheme aims to cumulatively train 50 lakh youth by 2020.[60] Figure 8-2 lists popular apprenticeships.

Informal Learning

Surveys estimate that as much as 80% of what employees learn on the job they learn through informal means, including performing their jobs while interacting every day with their colleagues.[61]

Employers can facilitate informal learning. For example, one Siemens plant places tools in cafeteria areas to take advantage of the work-related discussions taking place. Even installing whiteboards with markers can facilitate informal learning. Sun Microsystems implemented an informal online learning tool it called Sun Learning eXchange. This evolved into a platform containing more than 5,000 informal learning items/suggestions addressing topics ranging from sales to technical support.[62] Cheesecake Factory uses VideoCafé, a YouTube-type platform, to let employees "upload and share video snippets on job-related topics, including customer greetings and food preparation."

Job Instruction Training

job instruction training (JIT)
Listing each job's basic tasks, along with key points, in order to provide step-by-step training for employees.

Many jobs (or parts of jobs) consist of a sequence of steps best learned step-by-step. Such step-by-step training is called **job instruction training (JIT)**. First, list the job's required steps (let's say for using a mechanical paper cutter) each in its proper sequence. Then list a corresponding "key point" (if any) beside each step. The steps in such a *job instruction training sheet* show trainees what to do, and the key points show how it's to be done—and why, as follows:

Steps	Key Points
1. Start motor	None
2. Set cutting distance	Carefully read scale—to prevent wrong-sized cut
3. Place paper on cutting table	Make sure paper is even—to prevent uneven cut
4. Push paper up to cutter	Make sure paper is tight—to prevent uneven cut
5. Grasp safety release with left hand	Do not release left hand—to prevent hand from being caught in cutter
6. Grasp cutter release with right hand	Do not release right hand—to prevent hand from being caught in cutter
7. Simultaneously pull cutter and safety releases	Keep both hands on corresponding releases—avoid hands being on cutting table
8. Wait for cutter to retract	Keep both hands on releases—to avoid having hands on cutting table
9. Retract paper	Make sure cutter is retracted; keep both hands away from releases
10. Shut off motor	None

As another example, the "exit" steps UPS teaches drivers include: Shift into the lowest gear or into park; turn off the ignition; apply the parking brake; release the seatbelt with left hand; open the door; place the key on your ring finger.[63]

Lectures

Lecturing is a quick and simple way to present knowledge to large groups of trainees, as when the sales force needs to learn a new product's features.[64] Here are some guidelines for presenting a lecture:[65]

- Don't start out on the wrong foot, for instance, with an irrelevant joke.
- Speak only about what you know well.
- Give your listeners signals. For instance, if you have a list of items, start by saying something like,"There are four reasons why the sales reports are necessary.... The first...."
- Use anecdotes and stories to show rather than tell.
- Be alert to your audience. Watch body language for negative signals like fidgeting or boredom.
- Maintain eye contact with the audience.
- Make sure everyone can hear. Repeat questions that you get from trainees.
- Leave hands hanging naturally at your sides.
- Talk from notes or PowerPoint slides, rather than from a script.
- Break a long talk into a series of short talks. Don't give a short overview and then spend a 1-hour presentation going point by point through the material. Break the long talk into a series of 10-minute talks, each with its own introduction. Write brief PowerPoint slides, and spend about a minute on each. Each introduction highlights what you'll discuss, why it's important to the audience members, and why they should listen to you.[66]
- Practice. If possible, rehearse under conditions similar to those under which you will actually give your presentation.

Programmed Learning

programmed learning
A systematic method for teaching job skills, involving presenting questions or facts, allowing the person to respond, and giving the learner immediate feedback on the accuracy of his or her answers.

Whether the medium is a textbook, iPad, or the Internet, **programmed learning** is a step-by-step, self-learning method that consists of three parts:

1. Presenting questions, facts, or problems to the learner
2. Allowing the person to respond
3. Providing feedback on the accuracy of answers, with instructions on what to do next

Generally, programmed learning presents facts and follow-up questions frame by frame. What the next question is often depends on how the learner answers the previous question. The built-in feedback from the answers provides reinforcement.

Programmed learning reduces training time. It also facilitates learning by letting trainees learn at their own pace, get immediate feedback, and reduce their risk of error. Some argue that trainees do not learn much more from programmed learning than from a textbook. Yet studies generally support programmed learning's effectiveness.[67] In addition to the usual programmed learning, computerized *intelligent tutoring systems* learn what questions and approaches worked and did not work for the learner, and then adjust the instructional sequence to the trainee's unique needs.

Behavior Modeling

behavior modeling
A training technique in which trainees are first shown good management techniques in a film, are asked to play roles in a simulated situation, and are then given feedback and praise by their supervisor.

Behavior modeling involves (1) showing trainees the right (or "model") way of doing something, (2) letting trainees practice that way, and then (3) giving feedback on the trainees' performance. Behavior modeling is one of the most widely used, well-researched, and highly regarded psychologically based training interventions.[68] The basic procedure is as follows:

1. *Modeling.* First, trainees watch live or video examples showing models behaving effectively in a problem situation. Thus, the video might show a supervisor effectively disciplining a subordinate, if teaching "how to discipline" is the aim of the training program.
2. *Role-playing.* Next, the trainees get roles to play in a simulated situation; here they are to practice the effective behaviors demonstrated by the models.
3. *Social reinforcement.* The trainer provides reinforcement in the form of praise and constructive feedback.
4. *Transfer of training.* Finally, trainees are encouraged to apply their new skills when they are back on their jobs.

Audiovisual-Based Training

Although increasingly replaced by Web-based methods, audiovisual-based training techniques like DVDs, films, PowerPoint, and audiotapes are still used.[69] The Ford Motor Company uses videos in its dealer training sessions to simulate problems and reactions to various customer complaints, for example.

Vestibule Training

With vestibule training, trainees learn on the actual or simulated equipment but are trained off the job (perhaps in a separate room or *vestibule*). Vestibule training is necessary when it's too costly or dangerous to train employees on the job. Putting new assembly-line workers right to work could slow production, for instance, and when safety is a concern—as with pilots—simulated training may be the only practical alternative. As an example, UPS uses a life-size learning lab to provide a 40-hour, 5-day realistic training program for driver candidates.[70]

Electronic Performance Support Systems (EPSS)

electronic performance support systems (EPSS)
Sets of computerized tools and displays that automate training, documentation, and phone support; integrate this automation into applications; and provide support that's faster, cheaper, and more effective than traditional methods.

Electronic performance support systems (EPSS) are computerized tools and displays that automate training, documentation, and phone support.[71] When you call a Dell service rep, he or she is probably asking questions prompted by an EPSS; it takes you both, step by step, through an analytical sequence. Without the EPSS, Dell would have to train its service reps to memorize an unrealistically large number of solutions. Aetna Insurance cut its 13-week instructor-led training course for new call center employees by about 2 weeks by providing employees with performance support tools.[72]

Performance support systems are modern job aids. **Job aids** are sets of instructions, diagrams, or similar methods available at the job site to guide the worker.[73] Job aids work particularly well on complex jobs that require multiple steps, or where it's dangerous to forget a step. For example, airline pilots use job aids (a checklist of things to do prior to takeoff).

job aid
A set of instructions, diagrams, or similar methods available at the job site to guide the worker.

Videoconferencing

Videoconferencing involves delivering programs over broadband lines, the Internet, or satellite. Vendors such as Cisco offer videoconference products such as Webex and TelePresence.[74] Cisco's Unified Video Conferencing (CUVC) product line combines Cisco group collaboration and decision-making software with videoconferencing, video telephony, and realistic "TelePresence" capabilities.[75]

Computer-Based Training (CBT)

Computer-based training refers to training methods that use interactive computer-based systems to increase knowledge or skills. For example, employers use CBT to teach employees safe methods for avoiding falls. The system lets trainees replay the lessons and answer questions, and is especially effective when paired with actual practice under a trainer's watchful eye.[76]

Computer-based training is increasingly realistic. For example, *interactive multimedia training* integrates the use of text, video, graphics, photos, animation, and sound to create a complex training environment with which the trainee interacts.[77] In training a physician, for instance, such a system lets a medical student take a hypothetical patient's medical history, conduct an examination, and analyze lab tests. The student can then interpret the sounds and draw conclusions for a diagnosis. *Virtual reality training* takes this realism a step further, by putting trainees into a simulated environment.

Simulated Learning and Gaming

"Simulated learning" means different things to different people. A survey asked training professionals what experiences qualified as simulated learning experiences. The percentages of trainers choosing each experience were: Virtual reality-type games, 19%; Step-by-step animated guide, 8%; Scenarios with questions and decision trees overlaying animation, 19%; Online role-play with photos and videos, 14%; Software training including screenshots with interactive requests, 35%; and Other, 6%.[78]

Virtual reality puts the trainee in an artificial three-dimensional environment that simulates events and situations experienced on the job.[79] Sensory devices transmit how the trainee is responding to the computer, and the trainee "sees, feels and hears" what is going on, assisted by special glasses.[80] Facebook's recent purchase of virtual reality glasses maker Oculus VR Inc. highlights virtual reality's growing potential.[81]

Employers also increasingly use computerized simulations (sometimes called *interactive learning*) to inject realism into their training. Air India and DMRC are Indian companies that have established simulators for training their employees in various areas of operation. Others companies can also use these facilities on hire. Orlando-based Environmental Tectonics Corporation created an Advanced Disaster Management simulation for emergency medical response trainees. One simulated scenario involves a plane crash. So realistic that it's "unsettling," trainees including firefighters and airport officials respond to the simulated crash's sights and sounds via pointing devices and radios.[82] Cisco embedded the learning required to train thousands of Cisco trainees for Cisco certification exams within a video game–like program that includes music, graphics, and sound effects.[83] A Novartis pharmaceuticals division runs about 80 or so clinical trials per year, and must be sure each trial team is trained for this. Novartis uses a custom-made simulation*. For example, the simulation shows trainees "how their decisions affected the quality of the trial and whether their decision saved time or added time to the process."[84] The Cheesecake Factory uses a simulation that shows employees how to build the "perfect hamburger."

Training simulations are expensive to create, but for large companies the cost per employee is usually reasonable.[85] In general, interactive and simulated technologies reduce learning time by an average of 50%.[86] Other advantages include mastery of learning (if the trainee doesn't learn it, he or she generally can't move on to the next step), increased retention, and increased trainee motivation (resulting from responsive feedback).

Specialist multimedia software houses such as Graphic Media of Portland, Oregon, produce much of the content for these programs. They produce both custom titles and generic programs such as a $999 package for teaching workplace safety.

Lifelong and Literacy Training Techniques

lifelong learning
Provides employees with continuing learning experiences over their tenure with the firm, with the aims of ensuring they have the opportunity to learn the skills they need to do their jobs and to expand their occupational horizons.

Lifelong learning means providing employees with continuing learning experiences over their tenure with the firm, with the aim of ensuring they have the opportunity to learn the skills they need to do their jobs and to expand their horizons. Lifelong learning may thus range from basic remedial skills (for instance, English as a second language) to college. For example, one senior waiter at the Rhapsody restaurant in Chicago received his undergraduate degree and began work toward a master of social work using the lifelong learning account (LiLA) program his employer offers.

LITERACY TRAINING By one estimate, about 39 million people in the United States have learning disabilities.[87] Yet today's emphasis on teamwork and quality requires that employees read, write, and understand numbers.[88]

Employers often turn to private firms to provide the requisite education.[89] Another simple approach is to have supervisors teach basic skills by giving employees writing and speaking exercises.[90] For example, if an employee needs to use a manual to find out how to change a part, teach that person how to use the index to locate the relevant section. Some call in teachers from a local high school.

Diversity training can be important, as in the following feature.

▶ **IMPROVING PERFORMANCE:** *HR Practices Around the Globe*

Diversity Training at ABC Virtual Communications, Inc.

Diversity training aims to improve cross-cultural sensitivity, with the goal of fostering more harmonious working relationships among a firm's employees. Such training typically includes improving interpersonal skills, understanding and valuing cultural differences, improving technical skills, socializing employees into the corporate culture, indoctrinating new workers into the U.S. work ethic, improving English proficiency and basic math skills, and improving bilingual skills for English-speaking employees.[91] For example, IBM has online programs to educate managers regarding diversity, inclusive leadership, and sexual harassment. Training materials include interactive learning modules that enable trainees to practice what they've learned, testimonials from IBM executives, and self-assessment tools.[92]

Most employers opt for an off-the-shelf diversity training program such as *Just Be F.A.I.R.* from Vision-Point productions. It includes streaming video, a facilitator discussion guide, participant materials and workbook, a DVD with print materials, PowerPoint slides, and two videos (the purchase price for the program is about $1,000). Vignettes illustrate such things as the potential pitfalls of stereotyping people.[93]

ABC Virtual Communications, Inc. (www.abcv.com) is a Des Moines, Iowa, provider of customized software development and other solutions. It therefore requires qualified personnel, particularly software engineers. Recruiting such employees is particularly difficult in Iowa, where many recent graduates move away.

ABC therefore recruits foreign-born individuals. However, hiring these skilled employees wasn't enough: ABC needed a diversity management training program that could turn these new employees—and the firm's current employees—into productive colleagues.

Its program consists of several courses. New ABC employees, representing 14 countries and 45 ethnic groups, take a mandatory 8-hour orientation overview for new employees on the "American workplace." All ABC employees take an "effective communications" training course. Conversational English and accent reduction classes for employees and their families are available through Rosetta Stone language learning software. The company also partnered with Des Moines Area Community College to create specialized classes for individual needs. At ABC Virtual, a globally diverse workforce was the key to improved performance, and diversity training helped the firm manage its diversity.[94] ■

Source: Based on Matthew Reis, "Do-It-Yourself Diversity," Training & Development, March 2004, pp. 80–81.; www.prismdiversity.com/resource /diversity_training.html, accessed June 1, 2011.; Jennifer Salopek, "Trends: Lost in Translation," Training & Development, December 2003, p. 15; www.visionpoint.com/training-solutions/ title/just-be-fair-basic-diversity-training, accessed June 17, 2011.; Paraphrased from "Best Practice: Workforce Diversity Training," The Manufacturing Practices Center of Excellence, www.brmpcoe.org/bestpracticea/internal/ abev/abcv_15.html.

Team Training

Teamwork does not always come naturally. Companies devote many hours to training new employees to listen to each other and to cooperate. For example, a Baltimore Coca-Cola plant suffered from high turnover and absenteeism.[95] The new plant manager decided to address these problems by reorganizing around teams. He then used team training to support and improve team functioning.

Team training focused on technical, interpersonal, and team management issues. In terms of *technical training*, for instance, management encouraged team employees to learn each other's jobs, to encourage flexible team assignments. **Cross training** means training employees to do different tasks or jobs than their own; doing so facilitates flexibility and job rotation, as when you expect team members to occasionally share jobs.

Interpersonal problems often undermine teamwork. Team training here therefore included *interpersonal skills* training such as in listening, handling conflict, and

---

cross training
Training employees to do different tasks or jobs than their own; doing so facilitates flexibility and job rotation.

negotiating.[96] Effective teams also require *team management* skills, for instance, in problem-solving, meetings management, consensus decision making, and team leadership, and the teams received such training as well.

Many employers use team training to build stronger management teams. For example, some use outdoor "adventure" training such as Outward Bound programs to build teamwork. This usually involves taking a firm's management team out into rugged, mountainous terrain.[97] The aim is to foster trust and cooperation among trainees. One chief financial officer for a bank helped organize a retreat for 73 of his firm's financial employees. As he said, "They are very individualistic in their approach to their work…. What I have been trying to do is get them to see the power of acting more like a team."[98]

Internet-Based Training

Employers use Internet-based learning to deliver almost all the types of training we have discussed to this point. For example, ADP trains new salespeople online, using a Blackboard learning management system similar to one used by college students.[99] The Italian eyewear company Luxottica (whose brands include LensCrafters and Sunglass Hut) provides training to its 38,000 employees worldwide via instant online access to information on new products and regulations.[100] Recently, state-owned postal service China Post created a new center to manage its online training college, which now delivers about 9,000 hours of training annually, offering over 600 programs.[101]

LEARNING PORTALS A *learning portal* is a section of an employer's website that offers employees online access to training courses. Many employers arrange to have an online training vendor make its courses available via the employer's portal. Most often, the employer contracts with application service providers (ASPs). When employees go to their firm's learning portal, they actually access the menu of training courses that the ASP offers for the employer. A Google search for e-learning companies reveals many, such as SkillSoft, Plateau Systems, and Employment Law Learning Technologies.

Learning management systems (LMS) are special software tools that support Internet training by helping employers identify training needs and schedule, deliver, assess, and manage the online training itself. (Blackboard and WebCT are two familiar college-oriented learning management systems.) General Motors uses an LMS to help its dealers in Africa and the Middle East deliver training. The Internet-based LMS includes a course catalog, supervisor-approved self-enrollment, and pre- and post-course tests. The system then automatically schedules the individual's training.[102] Many employers integrate the LMS with the company's talent management systems. That way, skills inventories and succession plans automatically update as employees complete their training.[103]

Online learning doesn't necessarily teach individuals faster or better. In one review, Web-based instruction was a bit more effective than classroom instruction for teaching memory of facts and principles; Web-based instruction and classroom instruction were equally effective for teaching information about how to perform a task or action.[104] But, of course, the need to teach large numbers of students remotely, or to enable trainees to study at their leisure, often makes e-learning the logical choice.[105]

Some employers opt for *blended learning*. Here, trainees use multiple delivery methods (such as manuals, in-class lectures, and Web-based seminars or "webinars") to learn the material.[106] Intuit (which makes TurboTax) uses instructor-led classroom training for getting new distributors up to speed. Then it uses virtual classroom systems (see the following) for things like monthly meetings with distributors, and for classes on special software features.[107]

The Virtual Classroom

virtual classroom
Teaching method that uses special collaboration software to enable multiple remote learners, using their PCs or laptops, to participate in live audio and visual discussions, communicate via written text, and learn via content such as PowerPoint slides.

A **virtual classroom** uses collaboration software to enable multiple remote learners, using their PCs, tablets, or laptops, to participate in live audio and visual discussions, communicate via written text, and learn via content such as PowerPoint slides.

The virtual classroom combines the best of Web-based learning offered by systems like Blackboard and WebCT with live video and audio. Thus, Elluminate Live! lets learners communicate with clear, two-way audio; build communities with user profiles and live video; collaborate with chat and shared whiteboards; and learn with shared applications such as PowerPoint slides.[108]

TRENDS SHAPING HR: *DIGITAL AND SOCIAL MEDIA*

Mobile learning (or "on-demand learning") means delivering learning content, on the learner's demand, via mobile devices like cell phones, laptops, and tablets, wherever and whenever the learner has the time and desire to access it.[109] For example, trainees can take full online courses using dominKnow's (www.dominknow.com) iPhone-optimized Touch Learning Center Portal.[110]

Most large employers distribute internal communications and training via mobile devices.[111] Employees at CompuCom Systems Inc. access instruction manuals through mobile devices; the company subsidizes employee purchases of smart phones or tablets to facilitate this. Natural user interfaces such as Apple's Siri voice recognition system facilitate such training.[112]

Employers use mobile learning to deliver training and downloads on topics "from how to close an important sales deal to optimizing organizational change."[113] IBM uses mobile learning to deliver just-in-time information (for instance, about new product features) to its sales force. To facilitate this, its training department often breaks up, say, an hour program into easier-to-use 10-minute pieces. Some employers use blogs to communicate learning to trainees.[114] J.P. Morgan encourages employees to use instant messaging, for instance, to update colleagues about new products quickly.

Employers also use social media, such as LinkedIn, Facebook, and Twitter, and virtual worlds like Second Life to communicate company news and messages and to provide training.[115] For example, British Petroleum uses Second Life to train new gas station employees. The aim here is to show new gas station employees how to use the safety features of gasoline storage tanks. BP built three-dimensional renderings of the tank systems in Second Life. Trainees use these to "see" underground and observe the effects of using the safety devices.[116]

Web 2.0 learning
Training that uses online technologies such as social networks, virtual worlds (such as Second Life), and systems that blend synchronous and asynchronous delivery with blogs, chat rooms, bookmark sharing, and tools such as 3-D simulations.

Web 2.0 learning is learning that utilizes online technologies such as social networks, virtual worlds (such as Second Life), and systems that blend synchronous and asynchronous delivery with blogs, chat rooms, bookmark sharing, and tools such as 3-D simulations.[117] About 40% of learning professionals surveyed said their companies use Web 2.0 learning, and 86% said they anticipated doing so. One large firm uses Web 2.0 to deliver credit card sales training to its service representatives around the country. *Collaborative peer forums* require teams of six to eight trainees to virtually "sell" their sales problem and solution to an executive.[118]

The accompanying HR Tools feature shows how managers can create their own training programs. ■

▶ IMPROVING PERFORMANCE: *HR Tools for Line Managers and Small Businesses*

Creating Your Own Training Program

While it would be nice if supervisors in even the largest firms could expect their firms to provide packaged training programs to train the new people they hire, many times they cannot. However, you still have many options.

Create Your Own Five-Step Training Program

Remember ADDIE—analyze (is training the problem?), design (including learning objectives, and motivating the trainee), develop (what specific materials and methods will we use?), implement (train the person), and evaluate. For many types of jobs, start by *setting training objectives*—be specific about what your employee should be able to do after training. Write a job description—list of the job's duties—if not already available. Write (see Table 8-1, page 230) a *task analysis record form* showing the steps in each of the employee's tasks. Write a *job instruction training form*; here list a key point (such as "carefully read scale") for each step (such as "set cutting distance"). Finally, compile the objectives, job description, task analysis form, and job instruction form in a *training manual*. Also, include an introduction to the job and an explanation of how the job relates to other jobs in the company.

Use Private Vendors

The small business owner can tap hundreds of suppliers of prepackaged training solutions. These range from self-study programs from the American Management Association (www.amanet.org) and SHRM (www.shrm.org), to specialized programs. For example, the employer might arrange with PureSafety to have its employees take occupational safety courses from www.puresafety.com.

SkillSoft is another example (go to http://skillsoft.com and click "Products"). Its courses include software development, business strategy and operations, professional effectiveness, and desktop computer skills. As an example, the course "interviewing effectively" shows supervisors how to use behavioral questioning to interview candidates.[119]

The buyer's guide from the American Society of Training and Development (www.astd.org) is a good place to start to find a vendor (check under "Resources").

Check the SBA

The government's Small Business Administration (see www.SBA.gov/training) provides a virtual campus that offers online courses, workshops, publications, and learning tools aimed at supporting small businesses.[120] For example, the small business owner can link under "Small Business Planner" to "Writing Effective Job Descriptions," and "The Interview Process: How to Select the Right Person." See the site map at www.sba.gov/sitemap for examples of what it offers.

Check NAM

The National Association of Manufacturers (NAM) is the largest industrial trade organization in the United States. It represents about 14,000 member manufacturers, including 10,000 small and midsized companies.

NAM helps employees maintain and upgrade their work skills and continue their professional development. It offers courses and a skills certification process.[121] There are no long-term contracts to sign. Employers simply pay about $10–$30 per course taken by each employee. The catalog includes OSHA, quality, and technical training as well as courses in areas like customer service. ■

Source: Based on Based on Paul Harris, "Small Businesses Bask in Training's Spotlight," T&D, 59, no. 2, Fall 2005, pp. 46–52; Stephen Covey, "Small Business, Big Opportunity," Training, 43, no. 11, November 2006, p. 40; www.themanufacturinginstitute.org/Skills-Certification/Right-Skills-Now/Right-Skills-Now.aspx, accessed August 24, 2014.

Implementing Management Development Programs

Management development is any attempt to improve managerial performance by imparting knowledge, changing attitudes, or increasing skills. It thus includes in-house programs like courses, coaching, and rotational assignments; professional programs like those offered by the CII or NHRD; online programs from various sources; and university programs like executive MBAs or short-term courses offered by the IIMs, XLRI, MDI Gurgaon, and NIBM Pune.

Management development is important for several reasons. For one thing, promotion from within is a major source of management talent, and virtually all promoted managers require some development to prepare them for their new jobs. Furthermore, management development facilitates organizational continuity, by preparing employees and current managers to smoothly assume higher-level positions.

Strategy's Role in Management Development

Management development programs should reflect the firm's strategic plans.[122] For example, strategies to enter new businesses or expand overseas imply that the employer will need succession plans in place to obtain and/or develop managers who have the

LEARNING OBJECTIVE 8-5
List and briefly discuss four management development methods.

management development
Any attempt to improve current or future management performance by imparting knowledge, changing attitudes, or increasing skills.

skills to manage these new businesses. Management development programs then impart the knowledge, attitudes, and skills these managers will need to excel at their jobs.[123]

Some management development programs are company-wide and involve all or most new (or potential) managers. Thus, new MBAs may join GE's management development program and rotate through various assignments and educational experiences. The firm may then slot superior candidates onto a "fast track," a development program that prepares them more quickly for senior-level commands.

Other development programs aim to fill specific top positions, such as CEO. For example, GE will spend years developing, testing, and watching potential replacements for CEO Jeffrey Immelt.

Succession Planning

Management development is often part of the employer's *succession planning process*.[124] *Succession planning* involves developing workforce plans for the company's top positions; it is the ongoing process of systematically identifying, assessing, and developing organizational leadership to enhance performance.[125]

Succession planning programs involve several stages.[126] First, an organization projection is made. Here, based on the company's strategic and business plans, top management and the human resource director identify what the company's future key position needs will be. The employer anticipates its management needs based on factors like plant expansion or contraction. Next, HR and management review the firm's management skills inventory to identify the management talent now employed.[127] These inventories, you may recall, contain data on things like education and work experience, career preferences, and performance appraisals. At this stage, management replacement charts may be drawn (see Figure 5-3, page 131). These summarize potential candidates for each of your management slots, as well as each person's development needs. As in Figure 5-3, the development needs for a future division vice president might include job rotation (to obtain more experience in the firm's finance and production division), executive development programs (to provide training and strategic planning), and assignment for 2 weeks to the employer's in-house management development center. At this stage, management may decide that one or more outside candidates should be recruited as well.

Management then turns to the development stage of the succession planning process. This means providing possible candidates with the developmental experiences they require to be viable candidates. Employers develop high-potential employees through internal training and cross-functional experiences, job rotation, external training, and global/regional assignments.[128]

Finally, succession planning requires assessing all these candidates and selecting those who will actually fill the key positions.[129]

Improving Performance Through HRIS: Succession Systems

At Dole Foods, the new president's strategy involved improving financial performance by reducing redundancies and centralizing certain activities, including succession planning.[130] Web technology helped Dole do this. Dole contracted with application service providers (ASPs) to handle things like payroll management.[131] For succession management, Dole chose software from Pilat NAI. The Pilat system keeps all the data on its own servers for a monthly fee. Dole's managers access the program via the Web using a password. They fill out online résumés for themselves, including career interests, and note special considerations such as geographic restrictions.

The managers also assess themselves on four competencies. Once the manager provides his or her input, the program notifies that manager's boss, who assesses his or her subordinate and indicates whether the person is promotable. This assessment and the online résumés then go automatically to the division head and the divisional HR director. Dole's senior vice president for human resources then uses the information to create career development plans for each manager, including seminars and other programs.[132] ■

Candidate Assessment and the 9-Box Grid

Some high-potential managers fail in their jobs, while some apparently low-potential managers excel. How then does an employer choose who to send through an expensive development program?

The 9-Box Grid is one tool. It shows *Potential* from low to medium to high on the vertical axis, and *Performance* from low to medium to high across the bottom—a total of nine possible boxes.

The grid can simplify, somewhat, the task of choosing development candidates. At the extremes, for instance, low potentials/low performers would not move on. The high-potential/high-performance stars most assuredly would. Most employers focus their development resources on high-performance/high-potential stars, and secondarily on those rated high-potential/moderate-performance, or high-performance/moderate-potential.[133] Other employers focus development resources on the company's "mission-critical employees"—those central to the firm's success and survival. We'll see how later in this section.

In any case, individual assessment should always precede development. At frozen foods manufacturer Schwan, senior executives first whittle 40 or more development candidates down to about 10. Then the program begins with a 1-day assessment by outside consultants of each manager's leadership strengths and weaknesses. This assessment becomes the basis for each manager's individual development plan. Action-learning (practical) projects then supplement individual and group training activities.[134]

We'll look at some popular development activities next.

Managerial On-the-Job Training and Rotation

job rotation
A management training technique that involves moving a trainee from department to department to broaden his or her experience and identify strong and weak points.

Managerial on-the-job training methods include job rotation, the coaching/understudy approach, and action learning. **Job rotation** means moving managers from department to department to broaden their understanding of the business and to test their abilities. The trainee may be a recent college graduate, or a senior manager being groomed for further promotion. In addition to providing a well-rounded training experience, job rotation helps avoid stagnation through the constant introduction of new points of view in each department. It also helps identify the trainee's strong and weak points. Periodic job changing can also improve interdepartmental cooperation; managers become more understanding of each other's problems; rotation also widens the acquaintances among management. The accompanying HR Practices feature illustrates this.

▶ **IMPROVING PERFORMANCE:** *HR Practices Around the Globe*

Global Job Rotation

As firms expand globally, job rotation takes on a new meaning. At firms like Shell and BP, rotating managers globally is a primary means through which the firms maintain their flexibility and responsiveness even as they grow to an enormous size.

An advantage of global job rotation (rotating managers from, say, Sweden to New York) is that it builds a network of informal ties that ensures superior cross-border communication and mutual understanding as well as tight interunit coordination and control.

Improved communication and understanding stem from the personal relationships that are forged as managers work in the firm's various locations. These activities can also enhance organizational control. When employees from the firm's global locations are rotated or brought together at, say, the Harvard Business School or Europe's INSEAD for a management-training program, the aim is more than just teaching basic skills. It is also to build a stronger identification with the company's culture and values. By creating shared values and a consistent view of the firm and its goals, management development activities like these can facilitate communication. They ensure that through a sense of shared values and purpose the firm's policies are followed, even with a minimal reliance on other forms of control.[135] ■

Source: Based on Paul Evans, Yves Doz and Andre Laurent, Human Resource Management in International Firms, New York: St. Martin's Press, 1990, pp. 122–124; www.sony.net/SonyInfo/csr_report/employees/training/index3.html; www.mckinsey.com/insights/organization/how_multinationals_can_attract_the_talent_they_need.

COACHING/UNDERSTUDY APPROACH   Here the trainee works directly with a senior manager or with the person he or she is to replace; the latter is responsible for the trainee's coaching. Normally, the understudy relieves the executive of certain responsibilities, giving the trainee a chance to learn the job.

ACTION LEARNING   **Action learning** programs give managers released time to work analyzing and solving problems in departments other than their own. It is reportedly the fastest-growing leadership development technique today, used by companies ranging from Wells Fargo to Boeing.[136] Its basics include carefully selected teams of 5 to 25 members, assigning them real-world business problems that extend beyond their usual areas of expertise, and structured learning through coaching and feedback. The employer's senior managers usually choose the projects and decide whether to accept the teams' recommendations.[137]

> **action learning**
> A training technique by which management trainees are allowed to work full-time analyzing and solving problems in other departments.

For example, Pacific Gas & Electric Company's (PG&E) Action-Forum Process has three phases:

1. A 6- to 8-week *framework* phase, during which the team defines and collects data on an issue;
2. The *action forum*—2 to 3 days at PG&E's learning center discussing the issue and developing action-plan recommendations; and
3. *Accountability sessions*, where the teams meet with the leadership group at monthly intervals to review progress.

Off-the-Job Management Training and Development Techniques

There are also many off-the-job techniques for training and developing managers.

As most everyone knows, the **case study method** has trainees solve realistic problems after studying written or video case descriptions. The person then analyzes the case, diagnoses the problem, and presents his or her findings and solutions in a discussion with other trainees. *Integrated case scenarios* create long-term, comprehensive case situations. IIM Ahmedabad uses the case study method extensively in its executive education programs. The IIMA Case Center has a depository of 3000+ cases in the Indian context, which are available to case teachers (https://cases.iima.ac.in/index.php/). One FBI Academy scenario starts with "a concerned citizen's telephone call and ends 14 weeks later with a simulated trial. In between is the stuff of a genuine investigation...." Scriptwriters (often training team employees) write the scripts. The scripts include background stories, detailed personnel histories, and role-playing instructions; their aim is to develop specific skills, such as interviewing witnesses.[138]

> **case study method**
> A development method in which the manager is presented with a written description of an organizational problem to diagnose and solve.

Computerized **management games** enable trainees to learn by making realistic decisions in simulated situations. For example, *Interpret* is a team exercise that "explores team communication, the management of information and the planning and implementation of a strategy. It raises management trainees' communication skills, helps them to better manage the information flow between individuals and the team, and improves planning and problem-solving skills."[139] In other games each team might have to decide how much to spend on advertising, how much to produce, and how much inventory to maintain.

> **management game**
> A development technique in which teams of managers compete by making computerized decisions regarding realistic but simulated situations.

People learn best by being involved, and games gain such involvement. They also help trainees develop problem-solving skills, and focus attention on planning rather than just putting out fires. They can develop leadership skills and foster cooperation and teamwork.

Gamification of such training also reportedly improves learning, engagement, and morale and is fairly easy to achieve. For instance, inject point systems, badges, and leaderboards into the training.[140]

OUTSIDE SEMINARS Numerous companies and universities offer Web-based and traditional classroom management development seminars and conferences. The selection of 1- to 3-day training programs offered by Ahmedabad Management Association, All India Management Association (AIMA), and CII illustrate what's available. Annual meetings or conferences of professional associations like National Institute of Personnel Management (NIPM), NHRD, or Indian Medical Association (IMA) provide members ample learning opportunities. The Kerala Chapter of NIPM conducts bi-annual HR Conclave on a contemporary topic, where audience has the opportunity to listen to academics, practitioners, and consultants/service providers about the subject. In 2017, the HR Conclave addressed Health and Wellness in Organizations as its theme.[141] Recently, for instance, their offerings ranged from "developing your emotional intelligence" to "assertiveness training," "assertiveness training for managers," "assertiveness training for women in business," "dynamic listening skills for successful communication," and "fundamentals of cost accounting."[142] Specialized groups, such as SHRM, NIPM, and Institute of Chartered Accountants of India (ICAI), provide specialized seminars for their profession's members.[143]

UNIVERSITY-RELATED PROGRAMS Many universities provide executive education and continuing education programs in leadership, supervision, and the like. These can range from 1- to 4-day programs to executive development programs lasting 1 to 4 months. Some of the programs are open to different organizations, while others are customized to specific requirements of a company. IIM Ahmedabad offers more than 75 open programs every year. Sector specific institutions like NIBM Pune and NIA offer programs for specific sectors.

In one such program, Maruti Suzuki India Limited (MSIL) wanted to improve its executives' strategic thinking skills. IIM Ahmedabad took a custom approach to design a program that was built from the ground up to suit MSIL's specific needs. Similarly, Kholer India worked with IIM Bangalore to build capabilities of its dealers. XLRI Jamshedpur offers customized advanced HR program for the HR team members of Accenture India. The Advanced Management Program of Harvard's Graduate School of Business Administration is another such program.[144]

role-playing
A training technique in which trainees act out parts in a realistic management situation.

ROLE-PLAYING The aim of **role-playing** is to create a realistic situation and then have the trainees assume the parts (or roles) of specific persons in that situation. Each trainee gets a role, such as:

> You are the head of a crew of telephone maintenance workers, each of whom drives a small service truck to and from the various jobs. Every so often you get a new truck to exchange for an old one, and you have the problem of deciding to which of your crew members you should give the new truck. Often there are hard feelings, so you have a tough time being fair.[145]

When combined with the general instructions and other roles, role-playing can trigger spirited discussions among the trainees. The aim is to develop trainees' skills in areas like leadership and delegating. For example, a supervisor could experiment with both a considerate and an autocratic leadership style, whereas in the real world this isn't so easy. Role-playing may also help someone to be more sensitive to others' feelings.

in-house development center
A company-based method for exposing prospective managers to realistic exercises to develop improved management skills.

CORPORATE UNIVERSITIES Many firms, particularly larger ones, establish **in-house development centers** (often called *corporate universities*). Employers may collaborate with academic institutions, and with training and development program providers and Web-based educational portals, to create packages of programs and materials for their centers. The best corporate universities (1) actively align offerings with corporate goals, (2) focus on developing skills that support business needs, (3) evaluate learning and performance, (4) use technology to support learning, and (5) partner with academia.[146]

Many employers offer virtual—rather than brick-and-mortar—corporate university services. For example, Cerner offers its employees "Cerner KnowledgeWorks." This offers employees three types of knowledge. *Dynamic knowledge* "is real-time content ... such as e-mails, instant messages, or conference calls." *Moderated content* "includes best practices, such as case studies or wikis that capture information about situations where we did well and how we did it." *Codified content* "is more formal documentation of official company practices, and includes installation guides, help files, and formal training or courses."[147]

EXECUTIVE COACHES   Many firms retain executive coaches to help develop their top managers' effectiveness. An **executive coach** is an outside consultant who questions the executive's boss, peers, subordinates, and (sometimes) family in order to identify the executive's strengths and weaknesses, and to counsel the executive so he or she can capitalize on those strengths and overcome the weaknesses.[148] Executive coaching can cost ₹1 million to ₹2 million per executive. Experts recommend using formal assessments prior to coaching, to uncover strengths and weaknesses and to provide more focused coaching.[149]

Executive coaching can be effective. Participants in one study included about 1,400 senior managers who had received "360-degree" performance feedback from bosses, peers, and subordinates. About 400 worked with an executive coach to review the feedback. About a year later, these and about 400 managers who didn't receive coaching again received multisource feedback. The managers who received coaching were more likely to set more effective goals for their subordinates, and to have improved ratings from subordinates and supervisors.[150]

The coaching field is unregulated, so managers should do their due diligence. Check references, and consult the International Coach Federation, a trade group.

THE SHRM LEARNING SYSTEM   The Society for Human Resource Management (SHRM) encourages HR professionals around the world, including India, to qualify for certification by taking examinations. The society offers several preparatory training programs.[151] These include self-study, and a college/university option that includes classroom interaction with instructors and other learners.[152]

Leadership Development and Life-Cycle Learning at Bank of Baroda

Bank of Baroda (BoB), a leading public sector bank in India with international presence and 52,000 employees, has taken people development as an important activity. The bank has assessed that going forward, it has to seriously consider succession planning (as a majority of its current top management will retire by 2020), building leadership pipeline, and proactively preparing employees for next roles. The bank's Board now closely monitors the leadership development and succession planning activities.

The 'We Lead' initiative of BoB was conceptualized as a multi-year, four-stage program for identified employees. All programs have significant classroom learning, interactions with international and national business/community leaders, self-study, coaching, group assignments, and action learning from high-impact business projects. Some of the initiatives launched at BoB are as follows:

- Baroda Senior Leadership Program (SLP) for identified top managers
- Baroda Emerging Leaders Program (ELP) for senior managers expected to move to senior management roles
- Baroda Rising Star Program (RSP) for department managers (Chief Managers) heading branches or handling critical support roles
- Sayaji Rao Gaekwad Scholar Program for managers and officers at middle and junior management levels

BoB also introduced life-cycle learning concept where employees whose roles are changing (because of promotion or internal movement) attend training programs. The objective of this initiative was to make employees taking new roles be prepared and competent for the assignment. In addition, Baroda Academy and constituent internal training institutes provide regular training programs in general banking operations and specialist areas like credit, compliance and risk management, and NPA (non performing asset) management.[153]

Leadership Development at GE

General Electric is known for its success in developing its executive talent. GE's current mix of executive development programs illustrates what it offers:[154]

Leadership programs: These multiyear training programs rotate about 3,000 employees per year through various functions with the aim of enabling people to run a large GE business.

Session C: This is GE's intense multilevel performance appraisal process. The CEO personally reviews GE's top 625 officers every year.

Crotonville: This is GE's corporate training campus in New York and offers a mix of conventional classroom learning and team-based training and cultural trips.

Boca Raton: At this annual meeting of GE's top 625 officers, they network, share their best ideas, and get to understand the company's strategy for the coming year.

The next big thing: Whether it's productivity and quality improvement through "Six Sigma" or "innovation," GE focuses its employees on central themes or initiatives.

Monthly dinners: Jeffrey Immelt, GE's CEO, meets periodically at dinners and breakfasts to learn more about his top executives and to "strengthen his connections with his top team."[155]

TRENDS SHAPING HR: *CUSTOMIZED TALENT MANAGEMENT THROUGH DIFFERENTIAL DEVELOPMENT ASSIGNMENTS*

In today's competitive environment, the usual HR practice of allocating development opportunities and other scarce resources across the board or based solely on performance makes less sense. It often makes more sense to focus more of the employer's resources on the "mission-critical employees" who the employer deems most crucial to the its future growth.

We'll look closer at how employers do this in the following chapter, but several examples follow:

- High-potential trainees in Johnson & Johnson's special "LeAD" leadership development program receive advice and regular assessments from coaches brought in from outside the company.[156]
- Some companies share future strategies on a privileged basis with rising leaders. For example, they invite them to quarterly meetings with high-level executives, and let them access an online portal where the rising leaders can review the company's strategy and critical metrics.[157] ∎

Managing Organizational Change Programs

Companies often find it necessary to change how they do things. For example, Microsoft changed its CEO a few years ago, then reorganized, changed its strategy

LEARNING OBJECTIVE **8-6**

List and briefly discuss the importance of the steps in leading organizational change.

to include supplying hardware (tablets, etc.) as well as software, and made other personnel changes. As here, organizational change may impact a company's strategy, culture, structure, technologies, or the attitudes and skills of its employees.

Making changes is never easy, but the hardest part is often overcoming employee resistance. Individuals, groups, and even entire organizations tend to resist change, because they are accustomed to the usual way of doing things or because of perceived threats to their influence, for instance.[158]

Lewin's Change Process

Psychologist Kurt Lewin formulated a model to summarize the basic process for implementing a change with minimal resistance. To Lewin, all behavior in organizations was a product of two kinds of forces: those striving to maintain the status quo and those pushing for change. Implementing change thus means reducing the forces for the status quo or building up the forces for change. Lewin's process consists of three steps:

1. *Unfreezing* means reducing the forces that are striving to maintain the status quo, usually by presenting a provocative problem or event to get people to recognize the need for change and to search for new solutions.
2. *Moving* means developing new behaviors, values, and attitudes. The manager may accomplish this through organizational structure changes, through conventional training and development activities, and sometimes through the other organizational development techniques (such as team building) we'll discuss later.
3. *Refreezing* means building in the reinforcement to make sure the organization doesn't slide back into its former ways of doing things—for instance, change the incentive system.

In practice, to deal with employee intransigence, some experts suggest that the manager use a process such as the following to implement the change:[159]

To bring about a desired organizational change at work:

1. *Establish a sense of urgency.* Create a sense of urgency. For example, present employees with a (fictitious) analyst's report describing the firm's imminent demise.
2. *Mobilize commitment* through joint diagnoses of problems. Create a task force to diagnose the problems facing the department or the company.

Microsoft appointed Satya Nadella its new CEO a few years ago, then reorganized, changed its strategy, and made other personnel changes.

Bloomberg/Contributor/Getty Images

This can help to produce a shared understanding of what can and must be improved.

3. *Create a guiding coalition.* It's never easy to implement big changes alone. Therefore, create a "guiding coalition" of influential people. They'll act as missionaries and implementers.

4. *Develop and communicate a shared vision* of what you see coming from the change. Keep the vision simple (for example, "We will be faster than anyone at satisfying customer needs."), and lead by example.[160]

5. *Help employees make the change.* Eliminate impediments. For example, do current policies or procedures make it difficult to act? Do intransigent managers discourage employees from acting?

6. *Aim first for attainable short-term accomplishments.* Use the credibility from these to make additional changes.[161]

7. *Reinforce the new ways of doing things* with changes to the company's systems and procedures. For example, use new appraisal systems and incentives to reinforce the desired new behaviors.

8. *Monitor and assess progress.* In brief, this involves comparing where the company or department is with where it should be.

Using Organizational Development

Beyond this process, there are many other ways to reduce resistance. Among the many suggestions are that managers impose rewards or sanctions that guide employee behaviors, explain why the change is needed, negotiate with employees, give inspirational speeches, or ask employees to help design the change.[162] Organizational development (OD) taps into the latter. **Organizational development** is a change process through which employees formulate the change that's required and implement it, often with the assistance of trained consultants. OD has several distinguishing characteristics:

organizational development
A special approach to organizational change in which employees themselves formulate and implement the change that's required.

1. It usually involves *action research*, which means collecting data about a group, department, or organization, and feeding the information back to the employees so they can analyze it and develop hypotheses about what the problems might be.

2. It applies behavioral science knowledge to improve the organization's effectiveness.

3. It changes the organization in a particular direction—toward empowerment, improved problem-solving, responsiveness, quality of work, and effectiveness.

For example, according to experts French and Bell, one OD method, *team-building meetings*, begins with the consultant interviewing each of the group members and the leader before the meeting.[163] They are asked what their problems are, how they think the group functions, and what obstacles are keeping the group from performing better. The consultant then categorizes the interview data into themes (such as "inadequate communications") and presents the themes to the group at the start of the meeting. The group ranks the themes in terms of importance, and the most important ones become the agenda for the meeting. The group then explores and discusses the issues, examines the underlying causes of the problems, and begins devising solutions.

Survey research is one of many more OD options (see Table 8-2). It requires having employees throughout the organization complete attitude surveys. The facilitator then uses those data as a basis for problem analysis and action planning. Surveys are a convenient way to unfreeze a company's management and employees. They provide a comparative, graphic illustration of the fact that the organization does have problems to solve.[164]

TABLE 8-2 Categories of OD Interventions

Human Process	Human Resource Management
T-groups	Goal setting
Process consultation	Performance appraisal
Third-party intervention	Reward systems
Team building	Career planning and development
Organizational confrontation meeting	Managing workforce diversity
Survey research	Employee wellness

Technostructural	Strategic
Formal structural change	Integrated strategic management
Differentiation and integration	Culture change
Cooperative union–management projects	Strategic change
Quality circles	Self-designing organizations
Total quality management	
Work design	

Evaluating the Training Effort

With today's emphasis on measuring results, it is crucial that the manager evaluate the training program. There are several things you can measure: participants' *reactions* to the program, what (if anything) the trainees *learned* from the program, and to what extent their on-the-job *behavior* or *results* changed as a result of the program. In one survey of about 500 U.S. organizations, 77% evaluated their training programs by eliciting reactions, 36% evaluated learning, and about 10% to 15% assessed the program's behavior and/or results.[165] Computerization facilitates evaluation. For example, Bovis Lend Lease uses learning management system software to monitor which employees are taking which courses, and the extent to which they're improving their skills.[166]

There are two basic issues to address when evaluating training programs. One is the design of the evaluation study and, in particular, whether to use controlled experimentation. The second is, "What should we measure?"

Designing the Study

In deciding how to design the evaluation study, the basic concern is this: How can we be sure that the training (rather than, say, a company-wide wage increase) caused the results that we're trying to measure? The *time series design* is one option. Here, as in Figure 8-3, you take a series of performance measures before and after the training program. This can provide some insight into the program's effectiveness.[167] However, you can't be sure that the training (rather than, say, the raise) caused any change.

Controlled experimentation is therefore the gold standard. A controlled experiment uses a training group and a control group that receives no training. Data (for instance, on quantity of sales or quality of service) are obtained both before and after one group is exposed to training and before and after a corresponding period in the control group. This makes it easier to determine the extent to which any change in the training group's performance resulted from the training, rather than from some organizationwide change like a raise in pay. (The pay raise should have affected employees in both groups equally.)[168]

LEARNING OBJECTIVE 8-7
Explain why a controlled study may be superior for evaluating the training program's effects.

controlled experimentation
Formal methods for testing the effectiveness of a training program, preferably with before-and-after tests and a control group.

FIGURE 8-3 **Using a Time Series Graph to Assess a Training Program's Effects**

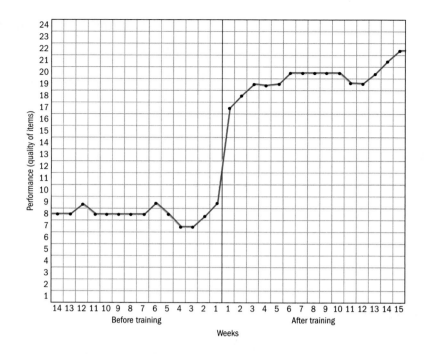

Training Effects to Measure

The manager can measure four basic categories of training outcomes or effects:

1. *Reaction.* Evaluate trainees' reactions to the program. Did they like the program? Did they think it worthwhile?
2. *Learning.* Test the trainees to determine whether they learned the principles, skills, and facts they were supposed to learn.
3. *Behavior.* Ask whether the trainees' on-the-job behavior changed because of the training program. For example, are employees in the store's complaint department more courteous toward disgruntled customers?
4. *Results.* Most important, ask, "What results did we achieve, in terms of the training objectives previously set?" For example, did the number of customer complaints diminish? Reactions, learning, and behavior are important. But if the training program doesn't produce measurable performance-related results, then it probably hasn't achieved its goals.[169]

Evaluating these is straightforward. Figure 8-4 presents one page from a sample evaluation questionnaire for assessing *reactions.* Or, you might assess trainees' *learning* by testing their new knowledge. For *behavioral change,* perhaps assess the effectiveness of a supervisory performance appraisal training program by asking that person's subordinates, "Did your supervisor provide you with examples of good and bad performance when he or she appraised your performance most recently?" Finally, directly assess a training program's *results* by measuring, say, the percentage of phone caller questions that call center trainees subsequently answered correctly.

A careful comparison of the training program's costs and benefits can enable the human resource team to compute the program's return on investment. Online calculators are available to facilitate such analyses.[170]

A program at MGM Resorts illustrates training evaluation.[171] In the hospitality industry, how likely guests are to return is a crucial metric, and is measured at MGM by "Net Promoter Scores" (NPS). With MGM's NPS scores not up to par, its training team concluded "guest facing" employees weren't sufficiently engaged. It created an Essentials of Hotel Management Program for front desk and assistant managers. The program emphasized skills like collaboration and communications. At the end of the approximately 1-year program, NPS scores had risen about 2% (which is considered a notable accomplishment).[172]

| OPM | *INSTRUCTOR HANDOUTS* | *United States Office of Personnel Management* |

TRAINING EVALUATION FORM

TITLE OF COURSE:
NAME OF INSTRUCTOR:
"Work and Family Issues — A Module for Supervisors and Managers"

DATE OF TRAINING
Started:_____
Ended:_____

| **NAME:** (Optional) | **POSITION TITLE/GRADE:** |

| **AGENCY:** | **OFFICE PHONE:** (Optional) | **OFFICE ADDRESS:** (Optional) |

Rate Your Knowledge and Skill Level
(Circle your rating)

Before this course Low -------------------------------------High
                     1   2   3   4   5

After this course   Low -------------------------------------High
                     1   2   3   4   5

Overall, how would you rate this course?

__ Excellent   __Very Good __ Good

__ Fair __ Poor

EVALUATION OF COURSE
(Check appropriate box)

ITEMS OF EVALUATION How did the course sharpen your knowledge or skills in:	Excellent	Very Good	Good	Fair	Poor	Not Applicable
1. What work and family programs are	∘	∘	∘	∘	∘	∘
2. Who uses work and family programs	∘	∘	∘	∘	∘	∘
3. How to recognize/solve work/family issues	∘	∘	∘	∘	∘	∘
4. Helping you take practical steps on the job	∘	∘	∘	∘	∘	∘

RATING OF INSTRUCTOR

1. Presentation, organization, delivery	∘	∘	∘	∘	∘	∘
2. Knowledge and command of the subject	∘	∘	∘	∘	∘	∘
3. Use of audio-visuals or other training aids	∘	∘	∘	∘	∘	∘
4. Stimulation of an open exchange of ideas, participation, & group interaction	∘	∘	∘	∘	∘	∘

STRONG POINTS OF THE COURSE
∘
∘

WEAK POINTS OF THE COURSE
∘
∘

ADDITIONAL DATA YOU WOULD LIKE TO HAVE COVERED IN COURSE
∘
∘
∘

ADDITIONAL COMMENTS/OR RECOMMENDATIONS

FIGURE 8-4 A Training Evaluation Form
Source: From Instructor Handouts: Training Evaluation Form, United States Office of Personnel Management.

Chapter Review

Chapter Section Summaries

8-1. Getting your new employee on board and up to speed begins with **orienting and training** him or her. Employee orientation means providing new employees with the information they need to function, and helping them start being emotionally attached to the firm. The four-step training process includes needs analysis, instructional design, implementation, and evaluation. Trainees need to be motivated to learn. Ensuring that they are motivated involves making the learning meaningful, making skills transfer easy, and reinforcing the learning.

8-2. There is more to orienting employees than introducing them to their coworkers. Even without a company-wide program like Toyota's, use the onboarding opportunity to begin instilling in the new employee the company values and traditions in which you expect the person to become **engaged**.

8-3. We used the acronym **ADDIE** to outline the **training process**: analyze, develop, design, implement, and evaluate. Before training employees, it's necessary to analyze their training needs and design the training program. In training new employees, employers use task analysis—basically, a detailed study of the job—to determine what skills the job requires. For current employees, performance analysis is required, specifically to verify that there is performance efficiency and to determine if training is the solution. Distinguishing between can't-do and won't-do problems is the main issue here. Once you understand the issues, you can design a training program, which means identifying specific training objectives, clarifying a training budget, and then actually designing the program in terms of the actual content.

8-4. With this in place, you can turn to **implementing the training program**. Specific training methods include on-the-job training, apprenticeship training, informal learning, job instruction training, lectures, programmed learning, audiovisual-based training, vestibule training, videoconferencing, electronic performance support systems, and computer-based training. Frequently, programs today are Internet-based, with employees accessing packaged online programs, backed up by learning management systems, through their company's learning portals. Employers also increasingly use mobile learning, for instance, delivering short courses and explanations to employees' smart phones. With increasing demands for technologically literate employees, lifelong learning can help ensure employees have the basic educational backgrounds they need to succeed on their jobs. Diversity training aims to create better cross-cultural sensitivity with the goal of fostering more harmonious working relationships.

8-5. Most training methods are useful for all employees, but some are particularly appropriate for **management development programs**. Like all employees, new managers often get on-the-job training, for instance, via job rotation and coaching. In addition, it's usual to supply various off-the-job training and development opportunities—for instance, using the case study method, management games, outside seminars, university-related programs, corporate universities, executive coaches, and (for human resource managers) the SHRM learning system.

8-6. When facing economic, competitive, or other challenges, managers have to execute **organizational change programs**. These may aim at changing the company's strategy, culture, structure, technologies, or the attitudes and skills of the employees. Often, the trickiest part of organizational change is overcoming employees' resistance to it. With that in mind, steps in an effective organizational change program include establishing a sense of urgency, mobilizing commitment, creating a guiding coalition, developing and communicating a shared vision, helping employees make the change, consolidating gains, reinforcing new ways of doing things, and monitoring and assessing progress. Organizational development involves action research, which means collecting data about a group and feeding the information back to the employees so they can analyze it and develop hypotheses about what the problems might be.

8-7. Whatever the training program, it's important to **evaluate the training effort**. You can measure reaction, learning, behavior, or results, ideally using a control group that is not exposed to training, in parallel with the group that you're training.

Discussion Questions

8-1. "A well-thought-out orientation program is essential for all new employees, whether they have experience or not." Explain why you agree or disagree with this statement.

8-2. Explain how you would apply our "motivation points" (pages 232–234) in developing a lecture, say, on orientation and training.

8-3. What are some typical on-the-job training techniques? What do you think are some of the main drawbacks of relying on informal on-the-job training for breaking new employees into their jobs?

What are some important advantages to using cloud-based training?

8-4. Describe the pros and cons of five management development methods.

8-5. Do you think job rotation is a good method to use for developing management trainees? Why or why not?

8-6. What is organizational development, and how does it differ from traditional approaches to organizational change?

8-7. List and briefly explain each of the steps in the training process.

Individual and Group Activities

8-8. You're the supervisor of a group of employees whose task is to assemble disk drives that go into computers. You find that quality is not what it should be and that many of your group's devices have to be brought back and reworked. Your boss says, "You'd better start doing a better job of training your workers."
   a. What are some of the staffing factors that could be contributing to this problem?
   b. Explain how you would go about assessing whether it is in fact a training problem.

8-9. Choose a task with which you are familiar—mowing the lawn, making a salad, or studying for a test—and develop a job instruction sheet for it.

8-10. Working individually or in groups, develop a short, programmed learning program on the subject "Guidelines for Giving a More Effective Lecture."

8-11. Find three or four actual examples of employers using social media for training purposes. At what levels of managers are the offerings aimed? What seem to be the most popular types of programs? Why do you think that's the case?

8-12. Working individually or in groups, develop several specific examples to illustrate how a professor teaching human resource management could use at least four of the techniques described in this chapter in teaching his or her HR course.

8-13. Working individually or in groups, develop an orientation program for high school graduates entering your university as freshmen.

8-14. Appendices A and B at the end of this book (pages 583–600) list the knowledge someone studying for the HRCI (Appendix A) or SHRM (Appendix B) certification exam needs to have in each area of human resource management (such as in Strategic Management, and Workforce Planning). In groups of several students, do four things: (1) review Appendix A and/or B; (2) identify the material in this chapter that relates to the Appendix A and/or B required knowledge lists; (3) write four multiple-choice exam questions on this material that you believe would be suitable for inclusion in the HRCI exam and/or the SHRM exam; and, (4) if time permits, have someone from your team post your team's questions in front of the class, so that students in all teams can answer the exam questions created by the other teams.

8-15. Perhaps no training task in Afghanistan was more pressing than that involved in creating the country's new railway system, which is an ongoing task. These were the people who were to help the newly elected government bring development in Afghanistan. However, many new recruits and even officers had no experience. There were language barriers between trainers and trainees. And some trainees found themselves quickly under fire from insurgents when they went as trainees out into the field. Based on what you learned about training from this chapter, list the five most important things you would tell the officer in charge of training to keep in mind as he designs the training program.

Experiential Exercise

Flying the Friendlier Skies

Purpose: The purpose of this exercise is to give you practice in developing a training program for the job of airline reservation clerk for a major airline.

Required Understanding: You should be fully acquainted with the material in this chapter and should read the following description of an airline reservation clerk's duties:

> Customers contact our airline reservation clerks to obtain flight schedules, prices, and itineraries. The reservation clerks look up the requested information on our airline's online flight schedule systems, which are updated continuously. The reservation clerk must deal courteously and expeditiously with the customer, and be able to quickly find alternative flight arrangements in order to provide the customer with the itinerary that fits his or her needs. Alternative flights and prices must be found quickly, so that the customer is not kept waiting, and so

that our reservations operations group maintains its efficiency standards. It is often necessary to look under various routings, since there may be a dozen or more alternative routes between the customer's starting point and destination.

You may assume that we just hired 30 new clerks, and that you must create a 3-day training program.

How to Set Up the Exercise/Instructions: Divide the class into teams of five or six students.

Airline reservation clerks obviously need numerous skills to perform their jobs. This airline has asked you to quickly design the outline of a training program for its new reservation clerks.

8-16. You may want to start by listing the job's main duties and by reviewing any work you may have done for the exercise at the end of Chapter 6.

8-17. In any case, please produce the requested outline, making sure to be very specific about what you want to teach the new clerks, and what methods and aids you suggest using to train them.

Application Case*

Reinventing the Wheel at Apex Door Company

Jim Delaney, president of Apex Door, has a problem. No matter how often he tells his employees how to do their jobs, they invariably "decide to do it their way," as he puts it, and arguments ensue between Jim, the employee, and the employee's supervisor. One example is the door-design department, where the designers are expected to work with the architects to design doors that meet the specifications. While it's not "rocket science," as Jim puts it, the designers invariably make mistakes—such as designing in too much steel, a problem that can cost Apex tens of thousands of wasted dollars, once you consider the number of doors in, say, a 30-story office tower.

The order processing department is another example. Jim has a very specific and detailed way he wants the order written up, but most of the order clerks don't understand how to use the multipage order form. They simply improvise when it comes to a detailed question such as whether to classify the customer as "industrial" or "commercial."

The current training process is as follows. None of the jobs has a training manual per se, although several have somewhat out-of-date job descriptions. The training for new people is all on the job. Usually, the person leaving the company trains the new person during the 1- or 2-week overlap period, but if there's no overlap, the new person is trained as well as possible by other employees who have filled in occasionally on the job in the past. The training is the same throughout the company—for machinists, secretaries, assemblers, engineers, and accounting clerks, for example.

Questions

8-18. What do you think of Apex's training process? Could it help to explain why employees "do things their way"? If so, how?

8-19. What role should job descriptions play in training at Apex?

8-20. Explain in detail what you would do to improve the training process at Apex. Make sure to provide specific suggestions, please.

Continuing Case

Carter Cleaning Company

The New Training Program

The Carter Cleaning Centers currently have no formal orientation or training policies or procedures, and Jennifer believes this is one reason why the standards to which she and her father would like employees to adhere are generally not followed.

The Carters would prefer that certain practices and procedures be used in dealing with the customers at the front counters. For example, all customers should be greeted with what Jack refers to as a "big hello." Garments they drop off should immediately be inspected for any damage or unusual stains so these can be brought to the customer's attention, lest the customer later return to pick up the garment and erroneously blame the store. The garments are then supposed to

*Source: Copyright Dr. Gary Dessler.

be placed together in a nylon sack immediately to separate them from other customers' garments. The ticket also has to be carefully written, with the customer's name and telephone number and the date clearly noted on all copies. The counter person is also supposed to take the opportunity to try to sell the customer additional services such as waterproofing, or simply notify the customer that "Now that people are doing their spring cleaning, we're having a special on drapery cleaning all this month." Finally, as the customer leaves, the counter person is supposed to make a courteous comment like "Have a nice day." Each of the other jobs in the stores—pressing, cleaning and spotting, and so forth—similarly contain certain steps, procedures, and, most importantly, standards the Carters would prefer to see upheld.

The company has had problems, Jennifer feels, because of a lack of adequate employee training and orientation. For example, two new employees became very upset last month when they discovered that they were not paid at the end of the week, on Friday, but instead were paid (as are all Carter employees) on the following Tuesday. The Carters use the extra 2 days in part to give them time to obtain everyone's hours and compute their pay. The other reason they do it, according to Jack, is that "frankly, when we stay a few days behind in paying employees it helps to ensure that they at least give us a few days' notice before quitting on us. While we are certainly obligated to pay them anything they earn, we find that psychologically they seem to be less likely to just walk out on us Friday evening and not show up Monday morning if they still haven't gotten their pay from the previous week. This way they at least give us a few days' notice so we can find a replacement."

There are other matters that could be covered during orientation and training, says Jennifer. These include company policy regarding paid holidays, lateness and absences, health benefits (there are none, other than workers' compensation), substance abuse, eating or smoking on the job (both forbidden), and general matters like the maintenance of a clean and safe work area, personal appearance and cleanliness, time sheets, personal telephone calls, and personal e-mail.

Jennifer believes that implementing orientation and training programs would help to ensure that employees know how to do their jobs the right way. And she and her father further believe that it is only when employees understand the right way to do their jobs that there is any hope their jobs will be accomplished the way the Carters want them to be accomplished.

Questions

8-21. Specifically, what should the Carters cover in their new employee orientation program, and how should they convey this information?

8-22. In the HR management course Jennifer took, the book suggested using a job instruction sheet to identify tasks performed by an employee. Should the Carter Cleaning Centers use a form like this for the counter person's job? If so, what should the form look like, say, for a counter person?

8-23. Which specific training techniques should Jennifer use to train her pressers, her cleaner/spotters, her managers, and her counter people? Why should these training techniques be used?

Translating Strategy into HR Policies and Practices Case*,§

*The overall map on page xxxviii of this book outlines the relationships involved.

Improving Performance at the Hotel Paris

The New Training Program

The Hotel Paris's competitive strategy is "To use superior guest service to differentiate the Hotel Paris properties, and to thereby increase the length of stay and return rate of guests, and thus boost revenues and profitability." HR manager Lisa Cruz must now formulate functional policies and activities that support this competitive strategy, by eliciting the required employee behaviors and competencies.

As she reviewed her company's training processes, Lisa had many reasons to be concerned. For one thing, the Hotel Paris relied almost exclusively on informal on-the-job training. New security guards attended a 1-week program offered by a law enforcement agency, but all other new hires, from assistant manager to housekeeping crew, learned the rudiments of their jobs from their colleagues and their supervisors, on the job. Lisa noted that the drawbacks of this informality were evident when she compared the Hotel Paris's performance on various training metrics with those of other hotels and service firms. For example, in terms of number of hours training per employee per year, number of hours training for new employees, cost per trainee hour, and percent of payroll spent on training, the Hotel Paris was far from the norm when benchmarked against similar firms.

As Lisa and the CFO reviewed measures of the Hotel Paris's current training efforts, it was clear that (when compared to similar companies) some changes were in order. Most other service companies provided at least 40 hours of training per employee per year, while the Hotel Paris offered, on average, no more than 5 or 6. Similar firms offered at least 40 hours of training per *new* employee, while the Hotel Paris offered, at most, 10. Even the apparently "good" metrics comparisons simply masked poor results. For example, whereas most service firms spend about 8% of their payrolls on training, the Hotel Paris spent less than 1%. The problem, of course, was that the Hotel Paris's training wasn't more efficient, it was simply nonexistent.

Given this and the commonsense links between (1) employee training and (2) employee performance, the CFO gave his go-ahead for Lisa and her team to design a comprehensive package of training programs for all Hotel Paris employees. They retained a training supplier to design a 1-day training program composed of lectures and audiovisual material for all new employees. This program covered the Hotel Paris's history, its competitive strategy, and its critical employee capabilities and behaviors, including the need to be customer oriented. With a combination of lectures and video examples of correct and incorrect behaviors, the behavior-modeling part of this program aimed to cultivate in new employees the company's essential values, including, "we endeavor to do everything we can to make the guests' stay 100% pleasant."

§Written by and copyright Gary Dessler, PhD.

The team developed separate training programs for each of the hotel's other individual job categories. For example, it retained a special vendor to create computer-based training programs, complete with interactive scenarios, for both the front-desk clerks and telephone operators. As with all the new training programs, they had these translated into the languages of the countries in which the Hotel Paris did business. The team chose to stay with on-the-job training for both the housekeeping and valet/door person job categories, but formalized this training with special handbooks for each job category's supervisory staff. For assistant managers, the team developed a new videoconference-based online training and development program. In this way, the new managers could interact with other assistant managers around the chain, even as they were learning the basics of their new jobs. Lisa and the CFO were not at all surprised to find that within a year of instituting the new training programs, scores on numerous employee capabilities and behavior metrics (including speed of check-in/out, percent of employees scoring at least 90% on Hotel Paris's values quiz, and percent room cleaning infractions) improved markedly. They knew from previous analyses that these improvements would, in turn, drive improvements in customer and organizational outcomes, and strategic performance.

Questions

8-24. Based on what you read in this chapter, what would you have suggested Lisa and her team do first with respect to training, particularly in terms of the company's strategy? Why?

8-25. Have Lisa and the CFO sufficiently investigated whether training is really called for? Why? What would you suggest?

8-26. Based on what you read in this Dessler *Human Resource Management* chapter and what you may access via the Web, develop a detailed training program for one of these hotel positions: security guard, housekeeper, or door person.

Key Terms

employee orientation, 235
training, 227
negligent training, 227
task analysis, 229
competency model, 229
performance analysis, 230
the cloud, 235
on-the-job training (OJT), 235

apprenticeship training, 236
job instruction training (JIT), 237
programmed learning, 238
behavior modeling, 238
electronic performance support systems (EPSS), 239
job aid, 239

lifelong learning, 240
cross training, 241
virtual classroom, 243
Web 2.0 learning, 243
management development, 244
job rotation, 246
action learning, 247
case study method, 247

management game, 247
role-playing, 248
in-house development center, 248
executive coach, 249
organizational development, 252
controlled experimentation, 253

Endnotes

1. Accessed on 21 August 2017 at https://www.peoplematters.in/article/hr-technology/how-mahindra-finance-beat-attrition-with-soap-opera-style-learning-15909.
2. Marjorie Derven, "Management Onboarding," *TD*, April 2008, pp. 49–52. See also www.roberthalf.com/onboarding, accessed August 23, 2014.
3. Sabrina Hicks, "Successful Orientation Programs," *Training & Development*, April 2000, p. 59. See also Howard Klein and Natasha Weaver, "The Effectiveness of an Organizational Level Orientation Program in the Socialization of New Hires," *Personnel Psychology* 53 (2000), pp. 47–66; Laurie Friedman, "Are You Losing Potential New Hires at Hello?" *Training & Development*, November 2006, pp. 25–27; and Talya N. Bauer, "Onboarding New Employees: Maximizing Success," *SHRM Foundation*, www.right.com/thought-leadership/research/shrm-foundations-effective-practice-guidelines-series-onboarding-new-employees-maximizing-success-sponsored-by-right-management.pdf, accessed March 2, 2014.

4. See, for example, John Kammeyer-Mueller and Connie Wanberg, "Unwrapping the Organizational Entry Process: Disentangling Multiple Antecedents and Their Pathways to Adjustments," *Journal of Applied Psychology* 88, no. 5 (2003), pp. 779–794.
5. www.right.com/thought-leadership/research/shrm-foundations-effective-practice-guidelines-series-onboardingnew-employees-maximizing-success-sponsored-by-right-management.pdf, accessed August 23, 2014.
6. www.shrm.org/templatestools/samples/hrforms/articles/pages/1cms_002153.aspx, http://hrweb.berkeley.edu/guides/managing-hr/recruiting-staff/new-employee/checklist, and www.go2hr.ca/articles/new-hire-orientation-checklist, all accessed March 30, 2015.
7. Mukta Kulkarni and Mark Lengnick–Hall, "Socialization of People with Disabilities in the Workplace," *Human Resource Management* 60, no. 4 (July–August 2011), pp. 521–540.
8. "Drug Rep Claims Handbook Protection from Retaliation,"

BNA Bulletin to Management, December 18, 2012, p. 8.
9. Ed Frauenheim, "IBM Learning Programs Get a 'Second Life,'" *Workforce Management*, December 11, 2006, p. 6. See also J. T. Arnold, "Gaming Technology Used to Orient New Hires," *HR Magazine* (2009 HR Trendbook supp), pp. 36, 38.
10. Jennifer Taylor Arnold, "Ramping Up Onboarding," *HR Magazine*, May 2010, pp. 75–78.
11. www.workday.com/company/news/workdaymobility.php, accessed March 24, 2009.
12. "Four Ways to Use QR Codes to Enliven Your Learning Event," *Training & Development*, January 2013, p. 19.
13. "New Survey Reveals One in Six Companies Using Gaming Techniques to Make Onboarding Fun," *Bloomberg BNA Bulletin to Management*, March 26, 2013, p. 99.
14. For example, IBM's "assimilation process" has three main steps: *affirming* (welcoming the new employee and assigning a coach); *beginning* (he or she is met in person, meets the team, is introduced on the intranet

onboarding platform, and learns his or her roles and responsibilities); and *connecting* (which includes having an "ask coach" make sure the employee is on track). www.right.com/thought-leadership/research/shrm-foundations-effective-practice-guidelines-series-onboarding-new-employees-maximizing-success-sponsored-by-right-management.pdf.
15. See, for example, Gary Dessler, *Winning Commitment: How to Build and Keep a Competitive Workforce* (New York: McGraw-Hill, 1993); and Gary Dessler, "How to Earn Your Employees' Commitment," *Academy of Management Executive* 13, no. 2 (1999).
16. Ibid., and see www.autonews.com/article/20050718/SUB/507180713/toyota-seeks-efficiency-training-for-all; http://thetoyotaway.org/excerpts.html; www.toyotageorgetown.com/tps1.asp; http://sloanreview.mit.edu/article/what-really-happened-to-toyota; and www.glassdoor.com/Reviews/Employee-Review-Toyota-Tsusho-America-RVW3553588.htm; all accessed February 28, 2014.

17. Ibid. While long respected for its commitment to these principles—and to the high-quality cars that its employee engagement produced—Toyota ran into problems a few years ago. In pursuing a new faster-growth strategy, Toyota's famed employee selection and on-boarding/training program may have faltered, possibly leading to some employee morale and vehicle quality problems. Soon under new top management, the company seems to have returned to its quality roots.

18. Laurie Miller, "2014 State of the Industry Report," *TD*, November 2014, pp. 30–34.

19. "Lack of Training Fuels Desire to Job Search," *Training & Development*, January 2013, p. 23.

20. Development Programs for Employees, www.coca-colaindia.com, (Navigation–Home–Topics–Sustainability), as accessed on 08 August 2017 at 4pm IST.

21. Laszlo Bock, *Work Rules!* (New York: Twelve, 2015), p. 60.

22. Ibid., p. 33.

23. Rita Smith, "Aligning Learning with Business Strategy," *Training & Development*, November 2008, pp. 41–43.

24. Christine Ellis and Sarah Gale, "A Seat at the Table," *Training*, March 2001, pp. 90–96.

25. Christopher Glynn, "Building a Learning Infrastructure," Training and Development, January 2008, pp.38-43.

26. Garry Karantz, ''More to Learn'', Workforce Management, January 2011, p.27.

27. Accessed on September 26, 2017 at http://www.mahindra.com/news-room/press-release/mahindra-and-mahindra-financial-services-wins-aon-best-employer-award-for-2017.

28. W. Clayton Allen, "Overview and Evolution of the ADDIE Training System," *Advances in Developing Human Resources* 8, no. 4 (November 2006), pp. 430–441.

29. www.intulogy.com/process, accessed April 20, 2011.

30. P. Nick Blanchard and James Thacker, *Effective Training: Systems, Strategies, and Practices* (Upper Saddle River, NJ: Prentice Hall, 1999), pp. 138–139. See also Matthew Casey and Dennis Doverspike, "Training Needs Analysis and Evaluation for New Technologies Through the Use of Problem Based Inquiry," *Performance Improvement Quarterly* 18, no. 1 (2005), pp. 110–124.

31. See also, for example, Jennifer Salopek, "The Power of the Pyramid," *Training & Development*, May 2009, pp. 70–73.

32. "Retooling Vocational Education," *The Economist*, August 23, 2014, p. 66.

33. Pat Galagan, "It's the Competency That Matters, Not the Course," *T + D*, January 2015, pp. 24–27.

34. Tom Barron, "When Things Go Haywire," *Training & Development*, February 1999, pp. 25–27; see also, for example, Bill Stetar, "Training: It's Not Always the Answer," *Quality Progress*, March 2005, pp. 44–49, http://performancetechnology.com/ptg_pdfs/qp0305stetar.pdf, accessed October 11, 2012.

35. Employers increasingly utilize learning content management systems (LCMS) to compile author training content. See, for example, Bill Perry, "Customized Content at Your Fingertips," *Training & Development*, June 2009, pp. 29–30.

36. P. Nick Blanchard and James Thacker, *Effective Training* (Upper Saddle River, NJ: Pearson, 2010), pp. 26–94, 153–199, 285–316; see also Bruno Neal," "e-ADDIE!," *T1D* 65, no. 3 (March 2011), pp. 76–77. Should be T+D.

37. Jay Bahlis, "Blueprint for Planning Learning," *Training & Development*, March 2008, pp. 64–67.

38. P. Nick Blanchard and James Thacker, *Effective Training: Systems, Strategies, and Practices* (Upper Saddle River, NJ: Prentice Hall, 2007), p. 8; and G. Sadri, "Boosting Performance Through Self-Efficacy," *T1D* 65 no. 6 (June 2011), pp. 30–31. Should be T+D.

39. Emily Baumann and Greta Ballentine, "Estimate Training Resources with Precision," *T + D*, February 2014, pp. 20–22.

40. Ibid.

41. Ibid., p. 90.

42. Kenneth Wexley and Gary Latham, *Developing and Training Human Resources in Organizations* (Upper Saddle River, NJ: Prentice Hall, 2002), p. 305.

43. Ibid.

44. Kathryn Tyler, "Focus on Training," *HR Magazine*, May 2000, pp. 94–102.

45. Janice A. Cannon-Bowers et al., "Framework for Understanding Pre-Practice Conditions and Their Impact on Learning," *Personnel Psychology* 51 (1998), pp. 291–320; see also J. S. Goodman et al., "Feedback Specificity, Information Processing, and Transfer of Training," *Organizational Behavior and Human Decision Processes* 115 no. 2 (July 2011), pp. 253–267.

46. Ibid., p. 305.

47. Ibid., and see Kendra Lee, "Reinforce Training," *Training* 48 no. 3 (May/June 2011), p. 24.

48. Eric Krell, "Get Sold on Training Incentives,"*HR Magazine*, February 2013, p. 57.

49. Stefanie Johnson,"Go for the Goal (as): Relationship Between Goal Setting and Transfer of Training Following Leadership Development," *Academy of Management Learning & Education* 11, no. 4 (2012), pp. 555–569.

50. Alan Saks and Monica Belcourt, "An Investigation of Training Activities and Transfer of Training in Organizations," *Human Resource Management* 45, no. 4 (Winter 2006), pp. 629–648. The percentage of managers transferring behaviors from training to the job may be as low as 10% to 20%. See George Vellios, "On the Level," *Training & Development*, December 2008, pp. 26–29. See also K. Lee, "Implement Training Successfully," *Training* 46, no. 5 (June 2009), p. 16.

51. Large training providers include Element K, Geo Learning, learn.com, Outsmart, Plateau, Saba People Systems, and SumTotal Systems. "Training Providers," *Workforce Management*, January 2011, p. 8. See also Jean Barbazette, "Take the Pain Out of Writing Training Materials," *T + D*, April 2013, pp. 108–110.

52. ASTD Infoline, "Planning and Organizing Training Events," August 2013; and Robert Hewes, "Step-by-Step," *T + D*, February 2014, pp. 56–61.

53. www.litmos.com/learning-management-system; www.talentlms.com; http://money.CNN.com/2014/09/03/technology/enterprise/what-is-the-cloud, both accessed March 31, 2015.

54. Wexley and Latham, *Developing and Training Human Resources in Organizations*, pp. 78–79.

55. Donna Goldwasser, "Me a Trainer?" *Training*, April 2001, pp. 60–66; http://employment.menswearhouse.com/ats/advantageSelector.action;jsessionid=C6EA17158451F5A2902F7195B678CF6A?type=training, accessed June 1, 2011.

56. See, for example, www.aps-online.net/consulting/structured_ojt.htm, accessed June 1, 2011; and Kathryn Tyler, "15 Ways to Train on the Job," *HR Magazine* 53 no. 9 (September 2008), pp. 105–108.

57. Valerie Davis-Howard, "Unleash Change Through a Peer-to-Peer Approach," *T + D*, July 2014, pp. 76–77.

58. The following four steps in on-the-job training based on William Berliner and William McLarney, *Management Practice and Training* (Burr Ridge, IL: McGraw-Hill, 1974), pp. 442–443. For the discussion of employee task analysis, see "Eight Steps to Better On-the-Job Training," *HR Focus* 80, no. 7 (July 2003), pp. 11, 13–14.

59. Cindy Waxer, "Steelmaker Revives Apprentice Program to Address Graying Workforce, Forge Next Leaders," *Workforce Management*, January 30, 2006, p. 40.

60. Robert Weintraub and Jennifer Martineau, "The Just in Time Imperative," *Training & Development*, June 2002, p. 52; Andrew Paradise, "Informal Learning: Overlooked or Over-hyped?" *Training & Development*, July 2008, pp. 52–53. In one survey, about one-third of respondents said they did not earmark training dollars for informal learning.

61. Accessed on 21 August 2017 at http://www.skilldevelopment.gov.in/assets/images/announcements/FAQ-NAPS.pdf.

62. Aparna Nancherla, "Knowledge Delivered in Any Other Form Is … Perhaps Sweeter," *Training & Development*, May 2009, pp. 54–60.

63. Nadira Hira, "The Making of a UPS Driver," *Fortune*, November 12, 2007, p. 120.

64. Arthur Winfred Jr. et al., "Effectiveness of Training in Organizations: A Meta Analysis of Design and Evaluation Features," *Journal of Applied Psychology* 88, no. 2 (2003), pp. 234–245.

65. Donald Michalak and Edwin G. Yager, *Making the Training Process Work* (New York: Harper & Row, 1979), pp. 108–111. See also Richard Wiegand, "Can All Your Trainees Hear You?" *Training & Development Journal* 41, no. 8 (August 1987), pp. 38–43; and "Dos and Don'ts at the Podium," *Journal of Accountancy* 200, no. 3 (September 2005).

66. Jacqueline Schmidt and Joseph Miller, "The Five-Minute Rule for Presentations," *Training & Development*, March 2000, pp. 16–17; and "Dos and Don'ts at the Podium," op cit.

67. G. N. Nash, J. P. Muczyk, and F. L. Vettori, "The Role and Practical Effectiveness of Programmed Instruction," *Personnel Psychology* 24 (1971), pp. 397–418; Duane Schultz and Sydney Ellen Schultz, *Psychology and Work Today* (Upper Saddle River, NJ: Prentice Hall, 1998), pp. 181–183; chemistry study based on N. Izzet Kurbanoglu, Yavuz Taskesenligil, and Mustafa Sozbilir, "Programmed Instruction Revisited: A Study on Teaching Stereochemistry," *Chemistry Education Research and Practice* 7, no. 1 (2006), pp. 13–21.

68. Paul Taylor et al., "A Meta-Analytic Review of Behavior Modeling Training," *Journal of Applied Psychology* 90, no. 4 (2005), pp. 692–719.

69. Wexley and Latham, *Developing and Training Human Resources in Organizations*, pp. 131–133. See also Teri O. Grady and Mike Matthews, "Video … Through the Eyes of the Trainee," *Training* 24, no. 7 (July 1987), pp. 57–62; "New ARTBA PPE Video and Laborers' Night Work Suggestions Highlight Construction Safety Advances," *EHS Today* 2, no. 7 (July 2009), p. 51.

70. Paula Ketter, "What Can Training Do for Brown?" *Training & Development*, May 2008, pp. 30–36.

71. Craig Marion, "What Is the EPSS Movement and What Does It Mean to Information Designers?" http://www.smnweb.com/e-hr/letture/perform/EPSS%20Movement.htm, August 20, 1999, accessed June 28, 2015.

72. Josh Bersin and Karen O'Leonard, "Performance Support Systems," *Training & Development*, April 2005, p. 68.

73. Blanchard and Thacker, *Effective Training*, 2010, p. 163.

74. www.cisco.com/en/US/products/ps10352/index.html, accessed June 28, 2015.

75. www.radvision.com/Support/cisco.htm, accessed June 1, 2011.

76. Dina Berta, "Computer-Based Training Clicks with Both Franchisees and Their Employees," *Nation's Restaurant News*, July 9, 2001, pp. 1, 18; and, "Is Online Fall Protection Training Effective?" *EHS Today* 3, no. 7 (July 2010).

77. P. Nick Blanchard and James Thacker, *Effective Training: Systems, Strategies, and Practices* (Upper Saddle River, NJ: Pearson, 2003), p. 247; see also Michael Laff, "Simulations: Slowly Proving Their Worth," *Training & Development*, June 2007, pp. 30–34.

78. Laff, "Simulations."

79. Blanchard and Thacker, *Effective Training*, 2003, p. 248.

80. Ibid., p. 249. See also Kim Kleps, "Virtual Sales Training Scores a Hit," *Training & Development*, December 2006, pp. 63–64.

81. www.reuters.com/article/2014/03/26/us-facebook-acquisition-idUSBREA2O1WX20140326, accessed June 28, 2015.

82. Jenni Jarventaus, "Virtual Threat, Real Sweat." T+D, May 2007, Vol. 61 Issue 5, p. 72

83. Clark Aldrich, "Engaging Mini-Games Find Niche in Training," *Training & Development*, July 2007, pp. 22–24; and "Cisco's Global Training Machine," *Workforce Management*, November 17, 2008, p. 30.

84. Drew Robb, "Let the Games Begin," *HR Magazine*, September 2012, p. 96.

85. "What Do Simulations Cost?" *Training & Development*, June 2007, p. 88; see also Paul Harris, "Immersive Learning Seeks a Foothold," *Training & Development*, January 2009, pp. 40–45; and R. S. Polimeni et al., "Using Computer Simulations to Recruit and Train Generation Y Accountants," *The CPA Journal* 79, no. 5 (May 2009), pp. 64–68.

86. Garry Kranz, "More to Learn," *Workforce Management*, January 2011, p. 27; quote is from Ann Pace, "Spurring Innovation and Engaging the Learners of the 2011 Workplace," *T+D* 65, no. 8 (August 2011), pp. 64–69.

87. Jeremy Smerd, "New Workers Sorely Lacking Literacy Skills," *Workforce Management*, December 10, 2008, p. 6.

88. Paula Ketter, "The Hidden Disability," *Training & Development*, June 2006, pp. 34–40.

89. Jennifer Salopek, "The Growth of Succession Management," *Training & Development*, June 2007, pp. 22–24; and Kermit Kaleba, "Businesses Continue to Push for Lifelong Learning," *Training & Development*, June 2007, p. 14.

90. Rita Zeidner, "One Workforce—Many Languages," *HR Magazine*, January 2009, pp. 33–37.

91. Matthew Reis, "Do-It-Yourself Diversity," *Training & Development*, March 2004, pp. 80–81.

92. www.prismdiversity.com/resources/diversity_training.html, accessed June 1, 2011.

93. Jennifer Salopek, "Trends: Lost in Translation," *Training & Development*, December 2003, p. 15; www.visionpoint.com/training-solutions/title/just-be-fair-basic-diversity-training, accessed June 17, 2011.

94. Paraphrased from "Best Practice: Workforce Diversity Training," Manufacturing Practices Center of Excellence, www.brmpcoe.org/bestpracticea/internal/abev/abcv_15.html.

95. Blanchard and Thacker, *Effective Training*, 2003, pp. 403–405.

96. Ibid., p. 404.

97. Holly Dolezalek, "Extreme Training," *Training* 47, no. 1 (January 2010), pp. 26–28.

98. Douglas Shuit, "Sound of the Retreat," *Workforce Management*, September 2003, p. 40.

99. Kevin Alansky, "Blackboard Pays Off for ADP," *T+D* 65, no. 6 (June 2011), pp. 68–69; see also Barbara Carnes, "The Ties That Bind," *Training & Development*, January 2013, pp. 38–40.

100. Greg Wright, "Retailers Buy into Relearning," *HR Magazine*, December 7, 2010, pp. 87–90.

101. Pat Galagan, "Made Fast in China," *Training & Development*, January 2013, p. 30.

102. John Zonneveld, "GM Dealer Training Goes Global," *Training & Development*, December 2006, pp. 47–51. See also "What's Next for the LMS?" *Training & Development*, September 2011, p. 16.

103. "The Next Generation of Corporate Learning," *Training & Development*, June 2003, p. 47.

104. Ibid.

105. For a list of guidelines for using e-learning, see, for example, Mark Simon, "E-Learning No How," *Training & Development*, January 2009, pp. 34–39. See also Sarah Gilbert, "E-learning Design with Ease," *T+D*, July 2014, pp. 70–71.

106. "The Next Generation of Corporate Learning," *Training & Development*, June 2004, p. 47; Jennifer Hofmann and Nanatte Miner, "Real Blended Learning Stands Up," *Training & Development*, September 2008, pp. 28–31; J. Hofmann, "Top 10 Challenges of Blended Learning," *Training* (Minneapolis, Minn.) 48, no. 2 (March/April 2011), pp. 12–13; and Lee Salz, "Use Webinars for Training and Revenue," *Training* 48, no. 2 (March/April 2011), p. 14.

107. Ruth Clark, "Harnessing the Virtual Classroom," *Training & Development*, November 2005, pp. 40–46.

108. Traci Sitzmann et al., "The Comparative Effectiveness of Web-Based and Classroom Instruction: A Meta-Analysis," *Personnel Psychology* 59 (2006), pp. 623–664.

109. Jennifer Taylor Arnold, "Learning On-the-Fly," *HR Magazine*, September 2007, p. 137; see also M. Donahue, "Mobile Learning Is the Next Generation in Training." *Hotel Management* 226, no. 4 (April 4, 2011), p. 17.

110. www.dominknow.com, accessed March 23, 2009.

111. Bill Roberts, "From IT Learning to Mobile Learning," *HR Magazine*, August 2012, pp. 61–65.

112. Chris Pirie, "Technology Plus Learning Equals Inspiration," *Training & Development*, December 2012, pp. 39–46.

113. Elizabeth Agnvall, "Just-in-Time Training," *HR Magazine*, May 2006, pp. 67–78.

114. For a similar program at Accenture, see Don Vanthournout and Dana Koch, "Training at Your Fingertips," *Training & Development*, September 2008, pp. 52–57. For a discussion of blogs in training see Becky Livingston, "Harnessing Blogs for Learning," *T+D* 65, no. 5 (May 2011), pp. 76–77.

115. Catherine Skrzypinski, "Social Media Changes Employee Expectations Regarding Communication," *HR Magazine*, January 2013, p. 14; see also Dan Steer, "Improve Formal Learning with Social Media," *Training & Development*, December 2012, pp. 31–33.

116. Pat Galagan, "Second That," *Training & Development*, February 2008, pp. 34–37.

117. Paraphrased from Manuel London and M. J. Hall, "Unlocking the Value of Web 2.0 Technologies for Training and Development: The Shift from Instructor-Controlled, Adaptive Learning to Learner-Driven, Generative Learning," *Human Resource Management* 50, no. 6 (November–December 2011), p. 761.

118. This is based on ibid., pp. 763–765.

119. Paul Harris, "Small Businesses Bask in Training's Spotlight," *T+D*, 59, no. 2, Fall 2005, pp. 46–52.

120. Ibid.

121. www.themanufacturinginstitute.org/Skills-Certification/Right-Skills-Now/Right-Skills-Now.aspx, accessed August 24, 2014.

122. For a discussion of leadership development tools, see John Beeson, "Building Bench Strength: A Tool Kit for Executive Development," *Business Horizons* 47, no. 6 (November 2004), pp. 3–9. See also Rita Smith and Beth Bledsoe, "Grooming Leaders for Growth," *T+D*, August 2006, pp. 47–50.

123. Paula Caligiuri, "Developing Global Leaders," *Human Resource Management Review* 16 (2006), pp. 219–228.

124. Ibid.

125. Whereas *succession planning* aims to identify and develop employees to fill specific slots, talent management is a broader activity. *Talent management* involves identifying, recruiting, hiring, and developing high-potential employees. Soonhee Kim, "Linking Employee Assessments to Succession Planning," *Public Personnel Management* 32, no. 4 (Winter 2003), pp. 533–547. See also Michael Laff, "Talent Management: From Hire to Retire," *T+D*, November 2006, pp. 42–48.

126. See, for example, David Day, "Developing Leadership Talent," *SHRM Foundation*, www.shrm.org/about/foundation/research/Documents/Developing%20Lead%20Talent-%20FINAL.pdf, accessed October 4, 2011.

127. Quoted in Susan Wells, "Who's Next," *HR Magazine*, November 2003, p. 43. See also Christee Atwood, "Implementing Your Succession Plan," *T+D*, November 2007, pp. 54–57; and Day, "Developing Leadership Talent."

128. See "Succession Management: Identifying and Developing Leaders," *BNA Bulletin to Management* 21, no. 12 (December 2003), p. 15; and Day, "Developing Leadership Talent."

129. Kim, "Linking Employee Assessments to Succession Planning."

130. Bill Roberts, "Matching Talent with Tasks," *HR Magazine*, November 2002, pp. 91–96.

131. www.sumtotalsystems.com/datasheets/sumt_succession_planning.pdf, accessed June 1, 2011.

132. Ibid., p. 34.

133. Gail Johnson Morris and Kim Rogers, "High Potentials Are Still Your Best Bet," *Training & Development*, February 2013, pp. 58–62.

134. Ann Pomeroy, "Head of the Class," *HR Magazine*, January 2005, p. 57. Of course, traits like cognitive ability and personality also mold job success, not just training. See, for example, Lisa Dragoni et al., "Developing Executive Leaders: The Relative Contribution of Cognitive Ability, Personality, and the Accumulation of Work Experience in Predicting Strategic Thinking Competency," *Personnel Psychology* 60, no. 4 (2011), pp. 829–861.

135. See Paul Evans, Yves Doz, and Andre Laurent, *Human Resource Management in International Firms* (New York: St. Martin's Press, 1990), pp. 122–124; www.sony.net/SonyInfo/csr_report/employees/training/index3.html; accessed March 4, 2014; and www.mckinsey.com/insights/organization/how_multinationals_can_attract_the_talent_they_need, accessed March 4, 2014.

136. Michael Marquardt, "Action Learning Around the World," *TD*, February 2015, pp. 45–49.

137. "Thrown into Deep End, Workers Surface as Leaders," *BNA Bulletin to Management*, July 11, 2002, p. 223. See also Michelle Peters, "Accomplish Two for One with Action Learning," *Training & Development*, February 2013, pp. 52–54.

138. Chris Whitcomb, "Scenario-Based Training at the FBI," *Training & Development*, June 1999, pp. 42–46. See also Michael Laff, "Serious Gaming: The Trainer's New Best Friend," *Training & Development*, January 2007, pp. 52–57.

139. http://teamcommunication.blogspot.com, accessed July 6, 2014.

140. Carol Leaman, "Boost Basic Job Skills Training," *Training & Development*, August 2014, pp. 34–39.

141. Bhuvan Gupta, "Happiness at Work: A Business Imperative," *People Matters*, August 2017, p. 76.

142. American Management Association, www.amanet.org, accessed July 6, 2014.

143. For information on the SHRM learning system, see www.shrm.org/Education/educationalproducts/learning/Pages/default.aspx?utm_campaign=LearningSystem_All_2012&utm_medium=mailing&utm_source=brochure, accessed July 21, 2013.

144. For a list of Harvard programs, see www.exed.hbs.edu/Pages/default.aspx, accessed July 21, 2013.

145. Norman Maier, Allen Solem, and Ayesha Maier, *The Role Play Technique* (San Diego, CA: University Associates, 1975), pp. 2–3. See also Karen Griggs, "A Role Play for Revising Style and Applying Management Theories," *Business Communication Quarterly* 68, no. 1 (March 2005), pp. 60–65.

146. Martha Peak, "Go Corporate U!" *Management Review* 86, no. 2 (February 1997), pp. 33–37; and Jessica Li and Amy Lui Abel, "Prioritizing and Maximizing the Impact of Corporate Universities," *T + D* 65, no. 5 (May 2011), pp. 54–57.

147. Russell Gerbman, "Corporate Universities 101," *HR Magazine*, February 2000, pp. 101–106; Holly Dolezalek, "University 2.0," *Training* 44, no. 8 (September 2007), pp. 22–23.

148. "Executive Coaching: Corporate Therapy," *The Economist*, November 15, 2003, p. 61. See also Steve Gladis, "Executive Coaching Builds Steam in Organizations," *Training & Development*, December 2007, pp. 59–61.

149. "As Corporate Coaching Goes Mainstream, Key Prerequisite Overlooked: Assessment," *BNA Bulletin to Management*, May 16, 2006, p. 153.

150. James Smither et al., "Can Working with an Executive Coach Improve Multisource Feedback Ratings over Time?" *Personnel Psychology* 56, no. 1 (Spring 2003), pp. 23–44.

151. www.shrm.org/Education/educationalproducts/learning/Pages/default.aspx.

152. For information on the SHRM learning system, see www.shrm.org/Education/educationalproducts/learning/Pages/default.aspx?utm_campaign=LearningSystem_All_2012&utm_medium=mailing&utm_source=brochure, accessed July 21, 2013.

153. Beena Parmar, "Bank of Baroda to Train 2,500 Employees to Build Future Leaders" Money Control, 2 June 2017.

154. This is based on Diane Brady, "Can GE Still Manage?" *Bloomberg Businessweek*, April 25, 2010, p. 29.

155. Ibid.

156. Quoted and abstracted from "Five Rules for Talent Management in the New Economy," May 2010, www.towerswatson.com/viewpoints/1988, accessed August 22, 2011.

157. Ibid.

158. See, for example, John Austin, "Mapping Out a Game Plan for Change," *HR Magazine*, April 2009, pp. 39–42.

159. The steps are based on Michael Beer, Russell Eisenstat, and Bert Spector, "Why Change Programs Don't Produce Change," *Harvard Business Review*, November–December 1990, pp. 158–166; Thomas Cummings and Christopher Worley, *Organization Development and Change*, Minneapolis, MN: West Publishing Company, 1993; John P. Kotter, "Leading Change: Why Transformation Efforts Fail," *Harvard Business Review*, March–April 1995, pp. 59–66; and John P. Kotter, *Leading Change* (Boston: Harvard Business School Press, 1996). See also Eric Abrahamson, "Change Without Pain," *Harvard Business Review*, July–August 2000, pp. 75–79; and David Herold et al., "Beyond Change Management: A Multilevel Investigation of Contextual and Personal Influences on Employees' Commitment to Change," *Journal of Applied Psychology* 92, no. 4 (2007), p. 949.

160. Kotter, "Leading Change," p. 85.

161. Beer, Eisenstat, and Spector, "Why Change Programs Don't Produce Change," p. 164.

162. Stacie Furst and Daniel Cable, "Employee Resistance to Organizational Change: Managerial Influence Tactics and Leader Member Exchange," *Journal of Applied Psychology* 3, no. 2 (2008), p. 453.

163. Wendell French and Cecil Bell Jr., *Organization Development* (Upper Saddle River, NJ: Prentice Hall, 1995), pp. 171–193. For examples of actual team-building programs, see, for example, www.teambuildinginc.com and www.teamcraft.com, both accessed August 24, 2014.

164. Benjamin Schneider, Steven Ashworth, A. Catherine Higgs, and Linda Carr, "Design Validity, and Use of Strategically Focused Employee Attitude Surveys," *Personnel Psychology* 49 (1996), pp. 695–705.

165. Wexley and Latham, *Developing and Training Human Resources in Organizations*, p. 128.

166. Todd Raphel, "What Learning Management Reports Do for You," *Workforce*, June 2001, pp. 56–58.

167. Wexley and Latham, *Developing and Training Human Resources in Organizations*, p. 153.

168. See, for example, Jack Phillips and Patti Phillips, "Moving From Evidence to Proof," *T + D* 65, no. 8 (August 2011), pp. 34–39, for a discussion of a process for gathering training assessment data.

169. However, see Phyllis Tharenou et al., "A Review and Critique of Research on Training and Organizational Level Outcomes," *Human Resource Management Review* 17 (2007), pp. 251–273.

170. For some examples, see, for instance, http://exceltemplates.net/images/2009/training-cost.jpg, www.tjtaylor.net/resources-tools2.htm, www.redhat.com/resourcelibrary/onlinetools/training-roi-calculator, and www.fastrak-consulting.co.uk/tactix/Features/tngroi/tngroi.htm. See also Tamar Elkeles, Patty Phillips, and Jack Phillips, "ROI Calculations for Technology-Based Learning," *TD*, January 2015, pp. 42–47.

171. Jennifer Salopek, "Showstopping Learning," *TD*, October 2014, pp. 56–59.

172. Ibid.

9

Performance Management and Appraisal

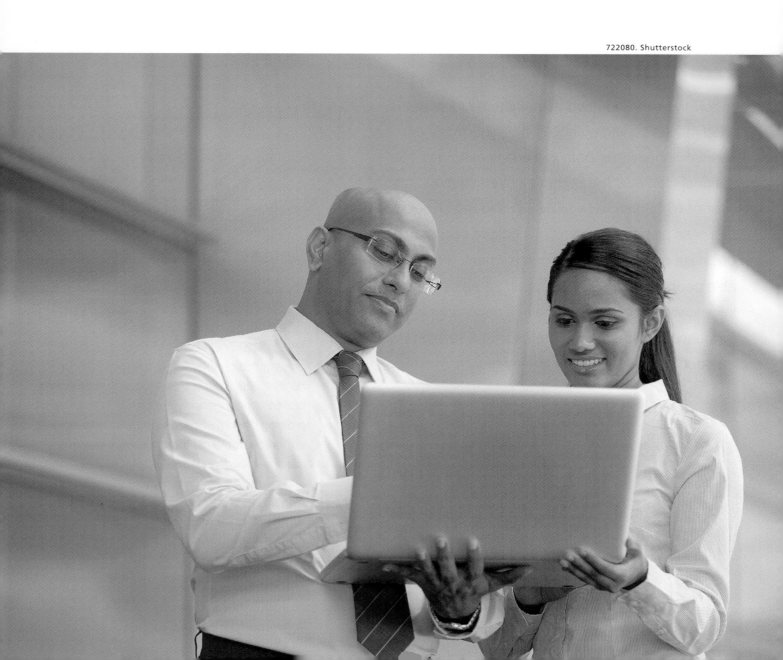

LEARNING OBJECTIVES

9-1 Describe the performance appraisal process.

9-2 Discuss the pros and cons of at least eight performance appraisal methods.

9-3 Give examples of potential appraisal problems and how to deal with them.

9-4 List steps to take in the appraisal interview.

9-5 Explain key points in how to use the appraisal interview to boost employee engagement.

9-6 Explain how you would take a performance management approach to appraisal.

Indofil Industries Limited manufactures, distributes, and markets a wide range of agrochemicals and specialty chemicals, both in the domestic and international markets. The company plans to reach a turnover of ₹6,000 crore by 2019-20 and has developed a business plan to that effect. To ensure success of the business plan, it had to be complemented by a suitable people strategy. To help bring employee actions in sync with Indofil's new goals, a new company performance management system (or PMS system) was introduced. We will see what they did.

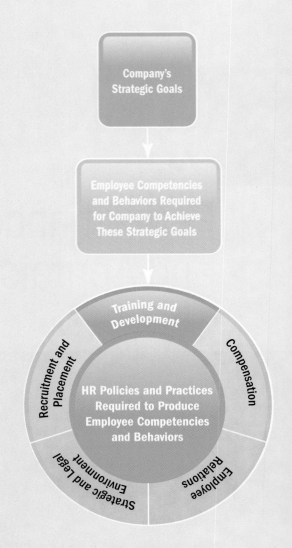

WHERE ARE WE NOW ...

Chapters 6–8 explained selecting, training, and developing employees. After employees have been on the job for some time, you should appraise their performance. The purpose of this chapter is to show you how to do that. The main topics we cover include the basics of performance appraisal, tools for appraising performance, dealing with rater error appraisal problems, the appraisal interview, employee engagement guide for managers, and performance management. Career planning is a logical consequence of appraisal: We'll turn to career planning in Chapter 10.

Basics of Performance Appraisal

Few things supervisors do are fraught with more peril than appraising subordinates' performance. Employees tend to be overly optimistic about their ratings. And they know their raises, careers, and peace of mind may hinge on how you rate them. As if that's not enough, few appraisal processes are as fair as employers think they are. Many obvious and not-so-obvious problems (such as the tendency to rate everyone "average") distort the process.[1] However, the perils notwithstanding, performance appraisal plays a big role in managing people. Performance appraisal/management systems, however, are not without criticisms. While acknowledging the significance of the same, a study among Indian employees showed the existence of a feeling of doubt about the ability of the system to distinguish superior performance and distribute rewards.

The Performance Appraisal Process

performance appraisal
Evaluating an employee's current and/or past performance relative to his or her performance standards.

Performance appraisal means evaluating an employee's current and/or past performance relative to his or her performance standards. You may equate appraisal forms like Figure 9-1 with "performance appraisal," but appraisal involves more than forms. It also requires setting performance standards, and assumes that the employee receives the training, feedback, and incentives required to eliminate performance deficiencies. Stripped to its essentials, performance appraisal always involves the three-step **performance appraisal process**: (1) setting work standards; (2) assessing the employee's actual performance relative to those standards (this often involves some rating form); and (3) providing feedback to the employee with the aim of helping him or her to eliminate performance deficiencies or to continue to perform above par.

performance appraisal process
A three-step appraisal process involving (1) setting work standards, (2) assessing the employee's actual performance relative to those standards, and (3) providing feedback to the employee with the aim of helping him or her to eliminate performance deficiencies or to continue to perform above par.

Effective appraisals actually begin before the actual appraisal, with the manager defining the employee's job and performance criteria. *Defining the job* means making sure that you and your subordinate agree on his or her duties and job standards and on the appraisal method you will use.

Why Appraise Performance?

There are five reasons to appraise subordinates' performance.

- First, most employers base pay, promotion, and retention decisions on the employee's appraisal.[2]
- Appraisals play a central role in the employer's *performance management* process. Performance management means continuously ensuring that each employee's performance makes sense in terms of the company's overall goals.
- The appraisal lets the manager and subordinate develop a plan for correcting any deficiencies, and to reinforce the subordinate's strengths.
- Appraisals provide an opportunity to review the employee's career plans in light of his or her exhibited strengths and weaknesses. We address career planning in Chapter 10.
- Finally, appraisals enable the supervisor to identify if there is a training need, and the remedial steps required.

FIGURE 9-1 Sample Faculty Evaluation Survey
Source: Copyright Gary Dessler, PhD.

Instructions: Thoughtful evaluations help the faculty member better understand and improve his or her teaching practices. For each of the following eight items, please assign a score, giving your highest score of 7 for Outstanding, a score of 4 for Average, your lowest score of 1 for Needs Improvement, and an NA if the question is not applicable:

Evaluation Items
_____ 1. The instructor was prepared for his/her lectures.
_____ 2. The course was consistent with the course objectives.
_____ 3. The instructor was fair in how he/she graded me.
_____ 4. The instructor carefully planned and organized this course.
_____ 5. The instructor was available during his/her posted office hours.
_____ 6. The instructor responded to online inquiries in a timely manner.
_____ 7. In terms of knowledge and/or experience, the instructor was competent to teach this course.
_____ 8. Overall how would you rate this course?

Defining the Employee's Goals and Performance Standards

The performance appraisal should compare "what should be" with "what is." Therefore, as noted, the first step in performance appraisal and management is to decide what should be—in other words, to let employees know what you expect of them in terms of performance standards. Managers use one or more of three bases—goals, job dimensions or traits, and behaviors or competencies—to establish ahead of time what the person's performance standards will be.

First, the manager can assess to what extent *the employee is attaining his or her numerical goals.* Such goals should derive from the company's overall profitability, cost reduction, or efficiency goals. For example, a company-wide goal of reducing costs by 10% should translate into goals for how individual employees and/or teams will cut costs. The HR as a Profit Center feature shows an example.

IMPROVING PERFORMANCE: *HR as a Profit Center*

Setting and Managing Performance Goals at Cigna TTK

Cigna TTK Health Insurance Company is a joint venture between Cigna Corporation USA and TTK Group, an Indian conglomerate. Though the firm only started operating in February 2014, it went on to win the Economic Times Best Promising Brands Award in 2015.[3] The management team wanted to make the company "irresistible" to employees. An internal research indicated that Cigna's employees looked for meaningful work, great work environment, and performance support. A new PMS system was, thus, introduced, which made the company shift away from the traditional model of fixed-term appraisals, rating, and documentation to challenging goal setting, developmental conversations, and informal documentation. Quality of interactions, which were more frequent and non-threatening, became features of this new system. The process grouped employees into two broad segments according to achievement of expectations as "on track" and "off track."[4] ∎

Source: Based on www.cignattkinsurance.in and www.hrkatha.com

Managers often say that effective goals should be "SMART." They are *specific*, and clearly state the desired results. They are *measurable*, and answer the question "how much?" They are *attainable*. They are *relevant*, and clearly derive from what the manager and company want to achieve. And they are *timely*, with deadlines and milestones.[5] Research provides insights into setting motivational goals. The accompanying HR Tools feature summarizes these findings.

IMPROVING PERFORMANCE: *HR Tools for Line Managers and Small Businesses*

How to Set Effective Goals

Behavioral science research studies suggest four guidelines for setting performance goals:

1. **Assign specific goals.** Employees who receive specific goals usually perform better than those who do not.
2. **Assign measurable goals.** Put goals in quantitative terms and include target dates or deadlines. If measurable results will not be available, then "satisfactory completion"—such as "satisfactorily attended workshop"—is the next best thing.
3. **Assign challenging but doable goals.** Goals should be challenging, but not so difficult that they appear unrealistic.
4. **Encourage participation.** Managers often face this question: Should I tell my employees what their goals are, or let them participate with me in setting their goals? The evidence suggests that participatively set goals do not consistently result in higher performance than assigned goals, nor do assigned goals consistently result in higher performance than participative ones. It is only when the participatively set goals are set higher than the assigned ones that the participatively set goals produce higher performance. Because it tends to be easier to set higher standards when your employees participate, participation tends to lead to improved performance.[6] ∎

Source: Based on E. A. Locke and G. P. Latham, "Building a Practically Useful Theory of Goal Setting and Task Motivation. A 35-Year Odyssey," American Psychologist 57, no. 9 (2002), pp. 705–717.

A *second* basis upon which to appraise someone is to use a form with *basic job dimensions* or *traits* such as such as "communication" or "teamwork." The assumption is that "good teamwork" is a useful standard for "what should be."

A third option is to appraise employees based *on their mastery of the competencies* (the skills, knowledge, and/or personal behaviors) performing the job requires. For example, we saw in Chapter 4 that BP's exploration division appraises employees' skills using a skills matrix (see Figure 4-9, page 118). This matrix shows the basic skills to be assessed (such as "technical expertise"), and the minimum level of each skill the job requires (what the minimum skill level "should be"). Employees appraised as having the requisite level of each skill are qualified to fill the position.

Who Should Do the Appraising?

Appraisals by the immediate supervisor are still the heart of most appraisal processes. Getting a supervisor's appraisal is relatively straightforward and makes sense. The supervisor is usually in the best position to observe and evaluate the subordinate's performance, and is responsible for that person's performance.

The human resources department serves an advisory role. Generally, they provide the advice on what appraisal tool to use, but leaves final decisions on procedures to operating managers. The human resource team should also train supervisors to improve their appraisal skills, monitor the appraisal system's effectiveness, and ensure that it complies with relevant laws.

However, relying only on supervisors' appraisals isn't advisable. For example, an employee's supervisor may not appreciate how customers and colleagues see the employee's performance. There is also always some danger of bias for or against the employee. If so, managers have several options.

PEER APPRAISALS AND 360 DEGREE   People often come across differently to their peers than they do to their boss. Peer appraisals—appraisals by one's peers—are therefore increasingly popular. In Indian academic institutes like IIM Ahmedabad (IIMA), peers actively participate in evaluating performance and providing developmental inputs. Facebook has employees compile peer reviews every 6 months.[7] Google employees receive annual feedback from both their supervisor and their peers.[8] (We'll discuss automated "crowd" appraisals later in this chapter.)

Typically, an employee due for a peer appraisal chooses an appraisal chairperson. The latter (perhaps with the employee's input) then selects a supervisor and several peers to evaluate the employee's work.

Peer appraisals can be effective. One's peers see aspects of the person that the boss may never see, so peers' opinions can be useful developmentally. Knowing your colleagues will appraise you can also change behavior. One study involved undergraduates placed into self-managing work groups. The researchers found that instituting peer appraisals had "an immediate positive impact on [improving] perception of open communication, task motivation, social loafing, group viability, cohesion, and satisfaction."[9]

RATING COMMITTEES   A rating committee usually consists of the employee's immediate supervisor and three or four other supervisors.[10]

Using multiple raters is advantageous. It helps cancel out problems such as bias on the part of individual raters.[11] It can also provide a way to include in the appraisal the different facets of an employee's performance observed by different appraisers. Studies often find that the ratings obtained from different sources rarely match.[12] It's therefore advisable to obtain ratings from the supervisor, his or her boss, and at least one other manager who is familiar with the employee's work.[13] At a minimum, employers require that the supervisor's boss sign off on any appraisals the supervisor does.

SELF-RATINGS   Some employers obtain employees' self-ratings, usually in conjunction with supervisors' ratings. The basic problem, of course, is that employees usually rate themselves higher than do their supervisors or peers.[14] One study found that, when

Many employers use rating committees to appraise employees.

Rehan Qureshi. Shutterstock

asked to rate their own job performances, 40% of employees in jobs of all types placed themselves in the top 10%, and virtually all remaining employees rated themselves at least in the top 50%.[15] In another study, subjects' self-ratings correlated negatively with their subsequent performance in an assessment center—the higher they appraised themselves, the worse they did in the center. In contrast, an average of the person's supervisor, peer, and subordinate ratings predicted the subjects' assessment center performance.[16]

APPRAISAL BY SUBORDINATES Many employers have subordinates rate their managers, usually for developmental rather than for pay purposes. Anonymity affects the feedback. Managers who receive feedback from subordinates who identify themselves view the upward feedback process more positively. However, subordinates who identify themselves tend to give inflated ratings.[17]

The evidence suggests that upward feedback improves managers' performance. One study focused on 252 managers during five annual administrations of an upward feedback program. Managers who were initially rated poor or moderate "showed significant improvements in [their] upward feedback ratings over the five-year period."[18] And, managers who met with their subordinates to discuss their upward assessment improved more than the managers who did not.[19]

Of course, employees no longer need their employers for upward evaluation systems—sites like Glassdoor and apps like Memo let employees post their own anonymous comments.[20]

360-DEGREE FEEDBACK With 360-degree feedback, the employer collects performance information all around an employee—from his or her supervisors, subordinates, peers, and internal or external customers—generally for developmental rather than pay purposes.[21] The usual process is to have the raters complete online ratee appraisal surveys. It's a combination of the different feedback sources discussed above. Computerized systems then compile this feedback into individualized reports to rates. Many Indian private firms and public sector undertakings (PSUs) use multisource feedback for developmental purposes, particularly for senior employees. Tata Group companies use 360-degree feedback to bring in change and to improve leadership effectiveness.[22] Bank of Baroda also envisages to introduce 360-degree feedback for leadership development.

Results are mixed. Participants seem to prefer this approach, but one study concluded that multisource feedback led to "generally small" improvements in subsequent ratings by supervisors, peers, and subordinates.[23] Such appraisals are more candid when subordinates know rewards or promotions are not involved.

Make sure the feedback the person receives is productive, unbiased, and development oriented.[24] And, it helps to collect multisource feedback by using a Web-based system that lets the rater rate the person along a series of dimensions.[25]

graphic rating scale
A scale that lists a number of traits and a range of performance for each. The employee is then rated by identifying the score that best describes his or her level of performance for each trait.

Techniques for Appraising Performance

We will see that many employers use digital tools to automate the appraisal/performance management process. With their digital dashboards, these tools monitor, report, and correct performance deviations in real time. Yet many employers still use traditional performance appraisal tools like those described next.

Graphic Rating Scale Method

The **graphic rating scale** is the simplest and most popular method for appraising performance. You'll find several varieties. As in the graphic rating scale in Figure 9-2, the scale may lists several *job dimensions or traits* (such as "communication" or "teamwork") and a range of performance values (from "below expectations" to "role model" or "unsatisfactory" to "outstanding") for each trait. The supervisor rates each subordinate by circling or checking the score that best describes the subordinate's performance for each trait, and totals the ratings.

Competency- (or skill- or behavior-) based graphic rating scales are another option. For example, Figure 9-3 shows a partial rating form for a pizza chef. This graphic rating form assesses the person's competencies and skills. Here the employer wants to appraise a pizza chef's job-related skills, one of which is: "Be able to maintain adequate inventory of pizza dough." As another example, Section I of Figure 9-4 focuses on behavioral competencies.[26] Here "Effectively leads and motivates nurses" is a required behavioral competency for a nurse supervisor.

Finally, the scale might rate (as in Section II of Figure 9-4) how well the employee did with respect to achieving specific profit, cost, or efficiency *goals*. "Nursing unit experienced zero patient medication errors in period" would be one example.

Alternation Ranking Method

alternation ranking method
Ranking employees from best to worst on a particular trait, choosing highest, then lowest, until all are ranked.

Ranking employees from best to worst on a trait or traits is another option. Since it is usually easier to distinguish between the worst and best employees, an **alternation ranking method** is most popular. First, list all subordinates to be rated, and then cross out the names of any not known well enough to rank. Then, on a form like that in Figure 9-5 (page 275), indicate the employee who is the highest on the performance dimension being measured and the one who is the lowest. Then choose the next highest and the next lowest, alternating between highest and lowest until all employees have been ranked.

Paired Comparison Method

paired comparison method
Ranking employees by making a chart of all possible pairs of the employees for each trait and indicating which is the better employee of the pair.

The **paired comparison method** makes the ranking method more precise. For every trait (quantity of work, quality of work, and so on), you compare every employee with every other employee. With, say, five employees to rate, you use a chart as in Figure 9-6 (page 275) of all possible pairs of employees for each trait. Then choose who the better employee of the pair is. In Figure 9-6, Maria ranked highest (has the most + marks) for quality of work, whereas Art was ranked highest for creativity.

Sample Performance Rating Form

Employee's Name _____   Level: Entry-level employee

Manager's Name _____

Key Work Responsibilities   Results/Goals to Be Achieved
1. _____   1. _____
2. _____   2. _____
3. _____   3. _____
4. _____   4. _____

Communication

1	2	3	4	5
Below Expectations		**Meets Expectations**		**Role Model**
Even with guidance, fails to prepare straightforward communications, including forms, paperwork, and records, in a timely and accurate manner; products require minimal corrections. Even with guidance, fails to adapt style and materials to communicate straightforward information.		With guidance, prepares straightforward communications, including forms, paperwork, and records, in a timely and accurate manner; products require minimal corrections. With guidance, adapts style and materials to communicate straightforward information.		Independently prepares communications, such as forms, paperwork, and records, in a timely, clear, and accurate manner; products require few, if any, corrections. Independently adapts style and materials to communicate information.

Organizational Know-How

1	2	3	4	5
Below Expectations		**Meets Expectations**		**Role Model**
<performance standards appear here>		<performance standards appear here>		<performance standards appear here>

Personal Effectiveness

1	2	3	4	5
Below Expectations		**Meets Expectations**		**Role Model**
<performance standards appear here>		<performance standards appear here>		<performance standards appear here>

Teamwork

1	2	3	4	5
Below Expectations		**Meets Expectations**		**Role Model**
<performance standards appear here>		<performance standards appear here>		<performance standards appear here>

Achieving Business Results

1	2	3	4	5
Below Expectations		**Meets Expectations**		**Role Model**
<performance standards appear here>		<performance standards appear here>		<performance standards appear here>

FIGURE 9-2 **Sample Graphic Performance Rating Form with Behavioral Examples**
Source: Reproduced with permission of the SHRM Foundation.

FIGURE 9-3 One Item from an Appraisal Form Assessing Employee Performance on Specific Job-Related Skills

Position: Pizza Cheif			
Skill 1: Be able to maintain adequate inventory of pizza dough		Rating	
Each round pizza dough must be between 12 and 14 ounces each, kneaded at least 2 minutes before being placed in the temperature and humidity-controlled cooler, and kept there for at least 5 hours prior to use. There should be enough, but no more for each day's demand.	Needs improvement	Satisfactory	Excellent

Forced Distribution Method

forced distribution method
Similar to grading on a curve; predetermined percentages of ratees are placed in various performance categories.

The **forced distribution method** is similar to grading on a curve. With this method, the manager places predetermined percentages of ratees into performance categories. At Lending Tree, the top 15% ratees are "1's," the middle 75% are "2's," and the bottom 10% are "3's" and the "first to go." GE used top 20%, middle 70%, and bottom 10% for its managers, and most of the bottom 10% lost their jobs.[27] (GE no longer strictly adheres to its 20/70/10 split, and today is experimenting with less stressful alternatives.)[28]

Forced distribution's big advantage is that it prevents supervisors from rating all or most employees "satisfactory" or "high." Forced distribution makes some sense. It reflects the fact that top employees often outperform average or poor ones by as much as 100%.[29] About a fourth of *Fortune* 500 companies use versions of it.[30]

But, as students know, with forced grading you're either in the top 5% or 10% (and get that "A"), or you're not. Forced distribution rating systems may also increase the risk of discriminatory adverse impact.[31] One survey found that 77% of responding employers were at least "somewhat satisfied" with forced ranking, while the remaining 23% were dissatisfied. The biggest complaints: 44% said it damages morale.[32] Some writers refer unkindly to it as "Rank and Yank."[33] Therefore, appoint a committee to review any employee's low ranking. And remember that distinguishing between top and bottom performers is usually not even the problem: "The challenge is to differentiate meaningfully between the other 80%."[34] For many years, Microsoft graded employees against one another in what employees called the "stack," ranking them from 1 to 5.[35] Microsoft recently substituted more frequent and qualitative appraisals. In India, in addition to multinational companies (MNCs), firms like Infosys, Airtel, TCS, and Cigna TTK have moved away from forced rating (bell curve) to a more qualitative and frequent appraisals system which has reduced stress on employees and support them to perform.[36]

Critical Incident Method

critical incident method
Keeping a record of uncommonly good or undesirable examples of an employee's work-related behavior and reviewing it with the employee at predetermined times.

With the **critical incident method**, the supervisor keeps a log of positive and negative examples (critical incidents) of a subordinate's work-related behaviors. Every 6 months or so, supervisor and subordinate meet to discuss the latter's performance, using the incidents as examples. One study involved 112 first-line supervisors. The conclusion of this and similar studies is that compiling critical incidents as they occur anchors the eventual appraisal in reality and thus improves appraisal outcomes.[37] It's thus advisable to keep a diary of employees' performances.[38]

Compiling incidents is useful. It provides examples the supervisor can use to explain the person's rating. It makes the supervisor think about the subordinate's appraisal all during the year (so the rating doesn't just reflect the employee's most recent performance). The downside is that it doesn't produce relative ratings for pay raise purposes. In Table 9-1, one of the assistant plant manager's duties was to supervise procurement and minimize inventory costs. The critical incident log shows that he or she let inventory storage costs rise 15%; this provides an example of what performance to improve.

Section I: Competencies: Does this employee exhibit the core competencies the job requires?

Exhibits Leadership Competency

Effectively leads and motivates nurses: Builds a culture that is open and receptive to improved clinical care; Sets clear goals for nurses; Is supportive of nurses; Motivates nurses to achieve their goals.

Generally exceeds expectations	Generally meets expectations	Generally fails to meet expectations
_____	_____	_____

Exhibits Technical Supervisory Competency

Effectively supervises nurses' technical activities: Exhibits the command of technical nursing knowledge and skills required to supervise nurses effectively, such as, assuring that nurses accurately administer medications, treat patients, intervene effectively to patients' expressions of symptoms, and accurately carry out physicians' instructions.

Generally exceeds expectations	Generally meets expectations	Generally fails to meet expectations
_____	_____	_____

Exhibits Managerial Supervisory Competency

Effectively manages unit: Develops annual, monthly, weekly, and daily plans within context of hospital's plans; effectively organizes and assigns nurses' work; maintains required nursing staffing levels and trains nurses; effectively monitors and controls nursing unit performance using hospital-approved metrics.

Generally exceeds expectations	Generally meets expectations	Generally fails to meet expectations
_____	_____	_____

Exhibits Communications Competency

Effectively communicates: Actively listens to and understands what others say; effectively conveys facts and ideas in writing and orally.

Generally exceeds expectations	Generally meets expectations	Generally fails to meet expectations
_____	_____	_____

Exhibits Decision-Making Competency

Effectively recognizes and solves problems and makes decisions: uses data to analyze alternatives and support conclusions; able to solve problems even of moderate to high complexity.

Generally exceeds expectations	Generally meets expectations	Generally fails to meet expectations
_____	_____	_____

Section II: Goals: Did this employee achieve his or her goals for the period you are appraising?

Primary goals employee was to achieve for this period (Note: list specific goals)	Rating 5 Exceeded goal 3 Met goal 1 Did not achieve goal	Explanations and/or examples
Goal 1	5 4 3 2 1	
Goal 2	5 4 3 2 1	
Goal 3	5 4 3 2 1	
Goal 4	5 4 3 2 1	
Goal 5	5 4 3 2 1	

Employee name and signature	Person doing appraisal	Date of appraisal

Source: Copyright Gary Dessler PhD

FIGURE 9-4 Pearson Pennsylvania Hospital Competencies and Goals-Based Appraisal Form for a Nurse-Supervisor

Source: Copyright Gary Dessler, PhD.

FIGURE 9-5 Alternation Ranking Method

ALTERNATION RANKING SCALE

Trait: _____

For the trait you are measuring, list all the employees you want to rank. Put the highest-ranking employee's name on line 1. Put the lowest-ranking employee's name on line 20. Then list the next highest ranking on line 2, the next lowest ranking on line 19, and so on. Continue until all names are on the scale.

Highest-ranking employee

1. _____	11. _____
2. _____	12. _____
3. _____	13. _____
4. _____	14. _____
5. _____	15. _____
6. _____	16. _____
7. _____	17. _____
8. _____	18. _____
9. _____	19. _____
10. _____	20. _____

Lowest-ranking employee

Narrative Forms

All or part of the written appraisal may be in narrative form, as in Figure 9-7. Here the person's supervisor assesses the employee's past performance and required areas of improvement. The supervisor's narrative assessment helps the employee understand where his or her performance was good or bad, and how to improve that performance.

FIGURE 9-6 Paired Comparison Method

Note: + means "better than." - means "worse than." For each chart, add up the number of +'s in each column to get the highest ranked employee.

Note: + means "better than." – means "worse than." For each chart, add up the number of +'s in each column to get the highest ranked employee.

FOR THE TRAIT "QUALITY OF WORK"

Employee rated:

As Compared to:	A Art	B Maria	C Chuck	D Diane	E José
A Art		+	+	−	−
B Maria	−		−	−	−
C Chuck	−	+		+	−
D Diane	+	+	−		+
E José	+	+	+	−	

Maria ranks highest here

FOR THE TRAIT "CREATIVITY"

Employee rated:

As Compared to:	A Art	B Maria	C Chuck	D Diane	E José
A Art		−	−	−	−
B Maria	+		−	+	+
C Chuck	+	+		−	+
D Diane	+	−	+		−
E José	+	−	−	+	

Art ranks highest here

TABLE 9-1 Examples of Critical Incidents for Assistant Plant Manager

Continuing Duties	Targets	Critical Incidents
Schedule production for plant	90% utilization of personnel and machinery in plant; orders delivered on time	Instituted new production scheduling system; decreased late orders by 10% last month; increased machine utilization in plant by 20% last month
Supervise procurement of raw materials and inventory control	Minimize inventory costs while keeping adequate supplies on hand	Let inventory storage costs rise 15% last month; overordered parts "A" and "B" by 20%; underordered part "C" by 30%
Supervise machinery maintenance	No shutdowns due to faulty machinery	Instituted new preventative maintenance system for plant; prevented a machine breakdown by discovering faulty part

FIGURE 9-7 Sample Narrative Appraisal Form

Source: Copyright Gary Dessler, PhD.

Supervisory Appraisal of Employee: Narrative Form		
Employee's Name	Department	Present Position
Appraisal Date	Supervisor Name/Title	Performance Period

Supervisor-Appraiser: First, briefly describe results for each of this employee's goals this year. Then, preferably using specific examples, describe the level of the employee's job knowledge, skills, and abilities. Then, jointly set goals for the coming period and describe required employee training and development in each area. Finally, describe your overall assessment of this employee's work this period.

Appraisal Criteria	Narrative Appraisal	Goals, Training, & Development
Job-Related Goals 1. _____ 2. _____ 3. _____	_____ _____ _____	_____ _____ _____
Employee Job Knowledge		
Employee Job Skills		
Employee Job Abilities		
Overall Assessment		

behaviorally anchored rating scale (BARS)

An appraisal method that aims at combining the benefits of narrative critical incidents and quantified ratings by anchoring a quantified scale with specific narrative examples of good and poor performance.

Behaviorally Anchored Rating Scales

A **behaviorally anchored rating scale (BARS)** is an appraisal tool that anchors a numerical rating scale with specific illustrative examples of good or poor performance. Developing a BARS typically involves five steps:

1. *Write critical incidents.* Ask the job's jobholders and/or supervisors to write specific illustrations (critical incidents) of effective and ineffective performance on the job.

2. *Develop performance dimensions.* Have these people cluster the incidents into 5 or 10 performance dimensions, such as "salesmanship skills."

3. *Reallocate incidents.* To verify these groupings, have another team who also knows the job reallocate the original critical incidents to the cluster they think it fits best. Retain a critical incident if most of this second team assigns it to the same cluster as did the first.

4. *Scale the incidents.* This second group then rates the behavior described by the incident as to how effectively or ineffectively it represents performance on the dimension.

5. *Develop a final instrument.* Choose about six or seven of the incidents as the dimension's behavioral anchors.[39] Figure 9-8 illustrates a BARS, for a car salesperson.

Three researchers developed a BARS for grocery checkout clerks.[40] They collected many checkout clerk critical incidents, and then grouped or clustered these into eight performance dimensions: Knowledge and Judgment; Conscientiousness; Skill in Human Relations; Skill in Operation of Register; Skill in Bagging; Organizational Ability of Checkstand Work; Skill in Monetary Transactions; and Observational Ability.

FIGURE 9-8 Behaviorally Anchored Rating Scale

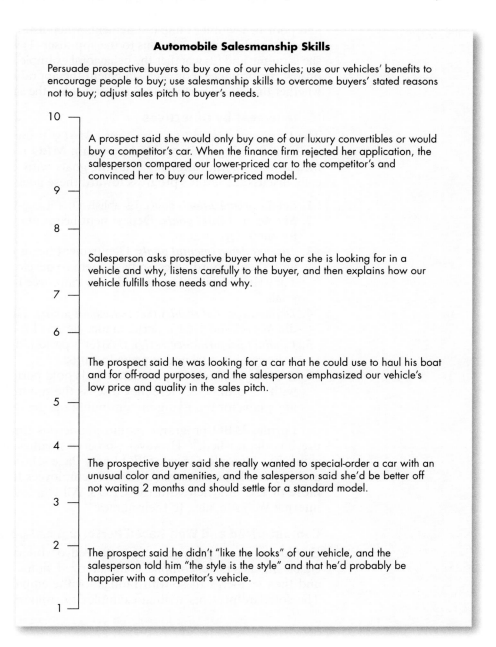

They then developed behaviorally anchored rating scales *for each of these eight dimensions*. Each contained a vertical scale (ranging from 1 to 9) for rating performance from "extremely poor" to "extremely good." Then they inserted specific critical incidents (such as "by knowing the price of items, this checker would be expected to look for mismarked and unmarked items") to anchor or illustrate each level of performance.

The BARS method has several advantages. Most notably, the critical incidents along the scale illustrate what to look for in terms of superior, average, and poor performance (an idea equally valuable when creating most other types of appraisal tools, including graphic rating scales). The critical incidents make it easier to explain the ratings to appraisees. And, clustering the critical incidents into five or six performance dimensions (such as "salesmanship skills") helps make the performance dimensions more independent of one another. (For example, a rater should be less likely to rate an employee high on all dimensions simply because he or she was rated high in "salesmanship skills.")[41] BARS is similar to another appraisal method, Behavioral Observation Scales (BOS), but the latter involves rating how frequently the ratees exhibit the illustrative behaviors.[42]

Mixed Standard Scales

Mixed standard scales are somewhat similar to behaviorally anchored scales. However they are called mixed scales because the employer "mixes" together sequentially the good and poor behavioral example statements when listing them. The aim is to reduce rating errors by making it less obvious to the appraiser (1) what performance dimensions he or she is rating; and (2) whether the behavioral example statements represent high, medium, or low performance. For each statement the appraiser rates the employee by indicating whether the latter's performance is better than, the same, or worse than the statement.

Management by Objectives

The term *management by objectives (MBO)* usually refers to a multistep company-wide goal-setting and appraisal program. MBO requires the manager to set specific measurable, organizationally relevant goals with each employee, and then periodically discuss the latter's progress toward these goals. The steps are:

1. *Set the organization's goals.* Establish a company-wide plan for next year and set goals.
2. *Set departmental goals.* Department heads and their superiors jointly set goals for their departments.
3. *Discuss departmental goals.* Department heads discuss the department's goals with their subordinates and ask them to develop their own individual goals. They should ask, "How could each employee help the department attain its goals?"
4. *Define expected results (set individual goals).* Department heads and their subordinates set short-term performance targets for each employee.
5. *Conduct performance reviews.* After a period, department heads compare each employee's actual and expected results.
6. *Provide feedback.* Department heads hold periodic performance review meetings with subordinates. Here they discuss the subordinates' performance and make any plans for rectifying or continuing the person's performance.

Formal MBO programs require numerous time-consuming meetings, and their use has diminished.[43] However, some companies successfully use streamlined versions. For example, Google CEO Larry Page sets company-wide "OKRs" (objectives and key results) quarterly. All Google employees then make sure their own goals are more or less in synch with the CEO's. All employees' goals are posted on Google's internal Web site, next to their names.[44]

Computerized and Web-Based Performance Appraisal

Employers increasingly use computerized or Internet-based appraisal systems. Most enable managers to compile comp\uterized notes on subordinates during the year, and then to merge these with ratings for the employee on several performance traits. The software presents written examples to support part of the appraisal. Most such appraisals combine several appraisal tools, usually graphic ratings anchored by critical incidents.[45]

For example, the cloud-based HR software, ZingHR (www.zinghr.com), allows users to customize appraisal and present a menu of evaluation dimensions. Within each dimension (such as communication), there are separate performance factors for things like writing, verbal communication, and receptivity to criticism. When a user clicks on a performance factor, he or she is presented with a scale. However, instead of numerical ratings, another software Employee Appraiser uses behaviorally anchored examples. Thus, for *verbal communication* there are six choices, ranging from "presents ideas clearly" to "lacks structure." The manager chooses the phrase that most accurately describes the worker. Then Employee Appraiser generates an appraisal with sample text. For small and medium enterprises (SMEs) in India, the HR function company Husys (www.Husys.net) offers a unique and simple to use technology solution, ApHusys (www.aphusys.com), which is available to SME managers and employees on mobile.

Successfactors, a subsidiary of software giant SAP, offers a Web-based employee appraisal solution. It includes performance review forms and approval processes, 51 competencies for most job types, a built-in writing assistant, and a legal scan.[46]

Electronic Performance Monitoring

electronic performance monitoring (EPM)
Having supervisors electronically monitor the amount of computerized data an employee is processing per day, and thereby his or her performance.

Electronic performance monitoring (EPM) systems use computer network technology to allow managers to monitor their employees' computers. They allow managers to monitor the employees' rate, accuracy, and time spent working online.[47]

EPM can improve productivity, but also seems to raise employee stress. However, one researcher concludes that electronic performance monitoring "represents the future of performance feedback where supervisors can electronically monitor the amount and quality of work an employee is producing and have objective indicators of employee performance immediately available and visible."[48]

Similarly, some employers digitally track workers' performance through wearables. For example, the British retailer Tesco has warehouse workers wear armbands. These track which specific goods each worker is moving and how long the task is taking to complete and quantify and report things like how long it takes each worker to fulfill each order.[49]

Conversation Days

When employees at Juniper Networks Inc. expressed concerns about their annual performance reviews and the lack of positive feedback, Juniper changed the process. Instead of once-a-year performance reviews, there are now semiannual "conversation days."

Many employers today make use of computerized or online appraisals for evaluating employee performance.

Studio 8. Pearson Education Ltd

The stress in these manager-employee conversations is on areas for improvement and growth, and on setting stretch goals that align with the employee's career interests. There are no explicit performance ratings. In 2015, GE similarly began experimenting with substituting frequent conversations for traditional appraisals.

Appraisal in Practice: Using Multiple Methods

Which appraisal method to use? In practice, the rating form will probably merge several approaches. For example, Figure 9-2 (page 272) has a numerical graphic rating scale anchored with behavioral incidents such as "Even with guidance, fails to…." The Strategic Context feature (page 281) shows how one employer created a new appraisal system.

TRENDS SHAPING HR: *CUSTOMIZED TALENT MANAGEMENT*

There has always been some customizing of appraisals. For example, rating a salesperson based on whether she attained her sales goals assumes she had her own customized goals to meet.

Today, some employers are customizing their appraisal in other ways. For example, it is increasingly common for companies to adapt their appraisals and rewards to how critical the employees are to the company's strategic success—their "mission-critical" employees. For example, GE prioritizes jobs and focuses on what it calls its employee "game changers."[50] Unilever includes 15% of employees per management level in its high-potential list each year.[51] Vodafone India develops its high potential senior leadership team members through a 12-month, customized leadership program in partnership with IIMA.[52] Companies like Infosys and Airtel, which abandoned the forced bell curve, have started giving emphasis on developmental conversations.[53] Tata Power has introduced a step-less performance management system, by comparing employees with peers at same level across different units and offices, and gives each employee a unique performance position—not grading into a category.[54] Shell China appoints "career stewards" to meet regularly with "emerging leaders."[55] McKinsey & Co. recommends limiting the "high potential group in whom the company invests heavily to no more than 10 to 20% of managerial and professional staff."[56]

Figure 9-9 illustrates one way to customize appraisals. Accenture uses a 4 × 4 matrix to plot employees by *Performance* (exceptional, high, medium, low) and *Value to the Organization* (mission-critical, core, necessary, nonessential). Consider a chemical engineering company. Here the firm's experienced engineers may be

Performance

	Exceptional	High	Average	Low
Mission-critical				
Core				
Necessary				
Non-essential				

Value to the organization

Provide additional rewards and experiences and provide development opportunities to benefit individual and organization

Provide training and experiences to prepare for mission-critical roles

Identify as at risk: Provide additional training and performance management attention to improve motivation and performance, and/or to move into necessary or core roles

Divest/seek alternative sourcing

FIGURE 9-9 **Accenture's Strategic Role Assessment Matrix**

Source: Reprinted by permission from "Accenture's Strategic Role Assessment Matrix", in "The New Talent Equation," Outlook, June 2009. © 2009 Accenture., © 2009.

"mission-critical," engineer-trainees "core," sales, accounting, and HR "necessary," and outsourceable employees such maintenance "nonessential."

This company would then tie each employee's pay, development, dismissal, and other personnel decisions to each employee's position in the matrix, in other words to both their performance rating and criticalness to the company (so that, not unreasonably, someone with more critical skills might get more slack and development then would someone who's "nonessential"). Hopefully, this employer would also design its incentives, promotions, and raises to support rather than turn off the mission critical engineers.[57] ■

IMPROVING PERFORMANCE: *The Strategic Context*

New Global Performance Appraisal/Management System of TRW and Infosys

As a global competitor facing stiff competition, TRW needed a performance appraisal system that was consistent and comprehensive.[58] It had to be *consistent* in that employees in all of TRW's far-flung organization could use the same system. It had to be *comprehensive* in that it consolidated the various components of performance management into a single cost-effective system. For TRW, these components included goal setting, performance appraisal, professional development, and succession planning.

TRW's team created an online system, one in which most TRW employees and supervisors worldwide could input and review their data electronically. (The team subsequently created an equivalent paper-based system, for use by certain employees abroad who didn't have easy access to the Web.) The Web-based performance management system included data such as biographical data, previous year's professional development activities, overall performance, and future potential/positions.

In practice, either the employee or the manager can trigger the process by completing the appraisal and sending it to the other (the employee usually begins the process). Once the employee finishes the online form, a system-generated e-mail notifies the manager that the form is ready for review. Then the two fine-tune the appraisal by meeting in person, and by interacting online.

The new system focuses everyone's attention on goal-oriented performance. It identifies development needs that are important to both TRW and the employee. It gives managers instantaneous access to employee performance-related data (by clicking the "managing employees" function, a manager sees an overview of the assessment status of each of his or her direct reports). It gives all managers access to an employee database so that, for instance, a search for a mechanical engineer with Chinese language skills takes just a few minutes. And the system lets the manager quickly review the development needs of all his or her employees.

Infosys is an Indian IT services company, which is currently facing shrinking margins, high competition, and employee turnover. It is getting its old PMS reworked. The old system, based on traditional approach and forced ranking (bell curve), was a subject of high levels of employee discontent and complaints of unfairness.

The company took a bold step to abolish the bell curve and empowered its managers to engage in discussions, setting clear goals, provide timely and regular feedback, and focus on success. Now, with the new system in place, managers had to justify their ratings to team members, which only a few of them found challenging.

A new online tool, iCount, was also introduced globally to manage performance. Employees were given specific, short-term goals and regular feedback, which helped in getting better outcomes. High performers were rewarded, while those who lagged received support for development. After the introduction of this new system, company officials reported that attrition rates came down significantly.[59] ■

Source: Based on D. Bradford Neary, "Creating a Company-Wide, Online, Performance Management System: A Case Study at TRW Inc.," Human Resource Management 41, no. 4 (Winter 2002), p. 495 and Besta Shankar, "Infosys Using New System iCount to Assess Employee Performance," *International Business Times*, 8 February 2016.

LEARNING OBJECTIVE 9-3

Give examples of potential appraisal problems and how to deal with them.

unclear standards

An appraisal that is too open to interpretation.

Dealing with Rater Error Appraisal Problems

In a perfect world, all employers would use performance appraisal systems with clear goals, fair appraisals, swift feedback, and useful coaching. Alas, that is rarely the case.[60] Graphic-type rating forms in particular are susceptible to several "rater error" problems; in other words, systematic errors in judgment that occur when people evaluate each other: unclear standards, halo effect, central tendency, leniency or strictness, and bias.

Potential Rating Problems

UNCLEAR STANDARDS Table 9-2 illustrates the **unclear standards** problem. This graphic rating scale seems objective. However, it might well result in unfair appraisals, because the traits and degrees of merit are ambiguous. For example, different supervisors might define "good" performance, "fair" performance, and so on, differently. The same is true of traits such as "quality of work."[61]

Supervisors must be familiar with appraisal techniques, understand and avoid problems that can cripple appraisals, and know how to conduct appraisals fairly.

Alex Stojanov / Alamy Stock Photo

The way to fix this problem is to include descriptive phrases that define or illustrate each trait, as in Figure 9-2. That form spells out what measures like "Role Model" or "Below Expectations" mean. This specificity results in more consistent and more easily explained appraisals.

halo effect

In performance appraisal, the problem that occurs when a supervisor's rating of a subordinate on one trait biases the rating of that person on other traits.

HALO EFFECT Experts define **halo effect** as "the influence of a rater's general impression on ratings of specific ratee qualities."[62] For example, supervisors often rate unfriendly employees lower on all traits, rather than just on "gets along well with others." Being aware of this problem is a step toward avoiding it. Supervisory training can also alleviate the problem, as can using a BARS (on which, recall, the performance dimensions are usually more independent of each other).

central tendency

A tendency to rate all employees the same way, such as rating them all average.

CENTRAL TENDENCY **Central tendency** means rating all employees average. For example, if the rating scale ranges from 1 to 7, raters tend to avoid the highs (6 and 7) and lows (1 and 2) and rate most of their people between 3 and 5. Doing so distorts the evaluations, making them less useful for promotion, salary, or counseling purposes. Ranking employees instead of using graphic rating scales can reduce this problem, since ranking means you can't rate them all average.

strictness/leniency

The problem that occurs when a supervisor has a tendency to rate all subordinates either high or low.

LENIENCY OR STRICTNESS Other supervisors tend to rate all their subordinates high or low, just as some instructors are notoriously high or low graders. This **strictness/leniency** problem is especially severe with graphic rating scales. *Ranking* forces supervisors to distinguish between high and low performers.

TABLE 9-2 **A Graphic Rating Scale with Unclear Standards**

	Excellent	Good	Fair	Poor
Quantity of work				
Quality of work				
Creativity				
Integrity				

Note: For example, what exactly is meant by "good," "quantity of work," and so forth?

There are other solutions. One is for the employer to recommend that supervisors avoid giving all their employees high (or low) ratings. A second is to require a distribution—that, say, about 10% of the people should be rated "excellent," 20% "good," and so forth. (But remember it may not be an error at all, as when all subordinates really are superior.)[63]

RECENCY EFFECTS   Recency means letting what the employee has done recently blind you to what his or her performance has been over the year. The main solution is to accumulate critical incidents all year long.

Diversity Counts: The Problem of Bias

Biased appraisals have a variety of causes. One study of **bias** (the tendency for individual differences to affect judgements) focused on rater personality. Raters who scored higher on "conscientiousness" tended to give their peers lower ratings—they were stricter, in other words; those more "agreeable" gave higher ratings—they were more lenient.[64] Managers also tend to be more lenient when appraising subordinates for administrative purposes like pay raises then for development purposes.[65] Furthermore, "performance ratings amplify the quality of the personal relationship between boss and employee. Good relationships tend to create good [appraisal] experiences, bad relationships bad ones."[66]

Unfortunately, subordinates' demographic traits (age, race, gender, and so on) also affect ratings. A 36-year-old supervisor ranked a 62-year-old subordinate at the bottom of the department's rankings, and then fired him. The court held that the younger boss's discriminatory motives might have prejudiced the dismissal decision.[67] In one study, promoted women had to have received higher performance ratings than promoted men to be promoted, "suggesting that women were held to stricter standards for promotion."[68] In another study, raters penalized successful women for their success.[69] The point is that the appraisal often says more about the appraiser than about the appraisee.[70] (Or, as one researcher said, "Rater idiosyncratic biases account for the largest percentage of the observed variances in performance ratings.")[71] Potential bias is one reason to use multiple raters, have the supervisor's boss review the rating, and/or have "calibration" meetings where supervisors discuss their reasons for the appraisals they gave each of their subordinates.[72] ■

The Need for Fairness

So, due to either the supervisor's ineptness or the method's inherent unfairness, many appraisals are unfair. Some managers ignore accuracy and instead use appraisals for political purposes (such as encouraging employees with whom they don't agree to leave the firm).[73] The employees' standards should be clear, employees should understand the basis on which you're going to appraise them, and the appraisal should be objective.[74] Make sure the employee has an opportunity to express his or her opinions.

In practice (as most students probably already know), the quality of the interpersonal relationship between the supervisor and employee will shape the appraisal's impact and worth. Supervisors should be trained in both the technical and interpersonal aspects of appraising employees and giving feedback.[75] They should understand how to build trust through open relationships, engage in continuous performance conversations, diagnose and productively address performance issues, and deliver and react to feedback conversations constructively.[76] To facilitate this, the employer should evaluate and reward supervisors partly based on their effectiveness in managing performance.[77]

bias
The tendency to allow individual differences such as age, race, and sex to affect the appraisal ratings employees receive.

FIGURE 9-10 Checklist of Best Practices for Administering Fair Performance Appraisals

- Base the performance review on duties and standards from a job analysis.
- Try to base the performance review on observable job behaviors or objective performance data.
- Make it clear ahead of time what your performance expectations are.
- Use a standardized performance review procedure for all employees.
- Make sure whoever conducts the reviews has frequent opportunities to observe the employee's job performance.
- Either use multiple raters or have the rater's supervisor evaluate the appraisal results.
- Include an appeals mechanism.
- Document the appraisal review process and results.
- Discuss the appraisal results with the employee.
- Let the employees know ahead of time how you're going to conduct the reviews.
- Let the employee provide input regarding your assessment of him or her.
- Indicate what the employee needs to do to improve.
- Train the supervisors who will be doing the appraisals. Make sure they understand the procedure to use, how problems (like leniency and strictness) arise, and how to deal with them.

Figure 9-10 lists best practices for ensuring fair appraisals. Table 9-3 summarizes each appraisal method's pros and cons.

TABLE 9-3 Important Advantages and Disadvantages of Appraisal Tools

Tool	Advantages	Disadvantages
Graphic rating scale	Simple to use; provides a quantitative rating for each employee.	Standards may be unclear; halo effect, central tendency, leniency, bias can also be problems.
BARS	Provides behavioral "anchors." BARS is very accurate.	Difficult to develop.
Alternation ranking	Simple to use (but not as simple as graphic rating scales). Avoids central tendency and other problems of rating scales.	Can cause disagreements among employees and may be unfair if all employees are, in fact, excellent.
Forced distribution method	End up with a predetermined number or % of people in each group.	Employees' appraisal results depend on your choice of cutoff points.
Critical incident method	Helps specify what is "right" and "wrong" about the employee's performance; forces supervisor to evaluate subordinates on an ongoing basis.	Difficult to rate or rank employees relative to one another.
MBO	Tied to jointly agreed-upon performance objectives.	Time-consuming.

LEARNING OBJECTIVE 9-4

List steps to take in the appraisal interview.

appraisal interview
An interview in which the supervisor and subordinate review the appraisal and make plans to remedy deficiencies and reinforce strengths.

Managing the Appraisal Interview or Discussion

The traditional periodic appraisal typically culminates in an **appraisal interview or discussion.** Here the manager and the subordinate review the appraisal and make plans to remedy deficiencies and reinforce strengths. These interviews are often uncomfortable. Few people like to receive—or give—negative feedback. Adequate preparation and effective implementation are essential. Supervisors face four types of appraisal situations, each with its unique objectives:[78]

- *Satisfactory—Promotable* is the easiest interview: The person's performance is satisfactory and promotion looms. Your objective is to develop specific development plans.
- *Satisfactory—Not promotable* is for employees whose performance is satisfactory but for whom promotion is not possible. The objective here is to maintain

satisfactory performance. The best option is usually to find incentives that are important to the person and sufficient to maintain performance. These might include extra time off, a small bonus, or recognition.

- When the person's performance is *unsatisfactory but correctable*, the interview objective is to lay out an action/development plan for correcting the unsatisfactory performance. This step is referred to as Personal Improvement Plans (PIP), where an employee is closely observed and helped to improve. In case of failure to improve, the employee invites action.
- Finally, the interview where the employee is *unsatisfactory* and the situation is *uncorrectable* may be particularly tense. Dismissal is often the preferred option, but the process has to be handled with care and human touch.
- Capability of managers or supervisor to engage in performance-related discussions is important. In a study conducted in India and China about talent management identified lack of capability related to communication and requisite HR competencies (like ability to spot talent) as managerial challenges.[79] As a result, many Indian organizations are increasingly developing such capabilities among their managers.

How to Conduct the Appraisal Interview

Useful interviews begin before the interview. Beforehand, review the person's job description, compare performance to the standards, and review any previous appraisals. Give the employee at least a week's notice to review his or her work. Set a time for the interview. Interviews with lower-level personnel like clerical workers should take less than an hour. Interviews with management employees often take 1 or 2 hours. Conduct the interview privately with no interruptions.

An effective review discussion requires effective coaching skills. Coaching doesn't mean telling someone what to do. Instead, it is a process.[80] *Preparation* means understanding the problem and the employee. Here the manager will watch the employee to see what he or she is doing, review productivity data, and observe the workflow.

Planning the solution is next. This requires reaching agreement on the problem, and laying out a change plan in the form of *steps to take, measures of success,* and *date to complete.*

With agreement on a plan, the manager can start the *actual coaching.* One writer says, "An effective coach offers ideas and advice in such a way that the subordinate can hear them, respond to them, and appreciate their value."[81] Useful guidelines include:

1. *Talk in terms of objective work data.* Use examples such as absences, tardiness, and productivity.
2. *Don't get personal.* Don't say, "You're too slow producing those reports." Instead, compare the person's performance to a standard. ("These reports should normally be done within 10 days.") Similarly, don't compare the person's performance to that of other people. ("He's quicker than you are.")
3. *Encourage the person to talk.* Stop and listen to what the person is saying; ask open-ended questions (such as, "What do you think we can do to improve the situation?"). Use a command such as "Go on." Restate the person's last point as a question, as in, "You don't think you can get the job done?"
4. *Get agreement.* Make sure the person leaves knowing specifically what he or she is doing right and doing wrong and with agreement on how things will be improved, and has an action plan with targets and dates.

Whether subordinates express satisfaction with their appraisal interview will depend on several things. These include not feeling threatened, having an opportunity to present their ideas and feelings and to influence the course of the interview, and having a helpful and constructive supervisor conduct the interview.

How to Handle a Defensive Subordinate

When a supervisor tells someone his or her performance is poor, the first reaction is often denial. Denial is a defense mechanism. By denying the fault, the person avoids having to question his or her own competence.

Therefore, dealing with defensiveness is an important appraisal skill. In his book *Effective Psychology for Managers*, psychologist Mortimer Feinberg suggests the following:

1. Recognize that defensive behavior is normal.
2. Never attack a person's defenses. Don't try to "explain someone to themselves" (as in, "You know the reason you're using that excuse is that you can't bear to be blamed."). Instead, concentrate on the fact ("sales are down").
3. Postpone action. Sometimes it's best to do nothing. Employees may react to sudden threats by hiding behind their defenses. Given sufficient time, a more rational reaction takes over.
4. Recognize your limitations. The supervisor is (probably) not a psychologist. Offering understanding is one thing; trying to deal with psychological problems is another.

How to Criticize a Subordinate

When necessary, criticize in a manner that lets the person maintain his or her dignity—in private, and constructively. Provide examples of critical incidents and specific suggestions. Avoid once-a-year "critical broadsides" by giving feedback periodically, so that the formal review contains no surprises. Never say the person is "always" wrong. Criticism should be objective and free of personal bias.

When the employee is not doing well, the manager will have to decide how candid to be. Former GE CEO Jack Welch once said it's cruel to tell someone who's mediocre that their work is satisfactory.[82] Someone who might have changed course may instead waste years in a dead-end job, only to be dismissed when a more demanding boss arrives.

Some managers do take a hard line. Not all employees are salvageable, and not all managers will spend time trying to overcome an employee's faults. For example, when one Netflix manager requested a performance improvement plan for a worker, the then-head of HR said basically, "Don't waste your time." Her position was, why waste time coaching this person if she'll probably never be able to do the job right anyway?[83]

On the other hand, many employers are now emphasizing praise over criticism. One tells its managers not to touch on more than two areas that need improvement but instead to emphasize their subordinates' strengths. In one recent year, almost all the *Fortune* 500 companies used the Gallup StrengthsFinder tool (www.gallupstrengthscenter.com) to help employees identify and build on their strengths. Facebook, for instance, has used StrengthsFinder to help train supervisors in a style that better fits its mostly Millennial-aged staff. It would seem that to attract, motivate, and retain today's new employees, a less critical appraisal approach may be advisable.[84]

GET AGREEMENT ON A PLAN The aim of the appraisal should be to improve unsatisfactory performance (and/or to reinforce exemplary performance). The appraisal should therefore result in a plan (Figure 9-11) for what the employee must do to improve his or her efforts.

How to Handle a Formal Written Warning

The employee's performance may be so weak that it requires a formal written warning. Such warnings serve two purposes: (1) to shake your employee out of his or her bad habits, and (2) to help you defend your rating to your own boss and (if needed) to the courts.

FIGURE 9-11 Sample Employee Development Plan

SAMPLE EMPLOYEE DEVELOPMENT PLAN			
Employee's Name	**Department**	**Employee's Job Title**	**Today's Date**
Employee's main Objectives for this period:	Did employee fully achieve objective (include rating from appraisal form, from Poor to Outstanding).	What training or other actions are required for improved performance on this objective?	Completion dates:
➤ 1 _____	_____	_____	_____
➤ 2 _____	_____	_____	_____
➤ 3 _____	_____	_____	_____
➤ 4 _____	_____	_____	_____
➤ 5 _____	_____	_____	_____

Employee Signature   Manager Signature
-----------------------------   ------------------------

Copyright Gary dessler, PhD

FIGURE 9-12 Appraisal Interview Checklist

Source: Copyight Gary Dessler, PhD.

Appraisal Interview Checklist		
Interview Item: Did you	Yes	No
1. Review the employee's job description, previous appraisals, goals, and current job standards prior to the interview?		
2. Provide adequate time and a private, cordial, non-threatening environment for the interview?		
3. Focus your discussion and comments on objective work data?		
4. Encourage the appraisee to talk (restate last comment as a question, etc.), and make it clear you are listening (nod, etc.)?		
5. Give the appraisee an opportunity to fully present his or her ideas and feelings?		
6. Consciously avoid attacking the appraisee's defenses?		
7. Criticize in a way that allowed the appraisee to maintain his or her dignity?		
8. Discuss your evaluation of each of the appraisee's job duties and/or goals?		
9. Reach agreement on the training and development required to improve the appraisee's performance?		
10. Discuss, as appropriate, the steps the employer may take if improvement goals are not met?		
11. Discuss the appraisee's performance in light of his or her career aspirations?		

Written warnings should list the employee's standards, make it clear that the employee was aware of the standard, specify any deficiencies relative to the standard, and show the employee had an opportunity to correct his or her performance.

Figure 9-12 provides an appraisal interview checklist.

LEARNING OBJECTIVE **9-5**

Explain key points in how to use the appraisal interview to boost employee engagement.

Employee Engagement Guide for Managers

Use the Appraisal Interview to Build Engagement

Managers can use the appraisal interview to improve their employees' engagement. Here are relevant findings and implications.

1. Employees who understand how they and their departments contribute to the company's success are more engaged.[85] Therefore, *take the opportunity to show the employee how his or her efforts contribute to the "big picture"—to his or her team's and the company's success.*

2. Another study found that employees' engagement rose when they experienced what the researchers called "psychological meaningfulness" (namely, the perception that one's role in the organization is worthwhile and valuable).[86] *Use the interview to emphasize the meaningfulness to the company of what the employee is doing.*

3. Employees who experience "psychological safety" (namely, the perception that it's safe to bring oneself to a role without fear of damage to self-image, status, or career) were more engaged.[87] A study by Gallup among Indian employees about PMS highlight that while Indian employees respect processes and procedures, their engagement levels are impacted by trust between members of a work group.[88] Therefore, *be candid and objective but do so supportively and without unnecessarily undermining the employee's self-image.*[89]

4. Efficacy drives engagement, so use the interview to make sure your employee *has what he or she needs* to do a good job.[90]

5. Managers should be candid and honest, but don't unnecessarily emphasize the negatives. Doing so undermines employee engagement. In a study of early career burnout among Indian knowledge workers, researchers found that poor management of work and fear of replacement resulted in disengagement and burnout.[91] In one survey, Gallup asked about 1,000 U.S. employees to respond to two statements: "My supervisor focuses on my strengths or positive characteristics" and "My supervisor focuses on my weaknesses or negative characteristics." It found that about three times more employees whose *managers focused on strengths* were engaged, compared with those whose managers focused on weaknesses.[92]

6. Research shows that involvement in decision making and letting employees voice their opinions improve employee engagement.[93] Use the interview as an opportunity to *show your employees that you listen to their ideas and value their contributions.*

7. Engagement rises when employees have an opportunity to improve their careers.[94] During the interview discuss the person's evaluation *in the context of where he or she sees himself or herself heading career-wise.*[95]

8. Research shows "a significant positive association between distributive [what rewards people get] and informational [what information they get] justice dimensions, and employee engagement."[96] Bottom line: *Make sure that the employee views the appraisal and the rewards or remedial actions as fair.*

Performance Management

Performance appraisal is fine in theory, but in practice, appraisals don't always go smoothly. Goals aren't set, the "appraisal" is a form from an office supply store, and the yearly feedback, if any, may be agonizing, with both participants fleeing before any coaching takes place. This runs counter to common sense. Employees should know what their goals are, performance feedback should be useful, and if there is a problem, the time to take action is right away, not 6 months later.

LEARNING OBJECTIVE **9-6**

Explain how you would take a performance management approach to appraisal.

Total Quality Management and Performance Appraisal

Management experts have long argued that most performance appraisals neither motivate employees nor guide their development.[97] Some proponents of the total quality management (TQM) movement even argued for eliminating performance appraisals altogether.[98] *Total quality management* (TQM) programs are organizationwide programs that integrate all functions and processes of the business such that all aspects of the business including design, planning, production, distribution, and field service are aimed at maximizing customer satisfaction through continuous improvements.[99] TQM programs are built on a philosophy encapsulated by several principles, such as: cease dependence on inspection to achieve quality; aim for continuous improvement; institute extensive training; drive out fear so that everyone may work effectively; remove barriers that rob employees of their pride of workmanship (in particular, the annual merit rating); and institute a vigorous program of self-improvement.[100] Basically, TQM advocates argue that the organization is a system of interrelated parts, and that employees' performance is more a function of things like training, communication, tools, and supervision than of their motivation.

What would performance appraisal look like in such a company? Visitors to Toyota Motor's Lexington, Kentucky, Camry plant would find such a system. Teams of employees monitor their own results, generally without managers' interventions. In frequent meetings, the team members continuously align those results with the work team's standards and with the plant's overall quality and productivity goals. Team members who need coaching and training receive it. Procedures that need changing are changed.

What Is Performance Management?

That is performance management in action. In comparing performance management and performance appraisal, "the distinction is the contrast between a year-end event—the completion of the appraisal form—and a process that starts the year with performance planning and is integral to the way people are managed throughout the year."[101] **Performance management** is the *continuous* process of identifying, measuring, and developing the performance of individuals and teams and *aligning* their performance with the organization's *goals*.[102] We can summarize performance management's six basic elements as follows:[103]

- *Direction sharing* means communicating the company's goals to all employees and then translating these into doable departmental, team, and individual goals.
- *Goal alignment* means having a method that enables managers and employees to *see* the link between the employees' goals and those of their department and company.
- *Ongoing performance monitoring* usually means computerized systems to measure the team's and/or employee's progress toward meeting performance goals.
- *Ongoing feedback* means providing face-to-face and computerized continuous feedback regarding progress toward goals.
- *Coaching and developmental support* should be part of the feedback process.
- *Recognition and rewards* should provide the incentives to keep the employee's goal-directed performance on track.

performance management
The *continuous* process of identifying, measuring, and developing the performance of individuals and teams and *aligning* their performance with the organization's *goals*.

TRENDS SHAPING HR: *DIGITAL AND SOCIAL MEDIA*

Employers increasingly use digital technologies including cloud computing, gaming, and social media to support performance management. For example, with Oracle TBE Performance Management Cloud Service, management would:

- First, *assign financial and nonfinancial goals* to each team's activities, goals which support the company's overall strategic goals. (Thus, an airline might measure ground crew aircraft turnaround time in terms of "improve turnaround time to 26 minutes per plane this year.")
- *Inform all teams and employees* of their goals.
- *Use IT-supported tools* (cloud-based performance management software, HR scorecards, and digital dashboards) to continuously display, monitor, and assess each team's and employee's performance (see Figure 9-13). Oracle TBE Performance Management Cloud Service illustrates this.[104] Because the goals

are "in the cloud" rather than embedded in documents, managers needn't wait until the annual or semiannual reviews to revise them. And the system's dashboards enable managers to continuously monitor each team or employee's performance, let employees update progress toward goal achievement, and let employees and managers log comments so the process is real-time and interactive. For more details, see www.oracle.com/taleo-tbe.

- Finally, if exceptions are noted, ensure you've *taken corrective action* before things swing out of control.

Beyond the cloud, employers are also adopting social media and gaming–based performance appraisal and management tools. Social media tools allow almost everyone in the company (the "crowd," as in "crowd appraisals") to continuously appraise each other's work. Workforce Rypple (subsequently bought by salesforce.com) is one such "social performance management platform."[105] Basically, it supplements traditional appraisals. Employees and managers use it to set goals, and to provide feedback and recognition as tasks get done.[106] For example,

FIGURE 9-13 Summary of Performance Management Report

Source: ZingHR.com

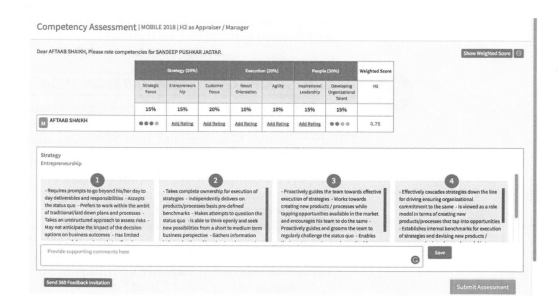

Washington-based LivingSocial employees use Rypple to comment on each other's work. LivingSocial then uses these comments as an input to its formal employee appraisals.[107] Solar energy company Sunrun also uses Rypple. A spokesman says: "It's great for putting ideas out there, you can unveil objectives to the whole team, ask for opinions and suggestions and then work on them together. We do 360 feedback each week."[108] Saba Social Performance Management Software is another such tool.[109] Employers often combine such ongoing reviews with Globoforce (www.globoforce. com) type rewards sites, which automate the process of instantaneously rewarding and recognizing colleagues.[110]

Dissatisfaction with its current performance appraisal process prompted Persistent Systems to have the gaming company eMee create a virtual appraisal game. Every Persistent Systems employee has a virtual avatar. Employees use them to give real-time feedback to each other, including virtual gifts and points (only immediate supervisors can give reprimands). The system apparently reduced turnover and improved performance.[111] ∎

The HR Practices Around the Globe feature shows how one company developed a company-wide performance management system.

IMPROVING PERFORMANCE: *HR Practices around the Globe*

Performance Management at General Dynamics Armament Systems (GDAS)

General Dynamics Armament Systems (GDAS) designs, develops, and produces high-performance products for the military, industrial, and commercial markets.[112] GDAS reorganized its various programs around teams. The teams and their team members have individual responsibility for income, sales, deliveries, and customer satisfaction. Organizing its programs around teams meant GDAS needed a better way to track the teams' performances and monitor and manage the company's performance.

Its new performance management reporting system uses a standard set of performance metrics processed and reported through a special business metrics scorecard. The scorecard displays the performance metrics for each team in three ways (actual, baseline plan, and current plan). It then calculates and displays a variance between the actual and the planned performances.

GDAS uses multiple scorecards to display performance metrics, such as for team and for divisional performance. The scorecards allow GDAS to maintain all of its crucial performance data in one system so managers can easily access the information anytime via the firm's intranet. The scorecards provide GDAS with approximately 450 performance reports and charts. To produce these charts manually would require 13 full-time employees. Instead, the performance measures reporting system, at a cost of $1 million, generates the reports and charts automatically. ∎

Source: Based on www.gdatp.com/about/; Best Practice: Performance Measures Reporting System," Best Manufacturing Practices Center of Excellence, www.bmpcoe.org/bestpractices/internal/gdas/gdas_11.html.

The Manager's Role in Performance Management

Technology, useful though it is, isn't mandatory for managers who want to take a performance management approach. What is mandatory is having the right philosophy and on-the-job behaviors. As a philosophy, performance management reflects nonthreatening TQM principles such as cease dependence on inspection to achieve quality, aim for continuous improvement, institute extensive training, and drive out fear so that everyone may work effectively. Behaviors include linking employees' goals to the company's goals, giving employees continuous feedback, providing required resources and coaching, rewarding good performance, and remembering that employees' performance reflects more than just whether they're "motivated."[113]

 HR in Practice at the Hotel Paris Both Lisa and the firm's CFO were concerned by the current disconnect between (1) what their current appraisal process was focusing on and (2) what the company wanted to accomplish in terms of its strategic goals. They wanted the firm's new performance management system to help breathe life into the firm's strategic performance. To see what they did, read the case on pages 295 of this chapter.

Chapter Review

Chapter Section Summaries

9-1. **Performance appraisal** means evaluating an employee's current or past performance relative to his or her performance standards. Managers appraise their subordinates' performance to obtain input on which promotion and salary raise decisions can be made, to develop plans for correcting performance deficiencies, and for career-planning purposes. Supervisory ratings are still at the heart of most appraisal processes.

9-2. The appraisal is generally conducted using one or more popular **appraisal methods or tools**. These include graphic rating scales, alternation ranking, paired comparison, forced distribution, critical incidents, behaviorally anchored rating scales, MBO, computerized performance appraisals, and electronic performance monitoring.

9-3. The appraisal process can be improved by eliminating chronic **problems** that often undermine appraisals and graphic rating scales in particular. These problems include unclear standards, halo effect, central tendency, leniency or strictness, and bias.

9-4. An appraisal typically culminates in an **appraisal interview**. Adequate preparation (including giving the subordinate notice, reviewing his or her job description and past performance, choosing the right place for the interview, and leaving enough time for it) is essential.

9-5. The manager can use the appraisal interview to improve the employees' level of **engagement**. For example, show the employee how his or her efforts contribute to the team's and the company's success; use the interview to emphasize the meaningfulness to the company of what the employee is doing; and emphasize support rather than threats.

9-6. **Performance management** is the *continuous* process of identifying, measuring, and developing the performance of individuals and teams and *aligning* their performance with the organization's *goals*. It means continuous interactions and feedback to ensure continuous improvement in the employee's and team's capacity and performance. Most importantly, it requires remembering that your employee's performance usually reflects more than just whether he or she is "motivated."

Discussion Questions

9-1. What is the purpose of a performance appraisal?

9-2. Answer the question, "Who should do the appraising?"

9-3. Discuss the pros and cons of four performance appraisal tools.

9-4. Explain how you would use the alternation ranking method, the paired comparison method, and the forced distribution method.

9-5. Explain in your own words how you would go about developing a behaviorally anchored rating scale.

9-6. Explain the problems to be avoided in appraising performance.

9-7. Compare and contrast performance management and performance appraisal.

Individual and Group Activities

9-8. Working individually or in groups, develop a graphic rating scale for the following jobs: secretary, professor, bus driver.

9-9. Working individually or in groups, describe the advantages and disadvantages of using the forced distribution appraisal method for college professors.

9-10. Working individually or in groups, develop, over the period of a week, a set of critical incidents covering the classroom performance of one of your instructors.

9-11. Appendices A and B at the end of this book (pages 583–600) list the knowledge someone studying for the HRCI (Appendix A) or SHRM (Appendix B) certification exam needs to have in each area of human resource management (such as in Strategic Management, and Workforce Planning).

In groups of several students, do four things: (1) review Appendix A and/or B; (2) identify the material in this chapter that relates to the Appendix A and/or B required knowledge lists; (3) write four multiple-choice exam questions on this material that you believe would be suitable for inclusion in the HRCI exam and/or the SHRM exam; and, (4) if time permits, have someone from your team post your team's questions in front of the class, so that students in all teams can answer the exam questions created by the other teams.

9-12. When he was doing his show The apprentice, Donald Trump often told apprentices "You're fired!" Review recent (or archived) episodes of Donald Trump's *The Apprentice* and answer this: What performance appraisal system did Mr. Trump use, and do you think it resulted in valid appraisals? What techniques discussed in this chapter did he seem to apply? How would you suggest he might change his appraisal system to make it more effective?

Experiential Exercise

Grading the Professor

Purpose: The purpose of this exercise is to give you practice in developing and using a performance appraisal form.

Required Understanding: You are going to develop a performance appraisal form for an instructor and should therefore be thoroughly familiar with the discussion of performance appraisals in this chapter.

How to Set Up the Exercise/Instructions: Divide the class into groups of four or five students.

9-13. First, based on what you now know about performance appraisal, do you think Figure 9-1 is an effective scale for appraising instructors? Why or why not?

9-14. Next, your group should develop its own tool for appraising the performance of an instructor. Decide which of the appraisal tools (graphic rating scales, alternation ranking, and so on) you are going to use, and then design the instrument itself.

9-15. Next, have a spokesperson from each group post his or her group's appraisal tool on the board. How similar are the tools? Do they all measure the same factors? Which factor appears most often? Which do you think is the most effective tool on the board?

9-16. The class should select the top 10 factors from all of the appraisal tools presented to create what the class perceives to be the most effective tool for appraising the performance of the instructor.

CHAPTER 9

Application Case

Appraising the Secretaries at Sweetwater U

Rob Winchester, newly appointed vice president for administrative affairs at Sweetwater State University, faced a tough problem shortly after his university career began. Three weeks after he came on board in September, Sweetwater's president, Rob's boss, told Rob that one of his first tasks was to improve the appraisal system used to evaluate secretarial and clerical performance at Sweetwater U. The main difficulty was that the performance appraisal was traditionally tied directly to salary increases given at the end of the year. Therefore, most administrators were less than accurate when they used the graphic rating forms that were the basis of the clerical staff evaluation. In fact, what usually happened was that each administrator simply rated his or her clerk or secretary as "excellent." This cleared the way for them to receive a maximum pay raise every year.

But the current university budget simply did not include enough money to fund another "maximum" annual raise for every staffer. Furthermore, Sweetwater's president felt that the custom of providing invalid feedback to each secretary on his or her year's performance was not productive, so he had asked the new vice president to revise the system. In October, Rob sent a memo to all administrators, telling them that in the future no more than half the secretaries reporting to any particular administrator could be appraised as "excellent." This move, in effect, forced each supervisor to begin ranking his or her secretaries for quality of performance. The vice president's memo met widespread resistance immediately—from administrators, who were afraid that many of their secretaries would begin leaving for more lucrative jobs, and from secretaries, who felt that the new system was unfair and reduced each secretary's chance of receiving a maximum salary increase. A handful of secretaries had begun picketing outside the president's home on the university campus. The picketing, caustic remarks by disgruntled administrators, and rumors of an impending slowdown by the secretaries (there were about 250 on campus) made Rob Winchester wonder whether he had made the right decision by setting up forced ranking. He knew, however, that there were a few performance appraisal experts in the School of Business, so he decided to set up an appointment with them to discuss the matter.

He met with them the next morning. He explained the situation as he had found it: The current appraisal system had been set up when the university first opened 10 years earlier. A committee of secretaries had developed it. Under that system, Sweetwater's administrators filled out forms similar to the one shown in Table 9-2. This once-a-year appraisal (in March) had run into problems almost immediately, since it was apparent from the start that administrators varied widely in their interpretations of job standards, as well as in how conscientiously they filled out the forms and supervised their secretaries. Moreover, at the end of the first year it became obvious to everyone that each secretary's salary increase was tied directly to the March appraisal. For example, those rated "excellent" received the maximum increases, those rated "good" received smaller increases, and those given neither rating received only the standard across-the-board cost-of-living increase. Since universities in general—and Sweetwater, in particular—have paid secretaries somewhat lower salaries than those prevailing in private industry, some secretaries left in a huff that first year. From that time on, most administrators simply rated all secretaries excellent in order to reduce staff turnover, thus ensuring each a maximum increase. In the process, they also avoided the hard feelings aroused by the significant performance differences otherwise highlighted by administrators.

Two Sweetwater experts agreed to consider the problem, and in 2 weeks they came back to the vice president with the following recommendations. First, the form used to rate the secretaries was grossly insufficient. It was unclear what "excellent" or "quality of work" meant, for example. They recommended instead a form like that in Figure 9-2. In addition, they recommended that the vice president rescind his earlier memo and no longer attempt to force university administrators to arbitrarily rate at least half their secretaries as something less than excellent. The two consultants pointed out

that this was unfair, since it was quite possible that any particular administrator might have staffers who were all or virtually all excellent—or conceivably, although less likely, all below standard. The experts said that the way to get all the administrators to take the appraisal process more seriously was to stop tying it to salary increases. In other words, they recommended that every administrator fill out a form as in Figure 9-2 for each secretary at least once a year and then use this form as the basis of a counseling session. Salary increases would have to be made on some basis other than the performance appraisal, so that administrators would no longer hesitate to fill out the rating forms honestly.

Rob thanked the two experts and went back to his office to ponder their recommendations. Some of the recommendations (such as substituting the new rating form for the old) seemed to make sense. Nevertheless, he still had serious doubts as to the efficacy of any graphic rating form, particularly compared with his original, preferred forced ranking approach. The experts' second recommendation—to stop tying the appraisals to automatic salary increases—made sense but raised at least one very practical problem: If salary increases were not to be based on performance appraisals, on what were they to be based? He began wondering whether the experts' recommendations weren't simply based on ivory tower theorizing.

Questions

9-17. Do you think that the experts' recommendations will be sufficient to get most of the administrators to fill out the rating forms properly? Why or why not? What additional actions (if any) do you think will be necessary?

9-18. Do you think that Vice President Winchester would be better off dropping graphic rating forms, substituting instead one of the other techniques we discussed in this chapter, such as a ranking method? Why or why not?

9-19. What performance appraisal system would you develop for the secretaries if you were Rob Winchester? Defend your answer.

Continuing Case

Carter Cleaning Company

The Performance Appraisal

After spending several weeks on the job, Jennifer was surprised to discover that her father had not formally evaluated any employee's performance for all the years that he had owned the business. Jack's position was that he had "a hundred higher-priority things to attend to," such as boosting sales and lowering costs, and, in any case, many employees didn't stick around long enough to be appraisable anyway. Furthermore, contended Jack, manual workers such as those doing the pressing and the cleaning did periodically get positive feedback in terms of praise from Jack for a job well done, or criticism, also from Jack, if things did not look right during one of his swings through the stores. Similarly, Jack was never shy about telling his managers about store problems so that they, too, got some feedback on where they stood.

This informal feedback notwithstanding, Jennifer believes that a more formal appraisal approach is required. She believes that there are criteria such as quality, quantity, attendance, and punctuality that should be evaluated periodically even if a worker is paid on piece rate. Furthermore, she feels quite strongly that the managers need to have a list of quality standards for matters such as store cleanliness, efficiency, safety, and adherence to budget on which they know they are to be formally evaluated.

Questions

9-20. Is Jennifer right about the need to evaluate the workers formally? The managers? Why or why not?

9-21. Develop a performance appraisal method for the workers and managers in each store.

Translating Strategy into HR Policies and Practices Case*,§

*The overall map on the page xxxviii of this book outlines the relationships involved.

Improving Performance at the Hotel Paris

The New Performance Management System

The Hotel Paris's competitive strategy is "To use superior guest service to differentiate the Hotel Paris properties, and to thereby increase the length of stay and return rate of guests, and thus boost revenues and profitability." HR manager Lisa Cruz must now formulate appraisal policies and activities that support this competitive strategy, by eliciting the required employee behaviors and competencies.

Lisa knew that the Hotel Paris's performance appraisal system was inadequate. When the founders opened their first hotel, they went to an office-supply store and purchased a pad of performance appraisal forms. The hotel chain used these. Each form was a two-sided page. Supervisors indicates whether the employee's performance in terms of various standard traits including quantity of work, quality of work, and dependability was excellent, good, fair, or poor. Lisa knew that, among other flaws, this appraisal tool did not force either the employee or the supervisor to focus the appraisal on the extent to which the employee was helping the Hotel Paris to achieve its strategic goals. She wanted a system that focused the employee's attention on taking those actions that would contribute to helping the company achieve its goals, for instance, in terms of improved customer service.

Both Lisa and the firm's CFO were concerned by the current disconnect between (1) what the current appraisal process was focusing on and (2) what the company wanted to accomplish in terms of its strategic goals. They wanted the firm's new performance management system to help breathe life into the firm's strategic performance, by focusing employees' behavior specifically on the performances that would help the Hotel Paris achieve its strategic goals.

Lisa and her team created a performance management system that focused on both competencies and objectives. In designing the new system, their starting point was the job descriptions they had created for the hotel's employees. These descriptions each included required competencies. Consequently, using a form similar to Figure 9-3, the front-desk clerks' appraisals now focus on competencies such as "able to check a guest in or out in 5 minutes or less." Most service employees' appraisals include the competency, "able to exhibit patience and guest support of this even when busy with other activities." There were other required competencies. For example, the Hotel Paris wanted all service employees to show initiative in helping guests, to be customer oriented, and to be team players (in terms of sharing information and best practices). Each of these competencies derives from the hotel's aim of becoming more service-oriented. Each employee now also receives one or more strategically relevant objectives for the coming year. (One, for a housecleaning crewmember, said, "Martha will have no more than three room cleaning infractions in the coming year," for instance.)

In addition to the goals- and competencies-based appraisals, other Hotel Paris performance management forms laid out the development efforts that the employee would undertake in the coming year. Instructions also reminded the supervisors that, in addition to the annual and semiannual appraisals, they should continuously interact with and update their employees. The result was a comprehensive performance management system: The supervisor appraised the employee based on goals and competencies that were driven by the company's strategic needs. And, the actual appraisal resulted in new goals for the coming year, as well as in specific development plans that made sense in terms of the company's and the employees' needs and preferences.

Questions

9-22. Choose one job, such as front-desk clerk. Based on any information you have (including job descriptions you may have created in other chapters), write a list of duties, competencies, and performance standards for that chosen job.

9-23. Based on that, and on what you read in this Dessler *Human Resource Management* chapter, create a performance appraisal form for appraising that job.

§Written by and copyright Gary Dessler, PhD.

Key Terms

Endnotes

1. See, for example, Howard Risher, "Performance Management Needs to Be Fixed," *Compensation & Benefits Review* 44, no. 4 (2014), pp. 191–194.
2. Experts debate the pros and cons of tying appraisals to pay decisions.

One side argues that doing so distorts the appraisals. A recent study concludes the opposite. Mary Jo Ducharme et al., "Exploring the Links Between Performance Appraisals and Pay Satisfaction," *Compensation and Benefits Review*,

September/October 2005, pp. 46–52. See also Robert Morgan, "Making the Most of Performance Management Systems," *Compensation and Benefits Review*, September/October 2006, pp. 22–27.

3. Accessed on 21 August 2017 at www.cignattkinsurance.in/overview
4. HRK News Bureau, Cigna TTK, "Engaging Workforce Through New Performance Management System," *HR Katha* (Nov, 2015),

HYPERLINK "http://www.hrkatha.com"www.hrkatha.com, 29 July 2017.

5. "Get SMART About Setting Goals," *Asia Africa Intelligence Wire,* May 22, 2005.

6. See, for example, E. A. Locke and G. P. Latham, "Building a Practically Useful Theory of Goal Setting and Task Motivation. A 35-Year Odyssey," *American Psychologist* 57, no. 9 (2002), pp. 705–717.

7. www.quora.com/What-does-Facebooks-performance-review-process-look-like, accessed April 2, 2015.

8. Bock, *Work Rules!,* p. 171.

9. Vanessa Druskat and Steven Wolf, "Effects and Timing of Developmental Peer Appraisals in Self-Managing Work-Groups," *Journal of Applied Psychology* 84, no. 1 (1999), pp. 58–74. For a recent review, see Erich Dierdorff and Eric Surface, "Placing Peer Ratings in Context: Systematic Influences beyond Ratee Performance," *Personnel Psychology* 60, no. 1 (Spring 2007), pp. 93–126.

10. See, for example, Brian Hoffman and David Woehr, "Disentangling the Meaning of Multisource Performance Rating Source and Dimension Factors," *Personnel Psychology* 62 (2009), pp. 735–765.

11. As one study concluded, "Far from being a source of nonmeaningful error variance, the discrepancies among ratings from multiple perspectives can in fact capture meaningful variance in multilevel managerial performance." In-Sue Oh and Christopher Berry, "The Five Factor Model of Personality and Managerial Performance: Validity Gains Through the Use of 360° Performance Ratings," *Journal of Applied Psychology* 94, no. 6 (2009), p. 1510.

12. Jeffrey Facteau and S. Bartholomew Craig, "Performance Appraisal Ratings from Different Rating Scores," *Journal of Applied Psychology* 86, no. 2 (2001), pp. 215–227.

13. See also Kevin Murphy et al., "Raters Who Pursue Different Goals Give Different Ratings," *Journal of Applied Psychology* 89, no. 1 (2004), pp. 158–164.

14. Such findings may be culturally related. One study compared self and supervisor ratings in "other-oriented" cultures (as in Asia, where values tend to emphasize teams). It found that self and supervisor ratings were related. M. Audrey Korsgaard et al., "The Effect of Other Orientation on Self: Supervisor Rating Agreement," *Journal of Organizational Behavior* 25, no. 7 (November 2004),

pp. 873–891. See also Heike Heidemeier and Klaus Mosar, "Self Other Agreement in Job Performance Ratings: A Meta-Analytic Test of a Process Model," *Journal of Applied Psychology* 94, no. 2 (2009), pp. 353–370.

15. Forest Jourden and Chip Heath, "The Evaluation Gap in Performance Perceptions: Illusory Perceptions of Groups and Individuals," *Journal of Applied Psychology* 81, no. 4 (August 1996), pp. 369–379. See also Sheri Ostroff, "Understanding Self-Other Agreement: A Look at Rater and Ratee Characteristics, Context, and Outcomes," *Personnel Psychology* 57, no. 2 (Summer 2004), pp. 333–375.

16. Paul Atkins and Robert Wood, "Self Versus Others Ratings as Predictors of Assessment Center Ratings: Validation Evidence for 360 Degree Feedback Programs," *Personnel Psychology* 55, no. 4 (Winter 2002), pp. 871–904.

17. David Antonioni, "The Effects of Feedback Accountability on Upward Appraisal Ratings," *Personnel Psychology* 47 (1994), pp. 349–355. For an anonymous online appraisal method, see, for example, http://work.com/perform, accessed October 12, 2012.

18. Alan Walker and James Smither, "A Five-Year Study of Upward Feedback: What Managers Do with Their Results Matters," *Personnel Psychology* 52 (1999), pp. 393–423; and Austin F. R. Smith and Vincent J. Fortunato, "Factors Influencing Employee Intentions to Provide Honest Upward Feedback Ratings," *Journal of Business Psychology* 22 (2008), pp. 191–207.

19. The evidence from another study suggests also that "upward and peer 360-degree ratings may be biased by rater affect [whether the rater likes the ratee]; therefore, at this point, these ratings should be used for the sole purpose of providing ratees with developmental feedback." David Antonioni and Heejoon Park, "The Relationship Between Rater Affect and Three Sources of 360-Degree Feedback Ratings," *Journal of Management* 27, no. 4 (2001), pp. 479–495.

20. Lindsay Gellman, "Memo Lets Workers Vent Anonymously About the Boss," *Wall Street Journal,* January 21, 2015, p. B7.

21. See, for example, "360-Degree Feedback on the Rise Survey Finds," *BNA Bulletin to Management,* January 23, 1997, p. 31; Leanne Atwater et al., "Multisource Feedback: Lessons Learned and Implications

for Practice," *Human Resource Management* 46, no. 2 (Summer 2007), p. 285. However, a small number of employers are beginning to use 360-degree feedback for performance appraisals, rather than just development. See, for example, Tracy Maylett, "360° Feedback Revisited: The Transition from Development to Appraisal," *Compensation & Benefits,* September/October 2009, pp. 52–59.

22. Accessed on 21 August 2017 at http://www.tata.in/article/inside/tata-aia-life-insurance-aon-best-employer-2016.

23. James Smither et al., "Does Performance Improve Following Multi-Score Feedback? A Theoretical Model, Meta Analysis, and Review of Empirical Findings," *Personnel Psychology* 58 (2005), pp. 33–36.

24. Jim Meade, "Visual 360: A Performance Appraisal System That's 'Fun,'" *HR Magazine,* July 1999, pp. 118–119, www.halogensoftware.com/landing/free-trial/360-multiraterfeedback?source=msn&c=Search-e360&kw=360%2520evaluations, accessed August 28, 2014.

25. www.sumtotalsystems.com/performance/index.html?e=001&sitenbr=156896193& keys=visual+360&submit.x=11&submit.y=11&submit=submit, accessed April 20, 2008.

26. Howard Risher, "Getting Serious about Performance Management," *Compensation & Benefits Review,* November/December 2005, pp. 18–26.

27. Leslie Kwoh, "Rank and Yank Retains Vocal Fans," *Wall Street Journal,* January 31, 2012, p. B12.

28. Jena McGregor, "The Struggle to Measure Performance," *BusinessWeek,* January 9, 2006, p. 26.

29. Steve Bates, "Forced Ranking," *HR Magazine,* June 2003, pp. 63–68.

30. Steven Cullen et al., "Forced Distribution Rating Systems and the Improvement of Workforce Potential: A Baseline Simulation," *Personnel Psychology* 58 (2005), p. 1.

31. Gary Giumetti, Amber Schroeder, and Fred Switzer III, "Forced Distribution Rating Systems: When Does 'Rank and Yank' Lead to Adverse Impact?" *Journal of Applied Psychology* 100, no. 1 (2015), pp. 180–193.

32. "Survey Says Problems with Forced Ranking Include Lower Morale and Costly Turnover," *BNA Bulletin to Management,* September 16, 2004, p. 297.

33. Steve Bates, "Forced Ranking: Why Grading Employees on a Scale Relative to Each Other Forces a Hard Look at Finding

Keepers, Losers May Become Weepers," *HR Magazine* 48, no. 6 (June 2003), p. 62. See also D. J. Schleicher et al., "Rater Reactions to Forced Distribution Rating Systems," *Journal of Management* 35, no. 4 (August 2009), pp. 899–927.

34. Clinton Wingrove, "Developing an Effective Blend of Process and Technology in the New Era of Performance Management," *Compensation & Benefits Review,* January/February 2003, p. 26.

35. Shira Ovide And Rachel Feintzeig, "Microsoft Abandons Dreaded 'Stack,'" *Wall Street Journal,* November 13, 2013, p. B1.

36. Accessed on September 26, 2017 at https://web.iima.ac.in/assets/snippets/workingpaper-pdf/6096466172015-10-04.pdf and http://telecom.economictimes.indiatimes.com/news/tcs-plans-to-straighten-out-the-bell-curve-with-new-appraisal-system/55612071.

37. Juan Sanchez and Phillip De La Torre, "A Second Look at the Relationship Between Rating and Behavioral Accuracy in Performance Appraisal," *Journal of Applied Psychology* 81, no. 1 (1996), p. 7. See also "How to ... Improve Appraisals," *People Management* 15, no. 3 (January 29, 2009), p. 57.

38. Angelo DeNisi and Lawrence Peters, "Organization of Information in Memory and the Performance Appraisal Process: Evidence from the Field," *Journal of Applied Psychology* 81, no. 6 (1996), pp. 717–737. See also A. Fox, "Curing What Ails Performance Reviews," *HR Magazine* 54, no. 1 (January 2009), pp. 52–56.

39. Based on Donald Schwab, Herbert Heneman III, and Thomas DeCotiis, "Behaviorally Anchored Scales: A Review of the Literature," *Personnel Psychology* 28 (1975), pp. 549–562. For a discussion, see also Uco Wiersma and Gary Latham, "The Practicality of Behavioral Observation Scales, Behavioral Expectation Scales, and Trait Scales," *Personnel Psychology* 30, no. 3 (Autumn 1986), pp. 619–689; and Neil M. A. Hauenstein, Reagan D. Brown, and Andrea L. Sinclair, "BARS and Those Mysterious, Missing Middle Anchors," *Journal of Business and Psychology,* 25, no.4, (2010), pp. 663-672.

40. Lawrence Fogli, Charles Hulin, and Milton Blood, "Development of First Level Behavioral Job Criteria," *Journal of Applied Psychology* 55 (1971), pp. 3–8. See also Joseph Maiorca, "How to Construct Behaviorally Anchored Rating Scales (BARS) for Employee

Evaluations," *Supervision*, August 1997, pp. 15–19; and Hauenstein et al., "BARS and Those Mysterious, Missing Middle Anchors."

41. Kevin R. Murphy and Joseph Constans, "Behavioral Anchors as a Source of Bias in Rating," *Journal of Applied Psychology* 72, no. 4 (November 1987), pp. 573–577; Aharon Tziner, "A Comparison of Three Methods of Performance Appraisal with Regard to Goal Properties, Goal Perception, and Ratee Satisfaction," *Group & Organization Management* 25, no. 2 (June 2000), pp. 175–191.

42. See for example, Richard D. Goffin et al., "Criterion Validation of Two Approaches to Performance Appraisal: The Behavioural Observation Scale and the Relative Percentile Scale," *Journal of Business and Psychology* 11, no. 1 (1996), pp. 23–33.

43. Many managers call MBO out of date. They say goal setting is no panacea, and and some jobs, for instance in R&D, may not be well measured by goals. Howard Risher, "Individual Performance Goals Can Be Problematic," *Compensation & Benefits Review* 45, no. 2, pp. 63–66.

44. Laszlo Bock, *Work Rules!* (New York: 12, 2015), p. 155.

45. However, one study concludes that Web-based performance management systems don't seem to improve performance management system effectiveness. Edward Lawler III et al., "What Makes Performance Appraisals Effective?" *Compensation & Benefits Review* 44, no. 4 (2012), p. 196.

46. www.successfactors.com/en_us/lp/ppc/employee-appraisal-software.html?Campaign_CRM=CRM-XJ14-HCM-1DG_GPPCPA&CmpLeadSource=Search%20Engine&source=Google_ppc&kw=Employee%20Appraisals%20Software&ad-%E2%80%90id=48484314803&adgroup=Google&gclid=CN2P2c233cQCFZEdgQodVnUA9w, accessed April 4, 2015.

47. See, for example, Stoney Alder and Maureen Ambrose, "Towards Understanding Fairness Judgments Associated with Computer Performance Monitoring: An Integration of the Feedback, Justice, and Monitoring Research," *Human Resource Management Review* 15, no. 1 (March 2005), pp. 43–67. For a more recent analysis of EPM, see Katherine J. S. Rogers, Michael J. Smith, and Pascale C. Sainfort, "Electronic Performance Monitoring, Job Design and Psychological Stress," paper available at www.igi-global.com/chapter/electronic-performance-monitoring-job-design/45284, accessed October 12, 2012.

48. Alder and Ambrose, "Towards Understanding Fairness Judgments"; and David T. Goomas, "Electronic Performance Self Monitoring and Engineered Labor Standards for 'Man-Up' Drivers in a Distribution Center," *Journal of Business and Psychology* 21 no. 4 (Summer 2007), pp. 541–558. Reprinted by permission from Springer Publishing. Cleared via Copyright Clearance Center.

49. H. James Wilson, "Wearables in the Workplace," *Harvard Business Review*, September 2013, pp. 23–25.

50. Adapted or quoted from "Next Generation Talent Management," Hewitt.com, accessed June 2010.

51. Ibid.

52. World of Opportunities, www.vodafone.in, (Navigation–Home–Careers at Vodafone–Why Work with Vodafone–World of Opportunities, as accessed on 08 August 2017 at 2pm IST.

53. Shrihari S and Varkkey B, (2015)Breaking Free from the bell curve: An alternate proposition for performance management , IIMA WP, accessible at https://web.iima.ac.in/assets/snippets/workingpaper-pdf/6096466172015-10-04.pdf

54. HRK News Bureau (2016), Tata Power Co-creates a new performance management system with employees, HR Katha www.hrkatha.com January.

55. Ibid.

56. Adapted or quoted from Gunter Stahl et al., "Global Talent Management: How Leading Multinationals Build and Sustain Their Talent Pipelines," Faculty and Research Working Paper, INSEAD, 2007.

57. Herman Aguinis and Ernest O'Boyle Jr., "Star Performers in 21st-Century Organizations," *Personnel Psychology* 67 (2014), pp. 313–315.

58. D. Bradford Neary, "Creating a Company-Wide, Online, Performance Management System: A Case Study at TRW Inc.," *Human Resource Management* 41, no. 4 (Winter 2002), p. 495.

59. Accessed on 21 August 2017 at http://www.dnaindia.com/money/report-infosys-terminates-using-bell-curve-to-assess-employees-performance-2129246.

60. See, for example, Jonathan Segal, "Performance Management Blunders," *HR Magazine*, November 2010, pp. 75–77.

61. See, for example, Adrienne Fox, "Curing What Ails Performance Reviews," *HR Magazine*, January 2009, pp. 52–55.

62. Andrew Solomonson and Charles Lance, "Examination of the Relationship Between True Halo and Halo Effect in Performance Ratings," *Journal of Applied Psychology* 82, no. 5 (1997), pp. 665–674.

63. Manuel London, Edward Mone, and John C. Scott, "Performance Management and Assessment: Methods for Improved Rater Accuracy and Employee Goal Setting," *Human Resource Management* 43, no. 4 (Winter 2004), pp. 319–336.

64. Ted Turnasella, "Dagwood Bumstead, Will You Ever Get That Raise?" *Compensation & Benefits Review*, September–October 1995, pp. 25–27. See also Solomonson and Lance, "Examination of the Relationship Between True Halo and Halo Effect," pp. 665–674.

65. I. M. Jawahar and Charles Williams, "Where All the Children Are Above Average: The Performance Appraisal Purpose Effect," *Personnel Psychology* 50 (1997), p. 921.

66. Annette Simmons, "When Performance Reviews Fail," *Training & Development* 57, no. 9 (September 2003), pp. 47–53.

67. "Flawed Ranking System Revives Workers' Bias Claim," *BNA Bulletin to Management*, June 28, 2005, p. 206.

68. Karen Lyness and Madeline Heilman, "When Fit Is Fundamental: Performance Evaluations and Promotions of Upper-Level Female and Male Managers," *Journal of Applied Psychology* 91, no. 4 (2006), pp. 767–775.

69. Madeleine Heilman et al., "Penalties for Success: Reactions to Women Who Succeed at Male Gender Type Tasks," *Journal of Applied Psychology* 89, no. 3 (2004), pp. 416–427. Managers may not rate successful female managers negatively (for instance, in terms of likability and boss desirability) when they see the woman as supportive, caring, and sensitive to their needs. Madeleine Heilmann and Tyler Okimoto, "Why Are Women Penalized for Success at Male Tasks? The Implied Communality Deficit," *Journal of Applied Psychology* 92, no. 1 (2007), pp. 81–92.

70. Wingrove, "Developing an Effective Blend of Process and Technology," pp. 25–30.

71. Gary Greguras et al., "A Field Study of the Effects of Rating Purpose on the Quality of Multisource Ratings," *Personnel Psychology* 56 (2003), pp. 1–21.

72. Joanne Sammer, "Calibrating Consistency," *HR Magazine*, January 2008, pp. 73–74. As one study recently concludes, "Far from being a source of non-meaningful error variance, the discrepancies among ratings from multiple perspectives can in fact capture meaningful variance in multilevel managerial performance." In-Sue Oh and Christopher Berry, "The Five Factor Model of Personality and Managerial Performance: Validity Gains Through the Use of 360° Performance Ratings," *Journal of Applied Psychology* 94, no. 6 (2009), p. 1510.

73. M. Ronald Buckley et al., "Ethical Issues in Human Resources Systems," *Human Resource Management Review* 11 (2001), pp. 11, 29. See also Ann Pomeroy, "The Ethics Squeeze," *HR Magazine*, March 2006, pp. 48–55; "10 Tips for Avoiding Liability in Conducting Evaluations." *The Legal Intelligencer* May 12, 2010, Academic OneFile, accessed October 13, 2012.

74. G. R Weaver and L. K. Treviño, "The Role of Human Resources in Ethics/Compliance Management: A Fairness Perspective," *Human Resource Management Review*, 2001, pp. 113–134. Also see, Julie McCarthy et al., "Progression Through the Ranks: Assessing Employee Reactions to High Stakes Employment Testing," *Personnel Psychology* 62 (2009), p. 826.

75. This is based on Howard Risher, "Getting Performance Management on Track," *Compensation & Benefits Review* 43, no. 5 (2011), pp. 273–281.

76. E. Pulakos and R. O'Leary, "Why Is Performance Management Broken? *Industrial and Organizational Psychology* 4 (2011), pp. 146–164.

77. Ibid.

78. Based on Robert Johnson, *The Appraisal Interview Guide* (New York: AMACOM, 1979), pp. 5–50; Judy Block, *Performance Appraisal on the Job: Making It Work for You* (New York: Executive Enterprises Publications, 1981), pp. 58–62.

79. Cooke Lee Fang, Saini S Debi and Wang Jue, "Talent Management in China and India: Comparison of Management Perceptions and HR practices," *Journal of World Business* (2014) , Volume 49, Issue 2, pp. 225-235.

80. This is based on Richard Luecke, *Coaching and Mentoring* (Boston: Harvard Business School Press, 2004), pp. 8–9.

81. Ibid., p. 9.

82. Jack Welch, broadcast interview at Fairfield University, C-SPAN, May 5, 2001.

83. Patty McCord, "How Netflix Reinvented HR," *Harvard Business Review,* January–February 2014, pp. 71–76.

84. Rachel Feintzeig, "You're Awesome! Firms Scrap Negative Feedback," *Wall Street Journal*, February 11, 2015, pp. B1, B5.

85. "Working Today: Understanding What Drives Employee

CHAPTER 9

Engagement," from the 2003 TowersPerrin Talent Report. Copyright TowersPerrin.

86. Jamie Gruman and Alan Saks, "Performance Management and Employee Engagement," *Human Resource Management Review* 21, no. 2 (2011), p. 123.

87. Ibid.

88. Pooja Lutra and Mala Jain (2012) India's performance management problem, Business Journal, May 3.

89. Ibid.

90. "Sustainable Employee Engagement," *Training & Development* 67, no. 2 (February 2013), p. 20.

91. Premalatha P, Manju M and Srinath J (2017) Burnout during early career: lived experiences of the knowledge worker in India, Journal of Enterprise Information Management, Vol 30 (1), pp 96-121.

92. "Driving Engagement by Focusing on Strengths," *Gallup Business Journal*: http://BusinessJournal.Gallup.com/content/124214/driving-engagement, accessed March 8, 2014.

93. D. Robinson, S. Perryman, and S. Hayday, "The Drivers of Employee Engagement," Institute for Employment Studies, April 2004.

94. Ibid.

95. Ibid.

96. Vishal Gupta and Sushil Kumar, "Impact of Performance Appraisal Justice on Employee Engagement: A Study of Indian Professionals," *Employee Relations* 35, no. 1, (2013), pp. 61–78.

97. Edward Lawler, "Performance Management: The Next Generation," *Compensation & Benefits Review*, May–June 1994, p. 16.

98. See, for example, Greg Boudreau, "Response: What TQM Says about Performance Appraisal," *Compensation & Benefits Review*, June 1994, pp. 20–24.

99. Based in part on Joel D. Ross, *Total Quality Management: Text, Cases, and Readings* (Delray Beach, FL: St. Lucie Press, 1993), p. 1.

100. Ibid., pp. 2–3, 35–36.

101. Howard Risher, "Getting Serious About Performance Management," *Compensation & Benefits Review*, November/December 2005, p. 19. See also Marie-Helene Budworth, "Performance Management: Where Do We Go from Here?" *Human Resource Management Review* 20, no. 1 (2011), pp. 81–84.

102. Peter Glendinning, "Performance Management: Pariah or Messiah," *Public Personnel Management* 31, no. 2 (Summer 2002), pp. 161–178. See also Herman Aguinis, *Performance Management* (Upper Saddle River, NJ: Prentice Hall, 2007), p. 2; "Performance Management Orientation Guide," *Workforce Management*, July 2012, pp. 20–22; and Angelo Kinicki, Kathryn Jacobson, Suzanne Peterson, and Gregory Prussia, "Development and Validation of the Performance Management Behavior Questionnaire," *Personnel Psychology* 60, no. 6 (2013), p. 4.

103. These are quoted or paraphrased from Risher, "Getting Serious About Performance Management," p. 19.

104. https://go.oracle.com/LP=3174?elqCampaignId=6310&src1=ad:pas:go:dg:tal&src2=wwmk14054343mpp012&SC=sckw=WWMK14054343MPP012, accessed April 4, 2015.

105. Leena Rao, "Salesforce Debuts 'Rypple-Powered Work.com' to Help Companies Manage Talent, Partners with Facebook," September 19, 2012, http://techcrunch.com/2012/09/19/salesforce-debuts-rypple-powered-work-com-to-help-companies-manage-talent/, accessed April 5, 2013; Eric Mosley, "The Power of the Crowd Sourced Performance Review," *Compensation & Benefits Review* 45, no. 6 (2013), pp. 320–323.

106. Rao, "Salesforce Debuts 'Rypple-Powered Work.com.'"

107. Rachel Silverman and Leslie Kwoh, "Performance Reviews Facebook Style," *Wall Street Journal*, August 1, 2012, p. B6.

108. Jenny Hill, "Could Social Media Revolutionise the Performance Appraisal Process?" www.hrmagazine.co.uk/hro/features/1073216/could-social-media-revolutionise-performance-appraisal-process, accessed April 5, 2013.

109. www.saba.com/blogs/2011/03/24/what-is-social-performance-management, accessed July 20, 2013.

110. Toni Veranges, "Held in High Regard," *HR Magazine*, November 2014, pp. 54–56.

111. "Game Changing Performance Management: A Software Company Makes a Game out of Yearly Performance Appraisals," *Training & Development* 68, no. 1 (January 2014), p. 80.

112. www.gdatp.com/about, accessed April 5, 2013.

113. Howard Risher, "Getting Serious About Performance Management," *Compensation & Benefits Review*, November/December 2005, p. 45.

10

Managing Careers and Retention

LEARNING OBJECTIVES

10-1 Discuss what employers and supervisors can do to support employees' career development needs.

10-2 Explain why career development can improve employee engagement.

10-3 Describe a comprehensive approach to retaining employees.

10-4 List and briefly explain the main decisions employers should address in reaching promotion and other employee life-cycle career decisions.

10-5 Explain each of the main grounds for dismissal.

Zydus Cadilla is a leading manufacturer and marketer of pharma products in India and abroad. In 2014, the ZyNext 2020 initiative was launched to make the company future ready. Multiple HR activities were launched, under which qualified and engaged employees were required to achieve the firm's ambitious growth plans. Zydus Cadilla's management takes talent development very seriously. We will see how companies like Zydus does this.

WHERE ARE WE NOW ...

Having invested time and resources in selecting, training, and appraising employees, the employer of course wants its employees to want to stay with the firm. The main purpose of this chapter is to explain how to support your employees' career development needs and improve employee retention. The main topics we'll address are career management, improving employee engagement through career management, managing employee turnover and retention, employee life-cycle management, and managing dismissals.

LEARNING OBJECTIVE 10-1
Discuss what employers and supervisors can do to support employees' career development needs.

Career Management

After appraising performance, it's often necessary to address career-related issues and to discuss these issues with subordinates.

Personnel activities like screening, training, and appraising serve two basic roles in organizations. First, their traditional role is to staff the organization—to fill its positions with employees who have the requisite interests, abilities, and skills. Often, however, these activities take on a second role, of ensuring that the long-run interests of the employees are supported by the organization and that, in particular, the employee is encouraged to grow and realize his or her full career potential. A basic assumption underlying the second role is that the employer has an obligation to utilize its employees' abilities to the fullest and to give all employees a chance to grow and to develop successful careers. Employers do this not just because they think that it's the right thing to do, but because by doing so both gain—the employee by having a more fulfilling career, and the employer by reaping the benefits of improved employee relations, engagement, and retention. One way this trend is manifesting itself is in the increased emphasis many firms are placing on career planning and development. We'll address career planning and related topics in this chapter.

Before proceeding, it would be useful to define some important terms we will be using throughout this chapter. We may define **career** as the occupational positions a person holds over the years. **Career management** is the process for enabling employees to better understand and develop their career skills and interests and to use these skills and interests most effectively both within the company and after they leave the firm. **Career development** is the lifelong series of activities (such as workshops) that contribute to a person's career exploration, establishment, success, and fulfillment. **Career planning** is the deliberate process through which someone becomes aware of personal skills, interests, knowledge, motivations, and other characteristics; acquires information about opportunities and choices; identifies career-related goals; and establishes action plans to attain specific goals.

career
The occupational positions a person has had over many years.

career management
The process for enabling employees to better understand and develop their career skills and interests, and to use these skills and interests more effectively.

career development
The lifelong series of activities that contribute to a person's career exploration, establishment, success, and fulfillment.

career planning
The deliberate process through which someone becomes aware of personal skills, interests, knowledge, motivations, and other characteristics and establishes action plans to attain specific goals.

HR in Practice at the Hotel Paris If the Hotel Paris wanted satisfied guests, they had to have engaged employees who did their jobs as if they owned the company, even when the supervisor was nowhere in sight. But for the employees to be engaged, Lisa knew the Hotel Paris had to make it clear that the company was also committed to its employees. To see what they did, see the case on page 332 of this chapter.

Careers Today

People once viewed careers as a sort of upward stairway from job to job, more often than not with one or at most a few firms. Today, many people do still move up, but many (or most) find themselves having to reinvent themselves. For example, the sales rep, laid off by a publishing firm that's just merged, may reinvent her career as an account executive at a media-oriented advertising firm.[1]

Careers today differ in other ways from a few years ago. With many more women pursuing professional and managerial careers, families must balance the challenges associated with dual career pressures. At the same time, what people want from their careers is changing. Baby boomers—those retiring in the next few years—tended to be job- and employer-focused. In India, the large number of young people entering the job market, have different aspirations. People entering the job market now often value more opportunities for balanced work–family lives. Many youngsters are choosing freelancing as a career option because freelancing not only gives them the work-life balance that they need but also helps to pursue hobbies and passions. According to Truelancer, an online marketplace for freelancers, India has around 15 million freelancers, and the numbers are growing.[2]

The Psychological Contract

One implication is that what employers and employees expect from each other is changing. What the employer and employee expect of each other is part of what psychologists call a *psychological contract.* This is "an unwritten agreement that exists between employers and employees."[3] The psychological contract identifies each party's mutual expectations. For example, the unstated agreement is that management will treat employees fairly and provide satisfactory work conditions, hopefully in a long-term relationship. Employees are expected to respond "by demonstrating a good attitude, following directions, and showing loyalty to the organization."[4]

The problem is that with today's tumultuous labor markets, neither the employer nor the employee can count on long-term commitments from each other. In India too, research has pointed to a shift from traditional expectations and obligations from both sides, specifically of employees towards the organization. The emerging psychological contract will be dynamic in nature, and Indian organizations have to be ready for a 'New Deal'.[5] That changes the psychological contract, and makes career management even more critical for the employee. One Indian study involving employees and functional heads shows that culture influences psychological contracts, and that employees and their supervisors differ in their understanding of mutual obligations.[6] Another study of Indian CPD (cutting and polishing of diamonds) industry shows that firms which retained or supported employees during recession, could later benefit from it.[7] Hence, Indian organizations need to move beyond focusing on compensation (which is important), and include relationship and growth variables.

The Employee's Role in Career Management

We will see that the employee, the manager, and the employer all have roles in the employee's career development. For example, the manager should provide timely and objective performance feedback, offer developmental assignments and support, and have career development discussions with the employee. He or she should act as a coach, appraiser, advisor, and mentor, listening to and clarifying the employee's career plans, giving feedback, generating career options, and linking the employee to organizational resources and career options. For its part, the employer should provide career-oriented training, development, and promotional opportunities, offer career information and career programs, and give employees a variety of career options.

Ultimately, however, it is the employee who must shoulder responsibility for his or her own career; assess interests, skills, and values; seek out career information resources; and generally take those steps that must be taken to ensure a happy and fulfilling career. For the employee, career planning means matching individual strengths and weaknesses with occupational opportunities and threats. In other words, the person wants to pursue occupations, jobs, and a career that capitalize on his or her interests, aptitudes, values, and skills. He or she also wants to choose occupations, jobs, and a career that make sense in terms of projected future demand for various occupations. Ideally, he or she should create in his or her mind an ideal future "self" to strive for.[8]

As one example, career-counseling expert John Holland says that personality (including values, motives, and needs) is an important career choice determinant. For example, a person with a strong social orientation might be attracted to careers that entail interpersonal rather than intellectual or physical activities and to occupations such as social work. Holland found six basic personality types or orientations. For a nominal fee, individuals can use his Self-Directed Search (SDS) test (available online at www.self-directed-search.com) to assess their occupational orientations and preferred occupations. The SDS has an excellent reputation, but one study of 24 no-cost online career assessment Web sites concluded that they were easy to use but suffered from insufficient validation and confidentiality. However, a number of online career assessment instruments such as Career Key (www.careerkey.org) do reportedly provide validated and useful information.[9] In India, two portals – Employment News (www.employmentnews.gov.in) and National Career Service portal (www.ncs.gov.in) – of the Union Ministry of Labor and Employment provide free information about careers and opportunities. Many private agencies and research portals (like www.paycheck.in) also provide related information. You will find other useful career tools in the next two exercises, and in the discussion in this chapter's appendix.

EXERCISE 1   One useful exercise for identifying occupational skills is to head a page "The School or Occupational Tasks I Most Enjoyed Doing." Then write a short essay describing the tasks. Provide as much detail as you can about your duties and responsibilities, and what you found enjoyable about each task. (It's not necessarily the most enjoyable *job* you've had, but the most enjoyable *task* you've had to perform within your jobs.) Next, on other pages, do the same thing for two other tasks. Now scrutinize the three essays. Underline the skills that you mentioned the most often. For example, did you especially enjoy the hours you spent on the Internet doing research for your boss when you worked one summer as an intern?[10]

EXERCISE 2   Another exercise can prove enlightening. On a page, answer the question: "If you could have any kind of job, what would it be?" Invent your own job if need be, and don't worry about what you *can* do—just what you want to do.[11]

The Employer's Role in Career Management

Along with the employee, the person's manager and employer have career management responsibilities. These depend partly on how long the employee has been with the firm.

For example, *before hiring*, realistic job interviews can help prospective employees more accurately gauge whether the job is a good fit for them. Especially for recent college graduates, *the first job* can be crucial for building confidence and a more realistic picture of what he or she can and cannot do: providing challenging first jobs and having an experienced mentor who can help the person learn the ropes are important. Some refer to this as preventing **reality shock**, a phenomenon that occurs when a new employee's high expectations and enthusiasm confront the reality of a boring, unchallenging job. Periodic *job rotation* can help the person develop a more realistic picture of what he or she is good at, and thus the career moves that might be best. Thus, Intuit offers new graduates entrée into its Rotational Development Programs.[12] These are comprehensive, 2-year programs in which employees first learn about Intuit's products, customers, employees, strategies, and values. Next the employees complete four 6-month rotations, getting experience in a range of Intuit business units and a variety of functions, for instance, product management, marketing, and human resources. All Rotational Development Program participants are paired with an executive advisor or mentor, who provides career coaching and mentoring.

Finally, we will see that once the person has been *on the job* for a while, career-oriented appraisals are important. Here the manager not only appraises the employee but helps the person to match his or her strengths and weaknesses with a feasible career path. For a number of reasons, employees may exit from formal careers paths, and, in India, many of them find it difficult to re-enter. Hindustan Unilever Limited (HUL), for instance, has initiated a program called 'Career by Choice.' It is especially tailored for female job seekers who were on a break in their careers due to various reasons such as marriage, child rearing, and taking care of their families.[13] Similarly, the Tata Group offers Tata SCIP or Second Carriers Inspiring Possibilities (www.tatasecondcareers.com) that provides women a platform to re-enter formal jobs. These programs give an opportunity to women to start back, if required, on a part-time basis.

Employer Career Management Methods

Employers including AFLAC, American Express, and Accenture recognize that it pays to help employees improve their careers. In a study of four Indian multinational firms (i.e., of Tata Motors, Infosys, Biocon, and ITC), a distinct preference for home-grown talent was observed. While the firms were developing global level operating competences and international careers for local employees, they also had to manage careers of international employees working with them.[14] For example, American Express recently opened several career counseling centers for its call-center workers, and both Genentech and AFLAC recently hired career counselors

reality shock
Results of a period that may occur at the initial career entry when the new employee's high job expectations confront the reality of a boring or otherwise unattractive work situation.

and are better preparing their line managers to give career advice.[15] Google has employees who volunteer to act as career coaches and mentors for other employees, and who Google officially designates "career gurus." In one recent year, over 1,000 Google employees (Googlers) used the gurus' services.[16] Some employers create Web-based or offline libraries of career development materials, and offer career workshops and perhaps individual career coaches for career guidance. One bank had an "Opportunity Knocks" program. Internal Job Posting (IJP) is an approach used by companies to fulfill their employees' career aspirations. Anand Group, a supplier of automobile systems and components and hospitality, is an Indian company with clear internal job posting policy. All vacancies across the group companies are floated and information is circulated to all employees. Aspiring employees need not take approval of their supervisor for applying, but after getting shortlisted, the HR department collects a No-Objection-Certificate.[17] In addition to career development training and follow-up support, the program included career development centers at work sites that employees could use on company time.[18]

A *career planning workshop* is "a planned learning event in which participants are expected to be actively involved, completing career planning exercises and inventories and participating in career skills practice sessions."[19] A typical workshop

FIGURE 10-1 Employee Career Development Plan

Source: "Reproduced with permission from the publisher BLR - Business & Legal Resources (www.HR.BLR.com).

Employee Career Development Plan

Employee: _____ Position: _____

Manager: _____ Department: _____

Date of Appraisal: _____

1. What is the next logical step up for this employee, and when do you think he or she will be ready for it?

Probable Next Job:	When Ready:			
	Now	6 Months	1 Year	2 Years
1.	☐	☐	☐	☐
2.	☐	☐	☐	☐
3.	☐	☐	☐	☐

2. What is the highest probable promotion within five years?

3. What does this employee need to prepare for promotion?

• Knowledge: _____
  _____

  Action Plan: _____
  _____

• Still Training: _____
  _____

  Action Plan: _____
  _____

• Management Training: _____
  _____

  Action Plan: _____
  _____

includes self-assessment exercises (skills, interests, values, and so on), an assessment of important occupational trends, and goal-setting and action-planning segments.

Career coaches generally help employees create 1- to 5-year plans showing where their careers with the firm may lead. Then, the employer and employee base the latter's development plans on what he or she will need to move up.[20] The coaches help individual employees identify their development needs and obtain the training, professional development, and networking opportunities that they require to satisfy those needs.[21]

Career development systems needn't be complicated. Even just receiving performance feedback from supervisors, having individual development plans, and having access to training is enough for many employees. Beyond that, job postings, formal career-oriented performance appraisals, formal counseling and mentoring with managers, and individual succession planning for high-potential employees are valuable.[22] Yet few respondents in one survey even had individual development plans.[23] Figure 10-1 illustrates a simple employee career planning form.[24]

Improving Performance Through HRIS: Integrating Talent Management and Career and Succession Planning

Consistent with best talent management practice, the employer should endeavor to integrate its career planning with its other HR activities efforts. As one example, an employee's career planning and development plans should reflect his or her performance appraisal ratings and training plans. Similarly, as explained in Chapter 5 (pages 133–134), succession plans should reflect employees' career interests.

Integrated talent management software helps to achieve such coordination. For example, the company that manages the trans-Alaska pipeline has an online portal that lets employees "see their full training history, development plans and upcoming deadlines, register for courses, or do career planning—usually without having to ask for help."[25] At the same time, "managers can get a quick picture of the training needs for a particular group, or see all the employees who have a specific qualification."[26] Bank of Baroda's online PMS system, Sparsh, allows every employee to plan their training requirements and view the training calendar. Similarly, Halogen eSuccession enables the employer to "identify the skills and competencies required to support your 3–5 year strategic plans and cultivate these in your high—potential employees with career and development planning...."[27] ■

Diversity Counts: Toward Career Success

People with disabilities tend to have less career success than do those without disabilities.[28] Some barriers may be self-imposed. For instance, some with disabilities may have lower career expectations, or may not proactively seek work-related help or support under the Indian laws (Rights for Persons with Disabilities Act, 2015), though Indian labor legislations are not explicit about the disabled in workplaces. However, the government of India has devised schemes for training/skill development of the disabled. These are Deendayal Disabled Rehabilitation Scheme (DDRS) for the upgradation of vocational training; skill training in identified national institutes; and financial support to state governments under the Scheme for Implementation of Persons with Disabilities Act (SPIDA).

However, most such problems reflect unfortunate assumptions and actions by managers and coworkers. Though well meaning, they may view those with disabilities as unable to perform various jobs, negatively evaluate them as being poor occupational fits, and assume that jobs designed for those without disabilities are inappropriate for those with disabilities. Figure 10-2 presents some positive strategies for people with disabilities. ■

FIGURE 10-2 **Career Guideline Suggestions for Those with Disabilities**

Source: "Career Management Strategies of People With Disabilities," Human Resource Management, may - June 2014, volume 53, number three, page 455-456. Reprinted by permission from John Wiley & Sons, Inc. Cleared via Copyright Clearance Center

Strategy	Key Import of Strategy
Espousing a positive mind-set and demonstrating extreme persistence	Overcome worries and focus on tasks at hand
Sensitizing people to ability over disability: • Signaling ability by learning new skills • Signaling ability by helping coworkers through newly gained skills • Signaling ability by trying to enhance performance through feedback seeking	Trounce stereotypes regarding competence
Engaging in disability advocacy: • Awareness building • Influencing organizational policymaking with regard to accommodation	Sensitize others to performance potential of all PWD and help all PWD perform
Building, leveraging, and contributing to relevant networks: • Forming networks comprising PWD • Seeking mentors who have a disability • Serving as role models or mentors to other PWD	Aid general adjustment and career growth of self and other PWD

The Manager as Mentor and Coach

Do not underestimate the impact that a supervisor can have on his or her employee's career development. With little or no additional effort than realistic performance reviews and candid career advice, a competent supervisor can help the employee get on and stay on the right career track. At the other extreme, an unsupportive supervisor may look back on years of having inhibited his or her employees' career development.

The manager can do several things to support subordinates' career development needs. When the subordinate first starts, make sure he or she develops the skills required to do the job well. Schedule regular performance appraisals, and at these reviews cover whether the employee's current skills and performance are consistent with his or her career aspirations. Indian companies are also expecting managers to be coaches to their subordinates. Dr Reddy's Laboratories considers a manager's commitment to leadership and coaching as one of the six leadership competencies. For senior level roles, including in Indian family-owned companies, hiring external coaches is preferred for training purposes. Traditionally, guidance or advice from elders was considered enough; however, with growing business complexity, formal coaching is welcomed.[29] Another study has indicated that Indian CEOs often get directly involved in identifying such coaches, and the external coach profile is mostly male (>75%) and highly educated.[30] Provide the employee with an informal development plan like that in Figure 10-1. Keep subordinates informed about how they can use the firm's current career-related benefits, and encourage them to do so.[31]

mentoring
Advising, counseling, and guiding.

In doing so the manager may act as mentor. **Mentoring** means having experienced senior people advising, counseling, and guiding employees' longer-term career development. An employee who agonizes over which career to pursue or how to navigate office politics may need mentoring.

Mentoring may be formal or informal. Informally, mid- and senior-level managers may voluntarily help less-experienced employees—for instance, by giving them career advice and helping them to navigate office politics. Many employers also have formal mentoring programs. For instance, the employer may pair protégés with potential mentors, and provide training to help mentor and protégé better understand their respective responsibilities. Studies show that having a mentor either formally or informally give career-related guidance and act as a sounding board can significantly enhance one's career satisfaction and success.[32]

coaching
Educating, instructing, and training subordinates.

For the supervisor, mentoring is both valuable and risky. It is valuable insofar as you can influence in a positive way the careers and lives of your less experienced subordinates and colleagues. The danger is it can backfire. **Coaching** focuses on teaching daily tasks that you can easily relearn, so coaching's downside is usually limited.

Mentoring focuses on relatively hard-to-reverse longer-term career issues, and often touches on the person's psychology (motives, and how one gets along with others, for instance). Because the supervisor is usually not a psychologist or trained career advisor, he or she must be extra cautious in the mentoring advice he or she gives.

Research on what supervisors can do to be better mentors reveals few surprises. Effective mentors *set high standards*, are willing to *invest the time* and effort the mentoring relationship requires, and actively *steer protégés* into important projects, teams, and jobs.[33] Effective mentoring requires *trust*, and the level of trust reflects the mentor's *professional competence, consistency, ability to communicate*, and readiness to *share control*.[34]

However, studies suggest that traditional mentoring is less effective for women than it is for men. For example, in one survey of employees who had "active mentoring relationships" in one recent year, 72% of the men received one or more promotions in the ensuing 2 years, compared with 65% of the women. A CEO or other senior executive mentored 78% of the men, compared with 69% of the women.[35]

Figures like these are prompting employers to assign female employees to mentors who have more organizational clout. For example, when Deutsche Bank discovered that several female managing directors had left the firm for better jobs at competitors, it began pairing them with mentor/sponsors from the bank's executive committee. The latter were in a position to advocate the women for promotion. Mentoring Indian managers, particularly women, has to be viewed in the cultural context as well. It is necessary that mentors offer diverse perspectives, and research has suggested using multiple mentors is favorable. While a male mentor can help break traditional glass ceilings and decode dimensions of organizational culture, women mentors can act as role models.[36]

▶ IMPROVING PERFORMANCE: *The Strategic Context*

Strategic human resource management means formulating HR policies and practices that produce the employee skills and behaviors the company needs to achieve its strategic aims. Cognizant Corporation requires its managers to enumerate the talent implications of each aspect of their strategic plans.[37] Because of this, it's no surprise that Cognizant has a well-thought-out career and talent development process. Each of Cognizant's 170,000 employees has his or her own development plan. Cognizant's Career Architecture Program enables employees to think through and choose Cognizant career tracks best suited to their capabilities and to the company's needs. Its Cognizant Academy provides training that serves both the company's needs today, as well as its projected longer-term talent and development needs. Cognizant's HR strategy has helped keep Cognizant a leader in its field, in part by ensuring that its employees get the career direction and development they need to be motivated to create the company's great products. ■

Source: Based on Kristen fyfe-mills, "commitment to talent development excellence," TD October 2014, pages 39–41. https://www.td.org/Publications/Magazines/TD/TD-Archive/2014/10/BEST-Cognizant; Http://Businesstoday.Intoday.In/Story/Malcolm-Frank-On-Cognizant-Strategy-Going-Forward/1/200337.Html; Http://Www.Cognizant.Com/Insightswhitepapers/Architecting-An-Enterprise-Content-Management-Strategy-A-Four-Pillar-Approach-Codex975.Pdf; Http://Www.Cognizant.Com/About-Cognizant/Company-Overview/Sustainability/Employee-Development.

LEARNING OBJECTIVE **10-2**

Explain why career development can improve employee engagement.

Employee Engagement Guide for Managers
Career Management

As mentioned earlier in this chapter, labor market turbulence has understandably prompted many people to ask why they should be loyal to their employers. "Why," they might ask, "should I be loyal to you if you're just going to dump me when you decide to cut costs again?" Employers today therefore have to think through how they're going to maintain employee engagement, and thereby minimize voluntary departures, and maximize employee effort. (Cognizant Corporation, above, is one example.)

Commitment-Oriented Career Development Efforts

Given the importance to most people of having a fulfilling and successful career, career planning and development can play an important role in engagement.

Managed effectively, the employer's career development process should send the signal that the employer cares about the employee's career success. As mentioned earlier, this doesn't necessarily have to be complicated. For example, the required performance appraisal can provide an easy opportunity to link the employee's performance, career interests, and developmental needs into a coherent career plan. With *career-oriented appraisals*, the supervisor and employee jointly merge the latter's past performance, career preferences, and developmental needs into a formal career plan.

Such appraisals needn't be automated but online systems are available. For example, ZingHR, a cloud-based software solution, allows managers and subordinates to identify development areas. Many Indian firms also handle development and engagement initiatives that coincide with the personal and social life of employees. For example, Larsen & Toubro runs different clubs for music, dance, and sports tournaments.

The JCPenney Management Career-Grid approach provides another good example of what is possible (although tumultuous management changes several years ago sidelined much of this effort). Penney's managerial performance appraisal form contained a listing of all the Penney's management and sales jobs by title, function, and level that employees could conceivably want to consider. The company trained its supervisors to consider the employee's performance, career interests, and Penney's needs, and to develop a career plan including development activities for the employee.

Here is how it worked. Prior to the annual appraisal, the associate and his or her manager reviewed Penney's career grid. The grid itemized all supervisory positions at Penney (grouped by operation jobs, merchandise jobs, personnel jobs, and general management jobs); it also included specific job titles such as "regional catalog sales manager." The firm also provided thumbnail job descriptions for all the grid's jobs.

The grid also identified typical promotional routes. For example, when considering the next assignment for a management associate, the supervisor could consider not only merchandise positions but also operations and personnel positions. Promotional projections could cross all four groups, as well as one or two job levels. For example, a senior merchandising manager might be projected for promotion to either assistant buyer or general merchandise manager. In sum, Penney's grid approach shows how employers can use a career-oriented appraisal process to guide the employee and manager to focus on the former's strengths, weaknesses, and career prospects and plans.[38]

Other employers use special training and development programs to facilitate their employees' career development. The accompanying HR Practices Around the Globe feature provides an example.

▶ **IMPROVING PERFORMANCE:** *HR Practices around the Globe*

Career Development at Medtronic[39]

Medtronic is a global medical technology company with more than 85,000 employees around the world. The company offers a wide range of career planning and development support tools aimed at helping employees understand their occupational strengths and weaknesses and reach their potential. These tools include customized development plans, self-assessment and feedback tools, mentoring programs, comprehensive on-site classes covering business, engineering, and science topics, tuition reimbursement scholarships, and online job listings so the employee can seek out new career opportunities within the company.

In addition, new MBA employees can participate in Medtronic's corporate Leadership Development Rotation Program. This is a 2- to 3-year program. It includes 12- to 18-month assignments in two different geographic locations, thus providing participants with both a broad understanding of Medtronics and in-depth functional experiences. Functional tracks include clinical, corporate development, finance, human resources, information technology, marketing/business development, operations, and regulatory.

In addition to their job assignments, participants engage in other developmental experiences including peer mentoring programs, functional training, and leadership workshops. Among other things, candidates for this program are required to have 3 to 5 years of professional and relevant work experience and an MBA (or other masters-level degree as appropriate) and to be mobile and willing to pursue opportunities in various geographic locations. ■

Source: Based on www.Medtronic.com/careers/develop-your-potential/, accessed March 12, 2013; http://www.medtronic.com/us-en/about-3/medtronic-plc facts.html?cmpid=mdt_plc_2015_US_about_3_story_panel_featured_company_facts_cta_text_link_learn_more.

Managing Employee Turnover and Retention

Not all employees' careers plans will coincide with the company's needs. *Turnover*—the rate at which employees leave the firm—varies markedly among industries. For example, turnover in the accommodation and food services industry is very high, with over half the industry's employees voluntarily leaving each year. Traditionally, the IT/ITES and the Banking and Finance (BFSI) sectors in India have seen very high employee turnover. A global study even placed India at the top of the world chart, with one in four employees changing jobs in 2013.[40] However, another study by Aon Hewitt in 2016 indicated that overall attrition was at a five-year low in India, and it was the lowest since the financial crisis in 2009.[41] In contrast, voluntary turnover in educational services in the US is about 12%.[42]

Furthermore, such figures only reflect employees who leave voluntarily, such as for better jobs. They don't include involuntary separations, such as for poor performance.[43] Combining voluntary and involuntary turnover produces some astounding statistics. For example, the turnover in many food service firms is around 100% per year. In other words, many restaurants need to replace just about all their employees every year! Turnover is expensive, as the HR as a Profit Center feature shows. Employees who are quitting voluntarily, are under notice period, or are planning to quit, may not contribute fully in their jobs. Research about intention-to-quit behavior among Indian IT professionals showed that the type of employees indicated above show lesser performance orientation, higher organizational deviance, and less organizational citizenship behaviors. Such behavior adds to the high cost of employee turnover.[44]

▶ IMPROVING PERFORMANCE: *HR as a Profit Center*

Turnover and Performance

What is the link between turnover and organizational performance? Perhaps surprisingly, the issue isn't clear (although it would seem obvious that firing an incompetent employee would be a positive).[45] The problem is that what might be a positive in individual cases becomes a negative when the employer repeatedly loses employees. One study concludes that *all* turnover, voluntary or involuntary, is associated with reduced organizational performance. The researchers say, "Organizations must recognize that when turnover rates rise, their workforce and financial performances are at risk. They should search for strategies to mitigate and eliminate turnover, recognizing that lower turnover [of all types] is always better."[46]

One study analyzed the tangible and intangible costs of turnover in a call center with 31 agents and 4 supervisors.[47] Tangible costs associated with an agent's leaving included the costs of recruiting, screening, interviewing, and testing applicants, as well as the cost of wages while the new agent was oriented and trained. Intangible costs included the cost of lost productivity for the new agent (who is less productive at first), the cost of rework for the new agent's errors, and the supervisory cost for coaching the new agent. The researchers' calculations estimated the cost of an agent leaving at about $21,551. This call center averaged 18.6 vacancies per year (about a 60% turnover rate). Therefore, the researchers estimated the total annual cost of agent turnover at $400,853. Taking steps to cut this turnover rate in, say, half could save this firm about $200,000 per year. How to cut turnover? Another study focused on turnover intentions among government technology workers. It concluded that human resource managers could influence turnover through practices such as promotion opportunities, training and development, pay and reward satisfaction, and family-friendly policies.[48] The bottom line is that HR practices can have a big influence on employee turnover, and thereby on the company's profitability. ∎

Source: Based on Tae–Youn Park and Jason Shaw, "Turnover Rates and Organizational Performance: A Meta-analysis," Journal of Applied Psychology 98, no. 2 (2013), pp. 268–309: Jolivette Wallace and Kristena Gaylor, "A Study of the Dysfunctional and Functional Aspects of Voluntary Employee Turnover," SAM Advanced Management Journal 77, no. 3 (Summer 2012), p. 27; Barbara Hillmer, Steve Hillmer, and Gale McRoberts, "The Real Costs of Turnover: Lessons from a Call Center," Human Resource Planning 27, no. 3 (2004), pp. 34–41; Kim Soonhee, "The Impact of Human Resource Management on State Government IT Employee Turnover Intentions," Public Personnel Management 41, no. 2 (Summer 2012), p. 257.

Reducing turnover requires identifying and managing the reasons for both voluntary and involuntary turnover.[49] We address managing voluntary turnover here, and managing involuntary turnover later in the chapter.

Managing Voluntary Turnover

In reducing turnover, the logical place to start is by measuring the number of employees (particularly top performers and high potentials) who leave the company.[50] SHRM recommends computing turnover as follows: "First calculate turnover for each month by dividing the number of [voluntary] separations during the month by the average number of employees during that month and multiplying by 100. Then calculate the annual turnover rate by adding the 12 months of turnover percentages together."[51]

However, identifying *why* employees voluntarily leave is not so easy. People who are dissatisfied with their jobs are more likely to leave, but the sources of dissatisfaction are many and varied. In one survey, the consultants collected data from 262 U.S. organizations having a minimum of 1,000 employees.[52] In this survey, the five top reasons that high-commitment/top-performing employees gave for leaving (ranked from high to low) were pay, promotional opportunities, work–life balance, career development, and health-care benefits. (In contrast, *employers* ranked the top five reasons employees left as promotion, career development, pay, relationship with supervisor, and work–life balance). Other reasons employees voluntarily leave include unfairness, not having their voices heard, and a lack of recognition.[53] Sometimes simply asking, "All things considered, how satisfied are you with your job?" can be as effective as soliciting employees' attitudes toward various facets of the job (such as supervision and pay).[54] Practical considerations also affect turnover. For example, high unemployment reduces voluntary turnover, and some locales have fewer job opportunities (and thus turnover) than do others.

Of course, losing low-performing employees isn't as problematic as losing high-performing ones. The U.S. chain Applebee's and many Indian IT/ITES companies give managers higher incentives or rewards for reducing turnover among top-performing employees.[55]

In any case, given the variety of things prompting employees to leave voluntarily, what can one do to manage voluntary turnover? A study conducted among Indian retail, frontline employees identified eight factors – quality of management practices; poor salary; lack of career growth; limited learning opportunities; lack of social support from co-workers, family, and supervisors; poor working conditions including safety at workplace; communication, and job insecurity – as the reasons that trigger the thought (intention to quit) in employees.[56] We'll list some tactics next, but there is no silver bullet. The manager should understand that retaining employees is a talent management issue, and that the best retention strategies are therefore multifunctional. For example, employees who aren't interested in their jobs, sense that they're not suited for their jobs, or feel undercompensated are more likely to leave. Employers can address such issues only by instituting effective and coordinated talent management (recruitment, selection, training, appraisal, and compensation) practices. Put another way, turnovers (both voluntary and involuntary) often start with poor selection decisions, compounded by inadequate training, insensitive appraisals, and inequitable pay. Trying to formulate a "retention strategy" without considering all of one's HR practices is futile.

A Comprehensive Approach to Retaining Employees

However identifying the problems is an important first step. Effectively conducted *exit interviews* provide useful insights into turnover problem areas. Many employers routinely administer *attitude surveys* to monitor employees about matters such as supervision and pay. Open-door policies and anonymous *"hotlines"* help management identify and remedy morale problems. Usually conducted by the employee's manager, the aim of a *stay interview* is to head off retention problems by finding out "how the employee is doing," and "what causes the employee to stick to the organization." Typical questions include "When you travel to work each day, what are you looking forward to?", "What are the factors you find attractive in this company?," and "How can I best support you?" Unlike anonymous group surveys, stay interviews are one on one, and reportedly provide useful information for reducing turnover and improving engagement.[57] Sometimes, analyzing the situation leads to simple solutions. To capitalize on the digital transformation business opportunity, Sapient India launched an unconventional talent management approach called "Trouble Makers" to seek creative, passionate, and risk-taking employees with sound technology background. With this approach, the company expected to reduce turnover while achieving results. Only those who can think out-of-the-box and are willing to experiment will find the job exciting and stay back.[58] Then, having identified potential problems, the employer can take steps like the following to boost employee retention.

RAISE PAY The most obvious explanation for why employees quit is often also the correct one: low pay. Particularly for high performers and key employees, enhanced pay has recently been the retention tool of choice for many employers.[59]

HIRE SMART "Retention starts up front, with the selection and hiring of the right employees."[60] This refers not just to the worker but also to hiring the right supervisors. For example, FedEx conducts periodic employee attitude surveys. The supervisor then meets to review the results with his or her employees to address any leadership problems the surveys raise.

DISCUSS CAREERS One expert says, "Professionals who feel their company cares about their development and progress are much more likely to stay."[61] Periodically discuss with employees their career preferences and prospects, and help them lay out career plans.[62] Long and stable career opportunities are used by most Indian firms, including the public sector undertakings to retain employees.

PROVIDE DIRECTION People can't do their jobs if they don't know what to do or what their goals are. Therefore, retaining employees requires making it clear what your expectations are regarding their performance and what their responsibilities are.

OFFER FLEXIBILITY In one survey, workers identified "flexible work arrangements" and "telecommuting" as the two top benefits that would encourage them to choose one job over another.

ATTRACTIVE EMPLOYEE WELFARE MEASURES Traditionally, Indian firms have retained employees by giving generous benefits to the employees and their families. These include education for children, healthcare, old-age support, celebration of events like birthdays, marriage anniversaries, etc., and support during period of grief like death, accidents, or sickness.

USE HIGH-PERFORMANCE HR PRACTICES In one study, call centers that made more use of high involvement work practices (for instance, employee empowerment, problem-solving groups, and self-directed teams) had lower rates of quits, dismissals, and total turnover. Idea Cellular Limited, an Indian mobile services operator, introduced Idea Participation Day, where its employees can give feedback to management and also participate in the action planning activity for implementing their inputs. This increased the level of employee ownership and, eventually, their performance.[63] So did those that "invested" more in employees (for instance, in terms of promotion opportunities, high relative pay, pensions, and full-time jobs).[64]

BONDS, LONG NOTICE PERIODS, AND BINDING CONTRACTS Although Indian companies, both in the public and private sectors, use service bonds, it's not very effective in controlling turnover. In India, bonds (specifying mandatory service) can be enforced only if the employer has made economic expense on the employee, e.g., training expenses. Otherwise, under the Indian Contract Act of 1872 (Section 27), an employee can resign from employment even if an agreement to serve an employer for a specific period has been signed[65], unless the employer proves that the employee can harm interests of the company, and the courts find that the bonds are reasonable and necessary.[66]

Many firms also use long notice periods to discourage job change and retain employees. An option is to buy out the notice period by paying the required amount. Some firms allow notice period adjustment against leaves. Recently, both IT/ITES employees (90 days is the common trend) and commercial pilots (one year as of 2016) in India have protested against notice period, and have petitioned the government.[67]

COUNTEROFFER? If a valued employee says he or she is leaving, should you make a counteroffer? Many argue against doing so, calling it a "Band-Aid for a head wound."[68] Employers who do allow counteroffers need a policy that specifies what people and positions are eligible for counteroffers, allowable compensation enhancements, and how to determine the offer.[69]

TRENDS SHAPING HR: *DIGITAL AND SOCIAL MEDIA*

Digital and social media tools can vastly improve the employee engagement/retention process. Software company SAS's employee-retention program sifts through employee data on traits like skills, tenure, performance, education, and friendships. It can predict which high-value employees are more likely to quit in the near future (allowing SAS to try to head that off).[70] Alliant Techsystems created a "flight risk model" to calculate the probability an employee would leave and to take corrective action.[71] Based on its analysis of previous survey results, Google's "Googlegeist" survey contains five questions aimed at identifying Googlers who are more likely to leave; if a team's responses fall below 70% favorable, Google knows to take corrective action.[72] Analytical software from Evolv (now Cornerstone, www.cornerstoneonde-mand.com/evolv) takes HR data analysis deeper than most. It can crunch more than 500 million data points on a vast array of items ranging from unemployment rates to a person's social media usage to help clients like Xerox improve retention.[73] For example, Evolv discovered that employees with two social media accounts perform much better than those with more or less, and that in call-center work, employees with criminal backgrounds perform better than those never arrested.[74]

Web sites such as Globoforce (www.globoforce.com) enable each employee's colleagues to comment on and to recognize and reward the person's contributions. Gujarat Gas Company Limited (GCCL) has introduced Sabash Cards which is a mode of instant recognition for its employees to anyone who has done good work. Vendors assert this leads to "dramatic improvements in employee engagement, retention and measurable adoption of corporate culture."[75]

Social media also enables an otherwise muted layoff to go viral. When UBS bank dismissed 10,000 employees recently, former employees quickly took to Twitter. Some claimed they discovered they were fired when they arrived to work and found their passes deactivated.[76] In the case of Mahindra Technologies, employee layoff, similar online outburst resulted in public apology by the company's leadership. The firm's chairman, Anand Mahindra, and the CEO extended personal apology on social media, and assured that all employees will be treated with dignity. While the apology helped to diffuse the situation, it bought back job losses in the Indian IT sector in focus.[77] ■

Job Withdrawal

Unfortunately, voluntary turnover is just one way that employees withdraw. Withdrawal in general means separating oneself from one's current situation—it's a means of escape for someone who is dissatisfied or fearful. At work, *job withdrawal* has been defined as "actions intended to place physical or psychological distance between employees and their work environments."[78]

Absences and voluntary turnover are two obvious types of job withdrawal. Others can be less obvious if no less corrosive. Some examples include "taking un-deserved work breaks, spending time in idle conversation and neglecting aspects of the job one is obligated to perform."[79] Other employees stop "showing up" mentally ("psychological withdrawal"), perhaps daydreaming at their desks while productivity suffers.[80] The employee is there, but mentally absent. In fact, the *job withdrawal process* tends to be incremental, often evolving from daydreaming to absences to quitting: "When an employee perceives that temporary withdrawal will not resolve his/her problems, then the employee is apt to choose a more permanent form of withdrawal (i.e., turnover, assuming that alternative work opportunities are available)."[81]

Studies confirm the high costs of job withdrawal behavior, so understanding its causes is important.[82] Absenteeism is a serious challenge in Indian industries. Organizations, managers, and the government have examined this issue at different points. Some suggested actions to control absences are initiatives like counseling, health checkup, involving families, and good employment relations. Another way to ensure absence control is planning leaves and breaks in advance. Many Indian firms also offer attractive financial and non-financial incentives (e.g., additional payment, compensatory leave, organizing celebrations within the company, etc.) to control mass absenteeism during festival and harvest seasons, when significant number of employees return to their villages.[83] Many people have experienced the desire to withdraw—to "get away" from some situation—so it's perhaps not difficult to empathize with those who feel they must escape. Some think of it in terms of pain versus pleasure. People tend to move toward situations that make them feel good, and away from those that make them feel bad.[84] People are repelled by situations that produce unpleasant, uncomfortable emotions, and are attracted to those that produce pleasant, comfortable ones.[85]

The manager can therefore think of withdrawal-reducing strategies in terms of reducing the job's negative effects, and/or of raising its positive effects. Because potential negatives and positives are virtually limitless, addressing withdrawal problems again requires a comprehensive human resource management approach. Illustrative potential negatives include, for instance, boring jobs, poor supervision, low pay, bullying, lack of career prospects, and poor working conditions. Potential positives include job enrichment, supportive supervision, equitable pay/family-friendly benefits, disciplinary/appeals processes, career development opportunities, safe and healthy working conditions, and having high-morale colleagues.[86] Interviews, surveys, and observation can help identify issues to address.

With more employees taking their jobs home via smart phones and iPads, employee "detachment" (not withdrawal) isn't always a bad thing. Two researchers found detaching oneself from work improves family life. They advise working out a system for ensuring some quality family time. For example, the employee and his or her partner might "agree on certain rules such as keeping the weekend free of work, or switching off the mobile phone after dinner."[87]

LEARNING OBJECTIVE 10-4
List and briefly explain the main decisions employers should address in reaching promotion and other employee life-cycle career decisions.

Employee Life-Cycle Career Management

An employee's tenure with a firm tends to follow a life cycle, from employment interview to first job, promotion, transfer, and perhaps retirement. We'll look here at the latter three.

Making Promotion Decisions

promotion
Advancement to a position of increased responsibility.

Promotions traditionally refer to advancements to positions of increased responsibility.

Most people crave promotions, which usually mean more pay, responsibility, and (often) job satisfaction. For employers, promotions can provide opportunities to reward exceptional performance, and to fill open positions with tested and loyal employees. Yet the promotion process isn't always a positive experience. Unfairness or secrecy can devalue the process. Furthermore, with more employers downsizing, some "promotions" take the form of more challenging but not necessarily higher-ranked or better-paid jobs.

Several decisions therefore loom large in any firm's promotion process.

DECISION 1: IS SENIORITY OR COMPETENCE THE RULE?   In setting promotion policies, one decision is whether to base promotion on seniority or competence, or some combination of the two.

Today's focus on performance favors competence. However, this depends on several things. Union agreements sometimes contain clauses emphasizing seniority. In many countries, including India, civil service regulations that stress seniority often govern promotions in many public-sector organizations.

DECISION 2: HOW SHOULD WE MEASURE COMPETENCE?   If the firm opts for competence, it must define and measure competence. Defining and measuring *past* performance is relatively straightforward. But promotions should rest on procedures for predicting the candidate's future performance.

For better or worse, most employers use prior performance as a guide, and assume that (based on exemplary prior performance) the person will do well on the new job. Many others use tests or assessment centers, or tools such as the 9-Box Grid (Chapter 8, page 246), to evaluate promotable employees and identify those with executive potential.

DECISION 3: IS THE PROCESS FORMAL OR INFORMAL?   Many firms have informal promotion processes. They may or may not post open positions, and key managers may use their own unpublished promotion criteria. Here employees (and courts) may conclude that factors like "who you know" are more important than performance, and that working hard to get ahead—at least in this firm—is futile.

Other employers set formal, published promotion policies and procedures. Employees receive a *formal promotion policy* describing the criteria by which the firm awards promotions. A *job posting policy* states the firm will post open positions and their requirements, and circulate these to all employees. As explained in Chapter 5 (Personnel Planning and Recruiting), many employers also maintain *employee qualification databanks* and use replacement charts and computerized employee information systems to assist in such planning.

DECISION 4: VERTICAL, HORIZONTAL, OR OTHER?   Promotions aren't necessarily upward. Thus some employees, such as engineers, may have little or no interest in promotion to managerial roles.

Several options are available. Some firms, such as the exploration division of British Petroleum (BP), create two parallel career paths, one for managers and another for "individual contributors" such as high-performing engineers. At BP, individual contributors can move up to nonsupervisory senior positions, such as "senior engineer." These jobs have most of the financial rewards attached to management-track positions at that level. Indian public sector banks have two career streams, i.e., generalist and specialists. Generalist officers move both vertically and horizontally. Based on their performance, the generalist officers are selected for board level director positions in any public sector bank or allied organizations. Specialist officers are individual contributors with limited mobility. However, exceptional specialists, who have experience in general banking roles, can also be promoted to board level positions.

Another option is to move the person horizontally. For instance, a production employee may move to human resources to develop his or her skills and to test and challenge his or her aptitudes. In a sense, "promotions" are possible even when leaving the person in the same job. For example, you might enrich the job and provide training to enhance the opportunity for assuming more responsibility.

In any case, there are practical steps to take in formulating promotion policies.[88] Establish eligibility requirements, for instance, in terms of minimum tenure and performance ratings. Require the hiring manager to review the job description, and revise if necessary. Vigorously review all candidates' performance and history. Preferably hire only those who meet the job's requirements. And reach out to employees who may have aspired to a promotion but who were not yet ready to be promoted. To paraphrase Google's chief HR officer, doing so is far better than having them quit or withdraw.[89]

Diversity Counts: The Gender Gap

Women still don't reach the top of the career ladder in numbers proportionate to their numbers in U.S. industry. Women constitute more than 40% of the workforce, but hold less than 2% of top management positions. Blatant or subtle discrimination may account for much of this. In one study, promoted women had to receive higher performance ratings than promoted men to get promoted, "suggesting that women were held to stricter standards for promotion."[90] Women report greater barriers (such as being excluded from informal networks) than do men, and more difficulty getting developmental assignments. Women have to be more proactive than men to get such assignments.

In India, representation of women in higher levels of governance and organizations is not very bright. According to the data from the Inter-Parliamentary Union and UN Women, India ranks 148th in representation of women in governance.[91] In the corporate sphere, the position of women at board-level positions is gradually increasing, according to the Building Diversity in Asia Pacific Boardrooms survey. From 5.8% in 2012, the percentage of women in board-level positions jumped to 8.6% in 2014, and this figure is expected grow. India, along with Australia and Malaysia, has shown significant improvement in board-level representation of women. In all the three countries, government initiatives (for example, The Companies Act, 2013, in India) have helped to accelerate the inclusion.[92] Another study of Indian IT sector boards showed that 80 percent of the listed companies have complied with the minimum requirement level, an indication of tokenism. This is in spite of the efforts to promote gender equality at lower levels.[93] An exception is the Indian banking sector, where during the 2015–17 period, many banks, both private and public, had women as CEOs or full-time board level executives. In the central and state governments, women have moved up the hierarchy to occupy critical positions of Secretaries to the government, Chief Secretary of different states, DGPs, etc.

Unfortunately, many career development programs are inconsistent with the needs of women. For example, many programs underestimate the role played by family responsibilities in many women's (and men's) lives. Similarly, some programs assume that career paths are continuous; yet the need to stop working for a time to attend to family needs often punctuates the career paths of many women (and perhaps men).[94] Some organizations have unwritten codes that prevent women from rising in the hierarchy. Many refer to this totality of subtle and not-so-subtle barriers to women's career progress as the *glass ceiling*. Employers need to eliminate the barriers that impede women's career progress. Some specific steps include the following.

ELIMINATE BARRIERS   Many practices (such as required late-night meetings) may seem gender neutral but in fact disproportionately affect women.

IMPROVE NETWORKING AND MENTORING   To improve female employees' networking opportunities, Marriott International instituted a series of leadership conferences for women. Speakers offered practical tips for career advancement, and shared their experiences. More important, the conferences provided informal opportunities—over lunch, for instance—for the Marriott women to meet and forge business relationships.

BREAK THE GLASS CEILING   As one expert puts it, "The roots of gender discrimination are built into a platform of work practices, cultural norms and images that appear unbiased.... People don't even notice them, let alone question them." These range from late meetings to golf course memberships.

ADOPT FLEXIBLE CAREER TRACKS   Inflexible promotional ladders (such as "You must work 8 years of 50-hour weeks to apply for partner") can put women—who often have more responsibility for child-raising chores or taking care of elderly—at a disadvantage.[95] One solution is to institute career tracks (including reduced hours and more flexible year-round work schedules) that enable women to periodically reduce their time at work, but remain on a partner track in an audit or consulting firm. For example, when the accounting firm Deloitte & Touche noticed it was losing female auditors, it instituted a new flexible/reduced work schedule. State Bank of India and ICICI Bank have allowed work-from-home for female employees in certain departments. To promote gender diversity, Cummins India has also introduced flexible work arrangements in their manufacturing plans. The company has also introduced childcare support and return-to-work initiatives. This enabled many working mothers who might otherwise have left to stay with the firm.[96] ■

Managing Transfers

transfers
Reassignments to similar positions in other parts of the firm.

A **transfer** is a move from one job to another, usually with no change in salary or grade. Employers may transfer a worker to vacate a position where he or she is no longer needed, to fill one where he or she is needed, or more generally to find a better fit for the employee within the firm. Many firms today boost productivity by consolidating positions. Transfers are a way to give displaced employees a chance for another assignment or, perhaps, some personal growth. Employees seek transfers for many reasons, including personal enrichment, more interesting jobs, greater convenience—better hours, location of work, and so on—or to jobs offering greater advancement possibilities. Transfers for the firm's convenience—once widely used—are used less of late.

Managing Retirements

Retirement planning is a significant issue for employers. In the United States, the number of 25- to 34-year-olds is growing relatively slowly, and the number of 35- to 44-year-olds is declining. So, with many employees in their 60s approaching retirement age, employers face a problem: "Companies have been so focused on downsizing to contain costs that they largely neglected a looming threat to their competitiveness … a severe shortage of talented workers."[97]

Shutterstock.India Picture

Employers are transferring employees less often, partly because of family resistance.

Many have wisely chosen to fill their staffing gaps in part with current or soon-to-be retirees. Fortuitously, 78% of employees in one survey said they expect to continue working in some capacity after normal retirement age (64% said they want to do so part-time). Only about a third plan to continue work for financial reasons; about 43% just want to stay active.[98]

The bottom line is that "retirement planning" is no longer just about helping current employees slip into retirement.[99] It should also help the employer to retain, in some capacity, the skills and brainpower of those who would normally retire and leave the firm.

A reasonable first step is to conduct numerical analyses of pending retirements. This should include a demographic analysis (including a census of the company's employees), determining the current average retirement age for the company's employees, and assessing how retirements will affect the employer's health-care and pension benefits. The employer can then determine the extent of the "retirement problem," and take fact-based steps to address it.[100]

Employers seeking to attract and/or retain retirees should take several steps. The general idea is to institute human resource policies that encourage and support older workers. Not surprisingly, studies show that employees who are more committed and loyal to the employer are more likely to stay beyond their normal retirement age.[101] It helps to create a culture that honors experience. In India, retired employees from different sectors like teaching, medical care, banking, etc., find re-employment in smaller companies and private sector. To overcome shortage of faculty, the government of India has permitted IITs and IIMs to employ retired faculty on contract. To cater to the welfare and reemployment of retirees from the Indian Armed forces (around 60,000 personnel are released or retire annually), the Directorate General of Resettlement (DGR) assist them in training and finding a second career. For officers, the DGR organizes a management course in IIMA, MDI, etc., which equips the officers to take up open market jobs. The Directorate's website (www.dgrindia.org) lists available jobs. Some companies modify selection procedures to suit retired persons. For example, one British bank stopped using psychometric tests, replacing them with role-plying exercises to gauge how candidates deal with customers.

Other techniques employers use to keep older workers include offering them part-time positions, hiring them as consultants or temporary workers, offering them flexible work arrangements, encouraging them to work past traditional retirement age, providing training to upgrade skills, and instituting a phased retirement program. The latter lets senior workers ease into retirement with gradually reduced work schedules.[102]

LEARNING OBJECTIVE 10-5

Explain each of the main grounds for dismissal.

dismissal

Involuntary termination of an employee's employment with the firm.

Managing Dismissals

Not all employee separations are voluntary. Some career plans and appraisals end not in promotion or graceful retirement but in **dismissal**—involuntary termination of an employee's employment with the firm. Many dismissals are avoidable. For example, many dismissals flow from bad hiring decisions. Using assessment tests, background checks, and clearly defined jobs can reduce such dismissals. Another safeguard is the judicious use of probation period, which is an opportunity for organizations to separate unfit employees or correct recruitment mistakes. Many Indian companies do not take advantage of this provision. At the same time, some employers treat employees unfairly by extending probationary period indefinitely. When brought to the notice of the Indian judiciary, this was termed as unacceptable, and the employer had to issue a confirmation.

The Indian law determines the nature of misconduct. The Employment Standing Orders, which governs workplace conduct, classifies offenses by employees into two categories – minor and major. This classification helps to deal with consequences proportionate to the magnitude of offence. The aim is to reform the person, and progressively allow more opportunities to perform.[103,104]

Grounds for Dismissal

There are four bases for dismissal: unsatisfactory performance, misconduct, lack of qualifications for the job, and changed requirements of (or elimination of) the job.

Unsatisfactory performance refers to a persistent failure to perform assigned duties or to meet prescribed standards on the job.[105] Specific reasons include excessive absenteeism, tardiness, a persistent failure to meet normal job requirements, or an adverse attitude.

Misconduct is deliberate and willful violation of the employer's rules and may include stealing and rowdy behavior. The types of misconduct and punishments are given as a part of the standing orders in case of Workmen and Service Regulations for officers. In the private sector, Codes of Conduct or Ethics Guidelines define the process.

Lack of qualifications and other requirements for the job is an employee's inability to do the assigned work, although he or she is diligent. Because this employee may be trying to do the job, it is reasonable to try to salvage him or her—perhaps through further training or by assigning the employee to another job. Fake qualifications and experience is a rampant problem in India. In the government service, a similar trend of giving fake caste certificate to take advantage of job reservation has been noticed. Government employees who gain employment through such means invite dismissal upon discovery. The Supreme Court of India has also ruled in favor of dismissal for securing employment based on forged caste certificate.[106]

Changed requirements of the job is an employee's incapability of doing the job after the nature of the job has changed. Similarly, you may have to dismiss an employee when his or her job is eliminated. Again, the employee may be industrious, so it is reasonable to retrain or transfer this person, if possible.

insubordination

Willful disregard or disobedience of the boss's authority or legitimate orders; criticizing the boss in public.

Insubordination, a form of misconduct, is sometimes the grounds for dismissal. The two basic categories of insubordination are unwillingness to carry out the manager's orders, and disrespectful behavior toward the manager. (This assumes that the orders were legitimate, and that the manager did not incite the reaction through his or her own extreme behavior.) Examples of insubordination include:[107]

1. Direct disregard of the boss's authority
2. Direct disobedience of, or refusal to obey, the boss's orders, particularly in front of others
3. Deliberate defiance of clearly stated company policies, rules, regulations, and procedures
4. Public criticism of the boss
5. Blatant disregard of reasonable instructions
6. Contemptuous display of disrespect
7. Disregard for the chain of command
8. Participation in (or leadership of) an effort to undermine and remove the boss from power

FAIRNESS SAFEGUARDS Dismissals are never easy. However, the manager can take steps to make them fair.[108] These are termed as following the principles of natural justice. First, allow the employee to explain why he (or she) did what he did. It could turn out, for instance, that the employee "disobeyed" the order because he or she did not understand it. Similarly, people who get *full explanations* of why and how termination decisions were made "were more likely to perceive their layoff as fair … and indicate that they did not wish to take the past employer to court."

Second, have a formal *multistep and a proportionate procedure* (including warning) and an appeal process.

Third, *the person who actually does the dismissing* is important. Employees in one study whose managers informed them of an impending layoff viewed the dismissal fairer than did those told by, say, a human resource manager.

Fourth, dismissed employees who feel they've been treated unfairly financially or handled without respect are more likely to sue or even raise the issue in social media. The much-publicized case of unfair dismissal of an employee in Tech Mahindra is such an example. The manner in which the employee was treated was discussed at length in the social media.[109] Many employers use severance pay to blunt a dismissal's sting.[110]

KNOW YOUR EMPLOYMENT LAW

Termination at Will in the US

terminate at will

In the absence of a contract, either the employer or the employee can terminate at will the employment relationship.

For more than 100 years, the prevailing rule in the United States has been that without an employment contract, either the employer or the employee can **terminate at will** the employment relationship. In other words, the employee could resign for any reason, at will, and the employer could similarly dismiss an employee for any reason, at will. Today, however, dismissed employees increasingly take their cases to court, and employers are finding that they no longer have a blanket right to fire.

Three main protections against wrongful discharge eroded the termination-at-will doctrine—*statutory exceptions, common law exceptions,* and *public policy exceptions.*

The Exit Process and Termination Interview

Dismissing an employee is one of the most difficult tasks you can face at work.[111] The dismissed employee, even if warned many times in the past, may still react with disbelief or even violence. In a unionized workplace, there is a possibility of unions resisting the move, and even calling a flash strike. In politically and socially-sensitive areas, the effect can spread outside the factory or office. Hence, in such cases, it will always be wise to take some precautions and, if possible, discuss the matter with the trade union leadership. Guidelines for the **termination interview or communication of the news** itself are as follows:

termination interview
The interview in which an employee is informed of the fact that he or she has been dismissed.

1. *Plan the interview carefully.* According to experts at Hay Associates, this includes:
   * Make sure the employee keeps the appointment time.
   * Never inform an employee over the phone.
   * Allow 10 minutes as sufficient time for the meeting.
   * Use a neutral site, not your own office.
   * Have employee agreements, the human resource file, and a release announcement prepared in advance.
   * Be available at a time after the interview in case questions or problems arise.
   * Have phone numbers ready for medical or security emergencies.
2. *Get to the point.* When the employee enters the office, give the person a moment to get comfortable and then inform him or her of your decision.
3. *Describe the situation.* Briefly, in three or four sentences, explain why the person is being let go. For instance, "Production in your area is down 4%, and we are continuing to have quality problems. We have talked about these problems several times in the past 3 months, and the solutions are not being followed through on. We have to make a change." Don't personalize the situation as in, "Your production is just not up to par." Emphasize the decision is irrevocable. Preserving the employee's dignity is crucial.[112]
4. *Listen.* Continue the interview until the person appears to be talking freely and reasonably calmly.
5. *Review the severance package.* Describe severance payments, benefits, access to office support people, and the way references will be handled. However, under no conditions make any promises of benefits beyond those already in the support package.
6. *Identify the next step.* The terminated employee may be disoriented and unsure what to do next. Explain where the employee should go next, upon leaving the interview. In Indian companies, it's also a common practice to allow such a person some time to search for alternate job, and then allow the person to resign. This will save the person from being affected by the social stigma connected with losing jobs.

outplacement counseling
A formal process by which a terminated person is trained and counseled in the techniques of self-appraisal and securing a new position.

OUTPLACEMENT COUNSELING With **outplacement counseling** the employer arranges for an outside firm to provide terminated employees with career planning and job search skills. *Outplacement firms* usually provide such outplacement services. Employees (usually managers or professionals) who are let go typically have office space and secretarial services they can use at local offices of such firms, plus the counseling services. The outplacement counseling is part of the terminated employee's support or severance package. Why not just give the person you're dismissing the outplacement fee as additional severance? In general, providing outplacement services seems to have positive effects for both the terminated employee and the employer.[113]

FOR THE EMPLOYEE What should you do if you get fired or passed over for a position?[114] Most people surrender to the usual stages of shock, denial, and anger. However, the better first step is usually to think through why you lost the job. Doing so isn't easy. Actively explore what (if anything) you did to contribute to the problem. Then objectively consider what you might do differently in the future, keeping in mind that you should view the loss (difficult though this may be) as an opportunity. Then evaluate your new options and be ready to seize the right opportunity.

exit interviews
Interviews with employees who are leaving the firm, conducted for obtaining information about the job or related matters, to give the employer insight about the company.

EXIT INTERVIEW Many employers conduct **exit interviews** with employees leaving the firm. These are interviews, usually conducted by a human resource professional just prior to the employee leaving, that elicit information aimed at giving employers insights into their companies. Exit interview questions include: How were you recruited? Was the job presented correctly and honestly? What was your supervisor's management style like? How do the employees on the team get along?[115]

The assumption is that because the employee is leaving he or she will be candid, but this is debatable.[116] In order to avoid offending the employer or manager, employees leaving the firm may not speak out the real reason. Researchers in the US found that at the time of separation, 38% of those leaving blamed salary and benefits, and 4% blamed supervision. Followed up 18 months later, 24% blamed supervision and 12% blamed salary and benefits.

Yet these interviews can be useful. When Blue Cross of Northeastern Pennsylvania laid off employees, many said, in exit interviews, "This is not a stable place to work." The firm took steps to address that concern for those who stayed with Blue Cross. Considering the sensitivity of exit interviews and the chances of losing focus, Indian companies have started using third parties to conduct the process. Marico Industries Limited outsourced the process to ensure confidentiality and be free of any prejudice. Marico was interested in identifying the real issues behind employee exits, and the process helped interested employees to return back. At present, 10% of employees in Marico are returnees.[117]

THE EXIT PROCESS The exit interview is just one part of a rational exit process. The employer should follow a checklist. Again ensure, for example, that the employee returns all keys and company equipment, that all computer and database password access is terminated, that proper communications are sent internally (for instance, to other employees if appropriate, and to payroll) and externally, that the employee leaves the premises in a timely fashion, and that if necessary precautions are followed to ensure security. It's also common in Indian companies to organize a farewell function with the team so that the positive connect remains.

Layoffs and the Plant Closing Law

Nondisciplinary separations may be initiated by either employer or employee. For the *employer*, reduced sales or profits or the desire for more productivity may require layoffs. *Employees* (as we've seen) may leave for better jobs, to retire, or for other reasons. In India, the Industrial Disputes Act of 1947 deals with layoffs and plant closures.

layoff
An employer sending employees home due to a lack of work; this is typically a temporary situation.

A **layoff**, in which the employer sends workers home for a time for lack of work, is usually not a permanent dismissal (although it may turn out to be). Rather, it is a temporary one, which the employer expects will be short term. However, some employers use the term *layoff* as a euphemism for discharge or termination.

CLOSURE OR DOWNSIZING EFFECTS It's not surprising that layoffs often result in "deleterious psychological and physical health outcomes" for those losing their jobs as well as for survivors.[118]

But not just the "victims" and "survivors" suffer. In one study, researchers "found that the more managers were personally responsible for handing out WARN notices to employees ... the more likely they were to report physical health problems, to seek treatment for these problems, and to complain of disturbed sleep."[119]

Given all this, many employers try to minimize layoffs and dismissals during downturns. Reducing everyone's work hours and mandating vacations are two options. Others reduce layoffs by offering financial bonuses for improved productivity.[120]

Ironically, when some employees most need employee assistance programs (such as counseling)—after they're downsized—they lose them. More firms are therefore extending these program benefits for a month or two to former employees.

Adjusting to Downsizings and Mergers

Downsizing means reducing, usually dramatically, the number of people employed by a firm. The basic idea is to cut costs and raise profitability. Downsizings (some call them "productivity transformation programs")[121] require careful consideration of several matters.

1. First is making sure *the right people* are let go; this requires having an effective appraisal system in place.
2. Second is *compliance with all applicable laws.*
3. Third is executing the seperations in a manner that is *just and fair.*
4. Fourth is *security,* for instance, retrieving keys and ensuring that those leaving don't take prohibited items with them.
5. Fifth is reducing the remaining *employees' uncertainty* and addressing their concerns. This typically involves a post-downsizing announcement and program, including meetings where senior managers field questions from the remaining employees.

Providing advanced notice regarding the impending downsizing can help cushion the otherwise negative effects. So can interpersonal sensitivity (in terms of the manager's demeanor during layoffs).[122] In the case of merger of State Bank of India with its associate banks, there were no forced downsizing. Instead, the Voluntary Retirement Scheme (VRS) was introduced, wherein employees who voluntarily choose to leave employment received good compensation and some benefits like normal retirement. (In case of resignation or dismissal, the employee would not have been eligible for such benefits.)

VRS is legally permitted in India as a more humane way to downsize, without any pressure on employees, while they are being compensated for the employment loss. Hence, trade unions also support VRS, if the compensation terms are favorable. The compensation received by the employee is also exempted from Income Tax (up to ₹5 lakh) under Section 10 (c) of the Income Tax Act. For exemption, vacancies created under the VRS scheme cannot be filled. For workmen covered under the Industrial Disputes Act of 1947, the scheme can be offered only with prior approval of the government.[123]

Supportiveness and creativity are especially important in high-performance-work-system-type firms. These rely heavily on employee engagement and teamwork.[124] Here, turnover is especially disruptive, so it may be particularly important to avoid layoffs. Options here include: implement pay freezes or cuts; introduce a hiring freeze before reducing the workforce; provide candid communications about the need for the downsizing; give employees an opportunity to express their opinions about the downsizing; and be fair and compassionate in implementing the downsizing.[125]

Chapter Review

Chapter Section Summaries

10-1. Employees are ultimately responsible for their own careers, but employers and managers also have roles in **career management**. These include establishing company-based career centers, offering career planning workshops, providing employee development budgets, and offering online career development programs. Perhaps the simplest is to make the appraisal itself career-oriented, by linking the appraisal feedback to the employee's aspirations and plans.

10-2. The employer's career planning and development process and practices (including career-oriented appraisal) help to foster **employee engagement**.

Managed effectively, the employer's career development process should send the signal that the employee cares about the employee's career success.

10-3. Managing voluntary turnover requires identifying its causes and then addressing them. A comprehensive approach to **retaining employees** should be multifaceted, and include improved selection, a well-thought-out training and career development program, assistance in helping employees lay out potential career plans, providing employees with meaningful work and recognition and rewards, promoting work–life balance, acknowledging employees' achievements, and providing all this within a supportive company culture.

10-4. Employers need to address employee **lifecycle career management** issues. Most notably, promotions can provide opportunities to reward exceptional performance, and to fill open positions with tested and loyal employees. Several decisions loom large in any firm's promotion process: Is seniority or competence the rule? How should we measure competence? Is the process formal or informal? Vertical, horizontal, or other? Women and people of color still experience relatively less career progress in organizations, and bias and more subtle barriers are often the cause. In general, the employer's promotion processes must comply with all the same antidiscrimination laws as do procedures for recruiting and selecting employees or any other HR actions. Transfers and retirements are other important career lifecycle issues.

10-5. **Managing dismissals** is an important part of any supervisor's job. Among the reasons for dismissal are unsatisfactory performance, misconduct, lack of qualifications, changed job requirements, and insubordination. In dismissing one or more employees, however, remember that termination at will as a policy has been weakened by exceptions in many states. Furthermore, care should be taken to avoid wrongful discharge suits.

Discussion Questions

10-1. Why is it advisable for an employee retention effort to be comprehensive? What activities would you say is involved in such a program?

10-2. What is the employee's role in the career development process? The manager's role? The employer's role?

10-3. What are the main decisions employers should address in reaching promotion decisions?

10-4. Discuss at least four procedural suggestions for managing dismissals effectively.

10-5. What would you as a supervisor do to avoid someone accusing you of wrongful dismissal?

Individual and Group Activities

10-6. Many rightfully offer Tata Steel and ITC Limited as examples of an employer that works hard to improve employee retention and engagement. Browse through the employment pages of both the companies' Web site. In this chapter, we discussed actions employers can take to improve employee retention and engagement. From the information on the Web pages, what is Tata Steel and ITC doing to support retention and engagement?

10-7. In groups of four or five students, meet with one or two administrators and faculty members in your college or university and, based on this, write a 2-page paper on the topic "the faculty promotion process at our college." What do you think of the process? Based on our discussion in this chapter, could you make any suggestions for improving it?

10-8. Working individually or in groups, choose two occupations (such as management consultant, HR manager, or salesperson) and use sources such as Industry Association and NSDC reports to size up the future demand for this occupation in the next 10 years or so. Does this seem like a good occupation to pursue? Why or why not?

10-9. In groups of four or five students, interview a small business owner or an HR manager with the aim of writing a 2-page paper addressing the topic "steps our company is taking to reduce voluntary employee turnover." What is this employer's turnover rate now? How would you suggest it improve its turnover rate?

10-10. Appendices A and B at the end of this book (pages 583–600) list the knowledge someone studying for the HRCI (Appendix A) or SHRM (Appendix B) certification exam needs to have in each area of human resource management (such as in Strategic Management, and Workforce Planning). In groups of several students, do four things: (1) review Appendix A and/or B; (2) identify the material in this chapter that relates to the Appendix A and/or B required knowledge lists; (3) write four multiple-choice exam questions on this material that you believe would be suitable for inclusion in the HRCI exam and/or the SHRM exam; and, (4) if time permits, have someone from your team post your team's questions in front of the class, so that students in all teams can answer the exam questions created by the other teams.

10-11. Several years ago, a survey of college graduates in the United Kingdom found that although many hadn't found their first jobs, most were already planning "career breaks" and to keep up their hobbies and interests outside work. As one report of the findings put it, "the next generation of workers is determined not to wind up on the hamster wheel of long hours with no play."[126] Part of the problem seems to be that many already see their friends "putting in more than 48 hours a week" at work. Career experts reviewing the results concluded that many of these recent college grads "are not looking for high-pay, high-profile jobs anymore."[127] Instead, they seem to be looking to "compartmentalize" their lives. They want to keep the number of hours they spend at work down, so they can maintain their hobbies and outside interests. If you were mentoring one of these people at work, what three bits of career advice would you give him or her? Why? What (if anything) would you suggest their employers do to accommodate these graduates' stated career wishes?

10-12. Web sites such as Sporting News occasionally run a story listing what they call the greatest coaches (for example, key "greatest coaches" into Google search).[128] Look at this list, and pick out two of the names. Then research these people online to determine what behaviors they exhibited that seem to account for why they were great coaches. How do these behaviors compare with what this chapter had to say about effective coaching?

Experiential Exercise

Where Am I Going ... and Why?

Purpose: The purpose of this exercise is to provide you with experience in analyzing your career preferences.

Required Understanding: Students should be thoroughly familiar with the "Employee's Role in Career Management" section in this chapter, as well as using Web resources extensively.

How to Set Up the Exercise/Instructions: Using Web resources and the "Employee's Role in Career Management" section in this chapter, analyze your career-related inclinations. Based on this analysis,

answer the following questions (if you wish, you may do this analysis in teams of three or four students).

10-13. What does your research suggest to you about what would be your preferable occupational options?

10-14. What are the prospects for these occupations?

10-15. Given these prospects and your own occupational inclinations, outline a brief, 1-page career plan for yourself, including current occupational inclinations, career goals, and an action plan listing four or five development steps you will need to take in order to get from where you are now career-wise to where you want to be, based on your career goals.

CHAPTER 10

Application Case

Google Reacts

On the face of it, Google would seem to be the last company that one would expect to have an employee retention problem. Google usually shows up in "Best Employers to Work For" lists; it's famous for full benefits, from dry cleaning to free Web-enabled transportation from San Francisco to great pensions; it offers great stock options; and, as a fast-growing company, it usually has many job applicants. So when its employee turnover began creeping up a few years ago, Google's human resource team had to decide what to do. Part of the problem is that as attractive as Google is to work for, Silicon Valley is filled with attractive employers, from Apple to Facebook. One of Google's first steps was to boost compensation. It gave all 23,000 Google employees a 10% raise,

plus a $1,000 tax-free holiday bonus.[129] But, still, Google management knew that pay was just part of the solution. It had to take other steps.

Questions

10-16. Without doing any research beyond what you learned in this chapter, what other steps would you suggest Google take to improve employee retention?

10-17. Was there any information in previous chapters of this book that would help to illustrate other steps Google took to improve retention?

10-18. Use other Internet sources, including Google.com, to finalize an answer to the question: What other steps should Google take to improve employee retention?

Continuing Case

Carter Cleaning Company

The Career Planning Program

Career planning has always been a pretty low-priority item for Carter Cleaning, since "just getting workers to come to work and then keeping them honest is enough of a problem," as Jack likes to say. Yet Jennifer thought it might not be a bad idea to give some thought to what a career planning program might involve for Carter. Many of their employees had been with them for years in dead-end jobs, and she frankly felt a little bad for them: "Perhaps we could help them gain a better perspective on what they want to do," she thought. And she definitely believed that career support would have an effect on improving Carter's employee retention.

Questions

10-19. What would be the advantages to Carter Cleaning of setting up a career planning program?

10-20. Who should participate in the program? All employees? Selected employees?

10-21. Outline and describe the career development program you would propose for the cleaners, pressers, counter people, and managers at the Carter Cleaning Centers.

Translating Strategy into HR Policies and Practices Case*,§

*The overall map on page xxxviii of this book outlines the relationships involved.

Improving Performance at the Hotel Paris

The New Career Management System

The Hotel Paris's competitive strategy is "To use superior guest service to differentiate the Hotel Paris properties, and to thereby increase the length of stay and return rate of guests, and thus boost revenues and profitability." HR manager Lisa Cruz must now formulate functional policies and activities that support this competitive strategy, by eliciting the required employee behaviors and competencies.

Lisa Cruz knew that, as a hospitality business, the Hotel Paris was uniquely dependent upon having engaged, high-morale employees. In a factory or small retail shop, the employer might be able to rely on direct supervision to make sure that the employees were doing their jobs. But in a hotel, just about every employee is "on the front line." There is usually no one there to supervise the limousine driver when he or she picks up a guest at the airport, or when the valet takes the guest's car, or the front-desk clerk signs the guest in, or the housekeeping clerk needs to handle a guest's special request. If the hotel wanted satisfied guests, they had to have engaged employees who did their jobs as if they owned the company, even when the supervisor was nowhere in sight. But for the employees to be engaged, Lisa knew, the Hotel Paris had to make it clear that the company was also committed to its employees.

From her experience, she knew that one way to do this was to help her employees have successful and satisfying careers, and she was therefore concerned to find that the Hotel Paris had no career management process at all. Supervisors weren't trained to discuss employees' developmental needs or promotional options during the performance appraisal interviews. Promotional processes were informal. And the firm made no attempt to provide any career development services that might help its employees to develop a better understanding of what their career options were, or should be. Lisa was sure that engaged employees were key to improving the experiences of the hotel's guests, and that she couldn't boost employee engagement without doing a better job of attending to her employees' career needs. In two hotels she began encouraging supervisors to at least engage in career-oriented appraisals with their subordinates, on a pilot project basis.

For Lisa and the CFO, their preliminary research left little doubt about the advisability of instituting a new career management system at the Hotel Paris. Based on their pilot project, employees in those Hotel Paris hotels who had been working under the new career management directive were more engaged, received more complimentary letters from guests, and received higher performance appraisal ratings than did employees who did not have career plans. The CFO therefore gave the go-ahead to design and institute a new Hotel Paris career management program.

Lisa and her team knew that they already had most of the building blocks in place, thanks to the new performance management system they had instituted just a few weeks earlier. For example, the new performance management system already required that the supervisor appraise the employee based on goals and competencies that were driven by the company's strategic needs; and the appraisal itself produced new goals for the coming year and specific development plans for the employee. These development plans had to make sense in terms of both the company's and the employee's needs and preferences.

In addition to the new performance management elements already in place, Lisa and her team created an online "Hotel Paris Career Center." With links to a choice of career assessment tools such as the Self-Directed Search (www.self-directed-search.com) and wizard-based templates for developing one's own career plan, the site went far toward providing the Hotel Paris's employees with the career assistance that they required. Also on the site, a new "International Job Openings" link made it easier for Hotel Paris employees to identify positions for which they might be qualified. The results exceeded Lisa and the CFO's expectations. Virtually every employee produced a career plan within the first 6 months. The appraisal interviews often turned into animated, career-oriented development sessions, and soon the various measures of employee commitment and guest service were trending up.

Questions

10-22. "Many hotel jobs are inherently 'dead end'; for example, maids, laundry workers, and valets either have no great aspirations to move up, or are just using these jobs temporarily, for instance, to help out with household expenses." First, do you agree with this statement? Why, or why not? Second, list three more specific career activities you would recommend Lisa implement for these employees.

10-23. Using what you learned in this chapter of Dessler *Human Resource Management*, build on the company's new system by recommending two more specific career development activities the hotel should implement.

10-24. What other specific career development activities would you recommend in light of the fact that the Hotel Paris's hotels and employees are dispersed around the world?

§Written by and copyright Gary Dessler, PhD.

Key Terms

career, 301
career management, 301
career development, 301
career planning, 301
reality shock, 303

mentoring, 306
coaching, 306
promotion, 313
transfers, 316
dismissal, 317

insubordination, 318
terminate at will, 318
termination interview, 319
outplacement counseling, 319
exit interviews, 320

layoff, 320
downsizing, 321

Endnotes

1. For example, see Phyllis Moen and Patricia Roehling, *The Career Mystique* (Boulder, CO: Rowman & Littlefield Publishers, 2005); and Geoff Williams, "3 Steps to Reinventing Your Career," U.*S. News & World Report,* June 5, 2013, http://money.usnews.com/money/personal-finance/articles/2013/06/05/3-steps-to-reinventing-your-career, accessed September 2, 2014.

2. Retrieved on 28 August 2017 from www.businesstoday.in/magazine/features/companies-are...freelancers.../230742.html.

3. Stephen Robbins and Timothy Judge, *Organizational Behavior* (Upper Saddle River, NJ: Pearson Education, 2011), p. 285.

4. Ibid., p. 284.

5. Promila Agarwal "State of Psychological Contract in India: Managing the New Deal", Global Business Review, 2015. V 16 (4), p 623 - 631.

6. Upasana Agarwal and S. Bhargava, "Exploring Psychological Contract Contents in India: The Employer and Employee Perspective," *Journal of Indian Business Research,* 2009, Vol. 1 (4), pp 238-251.

7. Biju Varkkey and Randhir Kumar, "Keeping the Sparkle On: Workforce Retention in Indian Diamond Cutting and Polishing Firms During Economic Recession," *International Journal of Organizational Analysis,* 2013, Vol. 21 (3) pp 454 – 470.

8. Karoline Strauss et al., "Future Work Selves: How Salient Hoped-For Identities Motivate Proactive Career Behaviors," *Journal of Applied Psychology* 97, no. 3, pp. 580–598.

9. Edward Levinson et al., "A Critical Evaluation of the Web-Based Version of the Career Key," *Career Development Quarterly* 50, no. 1 (September 1, 2002), pp. 26–36.

10. Richard Bolles, *What Color Is Your Parachute?* (Berkeley, CA: Ten Speed Press, 2003), pp. 5–6.

11. This example is based on Richard Bolles, *The Three Boxes of Life* (Berkeley, CA: Ten Speed Press, 1976). Richard Bolles updates his famous career book *What Color Is Your Parachute?* annually. It contains this and many other career exercises.

The 2015 edition is published by Ten Speed Press in Berkeley, California.

12. http://careers.intuit.com/university/new-grads, accessed March 12, 2013.

13. Retrieved on 29 August 2017 from https://www.hul.co.in/careers/professionals/career-by-choice.

14. Mohan Thite, 'From Local to Global HRM: Interviews with HR Heads in Emerging Indian Multinationals,' *International Journal of Indian Culture and Business Management,* 2014, Vol 9 (4), pp 151- 163.

15. Rachel Silverman, "Workers Get Help Climbing the Career Ladder," *Wall Street Journal,* January 14, 2015, p. B6.

16. Laszlo Bock, *Work Rules!* (New York: Twelve, 2015), pp. 217–218.

17. Retrieved on 29 August 2017 from www.anandgroupindia.com.

18. Patrick Kiger, "First USA Bank, Promotions and Job Satisfaction," *Workforce,* March 2001, pp. 54–56.

19. Fred Otte and Peggy Hutcheson, *Helping Employees Manage Careers* (Upper Saddle River, NJ: Prentice Hall, 1992), p. 143.

20. David Foote, "Wanna Keep Your Staff Happy? Think Career," *Computerworld,* October 9, 2000, p. 38. For an example, the U.S. Homeland Security Department's TSA has a career coaching/planning program. See http://tsacareercoaching.tsa.dhs.gov/index.php/faq-tsa-career-plan, accessed September 2, 2014.

21. Julekha Dash, "Coaching to Aid IT Careers, Retention," *Computerworld,* March 20, 2000, p. 52.

22. Yehuda Baruch, "Career Development in Organizations and Beyond: Balancing Traditional and Contemporary Viewpoints," *Human Resource Management Review* 16 (2006), p. 131.

23. Carla Joinson, "Employee, Sculpt Thyself with a Little Help," *HR Magazine,* May 2001, pp. 61–64.

24. See also Jim Bright, "Career Development: Empowering Your Staff to Excellence," *Journal of Banking and Financial Services* 17, no. 3 (July 2003), p.12.

25. Tim Harvey, "Enterprise Training System Is Trans Alaska Pipeline's Latest Safety Innovation," *Pipeline and Gas Journal* 229, no. 12 (December 2002), pp. 28–32.

26. Ibid.

27. www.halogensoftware.com/products/halogen-esuccession/, accessed August 27, 2012.

28. Mukta Kulkarni and K. V. Gopakumar, "Career Management Strategies of People with Disabilities," *Human Resource Management* 53, no. 3 (May–June 2014), pp. 445–466.

29. Padma R Nandi, 'Commitment to Learn and Coach,' *People Matters,* 2011.

30. H. Naidu, 'Challenges to Coaching in India,' *International Coach Academy Research Papers* (2012). www.coachcampus.com

31. Bill Hayes, "Helping Workers with Career Goals Boosts Retention Efforts," *Boston Business Journal* 21, no. 11 (April 20, 2001), p. 38.

32. Michael Doody, "A Mentor Is a Key to Career Success," *Health-Care Financial Management* 57, no. 2 (February 2003), pp. 92–94.

33. Richard Luecke, *Coaching and Mentoring* (Boston: Harvard Business School Press, 2004), pp. 100–101.

34. Ferda Erdem and Janset Özen Aytemur, "Mentoring—A Relationship Based on Trust: Qualitative Research," *Public Personnel Management* 37, no. 1 (Spring 2008), pp. 55–65.

35. Herminia Ibarra, Nancy Carter, and Christine Silva, "Why Men Still Get More Promotions Than Women," *Harvard Business Review,* September 2010, pp. 80–85.

36. Nisha Nair and Neharika Vohra, 'Mentoring As Means to Achieve Inclusion: A Focus on Practice and Research on Women in India, in Mentoring Diverse Leaders,' Edited by Audery J Murell and Stacey Blake Beard, 2017, Taylor and Francis.

37. Fyfe-Mills, "Commitment to Talent Development Excellence." See also http://businesstoday.intoday.in/story/malcolm-frank-on-cognizant-strategy-going-forward/1/200337.

html, www.cognizant.com/InsightsWhitepapers/architecting-an-enterprise-content-management-strategy-a-four-pillar-approach-codex975.pdf, and www.cognizant.com/about-cognizant/company-overview/sustainability/employee-development, all accessed April 9, 2015.

38. This is based on Gary Dessler, *Winning Commitment* (New York: McGraw-Hill, 1993), Chapter 10. See also www.glassdoor.com/Reviews/J-CPenney-Reviews-E361.htm, http://jobs.jcp.com/viewalljobs, and www.glassdoor.com/Reviews/Employee-Review-J-CPenney-RVW479729.htm, all accessed July 7, 2014.

39. www.Medtronic.com/careers/develop-your-potential, accessed March 12, 2013; www.medtronic.com/us-en/about-3/medtronic-plc-facts.html?cmpid=mdt_plc_2015_US_about_3_story_panel_featured_company_facts_cta_text_link_learn_more, accessed April 10, 2015.

40. Retrieved on 29 August 2017 from http://archive.indianexpress.com/news/india-no-1-in-world-on-attrition-chart-one-in-four-to-switch-jobs-hay-group/1126286/.

41. Retrieved on 29 August 2017 from ewww.business-standard.com/article/management/attrition-levels-in-india-at-five-year-low-says-aon-hewitt-survey-116021700702_1.html.

42. See, for example, www.nobscot.com/survey/index.cfm and www.bls.gov/jlt, accessed April 27, 2011. For computing turnover, see SHRM, "Executive Brief: Differences in Employee Turnover Across Key Industries," www.shrm.org, accessed August 30, 2012.

43. Jean Phillips and Stanley Gully, *Strategic Staffing* (Upper Saddle River, NJ: Pearson Education, 2012).

44. Sandeep Krishnana and Manjari Singh, "Outcomes of Intention to Quit of Indian IT Professionals," *Human Resource Management,* 2010, Vol 49 (1), pp. 421–437.

CHAPTER 10

45. Tae-Youn Park and Jason Shaw, "Turnover Rates and Organizational Performance: A Meta-analysis," *Journal of Applied Psychology* 98, no. 2 (2013), pp. 268–309.

46. Ibid., p. 283. See also Jolivette Wallace and Kristena Gaylor, "A Study of the Dysfunctional and Functional Aspects of Voluntary Employee Turnover," *SAM Advanced Management Journal* 77, no. 3 (Summer 2012), p. 27.

47. The following example is based on Barbara Hillmer, Steve Hillmer, and Gale McRoberts, "The Real Costs of Turnover: Lessons from a Call Center," *Human Resource Planning* 27, no. 3 (2004), pp. 34–41.

48. Kim Soonhee, "The Impact of Human Resource Management on State Government IT Employee Turnover Intentions," *Public Personnel Management* 41, no. 2 (Summer 2012), p. 257.

49. Park and Shaw, "Turnover Rates and Organizational Performance."

50. Adrienne Fox, "Drive Turnover Down," *HR Magazine*, July 2012, pp. 23–27.

51. SHRM, "Executive Brief."

52. www.worldatwork.org/waw/ adimLink?id=17180, accessed April 27, 2011.

53. Phillips and Gully, *Strategic Staffing*, p. 329.

54. Stephen Robbins and Timothy Judge, *Organizational Behavior* (Upper Saddle River, NJ: Pearson Education, 2011), p. 81.

55. Phillips and Gully, *Strategic Staffing*, p. 328.

56. Priyanka and S K Dubey, "Employees Turnover Intention in Indian Retail Industry - An exploratory study," (2016) *Business Perspectives*, Vol 16 (1), pp 7–20.

57. Katherine Tyler, "Who Will Stay and Who Will Go?" *HR Magazine*, December 2011, pp. 101–103.

58. Anumeha Chaturvedi, "Sapient India Launches New Hiring Campaign," *ET Bureau*, 07 April 2016.

59. "Employers Using Cash to Retain Key Talent," *BNA Bulletin to Management*, June 26, 2012, p. 202.

60. Max Messmer, "Employee Retention: Why It Matters Now," *CPA Magazine*, June/July 2009, p. 28; and "The Employee Retention Challenge," Development Dimensions International, 2009.

61. Messmer, "Employee Retention."

62. Ibid. See also Eric Krell, "Five Ways to Manage High Turnover," *HR Magazine*, April 2012, pp. 63–65.

63. Dun and Bradstreet, 'Sodexo: HR Best Practices 2017 – Transforming the Thinking,' Idea Cellular Ltd (2017), p 45.

64. Rosemary Batt and Alexander Colvin, "An Employment Systems Approach to Turnover:

65. Central Inland Water Transport Corporation vs Brojonath Ganguli, Supreme Court of India, 1986, *IILJ*, 171

66. Saurabh Mishra, 'Are Employment Bonds Legal in Indian Context or Not?', accessed in 2015 at blog.ipleaders.in.

67. Retrieved on March 2017 from http://www.business-standard.com/article/companies/get-rid-of-3-month-notice-period-techies-ask-govt-to-ease-quitting-process-117030200238_1.html, and retrieved on June 2017 from http://economictimes.indiatimes.com/industry/transportation/airlines-/-aviation/pilots-oppose-extension-of-notice-period-for-quitting/articleshow/58991637.cms.

68. "Counteroffers: Smart Move to Keep a Star or Waste of Time?" *BNA Bulletin to Management*, November 6, 2012, p. 358.

69. Ibid.

70. Baker, op cit. Stephen Baker, "Data Mining Moves to Human Resources" Bloomberg Business, March 11, 2009. See also "HR Analytics," *Workforce Management*, August 2012, p. 24.

71. Ed Frauenheim, "Numbers Game," *Workforce Management* 90, no. 3 (March 2011), p. 21.

72. Bock, *Work Rules!*, p. 142.

73. "The World's Top 10 Most Innovative Companies in Big Data," www.fastcompany.com/most-innovative-companies/2014/industry/big-data, accessed April 24, 2015.

74. Ibid.

75. From www.globoforce.com, accessed April 7, 2013. Used by permission from Globoforce.

76. "Shocked UBS Staff Take to Twitter," www.CNBC.com/ID/49617998/, accessed October 21, 2012.

77. Retrieved on 29 August 2017 from http://economictimes.indiatimes.com/tech/ites/anand-mahindras-apology-brings-it-layoffs-in-spotlight/articleshow/59497311.cms

78. David Wilson, "Comparative Effects of Race/Ethnicity and Employee Engagement on Withdrawal Behavior," *Journal of Managerial Issues* 21, no. 2 (Summer 2009), pp. 165–166, 195–215.

79. Paul Eder and Robert Eisenberger, "Perceived Organizational Support: Reducing the Negative Influence of Coworker Withdrawal Behavior," *Journal of Management* 34, no. 1 (February 2008), pp. 55–68.

80. Wilson, "Comparative Effects of Race/Ethnicity and Employee Engagement."

81. Lisa Hope Pelled and Katherine R. Xin, "Down and Out: An

Investigation of the Relationship Between Mood and Employee Withdrawal Behavior," *Journal of Management* 25, no. 6 (1999), pp. 875–895.

82. Ibid.

83. Ranjita Chattopadyay, "Managing Absenteeism in the Workplace," *Career Tips/Work an Pay*, www.paycheck.in available at https://blog.ipleaders.in/are-employment-bonds-legal-india/

84. Ibid.

85. Ibid.

86. See, for example, Margaret Shaffer and David Harrison, "Expatriates' Psychological Withdrawal from International Assignments: Work, Nonwork, and Family Influences," *Personnel Psychology* 51, no. 1 (Spring 1998), pp. 87–118; Karl Pajo, Alan Coetzer, and Nigel Guenole, "Formal Development Opportunities and Withdrawal Behaviors by Employees in Small and Medium-Sized Enterprises," *Journal of Small Business Management* 48, no. 3 (July 2010), pp. 281–301; and P. Eder et al., "Perceived Organizational Support: Reducing the Negative Influence of Coworker Withdrawal Behavior," *Journal of Management* 34 no. 1 (February 2008), pp. 55–68.

87. Verena Hahn and Christian Dormann, "The Role of Partners and Children for Employees' Psychological Detachment from Work and Well-Being," *Journal of Applied Psychology* 98, no. 1 (2013), pp. 26–36.

88. Pamela Babcock, quoting Terry Henley, SPHR, in "Promotions: Is There a 'New Normal'?" www.shrm.org/hrdisciplines/employeereltions/articles/Pages/PromotionsIsThereaNewNormal.aspx, accessed June 1, 2011.

89. Bock, *Work Rules!*, p. 358.

90. Karen Lyness and Madeline Heilman, "When Fit Is Fundamental: Performance Evaluations and Promotions of Upper-Level Female and Male Managers," *Journal of Applied Psychology* 91, no. 4 (2006), pp. 777–785.

91. Nasrin Sultana and Ragini Bhuam, 'Proportion of Women Directors Up 180%, But Gender Diversity Lags in India: Survey,' 2017, accessed at livemint.com.

92. Kornferry Institute, Building Diversity in Asia Pacific Board Rooms (2016), as accessed on 27 September, 2017 at www.kornferry.com.

93. Kamal Kishore, 'Representation of Women on Boards of Indian Companies: An Indian Story,' *Journal of Management and Public Policy*, 2016, Vol. 7 (2), pp. 29-26.

94. In Ellen Cook et al., "Career Development of Women of Color and White Women: Assumptions, Conceptualization, and Interventions from an Ecological Perspective," *Career*

Development Quarterly 50, no. 4 (June 2002), pp. 291–306.

95. Kathleen Melymuka, "Glass Ceilings & Clear Solutions," *Computerworld*, May 29, 2000, p. 56.

96. Robin Shay, "Don't Get Caught in the Legal Wringer When Dealing with Difficult to Manage Employees," www.shrm.org, http://moss07.shrm.org/Publications/hrmagazine/EditorialContent/Pages/0702toc.aspx, accessed July 28, 2009.

97. Ken Dychtwald et al., "It's Time to Retire Retirement," *Harvard Business Review*, March 2004, p. 49.

98. "Employees Plan to Work Past Retirement, but Not Necessarily for Financial Reasons," *BNA Bulletin to Management*, February 19, 2004, pp. 57–58. See also Mo Wang, "Profiling Retirees in the Retirement Transition and Adjustment Process: Examining the Longitudinal Change Patterns of Retirees' Psychological Well-Being," *Journal of Applied Psychology* 92, no. 2 (2007), pp. 455–474.

99. See, for example, Matt Bolch, "Bidding Adieu," *HR Magazine*, June 2006, pp. 123–127; and Claudia Deutsch, "A Longer Goodbye," *New York Times*, April 20, 2008, pp. H1, H10.

100. Luis Fleites and Lou Valentino, "The Case for Phased Retirement," *Compensation & Benefits Review*, March/April 2007, pp. 42–46.

101. Andrew Luchak et al., "When Do Committed Employees Retire? The Effects of Organizational Commitment on Retirement Plans Under a Defined Benefit Pension Plan," *Human Resource Management* 47, no. 3 (Fall 2008), pp. 581–599.

102. Eric Krell, "Ways to Phased Retirement," *HR Magazine*, October 2010, p. 90.

103. Khar Bhan Ram v/s Punjab National Bank and others Allahabad HC, 1194 LLR. and Subash Vithal Pise v/s Childrens Film Society of India, Bombay HC, 1198. LLR. 852.

104. Andrea Poe, "Make Foresight 20/20," *HR Magazine*, February 20, 2000, pp. 74–80. See also Nancy Hatch Woodward, "Smoother Separations," *HR Magazine*, June 2007, pp. 94–97.

105. Joseph Famularo, *Handbook of Modern Personnel Administration* (New York: McGraw Hill, 1982), pp. 65.3–65.5. See also Carolyn Hirschman, "Off Duty, Out of Work," *HR Magazine*, www.shrm.org/hrmagazine/articles/0203/0203hirschman.asp, accessed January 10, 2008.

106. Accessed on September 27, 2017 at https://www.ndtv.com/india-news/if-fake-caste-certificate-got-you-that-job-then-youll-be-punished-supreme-court-1721606.

107. Kenneth Sovereign, *Personnel Law* (Upper Saddle River, NJ: Prentice Hall, 1999), p. 148; "Disciplinary Issues: What Constitutes Insubordination?" www.shrm.org/TemplatesTools/hrqa/Pages/CMS_020144.aspx, accessed September 11, 2013.

108. C. R. Wanberg, L. W. Bunce, & M. B. Gavin, "Perceived fairness of layoffs among individuals who have been laid off: A longitudinal study" *Personnel Psychology*, 52, 1999, 59–84; Brian Klaas and Gregory Dell'omo, "Managerial Use of Dismissal: Organizational Level Determinants," *Personnel Psychology* 50 (1997), pp. 927–953; Nancy Hatch Woodward, "Smoother Separations," *HR Magazine*, June 2007, pp. 94–97.

109. Retrieved on 29 August 2017 from http://economictimes.indiatimes.com/tech/ites/anand-mahindra-apologises-over-tech-mahindra-employee-sacking/videoshow/59502351.cms.

110. "Fairness to Employees Can Stave Off Litigation," *BNA Bulletin to Management*, November 27, 1999, p. 377.

111. Based on Coil and Rice, "Three Steps to Creating Effective Employee Releases." See also Martha Frase-Blunt, "Making Exit Interviews Work," *HR Magazine*, August 2004, pp. 9–11.

112. William J. Morin and Lyle York, *Outplacement Techniques* (New York: AMACOM, 1982), pp. 101–131; F. Leigh Branham, "How to Evaluate Executive Outplacement Services," *Personnel Journal* 62 (April 1983), pp. 323–326; Sylvia Milne, "The Termination Interview," *Canadian Manager*, Spring 1994, pp. 15–16; and Matthew S. Wood and Steven J. Karau, "Preserving Employee Dignity During the Termination Interview: An Empirical Examination," *Journal of Business Ethics* 86, no. 4 (2009), pp. 519–534.

113. Bram Lowsky, "Inside Outplacement," *Workforce,* June 2014, pp. 36–39, 48.

114. Mitchell Lee Marks et al., "Rebounding from Career Setbacks," *Harvard Business Review*, October 2014, pp. 105–108.

115. Marlene Piturro, "Alternatives to Downsizing," *Management Review*, October 1999, pp. 37–42; "How Safe Is Your Job?" *Money*, December 1, 2001, p. 130.

116. Joseph Zarandona and Michael Camuso, "A Study of Exit Interviews: Does the Last Word Count," *Personnel* 62, no. 3 (March 1981), pp. 47–48. For another point of view, see "Firms Can Profit from Data Obtained from Exit Interviews," *Knight-Ridder/Tribune Business News*, February 13, 2001, Item 0104 4446.

117. Namrata Singh, 'India Inc Outsources Exit Interviews,' 11 May 2015, Times News Network (www.timesofindia.com).

118. Ibid.

119. Ibid.

120. "Adopting Laid-Off Alternatives Could Help Employers Survive, Even Thrive, Analysts Say," *BNA Bulletin to Management*, February 24, 2009, p. 57.

121. "Calling a Layoff a Layoff," *Workforce Management*, April 21, 2008, p. 41.

122. "Communication Can Reduce Problems, Litigation After Layoffs, Attorneys Say," *BNA Bulletin to Management*, April 14, 2003, p. 129.

123. Retrieved on 29 August 2017 from https://www.sbi.co.in/webfiles/uploads/files/1446462066513_CCP_HRD_PM_ENGLISH_402_1.pdf

124. Roderick Iversen and Christopher Zatzick, "The Effects of Downsizing of Labor Productivity: The Value of Showing Consideration for Employees' Morale and Welfare and High Performance Work Systems," *Human Resource Management* 50, no. 1 (January/February 2011), pp. 29–44.

125. Ibid., p. 40.

126. "New Trend in Career Hunt," *Europe Intelligence Wire*, February 10, 2004.

127. Ibid.

128. See, for example, http://aol.sportingnews.com/ncaabasketball/story/2009-07-29/sporting-news-50-greatest-coaches-all-time, accessed July 7, 2014.

129. http://abclocal.go.com/kgo/story?section=news/business&id=7775524, accessed June 1, 2011.

130. Brett Arends, "How Summer Can Change Your Future," *Wall Street Journal*, May 17–18, 2014, p. B8.

131. John Holland, *Making Vocational Choices: A Theory of Careers* (Upper Saddle River, NJ: Prentice Hall, 1973).

132. Bart Wille and Filip De Fruyt, "Vocations as a Source of Identity: Reciprocal Relations Between Big Five Personality Traits and RIASEC Characteristics Over 15 Years," *Journal of Applied Psychology* 99, no. 2 (2014), pp. 262–281.

133. 1Ibid., p. 5. Researchers and career specialists are working with the U.S. government's O*NET to devise a methodology that will enable individuals to make better use of O*NET in identifying and choosing career paths. See, for example, Patrick Converse et al., "Matching Individuals to Occupations Using Abilities and the O*NET: Issues and an Application in Career Guidance," *Personnel Psychology* 57 (2004), pp. 451–57.

134. Quoted or paraphrased from www.onetcenter.org/mynextmove.html, accessed April 8, 2013.

135. This is based on Edgar Schein, *Career Dynamics* (Reading, MA; Addison Wesley, 1978), pp. 128–129; and Edgar Schein, "Career Anchors Revisited: Implications for Career Development in the 21st Century," *Academy of Management Executive* 10, no. 4 (1996), pp. 80–88.

136. Ibid., pp. 257–262. For a test of Schein's career anchor concept, see Yvon Martineau et al., "Multiple Career Anchors of Québec Engineers: Impact on Career Path and Success," *Relations Industrielles/Industrial Relations* 60, no. 3 (Summer 2005), pp. 45, 455–482.

137. Deb Koen, "Revitalize Your Career," *Training and Development*, January 2003, pp. 59–60.

138. See John Wareham, "How to Make a Headhunter Call You," *Across-the-Board* 32, no. 1 (January 1995), pp. 49–50; and Deborah Wright Brown and Alison Konrad, "Job Seeking in a Turbulent Environment: Social Networks and the Importance of Cross-Industry Ties to an Industry Change," *Human Relations* 54, no. 8 (August 2001), p. 1018.

139. Erica Fry, "How to Land Your Dream Job," *Fortune*, September 22, 2014, pp. 104–105.

140. Dan Klamm, "3 Ways to Ace Your Job Interview with Social Media," http://mashable.com/2010/06/01/job-interview-social-media/, accessed April 1, 2013.

141. Rachel Silverman, "New Year, New Job? Read This First," *Wall Street Journal*, January 2, 2015, pp. B1, B4.

142. Erica Fry, "Start Up: You," *Fortune,* January 1, 2015, pp. 84–87.

143. Based on Phyllis Korkke, "How to Say 'Look at Me!' to an Online Recruiter," *New York Times*, January 20, 2013, p. 8; and Eilene Zimmerman, "Recruiting a Recruiter for Your Next Job," *New York Times*, April 7, 2013, p. 10.

144. Sheryl Jean, "Say Goodbye to Paper, Hello to Social Resume," *Miami Herald*, March 4, 2013, p. 19.

145. Susan Adams, "The 10 Best Websites for Your Career," *Forbes*, www.forbes.com/sites/susanadams/2012/09/14/the-10-best-websites-for-your-career, accessed April 10, 2015.

146. "Resume Banks Launched," *Financial Executives* 17, no. 6 (September 2001), p. 72; James Siegel, "The ACCA Launches Online Career Center," *A/C, Heating & Refrigeration News*, June 16, 2003, p. 5.

147. See, for example, "Job Search Tips" *The America's Intelligence Wire*, May 17, 2004; and "What to Do When Your Job Search Stalls," *BusinessWeek* online, March 16, 2004.

148. A classic but still one of the most useful job search guides available: Richard Payne, *How to Get a Better Job Quicker* (New York: Mentor, 1987), pp. 54–87.

149. "Read This Before You Put a Resume Online," *Fortune*, May 24, 1999, pp. 290–291.

150. Sara Needleman, "Posting a Job Profile Online? Keep It Polished," August 29, 2006, *Wall Street Journal*, p. B7.

151. Payne, *How to Get a Better Job Quicker*.

Appendix for Chapter 10

Managing Your Career and Finding a Job

The individual must be responsible for creating and managing his or her own career. And, in today's job marketplace, knowing how to find and get a job is crucial.

Making Career Choices

It is unfortunate but true that many people don't put much thought into their careers. Some choose majors based on class scheduling preferences, favorite professors, or unstated psychological motives. Others stumble into jobs because "that's all that was available." If there was ever anything that cried out for fact-based decisions, it is choosing your career. The first and essential step is to learn as much as possible about your interests, aptitudes, and skills. The most direct way to do this is through experience, preferably a roster of jobs, internships, and experiences that will help you crystallize what it is you like to do and are great at. Getting experience doesn't just help career planning: In one study, the researchers sent out 9,400 fictitious resumes for "applicants" that differed in things like grade point average, major, and university. On-the-job experience—for instance, via internships—seemed to be the single most important factor in getting a job interview.[130] Beyond that, there are career tests and exercises you can use.

Identify Your Occupational Orientation   Career-counseling expert John Holland says that personality (including values, motives, and needs) is one career choice determinant. For example, a person with a strong social orientation on Holland's Self-Directed Search (SDS) might be attracted to careers that entail interpersonal rather than intellectual or physical activities and to occupations such as social work. Based on research with his earlier Vocational Preference Test (VPT), Holland found six basic personality types or orientations (see www.self-directed-search.com).[131]

1. *Realistic orientation.* These people are attracted to occupations that involve physical activities requiring skill, strength, and coordination. Examples include forestry, farming, and agriculture.
2. *Investigative orientation.* Investigative people are attracted to careers that involve cognitive activities (thinking, organizing, understanding) rather than affective activities (feeling, acting, or interpersonal and emotional tasks). Examples include biologist, chemist, and college professor.
3. *Artistic orientation.* People here are attracted to careers that involve self-expression, artistic creation, expression of emotions, and individualistic activities. Examples include artists, advertising executives, and musicians.
4. *Social orientation.* These people are attracted to careers that involve interpersonal rather than intellectual or physical activities. Examples include clinical psychology, foreign service, and social work.
5. *Enterprising orientation.* Verbal activities aimed at influencing others characterize enterprising personalities. Examples include managers, lawyers, and public relations executives.
6. *Conventional orientation.* A conventional orientation favors careers that involve structured, rule-regulated activities, as well as careers in which it is expected that the employee subordinate his or her personal needs to those of the organization. Examples include accountants and bankers.

Most people have more than one "RIASEC" occupational orientation (they might be social, realistic, and investigative, for example), and Holland believes that the more similar or compatible these orientations are, the less internal conflict or indecision a person will face in making a career choice. You can take Holland's SDS online for a small fee (see www.self-directed-search.com). Of course, as someone gains experience, it is possible (or likely) that his or her RIASEC scores will change over time.[132]

Identify Your Skills   You may have a "conventional" orientation, but whether you have *the skills* to be an accountant, banker, or credit manager will affect which occupation you ultimately choose. Therefore, you have to identify your skills. We presented some exercises for this earlier in this chapter, on page 303.

Aptitudes and Special Talents   For career planning purposes, a person's aptitudes are usually measured with a test battery such as the general aptitude test battery (GATB), which most state one-stop career centers make available. This instrument measures various aptitudes including intelligence and mathematical ability. You can also use specialized tests, such as for mechanical comprehension. Holland's Self-Directed Search will also provide some insights into your aptitudes, as will O*NET.[133]

O*NET   O*NET offers a free online "My Next Move" occupation and career assessment system (www.onetcenter.org/mynextmove.html). It includes *O*NET Interest Profiler*, a tool that offers customized career suggestions on over 900 different careers based on a person's interests and level of education and work experience. Users obtain important information including skills, tasks, salaries, and employment outlook for occupations.[134]

Identify Your Career Anchors   Professor Edgar Schein says that career planning is a continuing process of discovery—one in which a person slowly develops a clearer occupational self-concept in terms of what his or her talents, abilities, motives, needs, attitudes, and values are. Schein also says that as you learn more about yourself, it becomes apparent that you have a dominant *career anchor*, a concern or value that you will not give up if a [career] choice has to be made.

Career anchors, as their name implies, are the pivots around which a person's career swings; a person becomes conscious of them because of learning, through experience, about his or her talents and abilities, motives and needs, and attitudes and values. Based on his research at the Massachusetts Institute of Technology, Schein believes that career anchors are difficult to predict because they are evolutionary and a product of a process of discovery. Some people may never find out what their career anchors are until they have to make a major choice—such as whether to take the promotion to the headquarters staff or strike out on their own by starting a business. It is at this point that all the person's past work experiences, interests, aptitudes, and orientations converge into a meaningful pattern that helps show what (career anchor) is the most important factor in driving the person's career choices. Based on his study of MIT graduates, Schein identified five career anchors.[135]

Technical/Functional Competence People who had a strong technical/functional career anchor tended to avoid decisions that would drive them toward general management. Instead, they made decisions that would enable them to remain and grow in their chosen technical or functional fields.

Managerial Competence Other people showed a strong motivation to become managers, and their career experience enabled them to believe they had the skills and values required. A management position of high responsibility is their ultimate goal. When pressed to explain why they believed they had the skills necessary to gain such positions, many in Schein's research sample answered that they were qualified because of what they saw as their competencies in a combination of three

areas: (1) *analytical competence* (ability to identify, analyze, and solve problems under conditions of incomplete information and uncertainty); (2) *interpersonal competence* (ability to influence, supervise, lead, manipulate, and control people at all levels); and (3) *emotional competence* (the capacity to be stimulated by emotional and interpersonal crises rather than exhausted or debilitated by them, and the capacity to bear high levels of responsibility without becoming paralyzed).

Creativity Some of the graduates had become successful entrepreneurs. To Schein these people seemed to have a need "to build or create something that was entirely their own product—a product or process that bears their name, a company of their own, or a personal fortune that reflects their accomplishments." For example, one graduate had become a successful purchaser, restorer, and renter of townhouses in a large city; another had built a successful consulting firm.

Autonomy and Independence Some seemed driven by the need to be on their own, free of the dependence that can arise when a person elects to work in a large organization where promotions, transfers, and salary decisions make them subordinate to others. Many of these graduates also had a strong technical/functional orientation.

As noted in the accompanying text, O*NET offers a free comprehensive online "My Next Move" occupation and career assessment system for building your future career (www.onetcenter.org/mynextmove.html).

Source: From O*NET website, www.onetonline.org.

Instead of pursuing this orientation in an organization, they had decided to become consultants, working either alone or as part of a relatively small firm. Others had become professors of business, freelance writers, and proprietors of a small retail business.

Security A few of the graduates were mostly concerned with long-run career stability and job security. They seemed willing to do what was required to maintain job security, a decent income, and a stable future in the form of a good retirement program and benefits. For those interested in *geographic security*, maintaining a stable, secure career in familiar surroundings was generally more important than pursuing superior career choices, if choosing the latter meant injecting instability or insecurity into their lives by forcing them to pull up roots and move to another city. For others, security meant *organizational security*. They might today opt for government jobs, where tenure still tends to be a way of life. They were much more willing to let their employers decide what their careers should be.

Assessing Career Anchors To help you identify career anchors, take a few sheets of blank paper and write out your answers to the following questions:[136]

1. What was your major area of concentration (if any) in high school? Why did you choose that area? How did you feel about it?
2. What is (or was) your major area of concentration in college? Why did you choose that area? How did you feel about it?
3. What was your first job after school? (Include military if relevant.) What were you looking for in your first job?
4. What were your ambitions or long-range goals when you started your career? Have they changed? When? Why?
5. What was your first major change of job or company? What were you looking for in your next job?
6. What was your next major change of job, company, or career? Why did you initiate or accept it? What were you looking for? (Do this for each of your major changes of job, company, or career.)
7. As you look back over your career, identify some times you have especially enjoyed. What was it about those times that you enjoyed?
8. As you look back, identify some times you have not especially enjoyed. What was it about those times you did not enjoy?
9. Have you ever refused a job move or promotion? Why?
10. Now review all your answers carefully, as well as the descriptions for the five career anchors (technical/functional competence, managerial competence, creativity and independence, autonomy, security). Based on your answers to the questions, rate, for yourself, each of the anchors from 1 to 5. 1 equals low importance, 5 equals high importance.

Technical/functional competence _____
Managerial competence _____
Creativity and independence _____
Autonomy _____
Security _____

What Do You Want to Do?

Identify High-Potential Occupations Learning about your skills and interests is only step one in choosing an occupation. You also have to identify those occupations that fit your occupational orientations, skills, career anchors, and occupational preferences, and that are (preferably) in high demand in the years to come.

Here, use the Internet. The U.S. Department of Labor's online *Occupational Outlook Handbook* (www.bls.gov/oco) is updated each year, and provides detailed descriptions and information on hundreds of occupations. O*NET (www.onetonline.org/) provides occupational demand projections. Figure 10A-1 lists some other sites to use both for occupational information and for information on where to turn to when searching for a job—the subject to which we now turn.

Selected Online Sources of Occupational Information

- All Star Jobs
- CampusCareeerCenter
- CareerBliss.com
- CareerOneSto
- CareerExplorer
- CareerOverview
- CityTownInfo
- College Central Network
- CollegeGrad.com
- Construct My Future (information about construction careers)
- Cool Works
- EducationPlanner
- eMedicalAssistants
- Explore Health Careers
- Green Jobs Ready
- hotjobs.com
- International Jobs
- Job Search Intelligence
- MyArtsCareer
- Occupational Outlook Handbook
- Professional Development for Teachers
- Quintessential Careers
- ResumeINDEX
- SalaryList
- Science Buddies—Careers
- Simply Hired
- Snag a Job

FIGURE 10A-1 **Selected Online Sources of Occupational Information**

Source: Based on http://mappingyourfuture.org/planyourcareer/careerresources.htm, accessed October 8, 2015.

Finding the Right Job

Your next step is to find a job that you want in the company and locale where you want to work.

Before leaving a current job, however, make sure leaving is what you want. Many people, dissatisfied at work, assume it must be the job or the occupation. But why switch from being a lawyer to a teacher, when it's not the profession but that law firm's 80-hour weeks that are the problem?

One must use a process of elimination. For example, you may like your occupation and employer, but not how your specific job is structured. Others may find their employers' ways of doing things are the problem. Or, it may in fact be the occupation.

In any case, the solution should fit the cause. For example, if, after thinking it through, you are satisfied with your occupation and where you work, but not with your job as it's organized now, try reconfiguring it. For example, consider alternative work arrangements such as flexible hours or telecommuting; delegate or eliminate the job functions you least prefer; and seek out a "stretch assignment" that will let you work on something you find more challenging.[137] If it's the specific employer, look elsewhere.

Job Search Techniques In Chapter 5 (Personnel Planning and Recruiting), we saw that employers use various tools to find recruits, so it shouldn't be surprising that job seekers should use basically the same tools.

Personal Contacts Generally, the most popular way to seek job leads and interviews is to rely on personal contacts (networking) such as friends and relatives.[138] So, let as many responsible people as possible know that you are looking for a job and also what kind of job you want. (Beware, though, if you don't want your job search getting back to your current boss. If that is the case, then just pick out two or three very close friends and ask them to be discreet in seeking a job for you.)

No matter how close your friends or relatives are to you, by the way, you do not want to impose too much on them. It is usually best to ask them for the name of someone they think you should talk to in the kind of firm in which you'd like to work, and then do the digging yourself.

Trends Shaping HR: Digital and Social Media Job searching is the flip side of recruiting, so for anyone who wants to attract recruiters, social media is obviously important. For example, it's been estimated that over 90% of recruiters use LinkedIn, so use this source wisely.[139] Don't turn off recruiters with sloppy photos or writing. Do include recommendations, document your accomplishments, and (if possible) send well-crafted updates and position statements on important issues to the members of your LinkedIn groups.

Once you get an interview, acing it means knowing as much as possible about the prospective employer and what it's looking for in employees, and here social media tools are excellent sources of such information.[140] For example, you will find lists of new hires and demographic information about employees on the employer's LinkedIn site. Following the employer's official Twitter accounts and blogs can reveal things like changes in the company's strategies, as well as show you did your homework. Its executives may also have their own "unofficial" Twitter accounts and blogs. Use these for insights into the issues they face. Similarly, use other social media including Twitter to help establish your brand, for instance, by sharing relevant news.

New Web sites aim to help employers find "passive candidates," plausible candidates who aren't actively looking for jobs.[141] For example, Poacht gleans employment information from people's LinkedIn profiles (without their names or other identifying information), and asks them if they're willing to switch jobs. Switch is an app that suggests jobs to users who then swipe right or left depending on whether they're interested in the jobs.

And remember that the head of Elance (which places millions of short-term professionals via its site) says those on its site are viewed as "mobile, independent bundles of skills," so keep updating your skills and remain adaptable.[142]

Employers scour social media, so make sure your name stands out. For example, job seekers can enhance their professional reputations by creating a Twitter presence. Those "Liking" a company on Facebook may receive early notice of job openings. Spend a few minutes every day on LinkedIn making new connections, and share links and advice with those in your LinkedIn network.[143] Join LinkedIn industry groups to build visibility. Make sure your résumé is in PDF format and readable on a smart phone screen. To bring yourself to recruiters' attention, follow up on comments they make on their blogs or in industry Web sites. Fewer job searchers are using paper résumés and are instead using social résumés. *Social résumés* provide snapshots of who the job searcher is by combining text material, photos, and samples of a person's work in infographic résumés posted on social media such as Twitter, LinkedIn, and blogs.[144] Finally, remember that the prospective employer will probably Google you before extending the offer, and may ask for access to your Facebook and LinkedIn pages. ■

Online Job Boards and Employer Web Sites Most large job search sites such as Monster.com have local-area search capabilities. Useful open-job aggregator sites include Indeed.com and SimplyHired.com. Idealist.com is good for nonprofit jobs, and there's USA Jobs for federal jobs.[145] Use the *Wall Street Journal*'s career Web site (www.careerjournal.com) to search for jobs by occupation and location. Most big-city newspapers also have their own (or links to) online local job listings. In addition to job boards like Monster and specialized ones (like www. theladder.com), virtually all large companies, industries, and crafts have their own specialized sites.[146] For example, the Air Conditioning Contractors in America (www. acca.org/careers) and Financial Executives International (www.fei.org) make it easy for industry employers and prospective employees to match their needs. Remember to use mobile services, for instance, accessing jobs via the Careerbuilder iPhone portal.

Answering Advertisements Answering ads tends to be a low-probability way to get a job, and this is particularly so as the level of jobs increases. Furthermore, automated applicant tracking services now crunch through thousands of résumés in seconds, making it even harder to stand out by answering ads. Nevertheless, good sources of classified ads for professionals and managers include the *New York Times*, the *Wall Street Journal*, and specialized journals in your field that list job openings. All these sources also post the positions online, of course.

Many employers don't even accept application letters or résumés anymore. For those who do, be sure to create the right impression with the materials you submit; check the style, grammar, neatness, and so forth, and check your résumé to make sure it's geared to the job for which you are applying. In your cover letter or email, be sure to specifically address why your background and accomplishments are appropriate to the advertised position; you must respond clearly to the company's identified needs.[147]

Be careful in replying to blind ads, however (such as those with just a post office box). Some executive search firms and employers will run ads even when no position exists just to gauge the market, and there is some risk that you blunder into responding to your own firm.

Employment Agencies Agencies are especially good at placing people in jobs paying up to about $80,000, but they can be useful for higher-paying jobs as well. The employer usually pays the fees for professional and management jobs. Assuming you know the job you want, review a few back issues of your paper's Sunday classified ads and sites like LinkedIn to identify agencies that handle the positions you want. Approach three or four initially, preferably in response to specific ads, and avoid signing any contract that gives an agency the exclusive right to place you.

States' one-stop career centers can be helpful. In them, job seekers can not only apply for unemployment benefits, but also register with the state job service, talk to career counselors, use computers to write résumés and access the Internet, take tests, and use career libraries offering books and videos on various employment topics.

In some centers job hunters can make use of free computers and photocopiers to facilitate job searches.

Executive Recruiters We've seen that employers retain executive recruiters to seek out top talent for their clients; employers always pay any fees. They do not do career counseling, but if you know the job you want, it pays to contact a few (keeping in mind however that most use LinkedIn to find passive candidates). Send/email your résumé and a cover note summarizing your objective in precise terms, including job title and the size of company desired, work-related accomplishments, current salary, and salary requirements. (Beware, because some firms call themselves executive search or career consultants but do no searches: In return for an (often hefty) fee they help you manage your search. Remember that with a search firm you never pay a fee.)

Career Counselors Career counselors will not help you find a job per se; rather, they specialize in aptitude testing, career counseling, and resume preparation. They are listed under "Career Counseling" or "Vocational Guidance." Their services usually cost $450 or so and include psychological testing and interviews with an experienced career counselor. Check the firm's services, prices, and history as well as the credentials of the person you will be dealing with.

Executive Search Consultants Executive marketing consultants manage your job-hunting campaign. They generally are not recruiters and do not have jobs to fill. Depending on the services you choose, your cost will range from $600 to $5,000 or more. The process may involve months of weekly meetings. Services include résumé and letter writing, interview skill building, and developing a full job-hunting campaign. Before approaching a consultant, it's advisable to do your own self-appraisal (as explained in this appendix) and read books like Richard Bolles's *What Color Is Your Parachute?*

Also make sure to do your due diligence, and remember these consultants are not recruiters and will not get you a job—you must do the legwork. Then check the Better Business Bureau, and decide which of these firms (if any) is for you.

Writing Your Résumé Your résumé is often still an important selling document, one that can determine whether you get offered a job interview. Of course, you should not produce a slipshod résumé: Avoid overcrowded pages, difficult-to-read copies, typographical errors, and other problems of this sort. And do not use a make-do résumé. Produce a new résumé for each job you are applying for, gearing your job objective and accomplishments to the job you want. Here are some résumé pointers, as offered by employment counselor Richard Payne and other experts.[148]

Start your résumé with your name, home and e-mail address, and home or cell phone number. Next, state your *job objective*. This should summarize in one sentence the specific position you want, where you want to do it (type and size of company), and a special reason an employer might have for wanting you to fill the job. For example, "Marketing manager in a medium-size e-commerce company in a situation in which strong creative skills would be valuable."

For each of your previous jobs, write a paragraph that shows job title, whom you reported to directly and indirectly, who reported to you, how many people reported to you, the operational and human resource budgets you controlled, and what your job entailed (in one sentence).

Your accomplishments should be the heart of your résumé. These show for each of your previous jobs: (1) a concrete action you took and why you took it and (2) the specific result of your action—the "payoff." For example, "As production supervisor, I introduced a new process to replace costly hand soldering of component parts. The new process reduced assembly time per unit from 30 to 10 minutes and reduced labor costs by over 60%." Use several of these statements for each job.

Keep your résumé to 2 pages or less, and list education, military service (if any), and personal background (hobbies, interests, associations) on the last page. For most job applications today, it's important to write a résumé that is electronically readable. Many applicant tracking systems use software to scan through large numbers of résumés, screening out those that don't seem to match (often based on the absence of certain key words). Therefore present your qualifications using powerful key words appropriate to the job or jobs for which you are applying. For example, a trainer might use key words and phrases such as: *computer-based training, interactive video*, and *group facilitator*.

If you post your résumé on the Web, experts suggest taking precautions. At a minimum, date your résumé (in case it lands on your boss's desk 2 years from now). Also insert a disclaimer forbidding unauthorized transmission by headhunters; check ahead of time to see who has access to the database on which you're posting your résumé; and consider cloaking your identity by listing your capabilities but not your name or employer—just an anonymous e-mail account to receive inquiries.[149]

Online Bios Employers often encourage or require their professionals and managers to post brief biographies on corporate intranets or Web sites. These bios let other employees know about their colleagues' expertise; they can also attract recruiters' inquiries. Tips for writing such bios include:[150]

Fill it with details. "The more information you enter, the more likely a person seeking someone with your background will find you...."
Avoid touchy subjects. For example, avoid religion and politics.

Look the part. Your profile may require posting photos. If so, dress in professional attire.
Make it search friendly. Make sure your profile contains the key words you think someone searching for someone with your background and expertise would be looking for, such as *manager, supervisor*, or *engineer*.
Use abbreviations. Abbreviations are important. For example, someone searching the site might more readily punch in "MBA" than "Masters in Business Administration."
Say it with numbers. Describe specifically how your work has contributed to your current employer's and past employer's bottom lines.
Proofread. Carefully proofread your online profile, as you would your résumé.

Handling the Interview

You have done all your homework, and now you have an interview scheduled with the person who is responsible for hiring for the job you want. What must you do to excel in the interview? Here are some suggestions.

Prepare, Prepare, Prepare First, preparation is essential. Before the interview, learn all you can about the employer, the job, and the people doing the recruiting. Search the Internet (or your library) to find out what is happening in the employer's field. Who is the competition? How are they doing?

Uncover the Interviewer's Needs Spend as little time as possible answering your interviewer's first questions and as much time as possible getting the person to describe his or her needs—what the person is looking to get accomplished and the type of person needed. Use open-ended questions, such as "Could you tell me more about that?"

Relate Yourself to the Person's Needs Once you understand the person your interviewer is looking for and the sorts of problems he or she needs solved, you are in a good position to describe your own accomplishments in terms of the interviewer's needs.[151] Start by saying something like, "One of the problem areas you've indicated is important to you is similar to a problem I once faced." Then state the problem, describe your solution, and reveal the results.

Make a Good Appearance and Show Enthusiasm Appearance, a firm handshake, and visual cues such as looking the interviewer in the eyes are crucial. Remember that studies of interviews show that in almost 80% of the cases, interviewers make up their minds about the applicant during the first few moments of the interview. A good first impression may turn bad during the interview, but it is unlikely. Bad first impressions, however, are almost impossible to overcome.

11

Establishing Strategic Pay Plans

LEARNING OBJECTIVES

11-1 List the basic factors determining pay rates.

11-2 Define and give an example of how to conduct a job evaluation.

11-3 Explain in detail how to establish a market-competitive pay plan.

11-4 Explain how to price managerial and professional jobs.

11-5 Explain the difference between competency-based and traditional pay plans.

11-6 Describe the importance of total rewards for improving employee engagement.

When new airline companies entered the Indian aviation market and started hiring employees, the already existing players faced a challenge. They had to review pay plans to retain their employees. Similarly, in the grocery business in the US, when Walmart opens a store, the other stores' usual reaction is to cut costs, particularly wages and benefits. So as Wegmans Food Markets, Inc., adds more stores and increasingly competes with Walmart, its management needs to decide this: Should we cut pay to better compete based on cost, or pursue a different compensation policy?[1] We'll see how Wegmans or Indian airline companies boosted profits by raising pay or by reviewing their pay plans.

WHERE ARE WE NOW …

Once you've appraised and coached your employees, they of course expect to be paid. Prudent employers don't set pay rates arbitrarily. Each employee's pay should make sense in terms of what other employees earn, and this requires a pay plan. The main purpose of this chapter is to show you how to establish a pay plan. The main topics we cover are basic factors in determining pay rates; job evaluation methods; how to create a market-competitive pay plan; pricing managerial and professional jobs; contemporary topics in compensation; and total rewards for employee engagement. The next chapter focuses specifically on pay-for-performance and incentive plans.

Basic Factors in Determining Pay Rates

Employee compensation includes all forms of pay going to employees and arising from their employment. It has two main components, **direct financial payments** (wages, salaries, incentives, commissions, and bonuses) and **indirect financial payments** (financial benefits like employer-paid insurance and vacations).

In turn, employers can make direct financial payments to employees based on increments of time or based on performance. Time-based pay still predominates. Blue-collar, clerical workers, and informal workers (like domestic helpers) receive daily or monthly wages, for instance. Others, like managers or Web designers, tend to be salaried and paid monthly, or yearly.

The second direct payment option is to pay for performance. For example, piece-work ties compensation to the amount of production (or number of "pieces") the worker turns out. Sales commissions tie pay to sales. Many employers' pay plans combine time-based pay and incentives.

In this chapter, we explain how to formulate plans for paying employees a time-based wage or salary. Subsequent chapters cover performance-based financial incentives and bonuses (Chapter 12) and employee benefits (Chapter 13).

Several factors should influence any pay plan's design. These include strategic policy considerations, as well as equity, legal, and union considerations.

Aligning Total Rewards with Strategy

The compensation plan should first advance the firm's strategic aims—management should produce an *aligned reward strategy.* This means creating a compensation package that produces the employee behaviors the firm needs to achieve its competitive strategy.[2] Put another way, the rewards should provide a clear pathway between each reward and specific business goals.[3]

We will see that many employers formulate a total rewards strategy to support their strategic aims. *Total rewards* encompass traditional pay, incentives, and benefits, but also "rewards" such as more challenging jobs (job design), career development, and recognition.

Table 11-1 lists illustrative questions to ask when crafting a strategy-oriented pay policy.

HR in Practice at the Hotel Paris Even a casual review by Lisa Cruz and the CFO made it clear that the Hotel Paris's compensation plan wasn't designed to support the firm's new strategic goals. To see how they handled this, see the case on page 370 of this chapter.

Equity and Its Impact on Pay Rates

In studies at Emory University, researchers investigated how capuchin monkeys reacted to inequitable pay. Some monkeys got sweet grapes in return for trading pebbles; others got cucumber slices. If a monkey receiving a cucumber slice saw a neighbor get grapes, it slammed down the pebble or refused to eat.[4] It seems even lower primates may demand fair treatment in pay.

Among humans, too, *the equity theory of motivation* postulates that people are motivated to maintain a balance between what they perceive as their contributions and their rewards. Equity theory states that if a person perceives an inequity,

TABLE 11-1 Do Our Compensation Policies Support Our Strategic Aims?

- What are our strategic aims?
- What employee behaviors and skills do we need to achieve our strategic aims?
- What compensation policies and practices—salary, incentive plans, and benefits—will help to produce the employee behaviors we need to achieve our strategic aims?

a tension or drive will develop that motivates him or her to reduce the tension and perceived inequity. Research tends to support equity theory, particularly as it applies to those underpaid.[5] For example, in one study turnover of retail buyers was significantly lower when the buyers perceived fair treatment in rewards and in how employers allocated rewards.[6] Overpaying can sometimes backfire, too, perhaps "due to feelings of guilt or discomfort."[7]

In compensation, one can address *external, internal, individual*, and *procedural* equity.[8]

- ● *External equity*   refers to how a job's pay rate in one company compares to the job's pay rate in other companies.
- ● *Internal equity*   refers to how fair the job's pay rate is when compared to other jobs within the same company (for instance, is the sales manager's pay fair, when compared to what the production manager earns?).
- ● *Individual equity*   refers to the fairness of an individual's pay as compared with what his or her coworkers are earning for the same or very similar jobs within the company, based on each person's performance.
- ● *Procedural equity*   refers to the "perceived fairness of the processes and procedures used to make decisions regarding the allocation of pay."[9]

Managers use various means to address such equity issues. For example, they use salary surveys (surveys of what other employers are paying) to monitor and maintain external equity. They use job analysis and comparisons of each job ("job evaluation") to maintain internal equity. They use performance appraisal and incentive pay to maintain individual equity. And they use communications, grievance mechanisms, and employees' participation to help ensure that employees view the pay process as procedurally fair. Some firms administer attitude surveys to monitor employees' pay satisfaction. Questions typically include, "How satisfied are you with your pay?" and "What factors do you believe are used when your pay is determined?"[10]

To head off discussions that might prompt feelings of internal inequity, some firms maintain strict secrecy over pay rates, while others publicize them.[11] However, "open pay" policies can backfire. In one firm, employees vigorously opposed paying a high salary to a great candidate unless everyone else's pay went up, too, for instance.[12] As of now, the research concerning pay secrecy is inconclusive, and most employers don't have open pay policies.[13] For external equity, online pay sites like Salary.com make it easy to see what one could earn elsewhere.

Legal Considerations in Compensation

Employers do not have free reign in designing pay plans. Various laws specify things like minimum wages, overtime rates, and benefits.[14]

Code of Wages Bill, 2017   In India, wage laws have been distributed across many legislations, which was creating difficulty in their implementation. Hence, the Indian government had constituted the Second National Commission on Labor to examine the existing labor laws and practices in the country. One of its recommendations was to consolidate the existing labor laws into five comprehensive codes.[15] On 10 August 2017, the government, thus, introduced the Code of Wages Bill, 2017, with the aim to amalgamate four major wage legislations, which are: Minimum Wages Act, 1948; Payment of Wages Act, 1936; Payment of Bonus Act, 1976; and Equal Remuneration Act, 1976.[16]

A number of Indian workers are employed in the unorganized sector. The Unorganized Worker's Social Security Act, 2008, was an effort by the government to legislate social security for unorganized workers. This act has been criticized for not addressing all pressing issues (like lack of training, gender justice, and ensuing living wages) of the unorganized sector.[17] Now, a new labor code on social security and welfare has been proposed, and it's expected to address some of the issues, though more serious concerns still remain.[18]

Davis-Bacon Act (1931)
A 1931 law that sets wage rates for laborers employed by contractors working for the federal government.

Walsh-Healey Public Contract Act (1936)
A 1936 law that requires minimum wage and working conditions for employees working on any government contract amounting to more than $10,000.

KNOWLEDGE BASE

Code on Wages Bill (2017)
This is expected to amalgamate four existing Indian laws:
(a) The Minimum Wages Act, 1948, (b) The Payment of Wages Act, 1936, (c) The Payment of Bonus Act, 1976, and (d) The Equal Remuneration Act, 1976.

One familiar provision, applicable in all countries, governs *overtime pay.* It says employers must pay overtime at a rate more than regular wages. The Factories Act of 1948 (Section 59) and the Minimum Wages Act of 1948 (Section 33) prescribe double the normal rate of pay for any hour worked over 48 hours in a workweek. Thus, if a worker covered by the act works 52 hours in one week, he or she must be paid for 4 of those hours at a rate equal to one-and-a-half times the hourly or weekly base rate the person would have earned for 48 hours.[19]

KNOW YOUR EMPLOYMENT LAW

The Workday

Employers need to be vigilant about employees who arrive early or leave late, lest the extra time spent on the employer's property obligate the employer to compensate the employee for that time. In India, the Factories Act of 1947 (Section 59), the Minimum Wages Act of 1948, and the Shops and Commercial Establishments Acts as applicable in different states (for example, Section XA of Kerala State), have specified overtime payment for additional work outside normal working hours. These laws also mandate an upper limit for the number of hours that an employee can work during a month or quarter. In unionized workplaces, working hours and overtime payment are part of union-management agreements. For example, a diligent employee may get dropped off at work early and spend, say, 20 minutes before his or her day actually starts doing work-related chores such as compiling a list of clients to call that day. While there is no hard and fast rule, some courts follow the rule that employees who arrive 15 or more minutes early are presumed to be working unless the employer can prove otherwise.[20] If using time clocks, employers should always instruct employees not to clock in more than 5–10 minutes early (or out 5–10 minutes late). Smart phones give employers further reason to meticulously record workers' hours.

The Indian legislations also set a *minimum wage.* The Minimum Wages Act, 1948, sets a floor for employees covered by it (both for the central and state governments). All Indian states have their own minimum wage. The Indian minimum wage (MW) framework is very complex because of the attempt it makes to accommodate the nature of jobs and regional requirements. Thus, the MW here can be fixed by hours, days, months, or any other period (including seasons). The legislation also permits setting wages for skill levels (highly skilled, skilled, semi-skilled, and unskilled) and geographies. With so many variables to be considered, the Indian MW system is considered as the most complex MW system in the world.[21] The proposed Indian wage code (i.e., the Code of Wages) is expected to reduce the complexity to some extent. It has recommended to make the central minimum wage or national floor, currently proposed as ₹18,000 per month, across all sectors. The state governments have to abide by the central minimum, but it can declare higher MW. (Note: As on 31 August 2017, the code is yet to be approved by the Indian parliament).

In the US, the Fair Labor Standards Act (FLSA) *child labor provisions* prohibit employing minors between 16 and 18 years old in hazardous occupations, and carefully restrict employment of those under 16.

A great many employers today pay people as "independent contractors" rather than as employees. Strictly speaking, these people are like consultants, and therefore are not covered by the Factories Act or Shops and Commercial Establishments Act. Many such workers in India are covered by the Contract Labor (Regulation and Abolition Act) of 1970. The Know Your Employment Law feature nearby explains about paying this type of worker.

EXEMPT/NONEXEMPT Specific categories of employees (workmen in the Indian context) are *exempt* from many legislations, including the Industrial Disputes Act, 1947, or certain provisions of the act, and particularly from overtime provisions.

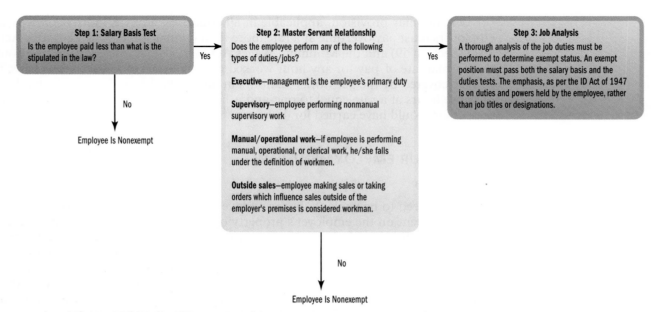

FIGURE 11-1 Who is Exempt?; Who is Not Exempt?

Source: Based on http://www.mondaq.com/india/x/434328/employee+rights+labour+relations/Workman+Under+Industrial+D isputes+Act+1947, accessed on September 3, 2017.

In the Indian context, exemptions are based on threshold wage/salary, master-servant relationship, and job characteristics or nature of job (Figure 11.1).

KNOW YOUR EMPLOYMENT LAW

The Independent Contractor in the US

Whether someone is an employee or an *independent contractor* is a continuing concern for employers.[22] For example, a federal court ruled that most of FedEx's roughly 15,000 owner-operator delivery people were independent contractors, not employees.[23]

Why claim that someone is an independent contractor? Because the FLSA's overtime and most other requirements do not apply, and the employer need not pay unemployment compensation; payroll taxes; Social Security taxes; or city, state, and federal income taxes or compulsory workers' compensation for that worker.

The problem is that many so-called independent contractor relationships aren't independent contractor relationships. In general, an individual is an independent contractor if the payer has the right to control or direct only the result of the work and not what will be done and how it will be done.[24] However, there is no single rule or test. Instead, the courts will look at the total situation. The major consideration is this: The more the employer controls what the worker does and how he or she does it, the more likely it is that the courts will find the worker to be an employee. The IRS lists rules at its Web site.[25] Uber faces lawsuits that its drivers are employees, not independent contractors.

To minimize the risks of independent contractor misclassification, employers should execute written agreements with all independent contractors; you'll find samples online.[26] Furthermore, employers should not impose work rules on or attempt to prohibit independent contractors from working for others. They should require independent contractors to provide their own tools and to be separately incorporated business entities.[27]

Because the Affordable Care Act covers employers with 50 or more employees, government agencies will be looking more closely at employers' independent contractors. To minimize problems, some employers are having staffing companies supply more of their workforce, thus staying below the 50-employee limit.[28] ∎

EQUAL REMUNERATION ACT (1979) This Indian legislation is considered as a gift of "The International Womens Year", to ensure the principle of equal pay for equal work [Section 4 (1)]. The act also mandates that women cannot be no discriminated against during recruitment (Section 5). Specifically, if the work requires equal skills, effort, and responsibility and involves similar working conditions, employees of both sexes must receive equal pay, unless the differences in pay stem from a seniority system, a merit system, the quantity or quality of production.

PAYMENT OF GRATUITY ACT (1972) Full-time employees working in firms with at least 10 employees having completed five years of service are eligible for gratuity payment. Gratuity is calculated at the rate of 15 days wages for each completed year of service. The employer is expected to arrange to pay gratuity amount within 30 days of leaving the service, from which it becomes due for payment. The proposal to raise the ceiling for gratuity to ₹20 lakh is under discussion. This has been a demand of the trade unions for a long time.

OTHER LEGISLATIONS REGARDING COMPENSATION IN INDIA Through the Employee Provident Fund Scheme, Family Pension, and Health Care and Insurance (provided by the Employees State Insurance Corporation), the Indian legislations provide for the social security of workers in the organized sector. By law, workers in the formal sector are eligible for gratuity (as per the Payment of Gratuity Act, 1972) and also for an annual bonus (according to the Payment of Bonus Act). The laws also provide compensation for workers who are affected by accidents, out of and in the course of employment. The proposed Code of Wages Bill, 2017, and Code on Social Security, 2017, are expected to consolidate the wage legislations in the country. We have also discussed features of the above laws in Chapter 2.

Union Influences on Compensation Decisions

Unions and labor relations laws also influence pay plan design. In India, the Trade Unions Act, 1926, allows workers the right to unionize and engage in collective bargaining. Historically, fixing wage rates have been one of the main issues in collective bargaining. Formal collective bargaining agreements between employers and workmen is the foundation of pay plan in India. Such agreements are found in public or formal private sector which have trade union. The following types of collective agreements happen in Indian firms.
• Agreements at industry level (like banking)
• Multi-unit agreements (one agreement for different units of the same company)
• Single company/plant/unit specific agreement, which also have legal sanctity when registered under the ID Act of 1947

In addition, wage boards and various pay commissions, as set up by the government, recommend pay scales and working conditions for specific groups. In this process, views of employee unions (if existing) or interest groups (like officers associations) are also invited.

Pay Policies

The employer's compensation strategy will manifest itself in *pay policies*. For example, a top hospital like Apollo or Aster might have a policy of paying nurses 20% above the prevailing market wage. Many Indian companies like the Tata Group, Delhi Metro Rail Corporation, and leading PSUs (like NTPC or oil companies) offer benefits, learning opportunities, and even company culture as a force to attract and retain talent. Pay policies can influence the employer's performance and profitability, as the accompanying feature on Wegmans Food Markets illustrates.

Two executives discuss a print layout; one happens to be in a wheelchair. law prohibits discrimination against qualified persons with disabilities in all aspects of employment, including compensation.

Javier Larrea/Pixtal/AGE Fotostock

Managers need pay policies on a range of issues. One is whether to emphasize *seniority* or *performance.* For example, it usually takes minimum 10 years for a faculty member in an Indian Institute of Technology (IIT) or Indian Institute of Management (IIM) to progress from Assistant Professor to full Professor of the government's pay scale. Such seniority-based pay may be advantageous to the extent that seniority is an objective standard. One disadvantage is that top performers may get the same raises as poor ones. Seniority-based pay might seem to be a relic reserved for some government agencies and unionized firms. The existing pay framework for officers of nationalized banks are divided into seven stages (JM I to TM VII), whereas board-level positions of executive directors and managing directors are separate appointments by the government. The PSUs also follow a similar system. In a shift from the current mechanism, the Indian government is thinking of allowing performing banks to have independent pay scales. However, one survey in the US found that 60% of employees responding thought high-seniority employees got the most pay. Only about 35% said their companies paid high performers more.[29]

How to distinguish between *high and low performers* is another policy issue. For example, for many years Indian companies have continued to give everyone the same raise. However, after seeing its market share drop over several years, management of various companies have decided on a turnaround strategy. This necessitated revising of compensation policies, to differentiate more aggressively between top performers and others. Other pay policies cover how to award salary increases and promotions, overtime pay, probationary pay, leaves for study, attending family functions, etc., and holidays.

▶ **IMPROVING PERFORMANCE:** *The Strategic Context*

Wegmans Food Markets

Strategic compensation management means formulating a total rewards package that produces the employee skills and behaviors that the company needs to achieve its strategic goals.

Wegmans exemplifies this. It competes in the retail food sector, where profit margins are thin and where online competitors and giants like Walmart drive costs and prices down. The usual competitor's reaction is to cut employee benefits and costs.[30] Wegmans takes a different approach. It views its workforce as an integral part of achieving Wegmans's strategic aims of *optimizing service while controlling costs by improving systems and productivity*. For example, one dairy department employee designed a new way to organize the cooler, thus improving ordering and inventory control.[31] The firm offers above-market pay rates, affordable health insurance, and a full range of employee benefits.[32] Wegmans's pay policies thus aim to produce exactly the sorts of high-productivity employee behaviors the company needs to achieve its strategic aims.

It's likely that its pay policies are one reason for Wegmans's exceptional profitability. For example, its employee turnover (about 38% for part-timers, 6%–7% for full-timers) is well below the industry's overall average of about 47%.[33] Its stores (which at about 120,000 square feet are much larger than competitors') average about $950,000 a week in sales (compared to a national average of $361,564), or about $49 million in sales annually, compared with a typical Walmart store's grocery sales of $23.5 million in sales.[34] As Wegmans's human resource head has said, good employees assure higher productivity, and that translates into better bottom-line results.[35] ■

Source: Based on Demby, "Two Stores Refused to Join the Race."; www.wegmans.com; Demby, "Two Stores Refuse to Join the Race," www.hoovers.com/company/Wegmans_Food_Markets_Inc/cfhtji-1.Html.

GEOGRAPHY   How to account for geographic differences in cost of living is another big pay policy issue. For example, the average pay for an office supervisor in the U.S. ranges from about $49,980 in Florida to $60,980 in New York.[36]

Employers handle cost-of-living differentials for transferees in several ways. One is to pay a differential for ongoing costs in addition to a one-time allocation. Paying of differential house rent allowance (HRA) is a common practice in India. This helps employees meet higher cost of housing in cities. As of 2017, the central government employees receive 24% (if residing in cities with more than 50 lakh population), 16% (if residing in cities between 5 and 50 lakh population), and 8% (if residing in cities with up to 5 lakh population) of their basic salary as HRA. Others simply raise the employee's base salary or give special allowances to take care of the cost differences. The accompanying feature on compensating expatriate employees expands on this.

▶ **IMPROVING PERFORMANCE:** *HR Practices Around the Globe*

Compensating Expatriate Employees

The question of cost-of-living differentials has particular significance to multinational firms, where pay rates range widely from, say, France to Zambia.

How should multinationals compensate expatriate employees—those it sends overseas? Two basic international compensation policies are popular: home-based and host-based plans.[37]

With a *home-based salary plan*, an international transferee's base salary reflects his or her home country's salary. The employer then adds allowances for cost-of-living differences—housing and schooling costs, for instance. This is a reasonable approach for short-term assignments, and avoids the problem of having to change the employee's base salary every time he or she moves.

In the *host-based plan*, the firm ties the international transferee's base salary to the host country's salary structure. In other words, the manager from New York who is sent to France would have his or her base salary changed to the prevailing base salary for that position in France, rather than keep the New York base salary. The firm usually tacks on cost-of-living, housing, schooling, and other allowances here as well.

Most multinational enterprises set expatriates' salaries according to the *home-based salary plan*. (Thus, a French manager assigned to Kiev by a U.S. multinational will generally have a base salary that reflects the salary structure in the manager's home country, in this case France.) In addition, the person typically gets allowances including cost-of-living, relocation, housing, education, and hardship allowances (for more challenging countries). The employer also usually pays any extra tax burdens resulting from taxes the manager is liable for over and above those he or she would have to pay in the home country. ■

Source: Based on Compensation Management.

Job Evaluation Methods

LEARNING OBJECTIVE **11-2**
Define and give an example of
how to conduct a job evaluation.

Employers use two basic approaches to setting pay rates: *market-based approaches* and *job evaluation methods*. Many firms, particularly smaller ones, simply use a *market-based* approach. Doing so involves conducting formal or informal salary surveys to determine what others in the relevant labor markets are paying for particular jobs. They then use these figures to price their own jobs. *Job evaluation methods* involve assigning values to each of the company's jobs. This process helps produce a pay plan in which each job's pay is equitable based on what other employers are paying for these jobs *and* based on each job's value to the employer.[38]

job evaluation
A systematic comparison done in order to determine the worth of one job relative to another.

Job evaluation is a formal and systematic comparison of jobs to determine the worth of one job relative to another. Job evaluation aims to determine a job's relative worth. Job evaluation eventually results in a *wage* or *salary structure* or hierarchy (this shows the pay rate for various jobs or groups of jobs). The basic principle of job evaluation is this: Jobs that require greater qualifications, more responsibilities, and more complex job duties should receive more pay than jobs with lesser requirements.[39] The basic job evaluation procedure is to compare jobs in relation to one another—for example, in terms of required effort, job complexity, and skills. Suppose you know (based on your job evaluation) the relative worth of the key jobs in your firm. You then conduct a salary survey to see what others are paying for similar jobs. By combining the information from the job evaluation and from the salary survey, you are on your way to being able to create a **market-competitive pay plan**—one where your pay rates are equitable both internally (based on each job's relative value) and externally (in other words when compared with what other employers are paying).

market-competitive pay plan
Pay plan where pay rates are equitable both internally (based on each job's relative value) and externally (in other words when compared with what other employers are paying).

Compensable Factors

You can use two basic approaches to compare the worth of several jobs. First, you might decide that one job is more important than another is, and not dig any deeper. As an alternative, you could compare the jobs by focusing on certain basic factors the jobs have in common. Compensation management specialists call these **compensable factors**. They are the factors that establish how the jobs compare to one another, and that determine the pay for each job.

compensable factor
A fundamental, compensable element of a job, such as skills, effort, responsibility, and working conditions.

The job evaluation committee typically includes at least several employees, and has the important task of evaluating the worth of each job using compensable factors.

Noel Hendrickson/Blend Images/AGE Fotostock

Some employers develop their own compensable factors. However, most U.S. companies use factors popularized by packaged job evaluation systems or by the U.S. federal legislation. For example, the Equal Pay Act in the US uses four compensable factors—skills, effort, responsibility, and working conditions. The method popularized by the Hay consulting firm emphasizes three factors: know-how, problem solving, and accountability. Walmart uses knowledge, problem-solving skills, and accountability requirements.

Choosing compensable factors plays a big role in job evaluation. You usually compare each job with all comparable jobs using the same compensable factors. However, the compensable factors you use depend on the job and the job evaluation method. For example, "decision making" might make sense for a manager's job, but not for a cleaner's job.[40]

Preparing for the Job Evaluation

Job evaluation is a judgmental process and demands close cooperation among supervisors, HR specialists, and employees and union representatives. The initial steps include identifying the need for the program, getting cooperation, and then choosing an evaluation committee. The committee then performs the actual evaluation.

Identifying the need for job evaluation shouldn't be difficult. For example, dissatisfaction reflected in high turnover, work stoppages, or arguments may result from paying employees different rates for similar jobs. Managers may express uneasiness with an informal way of assigning pay rates.

Employees may fear that a systematic evaluation of their jobs may reduce their pay rates, so *getting employees to cooperate* in the evaluation is important. For example, you can tell employees that because of the impending job evaluation program, pay rate decisions will no longer be made just by management whim, and that no current employee's rate will be adversely affected because of the job evaluation.

Finally, *choose a job evaluation committee*. The committee usually consists of about five members, most of whom are employees. Management has the right to serve on such committees, but employees may view this with suspicion. However, a human resource specialist can usually be justified to provide expert assistance. Union representation is possible. In most cases, though, the union's position is that it is accepting the results of the job evaluation only as an initial decision and is reserving the right to appeal actual job pricing decisions through grievance or bargaining channels.[41] Once appointed, each committee member should receive a manual explaining both the job evaluation process and how to conduct the job evaluation.

benchmark job
A job that is used to anchor the employer's pay scale and around which other jobs are arranged in order of relative worth.

The evaluation committee then performs three main functions. First, it usually identifies 10 or 15 key **benchmark jobs**. These will be the first jobs they'll evaluate and will serve as the anchors or benchmarks against which the relative importance or value of all other jobs is compared. Next, the committee may select *compensable factors* (although the human resources department will usually choose these). Finally, the committee performs its most important function—actually *evaluating the worth of each job*. For this, the committee will probably use one of the following methods: ranking, job classification, or point method.

Job Evaluation Methods: Ranking

ranking method
The simplest method of job evaluation that involves ranking each job relative to all other jobs, usually based on overall difficulty.

The simplest job evaluation method ranks each job relative to all other jobs, usually based on some overall factor like "job difficulty." There are several steps in the job **ranking method**.

1. *Obtain job information.* Job analysis is the first step. Here job descriptions for each job are prepared, and the information they contain about the job's duties is usually the basis for ranking jobs. (Sometimes job specifications are also prepared. However, the ranking method usually ranks jobs based on the whole job, rather than on several compensable factors. Therefore, job specifications, which tend to list job demands in terms of compensable factors such as problem solving, decision making, and skills, are not as important with ranking as they are for other job evaluation methods.)

2. *Select and group jobs.*   It is usually not practical to make a single ranking for all jobs in an organization. The usual procedure is to rank jobs by department or in clusters (such as factory workers or clerical workers). This removes the need for direct comparison of, say, factory jobs and clerical jobs.

3. *Select compensable factors.*   In the ranking method, it is common to use just one factor (such as job difficulty) and to rank jobs based on the whole job. However regardless of the number of factors you choose, explain the definition of the factor(s) to the evaluators carefully so that they all evaluate the jobs consistently.

4. *Rank jobs.*   For example, each rater gets a set of index cards, each of which contains a brief description of a job. Then they arrange these cards from lowest to highest. Some managers use an "alternation ranking method" to make this procedure more accurate. Here you take the cards, first choosing the highest and the lowest, then the next highest and next lowest, and so forth, until you've ranked all the cards. Table 11-2 illustrates such a job ranking. Jobs in this small health facility rank from orderly up to office manager. The corresponding current pay scales are shown in the column following the job titles. (After ranking, it is possible to slot additional jobs based on their difficulty between those already ranked and to assign each an appropriate wage rate.) The ranked listing of jobs enables us to compare each job's rank with its current pay, and decide if what we are currently paying is internally equitable; we may adjust a job's pay up or down, based on this. Online programs (for example, go to www.hr-guide.com, click under "Job Evaluation, Ranking," and then click "Interactive Ranking Program") can help you rank (and check the rankings of) your positions.[42]

5. *Combine ratings.*   Usually, several raters rank the jobs independently. Then the rating committee (or the employer) can simply average the raters' rankings.

6. *Compare current pay with what others are paying based on salary survey.*   Next, we show on the same table (in the middle column) what others in the community are paying for similar jobs, based on a salary survey that we conduct. This helps us ensure that our pay will be *externally* equitable.

7. *Assign a new pay scale.*   Finally, we compare what we are currently paying for each job with what others are paying, and decide (in this case) to adjust our pay scale by raising what we pay for each job. The last column therefore shows our new pay scale.

This is the simplest job evaluation method, as well as the easiest to explain. And it usually takes less time than other methods.

Drawbacks derive more from how managers use ranking than from the method itself. For example, there's a tendency to rely too heavily on "guesstimates" (of

TABLE 11-2 Job Ranking at Jackson Hospital

Ranking Order	Our Current Monthly Pay	What Others Pay: Salary Survey Pay	Our Final Assigned Pay
1. Office manager	₹43,000	₹45,000	₹44,000
2. Chief nurse	42,500	43,000	42,750
3. Accountant	34,000	36,000	35,000
4. Nurse	32,500	33,000	32,750
5. Specialist cook	31,000	32,000	31,500
6. Nurse's assistant	28,500	30,500	29,500
7. Ward assistant	5,500	7,000	7,000

Note: After ranking, it becomes possible to slot additional jobs (based on overall job difficulty, for instance) between those already ranked and to assign each an appropriate wage rate.

things like overall difficulty), since ranking usually does not use compensable factors. Similarly, ranking provides no yardstick for quantifying the value of one job relative to another. For example, job number 4 may in fact be five times "more valuable" than job number 5, but with the ranking method all you know is that one job ranks higher than the other. Ranking is usually more appropriate for small employers that can't afford the time or expense of a more elaborate method.

The *factor comparison method* is a special ranking method. It requires ranking each of a job's "factors" (such as education required, experience, and complexity), and then adding up the points representing the number of "degrees" of each factor each job has. Employers seldom use it today.

Job Evaluation Methods: Job Classification

job classification (or job grading)
A method for categorizing jobs into groups.

classes
Grouping jobs based on a set of rules for each group or class, such as amount of independent judgment, skill, physical effort, and so forth, required. Classes usually contain similar jobs.

grades
A job classification system like the class system, although grades often contain dissimilar jobs, such as secretaries, mechanics, and firefighters. Grade descriptions are written based on compensable factors listed in classification systems.

grade definition
Written descriptions of the level of, say, responsibility and knowledge required by jobs in each grade. Similar jobs can then be combined into grades or classes.

Job classification (or job grading) is a simple, widely used job evaluation method in which raters categorize jobs into groups; all the jobs in each group are of roughly the same value for pay purposes. We call these groups **classes** if they contain similar jobs, or **grades** if they contain jobs that are similar in difficulty but otherwise different. Thus, in the government's pay grade system, a "media assistant" and a "fire fighter" might both be graded "PB-2" (PB stands for "Pay Band"). On the other hand, in its job class system, the Tata Group might classify all "secretary IIs" in one class, all "maintenance engineers" in another, and so forth.

In practice, there are several ways to categorize jobs. One is to write class or grade summaries or descriptions (similar to job descriptions); you then place jobs into the classes or grades based on how well they fit these descriptions. Another is to write a set of compensable factor-based rules for each class (for instance, how much independent judgment, skill, and physical effort does the class of jobs require?). Then categorize each job according to these rules.

The usual procedure blends these two: the analysts choose compensable factors and then develop short class or grade descriptions that describe each class (or grade) in terms of the amount or level of the factors in those jobs. For example, the U.S. government's classification system uses eight compensable factors: (1) difficulty and variety of work, (2) supervision received and exercised, (3) judgment exercised, (4) originality required, (5) nature and purpose of interpersonal work relationships, (6) responsibility, (7) experience, and (8) knowledge required. Based on these compensable factors, raters write a **grade definition** like that in Figure 11-2. This one shows one grade description (for grade GS-7) for the federal government's pay grade system. Then the evaluation committee reviews all job descriptions and slots each job into its appropriate grade, by comparing each job description to the rules in each grade description. Thus, the federal government system classifies the positions *automotive mechanic, welder, electrician,* and *machinist* in grade GS-10.

The classification method has several advantages. The main one is that most employers usually end up grouping jobs into classes or grades anyway, regardless of the evaluation method they use. They do this to avoid having to price separately

FIGURE 11-2 Example of a Grade Definition

Source: From "Grade Level Guide for Clerical and Assistance Work" from U.S. Office of Personnel Management, June 1989.

Grade	Nature of Assignment	Level of Responsibility
GS-7	Performs specialized duties in a defined functional or program area involving a wide variety of problems or situations; develops information, identifies interrelationships, and takes actions consistent with objectives of the function or program served.	Work is assigned in terms of objectives, priorities, and deadlines; the employee works independently in resolving most conflicts; completed work is evaluated for conformance to policy; guidelines, such as regulations, precedent cases, and policy statements require considerable interpretation and adaptation.

dozens or hundreds of jobs. Of course, the job classification automatically groups the employer's jobs into classes. The disadvantages are that it isn't easy to write the class or grade descriptions, and considerable judgment is required to apply them. Yet many employers use this method with success.

Job Evaluation Methods: Point Method

point method

The job evaluation method in which a number of compensable factors are identified and then the degree to which each of these factors is present on the job is determined.

The **point method**'s overall aim is to determine the degree to which the jobs you're evaluating contain selected compensable factors. It involves identifying several compensable factors for the jobs, as well as the degree to which each factor is present in each job. Assume there are five degrees of the compensable factor "responsibility" a job could contain. Further, assume you assign a different number of points to each degree of each compensable factor. Once the evaluation committee determines the degree to which each compensable factor (like "responsibility" and "effort") is present in a job, it can calculate a total point value for the job by adding up the corresponding degree points for each factor. The result is a quantitative point rating for each job. The point method of job evaluation is the most popular job evaluation method today.[43]

"PACKAGED" POINT PLANS   A number of groups (such as the Hay Group) have developed standardized point plans. Many thousands of employers use these systems. They contain ready-made factor and degree definitions and point assessments for a wide range of jobs. Employers can often use them with little or no modification.

Computerized Job Evaluations

Using job evaluation methods such as the point method can be time-consuming. Accumulating the information about "how much" of each compensable factor the job contains is a tedious process. The evaluation committees must debate the level of each compensable factor in each job. They then write down their consensus judgments and compute each job's point values or rankings. Many employers therefore turn to computerized systems.

Most such computerized systems have two main components.[44] There is, first, a structured questionnaire. This contains items such as "enter total number of employees who report to this position." Second, such systems may use statistical models. These allow the computer program to price jobs more or less automatically, by assigning points based on the questionnaire responses.

Computer-aided job evaluation can streamline the job evaluation process

Source: Reprinted by permission from Computer-aided job evaluation can streamline the job evaluation process, in Screen capture: www.hrsoftware.netcgi/JobEvaluation.cgi.

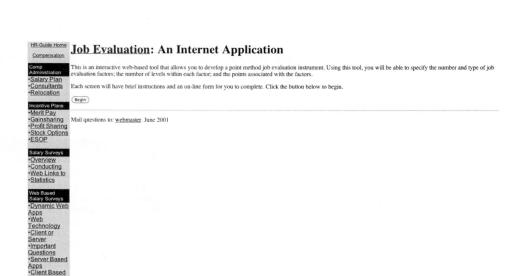

How to Create A Market-Competitive Pay Plan

LEARNING OBJECTIVE 11-3

Explain in detail how to establish a market-competitive pay plan.

As we said, many firms simply price their jobs based on what other employers are paying—they just use a market-based approach. However, most employers also base their pay plans on job evaluation methods like those just described. These evaluations assign values (such as point values) to each job. This helps to produce a pay plan in which each job's pay is internally equitable, based, as it is, on the job's value to the employer (as measured, for instance, by how many points it warrants). However, even with the job evaluation approach, managers must adjust pay rates to fit the market.[45] After all, you want employees' pay to be equitable internally—relative to what their colleagues in the firm are earning—but also competitive externally—relative to what *other employers* are paying. In a *market-competitive pay plan* a job's compensation reflects the job's value in the company, as well as what other employers are paying for similar jobs in the marketplace. Because the point method (or "point-factor method") is so popular, we'll use it as the centerpiece of our step-by-step example for creating a market-competitive pay plan.[46] The 16 steps in creating a market-competitive pay plan begin with choosing benchmark jobs.

1. Choose Benchmark Jobs

Particularly when an employer has dozens or hundreds of different jobs, it's impractical and unnecessary to evaluate each of them separately. Therefore, the first step in the point method is to select benchmark jobs. Benchmark jobs are representative of the jobs the employer needs to evaluate. Like "accounting clerk" they should be common among employers (thus making it easier to survey what competitors are paying for similar jobs).[47]

2. Select Compensable Factors

The choice of compensable factors depends on tradition (as noted, the Equal Pay Act of 1963 uses four compensable factors: skill, effort, responsibility, and working conditions), and on strategic and practical considerations. For example, if your firm's competitive advantage is quality, you might substitute "responsibility for quality" for working conditions, or simply add it as a fifth factor.[48] Similarly, using "working conditions" makes little practical sense for evaluating executive jobs.

The employer should carefully define each factor. This is to ensure that the evaluation committee members will each apply the factors with consistency. Figure 11-3 shows (on top) one such definition, in this case for the factor job complexity. The human resource specialist often draws up the definitions.

3. Assign Weights to Compensable Factors

Having selected compensable factors, the next step is to determine the relative importance (or weighting) of each factor (for instance, how much more important is "skill" than "effort"?). This is important because for each cluster of jobs some factors are bound to be more important than others are. Thus, for executive jobs the "mental requirements" factor would carry far more weight than would "physical requirements." To assign weights, we assume we have a total 100 percentage points to allocate for each job. Then (as an illustration), assign percentage weights of 60% for the factor job complexity, 30% for effort, and 10% for working conditions.[49]

4. Convert Percentages to Points for Each Factor

Next, we want to convert the percentage weights assigned to each compensable factor into point values for each factor (this is, after all, the point method). It is traditional to assume we are working with a total of 1,000 points (although one could use some other figure). To convert percentages to points for each compensable factor, *multiply the percentage weight for each compensable factor (from the previous step) by 1,000.*[50]

Factor Definition: What Is Job Complexity? Job complexity generally refers to the amount of judgment, initiative, ingenuity, and complex data analysis that doing the job requires. To what extent does the person doing this job confront unfamiliar problems, deal with complex decisions, and have to exercise discretion?

Degree	Points	Job Complexity Degree Definitions: What to Look for in the Job
First	120	Here the job is routine and consists of repetitive operations requiring little or no choice of action and the automatic application of easily understood rules and procedures. For example, a filing clerk.
Second	240	Here the employee follows detailed instructions but may have to make limited decisions based on previously prescribed instructions which lay our prescribed alternatives. For example, a billing clerk or a receptionist.
Third	360	Here the employee again follows detailed instructions but because the number of matters to consider is more varied the employee needs to exhibit initiative and independent judgment, under direct supervision. For example, a nurse's aide.
Fourth	480	Here the employee can generally follow standard practices but the presence of nonroutine problems requires that the employee be able to use initiative and judgment to analyze and evaluate situations, possibly modifying the standard procedures to adjust to the new situations. For example, a nurse.
Fifth	600	On this job, the employee needs to use independent judgment and plan and perform complex work under only general supervision, often working independently toward achieving overall results. For example, medical intern.

This will tell you the *maximum number of points* for each compensable factor. Doing so in this case would translate into $1{,}000 \times 0.60 = 600$ possible points for job complexity, $1{,}000 \times 0.30 = 300$ points for effort, and $1{,}000 \times 0.10 = 100$ points for working conditions.

5. Define Each Factor's Degrees

Next, split each factor into degrees, and define (write degree definitions for) each degree so that raters may judge the amount or degree of a factor existing in a job. Thus, for a compensable factor such as "job complexity" you might choose to have five degrees, ranging from "here the job is routine" to "uses independent judgment." (Our definitions for each degree are shown in Figure 11-3 under "Job Complexity Degree Definitions: What to Look For in the Job.") The number of degrees usually does not exceed five or six, and the actual number depends mostly on judgment. Thus, if all employees work either in a quiet, air-conditioned office or in a noisy, hot factory, then two degrees would probably suffice for the factor "working conditions." You need not have the same number of degrees for each factor, and you should limit degrees to the number necessary to distinguish among jobs.

6. Determine for Each Factor Its Factor Degrees' Points

The evaluation committee must be able to determine the number of points each job is worth. To do this, the committee must be able to examine each job and (from each factor's degree definitions) *determine what degree of each compensable factor*

TABLE 11-3 **Points Assigned to Factors and to Their Degrees (Revised)**

Factors	First-Degree Points	Second-Degree Points	Third-Degree Points	Fourth-Degree Points	Fifth-Degree Points
Job complexity (Total maximum points equal 600)	120	240	360	480	600
Effort (Total maximum points equal 300)	60	120	180	240	300
Working conditions (Total maximum points equal 100 points)	20	40	60	80	100

that job has. For them to do this, we must first assign points to *each degree of each compensable factor*. For example, in our illustration, we have five possible degrees of job complexity, and the job complexity compensable factor is worth up to 600 points maximum. In our case, we simply decide that the first degree level of job complexity is worth 120 (or one-fifth of 600) points, the second degree level is worth 240 points, the third degree level is worth 360 points, the fourth degree level is worth 480 points, and the fifth degree is worth the maximum 600 points (see Figure 11-3).[51] Do this for each factor (as in Table 11-3).

7. Review Job Descriptions and Job Specifications

The heart of job *evaluation* involves determining the amount or degree to which the job contains the selected compensable factors such as effort, job complexity, and working conditions. The team conducting the job evaluation will frequently do so by first reviewing each job's job description and job specification. As we explained in Chapter 4 (Job Analysis), it is through the job analysis that the manager identifies the job's duties and responsibilities and writes the job description and job specification. Ideally therefore, the job analyst included in the job description and specification information about the compensable factors (such as job complexity) around which the employer plans to build its compensation plan.[52]

8. Evaluate the Jobs

Steps 1–7 provide us with the information (for instance, on points and degrees) based on which we can evaluate the jobs. The committee has now gathered the job descriptions and job specifications for the benchmark jobs they will focus on.

Then, from their review of each job description and job specification, the committee *determines the degree to which each compensable factor is present in each job*. Thus for, say, a job of master mechanic, the team might conclude (after studying the job description and job specification) that the master mechanic's job deserves the third degree level of *job complexity* points, the first degree level of *effort*, and the first degree level of *working conditions*.

Knowing the job complexity, effort, and working conditions degrees for each job, *and knowing the number of points we previously assigned to each degree* of each compensable factor, we can now determine how many job complexity, effort, and working conditions points each benchmark job should contain. (We know the degree level for each factor for each job, so we merely check the corresponding points (see Table 11-3) that we previously assigned to each of these degrees.)

Finally, we add up these degree points for each job to determine each job's total number of points.[53] The master mechanic job gets 360 + 60 + 20 = 440 points from Table 11-3. This enables us to list a hierarchy of jobs, based upon each job's points. We can soon turn to assigning wage rates to each job (step 9). But first, we should define market-competitive pay plan and wage curve.

FIGURE 11-4 **Plotting a Wage Curve**

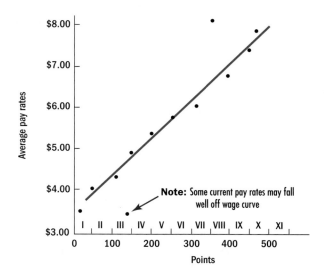

market-competitive pay system

A pay system in which the employer's actual pay rates are competitive with those in the relevant labor market.

wage curve

Shows the relationship between the value of the job and the average wage paid for this job.

What should the pay rate be for each job? Of course, jobs with more points should command higher pay. The question is what pay rate to use. Our company's current, "internal" pay rates? Or pay rates based on what the "external" market is paying?[54]

With a **market-competitive pay system**, the employer's actual pay rates are competitive with those in the relevant labor market, as well as equitable internally.[55] Put simply, the basic approach is to compare what the employer is *currently* paying for each job ("internal pay") with what the market is paying for the same or similar job ("external pay"), and then to combine this information to produce a market-competitive pay system.

WAGE CURVES   Wage curves play a central role in assigning wage rates to jobs. The wage curve typically shows the pay rates paid for jobs, relative to the points or rankings assigned to each job by the job evaluation. Figure 11-4 presents an example. Note that it shows pay rates for jobs on the vertical axis, and point values for these jobs along the horizontal axis. The purpose of the wage curve is to show the relationships between (1) the value of the job (expressed in points) as determined by one of the job evaluation methods and (2) the pay rates for the job. (We'll see that many employers may combine jobs into classes or grades. Here the wage curve would show the relationship between average pay rates for each grade, and each grade's average point value.) The pay rates on the wage curve are traditionally those now paid by the employer. However, if there is reason to believe the current pay rates are out of step with the market rates for these jobs, the employer will have to adjust them. One way to do this is to compare a wage curve that shows the jobs' *current* wage rates relative to the jobs' points, with a second curve that shows *market* wage rates relative to points. We do this as follows.

9. Draw the Current (Internal) Wage Curve

First, to study how each job's points relates to its current pay rate, we start by drawing an *internal wage curve*. Plotting each job's points and the wage rate the employer is now paying for each job (or wage rates, if there are several for each job) produces a scatter plot as in Figure 11-5 (left). We now draw a wage curve (on the right) through these plots that shows how point values relate to current wage rates. We can draw this wage line by just estimating a line that best fits the plotted points (by minimizing the distances between the plots and the curve). Or we can use regression, a statistical technique. Using the latter will produce a current/internal wage curve that best fits the plotted points. In any case, we show the results in Figure 11-5 (right).[56]

**FIGURE 11-5 The Current/
Internal Wage Curve**

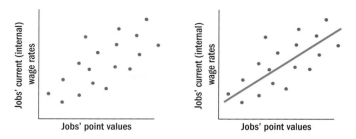

10. Conduct a Market Analysis: Salary Surveys

salary survey
A survey aimed at determining prevailing wage rates. A good salary survey provides specific wage rates for specific jobs. Formal written questionnaire surveys are the most comprehensive, but telephone surveys and newspaper ads are also sources of information.

Next, we must compile the information needed to draw an *external wage curve* for our jobs, based on what other employers are paying for similar jobs. **Salary surveys**—surveys of what others are paying—play a big role in pricing jobs.[57] Employers use salary surveys in three ways. First, they use survey data to price benchmark jobs. Benchmark jobs are the anchor jobs around which they slot their other jobs, based on each job's relative worth to the firm. Second, employers typically price 20% or more of their positions directly in the marketplace (rather than relative to the firm's benchmark jobs), based on a survey of what comparable firms are paying for comparable jobs. (Google might do this for jobs like systems engineer, whose salaries fluctuate widely and often.) Third, surveys also collect data on benefits like insurance, sick leave, and vacations for decisions regarding employee benefits.

Salary surveys can be formal or informal. *Informal* phone or Internet surveys are good for checking specific issues, such as when a bank wants to confirm the salary at which to advertise a newly open teller's job, or whether some banks are really paying tellers an incentive. Some large employers can afford to send out their own *formal* surveys to collect compensation information from other employers. These ask about things like number of employees, overtime policies, starting salaries, and paid vacations.

Many employers use surveys published by consulting firms, professional associations, or government agencies. For example, the U.S. Department of Labor's Bureau of Labor Statistics' (BLS) *National Compensation Survey (NCS)* provides comprehensive reports of occupational earnings, compensation cost trends, and benefits (www.bls.gov/bls/wages.htm). The salary comparison website, Paycheck. in, allows individuals to check salary ranges of occupations using its salary checker (http://www.paycheck.in/main/salary/salary-checker-1). PayCheck also has a minimum wage checker that allows checking official MW rates of the Center and the states (http://www.paycheck.in/main/salary/minimumwages).

In PayCheck India Project's national compensation survey, detailed occupational earnings are available through salary checker. Paycheck India also maintains a minimum wage database, where central and state minimum wages can be accessed free of cost.

Private consulting and/or executive recruiting companies like Hay & Associates, Towers Watson Global Data Services, and Aon/Hewitt (www.aon.com) publish data covering compensation for top and middle management and members of boards of directors. In the US, professional organizations like the Society for Human Resource Management and the Financial Executives Institute publish surveys of compensation practices among members of their associations.[58]

USING THE INTERNET TO DO COMPENSATION SURVEYS Internet-based options makes it easy for anyone to access published compensation survey information. Table 11-4 shows some popular salary survey Web sites.

Many of these sites, such as Paycheck.in, provide national salary levels for jobs that the site then arithmetically adjusts to each locale based on cost-of-living formulas. PayCheck India is a part of the global WageIndicator project (www.wageindicator.org), where salaries of more than 70 countries are collected and compared. In India,

TABLE 11-4 Some Pay Data Web Sites

Sponsor	Internet Address	What It Provides	Downside
Salary.com	www.salary.com	Salary by job and ZIP code, plus job and description, for hundreds of jobs	Adapts national averages by applying local cost-of-living differences
PayCheck India	www.paycheck.in	Salaries and wages for multiple Indian jobs, by location	Limited to Indian jobs based on voluntary web survey
Job Star	http://jobstar.org/tools/salary/sal-prof.php	Profession-specific salary surveys	Necessary to review numerous salary surveys for each profession

PayCheck has been active since 2007, and IIMA is the research partner to collect real-time picture of what employers in the region are actually paying for, say, accounting clerks, it's useful to access the online Internet sites of one or two of your local newspapers, or check the classified advertisement columns.

11. Draw the Market (External) Wage Curve

The current/internal wage curve from step 9 is helpful. For example showing, as it does, how a job's current pay rate compares with its points helps the employer identify jobs for which pay rates are currently too high or too low, relative to other jobs in the company. (For example, if a job's current wage rate is well above the internal wage curve, it suggests that the present wage rate for that job is inequitably high, given the number of points we've assigned to that job.)

What the current (internal) wage curve does *not* reveal is whether our pay rates are too high, too low, or just right relative to what other firms are paying. For this, we need to draw a *market* or *external wage* curve.

To draw the market/external wage curve, we produce a scatter plot and wage curve as in Figure 11-6 (left and right). However, instead of using our firm's current wage rates, we use market wage rates (obtained from salary surveys). The market/external wage curve thereby compares our jobs' points with market pay rates for our jobs.

12. Compare and Adjust Current and Market Wage Rates for Jobs

How different are the market rates other employers are paying for our jobs and the current rates we are now paying for our jobs? To determine this, we combine both the current/internal and market/external wage curves on one graph, as in Figure 11-7. The market wage curve might be higher than our current wage curve (suggesting that our current pay rates may be too low), or below our current wage curve (suggesting that our current wage rates might be too high). Or perhaps market wage rates are higher for some of our jobs and lower for others.[59]

FIGURE 11-6 **The Market/ External Wage Curve**

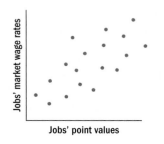

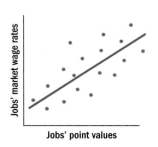

FIGURE 11-7 **Plotting Both the Market and Internal Wage Curves**

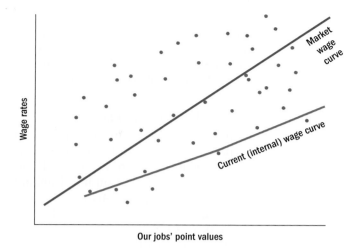

FIGURE 11-8 **Wage Structure**

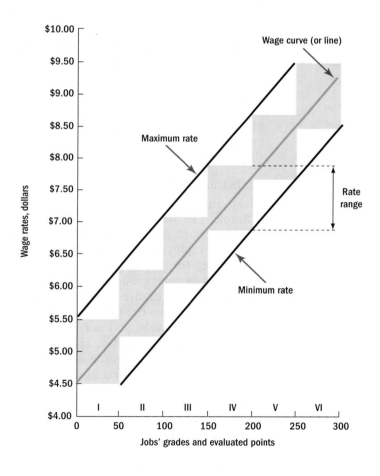

Based on comparing the current/internal wage curve and market/external wage curve in Figure 11-7, we must decide whether to adjust the current pay rates for our jobs, and if so how. This calls for a policy decision by management. Strategic considerations influence this decision. Do our strategic aspirations suggest we should pay more, the same, or less than competitors? For example, we might decide to move our current internal wage curve up (and thereby give everyone a raise), or down (and thereby perhaps withhold pay increases for some time), or adjust the slope of the internal wage curve to increase what we pay for some jobs and decrease what we pay for others. In any case, the wage curve we end up with (the orange line in Figure 11-8) should now be equitable internally (in terms of the point value of each job) and equitable externally (in terms of what other firms are paying).[60]

13. Develop Pay Grades

Employers typically group similar jobs (in terms of points) into grades for pay purposes. Then, instead of having to deal with hundreds of job rates, you might only have to focus on, say, pay rates for 10 or 12 pay grades. For example, Serco, a s ervices firm which operates a London, England, light railway system, set up pay grades after ranking jobs using a system based on knowledge, management complexity, and the job's magnitude and impact on the organization.[61]

pay (or wage) grade
A pay grade is composed of jobs of approximately equal difficulty.

A **pay (or wage) grade** is composed of jobs of approximately equal difficulty or importance as determined by job evaluation. If you used the point method of job evaluation, the pay grade consists of jobs falling within a range of points. If the ranking method was used, the grade consists of a specific number of ranks. If you use the classification system, then your jobs are already categorized into classes (or grades).

DETERMINING THE NUMBER OF PAY GRADES   It is standard to establish grades of equal point spread. (In other words, each grade might include all those jobs falling between 50 and 100 points, 100 and 150 points, 150 and 200 points, etc.) Since each grade is the same width, the main issue involves determining how many grades to have. There doesn't seem to be any optimal number, although 10 to 16 grades for a given job cluster (shop jobs, clerical jobs, etc.) seems to be common. You need more pay grades if there are, say, 1,000 jobs to be graded than if there are only 100.

14. Establish Rate Ranges

Most employers do not pay just one rate for all jobs in a particular pay grade. For example, GE Medical won't want to pay all its accounting clerks, from beginners to long tenure, at the same rate, even though they may all be in the same pay grade. Instead, employers develop vertical pay (or "rate") ranges for each of the horizontal pay grades (or pay classes). These **pay (or rate) ranges** often appear as vertical boxes within each grade, showing minimum, maximum, and midpoint pay rates for that grade, as in Figure 11-8. (Specialists call this graph a *wage structure*. Figure 11-8 graphically depicts the range of pay rates—in this case, per hour—paid for each pay grade.) Alternatively, you may depict the pay range for each class or grade as steps in a table, as in Table 11-5. Here you will have specific corresponding pay rates for each step within each grade in tabular form. Thus, Table 11-5 shows the pay rates and steps for most federal government grades. As of the time of this pay schedule, for instance, employees in positions classified in grade GS-10 could be paid annual salaries between $46,691 and $60,695, depending on the level or step at which they were hired into the grade, the amount of time they were in the grade, and any merit increases they've received.

pay (or rate) ranges
A series of steps or levels within a pay grade, usually based upon years of service.

DEVELOPING RATE RANGES   As in Figure 11-8, the wage curve usually anchors the average pay rate for each vertical pay range. The firm might then arbitrarily decide on a maximum and minimum rate for each grade, such as 15% above and below the wage curve. As an alternative, some employers allow the pay range for each grade to become taller (they include more pay rates) for the higher pay ranges, reflecting the greater demands and performance variability inherent in more complex jobs. As in Figure 11-8, most employers structure their rate ranges to overlap a bit, so an employee in one grade who has more experience or seniority may earn more than would someone in an entry-level position in the next higher pay grade.[62]

TABLE 11-5 Illustrative case of U.S. Federal Government.

SALARY TABLE 2015-GS
INCORPORATING THE 1% GENERAL SCHEDULE INCREASE
EFFECTIVE JANUARY 2015

Annual Rates by Grade and Step

Grade	Step 1	Step 2	Step 3	Step 4	Step 5	Step 6	Step 7	Step 8	Step 9	Step 10	Within Grade Amounts
1	$ 18,161	$ 18,768	$ 19,372	$ 19,973	$ 20,577	$ 20,931	$ 21,528	$ 22,130	$ 22,153	$ 22,712	Varies
2	20,419	20,905	21,581	22,153	22,403	23,062	23,721	24,380	25,039	25,698	Varies
3	22,279	23,022	23,765	24,508	25,251	25,994	26,737	27,480	28,223	28,966	743
4	25,011	25,845	26,679	27,513	28,347	29,181	30,015	30,849	31,683	32,517	834
5	27,982	28,915	29,848	30,781	31,714	32,647	33,580	34,513	35,446	36,379	933
6	31,192	32,232	33,272	34,312	35,352	36,392	37,432	38,472	39,512	40,552	1,040
7	34,662	35,817	36,972	38,127	39,282	40,437	41,592	42,747	43,902	45,057	1,155
8	38,387	39,667	40,947	42,227	43,507	44,787	46,067	47,347	48,627	49,907	1,280
9	42,399	43,812	45,225	46,638	48,051	49,464	50,877	52,290	53,703	55,116	1,413
10	46,691	48,247	49,803	51,359	52,915	54,471	56,027	57,583	59,139	60,695	1,556
11	51,298	53,008	54,718	56,428	58,138	59,848	61,558	63,268	64,978	66,688	1,710
12	61,486	63,536	65,586	67,636	69,686	71,736	73,786	75,836	77,886	79,936	2,050
13	73,115	75,552	77,989	80,426	82,863	85,300	87,737	90,174	92,611	95,048	2,437
14	86,399	89,279	92,159	95,039	97,919	100,799	103,679	106,559	109,439	112,319	2,880
15	101,630	105,018	108,406	111,794	115,182	118,570	121,958	125,346	128,734	132,122	3,388

Source: From Salary table 2015-gs Incorporating the 1% general schedule increase Effective january 2015, from http://www.opm.gov/policy-data-oversight/pay-leave/salaries-wages/salary-tables/pdf/2015/GS.pdf.

There are several reasons to use pay ranges for each pay grade. First, it lets the employer take a more flexible stance in the labor market. For example, it makes it easier to attract experienced, higher-paid employees into a pay grade at the top of the range, since the starting salary for the pay grade's lowest step may be too low to attract them. Pay ranges also let companies provide for performance differences between employees within the same grade or between those with different seniorities.

Compensation experts sometimes use *compa ratios*. The **compa ratio** equals an employee's pay rate divided by the pay range midpoint for his or her pay grade. A compa ratio of 1 means the employee is being paid exactly at the pay range midpoint. If the compa ratio is above 1 then the person's pay rate exceeds the midpoint pay for the job. If it is below then the pay rate is less than the midpoint. The compa ratio can help reveal how many jobs in each pay grade are paid above and below competitive market pay rates.[63]

compa ratio
Equals an employee's pay rate divided by the pay range midpoint for his or her pay grade.

15. Address Remaining Jobs

To this point, we have focused our job evaluation on a limited number of benchmark jobs, as is traditional. We now want to add our remaining jobs to the wage structure. We can do this in two ways. We can evaluate each of the remaining jobs using the same process we just went through. Or we can simply slot the remaining jobs into the wage structure where we feel they belong, without formally evaluating and assigning points to these jobs. Jobs similar enough to our benchmark jobs we can easily slot into the wage structure. Jobs we're not sure about should undergo the same job evaluation process; we assign points to them and precisely slot them into the wage structure.[64]

16. Correct Out-of-Line Rates

Finally, the wage rate the firm is now paying for a particular job may fall well off the wage curve or well outside the rate range for its grade, as illustrated in Figure 11-4 (page 352). This means that the average pay for that job is currently too high or too low, relative to other jobs in the firm. For underpaid jobs, the solution is clear: Raise the wages of underpaid employees to the minimum of the rate range for their pay grade.

Current pay rates falling above the rate range are a different story. These are "red circle," "flagged," or "overrates." There are several ways to cope with this problem. One is to freeze the rate paid to these employees until general salary increases bring the other jobs into line. A second option is to transfer or promote the employees involved to jobs for which you can legitimately pay them their current pay rates. The third option is to freeze the rate for 6 months, during which time you try to transfer or promote the overpaid employees. If you cannot, then cut the rate you pay these employees to the maximum in the pay range for their pay grade. The accompanying HR Tools feature explains a streamlined pay plan procedure for small businesses.

▶ **IMPROVING PERFORMANCE:** *HR Tools for Line Managers and Small Businesses*

Developing a Workable Pay Plan

Pay plans are as important for small firms as a large ones. Pay that is too high wastes money; too low triggers turnover; and internally inequitable causes endless demands for raises. The owner who wants to concentrate on major issues like sales needs a rational pay plan.

Surveying market rates come first. Sites like LinkedIn and Salary.com will show localized average pay rates for jobs in your geographic area. The Sunday newspaper classified ads (online and offline) will contain information on wages offered for jobs similar to those you're trying to price. Local job service "one-stop" offices can provide a wealth of information, as they compile extensive information on pay ranges and averages for many jobs. Employment agencies, always anxious to form ties with employers, will provide good data. Local college and university career centers will reveal prevailing pay rates for many jobs. Professional associations (such as the careers link for civil engineers at www.asce.org) are good sources of professionals' pay rates.

Smaller firms are making use of the Internet in other ways. StockHouse Media Corp (www.stockhouse.com) uses the Web for determining salaries for all the firm's personnel. For example, the HR manager surfs the Web to monitor rates and trends by periodically checking job boards, company Web sites, LinkedIn, and industry associations.[65]

If you employ more than 20 employees or so, conduct at least a rudimentary job evaluation (probably using the ranking method we covered on pages 345–347). You will need job descriptions (see, for example O*NET and jobdescription.com), since these will be the source of data regarding the nature and worth of each job.

You may find it easier to split your employees into three clusters—say, managerial/professional, office/clerical, and plant personnel. For each of the three groups, choose one or more compensable factors. Then rank (or assign points to) each job in that cluster based on, say, a ranking job evaluation. For each job you will then want to create a pay range. In general, you might choose as the midpoint of that range the average market salary for that job, or an average of the market rate and what you are currently paying. Then produce a total range of about 30% around this average, broken into five steps. (Thus, assemblers, one of the plant personnel jobs, might earn from $8.00 to $12.60 per hour, in five steps.)

Required compensation policies will include amount of holiday and vacation pay (as we explain in Chapter 13), overtime pay policy, method of pay (weekly, biweekly, monthly), garnishments, and time card or sign-in sheet procedures. Many examples are available online.[66] ∎

Pricing Managerial and Professional Jobs

LEARNING OBJECTIVE **11-4**
Explain how to price managerial and professional jobs.

Developing compensation plans for managers or professionals is similar in many respects to developing plans for any employee. The basic aim is the same: to attract, motivate, and retain good employees. And job evaluation is about as applicable to managerial and professional jobs (below the top executive levels) as to production and clerical ones.

There are some big differences though. Managerial jobs tend to stress harder-to-quantify factors like judgment and problem solving more than do production and clerical jobs. There is also more emphasis on paying managers and professionals based on their performance or on what they can do, rather than on static job demands like working conditions. And one must compete in the marketplace for executives who sometimes have rock star pay. So, job evaluation, although still important for management jobs, usually plays a secondary role to issues like bonuses, incentives, market rates, and benefits.

What Determines Executive Pay?

The traditional wisdom is that company size and performance significantly affect top managers' salaries. Yet early studies showed that these explained only about 30% of CEO pay: "In reality, CEO pay is set by the board taking into account a variety of factors such as the business strategy, corporate trends, and most importantly where they want to be in a short and long term."[67] One study concluded that three main factors, *job complexity* (span of control, the number of functional divisions over which the executive has direct responsibility, and management level), the employer's *ability to pay* (total profit and rate of return), and the executive's *human capital* (educational level, field of study, work experience), accounted for about two-thirds of executive compensation variance.[68] In practice, CEOs exercise influence over their boards of directors, so their pay sometimes doesn't reflect strictly arms-length negotiations.[69]

Many employers do use job evaluation for pricing managerial jobs (at least, below the top jobs). The basic approach is to classify executive and management positions into grades, each with a salary range.

As with nonmanagerial jobs, one alternative is to rank the executive and management positions in relation to each other, then group into classes those of similar value. However, firms also use the job classification and point methods, with compensable factors like position scope, complexity, and difficulty. As with any jobs, job analysis, salary surveys, and the fine-tuning of salary levels around wage curves play roles.

Shareholder activism and government oversight have tightened the restrictions on what companies pay top executives. For example, the banking giant HSBC shelved plans to raise its CEO's pay by over a third after shareholders rejected the proposals.[70]

Compensating Executives

Compensation for a company's top executives usually consists of four main elements.[71] *Base pay* includes the person's fixed salary as well as, often, guaranteed bonuses such as "10% of pay at the end of the fourth fiscal quarter, regardless of whether the company makes a profit." *Short-term incentives* are usually cash or stock bonuses for achieving short-term goals, such as year-to-year sales revenue increases. *Long-term incentives* aim to encourage the executive to take actions that drive up the value of the company's stock and include things like stock options; these generally give the executive the right to purchase stock at a specific price for a specific period. Finally, *executive benefits and perks* include things such as supplemental executive retirement pension plans. With so many complicated elements, employers must also be alert to the tax and securities law implications of their executive compensation decisions.[72]

Salary is traditionally the cornerstone of executive compensation. On it, employers layer benefits, incentives, and perquisites—all normally conferred in proportion to base pay. Procter & Gamble Co.'s CEO was paid $15.2 million recently, including a base salary of $1.6 million, a cash-based bonus of $2.4 million, stock options valued at $4.4 million, stock awards of $6.45 million, plus perks such as air travel.[73] Top executive compensation packages can be whoppers. The CEO of Oracle earned just over $96 million in one recent year, and the CEO of Walt Disney Corporation $37.1 million.[74] But overpaid as many critics may think they are, one expert says CEOs with the highest 20% of compensation produced stock returns 60% greater than those of other firms in their industries.[75]

Executive compensation emphasizes performance (discussed in Chapter 12) more than do other employees' pay plans, since organizational results reflect executives' contributions more directly than those of lower-echelon employees.[76] Indeed, boards are boosting the emphasis on performance-based pay (in part due to shareholder activism). The big issue here is identifying the appropriate performance measures. Typical short-term measures include revenue growth and operating profit margin. Long-term measures include rate of return above some predetermined base.

Executive Compensation in India

In Indian public-limited companies, law of the land has limited the payment of top management, but there has always been a debate about excessive payouts. Earlier, the Companies Act of 1956, which regulated top executive (i.e., director) compensation, had specified the framework for remuneration of top executives of Indian companies. Till 1991, an upper ceiling of ₹15,000 per month existed for top managerial remuneration. Similarly, there were caps on profit sharing and perquisites payable. The limits were later relaxed. However, the act was reworked, and a new version came into effect in 2013.

The Companies Act, 2013, has addressed a few contentious issues related to top management compensation. It specifies that every listed company has to constitute a nomination and remuneration committee. This committee has the mandate to ensure that the level and structure of compensation is such that it's able to attract, retain, and motivate directors. The law also mandates that there should be a balance between fixed and performance components in the remuneration paid to directors, key management personnel, and senior managers. The payment has to reflect the short- and long-term performance requirements of companies. The board has to approve the compensation policy, which is expected to bring in much required transparency and good governance.

Compensating Professional Employees

In compensating professionals, employers should first ensure that the person is actually a "professional". High compensation paid to professional managers has been a matter of concern in India. When Infosys appointed a new CEO, Vishal Sikka, from outside the company, his compensation package made headlines.[77] Later, when the board revised the top management compensation, the founders and other activists raised governance issues. Another point of contention was the high severance pay awarded to the previous CFO. Eventually, it led to resignations of board members, including the Chairman and the CEO.[78] In the US, the Fair Labor Standards Act "provides an exemption from both minimum wage and overtime pay for employees employed as bona fide executive, administrative, professional and outside sales employees."[79]

Beyond that, compensating professional employees like engineers presents unique problems.[80] Analytical jobs emphasize compensable factors such as creativity and problem solving, ones not easily compared or measured. Furthermore, how do you measure performance? For example, the success of an engineer's design depends on how the firm develops and markets it.

Employers can use job evaluation for professional jobs. Compensable factors here tend to focus on problem solving, creativity, job scope, and technical knowledge and expertise. Firms use the point method and job classification.

Yet, in practice, firms rarely rely on just job evaluation for pricing professional jobs. Factors like creativity (as noted) are hard to measure, and non-pay issues often influence professionals' job decisions. For example, a few years ago Google raised its employees' salaries by 10% in the face of defections by even their highest-paid professionals, such as the head of its Chrome OS team, to Facebook.[81] Many of these Google professionals, although well paid by most standards, still felt underpaid. Some moved to jobs they hoped would have more challenges. Others may have sought younger firms with new stock options.

Most employers therefore emphasize a market-pricing approach for these jobs. They price professional jobs in the marketplace as best they can, to establish the values for benchmark jobs. Then they slot these benchmark jobs and their other professional jobs into a salary structure. Each professional discipline (such as engineer) usually ends up having four to six grade levels, each with a broad salary range. This helps employers remain competitive when bidding for professionals who literally have global employment possibilities.[82]

Improving Performance Through HRIS: Payroll Administration

Payroll administration is one of the first functions most employers computerize or outsource, and for good reason. Administering the payroll system—keeping track of each employee's FLSA worker status, wage rate, dependents, benefits, overtime, tax status, and so on; computing each paycheck; and then directing the actual printing of checks or direct deposits is a time-consuming task, one complicated by the need to comply with many federal, state, and local wage, hour, and other laws.

Many employers do perform this function in-house, usually with a payroll processing software package. ZingHR, a cloud-based HR software application, has a payroll system that allows flexibility for employers.

On the other hand, many employers do outsource payroll administration to vendors like Husys which is an Indian service provider catering to small and medium enterprises. Many entrepreneurs and accounting firms also provide payroll services such as ADP. These vendors offer a range of payroll processing options. For instance, smaller employers may opt to call in their payroll data to the vendor's specialists, while larger ones may have this data processed automatically online. In deciding which vendor to use, the employer should consider its goals and the potential economic benefits, as well as factors such as the vendor's reputation. SHRM in the US recommends evaluating the initial list of prospective vendors based on the employer's goals for the relationship. Don't just consider the relative economic benefits of outsourcing the function (rather than doing it in-house), but also the desirability of integrating the employer's internal systems with the vendor's, streamlining tax compliance and filings, and increasing employee self-service.[83] ■

LEARNING OBJECTIVE **11-5**

Explain the difference between competency-based and traditional pay plans.

Contemporary Topics in Compensation

In this final section, we'll look at five important contemporary compensation topics: competency-based pay, broadbanding, comparable worth, board oversight of executive pay, and total rewards.

Competency-Based Pay

Some managers question whether job evaluations that slot jobs into narrow cubbyholes ("Machinist I," "Machinist II," and so on) might not actually be counterproductive. For example, high-performance work systems depend on flexible multiskilled job assignments and on teamwork, and there's no place here for employees to say, "That's not my job."

Many employers, such as General Mills, pay certain workers based on attained skill levels.

Mark Richard/PhotoEdit, Inc.

competency-based pay
Where the company pays for the employee's range, depth, and types of skills and knowledge, rather than for the job title he or she holds.

Competency-based pay aims to avoid that problem.[84] With competency (generally skill or knowledge-based) pay, you pay the employee for the skills and knowledge he or she is capable of using rather than for the responsibilities or title of the job currently held.[85] Experts variously call this competence-, knowledge-, or skill-based pay. With competency-based pay, an employee in a class I job who could (but may not have to at the moment) do class II work gets paid as a class II worker, not a class I. *Competencies* are demonstrable personal characteristics such as knowledge, skills, and personal behaviors such as leadership. Why pay employees based on the skill levels they achieve, rather than based on the jobs they're assigned to? With more companies organizing around teams, you want to encourage employees to get and to use the skills required to rotate among jobs.

In practice, competency-based pay usually comes down to pay for knowledge, or skill based pay.[86] Most such pay programs generally contain five elements. The employer *defines* specific required skills and chooses a *method* for basing the person's pay on his or her skills. A *training* system lets employees acquire skills. There is a formal competency *testing* system. And, the work is *designed* so that employees can easily move among jobs of varying skill levels. As an example, review Chapter 4's Figure 4-9 on page 118. For this job, BP lists the minimum level for each skill (such as Technical Expertise, and Problem Solving) someone holding this job must attain. As an employee achieves each level of each skill, he or she would receive a bump in pay. The accompanying JLG program feature shows another example.

▶ **IMPROVING PERFORMANCE:** *HR Practices Around the Globe*

JLG's Skill-Based Pay Program

JLG industries supplies access equipment such as aerial work platforms and mast booms.[87] The firm instituted a skill-based pay program to reward employees for the number of basic skills they can perform rather than for the jobs to which they are assigned.[88] JLG integrated the skill pay program into its existing payroll system, and supported it with a computerized reporting system.

As an employee acquires and masters a new skill, JLG increases his or her pay on a scheduled basis. Pay increases are directly proportional to employee "value" based on skill acquisition. Pay adjustment increments are $0.30 per hour and can be in addition to regularly scheduled merit increases. Qualified employees are eligible to receive a skill-based wage adjustment at three times. The first increase is available at the completion of an initial 6-month probationary employment period. An additional skill-based adjustment may come in conjunction with the employee's annual merit review. Other skill-based adjustments are allowed yearly and 6 months after the annual merit review.

JLG assigns hourly production and maintenance workers to a particular "job family." A job family consists of a group of employees performing similar activities and requiring similar skills. *Each job family has a set of required skills,* including certain job-related skills as well as skills related to quality and safety.

Skill assessment is ongoing. Formal evaluation begins at the end of the 6-month probationary period, at which time the employee is tested for mastery of *the minimum skills* required for the job family. (A 100% mastery of these minimum skills is required for successful completion of the probationary period.) Then, twice a year, the company analyzes the employee's progress toward more *advanced skills*, and sets training objectives. Overall responsibility for skills acquisition and career development rests with the employee. The employee determines his/her level of participation in acquiring new or additional skills. Supervisors assist by helping the employee identify and plan for new skills to be acquired, and by creating opportunities for cross-training and certifying the skills training.

To determine if an employee is qualified for a skill-based pay raise, a comparison is made between the employee's current wage rate and the skill-based target rate within the job family to which the employee is assigned. If the current wage rate is equal to or greater than the target rate, no pay adjustment is made. If the current rate is below the target rate, a skill-based adjustment is authorized for employees who mastered the job family's skills.

In place since the 1990s, JLG reports that the program is producing benefits. The skill mastery it fosters permits faster adaptation to technology and product mix changes. With a greater skill range, workers are better able to focus on problem areas and avoid idle time waiting for problems to be fixed, or for work done by others. Employees participate more actively in problem solving because of their wider perspective on total workflow. The program permits lower overall staffing levels by incorporating into job family skill requirements specialized tasks others might otherwise be hired to perform. The company has been able to raise minimum hiring qualifications. Overall increases in productivity have enabled expansion of capacity. ∎

Source: From "JLG Industries, Inc., "Information: Skill-Based Pay Program," www.bmpcoe.org/bestpractices/internal/jlg/jlg_14.html.

Broadbanding

Most firms end up with pay plans that slot jobs into classes or grades, each with its own vertical pay rate range. For example, the U.S. government's pay plan consists of 15 main grades (GS-1 to GS-15), each with its own pay range. For an employee whose job falls in one of these grades, the pay range for that grade dictates his or her minimum and maximum salary.

The question is, "How wide should the salary grades be, in terms of the number of job evaluation points they include?" (For example, should the U.S. government collapse its 15 salary grades into 5 or 6 broader bands.) There is a downside to having (say, 15) narrow grades. For instance, if you want someone whose job is in grade 2 to fill in for a time in a job that happens to be in grade 1, it's difficult to reassign that person without lowering his or her salary. Similarly, if you want the person to learn about a job that happens to be in grade 3, the employee might first want a corresponding raise to grade 3 pay. Traditional grade pay plans thus may tend to breed inflexibility.

> **broadbanding**
> Consolidating salary grades and ranges into just a few wide levels or "bands," each of which contains a relatively wide range of jobs and salary levels.

That is why some firms broadband their pay plans.[89] **Broadbanding** means collapsing salary grades into just a few wide levels or bands, each of which contains a relatively wide range of jobs and pay levels. Figure 11-9 illustrates this. Here, the company's previous six pay grades are consolidated into two broad grades or "broadbands."

A company may create broadbands for all its jobs, or for specific groups such as managers or professionals. The (vertical) pay rate range of each broadband is relatively large, since it ranges from the minimum pay of the lowest grade the firm merged into the broadband up to the maximum pay of the highest merged grade. Thus, for example, instead of having 10 salary grades, each of which contains a salary range of $15,000, the firm might collapse the 10 grades into three broadbands, each with a set of jobs such that the difference between the lowest- and highest-paid jobs might be $40,000 or more. For the jobs that fall in this broadband, there is therefore a much wider range of pay rates. You can move an employee from job to job within the broadband more easily, without worrying about the employee's moving outside the relatively narrow rate range associated with a traditional narrow pay grade.

Broadbanding injects greater flexibility into employee pay.[90] For example, "the employee who needs to spend time in a lower-level job to develop a certain skill set

FIGURE 11-9
Broadbanded Structure and How It Relates to Traditional Pay Grades and Ranges

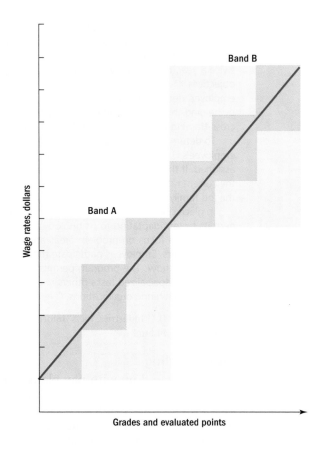

can receive higher-than-usual pay for the work, a circumstance considered impossible under traditional pay systems."[91] Conversely, employees assigned to traditional narrowly defined pay grades may take a "that's not my job" attitude and focus on their usual assigned duties.[92]

comparable worth
The concept by which women who are usually paid less than men can claim that men in comparable rather than in strictly equal jobs are paid more.

Comparable Worth

Comparable worth refers to the requirement to pay men and women equal wages for jobs that are dissimilar but of comparable value (for instance measured in points) to the employer. This may mean comparing dissimilar jobs, such as nurses to truck mechanics. The question "comparable worth" seeks to address is this: Should you pay women who are performing jobs *equal* to men's or just *comparable* to men's the same as men?

County of Washington v. Gunther (1981) was a pivotal case. It involved Washington County, Oregon, prison matrons who claimed sex discrimination. The county had evaluated roughly comparable (but different) men's jobs as having 5% more "job content" (based on a point evaluation system) than the women's jobs, but paid the men 35% more.[93] Why should there be such a pay discrepancy for roughly comparable jobs? After moving through the courts to the U.S. Supreme Court, Washington County finally agreed to pay 35,000 employees in female-dominated jobs almost $500 million in pay raises over 7 years to settle.

Comparable worth has implications for job evaluation. Virtually every comparable worth case that reached court involved the point method of job evaluation. By assigning points to dissimilar jobs, point plans facilitate comparability ratings among different jobs. Should employers still use point plans? Perhaps the wisest approach is for employers to price their jobs as they see fit (with or without point plans), but to also ensure that women have equal access to all jobs. In other words, eliminate sex-segregated jobs.

Diversity Counts: The Pay Gap

All this notwithstanding, women in the United States earn only about 81% as much as men.[94] In general, education may reduce the wage gap somewhat.[95] But gaps remain, even among the most highly trained. For example, new female medical doctors in the US recently earned about $17,000 per year less than their male counterparts did.[96] Reasons put forward for the male-female gap range from the outdated notion that employers view women as having less leverage, to the fact that professional men change jobs more often (gaining more raises in the process) and that women tend to end up in departments that pay less.[97] According to a study conducted by PayCheck India in collaboration with WageIndicator and published by the career website, Monster India, gender pay gap is a reality in India. In 2016, while Indian men working in the formal sector earned ₹288.68 per hour, women earned only ₹207.85. This accounts for a 27% difference. While the manufacturing sector recorded the highest gap (34.9%), banking and finance had the lowest (17.7%).[98] In any case, it's a problem employers should recognize and address. ■

Board Oversight of Executive Pay in the U.S. and India

There are various reasons why boards are scrutinizing their executives' pay more than in the past. The Dodd-Frank Law of 2010 requires that American companies give shareholders a "say on pay." Law firms are filing class-action suits demanding information from companies about their senior executive pay decisions.[99] The Financial Accounting Standards Board requires that most public companies recognize as an expense the fair value of the stock options they grant.[100] The Sarbanes-Oxley Act makes executives personally liable, under certain conditions, for corporate financial oversight lapses. The chief justice of Delaware's Supreme Court said that governance issues, shareholder activism, and other changes have "created a new set of expectations for directors."[101] The Securities and Exchange Commission (SEC) requires filing detailed compensation-related information, including a listing of all individual "perks" or benefits if they total more than $100,000.[102]

The net result is that lawyers specializing in executive pay suggest that boards of directors (whose compensation committees usually make these pay decisions in large firms) ask themselves these questions:[103]

- Has our compensation committee identified its duties and processes?
- Is our compensation committee using the appropriate compensation advisors?
- Are there particular executive compensation issues that our committee should address?[104]
- Do our procedures demonstrate diligence and independence (including careful deliberations and records)?
- Is our committee appropriately communicating its decisions? How will shareholders react?[105]

Executive Compensation in India

In India, the Companies Act, 2013, sets the broad framework for establishing managerial remuneration for board-level positions (managing director and full-time directors). The total amount is capped at 11% of the net profits. Any excess has to be authorized by the shareholders in its general body meeting and approved by the government of India, under Schedule V of the law.

The law, technically, does not place any restriction on compensation to top managers (non-board positions) like CEO, CFO, CHRO, etc., as the amount of compensation is a business decision. However, this act and Companies (Appointment and Remuneration of Managerial Personnel) Rules, 2014, expect companies listed in

India to publically disclose the compensation paid. Companies have to establish a duly approved remuneration policy which governs the compensation structure. Executive compensation disclosure was a mandated practice for Indian firms, since 2002.

Listed companies are also obliged under this act and SEBI regulations, i.e., SEBI (Listing Obligations and Disclosure Requirement) Regulations, 2015, to establish a Nomination and Remuneration Committee (NRC) of the board. The NRC is responsible for formulating the remuneration policy of the company and recommending it to the board for approval. This group has to be chaired by an independent director of the board, and remuneration details have to be reported by the company.

The global hot debate about unduly high compensation being paid to executives has been discussed in the Indian context also. A study of compensation paid by India's top 102 companies between 2007 and 2012 found a positive relationship between company size and compensation,[106] and this was a common trend in India.[107] A high level of stock market return positively influenced compensation (as it becomes easier to justify the payment to shareholders) than other indicators like PAT (Profit after Tax) which did not show any statistically significant influence.[108] Further, private companies (domestic, foreign, and dispersed ownership) paid more than government companies (government companies were considered the base). The research also found that the proportion of non-executive independent directors on the board positively impacted compensation levels, and at the same time raised concerns about independent functioning of compensation committees of the board. The above finding raises a question about "promoter capture" and real independence of independent directors. Another study of 51 listed companies in India reveals that executive remuneration tends to be linked more to market performance than accounting performance.[109]

Another research with data from 2003–2012 shows that managerial remuneration is linked with positive accounting performance, but market performance did not hold much influence. Foreign institutional investor (FII) shareholding was another variable that significantly and positively impacted remuneration.[110] Another study for the same period also indicated that pay for performance is popular in Indian firms, and it was more based on accounting performance rather than market performance. Though pay for performance was reported to be absent in business groups and small firms, it was significant in standalone and large firms.[111] A more recent analysis of 20 top-listed Indian companies showed that professional CEOs and top managers are getting better paid than owner or promoter CEOs in many companies.[112] However, the huge salary difference between top-level executives and others employees (estimated at 1200 times for 2016–17, based on publically disclosed median salary data) is a matter of concern.[113] The differential will be more if statutory minimum wages are considered. Another point of concern is the significantly visible prevalence of gender pay gap in India, which has not been addressed at the policy and governance levels. Some of the studies done by the PayCheck India team has also confirmed the presence of gender pay gap across most levels and sectors, though the gap is gradually narrowing.[114]

Like in other countries, remuneration in the Indian financial sector is also governed by an oversight from regulators like the Reserve Bank of India (RBI) for banks and Insurance Regulatory and Development Authority (IRDA) for insurance companies. For governing compensation of whole-time directors or CEOs, risk takers, and control function staff of private banks and foreign banks in India, the RBI has issued guidelines and reporting structures. As per the RBI, compensation issue is key to regulation and governance of banks, and it has to be consistent with the Companies Act.[115] Executives in public sector banks are governed by strict government norms, which creates significant differences for similar work.[116] For the insurance industry, in 2016, the sector regulator, IRDAI, imposed limits for compensation of MD/CEO and whole-time directors of private insurance companies.

It has been capped at ₹1.5 crore from policy–holders' fund, and any excess payment has to be funded from the shareholders fund.[117]

Employee Engagement Guide For Managers

Total Rewards Programs

Total rewards is an important concept in compensation management. People bring to their jobs many needs—for challenging work and for respect and appreciation, for instance—not all of which are satisfied by pay or bonuses. "'Total rewards' encompass not only compensation and benefits but also personal and professional growth opportunities and a motivating work environment."[118] It includes not just traditional financial rewards (wages and incentives plus benefits and perks), but also nonfinancial and intangible rewards such as recognition, the nature of the job/quality of work, career development opportunities,[119] good relationships with managers and colleagues, organizational justice, trust in employees, feeling of being valued and involved, opportunities for promotion,[120] and a great work climate.[121] Total rewards also include recognition programs and redesigned jobs (discussed in Chapter 4), telecommuting programs, health and well-being programs, and training and career development.

TRENDS SHAPING HR: *DIGITAL AND SOCIAL MEDIA*

Noncash recognition/appreciation rewards such as gift cards, merchandise, and recognition are important parts of such total compensation.[122]

New digital and social media tools enable employees to recognize and reward each other. For example, a West Virginia DuPont plant installed an online system that enabled employees to give each other recognition; 95% were soon using it.[123] International Fitness Holdings lets employees use a Facebook-type application to recognize peers by posting messages and sending private e-mails.[124] Employers contract with sites like Globoforce.com to provide online recognition systems. ■

Total Rewards and Employee Engagement

When it comes to employee engagement, both material and non-material rewards—total rewards—seem essential.[125] For example, one study found that base pay and benefits alone were weakly related to engagement.[126] However, intangible rewards (such as the nature of the job/quality of work and career development opportunities) had high or very high impacts on engagement and performance, when combined with base salary and short-term incentives or bonuses.[127]

It's therefore not surprising that many high-engagement employers do emphasize total rewards. For example, the values laid out in Toyota's famous "The Toyota Way" include mutual trust and respect, stable employment, helping employees to develop their technical skills, and "support for production staff combining work with childcare, career design support, and raising of corporate awareness." Disney emphasizes providing employees/cast members with a total rewards package that includes pay plus various benefits and career development opportunities.[128] Similarly, many "Best Companies to Work For" emphasize intangible rewards. For example, one top executive at NetApp takes an opportunity to call and thank several employees each day for their efforts, and Whole Foods emphasizes employee involvement, for instance letting employees vote on new hires and see what all Whole Foods employees earn.[129] At SAS there is stimulating work, an empowering management philosophy, flexible work, and an emphasis on being happy at work.[130]

In addition to encouraging such rewards, the employer should issue total reward statements periodically. List all the rewards—financial and nonfinancial—the company offers, and note their importance to the employees' overall well-being.[131] Doing so increases their impact.

Chapter Review

Chapter Section Summaries

11-1. In establishing strategic pay plans, managers first need to understand some **basic factors in determining pay rates**. Employee compensation includes both direct financial payments and indirect financial statements. The factors determining the design of any pay plan include legal, union, company strategy/policy, and equity. The Indian government is proposing a Code for Wages, where four wage related legislations will be amalgamated into a singe code. The code, when it comes into force, is expected to improve the efficiency of current wage legislation and administration.

11-2. Employers use two basic approaches to setting pay rates: *market-based approaches* and **job evaluation methods**. Many firms, particularly smaller ones, simply use a *market-based* approach. Job evaluation methods involve assigning values to each of the company's jobs. This helps to produce a pay plan in which each job's pay is equitable based on its value to the employer. Popular job evaluation methods include ranking, job classification, and the point method.

11-3. We said the process of **creating a market-competitive pay plan** while ensuring external, internal, and procedural equity consists of 16 steps as follows: (1) Choose benchmark jobs; (2) Select compensable factors; (3) Assign weights to compensable factors; (4) Convert percentages to points for each factor; (5) Define each factor's degrees; (6) Determine for each factor its factor degrees' points; (7) Review job descriptions and job specifications; (8) Evaluate the jobs; (9) Draw the current (internal) wage curve; (10) Conduct a market analysis: Salary surveys; (11) Draw the market (external) wage curve; (12) Compare and adjust current and market wage rates for jobs; (13) Develop pay grades; (14) Establish rate ranges; (15) Address remaining jobs; and (16) Correct out-of-line rates.

11-4. **Pricing managerial and professional jobs** involves some special issues. Managerial pay typically consists of base pay, short-term incentives, long-term incentives, and executive benefits and, particularly at the top levels, doesn't lend itself to job evaluation but rather to understanding the job's complexity, the employer's ability to pay, and the need to be competitive in attracting top talent.

11-5. We addressed five important **special topics in compensation**. More employers are moving from paying jobs based on their intrinsic duties toward paying jobs based on the competencies the job requires. Broadbanding means consolidating several rates and ranges into a few wide levels or "bands," each of which contains a relatively wide range of jobs in salary levels. Comparable worth refers to the requirement to pay men and women equal pay for jobs that are of comparable rather than strictly equal value to the employee. With many stockholders concerned with excessive executive remuneration, board oversight of executive pay has become an important issue, and boards of directors should use qualified advisors and exercise diligence and independence in formulating executive pay plans.

11-6. Research shows that if **employee engagement** is the aim, it makes sense to emphasize total rewards, not just financial rewards. For example, one study found that base pay and benefits alone had a weak relationship with employee engagement. However, total rewards including intangible rewards such as the nature of the job/quality of work, and career development opportunities had a high or very high impact on engagement and performance, when combined with base salary and short-term incentives or bonuses.

Discussion Questions

11-1. What is the difference between exempt and non-exempt jobs?

11-2. Should the job evaluation depend on an appraisal of the jobholder's performance? Why? Why not?

11-3. What is the relationship between compensable factors and job specifications?

11-4. Define and give an example of how to conduct a job evaluation.

11-5. The average pay for most Indian university's vice chancellors is around ₹18 lakh per year, but a few working in private universities earn much more. For example, the president of a newly-established private university in India may earn around ₹10 million in one year.

Discuss why you would (or would not) pay university presidents as much as or more than many corporate CEOs.

11-6. Do small companies need to develop a pay plan? Why or why not?

Individual and Group Activities

11-7. Working individually or in groups, conduct salary surveys for the following positions: entry-level accountant and entry-level chemical engineer. What sources did you use, and what conclusions did you reach? If you were the HR manager for a local engineering firm, what would you recommend that you pay for each job?

11-8. Working individually or in groups, develop compensation policies for the teller position at a local bank. Assume that there are four tellers: two were hired in May and the other two were hired in December. The compensation policies should address the following: appraisals, raises, holidays, vacation pay, overtime pay, method of pay, garnishments, and time cards.

11-9. Working individually or in groups, access relevant Web sites to determine what equitable pay ranges are for these jobs: chemical engineer, marketing manager, and HR manager, all with a bachelor's degree and 5 years' experience. Do so for the following cities: Mumbai, Delhi, Ahmedabad, Patna, Kochi, and Shillong. For each position in each city, what are the pay ranges and the average pay? Does geographical location impact the salaries of the different positions? If so, how?

11-10. Appendices A and B at the end of this book (pages 583–600) list the knowledge someone studying for the HRCI (Appendix A) or SHRM (Appendix B) certification exam needs to have in each area of human resource management (such as in Strategic Management, and Workforce Planning). In groups of several students, do four things: (1) review Appendix A and/or B; (2) identify the material in this chapter that relates to the Appendix A and/or B required knowledge lists; (3) write four multiple-choice exam questions on this material that you believe would be suitable for inclusion in the HRCI exam and/or the SHRM exam; and, (4) if time permits, have someone from your team post your team's questions in front of the class, so that students in all teams can answer the exam questions created by the other teams.

11-11. Working individually or in groups, use the point system described in steps 1 to 16 in this chapter. Do so for a job description that you find online—a list like that at http://hiring.monster.com/hr/hr-best-practices/recruiting-hiring-advice/job-descriptions/sample-job-descriptions.aspx is useful. To simplify things, assume there is only one compensable factor you have to use, and that it is job complexity, so that you can use Figure 11-3.

Experiential Exercise

Ranking the College's Administrators

Purpose: The purpose of this exercise is to give you experience in performing a job evaluation using the ranking method.

Required Understanding: You should be thoroughly familiar with the ranking method of job evaluation and obtain job descriptions for your college's dean, department chairperson, director of admissions, library director, registrar, and your professor.

How to Set Up the Exercise/Instructions: Divide the class into groups of four or five students. The groups will perform a job evaluation of the positions of dean, department chairperson, and professor using the ranking method.

Perform a job evaluation by ranking the jobs. You may use one or more compensable factors.

11-12. If time permits, a spokesperson from each group can put his or her group's rankings on the board. Did the groups end up with about the same results? How did they differ? Why do you think they differed?

CHAPTER 11

Application Case

Salary Inequities at AstraZeneca

More than 50 years after passage of the Equal Pay Act, women in America still earn about 80 cents for every dollar earned by a man. That adds up to a loss for the average female worker of about $380,000 over a lifetime.

Recently, the U.S. Department of Labor's Office of Federal Contract Compliance Programs (OFCCP) entered into an agreement with AstraZeneca, a large international pharmaceuticals firm, for the company to pay some of its female sales associates a total of $250,000.[132] AstraZeneca had a contract valued at over $2 billion with the U.S. Department of Veterans Affairs to provide drugs to hospitals around the country. That made it subject to Executive Order 11246, which aims to ensure that employees of U.S. contractors and subcontractors with federal contracts pay their employees fairly without regard to sex, race, color, religion, and national origin.

After conducting a compliance review, the OFCCP concluded that AstraZeneca violated Executive Order 11246 by failing to ensure certain women employees were paid fairly. According to the OFCCP lawsuit, an AstraZeneca Business Center had routinely paid some of its female "primary care" and "specialty care" level III pharmaceutical sales specialists an average of $1,700 less than men with the same positions.

Because of the company's pay secrecy policies, many of the women didn't know they were being paid less. In addition to the financial settlement, AstraZeneca and OFCCP will review records of the firm's female employees in 14 states. If they find additional statistical evidence of wage discrimination, the company must remedy it.

Questions

AstraZeneca has brought you in as a compensation consultant. Here are the questions they would like you to answer for them:

11-13. Although the case with OFCCP is closed, we wonder if there are any less discriminatory explanations possible for why our women sales reps on average earned less than men. If so, what are they?

11-14. Our own company now uses a point method to evaluate jobs for pay purposes, and each resulting job class also has a rate range associated with it. Sales associates are now paid a salary that is not based on incentive pay. List three specific things we can do to ensure that a similar problem (inequitable pay based on gender) does not arise again, assuming they continue using the point plan.

11-15. What sort of compensation plan would you recommend for us, and why?

Continuing Case

Carter Cleaning Company

The New Pay Plan

Carter Cleaning Centers does not have a formal wage structure nor does it have rate ranges or use compensable factors. Wage rates are based mostly on those prevailing in the surrounding community and are tempered with an attempt on the part of Jack Carter to maintain some semblance of equity between what workers with different responsibilities in the stores are paid.

Carter does not make any formal surveys when determining what his company should pay. He peruses the want ads almost every day and conducts informal surveys among his friends in the local chapter of the laundry and cleaners trade association. While Jack has taken a "seat-of-the-pants" approach to paying employees, his salary schedule has been guided by several basic pay policies. Although many of his colleagues adhere to a policy of paying minimum rates, Jack has always followed a policy of paying his employees about 10% above what he

feels are the prevailing rates, a policy that he believes reduces turnover while fostering employee loyalty. Of somewhat more concern to Jennifer is her father's informal policy of paying men about 20% more than women for the same job. Her father's explanation is, "They're stronger and can work harder for longer hours, and besides they all have families to support."

Questions

11-16. Is the company at the point where it should be setting up a formal salary structure based on a complete job evaluation? Why?

11-17. Is Jack Carter's policy of paying 10% more than the prevailing rates a sound one, and how could that be determined?

11-18. Similarly, is Carter's male–female differential wise? If not, why not?

11-19. Specifically, what would you suggest Jennifer do now with respect to her company's pay plan?

Translating Strategy into HR Policies and Practices Case*,§

*The overall map on page xxxviii of this book outlines the relationships involved.

Improving Performance at the Hotel Paris

The New Compensation Plan

The Hotel Paris's competitive strategy is "To use superior guest service to differentiate the Hotel Paris properties, and to thereby increase the length of stay and return rate of guests, and thus boost revenues and profitability." HR manager Lisa Cruz must now formulate functional

policies and activities that support this competitive strategy by eliciting the required employee behaviors and competencies.

Like several other HR systems at the Hotel Paris, the compensation program was unplanned and unsophisticated. The company has a narrow target range for what it will pay employees in each job category (front-desk clerk, security guard, and so forth). Each hotel manager decides where to start a new employee within that narrow pay range. The company has given little thought to tying general pay levels or individual employees' pay to the company's strategic goals. For example, the firm's policy is simply to pay its employees a "competitive salary," by which it means about average for what other hotels in the city are paying for similar jobs. Lisa knows that pay policies like these may actually run counter to what the company wants to achieve strategically, in terms of creating an extraordinarily service-oriented workforce. How can you hire and retain a top workforce, and channel its behaviors toward high-quality guest services, if you don't somehow link performance and pay? She and her team therefore turn to the task of assessing and redesigning the company's compensation plan.

Even the most casual review by Lisa Cruz and the CFO made it clear that the company's compensation plan wasn't designed to support the firm's new strategic goals. For one thing, they knew that they should pay somewhat more on average than did their competitors if they expected employees to exceed expectations when it came to serving guests. Yet their review of a variety of metrics (including the Hotel Paris's salary/competitive salary ratios, the total compensation expense per employee, and the target percentile for total compensation) suggested that in virtually all job categories the Hotel Paris paid no more than average and, occasionally, paid somewhat less.

The current compensation policies had also bred what one hotel manager called an "I don't care" attitude on the part of most employees. What she meant was that most Hotel Paris employees quickly learned that regardless of what their performance was, they always ended up getting paid about the same as employees who performed better and worse than they did. So, the firm's compensation plan actually created a disconnect between pay and performance: It was not channeling employees' behaviors toward those required to achieve the company's goals. In some ways, it was doing the opposite.

Lisa and the CFO knew they had to institute a new, strategic compensation plan. They wanted a plan that improved employee morale, contributed to employee engagement, reduced employee turnover, and rewarded (and thus encouraged) the sorts of service-oriented behaviors that boosted guest satisfaction. After meeting with the company's CEO and the board, the CFO gave Lisa the go-ahead to redesign the company's compensation plan, with the overall aim of creating a new plan that would support the company's strategic aims.

Lisa and her team (which included a consulting compensation expert) set numerous new measurable compensation policies for the Hotel Paris, and these new policies formed the heart of the new compensation plan. A new job evaluation study provided a more rational and fair basis upon which the company could assign pay rates. A formal compensation survey by the consultant established, for the first time at the Hotel Paris, a clear picture of what competitive hotels and similar businesses were paying in each geographic area, and enabled the Hotel Paris team to more accurately set targets for what each position at the hotel should be paying. Rather than just paying at the industry average, or slightly below, the new policy called for the Hotel Paris to move all its salaries into the 75th percentile over the next 3 years.

As they instituted the new compensation policies, Lisa and the CFO were pleased to learn from feedback from the hotel managers that they were already noting several positive changes. The number of applicants for each position had increased by over 50% on average, turnover dropped by 80%, and surveys of morale and commitment were producing higher results. Lisa and her team now began to consider how to inject more of a "pay for performance" element into the company's compensation plan, perhaps by instituting new bonuses and incentives. We will see what she did in Chapter 12.

Questions

11-20. Lisa knew little about setting up a new compensation plan. Based on what you learned here in Dessler *Human Resource Management*, what would you tell her if she asked, "How do I set up a new compensation plan for the Hotel Paris?"

11-21. Would you suggest that Hotel Paris implement a competency-based pay plan for its nonmanagerial staff? Why or why not? Outline what they need to do for one.

11-22. Devise a ranking job evaluation system for the Hotel Paris's nonmanagerial employees (housekeepers, valets, front-desk clerks, phone operators, waitstaff, groundskeepers, and security guards) and use it to show the worth of these jobs relative to one another.

---

§ Written and copyright by Gary Dessler, PhD.

Key Terms

employee compensation, 337
direct financial payments, 337
indirect financial payments, 337
Code of Wages Bill 2017, 338
Equal Remuneration Act (1979), 341
Payment of Gratuity Act (1972), 341

job evaluation, 344
market-competitive pay plan, 344
compensable factor, 344
benchmark job, 345
ranking method, 345
job classification (or job grading), 347
classes, 347

grades, 347
grade definition, 347
point method, 348
market-competitive pay system, 352
wage curve, 352
salary survey, 353
pay (or wage) grade, 356

pay (or rate) ranges, 356
compa ratio, 357
competency-based pay, 362
broadbanding, 363
comparable worth, 364

Endnotes

1. Elayne Robertson Demby, "Two Stores Refused to Join the Race to the Bottom for Benefits and Wages," *Workforce Management*, February 2004, pp. 57–59; www.wegmans.com/webapp/wcs/stores/servlet/CategoryDisplay?categoryId=284278&store Id=10052&langId=-1, accessed July 13, 2015.

2. Richard Henderson, *Compensation Management* (Reston, VA: Reston Publishing, 1980), pp. 101–127; and Stacey L. Kaplan, "Total Rewards in Action: Developing a Total Rewards Strategy," *Benefits & Compensation Digest* 42, no. 8 (August 2005), pp. 32–37.

3. Duncan Brown, "The Future of Reward Management: From Total Reward Strategies to Smart Rewards," *Compensation & Benefits Review* 46, no. 3, pp. 147–151.

4. Nicholas Wade, "Play Fair: Your Life May Depend on It," *New York Times*, September 12, 2003, p. 12.

5. Robert Bretz and Stephen Thomas, "Perceived Inequity,

Motivation, and Final Offer Arbitration in Major League Baseball," *Journal of Applied Psychology,* June 1992, pp. 280–282; Reginald Ell, "Addressing Employees' Feelings of Inequity: Capitalizing on Equity Theory in Modern Management," *Supervision* 72, no. 5 (May 2011), pp. 3–6.

6. James DeConinck and Duane Bachmann, "An Analysis of Turnover Among Retail Buyers," Journal of Business Research 58, no. 7 (July 2005), pp. 874–882

7. Michael Harris et al., "Keeping Up with the Joneses: A Field Study of the Relationships Among Upward, Lateral, and Downward Comparisons and Pay Level Satisfaction," *Journal of Applied Psychology* 93, no. 3 (2008), pp. 665–673.

8. David Terpstra and Andre Honoree, "The Relative Importance of External, Internal, Individual, and Procedural Equity to Pay Satisfaction," *Compensation & Benefits Review,* November/December 2003, pp. 67–74.

9. Ibid., p. 68.

10. Millicent Nelson et al., "Pay Me More: What Companies Need to Know About Employee Pay Satisfaction," *Compensation & Benefits Review,* March/April 2008, pp. 35–42.

11. Pay inequities manifest in unexpected ways. In one study, the researchers studied the impact of keeping pay rates secret, rather than publicizing them. They found that individuals with lower levels of tolerance for inequity reacted particularly harshly to pay secrecy in terms of weaker individual test performance. Peter Bamberger and Elena Belogolovsky, "The Impact of Pay Secrecy on Individual Test Performance," *Personnel Psychology* 60, no. 3 (2010), pp. 965–996.

12. Rachel Emma Silverman, "Psst.... This Is What Your Coworker Is Paid," *Wall Street Journal,* January 30, 2013, p. B6. Pay confidentiality may also violate the National Labor Relations Act, which permits workers to engage in concerted activities for collective bargaining "or other mutual aid or protection." Howard Risher, "Pay Transparency Is Coming," *Compensation & Benefits Review* 46, no. 1 (2014), pp. 3–5.

13. Frank Giancola, "What the Research Says About the Effects of Open Pay Policies on Employees' Pay Satisfaction and Job Performance," *Compensation & Benefits Review* 46, no. 3 (May/June 2014), pp. 161–168.

14. Henderson, *Compensation Management;* see also Barry Gerhart and Sara Rynes, *Compensation: Theory, Evidence, and Strategic Implications* (Thousand Oaks,

CA: Sage Publications, 2003); and Joseph Martocchio, *Strategic Compensation* (Upper Saddle River, NJ: Prentice Hall, 2006), pp. 67–94.

15. GOI, Report of Second National Commission on Labour (2002), as accessed on 20 September 2017 at http://www.prsindia. org/uploads/media/1237548159/ NLCII-report.pdf.

16. Accessed on October 9, 2017 from http://www.thehindu.com/ news/national/other-states/44-labour-laws-to-be-amalgamated-into-4-codes/article7762305. ece#!.

17. Paromita Goswami, "A Critique of the Unorganized Worker's Social Security Act, 2009," *Economic and Political Weekly,* Vol 44 (11) March 2000.

18. K R Shyamsunder, "Labour Exercise," *Business Line,* May 1, 2017.

19. We'll see that the federal government is pressing to expand employment overtime eligibility. See, for example, "Obama Signs Memo Telling Labor Department to Expand Employee Overtime Eligibility," *Bloomberg BNA Bulletin to Management,* March 18, 2014, pp. 81–82.

20. Ibid., p. 215.

21. Biju Varkkey, "India Chapter in Minimum Wages," Collective Bargaining and Economic Development in Asia and Europe, Eds by Economic and Political Weekly, Vol 44 (11) March. M Van Klaveran, Dennis Gregory, and T Schulten (2015).

22. Several state legislatures have moved to tighten regulations regarding misclassifying workers as independent contractors, some going so far as adding criminal penalties for violations. "Misclassification Cases Draw More Attention, Attorneys Say," *BNA Bulletin to Management,* December 15, 2009, p. 399. The U.S. Department of Labor is working with state agencies to challenge independent contractor worker misclassifications. "DOL, State Agencies, and Litigants Proceed with Challenges to Worker Misclassification," *BNA Bulletin to Management,* August 14, 2012, p. 257.

23. "Federal Court Mostly Rules for FedEx Ground in Driver Lawsuits Alleging Misclassification," *BNA Bulletin to Management,* December 21, 2010, p. 403. Different countries classify independent contractors in different ways, which requires knowledge of the specific local requirements. Eric Krell, "Status Check," *HR Magazine,* November 2011, pp. 63–66.

24. www.irs.gov/Businesses/Small-Businesses-&-Self-Employed/ Independent-Contractor-

Defined, accessed March 19, 2014.

25. http://www.irs.gov/Businesses/ Small-Businesses-&-Self-Employed/Independent-Contractor-Self-Employed-or-Employee, accessed July 13, 2015.

26. See, for instance, www.uschambersmallbusinessnation.com/ toolkits/tool/indcon_m.

27. This is based on Matthew Simpson, "Five Steps to Reduce the Risks of Miscalculation," *BNA Bulletin to Management,* February 21, 2012, p. 63.

28. Conrad De Aenlle, "Employee or Contractor? Healthcare Law Raises Stakes," *New York Times,* February 15, 2015, p. BU 11.

29. Peg Buchenroth, "Driving Performance: Making Pay Work for the Organization," *Compensation & Benefits Review,* May/June 2006, pp. 30–35.

30. Demby, "Two Stores Refused to Join the Race."

31. Ibid.

32. www.wegmans.com, accessed June 1, 2011.

33. Demby, "Two Stores Refuse to Join the Race"; www.hoovers. com/company/Wegmans_Food_ Markets_Inc/cfhtji-1.Html, accessed June 1, 2011.

34. Ibid.

35. Demby, "Two Stores Refuse to Join the Race."

36. www.bls.gov/oes/current/ oes431011.htm, accessed July 27, 2013.

37. This is based on compensation management.

38. See, for example, Joseph Martocchio, *Strategic Compensation* (Upper Saddle River, NJ: Pearson Education, 2011), p. 140; John Kilgour, "Job Evaluation Revisited: The Point-Factor Method," *Compensation & Benefits Review,* July/August 2008, pp. 37–46; and www.shrm.org/ TemplatesTools/Toolkits/Pages/ PerformingJobEvaluations.aspx, accessed April 5, 2014.

39. Martocchio, *Strategic Compensation,* 2006, p. 138. See also Nona Tobin, "Can Technology Ease the Pain of Salary Surveys?" *Public Personnel Management* 31, no. 1 (Spring 2002), pp. 65–78.

40. Job analysis (Chapter 4) can be a useful source of information on compensable factors, as well as on job descriptions and job specifications. For example, a quantitative job analysis technique like the position analysis questionnaire generates quantitative information on the degree to which the following five basic factors are present in each job: having decision-making/communication/social responsibilities, performing skilled activities, being physically active, operating vehicles or equipment, and processing information. As a result, a job analysis technique like the PAQ is actually as (or

some say, more) appropriate as a job evaluation technique (than for job analysis) in that jobs can be quantitatively compared to one another on those five dimensions and their relative worth thus ascertained.

41. Michael Carrell and Christina Heavrin, *Labor Relations and Collective Bargaining* (Upper Saddle River, NJ: Prentice Hall, 2004), pp. 300–303.

42. www.hr-guide.com/data/G909. htm, accessed July 10, 2014.

43. Kilgour, "Job Evaluation Revisited," p. 40.

44. See, for example, http://pristina. usembassy.gov/uploads/images/ TPAyt1xR9zbj_JQ2iG1tpw/ caje1.pdf.

45. Martocchio, *Strategic Compensation,* 2011, p. 140.

46. For a discussion, see Roger Plachy, "The Point Factor Job Evaluation System: A Step-by-Step Guide, Part I," *Compensation & Benefits Review,* July/August 1987, pp. 12–27; Roger Plachy, "The Case for Effective Point-Factor Job Evaluation, Viewpoint I," *Compensation & Benefits Review,* March/April 1987, pp. 45–48; Roger Plachy, "The Point-Factor Job Evaluation System: A Step-by-Step Guide, Part II," *Compensation & Benefits Review,* September/October 1987, pp. 9–24; and particularly Kilgour, "Job Evaluation Revisited," pp. 37–46.

47. Martocchio, *Strategic Compensation,* 2011, p. 141.

48. Kilgour, "Job Evaluation Revisited," pp. 37–46.

49. Ibid.

50. Ibid.

51. Ibid.

52. Ibid.

53. Ibid.

54. Ibid. Of course, the level of economic activity influences compensation expectations. Fay Hansen, "Currents in Compensation and Benefits," *Compensation & Benefits Review* 42, no. 6 (2010), p. 435.

55. Martocchio, *Strategic Compensation,* 2011, p. 151.

56. Kilgour, "Job Evaluation Revisited," pp. 37–46.

57. Henderson, *Compensation Management,* pp. 260–269. See also "Web Access Transforms Compensation Surveys," *Workforce Management,* April 24, 2006, p. 34.

58. See Judy Canavan, "Compensation Surveys: The Good, the Bad, and the Ugly," *Compensation & Benefits Review* 46, no. 2 (2014), pp. 74–79.

59. Kilgour, "Job Evaluation Revisited," pp. 37–46. See also William Liccione, "Linking the Market and Internal Values of Jobs: Rethinking the Market Line," *Compensation & Benefits Review* 46, no. 2 (2014), pp. 80–88.

60. Kilgour, "Job Evaluation Revisited," pp. 37–46.
61. David W. Belcher, *Compensation Administration* (Englewood Cliffs, NJ: Prentice Hall, 1974), pp. 257–276; and Nicola Sulliva, "Serco Introduces Pay Grade Structure for Senior Staff," *Employee Benefits*, July 2010, p. 5.
62. Martocchio, *Strategic Compensation,* 2011, p. 185.
63. Ibid., p. 189.
64. Kilgour, "Job Evaluation Revisited," pp. 37–46.
65. Susan Marks, "Can the Internet Help You Hit the Salary Mark?" *Workforce*, January 2001, pp. 86–93.
66. For sources of sample policies see, for example, sites such as http://hr.blr.com/timesavers?type=54 and the HR systems discussion on pages 000–000.
67. James Reda, "Executive Pay Today and Tomorrow," *Corporate Board* 22, no. 126 (January 2001), p. 18.
68. Syed Tahir Hijazi, "Determinants of Executive Compensation and Its Impact on Organizational Performance," *Compensation & Benefits Review* 39, no. 2 (March–April 2007), p. 58(9).
69. For example, some authors argue that executives of large companies use their power to have themselves compensated in ways that are not sufficiently related to performance. Lucian Bebchuk and Jesse Fried, *Pay Without Performance: The Unfulfilled Promise of Executive Compensation* (Boston: Harvard University Press, 2004).
70. http://uk.reuters.com/article/2010/02/23/uk-hsbc-idUKTRE61M6FT20100223, accessed June 23, 2011.
71. Mark Meltzer and Howard Goldsmith, "Executive Compensation for Growth Companies," *Compensation & Benefits Review*, November/December 1997, pp. 41–50; Martocchio, *Strategic Compensation,* 2011, pp. 421–428. See also Martin J. Conyon, "Executive Compensation and Incentives," *The Academy of Management Perspectives* 20, no. 1 (February 2006), p. 25(20); and "Realities of Executive Compensation—2006/2007 Report on Executive Pay and Stock Options," www.watson-wyatt.com/research/resrender.asp?id=2006-US-0085&page=1, accessed May 20, 2007.
72. Douglas Tormey, "Executive Compensation: Creating a 'Legal' Checklist," *Compensation & Benefits Review*, July/August 1996, pp. 12–36. See also Bruce Ellig, "Executive Pay: A Primer," *Compensation & Benefits Review*, January/February 2003, pp. 44–50.

73. http://finance.yahoo.com/news/p-gs-ceo-pay-slips-200307540.html, accessed February 8, 2013.
74. "At the Top of Their Industries," *New York Times*, April 7, 2013, p. B.8.
75. "American Chief Executives Are Not Overpaid," *The Economist*, September 8, 2012, p. 67.
76. See, for example, Fay Hansen, "Current Trends in Compensation and Benefits," *Compensation & Benefits Review* 36, no. 2 (March/April 2004), pp. 7–8.
77. http://www.businesstoday.in/magazine/cover-story/indian-ceo-salaries-changing-trend-vishal-sikka-infosys/story/211913.html
78. http://timesofindia.indiatimes.com/companies/inside-story-of-the-tensions-between-infy-ceo-founders/articleshow/57051249.cms
79. www.dol.gov/whd/regs/compliance/fairpay/fs17d_professional.pdf, accessed June 1, 2011.
80. See, for example, Martocchio, *Strategic Compensation* 2006; and Patricia Zingheim and Jay Schuster, "Designing Pay and Rewards in Professional Services Companies," *Compensation & Benefits Review*, January/February 2007, pp. 55–62.
81. Farhad Manjoo, "Engineers to the Valley: Pay Up," *Fast Company* 153, no. 38 (March 2011).
82. Dimitris Manolopoulos, "What Motivates Research and Development Professionals? Evidence from Decentralized Laboratories in Greece," *International Journal of Human Resource Management* 17, no. 4 (April 2006), pp. 616–647.
83. www.shrm.org/HRdisciplines/pages/CMS_012013.aspx, accessed May 20, 2012.
84. See, for example, Robert Heneman and Peter LeBlanc, "Development of and Approach for Valuing Knowledge Work," *Compensation & Benefits—Review*, July/August 2002, p. 47. A survey found that only about 12% of employers use skill-based pay, and 13% use competency-based pay. Frank Giancola, "Skill-Based Pay: Fad or Classic?" *Compensation & Benefits Review* 43, no. 4 (2011), pp. 220–226.
85. Gerald Ledford Jr., "Paying for the Skills, Knowledge, and Competencies of Knowledge Workers," *Compensation & Benefits Review*, July/August 1995, p. 56; see also P. K. Zingheim et al., "Competencies and Rewards: Substance or Just Style?" *Compensation and Benefits Review* 35, no. 5 (September/October 2003), pp. 40–44.
86. Martocchio, *Strategic Compensation,* 2011, p. 168.

87. www.jlg.com/en-US/Industries.html, accessed April 9, 2013.
88. Quoted or paraphrased from "JLG Industries, Inc., "Information: Skill-Based Pay Program," www.bmpcoe.org/bestpractices/internal/jlg/jlg_14.html, accessed April 9, 2013.
89. See, for example, www.shrm.org/hrdisciplines/compensation/articles/pages/salarystructures.aspx, accessed September 27, 2013.
90. David Hofrichter, "Broadbanding: A 'Second Generation' Approach," *Compensation & Benefits Review*, September/October 1993, pp. 53–58. See also "The Future of Salary Management," *Compensation & Benefits Review*, July/August 2001, pp. 7–12.
91. Ibid., p. 55.
92. For example, see Sandra Emerson, "Job Evaluation: A Barrier to Excellence?" *Compensation & Benefits Review*, January/February 1991, pp. 39–52; Nan Weiner, "Job Evaluation Systems: A Critique," *Human Resource Management Review* 1, no. 2 (Summer 1991), pp. 119–132; and Brian Klaas, "Compensation in the Jobless Organization," *Human Resource Management Review* 12, no. 1 (Spring 2002), pp. 43–62.
93. *County of Washington v. Gunther*, U.S. Supreme Court, no. 80–426, June 8, 1981.
94. Laura Fitzpatrick, "Why Do Women Still Earn Less Than Men?" www.time.com/time/nation/article/0,8599,1983185,00.html, accessed September 4, 2014.
95. Christopher Dougherty, "Why Are the Returns to Schooling Higher for Women Than for Men?" *Journal of Human Resources* 40, no. 4 (Fall 2005), pp. 969–988.
96. Rachel Silverman, "Women Doctors Face Pay Disparity," *Wall Street Journal*, February 8, 2011, p. D4.
97. "Women Still Earned Less Than Men, BLS Data Show," *BNA Bulletin to Management*, June 8, 2000, p. 72. See also E. Frazier, "Raises for Women Executives Match Those for Men, but Pay Gap Persists," *The Chronicle of Philanthropy* 20, no. 24 (October 2, 2008), p. 33.
98. Accessed on 20 September 2017 at http://economictimes.indiatimes.com/jobs/india-suffers-from-huge-gender-pay-gap-monster-salary-index/articleshow/52306658.cms.
99. "The Say on Pay Payday," *The Economist*, February 16, 2013, p. 65.
100. Mark Poerio and Eric Keller, "Executive Compensation 2005: Many Forces, One Direction," *Compensation & Benefits Review*, May/June 2005, pp. 34–40.

101. Ibid., p. 38.
102. Jennifer Dudley, "The New Executive Compensation Rule: The Tough Disclosures," *Compensation & Benefits Review*, July/August 2007, pp. 28–34.
103. Society for Human Resource Management, "Changing Leadership Strategies," *Workplace Visions*, no. 1 (2008), p. 3.
104. For a discussion of some of the issues that go into hammering out an executive employment agreement, see, for example, Jonathan Cohen and Laura Clark, "Is the Executive Employment Agreement Dead?" *Compensation & Benefits Review*, July/August 2007, pp. 50–55.
105. Ibid. See also Brent Longnecker and James Krueger, "The Next Wave of Compensation Disclosure," *Compensation & Benefits Review*, January/February 2007, pp. 50–54.
106. N Balasubramanian, Samir Kumar Barua, D Kartik, Corporate Governance Issues in Executive Compensation: The Indian Experience (2018-2012), IIMB working paper, No 426.
107. Chakrabarti R et.al Executive Compensation in India, in Handbook on Executive Compensation, (2011), Edgar Elgar, UK.
108. Ibid.,
109. Lakwinder Singh Kal , Payal Nanda " Independence of remuneration committee & Executive remuneration in India" 2016, Indian Journal of Industrial Relations and Human Resource Management, Col 52 (1) July p 17-36.
110. Lakwinder Singh Kang, Payal Nanda "How is managerial remuneration determined in India" Journal of Accounting in Emerging Economies, 2017, Vol 7 (2) p 154-172.
111. Mehul Raithatha and Surendrarao Komera, "Executive Compensation and firm performance: Evidence from Indian firms" 2016, IIMB Management Review, Vol 28 (3) p 160-169.
112. Accessed on 20 September 2017 at http://www.livemint.com/Opinion/0Xa18eFIQKYneZJmXXv3OJ/Rising-salaries-of-Indian-CEOs-are-a-healthy-trend.html.
113. Accessed on 20 September 2017 at http://profit.ndtv.com/news/trends/article-indian-ceos-earn-up-to-1-200-times-you-read-that-right-of-average-staff-1728211.
114. Monster India and Paycheck.in Gender pay report 2016 Ready reckoner, (2017), accessible at http://media.monsterindia.com/logos/research_report/MSI_Gender_Ready_Reckoner_March_2017.pdf.
115. Accessed on 20 September 2017 at https://www.rbi.org.

CHAPTER 11

in/scripts/NotificationUser.
aspx?Id=6938&Mode=0

116. Accessed on 20 September 2017 at http://www.moneylife.in/article/rbi-guidelines-on-bank-ceosrsquo-compensation-mdashare-they-missing-the-woods-for-the-trees/23249.html.

117. Accessed on 20 September 2017 http://economictimes.indiatimes.com/news/company/corporate-trends/irda-caps-ceos-salary-at-rs-1-5-crore-from-policyholders-fund/articleshow/53562984.cms.

118. Robert L. Heneman, "Implementing Total Rewards Strategies," www.shrm.org/hr-disciplines/benefits/Documents/07RewardsStratReport.pdf, accessed March 24, 2014.

119. Dow Scott and Tom McMullen, "The Impact of Rewards Programs on Employee Engagement," *WorldatWork: Survey of Rewards and Employee Engagement*, June 2010, www.worldatwork.org.

120. Duncan Brown and Peter Reilly, "Reward and Engagement: The New Realities," *Compensation & Benefits Review*, 45, no. 3, 2013, pp. 145–157.

121. Tom McMullen, "Eight Recommendations to Improve Employee Engagement," *Journal of Compensation and Benefits*, July/August 2013, p. 23.

122. Melissa Van Dyke and Mike Ryan, "Changing the Compensation Conversation on the Growing Utility of Non-Cash Rewards and Recognition," *Compensation & Benefits Review* 44, no. 5 (2013), pp. 276–279.

123. Meg Breslin, "Solid Rewards Program Can Be Rewarding for Businesses," *Workforce Management*, January 2013, p. 8.

124. Dave Zielinski, "Giving Praise," *HR Magazine*, October 2012, p. 77.

125. Scott and McMullen, "The Impact Rewards Programs on Employee Engagement."

126. Ibid.

127. While some total rewards elements contribute to engagement and performance, it is not clear that others do. For example, it's not clear that "programs such as pet insurance and working at home add anything to the business success of our organization." See Jay Schuster and Patricia Zingheim, "Recalibrating Best Practice," *Compensation & Benefits Review* 45, no. 3 (2013), pp. 134–135.

128. http://disneycareers.com/en/working-here/total-rewards, accessed March 24, 2014.

129. This is based on George Bradt, "How the Best Big Companies to Work for Drive Appreciation, Access and Rewards," www.forbes.com/sites/georgebradt/2014/03/12/how-the-best-fortune-500-companies-to-work-for-drive-appreciation- access-rewards-2, accessed March 24, 2014.

130. www.sas.com/en_us/careers.html, accessed March 24, 2014.

131. McMullen, "Eight Recommendations to Improve Employee Engagement."

132. This case based on www.nature.com/scitable/forums/women-in-science/astro-zeneca-settles-women-s-pay-inequality-20334719; www.dol.gov/opa/media/press/ofccp/OFCCP20110829.htm; and http://social.dol.gov/blog/astrazeneca-what-we-learned/, all accessed August 31, 2012.

12

Pay for Performance and Financial Incentives

LEARNING OBJECTIVES

12-1 Explain how you would apply four motivation theories in formulating an incentive plan.

12-2 Discuss the main incentives for individual employees.

12-3 Discuss the pros and cons of commissions versus straight pay for salespeople.

12-4 Describe the main incentives for managers and executives.

12-5 Name and describe the most popular organization-wide incentive plans.

12-6 Explain how to use incentives to improve employee engagement.

The owners of a fast-food franchise in Ahmedabad knew that their stores' performance and profits depended on their employees' performance. They had to face competition from local hotels, other established fast-food chains, and the roadside *Chai Kitlis*. They hoped a new employee incentive program could boost their employees' and their shops' performance. We'll see that they did.

WHERE ARE WE NOW ...

Chapter 11 focused on developing pay plans and on salaries and wages. Incentives are important in any pay plan. The main purpose of this chapter is to explain how managers use incentives to motivate employees. The main topics we'll discuss are money's role in motivation, individual employee incentive and recognition programs, incentives for salespeople, incentives for managers and executives, team and organization-wide incentive plans, and incentives and employee engagement. In Chapter 13, we'll turn to the financial and nonfinancial benefits that comprise the third component of employee compensation packages.

financial incentives
Financial rewards paid to workers whose production exceeds some predetermined standard.

productivity
The ratio of outputs (goods and services) divided by the inputs (resources such as labor and capital).

fair day's work
Output standards devised based on careful, scientific analysis.

scientific management movement
Management approach based on improving work methods through observation and analysis.

variable pay
Any plan that ties pay to productivity or profitability, usually as one-time lump payments.

Money's Role In Motivation

Frederick Taylor popularized using **financial incentives**—financial rewards paid to workers whose production exceeds some predetermined standard—in the late 1800s. As a supervisor at the Midvale Steel Company, Taylor was concerned with what he called "systematic soldiering"—the tendency of employees to produce at the minimum acceptable level. Some workers had the energy to run home and work on their houses after a 12-hour day. Taylor knew that if he could harness this energy at work, Midvale could achieve huge productivity gains. **Productivity** "is the ratio of outputs (goods and services) divided by the inputs (resources such as labor and capital)."[1]

In pursuing that aim, Taylor turned to financial incentives. At the time, primitive incentive plans were in use, but were generally ineffective (because employers arbitrarily changed incentive rates).

Taylor made three contributions. He saw the need for formulating a "**fair day's work**," namely precise output standards for each job. He spearheaded the **scientific management movement**, which emphasized improving work through observation and analysis. And he popularized using incentive pay to reward employees who produced over standard.

Incentive Pay Terminology

Managers often use two terms synonymously with incentive plans.[2] Traditionally, all incentive plans are *pay-for-performance* plans. They all tie employees' pay to the employees' performance. **Variable pay** is more specific: It is usually an incentive plan that ties a group's or team's pay to some measure of the firm's (or the unit's) overall profitability;[3] *profit-sharing plans* (discussed later) are one example.[4] However, confusing as it may be, some experts use the term *variable pay* to include incentive plans for individual employees.[5]

Linking Strategy, Performance, and Incentive Pay

In any case, incentive pay—tying workers' pay to their performance—is widely popular.[6] The problem is that linking pay to performance is easier said than done. (One plan, at Levi Strauss, is widely assumed to have been the last nail in the coffin of Levi's US-based production. The Supreme Court of India has criticized Food Corporation of India's (FCI) incentive scheme for its department workers. It appeared to the apex court that something was "seriously wrong" with the FCI scheme as 370 departmental laborers were paid ₹4.5 lakh a month, a salary which was much more than that of the President of India.[7] In spite of high incentive earnings, FCI's performance was a matter of concern to the government. As logical as it seems to link pay to performance, about 83% of companies with such programs say their programs are at best somewhat successful. One study found that just 28% of the 2,600 U.S. workers it surveyed said their companies' incentive plans motivated them. "Employees don't see a strong connection between pay and performance, and their performance is not particularly influenced by the company's incentive plan," said one expert.[8] Equally problematical is the fact that some incentives incentivize the wrong behavior.[9] Thus, incentivizing "number of cars sold" in a dealership might produce high performance (in numbers of cars sold) but low per-car profit, inadvertently undermining its strategy to boost dealer profits. A study of Indian health workers in the public and private sectors, working in two states, showed that both the groups rated job content and work environment as the most important motivators, higher than compensation. The public sector health workers gave higher ranking to good benefits and recognition of good work by supervisor than the workers in the private sector. Given the geographical and cultural diversity in India, managers and policy makers have to understand the unique motivating factors and local requirements while designing incentive schemes, particularly non-financial incentives.[10]

Another big reason for incentive plans' often-dismal results is the fact that incentives that may motivate some people won't motivate others.[11] Compensation experts therefore argue that managers should understand the motivational bases of incentive plans.[12] We'll review some motivation background next, and then go on to explain various incentive plans.

Motivation and Incentives

Several motivation theories have particular relevance to designing incentive plans.

MOTIVATORS AND FREDERICK HERZBERG   Frederick Herzberg said the best way to motivate someone is to organize the job so that doing it provides the challenge and recognition we all need to help satisfy "higher-level" needs for things like accomplishment and recognition. These needs are relatively insatiable, says Herzberg, so challenging work provides a sort of built-in motivation generator. Doing things to satisfy a worker's "lower-level" needs for things like better pay and working conditions just keeps the person from becoming dissatisfied.

Herzberg says the factors ("hygienes") that satisfy lower-level needs are different from those ("motivators") that satisfy or partially satisfy higher-level needs. If *hygiene* factors (factors outside the job itself, such as working conditions, salary, and incentive pay) are inadequate, employees become dissatisfied. However, adding more of these hygienes (like incentives) to the job (supplying what Herzberg calls "extrinsic motivation") is an inferior way to try to motivate someone, because lower-level needs are quickly satisfied. Inevitably the person says, in effect, "I want another raise."

Instead of relying on hygienes, says Herzberg, managers interested in creating a self-motivated workforce should emphasize "job content" or *motivator* factors. Managers do this by enriching workers' jobs so that the jobs are more challenging, and by providing feedback and recognition—by making doing the job intrinsically motivating, in other words. In organizational psychology, **intrinsic motivation** is motivation that derives from the pleasure someone gets from doing the job or task. It comes from "within" the person, rather than from externally, such as from a financial incentive plan. Intrinsic motivation means that just doing the task provides the motivation. Herzberg makes the point that relying exclusively on financial incentives is risky. The employer should also provide the recognition and challenging work that most people desire.

DEMOTIVATORS AND EDWARD DECI   Psychologist Edward Deci's work highlights another potential downside to relying too heavily on extrinsic rewards: They may backfire. Deci found that extrinsic rewards could at times actually detract from the person's intrinsic motivation.[13] The point may be stated thusly: Be cautious in devising incentive pay for highly motivated employees, lest you inadvertently demean and detract from the desire they have to do the job out of a sense of responsibility.

EXPECTANCY THEORY AND VICTOR VROOM   In general, people won't pursue rewards they find unattractive, or where the odds of success are very low. Psychologist Victor Vroom's expectancy motivation theory echoes these commonsense observations. He says a person's motivation to exert some level of effort depends on three things: the person's **expectancy** (in terms of probability) that his or her effort will lead to performance;[14] **instrumentality**, or the perceived connection (if any) between successful performance and actually obtaining the rewards; and **valence**, which represents the perceived value the person attaches to the reward.[15] In Vroom's theory:

$$\text{Motivation} = (E \times I \times V),$$

where E represents expectancy, I instrumentality, and V valence. If E or I or V is zero or inconsequential, there will be no motivation.

Vroom's theory has three implications for how managers design incentive plans.

- First, if employees don't *expect* that effort will produce performance, no motivation will occur. So, managers must ensure that their employees have the skills to do the job, and believe they can do the job. Thus, training, job descriptions, and confidence building and support are important in using incentives.
- Second, Vroom's theory suggests that employees must see the *instrumentality* of their efforts—they must believe that successful performance will in fact lead to

intrinsic motivation

Motivation that derives from the pleasure someone gets from doing the job or task.

expectancy

A person's expectation that his or her effort will lead to performance.

instrumentality

The perceived relationship between successful performance and obtaining the reward.

valence

The perceived value a person attaches to the reward.

getting the reward. Managers can accomplish this, for instance, by creating easy to understand incentive plans.

- Third, the reward itself must be of *value* to the employee. Ideally, the manager should take into account individual employee preferences.

behavior modification

Using contingent rewards or punishment to change behavior.

BEHAVIOR MODIFICATION/REINFORCEMENT AND B. F. SKINNER   Using incentives also assumes the manager understands how consequences affect behavior.[16] Psychologist B.F. Skinner's findings are useful here. Managers apply Skinner's principles by using *behavior modification*. **Behavior modification** means changing behavior through rewards or punishments that are contingent on performance. For managers, behavior modification boils down to two main principles. First, that behavior that appears to lead to a positive consequence (reward) tends to be repeated, whereas behavior that appears to lead to a negative consequence (punishment) tends not to be repeated; and second, that managers can therefore get someone to change his or her behavior by providing the properly scheduled rewards (or punishment).

To arrange our discussion, we will organize the following sections around individual employee incentive and recognition programs, sales compensation programs, management and executive incentive compensation programs, and team- and organization-wide incentive programs. First, however, we look at some legal aspects of incentive plan design.

KNOW YOUR EMPLOYMENT LAW

Employee Incentives and the Law

Various laws affect incentive and bonus pay. Under the Payment of Bonus Act of 1965 if the incentive the worker receives is in the form of a prize or cash award, the employer generally must *exclude the value of that award* when calculating the worker's overtime pay for that pay period.[17] So, unless you structure the incentive bonuses properly, the bonus itself becomes part of the wages. According to the Payment of Bonus Act, salary or wages means all remuneration (other than overtime pay) which can be expressed as money. However, it does not cover any allowances [Section 2.21.(i)]; value of house and amenities [Section 2.21.(ii)]; traveling concessions [2.21.(iii)]; any incentives, production, and attendance bonus (2.21.(iv)); social security or pension contribution by employer [Section 2.21.(v)]; payment for retrenchment, gratuity and retirement benefits [Section 2.21.(v)]; and commission paid to employee [Section 2.21.(vi)]. If an employee is given free food or paid an allowance for food, then the value of food is considered as a part of the salary for the calculation of bonus. Since 1 April 2014, workers who earn up to ₹21,000 per month are eligible for bonus. (Earlier, the eligibility was ₹10,000 per month).

LEARNING OBJECTIVE 12-2

Discuss the main incentives for individual employees.

piecework

A system of pay based on the number of items processed by each individual worker in a unit of time, such as items per hour or items per day.

Individual Employee Incentive and Recognition Programs

Several incentive plans are particularly suited for use with individual employees.

Piecework

Piecework is the oldest incentive plan and still the most commonly used. Earnings are tied directly to what the worker produces; the person is paid a piece rate for each unit he or she produces. Thus, if Rakesh Kumar gets ₹4 apiece for stamping out doorjambs, then he would get, say, ₹800 for stamping out 200.

Developing a workable piece rate plan requires both job evaluation and (strictly speaking) industrial engineering. Job evaluation enables you to assign an hourly wage rate to the job in question. But the crucial issue in piece rate planning is the production standard, and this standard is often developed by industrial engineers. The engineers state production standards in terms of a standard number of minutes per unit or a standard number of units per hour. In Rakesh's case, the job evaluation indicated that his doorjamb stamping job was worth `80 an hour. The industrial engineer determined that 20 jambs per hour was the standard production rate. Therefore, the engineered piece rate (for each doorjamb) was `80 divided by 20, which equals `4 per doorjamb.

straight piecework
An incentive plan in which a person is paid a sum for each item he or she makes or sells, with a strict proportionality between results and rewards.

With a **straight piecework** plan, Rakesh would be paid based on the number of doorjambs he produced; there would be no guaranteed minimum wage. However, today most employers must guarantee their workers a minimum wage. With a guaranteed piecework plan, Rakesh would be paid ₹40 per hour (as per the minimum wage of 2015) whether or not he stamped out 18 doorjambs per hour. But he would also get ₹4 for each unit over 18.

Piecework generally implies straight piecework, a strict proportionality between results and rewards regardless of the level of output. Thus, in Rakesh's case, he continues to get ₹4 apiece for stamping out doorjambs, even if he stamps out more than planned, say, 500 per day. However, certain piecework plans call for a sharing of productivity gains between worker and employer. Typically, the worker here receives reduced credit for all production above standard—perhaps ₹3.50 per piece over 200 units per day, for instance.[18] Conversely, some such plans boost the employee's share once a threshold is met—such as paying Rakesh ₹4.50 each once he reached 200 units per day.

standard hour plan
A plan by which a worker is paid a basic hourly rate but is paid an extra percentage of his or her rate for production exceeding the standard per hour or per day. Similar to piecework payment but based on a percent premium.

The **standard hour plan** is like the piecework plan, with one difference. Instead of getting a rate per piece, the worker gets a pay premium equal to the percent by which his or her performance exceeds the standard. So if Rakesh's standard is 160 doorjambs per day (₹640 per day), and he brings in 200 jambs, he'd get an extra 25% (40/160), or ₹800. Using this approach may reduce workers' tendency to link their production standard (18 jambs per hour) to pay. This makes it easier to change the standard.

ADVANTAGES AND DISADVANTAGES   Piecework incentive plans have several advantages. They are simple to calculate and easily understood by employees. Piecework plans appear equitable in principle, and their incentive value can be powerful since they tie pay directly to performance.

Piecework also has disadvantages. The main one is its unsavory reputation, based on some employers' habit of arbitrarily raising production standards whenever they found their workers earning "excessive" wages. A more subtle disadvantage is that since piece rates are quoted on a per piece basis, in worker's minds the production standard (in pieces per hour) becomes tied inseparably to the amount of money earned.

Piecework systems thus risk engendering rigidity. When the employer tries to revise production standards, resistance ensues.[19] Employees become preoccupied with producing the number of units needed. They can become less focused on quality and may resist switching jobs (since doing so could reduce productivity). Attempts to introduce new processes may more likely fail, insofar as they require adjusting engineered standards. Equipment maintenance tends to decline as employees focus on maximizing quantity.[20]

For such reasons, more employers are moving to other plans, such as those on the following pages.[21]

Merit Pay as an Incentive

merit pay (merit raise)
Any salary increase awarded to an employee based on his or her individual performance.

Merit pay or a **merit raise** is a salary increase the firm awards to an individual employee based on individual performance. It is different from a bonus in that it usually becomes part of the employee's base salary, whereas bonuses are generally one-time payments. Although the term *merit pay* can apply to the incentive raises given to any employee, the term is more often used for professional, office, and clerical employees. In the Indian context, particularly the private sector, meritorious employees are given higher annual increments, which permanently increases the basic pay.

Merit pay is the subject of much debate. Advocates argue that awarding pay raises across the board (without regard to individual merit) may detract from performance by showing employees they'll be rewarded regardless of how they perform.

Detractors present good reasons why merit pay can backfire. Most notably, since many appraisals are unfair, so too are the merit decisions you base them on.[22]

The evidence, while mixed, tends to support using merit pay. One study focused on 218 workers in a nuclear waste facility. The researchers found a "very modest relationship between merit pay increase and performance rating."[23] Research into tying merit pay increases to teachers' or faculty members' research and/or teaching performance suggest that merit pay is more clearly linked with research productivity than with teaching effectiveness.[24]

When they're not working, the solution is not to throw out merit raises, but to improve them. This starts with establishing effective appraisal procedures and ensuring that managers do in fact tie merit pay awards to performance.

Merit plan effectiveness also depends on differentiating among employees. In one survey, the highest-paid office clerical employees got short-term incentive payouts of about 13%, the lowest-rated got 3%, and mid-rated employees got 8%.[25]

Employers are experimenting with using crowdsourcing for awarding bonuses. For example, one small San Francisco–based company asked each employee to allocate 1,200 stock options among coworkers however they chose.[26] Allowing everyone to "vote" on each other's performance this way can help identify employees who are helpful team contributors but might otherwise slip under management's radar.

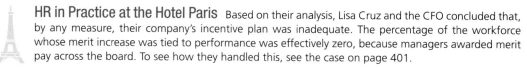

HR in Practice at the Hotel Paris Based on their analysis, Lisa Cruz and the CFO concluded that, by any measure, their company's incentive plan was inadequate. The percentage of the workforce whose merit increase was tied to performance was effectively zero, because managers awarded merit pay across the board. To see how they handled this, see the case on page 401.

MERIT PAY OPTIONS   Two adaptations of merit pay plans are popular. One awards merit raises in a lump sum once a year and does *not* make the raise part of the employee's salary (making them, in effect, short-term bonuses for lower-level workers). Traditional merit increases are cumulative, but these *lump-sum merit raises* are not. This produces two potential benefits. First, the merit raise is not baked into the employee's salary, so you need not pay it year after year. Lump-sum merit increases can also be more dramatic motivators than a traditional merit raise. For example, a 5% lump-sum merit payment to an employee with an annual salary of ₹5,00,000 is ₹50,000 annual cash, as opposed to a monthly merit payout of ₹4,166 for 12 months.

The other adaptation ties merit awards to both individual and organizational performance. Table 12-1 presents an example. In this example, you might measure the company's performance by, say, profits. Here, company performance and the employee's performance (using his or her performance appraisal) receive equal weight in computing the merit pay. In Table 12-1 an outstanding performer would receive 70% of his or her maximum lump-sum award even when the organization's performance was marginal. However, employees with marginal or unacceptable performance would get no lump-sum awards even when the firm's performance was outstanding. For example, at Discovery Communications executive assistants can receive bonuses of up to 10% of their salaries. The boss's evaluation of the assistant's individual performance accounts for 80% of the potential bonus, 10% is based on how the division does, and 10% on how the company does.[27]

Incentives for Professional Employees

Professional employees are those whose work involves the application of learned knowledge to the solution of the employer's problems, such as lawyers and engineers.

Making incentive pay decisions for professional employees is challenging. For one thing, firms usually pay professionals well anyway. For another, they're already driven by the desire to produce high-caliber work.

However, it is unrealistic to assume that people like Google engineers work only for professional gratification. Few firms, therefore, work harder to maintain competitive incentives for professionals. For example, Google reportedly pays higher incentives to engineers working on important projects. Those who choose the intrinsic motivation of working on more theoretical long-term projects are rewarded if their

TABLE 12-1 **Merit Award Determination Matrix (an Example)**

The Employee's Performance Rating (Weight = 0.50)	The Company's Performance (Weight = 0.50)				
	Outstanding	Excellent	Good	Marginal	Unacceptable
Outstanding	1.00	0.90	0.80	0.70	0.00
Excellent	0.90	0.80	0.70	0.60	0.00
Good	0.80	0.70	0.60	0.50	0.00
Marginal	—	—	—	—	—
Unacceptable	—	—	—	—	—

Note: To determine the dollar value of each employee's award: (1) multiply the employee's annual, straight-time wage or salary as of June 30 times his or her maximum incentive award (as determined by management or the board—such as, "10% of each employee's pay") and (2) multiply the resultant product by the appropriate percentage figure from this table. For example, if an employee had an annual salary of ₹4,00,000 on June 30 and a maximum incentive award of 7% and if her performance and the organization's performance were both "excellent," the employee's award would be ₹22,400 (₹40,000 × 0.07 × 0.80 = ₹22,400).

research pays off.[28] As at most Silicon Valley firms, Google's professionals also bask in the light of potentially millionaire-making stock option grants.

Dual-career ladders are another way to manage professionals' pay. At many employers, higher pay requires rerouting from, say, engineering into management. However, not all professionals want management. Indian public sector banks have created the specialist cadre, for those who wish to stay in domains and choose against general banking career track. Therefore, many employers institute one path for managers, and another for technical experts, allowing the latter to earn higher pay without switching to management.[29]

Nonfinancial and Recognition-Based Awards

Employers often supplement financial incentives with various nonfinancial and recognition-based awards. The term *recognition program* usually refers to formal programs, such as employee-of-the-month programs. Bank of Baroda has introduced a monthly, 'employee of the month' scheme for each branch. The name of selected employee is made public. *Social recognition program* generally refers to informal manager–employee exchanges such as praise, approval, or expressions of appreciation for a job well done. Tata Communications believe that young employees (the average age is 35 years in the company) have to be recognized differently. Thus, exceptional performers are promoted and given chances to demonstrate entrepreneurship and business impact.[30] *Performance feedback* means providing quantitative or qualitative information on task performance so as to change or maintain performance; showing workers a graph of how their performance is trending is an example.[31]

TRENDS SHAPING HR: *DIGITAL AND SOCIAL MEDIA*[32]

Employers are bulking up their recognition programs with digital support. For example, Baudville, a workplace recognition vendor, offers an e-card service called ePraise. Employers use this to tell employees they're appreciated. Intuit shifted its employee recognition, years of service, patent awards, and wellness awards programs to Globoforce, an online awards vendor. This "allowed us to build efficiencies and improved effectiveness" into the programs, says Intuit's vice president of performance, rewards, and workplace.[33] Management consultant Hewitt Associates uses www.bravanta.com to help its managers more easily recognize exceptional employee service with special awards. Other recognition sites include www.premierechoiceaward.com/secure/home.asp, and www.giveanything.com.

Various new apps let employees showcase their awards, contributions, and praise from coworkers. For example, go to http://quickbooks.intuit.com/r/, and key "7 mobile apps for recognizing and rewarding employees" into the search box, and click "search."[34] Apps also enable employees to praise each other.[35] For example, one lets employees "give recognition by picking out a badge and typing in a quick note to thank the people who matter most...." Others let users post the positive feedback they receive to their LinkedIn profiles.

Mobile technology is also changing how employers incentivize front-line service people. For example, while paying for an espresso in some coffeehouses with a credit card, the iPad screen will ask how big a tip you want to leave. ■

Most employers combine financial and nonfinancial awards. At American Skandia, which provides insurance and financial planning products and services, customer service reps who exceed standards receive a plaque, a $500 check, their photo and story on the firm's internal Web site, and a dinner for themselves and their teams.[36] IIM Ahmedabad gives special cash awards, certificates, and public appreciation to its faculty and staff members who excel in performance (teaching excellence and research for faculty, and work performance for staff). An Indian interior design firm rewards its employees by supporting them to attend activities of their interest, like dance classes, paining, etc.[37] Recently, Infosys rewarded top performers with iPhones, while HCL gave Mercedes cars and international vacations. After studying various Indian practices for rewards, *People Matters* concluded that high power or sensational rewards, generous medical benefits and health-related activities, and frequent recognitions are the top three trends.[38] One survey of 235 managers found that the most-used financial and nonfinancial rewards to motivate employees (from most used to least) were:[39] employee recognition, gift certificates, special events, cash rewards, merchandise incentives, e-mail/print communications, training programs, work/life benefits, variable pay, group travel, individual travel, and sweepstakes. The HR Tools feature elaborates.

▶ IMPROVING PERFORMANCE: *HR Tools for Line Managers and Small Businesses*

The supervisor should not rely just on the employer's financial incentive plans for motivating subordinates. Those plans may not be complete, plus there are simply too many opportunities to motivate employees every day to let those opportunities pass. What to do?

First, the best option for motivating an employee is also the simplest—*make sure the employee has a doable goal* and that he or she agrees with it. It makes little sense to try to motivate employees with financial incentives if they don't know their goals or don't agree with them. Psychologist Edwin Locke and his colleagues have consistently found that specific, challenging goals lead to higher task performance than do specific, unchallenging goals; vague goals; or no goals.

Second, *recognizing an employee's contribution* is a powerful motivation tool. Studies (and theories like those of Herzberg) show that recognition has a positive impact on performance, either alone or in combination with financial rewards. For example, in one study, combining financial rewards with recognition produced a 30% performance improvement in service firms, almost twice the effect of using each reward alone.

Third, use *social recognition* (such as compliments) as positive reinforcement on a day-to-day basis. Figure 12-1 presents a list.[40] ■

- Challenging work assignments
- Freedom to choose own work activity
- Having fun built into work
- More of preferred task
- Role as boss's stand-in when he or she is away
- Role in presentations to top management
- Job rotation
- Encouragement of learning and continuous improvement

- Being provided with ample encouragement
- Being allowed to set own goals
- Compliments
- Expression of appreciation in front of others
- Note of thanks
- Employee-of-the-month award
- Special commendation
- Bigger desk
- Bigger office or cubicle

FIGURE 12-1 **Social Recognition and Related Positive Reinforcement Managers Can Use**

Source: Based on Bob Nelson, *1001 Ways to Reward Employees* (New York: Workman Pub, 1994), p. 19; Sunny C. L. Fong and Margaret A. Shaffer, "The Dimensionality and Determinants of Pay Satisfaction: A Cross-Cultural Investigation of a Group Incentive Plan," *International Journal of Human Resource Management* 14, no. 4 (June 2003), p. 559 (22).

Job Design

Although not usually considered an "incentive," job design (discussed in Chapter 4) can significantly impact employee motivation and retention. A study by Harvard Business School researchers concluded that job design is a primary driver of employee engagement. A study by Sibson Consulting concluded that job responsibility and feedback were the fifth- and seventh-most important drivers of employee engagement. A study by Towers Watson concluded that challenging work ranked as the seventh-most important driver for attracting employees.[41] Job design is thus a useful part of an employer's total rewards program.

The Strategic Context feature illustrates how employers combine incentives to boost profits.

▶ IMPROVING PERFORMANCE: *The Strategic Context*

The Fast-Food Chain

The heart of just about any fast-food chain's strategy is to control performance: One chain wanted to know, "Can financial and nonfinancial incentives boost performance in our fast-food chain?"

Two researchers studied the impact of financial and nonfinancial incentives on business performance in 21 stores of a fast-food franchise in the Midwest.[42] The researchers compared performance over time in stores that did and did not use financial and nonfinancial incentives. Each store had about 25 workers and two managers. The researchers trained the managers to identify measurable employee behaviors that were currently deficient but that could influence store performance. Example behaviors included "keeping both hands moving at the drive-through window" and "repeating the customer's order back to him or her."[43] Then the researchers instituted financial and nonfinancial incentive plans. They measured store performance in terms of gross profitability (revenue minus expenses), drive-through time, and employee turnover.

Financial Incentives

Some employees in some of the stores received financial incentives for exhibiting the desired behaviors. The financial incentives consisted of lump-sum bonuses in the workers' paychecks. For example, if the manager observed a work team exhibiting up to 50 behaviors (such as "working during idle time") during the observation period, he or she added $25 to the paychecks of all store employees that period; 50 to 100 behaviors added $50 per paycheck, and more than 100 behaviors added $75 per paycheck. Payouts eventually rose over time as the employees learned to enact the behaviors they were to exhibit.

Nonfinancial Incentives

The researchers trained the managers in some stores to use nonfinancial incentives such as feedback and recognition. For example, for *performance feedback* managers maintained charts showing the drive-through times at the end of each day. They placed the charts by the time clocks. Thus, these store employees could keep track of their store's performance on measures like drive-through times. The researchers also trained managers to administer *recognition* to employees. For instance, "I noticed that today the drive-through times were really good."[44]

Results

Both the financial and nonfinancial incentives improved employee and store performance.[45] For example, store profits rose 30% for those units where managers used financial rewards. Store profits rose 36% for those units where managers used nonfinancial rewards. During the same 9-month period, drive-through times decreased 19% for the financial incentives group, and 25% for the nonfinancial incentives groups. Turnover improved 13% for the financial incentives group, and 10% for the nonfinancial incentives group.

Implications for Managers

Here is what these findings mean for managers designing incentive plans:[46]

1. Link the incentive to behavior that is crucial for achieving strategic goals.[47] For example, this chain wanted to boost store performance and profits. Incentivizing employees to work faster and smarter accomplished that.

2. The point of an incentive is to motivate the person to work better. Therefore, it makes more sense to use an incentive plan when (1) motivation (not ability) is the problem; (2) when the employee's effort and results are directly related; and (3) when the employee can actually control the results you plan to incentivize. Put another way, make sure there is a clear link between the person's *effort and performance* and between the *performance and reward*, that the incentive is *attractive* to the employee, and that the employee *has the skills* to do the job.

3. Don't just rely on material rewards. Support the incentive plan with performance feedback (as in the form of performance graphs) and with recognition.[48]

4. Set complete standards. For example, don't just pay for "repeating the customer's order" if speed is important too.

5. Be scientific. As in this study, *gather evidence* and analyze the effects of the incentive plan over time.[49] ∎

LEARNING OBJECTIVE 12-3

Discuss the pros and cons of commissions versus straight pay for salespeople.

Incentives for Salespeople

As one survey said, "the performance metrics given to the sales team must drive behaviors that will help the company's ... strategy to be successful."[50]

Unfortunately, the same survey also found that "30% of respondents believe their sales compensation program rewarded the right behaviors 'not well' or 'very poorly.'"[51]

Employers are therefore moving to align (1) how they measure and reward their salespeople with (2) their firms' strategic goals.[52]

Salary Plan

Sales compensation plans may focus on salary, commissions, or some combination to drive sales objectives.[53] Some firms pay salespeople fixed salaries (perhaps with occasional incentives in the form of bonuses, sales contest prizes, and the like).[54] Straight salary makes sense when the main task involves prospecting (finding new clients) or account servicing. Turnover is another reason. Faced with the difficulty of attracting and keeping good salespeople, a Buick–GMC dealership in Lincolnton, North Carolina, offers straight salary as an option to salespeople who sell an average of at least eight vehicles a month (plus a small "retention bonus" per car sold).[55]

The straight salary approach also makes it easier to switch salespersons' territories, and it can foster sales staff loyalty. The main disadvantage, of course, is that straight salary may demotivate potentially high-performing salespeople.[56]

Commission Plan

Straight commission plans pay salespeople for results, and only for results. Commission plans tend to attract high-performing salespeople who see that effort clearly produces rewards. Sales costs are proportionate to sales rather than fixed, and the company's fixed sales costs are thus lower. Such plans are easy to understand and compute. Commission plan alternatives include straight commissions, quota bonuses (for meeting particular quotas), management by objectives programs (pay is based on specific metrics), and ranking programs (these reward high achievers but pay little or no bonuses to the lowest-performing salespeople).[57]

However, problems abound. In poorly designed plans, salespeople may focus on making the sale, and neglect nonselling duties such as servicing small accounts and pushing hard-to-sell items. Wide variations in pay may occur; this can make some feel the plan is inequitable. Misjudging sales potential can lead to excessively high commissions and to the need to cut commission rates. Salespersons' pay may be excessive in boom times and low in recessions. Furthermore, sales performance—like any performance—reflects not just motivation, but ability. If the person can't sell, commissions won't produce sales.[58]

Combination Plan

Most companies pay salespeople a combination of salary and commissions, usually with a sizable salary component. An incentive mix of about 70% base salary/30% incentive seems typical; this cushions the salesperson's downside risk (of earning nothing), while limiting the risk that the commissions could get out of hand from the firm's point of view.[59]

Combination plans have pros and cons.[60] They give salespeople a floor to their earnings, let the company specify what services the salary component is for (such as servicing current accounts), and still provide an incentive for superior performance. However, the salary component isn't tied to performance, so the employer trades away some incentive value. Eureka Forbes has created attractive, contest-based incentives where those who achieve the set sales target are rewarded with international holidays and membership in exclusive, aspirational groups like the Hall of Fame.

Combination plans also tend to become complicated, and misunderstandings can result. This might not be a problem with a simple salary-plus-commission plan, but most plans are not so simple. For example, in a "commission-plus-drawing-account" plan, the salesperson is paid based on commissions. However, he or she can draw on future earnings during low sales periods. In the "commission-plus-bonus" plan, the firm pays its salespeople mostly based on commissions. However, they also get a small bonus for directed activities like selling slow-moving items.

Maximizing Sales Results

In setting sales quotas and commission rates, the goal is to motivate sales activity but avoid excessive commissions. Unfortunately, the tendency to set commission rates informally often reduces plans' effectiveness.[61]

Setting effective quotas is an art. Questions to ask include: Are quotas communicated to the sales force within 1 month of the start of the period? Does the sales force know how their quotas are set? Do you combine bottom-up information (like account forecasts) with top-down requirements (like the company business goals)? Are returns and de-bookings reasonably low?[62]

One expert suggests this rule as to whether the sales incentive plan is effective: 75% or more of the sales force achieving quota or better, 10% of the sales force achieving higher performance level (than previously), and 5% to 10% of the sales force achieving below-quota performance and receiving performance development coaching.[63] The employer should also consider the effect of sales carryover. In most firms, a significant portion of the sales in one year reflects a "carryover" (sales that would repeat even without any efforts by the sales force) of sales from the prior year. Paying the sales force a commission on all the current year's sales means the employer has paid a commission on last year's carryover sales, which the sales force had little or no role in bringing in this year.[64]

A survey of sales effectiveness reveals that salespeople at high-performing companies:

- Receive 38% of their total cash compensation in the form of *sale incentive pay* (compared with 27% for salespeople at low-performing companies)
- Are twice as likely to receive stock, *stock options*, or other equity pay as their counterparts at low-performing companies (36% versus 18%)
- Spend 264 more hours per year on *high-value sales activities* (e.g., prospecting, making sales presentations, and closing) than salespeople at low-performing companies
- Spend 40% more time each year with their *best potential customers*—qualified leads and prospects they know—than salespeople at low-performing companies
- Spend nearly 25% *less time on administration*, allowing them to allocate more time to core sales activities, such as prospecting leads and closing sales[65]

Distinguishing among performers is also important. For example, some companies distinguish among stars, laggards, and core performers. Some companies limit how much their salespeople can earn in commissions, but doing so can perversely encourage stars to quit selling when they reach their quotas. Laggards seem to do better with more frequent, quarterly bonuses and social pressure to improve their performance. Core performers—the vast midrange of the sales force—should have multitier targets. The first tier target is what sales agents historically attain. The second tier reflects what a small percentage of the sales force attains. The third tier target is usually only attained by the company's star salespeople.[66]

Sales Incentives in Action

Car salespersons' compensation ranges from 100% commission to a small base salary with commission accounting for most of total compensation. Traditionally, a car salesperson's commission is based on a percentage of the difference between the dealer's invoice cost and the amount the car is sold for, minus an amount to cover the "pack" or dealer overhead (the pack being perhaps ₹5,000 for a new car to ₹10,000 for a used car, and rising for pricier cars).[67]

This approach encourages the salesperson to hold firm on the retail price, and to push "after-sale products" like floor mats and side moldings. There may also be extra incentives to sell packages such as rustproofing. For selling slow-moving vehicles, the salesperson may get a "spiff"—an extra incentive bonus over commission. And there are bonuses, such as Salesperson of the Month.[68]

Commission plans like these still dominate, but not as much. Many dealers are substituting salary plus bonus plans for commissions. This reflects the growing emphasis on "one price no hassle" pricing.[69] But in either case, the pay plan's aim is to produce the salesperson behaviors the dealership needs to support its strategic aims.

Performance Pay for the Government of India

Rewarding performing employees in the government has always been a challenge. The Sixth Pay Commission suggested the Performance Related Incentive Scheme (PRIS) which included performance evaluation based higher annual increments and annual incentive payment. The Seventh Central Pay Commission (Seventh CPC) further refined it.

The Seventh CPC wanted incentives to be linked with departmental goals and annual appraisal of government employees (APAR) with 60% weightage given to work output and 40% to personal attributes. The scheme is yet to be fully implemented. The Commission also recommended that poor performers should not receive annual increase in base salary. The recommendations can impact 50 lakh central government employees.[70]

TRENDS SHAPING HR: *DIGITAL AND SOCIAL MEDIA*

Somewhat astonishingly, given the amount of money employers pay out in commissions, about 60% of employers track sales performance and sales commissions much as they did decades ago, using spreadsheets.[71] But to maximize performance, the sales manager typically needs evidence, such as: Do the salespeople know how we measure and reward performance? And, does our commission plan maximize sales of our most profitable products?[72] Spreadsheets don't easily support such analyses.[73] For example, with more than 1,000 sales representatives, First Tennessee Bank had problems managing its sales incentive programs.[74] Bank employees had to enter by hand sales information for each of the 1,000 sales reps onto Excel spreadsheets. The process "had begun to spiral out of control." Switching to an *enterprise incentive management* (EIM) software system solved the problem.[75]

Many employers therefore use such EIM software to track and control sales commissions.[76] Several vendors supply these. For example, Oracle Sales Cloud enables management to easily create scorecard metrics such as number of prospecting calls and sales contracts, and to monitor these in real-time on the system's dashboards.[77] Users can also gamify the sales incentive process with Oracle Sales Cloud, by creating rewards such as points or badges based on each salesperson's performance. ∎

Incentives for Managers and Executives

Managers play a crucial role in divisional and company-wide profitability, and employers therefore put considerable thought into how to reward them. Most managers get short-term and long-term incentives in addition to salary.[78] Of firms offering short-term incentive plans, virtually all—96% in one study—provided those incentives in cash. For those offering long-term incentives, about 48% offer them as stock options. The options aim to reward management for long-term growth in shareholder value.[79]

Strategy and the Executive's Long-Term and Total Rewards Package

Whether consolidating operations or pursuing growth, firms can't fully implement most strategies in just 1 or 2 years. Therefore, the long-term signals you send managers via their long-term incentives can determine whether the firm's strategy succeeds.

The executives' reward components—base salary, short- and long-term incentives, and benefits—must align with each other and with the company's strategic aims. Compensation experts suggest first specifying the strategic aims—"What is our strategy and what are our strategic goals?"—and then deciding what long-term behaviors (boosting sales, cutting costs, and so on) are important for achieving these strategic aims. Next shape each component of the executive total compensation package (base salary, short- and long-term incentives, and benefits) to encourage these required behaviors; then group the components into a balanced plan that makes sense in terms of motivating the executive to achieve the firm's aims. The point is this: Each pay component should help focus the manager's attention on the behaviors required to achieve the company's strategic goals.[80]

Using multiple, strategy-based performance criteria for incentivizing executives is best. Criteria include financial performance, number of strategic goals met, employee productivity measures, customer satisfaction surveys, and employee morale surveys.[81]

One expert estimates that the typical CEO's salary accounts for about one-fifth of his or her pay. A bonus based on explicit performance standards accounts for another fifth, and long-term incentive awards such as stock options and long-term performance plans account for the remaining three-fifths.[82] Ideally, the plan's performance standards should include a combination of market benchmarks (such as performance against competitors) as well as business performance standards (such as earnings per share growth).

Remuneration of Key Managerial Personnel in India

The compensation of executive management of a company (i.e., those who are responsible for day-to-day management) is governed by the Companies Act, 2013. This act along with the Companies (Appointment and Remuneration of Managerial Personnel), 2014, deals with both legal and process part of compensation for key managerial persons. The ceiling for key managerial remuneration (who is considered manager under the act is defined) is 11% of the net profit of the company (Section 197). In exceptional cases, with approval from the general body meeting (GBM) and the central government, higher payment is possible.

SARBANES-OXLEY ACT IN THE US The Sarbanes-Oxley Act of 2002 affects how employers formulate their executive incentive programs. Congress passed Sarbanes-Oxley to inject a higher level of responsibility into executives' and board members' decisions. It makes them personally liable for violating their fiduciary responsibilities to their shareholders. The act also requires CEOs and CFOs of a public company to repay any bonuses, incentives, or equity-based compensation received from the company during the 12-month period following the issuance of a financial statement that the company must restate due to material noncompliance with a financial reporting requirement stemming from misconduct.[83]

Short-Term Incentives and the Annual Bonus

For better or worse, employers are shifting away from long-term incentives to put more emphasis on short-term performance and incentives.[84] Most firms have **annual bonus** plans for motivating managers' short-term performance. Such short-term incentives can easily produce plus-or-minus adjustments of 25% or more to total pay. Three factors influence one's bonus: eligibility, fund size, and individual performance.

ELIGIBILITY   Employers first decide eligibility. Traditionally, most based annual bonus eligibility on job level/title, base salary, and/or officer status. Some simply based eligibility on job level or job title, or salary.[85] Recently, more employers are offering a broader range of employee annual incentive plans "… in which both executives and other employees participate."[86]

The trend is evident from surveys of what determines bonus plan eligibility. Rather than job title or officer status, *salary grade or band* was the most common eligibility determinant, reported by 42% of employers in one survey. This was followed by *title/reporting relationship* (24%), *officer status* (13%), *compensation committee approval* (11%), *discretionary* (6%), and *base salary* (2%).[87]

The percentage size of any bonus is typically greater for top executives. Thus, an executive earning $250,000 in salary may be able to earn another 80% of his or her salary as a bonus, while a manager in the same firm earning $100,000 can earn only another 30%. Recently, Microsoft's CEO was eligible for an annual bonus of up to 100% of his salary (but collected only half). A typical bonus percentage might be executives, 45% of base salary; managers, 25%; and supervisory personnel, 12%.

FUND SIZE   Second, one must determine how big the annual bonus fund should be. Most employers (33% in one survey) traditionally use the sum of targets approach.[88] This means they estimate the likely bonus for each eligible ("target") employee, and total these to arrive at the bonus pool's size.

However, more employers are funding the short-term bonus based on financial results. Here there are no fixed rules about the proportion of profits to pay out. One

annual bonus
Plans that are designed to motivate short-term performance of managers and that are tied to company profitability.

Even in retail stores, it's not unusual to compensate managers partly based on short-term sales and profits.

Blue Jean Images/Alamy Stock Photo

alternative is to reserve a minimal amount of the profits, say, 10%, for safeguarding stockholders' investments. Then establish a fund for bonuses equal to, say, 20% of the operating profit (profit from the company's core business) before taxes in excess of this safeguard amount. Suppose the operating profits were $200,000 (after putting away 10% to safeguard stockholders). Then the management bonus fund might be 20% of $200,000 or $40,000. Most employers use more than one financial measure on which to base the bonus fund, with sales, earnings per share, and cash flow the most popular.[89] Other illustrative formulas include:

- Twelve percent of net earnings after deducting 6% of net capital
- Ten percent of the amount by which net income exceeds 5% of stockholders' equity

Employers also use formulas to build their bonus pools on other measures they wish to emphasize. For example, Transocean Ltd., the firm that managed the Deepwater Horizon Gulf oil rig that sank in 2010, uses a formula that includes "safety" as 25% of the formula. After the Gulf explosion, senior Transocean executives donated any safety bonuses to the victims' families.[90]

Some firms don't use a formula to determine fund size at all, but make that decision on a discretionary basis.[91] Others, again, determine fund size by simply summing up the likely awards.

THE INDIVIDUAL AWARDS   Finally, one must decide the actual individual awards. Typically, the employer sets a target bonus (as well as maximum bonus, perhaps double the target bonus) for each eligible position. The actual bonus then reflects the manager's performance. For example, having previously decided which financial performance measures (return on assets, revenue growth, and so on) to use to measure each manager's performance, the employer computes preliminary total company bonus estimates, and compares the total amount of money required with the bonus fund available.[92] If necessary, it then adjusts the individual bonus estimates. In any case, outstanding managers should receive at least their target bonuses, and marginal ones should receive at best below-average awards. Use what you save on the marginal employees to supplement the outstanding employees.

One question is whether to give managers bonuses based on individual performance, corporate performance, or both. Firms usually tie top-level executive bonuses mostly to overall corporate results (or divisional results if the executive heads a major division). But as one moves farther down, corporate profits become a less accurate gauge of a manager's contribution. For supervisors or the heads of functional departments, it often makes more sense to gear the bonus more closely to individual performance. A study of CEOs of Standard & Poor's 1500 companies for one 3-year period found that 57% of the CEOs received pay increases although company performance (in terms of total shareholder return) did not improve.[93]

Many firms do end up tying short-term bonuses to both organizational and individual performance. Perhaps the simplest method is the *split-award plan*. This makes the manager eligible for two bonuses, one based on his or her individual effort and one

TABLE 12-2 Multiplier Approach to Determining Annual Bonus

Individual Performance (Based on Appraisal, Weight = 0.50)	Company Performance (Based on Sales Targets, Weight = 0.50)			
	Excellent	Good	Fair	Poor
Excellent	1.00	0.90	0.80	0.70
Good	0.80	0.70	0.60	0.50
Fair	0.00	0.00	0.00	0.00
Poor	0.00	0.00	0.00	0.00

Note: To determine the dollar amount of a manager's award, multiply the maximum possible (target) bonus by the appropriate factor in the matrix.

based on the organization's overall performance. Thus, a manager might be eligible for an individual performance bonus of up to $10,000, but receive only $2,000 at the end of the year, based on his or her individual performance evaluation. But the person might also receive a second bonus of $3,000, based on the firm's profits for the year.

One drawback to this approach is that it may give marginal performers too much—for instance, someone could get a company-based bonus, even if his or her own performance is mediocre. One way to avoid this is to use the *multiplier method*. As Table 12-2 illustrates, multiply the person's target bonus by 1.00, 0.80, or zero (if the firm's performance is excellent, and the person's performance is excellent, good, fair, or poor). A manager whose own performance is poor does not even receive the company-based bonus.

Employers use *long-term incentives* to inject a long-term perspective into their executives' decisions. With only short-term criteria to shoot for, a manager could conceivably boost profitability by reducing plant maintenance, for instance; this tactic might catch up with the company 3 or 4 years later. Popular long-term incentives include cash, stock options, stock, stock appreciation rights, and phantom stock.[94] PepsiCo's CEO was paid $13.2 million recently, including a base salary of $1.6 million, stock awards of $7.5 million, and a performance-based bonus of $4 million, plus perks such as air travel.[95]

Long-term incentives such as stock options, if well-designed, should only pay off if the firm achieves its strategic goals (such as "double our rate of return"), because the owners and investors should also benefit from the executives' efforts. Long-term incentives may also be "golden handcuffs," motivating executives to stay by letting them accumulate capital (usually options to buy company stock) that they can cash in only after a certain period. Again, popular long-term incentives include cash, stock, stock options, stock appreciation rights, and phantom stock.[96] We'll look at each.

stock option

The right to purchase a stated number of shares of a company stock at today's price at some time in the future.

STOCK OPTIONS   A **stock option** is the right to purchase a specific number of shares of company stock at a specific price during a specific period. The executive thus hopes to profit by exercising his or her option to buy the shares in the future but at today's price. This assumes the stock will go up. Unfortunately, this depends partly on considerations outside the manager's control.[97] When stock markets dropped a few years ago, many employers including Intel and Google modified option plans to boost the likely payout.[98] The HR Practices Around the Globe feature addresses one aspect of this.

▶ IMPROVING PERFORMANCE: *HR Practices Around the Globe*

"International human resource management" is important because cultural, political, legal, and economic differences mean that employees in one country often react differently to an HR practice than would employees in other countries.

For example, until January 2006, China basically prohibited publicly listed companies from offering stock incentive plans to their managers. At that point better economic conditions and an evolving political philosophy led to new regulations. Soon 42 Chinese-listed companies were permitting such plans.

A study focused on those 42 companies. It sought to determine how the new incentive plans affected company performance. To understand the findings it's important to know that managing in China still has unique characteristics. For example, prior to becoming publicly listed firms, the big firms were usually owned by the government. Furthermore, the government may well continue to retain certain ownership control rights even after the firms go on the stock market. In such cases, the goals of the owners and the management may diverge. For example, government owners might want to maximize employment, rather than profitability. The question is, given such cultural and political realities, do management stock option plans in China translate into improved company performance, as they often do in the United States?

The researchers compared the performance of the 42 Chinese companies that did adopt management stock-option plans with a control group of firms without such plans. One thing they found was that the stock-option plans did improve firm performance *in companies controlled by private shareholders*, but not in companies controlled by the government. In the latter, goals such as maximizing employment may have outweighed boosting profits, thus limiting managers' profit-boosting efforts.

The findings highlight why managing globally is challenging. In this case, a stock option plan that might improve financial performance in the United States might fail in China, where the government owners' goals may well differ from the desire of managers to boost profits. ■

Source: Based on Robert Boylan, Maggie Foley, and Yu-Jun Lian, "Are Equity Incentives Effective in Chinese Listed Firms? New Evidence from Propensity Score Matching (PSN)," *International Journal of Business Strategy* 10, no. 3 (September 2010).

The chronic problem with stock options is that they often reward even managers who have lackluster performance, but there are also other issues. Several years ago some executives allegedly lied about the dates they received their options to boost their returns. Options may also encourage executives to take perilous risks in pursuit of higher (at least short-term) profits.[99] Stock options provide an incentive to go for spectacular results, but since the managers haven't actually bought the stock yet, they don't risk their own money. One solution is to simply draft the option plan so it forces recipients to convert their options to stock more quickly.[100]

Employee stock ownership plans or ESOPs have been introduced in India, and companies have been using it to attract and retain talent in the country. Many Indian companies, specifically in the IT sector, have granted ESOPs to their employees. ESOPs are governed by the provisions of SEBI (ESOP guidelines), Companies Act, Income Tax Act, accounting guidelines, and Foreign Exchange Management Act (FEMA). Indian law also allows companies to grant sweat equity (discounted shares for considerations other than cash, like intellectual property, specific skills, etc.) which is different from ESOP as the later can be issued only against cash.

OTHER STOCK PLANS   Beyond that, the trend is toward tying rewards more explicitly to performance goals. Instead of stock options, more firms are granting various types of performance-based shares. With *performance-contingent restricted stock* the executive receives his or her shares only if he or she meets the preset performance targets.[101] With (time-based) *restricted stock plans*, the firm usually awards rights to the shares without cost to the executive but the employee is restricted from acquiring (and selling) the shares for, say, 5 years. The employer's aim is to retain the employee's services during that time.[102] With *indexed options*, the option's exercise price fluctuates with the performance of, say, a market index. Then, if the company's stock does no better than the index, the manager's options are worthless. With *premium priced options*, the exercise price is higher than the stock's closing price on the date of the grant, so the executive can't profit from the options until the stock makes significant gains.[103]

Stock appreciation rights (SARs) let the recipient exercise the stock option (by buying the stock) or to take any appreciation in the stock price in cash, stock, or some combination of these. Under *phantom stock plans*, executives receive not shares but "units" that are similar to shares of company stock. Then at some future time, they receive value (usually in cash) equal to the appreciation of the "phantom" stock they own. Both SARs and phantom stock essentially "are bonus plans that grant not stock but rather the right to receive an award based on the value of the company's stock."[104] A *performance achievement plan* awards shares of stock for the achievement of predetermined financial targets, such as profit or growth in earnings per share. Most employees seem to prefer cash bonuses to either stock options or restricted stocks. Due to differences in employee preferences, when possible, enable each employee to choose whether to receive stock options or restricted stock.[105]

ETHICS AND INCENTIVES   Anyone designing a long-term incentive plan should keep in mind the management truism "People put their efforts where they know they'll be rewarded." The problem is that simplistic incentives that focus on just one factor (such as cost-cutting) may inadvertently encourage managers to ignore other important factors (such as long-term investment). Similarly, in the absence of strong ethical standards, incentives may breed unethical behavior.[106] Examples are depressingly familiar. For example, *Forbes* alleged that one firm's culture now "rewards hard-nosed aggressiveness and doesn't put the client's interests before those of the firm."[107] For stock-option plan designers, the solution is to include a sufficient array of bonus-able criteria in the incentive plan, while fostering an ethical culture.

Some Other Executive Incentives

Companies also offer other executive incentives. Some incentivize executives to stay with the firm. This is especially important when executives might flee because another company is stalking the firm with intentions to buy it. **Golden parachutes** are extraordinary (large) payments companies make to executives in connection with a change in company ownership or control.[108]

Some firms use loans as incentives, for example by guaranteeing large loans to directors and officers to buy company stock. Thus, directors and officers of Conseco owed the company more than $500 million in loans when company shares tanked.[109]

Team and Organization-Wide Incentive Plans

We've focused so far on individual employee incentives (such as piecework, commissions, and executive bonuses). Let's look now at incentives for teams, and for all employees company-wide.

How to Design Team Incentives

Firms increasingly rely on teams to manage their work. They therefore need incentive plans that encourage teamwork and focus teams on performance. **Team (or group) incentive plans** pay incentives to the team based on the team's performance.

The main question here is how to reward the team's performance, and the wrong choice can prove lethal. Levi Strauss switched from an individual to a team incentive plan, one that rewarded the team as a whole for its output. Unfortunately, they neglected the fact that some employees worked harder than others. The slower ones (economists sometimes call them "free riders" because they take a free ride on others' efforts) were paid the same as the faster ones. The faster ones, no longer individually incentivized, slowed down, production declined, and Levi's closed its U.S. factories.

So, the main aim is to have all your team pulling together. Free riders notwithstanding, the usual approach is still to tie rewards to some overall standard (goal) of group performance, such as "20 total labor hours per car."[110] One company established such an overall standard for its teams. If the firm reached 100% of its goal, the employees would share in about 5% of the improvement (in labor costs saved).

---

golden parachute
A payment companies make in connection with a change in ownership or control of a company.

team (or group) incentive plan
A plan in which a production standard is set for a specific work group, and its members are paid incentives if the group exceeds the production standard.

Team incentives can foster a sense of cooperation and unanimity.

123rf.com

The firm divided the resulting bonus pool by the number of employees to compute the value of a "share." If the firm achieved less than 100% of its goal, the bonus pool was less. The results of this plan in terms of focusing teams on the firm's strategic goals were reportedly "extraordinary."[111] Firms such as Toyota that use team plans rely on employee selection, training, and peer pressure to minimize free riding.

While most employers just use experience to estimate what the team goal or standard should be ("20 total labor hours per car"), others carefully engineer their production standards. If so, the employer will typically base the team incentive on either the piece rate or standard hour plan. All team members then typically receive the same share of the team's incentive pay. Thus, the team might receive say, $5 for each wheel installed above the industrially engineered "standard" 10 wheels per hour.

Occasionally, the employer may want to pay team members according to some other formula. For instance, instead of paying each team member based on how well the team as a whole does, pay everyone based on how well the *best* team member does. This counterintuitive option may make sense when an employer has reason to believe the new team incentive plan might demotivate high-performing team members. That's what happened at Levi's, for instance.

Team incentives often make sense. They reinforce team planning and problem solving, and can help ensure cooperation. Team incentives also facilitate training, since each member has an interest in getting new members up to speed fast. The main disadvantage is the demotivating effects of free rider workers who share in the team-based pay but who don't put their hearts into it.

Evidence-Based HR: Inequities That Undercut Team Incentives

Although about 85% of large employers reportedly use some type of group-or team-based incentives, studies suggest that team incentives are often counterproductive. Why?

A researcher studied business students enrolled in a graduate online MBA program.[112] She devised a method for categorizing how they said they reacted to the team incentives they'd experienced in the past.

Inequity was the big problem.[113] Sometimes all team members' financial compensation was the same, although one or two people "did the lion's share of the work." In other cases, the employer chose one or two team members for promotion, leaving others to feel they'd worked hard to support someone else's career. The bottom line is that unless you take steps to minimize inequities, it may be best to pay employees based on their individual contributions, rather than on collective team performance.

organization-wide incentive plan
Incentive plan in which all or most employees can participate.

Many employers take the team incentive idea to the next logical level and institute incentive plans in which all or most employees participate. **Organization-wide incentive plans** are plans in which all or most employees can participate, and which generally tie the reward to some measure of company-wide performance. Also called *variable pay plans*, we'll look at them next.

Profit-Sharing Plans

profit-sharing plan
A plan whereby employees share in the company's profits.

Profit-sharing plans are plans in which all or most employees receive a share of the firm's annual profits. Research is sketchy. One study concluded that there is ample evidence that profit-sharing plans boost productivity and morale, but that their effect on profits is insignificant, once you factor in the costs of the plans' payouts.[114] A more recent study, conducted in Spain, concluded that profit-sharing plans improve employee commitment.[115]

There are several types of profit-sharing plans. With *current profit-sharing* or cash plans, employees share in a portion of the employer's profits quarterly or annually. Here the firm simply distributes a percentage of profits (usually 15% to 20%) as profit shares to employees at regular intervals. The Home Depot instituted such a cash program for all its store workers. It started paying store associates a bonus if their stores met certain financial goals. In one recent year, it distributed $90 million under that company-wide incentive plan.[116]

With *deferred profit-sharing* plans, the employer puts cash awards into trust accounts for the employees' retirement.[117] Employees' income taxes on the distributions are deferred until the employee retires or withdraws funds from the plan (thus "deferred profit sharing-plans"). Such plans are essentially pension plans "in which the employer has discretion to determine when and how much the company pays into the plan."[118] The employer generally distributes such awards based on a percentage of the employee's salary, or some measure of the employee's contribution to company profits.[119]

Scanlon Plans

Few would argue with the idea that one of the best ways of ensuring that employees are engaged and committed is to ensure that by pursuing his or her goals, the worker pursues the employer's goals as well. Experts have proposed many ways to achieve this. However, few have been as successful as the **Scanlon plan**, developed in 1937 by Joseph Scanlon, a United Steel Workers Union official.[120] It is still popular today.

The Scanlon plan is remarkably progressive, considering that it is now more than 75 years old. Scanlon plans have five basic features.[121] The first is Scanlon's *philosophy of cooperation.* This philosophy assumes that managers and workers must rid themselves of the "us" and "them" attitudes that normally inhibit employees from developing a sense of ownership in the company.

A second feature is what its practitioners call *identity.* This means that in order to focus employee involvement, the company must articulate its mission or purpose, and employees must understand how the business operates in terms of customers, prices, and costs. *Competence* is a third basic feature. The program, say three experts, "explicitly recognizes that a Scanlon plan demands a high level of competence from employees at all levels."[122] This suggests careful selection and training.

The fourth feature of the plan is the *involvement system.* Employees present improvement suggestions to the appropriate departmental-level committees, which transmit the valuable ones to the executive-level committee. It then decides whether to implement the suggestion.

The fifth element of the plan is the *sharing of benefits formula.* If a suggestion is implemented and successful, all employees usually share in 75% of the savings. For example, assume that the normal monthly ratio of payroll costs to sales is 50%. (Thus, if sales are ₹600,000, payroll costs should be ₹300,000.) Assume the firm implements suggestions that result in payroll costs of ₹250,000 in a month when sales were ₹550,000 and payroll costs therefore should have been ₹275,000 (50% of sales). The savings attributable to these suggestions is ₹25,000 (275,000 minus 250,000). Workers would typically split 75% of this (18,750), while 6,250 would go to the firm. In practice, the firm sets aside about one-quarter of the ₹18,750, for months when payroll costs exceed the standard.

Other Gainsharing Plans

The Scanlon plan is one early version of today's **gainsharing plans**. Gainsharing is an incentive plan that engages many or all employees in a common effort to achieve a company's productivity objectives, with any resulting cost-savings gains shared among employees and the company.[123] In addition to the Scanlon plan, other popular gainsharing plans include the Lincoln, Rucker, and Improshare plans.

The basic difference among these plans is how employers determine employee bonuses. The Scanlon formula divides payroll expenses by total sales (or, sometimes, by total sales plus increases in inventory). In one version of the *Lincoln incentive system*, first instituted at the Lincoln Electric Company of Ohio, employees work on a guaranteed piecework basis. The company then distributes total annual profits (less taxes, 6% dividends to stockholders, and a reserve) each year among employees based on their merit rating. Most firms customize their gainsharing plans.

Results—from programs in hospitals, as well as manufacturing plants—suggest that gainsharing improves productivity and patient care, and reduce grievances, but may also entail considerable implementation costs.[124] Based on positive results,

Scanlon plan
An incentive plan developed in 1937 by Joseph Scanlon and designed to encourage cooperation, involvement, and sharing of benefits.

gainsharing plan
An incentive plan that engages employees in a common effort to achieve productivity objectives and share the gains.

the U.S. Department of Health and Human Services approved certain hospital gainsharing plans. Here the hospital pays physicians a share of any cost savings attributable in part to the physicians' efforts.[125]

At-Risk Pay Plans

earnings-at-risk pay plan
Plan that puts some portion of employees' normal pay at risk if they don't meet their goals, in return for possibly obtaining a much larger bonus if they exceed their goals.

Pay for performance can support an employer's cost control efforts. Base pay and benefits represent the lion's share of labor costs, and normally neither varies much even when sales plummet.[126] (Pay cuts adversely affect morale, and if sales fall one year, it's generally hard to cut labor costs without downsizing.) Variable pay plans are one way around this. For example, in an **earnings-at-risk pay plan**, employees agree to put some portion (say, 10%) of their normal pay at risk (forego it) if they don't meet their goals, in return for possibly obtaining a much larger bonus if they exceed their goals. For example, put part of the employees' pay "at risk" by replacing (1) 10% of each worker's wages with (2) a 10% bonus if the company meets its goals plus an additional 3% bonus if it exceeds these goals.

Employee Stock Ownership Plans

employee stock ownership plan (ESOP)
A corporation contributes shares of its own stock to a trust in which additional contributions are made annually. The trust distributes the stock to employees on retirement or separation from service.

Employee stock ownership plans (ESOPs) are company-wide plans in which the employer contributes shares of its own stock (or cash to be used to purchase such stock) to a trust established to purchase shares of the firm's stock for employees. The firm generally makes these contributions annually in proportion to total employee compensation, with a limit of 15% of compensation. The trust holds the stock in individual employee accounts. It then distributes the stock to employees upon retirement (or other separation from service), assuming the person has worked long enough to earn ownership of the stock. (*Stock options*, as discussed earlier in this chapter, go directly to the employees individually to use as they see fit, rather than into a retirement trust.)

ESOPs are popular. The company receives a tax deduction equal to the fair market value of the shares it transfers to the trustee, and can claim an income tax deduction for dividends paid on ESOP-owned stock. Employees, as noted, aren't taxed until they receive a distribution from the trust, usually at retirement.

ESOPs can also help the shareholders of closely held corporations (for instance, a family owns all the shares) to diversify their assets. They place some of their own shares of the company's stock into the ESOP trust and (with the company compensating them for the shares they put in the trust) then purchase other marketable securities for themselves in their place.[127]

Studies suggest that ESOPs probably do encourage employees to develop a sense of ownership in and commitment to the firm, but their effects on motivation and performance are questionable. In any case, those responsible for the funds—usually, the firm's top executives—must be fastidious in executing their fiduciary responsibilities for the fund.[128]

BROAD-BASED STOCK OPTIONS   Some companies offer "broad-based stock option plans" in which all or most employees can participate. The basic thinking is that sharing ownership in the company with employees makes motivational and practical sense.[129]

Employers seem to be cutting back on these. For example, Time Warner, Microsoft, Aetna, and Charles Schwab discontinued distributing stock options to most employees. Some of them, including Microsoft, are instead awarding stock. With current tax laws, companies must show the options as an expense when awarded, reducing their attractiveness as a "costless" reward. Microsoft and others apparently feel awarding stock instead of stock options is a more direct and immediate way to link pay to performance.[130]

Incentive Plans in Practice: Nucor

Nucor Corp. is the largest steel producer in the United States. It also has the highest productivity and lowest labor cost per ton.[131] Employees can earn bonuses of 100%

or more of base salary, and all Nucor employees participate in one of four performance-based incentive plans. With the *production incentive plan*, operating and maintenance employees and supervisors get weekly bonuses based on their work groups' productivity. The *department manager incentive plan* pays department managers annual incentive bonuses based mostly on the ratio of net income to dollars of assets employed for their division. With the *professional and clerical bonus plan*, employees who are not in one of the two previous plans get bonuses based on their divisions' net income return on assets.[132] Finally, under the *senior officer incentive plan*, Nucor senior managers (whose base salaries are lower than those in comparable firms) get bonuses based on Nucor's annual overall percentage of net income to stockholders equity.[133] Nucor also divides 10% of its operating profits yearly among all employees (except senior officers). Depending on company performance, this may be from 1% to over 20% of an employee's pay.

LEARNING OBJECTIVE **12-6**
Explain how to use incentives to improve employee engagement.

Employee Engagement Guide for Managers

Incentives and Engagement

A survey provides some insights into the role of incentive pay in fostering employee engagement. Of approximately 6,300 compensations professionals the researchers solicited, 736 responded to the survey.[134] Here's what the researchers found.

First, although the compensation professionals believed that total rewards programs can influence employee engagement, many of them did *not* specifically include employee engagement as one of the goals of their compensation plans. About 60% agreed or strongly agreed that "employee engagement and performance metrics are incorporated into variable pay programs in our organization." Only 37% agreed or strongly agreed that "in the organization, engagement levels fostered by line managers are important factor in evaluating performance."

Second, they concluded that the most direct ways to encourage employee engagement with incentives are (1) to measure the extent to which *supervisors are encouraging their subordinates to be engaged,* and (2) to *use incentives to reward supervisors for improving employee engagement.*

Third, even more important than the rewards themselves, getting employees involved in developing the rewards programs was the "gold standard" for building employee cooperation and commitment. An Indian study of employee engagement and rewards conducted among corporate and non-corporate employees showed compensation and incentive as critical areas, along with career and developmental opportunities for employee development.[135] The Indian diamond cutting and polishing industry is also known for enhancing employee motivation and loyalty by giving liberal incentives.[136]

So in brief: Make improving employee engagement a formal target of your compensation plan; appraise and incentivize your supervisors partly based on whether they take steps to improve their subordinates' engagement; and if possible let employees participate in devising the compensation plan.

Chapter Review

Chapter Section Summaries

12-1. In designing an effective financial incentive plan, it's important to understand the relationship between **money and motivation**. Hertzberg said the best way to motivate someone is to organize the job so that it provides the feedback and challenge that help satisfy the person's higher-level needs. Deci found that extrinsic rewards may actually detract from a person's intrinsic motivation. Vroom's expectancy motivation theory says a person's motivation depends on expectancy, instrumentality, and valence. Skinner's behavior modification–based approach means changing behavior through rewards or punishments that are contingent on performance.

12-2. Piecework is an **individual employee incentives and recognition program** incentive plan in which a person is paid a sum for each item he or she makes. Merit pay is a salary increase awarded based on individual performance. Nonfinancial and recognition-based awards include awards in the form of employee recognition, gift certificates, and individual travel. Many employers use enterprise incentive management systems to automate the planning, analysis, and management of their incentive plans.

12-3. **Incentives for salespeople** are typically sales commissions. Although the percentage of pay in the form of sales commission may vary, a survey found that salespeople at high-performing companies receive about 38% of their total cash compensation in sales-related variable pay.

12-4. Managers take many things into consideration when formulating **incentives for managers and executives**. Most firms have annual bonus plans aimed at motivating managers' short-term performance. The actual award often depends on some combination of individual performance and organizational performance, so that, for instance, high-performing managers get a bonus even if the company itself underperforms. Long-term incentives include stock options, "golden parachutes," and stock appreciation rights.

12-5. With more employers organizing their efforts around teams, **team and organization-wide incentive plans are more important**. With team incentive plans, the main question is whether to reward members based on individual or team performance; both have pros and cons. Organization-wide incentive plans are plans in which all or most employees can participate. These include profit-sharing plans in which employees share in the company's profits; gainsharing plans, including the Scanlon plan, engage employees in a common effort to achieve productivity objectives and thereby share the gains. Employee stock ownership plans are company-wide plans in which the employer contributes shares of its own stock to a trust established to purchase shares of the firm's stock for employees.

12-6. Consciously make **employee engagement** a target of your compensation plan; appraise and incentivize supervisors partly based on their effectiveness in improving their subordinates' engagement; and if possible enable employees to participate in devising the compensation plan.

Discussion Questions

12-1. Compare and contrast six types of incentive plans.
12-2. Explain five reasons why incentive plans fail.
12-3. Describe the nature of some important management incentives.
12-4. You are applying for a job as a manager and are at the point of negotiating salary and incentives. What questions would you ask your prospective employer concerning incentives? Describe the incentives package you would try to negotiate for yourself.

12-5. In this chapter, we listed a number of guidelines for instituting a pay-for-performance plan. Do you think these points make sense in terms of motivation theory? Why or why not?
12-6. What is merit pay? Do you think it's a good idea to award employees merit raises? Why or why not?
12-7. Give four examples of when you would suggest using team or group incentive programs rather than individual incentive programs.

Individual and Group Activities

12-8. Working individually or in groups, create an incentive plan for the following positions: chemical engineer, plant manager, used-car salesperson. What factors did you have to consider in reaching your conclusions?
12-9. A private business school in India instituted a "Teacher Incentive Program" (TIP) for its faculty. Faculty chairs of each department were told to award ₹5,000 per month raises (not bonuses) to about 40% of their faculty members based on how good a job they did at teaching (based on student rating of courses), and how many courses they taught per year. What are the potential advantages and pitfalls of such an incentive program? How well do you think it was accepted by the faculty? Do you think it had the desired effect?

12-10. Appendices A and B at the end of this book (pages 583–600) list the knowledge someone studying for the HRCI (Appendix A) or SHRM (Appendix B) certification exam needs to have in each area of human resource management (such as in Strategic Management, and Workforce Planning). In groups of several students, do four things: (1) review Appendix A and/or B; (2) identify the material in this chapter that relates to the Appendix A and/or B required knowledge lists; (3) write four multiple-choice exam questions on this material that you believe would be suitable for inclusion in the HRCI exam and/or the SHRM exam; and, (4) if time permits, have someone from your team post your team's questions in front of the class, so that students in all teams can answer the exam questions created by the other teams.

12-11. Several years ago in the US, the pension plan of the Utility Workers Union of America proposed that shareholders change the corporate bylaws of Dominion Resources, Inc., so that in the future management had to get shareholder approval of executive pay exceeding $1 million, as well as detailed information about the firm's executive incentive plans. The union pointed out that, usually, under IRS regulations, corporations can't deduct more than $1 million in pay for any of a company's top five paid executives. Under the new rules the Utility Workers Union is pushing, boards of directors will no longer be able to approve executive pay above $1 million; instead, shareholders would have to vote on it. In terms of effectively running a company, what do you think are the pros and cons of the union's recommendations? Would you vote for or against the union's recommendation? Why?

Experiential Exercise

Motivating the Sales Force at Express Auto

Purpose: The purpose of this exercise is to give you practice developing an incentive plan.

Required Understanding: Be thoroughly familiar with this chapter, and read the following:

Express Auto, an automobile mega-dealership with more than 600 employees that represents 22 brands, has just received a very discouraging set of survey results. Customer satisfaction scores have fallen for the ninth straight quarter. Customer complaints include:

- It was hard to get prompt feedback from mechanics by phone.
- Salespeople often did not return phone calls.
- The finance people seemed "pushy."
- New cars were often not properly cleaned or had minor items that needed immediate repair or adjustment.

- Cars often had to be returned to have repair work redone.

Table 12-3 describes Express Auto's current compensation system.

How to Set Up the Exercise/Instructions: Divide the class into groups of four to five students. One or more groups should analyze each of the five teams in column one. Each student group should analyze the compensation package for its Express Auto team. Each group should address these questions:

12-12. In what ways might your team's compensation plan contribute to the customer service problems?

12-13. What recommendations would you make to improve the compensation system in a way that would likely improve customer satisfaction?

TABLE 12-3 Express Auto Compensation System

Express Auto Team	Responsibility of Team	Current Compensation Method
1. Sales force	Persuade buyer to purchase a car.	Very small salary (minimum wage) with commissions. Commission rate increases with every 20 cars sold per month.
2. Finance office	Help close the sale; persuade customer to use company finance plan.	Salary, plus bonus for each $10,000 financed with the company.
3. Detailing	Inspect cars delivered from factory, clean, and make minor adjustments.	Piecework paid on the number of cars detailed per day.
4. Mechanics	Provide factory warranty service, maintenance, and repair.	Small hourly wage, plus bonus based on (1) number of cars completed per day and (2) finishing each car faster than the standard estimated time to repair.
5. Receptionists/phone service personnel	Primary liaison between customer and sales force, finance, and mechanics.	Minimum wage.

CHAPTER 12

Application Case

Inserting the Team Concept into Compensation—or Not

In his new position at Hathaway Manufacturing, one of the first things Sandy Caldwell wanted to do was improve productivity through team-work at every level of the firm. As the new human resource manager for this plant, Sandy set out to change the culture to accommodate the team-based approach he had become so enthusiastic about in his most recent position.

Sandy started by installing the concept of team management at the highest level, to oversee the operations of the entire plant. The new management team consisted of manufacturing, distribution, planning, technical, and human resource plant managers. Together they developed a new vision for the 500-employee facility, which they expressed in the simple phrase "Excellence Together." They drafted a new mission statement for the firm that focused on becoming customer driven and team based, and that called upon employees to raise their level of commitment and begin acting as "owners" of the firm.

The next step was to convey the team message to employees throughout the company. The communication process went surpris-ingly well, and Sandy was happy to see his idea of a "workforce of owners" begin to take shape. Teams trained together, developed pro-duction plans together, and embraced the technique of 360-degree feedback, in which an employee's performance evaluation is obtained from supervisors, subordinates, peers, and internal or external cus-tomers. Performance and morale improved, and productivity began to tick upward. The company even sponsored occasional celebrations to reward team achievements, and the team structure seemed firmly in place.

Sandy decided to change one more thing. Hathaway's long-standing policy had been to give all employees the same annual pay

increase. But Sandy felt that in the new team environment, outstand-ing performance should be the criterion for pay raises. After consulting with CEO Regina Cioffi, Sandy sent a memo to all employees announc-ing the change to team-based pay for performance.

The reaction was immediate and 100% negative. None of the employees was happy with the change, and among their complaints, two stood out. First, because the 360-degree feedback system made everyone responsible in part for someone else's performance evaluation, no one was comfortable with the idea that pay raises might also be linked to peer input. Second, there was a widespread perception that the way the change was decided upon, and the way it was announced, put the firm's commitment to team effort in doubt. Simply put, employees felt left out of the decision process.

Sandy and Regina arranged a meeting for early the next morning. Sitting in her office, they began a painful debate. Should the new policy be rescinded as quickly as it was adopted, or should it be allowed to stand?

Questions

12-14. Does the pay-for-performance plan seem like a good idea? Why or why not?

12-15. What advice would you give Regina and Sandy as they con-sider their decision?

12-16. What mistakes did they make in adopting and communicat-ing the new salary plan? How might Sandy have approached this major compensation change a little differently?

12-17. Assuming the new pay plan is eventually accepted, how would you address the fact that in the new performance evaluation system, employees' input affects their peers' pay levels?

Note: The incident in this case is based on an actual event at Frito-Lay's Kirkwood, New York, plant, as reported in C. James Novak, "Proceed with Caution When Paying Teams," *HR Magazine,* April 1997, p. 73.

Continuing Case

Carter Cleaning Company

The Incentive Plan

The question of whether to pay Carter Cleaning Center employees an hourly wage or an incentive of some kind has always intrigued Jack Carter.

His basic policy has been to pay employees an hourly wage, except that his managers do receive an end-of-year bonus depending, as Jack puts it, "on whether their stores do well or not that year."

However, he is considering using an incentive plan in one store. Jack knows that a presser should press about 25 "tops" (jackets, dresses, blouses) per hour. Most of his pressers do not attain this ideal standard, though. In one instance, a presser named Walt was paid $8 per hour, and Jack noticed that regardless of the amount of work he had to do, Walt always ended up going home at about 3:00 P.M., so he earned about $300 at the end of the week. If it was a holiday week, for instance, and there were a lot of clothes to press, he might average 22 to 23 tops per hour (someone else did pants) and so he'd earn perhaps $300 and still finish each day in time to leave by 3:00 P.M. so he could pick up his children at school. But when things were very slow in the store, his productivity would drop to perhaps 12 to 15 pieces an hour, so that at the end of the week he'd end up earning

perhaps $280, and in fact not go home much earlier than he did when it was busy.

Jack spoke with Walt several times, and while Walt always prom-ised to try to do better, it gradually became apparent to Jack that Walt was simply going to earn his $300 per week no matter what. Though Walt never told him so directly, it dawned on Jack that Walt had a fam-ily to support and was not about to earn less than his "target" wage, regardless of how busy or slow the store was. The problem was that the longer Walt kept pressing each day, the longer the steam boilers and compressors had to be kept on to power his machines, and the fuel charges alone ran close to $6 per hour. Jack clearly needed some way short of firing Walt to solve the problem, since the fuel bills were eating up his profits.

His solution was to tell Walt that, instead of an hourly $8 wage, he would henceforth pay him $0.33 per item pressed. That way, said Jack to himself, if Walt presses 25 items per hour at $0.33 he will in effect get a small raise. He'll get more items pressed per hour and will therefore be able to shut the machines down earlier.

On the whole, the experiment worked well. Walt generally presses 25 to 35 pieces per hour now. He gets to leave earlier and, with the small increase in pay, he generally earns his target wage. Two problems have arisen, though. The quality of Walt's work has dipped a bit, plus his manager has to spend a minute or two each hour counting the number of pieces Walt pressed that hour. Otherwise, Jack is fairly pleased with the results of his incentive plan, and he's wondering whether to extend it to other employees and other stores.

Questions

12-18. Should this plan be extended to pressers in the other stores?

12-19. Should other employees (cleaner/spotters, counter people) be put on a similar plan? Why or why not? If so, how, exactly?

12-20. Is there another incentive plan you think would work better for the pressers? Describe it.

12-21. A store manager's job is to keep total wages to no more than 30% of sales and to maintain the fuel bill and the supply bill at about 9% of sales each. Managers can also directly affect sales by ensuring courteous customer service and by ensuring that the work is done properly. What suggestions would you make to Jennifer and her father for an incentive plan for store managers or front-desk clerks?

Translating Strategy into HR Policies and Practices Case*,§

The overall map on page xxxviii of this book outlines the relationships involved.

Improving Performance at the Hotel Paris

The New Incentive Plan

The Hotel Paris's competitive strategy is "To use superior guest service to differentiate the Hotel Paris properties, and to thereby increase the length of stay and return rate of guests, and thus boost revenues and profitability." HR manager Lisa Cruz must now formulate functional policies and activities that support this competitive strategy by eliciting the required employee behaviors and competencies.

One of Lisa Cruz's biggest pay-related concerns is that the Hotel Paris compensation plan does not link pay to performance in any effective way. Because salaries were historically barely competitive, supervisors tended to award merit raises across the board. So, employees who performed well got only about the same raises as did those who performed poorly. Similarly, there was no bonus or incentive plan of any kind aimed at linking employee performance to strategically relevant employee capabilities and behaviors such as greeting guests in a friendly manner or providing expeditious check-ins and check-outs. The bottom line for Lisa and the CFO was that the company's financial rewards system—potentially, the single-biggest tool they had for channeling employee performance toward accomplishing the Hotel Paris's goals—was totally inadequate. She and her team thus turned to the job of deciding what sort of incentive-based reward systems to install.

Based on their analysis, Lisa Cruz and the CFO concluded that, by any metric, their company's incentive plan had to be changed. The percentage of the workforce whose merit increase or incentive pay was tied to performance was effectively zero, because managers awarded merit pay across the board. No more than 5% of the workforce (just the managers) was eligible for incentive pay. And, the percentage difference in incentive pay between a low-performing and a high-performing employee was less than 2%. Lisa knew from industry studies that in top firms, over 80% of the workforce had merit pay or incentive pay tied to performance. She also knew that in high-performing firms, there was at least a 5% or 6% difference in incentive pay between a low-performing and a high-performing employee. The CFO authorized Lisa to design a new strategy-oriented incentive plan for the Hotel Paris's employees. Their overall aim was to incentivize the pay plans of just about all the company's employees.

Lisa and the company's CFO laid out three measurable criteria that the new incentive plan had to meet. First, at least 90% (and preferably

§ Written and copyright by Gary Dessler, PhD.

all) of the Hotel Paris's employees must be eligible for a merit increase or incentive pay that is tied to performance. Second, there must be at least a 10% difference in incentive pay between a low-performing and high-performing employee. Third, the new incentive plan had to include specific bonuses and evaluative mechanisms that linked employee behaviors in each job category with strategically relevant employee capabilities and behaviors. For example, front-desk clerks were to be rewarded in part based on the friendliness and speed of their check-ins and check-outs, and the housecleaning crew was to be evaluated and rewarded in part based on the percentage of room cleaning infractions.

With these criteria in mind, Lisa and her team turned to designing the new merit and incentive pay plan. They created a larger merit pay pool, and instructed supervisors that employees scoring in the lower 10% of performance were to receive no merit pay, while the difference in merit pay between the top category and medium category employees was to be 10%. They contracted with an online employee recognition firm and instituted a new "Hotel Paris instantaneous thank-you award program." Under this program, any guest or any supervisor could recommend any hotel employee for an instantaneous recognition award; if approved by the department manager, the employee could choose the recognition award by going to the company's Web site. The incentive structure for all the company's managers, including hotel managers, assistant managers, and departmental managers, now ties at least 10% of each manager's annual pay to the degree to which his or her hotel achieves its strategic aims. The plan measures this in terms of ratings on the guest satisfaction index, average length of guest stay, and frequency of guest returns. Ratings on all these metrics soon began to rise.

Questions

12-22. Discuss what you think of the measurable criteria that Lisa and the CFO set for their new incentive plan.

12-23. Given what you know about the Hotel Paris's strategic goals, list three or four specific behaviors you would incentivize for each of the following groups of employees: front-desk clerks, hotel managers, valets, housekeepers.

12-24. Based on what you learned in this chapter of Dessler *Human Resource Management*, lay out a complete incentive plan (including all long- and short-term incentives) for the Hotel Paris's hotel managers.

Endnotes

1. Jay Heizer and Barry Render, *Operations Management* (Upper Saddle River, NJ: Pearson, 2001), p. 15.
2. See, for example, Mary Ducharme and Mark Podolsky, "Variable Pay: Its Impact on Motivation and Organisation Performance," *International Journal of Human Resources Development and Management* 6 (May 9, 2006), p. 68.
3. Ibid.
4. "Employers Use Pay to Lever Performance," *BNA Bulletin to Management*, August 21, 1997, p. 272; and "Variable Pay Is Superior to Bonus," *People Management*, February 24, 2011, p. 14.
5. See, for example, Kenan Abosch, "Variable Pay: Do We Have the Basics in Place?" *Compensation & Benefits Review*, July/August 1998, pp. 2–22.
6. Even the traditional holiday bonus is being replaced by performance-based pay. "Cash Bonuses Are Ghosts of Holidays Past, Survey Says," *BNA Bulletin to Management*, December 13, 2005, p. 396.
7. Dhananjay Mahapatra | TNN | Jan 9, 2016, 02.13 AM IST, 'FCI loaders paid more than President, SC says it's fishy', *The Times of India*, timesofindia. indiatimes.com , [Navigation: News Home » India » Article], as accessed on 04 September 2017 at 5pm IST.
8. "Few Employees See the Pay for Performance Connection," *Compensation & Benefits Review* 17, no. 2 (June 2003); "Most Workers Not Motivated by Cash," *Incentive Today*, July–August 2004, p. 19; and "Pay-for-Performance Plans' Impact Uncertain: Study," *Modern Healthcare*, May 24, 2004, p. 34.
9. Kathy Chu, "Employers See Lackluster Results Linking Salary to Performance," *Wall Street Journal*, June 15, 2004, p. D2.
10. David Peters, Subrata Chakraborty, Prasant Mahapatra, and Laura Steinhardt, "Job Satisfaction and Motivation of Health Workers in Public and Private Sectors: Cross-Sectional Analysis from Two Indian States, Human Resources for Health, 2010.
11. Ted Turnasella, "Pay and Personality," *Compensation & Benefits Review*, March/April 2002, pp. 45–59.
12. Jason Shaw et al., "Reactions to Merit Pay Increases: A Longitudinal Test of a Signal Sensitivity Perspective," *Journal of Applied Psychology* 88, no. 3 (2003), pp. 538–544.
13. See, for example, Edward Deci, *Intrinsic Motivation* (New York: Plenum, 1975).
14. Ruth Kanfer, "Motivation Theory," in Harry C. Triandis, Marvin D. Dunnette, and Leaetta M. Hough, *Handbook of Industrial and Organizational Psychology* (Palo Alto, CA: Consulting Psychologists Press, 1994), p. 113. For a discussion about applying Vroom's principles, see B. Schaffer, "Leadership and Motivation." *Supervision* 69, no. 2 (February 2008), pp. 6–9.
15. For a discussion, see John P. Campbell and Robert Prichard, "Motivation Theory in Industrial and Organizational Psychology," in Marvin Dunnette (ed.), *Industrial and Organizational Psychology* (Chicago: Rand McNally, 1976), pp. 74–75; Kanfer, "Motivation Theory," pp. 115–116; and B. Schaffer, "Leadership and Motivation," op cit.
16. See, for example, Aubrey Daniels et al., "The Leader's Role in Pay Systems and Organizational Performance," *Compensation & Benefits Review*, May/June 2006, pp. 58–60; and Suzanne Peterson and Fred Luthans, "The Impact of Financial and Nonfinancial Incentives on Business Unit Outcomes Over Time," *Journal of Applied Psychology* 91, no. 1 (2006), pp. 156–165.
17. See, for example, Diane Cadrain, "Cash Versus Non-Cash Rewards," *HR Magazine*, April 2003, pp. 81–87.
18. Richard Henderson, *Compensation Management* (Reston, VA: Reston, 1979), p. 363.
19. David Belcher, *Compensation Administration* (Englewood Cliffs, NJ: Prentice Hall, 1973), p. 314.
20. These problems have been long known. See, for example, Thomas Wilson, "Is It Time to Eliminate the Piece Rate Incentive System?" *Compensation and Benefits Review*, March–April 1992, pp. 43–49.
21. William Atkinson, "Incentive Pay Programs That Work in Textile," *Textile World* 151, no. 2 (February 2001), pp. 55–57.
22. See, for example, "Bias Creeps into Bonus Process, MIT Study Finds," *Workforce Management*, September 20, 2008, pp. 8–9.
23. Michael Harris et al., "A Longitudinal Examination of a Merit Pay System: Relationships Among Performance Ratings, Merit Increases, and Total Pay Increases," *Journal of Applied Psychology* 83, no. 5 (1998), pp. 825–831. See also H. Risher, "Add Merit Pay for Performance," *Compensation and Benefits Review* 40, no. 6 (November/December 2008), pp. 22–29.
24. Eric R. Schulz and Denise Marie Tanguay, "Merit Pay in a Public Higher Education Institution: Questions of Impact and Attitudes," *Public Personnel Management* 35, no. 1 (Spring 2006), p. 71(18); Thomas S. Dee and Benjamin J. Keys, "Does Merit Pay Reward Good Teachers? Evidence from a Randomized Experiment," *Journal of Policy Analysis & Management* 23, no. 3 (Summer 2004), pp. 471–488. See also Sanghee Park and Michael Sturman, "How and What You Pay Matters: The Relative Effectiveness of Merit Pay, Bonuses and Long-Term Incentives on Future Job Performance," *Compensation & Benefits Review* 44, no. 2 (2012), pp. 80–85.
25. Fay Hansen, "Wage and Salary Trends," *Compensation & Benefits Review* 40, no. 5 (November/December 2008), p. 5.
26. Rachel Silverman, "My Colleague, My Paymaster," *Wall Street Journal*, April 4, 2012, pp. B1, B8.
27. Jonathan Glater, "Varying the Recipe Helps TV Operations Solve Morale Problem," *New York Times*, March 7, 2001, p. C1.
28. Steve Yegge, quoted in http:// glinden.blogspot.com/2006/09/ management-and-incentives-at-google.html, accessed June 1, 2011. See also Franck Giancola, "Should HR Professionals Devote More Time to Intrinsic Rewards?" *Compensation & Benefits Review* 46, no. 1 (2014), pp. 25–31.
29. Brian Skelton, "Dual-Career Tracks: Rewarding and Maintaining Technical Expertise," www.todaysengineer.org/2003/ May/dual-ladder.asp, accessed September 8, 2014.
30. Posted at: Oct 26, 2016, 12:35 AM; last updated: Oct 26, 2016, 12:35 AM (IST), 'India Inc wakes up to employee engagement', *The Tribune*, www.tribuneindia. com, [Navigation--Jobs Careers » Worklife], as accessed on 04 September 2017 at 3pm IST.
31. Peterson and Luthans, "The Impact of Financial and Nonfinancial Incentives," pp. 156–165.
32. "WorkSimple 'Praise' App Boosts Employee Recognition," *T+D* (January 2012) p. 21, *Academic OneFile*, accessed March 17, 2013.
33. Michelle V. Rafter, "Back in a Giving Mood," *Workforce Management* 88, no. 10 (September 14, 2009), pp. 25–29.
34. http://blog.intuit.com/ employees/6-mobile-apps-for-recognizing-and-rewarding-employees, accessed July 11, 2014.
35. Like those at http://blog.intuit. com/employees/6-mobile-apps-for-recognizing-and-rewarding-employees.
36. See, for example, Leslie Yerkes, *Fun Works: Creating Places Where People Love to Work* (San Francisco, CA: Berrett-Koehler Publishers, 2007).
37. "How to Reward Your Employees?" *Mumbai Mirror*, May 23, 2015.
38. Vikram Coudhury, "Top Reward Trends in India," People Matters, 2015.
39. Charlotte Huff, "Recognition That Resonates," *Workforce Management*, September 11, 2006, pp. 25–29. A survey of executives concluded that three nonfinancial incentives—praise and commendation from immediate managers, attention from leaders, and opportunities to lead project or task forces—all ranked higher in motivational effectiveness than did financial incentives including stock options. Daniel Morrell, "Employee Perceptions and the Motivation of Non-Monetary Incentives," *Compensation & Benefits Review* 43, no. 5 (September/October 2011), pp. 318–323.
40. Bob Nelson, *1001 Ways to Reward Employees* (New York: Workman Pub., 1994), p. 19. See also Sunny C. L. Fong and Margaret A. Shaffer, "The Dimensionality and Determinants of Pay Satisfaction: A Cross-Cultural Investigation of a Group Incentive Plan," *International Journal of Human Resource Management* 14, no. 4 (June 2003), p. 559(22).
41. www.deloitte.com/assets/ DcomUnitedStates/Local%20 Assets/Documents/us_consulting_ 2010StrategicSalesCompensationSurvey_072910.pdf, accessed September 8, 2014.
42. Peterson and Luthans, "The Impact of Financial and Nonfinancial Incentives," pp. 156–165.
43. Ibid., p. 159.
44. Ibid., p. 159.
45. Ibid., p. 162. See also "Delivering Incentive Compensation Plans That Work," *Financial Executive* 25, no. 7 (September 2009), pp. 52–54, and "Survey Finds Many Employers Not Satisfied with Their Pay-for-Performance Programs," *BNA Bulletin to Management*, January 7, 2014, p. 3.
46. For a checklist for determining when pay for performance is advisable, see Myron Glassman et al., "Evaluating Pay for Performance Systems: Critical Issues for Implementation," *Compensation & Benefits Review* 42, no. 4 (2010), p. 236.
47. "Two Frameworks for a More ROI-Minded Rewards Plan," *Pay for Performance Report*, February 2003, p. 1, www.ioma.com/issues/

PFP/2003_02/518132-1. html, accessed November 3, 2009; and Alan Robinson and Dean Schroeder, "Rewards That Really Work," *Security Management*, July 2004, pp. 30–34. See also Patricia Zingheim and Jay Schuster, "What Are Key Pay Issues Right Now?" *Compensation & Benefits Review*, May/June 2007, pp. 51–55.

48. Reed Taussig, "Managing Cash Based Incentives," *Compensation & Benefits Review*, March/April 2002, pp. 65–68. See also Nigel Nicholson, "How to Motivate Your Problem People," *Harvard Business Review*, January 2003, pp. 57–65; and "Incentives, Motivation and Workplace Performance," Incentive Research Foundation, www.incentivescentral.org/employees/whitepapers, accessed May 19, 2007.

49. Theodore Weinberger, "Evaluating the Effectiveness of an Incentive Plan Design Within Company Constraints," *Compensation & Benefits Review*, November/December 2005, pp. 27–33; and Howard Risher, "Adding Merit to Pay for Performance," *Compensation & Benefits Review*, November/December 2008, pp. 22–29.

50. www.deloitte.com/assets/Dcom-UnitedStates/Local%20Assets/Documents/us_consulting_2010StrategicSalesCompensationSurvey_072910.pdf, accessed June 1, 2011.

51. Ibid.

52. Deloitte Varicent, 2010 Strategic Sales Compensation Survey, p. 6, at www.deloitte.com/assets/Dcom-UnitedStates/Local%20Assets/Documents/us_consulting_2010Strategic SalesCompensationSurvey_072910.pdf, accessed August 29, 2011.

53. www.deloitte.com/assets/DcomUnitedStates/Local%20Assets/Documents/us-consulting_2010 StrategicSalesCompensationSurvey_072910.pdf, accessed September 8, 2014. See also Pankaj Madhani, "Managing Salesforce Compensation: A Lifecycle Perspective," *Compensation & Benefits Review* 44, no. 6, pp. 315–326.

54. Straight salary by itself is not, of course, an incentive compensation plan as we use the term in this chapter.

55. Donna Harris, "Dealers Rethink How They Pay Salespeople," *Automotive News*, June 14, 2010, www.autonews.com/article/20100614/RETAIL07/306149932?CSAuthResp=1%3A37354 836327014 7%3A423310% 3A4129%3A24%3Aapproved% 3A06E323F6579E1FCB 5665B3CC4B7C6C0B&=, accessed September 8, 2014.

56. Sonjun Luo, "Does Your Sales Incentive Plan Pay for Performance?" *Compensation &*

Benefits Review, January/February 2003, pp. 18–24.

57. Scott Ladd, "May the Sales Force Be with You," *HR Magazine*, September 2010, p. 105.

58. Luo, "Does Your Sales Incentive Plan Pay for Performance," pp. 331–345. See also James M. Pappas and Karen E. Flaherty, "The Moderating Role of Individual-Difference Variables in Compensation Research," *Journal of Managerial Psychology* 21, no. 1 (January 2006), pp. 19–35; and T. B. Lopez, C. D. Hopkins, and M. A. Raymond, "Reward Preferences of Salespeople: How Do Commissions Rate?" *Journal of Personal Selling & Sales Management* 26, no. 4 (Fall 2006), p. 381(10).

59. Bill O'Connell, "Dead Solid Perfect: Achieving Sales Compensation Alignment," *Compensation & Benefits Review*, March/April 1996, pp. 46–47. See also C. Albrech, "Moving to a Global Sales Incentive Compensation Plan," *Compensation & Benefits Review* 41, no. 4 (July/August 2009), p. 52.

60. See, for example, Pankaj Madhani, "Realigning Fixed and Variable Pay in Sales Organizations: An Organizational Lifestyle Approach," *Compensation & Benefits Review* 42, no. 6, pp. 488–498.

61. Leslie Stretch, "From Strategy to Profitability: How Sales Compensation Management Drives Business Performance," *Compensation & Benefits Review*, May/June 2008, pp. 32–37.

62. S. Scott Sands, "Ineffective Quotas: The Hidden Threat to Sales Compensation Plans," *Compensation & Benefits Review* (March/April 2000), pp. 35–42. See also "Driving Profitable Sales Growth: 2006/2007 Report on Sales Effectiveness," www. watsonwyatt.com/research/resrender.asp?id=2006-US-0060&page=1, accessed May 20, 2007.

63. Peter Gundy, "Sales Compensation Programs: Built to Last," *Compensation & Benefits Review* (September/October 2002), pp. 21–28. See also T. B. Lopez, C. D. Hopkins, and M. A. Raymond, "Reward Preferences of Salespeople: How Do Commissions Rate?" *Journal of Personal Selling & Sales Management* 26, no. 4 (Fall 2006), p. 381(10).

64. Pankaj Madhani, "Reallocating Fixed and Variable Pay in Sales Organizations: a Sales Carryover Perspective," *Compensation & Benefits Review* 43, no. 6, (2011) pp. 346–360.

65. "Driving Profitable Sales Growth: 2006/2007 Report on Sales Effectiveness," www.watsonwyatt.com/research/resrender.

asp?id=2006-US-0060&page=1, accessed May 20, 2007.

66. Thomas Steenburgh and Michael Ahearne, "Motivating Salespeople: What Really Works," *The Harvard Business Review*, July–August 2012, pp. 71–75.

67. "Car Salesman Commission the Way It Works," http://carsalesprofessional.com/car-salesman-commission/, accessed June 26, 2011.

68. Ibid.

69. Peter Glendinning, "Kicking the Tires of Automotive Sales Compensation," *Compensation & Benefits Review*, September/October 2000, pp. 47–53; and Michele Marchetti, "Why Sales Contests Don't Work," *Sales and Marketing Management* 156 (January 2004), p. 19. See also "Salary and Bonus Gain Favor in Sales Pay (for Motor Vehicle Salespeople)," *Automotive News* 75, no. 5915 (February 5, 2001), p. 50.

70. Government of India, Report of Seventh Central Pay Commission, 2015, November; accessed at doe.gov.in.

71. Varicent, "2010 Strategic Sales."

72. Bob Conlin, "Best Practices for Designing New Sales Compensation Plans," *Compensation & Benefits Review*, March/April 2008, p. 51.

73. Ibid., p. 53.

74. Jeremy Wuittner, "Plenty of Incentives to Use E.I.M. Software Systems," *American Banker* 168, no. 129 (July 8, 2003), p. 680.

75. Nina McIntyre, "Using EIM Technology to Successfully Motivate Employees," *Compensation & Benefits Review*, July/August 2001, pp. 57–60.

76. www.vuesoftware.com/Product/Compensation_Management. aspx, accessed September 8, 2014.

77. Oracle Fusion Incentive Compensation Data Sheet, http://www.oracle.com/us/products/applications/fusion/hcm-workforce-compensation-1543936. pdf, accessed July 14, 2015.

78. Mark Meltzer and Howard Goldsmith, "Executive Compensation for Growth Companies," *Compensation & Benefits Review*, November/December 1997, pp. 41–50; and Barbara Kiviat, "Everyone into the Bonus Pool," *Time* 162, no. 24 (December 15, 2003), p. A5.

79. www.mercer.com/pressrelease/details.jhtml/dynamic/idContent/1263210, accessed January 2, 2007.

80. Meltzer and Goldsmith, "Executive Compensation for Growth Companies," pp. 41–50. See also Patricia Zingheim and Jay Schuster, "Designing Pay and Rewards in Professional Companies," *Compensation &*

Benefits Review, January/February 2007, pp. 55–62; and Ronald Bottano and Russell Miller, "Making Executive Compensation Count: Tapping into the New Long-Term Incentive Portfolio," *Compensation & Benefits Review*, July/August 2007, pp. 43–47.

81. George Yancey, "Aligning the CEO's Incentive Plan with Criteria That Drive Organizational Performance," *Compensation & Benefits Review* 42, no. 3 (2010), pp. 190–196.

82. Richard Ericson, "Benchmarking for Executive Incentive Pay: The Importance of Performance Standards," *Compensation & Benefits Review* 43, no. 2, (2010), pp. 92–99.

83. See "The Impact of Sarbanes-Oxley on Executive Compensation," www.thelenreid.com, accessed December 11, 2003. See also Brent Longnecker and James Krueger, "The Next Wave of Compensation Disclosure," *Compensation & Benefits Review*, January/February 2007, pp. 50–54.

84. James Reda, "Executive Compensation: Balancing Risk, Performance and Pay," *Financial Executive* 25, no. 9 (November 2009), pp. 46–50. See also Bruce Ellig, "Short-Term Incentives: Top-Down or Bottom-Up?" *Compensation & Benefits Review* 43, no 3, (May/June 2011), pp. 179–183.

85. Meltzer and Goldsmith, "Executive Compensation for Growth Companies," pp. 44–45; See also Jennifer Wynter-Palmer, "Is the Use of Short-Term Incentives Good Organization Strategy?" *Compensation & Benefits Review* 44, no. 5, 2013, pp. 254–265.

86. Max Smith and Ben Stradley, "New Research Tracks the Evolution of Annual Incentive Plans," *Executive Compensation*, Towers Watson, 2010, Towerswatson.com, accessed August 28, 2011.

87. Ibid.

88. Ibid.

89. Ibid.

90. Dionne Searcey, "Transocean Executives to Donate Bonuses," *Wall Street Journal*, April 6, 2011, p. B1.

91. Meltzer and Goldsmith, "Executive Compensation for Growth Companies," p. 44. Fay Hansen, "Salary and Wage Trends," *Compensation & Benefits Review*, March/April 2004, pp. 9–10.

92. Bruce Ellig, "Executive Pay Financial Measurements," *Compensation & Benefits Review*, September/October 2008, pp. 42–49.

93. "Study: CEO Compensation Not Tied to Company Performance," *BNA Bulletin to Management*, March 22, 2011, p. 92.

94. See for example Bruce Ellig, "Long-Term Incentive Plan Combinations," *Compensation & Benefits Review* 46, no. 1 (2014), pp. 10–15.

95. www.usatoday.com/story/money/business/2014/03/21/pepsico-ceospay-bumped-to-132-million/6717929/, accessed April 3, 2014.

96. See, for example, Bruce Ellig, "Stock Awards Can Be a Powerful Executive Pay Element," *Compensation & Benefits Review* 45, no. 6 (2013), pp. 309–319.

97. Benjamin Dunford et al., "Underwater Stock Options and Voluntary Executive Turnover: A Multidisciplinary Perspective Integrating Behavioral and Economic Theories," *Personnel Psychology* 61 (2008), pp. 687–726.

98. Phred Dvorak, "Slump Yields Employee Rewards," *Wall Street Journal*, October 10, 2008, p. B2; Don Clark and Jerry DiCola, "Intel to Let Workers Exchange Options," *Wall Street Journal*, March 24, 2009, p. B3.

99. Wm. Gerard Sanders and Donald Hambrick, "Swinging for the Fences: The Effects of CEO Stock Options on Company Risk-Taking and Performance," *Academy of Management Journal* 50, no. 5 (2007), pp. 1055–1078.

100. "Study Finds That Directly Owning Stock Shares Leads to Better Results," *Compensation & Benefits Review*, March/April 2001, p. 7. See also Lucian A. Bebchuk and Jesse M. Fried, "Pay Without Performance: Overview of the Issues," *Academy of Management Perspective* 20, no. 1 (February 2006), p. 5(20).

101. www.mercer.com/press-release/details.jhtml/dynamic/idContent/1263210, accessed January 2, 2007.

102. www.nceo.org/main/article.php/id/43/, accessed June 1, 2011.

103. Louis Lavelle, "How to Halt the Options Express," *Business-Week*, September 9, 2002.

104. www.nceo.org/main/article.php/id/43/, accessed June 1, 2011.

105. Menahchem Abudy and Efrat Shust, "Employee's Attitudes Toward Equity-Based Compensation," *Compensation & Benefits Review* 44, no. 5 (2013), pp. 246–253.

106. Christine Bevilacqua and Parbudyal Singh, "Pay for Performance—Panacea or Pandora's Box? Revisiting an Old Debate in the Current Economic Environment," *Compensation & Benefits Review*, September/October 2009, pp. 21–26.

107. www.forbes.com/2010/06/14/goldman-sachs-paulson-markets-lloyd-blankfein.html, accessed May 21, 2011.

108. Under IRS regulations, companies cannot deduct all golden parachute payments made to executives, and the executive must pay a 20% excise tax on the golden parachute payments. "Final Regs Issued for Golden Parachute Payments," *Executive Tax and Management Report* 66, no. 17 (September 2003), p. 1.

109. "Conseco Not Alone on Executive Perks," *Knight-Ridder/Tribune Business News*, August 28, 2003, item 03240015. See also "Realities of Executive Compensation—2006/2007 Report on Executive Pay and Stock Options," www.watsonwyatt.com/research/resrender.asp?id=2006-US-0085&page=1, accessed May 20, 2007.

110. Other suggestions are as follows: equal payments to all members on the team; differential payments to team members based on their contributions to the team's performance; and differential payments determined by a ratio of each group member's base pay to the total base pay of the group. See Kathryn Bartol and Laura Hagmann, "Team Based Pay Plans: A Key to Effective Team Work," *Compensation & Benefits Review*, November–December 1992, pp. 24–29. See also Charlotte Garvey, "Steer Teams with the Right Pay," *HR Magazine*, May 2002, pp. 70–71; and K. Merriman, "On the Folly of Rewarding Team Performance, While Hoping for Teamwork," *Compensation & Benefits Review* 41, no. 1 (January/February 2009), pp. 61–66.

111. Richard Seaman, "The Case Study: Rejuvenating an Organization with Team Pay," *Compensation & Benefits Review*, September/October 1997, pp. 25–30. See also Peter Wright, Mark Kroll, Jeffrey A. Krug, and Michael Pettus, "Influences of Top Management Team Incentives on Firm Risk Taking," *Strategic Management Journal* 28, no. 1 (January 2007), pp. 81–89.

112. K. Merriman, "On the Folly of Rewarding Team Performance, While Hoping for Teamwork," *Compensation & Benefits Review*, January/February 2009, pp. 61–66.

113. As another example, see Bernd Irlenbusch and Gabriele K. Lünser, "Relative Rewards Within Team-Based Compensation," November 2006. IZA Discussion Paper No. 2423. Available at SSRN: http://ssrn.com/abstract=947075, accessed May 21, 2011.

114. Seongsu Kim, "Does Profit Sharing Increase Firms' Profits?" *Journal of Labor Research*, Spring 1998, pp. 351–371. See also Jacqueline Coyle-Shapiro et al., "Using Profit-Sharing to Enhance Employee Attitudes: A Longitudinal Examination of the Effects on Trust and Commitment," *Human Resource Management* 41, no. 4 (Winter 2002), pp. 423–449.

115. Alberto Bayo-Moriones and Martin Larraza-Kintana, "Profit Sharing Plans and Effective Commitment: Does the Context Matter?" *Human Resource Management* 48, no. 2 (March–April 2009), pp. 207–226.

116. Kaja Whitehouse, "More Companies Offer Packages Linking Pay Plans to Performance," *Wall Street Journal*, December 13, 2005, p. B4.

117. Under the U.S. tax code, "any arrangement that provides for the deferral of compensation in a year later than the year in which the compensation was earned may be considered a deferred compensation arrangement." Steven Friedman, "2008 Compliance Strategies for Employers in Light of Final 409A Regulations," *Compensation & Benefits Review*, March/April 2008, p. 27.

118. www.axa-equitable.com/retirement/how-do-company-profit-sharing-plans-work.html, accessed June 1, 2011.

119. Joseph Martocchio, *Strategic Compensation* (Upper Saddle River, NJ: Prentice Hall, 2006), pp. 163–165.

120. Brian Graham-Moore and Timothy Ross, *The Scanlon Way to Improved Productivity: A Practical Guide* (New York: Wiley, 1978), p. 2. For a review of potential problems, see Denis Collins, "Death of a Gainsharing Plan: Power Politics and Participatory Management," *Organizational Dynamics* 24 (Summer 1995), pp. 23–37. For an historical perspective on gainsharing's effectiveness, see Alexander Gardner, "Goal Setting and Gainsharing: The Evidence of Effectiveness," *Compensation & Benefits Review* 43, no 4 (July/August 2011), pp. 236–244.

121. These are based in part on Steven Markham, K. Dow Scott, and Walter Cox Jr., "The Evolutionary Development of a Scanlon Plan," *Compensation & Benefits Review*, March/April 1992, pp. 50–56. See also Woodruff Imberman, "Are You Ready to Boost Productivity with a Gainsharing Plan? To Survive and Prosper in Our Hyper-competitive Environment, Board Converters Must Motivate Employees at All Levels," *Official Board Markets* 82, no. 47 (November 25, 2006), p. 5(2); and James Reynolds and Daniel Roble, "Combining Pay for Performance with Gainsharing," *Healthcare Financial Management* 60, no. 11 (November 2006), p. 50(6).

122. Markham et al., "The Evolutionary Development of a Scanlon Plan," p. 51.

123. Barry W. Thomas and Madeline Hess Olson, "Gainsharing: The Design Guarantees Success," *Personnel Journal*, May 1998, pp. 73–79; and A. C. Gardner, "Goal Setting and Gainsharing: The Evidence on Effectiveness," *Compensation and Benefits Review* 43, no. 4 (July/August 2011), pp. 236–244.

124. Paraphrased from Woodruff Imberman, "Boosting Plant Performance with Gainsharing," *Business Horizons*, November–December 1992, p. 77. See also Max Reynolds and Joane Goodroe, "The Return of Gainsharing: Gainsharing Appears to Be Enjoying a Renaissance," *Healthcare Financial Management* 59, no. 11 (November 2005), p. 114(6); and hospital gainsharing discussion in Anjana Patel, "Gainsharing: Past, Present, and Future," *Healthcare Financial Management* 60, no. 9 (September 2006), pp. 124–128, 130.

125. Paul Rossler and C. Patrick Koelling, "The Effect of Gainsharing on Business Performance at a Paper Mill," *National Productivity Review*, Summer 1993, pp. 365–382; and Anjana Patel, "Gainsharing: Past, Present, and Future," *Healthcare Financial Management* 60, no. 9 (September 2006), pp. 124–128, 130.

126. Robert Greene, "Variable Compensation: Good Fit to Turbulent Environments," *Compensation & Benefits Review* 44, no. 6, November/December 2012, p. 308.

127. Steven Etkind, "ESOPs Create Liquidity for Share Holders and Help Diversify Their Assets," *Estate Planning* 24, no. 4 (May 1998), pp. 158–165. See also S. Coomes, "Employee Stock Plans Can Save Taxes, Attract Talent," *Nation's Restaurant News* 42, no. 36 (September 15, 2008), p. 12.

128. William Smith, Harold Lazarus, and Harold Murray Kalkstein, "Employee Stock Ownership Plans: Motivation and Moral Issues," *Compensation & Benefits Review*, September/October 1990, pp. 37–46. See also "ESOP Trustees Breached Their Fiduciary Duties Under ERISA by Failing to Make Prudent Investigation into Value of Stock Purchased by ESOP," *Tax Management Compensation Planning Journal* 30, no. 10 (October 4, 2002), p. 301(1); and J. D. Mamorsky, "Court Approves ERISA Action

Against ENRON Executives, Trustee, and Plan Auditor for Retirement Plan Losses," *Journal of Compensation and Benefits* 20, no. 1 (January–February 2004), p. 46(7).

129. James Sesil et al., "Broad-Based Employee Stock Options in U.S. New Economy Firms," *British Journal of Industrial Relations* 40, no. 2 (June 2002), pp. 273–294.

130. Eric Dash, "Time Warner Stops Granting Stock Options to Most of Staff," *New York Times*, February 19, 2005, item 128921996.

131. Janet Wiscombe, "Can Pay for Performance Really Work?" *Workforce*, August 2001, p. 30.

132. Susan Marks, "Incentives That Really Reward and Motivate," *Workforce*, June 2001, pp. 108–114.

133. Although not an issue at Nucor, the employer needs to beware of instituting so many incentive plans (cash bonuses, stock options, recognition programs, and so on) that employees don't have a clear priority of the employer's priorities. See, for example, Stephen Rubenfeld and Jannifer David, "Multiple Employee Incentive Plans: Too Much of a Good Thing?" *Compensation & Benefits Review*, March/April 2006, pp. 35–43.

134. This is based on Dow Scott and Tom McMullen, "The Impact of Rewards Programs on Employee Engagement," WorldatWork, June 2010

135. Tejvir Singh, Pankaj Kumar, and Pushpendra Priyadarsi, "Employee Engagement: A Comparative Study of Selected Indian Organizations," *International Journal of Management Practices and Contemporary Thoughts.*

136. Biju Varkkey and Randhir Kumar, "Keeping the Sparkle On," *International Journal of Organizational Analysis*, 2015.

13

Benefits and Services

LEARNING OBJECTIVES

13-1 Name and define each of the main pay for time not worked benefits.

13-2 Describe each of the main insurance benefits.

13-3 Discuss the main retirement benefits.

13-4 Outline the main employees' services benefits.

13-5 Explain the main flexible benefit programs.

13-6 Explain how to use benefits to improve engagement, productivity, and performance.

In 1983, three youngsters laid the foundation of Blue Dart, which is currently the largest express courier company in South Asia. The company emphasizes on customer service but also recognizes the value of engaged employees. While the courier industry is highly people intensive and experiences high employee turnover, Blue Dart could manage to control it. Many of its current managers joined the company as courier boys. Apart from a caring culture, employee benefits played an important part in its success. We will see what Blue Dart Management did.[1]

WHERE ARE WE NOW ...

Chapters 11 and 12 addressed salaries (or wages) and incentives. The main purpose of this chapter is to explain the third major pay component: employee benefits. The main topics we discuss are pay for time not worked benefits, insurance benefits, retirement benefits, employees' services benefits, flexible benefits, and using benefits to improve engagement and performance. This chapter completes our discussion of employee compensation. The next chapter starts a new part of this book, and focuses on managing employee relations.

Introduction: The Benefits Picture Today

"What are your benefits?" is the first thing many applicants ask. **Benefits**—indirect financial and nonfinancial payments employees receive for continuing their employment with the company—are an important part of just about everyone's compensation.[2] They include things like health and life insurance, pensions, paid time off, and child-care assistance.[3] In the Indian context, benefits can be classified into two parts: (i) mandatory benefits covering like Provident Fund, NPS, ESI Scheme, Gratuity, Leave/Vacation travel, and Employee Compensation, and (ii) non-mandatory or voluntary benefits (which are provided by an employer). The second category generally includes additional/topup health insurance, life insurance policies, accident insurances, and personal loans. Many Indian firms also provide employee welfare and wellness oriented benefits like gym memberships, employee discount on products, etc. Employee benefits account for about 37% of wages and salaries (or about 30% of total payrolls). Figure 13-1 summarizes the breakdown of benefits as a percentage of employee compensation in the U.S. context.

For most employees, *health benefits* are the 800-pound gorilla of the benefits package. In one U.S. survey, 78% of employees cited health-care benefits as most crucial to retaining them; 75% cited compensation. But the same survey found that only 34% are satisfied with their health-care benefits.[4] A survey in India found that Indian employees are not just looking at standard salary but for benefits that are conducive for high performance, including individual wellness and health. In giving benefits, Indian companies perceive challenges in keeping with competition, hiring and retention of talent, and collecting employee feedback about current benefits.[5] Even human resource managers sometimes underestimate benefits' attractiveness. The above study also identified communication of benefits as a challenge for Indian companies. One survey concluded that many human resource managers erroneously assume that things like job security and autonomy and independence are more important to employees than are benefits.[6]

Policy Issues

Employers therefore should design benefits packages carefully. The list of policy issues includes what benefits to offer, who receives coverage, whether to include retirees in the plan, whether to deny benefits to employees during initial "probationary" periods, how to finance benefits, cost-containment procedures, and how to communicate benefits options to employees.[7]

Legal issues loom large. Labor laws mandate some benefits (such as Social Security in the form of Employee Provident Fund) while other benefits are at the employer's discretion (see Table 13-1). However, law still affects discretionary benefits

FIGURE 13-1 Relative Importance of Employer Costs for Employee Compensation (private industry in the U.S.), June 2015

Source: Based on Employer Costs For Employee Compensation—June 2015, http://www.bls.gov/news.release/pdf/ecec.pdf accessed September 17, 2015.

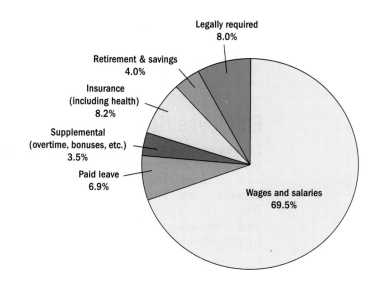

TABLE 13-1 **Some Required and Discretionary Benefits in India**

Benefits Required by Central or State Laws (applicable only to covered employees)	Benefits Discretionary on Part of Employer*
Social Security [Provident Fund/NPS, Gratuity, Health Plans/Insurance - ESIC or Central Government Health Scheme (CGHS) etc.]	Additional disability, health, life insurance, and pensions under private or top-up schemes
Medical facilities and hospital facilities under ESIC or CGHS	Medical care and insurance support for retired/former employees.
Workers' compensation for accidents/injury, etc.; death benefit, compassionate appointment for relatives in government/PSUs	Paid time off for vacations, holidays, sick leave, personal leave, etc.
Leaves under Maternity Benefit Act; Paternity leave for government/PSUs; Overtime pay as per law	Employee assistance and counseling programs; "family-friendly" benefits for child care, elder care, flexible work schedules, etc.; executive perquisites Educational support for self, support for children's education including freeship, tuition fee reimbursement.
	Company Housing, Leasing of houses, Provision for self-lease of accommodation, Housing loans, payment of full or part of interest on loans.
	Compensatory off days, encashment of unused accumulated leaves.
	Special leaves for occassions, like parent teachers meetings in schools, anniversaries, and leave for women during periods.

Note: *Although not required under law, some employers extend the same.

such as vacation leave. And employers must adhere to the laws of the states in which they do business.

There are many benefits and ways to classify them. One way is to categorize them as mandatory and non-mandatory benefits. More elaborate classifications are also possible. We will classify them as (1) pay for time not worked (such as vacations), (2) insurance benefits, (3) retirement benefits, (4) personal services benefits, and (5) flexible benefits. We will start our discussion with pay for time not worked.

HR in Practice at the Hotel Paris As they reviewed the benefits numbers, Lisa Cruz and the CFO became increasingly concerned. They computed several benefits-related metrics for their firm, including *benefits costs as a percentage of payroll* and *sick days per full-time equivalent employee per year.* The results were not what they should have been. They had to change their benefits plan. To see how they handled this, read the case on pages 432.

Employee Benefits in India

Employee benefits or perquisites are now an integral part of compensation packages offered by all companies. Relevant laws, location specific practices/requirements, and tax laws now determine the type and extent of perquisites given by Indian organizations. The law [for example, the Factories Act of 1948, Plantation Labor Act of 1951, Sales Promotion Employees (Conditions of Service) Act of 1976, Shops and Commercial Establishments Acts of different states, etc.] mandates employers to provide employee benefits like leave and employee welfare measures for free at nominal cost. The legal benefits and welfare provisions are applicable only for the category of workers who are covered by the legislation.

The welfare measures are intended to enhance the comfort level of workers, thus increasing their productivity. The Factories Act stipulates providing welfare benefits like childcare in the form of a crèche, health facilities for workmen, washing facilities, canteen, drinking water, etc. Other legislations for social security benefits like Provident Fund, health insurance, gratuity, etc., also exist in India. Some of these legislations have been discussed in Chapter 2. Traditionally, the cost incurred by the employer on welfare was not included as a direct part of employee compensation. At present, many firms have adopted cost-to-company (CTC) approach, and they include such costs to determine the total employment cost incurred for each employee.

In addition to the legislated benefits, many Indian companies provide additional privileges to their employees like soft loans for housing, transportation, schooling, etc. While the law on benefits do not include managerial employees, firms have extended the benefits to managers also. Despite lower salary level than MNCs and private sector, people are drawn towards public-sector and government employment because of the benefits such as residential township with facilities for recreation and entertainment; high quality schools where children of employees are guaranteed admissions; and state-run hospitals or contacts with leading hospitals.

The MNCs and private employers also offer attractive perquisites. For example, the Tata Group offers a wide range of benefits, which have been discussed in Chapter 1. Other multi-national players like IBM, Intel, and Accenture India offer a wide range of employee privileges to suit employee needs, business requirements, and local Indian laws. Today, most companies focuses on health and well-being of employees and dependents. Some companies have created gym and indoor-games facilities in the office so that employees are saved the trouble of driving down to a private gym. Nowadays, facilities for indoor sports like table tennis, carom, etc., as well as hi-tech gaming are available within the company premises. Other than these, healthy food options have been made available in the office canteens. Festivals and occasions are celebrated in offices, and employees and their families are invited for celebrations. Nowadays, companies also have certain assigned days meant for bringing family members to the office.

Pay For Time Not Worked

Pay for time not worked—also called **supplemental pay benefits**—is a very costly benefit, because of the large amount of time off most employees receive. Common time-off-with-pay benefits include holidays, vacations, funeral leave, military duty (in case employee has volunteered in Territorial Army of India), personal days, sick leave, sabbatical leave, maternity and paternity leave, and payments for laid-off or terminated employees.

Unemployment Insurance

In the US and Europe, all states have their own **unemployment insurance (or compensation)** laws. These provide benefits to eligible workers who become unemployed through no fault of their own. The benefits derive from a tax on employers that can range from 0.1% to 5% of taxable payroll in most states. An employer's unemployment tax rate reflects its rate of employee terminations. Unemployment tax rates are rising in many U.S. states.

In India, Employees State Insurance Corporation (ESIC) provides unemployment insurance to insured persons (IPs). Rajiv Gandhi Shramik Kalyan Yogana , a government scheme, mandates payment to employees affected by events like closure of factory/establishment, retrenchment (both under the provisions of Industrial Disputes Act, 1947), or permanent invalidity. The IP should have been registered for three or more years, and the allowance will be equivalent to 50% of wages for two years.

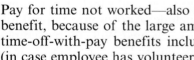

LEARNING OBJECTIVE 13-1
Name and define each of the main pay for time not worked benefits.

supplemental pay benefits
Benefits for time not worked such as unemployment insurance, vacation and holiday pay, and sick pay.

unemployment insurance (or compensation)
Provides benefits if a person is unable to work through some fault other than his or her own.

Such IPs receive financial support for skill upgradation, and they can avail medical care for themselves and families.[8] There is also news that the government of India is considering a national unemployment support scheme for the benefit of poor and unemployed.[9] Already, a few states like Kerala have introduced unemployment pay system for the unemployed. Firms aren't required to let everyone they dismiss receive unemployment benefits—only those released through no fault of their own. Thus, strictly speaking, a worker fired for chronic lateness can't legitimately claim benefits. But many managers are lackadaisical in protecting their employers and eventually end up paying compensation or even reinstating the dismissed employee.

The main rule is to keep a list of written warnings to demonstrate that poor performance caused the dismissal.

Vacations and Holidays

Most firms offer vacation and holiday benefits. In India, under the Factories Act of 1948, adult workers who have worked for 240 days in a year are eligible for one-day earned leave (or leave with wages) equal to one day for every 20 days worked (Section 79). This implies that almost 4 weeks of leave with wages. Many Indian firms provide 21 days to 30 days of annual paid leave to full-time employees, also termed as earned leave. In the US, about 90% of full-time workers and 40% of part-timers get paid holidays, an average of eight paid holidays off.[10] Common U.S. paid holidays include New Year's Day, Memorial Day, Independence Day, Labor Day, Thanksgiving Day, and Christmas Day.[11] On average, American workers get about 9 days of vacation leave after 1 year's employment, 14 days after 5 years, and 17 after 10 years.[12]

Compared to western countries, Indian employees get more annual holidays. The National and Festival Holiday Act (applicable to all states and establishments) mandates that three national holidays have to be observed in India. These are January 26 (Republic Day), August 15 (Independence Day), and October 2 (Gandhi Jayanti). Apart from these, employees are eligible for holidays according to the calendar decided by the government. The total number of holidays varies between states because of regional events. Some firms give some additional holiday on special days like their foundation day. For the government employees, 14 days are declared as holidays. In addition, depending on regional and religious events, two more days are allowed every year as restricted holidays (Table 13.1 and Table 13.2). Employees who work during holidays are eligible for double wages or, in some cases, a compensatory off. Firms should address several holiday- and vacation-related policy issues, such as how many days employees get, and which days (if any) are paid holidays. Other vacation policy decisions include: Are employees paid for accrued vacation time if they quit before taking their vacations? Will you pay employees for a holiday if they don't come to work the day before and the day after the holiday? And, should we pay some premium—such as time and a half—when employees must work on holidays?

More firms are taking a more flexible vacation leave approach. For example, IBM gives each employee at least 3 weeks' vacation, but doesn't track how much vacation each takes. Indian IT companies, TCS and Infosys, have introduced a new category of leave, titled bereavement leave, that allows employees to take paid off in case of loss of a near relative.[13] Microsoft India introduced the concept of paid caregiver leave of four weeks for employees who are caring for family members.[14] Employees sometimes just make informal arrangements with supervisors.[15]

In contrast, some employers emphasize centralized absence oversight (called "integrated absence management"). This starts with collecting data. For instance, how many people are on leave; how many days of work is the employer losing; how much is the employer spending to replace absent workers; and what units have the attendance problems?[16] These employers then closely monitor all aspects of their employees' leaves and absences. Wage surveys and Web sites[17] provide sample vacation policies for inclusion in the firm's employee manual. PayCheck India provides the required information in the Indian context.

Unemployment insurance/ compensation laws provide short-term benefits to people who lose their jobs through no fault of their own.

Mark Peterson/Corbis

TABLE 13-2 **The List of National Holidays in 2017 as Declared by the Government of India**

Sr. No	Holiday	Date	Saka Date	Day
1	Makar Sankrati	January 14	Pausha 15	Saturday
2	Republic Day	January 26	Magha 06	Thursday
3	Holy	March 13	Phalguna 22	Monday
4	Mahavir Jayanti	April 09	Chaitra 19	Sunday
5	Good Friday	April 14	Chaitra 24	Friday
6	Idu'I' Fitr	June 26	Ashadha 05	Monday
7	Raksha bandhan	August 07	Sravana 16	Monday
8	Independence Day	August 15	Sravana 24	Tuesday
9	Id-ul-Zuha(Bakrid)	September 02	Bhadra 11	Saturday
10	Dussehra	September 30	Asvina 08	Saturday
11	Muharram	October 01	Asvina 09	Sunday
12	Mahatma Gandhi's Birthday	October 02	Asvina 10	Monday
13	Diwali	October 19	Asvina 28	Thursday
14	Vikram Samvant New year	October 20	Kartika 01	Friday
15	Gurunanak Birthday	November 04	Kartika 13	Saturday
16	Id-e-Milad	December 02	Agrahayana 11	Saturday
17	Christmas	December 25	Pausha 04	Monday

(Continued)

TABLE 13-3 The List of Restricted Holidays in 2017 as Declared by the Government of India

Sr. No	Holiday	Date	Saka Date	Day
1	New year Day	January 01	Pausha 11	Sunday
2	Guru Nanak Govind Singh's Birthday	January 05	Pausha 15	Thursday
3	Makar Sankrati	January 14	Pausha 14	Saturday
4	Pongal	January 14	Pausha 14	Saturday
5	Basant Panchami	February 01	Magha 12	Wednesday
6	Guru Ravidas Birthday	February 10	Magha 21	Friday
7	Shivaji Jayanti	February 19	Magha 30	Sunday
8	Swami Dayand Saraswati Jayanti	February 21	Phalguna 02	Tuesday
9	Holika Dahan	March 12	Phalguna 21	Sunday
10	Chaitra sukadi/Gudi padva/ Cheti Chand	March 28	Chaitra 07	Tuesday
11	Hazarat Ali's Birthday	April 11	Chaitra 21	Tuesday
12	Vaisakhi	April 13	Chaitra 23	Thursday
13	Mesadi	April 14	Chaitra 24	Friday
14	Vaisakhadi (Bengal)Bahag Bihu (Assam)	April 15	Chaitra 25	Saturday
15	Easter Sunday	April 16	Chaitra 26	Sunday
16	Guru Rabindranath's Birthday	May 09	Vaisakha 19	Tuesday
17	Jamat-UL-Vida	June 23	Ashadha 02	Friday
18	Rath yatra	June 25	Ashadha 04	Sunday
19	Raksha Bandhan	August 07	Sravana 16	Monday
20	Janmashtami	August 15	Sravana 24	Tuesday
21	Parsi New year Day	August 17	Sravana 26	Thursday
22	Ganesh Chaturthi	August 25	Bhadra 03	Friday
23	Onam	September 04	Bhadra 13	Monday
24	Dussehra	September 27	Asvina 05	Wednesday
25	Dussehra (Maha Asthmi)	September 28	Asvina 06	Thursday
26	Dussehra (Maha navmi)	September 29	Asvina 07	Friday
27	Maharishi Valmiki's Birthday	October 05	Asvina 13	Thursday
28	Karaka Chaturthi	October 08	Asvina 16	Sunday
29	Deepavli (South India)	October 18	Asvina 26	Wednesday
30	Narka Chaturdasi	October 18	Asvina 26	Wednesday
31	Govardhan Puja	October 20	Asvina 28	Friday
32	Bhai Duj	October 21	Asvina 29	Saturday
33	Chhat puja	October 26	Kartika 04	Thursday
34	Gurtu Teg Bahadur martyrdom day	November 24	Agrahayana 03	Friday
35	Christmas Eve	December 24	Pausha 03	Sunday

Source: Government of India, Ministry of Personnel, Public Grievances & Pension (Department of Personnel & Training) Notification F.NO. 12/8/2016-JCA-2 dated 24.06.2016; available at http://document.ccis.nic.in/WriteReadData/CircularPortal/D2/D02est/12_8_2016-JCA-2-24062016A.pdf

KNOW YOUR EMPLOYMENT LAW

Some Legal Aspects of Vacations and Holidays

Although law doesn't require vacation benefits, the employer must still formulate its vacation policy with care. In India, the employer type (government or private), industry type, and company's HR policies and agreements with unions decide on the number and kind of vacations. Legally, the Factories Act of 1948 and Shops and Commercial Establishments Act have provisions for earned leave, which is akin to vacations. However, teachers of schools and universities can avail vacations in sync with student calendars. As an example, many employers' vacation policies say vacation pay accrues, say, on a biweekly basis. By doing so, these employers obligate themselves to pay new employees pro rata vacation pay if they leave the firm during their first year. But if the employer's vacation policy requires that a new employee pass his or her first employment anniversary *before becoming entitled* to a vacation, the employee gets no vacation pay if he or she leaves during that first year.

Another frequent question is whether the employer can cancel an employee's scheduled vacation, for instance, due to a rush of orders. Here it's important that the employer formulate its vacation policy so it's clear that the employer reserves the right to require vacation cancellation and rescheduling if production so demands. ■

Sick Leave

sick leave
Provides pay to an employee when he or she is out of work because of illness.

Sick leave provides pay to employees when they're out of work due to illness. Most policies grant full pay for a specified number of sick days—perhaps 12 or 15 per year (normal in Indian government and PSUs), usually accumulating at the rate of, say, 1 day per month of service.

The problem is that while many employees use their sick days only when sick, others use them whether they're sick or not. In many sectors, Indian blue-collar labor and migrant workers report sick as a way to get paid leave during festivals and harvest seasons. In one survey, personal illnesses accounted for about 45% of unscheduled sick leave absences. Family issues (27%), personal needs (13%), and "entitlement" (9%) were other reasons cited.[18] Such absenteeism costs U.S. employers perhaps $100 billion per year and similar high cost for Indian employers also, with personal illness accounting for about a third of the absences.[19]

COST-REDUCTION TACTICS Employers use several tactics to reduce excessive sick leave absence. Some repurchase unused sick leave at the end of the year by paying their employees a sum for each unused sick day. The problem is that legitimately sick employees may come to work. Others hold monthly lotteries in which only employees with perfect monthly attendance are eligible for a cash prize. Payment of attendance-based bonus is a common practice in many traditional Indian firms. At Marriott, employees can trade the value of some sick days for other benefits. Recognizing the leave pattern and advance planning can help in cost control. Indian cutting and polishing of diamonds industry (CPDs) close operations for a few weeks between October and November so that workers can participate in Diwali celebrations along with their family.[20] Many employers aggressively investigate all absences, calling absent employees at home.[21]

Many employers use *pooled paid leave plans* (or *"banks"*).[22] These plans lump together sick leave, vacation, and personal days into a single leave pool. For example, one hospital previously granted new employees 25 days off per year (10 vacation days, 3 personal days, and 12 sick days). Employees used, on average, 5 of those 12 sick days (as well as all vacations and personal days).[23] The pooled paid leave plan allowed new employees to accrue 18 days to use as they saw fit. (Special absences like serious short-term illnesses and bereavement leave were handled separately.) The pooled plan reduced absences. Most firms don't include federal holidays in their paid time off "banks."[24] The accompanying Profit Center feature shows how one employer cut costs.

▶ **IMPROVING PERFORMANCE:** *HR as a Profit Center*

Controlling Sick Leave

Sick leave often gets out of control because employers don't measure it. In one survey, only 57% of employers formally tracked sick days for their exempt employees.[25] Three-fourths of the employers couldn't provide an estimate of what sick pay was costing them. Therefore, the employer should first have a system for monitoring sick leaves and for measuring their financial impact.[26]

As an example, when she became director of the United Kingdom's Driver and Vehicle Licensing Agency, the new director knew steps were needed to address its absence rate.[27] The rate had peaked at 14 days out per employee in 2005, at a cost of about $20 million per year (then £10.3 million).

The new director organized a human resource absence initiative.[28] The agency set a goal of reducing absences by 30% by 2010. Agency directors received absence-reduction goals, and their progress was tracked. The agency introduced new policies on special leave, rehabilitation support, and monitoring absentees. They made it easier for employees to swap work shifts, and introduced a guaranteed leave day policy.

By 2010, the sickness absence rate was down to 7.5 days per employee and productivity was up, for multiyear savings of about $48 million dollars (£24.4 million). ∎

Source: Based on "Creating Holistic Time Off Programs Can Significantly Reduce Expenses," Compensation & Benefits Review, July/August 2007, pp. 18–19; Rita Zeidner, "Strategies for Saving in a Down Economy," HR Magazine, February 2009, p. 28. Judith Whitaker, "How HR Made a Difference," People Management 27 (October 28, 2010).

Paternity Leaves and the Maternity Benefit Act (1961)

Parental leave is an important benefit. About half of workers are women, about 80% will become pregnant during their work lives, and some workers are single parents. Earlier, the Maternity Benefit Act of 1961 (latest amendment was made in 2017) allowed 12 weeks of paid maternity benefit. The act is silent on the marital status of female employees. Other legislations that provide for maternity benefits are the Mines Maternity Benefit Act (1941), the Employees State Insurance Act (1948), and the Plantation Labor Act (1951).

The benefits of this act is applicable to all employees of any firm employing more than 10 workers during the past one year. In 2017, the act was amended to enhance the benefit of leave from 12 to 26 weeks, including 18 weeks after childbirth [Section 5 (3))]. As per the amended legislation, the benefit is admissible for two children, and from the third child, the previous provision of 12 weeks of paid maternity leave will be applicable.

The act also provides for paid leaves of (i) six weeks for miscarriage or medical termination of pregnancy and (ii) two weeks for women undergoing tubectomy operation (Section 9 and 9A). For nursing the child, the act mentions that women must be allowed to visit the crèche four times a day (Section 11). The amendment also saw the introduction of Commissioning Mother (mother who uses her egg to create an embryo in any other woman), who is now eligible for 12 weeks leave after the child is handed over [Section 5 (4)], and Adopting Mother, who is eligible for 12 weeks leave after receiving the child [Section 5(4)]. The act also encourages work-from-home facility based on understanding with employer [Section 5 (5)].

The Indian government had already introduced 180-day maternity leave following the recommendations of the Sixth Central Pay Commission. In addition, the government allows female employees to avail leave up to 2 years (i.e., 730 days) to take care of the needs of children up to 18 years. This includes leave for sickness and preparation for examinations. In 2014, the Supreme Court of India upheld this right, which allowed women employees to take uninterrupted 2 years leave.

While there is no provision for mandatory paternity leave in the Indian private sector, government employees can avail 15 days of paid leave (before and up to six months from birth of child, after which it lapses) for maximum two children [Rule 43-A, 43-AA of Central Civil Services (Leave) Rules, 1972]. Many private sector companies also provide paternity leaves, ranging from 1 day to 15 days. Cummins India raised its paternity leave benefit to one month, while Salesforce India's employees get 12 weeks paternity benefit, in line with their global policy.[29]

There is no legal provision for parental leave in India. Globally, employers are enriching their parental leave plans to make it more attractive for mothers to return from maternity leave. Tactics include keeping in touch during maternity leave, offering flexible jobs with reduced travel and hours, and longer leaves.[30]

Severance Pay

severance pay
A one-time payment some employers provide when terminating an employee.

Many employers, particularly in the US, provide **severance pay**, which can be over and above legal entitlements, as a one-time separation payment when terminating an employee. In India, the Industrial Disputes Act, 1947, sets the framework for retrenching employees, by paying retrenchment compensation. Companies employing more than 100 workers have to take prior permission from the authority, before retrenching. Most managers expect non-workmen employees to give them one month to three months notice if they plan to quit, so it seems appropriate to provide severance pay when dismissing an employee. Long notice periods, often 90 days, is a contentious matter in India. Many Indian companies extended notice period to control attrition.[31] Reducing the chances of litigation or bad public relations from disgruntled former employees is another reason. Severance pay also helps reassure employees who stay on after a downsizing that they'll receive some financial help if they're let go. In India, separation or termination of workmen/employees is possible under the provisions of the Industrial Disputes Act. The term "retrenchment" is used instead of words like termination or dismissal. (The term lay-off also has a different meaning under Section 25C of the act.) According to Section 2 (oo), retrenchment does not cover instances of separation of employee; dismissal of employee as punishment; leaving employment on grounds of VRS; expiry or non-renewal of employment contract; or termination because of ill health.

Lay-off (Section 25F) requires the employer to give one-month notice in writing with reasons for retrenchment. The information, along with reasons, have to be communicated to the government [Section 25F (c)]. Retrenched employees are eligible for retrenchment compensation at the rate of 15 days wages for each completed year's service (continuous). It's calculated from the date of appointment, with 240 days employment counted as one year.

However, if the establishment employs more than 100 workmen, the law is stricter. Under Section 25N, advance permission from the government has to be taken for retrenchment. The government has powers to refuse or allow retrenchment, and the decision has to be taken within 60 days of application. In the absence of any prior agreement between employer and workmen (through unions) about who will be retrenched first, Section 25G specifies that the last person to be employed will be retrenched first. Any deviation has to be justified to the government.

Apart from the Industrial Disputes Act of 1947, the Shops and Commercial Establishment Act (each Indian state has a separate law) also allows termination, with permission of the state government. Under these circumstances, termination is difficult in India, and the above legal clauses illustrate rigidity of the Indian employment system.

Supplemental Unemployment Benefits

supplemental unemployment benefits
Provide for a "guaranteed annual income" in certain industries where employers must shut down to change machinery or due to reduced work. These benefits are paid by the company and supplement unemployment benefits.

In some industries such as auto making, shutdowns to reduce inventories or change machines are common. **Supplemental unemployment benefits** are cash payments that supplement the employee's unemployment compensation, to help the person maintain his or her standard of living while out of work.

workers' compensation
Provides income and medical benefits to work-related accident victims or their dependents regardless of fault.

Insurance Benefits

Most employers also provide a number of required or voluntary insurance benefits, such as workers' compensation and health insurance.

Workers' Compensation

Workers' compensation laws (called the Employees Compensation Law of 1923 in India, which was earlier known as the Workmen Compensation Act, 1923) aim to provide sure, prompt income and medical benefits to work-related accident victims or their dependents, regardless of fault.

HOW BENEFITS ARE DETERMINED   Workers' compensation can be monetary or medical. In the event of a worker's death or disablement, the person's dependents receive a cash benefit based on prior earnings—usually one-half to two-thirds the worker's average weekly wage, per week of employment. The Employee's Compensation Act also covers certain diseases that workers may contract as a result of the work conditions. Such workers are deemed to have suffered an accident, and have to be compensated. The act also provides methodology for calculating compensation for death and permanent disability. For executives and managers who are outside the purview of this legislation, companies provide relief through group accident insurance schemes and group health insurance schemes. This a purely discretionary for a company. Hence, in case of failure of employer to cover the employee under accident insurance schemes, the burden will be on the employee, and compensation can be claimed after legal battle with the employer.

For workers' compensation to cover an injury or work-related illness, one must only prove that it arose while the worker was on the job. It doesn't matter that he or she may have been at fault. Suppose you instruct employees to wear safety goggles at their machines. One worker doesn't and has an eye injury on the job. The company must still provide workers' compensation benefits.

CONTROLLING WORKERS' COMPENSATION COSTS   It is important to control workers' compensation claims (and therefore costs). The employer's insurance company usually pays the claim, but the employer's premiums reflect the amount of claims.[32] Fewer claims also imply fewer accidents.

There are several ways to reduce workers' compensation claims. For example, screen out accident-prone workers. Reduce accident-causing conditions. And reduce the health problems that sometimes trigger these claims—for instance, by instituting effective safety and health programs, and complying with safety standards laws. Furthermore, some workers' compensation claims are not legitimate. Red flags include vague accident details, minor accidents resulting in major injuries, lack of witnesses, injuries occurring late Friday, and late reporting.[33]

Case management is a popular cost-control method. It is "the treatment of injured workers on a case-by-case basis by an assigned manager, usually a registered nurse, who coordinates with the physician and health plan to determine which care settings are the most effective for quality care and cost."[34]

Moving aggressively to support the injured employee and to get him or her back to work quickly is important too. The involvement of an attorney and the duration of the claim both influence the workers claim cost.[35] Many firms have programs such as physical therapy nursing assistance to help reintegrate claim recipients. Also, monitor health-care providers to confirm they're complying with their fee schedules.[36]

Hospitalization, Health, and Disability Insurance

Health insurance looms large in many people's choice of employer, because it's so expensive.[37] Hospitalization, health, and disability insurance helps protect employees against hospitalization costs and the income loss arising from off-the-job accidents or illness. Many employers purchase insurance from insurance companies. Others contract with health maintenance organizations or preferred provider organizations. The employer and employee usually both contribute to the plan.

Table 13-4 illustrates the prevalence of health-related benefits in the US.

TABLE 13-4 **Percentage of U.S. Employers Offering Some Popular Health Benefits**

Prescription drug program coverage	98%
Dental insurance	96%
Mail-order prescription program	90%
Mental health coverage	89%
Preferred provider organization (PPO)	86%
Accidental death and dismemberment insurance (AD&D)	83%
Vision insurance	82%
Contraceptive coverage	82%
Chiropractic coverage	80%
Employee assistance plan	77%
Long-term disability	77%

Source: Employee Benefits An Overview of Employee Benefits Offerings in the U.S (2013). www.shrm. org/Research/SurveyFindings/Articles/Documents/13-0245%202013_EmpBenefits_FNL.pdf, accessed April 4, 2014. SHRM Foundation.

HMOS Many employers offer membership in a **health maintenance organization (HMO)**, a medical organization consisting of specialists (surgeons, psychiatrists, and so on), often operating out of a health-care center. It provides routine medical services to employees who pay a nominal fee. Employees often have "gatekeeper" doctors who must approve appointments with specialist doctors. The HMO receives a fixed annual fee per employee from the employer (or employer and employee), regardless of whether it provides that person service.

PPOS Preferred provider organizations (PPOs) are a cross between HMOs and the traditional doctor–patient arrangement: They are "groups of health care providers that contract with employers, insurance companies, or third-party payers to provide medical care services at a reduced fee."[38] Unlike HMOs, PPOs let employees select providers (such as doctors) from a relatively wide list, and see them in their offices, often without gatekeeper doctor approval. Providers agree to discounts and to certain controls, for example, on testing.[39]

MENTAL HEALTH BENEFITS The World Health Organization estimated that more than 34 million people in the United States between the ages of 18 and 64 suffer from mental illness.[40] WHO also estimates that in 2015, five crore Indians suffered from depression and another three crore from anxiety-related disorders. Low- and middle-income countries, including India, account for 78% of the reported suicides, of which Indians account for 1.5%.[41] A study by a leading employee assistance program provider in 2016 reported that 46% of workers in India suffer from stress, which can lead to more severe form of mental illness.[42] A more recent survey among IT/ITES sector after the spate of layoffs and job-losses, placed the figures at 62.5%. The reason was mainly the feeling of job insecurity.[43] Mental illnesses represent about 24% of all reported disabilities, more than disabling injuries, cardiovascular diseases, and cancer combined.

Mental health costs are rising. Reasons include widespread drug and alcohol problems, an increase in demands and claims require employers to offer minimum mental health benefits, and the fact that mental health claims tend to trigger other health-care claims.

COBRA in the US

COBRA—the Consolidated Omnibus Budget Reconciliation Act—requires most private employers to continue to make health benefits available to separated employees and their families for a time, generally 18 months after separation.[44] The former employee must pay for the coverage.

Employers ignore COBRA's regulations at their peril. The employer does not want separated employees to leave and be injured, and then claim it never told them they could have continued their insurance coverage. Therefore, when a new employee first becomes eligible for the company's insurance plan, the person *must* receive (and acknowledge receiving) an explanation of his or her COBRA rights. And all employees separated from the company should sign a form acknowledging that they received and understand those rights.

Trends in Employer Health-Care Cost Control

A business with 50 employees might pay ₹1 million or more just for insurance coverage, before accounting for things like sick days. Health-care cost control is therefore one big way the HR department can improve profits.

Employers are endeavoring to rein in health-care costs.[45] Most cost-control efforts should start by instituting methods for measuring and auditing health-care costs.[46] It makes little sense to initiate cost cuts when employers are paying out thousands or millions of dollars in erroneous claims. One U.S. survey found that although the industry standard for percentage of claims errors is 3%, the *actual* percentage of claims with errors was about 6.3%. The U.S. industry standard for percentage of claims dollars actually paid in error was 1%; the *actual* percentage of claims dollars paid in error was 3.4%. So, setting standards for errors and then auditing all claims may be the most direct way to reduce employer health-care expenses.[47]

A study of healthcare cost of Indian companies by Towers Watson in 2015 indicated that healthcare costs are increasing and over 55% employers are spending more than 25% of payroll costs on healthcare.[48] It was also found that unlimited employee health coverage was the main attraction point for Indian PSUs. For workers, the Employees State Insurance Corporation (ESIC) provided health care through its hospital network, and additionally, it provided healthcare insurance to protect against loss of salary due to illness. Under the health benefits, coverage to a larger set of dependents, including parents, is a unique feature in India.[49] Many Indian companies have started to organize preventive annual medical checkups, for employees as well as their family members, through which they expect an early detection of health issues. In a bid to control costs, many employers are also asking employees to share part of the costs.[50]

WELLNESS PROGRAMS   Because various illnesses are preventable, many employers offer preventive programs.[51] For example, the top three health-care priorities of employers in a recent Aon Hewitt Health Care Survey report were, "Offer incentives or disincentives to motivate sustained health-care behavior change"; "Promote a culture of health in the workplace (e.g., healthy cafeteria, flexible schedules to allow time for physical activity)"; and "Move to rewarding improved health results or outcomes."[52] In one study "employers who undertook prevention programs aimed at cardiovascular disease … reported an average 28% reduction in sick leave, [and] a 26% reduction in direct health-care costs."[53]

Employers offer a variety of preventive services and incentives.[54] Some *link each employee's health-care premiums* to his or her healthy behaviors.[55] *Clinical prevention* programs include things like mammograms and routine checkups. Walgreens owns companies that provide *on-site health-care services* such as mammograms for employers.[56] *Health promotion and disease prevention* programs include seminars and incentives aimed at improving unhealthy behaviors.[57] Other wellness program trends include obesity management, stress management, senior health improvement, and tobacco cessation programs.[58] Incentives, for instance, $50–$100, can boost wellness program participation, but may backfire.[59] Whirlpool gives nonsmoker discounts on health-care premiums worth about $500. It suspended 39 workers it caught smoking outside the plant after claiming on their benefits enrollment forms that they were nonsmokers.

IMPROVING PERFORMANCE: *HR as a Profit Center*

The Doctor Is on the Phone

With more than 12,000 employees in its health plan, Rent-A-Center was looking for a better way to get its employees the medical advice they required, while also reducing health plan costs. The company signed an agreement with Teladoc, Inc. Teladoc's doctors provide medical consultations over the phone. In the first 16 months the new telemedicine program was in effect, Rent-A-Center saved more than $770,000 in doctor and hospital visits and in employee productivity that would have been lost.

The program seems to be win-win. The Teladoc consultation is free to employees, compared to a $20 office co-payment, and the doctors are available 24 hours per day, usually within 30 minutes. If necessary, they call in antibiotics prescriptions. And for Rent-A-Center, there's that extra $770,000 in their bottom line.[60] ■

Source: Based on Susan Galactica, "There's a Doctor on the Phone? Employers Dial-Up Telemedicine," Workforce Management, September 2012, p. 8. See also, "Speakers tout advantages, $6 billion potential of telemedicine," Bloomberg BNA bulletin to management, December 16, 2014, page 399.

Long-Term Care

Long-term care insurance—for things like nursing assistance to former employees in their old age—is a key employee benefit. Many Indian employers, particularly the PSUs and traditional Indian private companies, permit extension of healthcare facilities to retired employees and immediate family members. Employers can also provide insurance benefits for several types of long-term care, such as adult day care, assisted living, and custodial care.

Life Insurance

> **group life insurance**
> Provides lower rates for the employer or employee and includes all employees, including new employees, regardless of health or physical condition.

In addition to hospitalization and medical benefits, most employers provide **group life insurance** plans. The Group Insurance Scheme of the Life Insurance Corporation or LIC is a popular option. Such plans generally offer lower rates than individual plans, and usually accept all employees regardless of health or physical condition.

In general, there are three key personnel policies to address: the benefits-paid schedule (the amount of life insurance benefits is usually tied to the employee's annual earnings), supplemental benefits (continued life insurance coverage after retirement, for instance), and financing (the amount and percent the employee contributes).

Accidental death and dismemberment coverage provides a lump-sum benefit in addition to life insurance benefits when death is accidental. It also provides benefits in case of accidental loss of limbs or sight.

Retirement Benefits

> **LEARNING OBJECTIVE 13-3**
> Discuss the main retirement benefits.

The first contingent of baby boomers turned 65 a few years ago. This presents two challenges for employers. First (as we explained in Chapter 10 (Careers and Retention)), employers are taking steps to entice older workers to keep working in some capacity.[61] Second, retirement benefits such as federal Social Security and employer pension/retirement plans like the 401(k) are big issues.

Social Security

> **Social Security**
> Program that provides three types of benefits: retirement income, survivor's or death benefits payable to the employee's dependents regardless of age at time of death, and disability benefits payable to disabled employees and their dependents.

Most people assume that **Social Security** provides income only when they are older than 62, but it actually provides three types of benefits. The familiar *retirement benefits* provide an income if you retire and are insured under the the relevant acts. In India, the main social security institutions are: (i) Employees Provident Fund, (ii) dependent support provided by the ESIC, (iii) gratuity provided under the Payment of Gratuity Act, 1972, and (d) compensation in case of injury or disability under Employees Compensation Act, 1923. Second are *survivor's* or *death benefits.* These provide monthly payments to your dependents regardless of your age at death (assuming you're insured under Social Security). Finally, *disability payments* provide payments to employees who become disabled totally (and to their dependents) if they meet certain requirements.

pension plans
Plans that provide a fixed sum when employees reach a predetermined retirement age or when they can no longer work due to disability.

defined benefit pension plan
A plan that contains a formula for determining retirement benefits.

defined contribution pension plan
A plan in which the employer's contribution to employees' retirement savings funds is specified.

Pension Plans

Pension plans provide income to individuals in their retirement, and just over half of full-time workers participate in some type of pension plan at work.

We can classify pension plans as contributory versus noncontributory plans, qualified versus nonqualified plans, and defined contribution versus defined benefit plans.[62] The employee contributes to the contributory pension plan, while the employer makes all contributions to the noncontributory pension plan. Employers derive certain tax benefits (such as tax deductions) for contributing to qualified pension plans; nonqualified pension plans get less favorable tax treatment. As with all pay plan components, employers should ensure retirement benefits support their strategic needs. For example, set guiding principles such as "assist in attracting employees."[63]

With **defined benefit pension plans**, the employee's pension is specified ("defined"), in that the person knows in advance his or her pension benefits.

Defined contribution pension plans specify ("define") what *contribution* the employee and employer will make to the employee's retirement or savings fund. Here the contribution is defined, not the pension. With a *defined benefit* plan, the employee can compute what his or her retirement *benefits* will be upon retirement. With a *defined contribution* plan, the actual pension will depend on the amounts contributed to the fund *and* on the success of the fund's investment earnings. Defined contribution plans are popular among employers due to their relative ease of administration, favorable tax treatment, and other factors. **Portability**—making it easier for employees who leave the firm prior to retirement to take their accumulated pension funds with them—is easier with defined contribution plans.

In any case, CEO retirement packages tend to dwarf the average employee's.[64] For example, when Target's CEO stepped down recently after a huge credit card breach, he walked away with retirement plans worth more than $47 million, plus a $7.2 million severance payment and $4.1 million from vested stock awards.

401(K) PLANS IN THE US   The most popular defined contribution plans are based on section 401(k) of the Internal Revenue Code, and called **401(k) plans**. The employee authorizes the employer to deduct a sum from his or her paycheck before taxes, and to invest it in the bundle of investments in his or her 401(k) account. The deduction is pretax, so the employee pays no tax on those dollars until after he or she retires (or removes the money from the 401(k) plan). The person can deduct annually an amount up to the IRS maximum (about $15,000). Employers often match employee's 401(k) contributions dollar for dollar up to a set percentage. The employer arranges, usually with an investment company such as Fidelity Investments, to administer the 401(k) plan and to make investment options (typically mutual stock funds and bond funds) available to the plan. In the recent downturn, more employees made "hardship withdrawals" from their 401(k) plans.[65]

Employers must choose 401(k) providers with care. The employer has a fiduciary responsibility to its employees and must monitor the fund and its administration.[66] In addition to trustworthiness, the 401(k) plan provider should make it easy to enroll and participate in the plan.[67] Firms such as Vanguard, Fidelity, and others establish Web-based 401(k) plans with online tools—such as an "asset allocation planner"— even for small firms. Employers must also monitor 401(k) housekeeping issues such as late deposits and incorrect employer matching contributions.[68]

KNOW YOUR EMPLOYMENT LAW

National Pension Scheme, India

The National Pension Scheme (NPS) is a voluntary, defined contribution pension fund that has come into force from January 1, 2004. With the introduction of NPS, the government of India has replaced the existing Defined Benefit Pension System with a contribution-based one. All new employees (except for the Armed Forces) who joined employment from January 1, 2004, were covered by the NPS. At present, any

Indian citizen including self-employed professionals can join the NPS scheme. The scheme is offered by Pension Fund Managers (like SBI Pension Fund, LIC Pension Fund, Kotak Pension Fund, Reliance Capital Pension Fund, etc.), and it is regulated by the Pension Fund Regulatory and Development Authority of India (PFRDA).

TRENDS SHAPING HR: *DIGITAL AND SOCIAL MEDIA*

There was a time not too long ago when communicating with employees about their benefits required a ponderous and expensive process involving communiqués from the central HR office, but with digital and social media that's no longer the case.[69] First, as just noted, employers are using benefits systems such as Benelogic, and in-house benefits Web sites. Others are pulling their Twitter feeds into their benefits Web sites to keep those Web sites up-to-date. Others use their company blogs to communicate employee perks and benefits. Some use their Facebook and LinkedIn pages to publicize their benefits to a wider audience. Recently, Siemens created an internal social media Web site for its 13,000 UK employees. Among other things, Siemens UK uses it to keep its employees up-to-date about its latest employee benefits offerings, to run real-time employee feedback polls about Siemens benefits, and to remind employees about the availability of various benefits. (For example, that each employee has points to use as part of the Siemens employee recognition program.)

On the other hand, social media sites get some workers in trouble. In one case in the US, an employee took a sick day, saying that chronic pain prevented her from coming to work. Unfortunately, she posted pictures of herself dancing at a festival the day she was supposed to be home sick. One of her Facebook "friends" got the photo and showed it to a company supervisor. The company fired her for absence, and an appeals court upheld the employer's decision.[70] Similar cases have been reported in India also. ■

Personal Services and Family-Friendly Benefits

Although time off, insurance, and retirement account for the lion's share of benefits costs, most employers also provide various services benefits. These include personal services (such as legal and personal counseling), "family-friendly" services (such as child-care facilities), educational subsidies, and executive perquisites (such as company cars for its executives).

Challenging economic times mean employers are revamping their personal services benefits. Among the most-*dropped* benefits have been educational assistance, long-term care insurance, and job sharing. "Most-added" benefits included legal counseling, lactation rooms, work-at-home policies, and paid or subsidized off-site fitness.[71] For example, when the Dallas/Fort Worth International Airport found that its employee fitness and wellness facility wasn't producing the expected health cost savings, it instituted incentives to get employees to use it more regularly.[72]

LEARNING OBJECTIVE 13-4
Outline the main employees' services benefits.

Personal Services

Personal services benefits include credit unions, legal services, counseling, and social and recreational opportunities. (Some employers use the term *voluntary benefits* to cover personal services benefits that range from things like pet insurance to automobile insurance.[73]) We'll look at some of these.

employee assistance program (EAP)
A formal employer program for providing employees with counseling and/or treatment programs for problems such as alcoholism, gambling, or stress.

Employee assistance programs (EAPs) provide counseling and advisory services, such as personal legal and financial services, child- and elder care referrals, adoption assistance, mental health counseling, and life event planning.[74] EAPs are popular, with more than 60% of larger firms offering them. According to a survey in India, 46% of Indian employees suffer from stress, while 43% have skewed BMI (body mass index). Some of the issues faced by Indian employees are poor relationships, work performance, expectations, and lifestyle problems like unhealthy eating habits, lack of sleep, consumerist culture with pressures of bank loans, and living standards. Many Indian

Software giant SAS Institute, Inc., is one company that offers generous employee benefits. The North Carolina firm keeps turnover at 4% in an industry where 20% is typical, partly by offering family-friendly benefits like paid maternity leave, day care on site, lunchtime piano concerts, massages, and yoga classes like this one.

Diego Cervo/Shutterstock

organizations use services of EAP (employee assistance program) providers to support employees in these areas. PSUs like SAIL, NTPC, and IOCL have full-fledged medical departments with qualified doctors and referral tie-ups, which can be availed by employees in need. One study found that personal mental health was the most common problem addressed by employee assistance programs, followed by family problems.[75]

For employers, EAPs produce advantages, not just costs. For example, sick family members and problems like depression account for many sick days. Employee assistance programs can reduce such absences by providing expert advice on issues like elder care referrals.[76] Few but the largest employers establish their own EAPs.

In either case, everyone involved including supervisors and EAP staff must respect *confidentiality.* Also, keep files locked, limit access, and minimize identifying information. *Be aware of legal issues.* For example, in most states counselors must disclose suspicions of child abuse to state agencies. *Define* the program's purpose, employee eligibility, the roles and responsibilities of EAP and employer personnel, and procedures for using the plan. Ensure your EAP vendors fulfill *professional and state licensing requirements.*

Family-Friendly (Work–Life) Benefits

Several trends have changed the benefits landscape. There are more households where both adults work, more one-parent households, more women in the workforce, and more workers over age 65.[77]

Such trends lead many employers to bolster their **family-friendly (or "work–life") benefits.**[78] These include child care, elder care, fitness facilities, and flexible work schedules—benefits that help employees balance their family and work lives.[79] We'll look at some examples.

family-friendly (or work–life) benefits
Benefits such as child-care and fitness facilities that make it easier for employees to balance their work and family responsibilities.

SUBSIDIZED OR ON-SITE CHILD CARE The Factories Act, 1948, mandates that child-care facilities should be provided by the employer, if the number of women working are 30 or more. Many Indian companies have taken positive steps to provide child-care facilities within their premises. But, most working people make private provisions to take care of their children. Employers who want to reduce the distractions associated with finding reliable child care can help. Some employers simply investigate the day care facilities in their communities and recommend certain ones to employees. Others set up company-sponsored and subsidized day care facilities. For example, Cummins

India, which has more than 30% women employees, has set up high quality child-care facilities in their offices and factories. Other Indian companies providing similar facilities are ICICI Bank, HUL, EY, etc.[80] Among educational institutions, IIMA has a daycare center which provides child-care and after-school care for the children of the institute's staff. Abbott Laboratories built a $10 million child-care center at its headquarters north of Chicago, daytime home to about 400 children of Abbott employees.[81]

By establishing subsidized day care, employers assumedly can benefit in several ways. These include improved recruiting results, lower absenteeism, improved morale, favorable publicity, and lower turnover. But, good planning is required. This often starts with a questionnaire to employees to answer questions like, "What would you be willing to pay for care for one child in a child-care center near work?"

SICK CHILD BENEFITS   Unexpected absences accounted for a cost per absence to employers of about $700 per episode (for temp employees and reduced productivity, for instance). More employers are thus offering emergency child-care benefits, for example, when an employee's babysitter is a no-show. Texas Instruments built a Web database its employees use to find last-minute child-care providers. Others, like Canada's CIBC, are expanding their on-site child-care centers to handle last-minute emergencies.[82]

ELDER CARE   The responsibility for caring for aging relatives can affect employee performance.[83] One study found that, to care for an older relative, 64% of employees took sick days or vacation time, 33% decreased work hours, 22% took leaves of absence, 20% changed their job status from full- to part-time, 16% quit their jobs, and 13% retired early.

More employers in the US are therefore providing elder care services, though such facility has to gain acceptance in India. For example, the United Auto Workers and Ford provide elder care referral services for Ford's salaried employees, including assessments and recommendations on the best care.[84]

EDUCATIONAL SUBSIDIES   The percentage of employers offering education benefits is diminishing.[85] Such programs are expensive, and the employer may also be paying its best employees to leave. Researchers studied how the U.S. Navy's part-time college education reimbursements influenced job mobility. Taking tuition assistance decreased the probability the person stayed in the Navy.[86]

Payments may range from all tuition and expenses down to a fixed amount per year. Many employers also reimburse non–job-related courses (such as a Web designer taking an accounting class) that pertain to company business.[87] Many employers provide college programs on the employer's premises, or remedial work in basic literacy. BITS Pilani provides a range of technical courses, leading to BS or MS degrees. Companies like Cummins India, Zydus-Cadilla, L&T, etc., have tied up with IIMA and other B-schools to provide long duration programs. The ePGP program of IIMA, offered through satellite learning, is an option for companies to encourage employees to obtain formal management qualification.[88]

Other Personal Services Benefits

Employers provide other personal services benefits.[89] Google, perennially one of the "100 best companies to work for," is famous for its personal services benefits, and the remarkable thing is that most of them cost Google nothing. This is because Google arranges with local vendors to provide on-Google site programs such as ATMs, mobile libraries, bike repair, car wash and oil change, dry cleaning, haircuts and salons, and organic grocery delivery.[90] Free though they are to Google, why does Google even bother? Largely because their on-site availability boosts employees' efficiency by reducing the need for them to seek services off-site. (It also offers the Google Child Care Center, and free shuttle service from San Francisco, for instance.)[91] CVS Caremark, seeking to retain older employees, offers various elder-friendly benefits. Its "snowbird" program lets pharmacists winter in Florida and work in the Northeast when it's warmer, for instance.[92] Nestlé Purina Pet Care's St. Louis headquarters lets employees bring their dogs to work.[93]

Nonmonetary benefits are another option.[94] In one survey, the nonmonetary benefits most desired by employees were: allowing more flexibility with one's work schedule, making available additional training and development opportunities, offering additional paid time off, and providing opportunities to work abroad.[95]

Unfortunately, it's not easy to evaluate the "profitability" of personal services-type programs.[96] The bottom line is that employers are reviewing (and often reducing) these benefits. Even Google, long known for offering benefits that blow most other employers away, cut back a bit of late.

Diversity Counts

DOMESTIC PARTNER BENEFITS When employers provide *domestic partner benefits* to employees, the employees' same-sex or opposite-sex domestic partners are eligible to receive the same benefits (health care, life insurance, and so forth) as do the husband, wife, or legal dependent of one of the firm's employees. Many U.S. employers offer domestic partner benefits, while Indian employers are yet to openly extend partner benefits to LGBT couples. Godrej Industries is an Indian company which has started initiatives to support its LGBTQ employees and their partners, and make them more comfortable at workplace. Facilities like medical care are extended to the partners, and a three-month break for child adoption is also provided.[97] The company even encourages its employees to support and participate in public events connected with diverse groups like the Bangalore Parade 2015.[98]

The Strategic Context feature illustrates how one employer uses benefits to support its strategic goals.

▶ IMPROVING PERFORMANCE: *The Strategic Context*

Gary Erickson started Clif Bar as a small bakery and grew it into a company that's been growing 20% per year. Central to his "healthy foods" strategy is the idea that his hundreds of employees should live the values of sustainability, healthiness, and eco-friendliness.[99] Therefore, he put together a benefits package that encouraged just such values. For example, the company encourages eco-friendliness by reimbursing employees up to $6,500 if they buy hybrid or electric vehicles. Those who bike or walk to work receive $1,500 per year. Clif Bar's subsidized cafeteria serves meals cooked with local organic ingredients. Employees become eligible for 6-week paid sabbaticals after 7 years working for the company. With employee turnover only 3%, in one recent year Clif Bar received over 7,500 applications for 114 open jobs, so his benefits plan also seems to be helping keep workforce costs under control. ■

Source: Based on JP Mangalindan, "a healthier, more rewarding workplace," fortune, October 6, 2014, pages 49–50.

Executive Perquisites

When you reach the pinnacle of the organizational pyramid—or close to the top—you will find, waiting for you, the "executive perk." Perquisites (perks for short) are special benefits for top executives. They range from company planes to private bathrooms.

Most fall between these extremes. Perks include *management loans* (typically to exercise executives' stock options); *financial counseling*; and *relocation benefits*, often including subsidized mortgages, purchase of the executive's current house, and payment for the move. Publicly traded companies must itemize all executives' perks (if they total more than $100,000). Income tax rules in India clearly specifies the tax burden of executive perquisites. Good corporate governance also requires disclosure of such perquisites. For example, in the recent case of Infosys, excessive severance pay to the former CFO and use of private plane were the governance issues raised by its founders.

LEARNING OBJECTIVE **13-5**

Explain the main flexible benefit programs.

Flexible Benefits Programs

Employees prefer choice in their benefits plans. In one survey of working couples, 83% took advantage of flexible hours (when available); 69% took advantage of the flexible-style benefits we'll discuss next; and 75% said that they prefer flexible benefits plans.[100]

Given this, it is prudent to survey employees' benefits preferences, perhaps using a form like that in Figure 13-2. In any case, employers should provide for choice when designing benefits plans.

The Cafeteria Approach

One way to provide a choice is with an aptly named *cafeteria benefits plan.* (Pay specialists use **flexible benefits plan** and **cafeteria benefits plan** synonymously.) A *cafeteria plan* is one in which the employer gives each employee a benefits fund budget, and lets the person spend it on the benefits he or she prefers, subject to two constraints. First, the employer must of course limit the total cost for each employee's benefits package. Second, each employee's benefits plan must include certain required items such as Social Security, workers' compensation, and unemployment insurance. Employees can often make midyear changes to their plans if, for instance, their dependent care costs rise and they want to divert contributions.[101]

TYPES OF PLANS Cafeteria plans come in several varieties. To give employees more flexibility in what benefits they use, about 70% of employers offer *flexible spending accounts* for medical and other expenses. To encourage employees to use this option, some firms are offering *debit cards* that employees can use at their medical provider or pharmacy.[102] *Core plus option plans* establish a core set of benefits (such as medical insurance), which are usually mandatory for all employees. Beyond the core, employees can then choose various benefits options.[103]

The accompanying HR Tools feature explains how many smaller employers manage the costs of their various benefits.

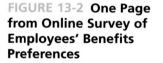

flexible benefits plan/ cafeteria benefits plan
Individualized plans allowed by employers to accommodate employee preferences for benefits.

FIGURE 13-2 One Page from Online Survey of Employees' Benefits Preferences
Reprinted with permission from GrapeVine solutions.

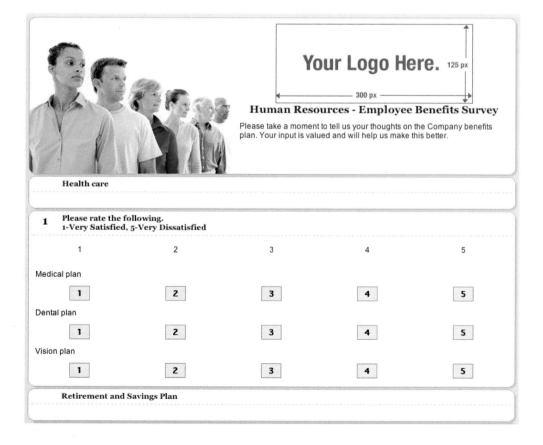

▶ **IMPROVING PERFORMANCE:** *HR Tools for Line Managers and Small Businesses*

Benefits and Employee Leasing

Many businesses—particularly smaller ones—don't have the resources or employee base to support the cost of many of the benefits we've discussed in this chapter. That's one big reason they turn to "employee leasing."

In brief, employee leasing firms (also called *professional employer organizations* or *staff leasing firms*) assume all or most of the employer's human resources chores. In doing so, they also become the employer of record for the employer's employees, by transferring them all to the employee leasing firm's payroll. The leasing firm thus becomes the employees' legal employer, and usually handles employee-related activities such as recruiting, hiring (with client firms' supervisors' approvals), and paying taxes (Social Security payments, unemployment insurance, and so on).

Insurance and benefits are usually the big attraction. Even group rates for life or health insurance can be quite high when only 20 or 30 employees are involved. That's where leasing comes in. Remember that the leasing firm is now the legal employer. The employees are thus part of a larger insurable group, along with other employers' former employees. The small business owner may get insurance it couldn't otherwise afford.

As in dealing with all vendors, the employer should have a detailed negotiated agreement with the employee leasing firm. Define what the services will be; include priorities, responsibilities, and warranties.[104] Understand that if the leasing firm merges into another firm, the new parent may require you to change your systems once the contract period expires.[105] ■

Source: Based on Bill Roberts, "Good Vendor Relations," HR Magazine, September 2011, p. 110.

Flexible Work Schedules

Flexible work schedules are popular.[106] Single parents use them for balancing work and family responsibilities. And for many millennial employees, flexible work schedules provide a way to pursue their careers without surrendering the quality of life they desire. There are several flexible work schedule options.

flextime
A work schedule in which employees' workdays are built around a core of midday hours, and employees determine, within limits, what other hours they will work.

Flextime is a plan whereby employees' workdays are built around a core of midday hours, such as 11:00 A.M. to 2:00 P.M. Thus, workers may opt to work from 7:00 A.M. to 3:00 P.M. or from 11:00 A.M. to 7:00 P.M. The number of employees in formal flextime programs—from 4% of operators to 17% of executive employees—doesn't tell the whole story. Many more employees take advantage of informal flexible work schedules.[107] Flexible timing is a much sought-after benefit by Indian employees. A survey indicated that 85% of Indians are not happy with their working hours. At the same time, more Indian companies are willing to offer flexi-time options to their employees.[108]. The effect of flextime for most employees is about 1 hour of leeway before 9:00 A.M. or after 5:00 P.M.[109]

Telecommuting—using technology to work away from the office—is popular. About 48% of employers offer ad hoc telecommuting options, while 17% offer them on a full-time basis.[110] Some jobs have much higher rates. For example, almost 45% of medical transcription is reportedly work from home.[111] Just over 13 million Americans work from home at least one day per week, with Fridays and Mondays the favorite days to stay home.[112] On the other hand, Yahoo! famously said a few years ago that it needed its employees "working side by side" and brought them back to the office.[113]

Employers that offer telecommuting must calculate the program's benefits and costs. Thus, Delta Airlines spends an initial $2,500 for each home-based reservation agent for computer and software licenses, but pays each such agent $1.50 per hour less than call-center counterparts. Less obvious expenses include having IT answer telecommuters' technical questions.[114] A telecommuting program at Capital One Bank apparently led to about a 41% increase in workplace satisfaction, and a 53% increase in those who say their workplace enhances group productivity.[115]

compressed workweek
Schedule in which employee works fewer but longer days each week.

COMPRESSED WORKWEEKS Many employees, like airline pilots, don't work conventional 5-day, 40-hour workweeks. Workers like these typically have **compressed workweek** schedules—they work fewer days each week, but each day they work longer hours. Some firms have four 10-hour day workweeks. Some workers—in hospitals, for instance—work three 12-hour shifts, and then take off for 4 days.[116] Some experts argue that 12-hour shifts increase fatigue and accidents. To reduce potential side effects, some employers install treadmills, exercise bikes, and special lights that mimic daylight.

job sharing
Allows two or more people to share a single full-time job.

work sharing
Refers to a temporary reduction in work hours by a group of employees during economic downturns as a way to prevent layoffs.

OTHER FLEXIBLE WORK ARRANGEMENTS **Job sharing** allows two or more people to share a single full-time job. For example, two people may share a 40-hour-per-week job, with one working mornings and the other working afternoons. About 22% of the firms questioned in one survey indicated that they allow job sharing.[117] Job sharing can be particularly useful for retirement-aged employees. It allows them to reduce their hours while the company retains their expertise.[118] **Work sharing** refers to a temporary reduction in work hours by a group of employees during economic downturns as a way to prevent layoffs. Thus, 400 employees may all agree to work (and be paid for) only 35 hours per week, to avoid a layoff of 30 workers.

EFFECTIVENESS OF FLEXIBLE WORK SCHEDULE ARRANGEMENTS Studies show that flexible work schedules have positive effects on employee productivity, job satisfaction, and employee absenteeism; the effect on absenteeism is generally greater than on productivity. Highly flexible programs were less effective than less flexible ones.[119]

LEARNING OBJECTIVE 13-6
Explain how to use benefits to improve engagement, productivity, and performance.

Employee Engagement Guide For Managers

Costco's Compensation Plan

Costco's HR strategy is to deflect Walmart's famously low costs and wages by paying employees more, and thereby producing improved employee engagement, productivity, and customer service.[120]

For example, Costco pays its employees on average about $21 per hour (not including overtime,) almost triple the federal minimum wage.[121] That compares with Walmart's average wage for full-time employees in the United States of $12.67 an hour.[122] Costco's *starting* pay is $11.50 per hour, again far above the minimum wage.[123]

Costco's employee benefits are also highly competitive, particularly compared with the typically sparse offerings in the retail industry.[124] For example, Costco pays about 90% of the health insurance costs of its over 90,000 domestic employees.[125] Its other benefits include (as examples) dental care, a pharmacy/prescriptions program, a vision program, a 401(k) plan, a dependent care assistance plan, an external network of professional counselors, voluntary short-term disability, long-term disability, and life insurance.[126] Costco also extends these benefits to employees' spouses, children, and domestic partners. To get the most from these plans, Costco employees can use www.costcobenefits.com, for instance, to find physicians in their areas.

Costco doesn't directly measure employee engagement; it says it tracks engagement by "byproducts," such as turnover and productivity.[127] By those criteria, Costco's engagement efforts seem to be working. Its sales per employee are about $500,000 a year versus $340,000 at Walmart's Sam's Club.[128] Costco's turnover is far below the retail industry average, and employee retention is higher.[129] Costco, by the way, is not alone. Other large chains with traditionally excellent customer service, like Nordstrom and the Container Store, also do well financially, in part by treating employees well and keeping engagement up.[130]

Chapter Review

Chapter Section Summaries

13-1. Employers provide numerous **pay for time not worked benefits**. These include unemployment insurance, vacation and other leave days, and sick pay. Minimizing sick leave pay is important, and here cost reduction tactics include paid leave plans that lump sick leave, vacation, and holidays into one leave pool.

13-2. Most employers also provide required or voluntary **insurance benefits**. Workers' compensation laws aim to provide sure, prompt medical benefits to work-related accident victims or their dependents, regardless of fault. Most employer health plans provide at least basic hospitalization and surgical and medical insurance for eligible employees. When an employee is terminated or terminates his or her employment, it is essential that the employer make the person aware of his or her rights. Employers generally work hard to keep the rising cost of health-care insurance under control.

13-3. **Retirement benefits** are important to employees today.

13-4. Most employers also provide various **personal services and family-friendly benefits**. These include credit unions, employee assistance programs, and subsidized child care and elder care.

13-5. Employees prefer choice in their benefits plans, so **flexible benefits programs** are important. Flexible benefits or cafeteria benefits plans are individual plans that accommodate employee preferences for benefits. Some employers turn to employee leasing companies to capitalize on the advantage of the leasing firm's large employee base to get better employee benefits for their employees. Employers also are implementing various types of flexible work schedules, including flextime, compressed workweeks, and other flexible work arrangements such as job sharing.

13-6. Costco's HR strategy is to deflect Walmart's low wages by paying employees more, thereby producing more **employee engagement**, higher productivity, and better customer service. As one example, Costco pays about 90% of the health insurance costs of its over 90,000 domestic employees.

Discussion Questions

13-1. What is unemployment insurance? Is an organization required to pay unemployment benefits to all dismissed employees? Explain how you would go about minimizing your organization's unemployment insurance tax.

13-2. Explain how ESIC protects employees' rights.

13-3. Describe the main retirement benefits.

13-4. What are the main provisions of the FMLA?

Individual and Group Activities

13-5. Working individually or in groups, research the unemployment laws of your state. Write a summary detailing your state's unemployment laws.

13-6. Assume you run a small business. Working individually or in groups, visit the Web sites www.paycheck.in and www.msme.gov.in. Write a two-page summary explaining: (1) the various social security and retirement savings programs available to small business employers, and (2) which type of benefits you would choose for your small business and why?

13-7. You are the HR consultant to a small business with about 40 employees. Now the firm offers only 5 days of vacation, 5 paid holidays, and legally mandated benefits such as unemployment insurance payments. Develop a list of other benefits you believe it should offer, along with your reasons for suggesting them.

13-8. Appendices A and B at the end of this book (pages 583–600) list the knowledge someone studying for the HRCI (Appendix A) or SHRM (Appendix B) certification exam needs to have in each area of human resource management (such as in Strategic Management, and Workforce Planning). In groups of several students, do four things: (1) review Appendix A and/or B; (2) identify the material in this chapter that relates to the Appendix A and/or B required knowledge lists; (3) write four multiple-choice exam questions on this material that you believe would be suitable for inclusion in the HRCI exam and/or the SHRM exam; and, (4) if time permits, have someone from your team post your team's

questions in front of the class, so that students in all teams can answer the exam questions created by the other teams.

Experiential Exercise

Revising the Benefits Package

Purpose: The purpose of this exercise is to provide practice in developing a benefits package for a small business.

Required Understanding: Be very familiar with the material presented in this chapter. In addition, review Chapter 11 to reacquaint yourself with sources of compensation survey information, and come to class prepared to share with your group the benefits package for the small business in which you work or in which someone with whom you're familiar works.

How to Set Up the Exercise/Instructions: Divide the class into groups of four or five students. Your assignment is

as follows: Rani Joseph runs a small personnel recruiting office in Mumbai and has decided to start offering an expanded benefits package to her 25 employees. At the current time, the only benefits are 15 paid holidays per year and 5 sick days per year. The firm works six days a week, and often employees have to attend calls from home or even on Sundays. In her company, there are 2 other managers, as well as 17 full-time recruiters and 5 secretarial staff members. Your assignment is as follows:

- In the time allotted, your group should create a benefits package in keeping with the size and requirements of this firm.

Application Case

Striking for Benefits

A few years ago, the strike by Southern California grocery workers against the state's major supermarket chains was almost 5 months old. The main issue was employee benefits, and specifically how much (if any) of the employees' health-care costs the employees should pay themselves. Based on their existing contract, Southern California grocery workers had unusually good health benefits. For example, they paid nothing toward their health insurance premiums, and paid only $10 co-payments for doctor visits. However, supporting these excellent health benefits cost the big Southern California grocery chains over $4 per hour per worker.

The big grocery chains were not proposing cutting health-care insurance benefits for their existing employees. Instead, they proposed putting any new employees hired after the new contract went into effect into a separate insurance pool, and contributing $1.35 per hour for their health insurance coverage. That meant new employees' health insurance would cost each new employee perhaps $10 per week. And, if that $10 per week wasn't enough to cover the cost of health care, then the employees would have to pay more, or do without some of their benefits.

It was a difficult situation for all involved. For the grocery chain employers, skyrocketing health-care costs were undermining their

competitiveness; the current employees feared any step down the slippery slope that might eventually mean cutting their own health benefits. The unions didn't welcome a situation in which they'd end up representing two classes of employees, one (the existing employees) who had excellent health insurance benefits, and another (newly hired employees) whose benefits were relatively meager, and who might therefore be unhappy from the moment they took their jobs and joined the union.

Questions

13-9. Assume you are mediating this dispute. Discuss five creative solutions you would suggest for how the grocers could reduce the health insurance benefits and the cost of their total benefits package without making any employees pay more.

13-10. From the grocery chains' point of view, what is the downside of having two classes of employees, one of which has superior health insurance benefits? How would you suggest they handle the problem?

13-11. Similarly, from the point of view of the union, what are the downsides of having to represent two classes of employees, and how would you suggest handling the situation?

Source: Based on "Settlement Nears for Southern California Grocery Strike," *Knight-Ridder/Tribune Business News*, February 26, 2004, item 04057052.

Continuing Case

Carter Cleaning Company

The New Benefit Plan

Carter Cleaning Centers has traditionally provided only legislatively required benefits for its employees. These include unemployment

compensation, Social Security, and workers' compensation (which is provided through the same insurance carrier that insures the stores for such hazards as theft and fire). The principals of the firm—Jack, Jennifer, and their families—have individual, family-supplied health and life insurance.

Jennifer can see several potential problems with the company's policies regarding benefits and services. One is turnover. She wants to study whether similar companies' experiences with providing health and life insurance benefits enable these firms to reduce employee turnover and perhaps pay lower wages. Jennifer is also concerned that her company has no formal vacation or paid days off or sick leave policies. Informally, at least, it is understood that employees get 1 week's vacation after 1 year's work, but in the past the policy regarding paid vacations for days such as New Year's Day and Thanksgiving Day has been very inconsistent. Sometimes employees who had been on the job only 2 or 3 weeks were paid fully for one of these holidays, while at other times employees who had been with the firm for 6 months or more had been paid for only half a day.

She also wonders whether it would be advisable to establish some type of day care center for the employees' children. Many of them have no place to go during the day (they are preschoolers) or have no place to go after school; she wonders whether a day care benefit would be in the best interests of the company.

Questions

13-12. Draw up a policy statement regarding vacations, sick leave, and paid days off for Carter Cleaning Centers.

13-13. What would you tell Jennifer are the advantages and disadvantages to Carter Cleaning Centers of providing its employees with health, hospitalization, and life insurance programs?

13-14. Would you advise establishing some type of day care center for the Carter Cleaning employees? Why or why not?

Translating Strategy into HR Policies and Practices Case*, §

*The overall map on page xxxviii of this book outlines the relationships involved.

Improving Performance at the Hotel Paris

The New Benefits Plan

The Hotel Paris's competitive strategy is "To use superior guest service to differentiate the Hotel Paris properties, and to thereby increase the length of stay and return rate of guests, and thus boost revenues and profitability." HR manager Lisa Cruz must now formulate functional policies and activities that support this competitive strategy by eliciting the required employee behaviors and competencies.

While the Hotel Paris's benefits (in terms of things like holidays and health care) were comparable to other hotels', Lisa knew they weren't good enough to support the high-quality service behaviors her company sought. Indeed, the fact that they were roughly comparable to those of similar firms didn't seem to impress the Hotel Paris's employees. Sixty percent of them consistently said they were dissatisfied with their benefits. Lisa's concern (with which the CFO concurred) was that dissatisfaction with benefits contributed to low morale and engagement, and thus to inhibiting the Hotel Paris from achieving its strategic aims. Lisa therefore turned to the task of assessing and redesigning the company's benefits plans.

As they reviewed the benefits numbers, Lisa and the CFO became concerned. They computed several benefits-related metrics for their firm, including benefits costs as a percentage of payroll, sick days per full-time-equivalent employee per year, benefits cost/competitor's benefits cost ratio, and workers' compensation experience ratings. The results, said the CFO, offered a "good news–bad news" situation. On the good side, as noted, the ratios were similar to most competing hotels'. The bad news was that the measures were well below those for high-performing service businesses. The CFO authorized Lisa to design and propose a new benefits plan.

Lisa knew there were several things she wanted to accomplish. She wanted a plan that contributed to improved employee morale and engagement. And, she wanted the plan to include elements that made it easier for her employees to do their jobs—so that, as she put it, "they could come to work and give their full attention to giving our guests great service, without worrying about child care and other family distractions."

The new plan's centerpiece was a proposal for much better family-friendly benefits. Because so many of each hotel's employees were single parents, and because each hotel had to run 24 hours a day, Lisa's team proposed, and the board approved, setting aside a room in each hotel for an on-site child-care facility and for hiring a trained professional attendant. They considered instituting a flexible work schedule program, but for most of the jobs, this was impractical, because each front-line employee simply had to be there at his or her appointed hour. However, they did institute a new job-sharing program. Now two people could share one housekeeping or front-desk clerk job, as long as the job was covered.

One of the metrics Lisa and her team specifically wanted to address was the relatively high absence rate at the Hotel Paris. Because so many of these jobs are front-line jobs—valets, limousine drivers, and front-desk clerks, for instance—absence had a particularly serious effect on metrics like overtime pay and temporary help costs. Here, at the urging of her compensation consultant, Lisa decided to opt for a system similar to Marriott's BENETRADE. With this benefit program, employees can trade the value of some sick days for other benefits. As Lisa put it, "I'd rather see our employees using their sick day pay for things like additional health-care benefits, if it means they'll think twice before taking a sick day to run a personal errand."

After just less than a year, Lisa and the CFO believe the new program is successful. Their studies suggest that the improved benefits are directly contributing to improved employee morale and commitment, sick days have diminished by 40%, and employee turnover is down 60%. And when they advertise for open positions, over 60% of the applicants cite "family-friendly benefits" as a top reason for applying to work at the Hotel Paris.

Questions

13-15. What is your opinion of the new Hotel Paris benefits plan?

13-16. Because employers typically make benefits available to all employees, they may not have the motivational effects of incentive plans. Given this, list five employee behaviors you believe Hotel Paris could try to improve through an enhanced benefits plan, and explain why you chose them.

13-17. Given your answer to question 13-16 and what you read in this chapter of Dessler *Human Resource Management*, explain specifically what other benefits you would recommend the Hotel Paris implement to achieve these behavioral improvements.

§Written by and copyright Gary Dessler, PhD.

Key Terms

benefits, 409
supplemental pay benefits, 411
unemployment insurance (or compensation), 411
sick leave, 415
severance pay, 417
supplemental unemployment benefits, 417

workers' compensation, 418
health maintenance organization (HMO), 419
group life insurance, 421
Social Security, 421
pension plans, 422
defined benefit pension plan, 422

defined contribution pension plan, 422
portability, 422
401(k) plan, 422
employee assistance program (EAP), 423
family-friendly (or work–life) benefits, 424

flexible benefits plan/cafeteria benefits plan, 427
flextime, 428
compressed workweek, 428
job sharing, 429
work sharing, 429

Endnotes

1. N V Madhavan, "Blue Dart: Providing Customer Satisfaction @ Express Speed, *Forbes India*, August 2016.

2. Based on Frederick Hills, Thomas Bergmann, and Vida Scarpello, *Compensation Decision Making* (Fort Worth, TX: The Dryden Press, 1994), p. 424. See also Fay Hansen, "The Cutting Edge of Benefit Cost Control," *Workforce*, March 2003, pp. 36–42; Crain's Benefits Outlook 2009, www.crainsbenefit.com/news/survey-finds-nearly-20-percent-of-employers-plan-to-drop-health-benefits.php, accessed July 28, 2009.

3. "Survey Finds 99 Percent of Employers Providing Health-Care Benefits," *Compensation & Benefits Review*, September/October 2002, p. 11. See also "National Compensation Survey: Employee Benefits in Private Industry in the United States, March 2006," U.S. Department of Labor, U.S. Bureau of Labor Statistics, August 2006.

4. "Trouble Ahead? Dissatisfaction with Benefits, Compensation," *HR Trendbook*, 2008, p. 16.

5. Pnb Metlife, "India Employee Benefit Study," 2015, as accessed on September 5, 2017, at www.pnbmetlife.com.

6. Frank Giancola, "Are Employee Benefit Programs Being Given Enough Credit for Their Effect on Employee Attitudes?" *Compensation & Benefits Review* 44, no. 5 (2012), pp. 291–297.

7. Joseph Martocchio, *Strategic Compensation* (Upper Saddle River, NJ: Prentice Hall, 2001), p. 262.

8. Accessed on September 20, 2017 at www.esic.nic.in/information-benefits.

9. Accessed on September 20, 2017 at http://www.india.com/news/india/budget-2017-narendra-modi-govt-planning-rs-1500-allowance-for-poor-unemployed-1763987/.

10. www.bls.gov/opub/perspectives/issue2.pdf, accessed September 8, 2014.

11. Ibid.

12. www.bls.gov/opub/perspectives/issue2.pdf, accessed June 1, 2011.

13. Accessed on September 20, 2017 at http://www.epaper.timesofindia.com/Repository/getFiles.asp?Style=OliveXLib:LowLevelEntityToPrint_TOINEW&Type=text/html&Path=TOIM/2010/09/07&ID=Ar02103.

14. Accessed on September 20, 2017 at http://economictimes.indiatimes.com/jobs/at-microsoft-india-caregivers-to-get-four-weeks-of-paid-leave/articleshow/58306250.cms.

15. Ken Belson, "At IBM, a Vacation Anytime, or Maybe No Vacation at All," *New York Times*, August 31, 2007, pp. A1–A18.

16. Robert Grossman, "Gone But Not Forgotten," *HR Magazine*, September 2011, p. 44; then put in place solutions such as rigorous absenteeism claims reviews.

17. See for instance, www.insperity.com/products/performance-management/policies.

18. "National Compensation Survey: Employee Benefits in Private Industry in the United States, March 2006," U.S. Bureau of Labor Statistics, August 2006, p. 116. See also "Spurious Sick-Notes Spiral Upwards," *The Safety and Health Practitioner* 22, no. 6 (June 2004), p. 3.

19. "Unscheduled Employee Absences Cost Companies More Than Ever," *Compensation & Benefits Review*, March/April 2003, p. 19; Robert Grossman, "Gone but Not Forgotten," *HR Magazine* 56, no. 9 (September 2011), pp. 34–46.

20. Biju Varkkey and Randhir Kumar 'Keeping the sparkle on: Workforce retention in Indian diamond cutting and polishing firms during economic recession', (2013) *International Journal of Organizational Analysis*, Vol. 21 Issue: 3, pp. 454 – 470.

21. "Making Up for Lost Time: How Employers Can Curb Excessive Unscheduled Absences," *BNA Human Resources Report*, October 20, 2003, p. 1097. See also W. H. J. Hassink et al., "Do Financial Bonuses Reduce Employee Absenteeism? Evidence from a Lottery," *Industrial and Labor Relations Review* 62, no. 3 (April 2009), pp. 327–342.

22. "SHRM Benefits Survey Finds Growth in Employer Use of Paid Leave Pools," *BNA Bulletin to Management*, March 21, 2002, p. 89.

23. See M. Michael Markowich and Steve Eckberg, "Get Control of the Absentee-Minded," *Personnel Journal*, March 1996, pp. 115–120; "Exploring the Pluses, Minuses, and Myths of Switching to Paid Time Off Banks," *BNA Bulletin to Management* 55, no. 25 (June 17, 2004), pp. 193–194.

24. Society for Human Resource Management 2009 Employee Benefits Survey, quoted in Martha Frase, "Taking Time Off to the Bank," *HR Magazine*, March 2010, p. 42. See also Marissa Warford, "Does Paid Time Off Pay Off?" *Workforce*, August 2014, pp. 26–29, 48.

25. "Creating Holistic Time Off Programs Can Significantly Reduce Expenses," *Compensation & Benefits Review*, July/August 2007, pp. 18–19.

26. See, for example, Rita Zeidner, "Strategies for Saving in a Down Economy," *HR Magazine*, February 2009, p. 28.

27. Judith Whitaker, "How HR Made a Difference," *People Management* 27 (October 28, 2010).

28. Ibid.

29. Accessed on September 20, 2017 at http://timesofindia.indiatimes.com/india/start-up-dads-at-tech-major-get-3-month-paternal-leave/articleshow/59624143.cms.

30. Sue Shellenbarger, "The Mommy Drain: Employers Beef Up Perks to Lure New Mothers Back to Work," *Wall Street Journal*, September 28, 2006, p. D1.

31. As accessed on September 20, 2017 at http://bangalore.com/bangalore/report-to-deal-with-attrition-companies-extending-notice-period-1873956

32. "Workers' Compensation Costs Are Rising Faster Than Wages," *BNA Bulletin to Management*, July 31, 2003, p. 244.

33. "Workers' Comp Claims Rise with Layoffs, but Employers Can Identify, Prevent Fraud," *BNA Bulletin to Management*, October 4, 2001, p. 313.

34. "Using Case Management in Workers' Compensation," *BNA Bulletin to Management*, June 6, 1996, p. 181; for other tactics, see, for example, H. Jorgensen, "Overhauling Claims Management." *Risk Management* 54, no. 7 (July 2007), p. 50. See also Donna Owens, "Back to Work," *HR Magazine*, November 2012, pp. 49–51.

35. "Workers Comp Research Provides Insight into Curbing Health Care Costs," *EHS Today*, February 2010, p. 18.

36. "Firms Cite Own Efforts as Key to Controlling Costs," *BNA Bulletin to Management*, March 21, 1996, p. 89. See also "Workers' Compensation Outlook: Cost Control Persists," *BNA Bulletin to Management*, January 30, 1997, pp.33–44; and Annmarie Lipold, "The Soaring Costs of Workers' Comp," *Workforce*, February 2003, p. 42ff.

37. In one recent survey, 53% of workers said they would trade some pay for better retirement benefits: "Employees Willing to Trade Pay for More Benefits, Survey Finds," *BNA Bulletin to Management*, March 6, 2012, p. 78.

38. Hills, Bergmann, and Scarpello, *Compensation Decision Making*, p. 137.

39. "Costs This Year Increased at Highest Rate Since 2004, Survey Reveals," *HR Focus* 88, no. 1 (January 10, 2011); "Health Costs," http://kff.org/health-costs/, accessed April 20, 2015.

40. Society for Human Resource Management, "Mental Health Trends," *Workplace Visions*, no. 2, http://moss07.shrm.org/Research/FutureWorkplaceTrends/ Pages/0303.aspx, accessed July 28, 2009.

41. WHO, "Depression and Other Common Mental Disorders-Global Health Estimates," (2017), accessed on October 9, 2017 at http://www.who.int/mental_health/management/depression/prevalence_global_health_estimates/en/.

42. Accessed on September 20, 2017 at http://economictimes.indiatimes.com/jobs/46-of-workforce-in-firms-in-india-suffer-from-some-or-the-other-form-of-stress-data/articleshow/52696795.cms.

43. Accessed on September 20, 2017 at http://www.news18.com/news/india/job-insecurity-cause-of-depression-and-anxiety-among-india-inc-says-survey-1464633.html.

44. See, for example, Karli Dunkelberger, "Avoiding COBRA's Bite: Three Keys to Compliance," *Compensation & Benefits Review*, March/April 2005, pp. 44–48. See also Patrick Muldowney, "Cobra and the Stimulus Act: A Sign of Things to Come?" *Compensation & Benefits Review* 42, no. 1 (January/February 2010), pp. 24–49.

45. http://insight.aon.com/?elqPURLPage=6567, accessed April 11, 2013.

46. James Curcio, "Creating Standardized Metrics and Benchmarking for Health, Absence and Productivity Management Programs: The EMPAQ Initiative," *Compensation & Benefits Review* 42, no. 2 (2010), pp. 109–126.

47. Vanessa Fuhrmanns, "Oops! As Health Plans Become More Complicated, They're Also Subject to a Lot More Costly Mistakes," *Wall Street Journal*, January 24, 2005, p. R4.

48. Towers Watson, "Asia Pacific Benefits Trend Survey," 2015.

49. Ibid

50. Ibid

51. "Employer Partners to Launch a Three-Year Wellness Initiative," *BNA Bulletin to Management*, August 7, 2007, p. 255.

52. http://insight.aon.com/?elqPURLPage?6567, accessed April 11, 2013.

53. Ron Finch, "Preventive Services: Improving the Bottom Line for Employers and Employees," *Compensation & Benefits Review*, March/April 2005, p. 18.

54. "Employer Partners to Launch a Three-Year Wellness Initiative," *BNA Bulletin to Management*, August 7, 2007, p. 255. See also Drew Robb, "Benefits Choices: Educating the Consumer," *HR Magazine*, March 2011, pp. 29–30.

55. Susan Wells, "Wellness Rewards," *HR Magazine*, February 2012, pp. 67–69.

56. "On-Site Clinics Aimed at Cutting Costs, Promoting Wellness," *BNA Bulletin to Management*, March 25, 2008, p. 103. See also Susan Wells, "Navigating the Expanding Wellness Industry," *HR Magazine*, March 2011, pp. 45–50.

57. Ibid. See also Josh Cable, "The Road to Wellness," *Occupational Hazards*, April 2007, pp. 23–27.

58. George DeVries, "The Top 10 Wellness Trends for 2008 and Beyond," *Compensation & Benefits Review*, July/August 2008, pp. 60–63.

59. Susan Wells, "Getting Paid for Staying Well," *HR Magazine*, February 2010, p. 59.

60. Susan Galactica, "There's a Doctor on the Phone? Employers Dial-Up Telemedicine," *Workforce Management*, September 2012, p. 8. See also "Speakers Tout Advantages, $6 Billion Potential of Telemedicine," *Bloomberg BNA Bulletin to Management,* December 16, 2014, p. 399.

61. Brenda Sunoo, "Millions May Retire," Workforce, December 1997, p. 48. See also "Many Older Workers Choose to 'Un-Retire' or Not Retire at All," *Knight Ridder/Tribune Business News*, September 28, 2003, item 03271012; and "For Many Seniors, a Job Beats Retirement," *Knight Ridder/ Tribune Business News*, February 9, 2003, item 3040001.

62. Martocchio, *Strategic Compensation*, pp. 245–248; and Lin Grensing-Pophal, "A Pension Formula That Pays Off," *HR Magazine* (February 2003), pp. 58–62.

63. For one recent example of how to do this, see Gail Nichols, "Reviewing and Redesigning Retirement Plans," *Compensation & Benefits Review*, May/June 2008, pp. 40–47.

64. "Target CEO's $47 Million Package Shows Gap with Workers," *Bloomberg BNA Bulletin to Management*, January 13, 2015, p. 12.

65. Jessica Marquez, "More Workers Yanking Money Out of 401(k)s," *Workforce Management*, August 11, 2008, p. 4.

66. Nancy Pridgen, "The Duty to Monitor Appointed Fiduciaries Under ERISA," *Compensation & Benefits Review*, September/October 2007, pp. 46–51; "Individual 401(k) Plan Participant Can Sue Plan Fiduciary for Losses, Justices Rule," *BNA Bulletin to Management*, February 20, 2008, p. 65.

67. "Benefit Trends: Automatic Enrollment Takes Off," *Compensation & Benefits Review*, September/October 2008, p. 14.

68. For a discussion, see Jewel Esposito, "Avoiding 401(k) ERISA Disasters," *Compensation & Benefits Review* 42, no. 1 (January/February 2010), pp. 39–45.

69. The following is based on www.tlnt.com/2012/04/26/ the-5-best-social-media-toolsfor- employee-benefitscommunication/, www.abenity.com/celebrate/how-touse-social-media-to-communicate-employee-perks-benefits/, www.benefitspro.com/2013/04/19/social-media-atool-to-boost-employeeengagement-p, and www .employeebenefits.co.uk/ benefits/communication/siemens-launches-social-medi-awebsite/ 105812.article, all accessed April 20, 2015.

70. "Employee Who's Facebook Photos Suggested Fraud Lacks FMLA Claims, Sixth Circuit Rules," *BNA Bulletin to Management*, November 20, 2012, p. 371.

71. Brad Reagan, "Perks with a Payoff," *Wall Street Journal*, October 24, 2011, p. r3.

72. Ibid.

73. Carolyn Hirschman, "Employees' Choice," *HR Magazine*, February 2006, pp. 95–99.

74. Joseph O'Connell, "Using Employee Assistance Programs to Avoid Crises," *Long Island Business News*, April 19, 2002, p. 10.

75. See Scott MacDonald et al., "Absenteeism and Other Workplace Indicators of Employee Assistance Program Clients and Matched Controls," *Employee Assistance Quarterly* 15, no. 3 (2000), pp. 51–58. See also Paul Courtis et al., "Performance Measures in the Employee Assistance Program," *Employee Assistance Quarterly* 19, no. 3 (2005), pp. 45–58.

76. See, for example, Donna Owens, "EAPs for a Diverse World," *HR Magazine*, October 2006, pp. 91–96.

77. "Fathers Fighting to Keep Work–Life Balance Are Finding Employers Firmly in their Corner," *BNA Bulletin to Management* 56, no. 24 (June 14, 2005), p. 185.

78. Susan Wells, "Are You Too Family-Friendly?" *HR Magazine*, October 2007, pp. 35–39.

79. Maureen Hannay and Melissa Northam, "Low-Cost Strategies for Employee Retention," *Compensation & Benefits Review*, July/August 2000, pp. 65–72. See also Roseanne Geisel, "Responding to Changing Ideas of Family," *HR Magazine*, August 2004, pp. 89–98.

80. Lipi Agarwal, "What makes Accenture, Deloitte, Cummins, EY, IBM, HUL among the best companies for women in India," *HR Katha*, Nov 14, 2016.

81. Patrick Kiger, "A Case for Childcare," *Workforce Management*, April 2004, pp. 34–40.

82. www.shrm.org/rewards/library, accessed December 23, 2006. See also Kathy Gurchiek, "Give Us Your Sick," *HR Magazine*, January 2007, pp. 91–93.

83. Kelli Earhart, R. Dennis Middlemist, and Willie Hopkins, "Elder Care: An Emerging Assistance Issue," *Employee Assistance Quarterly* 8, no. 3 (1993), pp. 1–10. See also "Finding a Balance Between Conflicting Responsibilities: Work and Caring for Aging Parents," *Monday Business Briefing*, July 7, 2004; and "Employers Feel Impact of Eldercare: Some Expanded Benefits for Workers," *Knight Ridder/Tribune Business News*, June 13, 2004, item 04165011.

84. Rudy Yandrick, "Elder Care Grows Up," *HR Magazine*, November 2001, pp. 72–77.

85. Jennifer Schramm, "Undereducated," *HR Magazine*, September 2011, p. 136.

86. Richard Buddin and Kanika Kapur, "The Effect of Employer-Sponsored Education on Job Mobility: Evidence from the U.S. Navy," *Industrial Relations* 44, no. 2 (April 2005), pp. 341–363.

87. Mary Burke, Euren Esen, and Jessica Cullison, "2003 Benefits Survey," SHRM/SHRM Foundation, 1800 Duke Street, Alexandria VA, 2003, p. 30. See also Michael Laff, "U.S. Employers Tighten Reins on Tuition Reimbursement," *Training & Development*, July 2006, p. 18.

88. Accessed on September 20, 2017 at www.iima.ac.in/web/epgp.

89. "Rising Gas Prices Prompting Employers to Consider Varied Computer Benefit Options," *BNA Bulletin to Management*, June 20, 2008, p. 201.

90. Laszlo Bock, *Work Rules!* (New York: 12, 2015), p. 274.

91. See "The 100 Best Companies to Work For," *Fortune*, February 6, 2012, p. 117.

92. Tamera Lionel, "Benefits for Older Workers," *HR Magazine*, March 2012, pp. 53–58.

93. "Perks at work," *Workforce*, September 2014, pp. 40–43.

94. Michael Custers, "Rethinking Existing HR Technologies for New Games in Employee Engagement and Benefits," *Compensation & Benefits Review* 44, no. 6, 2013, pp. 332–335.

95. Ibid.

96. Marcus Butts et al., "How Important Are Work-Family Support Policies? A Meta-Analytic Investigation of Their Effects on Employee Outcomes," *Journal of Applied Psychology* 98, no. 1 (2013), pp. 1–25.

97. Yogesh Pawar, "It's all about inclusion at Godrej," DNA, July 31, 2016.

98. Suman Layak, "How the Godrej Group is creating an Inclusive culture to accept its LGBT colleagues," *The Economic Times*, December 27, 2015.

99. Mangalindan, "A Healthier, More Rewarding Workplace."

100. "Couples Want Flexible Leave, Benefits," *BNA Bulletin to Management*, February 19, 1998, p. 53; SHRM, "2003 Benefits Survey," p. 14. See also Paul Harris, "Flexible Work Policies Mean Business," *Training & Development*, April 2007, pp. 32–36.

101. Carolyn Hirshman, "Kinder, Simpler Cafeteria Rules," *HR Magazine*, January 2001, pp. 74–79.

102. "Debit Cards for Health-Care Expenses Receive Increased Employer Attention," *BNA Bulletin to Management*, September 25, 2003, p. 305.

103. Martocchio, *Strategic Compensation*, p. 263.
104. Bill Roberts, "Good Vendor Relations," *HR Magazine*, September 2011, p. 110.
105. Ibid.
106. Elka Maria Torpey, "Flexible Work: Adjusting the When and Where of Your Job," *Occupational Outlook Quarterly*, Summer 2007, pp. 14–27.
107. "Slightly More Workers Are Skirting 9–5 Tradition," *BNA Bulletin to Management*, June 20, 2002, p. 197.
108. "More than half of Indian companies offering flexi time work: survey," (2017) accessed on October 9, 2017 at https://blog.wisdomjobs.com/half-indian-companies-offering-flexi-time-work-survey/.
109. The percentage of employers with flextime programs actually dropped from 2007 to 2011, from 58% to 53%. Joseph Coombs, "Flexibility Still Meeting Resistance," *HR Magazine*, July 2011, p. 72.
110. Dori Meinert, "Make Telecommuting Pay Off," *HR Magazine*, June 2011, pp. 33–37. See also Donna Dennis et al., "Effective Leadership in a Virtual Workforce," *Training & Development*, February 2013, pp. 47–49.
111. "Telework Among Full-Time Employees Almost Doubled in the Last Decade, Study Says," *BNA Bulletin to Management*, June 12, 2012, p. 187.
112. "13.4 Million Work from Home in 2010, Census Bureau Reports," *BNA Bulletin to Management*, October 16, 2012, p. 330.
113. Martha White, "One Part Gone: Yahoo Says No to Telecommuting," www.CNBC.com/ID/100492123, accessed February 25, 2013.
114. Dori Meinert, "Make Telecommuting Pay Off," *HR Magazine*, June 2011, pp. 33–37.
115. Ann Pomeroy, "The Future Is Now," *HR Magazine*, September 2007, pp. 46–52. See also "Telework Among Full-Time Employees Almost Doubled in the Last Decade, Study Says," *BNA Bulletin to Management*, June 12, 2012, p. 187.
116. See, for example, "Compressed Workweeks Gain Popularity, but Concerns Remain About Effectiveness," *BNA Bulletin to Management*, September 16, 2008, p. 297.
117. SHRM, "2003 Benefits Survey," p. 2.
118. "With Job Sharing Arrangements, Companies Can Get Two Employees for the Price of One," *BNA Bulletin to Management* 56, no. 47 (November 22, 2005), pp. 369–370.
119. Boris Baltes et al., "Flexible and Compressed Workweek Schedules: A Meta-Analysis of Their Effects on Work-Related Criteria," *Journal of Applied Psychology* 84, no. 4 (1999), pp. 496–513. See also Charlotte Hoff, "With Flextime, Less Can Be More," *Workforce Management*, May 2005, pp. 65–66.
120. http://articles.moneycentral.msn.com/Investing/Extra/CostcoTheAntiWalMart.aspx?page?1, accessed September 15, 2011; and, Hamilton Nolan, "The Anti-Wal-Mart," http://gawker.com/costco-the-anti-wal-mart-511739135, accessed August 7, 2013.
121. Tavia Grant, "How One Company Levels the Pay Slope of Executives and Workers," *Globe and Mail*, November 16, 2013, www.theGlobeandMail.com/news/national, accessed April 1, 2014.
122. Stone, "Costco CEO Craig Jelinek Leads the Cheapest, Happiest Company in the World."
123. Kevin Short, "11 Reasons to Love Costco That Have Nothing to Do with Shopping," November 19, 2013, www.HuffingtonPost.com/2013/11/19/reasons-love-Costco, accessed April 1, 2014.
124. www.Costco.com/benefits.HTML, accessed April 1, 2014.
125. Ibid.
126. Ibid.
127. Garry Kranz, "Special Report on Employee Engagement Losing Lifeblood," *Workforce*, July 21, 2011, www.workforce.com/articles/special-report-on-employee-engagement-losing-lifeblood, accessed April 10, 2014.
128. http://articles.moneycentral.msn.com/Investing/Extra/CostcoThe AntiWalMart.aspx?page?1, accessed September 15, 2011; and Hamilton Nolan, "The Anti-Wal-Mart," http://gawker.com/costco-the-anti-wal-mart-511739135, accessed August 7, 2013.
129. Ibid. See also Brad Stone, "Costco CEO Craig Jelinek Leads the Cheapest, Happiest Company in the World," *Bloomberg BusinessWeek*, June 6, 2013, www.BusinessWeek.com/articles/2013-06-06/Costco-CEO-Craig-Jelinek-leads-the-cheapest-happiest-company-in-the-world, accessed March 31, 2014.
130. Ibid

14

Building Positive Employee Relations

Qilai Shen/In Pictures/Corbis

LEARNING OBJECTIVES

14-1 Define *employee relations.*

14-2 Discuss at least four methods for managing employee relations.

14-3 Explain what is meant by ethical behavior.

14-4 Explain what is meant by fair disciplinary practices.

14-5 Answer the question, "How do companies become 'Best Companies to Work For'?"

Four days after more than 4,000 non-permanent workers of Tata Motors, Jamshedpur, went on strike, an agreement between the management and union was reached at. The pay difference between permanent and non-permanent staff for August 2017 was the point of clash. The four-day work stoppage led to significant loss of production.[1] We'll see what was done to improve the situation.

WHERE ARE WE NOW ...

Although people tend to view recruitment, selection, appraisal, training, and compensation as the heart of human resource management, most employees expect something more. For example, they expect to be treated fairly, and to have a safe work environment. Now, in Part Five, we therefore turn to ethics, employee fairness, safety, and union relations. The main purpose of this chapter is to explain the building blocks of positive employee relations. Our topics include what is employee relations, managing employee relations, using human resource management tools to promote ethics and fair treatment, managing employee discipline, and developing employee engagement and great places to work for.

LEARNING OBJECTIVE 14-1

Define *employee relations*.

employee relations

The activity that involves establishing and maintaining the positive employee–employer relationships that contribute to satisfactory productivity, motivation, morale, and discipline, and to maintaining a positive, productive, and cohesive work environment.

What Is Employee Relations?

Anyone who has worked knows that some companies are better to work for than are others. Some Indian companies such as Ujjivan Small Finance Bank Limited, Godrej Consumer Products Limited (GCPL), Lemon Tree Hotels Limited, and The Oberoi Group show up repeatedly on the list of "Best Indian Companies to Work for." Many others always seem to garner labor problems and negative press. This commonsense observation reflects the fact that some companies do have better employee relations than do others.

Employee relations (ER), also referred to as industrial relations (IR) when trade unions are involved, is the managerial activity that involves establishing and maintaining the positive employee–employer relationships that contribute to satisfactory productivity, motivation, morale, and discipline, and to maintaining a positive, productive, and cohesive work environment.[2] Whether you're recruiting employees, managing union organizing campaigns, asking employees to work overtime, or doing some other task, it obviously makes sense to have employees "on your side." Many employers therefore endeavor to build positive employee relations, on the sensible assumption that doing so beats building negative ones. Managing employee relations is usually assigned to HR, and is a topic that MBA students and HRM specialists learn in their curriculum. But, of late, the focus on studying ER has reduced extensively in India.

Employers can do many things to build positive employee relations. Some examples include providing good training, fair appraisals, and competitive pay and benefits (all of which we discussed in previous chapters). Cooperation between trade unions and managers is another powerful way to ensure positive employee relations. According to an observer, Bajaj Auto, Thermax Limited and Bosch (Pune) can be cited as examples where the trade union works as business partner to the management, with positive results for the company and workers.[3] Cochin Shipyard Limited, Kerala, is an example of a central PSU that has maintained positive ER through union–management relationship. Even the recent point of contention with unions about IPO (initial public offering), was handled through continuous dialogue.[4] However, most employers also institute special "employee relations programs" to maintain positive employee relations. These include employee fair treatment programs, improving employee relations through improved communications, developing employee recognition/relations programs, and having fair and predictable disciplinary procedures.

LEARNING OBJECTIVE 14-2

Discuss at least four methods for managing employee relations.

Employee Relations Programs For Building And Maintaining Positive Employee Relations

We'll begin with how to ensure fair treatment.

Ensuring Fair Treatment

Anyone who has suffered unfair treatment at work knows it is demoralizing. Unfair treatment reduces morale, poisons trust, and negatively impacts employee relations and performance.[5] Employees of abusive supervisors are more likely to quit, and to report lower job and life satisfaction and higher stress.[6] The effects on employees of such abusiveness are particularly pronounced where the abusive supervisors seem to have support from higher-ups.[7] Even when someone just witnesses abusive supervision— for instance, seeing a coworker abused—it triggers adverse reactions including further unethical behavior.[8] At work, **fair treatment** reflects concrete actions such as "employees are treated with respect," and "employees are treated fairly" (see Figure 14-1).[9]

fair treatment

Reflects concrete actions, such as "employees are treated with respect," and "employees are treated fairly."

There are many reasons why managers should be fair. The golden rule is one obvious reason. What may not be so obvious is that unfairness can backfire on the company. For example, victims of unfairness exhibit more workplace deviance, such as theft and sabotage.[10] Victims of unfairness also suffer a range of ill effects including poor health, strain, and psychological conditions.[11] Unfairness leads to increased tensions between the employee and his or her family or partner.[12]

FIGURE 14-1 Perceptions of Fair Interpersonal Treatment Scale

Source: "The Perceptions of Their Interpersonal Treatment Scale: Development and Validation of a Measure of Interpersonal Treatment in the Workplace" by Michelle A. Donovan, from *Journal of Applied Psychology* 83, no. 5 (1998).

What is your organization like most of the time? Circle yes if the item describes your organization, No if it does not describe your organization, and ? if you cannot decide.

IN THIS ORGANIZATION:

1. Employees are praised for good work	Yes	?	No
2. Supervisors yell at employees (R)	Yes	?	No
3. Supervisors play favorites (R)	Yes	?	No
4. Employees are trusted	Yes	?	No
5. Employees' complaints are dealt with effectively	Yes	?	No
6. Employees are treated like children (R)	Yes	?	No
7. Employees are treated with respect	Yes	?	No
8. Employees' question and problems are responded to quickly	Yes	?	No
9. Employees are lied to (R)	Yes	?	No
10. Employees' suggestions are ignored (R)	Yes	?	No
11. Supervisors swear at employees (R)	Yes	?	No
12. Employees' hard work is appreciated	Yes	?	No
13. Supervisors threaten to fire or lay off employees (R)	Yes	?	No
14. Employees are treated fairly	Yes	?	No
15. Coworkers help each other out	Yes	?	No
16. Coworkers argue with each other (R)	Yes	?	No
17. Coworkers put each other down (R)	Yes	?	No
18. Coworkers treat each other with respect	Yes	?	No

Note: R = the item is reverse scored

Abusive supervisors undermine their subordinates' effectiveness and may prompt them to act destructively.[13] In terms of employee relations, employees' perceptions of fairness relate positively to enhanced employee commitment; enhanced satisfaction with the company, job, and leader; and enhanced organizational citizenship behaviors.[14]

The employer and the manager are responsible for ensuring that the employee is treated fairly and with respect (and that its employees treat each other respectfully).[15] Techniques for minimizing unfairness (discussed in previous chapters) include hire competent and well-balanced employees and supervisors, ensure equitable pay, institute fair performance appraisal systems, and have policies requiring fair treatment of all employees. Communications systems (such as periodic attitude surveys), and disciplinary appeals programs (both discussed later in this chapter) can also reduce unfairness.

procedural justice
Refers to just procedures in the allocation of rewards or discipline, in terms of the actual procedures being evenhanded and fair.

distributive justice
Refers to a system of distributing rewards and discipline in which the actual results or outcomes of are evenhanded and fair.

RESEARCH INSIGHT A study illustrates the effects of unfairness. College instructors first completed surveys concerning the extent to which they saw their colleges as treating them with *procedural* and *distributive* justice. (**Procedural justice** refers to justice in the allocation of rewards or discipline, in terms of the procedures being evenhanded and fair; **distributive justice** refers to a system for distributing rewards and discipline in which *the actual results* or outcomes are evenhanded and fair.) Procedural justice items included, for example, "In general, the department/college's procedures allow for requests for clarification or for additional information about a decision." Distributive justice items included, "I am fairly rewarded considering the responsibilities I have."

Then the instructors completed organizational commitment questionnaires, with items such as "I am proud to tell others that I am part of this department/college." Their students then completed surveys, with items such as "The instructor was sympathetic to my needs," and "The instructor treated me fairly."

The results were impressive. Instructors who perceived high distributive and procedural justice were more committed. Furthermore, these instructors' students reported higher levels of instructor effort, prosocial behaviors, and fairness, and had more positive reactions to their instructors.[16] So in this case, treating some professors badly backfired on the university. Treating others fairly produced improved employee commitment and results.

The accompanying Strategic Context feature shows how one employer in China improved the fairness with which it treated employees.

▶ IMPROVING PERFORMANCE: *The Strategic Context*

A New HR Strategy at the Foxconn Plant in Shenzhen, China

social responsibility
Refers to the extent to which companies should and do channel resources toward improving one or more segments of society other than the firm's owners or stockholders.

The phrase *social responsibility* tends to trigger images of charitable contributions and helping the homeless, but it actually refers to much more. For example, it refers to the honesty of the company's ads; to the quality of the parts it builds into its products; and to the honesty, ethics, fairness, and "rightness" of its dealings with customers, suppliers, and, of course, employees. The basic question is always whether the company is serving all its constituencies (or "stakeholders") fairly and honestly. Corporate **social responsibility** thus refers to the extent to which companies should and do channel resources toward improving one or more segments of society other than the firm's owners or stockholders.[17]

A worker uprising at Apple's Foxconn iPhone assembly plant in Shenzhen, China, shows that workers around the globe want their employers to treat them in a fair and socially responsible manner.

Producing quality products as efficiently as possible was long the strategy at this plant. However, after the uprising over pay and work rules at the Foxconn plant, Apple asked the plant's owner to have the Fair Labor Association (FLA) survey the plant's workers. The FLA found "tons of issues."[18] For example, employees faced "overly strict" product-quality demands without adequate training: "Every job is tagged to time, there are targets on how many things must be completed within an hour," said Xie Xiaogang, 22, who worked at Foxconn's Shenzhen plant. "In this environment, many people cannot take it."[19] Heavy overtime work requirements and having to work through a holiday week were other examples.

To foster the improved behaviors that the plant's performance required, Hon Hai, the Foxconn plant's owner, tweaked its efficiency-first strategy and changed its plant human resource strategy and practices, for instance, by raising salaries and cutting mandatory overtime. Those changes were among 284 made at Foxconn after the audits uncovered violations of Chinese regulations.[20] The changes show that fair treatment is a global obligation. ■

Source: Based on Daniel Denison, Corporate Culture and Organizational Effectiveness, New York: Wiley, 1990, p. 155; "When the Jobs Inspector Calls," Economist, March 31, 2012, p. 73; Alexandra Ho and Tim Culpan, with assistance from Jun Yang in Seoul, Andrea Wong in Taipei, Tian Ying in Beijing, and Jasmine Wang in Hong Kong. "Foxconn Labor Disputes Disrupt IPhone Output for 2nd Time," Bloomberg News, October 8, 2012, www.bloomberg.com/news/ 2012-10-07/foxconn-labor-disputes-disrupt-iphone-output-for-2nd-time.html.

Non-Permanent Workers' Strike at Tata Motors, Jamshedpur

Tata Motors (TELCO) signed a wage revision agreement with its workers union on July 31, 2017. The Jameshedpur plant of TELCO employs both permanent and non-permanent workers, and the agreement specified an increase in wages for non-permanent workers as well. When the firm disbursed salary for the month of August, the non-permanent employees found that their remuneration increase was not as per the agreement. While the permanent workers received an increase of ₹12,500 per month, the temporary staff received between ₹1,500 and ₹3,000. TELCO attributed the error to a technical glitch, but the affected workers went on strike. This affected production of the plant, which declined below 20% of normal, though the company claimed that only a section of workers were on strike.

After reconciliatory meetings between the management and representatives of non-permanent workers, the four-day-old strike was called off. The agreement ensured that 200 non-permanent employees will be absorbed on permanent rolls of the company. To make up for the lost production, the union decided that workers will work during the next Sunday (i.e., September 10, 2017). ■

Source: BW Online Bureau, 'Tata Motors Union Calls off four day strike at Jamshedpur Plant,' *Business World*, 2017, September.

Indian General Strike of 2016

The Indian General Strike of September 2016 is an apt example of the rising expectations of the workforce from the government. The decision to organize the largest nationwide strike in the history of India, was jointly taken by all the Central Trade Unions in the country along with the Independent National Federations.

The strike brought economic activities in many sectors and areas to a halt. It saw a participation of over 150 million workers from various economic sectors, who united against the "anti-people, anti-worker policies" of the ruling NDA government and demanded higher wages and other working conditions. Some of the issues raised were falling real wages, dip in interest rates, rising cost of living, and job losses, which reflected general sentiment of the workers. ∎

Bullying and Victimization

Some workplace unfairness, such as bullying, is blatant. Bullying and victimization— singling out someone to harass and mistreat—is a serious problem. For example, one survey of 1,000 U.S. employees concluded that about 45% said they had worked for abusive bosses.[21] The U.S. government (www.stopbullying.gov) says most would agree that bullying involves three things:

- *Imbalance of power.* People who bully use their power to control or harm, and the people being bullied may have a hard time defending themselves.
- *Intent to cause harm.* Actions done by accident are not bullying; the person bullying has a goal to cause harm.
- *Repetition.* Incidents of bullying happen to the same person over and over by the same person or group, and that bullying can take many forms, such as:
  - *Verbal:* name-calling, teasing
  - *Social:* spreading rumors, leaving people out on purpose, breaking up friendships
  - *Physical:* hitting, punching, shoving
  - *Cyberbullying:* using the Internet, mobile phones, or other digital technologies to harm others

Workplace bullying has been studied in the Indian context. A study of 1036 IT/ITES workers from six Indian cities, showed that 44.3% of the respondents had experienced some sort of bullying and 19.7% had faced severe or moderate bullying. Superiors were identified as the predominant source of bullying.[22] As per another study covering different sectors, 46% of the surveyed employees were occasionally or frequently bullied at work.[23] A study of the responses of the targets points that exit is an actively adopted strategy, but there remains a negative feelings of defeat, victimization, and unfair treatment. This may lead to precipitation of maladaptation and low performance in future.[24] Undoubtedly, the perpetrator is to blame for bullying. However, how some people behave does make them more likely victims.[25] Those "more likely" include submissive victims (who seem more anxious, cautious, quiet, and sensitive), provocative victims (who show more aggressive behavior), and victims low in self-determination (who seem to leave it to others to make decisions for them). High performers can earn colleagues' envy and thus suffer victimization.[26] Building team cohesion through teambuilding training, social gatherings, and friendly inter-team competition can head off such envy and victimization.[27]

Beyond fairness, maintaining positive employee relations requires having special communications programs in place that let employees express their opinions, and let management know if there's a problem. We turn to these programs next.

Improving Employee Relations Through Communications Programs

Many employers use communications programs to bolster their employee relations efforts, on the reasonable assumption that employees feel better about their employers when they're "kept in the loop." Therefore, for example, one university's Web site says, "We believe in keeping our employees fully informed about our policies, procedures, practices and benefits."[28] This employer uses an *open-door policy* to encourage communication between employees and managers, an *employee handbook* covering basic employment information, and "the opportunity to keep abreast of University events and other information of interest through the *website, e-mail* and *hard copy memoranda.*"[29]

Two-way communication also helps management know what's bothering employees. To paraphrase one writer, no one likes getting complaints, but soliciting complaints is vital for employers who want to short-circuit inequitable treatment and maintain positive employee relations.[30] Approaches may include hosting employee *focus groups,* making available *ombudsman* and *suggestion boxes*, and implementing telephone, messaging, and Web-based *hotlines*. (Some employers use hotline providers to manage their hotlines. A vendor sets up the hotlines for the employer; it also receives the employees' comments, and provides ongoing feedback to the employer about employees' concerns, as well as periodic summaries of comments and trends.) *Exit interviews*, discussed in an earlier chapter, provide another opportunity to sample the quality of one's employee relations.[31] Managers also use *open-door policies* and "management by walking around" to informally ask employees "how things are going."

organizational climate
The perceptions a company's employees share about the firm's psychological environment, for instance, in terms of things like concern for employees' well-being, supervisory behavior, flexibility, appreciation, ethics, empowerment, political behaviors, and rewards.

USING ORGANIZATIONAL CLIMATE SURVEYS Similarly, employers use attitude, morale, or *climate surveys* to support employee relations efforts. They use the surveys to "take the pulse" of their employees' attitudes toward a variety of organizational issues including leadership, safety, role clarity, fairness, and pay, and to thereby get a sense of whether their employee relations need improvement. The dividing lines between attitude surveys, satisfaction or morale surveys, and climate surveys are somewhat arbitrary; several experts define **organizational climate** as the perceptions a company's employees share about the firm's psychological environment, for instance, in terms of things like concern for employees' well-being, supervisory behavior, flexibility, appreciation, ethics, empowerment, political behaviors, and rewards.[32]

Many employers use online surveys from firms like Know Your Company (http://knowyourcompany.com), focusing on questions such as "Are you proud to work here?"[33] Google conducts an annual "Googlegeist" survey. This focuses not on engagement per se but on its markers such as willingness to leave.[34] Other surveys are available off the shelf. For instance, one SHRM sample survey has employees use a scale from 1 ("to a very little extent") to 5 ("to a very great extent") to answer survey questions. Questions include, "Overall, how satisfied are you with your supervisor?," "Overall, how satisfied are you with your job?," and "Does doing your job well lead to things like recognition and respect from those you work with?"[35]

Develop Employee Recognition/Relations Programs

Opportunities for two-way communications like these improve employee relations, but there are other employee relations programs. Most notable here are the employee recognition and award programs we touched on in Chapters 10 and 11, particularly formal company-wide programs such as employee-of-the-month awards. For example, one trade journal notes how the Murray Supply Co. held a special dinner for all its employees, at which it gave out special awards for things like safe driving, tenure with the company, and branch employee of the year.[36] Bank of Baroda and Eureka Forbes have instituted variety of recognition programs for its branch- and field-based employees. As here, employers often distribute such awards with much fanfare at special events such as awards dinners. One SHRM survey found that 76% of organizations surveyed had such employee recognition programs, and another 5% planned to implement one soon.[37]

Instituting recognition and service award programs requires planning.[38] For example, instituting a *service award program* requires reviewing the tenure of existing employees and establishing meaningful award periods (1 year, 5 years, etc.). It also requires establishing a budget, selecting awards, having a procedure for monitoring what awards to actually award, having a process for giving awards (such as special dinners or staff meetings), and periodically assessing program success. Similarly, instituting a *recognition program* requires developing criteria for recognition (such as customer service, cost savings, etc.), creating forms and procedures for submitting and reviewing nominations, selecting meaningful recognition awards, and establishing a process for actually awarding the recognition awards.

Use Employee Involvement Programs

Employee relations also tend to improve when employees become involved with the company in positive ways, and so *employee involvement* is another useful employee relations strategy.

Employers encourage employee involvement in various ways. Some organize focus groups. A *focus group* is a small sample of employees who are presented with a specific question or issue and who interactively express their opinions and attitudes on that issue with the group's assigned facilitator. Various committees involved in the management of employee benefits like canteen, sports, entertainment, and transport are other popular involvement mechanisms in the Indian context. In case of unionized workplaces, unions are involved in identifying employee representatives.

TRENDS SHAPING HR: *DIGITAL AND SOCIAL MEDIA*

Many employers use *social media* such as the pinboard-style photo-sharing Web site Pinterest to encourage involvement.[39] One survey found that just over half of employers use social media tools to communicate with employees and to help develop a sense of community.[40] According to TeamLease's World of Work Report 2016, social media use in office impacts workplace productivity. Indian employees are found to spend 32% of their office time on social media for personal work. This amounts to an average of 2.35 hours every day, per employee.[41] Many Indian companies have institutionalized policies or given guidelines to employees to control social media use. Air India has warned employees and former employees against negative postings, and indicated that former employees who indulge in negative campaign against the former employer may lose their retirement benefits.[42] Godrej group uses social media tools to connect with employees across geographies. Celebrations and meetings are live-streamed across locations and group companies, instead of being restricted to one location.[43] ∎

suggestion teams
Temporary teams whose members work on specific analytical assignments, such as how to cut costs or raise productivity.

problem-solving teams
Teams that identify and research work processes and develop solutions to work-related problems.

quality circle
A special type of formal problem-solving team, usually composed of 6 to 12 specially trained employees who meet once a week to solve problems affecting their work area.

self-managing/self-directed work team
A small (usually 8 to 10 members) group of carefully selected, trained, and empowered employees who basically run themselves with little or no outside supervision, usually for the purpose of accomplishing a specific task or mission.

USING EMPLOYEE INVOLVEMENT TEAMS   Employers also use special teams to gain employees' involvement. **Suggestion teams** are temporary teams whose members work on specific analytical assignments, such as how to cut costs or raise productivity. One airline split employees (such as baggage handlers and ground crew) into separate teams, linking team members via its Web site for brainstorming and voting on ideas.[44] Some employers formalize this process by appointing semipermanent **problem-solving teams**. These identify and research work processes and develop solutions to work-related problems.[45] They usually consist of the supervisor and five to eight employees from a common work area.[46]

A **quality circle (QC)** is a type of formal problem-solving team, usually composed of 6 to 12 specially trained employees who meet weekly to solve problems affecting their work area.[47] The team gets training in problem-analysis techniques (including basic statistics). Then it applies these techniques to solve problems in its work area.[48] Quality circles are popular in Indian organizations, particularly in the manufacturing sector. Companies like Maruti Suzuki India, Honeywell, BHEL, etc., have strong QC movements. Introduction of quality circles has helped the state-owned India Gandhi Government Medical College and Hospital (IGGMCH) and other government hospitals to tackle routine administrative problems, improve service quality, and employee participation.[49]

In many facilities, specially trained teams of self-managing employees do their jobs with little or no oversight from supervisory personnel. A **self-managing/self-directed work team** is a small (usually 8 to 10 members) group of carefully selected, trained, and empowered employees who basically run themselves with little or no outside supervision, usually for the purpose of accomplishing a specific task or mission.[50] The task or mission might be an auto dashboard installed or a fully processed insurance claim. For example, the GE aircraft engine plant in Durham, North Carolina, is a self-managing team-based facility. Employees work in teams, all of which report to the factory manager.[51] In such teams, employees "train one another, formulate and track their own budgets, make capital investment proposals as needed, handle quality control and inspection, develop their own quantitative standards, improve every process and product, and create prototypes of possible new products."[52]

USING SUGGESTION SYSTEMS   Most employers understand that employee suggestions can produce significant savings (and, through involvement and rewards, improved employee relations). For example, one study several years ago of 47 companies concluded that the firms had saved more than $624 million in one year from their suggestion programs; more than 250,000 suggestions were submitted, of which employers adopted over 93,000 ideas.[53] Furthermore, employees like these programs. In one survey, 54% of the 497 employees surveyed said they made more than 20 suggestions per year, while another 24% said they made between 10 and 20 suggestions per year.[54] Maruti Suzuki India (MSIL) reported that during 2015–16, its suggestion scheme resulted in savings of ₹281 crore. Employee suggestions across the hierarchy were in the areas of safety, quality, and productivity improvement, process simplification, energy saving, and cost management.[55] The accompanying HR as a Profit Center feature provides an example.

▶ IMPROVING PERFORMANCE: *HR As A Profit Center*

The Cost-Effective Suggestion System[56]

A Lockheed Martin unit in Oswego, New York, developed its "Cost-Effectiveness Plus" suggestion program to encourage and recognize employees for streamlining processes. With the Cost-Effectiveness Plus program, employees electronically submit their ideas. These are then evaluated and approved by the local manager and the program's coordinator (and by higher management when necessary). This program reportedly saves this facility about $77,000 per implemented idea, or more than $100 million each year.

Today's suggestion systems are more sophisticated than the "suggestion boxes" of years ago.[57] The main improvements are in how the manager formalizes and communicates the suggestion process. The head of one company that designs and installs suggestion systems for employers lists the essential elements of an effective employee suggestion system as follows:[58]

✓ Senior staff support
✓ A simple, easy process for submitting suggestions
✓ A strong process for evaluating and implementing suggestions
✓ An effective program for publicizing and communicating the program
✓ A program focus on key organizational goals ■

Source: Based on Wells, "From Ideas to Results", HR Magazine.

<table>
<tr><td>LEARNING OBJECTIVE 14-3
Explain what is meant by ethical behavior.</td></tr>
</table>

The Ethical Organization

People face ethical choices every day. Is it wrong to use a company credit card for personal purchases? Is a $50 gift to a client unacceptable? Compare your answers by doing the quiz in Figure 14-2.

Most everyone reading this book rightfully views themselves as ethical people, so why include ethics in a human resource management book? For three reasons: First, ethics is not theoretical. Instead, it greases the wheels that make businesses work. Managers who promise raises but don't deliver, salespeople who say "The order's coming" when it's not, production managers who take kickbacks from suppliers—they all corrode the trust that day-to-day business transactions depend on.

Second, it is hard to even imagine an *un*ethical company with good employee relations.

Third, ethical dilemmas are part of human resource management. For example, your team shouldn't start work on the new machine until all the safety measures are checked, but your boss is pressing you start: What should you do? One survey found that 6 of the 10 most serious ethical work issues—workplace safety, employee records security, employee theft, affirmative action, comparable work, and employee privacy rights—were HR-related.[59]

ethics
The study of standards of conduct and moral judgment; also the standards of right conduct.

Ethics are "the principles of conduct governing an individual or a group"—the principles people use to decide what their conduct should be.[60] Of course, not all conduct involves ethics.[61] For example, buying an iPad usually isn't an ethical decision. Instead, ethical decisions are rooted in *morality*. Morality refers to society's accepted standards of behavior. To be more precise, morality (and therefore ethical decisions)

The spread of technology into the workshop has raised a variety of new ethical questions and many old ones still linger. Compare your answers with those of other Americans surveyed, on page 475.

Office Technology

1. Is it wrong to use company e-mail for personal reasons?
   ☐ Yes   ☐ No

2. Is it wrong to use office equipment to help your children or spouse do schoolwork?
   ☐ Yes   ☐ No

3. Is it wrong to play computer games on office equipment during the workday?
   ☐ Yes   ☐ No

4. Is it wrong to use office equipment to do Internet shopping?
   ☐ Yes   ☐ No

5. Is it unethical to blame an error you made on a technological glitch?
   ☐ Yes   ☐ No

6. Is it unethical to visit pornographic Web sites using office equipment?
   ☐ Yes   ☐ No

Gifts and Entertainment

7. What's the value at which a gift from a supplier or client becomes troubling?
   ☐ $25   ☐ $50   ☐ $100

8. Is a $50 gift to a boss unacceptable?
   ☐ Yes   ☐ No

9. Is a $50 gift *from* the boss unacceptable?
   ☐ Yes   ☐ No

10. Of gifts from suppliers: Is it OK to take a $200 pair of football tickets?
    ☐ Yes   ☐ No

11. Is it OK to take a $120 pair of theater tickets?
    ☐ Yes   ☐ No

12. Is it OK to take a $100 holiday food basket?
    ☐ Yes   ☐ No

13. Is it OK to take a $25 gift certificate?
    ☐ Yes   ☐ No

14. Can you accept a $75 prize won at a raffle at a supplier's conference?
    ☐ Yes   ☐ No

Truth and Lies

15. Due to on-the-job pressure, have you ever abused or lied about sick days?
    ☐ Yes   ☐ No

16. Due to on-the-job pressure, have you ever taken credit for someone else's work or idea?
    ☐ Yes   ☐ No

FIGURE 14-2 The *Wall Street Journal* Workplace Ethics Quiz

Source: Ethics and Compliance Officer Association, Waltham, MA, and the Ethical Leadership Group, Global Compliance's Expert Advisors, Wilmette, IL. (printed in the *Wall Street Journal,* October 21, 1999, pp. B1–B4). © 1999 by Ethics and Compliance Officer Association. Reprinted by permission. All rights reserved.

always involves the most fundamental questions of what is right and wrong, such as stealing, murder, and how to treat other people.

Ethics and Employee Rights

Societies don't rely on employers' ethics or sense of fairness or morality to ensure that they do what's right. Societies also institute various laws and procedures for enforcing these laws. These laws lay out what employers can and cannot do, for instance, in terms of discriminating based on race. In so doing, these laws also carve out explicit rights for employees. In India, the Industrial Disputes Act of 1947 allows individual employee to approach labor court for relief against cases of wrongful termination. Similarly, violation of provisions in the employment contract can be challenged in courts.

Protecting employee rights is thus part and parcel of all the employment laws we discuss in this book. In Indian companies, the employee code of conduct (or certified standing orders in case of workmen in industries) specify employee's rights. The Tata Code of Conduct is an illustrative example of strong code for a large business group. It is described as a "comprehensive document that serves as the ethical road map for Tata employees and companies, and provides the guidelines by which the group conducts its businesses." Violations of the Tata Code is taken seriously and promptly acted upon.[62] The bottom line is that although ethics, fairness, and morality help govern how employers treat their employees, the enforceable rights embedded in employment law also govern what employers and employees can do.

What Shapes Ethical Behavior at Work?

Why do people do bad things? It's complicated. However, one review of over 30 years of ethics research concluded that three factors combine to determine the ethical choices we make.[63] The authors titled their paper "Bad Apples, Bad Cases, and Bad Barrels." This title highlighted their conclusion that when

> "Bad apples" (people who are inclined to make unethical choices), must deal with "Bad cases" (ethical situations that are ripe for unethical choices), while working in "Bad barrels" (company environments that foster or condone unethical choices), … then people tend to act unethically.

Here's a closer look at what they found.

The Person (What Makes Bad Apples?)

First, because people bring to their jobs their own ideas of what is morally right and wrong, each person must shoulder much of the credit (or blame) for his or her ethical choices.

For example, researchers surveyed CEOs to study the CEOs' intentions to engage in two questionable practices: soliciting a competitor's technological secrets, and making illegal payments to foreign officials. The researchers concluded that the CEOs' personal predispositions more strongly affected their decisions than did outside pressures or characteristics of their firms.[64] The most principled people, with the highest level of "cognitive moral development," think through the implications of their decisions and apply ethical principles. How would you rate your own ethics? Figure 14-2 (page 446) presented a short self-assessment survey (you'll find typical survey takers' answers on page 465).

Which Ethical Situations Make for Ethically Dangerous Situations (Bad Cases)?

But, it's not just the person but the situation that's important. For example, the researchers found that "smaller" ethical dilemmas prompt more bad choices. What determines "small"? Basically, how much harm can befall victims of the choice, or the number of people potentially affected. People seemed more likely to "do the wrong thing" in "less serious" situations, in other words. That obviously doesn't mean that some people don't do bad things when huge consequences are involved; it just means that people cut more ethical corners on small things. The problem is that one thing leads to another; people start by doing small bad things and then "graduate" to larger ones.[65] And employees who worry about being excluded from a group may support the group's unethical behavior to stay in the group, compounding a bad situation.[66]

What Are the "Bad Barrels"?—The Outside Factors That Mold Ethical Choices

Finally, the study found that some companies produce more poisonous social environments (outside factors or "barrels") than do others; these bad environments in turn foster unethical choices.[67] For example, companies that promoted an "everyone for him- or herself" culture were more likely to suffer more unethical choices. Those that encouraged employees to consider the well-being of everyone had more ethical choices. Most importantly, companies whose managers put in place "a strong ethical culture that clearly communicates the range of acceptable and unacceptable behavior" suffered fewer unethical decisions.[68]

We can translate finding like these into the following specific steps managers can take to create more ethical environments.

How Managers Can Create More Ethical Environments

REDUCE JOB-RELATED PRESSURES If people did unethical things at work solely for personal gain or because they were "bad people," it perhaps would be understandable (though inexcusable). The scary thing is that it's often not personal interests but the pressures of the job. As one former executive said at his trial, "I took these actions, knowing they were wrong, in a misguided attempt to preserve the company to allow it to withstand what I believed were temporary financial difficulties."[69]

One study illustrates this. It asked employees to list their reasons for taking unethical actions at work.[70] For most of these employees, "meeting schedule pressures," "meeting overly aggressive financial or business objectives," and "helping the company survive" were the three top causes. "Advancing my own career or financial interests" ranked about last.[71] In any case, reducing such "outside" pressures helps head off ethical lapses.

"WALK THE TALK" It's hard to resist even subtle pressure from one's boss. So it's not surprising that in one report, "the level of misconduct at work dropped dramatically when employees said their supervisors exhibited ethical behavior."[72] Examples of how supervisors lead subordinates astray ethically include:

- Tell staffers to do whatever is necessary to achieve results.
- Overload top performers to ensure that work gets done.
- Look the other way when wrong doing occurs.
- Take credit for others' work or shift blame.[73]

Managers therefore have to walk the talk—not just talk ethics but behave ethically. Here some managers urge employees to apply a quick "ethics test" to evaluate whether what they're about to do fits the company's code of conduct. For example, Raytheon Co. asks employees who face ethical dilemmas to ask:

Is the action legal?

Is it right?

Who will be affected?

Does it fit Raytheon's values?

How will it "feel" afterward?

How will it look in the newspaper?

Will it reflect poorly on the company?[74]

How Human Resource Managers Can Create More Ethical Environments

There are also steps the HR group can take.

INSTITUTE ETHICS POLICIES AND CODES Employers use ethics policies and codes to signal that their companies are serious about ethics. For example, IBM's code of ethics says, in part:

> Neither you nor any member of your family may, directly or through others, solicit or accept from anyone money, a gift, or any amenity that could influence or could reasonably give the appearance of influencing IBM's business relationship with that person or organization. If you or your family members receive a gift (including money), even if the gift was unsolicited, you must notify your manager and take appropriate measures, which may include returning or disposing of what you received.[75]

ENFORCE THE RULES Codifying such rules without enforcing them is futile. To paraphrase one study, managers' statements can reduce unethical behavior on the part of employees, but knowing that behavior is actually being monitored and enforced has the biggest impact.[76] *Ethics audits* address topics like conflicts of interest, giving and receiving gifts, employee discrimination, and access to company information.[77]

One study found that fraud controls such as hotlines, surprise audits, fraud training for employees, and mandatory vacations can each reduce internal theft by around 50%.[78] More firms, such as Lockheed Martin Corp., also appoint chief ethics officers.[79]

ENCOURAGE WHISTLEBLOWERS   Some companies encourage employees to use hotlines and other means to "blow the whistle" on the company when they discover fraud. In complying with the Dodd-Frank Act, the U.S. SEC established a whistleblower reward for people who report unethical corporate behavior to it.[80] For Indian companies, SEBI and The Companies Act, 2013, have stipulated whistleblowing provisions. Though a bill to encourage whistleblowing and protect the whistleblowers was proposed in 2011, it's still to become a law. However, many Indian companies have established systems that allow employees to raise issues of ethical violations. In 2017, Indian market regulator SEBI receiving an anonymous complaint from someone at Infosys about the financial and corporate governance irregularities in the company, is a case example. It is also tracking possible incidents of retaliation against whistleblowers.[81]

FOSTER THE RIGHT CULTURE[82]   **Organizational culture** is the "characteristic values, traditions, and behaviors a company's employees share." A *value* is a basic belief about what is right or wrong, or about what you should or shouldn't do. ("Honesty is the best policy" would be a value.) Managing people and shaping their behavior depends on shaping the values they use as behavioral guides. For example, if management really believes "honesty is the best policy," the actions it takes should reflect this value. Managers therefore have to think through how to send the right signals to their employees—in other words, create the right culture. Doing so includes:

- *Clarifying expectations.* First, make clear what values you want subordinates to follow. For example, the IBM ethics statement shows the company takes ethics seriously.
- *Using signs and symbols. Symbolism*—what the manager actually does—ultimately does the most to create and sustain the company's culture. As we said earlier, managers need to "walk the talk." They can't say "don't falsify the financials" and then do so themselves.
- *Providing physical support.* The physical signs of the employer's values—its incentive plan, appraisal system, and disciplinary procedures, for instance—send strong signals regarding what employees should and should not do. For example, do the promotions employees get reward ethical behavior or penalize it?[83]

The accompanying HR Tools feature illustrates ethics management in small businesses.

organizational culture
The characteristic values, traditions, and behaviors a company's employees share.

▶ **IMPROVING PERFORMANCE:** *HR Tools For Line Managers And Small Businesses*

Small Business Ethics

When people think of unethical corporate behavior, big companies come to mind, because they're usually in the headlines. Yet studies show that small and midsize enterprises are prone to the same unethical corporate behavior as big firms.

For example, one study of 20 small to midsize firms found that bribery, corrupt dealings, payoffs to local gangsters, and a general tone of dishonesty were all "business as usual" at many of these firms.[84] Some were clever about their corrupt dealings. When doing business abroad, one U.S. business tried to keep its hands clean by forming a "strategic alliance" with a local firm. The latter then did the dirty work, for example, handling the local bribes, while the U.S. firm's managers looked the other way.

There are several reasons why smaller firms should be particularly alert to unethical behavior. Small firms don't have the resources for ethics officers, ethics hotlines, or the ethics training that big firms have. Furthermore, having an unethical accountant in a billion-dollar firm embezzle $10 million is a nuisance. Having the sales manager of a $10 million firm walk off with $1 million cash could be the end.

Small business owners can take several steps to establish a useful ethics program. First, *size up your company's current ethics-related activities*.[85] Even a self-audit based on guidelines like those in this chapter (the availability of an ethics code, ethics training, internal controls to monitor ethical behavior, and so on) can be worthwhile. Second, *create a code of conduct (Googling "code of conduct" will reveal thousands of examples)*, and make it clear that you take it seriously. Third, *train your people*. Training needn't be complicated. For example, one expert suggests having your managers develop scenarios, relevant to your business, illustrating which behaviors are ethical and which are not; then meet to discuss these. Fourth, make it easier to *solicit feedback* from your employees, so that they can more easily report suspicions of unethical behavior. ("Open door" polices and anonymous suggestion boxes are examples.) And, perhaps most importantly, *walk the talk*. In a small business, the owner is so visible that employees will take their ethical signals from him or her. ∎

Institutionalizing Ethical Culture: Case of Tata Power Delhi Distribution Ltd (TPDDL)

When Tata Power acquired a majority stake and management of the power distribution company of Delhi and formed TPDDL, the challenges were many. Power distribution in Delhi was the monopoly of Delhi Vidyut Board (DVB), the state-owned power utility company which was reeling under losses and poor management. In 2002, TPDDL had T&D losses of 53%, 100,000 pending customer complaints, and backlog of 20,000 new connection requests.

Among other challenges, building an ethical climate in the new JV was a challenge. Reportedly, the unethical bahavior of employees was a reason for the commercial losses of the company. Settling complaints or giving concessions for external considerations was a prevalent practice. In spite of lossess, employees continued to get paid and enjoyed job security.

Job security was a condition in the JV agreement, hence employees had to be retained. As a Tata Group company, strong on ethics, the Tata Code of ethics had to be implemented. This was a challenge before the new TPDDL leadership. Old employees had to be oriented to new ways of working in alignment with the Tata Code.[86]

The HR team started sending across strong communication and initiated training initiatives covering all employees, related to ethical working. At the same time, Voice of Employee meetings anchored by senior leaders were also held to listen to employee grievances and address them. An attractive voluntary retirement scheme was also introduced, which brought down employee strength.

The activity was anchored by the CEO, who was also the Chief Ethics Officer. Introduction of ethics policy was followed by intensive training for all employees. This was supported by HR policies, which sent a message about caring for them. A three-tier ethics management system was introduced to resolve ethical complaints, and the confidential whistleblower system, which was also instituted, ensured communication of concerns without the fear of retribution.

The results were also positive. While employee behavior improved as desired, business performance also improved, significantly in the area of commercial loss reduction. Other benefits were increase in employee engagement scores, decrease in customer complaints and reduction in reported cases of unethical conduct in the workplace.[87] ∎

HIRE RIGHT As one writer says, "The simplest way to tune up an organization, ethically speaking, is to hire more ethical people."[88] A study of ethics in Indian organizations based on Tata Steel indicated that ethical problems arise out of conflicting choices. Hence, hiring employees whose values fit to that of the firm's is very important.[89] Start by using recruitment materials that emphasize your firm's commitment to honest dealings and ethics. Then use screening tools like honesty tests, background checks, and interview questions (such as "Have you ever observed someone stretching the rules at work? What did you do about it?") to screen out problematical people.[90] Finally, treat job applicants fairly. "If prospective employees perceive that the hiring process does not treat people fairly, they may assume that ethical behavior is not important in the company."[91] Here, keep several things in mind:

- Applicants tend to view the *formal procedure* (such as the interview) as fair to the extent that it tests job-related criteria and provides an opportunity to demonstrate competence.
- Applicants expect respect. *Interpersonal treatment* reflects such things as the propriety of the questions, the politeness of interviewer, and the degree of two-way communication.
- Applicants see a selection system as fair to the extent that the employer provides *useful feedback* about the employee's or candidate's own performance.[92]

USE ETHICS TRAINING Ethics training usually involves showing employees how to recognize ethical dilemmas, how to apply codes of conduct to resolve problems, and how to use personnel activities like disciplinary practices in ethical ways.[93] The training should emphasize the moral underpinnings of the ethical choice and the company's deep commitment to integrity and ethics. Include participation by top managers in the program to emphasize that commitment.[94]

Ethics training is basically mandatory. In the US, since 1991, federal sentencing guidelines have prescribed reduced penalties for employers accused of misconduct who implement codes of conduct and ethics training.[95] The Sarbanes-Oxley Act of 2002 makes ethics training even more important. The Indian Companies Act of 2013 mandates imparting training to employees and directors, including independent/non-executive directors in various aspects of organizational governance.

Ethics training is often Internet-based. Online ethics training tools include *Business Ethics for Managers* from SkillSoft (www.skillsoft.com).[96] A study on ethics training conducted in the Indian IT industry shows that the sector uses both formal and informal methods for effective ethics training.[97] Lockheed Martin's 160,000 employees take ethics and legal compliance training via the firm's intranet. Lockheed's online ethics program software also keeps track of how well the company and its employees are doing in terms of maintaining high ethical standards.[98] Some employers are switching from packaged ethics training to more company-relevant customized programs. For example, Yahoo! had a vendor produce an animated package containing ethical scenarios set in Yahoo! company offices around the world. The 45-minute program covers Yahoo!'s code of conduct as well as issues like the Foreign Corrupt Practices Act.[99]

USE REWARDS AND DISCIPLINE   Employees expect you to punish unethical conduct and to reward ethical conduct.[100] The employer should discipline executives, not just underlings, who misbehave.[101]

INSTITUTE EMPLOYEE PRIVACY POLICIES[102]   Most employees probably view invasions of their privacy by their employers as unethical. At work, employee privacy violations include *intrusion* (such as locker room and e-mail surveillance), *publication* of private matters, *disclosure* of medical records, and *appropriation* of an employee's name or likeness for commercial purposes.[103] In practice, background checks, monitoring off-duty conduct and lifestyle, drug testing, workplace searches, and workplace monitoring trigger most privacy violations.[104]

KNOW YOUR EMPLOYMENT LAW

Electronic Monitoring

Electronic Communications Privacy Act (ECPA)
The ECPA is a federal law intended to help restrict interception and monitoring of oral and wire communications.

What can the employer do to balance privacy concerns with its need to protect itself? In the U.S., there are two main restrictions on workplace monitoring: the **Electronic Communications Privacy Act (ECPA)**, and *common-law protections* against invasion of privacy (protections that have evolved from court decisions, for instance, decisions against defaming employees by publicizing highly personal matters about them without their permission). The ECPA is a federal law intended to help restrict interception and monitoring of oral and wire communications. It contains two exceptions. The "business purpose exception" permits employers to monitor communications if they can show a legitimate business reason for doing so. The second, "consent exception," lets employers monitor communications if they have their employees' consent to do so.[105]

In India, Section 69 of the Information Technology (IT) Act, 2000, gives power to the government to intercept and monitor messages, though prior approval has to be sought. If an employee suffers loss due to the surveillance, under Section 43A of the IT Act, the employee is entitled for compensation. Under the current privacy laws in India, employers can take normal precautions and monitor workers. However, they should take note of these three points: a) consent in advance, b) degree of intrusion, and c) use of data (purpose limitations) and consequences.

With the Supreme Court of India pronouncing privacy as a fundamental right on August 24, 2017, the issue of privacy has become a matter of discussion in the country. The apex court has also observed that a stringent data protection law has to be made, taking into account the three factors described above.[106]

More employers are using
iris scanning to verify
employee identity.

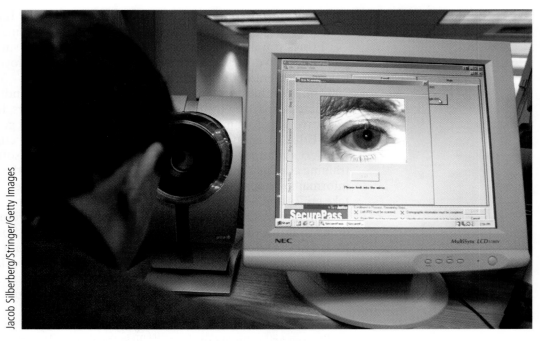

Electronic eavesdropping is thus legal—up to a point. For example, federal law
and most state laws allow employers to monitor employees' phone calls in the ordinary course of business. However, they must stop listening when it becomes clear the
conversation is personal. You can also intercept e-mail to protect the property rights
of the e-mail provider. However, court cases suggest employers may have fewer rights
to monitor e-mail than previously assumed.[107]

To be safe, employers issue e-mail and online service usage policies, which warn
employees that those systems should be used for business only. Employers also have
employees sign e-mail and telephone monitoring acknowledgment statements like
that in Figure 14-3. Many employees probably assume that their communications
using the corporate e-mail system are open to review, but that e-mails they send via the
employer's system but using personal e-mail accounts such as Gmail aren't. However,
that's not necessarily true. An attorney should review the company's e-mail policy, but,
at a minimum, make it clear that employees should have no expectation of privacy in
their e-mail and Internet usage.[108] Also emphasize that all messages sent and received
on the employer's e-mail system are company property and not confidential.[109]

Videotaped workplace monitoring requires more caution. Continuous video surveillance of employees in an office setting may not be a problem. ■

In one survey 41% of employers with more than 20,000 employees had someone
reading employee e-mails.[110] Ninety-six percent block access to adult Web sites, 61% to
game sites.[111] Some check employees' personal blogs or Facebook sites to see if
they're publicizing work-related matters.[112]

TRENDS SHAPING HR: *DIGITAL AND SOCIAL MEDIA*

Monitoring reflects in part a proliferation of online and smart devices and social
media tools.[113] For example, a New Jersey court found one employer liable when
one of its employees used his company computer at work to distribute child pornography.[114] Security is another problem: One "4-gigabyte MP3 player, such as the
first generation of iPod Mini … can take home a lot of corporate data," said one
employer (a process some graphically describe as "podslurping").[115] And, increasingly, disgruntled employees are using their companies' cloud services to hack into
and undermine their employers' computer systems.[116]

Jacob Silberberg/Stringer/Getty Images

FIGURE 14-3 Sample E-Mail Monitoring Acknowledgment Statement

I understand that XYZ Company periodically monitors any e-mail communications created, sent, or retrieved using this company's e-mail system. Therefore, I understand that my e-mail communications may be read by individuals other than the intended recipient. I also understand that XYZ Company periodically monitors telephone communications, for example to improve customer service quality.

_____   _____
Signature   Date

_____   _____
Print Name   Department

Monitoring today therefore goes far beyond listening in on phone lines. New York's Bronx Lebanon Hospital uses biometric scanners to ensure that employees who clock in really are who they say they are.[117] Iris scanning tends to be the most accurate authorization device. Some organizations like the Federal Aviation Administration use it to control employees' access to their network information systems.[118] UPS uses GPS to monitor their drivers' whereabouts—and therefore productivity.[119] One restaurant in Dallas digitally monitors most everything waiters do, for instance, tracking every ticket, dish, and drink that they process.[120] This not only makes it easier to track employee theft, but also helps identify exceptionally conscientious waiters. To keep productivity up, the British grocery chain Tesco has some distribution center employees wear "Motorola arm-mounted terminals" (armbands) that keep track of how quickly employees are unloading and scanning goods.[121]

Such monitoring, as we said, raises privacy issues.[122] The dilemma is that it can also boost profits. For example, employers routinely use software to monitor (usually secretly) what their employees are doing online. When one employer noticed high employee overtime claims, they installed new software, and discovered many employees spent hours each day shopping online instead of working.

Physicians often say that "every medicine contains a little poison," since anything, even aspirin, becomes dangerous if misused. For employers, the dilemma is to obtain the profit advantages of monitoring, while minimizing the ethical and privacy issues that it raises. ■

Managing Employee Discipline

The purpose of *discipline* is to encourage employees to behave sensibly at work (where *sensible* means adhering to rules and regulations). Discipline is necessary when an employee violates a rule.[123]

Proper disciplinary procedures are important for several reasons. For one thing, positive employee relations requires trust, and few personnel actions will undermine trust as will arbitrary discipline. Legal concerns are another reason. One study surveyed 45 published arbitration awards in which tardiness had triggered discipline and/or discharge. When arbitrators overturned employers' decisions, it was usually because of inadequate disciplinary procedures—for example, the employer had failed to clarify what "tardy" meant. Unfair disciplinary procedures can backfire in other ways. For example, unfair discipline can trigger retaliatory employee misbehavior. And, of course, it is hard to be seen as ethical when disciplinary actions are unfair.[124]

The Three Pillars of Fair Discipline

Disciplining employees is often unavoidable, but any such discipline should be rooted in the need to be fair. Fairness, in a way, means that the principles of natural justice are upheld during the entire process. The organization builds a fair discipline process on three pillars: rules and regulations, a system of progressive penalties, and an appeals process.[125]

RULES AND REGULATIONS An acceptable disciplinary process begins with a set of clear disciplinary rules and regulations. The rules should cover problems such as theft, destruction of company property, drinking on the job, and insubordination. Examples of rules include:

> *Poor performance is not acceptable.* Each employee is expected to perform his or her work properly and efficiently and to meet established standards of quality. For example, this has been aptly exemplified in the section on "Values" in the Infosys' *Code of Conduct and Ethics*, where excellence has been stated as one of the five core values that any employee is expected to instill in themselves.

> *Alcohol and drugs do not mix with work.* The use of either during working hours and reporting for work under the influence of either are both strictly prohibited.

The purpose of the rules is to inform employees ahead of time what is and is not acceptable behavior. Tell employees, preferably in writing, what is not permitted. The employee orientation handbook should contain the rules and regulations.

PENALTIES A system of progressive penalties is the second pillar of effective discipline. Hence, offences are classified as minor offences and major offences in India. The severity of the penalty usually depends on the offense and the number of times it has occurred. For example, most companies issue warnings for the first unexcused lateness. However, for a fourth offense, the usual disciplinary action may be initiated.

APPEALS PROCESS Third, an appeals process should be part of the disciplinary process. The aim here is to ensure that supervisors mete out discipline fairly. FedEx's *guaranteed fair treatment* multistep program illustrates this. We'll look at it in a moment.

An appeals process is essential but is no panacea. The employer can sometimes mitigate the effects of unfair discipline by catching it during an appeal. However, some supervisory behavior may be impossible to overcome. For example, behaviors that attack the employee's personal and/or social identity are difficult to remedy.[126]

Diversity Counts

COMPARING MALES AND FEMALES IN A DISCIPLINE SITUATION What several researchers sadly call the "Evil Woman Thesis" argues that when a woman doesn't act the way other men and women expect she should act, they tend to treat her more harshly than they might if a man acted unexpectedly.[127]

While such a thesis might seem preposterous, the research seems to support it. In one study, 360 graduate and undergraduate business school students reviewed a labor arbitration case. The case involved two employees, one male and one female, with similar work records and tenure with their employers. Both were discharged for violation of company rules related to alcohol and drugs. The case portrays one worker's behavior as a more serious breach of company rules: The more culpable worker (a male in half the study and a female in the other half) had brought the intoxicant to work. The students had to express their agreement with two alternative approaches (tough or not-so-tough) to settling the dispute that arose after the discharge.

The researchers found bias against the female "employee" by both the male and female students. Both the male and female students recommended harsher treatment for the "culpable" female employee in the case than they did for the "culpable" man. As the researchers conclude, "women, as decision makers, appear to be as willing as men to impose harsher discipline on women than upon men." The Indian law regulates disciplinary action against pregnant women. The Maternity Benefit Act of 1961 places restriction on terminating an expectant woman who is absent from work due to pregnancy (Section 12). ■

How to Discipline an Employee

Even if you're a manager in a *Fortune* 500 company, you may find yourself without company guidelines when you have to discipline an employee for violating company rules.

An error could trigger a costly appeal, or even litigation. To help head off errors, fair discipline guidelines would include:[128]

- Make sure the evidence supports the charge of employee wrongdoing.
- Make sure to protect the employees' due process rights.[129] For example, did the person have a chance to defend himself or herself?
- Adequately warn the employee of the disciplinary consequences of his or her alleged misconduct. Have the employee sign a form as in Figure 14-4
- The rule that allegedly was violated should be "reasonably related" to the efficient and safe operation of the particular work environment.
- Objectively investigate the matter before administering discipline.
- The investigation should produce substantial evidence of misconduct.
- Apply applicable rules, orders, or penalties *without discrimination*.
- Maintain the employee's right to counsel. For example, all union employees generally have the right to bring a representative to an interview that they reasonably believe might lead to disciplinary action.
- Don't rob your subordinate of his or her dignity, for instance by disciplining the person in public.
- Listen to what the person has to say.
- Remember that the burden of proof is on you. In U.S. society, a person is considered innocent until proven guilty.
- Get the facts. Don't base your decision on hearsay evidence or on your general impression.
- Don't act while angry.
- Adhere to your company's disciplinary appeals process.[130]

FIGURE 14-4 Report of Employee Discipline

Apex Telecommunications Corporation
Report of Disciplinary Action and Warning

Employee's Name_____
Employee's Department_____
Date of Misconduct_____   Today's Date_____

Description of Incident and misconduct (including witnesses, if any)_____

Witnesses to Incident_____

If the misconduct violated an Apex Co. policy or rule, state the policy or rule_____

Employee's explanation for misconduct, if any_____

Disciplinary action taken, if any_____

The employee was warned today that if misconduct such as this reoccurs at any time during the next_____ weeks, he or she may be subject to the following disciplinary action_____

_____   _____
Supervisor's signature   Employee's signature

_____   _____
Print name   Print name

Discipline Without Punishment

Traditional discipline processes have two main drawbacks. First, no one likes being punished. Second, punishment tends to gain short-term compliance, but not long-term cooperation.

Discipline without punishment (or alternative or nonpunitive discipline) aims to avoid these drawbacks by reducing the punitive nature of the discipline. Steps include:[131]

1. *Issue an oral reminder for a first infraction.*
2. *Should another incident arise within 6 weeks, issue a formal written reminder, and place a copy in the employee's personnel file.* Also, hold a second private discussion with the employee.
3. *Give a paid, one-day "decision-making leave."* If another incident occurs in the next 6 weeks or so, tell the employee to take a 1-day leave with pay, and to consider whether he or she wants to abide by the company's rules. When the employee returns to work, he or she meets with you and gives you a decision.
4. *If no further incidents occur in the next year or so, purge the 1-day paid suspension from the person's file.* If the behavior is repeated, the next step is dismissal.

The process would not apply to exceptional circumstances. Criminal behavior or in-plant fighting might be grounds for immediate dismissal, for instance. Delhi Metro Rail Corporation (DMRC) has employed positive discipline management which focuses on improving or changing behavior. The system also rewards employees for good behavior, such as returning lost goods, providing high quality of customer service, and averting accidents. For small errors, an employee is orally warned, and negative points are recorded against his/her name. If the employee accumulates more negative points, disciplinary action is initiated in accordance with DMRC's Conduct, Discipline, and Appeal Rules. Immediate disciplinary action is taken, if an employee engages in major misconduct or commits a serious offence like compromising safety.[132]

Employee Engagement Guide For Managers

How Companies Become "Best Companies to Work For"

We began this chapter by noting that some companies are better to work for than are others, and we therefore focused on programs managers use to cultivate the positive employee relations that contribute to being a best place to work. This final section zeroes in on three companies that are known in part for actually being best places to work.

LEARNING OBJECTIVE 14-5
Answer the question, "How do companies become 'Best Companies to Work For'?"

The "Best Companies to Work For"

Each year, several organizations publish "Best Companies to Work For" lists, the most notable of which is probably "Fortune Magazine's 100 Best Companies to Work For®."[133] Based on an extensive multinational survey of employees by the Great Place to Work® Institute (www.greatplacetowork.com), the survey seeks to identify the best companies to work for based on how the employees working in them actually feel about working there. The Great Place to Work Institute defines a great workplace "as one where employees trust the people they work for, have pride in the work they do, and enjoy the people they work with."[134] They say that the companies on their great companies list "have the highest levels of trust, strongest evidence of employee engagement and demonstrate the best applied management practices and programs" as defined by the institute's proprietary models.[135]

TABLE 14-1 India's Best Companies to Work for (2016)

S. No.	Name of the Company	Sector
1.	Intuit India	Information Technology
2.	American Express India	Financial Services and Insurance
3.	Google India Private Limited	Information Technology
4.	Lemon Tree Hotels Limited	Hospitality
5.	SAP Labs India Private Limited	Information Technology
6.	Adobe Systems India Private Limited	Information Technology
7.	NetApp India Private Limited	Information Technology
8.	Teleperformance India	Information Technology
9.	Pitney Bowes Software India Private Limited	Information Technology
10.	DHL Express (India) Private Limited	Transportation
11.	SAP India	Information Technology
12.	Marriott Hotels India Private Limited	Hospitality
13.	Ujjivan Small Finance Bank Limited	Financial Services and Insurance
14.	InterContinental Hotels Group	Hospitality
15.	Hyatt Hotels and Resort	Hospitality
16.	Bajaj Finance Limited	Financial Services and Insurance
17.	Cadence Design Systems –India	Information Technology
18.	Godrej Consumer Products Limited	Manufacturing and Production
19.	Federal Express Corporation	Transportation
20.	Reliance Capital – Commercial Finance and Home Finance Divisions	Financial Services and Insurance
21.	The Oberoi Group	Hospitality
22.	PayPal India Private Limited	Information Technology
23.	Mahindra and Mahindra Automotive and Farm Equipment Sectors	Manufacturing and Production
24.	BT Global Business Services (GBS)	Information Technology
25.	Hilton Worldwide	Hospitality
26.	Spicer India Private Limited	Manufacturing and Production
27.	Indian Oil Corporation Limited	Manufacturing and Production
28.	Indus Towers	Telecommunications
29.	Blue Dart Express Limited	Transportation
30.	Hardcastle Restaurants Private Limited	Retail

Source: ET Bureau (HYPERLINK "http://economictimes.indiatimes.com/articleshow/59419981. cms?utm_source=contentofinterest&utm_medium=text&utm_campaign=cppst" http://economic-times.indiatimes.com) 'India's best companies to work for 2017: The complete list', [Navigation--ET Home›News›Company›Corporate Trends], as accessed on 15 September 2017 at 6pm IST; and India's Best Companies to Work For: A Study by Economic Times, HYPERLINK "http://www. greatplacetowork.in" www.greatplacetowork.in , [Home---Best Companies---Article] , as accessed on 15 September 2017 at 7pm IST

SAS: Great Benefits, Trust, and Work-Life Balance

SAS, headquartered in Cary, North Carolina, is a leader in providing business analytics software and services to companies that include 90 of the top 100 companies on the *Fortune* global 500 list.[136] Founded in the 1970s, the company is privately owned and has long been known for the quality of its benefits and for the support it provides for its employees' work–life balance. It has annual revenues of over $2.3 billion, and a worldwide workforce of over 13,000 people, about half of whom work at the company's North Carolina campus.

When most people think about employee relations at SAS, the first thing that comes to mind is probably the company's employee benefits, which are extraordinary. They include (for example) 3 to 4 weeks per year company-paid vacations, paid sick days, flexible work schedules, 11 paid holidays, competitive pay, company-paid life insurance and accidental death and dismemberment insurance, retirement plans, an on-site recreation and fitness center, employee assistance programs, domestic partner benefits, and subsidized on-site child-care centers in Cary (eligibility is based on seniority).[137]

As impressive as these benefits are, they are in some respects just a symbol of SAS's approach to employee relations. While many employers talk about "putting their employees first," SAS has long put its money where its mouth is. For example, late in 2008, as the recession was gaining speed, most employers were laying off employees. SAS's founder and CEO, Dr. Jim Goodnight, held a special global webcast to announce to his employees that none of SAS's 13,000 worldwide employees would lose their jobs.[138] They have reportedly never laid off an employee.[139] SAS goes to great lengths to foster its employees' trust in other ways, for instance by giving them abundant freedom in the hours they work. They also have the Great Place to Work Institute independently survey SAS workers on important characteristics of trust including open communication, respect, career paths, and being treated as a human being.[140]

What does all this do for SAS? As one long-term employee put it, "I just can't imagine leaving SAS, and I felt that way for a very long time ... if somebody offered to double my salary, I wouldn't even think about it."[141] Employee turnover, about 20% in software companies, is about 3% at SAS, which highlights another important facet of the SAS benefits programs.[142] One person who has studied SAS estimates that the lower turnover alone saves SAS $60 million to $80 million a year. As another example, letting employees visit on-campus health professionals (as SAS does) can cut hours out of the average employee's time away from work for doctors' visits.[143] And, of course, the effect on engagement, morale, and productivity may be priceless.

Google: Happiness and People Analytics

When Google founders Larry Page and Sergey Brin began building Google, they wanted to make it a great place to work, and in doing so, they turned to SAS. They met with SAS executives and sent a team there to better understand what made SAS consistently a "Best Company to Work For."[144]

It's therefore not surprising that Google is one of the few employers whose employee benefits equal or exceed those at SAS. In addition to things like health-care benefits and flexible work hours (and the possibility of making millions on stock options), its benefits include on-site dry cleaners, bowling alleys, cafés, transportation to and from campus, and nap pods.[145] As Google puts it, "It's all about removing barriers so Googlers can focus on the things they love, both inside and outside of work. We're constantly searching for unique ways to improve the health and happiness of our Googlers."[146]

Aside from the breadth and depth of its benefits, what sets Google apart is the scientific way it goes about deciding how to "improve the health and happiness" of Google employees. At Google, maintaining positive employee relations is highly analytical (one writer calls Google "The Happiness Machine."[147] Google calls its human resource department, "People Operations" (employees call it "POPS"). It has hired social scientists to create what they call the People & Innovation Lab, with a Google "people analytics team" charged with finding out how to make Googlers happy.[148] Google "monitors its employees well-being to a degree that can seem absurd to those who work outside [Google's headquarters in] Mountain View [California]."[149] The social scientists run little experiments, for instance, to determine if successful middle managers have certain skills, and what's the best way to remind people to contribute to their 401(k)s.[150] In one case, when the analytics team found that women staffers' turnover was too high, they concluded that new mothers were leaving at twice Google's average departure rate.[151] The study led to a redesigned maternity leave plan that includes 5 months off at full pay and full benefits. The new plan cut female Googler turnover in half.[152] To support its analytical approach, Google "solicits employee feedback on everything from how they prefer to be compensated, to the design of new bicycles used throughout the expansive headquarters campus."[153] So, it's little wonder why Googlers are happy.

FedEx: Guaranteed Fair Treatment

FedEx has been one of the "Fortune Magazine's 100 Best Companies to Work For" for 12 of the past 15 years. Several things—excellent benefits, competitive salaries, and (as we discussed in Chapter 5) a focus on promoting from within (as embodied by its Job Change Applicant Tracking System [JCATS]) help to explain this; however, it may be FedEx's emphasis on building trust through communications that most sets it apart.

SURVEY FEEDBACK ACTION (SFA)   The FedEx survey feedback action (SFA) program is one example. SFA includes an anonymous survey that allows employees to express feelings about the company and their managers, and to some extent about service, pay, and benefits. Each manager then has an opportunity to use the results to help design a blueprint for improving workgroup engagement and commitment.[154]

SFA has three phases. First, the survey itself is a standard, anonymous questionnaire given each year to every employee. The questions are designed to gather information about what helps and hinders employees in their work environment. Sample items include: "I can tell my manager what I think" and "My manager tells me what was expected." A workgroup's survey results are compiled and sent anonymously to the manager.

The second phase is a feedback session between the manager and his or her workgroup. The goal here is to identify specific concerns or problems, examine causes for these problems, and devise action plans to correct the problems.

The feedback meeting should lead to a third, "action plan" phase. This produces a list of actions that the manager will take to address employees concerns and boost results. It includes: What is the concern? What's your analysis? What's the cause? and What should be done?

THE FEDEX GUARANTEED FAIR TREATMENT PROCESS   FedEx's Guaranteed Fair Treatment Process (GFTP) is a sort of turbocharged grievance process. It goes beyond most grievance procedures in several ways, perhaps most notably in that an appeal can go all the way to FedEx's top executives. The effect is twofold: Complaints don't get a chance to accumulate; and all managers think twice before acting unfairly.[155] GFTP is available to all permanent FedEx employees. It covers concerns regarding matters such as disputed performance reviews, disciplinary actions, and terminations.[156]

Employees use Guaranteed Fair Treatment Process packets, available from the HR department, to file GFTP complaints. These include a fact sheet listing the complainant's name and work history; a GFTP tracking sheet to track the complaint at each step; management's rationale (for instance, in terms of applicable policies and procedures); a write-up from the HR department; space for key documents (termination letters, and so on); and space for backup information including witness statements. The employee must try to resolve the problem with his or her supervisor before filing a GFTP appeal.

GFTP contains three steps.[157] In step one, *management review*, the complainant submits a written complaint to a manager, senior manager, or managing director, within seven calendar days of the occurrence of the eligible issue. Then the manager, senior manager, and managing director of the employee's group review all relevant information; hold a telephone conference and/or meeting with the complainant; make a decision to either uphold, modify, or overturn management action; and communicate their decision in writing to the complainant.

If turned down in step one, then in step two, *officer complaint*, the complainant submits a written complaint to an officer (VP or senior vice president) of the division within 7 calendar days of the step one decision.

Finally (if necessary), in step three, *executive appeals review*, the complainant submits a written complaint within seven calendar days of the step two decision to the employee relations department. This department investigates and prepares a GFTP case file for the appeals board executive review. The appeals board—the CEO, the COO, the chief personnel officer, and senior vice presidents—then reviews all relevant information and makes a decision to either uphold, overturn, or initiate a board of review or to take other appropriate action; the appeals board's decision is final. (See Table 14-1)

A "Best Company" Human Resource Philosophy?

SAS, Google, and FedEx are different from each other, and from other companies, and so there's no guarantee that what works for them will work for other firms. For example, SAS is privately owned. Its owners can therefore more easily absorb the short-term fluctuations in profits that great benefits and no layoffs engender than can most publicly traded companies. Google has grown fast through a series of smart strategic moves, and, when the economy turns down, its managers generally still have to focus more on retaining great employees than on laying them off. FedEx, still a "Best Company to Work For," has run into some labor relations problems recently, for instance, from drivers who don't want to be independent contractors.

However, there are several things that any manager intent on building positive employee relations can learn from studying any of these three companies. For example, their managers work hard to cultivate trust and to ensure—for instance, by monitoring employees' attitudes and by instituting open-door and guaranteed fair treatment–type grievance processes—that employees are treated fairly. And, in numerous ways (such as in their recognition programs, involvement programs, ethical standards, benefits, and climate surveys and other two-way communications programs), they all exhibit a deep and evident respect for their employees and to "putting employees first."

But perhaps the single most important thing a manager can glean from these three companies is the human resource philosophy on which they built their human resource management practices. In Chapter 1, we said that people's actions are always based in part on the basic assumptions they make, and that this is especially true in regard to human resource management. The basic assumptions you make about people—Can they be trusted? Do they dislike work? Why do they act as they do? How should they be treated?—together comprise your philosophy of human resource management. And every personnel decision you make—the people you hire, the training you provide, your leadership style, and the like—reflects (for better or worse) this basic philosophy.

One of the things molding your own philosophy is that of your organization's top management. While it may or may not be stated, it is usually communicated by their actions and permeates every level and department. Google's founders want their employees to be happy, and they've worked since Google's founding to make sure that they are. FedEx founder and CEO Frederick Smith is famous for (among many other things) his P-S-P mantra, namely that when you treat your People well they will provide great Service and Profits will follow.[158] Similarly, the founder and CEO of SAS has said, "We've worked hard to create a corporate culture that is based on trust between our employees and the company ... a culture that rewards innovation, encourages employees to try new things and yet doesn't penalize them for taking chances, and a culture that cares about employees' personal and professional growth."[159] Such HR philosophies may well be the "magic sauce" that explains why great companies to work for are great.

Chapter Review

Chapter Section Summaries

14-1. Employee relations is the activity that involves establishing and maintaining the positive employee–employer relationships that contribute to satisfactory productivity, motivation, morale, and discipline, and to maintaining a positive, productive, and cohesive work environment.

14-2. Managers and HR management use **programs to develop positive employee relations**. Unfair treatment reduces morale, increases stress, and has negative effects on employees and should be weeded out. Managers also use communications programs, recognition programs, and employee involvement programs to build positive employee relations.

14-3. Ethics refers to the principles of conduct governing an individual or a group, and specifically to the standards you use to decide what your conduct should be. Numerous factors shape ethical behavior at work. These include individual factors, organizational factors, the boss's influence, ethics policies and codes, and the organization's culture. HR management can influence ethical behavior. Having a fair and open selection process, establishing special ethics training programs,

and rewarding (or disciplining) ethical (or unethical) work-related behavior are some examples.

14-4. A fair and just **discipline** process is based on rules and regulations, a system of progressive penalties, and an appeals process. A number of discipline guidelines are important, including discipline should be in line with the way management usually responds to similar incidents, management must adequately investigate the matter, and do not rob a subordinate of his or her dignity.

14-5. There are several things that any manager intent on building positive employee relations and **employee engagement** can draw from studying "Best Companies to Work For" such as SAS, Google, and FedEx. Their managers cultivate trust and ensure that employees are treated fairly. They all exhibit a deep and evident respect for their employees and to "putting employees first." Their human resource philosophy emphasizes trust, respect, and caring about their employees' personal and professional growth.

Discussion Questions

14-1. Explain how you would ensure fairness in disciplining, discussing particularly the prerequisites to disciplining, disciplining guidelines, and the discipline without punishment approach.

14-2. Why is it important in our litigious society to manage electronic monitoring properly?

14-3. Provide two examples of behaviors that would probably be unethical but legal, and three that would probably be illegal but ethical.

14-4. List 10 things your college or university does to encourage ethical behavior by students and/or faculty.

14-5. You need to select a nanny for your or a relative's child, and want someone ethical. What would you do to help ensure you ended up hiring someone ethical?

14-6. You believe your coworker is being bullied. How would you verify this, and what would you do about it if it is true?

14-7. Define *employee relations* and discuss at least four methods for managing it.

Individual and Group Activities

14-8. Working individually or in groups, interview managers or administrators at your employer or college in order to determine the extent to which the employer or college endeavors to build two-way communication, and the specific types

of programs used. Do the managers think they are effective? What do the employees (or faculty members) think of the programs in use at the employer or college?

14-9. Working individually or in groups, obtain copies of the student handbook for your college and determine to what extent there is a formal process through which students can air grievances. Based on your contacts with other students, has it been an effective grievance process? Why or why not?

14-10. Working individually or in groups, determine the nature of the academic discipline process in your college. Do you think it is effective? Based on what you read in this chapter, would you recommend any modifications?

14-11. Appendices A and B at the end of this book (pages 583–600) list the knowledge someone studying for the HRCI (Appendix A) or SHRM (Appendix B) certification exam needs to have in each area of human resource management (such as in Strategic Management, and Workforce Planning). In groups of several students, do four things: (1) review Appendix A and/or B; (2) identify the material in this chapter that relates to the Appendix A and/or B required knowledge lists; (3) write four multiple-choice exam questions on this material that you believe would be suitable for inclusion in the HRCI exam and/or the SHRM exam; and, (4) if time permits, have someone from your team post your team's questions in front of the class, so that students in all teams can answer the exam questions created by the other teams.

14-12. In a research study at Ohio State University, a professor found that even honest people, left to their own devices, would steal from their employers.[160] In this study, the researchers gave financial services workers the opportunity to steal a small amount of money after participating in an after-work project for which the pay was inadequate. Would the employees steal to make up for the underpayment? In most cases, yes. Employees who scored low on an honesty test stole whether or not their office had an ethics program that said stealing from the company was illegal. Employees who scored high on the honesty test also stole, but only if their office did not have such an employee ethics program—the "honest" people didn't steal if there was an ethics policy.

Individually or in groups, answer these questions: Do you think findings like these are generalizable? In other words, would they apply across the board to employees in other types of companies and situations? If your answer is yes, what do you think this implies about the need for and wisdom of having an ethics program?

Experiential Exercise

Discipline or Not?

Purpose: The purpose of this exercise is to provide you with some experience in analyzing and handling an actual disciplinary action.

Required Understanding: Students should be thoroughly familiar with the facts of the following incident, titled "Botched Batch."

How to Set Up the Exercise/Instructions: Divide the class into groups of four or five students. Each group should take the enquiry officer's point of view and assume that they are to analyze the case and make the recommendation. Review the case again at this point, but please do not read the award and discussion sections.

Each group should answer the following questions:

14-13. Based on what you read in this chapter, including all relevant guidelines, what would your decision be if you were the HR Director of the company? Why?

14-14. Do you think that after their experience in this case. The parties involved will be more or less inclined to settle grievances by themselves without resorting to arbitration?

Botched Batch

Facts: A computer department employee made an entry error that botched an entire run of computer reports. Efforts to rectify the situation produced a second set of improperly run reports. Because of the series of errors, the employer incurred extra costs of ₹2 lakh, plus a weekend of overtime work by other computer department staffers. Management suspended the employee for 3 days for negligence, and revoked a promotion (she was on probation after the last promotion which was awarded two months before) for which the employee had previously been offered.

Protesting the action, the employee stressed that she had attempted to correct her error in the early stages of the run by notifying the manager of computer operations of her mistake. Maintaining that the resulting string of errors could have been avoided if the manager had followed up on her report and stopped the initial run, the employee argued that she had been treated unfairly because the manager had not been disciplined even though he compounded the problem, whereas she was severely punished. Moreover, citing her "impeccable" work record and management's acknowledgment that she had always been a "model employee," the employee insisted that the denial of her previously approved promotion was "unconscionable."

14-5. As a demonstration, the group may hold a disciplinary enquiry. One of the students can be made the enquiry officer.

Application Case

Enron, Ethics, and Organizational Culture

For many people, a company called Enron Corp. still ranks as one of history's classic examples of ethics run amok. During the 1990s and early 2000s, Enron was in the business of wholesaling natural gas and electricity. Enron made its money as the intermediary (wholesaler) between suppliers and customers. Without getting into all the details, the nature of Enron's business—and the fact that Enron didn't actually own the assets—meant that its profit statements and balance sheets listing the firm's assets and liabilities were unusually difficult to understand.

It turned out that the lack of accounting transparency enabled the company's managers to make Enron's financial performance look much better than it actually was. Outside experts began questioning Enron's financial statements in 2001. In fairly short order, Enron collapsed, and courts convicted several of its top executives of things like manipulating Enron's reported assets and profitability. Many investors (including former Enron employees) lost all or most of their investments in Enron. In Enron's case, this breakdown is perhaps more perplexing than usual. As one writer said,

> Enron had all the elements usually found in comprehensive ethics and compliance programs: a code of ethics, a reporting system, as well as a training video on vision and values led by [the company's top executives].[161]

Experts subsequently put forth many explanations for how a company that was apparently so ethical outwardly could actually have been making so many bad ethical decisions without other managers (and the board of directors) noticing. The explanations ranged from a "deliberate concealment of information by officers," to more psychological explanations (such as employees not wanting to contradict their bosses) and the "surprising role of irrationality in decision-making."[162]

But perhaps the most persuasive explanation of how an apparently ethical company could go so wrong concerns organizational culture. The reasoning here is that it's not the rules but what employees feel they should do that determines ethical behavior. For example (speaking in general, not specifically about Enron), the executive director of the Ethics Officer Association put it this way:

> We're a legalistic society, and we've created a lot of laws.
> We assume that if you just knew what those laws meant that you would behave properly. Well, guess what? You can't write enough laws to tell us what to do at all times every day of the week in every part of the world. We've got to develop the critical thinking and critical reasoning skills of our people because most of the ethical issues that we deal with are in the ethical gray areas.

Questions

14-15. Based on what you read in this chapter, summarize in one page or less how you would explain Enron's ethical meltdown.

14-16. It is said that when one securities analyst tried to confront Enron's CEO about the firm's unusual accounting statements, the CEO publicly used vulgar language to describe the analyst, and that Enron employees subsequently thought doing so was humorous. If true, what does that say about Enron's ethical culture?

14-17. This case and chapter had something to say about how organizational culture influences ethical behavior. What role do you think culture played at Enron? Give five specific examples of things Enron's CEO could have done to create a healthy ethical culture.

Continuing Case

Carter Cleaning Company

Guaranteeing Fair Treatment

Being in the laundry and cleaning business, the Carters feel strongly about not allowing employees to smoke, eat, or drink in their stores. Jennifer was therefore surprised to walk into a store and find two employees eating lunch at the front counter. There was a large pizza in its box, and the two of them were sipping colas and eating slices of pizza and submarine sandwiches off paper plates. Not only did it look messy, but there were grease and soda spills on the counter and the store smelled from onions and pepperoni, even with the exhaust fan pulling air out through the roof. In addition to being a turnoff to customers, the mess on the counter meant that a customer's order might actually become soiled in the store.

Although this was a serious matter, Jennifer didn't feel that what the counter people were doing was grounds for dismissal (partly because the store manager had apparently condoned their actions). It seemed to her that the matter called for more than just a warning but less than dismissal.

Questions

14-18. What would you do if you were Jennifer, and why?

14-19. Should a disciplinary system be established at Carter Cleaning Centers?

14-20. If so, what should it cover? How would you suggest it deal with a situation such as the one with the errant counter people?

14-21. How would you deal with the store manager?

Translating Strategy into HR Policies and Practices Case*' §

The overall map on page xxxviii of this book outlines the relationships involved.

Improving Performance at the Hotel Paris

The Hotel Paris's New Ethics, Justice, and Fair Treatment Process

The Hotel Paris's competitive strategy is "To use superior guest service to differentiate the Hotel Paris properties, and to thereby increase the length of stay and return rate of guests, and thus boost revenues and profitability." HR manager Lisa Cruz must now formulate functional policies and activities that support this competitive strategy, by eliciting the required employee behaviors and competencies.

As the head of HR for the Hotel Paris, Lisa Cruz was especially concerned about her company maintaining the highest ethical standards. Her concerns were twofold. First, there are, in any single hotel each day, at least a dozen people (including housekeepers, front-desk clerks, security guards, and so on) with easy access to guests' rooms, and to their personal belongings. Guests—many younger, and many unwary—are continually walking the halls unprotected. So, in a service company like this, there is simply no margin for ethical errors.

But she was concerned about ethics for a second reason. She knew that employees do not like being treated unfairly, and that unfairness in any form could manifest itself in low morale and in diminished performance. She wondered if her employees' low morale and engagement—as measured by her firm's attitude surveys—stemmed, in part, from what they perceived as unjust treatment. Lisa therefore turned to the task of assessing and redesigning the Hotel Paris's ethics, justice, and fair treatment practices.

When she sat with the CFO to discuss her proposal for the Hotel Paris's fairness, justice, and ethics system, Lisa came armed with some research. In 2003, the *Journal of Applied Psychology* published a study that showed how improving the level of interpersonal and procedural justice in a service company can lead to improved employee attitudes and performance and thus to improved hotel performance.[163] And the study was done in a hotel chain.

In this study, the researchers collected employee survey data from a hotel chain's 111 different hotels in the United States and Canada. The employee services department of this hotel chain obtained completed surveys from 8,832 of the hotel's employees. The researchers also obtained data on employee turnover as well as on the employees' commitment, employees' intentions to remain with the organization, and guest satisfaction.

Clearly, having fair and just procedures in place affected these hotels' employee morale and behavior, and thus company performance—they could even measure the links. For example, procedural justice and interpersonal justice were related to increased levels of employees' satisfaction with supervision.

For Lisa and the CFO, these results supported, in a measurably defensible way, the idea that spending the money required to improve procedural and interpersonal justice would likely improve employee attitudes and behaviors (employee commitment, discretionary service behavior, and employee turnover), and, thereby, improve guest satisfaction and company performance.

Lisa and her HR team took steps to institute new ethics, justice, and fair treatment practices at the Hotel Paris. Working with the company's general counsel, they produced and presented to the CEO a new Hotel Paris code of ethics, as well as a more complete set of ethical guidelines. These now appear on the Hotel Paris's careers Web site link, and are part of each new employee's orientation packet. They contracted with a vendor to provide a customized, Web-based ethics training program, and made it clear that the first employees to participate in it were the company's top executives.

Lisa and her team then proceeded methodically through the company's entire HR process, starting with recruitment and selection. The selection process now includes an honesty test. New guidelines ensure an open and fair performance appraisal process. The team completely revamped the hotel's disciplinary process. They instituted a new appeals process that included appeals to each hotel's manager, and then to Lisa Cruz, and finally to a top management executive appeals committee. They instituted a new discipline without punishment system.

After 6 months of operating under the new system, several changes are evident. Surveys Lisa took before the new program, and now, indicate a significant upward movement in the employees' perceptions of "consistent and equitable treatment of all employees." Grievances are down by 80%, 95% of employees are able to quote the ethics code, employee morale and commitment are up, and, in general, employee service–type behaviors (such as greeting guests in a friendly manner) have increased, too. Lisa and the CFO are pleased with the new system, and are optimistic it will also help to improve customer service satisfaction.

Questions

14-22. Based on what you learned in this chapter of Dessler *Human Resource Management*, what do you think of the adequacy and effectiveness of the steps Lisa has taken so far?

14-23. List three more specific steps Hotel Paris should take with respect to each individual human research function (selection, training, and so on) to improve the level of ethics in the company.

14-24. Based on what you learned in this chapter, write a short (less than one page) explanation Lisa can use to sell to top management the need to further improve the hotel chain's fairness and justice processes.

§ Written by and copyright Gary Dessler, PhD.

Key Terms

employee relations, 439
fair treatment, 439
procedural justice, 440
distributive justice, 440

social responsibility, 441
organizational climate, 443
suggestion teams, 444
problem-solving teams, 444

quality circle, 444
self-managing/self-directed work
   team, 444
ethics, 445

organizational culture, 449
Electronic Communications
   Privacy Act (ECPA), 451

Ethics Quiz Answers

Quiz is on page 457.

1. 34% said personal e-mail on company computers is wrong.
2. 37% said using office equipment for schoolwork is wrong.
3. 49% said playing computer games at work is wrong.
4. 54% said Internet shopping at work is wrong.
5. 61% said it's unethical to blame your error on technology.
6. 87% said it's unethical to visit pornographic sites at work.
7. 33% said $25 is the amount at which a gift from a supplier or client becomes troubling, while 33% said $50, and 33% said $100.

8. 35% said a $50 gift to the boss is unacceptable.
9. 12% said a $50 gift from the boss is unacceptable.
10. 70% said it's unacceptable to take the $200 football tickets.
11. 70% said it's unacceptable to take the $120 theater tickets.
12. 35% said it's unacceptable to take the $100 food basket.
13. 45% said it's unacceptable to take the $25 gift certificate.
14. 40% said it's unacceptable to take the $75 raffle prize.
15. 11% reported they lie about sick days.
16. 4% reported they take credit for the work or ideas of others.

Endnotes

1. Accessed on September 20, 2017, at http://www.hindustantimes.com /business-news/tata-motors-union-calls-off-four-day-strike-at-jamshedpur-plant/story-NlGPHMinu3e1ojc-0MV4JzI.html.

2. "Workforce Compensation and Performance Service, Office of Performance and Compensation Systems Design, Classification Programs Division," July 1999, HRCD-7; "Employee Relations," *HR Magazine* 55, no. 7 (July 2010), p. SS-4.

3. Accessed on September 21, 2017 at https://www.peoplematters.in/blog/employee-relations/trade-unions-as-business-partners-part-2-6800.

4. Accessed on September 21, 2017 at http://www.freepressjournal.in/business/csl-constantly-engages-with-trade-union-to-keep-them-on-board-with-ipo/1112776.

5. See, for example, Chris Long et al., "Fairness Monitoring: Linking Managerial Controls and Fairness Judgments in Organizations," *Academy of Management Journal* 54, no. 3 (2012), pp. 1045–1068.

6. Bennett Tepper, "Consequences of Abusive Supervision," *Academy of Management Journal* 43, no. 2 (2000), pp. 178–190. See also Samuel Aryee et al., "Antecedents and Outcomes of Abusive Supervision: A Test of a Trickle-Down Model," *Journal of Applied Psychology* 92, no. 1 (2007), pp. 191–201.

7. Mindy Shoss et al., "Blaming the Organization for Abusive Supervision: The Roles of Perceived Organizational Support and Supervisors Organizational Embodiment," *Journal of Applied Psychology* 98, no. 1 (2013), pp. 158–168.

8. Sean Hannah et al., "Joint Influences of Individual and Work Unit of Abusive Supervision on Ethical Intentions and Behaviors: A Moderated Mediation Model," *Journal of Applied Psychology* 98, no. 4 (2013), pp. 579–592.

9. Michelle Donovan et al., "The Perceptions of Fair Interpersonal Treatment Scale: Development and Validation of a Measure of Interpersonal Treatment in the Workplace," *Journal of Applied Psychology* 83, no. 5 (1998), pp. 683–692.

10. Bennett Tepper et al., "Abusive Supervision and Subordinates Organization Deviance," *Journal of Applied Psychology* 93, no. 4 (2008), pp. 721–732.

11. Jordan Robbins et al., "Perceived Unfairness and Employee Health: A Meta-Analytic Integration," *Journal of Applied Psychology* 97, no. 2 (2012), pp. 235–272.

12. Dawn Carlson et al., "The Fallout from Abusive Supervision: An Examination of Subordinates and Their Partners," *Personnel Psychology* 60, no. 4 (2011), pp. 937–961.

13. Marie Mitchell and Maureen Ambrose, "Employees Behavioral Reactions to Supervisor Aggression: An Examination of Individual and Situational Factors," *Journal of Applied Psychology* 97, no. 6 (2012), pp. 1148–1170.

14. Gary Weaver and Linda Treviño, "The Role of Human Resources in Ethics/Compliance Management: A Fairness Perspective," *Human Resource Management Review* 11 (2001), p. 117.

15. For example, monitor social media sites for evidence that one employee is harassing another. "Facebook Harassment: Social Websites May Prompt Need for New Policies, Procedures," *BNA Bulletin to Management*, July 20, 2010, p. 225.

16. Suzanne Masterson, "A Trickle-Down Model of Organizational Justice: Relating Employees' and Customers' Perceptions of and Reactions to Fairness," *Journal of Applied Psychology* 86, no. 4 (2001), pp. 594–601.

17. Based on Daniel Denison, *Corporate Culture and Organizational Effectiveness* (New York: Wiley, 1990), p. 155.

18. "When the Jobs Inspector Calls," *Economist,* March 31, 2012, p. 73.

19. Alexandra Ho and Tim Culpan, with assistance from Jun Yang in Seoul, Andrea Wong in Taipei, Tian Ying in Beijing, and Jasmine Wang in Hong Kong, "Foxconn Labor Disputes Disrupt IPhone Output for 2nd Time," *Bloomberg News*, October 8, 2012, www.bloomberg.com/news/2012-10-07/foxconn-labor-disputes-disrupt-iphone-output-for-2nd-time.html, accessed April 14, 2013.

20. Ibid.

21. Teresa Daniel, "Tough Boss or Workplace Bully?" *HR Magazine*, June 2009, pp. 83–86.

22. Premila D'Crux, Charlotte Rayner Bullying in the Indian Workplace: A study of ITES-BPO sector, (2012), Economic and Industrial Democracy, Sage V 34 (4) p-597-619.

23. Richa Gupta et.al Investigating Workplace Bullying in India: Psychometric Properties, Validity and Cutoff Scores of Negative Acts Questionneire - Revised. (2017), Sage Open, April-June.

24. Premilla D'Cruz, Ernesto Noronha The exit coping response to workplace bullying: The contribution of inclusivist and exclusivist HRM strategies. (2010) Employee Relations, Vol 32 (2), p 102-120.

25. Eugene Kim and Theresa Glomb, "Get Smarty-Pants: Cognitive Ability, Personality, and Victimization," *Journal of Applied Psychology* 95, no. 3 (2010), pp. 889–901. See also Jaclyn Jensen et al., "Is It Better to Be Average? High and Low Performance as Predictors of Employee Victimization," *Journal of Applied Psychology* 90, no. 2 (2014), pp. 296–309.

26. Eugene Kim and Teresa Glomb, "Victimization of High Performers: The Roles of Envy and Work Group Identification," *Journal of Applied Psychology* 9, no. 4 (2014), pp. 619–634.

27. Ibid.

28. http://view.fdu.edu/default. aspx?id?3529, accessed September 6, 2012.

29. Ibid.

30. Carolyn Hirschman, "Giving Voice to Employee Concerns: Encouraging Employees to Speak Out Requires Respectful Treatment and Appropriate Action," *HR Magazine* 53, no. 8 (August 2008), pp. 50–54.

31. Tschanen Niederkohr, "Use the Exit Interview to Gain Valuable Insight," *Aftermarket Business* 117, no. 11 (November 2007), p. 8.

32. J. G. Carr, A. M. Schmidt, J. K. Ford, and R. P. DeShon, "Climate Perceptions Matter: A Meta-Analytic Path Analysis Relating Molar Climate, Cognitive and Affective States, and Individual Level Work Outcomes," *Journal of Applied Psychology* 88 (2003), pp. 605–619; quoted in Stephen Robbins and Timothy Judge, *Organizational Behavior* (Upper Saddle River, NJ: Prentice Hall, 2011), p. 524; and www.yourerc.com/blog/post/ What-is-OrganizationalClimate. aspx, accessed September 8, 2014.

33. Rachel Silverman, "Are You Happy in Your Job? Bosses Push Weekly Surveys," *Wall Street Journal*, December 3, 2014, pp. B1, B4.

34. Laszlo Bock, *Work Rules!* (New York: 12, 2015), pp. 140–142.

35. "Survey: Employee Survey Number One," www.shrm.org/ templatestools/samples/HR-forms, accessed April 11, 2012.

36. Pat Lenius, "Murray Supply Host Recognition Dinner," *Supply House Times*, May 2011, p. 70.

37. SHRM Survey Findings: Employee Recognition Programs, Winter 2012. In collaboration with and commissioned by Globoforce (www.globoforce.com).

38. This is based on "Recognition: Service Award Checklist," www.shrm.org/templatestools/ samples/HR-forms, November 5, 2010, accessed April 14, 2012.

39. http://mashable.com/follow/ topics/pinterest, accessed April 15, 2012.

40. "Over Half of Employers Use Social Media for Internal Communications, Survey Reveals," *Bloomberg BNA Bulletin to Management*, June 4, 2013, p. 179.

41. PTI, "Social Media indulgence root cause of workplace unproductivity: Report," *Business Standard*, October 18, 2016.

42. PTI, "Air India warns former employees from speaking against airline on social media," 2017, LiveMint.com, June 29, 2017.

43. Accessed on October 6, 2017, at http://www.hungamadigitalservices.com/naval-godrejs-centenary-celebration-goes-digital-hungama-digital-services/.

44. Tamara Lytle, "Giving Employees a Say: Getting—and Acting on—Ideas Offered by Employees Can Save Employers Money and Build a Sense of Ownership among Workers," *HR Magazine* 56, no. 10 (October 2011), pp. 69–74.

45. James H. Shonk, *Team-Based Organizations* (Chicago: Irwin, 1997), pp. 27–33.

46. Ibid., p. 28.

47. John Katzenbach and Douglas Smith, "The Discipline of Teams," *Harvard Business Review*, March/April 1993, pp. 116–118.

48. Everett Adams Jr., "Quality Circle Performance," *Journal of Management* 17, no. 1 (1991), pp. 25–39.

49. Accessed on September 21, 2017 at http://timesofindia. indiatimes.com/city/nagpur/ Quality-circles-help-government-hospitals-improve-services/articleshow/48519508.cms.

50. See for example, Jack Orsburn et al., *Self-Directed Teams*, Homewood, IL: Business One Irwin, 1990, p. 8; http:// sloanreview.mit.edu/article/how-to-lead-a-selfmanaging-team/, accessed July 14, 2014.

51. Charles Fishman, "Engines of Democracy," *Fast Company*, October 1999, pp. 173–202.

52. Tom Peters, *Liberation Management* (New York: Alfred A. Knopf, 1992), pp. 238–239.

53. Susan Wells, "From Ideas to Results: To Get the Most from Your Company's Suggestion System, Move Ideas up the Ladder through a Formal Process," *HR Magazine* 50, no. 2 (February 2005), pp. 54–59.

54. Rebecca Hastings, "Survey: Employees Have Plenty of Suggestions," www.shrm.org/HR-disciplines/employeerelations/ articles, February 29, 2012, accessed April 15, 2012.

55. Accessed on September 21, 2017 at http://www.thehindubusinessline.com/companies/ employee-suggestions-saved-maruti-suzuki-281-crore-in-201516/article8528896.ece.

56. Based on Wells, "From Ideas to Results."

57. Ibid.

58. This is quoted from ibid.

59. Kevin Wooten, "Ethical Dilemmas in Human Resource Management: An Application of a Multidimensional Framework, A Unifying Taxonomy, and Applicable Codes," *Human Resource Management Review* 11 (2001), p. 161. See also Sean Valentine et al., "Employee Job Response as a Function of Ethical Context and Perceived Organization Support," *Journal of Business Research* 59, no. 5 (2006), pp. 582–588.

60. Manuel Velasquez, *Business Ethics: Concepts and Cases* (Upper Saddle River, NJ: Prentice Hall, 1992), p. 9.

See also O. C. Ferrell, John Fraedrich, and Linda Ferrell, *Business Ethics* (Boston: Houghton Mifflin, 2008).

61. For further discussion of ethics and morality, see Tom Beauchamp and Norman Bowie, *Ethical Theory and Business* (Upper Saddle River, NJ: Prentice Hall, 2001), pp. 1–19.

62. Accessed on September 21, 2017 at http://tata.com/ aboutus/articlesinside/ Tata-Code-of-Conduct.

63. Jennifer Kish-Gephart, David Harrison, and Linda Trevino, "Bad Apples, Bad Cases, and Bad Barrels: Meta-Analytic Evidence about Sources of Unethical Decisions at Work," *Journal of Applied Psychology* 95, no. 1 (2010), pp. 1–31.

64. Sara Morris et al., "A Test of Environmental, Situational, and Personal Influences on the Ethical Intentions of CEOs," *Business and Society*, August 1995, pp. 119–147. See also Dennis Moberg, "Ethics Blind Spots in Organizations: How Systematic Errors in Person's Perception Undermine Moral Agency," *Organization Studies* 27, no. 3 (2006), pp. 413–428; and Scott Reynolds et al., "Automatic Ethics: The Effects of Implicit Assumptions and Contextual Cues on Moral Behavior," *Journal of Applied Psychology* 95, no. 5 (2010), pp. 752–760.

65. David Welsh, Deidre Snyder, Michael Christian, and Lisa Ordonez, "The Slippery Slope: How Small Ethical Transgressions Pave the Way for Larger Future Transgressions," *Journal of Applied Psychology* 100, no. 1 (2015), pp. 114–127.

66. Stefan Thau et al., "Unethical for the Sake of the Group: Risk of Social Exclusion and Pro-group Unethical Behavior," *Journal of Applied Psychology* 100, no. 1 (2015), pp. 98–113.

67. Ibid., p. 21.

68. Ibid.

69. "Former CEO Joins WorldCom's Indicted," *Miami Herald*, March 3, 2004, p. 4C.

70. Ferrell and Fraedrich, *Business Ethics*, p. 28; adapted from Rebecca Goodell, *Ethics in American Business: Policies, Programs, and Perceptions* (Washington, DC: Ethics Resource Center, 1994), p. 54. For other insights into unethical behavior's causes, see, for example, F. Gino et al., "Nameless + Harmless = Blameless: When Seemingly Irrelevant Factors Influence Judgment of (Un)ethical Behavior," *Organizational Behavior and Human Decision Processes* 111, no. 2 (March 2010), pp. 93–101; and J. Camps et al., "Learning Atmosphere and Ethical Behavior, Does It Make Sense?" *Journal of Business Ethics* 94, no. 1 (June 2010), pp. 129–147.

71. A recent study suggests that people may not be so selfless. Elizabeth Umphress, John Bingham, and Marie Mitchell, "Unethical Behavior in the Name of the Company: The Moderating Effect of Organizational Identification and Positive Reciprocity Beliefs on Unethical Pro-organizational Behavior," *Journal of Applied Psychology* 95, no. 4 (2010), pp. 769–770.

72. "Ethics Policies Are Big with Employers, but Workers See Small Impact on the Workplace," *BNA Bulletin to Management*, June 29, 2000, p. 201.

73. Guy Brumback, "Managing Above the Bottom Line of Ethics," *Supervisory Management*, December 1993, p. 12. See also E. E. Umphress et al., "The Influence of Distributive Justice on Lying for and Stealing from a Supervisor," *Journal of Business Ethics* 86, no. 4 (June 2009), pp. 507–518; and S. Chen, "The Role of Ethical Leadership Versus Institutional Constraints: A Simulation Study of Financial Misreporting by CEOs," *Journal of Business Ethics* 93, part supplement 1 (June 2010), pp. 33–52.

74. Dayton Fandray, "The Ethical Company," *Workforce* 79, no. 12 (December 2000), pp. 74–77.

75. IBM Business Conduct Guidelines, www.ibm.com/investor/ pdf/BCG 2012.pdf, accessed August 2, 2013.

76. Richard Beatty et al., "HR's Role in Corporate Governance: Present and Prospective," *Human Resource Management* 42, no. 3 (Fall 2003), p. 268.

77. Eric Krell, "How to Conduct an Ethics Audit," *HR Magazine*, April 2010, pp. 48–51.

78. Betsy Shepherd, "Occupational Fraud," *Workforce Management*, April 2012, p. 18.

79. Dale Buss, "Corporate Compasses," *HR Magazine*, June 2004, pp. 127–132.

80. www.sec.gov/news/ press/2011/2011116.htm, accessed September 6, 2012.

81. "SEC Actively Tracking Conduct That Might Constitute Retaliation," *BNA Bulletin to Management*, October 23, 2012, p. 342.

82. David Mayer et al., "Who Displays Ethical Leadership, and Why Does It Matter? An Examination of Antecedents and Consequences of Ethical Leadership," *Academy of Management Journal* 55, no. 1 (2012), p. 167.

83. Sometimes the most straightforward way of changing a company's culture is to move fast to change its top management. See Jeremy Smerd, "A Stalled Culture Change?" *Workforce Management*, December 14, 2009, pp. 1, 3.

84. "Ethics: It Isn't Just the Big Guys," *The American*

Intelligence Wire, July 28, 2003, p. 10.

85. Based on "Ethics: It Isn't Just the Big Guys," *The American Intelligence Wire*, July 28, 2003, p. 10.

86. Joytsna Bhatnagar, & Saini, Debi. Human resource driven turnaround at North Delhi Power Limited: Transition from a public utility to a private enterprise. (2007) Asian Case Research Journal, 11(2), 163–213.

87. Jatinder Kumar Jha, Biju Varkkey et. al. Contribution of HR in development of ethical climate at workplace: A study, 2017, South Asian Journal of HRM, 4 (1), p 1-23.

88. Krohe Jr., "The Big Business of Business Ethics," *Across the Board* 34 (May 1997), pp. 23–29; Deborah Wells and Marshall Schminke, "Ethical Development and Human Resources Training: An Integrator Framework," *Human Resource Management Review* 11 (2001), pp. 135–158.

89. Sunil Kumar Maheshwari and M P Ganesh, "Ethics in Organizations: The case of Tata Steel," *Vikalpa* (2006), Vol 31(2), pp 75-87.

90. "Ethical Issues in the Management of Human Resources," *Human Resource Management Review* 11 (2001), p. 6; Joel Lefkowitz, "The Constancy of Ethics amidst the Changing World of Work," *Human Resource Management Review* 16 (2006), pp. 245–268; William Byham, "Can You Interview for Integrity?" *Across the Board* 41, no. 2 (March/April 2004), pp. 34–38; Evan Offstein and Ronald Dufresne, "Building Strong Ethics and Promoting Positive Character Development: The Influence of HRM at the United States Military Academy at West Point," *Human Resource Management* 46, no. 1 (Spring 2007), pp. 95–114.

91. Gary Weaver and Linda Treviño, "The Role of Human Resources in Ethics/Compliance Management: A Fairness Perspective," *Human Resource Management Review* 11 (2001), p. 123. See also Linda Andrews, "The Nexus of Ethics," *HR Magazine*, August 2005, pp. 53–58.

92. Russell Cropanzano and Thomas Wright, "Procedural Justice and Organizational Staffing: A Tale of Two Paradigms," *Human Resource Management Review* 13, no. 1 (2003), pp. 7–40.

93. "Ethical Issues in the Management of Human Resources," p. 6.

94. Weaver and Treviño, "The Role of Human Resources in Ethics/Compliance Management," p. 123.

95. Kathryn Tyler, "Do the Right Thing: Ethics Training Programs Help Employees Deal with Ethical Dilemmas," *HR Magazine*, February 2005, pp. 99–102.

96. Tom Asacker, "Ethics in the Workplace," *Training & Development*, August 2004, p. 44; www.skillsoft.com/catalog/detail.asp?CourseCode=pd_18_a01_bs_enus, accessed September 8, 2014.

97. Pratima Varma, Siddarth Mohapatra, and Jan Lowstedt, "Ethics Training in the Indian IT Sector: Formal, Informal or Both," *Journal of Business Ethics* (2016), Vol 133 (1), pp 73-93.

98. M. Ronald Buckley et al., "Ethical Issues in Human Resources Systems," *Human Resource Management Review* 11, no. 1, 2 (2001), pp. 11, 29. See also Ann Pomeroy, "The Ethics Squeeze," *HR Magazine*, March 2006, pp. 48–55.

99. Ed Finkel, "Yahoo Takes New Road on Ethics Training," *Workforce Management*, July 2010, p. 2.

100. Ibid., p. 125.

101. Robert Grossman, "Executive Discipline," *HR Magazine*, August 2005, pp. 46–51. See also Jean Thilmany, "Supporting Ethical Employees," *HR Magazine* 52, no. 9 (September 2007), pp. 105–106, 108, 110, 112.

102. Milton Zall, "Employee Privacy," *Journal of Property Management* 66, no. 3 (May 2001), p. 16.

103. Morris Attaway, "Privacy in the Workplace on the Web," *Internal Auditor* 58, no. 1 (February 2010), p. 30.

104. Declam Leonard and Angela France, "Workplace Monitoring: Balancing Business Interests with Employee Privacy Rights," *Society for Human Resource Management Legal Report,* May–June 2003, pp. 3–6.

105. *Vega-Rodriguez* v. *Puerto Rico Telephone Company*, CA1, #962061, 4/8/97, discussed in "Video Surveillance Withstands Privacy Challenge," *BNA Bulletin to Management*, April 17, 1997, p. 121. Also see, J. Greenwald, "Monitoring Communications? Know Legal Pitfalls," *Business Insurance* 45, no. 6 (February 7, 2011), pp. 1, 17.

106. Akhil Deo, "How right to privacy judgement will and won't impact India's data protection regime," *The Wire*, August 24, 2017.

107. *Quon* v. *Arch Wireless Operating Co.*, 529 F.3d 892 (9th Cir. 2008); "Employers Should Re-Examine Policies in Light of Ruling," *BNA Bulletin to Management*, August 12, 2008, p. 263.

108. Dionne Searcey, "Some Courts Raise Bar on Reading Employee E-mail," *Wall Street Journal*, November 19, 2009, p. A17.

109. "When Can an Employer Access Private E-Mail on Its System?" *BNA Bulletin to Management*, July 14, 2009, p. 224;

one employment lawyer says that courts look to whether the employer's process is reasonable when determining if the employer's monitoring practices are acceptable. Electronic monitoring is generally reasonable "where there is a legitimate business purpose, where policies exist to set the privacy expectations of employees, and where employees are informed of the rules and understand the methods used to monitor the workplace." Nicole Kamm, "Bodyguard for Electronic Information," *HR Magazine*, January 2010, pp. 57–58.

110. Fredric Leffler and Lauren Palais, "Filter Out Perilous Company E-Mails," *Society for Human Resource Management Legal Report*, August 2008, p. 3. A survey of 220 large U.S. firms suggests that about 38% of them have people reading or otherwise analyzing employees' outgoing e-mail. See Searcey, "Some Courts Raise Bar on Reading Employee Email."

111. Bill Roberts, "Stay Ahead of the Technology Use Curve," *HR Magazine*, October 2008, pp. 57–61.

112. One attorney notes that problems can arise with the Federal Stored Communications Act if the employer uses illicit or coercive means to access the employee's private social media accounts. *BNA Bulletin to Management*, July 21, 2009, p. 225.

113. "Twitter Is Latest Electronic Tool to Pose Challenges and Opportunities for Employers," *BNA Bulletin to Management*, June 16, 2009, p. 185. See also Sean Valentine et al., "Exploring the Ethicality of Firing Employees Who Blog," *Human Resource Management* 49, no. 1 (January/February 2010), pp. 87–108.

114. "After Employer Found Liable for Worker's Child Porn, Policies May Need to Be Revisited," *BNA Bulletin to Management*, March 21, 2006, p. 89.

115. Ibid.

116. "Disgruntled Workers' Hacking of Employers Is on the Rise, FBI–DHS Public Alert Says," *Bloomberg BNA Bulletin to Management*, October 7, 2014, p. 315.

117. "Time Clocks Go High Touch, High Tech to Keep Workers from Gaming the System," *BNA Bulletin to Management*, March 25, 2004, p. 97.

118. Andrea Poe, "Make Foresight 20/20," *HR Magazine*, February 2000, pp. 74–80.

119. Gundars Kaupin et al., "Recommended Employee Location Monitoring Policies," www.shrm.org, accessed January 2, 2007.

120. Steve Lohr, "Unblinking Eyes Track Employees," *New York Times*, June 22, 2014, pp. 1, 15.

121. Claire Suddath, "Tesco Monitors Employees with Motorola on Bands," www.BusinessWeek.com/articles/2013-02-13/Tescomonitors_employees-with-Motorola-arm-bands, accessed February 14, 2013.

122. Rita Zeidner, "New Face in the C-Suite," *HR Magazine*, January 2010, p. 39.

123. Lester Bittel, *What Every Supervisor Should Know* (New York: McGraw-Hill, 1974), p. 308; and Thomas Salvo, "Practical Tips for Successful Progressive Discipline," SHRM White Paper July 2004, www.shrm.org/hrresources/whitepapers_published/CMS_009030 asp, accessed January 5, 2008.

124. David Campbell et al., "Discipline Without Punishment—At Last," *Harvard Business Review*, July/August 1995, pp. 162–178; J. F. Mason, "Myspace, Yourspace: What Employers Must Know About Social-Media Risks," *National Underwriter* (P & C) 115, no. 11 (March 28, 2011), pp. 18, 20.

125. For fair discipline guidelines, see Bittel, *What Every Supervisor Should Know*, p. 308; Paul Falcone, "Fundamentals of Progressive Discipline," *HR Magazine*, February 1997, pp. 90–92; and "How to Discipline and Fire Employees," www.entrepreneur.com/article/79928, accessed May 3, 2012.

126. David Mayer et al., "When Do Fair Procedures Not Matter? A Test of the Identity Violation Effect," *Journal of Applied Psychology*, 94, no. 1, 2009, pp. 142–161.

127. Grossman, "Executive Discipline," pp. 46–51; "The Evil Women Theses," based on Sandra Hartman et al., "Males and Females in a Discipline Situation Exploratory Research on Competing Hypotheses," *Journal of Managerial Issues* 6, no. 1 (Spring 1994), pp. 57, 64–68; "A Woman's Place," *Economist* (August 19, 2000), p. 56.

128. For fair discipline guidelines, see Bittel, *What Every Supervisor Should Know*, p. 308; Falcone, "Fundamentals of Progressive Discipline," pp. 90–92; and "How to Discipline and Fire Employees."

129. George Bohlander, "Why Arbitrators Overturn Managers in Employee Suspension and Discharge Cases," *Journal of Collective Negotiations* 23, no. 1 (1994), pp. 76–77.

130. "Employers Turn to Corporate Ombuds to Defuse Internal Ticking Time Bombs," *BNA Bulletin to Management*, August 9, 2005, p. 249.

131. Dick Grote, "Discipline without Punishment," *Across the Board* 38, no. 5 (September 2001), pp. 52–57.

CHAPTER 14

132. Samar K Dutta, Biju Varkkey, Srijanpal Singh, and S. Nankar, "DMRC: The Saga of Excellence," UNDP, 2011, New Delhi.

133. http://money.cnn.com/ magazines/fortune/best-companies/2014/list/ accessed July 17, 2015.

134. http://www.greatplacetowork. com/best-companies#sthash. ECoNqRRH.dpbs, accessed July 17, 2015.

135. Ibid.

136. http://www.sas.com/en_us/ company-information/great-workplace.html, accessed July 17, 2015.

137. www.sas.com/content/dam/ SAS/en_us/doc/other1/benefits-brochure.pdf; also see www. sas.com/en_us/news/pressreleases/2014/january/greatworkplace-US-Fortune-2014.html, accessed September 8, 2014.

138. Mark Crowley, "How SAS Became the World's Best Place to Work," www.fastcompany. com/300-4953/how-SAS-became-worlds-best-place-to-work, accessed April 8, 2014.

139. Rebecca Leung, "Working the Good Life," www.CBSnews. com/news/working-the-good-life/, accessed July 17, 2015.

140. Ibid.

141. Ibid.

142. Ibid.

143. Ibid.

144. Mark Crowley, "Not a Happy Accident: How Google Deliberately Designed Workplace Satisfaction," www.fastcompany. com/300-7268/where-are-they-now, accessed April 8, 2014.

145. http://US.Greatrated.com/ Googlean, accessed April 6, 2014.

146. From "Benefits", Google Careers, https://www.google. co.in/about/careers/lifeatgoogle/ benefits/, accessed April 7, 2014. Used by permission from Google Press.

147. Farhad Manjoo, "The Happiness Machine," January 21, 2013, www.slate.com, accessed April 6, 2014.

148. Ibid.; and Greta Roberts, "Why Google's Employee Engagement Programs Are Bad for Your Business," www.talentanalytics. com/blog, accessed April 5, 2014.

149. Manjoo, "The Happiness Machine."

150. Ibid.

151. Ibid.

152. Ibid.

153. Crowley, "Not a Happy Accident: How Google Deliberately Designs Workplace Satisfaction."

154. This is based on Gary Dessler, *Winning Commitment*, New York: McGraw-Hill, 1993, pp. 37–51; "The Federal Express Employee Handbook," August 7, 1989, p. 89; and "FedEx Attributes Success to People-First Philosophy," www.fedex.com/ ma/about/overview/philosophy. html, accessed July 18, 2015.

155. Ibid.

156. Ibid.

157. Ibid.

158. http://www.fedex.com/cz_english/about/overview/philosophy. html, accessed July 14, 2014.

159. "Working at SAS: An Ideal Environment for New Ideas," SAS Web site, April 20, 2012.

Copyright © SAS Institute Inc., Cary, NC, USA. All Rights Reserved. Used with permission.

160. Based on "Theft Is Unethical," *HR Solutions* 34 (October 2002), p. 66.

161. David Gebler, "Is Your Culture a Risk Factor?" *Business and Society Review* 111, no. 3 (Fall 2006), pp. 337–362.

162. John Cohan, "'I Didn't Know' and 'I Was Only Doing My Job': Has Corporate Governance Careened Out of Control? A Case Study of Enron's Information Myopia," *Journal of Business Ethics* 40, no. 3 (October 2002), pp. 275–299.

163. Tony Simons and Quinetta Roberson, "Why Managers Should Care About Fairness: The Effects of Aggregate Justice Perceptions on Organizational Outcomes," *Journal of Applied Psychology* 88, no. 3 (2003), p. 432.

15
Labor Relations and Collective Bargaining

LEARNING OBJECTIVES

15-1 Give a brief history of the American labor movement.

15-2 Discuss the main features of at least three major pieces of labor legislation.

15-3 Present examples of what to expect during the union drive and election.

15-4 Illustrate with examples bargaining that is not in good faith.

15-5 Develop a grievance procedure.

15-6 Describe a strategy for cooperative labor relations.

Some people call Costco "The Anti-Walmart," because Costco treats its workers and unions so well.[1] Whereas Walmart is known for difficult labor relations (it said, for instance, it was eliminating health insurance for future employees working under 24 hours per week),[2] Costco actually keeps profits up in part with positive labor relations policies.[3] We'll see how they do it.

WHERE ARE WE NOW ...

Chapter 14 focused on employee relations, ethics and justice—important issues in determining employees' tendencies to join unions. The main purpose of this chapter is to help you deal effectively with unions and grievances. After briefly discussing the history of the American labor movement, we describe the basic labor law, including unfair labor practices. We explain labor negotiations, including the union actions you can expect during the union campaign and election. And we explain what you can expect during the actual bargaining sessions, and how to handle grievances.

LEARNING OBJECTIVE 15-1

Give a brief history of the American labor movement.

The Labor Movement in the US and India

Today, over 14 million U.S. workers belong to unions—about 11% of the total number of men and women working in America—and another 1.5 million work in places covered by union agreements but don't report being union members.[4] Almost 36% of public-sector workers belong to unions, including heavily unionized occupations such as teachers, police officers, and firefighters. In some private sector industries such as utilities (22.3 % unionization), transportation and warehousing (19.6 percent), and telecommunications (14.8 %), it can still be hard to get jobs without joining unions. And unionization also ranges widely by state, from a high of 24.6% in New York down to 1.9% in North Carolina.[5]

Furthermore, it's a mistake to assume that unions affect employers only negatively. For example, perhaps by professionalizing the staff and/or systematizing practices, heart attack mortality among patients in hospitals with unionized registered nurses was 5% to 9% lower than in nonunion hospitals.[6] Support for unions has always ebbed and flowed in America and India, and today pressures are building against unions. We'll look at unions and dealing with them in this chapter.

Why Do Workers Organize?

Experts have spent much time and money trying to figure out why workers unionize, and they've proposed many theories. Yet there is no simple answer.

It's not just about better pay or working conditions, though these are important. For example, recent median weekly wages for union workers the US was $970, versus $763 for nonunion workers.[7] Union workers also generally receive more holidays, sick leave, unpaid leave, insurance plan benefits, long-term disability benefits, and other benefits.

But it's not just money. The urge to unionize often comes down to the belief on the part of workers that it's only through unity that they can get their fair share of the "pie" and also protect themselves from the arbitrary whims of management. The bottom line is that low morale, fear of job loss, and poor communication (in other words, poor employee relations) also foster unionization. When Kaiser Permanente cut back on vacation and sick leave for its pharmacists, the Guild for Professional Pharmacists won back the lost vacation days. Said one, "Kaiser is a pretty benevolent employer, but there's always the pressure to squeeze a little."[8] One labor relations lawyer says, "The one major thing unions offer is making you a 'for cause' instead of an 'at will' employee, which guarantees a hearing and arbitration if you're fired."[9] So, in practice, low morale, fear of job loss, and arbitrary management actions help foster unionization.

In some respects, things have not changed in decades. Here is how one writer describes the motivation behind the early (1900s) unionization of automobile workers:

In the years to come, economic issues would make the headlines when union and management met in negotiations. But in the early years, … the principal grievances of the autoworkers were the speed-up of production and the lack of any kind of job security. As production tapered off, the order in which workers were laid off was determined largely by the whim of foremen and other supervisors…. Generally, what the workers revolted against was the lack of human dignity and individuality, and a working relationship that was massively impersonal, cold, and nonhuman. They wanted to be treated like human beings—not like faceless clock card numbers.[10]

Making fenders at an early Ford factory in Ypsilanti, Michigan. In addition to heavy physical labor, workers faced health hazards—poor lighting, dust, and dangerous machinery.

Employee Engagement and Unionization

Why else do workers unionize? *Modern Survey* conducted a study that measured items such as employees' interest in being represented by a union, confidence in senior management, and employee engagement. It concluded that 50% of "actively disengaged" employees would vote "yes" to unionization, while only 20% of such employees would vote "no union." It concludes that "paying attention to employee engagement levels within your organization helps to foster positive relationships between employees and management and decreases the likelihood of a workforce seeking union representation."[11]

Gallup conducts its own surveys that complements these conclusions. For example, among the over 500 organizations in which Gallup measures employee engagement, 45% of *non*union employees were engaged, while fewer—38%—of unionized employees were engaged.[12]

Findings like these don't prove that engaged employees are less likely to support a unionization effort in their companies, or that unionized employees are less engaged. The findings are correlational, so they only "prove" that when employee engagement goes up unionization goes down. It could be that the same management policies (such as guaranteed fair treatment systems) affect both employee engagement and non-unionization. But on the whole such findings do suggest that the same sorts of policies (such as good benefits, building trust, and guaranteeing fair treatment) that improve employee engagement may also reduce the likelihood of being unionized.

What Do Unions Want?

We can generalize by saying that unions have two sets of aims, for *union security* and for *improved wages, hours, working conditions*, and *benefits* for their members.

UNION SECURITY First and probably foremost, unions seek security for themselves. They fight hard for the right to represent a firm's workers, and to be the exclusive bargaining agent for all employees in the unit. (As such, they negotiate contracts for all employees, including those not members of the union.) Multiple unions in same firm often end up eroding their bargaining power, and there is always an inter-union rivalries. Employers also experience difficulties while dealing with multiple unions. Five types of union security are possible:

1. **Closed shop**.[13] The company can hire only current union members. In some Indian organizations, jobs like porters are given only to union members. The U.S. Congress outlawed closed shops in interstate commerce, but they still exist in some states for particular industries (such as printing).
2. **Union shop**. The company can hire nonunion people, but they must join the union after a prescribed period and pay dues. (If not, they can be fired.)
3. **Agency shop**. Employees who do not belong to the union still must pay the union an amount equal to union dues (on the assumption that the union's efforts benefit *all* the workers).
4. **Preferential shop**. Union members get preference in hiring, but the employer can still hire nonunion members.
5. **Maintenance of membership arrangement**. Employees do not have to belong to the union. However, union members employed by the firm must maintain membership in the union for the contract period.

Not all states give unions the right to require union membership as a condition of employment. **Right to work** is a term used to describe "state statutory or constitutional provisions banning the requirement of union membership as a condition of employment."[14] *Right-to-work laws* don't outlaw unions. They do outlaw (within those states) any form of union security. In India, the right to work without union membership is constitutionally guaranteed. Recently, in the US, there were 23 right-to-work states.[15] Right to work adversely affects union membership levels.[16]

IMPROVED WAGES, HOURS, AND BENEFITS Once the union ensures its security at the employer, it fights to improve its members' wages, hours, working conditions, and benefits. The typical labor agreement also gives the union a role in other human resource activities, including recruiting, selecting, compensating, promoting, training, and discharging employees.

closed shop
A form of union security in which the company can hire only union members.

union shop
A form of union security in which the company can hire nonunion people, but they must join the union after a prescribed period of time and pay dues. (If they do not, they can be fired.)

agency shop
A form of union security in which employees who do not belong to the union must still pay union dues on the assumption that union efforts benefit all workers.

preferential shop
Union members get preference in hiring, but the employer can still hire nonunion members.

right to work
A term used to describe state statutory or constitutional provisions banning the requirement of union membership as a condition of employment.

The AFL-CIO and the SEIU in the US

The American Federation of Labor and Congress of Industrial Organizations (AFL-CIO) is a voluntary federation of about 57 national and international labor unions in the United States. For many people in the United States, the AFL-CIO is still synonymous with the word *union*.

There are three layers in the AFL-CIO and most other U.S. unions. The worker joins the local union, to which he or she pays dues. The local is in turn a single chapter in the national union. For example, if you were a teacher in Detroit, you would belong to the local union there, which is one of hundreds of local chapters of the American Federation of Teachers, their national union (most unions actually call themselves international unions). The third layer is the national federation, in this case, the AFL-CIO.

The Service Employees International Union (SEIU) is a federation of more than 2.2 million members. It includes the largest health-care union, with more than 1.1 million members, including nurses, LPNs, and doctors, and the second-largest public employees union, with more than 1 million local and state government workers.[17]

Union federation membership is in flux. Some years ago, the SEIU, the International Brotherhood of Teamsters, and UNITE HERE left the AFL-CIO and established their own federation, called the Change to Win Coalition. Together, the departing unions represented over a quarter of the AFL-CIO's membership and budget. Change to Win plans to be more aggressive about organizing workers than they say the AFL-CIO was.[18] Then the UNITE HERE union left Change to Win and rejoined the AFL-CIO.

Unions And The Law: As in the US and India

The history of the American labor movement is one of expansion and contraction in response to public policy changes. Until about 1930, there were no special labor laws. Employers were not required to engage in collective bargaining with employees and were virtually unrestrained in their behavior toward unions; the use of spies and firing of union agitators were widespread. "Yellow dog" contracts, whereby management could require nonunion membership as a condition for employment, were widely enforced. Most union weapons—even strikes—were illegal.

> **LEARNING OBJECTIVE 15-2**
>
> Discuss the main features of labor legislation in USA and history of unions in India.

This situation lasted until the Great Depression (around 1930).[19] Since then, in response to changing public attitudes and economic conditions, labor law has gone through three clear periods: from "strong encouragement" of unions, to "modified encouragement coupled with regulation," and finally to "detailed regulation of internal union affairs."[20]

UNFAIR EMPLOYER LABOR PRACTICES The Wagner Act deemed "statutory wrongs" (but not crimes) five unfair labor practices used by employers:

1. It is unfair for employers to "interfere with, restrain, or coerce employees" in exercising their legally sanctioned right of self-organization.
2. It is unfair for company representatives to dominate or interfere with either the formation or the administration of labor unions. Among other specific management actions found to be unfair under these first two practices are bribing employees, using company spy systems, moving a business to avoid unionization, and blacklisting union sympathizers.
3. Employers are prohibited from discriminating in any way against employees for their legal union activities.
4. Employers are forbidden to discharge or discriminate against employees simply because the latter file unfair practice charges against the company.
5. Finally, it is an unfair labor practice for employers to refuse to bargain collectively with their employees' duly chosen representatives.

FROM 1935 TO 1947 Union membership increased quickly after passage of the Wagner Act. Other factors such as an improving economy and aggressive union leadership contributed to this rise. But by the mid-1940s, largely due to massive postwar strikes, public policy began to shift against what many viewed as union excesses. The stage was set for passage of the Taft-Hartley Act.

Period of Modified Encouragement Coupled with Regulation: The Taft-Hartley Act (1947)

Taft-Hartley Act of 1947

Also known as the *Labor Management Relations Act*, this law prohibited unfair union labor practices and enumerated the rights of employees as union members. It also enumerated the rights of employers.

The **Taft-Hartley** *(or Labor Management Relations)* **Act of 1947** reflected the public's less enthusiastic attitude toward unions. It amended the National Labor Relations (Wagner) Act by limiting unions in four ways: (1) prohibiting unfair union labor practices, (2) enumerating the rights of employees as union members, (3) enumerating the rights of employers, and (4) allowing the president of the United States to bar temporarily national emergency strikes.

Unfair Union Labor Practices

The Taft-Hartley Act enumerated several labor practices that unions were prohibited from engaging in:

1. First, it banned *unions* from *restraining or coercing employees* from exercising their guaranteed bargaining rights. (Some union actions that courts have held illegal include telling an anti-union employee that he or she will lose his or her job once the union gains recognition, and issuing patently false statements during union organizing campaigns.)
2. It is also an unfair labor practice for a union to *cause an employer to discriminate* in any way against an employee so as to encourage or discourage his or her union membership. For example, the union cannot try to force an employer to fire a worker because he or she doesn't attend union meetings or refuses to join a union. There is one exception: Suppose a closed or union shop prevails (and union membership is therefore a prerequisite to employment). Then the union may demand the discharge of someone who fails to pay his or her initiation fees and dues.
3. It is an unfair labor practice for a union to *refuse to bargain in good faith* with the employer about wages, hours, and other employment conditions.
4. It is an unfair labor practice for a union to engage in *featherbedding* (requiring an employer to pay an employee for services not performed).

RIGHTS OF EMPLOYEES The Taft-Hartley Act protected the rights of employees against their unions in other ways. For example, many people felt that compulsory unionism violated the right of freedom of association. Legitimized by Taft-Hartley, new right-to-work laws sprung up in 19 (now 23) states (mainly in the South and Southwest). In New York, for example, in many printing firms you can't work as a press operator unless you belong to a printers' union. In Florida, a right-to-work state, printing shops typically employ both union and nonunion operators. Even today, union membership varies widely by state, from a high of 26.8% in New York to a low of 3.2% in North Carolina.[21] The Taft-Hartley act also required the employee's authorization before the union could subtract dues from his or her paycheck.

In general, the Labor Relations (Taft-Hartley) Act does not restrain unions from unfair labor practices to the extent that the law does employers. It says unions may not restrain or coerce employees. However, "violent or otherwise threatening behavior or clearly coercive or intimidating union activities are necessary before the NLRB will find an unfair labor practice."[22] Examples include physical assaults or threats, economic reprisals, and mass picketing that restrains lawful entry or leaving.

RIGHTS OF EMPLOYERS IN THE US The Taft-Hartley Act also explicitly gave *employers* certain rights. First, it gave them full freedom to express their views concerning union organization. For example, as a manager you can tell your employees that in your opinion unions are worthless, dangerous to the economy, and immoral. You can even (generally) hint that unionization and high-wage demands might result in the permanent closing of the plant (but not its relocation). Employers can set forth the union's record concerning violence and corruption, if appropriate. In fact, the only major restraint is that employers must avoid threats, promises, coercion, and direct interference with workers who are trying to reach a decision. There can be no threat of reprisal or force or promise of benefit.[23]

Furthermore, the employer (1) cannot meet with employees on company time within 24 hours of an election or (2) suggest to employees that they vote against the union while they are at home or in the employer's office (although he or she can do so while in their work area or where they normally gather).

A Brief History of Union Movement in India

The Indian labor movement is more than 150 years old, with its origin in the 1850s. But it gained momentum in 1918, when the Madras Labor Union was formed with mill-workers as members. A series of protests and strikes were organized, leading to the formation of All India Trade Union Congress (AITUC) in 1920, which gave a fillip to the organized labor movement in India. The early years were turbulent, with a series of agitations and strikes in different parts of the country. The focus of the unions was to end exploitation of workers in factories and other workplaces like mines. Trade unions also participated in the freedom struggle against the colonial rule. National leaders like Mahatma Gandhi were active in the trade union movement. The introduction of Trade Union (TU) Act of 1926 provided the required legal framework for unions. The TU Act also provided immunity from civil suits and criminal prosecutions. It also allowed any seven members to register a union and also allowed external leadership. Both the above provisions have been criticized later. The legislations were also silent about the recognition of trade union as a representative of worker by the employer.

The changes in the political landscape of India resulted in the AITUC splitting into Indian National Trade Union Congress (INTUC) in 1947, followed by the formation of Hindustan Mazdoor Sabha (HMS) in 1948. Subsequent political events like the split in the Indian National Congress and the Communist Party also resulted in formation of corresponding unions. Thus, in India, politically affiliated unions became a feature, and many trade union leaders got elected to the parliament or state assemblies and even became ministers. The election of communist government in states like Kerala and West Bengal gave a fillip to the labor movement in these states. The economic planning model of Five Year Plans and the import substitution model led to the creation of public sector, under which unions thrived. It also led to the growth of private sector.

With the support of political parties and elected governments, the public sector and many private companies, particularly in manufacturing and services, became heavily unionized. What followed in the 1960s and 1970s was a rise in trade union activity leading to strikes and lockouts. The imposition of Emergency in 1975 led to the suspension of trade union rights, leading to a sudden fall in trade union activity (many prominent opposition trade union leaders were jailed during the emergency period); however, union activities picked up after the Emergency was lifted. Under pressure from trade unions, in 1976, the Industrial Disputes Act was amended making it mandatory for firms employing more than 300 workmen to take prior government permission before retrenching.

The failure of the Bombay Textile Strike (1981–1983) led by an independent trade union leader, Dutta Samant, marked another shift in labor unions in the country. The strike was initiated in a small scale over the issue of wages soon embraced the entire industry, but it failed to achieve its purpose. Thus, nonpolitical unions focusing on members' requirements without any political stance became a reality in India. In many places, they competed with traditional politically supported unions. Another significant event during the same time (1980–81) was the large PSU strike in Bangalore.

With the first wave of partial economic liberalization in 1984, the approach of unions also started to change. By that time, the profile of their members also changed with more workers wanting better living conditions, rather than those subscribing to a political ideology. Private sector unions became increasingly open to productivity-linked agreements that were later accepted by the public sector unions as well. The powerful banking sector trade unions allowed the introduction of computers on a limited scale. Though the unions extracted a price for this in terms of extra payment, their strength and ability to call for an industrial action started to diminish.

Soon both the employers and unions realized the need to achieve productivity gains and to maintain healthy bottom-line. They also understood the effects of competition and market forces. The focus also shifted from just increasing output to building a positive work culture and enhancing skills. In many firms, management and unions worked together to build better work culture and share the gains. There was a marked shift towards adopting a collaborative approach rather than a confrontationist one.

The next phase of economic reforms was introduced in 1992. These reforms focused on opening of the economy and its integration with global economic forces. Privatization of state-owned enterprises and closing down of unviable ones were part of the reform package. The voluntary retirement scheme (VRS) became a legal option for firms to separate excess employees on mutual agreement. The national renewal fund (NRF) was established to help firms adjust to the realities of this new economy. At present, many traditional unions, both in the public and private sectors, have recognized the significance of market forces and competition, and are prepared to work with the management to increase competitiveness. While the industry and investors demanded reforming the labor laws to introduce more flexibility and the right to hire and fire, due to opposition from national unions, much progress could not be made.

The emerging new-generation IT/ITES sector did not have labor union activity. The career and professional growth focused employees showed antipathy toward unions, and their employers went ahead to ensure good work conditions. Union of Information Technology Professionals (UNITES Pro.), based in Bengaluru, has been campaigning for employee rights in this sector, but its acceptance levels are low. However, in recent times, the rising job insecurity in the IT/ITES sector has changed the outlook of knowledge workers, who are generally non-inclined to unions and its methods of asserting for rights. Confronted with withdrawal of job offers, the prospective employees of Satyam Computers attempted unionization.[24] Non-union firms have also become a norm in the traditionally unionized sectors like manufacturing and services (e.g., the new private banks are completely trade-union free). These non-union firms employ lesser number of blue-collar workers, outsource many such activities, relocate their operations, and practice innovative people management practices. In some cases, maintaining non-union status is made a part of the performance goals of the HR team.

The marginalization of mainstream trade unions and the rising insecurity of jobs, lead to backlashes in many firms. Between 2009 and now, there has been increasing incidents of strikes and agitations, including efforts from employees to unionize in many private companies and MNCs. Employees of HMSI and Rico Motors went on a strike demanding, among others, the right to unionize, and there were incidents of violence associated with the strike. During the same period, the ground staff and cabin crew of Jet Airways went on a strike after many of them were removed from jobs citing economic difficulties. Jet Airways' pilots also protested against the sacking of two senior pilots. In the case of Pricol Industries Coimbatore and Maruti Suzuki India, senior executives were unfortunate victims of violent unions. A few similar incidents happening across India, have invited the attention to the increasing cases of union militancy in some pockets and sectors.

Formal trade unions have traditionally stayed away from actively organizing the non-formal sector, which provides employment to a large section of the Indian population. States like Kerala or West Bengal are exceptions, as they have strong leftist political activity at the grass-roots level. Recently, the Self Employed Women's Association (SEWA), which works to organize informal sector workers, mostly women, has been given the status of a central trade union. The recognition will help SEWA raise issues of informal sector work at the national stage.

LABOR LAW TODAY   As we'll see toward the end of this chapter, it isn't quite clear whether the pressures toward a more encouraging or a more discouraging climate for labor law will prevail for the next few years. On the one hand, we'll see that unions are pushing for new legislation that would substantially improve unions' efforts. On the other hand, economic realities (shrinking state budgets, for instance) have undoubtedly reduced union membership.[25] At present, the Indian government has initiated steps to rationalize the labor laws and consolidate them to four major labor codes (discussed in Chapter 2).

The Union Drive and Election: The U.S. experience

It is through the union drive and election that a union tries to be recognized to represent employees. To protect themselves and their employers, supervisors need to understand this process. It has five basic steps.[26]

LEARNING OBJECTIVE 15-3

Present examples of what to expect during the union drive and election.

Step 1. Initial Contact

During the initial contact stage, the union determines the employees' interest in organizing, and establishes an organizing committee.

The initiative for the first contact between the employees and the union may come from the employees, from a union already representing other employees of the firm, or from another union. In any case, there is an initial contact.

Once an employer becomes a target, a union official usually assigns a representative to assess employee interest. The representative visits the firm to determine if enough employees are interested in a campaign, identifies employees who would make good leaders in the organizing campaign, and creates an organizing committee. The aim is to educate the committee about the benefits of forming a union and the law and procedures for forming a local union.

The union must follow certain rules when it starts contacting employees. The law allows organizers to solicit employees for membership as long as the effort doesn't endanger the performance or safety of the employees. Therefore, much contact takes place off the job, perhaps at home or at places near work. Organizers can also safely contact employees on company grounds during off hours (such as lunch or break time). Yet, in practice, there will be much informal organizing going on at the workplace as employees debate organizing. Sometimes the first inkling management has is the distribution of handbills soliciting union membership.

LABOR RELATIONS CONSULTANTS   Both management and unions typically use "labor relations consultants." These may be law firms, researchers, psychologists, labor relations specialists, or public relations firms. Some are former union organizers.[27]

For the employer, the consultant's services may range from ensuring that the firm properly fills out routine labor relations forms to managing the union campaign. Unions may use public relations firms to improve their image, or specialists to manage corporate campaigns. (These pressure shareholders and creditors to get management to agree to the union's demands.)

union salting
A union organizing tactic by which workers who are in fact employed full-time by a union as undercover organizers are hired by unwitting employers.

UNION SALTING   Unions are not without creative ways to win elections. In the US, the National Labor Relations Board defines **union salting** as "placing of union members on nonunion job sites for the purpose of organizing." Critics claim that "salts" interfere with business operations and harass employees.[28] The solution is to know whom you're hiring. However, not hiring someone solely because he or she might be pro-union or a union salt, but otherwise qualified would be discriminatory, and the company might lose a good employee.[29]

Step 2. Obtaining Authorization Cards

For the union to petition the company for the right to hold an election, it must show that a sizable number of employees may be interested in organizing. Therefore, the next step for union organizers is to try to get the employees to sign **authorization cards**. Signatures of minimum number of employees, among other things, usually authorize the union to seek a representation election and state that the employee has applied to join the union.

This is a challenging time for supervisors. During this stage, both union and management use propaganda. The union claims it can improve working conditions, raise wages, increase benefits, and generally get the workers better deals. Management can attack the union on ethical and moral grounds and cite the cost of union membership. Management can also explain its accomplishments, express facts and opinions, and explain the law applicable to organizing campaigns. However, neither side can threaten, bribe, or coerce employees. And an employer (or supervisor) may not make promises of benefits to employees or make unilateral changes in terms and conditions of employment that were not planned to be implemented prior to the onset of union organizing activity.

STEPS TO TAKE   Management can take several steps with respect to union formation. Some employers welcome it, but many look at it with suspicion. However, Indian workers have the right to register their trade union, as per the provisions of Trade Union Act of 1926.

Similarly, it is an unfair labor practice to tell employees they can't sign a card. What you *can* do is prepare supervisors so they can explain what the card actually authorizes the union to do—including subjecting the employee to union rules. The union, for instance, may force the employee to picket and fine any member who does not comply. Such explanations can be an effective weapon.

One thing managers should *not* do is look through signed authorization cards if confronted with them by union representatives. The NLRB in the US could construe that as an unfair labor practice, as spying on those who signed. Doing so could also later form the basis of a charge alleging discrimination due to union activity, if the firm subsequently disciplines someone who signed a card.

In the US, during this stage, unions can picket the company, subject to three constraints: (1) The union must file a petition for an election within 30 days after the start of picketing; (2) the firm cannot already be lawfully recognizing another union; and (3) there cannot have been a valid NLRB election during the past 12 months.

Step 3. Hold a Hearing

Once the union collects the authorization cards, one of three things can occur. If the employer chooses *not to contest union recognition* at all, then the parties need no hearing, and a special "consent election" is held. If the employer chooses not to contest the union's *right to an election*, and/or the scope of the bargaining unit, and/or which employees are eligible to vote in the election, no hearing is needed and the parties can stipulate an election. If an employer *does* wish to contest the union's right, it can insist on a hearing to determine those issues. An employer's decision about whether to insist on a hearing is a strategic one. Management bases it on the facts of each case, and on whether it feels it needs more time to try to persuade employees not to elect a union.

Most companies do contest the union's right to represent their employees, claiming that a significant number don't really want the union. It is at this point that the NLRB gets involved. The union usually contacts the NLRB, which requests a hearing. It then sends a hearing officer to investigate. The examiner sends both management and union a notice of representation hearing (NLRB Form 852) that states the time and place of the hearing.

The hearing addresses several issues. First, does the record indicate there is enough evidence to hold an election? (For example, did 30% or more of the employees in an appropriate bargaining unit sign the authorization cards?) Second, the examiner decides what the bargaining unit will be. The **bargaining unit** is the group of employees that the union will be authorized to represent and bargain for collectively. If the entire organization is the bargaining unit, the union will represent all nonsupervisory, nonmanagerial, and nonconfidential employees, even though the union may be oriented mostly toward blue-collar workers. (Professional and nonprofessional employees can be included in the same bargaining unit only if the professionals agree.) If your firm disagrees with the examiner's bargaining unit decision, it can challenge the decision. This will require a separate NLRB ruling.

bargaining unit
The group of employees the union will be authorized to represent.

The NLRB hearing addresses other issues. These include, "Does the employer qualify for coverage by the NLRB?" and "Is the union a labor organization within the meaning of the National Labor Relations Act?"

If the results of the hearing are favorable for the union, the NLRB will order holding an election. It will issue a Notice of Election (NLRB Form 707) to that effect for the employer to post.

Step 4. The Campaign

During the campaign that precedes the election, union and employer appeal to employees for their votes. The union will emphasize that it will prevent unfairness, set up grievance and seniority systems, and improve wages. Union strength, they'll say, will give employees a greater voice in disciplinary matters and in determining wages and working conditions. Management will stress that improvements like those don't require unions and that wages are equal to or better than with a union. Management will also emphasize the cost of union dues; the fact that the union is an "outsider"; and that if the union wins, a strike may follow. It can even attack the union on ethical and moral grounds, while insisting that employees will not be as well off and may lose freedom. But neither side can threaten, bribe, or coerce employees.

Step 5. The Election

The election occurs within 30 to 60 days after the NLRB issues its Decision and Direction of Election. The election is by secret ballot; the NLRB provides the ballots, voting booth, and ballot box; counts the votes; and certifies the results.

The union becomes the employees' representative if it wins the election, and winning means getting a majority of the votes *cast*, not a majority of the total workers in the bargaining unit. (Also keep in mind that if an employer commits an unfair labor practice, the NLRB may reverse a "no union" election. Supervisors must therefore be careful not to commit unfair practices.)

Several things influence whether the union wins the certification election. Unions have a higher probability of success in geographic areas with a higher percentage of union workers. High unemployment seems to lead to poorer results for the union, perhaps because employees fear that unionization efforts might result in reduced job security or employer retaliation. Unions usually carefully pick the size of their bargaining unit (all clerical employees in the company, only those at one facility, and so on) because the larger the bargaining unit, the smaller the probability of union victory. The more workers vote, the less likely a union victory, probably because more workers who are not strong supporters vote.

Evidence-Based HR: What to Expect the Union to Do to Win the Election

The other side of the coin is this: What can unions do to boost their chances they'll win the election? A researcher analyzed data from 261 NLRB elections. She found that the best way for unions to win is a "rank-and-file strategy." It includes union tactics such as the following:[30]

1. "Reliance on a slow, underground, person-to-person campaign using house calls, small group meetings, and pre-union associations to develop leadership and union commitment, and prepare workers for employer anti-union strategies before the employer becomes aware of the campaign."
2. The union will focus on building active rank-and-file participation, including an organizing committee reflecting the different interest groups in the bargaining unit.
3. The union will press for a first contract early in the organizing process.
4. The union will use "inside and outside pressure tactics to build worker commitment and compel the employer to run a fair campaign."
5. There will be an emphasis during the organizing campaign on issues such as respect, dignity, and fairness, not just traditional bread-and-butter issues like wages.

The Supervisor's Role

Target recently won a unionization election at a New York store, but a U.S. federal judge overturned it and required a new election. The judge found that Target managers had violated labor law by telling employees they couldn't wear union buttons or distribute flyers, and by threatening to discipline workers who discussed union matters.[31]

Supervisors are an employer's first line of defense in the unionizing effort. They are often in the best position to sense employee attitude problems, and to discover the first signs of union activity. However, supervisors can also inadvertently undermine their employer's union efforts.

For example, one plant superintendent reacted to a union's initial organizing attempt by prohibiting distribution of union literature in the plant's lunchroom. Since solicitation of off-duty workers in nonwork areas is generally legal, the company subsequently allowed the union to post literature on the company's bulletin board and to distribute literature in nonworking areas inside the plant. However, the NLRB still ruled that the initial act of prohibiting distribution of the literature was an unfair labor practice, one not "made right" by the company's subsequent efforts. The NLRB used the superintendent's action as one reason for invalidating an election that the company had won.[32] (Today certain "supervisors" may no longer be excluded from the bargaining unit. The employer could trigger an unfair labor practice charge if it tries to use those people to assist in its campaign.)[33]

SOME TIPS   Supervisors can use the acronym TIPS to remember what *not* to do during the campaigns.[34] *Do not* Threaten, Interrogate, make Promises to, or Spy on employees (for instance, do not threaten that you will close or move the business, cut wages, reduce overtime, or lay off employees). FORE outlines what you may do. *You may* give employees Facts (like what signing the authorization card means), express your Opinion about unions, explain factually correct Rules (such as that the law permits permanently replacing striking employees), and share your Experiences about unions. The Know Your Employment Law feature expands on this.

Decertification Elections: Ousting the Union

The lifespan of a union at any organization is not merely determined by its ability to win favor with the employees and subsequently the elections. In the US, the same law that grants employees the right to unionize has also made provisions for certain ways in which they may terminate legally (in other words, 'decertify') their union's right to represent them. In India, Section 10 of the Trade Unions Act, 1926, specifies that the registrar of trade unions can withdraw or cancel registration of trade unions in specific circumstances. These circumstances are obtaining certificate by fraud or mistake, the union not following the law, or if membership falls below the requisite numbers. A point to note here is that, in India, registration of unions and its recognition as bargaining agent are separate.

It is interesting to note that decertification campaigns are similar to certification campaigns with respect to several aspects like organization of membership meetings by the union, house-to-house visits, mailing literature into homes, usage of mediums such as phone calls, e-mails, and (sometimes) even threats so as to win the election.

Against the backdrop of globalization, the entire matter of employer's challenges with respect to the unions is more complicated.

▶ **IMPROVING PERFORMANCE:** *HR Practices Around The Globe*

France Comes to the Workers' Aid

Employers planning to expand abroad should ponder the recent experience of drug maker Sanofi SA, in France. Because of the relatively high cost of running its research facility in southwestern France, Sanofi told its researchers there it was closing their facility.[35] Employees began staging weekly protests, supported by the French government, which opposes profitable companies slashing jobs. After 9 months, the company was still waiting for a government report on the situation so it could finish negotiating with its unions and try to get some of them other jobs elsewhere. As one Sanofi manager said, "In France, the politics, the labor laws are extremely different than in any other regions…. It means that for sites like Toulouse … anything you want to do differently gets to be a confrontational issue."[36] ■

Source: Based on Nick Wingfield and Melissa Eddy, "In Germany, Union Culture Clashes with Amazons' Labor Practices," New York Times, August 5, 2013, pp. B1, B4.

The Collective Bargaining Process

Once a union is formed to represent employees at a company or an institute, the first step towards a collaborative effort between the management and labor is when they meet to discuss a labor agreement. Containing specific provisions which discuss aspects pertaining to wages, work hours, and working conditions, the agreement is formed as a result of discussions and negotiations between the management and the union–a process which is known as collective bargaining.

While the Supreme Court defines it as "the technique by which dispute as to conditions of employment is resolved amicably by agreement rather than by coercion," the National Labor Relations Act states: "For the purpose of (this act) to bargain collectively is the performance of the mutual obligation of the employer and the representative of the employees to meet at reasonable times and confer in good faith with respect to wages, hours, and terms and conditions of employment, or the negotiation of an agreement, or any question arising thereunder and the execution of a written contract incorporating any agreement reached if requested by either party, but such obligation does not compel either party to agree to a proposal or require the making of a concession." Simply put, both the management and labor are required by the law to negotiate wage, working hours, and working conditions in "good faith".

What Is Good Faith?

Good faith bargaining is the cornerstone of effective labor–management relations. It implies that both parties can communicate and negotiate, match proposals with counterproposals, and make a reasonable effort to arrive at an agreement; and it does not mean that any of the parties is compelled to agree with the other or that either party make any specific concessions (although some may be deemed as necessary to arrive at a favorable conclusion). In order to gauge whether the bargaining is in "good faith" or not, certain instances that can be looked at are as follows:

Surface bargaining Going through the motions of bargaining without any real intention of completing an agreement.

Inadequate concessions Unwillingness to compromise.

Inadequate proposals and demands The advancement of proposals to be a positive factor in determining overall good faith.

Dilatory tactics Good CB requires that the parties meet and "confer at reasonable times and intervals." Obviously, refusal to meet with the union does not satisfy the positive duty imposed on the employer.

Imposing conditions Attempts to impose conditions that are so onerous or unreasonable so as to indicate bad faith.

Making unilateral changes in conditions This is a strong indication that the employer or union is not bargaining with the required intent of reaching an agreement.

A History of Collective Bargaining in India

Sydney Webb and Beatric Webb e had coined the term collective bargaining (1891) after which it was widely accepted in the US and other countries, including India, as a conduit for settling industrial disputes, thereby conferring upon the US the title of "motherland of collective bargaining". Against the backdrop of the Indian economy, however, collective bargaining represents a more recent phenomenon. The Supreme Court of India has defined collective bargaining as the technique by which dispute as to conditions of employment is resolved amicably rather than coercion.[37]

Despite the fact that the very First Five-Year Plan in India identified the need for collective bargaining in order to resolve labor disputes as well as maintain a peaceful industrial environment across the nation, the laws regarding this were not structured enough. The Second Five-Year Plan saw an increasing amount of concern with respect to this matter as industrial peace came to be regarded as "indispensable for the development of an undertaking or an industry". The issue was addressed with the same zeal in the Third Five-Year Plan wherein the focus lay on "the adoption of voluntary arbitrations in the place of compulsory adjudication". Furthermore, the Fourth Five-Year Plan drew upon the need for collective bargaining amidst a stronger trade union scenario in the country.

However, it was only with the formation of the National Commission on Labor in 1966 that the need for collective bargaining in India actually came to the forefront. Indulging in extensive investigations regarding the plethora of labor issues across the nation, a series of recommendations were made to make collective bargaining a more effective endeavor in the future. Even after these efforts, the scenario of collective bargaining could not make much headway due to various factors such as lack of strong trade unions and willingness of employer's organizations for the process to unfold smoothly, union-rivalry due to the multiplicity of trade unions, and inclination towards compulsory adjudication as opposed to the system of voluntary arbitration that had been initially proposed.

The Negotiating Team

Both union and management send negotiating teams to the bargaining table, and both go into the bargaining sessions having "done their homework."

First, they acquire data on which to build their bargaining positions.[38] From compensation surveys they compile data on pay and benefits, including comparisons with local pay rates and to rates for similar jobs in the industry. Data on the distribution of the workforce (in terms of age, sex, and seniority, for instance) are important, because it determines benefits. Internal economic data regarding benefits, earnings, and the cost of overtime are important too. Union representatives will have sounded out union members on their desires and conferred with representatives of related unions.

Management will also "cost" the current labor contract and determine the increased cost—total, per employee, and per hour—of the union's demands. It will use information from grievances and feedback from supervisors to determine what the union's demands might be, and prepare counteroffers and arguments.[39] Other popular tactics include attitude surveys to test employee reactions to various sections of the contract that management may feel require change, and informal conferences with local union leaders to discuss the operational effectiveness of the contract and to send up trial balloons on management ideas for change.

Costing the Contract

Collective bargaining experts emphasize the need to cost the union's demands carefully. One says,

> The mistake I see most often is [HR professionals who] enter the negotiations without understanding the financial impact of things they put on the table. For example, the union wants three extra vacation days. That doesn't sound like a lot, except that in some states, if an employee leaves, you have to pay them for unused vacation time. [So] now your employer has to carry that liability on their books at all times.[40]

Bargaining Items

Labor law sets out categories of specific items that are subject to bargaining: These are mandatory, voluntary, and illegal items.

Voluntary (or permissible) bargaining items are neither mandatory nor illegal; they become a part of negotiations only through the joint agreement of both management and union. Neither party can compel the other to negotiate over voluntary items. You cannot hold up signing a contract because the other party refuses to bargain on a voluntary item, such as benefits for retirees.

Illegal bargaining items are forbidden by law. A clause agreeing to hire union members exclusively would be illegal in a right-to-work context, for example.

Building Negotiating Skills

Hammering out a satisfactory labor agreement requires negotiating skills. Experienced negotiators use *leverage, desire, time, competition, information, credibility*, and *judgment* to improve their bargaining positions.[41] Things you can *leverage* include *necessity, desire, competition*, and *time*.[42] For example, the union knows that an employer who must fill a big order fast (*necessity*) is at a disadvantage.

Similarly, the employer who makes its *desires* too obvious undercuts its position. *Competition* is important too. There is no more convincing ploy than subtly hinting you've got an alternative (like shifting services abroad). *Time* (particularly deadlines) can also tilt things for or against you.

"Knowledge is power" when negotiating, so having *information* is advantageous, as is *credibility*. Finally, good negotiators need *judgment:* the ability to "strike the right balance between gaining advantages and reaching compromises, in the substance as well as in the style of [their] negotiating technique."[43]

Bargaining Hints

Expert Reed Richardson has the following advice for bargainers:

1. Be sure to set clear objectives for every bargaining item, and be sure you understand the reason for each.
2. Do not hurry.
3. When in doubt, caucus with your associates.
4. Be well prepared with firm data supporting your position.
5. Strive to keep some flexibility in your position.
6. Don't concern yourself just with what the other party says and does; find out why.
7. Respect the importance of face saving for the other party.
8. Be alert to the real intentions of the other party—not only for goals, but also for priorities.
9. Be a good listener.
10. Build a reputation for being fair but firm.

---

voluntary (or permissible) bargaining items
Items in collective bargaining over which bargaining is neither illegal nor mandatory—neither party can be compelled against its wishes to negotiate over those items.

illegal bargaining items
Items in collective bargaining that are forbidden by law; for example, a clause agreeing to hire "union members exclusively" would be illegal in a right-to-work state.

mandatory bargaining items
Items in collective bargaining that a party must bargain over if they are introduced by the other party—for example, pay.

11. Learn to control your emotions and use them as a tool.
12. As you make each bargaining move, be sure you know its relationship to all other moves.
13. Measure each move against your objectives.
14. Remember that collective bargaining is a compromise process. There is no such thing as having all the pie.
15. Try to understand the people and their personalities.[44]
16. Remember that excessive bargainer transparency and openness can backfire.[45]

Impasses, Mediation, and Strikes

In collective bargaining, an **impasse** (or stalemate) occurs when the parties are not able to move further toward settlement. While unions may threaten to strike work or even declare a strike, management may counter it with lockout. Both are legal in India (as per the Industrial Disputes Act of 1947) and are subject to conditions prescribed by the law. This usually occurs because one party is demanding more than the other will offer. Sometimes a third party, such as a mediator or a conciliator who receives a notice for strike (Section 4 of the ID Act, 1947) can resolve an impasse. Alternatively, the central or state government can appoint a Board of Conciliation with equal representation from both sides (Section 5 of the ID Act, 1947). While the conciliation is in progress, no strikes or lockouts can be enforced. If the impasse is not resolved, the union may call a work stoppage, or strike.[46]

THIRD-PARTY INVOLVEMENT   Negotiators use three types of third-party interventions to overcome an impasse. With **mediation**, a neutral third party tries to assist the principals in reaching agreement. The mediator meets with each party to determine where each stands, and then uses this information to find common ground for bargaining. When Hostess Brands couldn't reach agreement with its unions, its bankruptcy judge had them join him for a mediation session, where he tried (unsuccessfully) to broker a new contract.[47]

In certain situations, as in a national emergency dispute, a **fact finder** is a neutral party who studies the issues in a dispute and makes a public recommendation for a reasonable settlement.[48] Presidential emergency fact-finding boards resolved impasses in certain critical transportation disputes.

Arbitration is the most definitive third-party intervention, because the arbitrator may have the power to determine and dictate the settlement terms. With *binding arbitration*, both parties are committed to accepting the arbitrator's award. With *non-binding arbitration*, they are not. Arbitration may also be voluntary or compulsory (imposed by a government agency). In the United States, voluntary binding arbitration is the most prevalent.

There are two main topics of arbitration. **Interest arbitration** centers on working out a labor agreement; the parties use it when such agreements do not yet exist or when one or both parties are seeking to change the agreement. **Rights arbitration** really means "contract interpretation arbitration." It usually involves interpreting existing contract terms, for instance, when an employee questions the employer's right to have taken some disciplinary action.[49]

SOURCES OF THIRD-PARTY ASSISTANCE   Various public and professional agencies make arbitrators and mediators available. For example, the American Arbitration Association (AAA) represents and provides the services of thousands of arbitrators and mediators to employers and unions. The U.S. government's Federal Mediation and Conciliation Service provides both arbitrators and mediators.[50] In addition, most states provide arbitrator and mediation services.

STRIKES   A **strike** is a withdrawal of labor. The Industrial Disputes Act of 1947 defines strike as "cessation of work by a body of persons employed in any industry acting in combination, or a concerted refusal, under a common understanding of any number of persons who are or have been so employed to work or accept employment [Section 2 (q)]."

impasse
Collective bargaining situation that occurs when the parties are not able to move further toward settlement, usually because one party is demanding more than the other will offer.

mediation
Intervention in which a neutral third party tries to assist the principals in reaching agreement.

fact finder
A neutral party who studies the issues in a dispute and makes a public recommendation for a reasonable settlement.

arbitration
The most definitive type of third-party intervention, in which the arbitrator usually has the power to determine and dictate the settlement terms.

interest arbitration
Arbitration enacted when labor agreements do not yet exist or when one or both parties are seeking to change the agreement.

rights arbitration
Arbitration that interprets existing contract terms, for instance, when an employee questions the employer's right to have taken some disciplinary action.

strike
A withdrawal of labor.

economic strike
A strike that results from a failure to agree on the terms of a contract that involves wages, benefits, and other conditions of employment.

unfair labor practice strike
A strike aimed at protesting illegal conduct by the employer.

wildcat strike
An unauthorized strike occurring during the term of a contract.

sympathy strike
A strike that takes place when one union strikes in support of the strike of another.

picketing
Having employees carry signs announcing their concerns near the employer's place of business.

corporate campaign
An organized effort by the union that exerts pressure on the corporation by pressuring the company's other unions, shareholders, directors, customers, creditors, and government agencies, often directly.

boycott
The combined refusal by employees and other interested parties to buy or use the employer's products.

The law [Section 22 (1)] also places restrictions on strike for public service employees giving six weeks notice, and not striking work within 14 days of giving notice and striking while conciliation proceedings are in progress before conciliation officer or seven days after conclusion of proceedings. There are four main types of strikes. An **economic strike** results from a failure to agree on the terms of a contract. Unions call **unfair labor practice strikes** to protest illegal conduct by the employer. A **wildcat strike** is an unauthorized strike occurring during the term of a contract. A **sympathy strike** occurs when one union strikes in support of the strike of another union.[51]

The likelihood of and severity of a strike depend partly on the parties' willingness to "take a strike."[52]

Picketing, or having employees carry signs announcing their concerns near the employer's place of business, is one of the first activities to appear during a strike. Its purpose is to inform the public about the existence of the labor dispute and often to encourage them to refrain from doing business with the struck employer.

Employers sometimes choose several options when employees strike. However, in India, the question about legality of action has to be decided by thecourts. One is to temporarily shut down the affected area and halt operations. A second is to contract out work to blunt the effects of the strike. A third is to continue operations, perhaps using supervisors and other nonstriking workers. A fourth alternative is hiring replacements for the strikers.

Diminished union influence plus competitive pressures now prompt more employers to replace (or consider replacing) strikers with permanent replacement workers. When the United Steel Workers struck refineries recently, BP quickly began training replacement workers.[53] And in a labor dispute a few years ago, the NFL implied even they might use replacement players.[54]

OTHER "WEAPONS" Management and labor each have other weapons to break an impasse. The union, for example, may resort to a corporate campaign. A **corporate or public campaign** is an organized effort by the union to exert pressure on the employer by pressuring the company's other unions, shareholders, corporate directors, customers, creditors, and government agencies.[55] Thus, the union might surprise members of the board of directors by picketing their homes and organizing a **boycott** of the company's banks or other collaborators.[56]

TRENDS SHAPING HR: *DIGITAL AND SOCIAL MEDIA*

UNIONS GO DIGITAL When it comes to organizing just about any sort of campaign, communication is king, a fact that hasn't been lost on unions. For example, in one survey, 49% of unions said they used Facebook to communicate with members and employees, 23% used Twitter, and 13% used YouTube.[57] About 92% of unions have a Web site, while 78.1% use e-mail newsletters.[58] The group trying to organize Starbucks workers (the *Starbucks Workers' Union*) started their own Web site (www.starbucksunion.org).[59] In another recent campaign, the employer restricted the use of its electronic systems (including e-mail) to "business purposes only." The union filed objections. The NLRB held that nonmanagement employees who normally have access to an employer's e-mail system as part of their jobs may use the system to communicate about union matters when not working, such as during lunch or break times.[60] ∎

inside games
Union efforts to convince employees to impede or to disrupt production—for example, by slowing the work pace.

lockout
A refusal by the employer to provide opportunities to work.

Inside games are union efforts to convince employees to impede or to disrupt production—for example, by slowing the work pace or refusing to work overtime.[61] Inside games are basically strikes—albeit "strikes" in which the company continues to pay the employees. In one inside game at a Caterpillar plant, UAW grievances rose from 22 to 336. This tied up workers and management in unproductive endeavors on company time.[62]

For their part, employers can try to break an impasse with lockouts. A **lockout** is a refusal by the employer to provide opportunities to work. It (sometimes literally) locks out employees and prohibits them from doing their jobs (and being paid). Section 2 (1) of the Industrial Disputes Act of 1947 defines lockout and Section 22 (2) sets conditions for lockout in public services, which are similar to provisions that prohibit strikes. By making similar conditions applicable to both workers/unions and employers, the law ensures fairness to both parties.

Both employers and unions can seek a court injunction if they believe the other side is causing irreparable harm to the other party. An **injunction** is a court order compelling a party or parties either to resume or to desist from a certain action.[63]

injunction
A court order compelling a party or parties either to resume or to desist from a certain action.

The Contract Agreement or Settlement

The actual contract agreement [also called Collective Bargaining Agreement, Long Term Agreement/Settlement (LTA or S)] may be a 20- or 30-page document, or longer. It may contain just general declarations of policy, or detailed rules and procedures. The tendency today is toward the longer contract.

The main sections of a typical contract cover subjects such as these: (1) management rights, obligations, worker rights and obligations; (2) union security and automatic payroll dues deduction; (3) grievance procedures; (4) arbitration of grievances; (5) disciplinary procedures; (6) compensation rates; (7) hours of work and overtime; (8) benefits: vacations, holidays, insurance, pensions; (9) health and safety provisions; (10) employee security seniority provisions; and (11) contract expiration date.

Dealing With Disputes And Grievances

LEARNING OBJECTIVE 15-5
Develop a grievance procedure.

Signing the labor agreement is not the last step in collective bargaining. No labor contract can cover all contingencies and answer all questions. For example, suppose the contract says you can only discharge an employee for "just cause." You subsequently discharge someone for speaking back to you. Was speaking back to you "just cause"?

The *grievance process* is the process or steps that the employer and union agreed to follow to ascertain whether some action violated the collective bargaining agreement. It is the vehicle for administering the contract day to day. However, this usually involves interpretation only, not negotiating new terms or altering existing ones. The aim is to clarify what those contract points really mean, in the context of addressing grievances regarding things like time off, disciplinary action, and pay. In India, the Department of Administrative Reforms and Public Grievances has been established to provide the citizens as well as the workers with a platform to address their grievances.

Sources of Grievances

In practice, it is probably easier to list those items that *don't* precipitate grievances than the ones that do. Employees may use just about anything involving wages, hours, or conditions of employment as the basis of a grievance.

Discipline cases and seniority problems including promotions, transfers, and layoffs would top this list. Others would include grievances growing out of job evaluations and work assignments, overtime, vacations, incentive plans, and holidays.[64] Here are three examples of grievances:

- *Absenteeism.* An employer fired an employee for excessive absences. The employee filed a grievance stating that there had been no previous warnings related to excessive absences.
- *Insubordination.* An employee on two occasions refused to obey a supervisor's order to meet with him, unless a union representative was present at the meeting. As a result, the employee was discharged and subsequently filed a grievance protesting the discharge.
- *Plant rules.* The plant had a posted rule barring employees from eating or drinking during unscheduled breaks. The employees filed a grievance claiming the rule was arbitrary.[65]

Grievances are often symptoms of underlying problems. Sometimes bad relationships between supervisors and subordinates are to blame: This is often the cause of grievances over "fair treatment," for instance. Organizational factors like ambiguous instructions also cause frustration and grievances. Union activism is another cause; the union may solicit grievances from workers to underscore ineffective supervision. Some individuals are by their nature negative, dissatisfied, and prone to complaints. Discipline and dismissal are two major sources of grievances.

The Grievance Procedure

grievance procedure
Formal process for addressing any factor involving wages, hours, or conditions of employment that is used as a complaint against the employer.

Most collective bargaining contracts contain a **grievance procedure**. It lists the steps in the procedure, time limits associated with each step, and specific rules such as "all charges of contract violation must be reduced to writing." Nonunionized employers need such procedures, too.

Grievance procedures differ from firm to firm. Some contain simple, two-step procedures. Here, the grievant, union representative, and company representative meet to discuss the grievance. If they don't find a satisfactory solution, the grievance goes before a third-party arbitrator who hears the case, writes it up, and makes a decision.

At the other extreme, the grievance procedure may contain six or more steps. The first step might be for the grievant and shop steward to meet informally with the supervisor of the grievant to try to find a solution. The next steps involve the grievant and union representatives meeting with higher-level managers. Finally, if top management and the union can't reach agreement, the grievance may go to arbitration.

Guidelines for Handling Grievances

The best way for a supervisor to handle a grievance is to develop a work environment in which grievances don't arise in the first place. Hone your ability to avoid, recognize, diagnose, and correct the causes of potential employee dissatisfaction (such as unfair appraisals or poor communications) before they become grievances.

Given that many factors including union pressures prompt grievances, it would be naïve to think that grievances arise only due to supervisor unfairness. However, there's little doubt that the quality of the interpersonal relations among you and your subordinates will influence your team's grievance rate. The supervisor is on the firing line and must steer a course between treating employees fairly and maintaining management's rights and prerogatives. The HR Tools feature presents some guidelines.

▶ IMPROVING PERFORMANCE: *HR Tools For Line Managers And Small Businesses*

How to Handle a Grievance Situation

Grievances cost money, in terms of lost work time, productivity, and (possibly) arbitrators' fees. One expert has developed a list of supervisor do's and don'ts as useful guides in handling grievances.[66] Some critical ones include:

Do:

1. Investigate and handle each case as though it may eventually result in arbitration.
2. Talk with the employee about his or her grievance; give the person a full hearing.
3. Require the union to identify specific contractual provisions allegedly violated.
4. Comply with the contractual time limits for handling the grievance.
5. Visit the work area of the grievance.
6. Determine whether there were any witnesses.
7. Examine the grievant's personnel record.
8. Fully examine prior grievance records.
9. Treat the union representative as your equal.
10. Hold your grievance discussions privately.
11. Fully inform your own supervisor of grievance matters.

Don't:

1. Discuss the case with the union steward alone—the grievant should be there.
2. Make arrangements with individual employees that are inconsistent with the labor agreement.

3. Hold back the remedy if the company is wrong.
4. Admit to the binding effect of a past practice.
5. Relinquish to the union your rights as a manager.
6. Settle grievances based on what is "fair." Instead, stick to the labor agreement.
7. Bargain over items not covered by the contract.
8. Treat as subject to arbitration claims demanding the discipline or discharge of managers.
9. Give long written grievance answers.
10. Trade a grievance settlement for a grievance withdrawal.
11. Deny grievances because "your hands have been tied by management."
12. Agree to informal amendments in the contract. ■

Tomas Abad/AGE Fotostock

One union's aims include making "… it our first priority to help millions more workers form unions so we can build a strong movement for rewarding work in America…".

LEARNING OBJECTIVE 15-6

Describe a strategy for cooperative labor relations.

The Union Movement Today And Tomorrow

Union membership has gradually declined in America from about 20% of the workforce in 1983 (when 17.8 million workers belonged to unions), to about 11% (just over 14 million workers) recently.[67]

Several factors contributed to the decline in union membership over the past 50 or so years. Unions traditionally appealed mostly to blue-collar workers, and the proportion of blue-collar jobs has been decreasing. Globalization increased competition and pressures on employers to cut costs and boost productivity, further squeezing unions. Other factors pressuring employers and unions include the deregulation of trucking, airlines, and communications; outdated equipment and factories; mismanagement; new technology; and laws (such as occupational safety) that somewhat substituted for and reduced the need for unions. As noted, the recent recession triggered budget cuts in both the public and private sectors, prompting anti-union public policy attitudes, and the loss of about 1 million public sector union jobs. Bankruptcies, such as those that swept the U.S. airline industry, often end with courts imposing less favorable contract terms on union employees.[68] For example, a bankruptcy court judge recently gave Patriot Coal Corp. the right to drastically reduce pay and benefits for thousands of miners, retirees, and dependents.[69]

The net effect has been the permanent layoff of hundreds of thousands of union members, the permanent closing of company plants, the relocation of companies to nonunion settings (either in the United States or abroad), and mergers and acquisitions that eliminated union jobs and affected collective bargaining agreements. That's why union membership as a percentage of people working has actually dropped by about two-thirds over 50 years, to about 11%.[70]

What Are Unions Doing About It?

Of course, unions aren't sitting idly by. For example, the priorities of the Change to Win Coalition (whose members broke off from the AFL-CIO) include making "… it our first priority to help millions more workers form unions so we can build a strong movement for rewarding work in America [and] unite the strength of everyone who works in the same industry so we can negotiate with today's huge global corporations for everyone's benefit."[71]

In practice, they'll do several things. Change to Win will be very aggressive about trying to organize workers, will focus on organizing women and minority workers, will focus more on organizing temporary or contingent workers, and will target specific multinational companies for international campaigns.[72]

Unions are in fact becoming more aggressive. For example, they are pushing Congress to pass the *Employee Free Choice Act*. This would make it easier for employees to unionize. Instead of secret-ballot elections, the act would institute a "card check" system. Here the union would win recognition when a majority of workers signed authorization cards saying they want the union. Several large companies, including Cingular Wireless, have already agreed to the card check process.[73] The act would also require binding arbitration to set a first contract's terms if the company and union can't negotiate an agreement within 120 days.[74] Unions are also using *class action lawsuits* to support employees in nonunionized companies to pressure employers.[75] And, unions are cooperating more with so-called alternative labor groups, which advocate for improved worker benefits and working conditions, but are not unions themselves.[76]

Finally, unions are becoming more proactive in coordinating their efforts.[77] For example, in its "Union Cities" campaigns, AFL-CIO planners work with local labor councils and individual unions to gain the support of a target city's elected officials. In Los Angeles, this helped the service workers' union organize janitors in that city.

Similarly, unions are extending their efforts abroad. For example, UNITE (now part of UNITE HERE) used a campaign to coordinate 800 workers at one foreign employer's distribution center with other workers at the employer's New York City headquarters, and with local activists and international unions throughout Europe. This forced the employer's parent company, a French conglomerate, to cease resisting the union's organizing efforts. To support its efforts to unionize autoworkers in the United States, the UAW enlisted thousands of union members in Brazil to picket Nissan dealerships there.[78] The same is happening in reverse. When Daimler said it was going to phase out producing its "C" cars in Germany and begin producing them in the United States, its German union, IG Metall, began cooperating with the UAW to unionize Daimler's American plants.[79]

Cooperative Clauses

When AT&T's workers threatened to strike if the company insisted on raising workers' health-care premiums, AT&T began training managers to fill in for workers.[80]

However, labor–management relations history is also sprinkled with cooperation. For example, more than 50 years ago, General Motors and Toyota created a joint venture they called New United Motor Manufacturing Inc. (NUMMI). The partners hoped to merge GM's marketing expertise with Toyota's famous team-based management system.[81] NUMMI and the United Auto Workers (UAW) agreed that management and labor would work together as a team, give workers a voice in decision making, and build high-quality cars at low cost. NUMMI and the UAW installed a new labor–management system in their plant. NUMMI's 2,400 hourly workers were organized around teams of 5 to 10 members. NUMMI reduced the number of supervisors.[82] The plant was soon very successful (although both parties eventually ended their joint venture).

Since then, many labor–management agreements have included so-called cooperative agreements. These agreements generally commit union and management to adopt one or more cooperative themes. One analysis of labor contracts expiring between 1997 and 2007 found that roughly half of the 1,041 contracts studied contained cooperative clauses. Parties commit to adhere to one or more of these cooperative themes (in descending order of frequency-of-mention in the agreements):[83]

- Intent to cooperate
- A statement of commitment to cooperate
- Committees to review mutual concerns that arise
- Decisions on traditional issues
- Guarantees of employment security

- Commitments to high-performance practices
- Decisions on strategic issues
- Full cooperation

At one extreme, for example, Alcoa's agreement contained a full "Cooperative Partnership Clause." This included provisions for joint management–labor decision-making committees, and a commitment to maintain employee security under catastrophic market conditions.[84] At the other extreme, many contain only a statement of intent to cooperate, such as on traditional issues like drug abuse, health care, and safety. The HR Around The Globe feature illustrates cooperation abroad.

There's little doubt, as a study argues, that unions "that have a cooperative relationship with management can play an important role in overcoming barriers to the effective adoption of practices that have been linked to organizational competitiveness."[85] But employers who want to capitalize on that potential must change how they think, by emphasizing a cooperative partnership.[86]

▶ IMPROVING PERFORMANCE: *HR Around The Globe*

Labor-Management Cooperation and Works Councils

When the United Auto Workers lost an effort to unionize the Volkswagen plant outside Chattanooga, Tennessee, the vote of 712 to 626 against joining the UAW surprised even Volkswagen management.

Perhaps the biggest reason for the surprise was that Volkswagen actually supported unionizing the plant. Part of the reason Volkswagen supported unionization is because it said it wanted to bring to Chattanooga the works councils that it uses successfully in Germany. A *works council* is an employee committee that elects representatives who work with management to establish policies on things like work hours and dismissal procedures.[87] The works councils meet monthly with managers to discuss topics ranging from no-smoking policies to layoffs.[88] (*Co-determination* is also the rule in Germany and several other countries. **Co-determination** means employees have the legal right to a voice in setting company policies. Workers elect their own representatives to the supervisory board of the employer.)[89] As the CEO of Volkswagen Chattanooga said, works councils are the "key to our success and productivity."[90]

Co-determination

An employee representation system in which workers elect their own representatives to the supervisory (management) board of the employer and have the legal right to a voice in setting company policies on matters such as company organization, hiring, and performance appraisal.

Volkswagen still hopes to bring works councils to its Chattanooga plant, but U.S. labor law may stand in the way, unless the plant's workers vote for a union. Many years ago, some employers tried to neutralize legitimate unions by setting up company backed "faux unions," a practice Congress soon outlawed. While works councils are legitimate, most experts believe that having nonunion employee representatives bargaining on matters such as pay and dismissals won't pass muster with American labor law. In recent years, there has been a recognition of the need for a cooperative framework on the basis of which countries across the globe can align their industrial policy.

With the advent of organizations like Trade Union Development Cooperation Network (TUDCN), efforts in this direction have gained momentum. However in the Indian scenario, several companies such as those hailing from the IT and ITES background, have found little ground to unite. One of the major steps in this direction came via National Confederation of United Founding Conference in 2014, where the first union for the benefit of workers in the IT sector was formed.

Registered as a trade union under the Indian Trade Unions Act of 1926, the Self-Employed Women's Association (SEWA) has paved a benchmark for other trade unions across the nation to look upto. The Union is open for membership to all self-employed women, whether in the rural or urban setups, across the nation with a nominal membership fee. An elected representation of two-tiers governs the Union. While the structure is interesting to note, what is worth noting is that members of SEWA have no fixed employer-employee relationship or any rules governing it as well. With barely any assets serving them as working capital, the main motive is to enable these women to remain economically active so as to be able to contribute to their families and societies significantly while also empowering them. ∎

Chapter Review

Chapter Section Summaries

15-1. The **labor movement** is important. About 14 million U.S. workers belong to unions—about 11% of the total. Workers unionize not just to get more pay or better working conditions; employer unfairness and the union's power are also important. Unions aim for union security, and then for improved wages, hours, and working conditions and benefits for their members. Union security options include the closed shop, union shop, agency shop, preferential shop, and maintenance of membership arrangement.

15-2. To understand unions and their impact, one should understand the interplay between **unions and the law**. In brief, labor law has gone through periods of strong encouragement of unions, to modified encouragement coupled with regulation, and finally to detailed regulation of internal union affairs.

15-3. When unions begin organizing, all managers and supervisors usually get involved, so it's essential to understand the mechanics of **the union drive and election**. The main steps include initial contact, obtaining authorization cards, holding a hearing, the campaign itself, and the election. Supervisors need to understand their role at each step in this process. Follow the acronym TIPS—do not Threaten, Interrogate, make Promises, or Spy. And follow FORE—provide Facts, express your Opinions, explain factually correct Rules, and share your Experiences.

15-4. The employer and union hammer out an agreement via the **collective bargaining process**. The heart of collective bargaining is good faith bargaining, which means both parties must make reasonable efforts to arrive at agreement, and proposals are matched with counterproposals. In the actual bargaining sessions, there are mandatory bargaining items such as pay, illegal bargaining items, and voluntary bargaining items such as benefits for retirees. If things don't go smoothly during collective bargaining, the parties may utilize third-party intermediaries, including mediators, fact finders, and arbitrators. Strikes represent a withdrawal of labor.

15-5. Most managers become involved with **disputes and grievances** during their careers. Collective bargaining agreements contain a specific grievance procedure listing the steps in the procedure. In general, the best way to handle a grievance is to create an environment in which grievances don't occur. However, if a grievance does occur, things to do include investigate, handle each case as though it may eventually result in arbitration, talk with the employee about the grievance, and comply with the contractual time limits for handling the grievance.

15-6. Membership is down but unions are still influential today, so it's important to understand the **union movement today and tomorrow**.

Discussion Questions

15-1. Why do employees join unions? What are the advantages and disadvantages of being a union member?

15-2. Briefly illustrate how labor law has gone through a cycle of repression and encouragement.

15-3. Explain in detail each step in a union drive and election.

15-4. Define impasse, mediation, and strike, and explain the techniques that are used to overcome an impasse.

Individual and Group Activities

15-6. You are the manager of a small manufacturing plant. The union contract covering most of your employees is about to expire. Working individually or in groups, discuss how to prepare for union contract negotiations.

15-7. Working individually or in groups, use Internet resources to find situations where company management and the union reached an impasse at some point during their negotiation process, but eventually resolved the impasse. Describe the issues on both sides that led to the impasse. How did they move past the impasse? What were the final outcomes?

15-8. Appendices A and B at the end of this book (pages 583–600) list the knowledge someone studying for the HRCI (Appendix A) or SHRM (Appendix B) certification exam needs to have in each area of human resource management (such as in Strategic Management, and Workforce Planning). In groups of several students, do four things: (1) review Appendix A and/or B; (2) identify the material in this chapter that relates to the Appendix A and/or B required knowledge lists; (3) write four multiple-choice exam questions on this material that you believe would be suitable for inclusion in the HRCI exam and/or the SHRM exam; and, (4) if time permits, have someone from your team post your team's questions in front of the class, so that students in all teams can answer the exam questions created by the other teams.

15-9. Several years ago, 8,000 Amtrak workers agreed not to disrupt service by walking out, at least not until a court hearing was held. Amtrak had asked the courts for a temporary restraining order, and the Transport Workers Union of America was actually pleased to postpone its walkout. The workers were apparently not upset at Amtrak, but at Congress for failing to provide enough funding for Amtrak. What, if anything, can an employer do when employees threaten to go on strike, not because of what the employer did, but what a third party—in this case, Congress—has done or not done? What laws would prevent the union from going on strike in this case?

Experiential Exercise

The Organizing Campaign at Sam's Cupcake Shop

Purpose: The purpose of this exercise is to give you practice in dealing with some of the elements of a union-organizing campaign.[91]

Required Understanding: You should be familiar with the material covered in this chapter, as well as the following incident, "The Organizing campaign at Sam's Cupcake Shop."

Incident: Sam's Cupcake Shop sells baked goods (croissants, cupcakes, rolls, cakes, etc.) and serves light meals such as breakfast and salads through its chain of ten small retail stores in the borough of Manhattan, in New York City. Each store is staffed with about 9 employees (plus one manager), some of whom do the cooking and some of whom staff the counter and sell the food items. As with Sam's other stores, the Sam's Cupcake Shop on First Avenue is staffed primarily with recent (legal) immigrants to America, all of whom are paid at or just above the minimum wage. It was no secret that at least one New York City agency was pressing (in 2015) for food service owners to raise the minimum wage for food service employees to $15 per hour.[92] Everything at the First Avenue store seemed to be going smoothly, but that apparent tranquility ended abruptly in July 27, 2015. That was the day that Anesha, the First Avenue store's manager called Taylor Brooke, Sam's Cupcake's human resource manager, to tell her that they had "an employee problem."

The problem, Anesha said, was that she'd heard from a few employees that the Service Employees International Union was trying to organize Sam's Cupcake Stores employees. Taylor's first reaction was one of caution, particularly because food service employees are historically difficult to organize—"they don't stay in their jobs long enough to unionize them," to paraphrase one union leader.[93] Unfortunately, Anesha said she had already taken what she called "sensible steps" to blunt the unionization effort. She had, first, explained to her employees that if costs went up because they unionized, then "we'd probably have to close this shop." She said she also promised better work schedules if they "ignored" the union, and told them they were prohibited from discussing union matters during work time. "And don't worry" she said to Taylor, "I've got a list of the employees who are pushing for the union."

The more Anesha talked, the more concerned Taylor became, not just with the union but with the possible consequences of Anesha's efforts. She wondered particularly if Anesha's actions could cause problems down the road for Sam's Cupcakes with the NLRB.

As it turned, she didn't have long to wait for an answer. The following week pickets from the union and its supporters appeared in front of the First Avenue store carrying signs decrying the company's "unfair labor practices." At that point Sam came into Taylor's office and said, "If they think they can railroad me into giving them big raises they are wrong; I am closing that store down." Taylor was in a quandary as to how to reply to Sam, and in general, what she should do.

How to Set Up the Exercise/Instructions: Divide the class into groups of several students. Assume that you are labor relations consultants retained by Taylor to identify the problems and issues involved and to advise Taylor and Sam of the company's rights and obligations, as well as the implications of what's transpired so far, add finally what to do next. Each group will spend the time allotted discussing the issues. Then, outline those issues, as well as an action plan for Taylor and Sam. What should they do next? Can Sam really close the store down?

If time permits, a spokesperson from each group should list on the board the issues involved and the group's recommendations.

Application Case

Negotiating with the Writers Guild of America

The talks between the Writers Guild of America (WGA) and the Alliance of Motion Picture & Television Producers (producers) began tense, and then got tenser.[94]

The biggest issue was how to split revenue from new media, such as when television shows move to the Internet. The producers said they wanted a profit-splitting system rather than the current residual system. Under the residual system, writers continue to receive "residuals" or income from shows they write every time they're shown (such as when *Seinfeld* appears in reruns). Writers Guild executives argued producers' revenues from advertising and subscription fees had recently jumped by about 40%.[95]

The situation grew tenser.[96] Even after meeting six times, it seemed that the parties had made no progress in resolving the dispute.[97]

Soon, the Writers Guild asked its members for strike authorization, and the producers were claiming that the guild was just trying to delay negotiations until the current contract expired (at the end of October). To paraphrase the president of the producers' group said, the WGA leadership seemed unwilling to bargain in good faith.[98] As evidence, the producers claimed that the WGA negotiating committee left one meeting after less than an hour.

Both sides knew timing was very important. During the fall and spring, television series production is in full swing. So, a writers' strike now would have a bigger impact than waiting until, say, the summer to strike. Perhaps not surprisingly, some movement was soon discernible.[99] Then the WGA and producers reached agreement. The new contract was signed soon after the two sides—including top union and industry officials like the head of Walt Disney Co.—began marathon bargaining sessions.[100]

Questions

15-10. The producers said the WGA was not bargaining in good faith. What did they mean by that, and do you think the evidence is sufficient to support the claim?

15-11. The WGA did eventually strike. What tactics could the producers have used to fight back once the strike began? What tactics do you think the WGA used?

15-12. This was a conflict between professional and creative people (the WGA) and TV and movie producers. Do you think the conflict was therefore different in any way than are the conflicts between, say, the Autoworkers or Teamsters unions against auto and trucking companies? Why?

15-13. What role (with examples) did negotiating skills seem to play in the WGA producers' negotiations?

Continuing Case

Carter Cleaning Company

The Grievance

On visiting one of Carter Cleaning Company's stores, Jennifer was surprised to be taken aside by a long-term Carter employee, who met her as she was parking her car. "Murray (the store manager) told me I was suspended for 2 days without pay because I came in late last Thursday," said George. "I'm really upset, but around here the store manager's word seems to be law, and it sometimes seems like the only way anyone can file a grievance is by meeting you or your father like this in the parking lot." Jennifer was very disturbed by this revelation and promised the employee she would look into it and discuss the situation with her father. In the car heading back to headquarters,

she began mulling over what Carter Cleaning Company's alternatives might be.

Questions

15-14. Do you think it is important for Carter Cleaning Company to have a formal grievance process? Why or why not?

15-15. Based on what you know about the Carter Cleaning Company, outline the steps in what you think would be the ideal grievance process for this company.

15-16. In addition to the grievance process, can you think of anything else that Carter Cleaning Company might do to make sure grievances and gripes like this one are expressed and are heard by top management?

Translating Strategy into HR Policies and Practices Case[*,§]

* The overall map on page xxxviii of this book outlines the relationships involved.

Improving Performance At The Hotel Paris

The Hotel Paris's New Labor Relations Practices

The Hotel Paris's competitive strategy is "To use superior guest service to differentiate the Hotel Paris properties, and to thereby increase the length of stay and return rate of guests, and thus boost revenues and profitability." HR manager Lisa Cruz must now formulate functional policies and activities that support this competitive strategy and boost performance by eliciting the required employee behaviors and competencies.

Lisa Cruz's parents were union members, and she had no strong philosophical objections to unions, per se. However, as the head of HR for the Hotel Paris, she did feel very strongly that her employer

should do everything legally possible to remain union-free. She knew that this is what the hotel chain's owners and top executives wanted, and that achieving their strategic goals would be best accomplished by staying union free. Furthermore, the evidence seemed to support their position. At least one study that she'd seen concluded that firms with 30% or more of their eligible workers in unions were in the bottom 10% in terms of performance, while those with 8% to 9% of eligible workers in unions scored in the top 10%.[101] The problem was that the Hotel Paris really had no specific policies and procedures in place to help its managers and supervisors deal with union activities. With all the laws regarding what employers and their managers could and could not do to respond to a union's efforts, Lisa knew her company was "a problem waiting to happen." She turned her attention to

§ Written and copyright by Gary Dessler, PhD.

deciding what steps she and her team should take with regard to labor relations and collective bargaining.

Lisa and the CFO knew that unionization was a growing reality for the Hotel Paris. Some of the hotel chain's U.S. employees were already unionized, and unions in this industry were quite active. For example, as they were surfing the Internet to better gauge the situation, Lisa and the CFO came across the Web site from the Hotel Employees Restaurant Union, local 26. It describes their success in negotiating a contract at several local hotels including ones managed by the Westin and Hilton chains. The CFO and Lisa agreed that it was important that she and her team develop and institute a new set of policies and practices that would enable the Hotel Paris to deal more effectively with unions.

Together with a labor–management attorney, the team developed a 20-page "What You Need to Know When the Union Calls" manual for Hotel Paris managers and supervisors. This contained three sets of information. First, it provided a succinct outline of *labor relations law*, particularly as it relates to the company's managers. Second, it laid a *detailed set of guidelines* regarding what supervisors could and could not do with respect to union organizing activities. Third, it identified all line supervisors as the company's *"front-line eyes and ears"* with respect to union organizing activity. Here, the manual provided examples of activities that might suggest that a union was trying to organize the hotel's employees, and whom the supervisor should notify.

Lisa and her team also decided to ensure that the company was responsive to its employees' concerns. Lisa and her team believed that many of the steps they'd taken earlier should help. For example, improving salaries and wages, providing financial incentives, and instituting the new ethics, justice, and fairness programs already seemed to be having a measurable effect on employee morale.

Questions

15-17. List and briefly describe what you believe are the three most important steps Hotel Paris management can take now to reduce the likelihood unions will organize more of its employees.

15-18. Write a detailed two-page outline for a "What You Need to Know When the Union Calls" manual. Lisa will distribute this manual to her company's supervisors and managers, telling them what they need to know about looking out for possible unionizing activity, and how to handle actual organizing process–related supervisory tasks.

Key Terms

closed shop, 472
union shop, 472
agency shop, 472
preferential shop, 472
right to work, 472
Taft-Hartley Act of 1947, 474
union salting, 478
bargaining unit, 479

voluntary (or permissible) bargaining items, 483
illegal bargaining items, 483
mandatory bargaining items, 483
impasse, 484
mediation, 484
fact finder, 484
arbitration, 484

interest arbitration, 484
rights arbitration, 484
strike, 484
economic strike, 485
unfair labor practice strike, 485
wildcat strike, 485
sympathy strike, 485
picketing, 485

corporate campaign, 485
boycott, 485
inside games, 485
lockout, 485
injunction, 486
grievance procedure, 487
Co-determination, 490

Endnotes

1. For example, see http://articles.moneycentral.msn.com/Investing/Extra/CostcoTheAntiWalMart.aspx?page=1, accessed June 29, 2011; and Hamilton Nolan, "The Anti-Wal-Mart," http://gawker.com/costco-the-anti-walmart-511739135, accessed August 7, 2013.

2. Christine Frey, "Costco's Love of Labor: Employees' Well-Being Key to Its Success," www.seattlepi.com/default/article/Costco-s-love-of-labor-Employees-well-being-key-1140722.php, accessed June 29, 2011; Steven Greenhouse and Reed Abelson, "Wal-Mart Cuts Some Health Care Benefits," *New York Times*, October 21, 2011, pp. B1, B5.

3. See, for example, www.costcobenefits.com/cms/ what-you-need-to-know-about-costco-benefits/, accessed April 25, 2015.

4. Steven Greenhouse, "Share of the Workforce in a Union Falls to a 97 Year Low, 11.3%," *New York Times*, January 24, 2013, B1; www.bls.gov/news.release/union2.nr0.htm, accessed July 22, 2015.

5. www.bls.gov/news.release/union2.nr0.htm, accessed July 22, 2015.

6. Michael Ash and Jean Seago, "The Effect of Registered Nurses' Unions on Heart Attack Mortality," *Industrial and Labor Relations Review* 57, no. 3 (April 2004), pp. 422–442.

7. www.bls.gov/news.release/union2.nr0.htm, accessed July 22, 2015.

8. Kris Maher, "The New Union Worker," *Wall Street Journal*, September 27, 2005, pp. B1, B11.

9. Robert Grossman, "Unions Follow Suit," *HR Magazine*, May 2005, p. 49.

10. Warner Pflug, *The UAW in Pictures* (Detroit: Wayne State University Press, 1971), pp. 11–12.

11. "Employee Engagement: A New Union Avoidance Strategy," June 28, 2011, www.modernsurvey.com, accessed April 12, 2014.

12. This is based on Jessica Tyler, "Employee Engagement and Labor Relations," *Gallup Business Journal.* http://businessJournal.Gallup.com, accessed April 9, 2014.

13. Arthur Sloane and Fred Witney, *Labor Relations* (Upper Saddle River, NJ: Prentice Hall, 2007), pp. 335–336.

14. Benjamin Taylor and Fred Witney, *Labor Relations Law* (Upper Saddle River, NJ: Prentice Hall, 1992), pp. 170–171; www.dol.gov/whd/state/righttowork.htm, accessed June 5, 2010.

15. www.dol.gov/whd/state/righttowork.htm, accessed September 11, 2014. Indiana's law applies only to school teachers; without Indiana, there are 22 right-to-work states.

16. "Research Inconclusive About Effective Right to Work on Economy," *BNA Bulletin to Management*, January 8, 2013, p. 14.

17. www.seiu.org/our-union/, accessed June 1, 2011.

18. Steven Greenhouse, "4th Union Quits AFL-CIO in a Dispute Over Organizing," *New York Times*, September 15, 2005, p. A14.

CHAPTER 15

19. Some trace early U.S. labor relations legislation back to a fire at the Triangle Shirtwaist factory in 1911. Following that tragedy, New York City and New York State soon adopted 36 new laws, and many view these laws as the basis for and precursor to the U.S. labor legislation efforts that began in earnest in the 1930s. "The Birth of the New Deal," *The Economist*, March 19, 2011, p. 39.

20. The following material is based on Sloane and Witney, *Labor Relations*, pp. 46–124.

21. www.bls.gov/news.release/union2.nr0.htm, accessed June 1, 2011.

22. Michael Carrell and Christina Heavrin, *Labor Relations and Collective Bargaining* (Upper Saddle River, NJ: Prentice Hall, 2004), p. 180.

23. Sloane and Witney, *Labor Relations*, p. 121.

24. Kurmanath K, "Satyam Freshers Attempt Unions," March 11, 2009, *The Hindu Business Line*, http://www.blonnet.com/2009/03/11/stories/2009031151230400.htm.

25. See, for example, Steven Greenhouse, "High Court to Weigh Union Cases," *New York Times*, November 11, 2013, pp. B1, B2.

26. For organizing examples from the unions' point of view, see www.twu.org/international/steps, accessed June 29, 2011; www.opeiu.org/NeedAUnion/StepstoCreatingaUnionWorkplace/tabid/71/Default.aspx, accessed June 29, 2011; and particularly http://ufcwone.org/steps-form-union, accessed August 7, 2013.

27. Kris Maher, "Unions' New Foe: Consultants," *Wall Street Journal*, August 15, 2005, p. B1.

28. "Some Say Salting Leaves Bitter Taste for Employers," *BNA Bulletin to Management*, March 4, 2004, p. 79; www.nlrb.gov/global/search/index.aspx?mode=s&qt=salting&col=nlrb&gb=y, accessed January 14, 2008. For a management lawyer's perspective, see www.fklaborlaw.com/union_salt-objectives.html, accessed May 25, 2007.

29. D. Diane Hatch and James Hall, "Salting Cases Clarified by NLRB," *Workforce*, August 2000, p. 92. See also www.fklaborlaw.com/union_salt-objectives.html, accessed May 25, 2007.

30. The following are adapted and/or quoted from Kate Bronfenbrenner, "The Role of Union Strategies in NLRB Certification Elections," *Industrial and Labor Relations Review* 50 (January 1997), pp. 195–212; see also J. Fiorito et. al., "Understanding Organising Activity Among US National Unions," *Industrial Relations Journal* 41, no. 1 (January 2010), pp. 74–92.

31. Stephen Greenhouse, "Union Gets New Election at a Target," *New York Times*, May 22, 2012, B3.

32. Frederick Sullivan, "Limiting Union Organizing Activity Through Supervisors," *Personnel* 55 (July/August 1978), pp. 55–65. See also Edward Young and William Levy, "Responding to a Union-Organizing Campaign: Do You and Your Supervisors Know the Legal Boundaries in a Union Campaign?" *Franchising World* 39, no. 3 (March 2007), pp. 45–49.

33. www.hreonline.com/HRE/view/story.jhtml?id=534358235, accessed April 25, 2015.

34. Carrell and Heavrin, *Labor Relations and Collective Bargaining*, pp. 167–168.

35. Karol Leather, Karmachari Sangh v/s Liberty Footwear Company, 1989, SCC 448.

36. Mimosa Spencer and Jeanne Whalen, "Change France? Sanofi Find It Can't," *Wall Street Journal*, April 11, 2013, pp. B1, D5.

37. Ibid., B1. Similarly, workers in Germany are resisting what they call Amazon's American-style business practices. Nick Wingfield and Melissa Eddy, "In Germany, Union Culture Clashes with Amazons' Labor Practices," *New York Times*, August 5, 2013, pp. B1, B4.

38. John Fossum, *Labor Relations* (Dallas: BPI, 1982), pp. 246–250; Sloane and Witney, *Labor Relations*, pp. 197–205.

39. *Boulwareism* is the name given to a strategy, now held in disfavor, by which the company, based on an exhaustive study of what it believed its employees wanted, made but one offer at the bargaining table and then refused to bargain any further unless convinced by the union on the basis of new facts that its original position was wrong. Fossum, *Labor Relations*, p. 267.

40. Kathryn Tyler, "Good-Faith Bargaining," *HR Magazine*, January 2005, p. 52.

41. These are based on James C. Freund, *Smart Negotiating* (New York: Simon & Schuster, 1992), pp. 42–46.

42. James C. Freund, *Smart Negotiating* (New York: Simon & Schuster, 1992), pp. 42–46.

43. Ibid., 33. One interesting observation: Communicating threats is more effective than communicating anger. See Marwan Sineceure et al., "Hot or Cold: Is Communicating Anger or Threats More Effective in Negotiation?" *Journal of Applied Psychology* 96, no. 5 (2011), pp. 1019–1032.

44. Reed Richardson, *Collective Bargaining by Objectives* (Upper Saddle River, NJ: Prentice Hall, 1977), p. 150. Both sides will try to manipulate the media to jockey for better positions; for example, see J. McCafferty,

"Labor-Management Dispute Resolution and the Media," *Dispute Resolution Journal* 56, no. 3 (August/October 2001), pp. 40–47.

45. Many negotiators pride themselves on being open, honest, and straightforward in their negotiations, but at least one study suggests that this can lead to excessive concessions. D. Scott DeRue et al., "When Is Straightforwardness a Liability in Negotiations? The Role of Integrative Potential and Structural Power," *Journal of Applied Psychology* 94, no. 4 (2009), pp. 1032–1047.

46. With or without reaching a solution, impasses and union–management conflict can leave union members demoralized. See, for example, Jessica Marquez, "Taking Flight," *Workforce,* June 9, 2008, pp. 1, 18.

47. Jacqueline Palank et al., "Last Chance to Save the Twinkie," *Wall Street Journal*, November 20, 2012, p. B1.

48. Fossum, *Labor Relations*, p. 312.

49. Carrell and Heavrin, *Labor Relations and Collective Bargaining*, p. 501.

50. http://fmcs.gov/assets/files/annual%20reports/FY2006_Annual_Report.pdf, accessed January 14, 2008.

51. Fossum, *Labor Relations*, p. 317.

52. This is based on Sloane and Whitney, *Labor Relations*, p. 213.

53. http://fuelfix.com/blog/2015/02/18/strike-update-bp-training-additional-replacement-workers/#30249101=0, accessed July 24, 2015.

54. http://profootballtalk.nbcsports.com/2011/03/21/league-doesnt-rule-out-replacement-players-during-lockout/, accessed June 29, 2011.

55. Some labor lawyers report an increase in the use by unions of corporate campaigns. Janet Walthall, "Unions Increasingly Using Corporate Campaigns," *BNA Bulletin to Management*, February 16, 2010, p. 55.

56. For a discussion, see Herbert Northrup, "Union Corporate Campaigns and Inside Games as a Strike Form," *Employee Relations Law Journal* 19, no. 4 (Spring 1994), pp. 507–549.

57. www.blogging4jobs.com/wp-content/uploads/2012/02/unions-social-media.png, accessed April 25, 2015.

58. www.bna.com/social-media-new-b17179923064/, accessed April 25, 2015.

59. www.starbucksunion.org, accessed August 7, 2013.

60. www.hreonline.com/HRE/view/story.jhtml?id=534358235, accessed April 25, 2015.

61. Northrup, "Union Corporate Campaigns and Inside Games," p. 513.

62. Ibid., p. 518.

63. Clifford Koen Jr., Sondra Hartman, and Dinah Payne, "The NLRB Wields a Rejuvenated Weapon," *Personnel Journal*, December 1996, pp. 85–87; D. Silverman, "The NLRA at 70: A New Approach to Processing 10(j)s [NLRA at Seventy conference in New York City, 2005]," *Labor Law Journal* 56, no. 3 (Fall 2005), pp. 203–206.

64. Carrell and Heavrin, *Labor Relations and Collective Bargaining*, pp. 417–418.

65. Richardson, *Collective Bargaining by Objectives*.

66. Based on M. Gene Newport, *Supervisory Management* (St. Paul, MN: West Group, 1976), p. 273; see also Walter Baer, "Grievance Handling: 101 Guides for Supervisors" (New York: American Management Association, 1970); and Mark Lurie, "The Eight Essential Steps in Grievance Processing," *Dispute Resolution Journal* 54, no. 4 (November 1999), pp. 61–65.

67. www.bls.gov/news.release/pdf/union2.pdf, accessed April 11, 2014.

68. Susan Carey and Jack Nicas, "AMR Will Ask the Judge to Toss Labor Pacts," *Wall Street Journal,* March 23, 2012, p. B3.

69. Kris Maher and Jacqueline Palank, "Patriot Coal Allowed to Win Union PACs," *Wall Street Journal*, May 30, 2013, p. B1.

70. www.bls.gov/news.release/union2.nr0.htm, accessed April 2, 2009.

71. Jennifer Schramm, "The Future of Unions," *Society for Human Resource Management, Workplace Visions* 4 (2005), pp. 1–8.

72. Ibid. See also www.changetowin.org/about-us.html, accessed February 13, 2010.

73. "The Limits of Solidarity," *Economist*, September 23, 2006, p. 34.

74. Chris Maher, "Specter Won't Support Union-Backed Bill," *Wall Street Journal*, March 25, 2009, p. A3.

75. "Unions Using Class Actions to Pressure Nonunion Companies," *BNA Bulletin to Management*, August 22, 2006, p. 271. See also Robert Grossman, "We Organized Labor and Code," *HR Magazine,* January 2008, pp. 37–40.

76. "New labour, alt–labour," *Economist*, September 14, 2013, pp. 33–34.

77. Dean Scott, "Unions Still a Potent Force," *Kiplinger Business Forecasts*, March 26, 2003.

78. Steven Greenhouse, "At a Nissan Plant in Mississippi, a Battle to Shape the UAW's Future," *New York Times*, October 7, 2013, pp. B1, B3.

79. Neal Boudette, "A New Alliance: UAW in Germany," *Wall Street Journal*, November 8, 2013, pp. B1, B2.

CHAPTER 15

80. Shalini Rankchandran and Anton Troianovski, "AT&T's Strike Camp," *Wall Street Journal,* April 5, 2012, pp. B1–B2.

81. Carrell and Heavrin, *Labor Relations and Collective Bargaining,* pp. 62–63.

82. Ibid.

83. George Gray, Donald Myers, and Phyllis Myers, "Cooperative Provisions in Labor Agreements: A New Paradigm?" *Monthly Labor Review,* January 1, 1999. See also Mark Schoeff Jr., "Labor on the March," *Workforce Management,* February 2010, pp. 1, 18–19.

84. Gray et al., "Cooperative Provisions in Labor Agreements."

85. Carol Gill, "Union Impact on the Effective Adoption of High Performance Work Practices,"

Human Resource Management Review 19 (2009), pp. 39–50.

86. See also Thomas Kochan, "A Jobs Compact for America's Future," *Harvard Business Review,* March 2012, pp. 64–70.

87. Based on ibid.

88. See, for example, www.fedee.com/ewc1.html, accessed November 4, 2009.

89. This is discussed in Eduard Gaugler, "HR Management: An International Comparison," *Personnel* 65, no. 8 (1988), p. 28. See also E. Poutsma et al., "The Diffusion of Calculative and Collaborative HRM Practices in European Firms," *Industrial Relations* 45, no. 4 (October 2006), pp. 513–546.

90. Steven Greenhouse, "Labor Regroups in South after

Volkswagen Vote," *New York Times,* February 17, 2004, p. B3.

91. © Gary Dessler, Ph.D. For information on what employers should not do see https://www.nlrb.gov/rights-we-protect/whats-law/employers/interfering-employee-rights-section-7-8a1, accessed July 26, 2015.

92. http://www.nytimes.com/2015/07/27/nyregion/proposed-minimum-wage-increase-for-fast-food-employees-divides-low-wage-workers.html?_r=0, accessed July 26, 2015.

93. Ibid.

94. Chris Pursell, "Rhetoric Flying in WGA Talks," *Television-Week,* July 23, 2007, pp. 3, 35; Peter Sanders, "In Hollywood, a Tale of Two Union

Leaderships," *Wall Street Journal,* January 7, 2008, p. B2.

95. Pursell, "Rhetoric Flying in WGA Talks."

96. Ibid.

97. James Hibberd, "Guild Talks Break with No Progress," *TVWeek* 26, no. 38 (October 8, 2007), pp. 1, 30.

98. Ibid.

99. "DGA Deal Sets the Stage for Writers," *Television Week,* January 21, 2008, pp. 3, 33.

100. "WGA, Studios Reach Tentative Agreement," *UPI NewsTrack,* February 3, 2008.

101. Brian Becker et al., *The HR Scorecard* (Boston: Harvard Business School Press, 2001), p. 16.

16

Safety, Health, and Risk Management

LEARNING OBJECTIVES

16-1 Explain the supervisor's role in safety.

16-2 Explain the basic facts about safety law and OSHA.

16-3 Answer the question, "What causes accidents?"

16-4 List and explain five ways to prevent accidents at work.

16-5 Describe how one company uses employee engagement to improve workplace safety.

16-6 List five workplace health hazards and how to deal with them.

16-7 Discuss the prerequisites for a security plan and how to set up a basic security program.

When it comes to safety strategy, the, explosion and fire on British Petroleum's (BP's) Deepwater Horizon rig in the Gulf of Mexico back in 2010 still stands out for what can go wrong. The blast took the lives of 11 workers.[2] Reports from the scene said a malfunctioning blowout preventer failed to activate, causing the disaster. Past critics of BP's safety practices weren't so sure.

WHERE ARE WE NOW ...

Over 80% of the workers in one survey ranked workplace safety more important than minimum wages, sick days, and maternity leave.[1] The main purpose of this chapter is to provide you with knowledge managers need to reduce workplace safety and health problems. The main topics we discuss are safety and the manager; manager's briefing on occupational safety law; what causes accidents; how to prevent accidents; employee engagement–based safety programs; workplace health hazards—problems and remedies; and occupational security and risk management.

LEARNING OBJECTIVE **16-1**

Explain the supervisor's role in safety.

Introduction: Safety and the Manager

Why Safety Is Important

Safety and accident prevention concern managers for several reasons, one of which is the staggering number of workplace accidents. In India, the Ministry of Labor's Indian Labor Statistics reported that about 1,400 fatal and over one lakh non-fatal accidents occur in non-domestic workplaces annually, thereby raising serious questions about the safety provisions for workers in their workplace. Furthermore, a study also went on to show that the number of fatal or non-fatal physical injuries caused at the workplace due to accidents, occupational diseases caused due to toxic exposures as well as health effects caused by environmental factors, are far more than the injuries caused by other mannerisms of manmade violence.[3] And they ignore the suffering the accidents cause the employee and his or her loved ones. Safety also affects costs and profits, as the accompanying Profit Center feature illustrates.

▶ IMPROVING PERFORMANCE: *HR as a Profit Center*

Improving Safety Boosts Profits

Many people assume that when employers economize on safety programs the money they save improves profits, but that's not the case. For one thing, poor safety practices raise wage rates, because wage rates are higher on jobs with riskier working conditions, other things equal.[4] And poor safety and the injuries and illnesses it begets actually drive up costs, including medical expenses, workers' compensation, and lost productivity.[5]

Consider the evidence. One study found a 9.4% drop in injury claims and a 26% average savings on workers' compensation costs over 4 years in companies inspected by California's occupational safety and health agency.[6] A survey of chief financial officers concluded that for every one dollar invested in injury prevention, the employer earns two dollars; 40% said "productivity" was the top benefit of effective workplace safety.[7] One forest products company saved over $1 million over 5 years by investing only about $50,000 in safety improvements and employee training. In the United States, work-related hearing loss costs employers about $242 million a year in workers' compensation claims alone, costs that are probably avoidable through earmuffs, earplugs, and training.[8] So one of the easiest ways to cut costs and boost profits is to spend money improving safety. ■

Source: Based on Russell Sobel, "Occupational Safety and Profit Maximization: Friends or Foes?," The Journal of Socioeconomics 30, no. 9 (2010), pp. 429–433; David Levine et al., "Randomized Government Safety Inspections Reduce Worker Injuries with No Detectable Job Loss," Science 336 (May 18, 2012), pp. 907–911; Chief Financial Officer Survey, Liberty Mutual Insurance Co., 2005; Mike Rich, "Preventing Hearing Loss," www.adhesivesmag.com, January 2012, pp. 40–41.

Injuries aren't just a problem in dangerous industries like construction. For example, computers contribute to airtight "sick building" symptoms like headaches. And office work is susceptible to problems like repetitive trauma injuries.

Management's Role in Safety

We will see that reducing accidents often boils down to reducing accident-causing conditions and accident-causing acts. However, telling employees to "work safely" is futile unless everyone knows management is serious about safety.[9] Management's attitude is crucial.

Historically, for instance, DuPont's accident rate has been much lower than that of the chemical industry as a whole. This good safety record is partly due to an organizational commitment to safety, which is evident in the following description:

> One of the best examples I know of in setting the highest possible priority for safety takes place at a DuPont Plant in Germany. Each morning at the DuPont Polyester and Nylon Plant, the director and his assistants meet at 8:45 to review the past 24 hours. The first matter they discuss is not production, but safety. Only after they have examined reports of accidents and near misses and satisfied themselves that corrective action has been taken do they move on to look at output, quality, and cost matters.[10]

Safety therefore starts at the top.[11] The Strategic Context feature illustrates this.

▶ **IMPROVING PERFORMACE:** *The Strategic Context*

Deepwater Horizon

To critics of BP's safety practices, the Deepwater Horizon disaster in the Gulf wasn't just due to a malfunctioning blowout preventer. To them, rightly or wrongly, the accident reflected the fact that BP's corporate strategy had long emphasized cost-cutting and profitability at the expense of safety. For example, 5 years earlier, a report by the Chemical Safety Board blamed a huge blast at BP's Texas City, Texas, oil refinery on cost-cutting, and on a safety strategy that aimed to reduce accidents but left in place "unsafe and antiquated equipment." To the board and to some others who studied BP's safety practices, Deepwater was another example of how encouraging safe employee behavior must start at the top, and how top management's strategy can trump even earnest efforts to improve employee safety behaviors.[12] ■

Source: Based on Chip Cummins, U.S. Cites Cost Cuts' Role In BP Refinery Blast, Safety Board Lays Blame With Top-Level Decisions, Raising Firm's Legal Risks, www.wsj.com/articles/SB116222460245007872.

In sum, employers should institutionalize their commitment with a safety policy, publicize it, and give safety matters high priority. For instance, at Larsen and Toubro Limited (L&T), dealing with workplace safety is inculcated in the very culture of the place, and it is evident through the portrayal of their three pillars – environment, health, and safety – which seek to ensure "living injury free everyday." Georgia-Pacific reduced its workers' compensation costs by requiring that managers halve accidents or forfeit 30% of their bonuses. ABB Inc. requires its top executives to make safety observation tours of the company's facilities, sites, and projects at least quarterly.[13]

The Supervisor's Role in Accident Prevention

After inspecting a work site in which workers were installing sewer pipes in a 4-foot trench, the Occupational Safety & Health Administration (OSHA) inspector cited the employer for violating the OSHA rule requiring employers to have a "stairway, ladder, ramp or other safe means of egress."[14] In the event the trench caved in, workers needed a quick way out. While this case has happened in the US, the same holds true for India as well.

As in most such cases, the employer had the primary responsibility for safety, but the local supervisor was responsible for day-to-day inspections. Here, the supervisor did not properly do his daily inspection. The trench did cave in, injuring workers (and, secondarily, costing his company many thousands of dollars).

Whether you're the manager in the IT department of a *Fortune* 500 company or managing an excavation or dry cleaning store, daily safety inspections should be part of your routine. As one safety recommendation put it, "a daily walk-through of your workplace—whether you are working in outdoor construction, indoor manufacturing, or any place that poses safety challenges—is an essential part of your work."[15]

What to look for depends on the workplace for which you're responsible. For example, construction sites and dry cleaning stores have hazards all their own. But in general you can use a checklist of unsafe conditions (Note: Please stop what you are reading and look around where you are now: Can you list four potential safety hazards?)

Occupational Health and Safety in India: An Overview

Safety and health of workers have been enshrined in the Constitution of India. Articles 24, 39 (E and F), and 42 specify the same. Both the central and state governments are responsible for ensuring worker's safety. Different aspects of health and safety have been included in the Union List (meant for the central government) and the Concurrent List (both the central and state governments are responsible). While health and safety in mines, oil fields, etc., have been included in the Union List, topics like working hours, conditions of work, social security (e.g., provident fund, compensation, old-age pension) and maternity have been included in the Concurrent List. While many legislations related to different aspects of safety exist in India (for example, the Factories Act has provisions related to safety, and it gets amended regularly), the Ministry of Labor, under the Union government, has announced the National Policy on safety, health, and environment at workplace, which gives the broad framework.

Safety is also a concern in the fast-growing construction sector. One of the widely discussed cases was the accident that happened at the construction site of BALCO in Korba.[16] Fatal accidents also occurred at DMRC's construction site, though the corporation followed stringent safety protocols. Employee safety is of high concern in the mining and oil and gas sectors. For example, the coal-mine safety legislation comprising the Mines Act of 1952, the Mines Rules of 1955, the Coal Mine Regulation of 1957, and other laws form a comprehensive and stringent framework aimed to prevent accidents and ensure safe working conditions in coal mines.

The growth of service sector in India, including that of the IT and ITES industry, has called attention to workplace safety in the service sector as well. In addition to legislations that insist on safety and health provisions of employees, the government of India has set up the National Safety Council (NSC), a voluntary organization, to develop and sustain different initiatives to improve safety and health at the workplace.[17] NSC is a tripartite body with representatives of employers, workers, and government.

At the ground level, safety and health remain a grave concern in India. According to the UN, about 6,300 people die each day in the country because of occupational accidents or work-related health issues. As per their data, around 317 million non-fatal accidents happen annually in India, which result in absences and loss of productivity as well as earnings. The economic burden of the same is estimated to be 4% of the annual GDP.[18] Another survey conducted by the Director General of Mines Safety, under the central Indian government, shows that 170 mine workers were affected by occupational diseases across seven states in silicosis-prone industries.[19] Another startling fact is the lack of coverage of any occupational law to the agricultural sector and unorganized work, where a large number of workers are affected without relief.

While poor implementation of safety law is often cited as a reason for poor safety records, there is also the need to align laws to meet requirements of the modern times. Proper and timely training in safety is another requirement, since lack of training is another reason for increasing incidences.[20] The government currently plans to make safety training mandatory for workers.[21]

Though there have been efforts by the government to ensure occupational health standards in India, the common complaint is that implementation is less than desired. A review of published studies on occupational health showed that occupational health management is a complex issue in India.[22] It includes child labor (even though employment of children below 14 years is prohibited), an informal sector spread across the country, lack of awareness and training, and inadequate attention given to occupational hygiene. The study concludes that the efficacy of the enforcement machinery operated by the government is less than desired. Occupational health concerns have been rising in the growing IT and ITES sector, with the government of India contemplating introducing a separate legislation for the BPOs and the services sector.

Recognizing the importance of high occupational health standards and the strategic advantage of having a healthy workforce, many Indian firms invest in wellness programs. Work places are regularly screened for safety hazards, and ergonomic aspects are given due consideration during the design of workplaces. Companies like Accenture India, Infosys, and Pfizer India have health clubs equipped with modern equipment and qualified trainers in the company premises itself. PSUs like NTPC, SAIL, BHEL, etc., provide such facilities in their residential townships for employees. Sessions on yoga, meditation, and other relaxation techniques are introduced in the workplace as stress busters. Employees at all levels have to attend regular medical screening to identify health-related symptoms.

Here is a list of important Indian legislations covering safety and health, and the administrative mechanisms:

- The Factories Act, 1948
- The Mines Act, 1952
- The Contract Labor (Regulation and Abolition) Act, 1970
- The Dock Workers (Safety, Health and Welfare) Act, 1986
- The Apprentices Act, 1961
- The Plantation Labor Act, 1951
- The Explosives Act, 1884
- The Petroleum Act, 1933
- Indian Electricity Act, 1910
- The Dangerous Machines (Regulations) Act, 1983
- Indian Atomic Energy Act, 1962
- Radiological Protection Rules, 1971
- Manufacture, Storage, and Import of Hazardous Chemicals Rules, 1989

In addition, there are three key legislations covering payment of compensation to workers and providing health services. They are:

- The Employee's Compensation Act, 1923
- The Employees State Insurance Corporation Act, 1948
- The Maternity Benefits Act, 1961

The important features related to safety in some of the above legislations are discussed below.

THE FACTORIES ACT, 1948 This act regulates the health, safety, welfare, and other working conditions of workers in factories. It requires factories employing more than the prescribed numbers to appoint qualified safety officer and medical officer. Safeguards have been prescribed to prevent and report instances of accidents. The legislation also makes pre-medical checkup and periodic medical examination during course of employment mandatory for all workers.

The state governments enforce this act through their factory inspectorates. The Directorate General Factory Advice Service and Labor Institutes (DGFASLI) coordinates matters concerning the safety, health, and welfare of workers in the factories along with their respective state governments. DGFASLI also conducts training, studies, and surveys on various aspects relating to the safety and health of workers through the Central Labor Institute in Mumbai and three other regional labor institutes located in Kolkata, Chennai, and Kanpur.

In case of apprentices engaged under the Apprentices Act of 1961, when they undergo training in factories, the relevant provisions (Chapters III, IV, and V) of the Factories Act are applicable to them, as if they are workers.

THE MINES ACT, 1952 The act has provisions related to the health, safety, and welfare of workers engaged in the coal, metal, and oil mines industries. The Directorate General of Mines Safety conducts inspections and inquiries; issues competency tests for the purpose of appointment to various posts in the mines; and organizes seminars or conferences on various aspects of workers' safety. The central government sets up courts of Inquiry to investigate those accidents that result in the death of 10 or above miners. Both penal and pecuniary punishments are prescribed for contravention of obligation and duties under the act. Apprentices undergoing training in mines are also be covered under the legislation, for safety and health purposes.

THE DOCK WORKERS (SAFETY, HEALTH, AND WELFARE) ACT, 1986 This act contains provisions for the health, safety, and welfare of workers working at ports or docks. The overall emphasis on the activities of the inspectorates constituted under this act is to contain the accident rates and the number of accidents at the ports.

THE CONTRACT LABOR (REGULATION AND ABOLITION) ACT, 1970   As per this legislation, first-aid boxes have to be provided with prescribed contents at every place where contract labor is deployed (Section 19). In case of violation by the contractor, the law requires the principal employer to directly provide for the damages, and the expenses can be deducted from contractor's payment.

THE EMPLOYEES COMPENSATION ACT, 1923   This renamed and amended act (previously known as Workmen's Compensation Act of 1923) has the dual objective of reducing workplace accidents and providing relief to those who are victims of accidents. With the change from workman to employee, clerical work has also been covered under this law. Those affected or their families receive compensation from the employer, in proportion to the injury. In case of death of an employee due to injury, dependents of the worker will receive compensation. Minimum compensation payable for death from injury has been enhanced to ₹1,20,000 from ₹80,000 previously, or 50% of the monthly wages of the deceased multiplied by the relevant factor. Even in case of a contract worker succumbing to an accident, the principal employer is liable to pay the compensation. To administer this legislation, the government appoints commissioners (Section 20), with powers to determine the amount of compensation and settle differences.

THE EMPLOYEES SATE INSURANCE ACT (ESI ACT), 1948   This act provides for a contributory social insurance scheme to support workers in contingencies such as sickness, maternity, employment injury causing temporary or permanent physical disability or death, and loss of wages or loss of earning capacity. Both workers and employers make contribution to the scheme, and the benefits are disbursed through the network of ESIC offices and hospitals across the country.

THE SHOPS AND COMMERCIAL ESTABLISHMENTS ACT (FOR DIFFERENT STATES)   This state level law (each state has independent law, which can be marginally different from other states) also has provisions related to health and safety. The provisions (as per Kerala State Act) include responsibilities for cleanliness, ventilation and lightening, and precaution against fire.

Employing female workers during night is another aspect, where safety concerns have been voiced. The Karnataka Shops and Commercial Establishments Act of 1961 allows employers to let women employees work in night shift, though subject to certain conditions which are:

- Providing transport from residence to workplace and back, which should be free of cost and with safety.
- Employing women in night shift on rotation basis.
- Posting adequate number of security guards during night shift.
- Pre-employment screening of support staff like drivers and guards.
- Scheduling transportation such that a female employee is not alone in the vehicle.

FIRM-LEVEL SAFETY MANAGEMENT: SAFETY OFFICERS AND COMMITTEES   Legislations like the Factories Act of 1948 require that in companies regularly employing more than 1,000 people, or in cases of risky process, upon the decision of the state government, qualified safety officer has be appointed (Section 40B). This safety officer directly reports to the head of the organization, and has to be given sufficient powers. With employee health and safety issues becoming a critical concern for the top management, non-manufacturing organizations have started giving importance to safety at work.

Many Indian firms, particularly in the manufacturing sector, have constituted participatory safety committees, with representation from employers and employees. In large multidivisional firms, like ECIL, multi-tier safety committees are constituted. In ECIL, the corporate-level safety committee looks into broader safety policy and development of a safety culture, while the next level of divisional safety committee deals with operational aspects of safety.[23] In an MNC, ABB India, approach to safety is taken in a participatory manner, taking into consideration the local requirements of different operations. Participatory forums include health and safety committee and employee forums.[24]

In the case of Coal India Limited (CIL), the participatory organization for safety is rather elaborate. At the apex level is the Standing Committee on Safety in Coal Mines, chaired by the minister for Coal and Mines. The Coal India Safety Board, headed by the Chairman of CIL, has workers and management representatives. A tripartite safety committee of workers, management, and government is constituted for each subsidiary company. Area committees and mine committees are also constituted with representatives of workers and management. At the tail-end point, designated and trained worker representatives monitor safety status of mines, on monthly basis.[25]

Manager's Briefing on Occupational Safety Law in the US

The U.S. Congress passed the **Occupational Safety and Health Act of 1970**[26] "to assure so far as possible every working man and woman in the nation safe and healthful working conditions and to preserve our human resources."[27] In India, the Factories Act, 1948, serves as one of the key paradigms underlying the decisions pertaining to safety, health, and working conditions of laborers in the country. Training as well as surveys and studies pertaining to all those aspects which directly or indirectly contribute to the well-being of workers in their workplace are conducted on a periodic basis by regional offices located in Kolkata, Chennai, and Kanpur along with the Central Labor Institute in Mumbai. The only employers it doesn't cover are self-employed persons, farms in which only immediate members of the employer's family work, and some workplaces already protected by other federal agencies or statutes. The act covers federal agencies, but usually not state and local governments.

Occupational Safety and Health Act of 1970
The law passed by Congress in 1970 "to assure so far as possible every working man and woman in the nation safe and healthful working conditions and to preserve our human resources."

OSHA Standards and Record Keeping

OSHA operates under the "general" standard clause that each employer:

> ... shall furnish to each of his [or her] employees employment and a place of employment which are free from recognized hazards that are causing or are likely to cause death or serious physical harm to his [or her] employees.

To carry out this basic mission, OSHA promulgates detailed legally enforceable standards. The regulations don't just list standards to which employers should adhere, but "how." For example, OSHA's respiratory protection standard also covers employee training.

Under OSHA, employers with 11 or more employees must maintain records of and report certain occupational injuries and occupational illnesses. An **occupational illness** is any abnormal condition or disorder caused by exposure to environmental factors associated with employment. This includes acute and chronic illnesses caused by inhalation, absorption, ingestion, or direct contact with toxic substances or harmful agents.

occupational illness
Any abnormal condition or disorder caused by exposure to environmental factors associated with employment.

WHAT THE EMPLOYER MUST REPORT As in Figure 16-1, employers must report all occupational illnesses.[28] They must also report most occupational injuries, specifically those that result in medical treatment (other than first aid), loss of consciousness, restriction of work (one or more lost workdays), restriction of motion, or transfer to another job.[29] If an on-the-job accident results in the death of an employee, all employers, regardless of size, must report the accident to the nearest office of the designated inspector and also the police for legal formalities. As of 2015, in the US, if even one employee is hospitalized for inpatient treatment because of a work-related incident, the employer must notify OSHA within 24 hours.[30]

FIGURE 16-1 What Accidents Must Be Reported Under the Occupational Safety and Health Act (OSHA)?

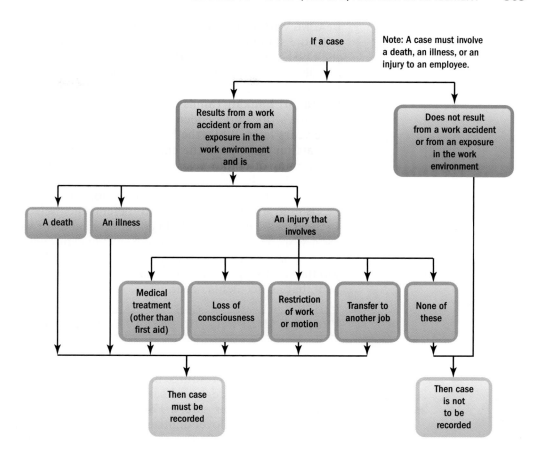

OSHA's current record-keeping rules allow the employer to conclude that an event needn't be reported if the facts so warrant—such as if a worker slips and falls after catching his foot on his car's seat belt when not at work on the company lot.[31]

However, OSHA's record-keeping requirements are still broad.[32] Examples of recordable conditions include food poisoning suffered by an employee in the employer's cafeteria and ankle sprains that occur during voluntary participation in a company softball game at a picnic the employee was required to attend.

Responsibilities and Rights of Employers and Employees

Both employers and employees have responsibilities and rights under the law. *Employers* are responsible for providing "a workplace free from recognized hazards," for being familiar with mandatory standards, and for examining workplace conditions to make sure they conform to standards.[33] Employers have the right to seek advice and off-site consultation from the authorities (it can be the Factories Inspector in case of factories in India, the Director General of Mines Safety for Mines, or the OSHA in the US), request and receive proper identification of the OSHA compliance officer before inspection, and to be advised by the compliance officer of the reason for an inspection.

Employees also have rights and responsibilities. Employees are responsible, for example, for complying with all applicable standards, for following all employer safety and health rules and regulations, and for reporting hazardous conditions to the supervisor. They have the right to demand safety and health on the job without fear of punishment. In Indian companies, not obeying mandatory safety provisions is an offence under the Standing Orders or Employee Code of Conduct. Safety concerns are also raised in union management meetings and are a part of collective bargaining agreements in India.

DEALING WITH EMPLOYEE RESISTANCE   Although employees are responsible to comply with the standards as laid down by the constitutional provisions of their country – the OSHA in the US and the Factories Act in India – they often resist; the employer usually remains liable for any penalties. The refusal of some workers to wear hard hats typifies this problem. What started in 2008 as an agitation against the killing of several Sri Lankan Tamils during the nation's civil war, has resulted in the formation of India's first independent union for workers involved in the IT and ITES sector nine years later. While the large-scale layoffs in the sector are chiefly responsible for this action on part of the employees, it also provides an interesting insight into the functioning of employees, wherein on the one hand they are expected to comply with rules and regulations at the workplace or as have been laid down by the Factories Act, whereas on the other, resistance in one form or the other becoming unavoidable.

Employers have attempted to defend themselves by citing worker intransigence. In most cases, courts still hold employers liable for workplace safety violations. Cited for a workplace injury, the employer may claim employee misconduct. The key here is to provide documented evidence that the employee was properly trained to do the job the right way but did not.[34] But the only sure way to eliminate liability is to make sure that no accidents occur.

TRENDS SHAPING HR: *DIGITAL AND SOCIAL MEDIA*

SITEDOCS DIGITAL WORKPLACE SAFETY   Safety compliance usually has been managed centrally, by human resource managers or by a specialized safety unit. However, new digital mobile device–based safety systems now give managers and even employees more influence over safety. For example, the SiteDocs digital safety management system lets the employer digitize, move, store, work with, and access safety documents via mobile devices (iPad) and the Web.[35] Employees can login via the mobile device and view and complete their safety documentation (such as OSHA reports). These become available immediately to management.

A system such as SiteDocs produces many benefits. For example, it enables management to monitor in real time whether employees are completing their documentation and to identify almost at once workplace hazards and incidents. It facilitates due diligence—for example, management knows at once who signed a document and when, and what corrective action was taken. Safety documents can be updated online, without the time and cost of updating hard copies. And the system gives employees instant access to available safety procedures, and automatically files safety forms. ■

LEARNING OBJECTIVE 16-3
Answer the question, "What causes accidents?"

unsafe conditions
The mechanical and physical conditions that cause accidents.

What Causes Accidents?

There are three basic causes of workplace accidents: chance occurrences, unsafe conditions, and employees' unsafe acts. Chance occurrences (such as walking past a tree just when a branch falls) are more or less beyond management's control. We will therefore focus on unsafe conditions and unsafe acts.

What Causes Unsafe Conditions?

Unsafe conditions are a main cause of accidents. They include:

- Improperly guarded equipment
- Defective equipment
- Hazardous procedures around machines or equipment
- Unsafe storage—congestion, overloading
- Improper illumination—glare, insufficient light
- Improper ventilation.[36]

The solution here is to identify and eliminate the unsafe conditions. The main aim of the Factories Act, 1948, is to ensure that adequate safety measures are taken on factory sites as well as areas undergoing any kind of industrial activity that may pose a threat to the overall safety and well-being of the workers engaged in work there. It, therefore, seeks to promote health, safety, and welfare of the workers employed in factories. The employer's safety department (if any) and its human resource managers and top managers should take responsibility for identifying unsafe conditions.

While accidents can happen anywhere, there are some high-danger zones. About one-third of industrial accidents occur around forklift trucks, wheelbarrows, and other handling and lifting areas. The most serious accidents usually occur by metal and woodworking machines and saws, or around transmission machinery like gears, pulleys, and flywheels.[37] Construction accounts for a disproportionate share of accidents, with falls the major problem.[38]

SAFETY CLIMATE   Work schedules and fatigue also affect accident rates. Accident rates usually don't increase too noticeably during the first 5 or 6 hours of the workday. But after that, the accident rate increases faster. This is due partly to fatigue and partly to the fact that accidents occur more often during night shifts. With reduced headcount and more people with second jobs, employee fatigue is a growing problem today.[39] Many employers are therefore taking steps to reduce employee fatigue, such as banning mandatory overtime.

The workplace "climate" or psychology is very important. One researcher reviewed the fatal accidents offshore oil workers suffered in the British North Sea.[40] A strong pressure to complete the work as quickly as possible, employees who are under stress, and a poor safety climate—for instance, supervisors who never mentioned safety—were some of the psychological conditions leading to accidents. Similarly, accidents occur more frequently in plants with high seasonal layoff rates, hostility among employees, many garnished wages, and blighted living conditions.

What Causes Unsafe Acts?

Unsafe employee acts (such as running) will undo your efforts to banish unsafe conditions, but there are no easy answers to what causes people to act that way.

It may seem obvious that some people are simply accident prone, but the research isn't clear.[41] On closer inspection it turns out some "accident repeaters" were just unlucky, or may have been more meticulous about reporting their accidents.[42] However, there is evidence that people with specific traits may indeed be accident prone. For example, people who are impulsive, sensation seeking, extremely extroverted, and less conscientious (in terms of being less fastidious and dependable) have more accidents.[43]

Furthermore, the person who is accident prone on one job may not be so on another. For example, personality traits that correlate with filing vehicular insurance claims include *entitlement* ("think there's no reason they should not speed"), *impatience* ("were 'always in a hurry'"), *aggressiveness* ("the first to move when the light turns green"), and *distractibility* ("frequently distracted by cell phones, eating, and so on").[44]

 HR in Practice at the Hotel Paris   Lisa and the CFO reviewed their company's safety records, and what they found disturbed them deeply. In terms of every safety-related metric they could find, including accident costs per year, lost time due to accidents, workers' compensation per employee, and number of safety training programs per year, the Hotel Paris compared unfavorably with most other hotel chains and service firms. To see how they handled this, see the case on page 530–531 of this chapter.

How to Prevent Accidents

In practice, accident prevention boils down to reducing unsafe conditions and reducing unsafe acts. In large firms, the chief safety officer (often called the "environmental health and safety officer") is responsible.[45] In smaller firms, managers, including those from human resources, plant management, and first-line managers, share these responsibilities.

LEARNING OBJECTIVE 16-4
List and explain five ways to prevent accidents at work.

Reducing Unsafe Conditions

Reducing unsafe conditions like the ones OSHA and the Factories Act of 1948 address are the employer's first line of defense. Safety engineers should design jobs to remove or reduce physical hazards. Supervisors play a critical role here, as outlined in the Factories Act as well. The Factories Act, 1948, requires that all factories (where more than 1,000 workers are employed) should have safety officers. (Section 40B). In case the manufacturing process carries the risk of harm, poisoning, or diseases, the state government can mandate appointment of safety officer [Section 40B (ii)]. The safety officer is given the status of a senior executive or department head in the factory, and has to report to the chief executive (*BHEL vs Vijay, 2006 (108) FLR 113*). Checklists can help identify and remove potential hazards.

Employers also use computerized tools to design safer equipment. For example, Designsafe helps to automate hazard analysis, risk assessment, and safety options identification. Designsafe helps the safety designer choose the most appropriate safety control device for keeping the worker safe, such as adjustable enclosures, presence-sensing devices, and personal protective equipment.[46]

Sometimes the solution for an unsafe condition is obvious, and sometimes it's not. For example, slippery floors often cause slips and falls.[47] Obvious remedies include floor mats and better lighting. Perhaps less obviously, personal safety gear, like slip-resistant footwear with grooved soles, can also reduce slips and falls. Cut-resistant gloves reduce the hazards of working with sharp objects.[48] (Hand injuries account for about 1 million emergency department visits annually by U.S. workers.)[49] Wearable digital devices such as motion monitors present new safety challenges.[50] The employer should determine the device's usability and ascertain that it won't cause an unanticipated safety problem.

Reducing unsafe conditions is important in offices too.[51] For example, get written confirmation that the space meets all building codes; make sure the builder, contractors, and/or landlord follow standards in the design and construction of facilities (for instance, unblocked exits); make sure the lease lets you compel the landlord to fix safety problems if ones surface; and make sure air ducts are cleaned of dust and allergens.

job hazard analysis
A systematic approach to identifying and eliminating workplace hazards before they occur.

JOB HAZARD ANALYSIS   A Yale University science student, working late in a lab, was critically injured when her hair became caught in a spinning lathe. **Job hazard analysis** involves a systematic approach to identifying and eliminating such hazards before they cause accidents. According to OSHA, job hazard analysis "focuses on the relationship between the worker, the task, the tools, and the work environment," and ends by reducing the potential risks to acceptable levels.[52]

Consider a safety analyst looking at the Yale science lab, with the aim of identifying potential hazards. Performing a job hazard analysis here might involve looking at the situation and asking these questions:

- *What can go wrong?* A student's hair or clothing could become caught in the lathe, a rotating object that "catches" it and pulls it into the machine.
- *What are the consequences?* The student could receive a severe injury as his or her body part or hair is caught and drawn into the spinning lathe.
- *How could it happen?* The accident could happen as a result of the student leaning too close to the lathe while working at the bench, or walking too close to the lathe, or bending to reach for an article that fell close to the lathe.
- *What are other contributing factors?* Speed is one contributing factor. The problem would occur so quickly that the student would be unable to take evasive action once the lathe ensnarled the hair.

The job hazard analysis should provide the basis for creating countermeasures. For example, given the speed with which such a lathe accident would occur, it's unlikely that training by itself would suffice. Instead, the lathe area here should be ensconced in its own protective casing, and changes made to ensure that the lathe can't spin unless the student takes action via a foot pedal to keep the lathe power on.

OPERATIONAL SAFETY REVIEWS   After Japan's Fukushima nuclear power plant exploded several years ago, many wondered if the International Atomic Energy

operational safety reviews
Reviews conducted by agencies to ascertain whether units under their jurisdiction are complying with all the applicable safety laws, regulations, orders, and rules.

Agency (IAEA) had conducted the necessary operational safety reviews. **Operational safety reviews** (or safety operations reviews) are conducted by agencies to ascertain whether units under their jurisdiction are complying with all the applicable safety laws, regulations, orders, and rules. For example, under IAEA's Operational Safety Review Program, "international teams of experts conduct in-depth reviews of operational safety performance at a nuclear power plant."[53]

PERSONAL PROTECTIVE EQUIPMENT Getting employees to wear personal protective equipment (PPE) like hard hats is famously difficult.[54] Wearability is important. In addition to providing reliable protection, protective gear should fit properly; be easy to care for, maintain, and repair; be flexible and lightweight; provide comfort and reduce heat stress; have rugged construction; be relatively easy to put on and take off; and be easy to clean, dispose of, and recycle.[55] Many employers, such as Kimberly-Clark and MCR Safety, are tapping into new fibers and fabrics to design easier-wearing high-tech solutions.[56] Including employees in planning the safety program and addressing comfort issues contribute to employees' willingness to use the protective gear.[57]

Of course, the manager should require wearing the protective equipment before the accident, not just after it. For example, a combustible dust explosion at a sugar refinery killed 14 employees and burned many others. The employer subsequently required that all employees wear fire-resistant clothing, unfortunately too late for the victims.[58]

Similarly, cold weather means employers must help protect their outdoor workers.[59] This should include, among other things, monitoring temperature and wind chill conditions, making sure workers are supplied with adequate cold-weather apparel, monitoring workers for signs of frostbite, and providing adequate indoor breaks.

But again, reducing unsafe conditions is always the first line of defense. Next use administrative controls (such as job rotation to reduce long-term exposure to the hazard). Only then turn to PPE.[60]

Diversity Counts: Protecting Vulnerable Workers

In designing safe and healthy environments, employers should pay special attention to vulnerable workers, such as young, immigrant, aging, and women workers.[61] For example, as the CEO of one safety engineering company said, "For decades, women essentially were ignored when it came to designing eye and face protection." Today, more products are available in smaller sizes.[62]

Similarly, with more workers postponing retirement, older workers are doing more manufacturing jobs.[63] They can do these jobs effectively. However, there are numerous potential physical changes associated with aging, including loss of strength, loss of muscular flexibility, and reduced reaction time.[64] This means that employers should make special provisions such as designing jobs to reduce heavy lifting, and boosting lighting levels.[65] The fatality rate for older workers is about three times that of younger workers.[66] ∎

Reducing Unsafe Acts

While reducing unsafe conditions is the first line of defense, human misbehavior will short-circuit even the best safety efforts.[67] Sometimes the misbehavior is intentional, but often it's not. Unfortunately, just telling employees to "pay attention" usually isn't enough. First identify and try to eliminate potential risks, such as unguarded equipment. Next, reduce potential distractions, such as noise, heat, and stress. Then, carefully screen and train employees, as we explain next.

Reducing Unsafe Acts Through Screening

Proper employee screening and placement reduce unsafe acts. Here the employer's aim is to identify the traits that might predict accidents on the job in question, and then screen candidates for this trait. For example, the Employee Reliability Index (ERI)[68] measures reliability dimensions such as emotional maturity, conscientiousness, and safe job performance.[69] Though not definitive, using the ERI in selection did seem to be associated with reductions in work-related accidents in one study. Others use *job simulation tests* (which attempt to assess the applicant by simulating physically demanding work activities) and *physical capabilities tests* (which measure muscle strength and motion) to predict who will have more accidents.[70]

Similarly, behavioral interview questions can be revealing. For example, ask, "What would you do if you saw another employee working in an unsafe way?" and "What would you do if your supervisor gave you a task, but didn't provide any training on how to perform it safely?"[71]

Reducing Unsafe Acts Through Training

Safety training reduces unsafe acts, especially for new employees. You should instruct employees in safe practices and procedures, warn them of potential hazards, and work on developing a safety-conscious attitude. OSHA's standards require more than training. Employees must demonstrate that they actually learned what to do. Because temporary workers account for a disproportionate share of workplace accidents, the employer should take particular care to train them.[72]

The main aim of safety training is not to meet government-specified training standards; it is to impart the knowledge and skills required to reduce accidents. The National Safety Council of India (nsc.org.in) and private agencies like the NIST (nistinstitute.com) provide safety training in India. The Directorate General of Factory Advice Service and Labor Institutes (DGFASI) conducts training programs for managers, trade union leaders, and workers, including a diploma in industrial safety, which qualifies participants for safety officer position. Specialized courses are also offered for inspectors under the Factories Act and other legislations.

The nature of the safety training is important. One study found that the most effective safety training demanded high employee engagement.[73] In this study, the "least engaging" programs included lectures, films, reading materials, and video-based training. Moderately engaging programs included computer interface instruction with feedback. "Engaging" ones included behavioral modeling, simulation, and hands-on training.

Emergency stop devices, such as buttons, override other machine controls to remove power from hazardous machine motion.

Valery Voennyy/Alamy

Improving Performance Through HRIS Online Safety Training

Employers also turn to the Web to support their safety training programs.[74] For example, PureSafety (www.ulworkplace.com) enables firms to create their own training Web sites, complete with a "message from the safety director." Once an employer installs the PureSafety Web site, it can populate the site with courses from companies that supply health and safety courses via that site.[75] When the University of California system wanted to deliver mandated safety training to its 50,000 employees on 10 different campuses, it developed a program with the vendor Vivid Learning Systems to deliver online. ■

Reducing Unsafe Acts Through Posters, Incentives, and Positive Reinforcement

Employers also use various tools to motivate worker safety.[76] Safety posters are one, but are no substitute for comprehensive safety programs. Employers should combine them with other techniques (like screening and training) to reduce unsafe conditions and acts, and change the posters often. Posters should be easily visible, legible, and well-lit.[77]

Incentive programs are also useful.[78] Management at Tesoro Corporation's Golden Eagle refinery in California instituted one such plan. Employees earn "WINGS" (an acronym for Willing Involvement Nurtures Greater Safety) points for engaging in one or more specific safety activities, such as taking emergency response training. Employees can each earn up to $20 per month by accumulating points.[79] The Profit Center feature shows another example.

OSHA has argued that such programs don't cut down on actual injuries or illnesses, but only on injury and illness *reporting*. OSHA might question any safety incentive payment that is so high that the award might dissuade reasonable workers from reporting safety problems.[80] One option (see accompanying Profit Center feature) is to emphasize nontraditional incentives, like recognition.[81] In any case, the incentive program needs to be part of a comprehensive safety program.[82]

▶ IMPROVING PERFORMANCE: *HR as a Profit Center*

Using Positive Reinforcement

Many employers successfully use *positive reinforcement programs* to improve safety. Such programs provide workers with continuing positive feedback, usually in the form of graphical performance reports and supervisory support, to shape the workers' safety-related behavior.

Researchers introduced one program in a wholesale bakery.[83] The new safety program included training and positive reinforcement. The researchers set and communicated a reasonable safety goal (in terms of observed incidents performed safely). Next, employees participated in a 30-minute training session by viewing pairs of slides depicting scenes that the researchers staged in the plant. One slide, for example, showed the supervisor climbing over a conveyor; the parallel slide showed the supervisor walking around the conveyor. After viewing an unsafe act, employees had to describe, "What's unsafe here?" Then the researchers demonstrated the same incident again but performed in a safe manner, and explicitly stated the safe-conduct rule ("go around, not over or under, conveyors").

At the conclusion of the training phase, supervisors showed employees a graph with their pretraining safety record (in terms of observed incidents performed safely) plotted. Supervisors then encouraged workers to consider increasing their performance to the new safety goal for their own protection, to decrease costs, and to help the plant get out of its last-place safety ranking. Then the researchers posted the graph and a list of safety rules.

Whenever observers walked through the plant collecting safety data, they posted on the graph the percentage of incidents they had seen performed safely by the group as a whole, thus providing the workers with positive feedback. Workers could compare their current safety performance with both their previous performance and their assigned goal. In addition, supervisors praised workers when they performed selected incidents safely. Safety in the plant subsequently improved markedly. ■

Workplace Safety in Services Sector: Vodafone India and Its 8 Absolute Rules

Vodafone India has introduced a safety policy (as part of its Health, Safety, Well Being of Employees and Partners or HSWB policy) aimed to improve safety and wellness in the organization. Unlike a manufacturing firm, Vodafone India focuses on safety of its sales, service, and support employees through eight safety rules which are applicable during office timing and even outside. Since most of the employees are mobile, road safety and driving related rules have been included in this protocol.

- Always wear a seat belt while driving and ensure that others wear one too.
- Never exceed speed limit.
- Always wear helmet while riding and ensure that pillion rider wears it as well.
- Never use mobile phone while driving.
- Never drive under the influence of alcohol or drugs that influence driver performance.
- Electrical work should be carried out only by qualified individuals.
- Always use suitable personal protective equipment and attach safety harnesses while working at heights.
- Never undertake any street or underground work activities unless competent to do so.

This code applies to Vodafone India's vendors supplying services and visitors to its offices as well. Visitors are given quick briefing on safety precautions, before they move for a meeting in the premises.

The company refers to the above rules as Absolute Code, which has to be followed mandatorily. Violations have invited action, including dismissals and warnings or termination of vendor contracts.[84]

The safety concern is extended to families too. The firm sends a kit consisting of safety equipment like gloves and electric socket cover and a safety message to all its employees' homes. Regular training programs are also held to reinforce the safety message.[85] ■

Particularly in situations like this where employees are relatively unsupervised, employers should create a safety-conscious culture by showing that they take safety seriously.

John Panella/Shutterstock

Reducing Unsafe Acts by Fostering a Culture of Safety

Employers and supervisors should create a safety-conscious culture by showing that they take safety seriously. One study measured safety culture in terms of questions like "my supervisor says a good word whenever he sees the job done according to the safety rules" and "my supervisor approaches workers during work to discuss safety issues."[86]

According to one safety expert, a workplace with a safety-oriented culture exhibits:

1. *Teamwork,* in the form of management and employees both involved in safety;
2. Highly visible and interactive *communication and collaboration* on safety matters;
3. A *shared vision* of safety excellence (specifically, an overriding attitude that all accidents and injuries are preventable);
4. *Assignment* of critical safety functions to specific individuals or teams;
5. A *continuous effort* toward identifying and correcting workplace safety problems and hazards;[87] and,
6. *Encouragement* of incident reporting.[88]

Reducing Unsafe Acts by Creating a Supportive Environment

Supportive supervisors' teams seem to have better safety records. "Organizations can develop a supportive environment by training supervisors to be better leaders, emphasizing the importance of teamwork and social support, and establishing the value of safety."[89]

Reducing Unsafe Acts by Establishing a Safety Policy

The company's written safety policy should emphasize that accident prevention is of the utmost importance at your firm, and that the firm will do everything practical to eliminate or reduce accidents and injuries.

Reducing Unsafe Acts by Setting Specific Loss Control Goals

Set specific safety goals to achieve. For example, set safety goals in terms of frequency of lost-time injuries per number of full-time employees.

Reducing Unsafe Acts Through Behavior-Based Safety and Safety Awareness Programs

behavior-based safety
Identifying the worker behaviors that contribute to accidents and then training workers to avoid these behaviors.

Behavior-based safety means identifying the worker behaviors that contribute to accidents and then training workers to avoid these behaviors. Tenneco Corporation (which manufactures Monroe shock absorbers) implemented one such program. The firm selected internal consultants from among its quality managers, training managers, engineers, and production workers. After training, the internal consultants identified five critical behaviors for Tenneco's first safety program, such as *Eyes on task: Does the employee watch his or her hands while performing a task?* The consultants made observations and collected data on the behaviors. Then they instituted training programs to get employees to perform these five behaviors properly.[90]

safety awareness program
Program that enables trained supervisors to orient new workers arriving at a job site regarding common safety hazards and simple prevention methods.

Employers also use *safety awareness* programs to improve employee safe behavior. A **safety awareness program** means trained supervisors orient new workers arriving at a job site regarding common safety hazards and simple prevention methods. For example, the Roadway Safety Awareness Program of the US covers trucker safety issues such as stopping distances required at various speeds (see the accompanying screen grab). In India, for instance, Ashok Leyland, an automotive company, has set up Road Safety Institutes that train truck drivers in safe driving practices. The aim is to reduce accidents and on-road fatalities by improving traffic discipline.

Reducing Unsafe Acts Through Employee Participation

Employees are an excellent source of insights about safety problems and solutions. For example, when the International Truck and Engine Corp. began designing a new robot-based plant, management appointed joint labor–management safety

The Roadway Safety Awareness Program covers trucker safety issues such as stopping distances required at various speeds.

Source: National Work Zone Safety Information Clearinghouse, a project of the American Road & Transportation Builders Association—Transportation Development Foundation.

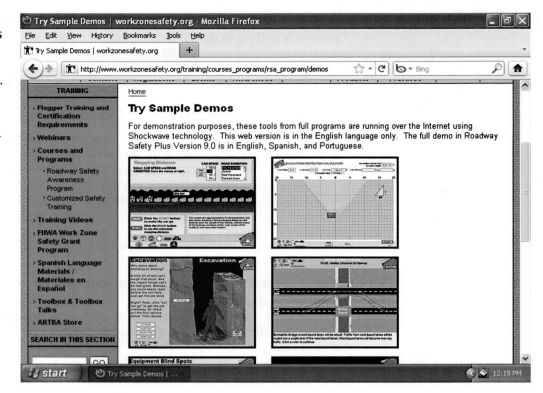

teams for each department.[91] The teams worked with project engineers to design safeguards for the robot equipment. The company sent one safety team to Japan to watch the robot machines in action, and to identify items teams needed to address. This team worked with employees to identify possible hazards and to develop new devices (such as color-coded locks) to protect the employees.[92]

TRENDS SHAPING HR: *DIGITAL AND SOCIAL MEDIA*

Conducting Safety and Health Audits and Inspections

Safety-conscious managers know that good intentions aren't enough: the employer must audit safety compliance. Companies (such as Milliken, discussed pages 515–516) therefore create safety committees to evaluate safety adequacy, to conduct and monitor safety audits, and to suggest ways for improving safety.[93] Line managers should routinely inspect for problems using safety audit/checklists, including investigating all accidents and "near misses."

Employers expedite and enable employee-generated "distributed" safety audits by using mobile digital tools. For example, managers and employees use iAuditor—Safety Audit and Checklist App,[94] available via iTunes from SafetyCulture Pty Ltd., to facilitate safety audits. iAuditor contains numerous safety checklists and tools that let employers create actions depending on the checklist response.[95] As another example, AssessNET is cloud-based safety software that lets employers remotely manage risk assessments, accident records, and safety audits.[96] Employees use AssessNET from their desktops and mobile devices. It provides them with quick access to safety records, lets them quickly report hazards, and alerts management of safety incidents.[97] With both tools, security-related metrics would include, for instance, injury and illness rates, workers' compensation cost per employee, at-risk behavior reduction, and safety training exercises.[98] To ensure that audits result in improvements, *trend the audit data* (for instance, to see if accident rates are rising or falling or steady), and *track the corrective actions* through to completion.[99] ∎

TABLE 16-1 Reducing Unsafe Conditions and Acts: A Summary

Reduce Unsafe Conditions

Identify and eliminate unsafe conditions.

Use administrative means, such as job rotation.

Use personal protective equipment.

Reduce Unsafe Acts

Emphasize top management commitment.

Emphasize safety.

Establish a safety policy.

Reduce unsafe acts through selection.

Provide safety training.

Use posters and other propaganda.

Use positive reinforcement.

Set specific safety goals to achieve.

Use behavior-based safety programs.

Encourage worker participation.

Conduct safety and health audits and inspections regularly.

Table 16-1 summarizes suggestions for reducing unsafe conditions and acts.[100]

LEARNING OBJECTIVE 16-5

Describe how one company uses employee engagement to improve workplace safety.

Employee Engagement Guide for Managers

Milliken & Company—World-Class Safety Through Employee Engagement

Milliken & Company, founded in 1865, designs, manufactures, and markets chemicals, floor coverings, protective fabrics, and textiles. The company has about 7,000 employees in more than 39 facilities around the world. The privately owned Milliken has received widespread recognition for the quality of its innovative products, for its high employee engagement, and for its world-class employee engagement-based occupational safety program; it's also the only company to consistently rank as a "most ethical company" for 15 years running.[101] A survey of Milliken's employees found an 80% positive engagement level, based on questions concerning employees' commitment, pride in company, and empowerment efforts.[102] Its extraordinarily low workplace illness and injury rates mean it consistently rates as one of the safest companies in which to work.[103]

Involvement-Based Employee Engagement

The centerpiece of Milliken's safety process is its *involvement-based employee engagement* program. For example, employees staff the safety steering and safety subcommittee system, submit "opportunity for improvement" suggestions weekly, review each of these suggestions, and provide feedback on every suggestion.[104] The safety process depends on *cascading goals* deriving from federal, state, and Milliken-based safety guidelines. These goals are translated through weekly meetings into specific metrics (for instance, "accidents per employee hour worked") to be achieved by each plant's subcommittees. Each safety subcommittee then performs weekly *audits,* to ensure compliance and to ensure the plant's safety activities are continuously improved.

The Milliken safety program quantifies each employee's involvement, for instance, in terms of serving on safety subcommittees, being a trainer or safety subject matter expert, or conducting safety audits.[105] Also to help win engagement, the program *empowers* employees, for instance, by training each to do his or her "safety job" (such as being knowledgeable about OSHA safety regulations). All plant employees are also trained to give and receive peer-to-peer safety comments. Each is authorized to act on what he or she observes by providing "constructive feedback" or "appreciative feedback" when observing another employee doing something safely (or not). Each employee is also trained to use Milliken's safety tracking mechanism. This tool helps employees make sure that safety suggestions, safety audit findings, or other safety agenda items are tracked and finalized, by giving each item a number, date, and the name of the responsible Milliken employee.[106]

Members of each plant's employee safety steering committee investigate all safety incidents to help discover the causes.[107] Milliken recognizes employees' safety efforts in formal celebratory events throughout the year, such as having "cheerleaders" provide safety cheers as engineers enter the plant.[108]

<table>
<tr><td>

LEARNING OBJECTIVE **16-6**

List five workplace health hazards and how to deal with them.

</td></tr>
</table>

Workplace Health Hazards: Problems and Remedies

Most workplace hazards aren't as obvious as unguarded equipment or slippery floors. Many are unseen hazards that the company inadvertently produces as part of its production processes. Typical workplace exposure hazards include chemicals and other hazardous materials, temperature extremes, biohazards (including naturally occurring, such as mold, and manmade, such as anthrax), and ergonomic hazards (such as uncomfortable equipment).[109]

Chemicals and Industrial Hygiene

OSHA standards list exposure limits for about 600 chemicals, such as asbestos, lead, cadmium, and formaldehyde. Hazardous substances like these require air sampling and other preventive and precautionary measures.

Managing such hazards comes under the area of *industrial hygiene* and involves recognition, evaluation, and control. First, the facility's health and safety officers (possibly working with teams of supervisors and employees) must *recognize* possible exposure hazards. This typically involves conducting plant/facility walk-around surveys, employee interviews, records reviews, and reviews of government (OSHA) and nongovernmental standards.

Once the manager identifies a possible hazard, *evaluation* involves determining how severe the hazard is. This requires measuring the exposure, comparing the measure to some benchmark (such as 0.10 fibers per cubic centimeter for asbestos), and determining if the risk is within standard.[110]

Hazard *control* involves eliminating or reducing the hazard. Note that personal protective gear is generally the *last* option for dealing with such problems. The employer must first install engineering controls (such as process enclosures or ventilation) and administrative controls (including training and improved housekeeping).

The accompanying HR Practices Around the Globe feature shows one safety program abroad.

▶ **IMPROVING PERFORMANCE:** *HR Practices Around the Globe*

Safety at Saudi Petrol Chemical

The industrial safety and security manager for the Saudi Petrol Chemical Co., in Jubail City, Saudi Arabia, says that his company's excellent safety record results from the fact that "our employees are champions of safety."[111] Employees serve on safety committees, develop and lead daily and monthly safety meetings, and conduct job safety analyses, for instance.

Safety begins with top management. Senior management representatives serve on the company's Management Health and Safety Committee. This committee meets monthly to review incident reports, establish health and safety goals, review safety statistics, and endorse and sponsor safety programs.

The firm cultivates its "safety first" culture from the day a new employee arrives at work. For example, new employees are encouraged to participate in the safety process during orientation. Then (about 6 weeks later) they attend a one-day orientation where company officials emphasize the importance of the company's health, safety, and environmental policies and programs. Employees also participate in monthly departmental training sessions to discuss departmental safety issues and safety suggestions. They work with their departmental committees to conduct monthly safety audits, to review and document departmental job safety, and to submit safety suggestions (about 60 suggestions are submitted per month). Employees are required to report every safety incident and near miss, and more than 600 reports are submitted each year. ■

Exposure to asbestos is a major potential source of occupational respiratory disease. This worker wears protective clothing and a respirator to remove asbestos from ceiling panels in a classroom.

Ashley Cooper/Corbis

KNOW YOUR EMPLOYMENT LAW

Hazard Communication

In, say, a dry cleaning store, it might not be apparent just by looking at it that the clear cleaning chemical hydrofluoric acid will eat through glass and blind an unsuspecting worker. Under OSHA's regulations, employers must communicate the presence and nature of hazards to which workers might be exposed. OSHA's *hazard communication standard,* recently revised, states that "in order to ensure chemical safety in the workplace, information about the identities and hazards of the chemicals must be available and understandable to workers." In line with this, chemical manufacturers and importers must label and provide hazard safety data sheets to their customers. All employers must have labels and safety data sheets available for their exposed workers, and train workers to handle the chemicals appropriately.[112] ■

Asbestos Exposure at Work and Air Quality

Asbestos is a major source of occupational respiratory disease. Efforts are still under way to rid old buildings of the substance.

Alcoholism and Substance Abuse

About two-thirds of people with an alcohol disorder work full-time.[113] Some estimate that almost 13 million U.S. workers use drugs illicitly.[114] According to a report by the Ministry of Social Justice, government of India, "Substance abuse has emerged as a serious concern, adversely affecting the physical and socio-economic well-being of the country." Further studies also show the increased use of substances among women as well as children in addition to the increase in pharmaceutical substance abuse, especially among street children, across the country.[115] In the US, employee alcoholism may cost employers about $226 billion per year, for instance, in higher absenteeism and accidents.[116]

For many employers, dealing with substance abuse begins with substance abuse testing.[117] It's unusual to find employers who don't at least test job candidates for substance abuse before formally hiring them. And many states are instituting mandatory random drug testing for high-hazard workers.

DEALING WITH SUBSTANCE ABUSE   Ideally, a drug-free workplace program includes five components:[118]

1. A drug-free workplace policy
2. Supervisor training
3. Employee education
4. Employee assistance
5. Drug testing

The policy should state, at a minimum, "The use, possession, transfer, or sale of illegal drugs by employees is prohibited." It should also explain the policy's rationale, and the disciplinary consequences. Supervisors should be trained to monitor employees' performance, and to stay alert to drug-related performance problems.

Several tools are available to screen for alcohol or drug abuse. The most widely used self-reporting screening instruments for alcoholism are the 4-item CAGE and the 25-item Michigan Alcoholism Screening Test (MAST). The former asks questions like these: Have you ever (1) attempted to Cut back on alcohol, (2) been Annoyed by comments about your drinking, (3) felt Guilty about drinking, (4) had an Eye-opener first thing in the morning to steady your nerves?[119] As in Table 16-2, alcohol-related symptoms range from tardiness in the earliest stages of alcohol abuse to prolonged, unpredictable absences in its later stages.[120]

Preemployment drug testing discourages those on drugs from applying for jobs or coming to work for employers who do testing.[121]

TABLE 16-2 Observable Behavior Patterns Indicating Possible Alcohol-Related Problems

Alcoholism Stage	Some Possible Signs of Alcoholism Problems	Some Possible Alcoholism Performance Issues
Early	Arrives at work late	Reduced job efficiency
	Untrue statements	Misses deadlines
	Leaves work early	
Middle	Frequent absences, especially Mondays	Accidents
	Colleagues mentioning erratic behavior	Warnings from boss
	Mood swings	Noticeably reduced performance
	Anxiety	
	Late returning from lunch	
	Frequent multi-day absences	
Advanced	Personal neglect	Frequent falls, accidents
	Unsteady gait	Strong disciplinary actions
	Violent outbursts	Basically incompetent performance
	Blackouts and frequent forgetfulness	
	Possible drinking on job	

Source: Based on Gopal Patel and John Adkins Jr., "The Employer's Role in Alcoholism Assistance," *Personnel Journal* 62, no. 7 (July 1983), p. 570; Mary-Anne Enoch and David Goldman, "Problem Drinking and Alcoholism: Diagnosis and Treatment," *American Family Physician,* February 1, 2002, www.aafp.org/afp/20020201/441.html, accessed July 20, 2008; and Ken Pidd et al., "Alcohol and Work: Patterns of Use, Workplace Culture, and Safety," www.nisu.flinders.edu.au/pubs/reports/2006/injcat82.pdf, accessed July 20, 2008.

Preemployment tests pick up only about half the workplace drug users, so ongoing random testing is advisable. One study concluded that preemployment drug testing had little effect on workplace accidents. However, a combination of preemployment and random ongoing testing was associated with a significant reduction in workplace accidents.[122]

Disciplining, discharge, in-house counseling, and referral to an outside agency are the four traditional prescriptions when a *current* employee tests positive. Most professionals seem to counsel treatment rather than outright dismissal, at least initially. Employers often make available the necessary counseling so as to support employees with alcohol or drug abuse problems.

Whether the alcohol abuse reflects a "disability" under the ADA depends on several things.[123] In general, employers can hold alcohol-dependent employees to the same performance standards as they hold nonalcoholics. However, there are legal risks. Employees have sued for invasion of privacy, wrongful discharge, defamation, and illegal searches. Therefore, before implementing a drug control program, employers should use employee handbooks and the like to publicize their substance abuse plans. Make sure to explain the conditions under which testing might occur and what accommodations you made for employees who voluntarily seek treatment.

Stress, Burnout, and Depression

Problems such as alcoholism sometimes reflect stress and depression. In turn, a variety of workplace factors can lead to stress. These include work schedule, pace of work, job security, route to and from work, workplace noise, poor supervision, and the number and nature of customers or clients.[124]

Personal factors also influence stress. For example, Type A personalities—workaholics who feel driven to be on time and meet deadlines—normally place themselves under greater stress. Add to job stress the stress caused by nonjob problems like divorce, and many workers are problems waiting to happen.

Human consequences of job stress include anxiety, depression, anger, cardio-vascular disease, headaches, accidents, and even early onset Alzheimer's disease.[125] A Danish study found that nurses working under excessive pressure had double the risk for heart attacks.[126]

For the employer, consequences include diminished performance and increased absenteeism and turnover. In India, the recent realization that a large part of the labor force is characterized by some or the other form of mental disorder has led the government to establish general and primary health services. A large number of NGOs have also initiated a number of activities related to rehabilitation, and they have been promoting human rights of the mentally-challenged people, with special focus on garnering employability for them and developing training institutes for them.[127]

REDUCING JOB STRESS   There are a number of ways to alleviate dysfunctional stress. These range from commonsense remedies (getting more sleep) to remedies like bio-feedback and meditation. Finding a more suitable job, getting counseling, and planning and organizing each day's activities are other sensible responses.[128] In his book *Stress and the Manager*, Dr. Karl Albrecht suggests the following ways for a person to reduce job stress:[129]

- Build rewarding, pleasant, cooperative relationships with colleagues and employees.
- Don't bite off more than you can chew.
- Build an especially effective and supportive relationship with your boss.
- Negotiate with your boss for realistic deadlines on important projects.
- Learn as much as you can about upcoming events and get as much lead time as you can to prepare for them.
- Find time every day for detachment and relaxation.
- Take a walk around the office to keep your body refreshed and alert.
- Find ways to reduce unnecessary noise.
- Reduce the amount of trivia in your job; delegate routine work when possible.
- Limit interruptions.
- Don't put off dealing with distasteful problems.
- Make a constructive "worry list" that includes solutions for each problem.
- Get more and better quality sleep.[130]

Meditation is an option. Choose a quiet place with soft light and sit comfortably. Then meditate by focusing your thoughts (for example, count breaths or visualize a calming location such as a beach). When your mind wanders, bring it back to focusing your thoughts on your breathing or the beach.[131]

WHAT THE EMPLOYER CAN DO   The employer and its supervisors play roles in reducing stress. Supportive supervisors and fair treatment are important; reign in bullying-prone supervisors. Other steps include reducing personal conflicts on the job and encouraging open communication between management and employees. Some employers use "resilience training" to help employees deal with stress. As one example, "participants consider previous stressful situations in their lives that they have overcome and identify factors that made the situations manageable."[132]

One British firm has a three-tiered employee stress-reduction program.[133] First is *primary prevention*. This focuses on ensuring that things like job designs and workflows are correct. Second is *intervention*. This includes individual employee assessment, attitude surveys to find sources of stress, and supervisory intervention. Third is *rehabilitation*, which includes employee assistance programs and counseling.

burnout
The total depletion of physical and mental resources caused by excessive striving to reach an unrealistic work-related goal.

BURNOUT   Experts define **burnout** as the total depletion of physical and mental resources caused by excessive striving to reach an unrealistic work-related goal. Burnout manifests itself in symptoms such as irritability, discouragement, exhaustion, cynicism, entrapment, and resentment.[134]

Employers can head off burnout, for instance, by monitoring employees in potentially high-stress jobs.[135] What can a burnout candidate do? In his book *How to Beat the High Cost of Success*, Dr. Herbert Freudenberger suggests:

- ***Break your patterns.*** First, the more well-rounded your life is, the better protected you are against burnout.
- ***Get away from it all periodically.*** Schedule occasional periods of introspection where you can get away from your usual routine. Another way to reduce burnout is to (try to) put your job aside once you go home.[136]
- ***Reassess your goals in terms of their intrinsic worth.*** Are the goals you've set for yourself attainable? Are they really worth the sacrifices?
- ***Think about your work.*** Could you do as good a job without being so intense?
- ***Stay active.*** One recent study concluded that "the increase in job burnout and depression was strongest among employees who did not engage in physical activity and weakest to the point of non-significance among those engaging in high physical activity."[137]

EMPLOYEE DEPRESSION *Employee depression* is a serious problem at work. Results from a recent study conducted on the Indian workforce showed that one out of every two employees in corporate India suffers from anxiety or depression. The main reason for this was identified to be "prolonged, ongoing stress due to personal and work contexts" with over 80% of the employees waiting for a year at the least before seeking professional help for it. A staggering 42.5% employees in the private sector were found to be afflicted with depression or general anxiety disorder.[138] Depressed people also tend to have worse safety records.[139]

Employers should work harder to ensure that depressed employees utilize available support services.

In order to ensure that the impacted employees utilize the services available to them, the employers therefore need to train supervisors to identify depression's warning signs and to counsel those who may need such services to use the firm's employee assistance program.[140] Depression is a disease. It does no more good to tell a depressed person to "snap out of it" than it would to tell someone with a heart condition to stop acting tired. Typical depression warning signs (if they last for more than 2 weeks) include persistent sad, anxious, or "empty" moods; sleeping too little; reduced appetite; loss of interest in activities once enjoyed; restlessness or irritability; and difficulty concentrating.[141]

Solving Computer-Related Ergonomic Problems

OSHA has no specific standards for computer workstations. It does have general standards that might apply, regarding, for instance, radiation, noise, and electrical hazards.[142]

In the US, NIOSH has provided general recommendations. Most relate to *ergonomics* or design of the worker–equipment interface. These include:

- Employees should take a 3- to 5-minute break from working at the computer every 20–40 minutes, and use the time for other tasks.
- Design maximum flexibility into the workstation so it can be adapted to the individual operator. For example, use adjustable chairs with midback supports. Don't stay in one position for long periods.
- Reduce glare with devices such as shades over windows and indirect lighting.
- Give workers a complete preplacement vision exam to ensure properly corrected vision for reduced visual strain.[143]
- Allow the user to position his or her wrists at the same level as the elbow.
- Put the screen at or just below eye level, at a distance of 18 to 30 inches from the eyes.
- Let the wrists rest lightly on a pad for support.
- Put the feet flat on the floor or on a footrest.[144]

Repetitive Motion Disorders

Repetitive motion disorders include disorders such as carpal tunnel syndrome and tendonitis, and result from too many uninterrupted repetitions of an activity or motion, or from unnatural motions such as twisting the arm or wrist. It affects people who perform repetitive tasks such as assembly line or computer work. Employers can reduce the problem, for instance, with programs to help workers adjust their pace of work.[145]

Infectious Diseases

With many employees traveling to and from international destinations, monitoring and controlling infectious diseases is an important safety issue.[146]

Employers can take steps to prevent the entry or spread of infectious diseases. These steps include:

1. Closely monitor the Centers for Disease Control and Prevention (CDC) travel alerts. Access this information at www.cdc.gov.
2. Provide daily medical screenings for employees returning from infected areas.
3. Deny access for 10 days to employees or visitors who have had contact with suspected infected individuals.
4. Tell employees to stay home if they have a fever or respiratory system symptoms.
5. Clean work areas and surfaces regularly. Make sanitizers containing alcohol easily available.
6. Stagger breaks. Offer several lunch periods to reduce overcrowding.[147]

Workplace Smoking

Smoking is a serious health and cost problem. The Indian government implemented the Prohibition of Smoking in Public Places Rules, 2008, which prohibits smoking in public places across the nation. This rule allows the owner or in-charge of a public space to register a complaint against as well as display the names of those persons involved in such activities.[148] For employers, these costs derive from higher health and fire insurance, increased absenteeism, and reduced productivity (as when a smoker takes a 10-minute break behind the store). Furthermore, the law regarding cigarettes and tobacco is proposed to be made more stringent by the Union government that has been discussing increasing the minimum age of a person allowed to buy cigarettes from 18 to 21 or even 25 years.

Occupational Security and Risk Management

Workplace safety relates to risks of injury or illness to employees. *Workplace security* relates to protecting employees from internal and external security risks such as criminal acts by outside perpetrators and terrorism.[149] An employer's workplace security plans should address things like establishing a formal security function, protecting the firm's intellectual property (for instance, through noncompete agreements), developing crisis management plans, establishing theft and fraud prevention procedures, preventing workplace violence, and installing facility security systems.[150] A SHRM survey found that about 85% of responding organizations now have some type of formal disaster plan.[151] Many firms of course also have special handling procedures for mail packages and hold regular emergency evacuation drills.

LEARNING OBJECTIVE 16-7
Discuss the prerequisites for a security plan and how to set up a basic security program.

Enterprise Risk Management

Enterprise risk management is "the process of assessing exposures to loss within an operation and determining how best to eliminate, manage or otherwise reduce the risk of an adverse event from having a negative impact on the business."[152]

Companies face a wide variety of risks, only some of which are OSHA-type direct risks to employees' health and safety. Specific risks include, for instance, natural disaster risks, financial risks, and risks to the firm's computer systems. *Human capital risks* would rank high. These include not just safety risks like those we discussed earlier in this chapter but also for instance, "risks" from unionization and from inadequate staffing plans.[153]

How the employer manages a specific risk depends on the class of risk it falls in. For example, *internal preventable* risks arise from actions within the company and include things like employees' illegal conduct or workplace accidents.[154] Employers manage these risks with methods such as codes of conduct, disciplinary procedures, and safety rules. *Strategy risks* are risks that managers accept as part of executing their strategies, such as the risk a banker takes that a borrower defaults. Employers manage some strategy risks with independent experts (like those who assess insurance risks) and with internal experts, like the risk managers who help to oversee banks' loan portfolios. *External risks* come from outside the company and include things like political and natural disasters and terrorism. Managing external risks might involve methods like scenario planning, in which the company endeavors to identify, analyze, and plan for multiple possible eventualities.

Preventing and Dealing with Violence at Work

Violence against employees is one internal preventable enterprise risk, and a huge problem.[155] Customers are often the perpetrators.[156] However, many assaults involve coworkers or a current or former partner or spouse.[157]

Workplace violence incidents by coworkers are predictable and avoidable. *Risk Management Magazine* estimates that about 86% of past workplace violence incidents were anticipated by coworkers, who had brought them to management's attention prior to the incidents actually occurring. Yet management usually did little or nothing.[158] Human resource managers can take several steps to reduce workplace violence risks.

HEIGHTEN SECURITY MEASURES Heightened security measures are the first line of defense, whether the violence is from coworkers, customers, or outsiders. According to OSHA, measures should include those in Figure 16-2.

IMPROVE EMPLOYEE SCREENING With about 30% of workplace attacks committed by coworkers, screening out potentially violent applicants is the employer's next line of defense.

Personal and situational factors correlate with workplace aggression. Men and individuals scoring higher on "trait anger" (the predisposition to respond to situations with hostility) are more likely to exhibit aggression. In terms of the situation, interpersonal injustice and poor leadership predict aggression against supervisors.[159]

FIGURE 16-2 How to Heighten Security in Your Workplace

Source: Based on "Creating a Safer Workplace: Simple Steps Bring Results," *Safety Now, September 2002,* pp. 1–2. See also www.osha.gov/SLTC/etools/hospital/hazards/workplaceviolence/ checklist.html, and www.osha.gov/Publications/osha3153.pdf, both accessed September 6, 2013.

- Improve external lighting.
- Use drop safes to minimize cash on hand.
- Post signs noting that only a limited amount of cash is on hand.
- Install silent alarms and surveillance cameras.
- Increase the number of staff on duty.
- Provide staff training in conflict resolution and nonviolent response.
- Close establishments during high-risk hours late at night and early in the morning.
- Issue a weapons policy; for instance, "firearms or other dangerous or deadly weapons cannot be brought onto the facility either openly or concealed."

Source: see "Creating a Safer Workplace: Simple Steps Bring Results," *Safety Now September 2002,* pp. 1–2. See also www.osha.gov/OshDoc/data_General_Facts/factsheet-workplace-violence.pdf, accessed September 22, 2015.

Employers can screen out potentially violent workers before they're hired. Obtain an employment application, and check the applicant's employment history, education, and references.[160] Sample interview questions include "What frustrates you?" and "Who was your worst supervisor and why?"[161] Certain background circumstances, such as the following, may call for a more in-depth background checking:[162]

- An unexplained gap in employment
- Incomplete or false information on the résumé or application
- A negative, unfavorable, or false reference
- Prior insubordinate or violent behavior on the job[163]
- A criminal history involving harassing or violent behavior
- A prior termination for cause with a suspicious (or no) explanation
- History of drug or alcohol abuse
- Strong indications of instability as indicated, for example, by frequent job changes or geographic moves
- Lost licenses or accreditations[164]

USE WORKPLACE VIOLENCE TRAINING   You can also train supervisors to notice the clues that typify potentially violent current employees. Common clues include:[165]

- An act of violence on or off the job
- Erratic behavior evidencing a loss of perception or awareness of actions
- Overly confrontational or antisocial behavior
- Sexually aggressive behavior
- Isolationist or loner tendencies
- Insubordinate behavior with a threat of violence
- Tendency to overreact to criticism
- Exaggerated interest in war, guns, violence, mass murders, catastrophes, and so on
- Commission of a serious breach of security
- Possession of weapons, guns, knives, or like items in the workplace
- Violation of privacy rights of others, such as searching desks or stalking
- Chronic complaining and the raising of frequent, unreasonable grievances
- A retributory or get-even attitude

GUIDELINES FOR FIRING A HIGH-RISK EMPLOYEE   When firing a high-risk employee:

- Plan all aspects of the meeting, including its time, location, the people to be present, and agenda.
- Involve security enforcement personnel.
- Advise the employee that he or she is no longer permitted onto the employer's property.
- Conduct the meeting in a room with a door leading to the outside of the building.
- Keep the termination brief and to the point.
- Make sure he or she returns all company-owned property at the meeting.
- Don't let the person return to his or her workstation.
- Conduct the meeting early in the week and early in the morning so he or she has time to meet with employment counselors or support groups.
- Offer as generous a severance package as possible.
- Protect the employee's dignity by not advertising the event.[166]

VIOLENCE TOWARD WOMEN AT WORK   Men have more fatal occupational injuries than do women, but the proportion of women who are victims of assault is much higher. The Gender-Motivated Violence Act (part of the Violence Against Women Act) imposes liabilities on employers whose women employees become violence victims.[167] Of all females murdered at work, more than three-fourths are victims of random criminal violence carried out by an assailant unknown to the victim. Family members, coworkers, or acquaintances commit the rest. Tangible security improvements including better lighting, cash-drop boxes, and similar steps can help. Women (and men) should have access to domestic crisis hotlines,[168] and to employee assistance programs.

Securing the Facility

In simplest terms, instituting a basic facility security program requires four steps: analyzing the current *level* of risk, and then installing *mechanical, natural,* and *organizational* security systems.[169] Many employers establish cross-functional threat assessment teams.[170] At one university, for instance, team members meet periodically to review potential threats to university students and employees.[171]

Such teams ideally start with an analysis of the facility's *current level of risk.* Here, start with the obvious. For example, what is the neighborhood like? Does your facility (such as the office building you're in) house other businesses or individuals that might bring unsafe activities to your doorstep? As part of this initial threat assessment, also review these six matters:

1. *Reception area access*, including need for a "panic button";
2. *Interior security*, including secure restrooms, and better identification of exits;
3. *Authorities' involvement*, in particular emergency procedures developed with local law enforcement;
4. *Mail handling*, including screening and opening mail;
5. *Evacuation*, including evacuation procedures and training; and
6. *Backup systems*, such as storing data off site.

Having assessed the potential current level of risk, the employer then turns to assessing and improving natural, mechanical, and organizational security.[172]

Natural security means capitalizing on the facility's natural or architectural features to minimize security problems. For example, do too many entrances hamper controlling facility access?

Mechanical security is the utilization of security systems such as locks, intrusion alarms, access control systems, and surveillance systems to reduce the need for continuous human surveillance.[173]

Many employers install video security cameras to monitor areas in and around their premises.

Andrey Popov/Shutterstock

Finally, *organizational security* means using good management to improve security. For example, it means properly training and motivating security staff and lobby attendants. Ensure that the security staff has written orders that define their duties, especially in situations such as fire, elevator entrapment, hazardous materials spills, medical emergencies, hostile intrusions, suspicious packages, civil disturbances, and workplace violence.[174] Also ask, "Are you properly investigating the backgrounds of new hires and contractors?"

As one corporate security summary put it, "workplace security involves more than … installing an alarm system."[175] Ideally, a comprehensive corporate anticrime program should start with the following:[176]

1. *Company philosophy and policy on crime.* Make sure employees understand that the employer has a zero-tolerance policy with respect to workers who commit any crimes.
2. *Investigations of job applicants.* Always conduct full background checks.
3. *Crime awareness training.* Make it clear during training and orientation that the employer is tough on workplace crime.
4. *Crisis management.* Establish and communicate what to do in the event of a bomb threat, fire, or other emergency.

Company Security and Employee Privacy

Security programs often entail monitoring employee communications and workplace activities. Ideally, employers should get employees' consent for monitoring. However, the employer may also monitor if it's clear from existing policies and notices that employees should have known monitoring might take place. Steps include:[177]

1. Distribute a policy that (a) says the company reserves the right to inspect and search employees as well as their personal property, electronic media, and files; and (b) that lockers and desks remain the property of the company and are subject to search.
2. Train investigators to focus on the facts and avoid making accusations.
3. Remember that employees can request that an employee representative be present during the investigative interview.
4. Make sure all investigations and searches are evenhanded and nondiscriminatory.

Business Continuity and Emergency Plans

One source estimates that 40% of companies never reopen after suffering business disruptions from a major catastrophe, so putting a disaster plan in place is imperative.[178] Emergency preparedness resources include www.ready.gov and the National Institute for Occupational Safety and Health (www.cdc.gov/niosh/).[179] To help the organization prepare for potential disasters, the human resource department should develop a plan and identify key responsibilities, make sure all employees are aware of the plan, and train employees regularly.[180] Such plans should cover *early detection of a problem, methods for communicating the emergency externally*, and *communications plans for initiating an evacuation*. The initial alarm should come first. The employer should then follow that with an announcement providing specific information about the emergency and letting employees know what action they should take.[181]

One also needs plans for dealing with health issues.[182] Thus, in the case of a cardiac arrest emergency, early CPR and an automated external defibrillator are essential. These devices should be available and one or more local employees trained in their use.[183]

Plans are also required for *business continuity* in the event of a disaster. The employer can designate a secure area of the company Web site for emergency employee communications, listing such things as expected hours of operation, facilities opening schedules, and alternative work locations.[184] The disaster plans should include establishing a command center and identifying employees considered essential in the event of a disaster, including responsibilities for each. Business continuity information is available at www.preparemybusiness.org.

TRENDS SHAPING HR: *DIGITAL AND SOCIAL MEDIA*

Twitter Notifications

Social media such as Twitter are obvious choices for quickly communicating emergency information to large numbers of dispersed individuals. When a tornado hit Bridgeport, Connecticut, a few years ago, the city's administrators used Twitter to tell citizens about things like power outages and blocked roads. The Canadian Red Cross uses social media to publicize preparedness information and respond to questions from affected communities. And emergency managers, utility companies, and the public used social media to share updates on things like shelter locations when Hurricane Sandy struck the Northeast.[185] ■

Terrorism

The employer can take several steps to protect its employees and physical assets from the risk of terrorist attack. These steps, now familiar at many workplaces, include:

- Screen the identities of everyone entering the premises.[186]
- Check mail carefully.
- Identify ahead of time a lean interim "crisis organization" that can run the company after a terrorist threat.
- Identify in advance under what conditions you will close the company down, as well as the shutdown process.
- Institute a process to put a crisis management team together.
- Prepare evacuation plans and make sure exits are well marked and unblocked.
- Designate an employee who will communicate with families and off-site employees.
- Identify an upwind, off-site location near your facility as a staging area for all evacuated personnel.
- Designate in advance several employees who will do headcounts at the staging area.
- Establish an emergency text-messaging procedure to notify affected individuals that an emergency may exist.[187]

Chapter Review

Chapter Section Summaries

16-1. The subject **safety and the manager** concerns managers for several reasons, one of which is the number of workplace accidents. Reducing accidents often boils down to reducing accident-causing conditions and accident-causing acts. However, safety always starts at the top.

16-2. Because of this, all managers need to be familiar with **occupational safety law**.

16-3. There are three basic **causes of workplace accidents**: chance occurrences, unsafe conditions,

and employees' unsafe acts. Unsafe conditions include things like improperly guarded equipment and hazardous procedures. Unsafe acts sometimes reflect personality traits such as impatience and distractibility.

16-4. In practice, **how to prevent accidents** boils down to reducing unsafe conditions and reducing unsafe acts. Reducing unsafe conditions is always the first line of defense and includes using checklists and following OSHA standards. There are then several basic approaches to reducing unsafe acts, for instance, through proper selection and placement, training, motivation and positive reinforcement, behavior-based safety, employee participation, and conducting safety and health audits.

16-5. The centerpiece of Milliken's safety process is its *involvement-based* employee engagement **program**. Milliken's employees staff the steering and safety subcommittee system, submit "opportunity for improvement" suggestions weekly, review each of these suggestions, and provide feedback on every suggestion.

16-6. Most **workplace health hazards** aren't obvious, like unguarded equipment. Typical exposure hazards include, for instance, chemicals, biohazards, and improperly designed equipment. Managing exposure hazards like these comes under the area of industrial hygiene, and involves recognition, evaluation, and control. Stress, burnout, and depression are more serious at work than many people realize, and both the employee and employer can take steps to deal with them. Employers especially need to train supervisors to identify depression's warning signs and to counsel those who may need special services.

16-7. Most employers today have **occupational security and risk management programs**. Heightened security measures are an employer's first line of defense against attacks on workers, and include, for instance, improving external lighting. Screening can reduce the risk of hiring potentially violent employees. Instituting a basic facility security program involves analyzing the current level of risk, and then installing mechanical, natural, and organizational security systems.

Discussion Questions

16-1. Explain how to reduce the occurrence of unsafe acts on the part of your employees.

16-2. Explain the supervisor's role in safety.

16-3. Explain what causes unsafe acts.

16-4. Describe at least five techniques for reducing accidents.

16-5. Explain how you would reduce stress at work.

Individual and Group Activities

16-6. Working individually or in groups, answer the question, "Is there such a thing as an accident-prone person?"

16-7. Working individually or in groups, compile a list of the factors at work or in school that create stress for you. What methods do you use for dealing with the stress?

16-8. Appendices A and B at the end of this book (pages 583–600) list the knowledge someone studying for the HRCI (Appendix A) or SHRM (Appendix B) certification exam needs to have in each area of human resource management (such as in Strategic Management, and Workforce Planning). In groups of several students, do four things: (1) review Appendix A and/or B; (2) identify the material in this chapter that relates to the Appendix A and/or B required knowledge lists; (3) write four multiple-choice exam questions on this material that you believe would be suitable for inclusion in the HRCI exam and/or the SHRM exam; and, (4) if time permits, have someone from your team post your team's questions in front of the class, so that students in all teams can answer the exam questions created by the other teams.

16-9. A safety journal presented some information about what happens when OSHA refers criminal complaints about willful violations of OSHA standards to the U.S. Department of Justice (DOJ). In one 20-year period, of the 119 cases OSHA referred to the DOJ, only 9 resulted in prison time for at least one of the defendants. "The Department of Justice is a disgrace," charged the founder of an organization for family members of workers killed on the job. One possible explanation for this low conviction rate is that the crime in cases like these is generally a misdemeanor, not a felony, and the DOJ generally tries to focus its attention on felony cases. Given this information, what implications do you think this has for how employers and their managers should manage their safety programs, and why do you take that position?

16-10. In the construction site of high-end apartments at Navi Mumbai, two workers who were working on suspended metal plank doing plastering work fell down and died. Do you think catastrophic failures like this are avoidable? If so, what steps would you suggest the general contractor take to avoid a disaster like this?

Experiential Exercise

How Safe Is the Small Industry Near Your Institution?

Purpose: The purpose of this exercise is to give you practice in identifying unsafe conditions.

Required Understanding: You should be familiar with material covered in this chapter, particularly that on unsafe conditions.

How to Set Up the Exercise/Instructions: Divide the class into groups of four. Assume that each group is a safety committee retained by your college's or university's safety engineer to identify and report on any possible unsafe conditions in and around the neighborhood. Each group will spend about 45 minutes in and around the building you are now in for the purpose of identifying and listing possible unsafe conditions.

Return to the class in about 45 minutes. A spokesperson for each group should list on the board the unsafe conditions you have identified. How many were there? Do they violate any legal processes as have been laid down by the Factories Act, 1948, in India? How would you go about checking?

Application Case

The New Safety and Health Program

At first glance, a dot-com company is one of the last places you'd expect to find potential safety and health hazards—or so the owners of LearnInMotion.com thought. There's no danger of moving machinery, no high-pressure lines, no cutting or heavy lifting, and certainly no forklift trucks. However, there are safety and health problems.

In terms of accident-causing conditions, for instance, the one thing dot-com companies have are cables and wires. Even with extensive use of Wi-Fi and Bluetooth, there are cables connecting computers to screens and to servers, and in many cases cables running from some computers to separate printers. There are 10 telephones in this particular office, all on 15-foot power lines that always seem to be snaking around chairs and tables. There is, in fact, an astonishing amount of cable considering this is an office with so-called wireless connections and with fewer than 10 employees. When the installation specialists wired the office (for electricity, high-speed cable, phone lines, burglar alarms, and computers), they estimated they used well over 5 miles of cables of one sort or another. Most of these are hidden in the walls or ceilings, but many of them snake their way from desk to desk, and under and over doorways. Several employees have tried to reduce the nuisance of having to trip over wires whenever they get up by putting their plastic chair pads over the wires closest to them. However, that still leaves many wires unprotected. In other cases, they brought in their own packing tape and tried to tape down the wires in those spaces where they're particularly troublesome, such as across doorways.

The cables and wires are only one of the more obvious potential accident-causing conditions. The firm's programmer, before he left the firm, had tried to repair the main server while the unit was still electrically alive. To this day, they're not sure exactly where he stuck the screwdriver, but the result was that he was "blown across the room," as one manager put it. He was all right, but it was still a scare. And while they haven't received any claims yet, every employee spends hours at his or her computer, so carpal tunnel syndrome is a risk, as are a variety of other problems such as eyestrain and strained backs.

One recent accident particularly scared the owners. The firm uses independent contractors to deliver the firm's books and DVD-based courses in New York and two other cities. A delivery person was riding his bike east at the intersection of Second Avenue and East 64th Street in New York when he was struck by a car going south on Second Avenue. Luckily, he was not hurt, but the bike's front wheel was wrecked, and the narrow escape got the firm's two owners, Mel and Maria, thinking about their lack of a safety program.

It's not just the physical conditions that concern the two owners. They also have some concerns about potential health problems such as job stress and burnout. Although the business may be (relatively) safe with respect to physical conditions, it is also relatively stressful in terms of the demands it makes in hours and deadlines. It is not unusual for employees to get to work by 7:30 or 8 in the morning and to work through until 11 or 12 at night, at least 5 and sometimes 6 or 7 days per week.

The bottom line is that both Maria and Mel feel quite strongly that they need to do something about implementing a health and safety plan. Now, they want you, their management consultants, to help them do it. Here's what they want you to do for them.

Questions

16-11. Based upon your knowledge of health and safety matters and your actual observations of operations that are similar to theirs, make a list of the potential hazardous conditions employees and others face at LearnInMotion.com. What should they do to reduce the potential severity of the top five hazards?

16-12. Would it be advisable for them to set up a procedure for screening out stress-prone or accident-prone individuals? Why or why not? If so, how should they screen them?

16-13. Write a short position paper on the subject, "What should we do to get all our employees to behave more safely at work?"

16-14. Based on what you know and on what other dot-coms are doing, write a short position paper on the subject, "What can we do to reduce the potential problems of stress and burnout in our company?"

Continuing Case

Carter Cleaning Company

The New Safety Program

Employees' safety and health are very important matters in the laundry and cleaning business. Each facility is a small production plant in which machines, powered by high-pressure steam and compressed air, work at high temperatures washing, cleaning, and pressing garments, often under very hot, slippery conditions. Chemical vapors are produced continually, and caustic chemicals are used in the cleaning process. High-temperature stills are almost continually "cooking down" cleaning solvents in order to remove impurities so that the solvents can be reused. If a mistake is made in this process—like injecting too much steam into the still—a boilover occurs, in which boiling chemical solvent erupts out of the still and over the floor, and on anyone who happens to be standing in its way.

As a result of these hazards and the fact that chemically hazardous waste is continually produced in these stores, several government agencies (including OSHA and the Environmental Protection Agency) have instituted strict guidelines regarding the management of these plants. For example, posters have to be placed in each store notifying employees of their right to be told what hazardous chemicals they are dealing with and what the proper method for handling each chemical is. Special waste-management firms must be used to pick up and properly dispose of the hazardous waste.

A chronic problem the Carters (and most other laundry owners) have is the unwillingness on the part of the cleaning/spotting workers to wear safety goggles. Not all the chemicals they use require safety goggles, but some—like the hydrofluoric acid used to remove rust stains from garments—are very dangerous. The latter is kept in special plastic containers, since it dissolves glass. The problem is that wearing safety goggles can be troublesome. They are somewhat uncomfortable, and they become smudged easily and thus cut down on visibility. As a result, Jack has always found it almost impossible to get these employees to wear their goggles.

Questions

16-15. How should the firm go about identifying hazardous conditions that should be rectified? Use checklists to list at least 10 possible dry cleaning store hazardous conditions.

16-16. Would it be advisable for the firm to set up a procedure for screening out accident-prone individuals? How should they do so?

16-17. How would you suggest the Carters get all employees to behave more safely at work? Also, how would you advise them to get those who should be wearing goggles to do so?

Translating Strategy into HR Policies and Practices Case*,§

*The overall map on page xxxviii of this book outlines the relationships involved.

Improving Performance at the Hotel Paris

The New Safety and Health Program

The Hotel Paris's competitive strategy is "To use superior guest service to differentiate the Hotel Paris properties, and to thereby increase the length of stay and return rate of guests, and thus boost revenues and profitability." HR manager Lisa Cruz must now formulate functional policies and activities that support this competitive strategy and boost performance, by eliciting the required employee behaviors and competencies.

While "hazardous conditions" might not be the first thing that comes to mind when you think of hotels, Lisa Cruz knew that hazards and safety were in fact serious issues for the Hotel Paris. Indeed, everywhere you look—from the valets leaving car doors open on the driveways to slippery areas around the pools, to thousands of pounds of ammonia, chlorine, and other caustic chemicals that the hotels use each year for cleaning and laundry, hotels provide a fertile environment for accidents. Obviously, hazardous conditions are bad for the Hotel Paris. They are inhumane for the workers. High accident rates probably reduce employee morale and thus service. And accidents raise the company's costs and reduce its profitability, for instance, in terms of workers' compensation claims and absences. Lisa knew that she had to clean up her firm's occupational safety and health

systems, for its employees' well-being, and to achieve the company's strategic goals.

Lisa and the CFO reviewed their company's safety records, and what they found disturbed them. In terms of every safety-related metric they could find, including accident costs per year, lost time due to accidents, workers' compensation per employee, and number of safety training programs per year, the Hotel Paris compared unfavorably with most other hotel chains and service firms. "Just in terms of extra workers' compensation costs, the Hotel Paris must be spending $500,000 a year more than we should be," said the CFO. And that didn't include lost time due to accidents, or the negative effect accidents had on employee morale, or the cost of litigation (as when, for instance, one guest accidentally burned himself with chlorine that a pool attendant had left unprotected). The CFO authorized Lisa to develop a new safety and health program.

Lisa and her team began by hiring a safety and health consultant, someone who had been an inspector and then manager with OSHA. Based on the analysis, the team then took numerous steps, including the following. First, specially trained teams consisting of someone from Lisa's HR group, the local hotel's assistant manager, and three local hotel employees went through each local hotel "with a fine tooth comb," as Lisa put it. They used an extensive checklist to identify and eliminate unsafe conditions.

---

§Written by and copyright Gary Dessler, PhD.

Lisa's team took other steps. They convinced the Hotel Paris's board of directors and chairman and CEO to issue a joint statement emphasizing the importance of safety, and the CEO, during a one-month period, visited each hotel to meet with all employees and emphasize safety. The Hotel Paris also contracted with a safety training company. This firm created special online safety programs for the company's managers, and developed five-day training seminars for the hotels' staffs.

The new programs seem to be effective. Lisa and the CFO were pleased to find, after about a year, that accident costs per year, lost time due to accidents, and workers' compensation expenses were all down at least 40%. And anecdotal evidence from supervisors suggested that employees feel better about the company's commitment to them and were providing better service as a result.

Questions

16-18. Based on what you read in this chapter of Dessler *Human Resource Management*, what's the first step you would have advised the Hotel Paris to take as part of its new safety and health program, and why?

16-19. List 10 specific high-risk areas in a typical hotel you believe Lisa and her team should look at now, including examples of the safety or health hazards that they should look for there.

16-20. Give three specific examples of how Hotel Paris can use HR practices to improve its safety efforts.

16-21. Write a one-page summary addressing the topic, "How improving safety and health at the Hotel Paris will contribute to us achieving our strategic goals."

Key Terms

Occupational Safety and Health Act of 1970, 504
occupational illness, 504
unsafe conditions, 506
job hazard analysis, 508
operational safety reviews, 509
behavior-based safety, 513
safety awareness program, 513
burnout, 520

Endnotes

1. "Workers Rate Safety Most Important Workplace Issue," *EHS Today*, October 2010, p. 17.
2. "BP Oil Spill Timeline," July 22, 2010, www.guardian.co.uk/environment/2010/jun/29/bp-oil-spill-timeline-deepwater-horizon, accessed June 29, 2011.
3. Accessed on September 25, 2017 at http://www.thehindu.com/2000/04/19/stories/0619000e.htm.
4. Russell Sobel, "Occupational Safety and Profit Maximization: Friends or Foes?" *The Journal of Socioeconomics* 30, no. 9 (2010), pp. 429–433.
5. www.osha.gov/dcsp/products/topics/businesscase/, accessed April 16, 2013.
6. David Levine et al., "Randomized Government Safety Inspections Reduce Worker Injuries with No Detectable Job Loss," *Science* 336 (May 18, 2012), pp. 907–911.
7. Chief Financial Officer Survey, Liberty Mutual Insurance Co., 2005.
8. Mike Rich, "Preventing Hearing Loss," www.adhesivesmag.com, January 2012, pp. 40–41.
9. One study recently concluded that "employee perceptions of the extent to which managers and supervisors are committed to workplace safety likely influence employee safety behavior and, subsequently, injuries." Jeremy Beus et al., "Safety Climate and Juries: An Examination of Theoretical and Empirical Relationships," *Journal of Applied Psychology* 95, no. 4 (2010), pp. 713–727.
10. Willie Hammer, *Occupational Safety Management and Engineering* (Upper Saddle River, NJ: Prentice Hall, 1985), pp. 62–63. See also "DuPont's 'STOP' Helps Prevent Workplace Injuries and Incidents," *Asia Africa Intelligence Wire*, May 17, 2004.
11. F. David Pierce, "Safety in the Emerging Leadership Paradigm," *Occupational Hazards*, June 2000, pp. 63–66. See also, for example, Josh Williams, "Optimizing the Safety Culture," *Occupational Hazards*, May 2008, pp. 45–49.
12. See the BP case in the Appendix for further discussion.
13. Sandy Smith, "ABB Inc. Relies on Leadership and Accountability for Safety Performance," *EHS Today*, November 2012, p. 38.
14. "Did This Supervisor Do Enough to Protect Trench-Workers?" *Safety Compliance Letter*, October 2003, p. 9.
15. Ibid.
16. Kranthi Kumara "India: Chhattisgarh government to call probe into Industrial Accident," as accessed on October 13, 2009 at www.wsws.org/articles/2009/oct2009/indi-o12.shtml.
17. Accessed on September 25, 2017 at www.nsc.org.in/links/aboutus.htm.
18. Zee Media Beuro, "World Day for Safety and Health at work: Tips for a healthier, secure environment at the workplace." (2017), accessed at HYPERLINK "http://www.zeenews.india.com" www.zeenews.india.com.
19. DNA correspondent, "Occupational health survey revels alarming numbers," as accessed on July 25, 2017 at dnaindia.com.
20. Tehelka, "Lack of occupational safety kills workers," as accessed on September 25, 2017 at HYPERLINK "http://www.tehelka.com" www.tehelka.com.
21. TNN, "Safety Training must for workers in industries," , *The Times of India*, May 4, 2017.
22. Ramakumar V. Agnihotaram, "An overview of occupational health research in India", *Indian Journal of Occupational and Environmental Medicine*," April 2009, V9(1), pp. 10 – 14.
23. Accessed on September 25, 2017 at HYPERLINK "http://www.ecil.co.in/saftey.php" www.ecil.co.in/saftey.php.
24. "Occupational Safety and Health Performance," as accessed on September 25, 2017, at HYPERLINK "http://www.abb.co.in" www.abb.co.in.
25. Safety Monitoring in Coal India Limited, as accessed on September 25, 2017, at http//coal.nic.in/weboflife-minesafety/safetymon.htm.
26. Based on "All About OSHA," rev. ed. (Washington, DC: U.S. Department of Labor, 1980), www.osha.gov/law-regs.html, accessed September 11, 2014.
27. Ibid.
28. "OSHA Hazard Communication Standard Enforcement," *BNA Bulletin to Management*, February 23, 1989, p. 13. See also William Kincaid, "OSHA vs. Excellence in Safety Management," *Occupational Hazards*, December 2002, pp. 34–36. Flow diagram based on *What Every Employer Needs to Know About OSHA Recordkeeping* (Washington, DC: U.S. Department of Labor, 1978), p. 3.
29. "What Every Employer Needs to Know about OSHA Record Keeping," U.S. Department of Labor, Bureau of Labor Statistics, Washington, DC, report 412–413, p. 3, www.osha.gov/recordkeeping/index.html, accessed September 11, 2014.
30. "New OSHA Recordkeeping Rule in Effect with the New Year," *Bloomberg BNA Bulletin to Management,* January 6, 2015, p. 2.
31. Arthur Sapper and Robert Gombar, "Nagging Problems Under OSHA's New Record Keeping Rule," *Occupational Hazards*, March 2002, p. 58.
32. Brian Jackson and Jeffrey Myers, "Just When You Thought You Were Safe: OSHA Record-Keeping Violations," *Management Review*, May 1994, pp. 62–63; www.osha.gov/recordkeeping/index.html, accessed October 26, 2011.
33. Knowing OSHA's rules is not enough. The employer should develop and communicate its own written safety and health rules to employees, monitor violations, and discipline employees who violate the rules. Michael Taylor, "OSHA Compliance Mistakes," *EHS Today*, July 2012, pp. 29–31.
34. Courtney Malveaux and J. A. Rodriguez Jr., "Can You Claim

Employee Misconduct? Take the Legal Test," *EHS Today,* November 2014, pp. 37–41.

35. The following is based on www.sitedocs.com, accessed May 5, 2015.

36. "A Safety Committee Man's Guide," Aetna Life and Casualty Insurance Company, Catalog 87684. See also Dan Petersen, "The Barriers to Safety Excellence," *Occupational Hazards,* December 2000, pp. 37–39.

37. "Did This Supervisor Do Enough to Protect Trench Workers?" *Safety Compliance Letter,* October 2003, p. 9.

38. "Four Ways a Construction Job Can Kill You," *EHS Today,* February 2015, pp. 23–24.

39. "The Dawning of a New Era," *Workforce Management,* December 2010, p. 3.

40. For a discussion, see David Hofmann and Adam Stetzer, "A Cross-Level Investigation of Factors Influencing Unsafe Behaviors and Accidents," *Personnel Psychology* 49 (1996), pp. 307–308. See also David Hofman and Barbara Mark, "An Investigation of the Relationship Between Safety Climate and Medication Errors as Well as Other Nurse and Patient Outcomes," *Personnel Psychology* 50, no. 9 (2006), pp. 847–869.

41. Duane Schultz and Sydney Schultz, *Psychology and Work Today* (Upper Saddle River, NJ: Prentice Hall, 2002), p. 332.

42. Robert Pater and Robert Russell, "Drop That 'Accident Prone' Tag: Look for Causes Beyond Personal Issues," *Industrial Safety and Hygiene News* 38, no. 1 (January 2004), p. 50, http://findarticles.com/p/articles/mi_hb5992/is_200401/ai_n24195869/, accessed August 11, 2009.

43. Discussed in Douglas Haaland, "Who's the Safest Bet for the Job? Find Out Why the Fun Guy in the Next Cubicle May Be the Next Accident Waiting to Happen," *Security Management* 49, no. 2 (February 2005), pp. 51–57.

44. "Thai Research Points to Role of Personality in Road Accidents," www.driveandstayalive.com/info%20section/news/individual%20news%20articles/x_050204_personality-in-crash-causation_thailand.htm, February 2, 2005, accessed August 11, 2009; Donald Bashline et al., "Bad Behavior: Personality Tests Can Help Underwriters Identify High-Risk Drivers," *Best's Review* 105, no. 12 (April 2005), pp. 63–64.

45. Todd Nighswonger, "Threat of Terror Impacts Workplace Safety," *Occupational Hazards,* July 2002, pp. 24–26.

46. Michael Blotzer, "Safety by Design," *Occupational Hazards,* May 1999, pp. 39–40; www.designsafe.com/dsesoftware.php, accessed May 26, 2007.

47. Susannah Figura, "Don't Slip Up on Safety," *Occupational Hazards,* November 1996, pp. 29–31. See also Russ Wood, "Defining the Boundaries of Safety," *Occupational Hazards,* January 2001, pp. 41–43.

48. See, for example, Laura Walter, "What's in a Glove?" *Occupational Hazards,* May 2008, pp. 35–36.

49. Donald Groce, "Keep the Gloves On!" *Occupational Hazards,* June 2008, pp. 45–47.

50. Tracy Moon Junior, "Wearable Technology in the Workplace," *EHS Today,* December 2014, pp. 28–29.

51. Howard Mavity, "What Should Be Your Safety Concerns When Buying or Leasing Office Space?" *EHS Today,* July 2014, pp. 20–22.

52. www.osha.gov/Publications/osha3071.pdf, accessed April 21, 2011.

53. www-ns.iaea.org/reviews/op-safety-reviews.asp, accessed April 21, 2011.

54. For example, when asked what accounted for injuries such as cuts and lacerations, contusions, and chemical exposure at their facilities, most employees concluded either that workers were not wearing the proper protective equipment or had been given the wrong protection for the task. Brian Perry, "Don't Invite an OSHA Citation with Lower Quality PPE," *EHS Today,* January 2011, p. 23.

55. James Zeigler, "Protective Clothing: Exploring the Wearability Issue," *Occupational Hazards,* September 2000, pp. 81–82. See also Judy Smithers, "Use OSHA's Compliance Directive to Evaluate Your PPE Program," *EHS Today,* January 2012, pp. 43–45.

56. Sandy Smith, "Protective Clothing and the Quest for Improved Performance," *Occupational Hazards,* February 2008, pp. 63–66. Note that the vast array of available personal protective equipment makes choosing the appropriate equipment what one expert calls "complex and sometimes confusing." See Scott Larsen, "Integrated Use of Personal Protective Equipment," *EHS Today,* June 2012, p. 31.

57. Tim Andrews, "Getting Employees Comfortable with PPE," *Occupational Hazards,* January 2000, pp. 35–38. However, "Making a job safer with machine guards or PPE lowers people's risk perceptions and thus can lead to an increase in at-risk behavior." E. Scott Geller, "The Thinking and Seeing

Components of People-Based Safety," *Occupational Hazards,* December 2006, pp. 38–40.

58. Laura Walter, "FR Clothing: Leaving Hazards in the Dust," *EHS Today,* January 2010, pp. 20–22.

59. Roger Paquette, "Staying Safe and Warm in Cold Weather Environments," *EHS Today,* January 2015, pp. 19–22.

60. "The Complete Guide to Personal Protective Equipment," *Occupational Hazards,* January 1999, pp. 49–60. See also Edwin Zalewski, "Noise Control: It's More Than Just Earplugs: OSHA Requires Employers to Evaluate Engineering and Administrative Controls Before Using Personal Protective Equipment," *Occupational Hazards* 68, no. 9 (September 2006), p. 48(3). You can find videos about personal protective products at "SafetyLive TV" at www.occupationalhazards.com, accessed March 14, 2009.

61. Sandy Smith, "Protecting Vulnerable Workers," *Occupational Hazards,* April 2004, pp. 25–28.

62. J. P. Sankpill, "A Clear Vision for Eye and Face Protection," *EHS Today,* November 2010, p. 29.

63. See, for instance, Laura Walter, "Training the Older Worker," *EHS Today,* February 2011, p. 39.

64. Robert Pater, "Boosting Safety with an Aging Workforce," *Occupational Hazards,* March 2006, p. 24.

65. Michael Silverstein, M.D., "Designing the Age Friendly Workplace," *Occupational Hazards,* December 2007, pp. 29–31.

66. Elizabeth Rogers and William Wiatrowski, "Injuries, Illnesses, and Fatalities Among Older Workers," *Monthly Labor Review* 128, no. 10 (October 2005), pp. 24–30.

67. Bill Sims Jr., "Employee Engagement and Commitment: The Super Bowl of Safety," *EHS Today,* July 2014, pp. 28–29.

68. See www.ramsaycorp.com/catalog/view/?productid=208.

69. Gerald Borofsky, Michelle Bielema, and James Hoffman, "Accidents, Turnover, and the Use of a Preemployment Screening Inventory: Further Contributions to the Validation of the Employee Reliability Inventory," *Psychological Reports,* 1993, pp. 1067–1076; www.ramsaycorp.com/catalog/view/?productid=208, accessed October 26, 2011.

70. Ibid., p. 1072. See also Keith Rosenblum, "The Companion Solution to Ergonomics: Pretesting for the Job," *Risk Management* 50, no. 11 (November 2003), p. 26(6).

71. Dan Hartshorn, "The Safety Interview," *Occupational Hazards,* October 1999, pp. 107–111.

72. Kathryn Tyler, "Better Safe Than Sorry," *HR Magazine,* December 2014, pp. 44–45.

73. Michael Burke et al., "The Dread Factor: How Hazards and Safety Training Influence Learning and Performance," *Journal of Applied Psychology* 96, no. 1 (2011), pp. 46–70.

74. See, for example, Ron Bruce, "Online from Kazakhstan to California," *Occupational Hazards,* June 2008, pp. 61–65.

75. Michael Blotzer, "PDA Software Offers Auditing Advances," *Occupational Hazards,* December 2001, p. 11. See also Erik Andersen, "Automating Health & Safety Processes Creates Value," *Occupational Hazards,* April 2008, pp. 53–63.

76. In a survey of about 2,600 employees, roughly one-fourth said they would not intervene if they saw a coworker acting unsafely, for fear the coworker would be defensive or angry. Phillip Ragain et al., "The Causes and Consequences of Employees' Silence," *EHS Today,* July 2011, pp. 36–38.

77. Jack Rubinger, "Signs, Labels and Lighting for a Safe and Productive Workplace," *EHS Today,* October 2012, p. 67.

78. See, for example, Josh Cable, "Seven Suggestions for a Successful Safety Incentive Program," *EHS Today,* March 23, 2005: http://ehstoday.com/safety/incentives/ehs_imp_37488, accessed July 24, 2015. See also J. M. Saidler, "Gift Cards Make Safety Motivation Simple," *Occupational Health & Safety* 78, no. 1 (January 2009), pp. 39–40.

79. Don Williamson and Jon Kauffman, "From Tragedy to Triumph: Safety Grows Wings at Golden Eagle," *Occupational Hazards,* February 2006, pp. 17–25; www.tsocorp.com/TSOCorp/SocialResponsibility/HealthandSafety/Healthand-Safety, accessed June 30, 2011.

80. "Are Traditional Incentive Programs Illegal?" *EHS Today,* April 2012, p. 12. See also Howard Mavity, "OSHA: Don't Get Caught in the Trap of Rewarding Employees for Reducing Recordables!" *EHS Today,* September 2012, pp. 39–41; and James Stanley, "OSHA's Warning on Safety Incentive Programs Are Wide of the Mark," *EHS Today,* October 2012, p. 63.

81. James Nash, "Construction Safety: Best Practices in Training Hispanic Workers," *Occupational Hazards,* February 2004, pp. 35–38.

82. Ibid., p. 37.

83. Based on Judi Komaki, Kenneth Barwick, and Lawrence Scott, "A Behavioral Approach to

Occupational Safety: Pinpointing and Reinforcing Safe Performance in a Food Manufacturing Plant," *Journal of Applied Psychology* 63 (August 1978), pp. 434–445. See also Anat Arkin, "Incentives to Work Safely," *Personnel Management* 26, no. 9 (September 1994), pp. 48–52; Sandy Smith, "Why Cash Isn't King," *Occupational Hazards*, March 2004, pp. 37–38.

84. Deepali Gupta, "7 New rules Vodafone's employees have to follow to avoid being fired," *The Economic Times*, December 18, 2012.

85. "Vodafone India has robust policies on Health, Safety, Well-Being of employees and partners," as accessed on September 25, 2017, at HYPERLINK "http://www.vodafone.in"www.vodafone.in.

86. Dov Zohar, "A Group Level Model of Safety Climate: Testing the Effect of a Group Climate on Students in Manufacturing Jobs," *Journal of Applied Psychology* 85, no. 4 (2000), pp. 587–596. See also Steven Yule, Rhona Flin, and Andy Murdy, "The Role of Management and Safety Climate in Preventing Risk-Taking at Work," *International Journal of Risk Assessment and Management* 7, no. 2 (December 20, 2006), p. 137; and Judy Agnew, "Building the Foundation for a Sustainable Safety Culture," *EHS Today*, February 2013, pp. 41–43.

87. Quoted from Sandy Smith, "Breakthrough Safety Management," *Occupational Hazards*, June 2004, p. 43. For a discussion of developing a safety climate survey, see also Sara Singer et al., "Workforce Perceptions of Hospital Safety Culture: Development and Validation of the Patient Safety Climate in Healthcare Organizations Survey," *Health Services Research* 42, no. 5 (October 2007), pp. 19–23.

88. "Encourage Incident Reporting to Improve Safety Culture," *EHS Today*, December 2012, p. 16.

89. Jennifer Nahrgang et al., "Safety at Work: A Meta-Analytic Investigation of the Link Between Job Demands, Job Resources, Burnout, Engagement, and Safety Outcomes," *Journal of Applied Psychology* 96, no. 1 (2011), p. 86.

90. Stan Hodson and Tim Gordon, "Tenneco's Drive to Become Injury Free," *Occupational Hazards*, May 2000, pp. 85–87. For another example, see Terry Mathis, "Lean Behavior-Based Safety," *Occupational Hazards*, May 2005, pp. 33–34.

91. Tim McDaniel, "Employee Participation: A Vehicle for Safety

by Design," *Occupational Hazards*, May 2002, pp. 71–76.

92. For another good example, see Christopher Chapman, "Using Kaizen to Improve Safety and Ergonomics," *Occupational Hazards*, February 2006, pp. 27–29.

93. Lisa Cullen, "Safety Committees: A Smart Business Decision," *Occupational Hazards*, May 1999, pp. 99–104. See also www.osha.gov/Publications/osha2098.pdf, accessed May 26, 2007; and D. Kolman, "Effective Safety Committees," *Beverage Industry* 100, no. 3 (March 2009), pp. 63–65.

94. https://itunes.apple.com/us/app/iauditor-safety-audit-checklist/id499999532?mt=8, accessed May 6, 2015.

95. http://download.cnet.com/iAuditor-Safety-Audit-and-Checklist/3000-2064_4-75728239.html, accessed May 6, 2015.

96. www.digitalmarketplace.service.gov.uk/service/5-g1-0377-007, accessed May 6, 2015.

97. www.assessnet.co.uk, accessed May 6, 2015.

98. John Garber, "Introduction to the Human Resource Discipline of Safety and Security," www.shrm.org/templates_tools/toolkits, accessed May 27, 2012.

99. Mike Powell, "Sustaining Your Safety Sweep Audit Process," *EHS Today*, December 2012, pp. 35–36.

100. Note that the vast majority of workers' injury-related deaths occur not at work, but when the employees are off the job, often at home. More employers are therefore implementing safety campaigns encouraging employees to apply safe practices at home. Katherine Torres, "Safety Hits Home," *Occupational Hazards*, July 2006, pp. 19–23.

101. "World-Class Safety: DuPont and Milliken Share Their Proven Successes," BLR, August 23, 2013, http://safety.blr.com/, accessed April 15, 2014.

102. Carey Tebbetts and Robert Allen, "Milliken's Keys to Employee Engagement, Increased Workplace Safety and Productivity," *EHS Today*, January 9, 2013: http://ehstoday.com/safety/millikens-keys-employee-engagement-increased-workplace-safety-and-productivity, accessed July 24, 2015.

103. Ibid
104. Ibid.
105. Ibid.
106. Ibid.

107. Mike Powell, "Harness the Full Power of Your Incident Investigation Process," *EHS Today*, September 2013, p. 71.

108. www.performancesolutionsbymilliken.com, accessed April 15, 2014. As part of its safety program, Milliken has partnered with the Occupational Safety and Health Administration and

follows the latter's voluntary protection program's (VPP's) guidelines to help it reach its safety goals. "Milliken and Company VPP Star Site Elm Facility Receiving VPP Recognition," www.osha.gov, accessed April 14, 2014. For another example of how employee engagement impacts occupational safety, see "How Employee Engagement Can Improve the Hospital's Health," *Gallup Business Journal*, http://businessjournal.gallup.com, accessed April 14, 2014.

109. This is based on Paul Puncochar, "The Science and Art to Identifying Workplace Hazards," *Occupational Hazards*, September 2003, pp. 50–54.

110. Ibid., p. 52. See also David Wagner, "The Role of Real-Time Detection in Industrial Hygiene," *EHS Today*, August 2014, pp. 29–30.

111. Based on S. L. Smith, "Sadaf Drives for Safety Excellence," *Occupational Hazards*, November 1998, p. 41. For further discussion, see also Kathy Seabrook, "10 Strategies for Global Safety Management," *Occupational Hazards*, June 1999, pp. 41–43.

112. "Hazard Communication," www.osha.gov/dsg/hazcom/index.HTML, accessed May 26, 2012.

113. Based on the report "Workplace Screening and Brief Intervention: What Employers Can and Should Do About Excessive Alcohol Use," www.ensuringsolutions.org/resources/resources_show.htm?doc_id=673239, accessed August 11, 2009.

114. "Employers Can Play Key Role in Preventing Painkiller Abuse, but Many Remain Reluctant," *BNA Bulletin to Management*, February 15, 2011, p. 49.

115. Accessed on September 25, 2017 at http://www.nisd.gov.in/content/231_1_DrugAbusePrevention.aspx.

116. Samuel Bacharach et al., "Alcohol Consumption and Workplace Absenteeism: The Moderating Effect of Social Support," *Journal of Applied Psychology* 95, no. 2 (2010), pp. 334–348.

117. See, for example, L. Claussen, "Can You Spot the Meth Addict?" *Safety & Health* 179, no. 4 (April 2009), pp. 48–52.

118. See for example, http://workplacedrugpolicy.com/program-components.htm; http://www.workingpartners.com/understanding-dfwp/elements-of-dfwp.asp; and http://www.dol.gov/elaws/asp/drugfree/drugs/screen15.asp, accessed July 27, 2015.

119. www.dol.gov/asp/programs/drugs/workingpartners/sab/screen.asp, accessed April 27, 2008; www.dol.gov/whd/FOH/

ch64/64a01.htm, accessed September 11, 2014.

120. Gopal Pati and John Adkins Jr., "The Employer's Role in Alcoholism Assistance," *Personnel Journal* 62, no. 7 (July 1983), p. 570. See also Commerce Clearing House, "How Should Employers Respond to Indications an Employee May Have an Alcohol or Drug Problem?" *Ideas and Trends*, April 6, 1989, pp. 53–57; "The Employer's Role in Alcoholism Assistance," *Personnel Journal* 62, no. 7 (July 1983), pp. 568–572.

121. William Current, "Pre-Employment Drug Testing," *Occupational Hazards*, July 2002, p. 56. See also William Current, "Improving Your Drug Testing ROI," *Occupational Health & Safety* 73, no. 4 (April 2004), pp. 40, 42, 44.

122. Frank Lockwood et al., "Drug Testing Programs and Their Impact on Workplace Accidents: A Time Series Analysis," *Journal of Individual Employment Rights* 8, no. 4 (2000), pp. 295–306; Roberts, "Random Drug Testing Can Help Reduce Accidents."

123. Beth Andrus, "Accommodating the Alcoholic Executive," *Society for Human Resource Management Legal Report*, January 2008, pp. 1, 4.

124. Eric Sundstrom et al., "Office Noise, Satisfaction, and Performance," *Environment and Behavior* no. 2 (March 1994), pp. 195–222; "Stress: How to Cope with Life's Challenges," *American Family Physician* 74, no. 8 (October 15, 2006).

125. "Failing to Tackle Stress Could Cost You Dearly," *Personnel Today*, September 12, 2006; www.sciencedaily.com/releases/2007/06/070604170722.htm, accessed November 3, 2009.

126. Tara Parker-Pope, "Time to Review Workplace Reviews?" *New York Times*, May 18, 2010, p. D5.

127. Accessed on September 25, 2017 at http://www.tandfonline.com/doi/abs/10.1080/09540260310001635177.

128. See, for example, Elizabeth Bernstein, "When a Coworker Is Stressed Out," *Wall Street Journal*, August 26, 2008, pp. B1, B2.

129. Karl Albrecht, *Stress and the Manager* (Englewood Cliffs, NJ: Spectrum, 1979). For a discussion of the related symptoms of depression, see James Krohe Jr., "An Epidemic of Depression?" *Across-the-Board*, September 1994, pp. 23–27; and Todd Nighswonger, "Stress Management," *Occupational Hazards*, September 1999, p. 100.

130. Sabine Sonnentag et al., "'Did You Have a Nice Evening?' A Day-Level Study on Recovery

Experiences, Sleep, and Affect," *Journal of Applied Psychology* 93, no. 3 (2008), pp. 674–684.

131. "Meditation Gives Your Mind Permanent Working Holiday; Relaxation Can Improve Your Business Decisions and Your Overall Health," discussed in *Investors Business Daily*, March 24, 2004, p. 89. See also "Meditation Helps Employees Focus, Relieve Stress," *BNA Bulletin to Management*, February 20, 2007, p. 63.

132. William Atkinson, "Turning Stress into Strength," *HR Magazine*, January 2011, p. 51.

133. "Going Head to Head with Stress," *Personnel Today*, April 26, 2005, p. 1.

134. See, for example, Christina Maslach and Michael Leiter, "Early Predictors of Job Burnout and Engagement," *Journal of Applied Psychology* 93, no. 3 (2008), pp. 498–512.

135. Christina Maslach and Michael Leiter, "Early Predictors of Job Burnout and Engagement," *Journal of Applied Psychology* 93, no. 3 (2008), pp. 498–512.

136. Sabine Sonnentag et al., "Staying Well and Engaged When Demands Are High: The Role of Psychological Detachment," *Journal of Applied Psychology* 95, no. 5 (2010), pp. 965–976.

137. Sharon Toker and Michael Biron, "Job Burnout and Depression: Unraveling Their Temporal Relationship and Considering the Role of Physical Activity," *Journal of Applied Psychology* 97, no. 3 (2012), p. 699.

138. Accessed on September 25, 2017 at https:// yourstory.com/2016/09/ depression-corporate-india/.

139. Ibid., p. 40.

140. See, for example, Felix Chima, "Depression and the Workplace: Occupational Social Work Development and Intervention," *Employee Assistance Quarterly* 19, no. 4 (2004), pp. 1–20.

141. Ibid.

142. www.osha.gov, accessed May 28, 2005. See also Jennifer Sinkwitts, "Five Steps to Improve Ergonomics in the Office," *EHS Today*, January 2014, pp. 33–34.

143. Anne Chambers, "Computer Vision Syndrome: Relief Is in Sight," *Occupational Hazards*, October 1999, pp. 179–184; www.osha.gov/etools/computerworkstations/index.html, accessed May 28, 2005.

144. Sandra Lotz Fisher, "Are Your Employees Working Ergosmart?," *Personnel Journal*, December 1996, pp. 91–92. See also www.cdc.gov/od/ohs/Ergonomics/compergo.htm, accessed May 26, 2007.

145. www.ninds.nih.gov/disorders/repetitive_motion/repetitive_motion.htm, accessed February 28, 2010.

146. Sandy Smith, "SARS: What Employers Need to Know," *Occupational Hazards*, July 2003, pp. 33–35.

147. "CDC Recommends Respirators in Revised H1N1 Flu Guidance for Healthcare Workers," *BNA Bulletin to Management*, October 20, 2009, pp. 329–336; Pamela Ferrante, "H1N1: Spreading the Message," *EHS Today*, January 2010, pp. 25–27.

148. Accessed on September 25, 2017 at https://blog.ipleaders.in/smoking-ban-in-india-complaint/.

149. Garber, "Introduction to the Human Resource Discipline of Safety and Security."

150. Ibid. See also, "New Challenges for Health and Safety in the Workplace," *Workplace Visions* (Society for Human Resource Management), no. 3 (2003), pp. 2–4, and J. L. Nash, "Protecting Chemical Plants from Terrorists: Opposing Views," *Occupational Hazards*, February 2004, pp. 18–20.

151. "Survey Finds Reaction to September 11 Attacks Spurred Companies to Prepare for Disasters," *BNA Bulletin to Management*, November 29, 2005, p. 377.

152. Garber, "Introduction to the Human Resource Discipline of Safety and Security."

153. "Study: Don't Silo Human Capital Risk," www.shrm.org/hrdisciplines/ethics/articles, accessed May 27, 2012.

154. Robert Kaplan and Anette Mikes, "Managing Risks: A New Framework," *Harvard Business Review*, June 2012, pp. 48–60.

155. "Workplace Violence Takes a Deadly Toll," *EHS Today*, December 2009, p. 17; "Workplace Violence," www.osha.gov/SLTC/workplaceviolence, accessed September 11, 2014.

156. Jerry Hoobler and Jennifer Swanberg, "The Enemy Is Not Us," *International Personnel Management Association for HR* 35, no. 3 (Fall 2006), pp. 229–246.

157. www.cdc.gov/ncipc/dvp/ipv_factsheet.pdf, accessed August 8, 2013.

158. Paul Viollis and Doug Kane, "At-Risk Terminations: Protecting Employees, Preventing Disaster," *Risk Management Magazine* 52, no. 5 (May 2005), pp. 28–33.

159. M. Sandy Hershcovis et al., "Predicting Workplace Aggression: A Meta-Analysis," *Journal of Applied Psychology* 92, no. 1 (2007), pp. 228–238.

160. Alfred Feliu, "Workplace Violence and the Duty of Care: The Scope of an Employer's Obligation to Protect Against the Violent Employee," *Employee Relations Law Journal* 20, no. 3 (Winter 1994/95), p. 395.

161. Dawn Anfuso, "Deflecting Workplace Violence," *Personnel Journal*, October 1994, pp. 66–77.

162. Feliu, "Workplace Violence and the Duty of Care," p. 395.

163. See, for example, James Thelan, "Is That a Threat?" *HR Magazine*, December 2009, pp. 61–63.

164. Feliu, "Workplace Violence and the Duty of Care."

165. Ibid., pp. 401–402.

166. Viollis and Kane, "At-Risk Terminations," pp. 28–33.

167. Kenneth Diamond, "The Gender-Motivated Violence Act: What Employers Should Know," *Employee Relations Law Journal* 25, no. 4 (Spring 2000), pp. 29–41; "Bush Signs 'Violence Against Women Act'; Funding Badly Needed Initiatives to Prevent Domestic & Sexual Violence, Help Victims," *The America's Intelligence Wire*, January 5, 2006.

168. For example, see www.womenshealth.gov/violence-against-women/get-help-for-violence/violence-help-hotlines.html.

169. Unless otherwise noted, the following including the six matters to address is based on Richard Maurer, "Keeping Your Security Program Active," *Occupational Hazards*, March 2003, pp. 49–52.

170. Ibid.

171. http://view.fdu.edu/default.aspx?id=3705, accessed February 28, 2010.

172. Maurer, "Keeping Your Security Program Active," p. 50.

173. Ibid.

174. Maurer, "Keeping Your Security Program Active," p. 52.

175. "Focus on Corporate Security," *BNA HR Executive Series*, Fall 2001, p. 4.

176. Ibid.

177. Louis Obdyke, "Investigating Security Breaches, Workplace Theft, and Employee Fraud," *Society for Human Resource Management Legal Report*, January/February 2003, pp. 1–2.

178. Craig Schroll, "Evacuation Planning: A Matter of Life and Death," *Occupational Hazards*, June 2002, pp. 49–51. See also "Thorough Preparation for Natural Disasters Is Most Effective Way to Reduce Risks, Costs," *BNA Bulletin to Management*, November 20, 2012, p. 369.

179. Sandy Smith, "Are You Prepared?" *EHS Today*, March 2012, pp. 33–36.

180. "HR Plays Key Role in Preparing Organizations for Disasters," *Bloomberg BNA Bulletin to Management*, June 25, 2013, p. 206.

181. Maurer, "Keeping Your Security Program Active," p. 52; Li Yuan et al., "Texting When There's Trouble," *Wall Street Journal*, April 18, 2007, p. B1.

182. "Swine Flu Tests Employer Emergency Plan; Experts Urge Communicating Best Practices," *BNA Bulletin to Management*, May 5, 2009, pp. 137–144.

183. Sandy Devine, "Are You Ready for a Sudden Cardiac Arrest Emergency?" *EHS Today*, April 2009, pp. 26–29.

184. "Business Continuity: What Is the Best Way to Plan for Disasters That May Affect Our Business, Like the Gulf Oil Spill?" www.shrm.org/templates_tools, accessed May 27, 2012.

185. *PR Newswire*, April 2, 2013 pNA; "Get Tips on Using Social Media for Disaster Recovery," *The Public Manager* 42, no. 1 (Spring 2013), p. 35(3); Joseph Porcelli, "How FEMA Drove 23,000 People to Join Its Online Community," *The America's Intelligence Wire*, October 28, 2012; "Officials Take to Social Media to Share Emergency Information: Canadians Tapped into Social Networks, Expect Emergency Responders to Use Social Media: New Red Cross Survey," *CNW Group*, October 9, 2012.

186. See also Shari Lau, "Terrorist Screening, Bonus Pay, Labor Department Audits," *HR Magazine*, October 2012, p. 28.

187. Lloyd Newman, "Terrorism: Is Your Company Prepared?" *Business and Economic Review* 48, no. 2 (February 2002), pp. 7–10; Yuan et al., "Texting When There's Trouble."

17
Managing Global Human Resources

LEARNING OBJECTIVES

17-1 List the HR challenges of international business.

17-2 Illustrate with examples how intercountry differences affect HRM.

17-3 List and briefly describe the main methods for staffing global organizations.

17-4 Discuss some important issues to keep in mind in training, appraising, and compensating international employees.

17-5 Discuss similarities and differences in employee engagement around the globe.

17-6 Explain with examples how to implement a global human resource management program.

A few years ago the Japanese industrial giant Hitachi embarked on a strategy to streamline its business into six market-based but integrated groups around the world, and to meld these into what it called "One Hitachi."[1] Its HR group needed a new human resource strategy to support this. We'll see what they did.

WHERE ARE WE NOW ...

More managers today are managing people internationally. The purpose of this chapter is to improve your effectiveness at applying your human resource knowledge and skills when global challenges are involved. The topics we'll discuss include the manager's global challenge, adapting human resource activities to intercountry differences, staffing the global organization, training and maintaining employees abroad, employee engagement globally, and managing HR locally: how to implement a global HR system.

LEARNING OBJECTIVE 17-1

List the HR challenges of international business.

The Manager's Global Challenge

You don't have to dig very far to see how important international business is to companies here and abroad. For example, the total sum of US imports and exports rose about nine times in the past 30 years, to about $4.7 trillion recently.[2] That growth has been great for all sorts of businesses, but also confronts managers with special challenges. For one thing, managers have to formulate and execute their market, product, and production plans on a global basis. Ford Motor, for instance, has a "One Ford" strategy aimed at offering similar Ford cars globally.

"Going global" also means employers must address international human resource management issues. For example, "Should we staff our local offices in Europe with local or US managers?" And, "How should we appraise and pay our Asia employees?"[3]

The challenging thing about managing globally is that what works in one country may not work in another. The employer faces an array of political, social, legal, and cultural differences among countries and people abroad. Therefore, for instance, an incentive plan may work in the United States, but backfire in some Eastern European country where workers need a predictable weekly wage to buy necessities. However, in spite of such intercountry differences, the employer must create, for each country's local facility and for the company as a whole, a workable set of human resource policies and practices.[4] Distance adds to the challenge. For example, how should Starbucks' chief HR officer, based in Seattle, monitor Starbucks' HR managers in China?

What Is International Human Resource Management?

international human resource management (IHRM)
The human resource management concepts and techniques employers use to manage the human resource challenges of their international operations.

Employers rely on **international human resource management (IHRM)** to deal with global HR challenges like these. We can define IHRM as the human resource management concepts and techniques employers use to manage the human resource challenges of their international operations. IHRM generally focuses on three main topics:[5]

1. *Managing human resources in global companies* (for example, selecting, training, and compensating employees who work abroad)
2. *Managing expatriate employees* (those the employer sends abroad)
3. *Comparing human resource management practices* in different countries

Adapting Human Resource Activities to Intercountry Differences

LEARNING OBJECTIVE 17-2

Illustrate with examples how intercountry differences affect HRM.

As we said, the challenges of international human resource management don't just stem from the distances involved (though this is important). The bigger issue is dealing with the cultural, political, legal, and economic differences among countries and their people. Their result is that what works in one country might fail in another.

Companies operating only within the United States generally have the luxury of dealing with a relatively limited set of economic, cultural, and legal variables. Economically the United States is a capitalist, competitive society. And while the U.S. workforce reflects a multitude of cultural and ethnic backgrounds, shared values (such as an appreciation for democracy) help to blur cultural differences. Different states and municipalities certainly have their own employment laws. However, a basic federal framework helps produce a predictable set of legal guidelines regarding matters such as employment discrimination and labor relations.

A company operating multiple units abroad doesn't face such homogeneity. For example, minimum legally mandated holidays range from none in the United Kingdom to 5 weeks in Luxembourg. Italy has no formal requirements for employee representatives on boards of directors, but they're usually required in

FIGURE 17-1 **Critical Intercountry Differences That Influence International HR Practices**

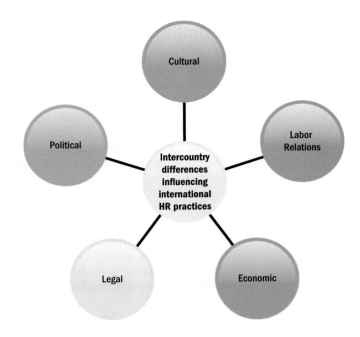

Denmark. The point is that managers have to adapt their human resource policies and practices to the countries in which they're operating. Figure 17-1 sums up critical intercountry differences.

Cultural Factors

For example countries differ widely in their *cultures*—in other words, in the basic values their citizens adhere to, and in how these values manifest themselves in the nation's arts, social programs, and ways of doing things.[6] Cultural differences manifest themselves in differences in how people from different countries think, act, and expect others to act. For example, the head of group purchasing at Michelin says that when he gives performance feedback in France employees don't think it's necessary to mention what's right because they know what they've done right. He focuses instead on what's wrong.[7] That approach would surprise most US employees, so there's a tendency for US managers to sugarcoat what's wrong. In China, heads of companies are inclined to see employees as members of their family, but in turn demand much of them.[8]

THE HOFSTEDE STUDY Studies by Professor Geert Hofstede illustrate international cultural differences. Hofstede says societies differ in five values, which he calls *power distance, individualism, masculinity, uncertainty avoidance,* and *long-term orientation.* For example, power distance represents the degree to which less powerful people accept the unequal distribution of power in society.[9] He concluded that acceptance of such inequality was higher in some countries (such as Mexico) than in others (such as Sweden).[10] In turn, such differences manifest themselves in different behaviors. To see how your country's culture compares with others, go to www.geert-hofstede.com/hofstede_dimensions.php.

Such cultural differences influence human resource policies and practices. For example, Americans' emphasis on individuality may help explain why European managers have more constraints, such as in dismissing workers.[11] As another example, in countries with a history of autocratic rule, employees often had to divulge information. Here, whistle-blower rules are less popular.[12]

LEGAL FACTORS Employers expanding abroad must also be familiar with the labor laws in the countries they're entering. For example, in India, companies with more

KNOWLEDGE BASE

Employers need to adapt their HR practices to the cultures of the countries where they do business.

McPHOTOs/Blickwinkel/AGE Fotostock

than 100 workers need government permission to fire anyone.[13] In Brazil, firing someone without "just cause" could trigger a fine of 4% of the total amount the worker ever earned.[14]

Similarly, the US practice of employment at will doesn't exist in Europe, where firing or laying off workers is usually expensive. And in many European countries, **works councils**—formal, employee-elected groups of worker representatives—meet monthly with managers on topics ranging from no-smoking policies to layoffs.[15]

Codetermination is the rule in Germany and several other countries. **Codetermination** means employees have the legal right to a voice in setting company policies. Workers elect their own representatives to the supervisory board of the employer.[16]

works councils
Formal, employee-elected groups of worker representatives.

codetermination
Employees have the legal right to a voice in setting company policies.

Economic Systems

Similarly, differences in *economic systems* translate into differences in intercountry HR practices. In *market* economies (such as the United States), governments play a relatively restrained role in deciding what will be produced and sold at what prices. In *planned* economies (such as North Korea), the government decides and plans what to produce and sell at what price. In *mixed* economies (such as China), many industries are still state-owned, while others make decisions based on market demand.

Differences in economic systems tend to translate into differences in human resource management policies. For instance, dismissing employees in China or Europe is more difficult than in the United States. Labor costs also vary widely. For example, hourly compensation costs (in US dollars) for production workers range from $2.01 in the Philippines to $9.34 in Taiwan, $35.53 in the United States, $47.38 in Germany, to $64.15 in Norway.[17]

HR Abroad Example: The European Union

To appreciate the employment effects of cultural, economic, and legal differences like these, consider Europe and China. The separate countries of the former European Community (EC) unified into a common market for goods, services, capital, and even labor called the *European Union (EU)*. Tariffs for goods moving across borders from one EU country to another generally disappeared, and employees generally move freely between jobs in EU countries. The introduction of a single currency (the euro) by a subset of EU countries further blurred differences. Despite (or perhaps partly because of) Greece's recent fiscal problems, EU countries today are moving towards increased economic integration.

Companies doing business in Europe must adjust their human resource policies and practices to EU directives (laws), as well as to country-specific employment laws. The directives are binding on all member countries, but each country can implement them as they wish. For example, the EU directive on confirmation of employment requires employers to provide employees with written terms and conditions of their employment.[18] In England, a detailed written statement is required, including things like rate of pay, date employment began, and hours of work. Germany doesn't require a written contract.

This interplay of EU directives and country laws means that an employer's human resource practices must vary from country to country. For example:[19]

- *Minimum EU wages.* Most EU countries have minimum wage systems. Some set national limits. Others allow employers and unions to work out their own minimum wages.
- *Working hours.* The EU sets the workweek at 48 hours, but most EU countries set it at 40 hours.
- *Termination of employment.* Required notice periods in Europe impede dismissals (which from employees' perspective is a good thing). For example, Whirlpool Corporation spent more than 3 years trying to eliminate 500 jobs in Italy, while (for better or worse) it took them less than a year to dismiss 1,000 people in Arkansas.[20]

HR Abroad Example: China

For years, employers relied on China's huge workforce to provide products and services at low cost. Part of the reason for the low labor cost was the dearth of labor laws on things like severance pay, minimum wages, and benefits.

But things are changing. For one thing, China's workforce, while still huge, is growing less quickly. For another, China has a new labor contract law. This adds many new employment protections for employees, and makes it more expensive for employers in China to implement personnel actions such as layoffs. Multinational companies doing business in China argue that the new law will raise labor costs and make it difficult to lay off employees, by instituting new severance package rules.[21] Local firms, including the remaining state-owned enterprises, tend to use fewer modern human resource management tools than do private Chinese multinationals like Lenovo, but must also deal with the fallout of the new labor law. There are therefore wide variations in how companies in China deal with HR issues such as the following.[22]

RECRUITING   Compared to some Western countries, it is relatively difficult to recruit, hire, and retain good employees. China's employment contract law requires, among many other things, that employers report the names, sexes, identification numbers, and contract terms for all employees they hire within 30 days of hiring to local labor bureaus.[23]

In China, recruiting effectiveness depends on nonrecruitment human resource management issues. Employees gravitate toward employers that provide the best career advancement training and opportunities.[24] Firms like Siemens China, with impressive training and development programs, have the least difficulty attracting good candidates. Poaching employees is a serious matter in China. The employer must verify that the applicant is free to sign a new employment agreement.

SELECTION   The dominant employee selection method involves analyzing the applicant's résumé and then interviewing him or her. The ideal way to do this is to institute a structured interview process, as many of the foreign firms in China have done.

COMPENSATION   Although many managers endorse performance-based pay in China, other employers, to preserve group harmony, make incentive pay a small part of the pay package. And, as in other parts of Asia, team incentives are advisable.[25]

LABOR UNIONS   Recently, Chinese facilities of IBM, PepsiCo, Walmart, and others have seen extensive strikes by Chinese workers.[26] Several things may be contributing to the strikes. China's new labor law expands workers' rights. An aging population in China means a diminishing supply of factory workers. And China's government may see the strikes as a way of raising workers' incomes and thus supporting its desire to boost consumer spending.

The accompanying HR Around the Globe feature compares how smaller US and Chinese employers deal with various HR issues.

▶ **IMPROVING PERFORMANCE:** *HR Practices Around the Globe*

Comparing Small Businesses, HR Practices in the United States and China

Cross-country differences tend to manifest themselves in small businesses, too. For example, one study compared practices in 248 small U.S. companies with those in 148 small Chinese companies.[27] First, in terms of *job analysis*, jobs in small Chinese companies tend to be more narrowly defined and set in stone than those in small US businesses. For example, the small Chinese firms have more up-to-date job descriptions, their employees deviate from their assigned job duties less frequently, their job descriptions tend to cover all the job's duties, and the job descriptions shape what the workers do.

Similarly, the researchers found significant differences in *performance appraisal practices* between U.S. and Chinese firms. In Chinese firms, compared to the United States, performance appraisals more often focus on the bottom line; appraisal feedback is evaluative rather than developmental; the appraisal focuses on objective, quantifiable results; and the main objective is to improve performance (rather than to develop the employee). Perhaps surprisingly, therefore, performance appraisals in small Chinese companies tend to be more hard-nosed than are those in the United States.

Finally (perhaps surprisingly given China's communist roots), there's more emphasis on incentive pay than guaranteed salaries in China's small businesses. Employees in the Chinese firms are more likely to receive bonuses based on the company's profits, to receive bonuses based on company-wide gainsharing plans, to get stock or stock options as incentives, and to be paid based mostly on an incentive plan rather than on a guaranteed income plan. On the other hand, there tends to be less variation among Chinese employees in pay, and more emphasis on seniority. ■

LEARNING OBJECTIVE 17-3
List and briefly describe the main methods for staffing global organizations.

Staffing the Global Organization

Employers' focus today is increasingly on managing human resource activities locally. In other words, their main concern is on selecting, training, appraising, and managing the in-country employees where they do business.

However, deciding whether to fill local positions with local versus expatriate ("imported") employees remains a major concern.

HR in Practice at the Hotel Paris On reviewing the data, it was apparent to Lisa and the CFO that the company's global human resource practices were probably inhibiting the Hotel Paris from being the world-class guest services company that it sought to be. To see how they handled this, see the case on page 559 of this chapter.

expatriates (expats)
Noncitizens of the countries in which employees are working.

home-country nationals
Citizens of the country in which the multinational company has its headquarters.

locals
Citizens of the countries in which employees are working; also called *host-country nationals*.

International Staffing: Home or Local?

In general, we can classify an international company's employees as *expatriates, home-country nationals, locals (host-country nationals),* or *third-country nationals*.[28] **Expatriates (expats)** are noncitizens of the countries in which they are working. Expatriates may also be **home-country nationals**, citizens of the country in which the company is headquartered. **Locals** (also known as *host-country nationals*) work for the company abroad and are citizens of the countries where they are working. **Third-country nationals** are citizens of a country other than the parent or the host country—for example, a French executive working in the Shanghai branch of a U.S. multinational bank.[29]

USING LOCALS   Most employees will be locals, for good reason. First, the cost of using expatriates is usually far greater than the cost of using local workers.[30] Some companies are surprised at the cost of posting someone abroad. Agilent Technologies estimated that it cost about three times the expatriate's annual salary to keep the person abroad for 1 year. When it outsourced its expatriate program, it discovered the costs were much higher. The firm then dramatically reduced the number it sent abroad, from about 1,000 to 300 per year.[31]

There are other reasons. In one survey, employers reported a 21% attrition rate for expatriate employees, compared with 10% for their general employee populations.[32] Local people may view the multinational as a "better citizen" if it uses local management talent; some governments even press for staffing with local management.[33] Some expatriates overemphasize short-term results (knowing they will soon move on).[34] It's also more difficult to bring workers into the United States from abroad. U.S. employers must vigorously recruit U.S. workers before filing foreign labor certification requests with the Department of Labor.[35]

USING EXPATS   Yet there are also reasons for using expatriates—either home-country or third-country nationals. Employers often can't find local candidates with the required qualifications. Multinationals also view a successful stint abroad as a required step in developing top managers. Furthermore, the assumption is that home-country managers are already steeped in the firm's policies and culture, and thus more likely to apply headquarters' ways of doing things.

However, the trend has been toward using locals or other (non-expat) solutions. Posting expatriates abroad is expensive, security problems give potential expatriates' pause, returning expatriates often leave for other employers within a year or two, and educational facilities are turning out top-quality candidates abroad. As a result, new expatriate postings tend to be down, and many employers are bringing them home early.[36] A survey found that about 47% of U.S. multinationals were maintaining the size of their expat workforces, 18% were increasing it, and 35% were decreasing it.[37] However about half the global companies in one recent survey said they were doubling the number of expats they send to countries like China.[38]

OTHER SOLUTIONS   The choice is not just between expatriate versus local employees. For example, there are "commuter" solutions, involving frequent international travel but no formal relocation.[39]

One survey found that about 78% of surveyed employers had some form of "localization" policy. This is a policy of transferring a home-country national employee to a foreign subsidiary as a "permanent transferee."[40] For example, U.S. IBM employees originally from India eventually filled many of the 5,000 jobs that IBM recently shifted from the United States to India. These employees chose to move back to India, albeit at local India pay rates. The human resource team needs to control expat expenses, as the accompanying Profit Center feature explains.

▶ **IMPROVING PERFORMANCE:** *HR as a Profit Center*

Reducing Expatriate Costs

Given the expense of sending employees abroad for overseas assignments, the employer's human resource team plays a big role in controlling and reducing expatriate costs. A survey shows some of the steps HR managers are taking to reduce these expenses.[41] First, companies are upping the numbers of short-term assignments they make. This lets them use short-term expats to replace some long-term expats (and their families) who the company must maintain abroad for extended periods. Fifty percent of the companies surveyed are also replacing some expatriate postings with local hires. With an eye on cutting costs, many employers were also reviewing their firms' policies regarding such things as housing, education, and home leave, along with expatriate allowances and premiums (cost-of-living allowance and mobility/quality-of-living premiums).[42] The bottom line is that there's a lot human resource managers can do to cut costs and boost profits by better managing expat assignments. ■

Source: Based on "Mercer's International Assignments Survey 2010," www.imercer.com/products/2010/intl-assignments-survey.aspx, accessed June 2, 2011; "Companies Juggle Cost Cutting with Maintaining Competitive Benefits for International Assignments, www.amanet.org/training/articles/Companies-Juggle-cost-cutting-with-Maintaining-Competitive-Benefits-for-International-Assignments.aspx.

OFFSHORING   As we explained in Chapter 5, *offshoring*—moving business processes such as manufacturing or call-center operations abroad, and thus having local employees abroad do jobs that the firm's domestic employees previously did in-house—is another globalization option.[43]

IBM Business Consulting Services surveyed employers to see what roles HR was playing in offshoring decisions.[44] Here, human resource managers help top management:[45]

- To understand the *local labor markets*, for example, in terms of their size, education levels, and unions.
- To understand how the firm's current *employment-related reputation* in the locale may affect outsourcing to here.
- To decide how much the firm should *integrate the local workforce* into the parent firm's corporate organization. For example, engineers might best become employees. Others (such as call centers) might best remain employees of vendor firms.
- To deal with skill shortages.[46] This often requires using signing bonuses, higher wages, and improved promotion opportunities.
- To identify how to reduce attrition. This might include more training and development, better compensation, and improved career opportunities.

TRENDS SHAPING HR: *DIGITAL AND SOCIAL MEDIA*

USING TRANSNATIONAL AND VIRTUAL TEAMS Managing internationally may also involve organizing "transnational" teams, composed of employees located in various countries.[47]

Such teams of course often "meet" in virtual environments. **Virtual teams** are groups of geographically dispersed coworkers who interact using a combination of telecommunications and information technologies to accomplish an organizational task. To facilitate the merger of Marion Laboratories and Merrell Dow Pharmaceuticals, the companies created a transnational virtual team composed of members from production sites in Asia, Europe, and North America.[48] The team helped deal with potential merger integration problems.[49]

In a Skype and FaceTime world, virtual teams are both practical and popular. Collaborative software systems such as Microsoft NetMeeting conference system,[50] Cisco WebEx,[51] and GoToMeeting[52] enable virtual teams to hold live project reviews and discussions, share documents and exhibits, and store the sessions on the project's Web site. Cloud-based tools such as Huddle[53] allow team members to attend from wherever they are using mobile devices, Microsoft Project lets project team members manage tasks and flag issues and risks,[54] and Dropbox[55] facilitates cloud-based document storage. If necessary, large-screen tools such as Cisco Immersive TelePresence[56] make it seem as if team members are together in the same room, although they may be thousands of miles apart.

The main challenges virtual teams face are often people related. Challenges include building trust, cohesion, and team identity, and overcoming the isolation among team members.

virtual teams
Groups of geographically dispersed coworkers who interact using a combination of telecommunications and information technologies to accomplish an organizational task.

Success therefore depends on human resource management actions. In particular, *train* virtual team members in leadership, conflict management, and meetings management, and to respond swiftly to virtual teammates.[57] Be scrupulous about answering e-mails and being positive.[58] *Select* virtual team members using behavioral and situational interviews, where they describe how they'd respond to illustrative virtual team situations. Use current virtual team members to help *recruit* and select new team members.[59] ■

Management Values and International Staffing Policy

It's not just hard facts that influence international staffing decisions. The top executives' personal inclinations and values also play a role. Some executives are just more "expat-oriented." Experts classify top executives' values as *ethnocentric, polycentric,* or *geocentric.*

In an ethnocentrically oriented corporation, "the prevailing attitude is that home-country attitudes, management style, knowledge, evaluation criteria, and managers are superior to anything the host country might have to offer."[60]

Such values translate into employment practices. With an **ethnocentric** staffing policy, the firm fills key management jobs with parent-country nationals.[61] Reasons given for ethnocentric staffing policies include lack of qualified host-country management talent, a desire to maintain a unified corporate culture and tighter control, and the desire to transfer the parent company's core competencies (such as a specialized manufacturing skill) to a foreign subsidiary more expeditiously.[62]

In the **polycentric** corporation, "there is a conscious belief that only host-country managers can ever really understand the culture and behavior of the host-country market; therefore, the foreign subsidiary should be managed by local people."[63]

A polycentric-oriented firm staffs its foreign subsidiaries with host-country nationals, and its home office with parent-country nationals. Such policies may reduce the local cultural misunderstandings that might occur if it used expatriate managers, and be less expensive.[64]

A **geocentric** staffing policy "seeks the best people for key jobs throughout the organization, regardless of nationality."[65] This global firm will transfer the best person to the open job, wherever he or she may be. This can optimize placements and help build a more consistent culture among the global management team members.

Ethics and Codes of Conduct

Employers also need to make sure their employees abroad are adhering to their firm's ethics codes. However, exporting a firm's ethics rules requires more than giving employees abroad versions of a U.S. employee handbook. For example, few countries abroad adhere to "employment at will." Therefore, even handbooks that say, "We can fire employees at will" won't enable one to dismiss employees.[66] Instead of exporting the employee handbook, some distribute and publicize a global code of conduct.

Often, the employer's main concern is establishing global standards for adhering to U.S. laws that have cross-border impacts. For example, IBM paid $10 million to settle accusations that it had bribed Chinese and South Korean officials to get $54 million in government contracts.[67] Global employers need global codes of conduct on things like discrimination, harassment, bribery, and Sarbanes-Oxley.

Selecting International Managers

In most respects, screening managers for jobs abroad is similar to screening them for domestic jobs. For either assignment, candidates need the technical knowledge and skills to do the job, and the intelligence and people skills to be successful managers.[68] Testing, interviewing, and background checks are as applicable for selecting expatriates as for domestic assignments.

---

ethnocentric
The notion that home-country attitudes, management style, knowledge, evaluation criteria, and managers are superior to anything the host country has to offer.

polycentric
A conscious belief that only the host-country managers can ever really understand the culture and behavior of the host-country market.

geocentric
The belief that the firm's whole management staff must be scoured on a global basis, on the assumption that the best manager of a specific position anywhere may be in any of the countries in which the firm operates.

However, selection for foreign assignments is different. For example, there is the problem of being alone in a foreign land. Furthermore, the person's adaptability is important. Some people adapt anywhere; others fail to adapt anywhere.[69]

How do firms select global managers? Analyses of expatriate practices suggest several things. Traditionally, most selection of expatriates was done "... solely on the basis of successful records of job performance in the home country."[70] Today, however, best practices in international assignee selection include providing *realistic previews* to prospective assignees, facilitating *self-selection* to enable expatriate candidates to decide for themselves if the assignments are right for them, and using *traditional selection procedures* focusing on personal traits such as openness.[71] Employers now also use more expatriate selection criteria. Selection criteria include technical/professional skills, expatriates' willingness to go, experience in the country, personality factors (including flexibility), leadership skills, the ability to work with teams, and previous performance appraisals in the selection process. There seems to be a decline in U.S. companies' premature return rates, suggesting that employers are more successful at sending expatriates abroad.[72]

TESTING   As noted, employers can take steps to improve the expat selection process, and testing is an obvious tool. For example, Brookfield Global Relocation Services Intercultural Group has used its Overseas Assignment Inventory (OAI) for over 40 years to help employers do a better job of selecting candidates for assignments abroad. It says, "Proper assessment and selection of employees for international assignments can mean the difference between success and a missed opportunity. The Overseas Assignment Inventory (OAI)—our proprietary assessment tool—can be used for: assessment and selection of candidates, development of chosen expatriates, self-assessment, and building candidate pools." The OAI is an online assessment that measures nine attributes and six context factors crucial for successful adaptation to another culture. Brookfield Global Relocation Services establishes global norms and conducts ongoing validation studies of the OAI.[73]

In terms of personality, successful expatriate employees tend to be extroverted, agreeable, and emotionally stable.[74] So not surprisingly, sociable, outgoing, conscientious people seem more likely to fit into new cultural settings.[75]

Intentions are important, too: For example, people who want expatriate careers try harder to adjust to such a life.[76] Similarly, expatriates who are more satisfied with their jobs abroad are more likely to adapt to the foreign assignment.[77]

REALISTIC PREVIEWS   Even in familiar foreign postings there will be language barriers, bouts of homesickness, and new friends. Realistic previews about the problems as well as about the country's cultural benefits are thus an important part of screening. The rule is always "spell it all out" ahead of time.[78]

ADAPTABILITY SCREENING   With flexibility and adaptability very important, **adaptability screening** should be part of the screening process. Such screening aims to assess the assignee's (and spouse's) probable success in handling the foreign transfer, and to alert them to issues (such as the impact on children) the move may involve. Employers often use specially trained psychologists for this.

Here, companies often look for overseas candidates whose work and nonwork experience, education, and language skills already demonstrate ability for living and working with different cultures. Even several successful summers spent traveling overseas or in foreign student programs might provide some basis to believe the potential transferee can adjust abroad.

adaptability screening
A process that aims to assess the assignees' (and spouses') probable success in handling a foreign transfer.

Diversity Counts: Sending Women Managers Abroad

While women represent about 50% of the middle management talent in U.S. companies, they represent only about 20% of managers sent abroad.[79] That's up from about 3% in the 1980s and 15% in 2005, but still low.[80] What accounts for this?

Many misperceptions still exist.[81] Line managers make these assignments, and many assume that women don't want to work abroad, are reluctant to move their families abroad, or can't get their spouses to move.[82] In fact, this survey found, women do want international assignments, they are not less inclined to move their families, and their male spouses are not necessarily reluctant.

Safety is another issue. Employers tend to assume that women abroad are more likely to become crime victims. However, most surveyed women expats said that safety was no more an issue with women than it was with men.[83]

Fear of cultural prejudices against women is another issue. In some cultures, women do have to follow different rules, for instance, in terms of attire. But as one expat said, "Even in the more harsh cultures, once they recognize that the women can do the job ... it becomes less of a problem."[84]

Employers take several steps to identify more women to assign abroad. For example, *formalize a process* for identifying employees who are willing to take assignments abroad. (At Gillette, for instance, supervisors use the performance review to identify the subordinate's career interests, including for assignments abroad.) *Train managers* to understand how employees really feel about going abroad, and what the real safety and cultural issues are. Let successful female expats *help recruit* prospective female expats. And provide the expat's spouse with *employment assistance*.[85] ∎

LEGAL ISSUES   In selecting employees for international assignments, managers should consider the legal issues. The government of India allows foreign passport holders to be employed in the country under certain conditions. Foreign nationals are issued an employment visa or E category visa to work in India. This visa is given only to highly skilled persons, for which comparable Indian talent is not available. The person should be earning more than US$ 25,000 per annum, in India.[86] Similarly, each country has specific laws related to employment of foreigners. If equal employment opportunity laws conflict with the laws of the country in which the U.S. employer is operating, the laws of the local country generally take precedence.[87]

Avoiding Early Expatriate Returns

You know the expatriate's assignment probably failed when he or she makes an early, unplanned return.

Systematizing the entire expatriate management process is one way to avoid such early returns. For example, employers should have an expatriate policy covering matters such as compensation and travel costs. Include procedures, for instance, requiring that the manager responsible for the expat's costs obtain all chain of command approvals.[88] Another step in avoiding early returns is to test and select people who have the necessary traits and adaptability (as discussed earlier). And perhaps most importantly consider the expat's family situation.

FAMILY PRESSURES   In one study, U.S. managers listed, in descending order of importance, reasons for expatriates leaving early: inability of spouse to adjust, managers' inability to adjust, other family problems, managers' personal or emotional immaturity, and inability to cope with larger overseas responsibility.[89]

Such findings underscore a truism about selecting international assignees: The problem is usually not incompetence, but family and personal problems. Yet, many employers still often select expatriates mostly based on technical competence.[90]

Given the role of family problems in expatriate failures, the employer should understand just how unhappy and cut off the expatriate manager's spouse can feel abroad. As one spouse said,[91]

> It's difficult to make close friends. So many expats have their guard up, not wanting to become too close. Too many have been hurt, too many times already, becoming emotionally dependent on a friend only to have the inevitable happen—one or the other gets transferred. It's also difficult to watch your children get hurt when their best friend gets transferred.[92]

Three things make it easier. First is *language fluency*, since spouses will feel even more cut off if they can't communicate. Second, having *preschool-age children* seemed to make it easier for the spouse to adjust. "This suggests that younger children, perhaps because of their increased dependency, help spouses retain that part of their social identities ..."[93] Third, it helps if there is a *strong bond of closeness* between spouse and expat partner. This provides the continuing emotional support many spouses find lacking abroad.

Keep in mind that it's usually not how different culturally the host country is from the person's home country that causes problems; it's the person's ability to adapt.[94] As noted earlier, some people are so culturally at ease that they're fine transferred anywhere; others will fail anywhere.[95] The HR Tools feature sums up some suggestions.

▶ **IMPROVING PERFORMANCE:** *HR Tools for Line Managers and Small Businesses*

Some Practical Solutions to the Expatriate Challenge

Expat failure is expensive; managers can take several practical steps to improve the expat's success abroad.

- ✓ *Provide realistic previews* of what to expect abroad, *careful screening* (of both the prospective expat and his or her spouse), *improved orientation,* and *improved benefits* packages.
- ✓ *Shorten the length* of the assignment.
- ✓ Use Internet-based *video technologies* and group decision-making software to enable global virtual teams to conduct business without relocation.[96]
- ✓ Form *"global buddy"* programs. Here local managers assist new expatriates with advice on things such as office politics, norms of behavior, and where to receive emergency medical assistance.[97]
- ✓ *Use executive coaches* to mentor and work with expatriate managers.[98] ■

Source: Based on M. Harvey et al., "Global Virtual Teams: A Human Resource Capital Architecture," International Journal of Human Resource Management 16, no. 9 (September 2005), pp. 1583–1599; Eric Krell, "Budding Relationships," HR Magazine 50, no. 6 (June 2005), pp. 114–118.

Social media such as www.linkedin.com (see their global expat network) and www.expatfinder.com are excellent sources of information, suggestions, support, and employment leads and connections for expats or for those considering a job abroad. A typical link you'll find at those sites is www.linkedin.com/title/expatriate+transfer+advisor.[99]

Training and Maintaining Employees Abroad

Orienting and Training Employees on International Assignment

LEARNING OBJECTIVE 17-4

Discuss some important issues to keep in mind in training, appraising, and compensating international employees.

When it comes to the orientation and training required for expatriate success abroad, the practices of many U.S. employers reflect more talk than substance. Executives agree that international assignees do best when they receive the special training (in things like language and culture) that they require. Few provide it.

Many vendors offer packaged pre-departure training. In general, the programs use on-and offline lectures, simulations, videos, and readings to prepare trainees. Their offerings illustrate the aim and content of such programs. One program aims to provide the trainee with (1) the basics of the new country's history, politics, business norms, education system, and demographics; (2) an understanding of how cultural values affect perceptions, values, and communications; and (3) examples of why moving to a new country can be difficult, and how to manage these challenges.[100] Others aim to boost self-awareness and cross-cultural understanding, and to reduce stress and provide coping strategies.[101] A third prepares individuals and their families "to interact successfully in daily life and business situations abroad; understand the impact various factors have on cultural behaviors and attitudes to make the most of the living abroad experience; and to raise awareness of the challenges of moving abroad, culture shock and how to deal with exposure to new cultural experiences."[102]

Some employers use returning managers to cultivate the global mind-sets of those departing. For example, Bosch holds regular seminars, where new arrived returnees pass on their experience to managers and their families going abroad.

ONGOING TRAINING Beyond such pre-departure training, more firms provide continuing, in-country cross-cultural training during the early stages of an overseas assignment.

For example, managers abroad (both expats and locals) continue to need traditional skills-oriented development. At many firms, including IBM, such development includes rotating assignments to help overseas managers grow professionally. IBM and other firms also have management development centers around the world where executives can hone their skills. And classroom programs (such as those at the London Business School or at INSEAD in France) provide overseas executives the educational opportunities (to acquire MBAs, for instance) that stateside colleagues have. Bank of Baroda (BoB) and State Bank of India (SBI), which have branches abroad, organize regular training programs for their Indian staff posted in foreign locations. International staff (i.e., locally recruited employees) are also trained, and occasionally BoB invites them to attend training programs in India. Many UAE-based companies promoted by Indians, encourage their employees to enroll for IIMA programs conducted in the UAE.

PepsiCo encourages expatriates to engage in local social activities, such as table tennis tournaments in China, to help them become acclimated faster to local cultures.[103]

International development activities hopefully have other, less tangible benefits. For example, rotating assignments can help managers form bonds with colleagues around the world. These can help the managers form the informal networks they need to make cross-border decisions more expeditiously.

Performance Appraisal of International Managers

Several things complicate appraising an expatriate's performance. Cultural differences are one. For example, a candid exchange is often the norm in the United States, but sometimes less so in China, where "face" is a concern.

Furthermore, who does the appraisal? Local management must have some input, but, again, cultural differences may distort the appraisals. (Thus, host-country bosses in Peru might evaluate a U.S. expatriate manager there somewhat negatively if they

Many global employers bring their international managers together periodically for training seminars.

Monkey Business Images/Thinkstock

find his or her use of participative decision making culturally inappropriate.) On the other hand, home-office managers may be so out of touch that they can't provide useful appraisals. In one survey, the managers knew that having appraisers from both the host and home countries produced the best appraisals. But, in practice, most didn't. Instead, they had raters from the host or the home countries do them.[104]

Suggestions for improving the expatriate appraisal process include:

1. Adapt the performance criteria to the local job and situation.
2. Weigh the evaluation more toward the on-site manager's appraisal than toward the home-site manager's.
3. If the home-office manager does the actual written appraisal, have him or her use a former expatriate from the same overseas location for advice.

Compensating Managers Abroad

In compensating those it transfers abroad, an employer such as accounting and advisory firm KPMG has basically three choices—continue paying based on the person's current home-country pay, pay based on what locals in the new country are paid, or pay so the person's home—country standard of living stays the same. [105]

There is some logic in maintaining the person's *home country pay*, particularly if the assignment will be brief. On the other hand paying the new expat based solely on what his or her new *local peers* are earning could be a shock if it means the person's former home-country standard of living (for children's schools, and so forth) can't be maintained under strictly local pay rates. The fact is it can be enormously more expensive to live in some countries (like Japan) than others (like India); if these cost-of-living differences aren't considered, it will be almost impossible to get managers to take "high-cost" assignments. It's common for Indian companies that depute employees abroad for certain duration to compensate them with a per-diem allowance, while the actual salary remains unchanged. However, for longer assignments the foreign country rules are applicable, with additional allowances as applicable. Therefore the more popular approach is to use the third option, namely by paying expats so that on their new jobs their pay is sufficient to maintain their former home-country *standard of living*; here most employers use what is called the balance sheet approach.

THE BALANCE SHEET APPROACH   The most common approach to formulating expatriate pay is to equalize purchasing power across countries, a technique known as the *balance sheet approach.*[106]

The basic idea is that each expatriate should enjoy the same standard of living he or she would have had at home. The balance sheet approach addresses four groups of expenses—income taxes, housing, goods and services, and discretionary expenses (child support, car payments, and the like). The employer estimates each of these four expenses in the expat's home country, and in the host country. The employer then pays any differences—such as additional income taxes or housing expenses. (Multiple-nation taxation can be a problem. Respondents often list "tax compliance" as the top challenge in sending employees abroad.)[107]

The base salary will normally be in the same range as the manager's home-country salary. In addition, however, there might be an overseas or foreign service salary premium. The executive receives this as a percentage of base salary, to compensate for the adjustments he or she will have to make.[108] There may also be several allowances, including a housing allowance and an education allowance for the expatriate's children. To help the expatriate manage his or her home and foreign financial obligations, most employers use a *split pay* approach; they pay, say, half a person's actual pay in home-country currency and half in the local currency.[109]

Table 17-1 illustrates the balance sheet approach. In this case, the manager's annual earnings are $160,000, and she faces a U.S. income tax rate of 28%. Other costs are based on the index of living costs abroad published in the "U.S. Department of State Indexes of Living Costs Abroad, Quarters Allowances, and Hardship Differentials," available via the www.state.gov Web site.[110]

TABLE 17-1 The Balance Sheet Approach
(Assumes U.S. Base Salary of $160,000)

Annual Expense	Chicago, U.S.	Shanghai, China (US$ Equivalent)	Allowance
Housing & utilities	$35,000	$44,800	$9,800
Goods & services	6,000	7,680	1,680
Taxes	44,800	57,344	12,544
Discretionary income	10,000	12,800	2,800
Total	$95,800	$122,624	$26,824

Determining rates abroad isn't always easy. Although there is a wealth of packaged compensation survey data available in the United States, such data are not quite as easy to come by overseas. Some multinational companies therefore conduct their own local annual compensation surveys. For example, Kraft has conducted one of total compensation in Belgium, Germany, Italy, Spain, and the United Kingdom. Realistically, however, most employers abroad do probably purchase one or more of various international salary surveys such as the Call Centre Remuneration Report – Australia, from Aon Hewitt, or the International Salary Survey Database—United Arab Emirates, from Executive Resources Limited.[111]

EXPATRIATE PAY EXAMPLE   As one expat pay example, those working for the company CEMEX (a multinational building supplies company)

> ... get foreign service premium equal to a 10% increase in salary. Some get a hardship premium, depending on the country; it ranges from zero in a relatively comfortable posting to, for example, 30% in Bangladesh. We pay for their housing. We pay for their children's schooling up to college. There's home leave—a ticket back to their home country for the entire family once a year. There are language lessons for the spouse. And we gross up the pay of all expats, to take out the potential effects of local tax law. Say you have an executive earning $150,000. This person would cost close to $300,000 as an ex-pat.[112]

foreign service premiums
Financial payments over and above regular base pay, typically ranging between 10% and 30% of base pay.

hardship allowances
Payments that compensate expatriates for exceptionally hard living and working conditions at certain locations.

mobility premiums
Typically, lump-sum payments to reward employees for moving from one assignment to another.

INCENTIVES   Employers pay various incentives to encourage the employee to take the job abroad. For example, **foreign service premiums** are financial payments over and above regular base pay. These typically range from 10% to 30% of base pay, and appear as weekly or monthly salary supplements. **Hardship allowances** compensate expatriates for hard living and working conditions at certain foreign locations. (U.S. diplomats posted to Iraq receive about a 70% boost in base salary, among other incentives.)[113] **Mobility premiums** are typically lump-sum payments to reward employees for moving from one assignment to another. In at least one way, executive compensation systems around the world are becoming more similar.[114] U.S. firms that offer overseas managers long-term incentives often use overall corporate performance criteria (like worldwide profits) when awarding incentive pay.

STEPS IN ESTABLISHING A GLOBAL PAY SYSTEM   Balancing global consistency in compensation with local considerations starts with establishing a rewards program that makes sense in terms of the employer's strategic aims.[115] Then the employer turns to more micro issues, such as, is how we're paying our employees abroad competitive?[116] Steps to follow in creating a global pay system include these:[117]

Step 1. **Set strategy.** First, formulate longer term strategic goals, for instance, in terms of improving productivity or boosting market share.

Step 2. **Identify crucial executive behaviors.** Next, list the actions you expect your executives to exhibit in order to achieve these strategic goals.

Step 3. **Global philosophy framework.** Next, step back and ask how you want *each pay component* (salary, bonus, incentives, and so forth) to contribute to prompting those executive actions.

Step 4. **Identify gaps.** Next, ask, "To what extent do our pay plans around the world now support these actions and what changes if any are required?"

Step 5. **Systematize pay systems.** Next, create more consistent performance assessment practices, and establish consistent job requirements and performance expectations for similar jobs worldwide.

Step 6. **Adapt pay policies** Finally, review your global pay policies (for setting salary levels, incentives, and so forth). Conduct surveys and analyses to assess local pay practices. Then fine-tune the firm's global pay policies so they make sense for each location.

Union Relations Abroad

Firms opening subsidiaries abroad face differing union-management relations practices among countries and regions. Walmart successfully neutralized unionization attempts in the United States, but had to accept unions in China.

As another example, the 2007–2009 recession and ongoing sovereign-debt crises in countries like Greece pushed up unemployment and understandably reduced unions' clout throughout Europe.[118] However, unions in Europe are still comparatively influential, and labor–management bargaining and relations reflect this.[119] For example, collective bargaining in Western Europe tends to be industry-wide, whereas in the United States it generally occurs at the company or plant level. And, union recognition in Europe is less restrictive than in the United States. For example, even if one union represents 80% of an employer's workers, another union in Europe can try to organize the other 20%.

Terrorism, Safety, and Global HR

Terrorism abroad is a serious issue. Even stationing employees in assumedly safe countries is no guarantee. A few years ago workers in French factories of Sony Corp. and 3M Co. took their managers hostage to negotiate better benefits.[120] When protests erupted in Egypt in February 2011, Medex Global Solutions evacuated more than 500 of its clients' people from Egypt; Medex had already been advising their clients about the possibilities for political unrest.[121] War and terrorist attacks in Kuwait, and recently in Syria, prompted the Indian government to act and plan evacuation of stranded Indian citizens. While the news of terror attacks have made employment in certain countries unattractive, some employers offer generous hardship allowance to Indians who are ready to work in such conditions. According to reports, IBM, Accenture, and Cognizant pay such allowances. Some Indian companies send senior executives to troubled areas by paying significantly high salaries.[122]

TAKING PROTECTIVE MEASURES Employers have thus had to institute more comprehensive safety plans abroad, including, for instance, evacuation plans to get employees to safety. (Legally, employers also have a duty of care for protecting international assignees and their dependents and international business travelers.)[123] Indian IT companies like NIIT and Tech Mahindra have established protocols to deal with such situations. Tech Mahindra has developed a mobile application. The company sends regular alerts through this app. NIIT also send alerts to its staff in difficult locations, and supports their interactions with families.[124] Many employers use intelligence services for monitoring potential terrorist threats abroad. The head of one intelligence firm estimates such services cost $6,000–$10,000 per year.[125] Some employers retain crisis management teams' services. They then call on these teams, for instance, when criminals kidnap one of their managers. As one executive said, "When you have a specialist, there's a better chance to get the person back."[126]

KIDNAPPING AND RANSOM (K&R) INSURANCE Hiring crisis teams and paying ransoms can be prohibitively expensive for all but the largest firms, so many employers buy kidnapping and ransom (K&R) insurance. Various events may trigger payments under such policies. The obvious ones are kidnapping (for instance, the employee is a hostage until the employer pays a ransom), extortion (threatening bodily harm),

and detention (holding an employee without any ransom demand). Tech Mahindra provides comprehensive insurance to all its international employees.[127]
The insurance typically covers several costs associated with kidnappings, abductions, or extortion. These include hiring a crisis team, the actual ransom payment, insuring the ransom money in transit, legal expenses, and employee death or dismemberment.[128] The HR Practices Around the Globe feature provides some practical examples.

▶ **IMPROVING PERFORMANCE:** *HR Practices Around The Globe*

Business Travel

Keeping business travelers safe is a specialty all its own, but suggestions here include:[129]

✓ Provide expatriates with training about the place they're going to, so they're more oriented.
✓ Tell them not to draw attention to the fact they're Americans—by wearing T-shirts with American names, for instance.
✓ Have travelers arrive at airports as close to departure time as possible and wait in areas away from the main flow of traffic.
✓ Equip the expatriate's car and home with security systems.
✓ Tell employees to vary their departure and arrival times and take different routes.
✓ Keep employees current on crime and other problems by regularly checking, for example, the State Department's travel advisories and warnings at http://travel.state.gov.[130] Click on "Travel Alerts" and "Country Information."
✓ Advise employees to act confident at all times. Body language can attract perpetrators, and those who look like victims often become victimized.[131]

Increased terrorism worldwide is causing more employers to use special travel safety tools to track and communicate with workers in real time.[132] For example, International SOS provides its clients with online and smart phone tools. These let the client quickly notify employees traveling abroad of potential problems and what to do about them. ■

AT&T makes sure that the employee always feels that he or she is still "in the loop" with what's happening back at the home office.

Squaredpixels/Getty Images

Repatriation: Problems and Solutions

One of the most worrisome facts about sending employees abroad is that 40% to 60% of them will probably quit within 3 years of returning home.[133] Given the investment the employer makes in training and sending these high-potential people abroad, it makes sense to try to retain them. For this, formal repatriation programs can be useful.[134] One study found that about 5% of returning employees resigned if their firms had formal repatriation programs, while about 22% of those left if their firms had no such programs.[135]

Probably the simplest way to improve retention is to value their experience. As one returnee put it: "My company was, in my view, somewhat indifferent to my experience in China as evidenced by a lack of monetary reward, positive increase, or leverage to my career in any way."[136]

The guiding principle of any repatriation program is this: Make sure the expatriate and his or her family don't feel the company has forgotten them. To that end, AT&T has a three-part repatriation program.[137] First, AT&T *matches the expat and his or her family with a psychologist* trained in repatriation issues. The psychologist meets with the family before they go abroad. The psychologist discusses the challenges they will face, assesses with them how well he or she thinks they will adapt, and stays in touch with them throughout their assignment.

Second, AT&T makes sure *the employee always feels that he or she is still "in the loop"* with the home office. For example, AT&T assigns the expatriate a mentor. It also periodically brings the expat back to the home office to meet with and to socialize with colleagues.

Third, AT&T *provides formal repatriation services.* About 6 months before the overseas assignment ends, the psychologist and an HR representative meet with the expat and the family, to start preparing them. For example, they help plan the employee's next career move, help the person update his or her résumé, and begin putting the person in contact with supervisors back home. They work with the person's family on the logistics of the move back. Then, about a month after returning home, the expat and family attend a "welcome home" seminar to discuss matters like the stress of repatriation.[138]

LEARNING OBJECTIVE **17-5**

Discuss similarities and differences in employee engagement around the globe.

Employee Engagement Guide for Managers

Engagement Around the Globe

A recent survey of employee engagement around the globe provides some useful observations.[139]

On average, the percent of engaged employees (including highly engaged and moderately engaged) was 70% in Latin America, 65% in North America, 61% in Asia/Pacific and Africa/Middle East, and 57% in Europe. The percentage of actively disengaged employees was highest in Europe (19%), lowest in Latin America (12%), and 15%–16% in North America, Asia/Pacific, and Africa/Middle East. Recently, the trend was for employee engagement (highly and moderately engaged) in all regions of the world to be converging around the current global average of about 61% of employees engaged. So, workers everywhere are becoming about equally engaged.

What are the top drivers of employee engagement around the globe? Career opportunities was the number-one key driver of employee engagement in all regions of the world, underscoring the universal importance of providing such opportunities. But beyond that point of agreement, the other key drivers varied by geographic area. For example, setting goals/managing performance was the number two key driver of employee engagement in North America but was much less important in Europe; the reputation of the organization was number two in Europe, pay was number two in Asia/Pacific, and recognition was number two in Latin America. So, the management actions that drive engagement vary somewhat by region.

One thing that did not seem to vary much was the global importance of employee engagement. The best performing companies' employees were in the top quartile in employee engagement.

LEARNING OBJECTIVE **17-6**

Explain with examples how to implement a global human resource management program.

Managing HR Locally: How to Put into Practice a Global HR System

Years ago international businesses often ran their international operations from "international" units within their corporate headquarters.[140] That structure evolved into a "multinational" structure; here subsidiary units (often with their own HR units) abroad largely controlled themselves. Now the trend is toward the "global" company. Global companies seek to be fully integrated. For example, a car to be sold in the United States might be designed in France and manufactured in China with parts from Japan.

This global approach has at least two big implications for human resource management. For one thing, it generally means that the company as a whole will want to be able to redeploy their best employees anywhere the firm does business (although most employers still rely most heavily on local employees). For example, one bank has a sort of global SWAT team of employees who are willing to be assigned to work anywhere on short notice. Hilton Worldwide's databanks contain information on every employee's skills, affiliations, language proficiency, and local market connections. Hilton can therefore easily transfer willing employees wherever necessary.

Second, being "global" also affects how the company organizes and manages its human resource management function, with the emphasis often on standardizing HR practices worldwide. The Strategic Context feature shows how one company did this.

▶ **IMPROVING PERFORMANCE:** *The Strategic Context*

Hitachi

A few years ago, the Japanese conglomerate Hitachi embarked on a strategy to streamline its business into six market-based but integrated groups around the world, and to meld them into what the company called "One Hitachi."[141] Takeo Yamaguchi, Hitachi's top human resource officer, knew Hitachi needed a new human resource strategy to support the One Hitachi strategy. He therefore set out to standardize Hitachi's human resource practices around the world. For example, he built a global HR database including data on things like employee name and performance history. To further support One Hitachi, he also standardized appraisal and compensation policies worldwide. So, for instance, now a manager in one region of the world is graded and compensated using the same processes and standards as a comparable manager in another region. ■

Source: Based on "Voices from the front lines," Harvard business review, September 2014, pages 77–83.

However, given cross-cultural and other differences, one could reasonably ask, "Is it realistic for a company to try to institute a standardized human resource management system in its facilities around the world, particularly since doing so usually means transferring one's selection, training, appraisal, pay, and other human resource practices abroad?"

A study suggests "yes." In brief, the study's results show that employers may have to defer to local managers on some specific human resource management policy issues. However, they also suggest that big intercountry HR differences are often not necessary. The important thing is how you implement the global human resource management system.

In this study, the researchers interviewed human resource personnel from six global companies—Agilent, Dow, IBM, Motorola, Procter & Gamble, and Shell Oil Co.—as well as international human resources consultants.[142] The study's overall conclusion was that employers who successfully implement global HR systems do so by applying several best practices. The basic idea is to *develop* systems that are *acceptable* to employees in units around the world, and ones that the employers can *implement* more effectively. Figure 17-2 summarizes this.

FIGURE 17-2 Best Practices for Creating Global HR Systems

Implement the international HR system and practices, such as by allocating adequate resources

Develop the international HR system, such as by forming global networks

Take steps to ensure the system is **acceptable** to those who must implement it, such as by investigating pressures to differentiate practices

Developing a More Effective Global HR System

First, these employers engage in two best practices in developing their worldwide human resource policies and practices.

Form global HR networks. To head off resistance, human resource managers around the world should feel part of the firm's global human resource management team. Treat the local human resource managers as equal partners. For instance, form global teams to develop the new human resources system. Create "an infrastructure of partners around the world that you use for support, for buy-in, for organization of local activities, and to help you better understand their own systems and their own challenges."[143]

Remember that it's more important to standardize ends and competencies than specific methods. For example, IBM uses a basically standardized recruitment and selection process worldwide. However, "details such as who conducts the interview (hiring manager vs. recruiter), or whether the prescreen is by phone or in person, differ by country."[144]

Making the Global HR System More Acceptable

Next, employers engage in three best practices so that the global human resource systems they develop will be *acceptable* to local managers around the world. These practices are:

Remember that truly global organizations find it easier to install global systems. For example, their managers work on global teams, and the firms identify, recruit, and place employees globally. As one Shell manager said, "If you're truly global, then you are hiring here [the United States] people who are going to immediately go and work in the Hague, and vice versa."[145] Doing so makes it easier for managers everywhere to accept the wisdom of having a standardized human resource management system.

Investigate pressures to differentiate and determine their legitimacy. Local managers will insist, "You can't do that here, because we are different culturally." These "differences" aren't usually persuasive. For example, when Dow wanted to implement an online recruitment and selection tool abroad, the hiring managers there said that their managers would not use it. After investigating the supposed cultural roadblocks, Dow successfully implemented the new system.[146]

However, first carefully assess whether the local culture or other differences might in fact undermine the new system. Be knowledgeable about local legal issues, and be willing to differentiate where necessary.

Try to work within the context of a strong corporate culture. Companies that do so find it easier to obtain agreement among far-flung employees. For example, because of how P&G recruits, selects, trains, and rewards them, its managers have a strong sense of shared values. For instance, new recruits quickly learn to think in terms of "we" instead of "I." They learn to value thoroughness, consistency, self-discipline, and a methodical approach. Having such global unanimity makes it easier to implement standardized human resource practices.

Implementing the Global HR System

Finally, two best practices helped ensure success in actually *implementing* the globally consistent human resource policies and practices.

"You can't communicate enough." "There's a need for constant contact with the decision makers in each country, as well as the people who will be implementing and using the system."[147]

Dedicate adequate resources. For example, don't require the local human resource management offices to implement new job analysis procedures unless the head office provides adequate resources for these additional activities.

Chapter Review

Chapter Section Summaries

17-1. Dealing with **global human resource challenges as a manager** isn't easy. The employer faces an array of political, social, legal, and cultural differences among countries abroad. What works in one country may not work in another.

17-2. **The need for adapting human resource activities to intercountry differences** influences employers' HR processes. For example, citizens of different countries adhere to different values, and countries have differing economic systems as well as different legal, political, and labor relations systems.

17-3. **Staffing the global organization** is a major challenge. Companies may use expatriates, home-country nationals, locals, or third-country nationals. Ethnocentric companies tend to emphasize home-country attitudes, polycentric companies focus more on host-country employees, and geocentric employers try to pick the best candidates from wherever they might be. Selecting employees to successfully work abroad depends on several things, most importantly on adaptability screening and on making sure that each employee's spouse and family get the realistic previews and support necessary to make the transition.

17-4. After selecting the employees to send abroad, attention turns to **training and maintaining your expatriate employees**.
In terms of pre-departure preparation, training efforts ideally first cover the impact of cultural differences; then, the focus moves to getting participants to understand how attitudes influence behavior, providing factual knowledge about the target country, and developing skills in areas like language and adjustment.

In compensating expatriates, most employers use the balance sheet approach; this focuses on four groups of expenses: income taxes, housing, goods and services, and discretionary expenses, and aims to ensure that the employee's standard of living abroad is about what it would have been at home.

With terrorism a threat, most employers today take protective measures, including buying kidnapping and ransom insurance.

Well-thought-out repatriation programs emphasize keeping employees in the loop as far as what's happening in their home offices, bringing them back to the office periodically, and providing formal repatriation services for the expatriate and his or her family to start preparing them for the return.

17-5. The worldwide trend is for employee engagement to converge around the current global average of about 61% of employees engaged. Career opportunities was the number-one key driver of employee engagement in all regions of the world, underscoring its universal importance.

17-6. With employers increasingly relying on local rather than expatriate employees, it's important for managers to understand **how to implement a global HR system**. The basic approach involves: (1) Develop a more effective global HR system; (2) Make the global HR system more acceptable; and (3) Implement the global system.

Discussion Questions

17-1. You are the president of a small business. What are some of the ways you expect "going international" will affect HR activities in your business?

17-2. What are some of the specific, uniquely international activities an international HR manager typically engages in?

17-3. What intercountry differences affect HRM? Give several examples of how each may affect HRM.

17-4. You are the HR manager of a firm that is about to send its first employees overseas to staff a new subsidiary. Your boss, the president, asks you why such assignments often fail, and what you plan to do to avoid such failures. How do you respond?

17-5. As an HR manager, what program would you establish to reduce repatriation problems of returning expatriates and their families?

Individual and Group Activities

17-6. Working individually or in groups, outline an expatriation and repatriation plan for an IT company employee from India, who is traveling to China for the next three years.

17-7. Give three specific examples of multinational corporations in your area. Check on the Internet or with each firm to determine in what countries these firms have operations. Explain the nature of some of their operations, and summarize whatever you can find out about their international employee selection and training HR policies.

17-8. Choose three traits useful for selecting international assignees, and create a straightforward test to screen candidates for these traits.

17-9. Use a library or Internet source to determine the relative cost of living in five countries as of this year, and explain the implications of such differences for drafting a pay plan for managers being sent to each country.

17-10. Appendices A and B at the end of this book (pages 583–600) list the knowledge someone studying for the HRCI (Appendix A) or SHRM (Appendix B) certification exam needs to have in each area of human resource management (such as in Strategic Management, and Workforce Planning). In groups of several students, do four things: (1) review Appendix A and/or B; (2) identify the material in this chapter that relates to the Appendix A and/or B required knowledge lists; (3) write four multiple-choice exam questions on this material that you believe would be suitable for inclusion in the HRCI exam and/or the SHRM exam; and, (4) if time permits, have someone from your team post your team's questions in front of the class, so that students in all teams can answer the exam questions created by the other teams.

17-11. An issue of *HR Magazine* contained an article titled "Aftershocks of War," which said that soldiers returning to their jobs from Iraq would likely require HR's assistance in coping with "delayed emotional trauma." The term *delayed emotional trauma* refers to the personality changes such as anger, anxiety, or irritability that exposure to the traumatic events of war sometimes triggers in returning veterans. Assume you are the HR manager for the employer of Ravi Menon, who is returning from an assignment in Afghanistan. Based on what you read in this chapter, what steps would you take to help smooth Ravi's reintegration into your workforce?

Experiential Exercise

A Taxing Problem for Expatriate Employees

Purpose: The purpose of this exercise is to give you practice identifying and analyzing some of the factors that influence expatriates' pay.

Required Understanding: You should be thoroughly familiar with this chapter and with the Web site www.irs.gov.

How to Set Up the Exercise/Instructions: Divide the class into teams of four or five students. Each team member should read the following: One of the trickiest aspects of calculating expatriates' pay relates to the question of the expatriate's U.S. federal income tax liabilities. Your team is the expatriate-employee compensation task force for your company, and your firm is about to send several managers and engineers to Japan, England, and Hong Kong. What information did you find on the site that will help your team formulate expat tax and compensation policies? Based on that, what are the three most important things your firm should keep in mind in formulating a compensation policy for employees you're about to send to Japan, England, and Hong Kong?

Application Case*

"Boss, I Think We Have a Problem"

Central Steel Door Corporation has been in business for about 20 years, successfully selling a line of steel industrial-grade doors.[145] The company had gradually increased its presence from the New York City area, first into New England and then down the Atlantic Coast, then through the Midwest and West, and finally into Canada. The company's basic expansion strategy was always the same: Choose an area, open a distribution center, hire a regional sales manager, and then let that regional sales manager help staff the distribution center and hire local sales reps.

Unfortunately, the company's traditional success in finding sales help did not extend to its overseas operations, when Mel Fisher, president of Central Steel Door, decided to expand his company into Europe. He tried for 3 weeks to find a sales manager by advertising in the *International New York Times*, which is read by businesspeople in Europe and by American expatriates living and working in Europe. Although the ads placed in the *Times* also ran for about a month on the *Times*'s Web site, Mr. Fisher so far has received only five applications. One came from a possibly viable candidate, whereas four came from candidates whom Mr. Fisher refers to as "lost souls"—people who seem to have spent most of their time traveling aimlessly from country to country, sipping espresso in sidewalk cafés. When asked what he had done for the last 3 years, one told Mr. Fisher he'd been on a "walkabout."

Other aspects of his international HR activities have been equally problematic. Fisher alienated two of his U.S. sales managers by sending them to Europe to temporarily run the European operations, but neglecting to work out a compensation package that would cover their relatively high living expenses in Germany and Belgium. One ended up staying the better part of the year, and Mr. Fisher was rudely surprised to be informed by the Belgian government that his sales manager owed thousands of dollars in local taxes. The two managers had hired about 10 local people to staff each of the two distribution centers. However, the level of sales was disappointing, so Fisher decided to fire about half the distribution center employees. That's when he got an emergency phone call from his temporary sales manager in Germany: "I've just been told that all these employees should have had written employment agreements and that in any case we can't fire anyone without at least 1 year's notice, and the local authorities here are really up in arms. Boss, I think we have a problem."

Questions

17-12. Based on this chapter and the case incident, compile a list of 10 international HR mistakes Mr. Fisher has made so far.

17-13. How would you have gone about hiring a European sales manager? Why?

17-14. What would you do now if you were Mr. Fisher?

Continuing Case

Carter Cleaning Company

Going Abroad

Jack Carter decided to take his first long vacation in years and go to Mexico for a month a few years ago. What he found surprised him: He spent time in Mexico City and was surprised at the dearth of cleaning stores, particularly considering the amount of air pollution. Traveling north, he passed through Juarez, Mexico, and was similarly surprised at the relatively few cleaning stores he found there. As he drove back into Texas, and back toward home, he began to think about whether it would be advisable to consider expanding his chain of stores into Mexico.

Aside from the possible economic benefits, he liked what he saw in Mexico. Starting a new business again also appealed to him. "I guess entrepreneurship is in my blood," is the way he put it.

As he drove home to have dinner with Jennifer, he began to formulate the questions he would have to ask before deciding whether to expand abroad.

Questions

17-15. Assuming they began by opening just one or two stores in Mexico, what do you see as the main HR-related challenges Jack and Jennifer would have to address?

17-16. How would you go about choosing a manager for a new Mexican store if you were Jack or Jennifer? For instance, would you hire someone locally or send someone from one of your existing stores? Why?

17-17. The cost of living in Mexico is substantially below that of where Carter is now located: How would you go about developing a pay plan for your new manager if you decided to send an expatriate to Mexico?

17-18. Present a detailed explanation of the factors you would look for in your candidate for expatriate manager to run the stores in Mexico.

*Copyright Gary Dessler PhD.

Translating Strategy into HR Policies and Practices Case^{*,§}

*The overall map on page xxxviii of this book outlines the relationships involved.

Improving Performance at The Hotel Paris

Managing Global Human Resources

The Hotel Paris's competitive strategy is, "To use superior guest service to differentiate the Hotel Paris properties, and to thereby increase the length of stay and return rate of guests, and thus boost revenues and profitability." HR manager Lisa Cruz must now formulate functional policies and activities that support this competitive strategy and boost performance by eliciting the required employee behaviors and competencies.

With hotels in 11 cities in Europe and the United States, Lisa knew that the company had to do a better job of managing its global human resources, Lisa knew. For example, there were no formal means of identifying or training management employees for duties abroad (for those going either to the United States or to Europe). As another example, recently, after spending upward of $200,000 on sending a U.S. manager and her family abroad, they had to return her abruptly when the family complained of missing their friends back home. Lisa knew this was no way to run a multinational business. She turned her attention to developing the HR practices her company required to do business more effectively internationally.

On reviewing the data, it was apparent to Lisa and the CFO that the company's global human resource practices were probably inhibiting the Hotel Paris from being the world-class guest services company that it sought to be. For example, high-performing service and hotel firms had formal departure training programs for at least 90% of the employees they sent abroad; the Hotel Paris had no such programs. Similarly, with each city's hotel operating its own local hotel HR information system, there was no easy way for Lisa, the CFO, or the company's CEO to obtain reports on metrics like turnover, absences, or workers' compensation costs across all the different hotels. As the CFO summed it up, "If we can't measure how each hotel is doing in terms of human resource metrics like these, there's really no way to manage these activities, so there's no telling how much lost profits and wasted efforts are dragging down each hotel's performance." Lisa received approval to institute new global human resources programs and practices.

In instituting these new programs and practices, Lisa had several goals in mind. She wanted an integrated human resource information system (HRIS) that allowed her and the company's top managers to monitor and assess, on an ongoing basis, the company's global performance on strategically required employee competencies and behaviors such as attendance, morale, commitment, and service-oriented behavior. To address this need, she received approval to contract with a company that integrated, via the Internet, the separate hotels' HR systems, including human resource and benefits administration, applicant tracking and résumé scanning, and employee morale surveys and performance appraisals.

She also contracted with an international HR training company to offer expatriate training for Hotel Paris employees and their families before they left for their foreign assignments, and to provide short-term support after they arrived. That training company also helped create a series of weeklong "Managers' Seminars." Held once every 6 months at a different hotel in a different city, these gave selected managers from throughout the Hotel Paris system an opportunity to meet and to learn more about the numerous new HR programs and practices that Lisa and her team had been instituting for the purpose of supporting the company's strategic aims. With the help of their compensation specialist, Lisa and her team also instituted a new incentive program for each of the company's local managers, to focus their attention more fully on the company's service-oriented strategic aims. By the end of the year, the Hotel Paris's performance on metrics such as percent of expatriates receiving pre-departure screening, training, and counseling were at or above those of high-performing similar companies. She and the CFO believed, rightly, that they had begun to get their global HR system under control.

Questions

17-19. Provide a one-page summary of what individual hotel managers should know in order to make it more likely incoming employees from abroad will adapt to their new surroundings.

17-20. In previous chapters of Dessler *Human Resource Management* you recommended various human resource practices the Hotel Paris should use. Choose one of these, and explain why you believe they could take this program abroad, and how you suggest they do so.

17-21. Choose one Hotel Paris human resource practice that you believe is essential to the company specifically for achieving its high-quality-service goal, and explain how you would implement that practice in the firm's various hotels worldwide.

---

§Written by and copyright Gary Dessler, PhD.

Key Terms

international human resource management (IHRM), 537	expatriates (expats), 541	virtual teams, 543	adaptability screening, 545
works councils, 539	home-country nationals, 541	ethnocentric, 544	foreign service premiums, 550
codetermination, 539	locals, 541	polycentric, 544	hardship allowances, 550
	third-country nationals, 542	geocentric, 544	mobility premiums, 550

Endnotes

1. "Voices from the Front Lines," *Harvard Business Review,* September 2014, pp. 77–83.
2. www.census.gov/foreign-trade/statistics/historical/gands.pdf, accessed September 16, 2014.
3. See, for example, Helen Deresky, *International Management* (Upper Saddle River, NJ: Pearson, 2008); and Anne Marie Francesco and Barry Allen Gold, *International Organizational Behavior* (Upper Saddle River, NJ: Pearson, 2005).
4. Nancy Wong, "Mark Your Calendar! Important Task for International HR," *Workforce,* April 2000, pp. 72–74.
5. Anne Marie Francesco and Barry Gold, *International Organizational Behavior* (Upper Saddle River, NJ: Prentice Hall, 2004), p. 145.
6. A. L. Lytle, J. M. Brett, Z. Barsness, C. H. Tinsley, and M. Janssens, "A Paradigm for Quantitative Cross-Cultural Research in Organizational Behavior," in B. M. Staw and L. L. Cummings (Eds), *Research in Organizational Behavior* 17 (1995), pp. 167–214. See also, as an example, Alsoruodan Shao and Daniel Skarlicki, "Service Employees' Reactions to Mistreatment by Customers: A Comparison Between North America and East Asia," *Personnel Psychology* 67 (2014), pp. 23–59.
7. "Voices from the Front Lines."
8. Thomas Hout and David Michael, "A Chinese Approach to Management," *Harvard Business Review,* September 2014, pp. 103–107.
9. www.geert-hofstede.com/, accessed August 12, 2013.
10. See Vas Taras, Bradley Kirkman, and Piers Steel, "Examining the Impact of Culture's Consequences: A Three-Decade, Multilevel, Multi-Analytic Review of Hofstadter's Cultural Value Dimensions," *Journal of Applied Psychology* 95, no. 3 (2010), pp. 405–439.
11. Chris Brewster, "European Perspectives on Human Resource Management," *Human Resource Management Review* 14 (2004), pp. 365–382.
12. "SOX Compliance, Corporate Codes of Conduct Can Create Challenges for U.S. Multinationals," *BNA Bulletin to Management,* March 28, 2006, p. 97.
13. "In India, 101 Employees Pose Big Problems," *Bloomberg Businessweek,* January 17–23, 2011, p. 13.
14. "Employer Beware," *The Economist,* March 12, 2011, p. 43.
15. See, for example, www.fedee.com/ewc1.html, accessed August 12, 2013. Similarly,

the European Union is in the process of introducing a stronger and more consistent data protection directive for all of its 28 nations. See Bill Roberts, "Tougher Data Privacy Law on EU Horizon," *HR Magazine,* January/February 2015, pp. 68–70.
16. This is discussed in Eduard Gaugler, "HR Management: An International Comparison," *Personnel* 65, no. 8 (1988), p. 28. See also E. Poutsma et al., "The Diffusion of Calculative and Collaborative HRM Practices in European Firms," *Industrial Relations* 45, no. 4 (October 2006), pp. 513–546.
17. 2011 figures, www.bls.gov/news.release/pdf/ichcc.pdf, accessed August 12, 2013.
18. Phillips Taft and Cliff Powell, "The European Pensions and Benefits Environment: A Complex Ecology," *Compensation & Benefits Review,* January/February 2005, pp. 37–50.
19. Ibid.
20. Deborah Ball and James Haggerty, "How to Cut a Job in Italy? Wait, and Wait Some More," *Wall Street Journal,* May 21, 2013, pp. B1, B2.
21. Lisbeth Claus, "What You Need to Know About the New Labor Contract Law of China," *SHRM Global Law Special Report,* October–November 2008.
22. See, for example, Syed Akhtar et al., "Strategic HRM Practices and Their Impact on Company Performance in Chinese Enterprises," *Human Resource Management* 47, no. 1 (Spring 2008), pp. 15–32.
23. Andreas Lauffs, "Chinese Law Spurs Reforms," *HR Magazine,* June 2008, pp. 92–98.
24. See, for example, Kathryn King-Metters and Richard Metters, "Misunderstanding the Chinese Worker," *Wall Street Journal,* July 7, 2008, p. R11.
25. Gary Dessler, "Expanding into China? What Foreign Employers Entering China Should Know About Human Resource Management Today," *SAM Advanced Management Journal,* August 2006. See also Joseph Gamble, "Introducing Western-Style HRM Practices to China: Shop Floor Perceptions in a British Multinational," *Journal of World Business* 41, no. 4 (December 2006), pp. 328–340; and Adrienne Fox, "China: Land of Opportunity and Challenge," *HR Magazine,* September 2007, pp. 38–44.
26. "Striking Chinese Workers Are Headache for Nike, IBM, Secret Weapon for Beijing," *Bloomberg News,* May 6, 2014.

27. Based on Robert Heneman et al., "Compensation Practices in Small Entrepreneurial and High-Growth Companies in the United States and China," *Compensation and Benefits Review,* July/August 2002, pp. 15–16.
28. Francesco and Gold, *International Organizational Behavior,* 2005, p. 145.
29. Ibid., p. 106.
30. Ibid., p. 769; Arvind Phatak, *International Dimensions of Management,* (South-Western College Publishing, 1995) p. 106.
31. Leslie Klass, "Fed Up with High Costs, Companies Winnow the Ranks of Career Expats," *Workforce Management,* October 2004, pp. 84–88.
32. "Survey Says Expatriates Twice as Likely to Leave Employer as Home-Based Workers," *BNA Bulletin to Management,* May 9, 2006, p. 147.
33. Phatak, *International Dimensions of Management,* p. 108.
34. John Daniels and Lee Radebaugh, *International Business,* (Upper Saddle River, NJ: 2001) p. 769.
35. "DOL Releases Final Rule Amending Filing, Processing of Foreign Labor Certifications," *BNA Bulletin to Management,* January 11, 2005, p. 11.
36. Michelle Rafter, "Return Trip for Expats," *Workforce,* March 16, 2009, pp. 1, 3.
37. See "Workforce Trends: Companies Continue to Deploy Ex-Pats," *Compensation & Benefits Review* 42, no. 1 (January/February 2010), p. 6.
38. "Expatriate Assignments in Growth Markets to Soar," *HR Magazine,* January 2013, p. 20.
39. Helene Mayerhofer et al., "Flexpatriate Assignments: A Neglected Issue in Global Staffing," *International Journal of Human Resource Management* 15, no. 8 (December 2004), pp. 1371–1389; and Martha Frase, "International Commuters," *HR Magazine,* March 2007, pp. 91–96.
40. Timothy Dwyer, "Localization's Hidden Costs," *HR Magazine,* June 2004, pp. 135–144.
41. "Mercer's International Assignments Survey 2010," www.imercer.com/products/2010/intl-assignments-survey.aspx, accessed June 2, 2011; "Companies Juggle Cost Cutting with Maintaining Competitive Benefits for International Assignments," www.amanet.org/training/articles/Companies-Juggle-cost-cutting-with-Maintaining-Competitive-Benefits-for-International-Assignments.aspx, accessed June 2, 2011.

42. "Mercer's International Assignments Survey 2010"; "Companies Juggle Cost Cutting with Maintaining Competitive Benefits for International Assignments."
43. Based on Pamela Babcock, "America's Newest Export: White Collar Jobs," *HR Magazine,* April 2004, pp. 50–57.
44. The following is based on "Back-Office and Customer Care Centers in Emerging Economies: A Human Capital Perspective," IBM Business Consulting Services, www-935.ibm.com/services/us/imc/pdf/ge510-3967-back-office-asiapac.pdf, accessed September 16, 2014.
45. Ibid., pp. 3, 4.
46. Ibid., pp. 5, 6.
47. Charles Snow, Scott Snell, Sue Canney Davison, and Donald Hambrick, "Use Transnational Teams to Globalize Your Company," *Organizational Dynamics,* Spring 1996, pp. 50–67.
48. Anthony Townsend, Samuel DiMarie, and Anthony Hendrickson, "Virtual Teams: Technology and the Workplace of the Future," *Academy of Management Executive* 12, no. 3 (1998), pp. 17–29; Christina Gibson and Susan Cohen, *Virtual Teams That Work: Creating Conditions for Virtual Team Effectiveness* (Jossey-Bass: San Francisco, 2004), provides practicing managers with valuable insights into organizing and managing virtual teams. See also Bjorn Ambos and Bodo Schlemglmich, "The Use of International R&D Teams: An Empirical Investigation of Selected Contingency Factors," *Journal of World Business* 39, no. 1 (February 2004), pp. 37–48.
49. Michael Harvey et al., "Challenges to Staffing Global Virtual Teams," *Human Resource Management Review* 14 (2004), p. 281.
50. www.microsoft.com/en-us/download/details.aspx?id=23745, accessed May 6, 2015.
51. https://signup.webex.com/webexmeetings/US/sem_acquisition.html?CPM=KNC-sem&TrackID=1031986&country=US&psearchID=webex%20collaboration%20meeting%20room, accessed May 6, 2015.
52. www1.gotomeeting.com/m/g2msem3.tmpl?Portal=www.gotomeeting.com&c_name=msns&c_mark=NAPPC&c_kwd=go_to_meeting_software_download-Broad&c_prod=GTM&c_cmp=sf-70150000000add7&c_

date=CATnumber&c_cell=CM jwmL3KrcUCFUIZ7AodlRIA gQ&gclid=CMjwmL3KrcUCF UIZ7AodlRIAgQ&gclsrc=ds, accessed May 6, 2015.

53. www.huddle.com, accessed May 6, 2015.

54. https://products.office.com/en-us/project?legRedir=true&Corr elationId=20cd3b87-4cc5-4e30-ad86-c713d2a47abd, accessed May 6, 2015.

55. www.dropbox.com, accessed May 6, 2015.

56. www.cisco.com/c/en/us/prod-ucts/collaboration-endpoints/ immersive-telePresence/index. html, accessed May 6, 2015.

57. Except as noted, this is based on information in Bradley Kirkman et al., "Five Challenges to Virtual Team Success: Lessons from Sabre, Inc.," *Academy of Management Executive* 16, no. 3 (2002), p. 70.

58. Paul Berry, "Communication Tips for Global Virtual Teams," *Harvard Business Review,* October 30, 2014, https://hbr. org/2014/10/communication-tips-for-global-virtual-teams, accessed April 30, 2015.

59. This item is based on Bradley Kirkman et al., "The Impact of Team Empowerment on Virtual Team Performance: The Moderating Role of Face-To-Face Interaction," *Academy of Management Journal* 47, no. 2 (2004), pp. 175–192.

60. Phatak, *International Dimensions of Management,* p. 129.

61. Charles Hill, *International Business: Competing in the Global Marketplace* (Burr Ridge, IL: Irwin, 1994), p. 507.

62. Ibid., pp. 507–510.

63. Ibid.

64. Ibid., p. 509.

65. Ibid. See also M. Harvey et al., "An Innovative Global Management Staffing System: A Competency-Based Perspective," *Human Resource Management* 39, no. 4 (Winter 2000), pp. 381–394.

66. Donald Dowling Jr., "Export Codes of Conduct, Not Employee Handbooks," *Society for Human Resource Management Legal Report,* January/ February 2007, pp. 1–4.

67. www.nytimes.com/2011/03/19/ business/global/19blue.html, accessed June 30, 2011.

68. Mason Carpenter et al., "International Assignment Experience at the Top Can Make a Bottom-Line Difference," *Human Resource Management* 30, no. 223 (Summer–Fall 2000), pp. 277–285. See also Gunter Stahl and Paula Caligiuri, "The Effectiveness of Expatriate Coping Strategies: The Moderating Role of Cultural Distance, Position Level, and Time on the International Assignment," *Journal of Applied Psychology* 90, no. 4 (2005), pp. 603–615.

69. Sunkyu Jun and James Gentry, "An Exploratory Investigation of the Relative Importance of Cultural Similarity and Personal Fit in the Selection and Performance of Expatriates," *Journal of World Business* 40, no. 1 (February 2005), pp. 1–8. See also Jan Selmer, "Cultural Novelty and Adjustment: Western Business Expatriates in China," *International Journal of Human Resource Management* 17, no. 7 (2006), pp. 1211–1222.

70. Mary G. Tye and Peter Y. Chen, "Selection of Expatriates: Decision-Making Models Used by HR Professionals," *Human Resource Planning* 28, no. 4 (December 2005), p. 15(6).

71. Paula Caligiuri et al., "Selection for International Assignments," *Human Resource Management Review* 19 (2009), pp. 251–262.

72. Zsuzsanna Tungli and Maury Peiperl, "Expatriate Practices in German, Japanese, UK and US Multinational Companies: A Comparative Survey of Changes," *Human Resource Management* 48, no. 1 (January–February 2009), pp. 153–171. See also Zsuzsanna Tungli and Maury Peiperl, "Expatriate Practices in German, Japanese, UK and US Multinational Companies: A Comparative Survey of Changes," *Human Resource Management* 48, no. 1 (January/February 2009), pp. 153–171.

73. www.brookfieldgrs.com/inter-cultural, accessed September 7, 2013.

74. P. Caligiuri, "The Big Five Personality Characteristics as Predictors of Expatriates' Desire to Terminate the Assignment and Supervisor-Rated Performance," *Personnel Psychology* 53, no. 1 (Spring 2000), pp. 67–88. See also Margaret A. Shaffer et al., "You Can Take It with You: Individual Differences and Expatriate Effectiveness," *Journal of Applied Psychology* 91, no. 1 (January 2006), pp. 109–125.

75. Quoted in Meredith Downes, Iris I. Varner, and Luke Musinski, "Personality Traits as Predictors of Expatriate Effectiveness: A Synthesis and Reconceptualization," *Review of Business* 27, no. 3 (Spring/Summer 2007), p. 16.

76. Jan Selmer, "Expatriation: Corporate Policy, Personal Intentions and International Adjustment," *International Journal of Human Resource Management* 9, no. 6 (December 1998), pp. 997–1007. See also Barbara Myers and Judith K. Pringle, "Self-Initiated Foreign Experience as Accelerated Development: Influences of Gender," *Journal of World Business* 40, no. 4 (November 2005), pp. 421–431.

77. Hung-Wen Lee and Ching-Hsing, "Determinants of the Adjustment of Expatriate Managers to Foreign Countries: An Empirical Study," *International Journal of Management* 23, no. 2 (2006), pp. 302–311.

78. P. Blocklyn, "Developing the International Executive," *Personnel,* March 1989, p. 45. See also Paula M. Caligiuri and Jean M. Phillips, "An Application of Self-Assessment Realistic Job Previews to Expatriate Assignments," *International Journal of Human Resource Management* 14, no. 7 (November 2003), pp. 1102–1116.

79. "More Women, Young Workers on the Move," *Workforce Management,* August 20, 2007, p. 9; Andy Smailes, "Women Abroad – How to Get the Most from an International Assignment", *Living Abroad,* January 18, 2013, www.livingabroad. com/women-abroad-how-to-get-the-most-from-an-international-assignment/, accessed July 28, 2015.

80. "More Women…", op. cit.; Tina Vasquez, "Women Abroad: How to Get the Most from an International Assignment," May 31, 2012, www.theglasshammer. com/news/2012/05/31/ women-abroad-%E2%80%93-how-to-get-the-most-from-an-international-assignment/, accessed July 17, 2014.

81. For a good discussion of this, see Yochanan Altman and Susan Shortland, "Women and International Assignments: Taking Stock—A 25 Year Review," *Human Resource Management* 47, no. 2 (Summer 2008), pp. 199–216.

82. Kathryn Tyler, "Don't Fence Her In," *HR Magazine* 46, no. 3 (March 2001), pp. 69–77.

83. Ibid.

84. Ibid.

85. See Nancy Napier and Sully Taylor, "Experiences of Women Professionals Abroad," *International Journal of Human Resource Management* 13, no. 5 (August 2002), pp. 837–851; Iris Fischlmayr, "Female Self-Perception as a Barrier to International Careers?" *International Journal of Human Resource Management* 13, no. 5 (August 2002), pp. 773–783; Wolfgang Mayrhofer and Hugh Scullion, "Female Expatriates in International Business: Evidence from the German Clothing Industry," *International Journal of Human Resource Management* 13, no. 5 (August 2002), pp. 815–836; and Altman and Shortland, "Women and International Assignments."

86. Accessed on 23 August 2017 at http://mha1.nic.in/pdfs/ ForeigD-work_visa_faq.pdf

87. See Donald Dowling Jr., "Choice of Law Contract Clauses May Not Fly Abroad," *Society for Human Resource Management Legal Report,* October–November 2008, pp. 1–2.

88. Chuck Csizmar, "Does Your Expatriate Program Follow the Rules of the Road?" *Compensation & Benefits Review,* January/ February 2008, pp. 61–69.

89. Discussed in Hill, *International Business,* pp. 511–515.

90. Barbara Anderson, "Expatriate Selection: Good Management or Good Luck?" *International Journal of Human Resource Management* 16, no. 4 (April 2005), pp. 567–583.

91. Margaret Shaffer and David Harrison, "Forgotten Partners of International Assignments: Development and Test of a Model of Spouse Adjustment," *Journal of Applied Psychology* 86, no. 2 (2001), pp. 238–254.

92. Ibid., p. 251.

93. Ibid., p. 250.

94. Deresky, *International Management,* p. 90.

95. Sunkyu Jun and James Gentry, "An Exploratory Investigation of the Relative Importance of Cultural Similarity and Personal Fit in the Selection and Performance of Expatriates," *Journal of World Business* 40, no. 1 (February 2005), pp. 1–8. See also Jan Selmer, "Cultural Novelty and Adjustment: Western Business Expatriates in China," *International Journal of Human Resource Management* 17, no. 7 (2006), pp. 1211–1222.

96. M. Harvey et al., "Global Virtual Teams: A Human Resource Capital Architecture," *International Journal of Human Resource Management* 16, no. 9 (September 2005), pp. 1583–1599.

97. Eric Krell, "Budding Relationships," *HR Magazine* 50, no. 6 (June 2005), pp. 114–118. See also Jill Elswick, "Worldly Wisdom: Companies Refine Their Approach to Overseas Assignments, Emphasizing Cost-Cutting and Work–Life Support for Expatriates," *Employee Benefit News,* June 15, 2004, Item 0416600B.

98. Geoffrey Abbott et al., "Coaching Expatriate Managers for Success: Adding Value Beyond Training and Mentoring," *Asia-Pacific Journal of Human Resources* 44, no. 3 (December 2006), pp. 295–317.

99. For others, see www.linkedin. com/groups/Global-Expat-Professional-Network-4763493 and www.linkedin.com/groups/ Forum-Expatriate-Management-1056387, both accessed July 29, 2015.

100. Adapted from www.inter-changeinstitute.org/html/ cross_cultural.htm, accessed July 1, 2011.

101. Adapted from www.kwintes-sential.co.uk/cultural-services/

articles/expat-cultural training. html, accessed July 1, 2011. See also www.global-lt.com/en/us/ cultural-training/expatriate-training.html#60Countries, accessed July 28, 2015.

102. www.global-lt.com/en/us/ cultural-training/cultural-train-ing-expatriate-training-courses. html#60Countries, accessed July 1, 2011.

103. Lynette Clemetson, "The Pepsi Challenge: Helping Ex-Pats Feel at Home," *Workforce Management*, December 2010, p. 36.

104. Hal Gregersen et al., "Expatriate Performance Appraisal in U.S. Multinational Firms," *Journal of International Business Studies* 27, no. 4 (Winter 1996), pp. 711–739. See also Hsi-An Shih, Yun-Hwa Chiang, and In-Sook Kim, "Expatriate Performance Management from MNEs of Different National Origins," *International Journal of Manpower* 26, no. 2 (February 2005), pp. 157–175; and Francesco and Gold, *International Organizational Behavior*, 2004, pp. 152–153.

105. See for example, www.kpmg. com/Global/en/IssuesAndIn-sights/ArticlesPublications/ Documents/your-assignment-abroad.pdf?sf11313026=1, page 5, accessed July 29, 2015.

106. Stephenie Overman, "Focus on International HR," *HR Magazine*, March 2000, pp. 87–92; Sheila Burns, "Flexible International Assignee Compen-sation Plans," *Compensation & Benefits Review*, May/June 2003, pp. 35–44; Thomas Shelton, "Global Compensation Strate-gies: Managing and Administer-ing Split Pay for an Expatriate Workforce," *Compensation & Benefits Review*, January/Febru-ary 2008, pp. 56–59.

107. "Expatriate Assignments in Growth Markets to Soar," *HR Magazine*, January 2013, p. 20.

108. Phatak, *International Dimen-sions of Management*, p. 134. See also "China to Levy Income Tax on Expatriates," *Asia Africa*

Intelligence Wire, August 3, 2004, Item A120140119.

109. Shelton, "Global Compensation Strategies."

110. http://aoprals.state.gov/content. asp?content_id=186&menu_ id=81, accessed May 8, 2014.

111. www.erieri.com/SurveySources/ International, accessed July 28, 2015.

112. Luis Hernandez, "On Why Ex-Pat Assignments Succeed—or Fail," *Harvard Business Review*, March 2011, p. 73.

113. Mark Schoeff Jr., "Danger and Duty," *Workforce*, November 19, 2007, pp. 1, 3.

114. See, for example, "More Mul-tinational Organizations Are Taking a Global Approach to Compensation," *Compensation & Benefits Review*, May/June 2008, p. 5.

115. Robin White, "A Strategic Ap-proach to Building a Consistent Global Rewards Program," *Compensation & Benefits Re-view*, July/August 2005, p. 25.

116. "Recommendations for Managing Global Compensa-tion Clause in a Changing Economy," Hewitt Associates, www.hewittassociates.com/_Me-taBasicCMAssetCache_/Assets/ Articles/2009/hewitt_pov_glo-balcomp_0109.pdf, accessed March 22, 2009.

117. White, "A Strategic Approach," pp. 23–40.

118. Asbjørn Wahl, "Political and Ideological Crisis in an Increas-ingly More Authoritarian Euro-pean Union," *Monthly Review* 65, no. 8 (January 2014).

119. Robert Sauer and Keith Voelker, *Labor Relations: Structure and Process* (New York: Macmillan, 1993), pp. 510–525; see also Ma-rino Regini, "Human Resource Management and Industrial Relations in European Compa-nies," *International Journal of Human Resource Management* 4, no. 3 (September 1993), pp. 555–568 and www.worker-par-ticipation.eu/National-Indus-trial-Relations/Across-Europe/ Trade-Unions2, accessed April 30, 2015.

120. Jessica Marquez, "Hostage-Taking in France Has U.S. Observers on Their Guard," *Workforce Management*, April 20, 2009, p. 10.

121. Lisbeth Claus, "International Assignees at Risk," *HR Maga-zine*, February 2010, p. 73.

122. Varun Aggarwal and KV Kur-manath, "How Terror is Affect-ing Indian Techies Overseas," 31 March 2016, *The Hindu, Business Line*, as accessed on 08 August 2017 at 3pm IST-www.thehindubusinessline. com, [Navigation--Home--Info Tech--Article].

123. Fay Hansen, "Skirting Danger," Workforce Magazine, January 19, 2009, pp. 1, 3.

124. Ibid., p.551.

125. Frank Jossi, "Buying Protection from Terrorism," *HR Magazine*, June 2001, pp. 155–160.

126. Frank Jossi, "Buying Protection from Terrorism," op cit.

127. Aggarwal, op.cit., p.551.

128. Based on Samuel Greengard, "Mission Possible: Protecting Employees Abroad," *Work-force,* August 1997, pp. 30–32. See also Z. Phillips, "Global Firms Consider Additional Cover for Overseas Execs," *Business Insurance* 43, no. 23 (June 15–22, 2009), pp. 4, 22.

129. http://travel.state.gov/content/ passports/english/alertswarn-ings.html, accessed September 11, 2014.

130. Greengard, "Mission Possible," p. 32.

131. Jane Levere, "Putting Safety First," *New York Times*, January 27, 2015, p. B4.

132. Carla Joinson, "Save Thousands per Expatriate," *HR Magazine*, July 2002, p. 77. A survey by accountants KPMG found that only about 4% of the 430 human resource executives surveyed believed they were effectively managing the repa-triation process. Tanya Mohn, "The Long Trip Home," *New York Times*, March 10, 2009, www.nytimes.com/2009/03/10/ business/worldbusiness/10iht-

10home.20715091.html, ac-cessed October 15, 2013.

133. Kathryn Tyler, "Retaining Re-patriates," *HR Magazine*, March 2006, pp. 97–102.

134. Quoted in Leslie Klaff, "The Right Way to Bring Expats Home," *Workforce*, July 2002, p. 43.

135. Maria Kraimer et al., "The Influence of Expatriate and Re-patriate Experiences on Career Advancement and Repatriate Retention," *Human Resource Management* 48, no. 1 (January–February 2009), pp. 27–47.

136. Ibid., p. 43.

137. Ibid.

138. "2014 Global Trends in Employee Engagement," Aon Hewitt, www.aon.com/ attachments/human-capital-consulting/2014-trends-in-global-employee-engagement-report .pdf, accessed May 5, 2015.

139. Yaarit Silverstone, Claira Yang, Colin Sloman, and Susan Cantrell, "Trends Reshaping the Future of HR: Reconfiguring the Global Talent Landscape," *Top Trends That Will Reshape the Future of HR: The Future of HR*, Accenture, www.Accenture .com/us-en/Pages/insight-future-HR.aspx, accessed March 6, 2015.

140. "Voices from the Front Lines."

141. Ann Marie Ryan et al., "Design-ing and Implementing Global Staffing Systems: Part 2—Best Practices," *Human Resource Management* 42, no. 1 (Spring 2003), pp. 85–94.

142. Ibid., p. 89.

143. Ibid., p. 90.

144. Ibid., p. 86. See also M. Schoeff, "Adopting an HR Worldview," *Workforce Management* 87, no. 19 (November 17, 2008), p. 8.

145. Ryan et al., "Designing and Implementing Global Staffing Systems," p. 87.

146. Ibid., p. 92.

147. Written by and copyrighted by Gary Dessler, PhD.

18

Managing Human Resources in Small and Entrepreneurial Firms

LEARNING OBJECTIVES

18-1 Explain why HRM is important to small businesses and how small business HRM is different from that in large businesses.

18-2 Give four examples of how entrepreneurs can use Internet and government tools to support the HR effort.

18-3 List five ways entrepreneurs can use their small size to improve their HR processes.

18-4 Discuss how you would choose and deal with a professional employer organization.

18-5 Describe how you would create a start-up human resource system for a new small business.

Popular Vehicles and Services Limited (PVSL), based in Kochi, is a top performing Maruti Suzuki dealer, with footprints in many south Indian states. It is a part of the Kuttukaran Group that has a combined turnover of ₹3,500 crore in 2017. The owners attribute PVSL's success to its human resource management (HRM) practices, which help in business performance and customer satisfaction. The HR department has a tag line: "Popular HR: We care."[1] But fast growth and hiring sociable employees require effective hiring. We'll see what they did.

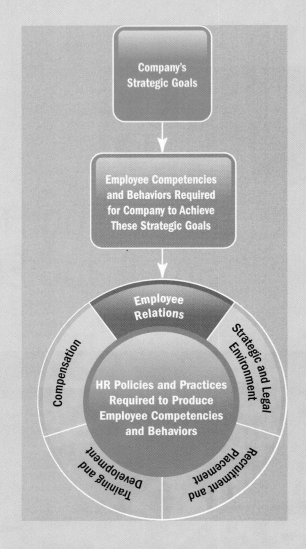

WHERE ARE WE NOW ...

Small businesses have special human resource management needs. The main purpose of this chapter is to help you apply what you know about human resource management to running a small business. The main topics we'll address include the small business challenge; using Internet and government tools to support the HR effort; leveraging small size with familiarity, flexibility, fairness, and informality; using professional employer organizations; and managing HR systems, procedures, and paperwork.

LEARNING OBJECTIVE **18-1**
Explain why HRM is important to small businesses and how small business HRM is different from that in large businesses.

The Small Business Challenge

There's nothing small about *small business*. Experiencing several highs and lows in the past few years, the small and medium enterprises (SMEs) of India have finally been recognized as one of the key sectors essential for the country's economic growth. The current government has facilitated several programs, such as, Public Procurement Policy, Pradhan Mantri MUDRA Yojana, Make in India, Startup India, and Skill India, which have aided in furthering the cause of SMEs. The SME footprint in India is projected to be US$ 25.8 billion equivalent by 2020, with a very high employment potential. Small businesses as a group also account for most of the new businesses created each year, as well as for most business growth (small firms grow faster than big ones). And small firms create most of the new jobs in the United States.[2]

Statistically speaking, therefore, most people graduating from college in the next few years will work for small businesses—those with less than about 200 employees. So, most everyone reading this book should know something about human resource management in small businesses.

How Small Business Human Resource Management Is Different

Managing human resources in small firms is different for four main reasons: *size, priorities, informality*, and the nature of the *entrepreneur*.

SIZE   For one thing, it's very unusual to find a business under 90 or so employees with a dedicated human resource management professional.[3] As a rule, it's not until a company reaches the 100-employee milestone that it can afford an HR specialist. Yet even five- or six-person retail shops must recruit, select, train, and compensate employees. So it's the owner or his or her assistant that does the HR paperwork and tasks. SHRM found, for instance, that even firms with under 100 employees often spend the equivalent of two or so people's time each year addressing human resource management issues.[4] That time usually comes out of the owner's long workday.

PRIORITIES   It's not just size but business realities that drive many small business managers and entrepreneurs (the men and women who provide the vision and "spark" that starts a new business) to focus on non-HR issues. After studying small e-commerce firms in the United Kingdom, one researcher concluded that, as important as human resource management is, it just wasn't a high priority for these firms:

> Given their shortage of resources in terms of time, money, people and expertise, a typical SME [*small- and medium-size enterprise*] manager's organizational imperatives are perceived elsewhere, in finance, production and marketing, with HR of diminished relative importance.[5]

INFORMALITY   One effect of this is that human resource management tends to be more informal in smaller firms. Thus, one study analyzed training practices in about 900 family and nonfamily small companies.[6] Training tended to be informal, with an emphasis on methods like coworker and supervisory on-the-job training. A study of HRM practices in Indian SMEs has revealed that for the owners, the willingness to formalize is sometimes constrained. Many believe that what they are doing is fine.[7] Another study found that direct involvement of owner managers (i.e., managers who are also managers) stand in the way of formalization of HR in Indian SMEs.[8]

Such informality isn't just due to a lack of resources, it's a "matter of survival." Entrepreneurs must react fast to changing competitive conditions. So, there's logic in keeping things like compensation policies flexible. Increasingly, more Indian SMEs are choosing to adopt formal HRM practices, and even take help of HR outsourcing firms like Husys (see www.Husys.net). The need for small businesses to adapt quickly often means handling matters like raises, appraisals, and time off "on an informal, reactive basis with a short time horizon."[9]

THE ENTREPRENEUR *Entrepreneurs* are people who create businesses under risky conditions. Researchers believe that small firms' relative informality partly stems from entrepreneurs' tendency to want to control things. "Owners tend to want to impose their stamp and personal management style on internal matters, including the primary goal and orientation of the firm, its working conditions and policies, and the style of internal and external communication and how this is communicated to the staff."[10]

IMPLICATIONS What does all this mean for the typical small firm's human resource management practices?

- First, rudimentary human resource practices may put small business owners at a *competitive disadvantage*. A small business owner not using tools like Web-based recruiting is incurring unnecessary costs, and probably deriving inferior results.
- Second, there is a *lack of specialized HR expertise*.[11] Even in larger small businesses, there are at most one or two human resource management people. This makes missing problems in specific areas such as equal employment law more likely. For example, managers in the smaller firm may not have the expertise to understand the legal implications of inappropriately asking a female job candidate if she's thinking of "starting a family."
- Third, the small business owner may not be fully complying with *compensation regulations and laws*. Examples include paying for overtime hours worked, and distinguishing between employees and independent contractors or contract labor.
- Fourth, paperwork duplication creates *data entry errors*. Small businesses often don't use human resource information systems. That means employee data (name, address, marital status, and so on) often appears on multiple human resource forms (medical insurance enrollment forms, PF forms, and so on). Any personal data change then requires manually changing all forms. This is inefficient, and triggers errors.

Diversity Counts: Necessity and the Entrepreneur

More men than women start new businesses, but according to one study, about 100 million women in 59 countries still started new businesses in one recent year.[12] Interestingly, most of the women who did start businesses were not in the developed world. The most likely countries for women to start businesses were in Latin America and sub-Saharan Africa. This may be because in developed economies, women have more career options. In developing economies such as Ghana, necessity infuses a confidence that drives more women to make it on their own.

According to the United Nations Industrial Development Organization (UNIDO), the involvement of women in entrepreneurial activities not only has economic benefits for the society but also has positive social repercussions for the women and their environment. Today, developing countries such as India and China witness a greater rise in women-driven entrepreneurial activities at the small and medium scale as compared to developed nations of the world. Improved awareness in society and support from the government for women entrepreneurs have led to this increase in numbers. Despite the surge, there are some limiting factors for women entrepreneurs in India, of which the main ones are fewer business contacts; less knowledge of how to deal with the government bureaucracy; and less bargaining power. ■

Why HRM Is Important to Small Businesses

Recently, a small software start-up experienced turmoil when social media postings from one employee accused another of harassment. The moral, says one expert, is that start-ups can't assume that all they need is an employee handbook; they also need a functioning HR system.[13]

Indeed, small firms that have effective HR practices do better than those that don't.[14] For example, researchers studied 168 family-owned high-growth SMEs. They concluded that successful high-growth SMEs placed more stress on training and development, performance appraisals, recruitment packages, maintaining morale, and setting competitive compensation levels than did less successful ones: "These findings suggest that these human resource activities do in fact have a positive impact on performance [in smaller businesses]."[15]

For many small firms, effective human resource management is also required for getting and keeping big customers. For example, to comply with international ISO-9000 quality standards, many large customers check that their small vendors follow the necessary HR standards.[16]

We devote this chapter to methods small business managers can use to improve their human resource management practices, starting with Internet and government tools.

<table>
<tr><td>

LEARNING OBJECTIVE **18-2**

Give four examples of how entrepreneurs can use Internet and government tools to support the HR effort.

</td></tr>
</table>

Using Internet and Government Tools to Support the HR Effort

No small business need cede the "HR advantage" to big competitors. Knowledgeable small business managers can level the terrain by using Internet-based HR resources, including free online resources from the government.

Complying with Employment Laws

Complying with federal (and state and local) employment law is a thorny issue for entrepreneurs. For example, the entrepreneur needs to know, "Must I pay this person overtime?" and, "Must I report this injury?"

Start by knowing which federal employment laws apply. For example, Indian SMEs should know that the Factories Act, 1948, is applicable to any factory where ten or more workers are employed on any one day of preceding 12 months, with the aid of power, or if minimum twenty workers are employed without power. Similarly, shops and commercial enterprises (including IT/ITES firms) are generally covered by the Shops and Commercial Establishments Act, which is specific for each state. Small business owners will find the legal answers they need to answer questions like these online.

HEALTH AND SAFETY   The Factories Act and other legislations have provisions related to occupational safety and health, which can be accessed by the Indian SMEs through the official website of the Ministry of Labor (labour.gov.in), or sites like Paycheck.in (See Figure 18.1). These sites contain the laws and practical information.

FIGURE 18-1 Paycheck India labour law section.

Source: From http://www.paycheck.in/main/labour-law-india as accessed on September 13, 2017.

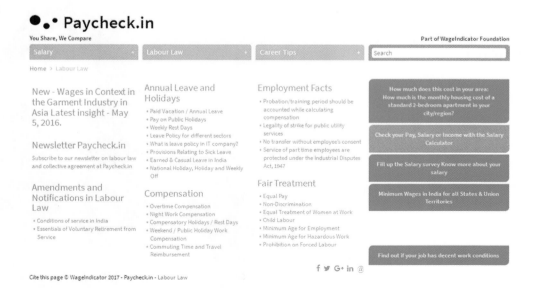

Employment Planning and Recruiting

Online tools can make small business owners as effective as their large competitors at writing job descriptions and recruiting applicants. It enables business owners to create accurate job descriptions and job specifications quickly.

WEB-BASED RECRUITING Similarly, small business owners can use the online recruiting tools we discussed in Chapter 5. For example, it's easy to scour LinkedIn.com, and to post jobs on Careerbuilder.com, and on professional associations' job boards.

TRENDS SHAPING HR: *DIGITAL AND SOCIAL MEDIA* [17]

Many small businesses use social media to recruit applicants. For example, LinkedIn lets employers post job openings and facilitates business networking. One recruiter reportedly looks for LinkedIn members with compelling summaries, excellent recommendations, and memberships in industry groups. On Twitter, recruiters see if a potential candidate has an appropriate username and photos. But also check Twitter for things like the person's status updates and retweets, to see (for instance) if he or she shares useful information. Small business recruiters should also focus on the social media that makes sense for them. For example, if you're looking for a Facebook marketing expert, look on Facebook. Or look for a photographer on Instagram. And on Facebook and LinkedIn, focus recruiting efforts on industry groups that make sense for your company. Check to see how your competitors use social media, and which communities they use.

Social media recruiting entails risks. For example, conversing with someone whose Facebook profile reveals ethnic background could expose the employer to a discrimination suit if that applicant isn't hired. And many agree that at the end of the day, social media recruiting can't substitute for in-person interactions. ∎

Employment Selection

Some tests are so easy to use they are particularly good for smaller firms. An example is the *Wonderlic Personnel Test*, which measures general mental ability. With questions somewhat similar to the SAT, it takes less than 15 minutes to administer

Use online tests, for instance, to test an applicant's typing speed, proficiency at QuickBooks, or even ability to sell over the phone.

Troels Graugaard/Getty Images

the four-page booklet. The tester reads the instructions, and then keeps time as the candidate works through the 50 problems. The tester scores the test by totaling the number of correct answers. Comparing the person's score with the minimum scores recommended for various occupations shows whether the person achieved the minimally acceptable score for the job in question.

The *Predictive Index* is another example. It measures work-related personality traits, drives, and behaviors—in particular, dominance, extroversion, patience, and blame avoidance. A template makes scoring simple. The Predictive Index program includes 15 standard benchmark personality patterns. For example, there is the "social interest" pattern, for a person who is generally unselfish, congenial, persuasive, patient, and unassuming. This person would be a good personnel interviewer, for instance.

Many vendors, including Wonderlic and the Predictive Index, offer online applicant testing and screening services. Wonderlic's service (which costs about $8,500 per year for a small firm) first provides job analyses for the employer's jobs. Wonderlic then provides a Web site the small business applicants can log into to take one or several selection tests (including the Wonderlic Personnel Test). Similarly, Indian SMEs can approach service providers who can help them with developing such tests. Pearson Clinical (www.pearsonclinical.in) and NPC India (npcindia.com) are such resources that can be consulted for this purpose.

The following are suggestions from *Inc.* magazine for supercharging a small business's recruiting and screening processes.

- *Keep it in the industry.* Use online job boards that target a particular industry or city to minimize irrelevant applicants.[18] For example, Naukri.com maintains city-specific job sites in over 19 states.[19] Beyond.com hosts more than 15,000 industry-specific communities.
- *Automate the process.* Automated applicant processing systems are inexpensive enough for small employers. For example, systems from Taleo, NuView Systems, and Accolo accept résumés and help automate the screening process.
- *Test online.* Use online tests, for instance, to test an applicant's proficiency at Tally, or even ability to sell over the phone.
- *Poll your inner circle.* Tap friends and employees for recommendations and use social networking sites such as LinkedIn, Facebook, and Twitter. Many employers announce job openings through LinkedIn. One says, "I get people vouching for each applicant, so I don't have to spend hours sorting through résumés."[20]
- *Send a recording.* InterviewStream records online video interviews. It sends the candidate an e-mail invitation with a link. When he or she clicks the link, a video interviewer asks the company's prerecorded questions. A Webcam captures the candidate's answers. Employers can allow candidates to rerecord their answers. Hiring managers can review the videos at their leisure.[21]

Employment Training

Online training can provide employee training that used to be beyond most small employers' reach.

PRIVATE VENDORS   The small business owner can tap hundreds of suppliers of prepackaged training solutions. These range from self-study programs from the All India Management Association (aima.org) and SHRM (www.shrm.org), to specialized programs. For example, the employer might arrange with NIIT to have its employees take computer courses.

SkillSoft is another example (http://skillsoft.com/catalog/default.asp). Its courses include business strategy and operations, professional effectiveness, and computer skills. For example, the course "interviewing effectively" is for managers, team leaders, and human resource professionals. About 2 1/2 hours long, it shows trainees how to use behavioral questioning to interview candidates.[22]

Employment Appraisal and Compensation

Small employers have easy access to computerized and online appraisal and compensation services. For example, Oracle Corporation's ePerformance[23] facilitates performance management by enabling managers to formalize the employee's goals and then assess progress toward meeting those goals. The eAppraisal system from Halogen Software[24] is another example. ZingHR is an Indian supplier of Human Capital Software, which can be customized and used by the SMEs as well.

Similarly, lack of easy access to high-priced salary surveys once made it difficult and time-consuming for smaller businesses to fine-tune their pay scales. Today, sites like www.salary.com makes it easy to determine local pay rates.

Employment Safety and Health

Safety is an important issue for small employers. One European study found that the majority of all workplace accidents occur in firms with less than 50 employees.[25] (Which is not surprising, since most people work for smaller businesses.) Indian SMEs have to follow provisions of the Factories Act, 1948, or other applicable laws like the Shops and Commercial Establishment Act. For compensating workers involved in accidents, the Workmen's Compensation Act of 1923, is applicable.

LEARNING OBJECTIVE 18-3

List five ways entrepreneurs can use their small size to improve their HR processes.

Leveraging Small Size with Familiarity, Flexibility, Fairness, and Informality

Because small businesses need to capitalize on their strengths, it makes sense for them to capitalize on their smallness when dealing with employees. For example, smallness can mean more personal *familiarity* with each employee's strengths, needs, and family situation. And it can mean being *flexible* and *informal* in its human resource management policies and practices.[26]

Simple, Informal Employee Selection Procedures

In addition to online recruitment and selection tools,[27] small business managers shouldn't forget simple, low-tech selection aids. For example, the Work Sampling Test we explained in Chapter 6 involves having the candidate show how he or she would actually do one of the job's tasks—such as a marketing candidate spending 30 minutes outlining an ad for a product. The accompanying HR Tools feature presents a more informal selection interview procedure the small business manager may find useful.

▶ IMPROVING PERFORMANCE: *HR Tools for Line Managers and Small Businesses*

A Streamlined Interviewing Process

The small business owner, pressed for time, may use the following practical, streamlined employment interview process.[28] One way to do so is to focus on four basic required factors: knowledge and experience, motivation, intellectual capacity, and personality. To proceed this way, interviewing expert John Drake suggests asking the following questions:

- ✓ **Knowledge and experience.** What must the candidate know to perform the job? What experience is necessary to perform the job? For example, ask a combination of situational questions plus open-ended questions to probe the candidate's suitability for the job, such as "How would you organize such a sales effort?" or "How would you design that kind of Web site?"
- ✓ **Motivation.** What should the person like doing to enjoy this job? Is there anything the person should not dislike? Are there any essential goals or aspirations the person should have? For example, probe such areas as the person's likes and dislikes (for each thing done, what he or she liked or disliked about it).
- ✓ **Intellectual capacity.** Are there any specific intellectual aptitudes required (mathematical, mechanical, and so on)? How complex are the problems the person must solve? What must a person be able to demonstrate intellectually? For example, ask questions that judge such things as complexity of tasks the person has performed, and grades in school.

✓ **Personality.** What are the critical personality qualities needed for success on the job (ability to withstand boredom, decisiveness, stability, and so on)? How must the job incumbent handle stress, pressure, and criticism? What kind of interpersonal behavior is required in the job? For example, probe by looking for self-defeating behaviors (aggressiveness, compulsive fidgeting, and so on) and by exploring the person's past interpersonal relationships, such as leading the work team on the last job. Is the candidate personable? Shy? Outgoing?

How to Organize the Interview

✓ Have a plan. Devise and use a plan to guide the interview. Drake says that significant areas to touch on include the candidate's:
  ✓ College experiences
  ✓ Work experience—summer, part-time
  ✓ Work experience—full-time (one by one)
  ✓ Goals and ambitions
  ✓ Reactions to the job you are interviewing for
  ✓ Self-assessments (by the candidate of his or her strengths and weaknesses)
  ✓ Military experiences
  ✓ Present outside activities[29]
✓ Follow your plan. Start with an open-ended question for each topic, such as "Could you tell me about what you did in college?" Then probe for information about the person's knowledge and experience, motivation, intelligence, and personality.

Match the Candidate to the Job

You should now be able to draw conclusions about the person's knowledge and experience, motivation, intellectual capacity, and personality, and to summarize the candidate's strengths and limits. This should provide a rational basis for matching the candidate to the job—one based on the traits and aptitudes the job actually requires. ■

Source: Based on John Drake, Interviewing for Managers: A Complete Guide to Employment Interviewing (New York, AMACOM, 1982).

Flexibility in Training

One study of 191 small and 201 large firms in Europe found that the small firms were relatively informal in their training and development.[30] Many didn't systematically monitor their managers' skill needs, and fewer than 50% (as opposed to 70% of large firms) had career development programs. The smaller firms also tended to focus any management development they did on teaching specific firm-related competencies (such as how to sell the firm's products).[31] The simplified training process we explained on page 228 (Chapter 8) is one good option for the small business. Informal methods such as the following work well, too.

INFORMAL TRAINING METHODS   Training expert Stephen Covey says small businesses can do many things to provide job-related training without establishing expensive formal training programs. His suggestions include:[32]

- Offer to cover the tuition for special classes
- Identify online training opportunities
- Provide a library of tapes and DVDs for systematic, disciplined learning during commute times
- Encourage the sharing of best practices among associates
- When possible, send people to special seminars and association meetings for learning and networking
- Create a learning ethic by having everyone teach each other what they are learning

Source: Questions for Covey: Small Business, Big Opportunity, Nov 2006, Training Magazine. www.Trainingmag.com. Used by permission from Lakewood Media Group.

Flexibility in Benefits and Rewards

The Family and Work Institute surveyed the benefits practices of about 1,000 small and large companies.[33] Not surprisingly, they found that large firms offer more *extensive* benefits packages than do smaller ones. However, many small firms overcame this by offering more flexibility. "They've discovered how to turn tiny into tight-knit, earning employees' trust by keeping them in the loop on company news and financials, and their loyalty by providing frequent feedback on performance."[34] At ID Media, with 90 employees, CEO Lynn Fantom gives all new employees a welcome breakfast on their first day. Internet start-up appssavvy Inc.'s CEO foregoes PowerPoint presentations in favor of humorous YouTube videos.[35]

Basically, the study found that small business owners, by personally interacting with all employees each day, did a better job of "understanding when work/life issues emerge."[36] Chicago Tea Stall in Adayar, Chennai, is an example of how employees of a small tea stall can be treated. Here, all employees are given free food, accommodation, and clothing allowances annually. They get good salary, paid leaves, and holidays, and they work only close to nine hours a day.[37]

Here are other examples of what small employers can offer:[38]

- *Extra time off.* For example, Friday afternoons off in the summer or school holidays or five day working week.
- *Compressed workweeks.* For example, compressed summer workweeks.
- *Bonuses at critical times.* Small business owners are more likely to know what's happening in their employees' lives. Use this knowledge to provide special bonuses, for instance, if an employee has a new baby or during festivals.
- *Flexibility.* For example, "If an employee is having a personal problem, help create a work schedule that allows the person to solve problems without feeling like they're going to be in trouble."[39]
- *Sensitivity to employees' strengths and weaknesses.* The small business owner should stay attuned to his or her employees' strengths, weaknesses, and aspirations. For example, give them an opportunity to train for and move into the jobs they desire.
- *Help them better themselves.* For example, pay employees to take a class to help them develop their job skills.
- *Feed them.* Provide free meals occasionally, perhaps by taking your employees to lunch.
- *Make them feel like owners.* For example, give employees input into major decisions, let them work directly with clients, get them client feedback, share company performance data with them, and let them share in the company's financial success.
- *Make sure they have what they need to do their jobs.* Having motivated employees is only half the challenge. Also ensure they have the necessary training, procedures, computers, and so on.
- *Constantly recognize a job well done.* Capitalize on your day-to-day interactions with employees to "never miss an opportunity to give your employees the recognition they deserve."[40]

SIMPLE RETIREMENT BENEFITS Access to retirement benefits is more prevalent in large firms than small ones. About 75% of large firms offer them, while only about 35% of small ones do.[41]

There are several ways for small firms to provide retirement plans. The National Pension Scheme (NPS), which is a government-approved scheme for Indian citizens aged 18–60 years, can be a good pension scheme for employees of SMEs.

Fairness and the Family Business

Most small businesses are "family businesses," since the owner (and often one or more employees) are family members.

Being a nonfamily employee here isn't easy. The tendency is to treat family and nonfamily employees differently. If so, as one writer puts it, "It's a sure bet that their lower morale and simmering resentments are having a negative effect on your operations and sapping your profits."[42] Reducing such "fairness" problems involves several steps, including:[43]

- *Set the ground rules.* One family business consultant says, During the hiring process the [management] applicant should be informed as to whether he or she will be essentially a placeholder, or whether there will be potential for promotion. At a minimum, make the expectations clear, regarding matters such as the level of authority and decision-making the person can expect to attain.[44]
- *Treat people fairly.* Work hard to avoid "any appearance that family members are benefiting unfairly from the sacrifice of others."[45]
- *Confront family issues.* Discord and tension among family members distract and demoralize employees. Family members must confront and work out their differences.
- *Erase privilege.* Family members "should avoid any behavior that would lead people to the conclusion that they are demanding special treatment in terms of assignments or responsibilities."[46] Family employees should come in earlier, work harder, and stay later than other employees stay.

LEARNING OBJECTIVE **18-4**
Discuss how you would choose and deal with a professional employer organization.

Using Professional Employer Organizations

As we explained in Chapter 13 (Benefits and Services), many small business owners look at the issues involved with managing personnel, and decide to outsource most of their human resource functions to vendors.[47] These vendors go by the names *professional employer organizations* (PEOs), *human resource outsourcers* (HROs), or sometimes *employee* or *staff leasing firms.* Husys is an Indian HRFO (Human Resource Function Outsource), working exclusively with SME clients.

How Do PEOs Work?

These vendors range from specialized payroll companies to those that handle all an employer's human resource management requirements.[48] At a minimum, these firms take over the employer's payroll tasks.[49] Usually, however, PEOs assume most of the employer's human resources chores. By transferring the client firm's employees to the PEO's payroll, PEOs become co-employers of record for the employer's employees. The PEO can then fold the client's employees into the PEO's insurance and benefits program, usually at a lower cost. The PEO usually handles employee-related activities such as recruiting, hiring (with client firms' supervisors' approvals), and payroll and taxes. Most PEOs focus on employers with under 100 employees, and charge fees of 2% to 4% of a company's payroll. HROs usually handle these functions on an "administrative services only"—they're basically your "HR office," but your employees still work for you.[50]

Why Use a PEO?

Employers turn to PEOs for several reasons.

LACK OF SPECIALIZED HR SUPPORT   Small firms with fewer than about 100 employees typically have no dedicated HR managers. The owner has most of the human resource management burden on his or her shoulders.

PAPERWORK   The Small Business Administration estimates that small business owners spend up to 25% of their time on personnel-related paperwork, such as background checks and benefits sign-ups.[51] Because the PEO takes over most of this, many small businesses conclude that it's cheaper for them just to pay the employee leasing firm's fees.

BENEFITS   Insurance and benefits are often the big PEO attraction. Getting health and other insurance is a problem for smaller firms. That's where leasing comes in. Leasing may get a small business insurance for its people that it couldn't otherwise.[52]

PERFORMANCE   Finally, the professionalism that the PEO brings to recruiting, screening, training, compensating, and maintaining employee safety and welfare will hopefully translate into improved employee and business results.

Caveats

There are several potential downsides. "If your PEO is poorly managed, or goes bankrupt, you could find yourself with an office full of uninsured workers."[53] Many employers view their human resource management practices (like training new engineers) as strategic, and aren't inclined to turn over such tasks to outsiders. Another potential problem is determining who's responsible. For example, who is responsible for an employee's injuries, the PEO or the employer? The contract should address this.[54]

WARNING SIGNS   Several things may signal problems with the prospective PEO. One is *lax due diligence*. For example, because they share liability with the employer, they should question you extensively about your firm's workplace safety and human resource policies and practices.[55] Figure 18-2 summarizes guidelines for finding and working with PEOs.

LEARNING OBJECTIVE **18-5**

Describe how you would create a start-up human resource system for a new small business.

Managing HR Systems, Procedures, and Paperwork

Introduction

Consider the paperwork required to run a five-person retail shop. Just to start with, recruiting and hiring an employee might require a help wanted advertising listing, an employment application, an interviewing checklist, various verifications—of education and immigration status, for instance—and a telephone reference checklist. You then might need an employment agreement, confidentiality and noncompetition agreements, and an employer indemnity agreement. To process the new employee

FIGURE 18-2 Guidelines for Finding and Working with PEOs

Source: Based on Robert Beck and J. Starkman, "How to Find a PEO That Will Get the Job Done," *National Underwriter* 110, no. 39 (October 16, 2006), pp. 39, 45; Lyle DeWitt, "Advantages of Human Resource Outsourcing," *The CPA Journal* 75, no. 6 (June 2005), p. 13; www.peo.com/dmn, accessed April 28, 2008; Layne Davlin, "Human Resource Solutions for the Franchisee," *Franchising World* 39, no. 10 (October 2007), p. 27; and see for example, www.adp.com/solutions/employer-services/totalsource/what-is-a-peo.aspx, accessed September 24, 2015.

Employers should choose and manage the PEO relationship carefully. Guidelines for doing so include:

- *Conduct a needs analysis.* Know ahead of time exactly what human resource concerns your company wants to address.
- *Review the services* of all PEO firms you're considering. Determine which can meet all your requirements.
- *Determine if the PEO is accredited.* There is no rating system. However, the Employer Services Assurance Corporation of Little Rock, Arkansas (www.Escorp.org), imposes higher financial, auditing, and operating standards on its members. Also check the National Association of Professional Employer Organizations (www.NAPEO.org), and www.PEO.com.
- Check the provider's bank, credit, insurance, and professional references.
- Understand how the *employee benefits will be funded.* Is it fully insured or partially self-funded? Who is the carrier? Confirm that employers will receive first-day coverage.
- See if the contract assumes the *compliance liabilities in the applicable states.*
- *Review the service agreement carefully.* Are the respective parties' responsibilities and liabilities clear?
- Investigate how long the *PEO has been in business.*
- *Check out the prospective PEO's staff. Do they seem to have the expertise to deliver on its promises?*
- Ask, *how will the firm deliver its services?* In person? By phone? Via the Web?
- Ask about upfront fees and how these are determined.
- *Periodically get proof that payroll taxes and insurance premiums are being paid properly* and that any legal issues are handled correctly.

you might need a background verification, a new employee checklist, and forms for withholding tax and to obtain new employee data. And to keep track of the employee once on board, you'd need—just to start—a personnel data sheet, daily and weekly time records, an hourly employee's weekly time sheet, and an expense report. Then come all the performance appraisal forms, a disciplinary notice, an employee orientation record, separation notice, and employment reference response.

In fact, this list barely scratches the surface of the policies, procedures, and paperwork you'll need to run the human resource management part of your business. Perhaps with just one or two employees you could track everything in your head, or just write a separate memo for each HR action, placing it in a folder for each worker. But with more employees, you'll need a human resource system comprised of standardized forms. Then as the company grows, you'll computerize various parts of the HR system—payroll, or appraising, for instance. The Strategic Context feature illustrates this.

▶ IMPROVING PERFORMANCE: *The Strategic Context*

City Garage in the US

City Garage's hiring system was inconsistent with its fast-growth strategy.[56] The firm's managers needed mechanics who were comfortable interacting directly with customers in City Garage's "open service area" format (where customers could watch and interact with their mechanics). The old hiring process was a paper-and-pencil application and one interview, followed by a hire/don't hire decision. The process ate up management time and was ineffective. City Garage's solution was to purchase the Personality Profile Analysis (PPA) online test from Thomas International USA. Now, after a quick application and background check, candidates take the 10-minute, 24-question PPA. City Garage staff then enter the answers into the PPA Software system, and receive test results almost at once. These show whether the applicant is right for the job, based on four personality characteristics. Computerizing its testing system improved City Garage's performance and profits, and helped it achieve its fast-growth "open service area" strategic goals. ■

Source: Based on Gilbert Nicholson, "Automated Assessments for Better Hires," Workforce (December 2000), pp. 102–107; http://www.citygaragedfw.com/.

Basic Components of Manual HR Systems

Very small employers (say, with 10 employees or less) will probably start with a manual human resource management system. From a practical point of view, this generally means obtaining and organizing a set of standardized personnel forms covering each important aspect of the HR process—recruitment, selection, training, appraisal, compensation, legal compliances and returns, safety—as well as some means for organizing all this information for each employees.

The number of forms you would conceivably need even for a small firm is quite large, as the illustrative list in Table 18-1 shows.[57] One simple way to obtain the basic forms of a manual HR system is from Web sites or books or CDs that provide compilations of HR forms. The forms you want can then be adapted from these sources for your particular situation.

OTHER SOURCES Several direct-mail catalog companies similarly offer HR materials. For example, Husys.net and other SME consultants offer packages of personnel forms. These include, for instance, Short- and Long-Form Employee Applications, Applicant Interviews, Employee Performance Reviews, and Absentee Calendars and Reports. Also available with different vendors are various legal-compliance forms, including standardized Harassment Policy and legal forms, as well as posters (for instance, covering legally required postings for matters such as Minimum Wages Act and Provident Fund).

Automating Individual HR Tasks

As the small business grows, it becomes impractical to rely on manual HR systems. It is at this point that most small- to medium-sized firms begin computerizing individual human resource management tasks.

TABLE 18-1 **Some Important Employment Forms**

New Employee Forms	Current Employee Forms	Employee Separation Forms
Application	Employee Status Change Request	Retirement Checklist
New Employee Checklist	Employee Record	Termination Checklist
Employment Interview	Performance Evaluation	Nomination Forms
Reference Check	Warning Notice	Unemployment Claim
Telephone Reference Report	Leave and Vacation Request	Employee Exit Interview
Employee Manual Acknowledgment	Probation Notice	
Employment Agreement	Job Description	
Employment Application Disclaimer	Probationary Evaluation Format	
Employee Secrecy Agreement	Security Deposit Acknowledgment	
	Absence Report	
	Disciplinary Notice	
	Grievance Form	
	Expense Report	
	Provident Fund/ESI or Insurance application and Acknowledgment	
	Injury Report	

HR in Practice at the Hotel Paris Lisa had managed to install several separate information systems, such as for performance appraisals. However, as she discussed one day over lunch with the CFO, these systems were not integrated. To see how she handled this, see the case on pages 605–606 of this chapter.

PACKAGED SYSTEMS   Here again, there are many resources available. For example, various Web sites contain categorical lists of HR software vendors.[58] These vendors provide software solutions for virtually all personnel tasks, ranging from benefits management to compensation, compliance, employee relations, outsourcing, payroll, and time and attendance systems.

Zoho People and ZingHR sell software packages for monitoring attendance, employee record keeping, writing employee policy handbooks, and conducting computerized employee appraisals. Husys.net, www.hrdirect.com, www.effortleshr.com, and others offer software and online solutions (Husys also provides consulting support) for writing employee policy manuals, maintaining employee records (including name, address, marital status, number of dependents, emergency contact and phone numbers, hire date, and job history), writing performance reviews, creating job descriptions, tracking attendance and hours worked for each employee, employee scheduling, writing organizational charts, managing payroll, conducting employee surveys, scheduling and tracking employee training activities, and managing labor law compliance, often cloud-based.[59]

Human Resource Information Systems (HRIS)

As the company grows, a more comprehensive system becomes necessary. We can define an integrated human resource information system (HRIS) as interrelated components working together to collect, process, store, and disseminate information to support decision making, coordination, control, analysis, and visualization of an organization's human resource management activities.[60] There are several reasons for installing an HRIS. The first is improved transaction processing.

Improved Transaction Processing

The day-to-day minutiae of maintaining and updating employee records take an enormous amount of time. One study found that 71% of HR employees' time was devoted to transactional tasks like checking leave balances, maintaining address records, and monitoring employee benefits distributions.[61] HRIS packages substitute powerful computerized processing for a wide range of the firm's HR transactions.

Online Self-Processing

HR information systems also facilitate employee self-processing. For example, at Provident Bank, the benefits system Benelogic lets employees self-enroll in all their desired benefits programs over the Internet at a secure site. It also "support[s] employees' quest for 'what if' information relating to, for example, the impact on their take-home pay of various benefits options."[62] That's all work that HR employees would previously have had to do for Provident's employees.

Improved Reporting Capability

By integrating numerous individual HR tasks (training records, appraisals, employee personal data, and so on), the HRIS improves HR's reporting capabilities. For example, reports might be available (company-wide and by department) for health-care cost per employee, pay and benefits as a percent of operating expense, cost per hire, report on training, volunteer turnover rates, turnover costs, time to fill jobs, and return on human capital invested (in terms of training and education fees, for instance).

HR System Integration

Because the HRIS's software components (record keeping, payroll, appraisal, and so forth) are integrated, they enable the employer to reengineer its HR function. For example, PeopleSoft's HRIS electronically routes salary increases, transfers, and other e-forms through the organization to the proper managers for approval. As one person signs off, it's routed to the next. If someone forgets to process a document, a smart agent issues reminders. The HRIS thus automates what might otherwise be a time-consuming manual process.

HRIS Vendors

Many firms today offer HRIS packages. Capterra.com, mentioned earlier, is one good source. Husys has a cloud HRIS application (named appHus) which can be customized for individual SMEs.

TRENDS SHAPING HR: *DIGITAL AND SOCIAL MEDIA*

HR on the Cloud

Most suppliers of human resource management systems, such as ADP, Ceridian, Kronos, Oracle, and SAP, offer totally cloud-based systems. For small business owners particularly, the advantages of cloud systems are that the vendors can more easily update them with the latest features—saving the small business owner much time and expense—and that the owner and employees can easily access the information from wherever they are.[63]

BambooHR illustrates an HR system especially designed for small and medium-sized businesses (www.bamboohr.com). A dramatic improvement over spreadsheets and other paper-based systems, bambooHR enables authorized managers and employees to securely and remotely access company information on matters like time off and personal information, and to produce reports and/or follow trends on the system's customizable dashboards. Furthermore, the bambooHR system was designed to be integrated with compatible applications. It can therefore be seamlessly integrated with the small business' payroll systems, applicant tracking systems, benefits enrollment systems, and performance review systems.[64] ■

Chapter Review

Chapter Section Summaries

18-1. Many people reading this book will work for or own their own small businesses, so it's important to understand **the small business challenge**. Without effective human resource management, small business owners run the risk that they'll be at a competitive disadvantage or that without the necessary HR expertise they may commit mistakes that lead to litigation.

18-2. Being small, small businesses can particularly capitalize on freely available **Internet and government tools to support their HR efforts**. For example, you can use Department of Labor elaws Advisors to answer overtime questions, the EEOC's Web sites for answers on questions like "How can we resolve the charge?" and the Department of Labor's OSHA Web site to review, for instance, your small business handbook. To better compete, small business owners can also use online recruiting tools like those we discussed in Chapter 5 and training programs available online from companies such as PureSafety.

18-3. Small businesses need to capitalize on their strengths, and in this case, it means capitalizing on **familiarity, flexibility, and informality**. For example, be flexible about extra time off, compressed workweeks, and job enrichment. They can also use relatively informal but still effective

employee selection procedures such as a work-sampling test. Informal training methods include online training opportunities, encouraging the sharing of best practices among associates, and sending employees to seminars. Because small businesses are often family businesses, it's important to treat nonfamily members fairly.

18-4. After reviewing all the challenges of managing human resources, many small business owners turn to **using professional employer organizations**. Also called *human resource outsourcers* or *employee or staff leasing firms*, these firms generally transfer the client firm's employees to the PEO's own payroll and thus become the employer of record for the employer's employees.

18-5. Small business managers need to understand how their **HR systems, procedures, and paperwork** will evolve. At first, there may be a simple manual human resource management system, for instance, with employee records compiled on forms from office supply companies and maintained in manual files. The employer then may purchase one or more packaged systems for automating individual HR tasks, for instance, such as applicant tracking and performance appraisal. As companies grow, they will look to integrate the separate systems with a human resource information system.

Discussion Questions

18-1. How and why is HR in small businesses different than that in large firms?

18-2. Explain why HRM is important to small businesses.

18-3. Explain and give at least five examples of ways entrepreneurs can use small size—familiarity,

flexibility, and informality—to improve their HR processes.

18-4. Describe with examples how you would create a start-up, paper-based human resource system for a new small business.

Individual and Group Activities

18-5. Form teams of five or six persons, each with at least one person who owns or has worked for a small business. Based on their experiences, make a list of the "inadequate-HR risks" the business

endured, in terms of competitive disadvantage, lack of specialized HR expertise, workplace litigation, compensation laws compliance, and paperwork/data-entry errors.

18-6. You own a small business, and you are confused about which of your employees is eligible for overtime pay. The employees in question include your secretary, two accounting clerks, one engineer, and two inside salespeople. Individually or in groups of four or five students, see Indian labor law sites or Paycheck India (www.paycheck.in) to determine who gets overtime pay.

18-7. You have about 32 employees working in your factory. Working individually or in teams of four or five students, find and create a list of five online sources you could use to provide training to them, at no cost to you or to them.

18-8. Appendices A and B at the end of this book (pages 583–600) list the knowledge someone studying for the HRCI (Appendix A) or SHRM (Appendix B) certification exam needs to have in each area of human resource management (such as in Strategic Management, and Workforce Planning). In groups of several students, do four things: (1) review Appendix A and/or B; (2) identify the material in this chapter that relates to the Appendix A and/or B required knowledge lists; (3) write four multiple-choice exam questions on this material that you believe would be suitable for inclusion in the HRCI exam and/or the SHRM exam; and, (4) if time permits, have someone from your team post your team's questions in front of the class, so that students in all teams can answer the exam questions created by the other teams.

Experiential Exercise

Building an HRIS

Purpose: The purpose of this exercise is to give you practice in creating a human resource management system (HRIS).

Required Understanding: You should be fully acquainted with the material in this chapter.

How to Set Up the Exercise/Instructions: Divide the class into teams of several students. Each team will need access to the Internet.

Assume that the owners of a small business come to you with the following problem. They have a company with less than 40 employees. They have been taking care of all HR paperwork informally, mostly on slips of paper and with memos. They want you to supply them with a human resource management information system—how computerized it is will be up to you, but they can only afford a budget of ₹50,000 upfront (not counting your consulting), and then about ₹5,000 per year for maintenance. You know from your HR training that there are various sources of paper-based and online systems. Write a two-page proposal telling them exactly what your team would suggest, based on its accumulated existing knowledge, and from online research.

Application Case

Netflix Breaks the Rules[65]

Why did Netflix survive as a start-up when the dot-com bubble burst in the late 1990s? Probably because, from the day he started Netflix, founder Reed Hastings believed in breaking the rules. His direct-to-consumer mail and video streaming business model certainly helped Netflix to survive. But the firm's unorthodox human resource management practices helped the company to attract and keep the high producers who design the products that are the firm's lifeblood. Hastings knew that top Silicon Valley workers could choose where they worked, and high pay is pretty much standard throughout the Valley's industries. How to set oneself apart? Hastings and his start-up colleagues believed that a culture that balanced a flexible work environment with few constraints and high responsibility was the answer. They called the policy "Freedom and Responsibility."

Just how unorthodox are the Netflix HR practices? Consider this: As a Netflix professional you get unlimited vacations. One engineer takes 5-week vacations to Europe, because he likes (as he says) to take his time off in big chunks. (An HR officer must approve time off in excess of 30 days annually.) As a Netflix employee, your pay isn't tied to performance appraisals, or even to a compensation plan. Frequent market salary surveys and pay hikes keep everyone's pay aligned with Silicon Valley competitors'. Each employee decides whether to take his or her pay in cash or in Netflix stock. Options vest immediately. Netflix doesn't recruit much at college job fairs, instead hiring mostly highly experienced professionals. There's no training, professional development, or career planning at Netflix (except for legally required training, such as diversity training). You're in charge of your own career.

But with freedom like that comes responsibilities. The company expects its salaried employees to work hard—to "do the jobs of three or four people," as one report put it. And Netflix doesn't have the "frat party" free-wheeling atmosphere that many dot-coms do. It's an adult environment. Netflix does not coddle underperformers. Yearly 360-degree performance reviews provide "direct and honest feedback." Those that aren't cutting it are quickly let go, but (whenever possible) amicably. Rather than the sorts of litigiousness that often characterizes dismissals in other firms (having to prove the person was incompetent, for instance), Netflix writes a check. The company believes that a handsome severance payment helps maintain the person's dignity, makes it easier for supervisors to make tough calls with underperformers, and, of course, minimizes blowback from those it dismisses. It's more like a "no-fault divorce," as one observer put it.

CHAPTER 18

Questions

In many respects, the Netflix HR strategy seems like a dream come true for small businesses. You don't need a pay plan; instead, you just update each person's pay every few months based on market surveys. You offer no training and development. And you don't track vacation time, more or less. If someone's not doing well, you just pay him or her to leave, with no hassles. Netflix seems to have hit upon its own version of "Netflix High-Performance Work Practices." Given that, answer the following questions (please be specific).

18-9. What (if anything) is it about Netflix that makes its HR practices work for it?

18-10. Would you suggest using similar practices in other businesses, such as, say, a new restaurant? Why?

18-11. List the criteria you would use for deciding whether another company is right for Netflix-type HR practices.

18-12. What argument would you make in response to the following: "Netflix just lucked out; they'd have done even better with conventional HR practices."

Source: Based on information in Michelle Conlin, "Netflix: Flex to the Max," September 24, 2007, www.businessweek.com/magazine/content/07_39/b4051059.htm, accessed July 3, 2011; Robert J. Grossman, "Tough Love at Netflix," April 1, 2010, www.shrm.org/Publications/hrmagazine/Editorial Content/2010/0410/Pages/0410grossman3.aspx, accessed July 3, 2011; and David F. Larcker, Allan McCall, and Brian Tayan, "Equity on De-mand: The Netflix Approach to Compensation," January 15, 2010, http://hbr.org/product/equity-on-demand-the-netflix-approach-to-compensat/an/CG19-PDF-ENG.

Continuing Case

Carter Cleaning Company

Cleaning in Challenging Times

As the economic downturn worsened a few years ago, revenues at the Carter stores fell steeply. Many of their customers were simply out of work and didn't need (or couldn't afford) dry cleaning. The Carters actually found themselves giving away some free cleaning services. They started a new program wherein existing customers could get one suit or dress cleaned free each month if they needed it for a job interview.

In the midst of this downturn, the Carters knew they had to get their employment costs under control. The problem was that, realistically, there wasn't much room for cutting staffing in a store. Of course, if a store got very slow, they could double up by having a cleaner/spotter spend some time pressing, or having the manager displace the counter person. But if sales only fell 15% to 20% per store, there really wasn't much room for reducing employee head count because each store never employed many people in the first place.

The question therefore naturally arose as to whether the Carters could cut their employment expenses without dismissing too many people. Jennifer Carter has several questions for you.

Questions

18-13. Assume that we don't want to terminate any of our employees. What work-scheduling-related changes could we make that would reduce our payrolls by, say, 20% per week but still keep all our employees on board?

18-14. We are currently handling most of our personnel-related activities, such as sign-ons, benefits administration, and appraisals, manually. What specific suggestions would you have for us in terms of using software systems to automate our HR processes?

18-15. Suggest at least five free Internet-based sources we could turn to for helping us to lower our total employment costs.

Translating Strategy into HR Policies and Practices Case[*,§]

The overall map on page xxxviii of this book outlines the relationships involved.

Improving Performance at the Hotel Paris

The New HRIS

The Hotel Paris's competitive strategy is "To use superior guest service to differentiate the Hotel Paris properties, and to thereby increase the length of stay and return rate of guests, and thus boost revenues and profitability." HR manager Lisa Cruz must now formulate functional policies and activities that support this competitive strategy and boost performance by eliciting the required employee behaviors and competencies.

Challenging economic times in the past few years brought the drawbacks of the Hotel Paris's relatively small size into sharp relief. Large chains like Marriott had vast online reservations capabilities with huge centralized systems that easily and economically handled reservations requests from throughout the world. By comparison, the Hotel Paris still handled reservations much as hotels did 15 years ago, either with separate Web sites for each of their hotel locations, e-mail, or an 800 number.

Their human resource management information systems were similarly primitive. Lisa had managed to install several separate information systems, such as for performance appraisals. However, as she discussed one day over lunch with the CFO, the HR systems were not integrated. Therefore, if an employee changed his or her name, for instance, through marriage, people in Lisa's office had to execute all those name changes manually on all the various employee rosters and benefits plans.

This lack of integration was bad enough in boom times, but was worse as the economy soured. The CFO pointed out to her that the amount of money they were spending on human resource management administration was about 30% higher than it was at larger chains such as Marriott. He understood that large size brings economies of scale. But he believed there had to be something they could do to reduce the cost of administering human resource management.

Lisa's solution was to get the CFO's approval to have several software consulting firms including IBM, Accenture, and Oracle provide

§Written by and copyright Gary Dessler, PhD.

CHAPTER 18

proposals for how to integrate the hotel's HR information systems. After getting the CFO's and CEO's approval, they contracted with one vendor and installed the system.

Questions

18-16. Using any benchmark data that you can find, including information from this textbook, what are some benchmark metrics that Lisa could be using to assess the efficiency of her human resource management operations? To what extent does the Hotel Paris's quality service orientation enter into how Lisa's metrics should compare?

18-17. Throughout this textbook, we've discussed various specific examples of how human resource management departments have been reducing the cost of delivering their services.

Keeping in mind the Hotel Paris's quality service orientation, please list and explain with examples how Lisa Cruz could use at least five of these.

18-18. Focusing only on human resource information systems for a moment, what sorts of systems would you suggest Lisa consider recommending for the Hotel Paris? Why?

18-19. Explain with detailed examples how Lisa can use free online and governmental sources to accomplish at least part of what you propose in your previous answers.

18-20. Give three examples of fee-based online tools you suggest Lisa use.

18-21. Based on what you read in this chapter of Dessler, *Human Resource Management*, do you suggest Lisa use a PEO? Why?

Endnotes

1. Accessed on September 13, 2017, at http://auto.economictimes.indiatimes.com/news/aftermarket/this-dealerships-success-is-part-of-case-studies-at-iim-harvard-while-its-unique-outlet-idea-was-adopted-by-maruti/60269709.
2. "Small Business Economic Indicators 2000," Office of Advocacy, U.S. Small Business Administration (Washington, DC, 2001), p. 5. See also "Small Business Laid Foundation for Job Gains," www.sba.gov/advo, accessed March 9, 2006.
3. Business size affects human resource activities such as executive compensation. Peter Hausdorf and Dale Duncan, "Firm Size and Internet Recruiting in Canada: A Preliminary Investigation," *Journal of Small-Business Management* 42, no. 3 (July 2004), pp. 325–334.
4. *SHRM Human Capital Benchmarking Study 2009*, Society for Human Resource Management, p. 12, www.shrm.org/research/surveyfindings/articles/documents/09-0620_human_cap_benchmark_full_fnl.pdf, accessed July 17, 2014.
5. Graham Dietz et al., "HRM Inside UK E-commerce Firms," *International Small Business Journal* 24, no. 5 (October 2006), pp. 443–470.
6. Bernice Kotey and Cathleen Folker, "Employee Training in SMEs: Effect of Size and Firm Type—Family and Nonfamily," *Journal of Small-Business Management* 45, no. 2 (April 2007), pp. 14–39.
7. Debi S. Saini and Pawan Budhwar, "Managing the Human Resource in Indian SMEs: The Role of Indigenous Realities," (2008) *Journal of World Business*, Vol 23 (4) P 417-434.
8. Manjari Singh and Neharika Vohra, "Level of Formalization of HRM in SMEs in India," *The Journal of*

Entrepreneurship, Vol 18 (1) March 2009, pp. 95-116.
9. Dietz et al., "HRM Inside UK E-commerce Firms."
10. Ibid. See also Wasserman, "Planning a Start-Up? Seize the Day ... Then Expect to Work All Night," *Harvard Business Review* 87, no. 1 (January 2009), pp. 27.
11. Points 2–5 based on Kathy Williams, "Top HR Compliance Issues for Small Businesses," *Strategic Finance* (February 2005), pp. 21–23.
12. "Entrepreneurs: The Gender Gap," http://diversitywoman.com/entrepreneurs-the-gender-gap, accessed April 20, 2013.
13. Evelyn Rusli, "Torment Claims Make GitHub Grow Up," *Wall Street Journal*, July 18, 2014, pp. B1, B5.
14. However, see Luc Sels et al., "Unraveling the HRM–Performance Link: Value Creating and Cost Increasing Effects of Small-Business HRM," *Journal of Management Studies* 43, no. 2 (March 2006), pp. 319–342. For supporting evidence of HR's positive effects on small companies, see also Andrea Rauch et al., "Effects of Human Capital and Long-Term Human Resources Development and Utilization on Employment Growth of Small-Scale Businesses: A Causal Analysis," *Entrepreneurship Theory and Practice* 29, no. 6 (November 2005), pp. 681–698; Andre Grip and Inge Sieben, "The Effects of Human Resource Management on Small Firms' Productivity and Employee's Wages," *Applied Economics* 37, no. 9 (May 20, 2005), pp. 1047–1054.
15. Dawn Carlson et al., "The Impact of Human Resource Practices and Compensation Design on Performance: An Analysis of Family-Owned SMEs," *Journal of Small Business Management* 44, no. 4 (October 2006), pp.

531–543. See also Jake Messersmith and James Guthrie, "High Performance Work Systems in Emergent Organizations: Implications for Firm Performance," *Human Resource Management* 49, no. 2 (March–April 2010), pp. 241–264.
16. Dietz et al., "HRM Inside UK E-commerce Firms." See also, Diana Wicks, "Checklist of Audit Questions for ISO Internal Audits of Human Resources", http://smallbusiness.chron.com/checklist-audit-questions-iso-internal-audits-human-resources-12265.html, accessed July 30, 2015.
17. "Six Common Mistakes Small Businesses Make When Incorporating Social Media into Their Recruiting Efforts," www.roberthalf.us/SocialMediaRecruitingMistakes; Rieva Lesonsky, "Find the Perfect Hire by Tapping into Social Media," *Employment Trends*, January 30, 2013, http://smallbiztrends.com/2013/01/3-ways-find-perfect-hire-social-media.html; and Emily Bennington, "Social Media Recruitment: Social Media Platforms and Your Next Hire," http://hiring.monster.com/hr/hr-best-practices/small-business/social-media-trends/social-media-recruitment.aspx, all accessed April 20, 2013.
18. Daren Dahl, "Recruiting: Tapping the Talent Pool ... Without Drowning in Resumes," *Inc.* 31, no. 3 (April 2009), pp. 121–122.
19. http://miamidade.jobing.com/jobs, accessed July 30, 2015.
20. Dahl, op. cit.
21. Dahl, op. cit.
22. Paul Harris, "Small Businesses Bask in Training's Spotlight," *T&D* 59, no. 2 (Fall 2005), pp. 46–52.
23. www.oracle.com/us/products/applications/peoplesoft-enterprise/hcm-resource-library/051027.pdf Accessed July 29, 2015.

24. www.halogensoftware.com/products/halogen-eappraisal, accessed August 17, 2013.
25. Jan de Kok, "Precautionary Actions within Small-and Medium-Sized Enterprises," *Journal of Small Business Management* 43, no. 4, October 2005, pp. 498–516.
26. Dietz et al., "HRM Inside UK E-commerce Firms."
27. Adrienne Fox, "McMurray Scouts Top Talent to Produce Winning Results," *HR Magazine* 51, no. 7 (July 2006), pp. 57.
28. This is based on John Drake, *Interviewing for Managers: A Complete Guide to Employment Interviewing* (New York: AMACOM, 1982).
29. Ibid.
30. Colin Gray and Christopher Mabey, "Management Development: Key Differences Between Small and Large Businesses in Europe," *International Small Business Journal* 23, no. 5 (October 2005), pp. 467–485.
31. Ibid. See also Essi Saru, "Organizational Learning and HRD: How Appropriate Are They for Small Firms?" *Journal of European Industrial Training* 31, no. 1 (January 2007), pp. 36–52.
32. From Stephen Covey, "Small Business, Big Opportunity," *Training* 43, no. 11 (November 2006), p. 40 www.Trainingmag.com. Used by permission from Lakewood Media Group.
33. Gina Ruiz, "Smaller Firms in Vanguard of Flex Practices," *Workforce Management* 84, no. 13 (November 21, 2005), p. 10.
34. Kira Bindrum, "Little Firms Redefine Culture of Work," *Crain's New York Business* 25, no. 49 (December 7–13, 2009), p. 20.
35. Ibid., pp. 7–13.
36. Ruiz, "Smaller Firms in Vanguard of Flex Practices."
37. Priyanka T, "Employee perks at this Chennai Tea staff are probably better than at your company," accessed on September

13, 2017 at HYPERLINK "http://www.thenewsminute.com"www.thenewsminute.com.

38. These are from Ty Freyvogel, "Operation Employee Loyalty," *Training Media Review*, September–October 2007.

39. Ibid.

40. Ibid.

41. Jeffrey Marshall and Ellen Heffes, "Benefits: Smaller Firm Workers Often Getting Less," *Financial Executive* 21, no. 9 (November 1, 2005), p. 10.

42. Phillip Perry, "Welcome to the Family," *Restaurant Hospitality* 90, no. 5 (May 2006), pp. 73, 74, 76, 78. Used by permission from Phillip Perry.

43. Ibid.

44. Ibid.

45. Ibid.

46. Ibid.

47. Jane Applegate, "Employee Leasing Can Be a Savior for Small Firms," *Business Courier Serving Cincinnati–Northern Kentucky* (January 28, 2000), p. 23.

48. Robert Beck and Jay Starkman, "How to Find a PEO That Will Get the Job Done," *National Underwriter* 110, no. 39 (October 16, 2006), pp. 39, 45.

49. Layne Davlin, "Human Resource Solutions for the Franchisee," *Franchising World* 39, no. 10 (October 2007), pp. 27–28.

50. Beck and Starkman, "How to Find a PEO."

51. Lyle DeWitt, "Advantages of Human Resources Outsourcing," *The CPA Journal* 75, no. 6 (June 2005), p. 13.

52. Ibid.

53. Ibid. For a useful summary of PEOs' pros and cons, see the discussion at www.proformative.com/questions/peo-pros-and-cons, accessed July 30, 2015.

54. Diana Reitz, "Employee Leasing Breeds Liability Questions," *National Underwriter Property and Casualty Risk and Benefits Management* 104, no. 18 (May 2000), p. 12.

55. Chafkin, "Fed Up with HR?"

56. Gilbert Nicholson, "Automated Assessments for Better Hires," *Workforce* (December 2000), pp. 102–107. See also www.citygaragedfw.com, accessed May 5, 2015.

57. For a more complete list, see, for example, Sondra Servais, *Personnel Director* (Deerfield Beach, FL: Made E-Z Products, 1994); www.hr.com/en/free_forms/, accessed September 10, 2012; and www.entrepreneur.com/formnet/hrcareers.html, accessed September 10, 2012.

58. www.ihrim.org, accessed April 28, 2008; www.pmihrm.com/hr_software_vendors.html, accessed July 18, 2014.

59. See, for example, www.effortlesshr.com/hr-software/online-employee-management-software and www.capterra.

com/human-resource-software, both accessed July 18, 2014.

60. Adapted from Kenneth Laudon and Jane Laudon, *Management Information Systems: New Approaches to Organization and Technology* (Upper Saddle River, NJ: Prentice Hall, 1998), p. G7. See also Michael Barrett and Randolph Kahn, "The Governance of Records Management," *Directors and Boards* 26, no. 3 (Spring 2002), pp. 45–48; Anthony Hendrickson, "Human Resource Information Systems: Backbone Technology of Contemporary Human Resources," *Journal of Labor Research* 24, no. 3 (Summer 2003), pp. 381–395; and Mike Harmer, "10 Secrets of Successful Software Implementations," *HR Magazine*, November 2014, pp. 40–43.

61. "HR Execs Trade Notes on Human Resource Information Systems," *BNA Bulletin to Management* (December 3, 1998), p. 1. See also Brian Walter, "But They Said Their Payroll Program Complied with the FLSA," *Public Personnel Management* 31, no. 1 (Spring 2002), pp. 79–94.

62. "HR Execs Trade Notes on Human Resource Information Systems," *BNA Bulletin to Management* (December 3, 1998), p. 2. See also Ali Velshi, "Human Resources Information," *The*

Americas Intelligence Wire (February 11, 2004).

63. www.comparehris.com/BambooHR and www.bamboohr.com/tour.php, both accessed May 4, 2015; Sarah Fister Gale, "Hey, You, Get Onto My Cloud…," *Workforce*, August 2014, pp. 44–45.

64. "HR Execs Trade Notes on Human Resource Information Systems," *BNA Bulletin to Management* (December 3, 1998), p. 2. See also Ali Velshi, "Human Resources Information," *The Americas Intelligence Wire* (February 11, 2004).

65. Copyright Gary Dessler, PhD, 2011; based on information in Michelle Conlin, "Netflix: Flex to the Max," September 24, 2007, www.businessweek.com/magazine/content/07_39/b4051059.htm, accessed July 3, 2011; Robert J. Grossman, "Tough Love at Netflix," April 1, 2010, www.shrm.org/Publications/hrmagazine/EditorialContent/2010/0410/Pages/0410grossman3.aspx, accessed July 3, 2011; and David F. Larcker, Allan McCall, and Brian Tayan, "Equity on Demand: The Netflix Approach to Compensation," January 15, 2010, http://hbr.org/product/equity-on-demand-the-netflix-approach-to-compensat/an/CG19-PDF-ENG, accessed July 3, 2011.

APPENDIX A

HRCI PHR® and SPHR® Certification Body of Knowledge

ABOUT THE HR CERTIFICATION INSTITUTE PHR AND SPHR BODY OF KNOWLEDGE

The HRCI PHR (Professional in Human Resources) and SPHR (Senior Professional in Human Resources) exams are created using the Institute's PHR and SPHR Body of Knowledge, which outlines the responsibilities of, and knowledge needed by, today's HR professional. The PHR and SPHR Body of Knowledge is updated periodically to ensure it is consistent with current practices in the HR field. All questions appearing on the exams are linked to the Body of Knowledge's responsibility and knowledge statements. The HRCI organizes its PHR and SPHR Body of Knowledge into six functional areas (such as Functional Area 01: Business Management and Strategy), each listing various responsibilities and knowledge statements. For brevity, we list just the required knowledge items here, alongside the corresponding chapters in this book that address each particular knowledge area. To see the entire Body of Knowledge (including responsibilities), please go to certification-handbook at HRCI.org.[1]

You'll find two numbers after each functional area heading. The first number is the percentage of the PHR exam that is about that topic. The second number is the percentage of the SPHR exam that is about that topic.

Functional Area 01: Business Management and Strategy (PHR: 11%, SPHR: 30%)

Developing, contributing to and supporting the organization's mission, vision, values, strategic goals and objectives; formulating policies; guiding and leading the change process; and evaluating organizational effectiveness as an organizational leader.

ADDRESSED IN THIS BOOK IN CHAPTER(S):	KNOWLEDGE OF	
1, 3	01	The organization's mission, vision, values, business goals, objectives, plans and processes
2, 11, 14, 15, 16, and Know Your Employment Law features in Chapters 2–16	02	Legislative and regulatory processes
1, 3, strategic Hotel Paris cases in Chapters 3–18 with in-chapter call-outs, "strategic" chapter openers, and *Improving Performance: The Strategic Context* features in most chapters	03	Strategic planning process, design, implementation and evaluation
1, 3	04	Management functions, including planning, organizing, directing and controlling
12, 14	05	Corporate governance procedures and compliance (for example: Sarbanes-Oxley Act)
1, 3, 5	06	*SPHR only* Due diligence processes (for example: M&A, divestitures)

---

[1] The exact URL is https://www.hrci.org/docs/default-source/web-files/phrsphrbodyofknowledge.pdf?sfvrsn=2, accessed September 30, 2015.

1, 3, 5	07	*SPHR only* Transition techniques for corporate restructuring, M&A off-shoring and divestitures
	08	Elements of a cost-benefit analysis during the life cycle of the business (such as scenarios for growth, including expected, economic stressed and worst-case conditions) and the impact to net worth/earnings for short-, mid- and long-term horizons
3, 12, 14	09	Business concepts (for example: competitive advantage, organizational branding, business case development, corporate responsibility)
3, 14, 16, 18	10	Business processes (for example: operations, sales and marketing, data management)

Functional Area 02: Workforce Planning and Employment (PHR: 24%, SPHR: 17%)

Developing, implementing and evaluating sourcing, recruitment, hiring, orientation, succession planning, retention and organizational exit programs necessary to ensure a workforce's ability to achieve the organization's goals and objectives.

ADDRESSED IN THIS BOOK IN CHAPTER(S):

KNOWLEDGE OF

2, 4, 5, 6, 7, and Know Your Employment Law features in Chapters 1–17	11	Applicable federal laws and regulations related to workforce planning and employment activities (for example: Title VII, ADA, EEOC Uniform Guidelines on Employee Selection Procedures, Immigration Reform and Control Act)
3, 4, 5, 6, 7, and HR as a Profit Center features in Chapters 1–17	12	Methods to assess past and future staffing effectiveness (for example: costs per hire, selection ratios, adverse impact)
5	13	Recruitment sources (for example: employee referral, social networking/ social media) for targeting passive, semi-active and active candidates
5	14	Recruitment strategies
1, 5	15	Staffing alternatives (for example: outsourcing, job sharing, phased retirement)
3, 4, 5	16	Planning techniques (for example: succession planning, forecasting)
2, 6, 7	17	Reliability and validity of selection tests/tools/ methods
6	18	Use and interpretation of selection tests (for example: psychological/personality, cognitive, motor/physical assessments, performance, assessment center)
7	19	Interviewing techniques (for example: behavioral, situational, panel)
5, 10, 11, 12, 13, 14	20	Impact of compensation and benefits on recruitment and retention
5, 17, and HR Practices Around the Globe features in Chapters 4–17	21	*SPHR only* International HR and implications of global workforce for workforce planning and employment.
5, 10, 14	22	Voluntary and involuntary terminations, downsizing, restructuring and out-placement strategies and practices
4, 5, 6, 7, 8, 9, 10	23	Internal workforce assessment techniques (for example: skills testing, skills inventory, workforce demographic analysis)
3, 8, 10, 18	24	Employment policies, practices and procedures (for example: orientation, on-boarding and retention)
5	25	Employer marketing and branding techniques
15	26	Negotiation skills and techniques

Functional Area 03: Human Resource Development (PHR: 18%, SPHR: 19%)

Developing, implementing and evaluating activities and programs that address employee training and development, performance appraisal and talent and performance management to ensure that the knowledge, skills, abilities and performance of the workforce meet current and future organizational and individual needs.

ADDRESSED IN THIS BOOK IN CHAPTER(S):	KNOWLEDGE OF

8 and in Know Your Employment Law features in this chapter and Chapters 2–18

27 Applicable federal laws and regulations related to HR development activities (for example: Title VII, ADA, Title 17 [Copyright law])

5, 8, 9, 10

28 Career development and leadership development theories and applications (for example: succession planning, dual career ladders)

8

29 Organizational development (OD) theories and applications

8

30 Training program development techniques to create general and specialized training programs

8

31 Facilitation techniques, instructional methods and program delivery mechanisms

4, 8

32 Task/process analysis

9

33 Performance appraisal methods (for example: instruments, ranking and rating scales)

9, 11, 12

34 Performance management methods (for example: goal setting, relationship to compensation, job placements/promotions)

HR Practices Around the Globe features in most chapters and Chapter 17 (Global HR)

35 *SPHR only* Applicable global issues (for example: international law, culture, local management approaches/practices, societal norms).

8

36 Techniques to assess training program effectiveness, including use of applicable metrics (for example: participant surveys, pre- and post-testing)

8, 10

37 Mentoring and executive coaching

Functional Area 04: Compensation and Benefits (PHR: 19%, SPHR: 13%)

Developing/selecting, implementing/administering and evaluating compensation and benefits programs for all employee groups in order to support the organization's goals, objectives and values.

ADDRESSED IN THIS BOOK IN CHAPTER(S):

KNOWLEDGE OF

2, 11, 12, 13, 15, and Know Your Employment Law features

38 Applicable federal laws and regulations related to compensation, benefits, and tax (for example: FLSA, ERISA, FMLA, USERRA)

11, 12, 13

39 Compensation and benefits strategies

40 Budgeting and accounting practices related to compensation and benefits

11

41 Job evaluation methods

11

42 Job pricing and pay structures

5, 11

43 External labor markets and/or economic factors

11, 12

44 Pay programs (for example: variable, merit)

11, 12, 13

45 *SPHR only* Executive compensation methods.

11, 12, 13, 14

46 Noncash compensation methods (for example: equity programs, noncash rewards)

13

47 Benefits programs (for example: health and welfare, retirement, Employee Assistance Programs [EAPs])

11, 12, 13, 17, and HR Around the Globe features

48 *SPHR only* International compensation laws and practices (for example: expatriate compensation, entitlements, choice of law codes).

11, 12, 13

49 Fiduciary responsibilities related to compensation and benefits

Functional Area 05: Employee and Labor Relations (PHR: 20%, SPHR: 14%)

Developing, implementing/administering and evaluating the workplace in order to maintain relationships and working conditions that balance employer/employee needs and rights in support of the organization's goals and objectives.

KNOWLEDGE OF

50 Applicable federal laws affecting employment in union and nonunion environments, such as laws regarding antidiscrimination policies, sexual harassment, labor relations, and privacy (for example: WARN Act, Title VII, NLRA)

51 Techniques and tools for facilitating positive employee relations (for example: employee surveys, dispute/ conflict resolution, labor/management cooperative strategies)

52 Employee involvement strategies (for example: employee management committees, self-directed work teams, staff meetings)

53 Individual employment rights issues and practices (for example: employment at will, negligent hiring, defamation)

54 Workplace behavior issues/practices (for example: absenteeism and performance improvement)

55 Unfair labor practices

56 The collective bargaining process, strategies and concepts (for example: contract negotiation, costing and administration)

57 Legal disciplinary procedures

58 Positive employee relations strategies and non-monetary rewards

59 Techniques for conducting unbiased investigations

60 Legal termination procedures

Functional Area 06: Risk Management (PHR: 8%, SPHR: 7%)

Developing, implementing/administering and evaluating programs, procedures and policies in order to provide a safe, secure working environment and to protect the organization from potential liability.

KNOWLEDGE OF

61 Applicable federal laws and regulations related to workplace health, safety, security and privacy (for example: OSHA, Drug-Free Workplace Act, ADA, HIPAA, Sarbanes-Oxley Act)

62 Occupational injury and illness prevention (safety) and compensation programs

63 Investigation procedures of workplace safety, health and security enforcement agencies

64 Return to work procedures (for example: interactive dialog, job modification, accommodations)

65 Workplace safety risks (for example: trip hazards, blood-borne pathogens)

66 Workplace security risks (for example: theft, corporate espionage, sabotage)

67 Potential violent behavior and workplace violence conditions

16	68	General health and safety practices (for example: evacuation, hazard communication, ergonomic evaluations)
16	69	Organizational incident and emergency response plans
14, 16	70	Internal investigation, monitoring and surveillance techniques
13, 14, 16	71	Employer/employee rights related to substance abuse
16, 18	72	Business continuity and disaster recovery plans (for example: data storage and backup, alternative work locations, procedures)
14, 16, 18	73	Data integrity techniques and technology (for example: data sharing, password usage, social engineering)
3, 4, 5, 18, and *Trends Shaping HR: Digital and Social Media and Improving Performance Through HRIS* features in Chapters 3–16	74	Technology and applications (for example: social media, monitoring software, biometrics)
	75	Financial management practices (for example: procurement policies, credit card policies and guidelines, expense policies)

CORE KNOWLEDGE

3, 8	76	Needs assessment and analysis
13, 18	77	Third-party or vendor selection, contract negotiation and management, including development of requests for proposals (RFPs)
9, 10, 14	78	Communication skills and strategies (for example: presentation, collaboration, sensitivity)
2, 4, 6, 9, 15, 16, 18, and *Know Your Employment Law* features in Chapters 2–16	79	Organizational documentation requirements to meet federal and state guidelines
8	80	Adult learning processes
8, 12, 13, 14	81	Motivation concepts and applications
8	82	Training techniques (for example: virtual, classroom, on-the-job)
	83	Leadership concepts and applications
	84	Project management concepts and applications
2 and *The New Workforce* features in most chapters	85	Diversity concepts and applications (for example: generational, cultural competency, learning styles)
14	86	Human relations concepts and applications (for example: emotional intelligence, organizational behavior)
1, 14	87	Ethical and professional standards
3–18 plus *Trends Shaping HR: Digital and Social Media and Improving Performance Through HRIS* features in most chapters	88	Technology to support HR activities (for example: HR Information Systems, employee self-service, E-learning, applicant tracking systems)
1, 3, and *HR as a Profit Center* features in most chapters	89	Qualitative and quantitative methods and tools for analysis, interpretation and decision-making purposes (for example: metrics and measurements, cost/benefit analysis, financial statement analysis)
8	90	Change management theory, methods and application
4	91	Job analysis and job description methods
4, 5, 18	92	Employee records management (for example: electronic/paper, retention, disposal)
3, 4, *Improving Performance: The Strategic Context* features in most chapters, a continuing strategic *Hotel Paris* case with in-chapter callouts in Chapters 3–16, and "strategic" chapter openers	93	Techniques for forecasting, planning and predicting the impact of HR activities and programs across functional areas

APPENDIX B

About the Society for Human Resource Management (SHRM) Body of Competency and Knowledge™ Model and Certification Exams

SHRM recently introduced the SHRM Body of Competency and Knowledge™, and announced that it would offer its own certification exams for human resource management professionals.[1] In brief, the SHRM Body of Competency and Knowledge™ model is built on a foundation of 15 functional "HR Expertise (HR Knowledge)" areas such as talent acquisition and retention, which SHRM in turn divides into four main domains—people, workplace, organization, and strategy. The SHRM Body of Competency and Knowledge™ (SHRM) model then layers, on top of these 15 functional knowledge areas, eight HR manager required competencies, such as leadership and navigation, and ethical practice.

SECTION 1: SHRM COMPETENCIES:[2]

The SHRM exams test for these eight managerial competencies as well as for the items in its 18 functional HR knowledge functional areas. Many students will hopefully develop many of these eight competencies as part of their other experiences and courses (management, strategic management, quantitative methods, OB, etc.) as well as in their HR courses. However, Dessler, *Human Resource Management*, 15th ed., touches on many of these competencies. For some examples, see the following table:

Full List of SHRM Competencies	Examples of Pages in Dessler, *Human Resource Management*, 15th ed.
Leadership & Navigation	2, 255, Improving Performance: The Strategic Context features throughout book, as on pages 15–16.
Ethical Practice	19, 456–458, 460, 462.
Business Acumen	68–84, Improving Performance: The Strategic Context features throughout book.
Relationship Management	256, 290, 292–296, 311, 313, 314
Consultation	For example, Employee Engagement Guide for Managers features as on pages 84–87 illustrate how HR managers provide data-based guidance to change organizations.
Critical Evaluation	72–84, 100, 181, 260–264 (HR metrics and evidence-based HR and the scientific way of doing things), 100, 181, 260–264
Global & Cultural Effectiveness	Chapter 17, and Improving Performance: HR Practices Around the Globe features as on page 401 throughout book
Communication	Chapter 14, (employee relations tools), 454, 537

---

[1] http://shrm.org/certification/Documents/SHRM-BoCK-FINAL4.pdf
[2] Source: Competencies and HR Knowledge from The SHRM Body of Competency and Knowledge, http://shrm.org/certification/Documents/SHRM-BoCK-FINAL4.pdf, accessed February 13, 2015.

SECTION 2: SHRM HR FUNCTIONAL HR AREAS

SHRM's 15 functional areas each include required HR expertise (HR Knowledge) as well as HR manager responsibilities. For brevity, we list below just the required knowledge items, alongside the corresponding chapters in this book that address each particular knowledge area. To see the entire SHRM Body of Competency and Knowledge™ (including Responsibilities), please go to http://shrm.org/certification/Documents/SHRM-BoCK-FINAL4.pdf

DOMAIN 1: PEOPLE

Functional Area #1: Talent Acquisition & Retention

Definition: *Talent Acquisition & Retention* encompasses the activities involved in building and maintaining a workforce. HR demonstrates value by developing, implementing, and measuring the individual and organizational success of activities and programs for sourcing, recruiting, hiring, onboarding, orientation, and retention.

ADDRESSED IN THIS BOOK IN CHAPTER(S):

KNOWLEDGE TOPICS

Chapters	Topic
10	• Employee lifecycle phases
10, 14	• Employee retention techniques
3 and Improving Performance: HR as a Profit Center features in many chapters	• Employer value proposition techniques
5	• Employment branding approaches
5	• External labor market PEST factors
5	• External and internal recruitment approaches
3, 9	• Evaluation techniques
9	• Formal assessment methods and tools
2, 4, 6	• Identification of bona fide occupational qualifications (BFOQs)
7, 9	• Interviewing techniques
4	• Job analysis, evaluation, and design of job descriptions
7	• Job offer contingencies
1, 3	• Metrics (e.g., cost per hire, days to fill)
5	• Recruitment approaches
6, 7	• Selection approaches
5	• Sourcing approaches
5	• Staffing projection approaches

Functional Area #2: Employee Engagement

Definition: *Employee Engagement* solidifies the connection among employee, manager, and the organization's mission, vision, values, and goals. HR demonstrates value by understanding and leveraging the employer employee relationship from both individual and organizational perspectives, developing effective strategies to address appropriate expectations for performance and behavior from employees at all levels.

ADDRESSED IN THIS BOOK IN CHAPTER(S):

KNOWLEDGE TOPICS

Chapters	Topic
2	• Alternative dispute resolution techniques
10, 14	• Analysis of organizational culture and climate
9, 10	• Coaching and counseling

9	• Cognitive biases (e.g., halo bias, similar-to-me bias)
9, 10, 14	• Complaint resolution procedures
	• Conflict management theory and approaches
9, 14, 15	• Disciplinary procedures and approaches
10	• Employee lifecycle phases
5, 18	• Employee recordkeeping and retention
14	• Investigation techniques
1,3,7,9,10,12,14,17	• Management of people
3 and HR as a Profit Center features in many chapters	• Metrics
12	• Motivational theories
8, 14	• Organizational culture influences
8	• Organizational change management
9	• Performance management systems
9	• Principles of effective performance appraisal techniques (e.g., goal-setting, giving feedback)
14	• Principles of survey creation, administration, and evaluation
11, 12, 14	• Recognition approaches
14, 16	• Retaliation prevention approaches
4, 13, 14	• Workplace flexibility

Functional Area #3: Learning & Development

Definition: *Learning & Development* aligns organizational business needs with employees' competencies, knowledge, and skills, effectively closing the gap between them. HR demonstrates value by identifying and creating learning opportunities that increase employee capability and organizational knowledge.

ADDRESSED IN THIS BOOK IN CHAPTER(S):	KNOWLEDGE TOPICS
10	• Career development techniques
10	• Career management philosophies
8, 10	• Change management approaches
9, 10	• Coaching styles and approaches
1, 3–7	• Competency models
10	• Employee lifecycle phases
8	• Knowledge-sharing techniques
8	• Learning evaluation approaches
10	• Mentoring options
3 and HR as a Profit Center features in many chapters	• Metrics
8	• Organizational intervention design and implementation approaches
8	• Leadership development techniques
8	• Learning theories
8	• Needs assessment techniques (e.g., organizational, training)
8	• Skill and competency development approaches
8	• Training design and implementation (e.g., ADDIE model)
8	• Training and development techniques and solutions

Functional Area #4: Total Rewards

Definition: *Total Rewards* encompasses direct and indirect remuneration approaches that employers use to attract, recognize, and retain workers. HR demonstrates value by designing and administering systems and programs (e.g., base pay, benefits, incentive pay, leave, perquisites, retirement) that support recruitment and retention efforts.

KNOWLEDGE TOPICS

- Accounting practices and principles
- Benefits (e.g., disability insurance, domestic partners, education, employee assistance programs, families, life insurance, retirement plans, unemployment insurance, wellness programs, workers' compensation)

- Employee lifecycle phases

- External labor markets PEST factors

- Fiduciary responsibilities

- Income replacement programs

- Job analysis, job design, job descriptions

- Metrics

- Perquisites

- Pay practices, policies, approaches, systems, and issues (e.g., base pay, minimum wage determinations, pay compression, pay equity, pay increases, pay levels and banding), and special provisions (e.g., overtime)

- Remuneration data analysis (collecting, analyzing, making recommendations)

- Time-off plans and approaches (e.g., paid and unpaid leave, vacation/

DOMAIN 2: ORGANIZATION

Functional Area #5: Structure of the HR Function

Definition: *Structure of the HR Function* encompasses the people-related processes, theories, and activities used to deliver HR services that create and drive organizational effectiveness. HR demonstrates value by selecting the appropriate delivery model (e.g. Center of Excellence/COE, generalist, shared services) with an understanding of stakeholder needs and the impact of decisions on the overall workforce.

KNOWLEDGE TOPICS

- Balanced scorecard philosophy

- Centralization versus decentralization

- Defined approaches to roles and functions for generalists and specialists

- Due diligence methodologies

- HR organizational structure and design

- HR functional integration approaches

- Negotiation and influence techniques
- Stakeholder analysis techniques

- Strategy design and implementation

- Structural model approaches to HR (e.g., Center of Excellence/COE, HR business partner, shared services)

Functional Area #6: Organizational Effectiveness & Development

Definition: *Organizational Effectiveness & Development* deals with the overall structure and functionality of the organization — that is, measuring the effectiveness and growth of people and processes from long- and short-term perspectives, and leading necessary organizational change initiatives. HR demonstrates value by aligning the organization's vision, mission, and goals with day-to-day Operational activities, including organizational design, development, performance measures, and standards.

ADDRESSED IN THIS BOOK IN CHAPTER(S):

KNOWLEDGE TOPICS

Chapter(s)	Topic
3	• Business solution and performance analysis
3	• Change and culture metrics
8	• Change management theories and approaches
	• Consulting techniques
4, 12	• Design approaches for a motivational work environment
4	• Design approaches for work activity
	• Group dynamics
14	• How employees learn culture
14	• How organizational cultures are created
	• Influence techniques
	• Knowledge management approaches (e.g., organizational storytelling techniques)
4, 5	• Labor supply and demand analysis
12	• Motivational theories
	• Organizational behavior theories
	• Organizational culture versus national culture
	• Organizational design structures and approaches (e.g., customer, functional, geographic, matrix, program)
8	• Organizational learning approaches
8	• Organizational needs analysis techniques
9	• Performance management theories, structures, and approaches
	• Project management approaches
4	• Roles and responsibilities (e.g., chain of command, span of control)
1, 3, strategic Hotel Paris cases in chapters 3–18 with in-chapter callouts, "strategic" chapter openers, and *Improving Performance: The Strategic Context* features in most chapters	• Strategic-tactical alignment
14	• Types of cultures (e.g., authoritarian, dominant cultures, mechanistic, participative, subcultures)
6, 7	• Understanding individual differences and Perceptions

Functional Area #7: Workforce Management

Definition: *Workforce Management* enables the organization to meet its talent needs and close critical skill gaps using data-driven processes (e.g., workforce planning, succession planning) that inform HR initiatives. HR demonstrates value by facilitating financial and operational growth, continuity, or stability.

KNOWLEDGE TOPICS

- Communication techniques
- Employee development techniques and approaches
- Knowledge management, retention, and transfer techniques
- Learning theories and philosophies
- Needs assessment techniques (e.g., organizational, training)
- Restructuring approaches
- Succession planning techniques
- Workforce planning techniques and analyses (e.g., gap and solution, implementation and evaluation, supply and demand, workforce profile)

Functional Area #8: Employee Relations

Definition: *Employee Relations* refers to any dealings between the organization and its employees regarding the terms and conditions of employment. HR demonstrates value by ensuring that the appropriate framework, mindset, and practices are in place to embrace or react or respond to the employment relationship, including relationships with employee representatives.

KNOWLEDGE TOPICS

- Alternative dispute resolution techniques
- Causes of strikes, boycotts, and work stoppages
- Child labor
- Collective bargaining process
- Communication approaches
- Contract administration techniques
- Contract negotiation approaches
- Disciplinary techniques
- Standard workday
- Employee engagement approaches

- Governmental labor parties and party relations by nation
- Grievance, complaint, and conflict resolution techniques
- Industrial relations
- International Labor Organization (ILO) core labor standards
- International labor practices
- Investigation techniques
- Labor economics
- Labor environments (e.g., pluralism, radicalism, unitarianism)
- Labor rights
- Living and fair wage concepts
- People-management techniques
- Positive union/management relations approaches
- Recognition approaches
- Service award approaches
- Social movement unionism, new unionism, proletariat

- Socialism, syndicalism, anarcho-syndicalism
- Strike actions, secondary actions, general strikes, sit-down strikes, work-to-rule
- Survey techniques
- Trade unions by nation
- Trade union federations
- Unfair labor practices
- Union acceptance and avoidance approaches
- Union attractiveness
- Union membership
- Union structures
- Unionized labor history
- Works councils structures and approaches
- World Trade Organization

Functional Area #9: Technology & Data

Definition: *Technology & Data* deals with the use of tools, technologies, and systems that support the gathering, analysis, and reporting of workforce information, as well as effective and efficient collaboration and communication throughout the organization. HR demonstrates value by developing knowledge about technology uses, trends, and innovations applicable to HR's strategic goals.

KNOWLEDGE TOPICS

- Business process integration approaches
- Data analytic techniques

- Data management protection approaches
- Electronic recordkeeping approaches
- Electronic signature acceptance
- HR information systems and sources

- HR management and information system design

- Information management theory

- Procurement approaches
- Product development
- Project management theories
- Social media practices and usage

- Systems integration approaches
- Technology use policies and practices

DOMAIN 3: WORKPLACE
Functional Area #10: HR in the Global Context

Definition: *HR in the Global Context* focuses on organizational growth and workforce-related issues and impacts, viewed from domestic, multinational, transnational, and global perspectives. HR demonstrates value by understanding how global PEST factors influence business decisions, and by applying this knowledge to day-to-day HR activities, policy creation, and business solution recommendations.

KNOWLEDGE TOPICS

- Creating a global organizational culture
- Cross-border HR management techniques
- Cultural models (e.g., Hall, Hofstede, Schein, Trompenaars)
- Global discrimination prevention practices
- Global legal systems (e.g., different nations' approaches to government-mandated, government provided, and voluntary benefits, extra-territoriality of laws and legislation)
- Global mindset techniques (e.g., communication barrier removal, cultural awareness training and assimilation, understanding PEST factors)

- Global trends in benefits, compensation, diversity and inclusion, employment laws, ethics and sustainability, labor markets, labor relations, safety and security, staffing management
- Managing international assignments (e.g., approaches and trends, effective performance, compensation adjustments, employee repatriation)
- Moving work (e.g., co-sourcing, near-shoring, offshoring, on-shoring)
- Taxation approaches
- Totalization agreements
- Visa and work permit considerations

Functional Area #11: Diversity & Inclusion

Definition: *Diversity & Inclusion* encompasses the qualities, life experiences, personalities, education, skills, competencies, and collaboration of the many different types of people who are necessary to propel an organization to success. HR demonstrates value by creating opportunities that leverage the human experience to address organizational needs or solve issues on a global basis.

KNOWLEDGE TOPICS

- Approaches to a multi-generational workforce

- Developing cross-cultural relationships

- Effective approaches to building trust and relationships
- Emotional intelligence
- Glass-ceiling prevention
- High- and low-context cultures
- Inclusive leadership
- Influence of the 4 T's (travel, training, transfers, and teams)
- Intercultural wisdom
- Issues related to disability, ethnicity, gender, language, race, sexual orientation

- Level of global acceptance of diversity (e.g., disability, ethnicity, gender, language, race, religion, sexual orientation)
- Mindful communication
- Religious influences and accommodation
- Techniques for cultural awareness and respect

Functional Area #12: Risk Management

Definition: *Risk management* is the identification, assessment, and prioritization of risks (defined in ISO 31000 as the effect of uncertainty on objectives), followed by the coordinated and economical application of resources to minimize, monitor, and control the probability and/or impact of unfortunate events or to maximize the realization of opportunities.

ADDRESSED IN THIS BOOK IN CHAPTER(S):

KNOWLEDGE TOPICS

16	• Business recovery planning
16	• Continuity of operations planning
16	• Corporate espionage and sabotage prevention
16	• Data integrity mechanisms and practices
	• Data management protection and disclosure approaches
13, 16	• Drug prevention
16, 17	• Duty of care
16	• Emergency/incident response plans
16	• Health and safety practices and procedures
18 and Improving Performance Through HRIS features	• Information management theory
16	• Kidnapping and ransom prevention
16	• Natural disaster and severe weather emergency preparation
16	• Occupational injury and illness prevention, compensation, and accommodations
16	• Public health preparedness and response
16	• Safety auditing techniques
16	• Terrorism prevention and responses
16	• Theft and fraud prevention approaches
14, 16	• Whistleblower protection approaches
16	• Workplace incident investigations
16	• Workplace safety risks and hazards
14, 16	• Workplace violence prevention techniques

Functional Area #13: Corporate Social Responsibility

Definition: *Corporate Social Responsibility* represents the organization's commitment to operate its business in an ethical and sustainable manner. HR demonstrates value by understanding the societal impacts to business decisions and using this insight to improve the quality of life for the community—people, organization, and planet—through philanthropy, ethics and governance, and environmentally sound practices, respectively.

ADDRESSED IN THIS BOOK IN CHAPTER(S):

KNOWLEDGE TOPICS

14, 17	• Anti-bribery approaches
	• Caux principles
	• Charitable/community giving approaches
14	• Code of conduct development

	• Community inclusion approaches
2, 3, 9, 15, 16, 17, 18	• Compliance program evaluation
2, 6, 10, 11, 13, 18	• Confidentiality measures and approaches
10, 13, 14, 15	• Conflicts-of-interest avoidance
	• Corporate citizenship and governance programs and legislation
	• Corporate philanthropy approaches
14	• Corporate social responsibility best practices
3, 5	• Economic trend analysis
14, 17	• Ethical decision-making in a global context
14	• Ethical employee management practices
14	• Investigation techniques
18	• ISO standards
1, 3, and Improving Performance: HR as a Profit Center features	• Key performance indicators
3	• PEST factors
14	• Privacy concerns
	• Social auditing techniques
5 and Trends Shaping HR: Digital and Social Media features in most chapters	• Social media usage
	• Transparent decision making
	• Volunteer programming

Functional Area #14: U.S. Employment Law & Regulations

Important Note: This Area is applicable only to examinees testing within the United States; examinees outside the U.S. will not be tested on it.

Definition: *U.S. Employment Law & Regulations* deals with the knowledge and application of all relevant laws and regulations in the United States relating to employment. These provisions set the parameters and limitations for each HR Functional Area and for organizations overall. HR demonstrates value by ensuring the organization's compliance with laws and regulations domestically and globally (including extraterritorially).

KNOWLEDGE TOPICS

Listed below are six broad categories of U.S. laws, regulations, and cases relating to employment, together with examples. (This is *not* an exhaustive list of categories *or* examples.) Local laws and regulations, such as those on the state or municipal level, are not included.

ADDRESSED IN THIS BOOK IN CHAPTER(S):

2, 11, 12, 13, and Know Your Employment Law features in most chapters

• ***Compensation*** *Examples*: Employee Retirement Income Security Act of 1974 (ERISA); Fair Labor Standards Act of 1938 (FLSA; Wage-Hour Bill; Wagner-Connery Wages and Hours Act) and amendments; Equal Pay Act of 1963 (amending FLSA); Lilly Ledbetter Fair Pay Act of 2009; *Ledbetter v. Goodyear Tire & Rubber Co.* (2007).

2, 3, 14, 15, and Know Your Employment Law features in most chapters

• ***Employee relations*** *Examples*: Labor Management Relations Act of 1947 (LMRA; Taft-Hartley Act); National Labor Relations Act of 1935 (NLRA; Wagner Act; Wagner-Connery Labor Relations Act); *NLRB v. Weingarten* (1975); *Lechmere, Inc. v. NLRB* (1992).

2, 4, 5, 6, 7, 8, 9, 10, and Know Your Employment Law features in most chapters

• ***Equal employment opportunity*** *Examples*: Age Discrimination in Employment Act of 1967 (ADEA) and amendments; Americans with Disabilities Act of 1990 (ADA) and ADA Amendments Act of 2008; Civil Rights Acts; Equal

Employment Opportunity Act of 1972 (amending Civil Rights Act); Uniform Guidelines on Employee Selection Procedures (1978) (29 CFR Part 1607); *Griggs v. Duke Power Co.* (1971); *Phillips v. Martin Marietta Corp.* (1971).

- *Job safety and health* *Examples*: Drug-Free Workplace Act of 1988; Guidelines on Sexual Harassment; Occupational Safety and Health Act of 1970.

- *Leave and benefits* *Examples*: Family and Medical Leave Act of 1993 (FMLA; expanded 2008, 2010); Patient Protection and Affordable Care Act (PPACA; ACA; "Obamacare"); *National Federation of Independent Business v. Sebelius* (2012).

- *Miscellaneous protection laws* *Examples*: Employee Polygraph Protection Act of 1988; Genetic Information Nondiscrimination Act of 2008 (GINA).

DOMAIN 4: STRATEGY
Functional Area #15: Business & HR Strategy

Definition: *Business & HR Strategy* involves organizational planning to achieve success and create value for stakeholders. HR demonstrates value by contributing its perspective and expertise to development of the enterprise strategy, and by developing, implementing, and evaluating an HR strategy aligned with the organization's goals, values, and tactics, as defined in the enterprise strategy.

KNOWLEDGE TOPICS

- Approaches for linking organizational and HR strategies

- Balanced scorecard utilization
- Business intelligence factors
- Change management techniques
- Competitive analysis techniques
- Conflict management techniques
- Due diligence techniques
- Effective communication techniques
- Ethical decision-making framework
- Goal-setting approaches
- HR systems integration approaches

- Labor market analysis
- Leadership theories, approaches, and evaluation
- Leading and lagging indicators
- Mission, vision, and values creation
- Organizational growth strategies, evolution stages, and success factors
- Project management methods

2, 13,16, and Know Your Employment Law features in most chapters

2, 11,13, and Know Your Employment Law features in most chapters

2, 4–16, and Know Your Employment Law features in most chapters

ADDRESSED IN THIS BOOK IN CHAPTER(S):

1, 3, strategic Hotel Paris cases in chapters 3–18, with in-chapter callouts, "strategic" chapter openers, and *Improving Performance: The Strategic Context* features in most chapters

3

3, 5

3, 8

3

8, 13, 14

3

7, 8, 9, 10, 14, 15

1, 14

3, 9

18 and Improving Performance Through HRIS features in most chapters

4, 5, 11, 15

1, 3

1, 3, strategic Hotel Paris cases in Chapters 3–18 with in-chapter callouts, "strategic" chapter openers, and *Improving Performance: The Strategic Context* features in most chapters

3, 14	• Quality assurance techniques
1, 3, strategic Hotel Paris cases in Chapters 3–18 with in-chapter call-outs, "strategic" chapter openers, and *Improving Performance: The Strategic Context* features in most chapters	• Strategic management considerations
3	• Strategic planning stages (i.e., strategy formulation, development, implementation, and evaluation)
3	• PEST factors
3	• SWOT and environmental scanning techniques

APPENDIX C

Comprehensive Cases

BANDAG AUTOMOTIVE*

Jim Bandag took over his family's auto supply business in 2012, after helping his father, who founded the business, run it for about 10 years. Based in Illinois, Bandag employs about 300 people, and distributes auto supplies (replacement mufflers, bulbs, engine parts, and so on) through two divisions, one that supplies service stations and repair shops, and a second that sells retail auto supplies through five "Bandag Automotive" auto supply stores.

Jim's father, and now Jim, have always endeavored to keep Bandag's organization chart as simple as possible. The company has a full-time controller, managers for each of the five stores, a manager who oversees the distribution division, and Jim Bandag's executive assistant. Jim (along with his father, working part-time) handles marketing and sales.

Jim's executive assistant administers the firm's day-today human resource management tasks, but the company outsources most HR activities to others, including an employment agency that does its recruiting and screening, a benefits firm that administers its 401(k) plan, and a payroll service that handles its paychecks. Bandag's human resource management systems consist almost entirely of standardized HR forms purchased from an HR supplies company. These include forms such as application and performance appraisal forms, as well as an "honesty" test Bandag uses to screen the staff that works in the five stores. The company performs informal salary surveys to see what other companies in the area are paying for similar positions, and use these results for awarding annual merit increases (which in fact are more accurately cost-of-living adjustments).

Jim's father took a fairly paternal approach to the business. He often walked around speaking with his employees, finding out what their problems were, and even helping them out with an occasional loan—for instance, when he discovered that one of their children was sick, or for part of a new home down payment. Jim, on the other hand, tends to be more abrupt, and does not enjoy the same warm relationship with the employees as did his father. Jim is not unfair or dictatorial. He's just very focused on improving Bandag's financial performance, and so all his decisions, including his HR-related decisions, generally come down to cutting costs. For example, his knee-jerk reaction is usually to offer fewer days off rather than more, fewer benefits rather than more, and to be less flexible when an employee needs, for instance, a few extra days off because a child is sick.

It's therefore perhaps not surprising that over the past few years Bandag's sales and profits have increased markedly, but that the firm has found itself increasingly enmeshed in HR/equal employment–type issues. Indeed, Jim now finds himself spending a day or two a week addressing HR problems. For example, Henry Jaques, an employee at one of the stores, came to Jim's executive assistant and told her he was "irate" about his recent firing and was probably going to sue. Henry's store manager stated on his last performance appraisal that Henry did the technical aspects of his job well, but that he had "serious problems interacting with his coworkers." He was continually arguing with them, and complaining to the store manager about working conditions. The store manager had told Jim that he had to fire Henry because he was making "the whole place poisonous,"

*© Gary Dessler, PhD.

and that (although he felt sorry because he'd heard rumors that Henry suffered from some mental illness) he felt he had to go. Jim approved the dismissal.

Gavin was another problem. Gavin had worked for Bandag for 10 years, the last two as manager of one of the company's five stores. Right after Jim Bandag took over, Gavin told him he had to take a Family and Medical Leave Act medical leave to have hip surgery, and Jim approved the leave. When Gavin returned from leave, Jim told him that his position had been eliminated. Bandag had decided to close his store and open a new, larger store across from a shopping center about a mile away, and had appointed a new manager in Gavin's absence. However, the company did give Gavin a (nonmanagerial) position in the new store as a counter salesperson, at the same salary and with the same benefits as he had before. Even so, "This job is not similar to my old one," Gavin insisted. "It doesn't have nearly as much prestige." His contention is that the FMLA requires that the company bring him back in the same or equivalent position, and that this means a supervisory position, similar to what he had before he went on leave. Jim said no, and they seem to be heading toward litigation.

In another sign of the times at Bandag, the company's controller, Miriam, who had been with the company for about six years, went on pregnancy leave for 12 weeks in 2012 (also under the FMLA), and then received an additional three weeks' leave under Bandag's extended illness days program. Four weeks after she came back, she asked Jim Bandag if she could arrange to work fewer hours per week, and spend about a day per week working out of her home. He refused, and about two months later fired her. Jim Bandag said, "I'm sorry, it's not anything to do with your pregnancy-related requests, but we've got ample reasons to discharge you—your monthly budgets have been several days late, and we've got proof you may have forged documents." She replied, "I don't care what you say your reasons are; you're really firing me because of my pregnancy, and that's illegal."

Jim felt he was on safe ground as far as defending the company for these actions, although he didn't look forward to spending the time and money that he knew it would take to fight each. However, what he learned over lunch from a colleague undermined his confidence about another case that Jim had been sure would be a "slam dunk" for his company. Jim was explaining to his friend that one of Bandag's truck maintenance service people had applied for a job driving one of Bandag's distribution department trucks, and that Jim had turned him down because the worker was deaf. Jim (whose wife has occasionally said of him, "No one has ever accused Jim of being politically correct") was mentioning to his friend the apparent absurdity of a deaf person asking to be a truck delivery person. His friend, who happens to work for UPS, pointed out that the U.S. Court of Appeals for the Ninth Circuit had recently decided that UPS had violated the Americans with Disabilities Act by refusing to consider deaf workers for jobs driving the company's smaller vehicles.

Although Jim's father is semiretired, the sudden uptick in the frequency of such EEO-type issues troubled him, particularly after so many years of labor peace. However, he's not sure what to do about it. Having handed over the reins of the company to his son, he was loath to inject himself back into the company's operational decision making. On the other hand, he was afraid that in the short run these issues were going to drain a great deal of Jim's time and resources, and that in the long run they might be a sign of things to come, with problems like these eventually overwhelming Bandag Automotive. He comes to you, who he knows consults in human resource management, and asks you the following questions.

Questions

1. Given Bandag Automotive's size, and anything else you know about it, should we reorganize the human resource management function, and if so, why and how?

2. What, if anything, would you do to change and/or improve upon the current HR systems, forms, and practices that we now use?

3. Do you think that the employee whom Jim fired for creating what the manager called a poisonous relationship has a legitimate claim against us, and if so, why and what should we do about it?

4. Is it true that we really had to put Gavin back into an equivalent position, or was it adequate to just bring him back into a job at the same salary, bonuses, and benefits as he had before his leave?

5. Miriam, the controller, is basically claiming that the company is retaliating against her for being pregnant, and that the fact that we raised performance issues was just a smokescreen. Do you think the EEOC and/or courts would agree with her, and, in any case, what should we do now?

6. An employee who is deaf has asked us to be one of our delivery people and we turned him down. He's now threatening to sue. What should we do, and why?

7. In the previous 10 years, we've had only one equal employment complaint, and now in the last few years we've had four or five. What should I do about it? Why?

Based generally on actual facts, but Bandag is a fictitious company. Bandag source notes: "The Problem Employee: Discipline or Accommodation?" *Monday Business Briefing*, March 8, 2005; "Employee Says Change in Duties after Leave Violates FMLA," *BNA Bulletin to Management*, January 16, 2007, p. 24; "Manager Fired Days After Announcing Pregnancy," *BNA Bulletin to Management*, January 2, 2007, p. 8; "Ninth Circuit Rules UPS Violated ADA by Barring Deaf Workers from Driving Jobs," *BNA Bulletin to Management*, October 17, 2006, p. 329.

ANGELO'S PIZZA*

Angelo Camero was brought up in the Bronx, New York, and basically always wanted to be in the pizza store business. As a youngster, he would sometimes spend hours at the local pizza store, watching the owner knead the pizza dough, flatten it into a large circular crust, fling it up, and then spread on tomato sauce in larger and larger loops. After graduating from college as a marketing major, he made a beeline back to the Bronx, where he opened his first Angelo's Pizza store, emphasizing its clean, bright interior; its crisp green, red, and white sign; and his all-natural, fresh ingredients. Within five years, Angelo's store was a success, and he had opened three other stores and was considering franchising his concept.

Eager as he was to expand, his four years in business school had taught him the difference between being an entrepreneur and being a manager. As an entrepreneur/small business owner, he knew he had the distinct advantage of being able to personally run the whole operation himself. With just one store and a handful of employees, he could make every decision and watch the cash register, check in the new supplies, oversee the takeout, and personally supervise the service.

When he expanded to three stores, things started getting challenging. He hired managers for the two new stores (both of whom had worked for him at his first store for several years) and gave them only minimal "how to run a store"–type training, on the assumption that, having worked with him for several years, they already knew pretty much everything they needed to know about running a store. However, he was already experiencing human resource management problems, and he knew there was no way he could expand the number of stores he owned, or (certainly) contemplate franchising his idea, unless he had a system in place that he could clone in each new store to provide the managers (or the franchisees) with the necessary management knowledge and expertise to run their stores. Angelo had no training program in place for teaching his store managers how to run their stores. He simply (erroneously, as it turned out) assumed that by working with him they would learn how to do things on the job. Since Angelo had no system in place, the new managers were, in a way, starting off below zero when it came to how to manage a store.

*© Gary Dessler, PhD.

There were several issues that particularly concerned Angelo. Finding and hiring good employees was number one. He'd read the new National Small Business Poll from the National Federation of Independent Business Education Foundation. It found that 71% of small business owners believed that finding qualified employees was "hard." Furthermore, "the search for qualified employees will grow more difficult as demographic and education factors" continue to make it more difficult to find employees. Similarly, reading the *Kiplinger Letter* one day, he noticed that just about every type of business couldn't find enough good employees to hire. Small firms were particularly in jeopardy; the *Letter* said that giant firms can outsource many (particularly entry-level) jobs abroad, and larger companies can also afford to pay better benefits and to train their employees. Small firms rarely have the resources or the economies of scale to allow outsourcing or to install the big training programs that would enable them to take untrained new employees and turn them into skilled ones.

Although finding enough employees was his biggest problem, finding enough honest ones scared him even more. Angelo recalled from one of his business school courses that companies in the United States are losing a total of well over $400 billion a year in employee theft. As a rough approximation, that works out to about $9 per employee per day and about $12,000 lost annually for a typical company. Furthermore, it was small companies like Angelo's that were particularly in the crosshairs, because companies with fewer than 100 employees are particularly prone to employee theft. Why are small firms particularly vulnerable? Perhaps they lack experience dealing with the problem. More importantly: Small firms are more likely to have a single person doing several jobs, such as ordering supplies and paying the delivery person. This undercuts the checks and balances managers often strive for to control theft. Furthermore, the risk of stealing goes up dramatically when the business is largely based on cash. In a pizza store, many people come in and buy just one or two slices and a cola for lunch, and almost all pay with cash, not credit cards.

And, Angelo was not just worried about someone stealing cash. They can steal your whole business idea, something he learned from painful experience. He had been planning to open a store in what he thought would be a particularly good location, and was thinking of having one of his current employees manage the store. Instead, it turned out that this employee was, in a manner of speaking, stealing Angelo's brain: what Angelo knew about customers, suppliers, where to buy pizza dough, where to buy tomato sauce, how much everything should cost, how to furnish the store, where to buy ovens, store layout—everything. This employee soon quit and opened up his own pizza store, not far from where Angelo had planned to open his new store.

That he was having trouble hiring good employees, there was no doubt. The restaurant business is particularly brutal when it comes to turnover. Many restaurants turn over their employees at a rate of 200% to 300% per year—so every year, each position might have a series of two to three employees filling it. As Angelo said, "I was losing two to three employees a month," adding, "We're a high-volume store, and while we should have about six employees per store [to fill all the hours in a week], we were down to only three or four, so my managers and I were really under the gun."

The problem was bad at the hourly employee level: "We were churning a lot at the hourly level," said Angelo. "Applicants would come in, my managers or I would hire them and not spend much time training them, and the good ones would leave in frustration after a few weeks, while often it was the bad ones who'd stay behind." But in the last two years, Angelo's three company-owned stores also went through a total of three store managers—"They were just blowing through the door," as Angelo put it, in part because, without good employees, their workday was brutal. As a rule, when a small business owner or manager can't find enough employees (or an employee doesn't show up for work), about 80% of the time the owner or manager does the job himself or herself. So, these managers often ended up working seven days a week, 10 to 12 hours a day, and many just burned out in the end. One night, working three jobs himself with customers leaving in anger, Angelo decided he'd never just hire someone because he was desperate again, but would start doing his hiring more rationally.

Angelo knew he should have a more formal screening process. As he said, "If there's been a lesson learned, it's much better to spend time up front screening out candidates who don't fit than to hire them and have to put up with their ineffectiveness." He also knew that he could identify many of the traits that his employees needed. For example, he knew that not everyone has the temperament to be a waiter (he has a small pizza/Italian restaurant in the back of his main store). As Angelo said, "I've seen personalities that were off the charts in assertiveness or overly introverted, traits that obviously don't make a good fit for a waiter or waitress."

As a local business, Angelo recruits by placing help wanted ads in two local newspapers, and he's been "shocked" at some of the responses and experiences he's had in response to the ads. Many of the applicants left voicemail messages (Angelo or the other workers in the store were too busy to answer), and some applicants Angelo "just axed" on the assumption that people without good telephone manners wouldn't have very good manners in the store, either. He also quickly learned that he had to throw out a very wide net, even if hiring only one or two people. Many people, as noted, he eliminated from consideration because of the messages they left, and about half the people he scheduled to come in for interviews didn't show up. He'd taken courses in human resource management, so (as he said) "I should know better," but he hired people based almost exclusively on a single interview (he occasionally made a feeble attempt to check references). In total, his HR approach was obviously not working. It wasn't producing enough good recruits, and the people he did hire were often problematic.

What was he looking for? Service-oriented courteous people, for one. For example, he'd hired one employee who used profanity several times, including once in front of a customer. On that employee's third day, Angelo had to tell her, "I think Angelo's isn't the right place for you," and he fired her. As Angelo said, "I felt bad, but also knew that everything I have is on the line for this business, so I wasn't going to let anyone run this business down." Angelo wants reliable people (who'll show up on time), honest people, and people who are flexible about switching jobs and hours as required. He calls his management style "trust and track." "I coach them and give them goals, and then carefully track results."

Angelo's Pizza business has only the most rudimentary human resource management system. Angelo bought several application forms at a local Office Depot, and rarely uses other forms of any sort. He uses his personal accountant for reviewing the company's books, and Angelo himself computes each employee's paycheck at the end of the week and writes the checks. Training is entirely on-the-job. Angelo personally trained each of his employees. For those employees who go on to be store managers, he assumes that they are training their own employees the way that Angelo trained them (for better or worse, as it turns out). Angelo pays "a bit above" prevailing wage rates (judging by other help wanted ads), but probably not enough to make a significant difference in the quality of employees whom he attracts. If you asked Angelo what his reputation is as an employer, Angelo, being a candid and forthright person, would probably tell you that he is a supportive but hard-nosed employer who treats people fairly, but whose business reputation may suffer from disorganization stemming from inadequate organization and training. He approaches you to ask you several questions.

Questions

8. My strategy is to (hopefully) expand the number of stores and eventually franchise, while focusing on serving only high-quality fresh ingredients. What are three specific human resource management implications of my strategy (including specific policies and practices)?

9. Identify and briefly discuss five specific human resource management errors that I'm currently making.

10. Develop a structured interview form that we can use for hiring (1) store managers, (2) wait staff, and (3) counter people/pizza makers.

11. Based on what you know about Angelo's, and what you know from having visited pizza restaurants, write a one-page outline showing specifically how you think Angelo's should go about selecting employees.

Based generally on actual facts, but Angelo's Pizza is a fictitious company. Angelo's Pizza source notes: Dino Berta, "People Problems: Keep Hiring from Becoming a Crying Game," *Nation's Business News*, 36, no. 20, May 20, 2002, pp. 72–74; Ellen Lyon, "Hiring, Personnel Problems Can Challenge Entrepreneurs," *Patriot-News*, October 12, 2004; Rose Robin Pedone, "Businesses' $400 Billion Theft Problem," *Long Island Business News*, 27, July 6, 1998, pp. 1B–2B; "Survey Shows Small-Business Problems with Hiring, Internet," *Providence Business News*, 16, September 10, 2001, pp. 1B; "Finding Good Workers Is Posing a Big Problem as Hiring Picks Up," *Kiplinger Letter*, 81, February 13, 2004; Ian Mount, "A Pizzeria Owner Learns the Value of Watching the Books," *New York Times*, October 25, 2012, p. B8.

GOOGLE*

Fortune magazine named Google the best of the 100 best companies to work for, and there is little doubt why. Among the benefits it offers are free shuttles equipped with Wi-Fi to pick up and drop off employees from San Francisco Bay Area locations, unlimited sick days, annual all-expense-paid ski trips, free gourmet meals, five on-site free doctors, $2,000 bonuses for referring a new hire, free flu shots, a giant lap pool, on-site oil changes, on-site car washes, volleyball courts, TGIF parties, free on-site washers and dryers (with free detergent), Ping-Pong and foosball tables, and free famous people lectures. For many people, it's the gourmet meals and snacks that make Google stand out. For example, human resources director Stacey Sullivan loves the Irish oatmeal with fresh berries at the company's Plymouth Rock Cafe, near Google's "people operations" group. "I sometimes dream about it," she says. Engineer Jan Fitzpatrick loves the raw bar at Google's Tapis restaurant, down the road on the Google campus. Then, of course, there are the stock options—each new employee gets about 1,200 options to buy Google shares (recently worth about $480 per share). In fact, dozens of early Google employees ("Googlers") are already multimillionaires thanks to Google stock. The recession that began back in 2008 did prompt Google and other firms to cut back on some of these benefits (cafeteria hours are shorter today, for instance), but Google still pretty much leads the benefits pack.

For their part, Googlers share certain traits. They tend to be brilliant, team oriented (teamwork is the norm, especially for big projects), and driven. *Fortune* describes them as people who "almost universally" see themselves as the most interesting people on the planet, and who are happy-go-lucky on the outside, but type A—highly intense and goal directed—on the inside. They're also super-hardworking (which makes sense, since it's not unusual for engineers to be in the hallways at 3 A.M. debating some new mathematical solution to a Google search problem). They're so team oriented that when working on projects, it's not unusual for Google team members to give up their larger, more spacious offices and to crowd into a small conference room, where they can "get things done." Historically, Googlers generally graduate with great grades from the best universities, including Stanford, Harvard, and MIT. For many years, Google wouldn't even consider hiring someone with less than a 3.7 average—while also probing deeply into the why behind any B grades. Google also doesn't hire lone wolves, but wants people who work together and people who also have diverse interests (narrow interests or skills are a turnoff at Google). Google also wants people with growth potential. The company is expanding so fast that it needs to hire people who are capable of being promoted five or six times—it's only, the company says, by hiring such overqualified people that it can be sure that the employees will be able to keep up as Google and their own departments expand.

---

*© Gary Dessler, PhD.

The starting salaries are highly competitive. Experienced engineers start at about $130,000 a year (plus about 1,200 shares of stock options, as noted), and new MBAs can expect between $80,000 and $120,000 per year (with smaller option grants). Most recently, Google had about 10,000 staff members, up from its beginnings with just three employees in a rented garage.

Of course, in a company that's grown from 3 employees to 10,000 and from zero value to hundreds of billions of dollars, it may be quibbling to talk about "problems," but there's no doubt that such rapid growth does confront Google's management, and particularly its "people operations" group, with some big challenges. Let's look at these.

For one, Google, as noted earlier, is a 24-hour operation, and with engineers and others frequently pulling all-nighters to complete their projects, the company needs to provide a package of services and financial benefits that supports that kind of life-style, and that helps its employees maintain an acceptable work–life balance.

As another challenge, Google's enormous financial success is a two-edged sword. Although Google usually wins the recruitment race when it comes to competing for new employees against competitors like Microsoft or Yahoo!, Google does need some way to stem a rising tide of retirements. Most Googlers are still in their 20s and 30s, but many have become so wealthy from their Google stock options that they can afford to retire. One 27-year-old engineer received a million-dollar founder's award for her work on the program for searching desktop computers, and wouldn't think of leaving "except to start her own company." Similarly, a former engineering vice president retired (with his Google stock profits) to pursue his love of astronomy. The engineer who dreamed up Gmail recently retired (at the age of 30).

Another challenge is that the work involves not only long hours but can also be very tense. Google is a very numbers-oriented environment. For example, consider a typical weekly Google user interface design meeting. Marisa Meyer, the company's vice president of search products and user experience, runs the meeting, where her employees work out the look and feel of Google's products. Seated around a conference table are about a dozen Googlers, tapping on laptops. During the 2-hour meeting, Meyer needs to evaluate various design proposals, ranging from minor tweaks to a new product's entire layout. She's previously given each presentation an allotted amount of time, and a large digital clock on the wall ticks off the seconds. The presenters must quickly present their ideas, but also handle questions such as "what do users do if the tab is moved from the side of the page to the top?" Furthermore, it's all about the numbers—no one at Google would ever say, for instance, "the tab looks better in red"—you need to prove your point. Presenters must come armed with usability experiment results, showing, for instance, that a certain percentage preferred red or some other color. While the presenters are answering these questions as quickly as possible, the digital clock is ticking, and when it hits the allotted time, the presentation must end, and the next team steps up to present. It is a tough and tense environment, and Googlers must have done their homework.

Growth can also undermine the "outlaw band that's changing the world" culture that fostered the services that made Google famous. Even cofounder Sergi Brin agrees that Google risks becoming less "zany" as it grows. To paraphrase one of its top managers, the hard part of any business is keeping that original innovative, small business feel even as the company grows.

Creating the right culture is especially challenging now that Google is truly global. For example, Google works hard to provide the same financial and service benefits every place it does business around the world, but it can't exactly match its benefits in every country because of international laws and international taxation issues. Offering the same benefits everywhere is more important than it might initially appear. All those benefits make life easier for Google staff, and help them achieve a work–life balance. Achieving the right work–life balance is the centerpiece of Google's culture, but this also becomes more challenging as the company grows. On the one hand, Google does expect all of its employees to work super hard; on the other hand, it realizes that it needs to help them maintain some sort of balance. As one manager says, Google acknowledges "that we work hard but that work is not everything."

Recruitment is another challenge. While Google certainly doesn't lack applicants, attracting the right applicants is crucial if Google is to continue to grow successfully. Working at Google requires a special set of traits, and screening employees is easier if it recruits the right people to begin with. For instance, Google needs to attract people who are super-bright, love to work, have fun, can handle the stress, and who also have outside interests and flexibility.

As the company grows internationally, it also faces the considerable challenge of recruiting and building staff overseas. For example, Google now is introducing a new vertical market–based structure across Europe to attract more business advertisers to its search engine. (By vertical market–based structure, Google means focusing on key vertical industry sectors such as travel, retail, automotive, and technology.) To build these industry groupings abroad from scratch, Google promoted its former head of its U.S. financial services group to be the vertical markets director for Europe; he moved there recently. Google is thus looking for heads for each of its vertical industry groups for all of its key European territories. Each of these vertical market heads will have to educate their market sectors (retailing, travel, and so on) so Google can attract new advertisers. Google already has offices across Europe, and its London office had tripled in size to 100 staff in just two years.

However, one of the biggest challenges Google still faces is gearing up its employee selection system, given that the company must hire thousands of people per year. When Google started in business, job candidates typically suffered through a dozen or more in-person interviews, and the standards were so high that even applicants with years of great work experience often got turned down if they had just average college grades. But a few years ago, even Google's cofounders acknowledged to security analysts that setting such an extraordinarily high bar for hiring was holding back Google's expansion. For Google's first few years, one of the company's cofounders interviewed nearly every job candidate before he or she was hired, and even today one of them still reviews the qualifications of everyone before he or she gets a final offer.

The experience of one candidate illustrates what Google was up against. A 24-year-old was interviewed for a corporate communications job at Google. Google first made contact with the candidate in May, and then, after two phone interviews, invited him to headquarters. There he had separate interviews with about six people and was treated to lunch in a Google cafeteria. They also had him turn in several "homework" assignments, including a personal statement and a marketing plan. In August, Google invited the candidate back for a second round, which it said would involve another four or five interviews. In the meantime, he decided he'd rather work at a start-up, and accepted another job at a new Web-based instant messaging provider.

Google's head of human resources, a former GE executive, says that Google is trying to strike the right balance between letting Google and the candidate get to know each other while also moving quickly. To that end, Google administered a survey to all Google's current employees in an effort to identify the traits that correlate with success at Google. In the survey, employees responded to questions relating to about 300 variables, including their performance on standardized tests, how old they were when they first used a computer, and how many foreign languages they speak. The Google survey team then went back and compared the answers against the 30 or 40 job performance factors they keep for each employee. They thereby identified clusters of traits that Google might better focus on during the hiring process. Google is also moving from the free-form interviews it used in the past to a more structured process.

Questions

12. What do you think of the idea of Google correlating personal traits from the employees' answers on the survey to their performance, and then using that as the basis for screening job candidates? In other words, is it or is it not a good idea? Please explain your answer.

13. The benefits that Google pays obviously represent an enormous expense. Based on what you know about Google and on what you read in this text, how would you defend all these benefits if you're making a presentation to the security analysts who were analyzing Google's performance?

14. If you wanted to hire the brightest people around, how would you go about recruiting and selecting them?

15. To support its growth and expansion strategy, Google wants (among other traits) people who are super-bright and who work hard, often round-the-clock, and who are flexible and maintain a decent work–life balance. List five specific HR policies or practices that you think Google has implemented or should implement to support its strategy, and explain your answer.

16. What sorts of factors do you think Google will have to take into consideration as it tries transferring its culture and reward systems and way of doing business to its operations abroad?

17. Given the sorts of values and culture Google cherishes, briefly describe four specific activities you suggest it pursue during new-employee orientation.

Source: Notes for Google: "Google Brings Vertical Structure to Europe," *New Media Age*, August 4, 2005, p. 2; Debbie Lovewell, "Employer Profile—Google: Searching for Talent," *Employee Benefits*, October 10, 2005, p. 66; "Google Looking for Gourmet Chefs," *Internet Week*, August 4, 2005; Douglas Merrill, "Google's 'Googley' Culture Kept Alive by Tech," *eWeek*, April 11, 2006; Robert Hof, "Google Gives Employees Another Option," *BusinessWeek Online*, December 13, 2005; Kevin Delaney, "Google Adjusts Hiring Process as Needs Grow," *Wall Street Journal*, October 23, 2006, pp. B1, B8; Adam Lishinsky, "Search and Enjoy," *Fortune*, January 22, 2007, pp. 70–82; www.nypost.com/seven/10302008/business/frugal_google_cuts_perks_136011.htm, accessed July 12, 2009; Adam Bryant, "The Quest to Build a Better Boss," *New York Times,* March 13, 2011, pp. 1, 7; Mark C. Crowley, "Not a Happy Accident: How Google Deliberately Designs Workplace Satisfaction", www.fastcompany.com/3007268/where-are-they-now/not-happy-accident-how-google-deliberately-designs-workplace-satisfaction, accessed September 16, 2014; Laszlo Bock, Work Rules!: Insights from Inside Google That Will Transform How You Live and Lead (New York, NY: Twelve, 2015).

MUFFLER MAGIC*

Muffler Magic is a fast-growing chain of 25 automobile service centers in Nevada. Originally started 20 years ago as a muffler repair shop by Ronald Brown, the chain expanded rapidly to new locations, and as it did so Muffler Magic also expanded the services it provided, from muffler replacement to oil changes, brake jobs, and engine repair. Today, one can bring an automobile to a Muffler Magic shop for basically any type of service, from tires to mufflers to engine repair.

Auto service is a tough business. The shop owner is basically dependent upon the quality of the service people he or she hires and retains, and the most qualified mechanics find it easy to pick up and leave for a job paying a bit more at a competitor down the road. It's also a business in which productivity is very important. The single largest expense is usually the cost of labor. Auto service dealers generally don't just make up the prices that they charge customers for various repairs; instead, they charge based on standardized industry rates for jobs like changing spark plugs or repairing a leaky radiator. Therefore, if someone brings a car in for a new alternator and the standard number of hours for changing the alternator is an hour, but it takes the mechanic 2 hours, the service center's owner may end up making less profit on the transaction.

---

*© Gary Dessler, PhD.

Quality is a persistent problem as well. For example, "rework" has recently been a problem at Muffler Magic. A customer recently brought her car to a Muffler Magic to have the car's brake pads replaced, which the service center did for her. Unfortunately, when she left she drove only about two blocks before she discovered that she had no brake power at all. It was simply fortuitous that she was going so slowly she was able to stop her car by slowly rolling up against a parking bumper. It subsequently turned out that the mechanic who replaced the brake pads had failed to properly tighten a fitting on the hydraulic brake tubes and the brake fluid had run out, leaving the car with no braking power. In a similar problem the month before that, a (different) mechanic replaced a fan belt, but forgot to refill the radiator with fluid; that customer's car overheated before he got four blocks away, and Muffler Magic had to replace the whole engine. Of course problems like these not only diminish the profitability of the company's profits, but, repeated many times over, have the potential for ruining Muffler Magic's word-of-mouth reputation.

Organizationally, Muffler Magic employs about 300 people, and Ron runs his company with eight managers, including himself as president, a controller, a purchasing director, a marketing director, and the human resource manager. He also has three regional managers to whom the eight or nine service center managers in each area of Nevada report. Over the past two years, as the company has opened new service centers, company-wide profits have diminished rather than increased. In part, these diminishing profits probably reflect the fact that Ron Brown has found it increasingly difficult to manage his growing operation. ("Your reach is exceeding your grasp" is how Ron's wife puts it.)

The company has only the most basic HR systems in place. It uses an application form that the human resource manager modified from one that he downloaded from the Web, and the standard employee status change request forms, sign-on forms, I-9 forms, and so on, that it purchased from a human resource management supply house. Training is entirely on-the-job. Muffler Magic expects the experienced technicians that it hires to come to the job fully trained; to that end, the service center managers generally ask candidates for these jobs basic behavioral questions that hopefully provide a window into these applicants' skills. However, most of the other technicians hired to do jobs like rotating tires, fixing brake pads, and replacing mufflers are untrained and inexperienced. They are to be trained by either the service center manager or by more experienced technicians, on-the-job.

Ron Brown faces several HR-type problems. One, as he says, is that he faces the "tyranny of the immediate" when it comes to hiring employees. Although it's fine to say that he should be carefully screening each employee and checking his or her references and work ethic, from a practical point of view, with 25 centers to run, the centers' managers usually just hire anyone who seems to be breathing, as long as he or she can answer some basic interview questions about auto repair, such as, "What do you think the problem is if a 2001 Camry is overheating, and what would you do about it?"

Employee safety is also a problem. An automobile service center may not be the most dangerous type of workplace, but it is potentially dangerous. Employees are dealing with sharp tools, greasy floors, greasy tools, extremely hot temperatures (for instance, on mufflers and engines), and fast-moving engine parts including fan blades. There are some basic things that a service manager can do to ensure more safety, such as insisting that all oil spills be cleaned up immediately. However, from a practical point of view, there are few ways to get around many of the problems—such as when the technician must check out an engine while it is running.

With Muffler Magic's profits going down instead of up, Brown's human resource manager has taken the position that the main problem is financial. As he says, "You get what you pay for" when it comes to employees, and if you compensate technicians better than your competitors do, then you get better technicians, ones who do their jobs better and stay longer with the company—and then profits will rise. So, the HR manager scheduled a meeting between himself, Ron Brown, and a professor of business who teaches compensation management at a local university. The HR manager has asked this professor to spend about a week looking at each of the service centers, analyzing the situation, and coming up with a compensation plan that will address Muffler Magic's quality and productivity problems. At this meeting, the professor makes three basic recommendations for changing the company's compensation policies.

Number one, she says that she has found that Muffler Magic suffers from what she calls "presenteeism"—in other words, employees drag themselves into work even when they're sick, because the company does not pay them if they are out; the company offers no sick days. In just a few days the professor couldn't properly quantify how much Muffler Magic is losing to presenteeism. However, from what she could see at each shop, there are typically one or two technicians working with various maladies like the cold or flu, and it seemed to her that each of these people was probably really only working about half of the time (although they were getting paid for the whole day). So, for 25 service centers per week, Muffler Magic could well be losing 125 or 130 personnel days per week of work. The professor suggests that Muffler Magic start allowing everyone to take three paid sick days per year, a reasonable suggestion. However, as Ron Brown points out, "Right now, we're only losing about half a day's pay for each employee who comes in and who works unproductively; with your suggestion, won't we lose the whole day?" The professor says she'll ponder that one.

Second, the professor recommends putting the technicians on a skill-for-pay plan. Basically, she suggests the following. Give each technician a letter grade (A through E) based upon that technician's particular skill level and abilities. An "A" technician is a team leader and needs to show that he or she has excellent diagnostic troubleshooting skills, and the ability to supervise and direct other technicians. At the other extreme, an "E" technician would typically be a new apprentice with little technical training. The other technicians fall in between those two levels, based on their individual skills and abilities.

In the professor's system, the "A" technician or team leader would assign and supervise all work done within his or her area but generally not do any mechanical repairs himself or herself. The team leader does the diagnostic troubleshooting, supervises and trains the other technicians, and test drives the car before it goes back to the customer. Under this plan, every technician receives a guaranteed hourly wage within a certain range, for instance:

A tech = $25–$30 an hour
B tech = $20–$25 an hour
C tech = $15–$20 an hour
D tech = $10–$15 an hour
E tech = $8–$10 an hour

Third, to directly address the productivity issue, the professor recommends that each service manager calculate each technician-team's productivity at the end of each day and at the end of each week. She suggests posting the running productivity total conspicuously for daily viewing. Then, the technicians as a group get weekly cash bonuses based upon their productivity. To calculate productivity, the professor recommends dividing the total labor hours billed by the total labor hours paid to technicians; in other words, total labor hours billed *divided by* total hours paid to technicians.

Having done some homework, the professor says that the national average for labor productivity is currently about 60%, and that only the best-run service centers achieve 85% or greater. By her rough calculations, Muffler Magic was attaining about industry average (about 60%—in other words, they were billing for only about 60 hours for each 100 hours that they actually had to pay technicians to do the jobs). (Of course, this was not entirely the technicians' fault. Technicians get time off for breaks and for lunch, and if a particular service center simply didn't have enough business on a particular day or during a particular week, then several technicians may well sit around idly waiting for the next car to come in.) The professor recommends setting a labor efficiency goal of 80% and posting each team's daily productivity results in the workplace to provide them with additional feedback. She recommends that if at the end of a week the team is able to boost its productivity ratio from the current 60% to 80%, then that team would get an additional 10% weekly pay bonus. After that, for every 5% boost of increased productivity above 80%, technicians would receive an additional 5% weekly bonus. So, if a technician's normal weekly pay is $400, that employee would receive an extra $40 at the end of the week when his team moves from 60% productivity to 80% productivity.

After the meeting, Ron Brown thanked the professor for her recommendations and told her he would think about it and get back to her. After the meeting, on the drive home, Ron was pondering what to do. He had to decide whether to institute the professor's sick leave policy, and whether to implement the professor's incentive and compensation plan. Before implementing anything, however, he wanted to make sure he understood the context in which he was making his decision. For example, did Muffler Magic really have an incentive pay problem, or were the problems more broad? Furthermore, how, if at all, would the professor's incentive plan impact the quality of the work that the teams were doing? And should the company really start paying for sick days? Ron Brown had a lot to think about.

Questions

18. Write a one-page summary outline listing three or four recommendations you would make with respect to each HR function (recruiting, selection, training, and so on) that you think Ron Brown should be addressing with his HR manager.

19. Develop a 10-question structured interview form Ron Brown's service center managers can use to interview experienced technicians.

20. If you were Ron Brown, would you implement the professor's recommendation addressing the presenteeism problem—in other words, start paying for sick days? Why or why not?

21. If you were advising Ron Brown, would you recommend that he implement the professor's skill-based pay and incentive pay plan as is? Why? Would you implement it with modifications? If you would modify it, please be specific about what you think those modifications should be, and why.

Based generally on actual facts, but Muffler Magic is a fictitious company. This case is based largely on information in Drew Paras, "The Pay Factor: Technicians' Salaries Can Be the Largest Expense in a Server Shop, as Well as the Biggest Headache. Here's How One Shop Owner Tackled the Problem," *Motor Age*, November 2003, pp. 76–79; see also Jennifer Pellet, "Health Care Crisis," *Chief Executive*, June 2004, pp. 56–61; "Firms Press to Quantify, Control Presenteeism," *Employee Benefits*, December 1, 2002.

BP TEXAS CITY*

When British Petroleum's (BP) Horizon oil rig exploded in the Gulf of Mexico in 2010, it triggered tragic reminders for experts in the safety community. In March 2005, an explosion and fire at BP's Texas City, Texas, refinery killed 15 people and injured 500 people in the worst U.S. industrial accident in more than 10 years. That disaster triggered three investigations: one internal investigation by BP, one by the U.S. Chemical Safety Board, and an independent investigation chaired by former U.S. Secretary of State James Baker and an 11-member panel that was organized at BP's request.

To put the results of these three investigations into context, it's useful to understand that under its current management, BP had pursued, for the past 10 or

---

*© Gary Dessler, PhD.

so years before the Texas City explosion, a strategy emphasizing cost-cutting and profitability. The basic conclusion of the investigations was that cost-cutting helped compromise safety at the Texas City refinery. It's useful to consider each investigation's findings.

The Chemical Safety Board's (CSB) investigation, according to Carol Merritt, the board's chair, showed that "BP's global management was aware of problems with maintenance, spending, and infrastructure well before March 2005." Apparently, faced with numerous earlier accidents, BP did make some safety improvements. However, it focused primarily on emphasizing personal employee safety behaviors and procedural compliance, and thereby reducing safety accident rates. The problem (according to the CSB) was that "catastrophic safety risks remained." For example, according to the CSB, "unsafe and antiquated equipment designs were left in place, and unacceptable deficiencies in preventive maintenance were tolerated." Basically, the CSB found that BP's budget cuts led to a progressive deterioration of safety at the Texas City refinery. Said Merritt, "In an aging facility like Texas City, it is not responsible to cut budgets related to safety and maintenance without thoroughly examining the impact on the risk of a catastrophic accident."

Looking at specifics, the CSB said that a 2004 internal audit of 35 BP business units, including Texas City (BP's largest refinery), found significant safety gaps they all had in common, including, for instance, a lack of leadership competence, and "systemic underlying issues" such as a widespread tolerance of noncompliance with basic safety rules and poor monitoring of safety management systems and processes. Ironically, the CSB found that BP's accident prevention effort at Texas City had achieved a 70% reduction in worker injuries in the year before the explosion. Unfortunately, this simply meant that individual employees were having fewer accidents. The larger, more fundamental problem was that the potentially explosive situation inherent in the depreciating machinery remained.

The CSB found that the Texas City explosion followed a pattern of years of major accidents at the facility. In fact, there had apparently been an average of one employee death every 16 months at the plant for the last 30 years. The CSB found that the equipment directly involved in the most recent explosion was an obsolete design already phased out in most refineries and chemical plants, and that key pieces of its instrumentation were not working. There had also been previous instances where flammable vapors were released from the same unit in the 10 years prior to the explosion. In 2003, an external audit had referred to the Texas City refinery's infrastructure and assets as "poor" and found what it referred to as a "checkbook mentality," one in which budgets were not sufficient to manage all the risks. In particular, the CSB found that BP had implemented a 25% cut on fixed costs between 1998 and 2000 and that this adversely impacted maintenance expenditures and net expenditures, and refinery infrastructure. Going on, the CSB found that in 2004, there were three major accidents at the refinery that killed three workers.

BP's own internal report concluded that the problems at Texas City were not of recent origin, and instead were years in the making. It said BP was taking steps to address them. Its investigation found "no evidence of anyone consciously or intentionally taking actions or making decisions that put others at risk." Said BP's report, "The underlying reasons for the behaviors and actions displayed during the incident are complex, and the team has spent much time trying to understand them—it is evident that they were many years in the making and will require concerted and committed actions to address." BP's report concluded that there were five underlying causes for the massive explosion:

- A working environment had eroded to one characterized by resistance to change, and a lack of trust.
- Safety, performance, and risk reduction priorities had not been set and consistently reinforced by management.
- Changes in the "complex organization" led to a lack of clear accountabilities and poor communication.

- A poor level of hazard awareness and understanding of safety resulted in workers accepting levels of risk that were considerably higher than at comparable installations.
- Adequate early warning systems for problems were lacking, and there were no independent means of understanding the deteriorating standards at the plant.

The report from the BP-initiated but independent 11-person panel chaired by former U.S. Secretary of State James Baker contained specific conclusions and recommendations. The Baker panel looked at BP's corporate safety oversight, the corporate safety culture, and the process safety management systems at BP at the Texas City plant as well as at BP's other refineries.

Basically, the Baker panel concluded that BP had not provided effective safety process leadership and had not established safety as a core value at the five refineries it looked at (including Texas City).

Like the CSB, the Baker panel found that BP had emphasized personal safety in recent years and had in fact improved personal safety performance, but had not emphasized the overall safety process, thereby mistakenly interpreting "improving personal injury rates as an indication of acceptable process safety performance at its U.S. refineries." In fact, the Baker panel went on, by focusing on these some what misleading improving personal injury rates, BP created a false sense of confidence that it was properly addressing process safety risks. It also found that the safety culture at Texas City did not have the positive, trusting, open environment that a proper safety culture required. The Baker panel's other findings included the following.

- BP did not always ensure that adequate resources were effectively allocated to support or sustain a high level of process safety performance.
- BP's refinery personnel are "overloaded" by corporate initiatives.
- Operators and maintenance personnel work high rates of overtime.
- BP tended to have a short-term focus and its decentralized management system and entrepreneurial culture delegated substantial discretion to refinery plant managers "without clearly defining process safety expectations, responsibilities, or accountabilities."
- There was no common, unifying process safety culture among the five refineries.
- The company's corporate safety management system did not make sure there was timely compliance with internal process safety standards and programs.
- BP's executive management either did not receive refinery-specific information that showed that process safety deficiencies existed at some of the plants, or did not effectively respond to any information it did receive.
- These findings and the following suggestions are based on "BP Safety Report Finds Company's Process Safety Culture Ineffective," *Global Refining & Fuels Report*, January 17, 2007.

The Baker panel made several safety recommendations for BP, including the following.

1. The company's corporate management must provide leadership on process safety.
2. The company should establish a process safety management system that identifies, reduces, and manages the process safety risks of the refineries.
3. The company should make sure its employees have an appropriate level of process safety knowledge and expertise.
4. The company should involve "relevant stakeholders" in developing a positive, trusting, and open process safety culture at each refinery.
5. BP should clearly define expectations and strengthen accountability for process safety performance.
6. BP should better coordinate its process safety support for the refining line organization.

7. BP should develop an integrated set of leading and lagging performance indicators for effectively monitoring process safety performance.

8. BP should establish and implement an effective system to audit process safety performance.

9. The company's board should monitor the implementation of the panel's recommendations and the ongoing process safety performance of the refineries.

10. BP should transform itself into a recognized industry leader in process safety management.

In making its recommendations, the panel singled out the company's chief executive at the time, Lord Browne, by saying, "In hindsight, the panel believes if Browne had demonstrated comparable leadership on and commitment to process safety [as he did for responding to climate change] that would have resulted in a higher level of safety at refineries."

Overall, the Baker panel found that BP's top management had not provided "effective leadership" on safety. It found that the failings went to the very top of the organization, to the company's chief executive, and to several of his top lieutenants. The Baker panel emphasized the importance of top management commitment, saying, for instance, that "it is imperative that BP leadership set the process safety tone at the top of the organization and establish appropriate expectations regarding process safety performance." It also said BP "has not provided effective leadership in making certain its management and U.S. refining workforce understand what is expected of them regarding process safety performance."

Lord Browne, the chief executive, stepped down about a year after the explosion. About the same time, some BP shareholders were calling for the company's executives and board directors to have their bonuses more closely tied to the company's safety and environmental performance in the wake of Texas City. In October 2009, OSHA announced it was filing the largest fine in its history for this accident, for $87 million, against BP. One year later, BP's Horizon oil rig in the Gulf of Mexico exploded, taking 11 lives. In September 2014, the U.S. District judge presiding over negligence claims in the ensuing case found BP guilty of gross negligence, basically reckless and extreme behavior; the company will appeal his ruling.

Questions

22. The text defines ethics as "the principles of conduct governing an individual or a group," and specifically as the standards one uses to decide what his or her conduct should be. To what extent do you believe that what happened at BP is as much a breakdown in the company's ethical systems as it is in its safety systems, and how would you defend your conclusion?

23. Are the Occupational Safety and Health Administration's standards, policies, and rules aimed at addressing problems like the ones that apparently existed at the Texas City plant? If so, how would you explain the fact that problems like these could have continued for so many years?

24. Since there were apparently at least three deaths in the year prior to the major explosion, and an average of about one employee death per 16 months for the previous 10 years, how would you account for the fact that mandatory OSHA inspections missed these glaring sources of potential catastrophic events?

25. The text lists numerous suggestions for "how to prevent accidents." Based on what you know about the Texas City explosion, what do you say Texas City tells you about the most important three steps an employer can take to prevent accidents?

26. Based on what you learned in Chapter 14, would you make any additional recommendations to BP over and above those recommendations made by the Baker panel and the CSB? If so, what would those recommendations be?

27. Explain specifically how strategic human resource management at BP seems to have supported the company's broader strategic aims. What does this say about the advisability of always linking human resource strategy to a company's strategic aims?

Source: Notes for BP Texas City: Sheila McNulty, "BP Knew of Safety Problems, Says Report," *Financial Times*, October 31, 2006, p. 1; "CBS: Documents Show BP Was Aware of Texas City Safety Problems," *World Refining & Fuels Today*, October 30, 2006; "BP Safety Report Finds Company's Process Safety Culture Ineffective," *Global Refining & Fuels Report*, January 17, 2007; "BP Safety Record Under Attack," *Europe Intelligence Wire*, January 17, 2007; Mark Hofmann, "BP Slammed for Poor Leadership on Safety, Oil Firm Agrees to Act on Review Panel's Recommendations," *Business Intelligence*, January 22, 2007, p. 3; "Call for Bonuses to Include Link with Safety Performance," *Guardian*, January 18, 2007, p. 24; www.bp.com/genericarticle.do?categoryId=9005029&contentId=7015905, accessed July 12, 2009; Steven Greenhouse, "BP Faces Record Fine for '05 Blast," *New York Times*, October 30, 2009, pp. 1, 6; Kyle W. Morrison, "Blame to Go Around," *Safety & Health*, 183, no. 3, March 2011, p. 40; Ed Crooks, "BP Had Tools to End Spill Sooner, Court Told," www.ft.com/cms/s/0/40d7b076-2ae8-11e3-8fb8-00144feab7de.html?ftcamp=published_links%2Frss%2Fhome_uk%2Ffeed%2F%2Fproduct#axzz2gZshHFOc, accessed October 2, 2013; Daniel Gilbert and Justin Scheck, "Judge Hammers BP for Gulf Disaster", *Wall Street Journal*, September 5, 2014, pp. B1, B2.

SOCIAL NETWORKING DURING OFFICE HOURS*

"Sir, I am a regular patient of this clinic, and highly respect all your staff and doctors. However, I regrettably say that I have been misguided by Minu many times. On one occasion, I was guided towards the payment window instead of the consultation room, and now I am denied appointment at the date and time recommended by the doctor himself. I had a word with other patients and they are also facing similar problems. I understand that such problems do occur once in a while, but being a well wisher of the clinic, I feel the matter should be brought to your notice. Do look into the matter or I am concerned the hospital's reputation will be at stake."

– Mr. Shyamji Rana, a reputed businessman of Ahmedabad

These words made Sargi Desai the HRA (HR and Administration) manager of Bless Eye Clinic, Ahmedabad, Gujarat ponder over what might have gone wrong. The deteriorating performance of the front office was a cause of concern. What worried him more was the fact that the complaint was against Minu, who was promoted from the post of reception-in-charge to front office coordinator on account of her star performance. He had noticed that of late something kept her preoccupied, affecting her performance.

Determined to have a word with her, Sargi Desai walked towards the front office. It was lunch time and the clinic provided staggered break to staff members. Minu was expected to be dealing with walk-in patients and other visitors till someone would replace her at the front desk. He reached Minu's desk, facing her back. The reception was more or less empty at that time, and she was sitting at the front desk and operating her Facebook account with two open chat windows. It seemed that Minu had not understood the importance of being front-face of the clinic. Even a minor error made by her would directly affect the clinic's goodwill and business.

The Bless Eye Clinic

Bless Eye Clinic was set up in mid 1990's by Dr. Mukherjee, an eye surgery specialist trained in Germany. Dr. Mukherjee, along with his three friends, of which two were doctors and another, a Chartered Accountant established the clinic. The major stake was held by Dr. Mukherjee[1]. The clinic was initially a small set-up and grew many times in one decade. In 2002, the clinic was shifted to a new and bigger premise.

---

[1] Dr. Mukherjee had 50% stake in the hospital while others held the balance.

* Prepared by Professor. Biju Varkkey with assistance from Research Associate Sanjana Srivastava, Indian Institute of Management, Ahmedabad.
  © 2012 by the Indian Institute of Management, Ahmedabad.

In addition to out-patient services, the clinic now has an attached in-patient wing that could accommodate ten patients and bystanders. A team of 54 regular on-roll employees, including seven doctors and five employees on temporary/trainee roles were employed there.

Awareness about the clinic was high in and even outside India. Apart from the stature of doctors and positive word of mouth, the Business Development and Social Media executive of the clinic, working under the guidance of one of the partners Dr. Sheth, had also helped to build the image. Lately, the owners were evaluating plans for further expansion of the clinic to cater to the growing segment of medical tourists. The government of Gujarat too was promoting medical tourism as a priority area for investments. In addition, the "Bless Eye Clinic Store" was also doing brisk business, and had diversified into sales and distribution of large range of pharmaceutical equipment, medicines, and eye wears.

During the initial three years, Bless Eye Clinic remained a small entity with three doctors and five administrative staff, including an accountant who handled administration, HR, and external relations. As patient inflow grew, more doctors with expertise in varied ophthalmological areas were recruited. At present, while Dr. Mukherjee is the Chief Surgeon and Managing Director, the other two co-founders are designated "Director and Senior Consultant." Other doctors are designated Junior Consultants, and they report directly to Dr. Mukherjee.

With growth, new positions of Finance Manager (FM) and HR and Administration Manager (HRA) were created. For administrative purposes, the FM reported to Dr. Sheth, a co-founder and director, and the HRA reported the other director, Dr. Shah. However, both FM and HRA were given full freedom to function. The fourth partner and co-founder, a chartered accountant who also owned an independent financial services firm, oversaw the administrative activities without holding any formal role. He would interact with the FM and HRA regularly. In addition, the nursing department was looked after by Devika, the Nursing Supervisor, who reported to Dr. Shah and managed a team of nine nurses.

All routine problems, except those financial in nature, faced by any nurse or patient were reported to Devika. There were 20 floor assistants, who helped the doctors and nurses in all activities including guiding patients from consultation or check-up rooms, handling stores and purchases as well as upkeeping the medical records. Some of these floor assistants were attached to the front office. Two assistants and all five housekeeping staff were supervised by Minu, and she was directly accountable to the HRA manager. The HRA manager was responsible for employee related issues like leave, salary, benefits, performance complaints, general administrative issues, and other requirements. While he had an assistant to help him, the FM had two accountants working under him. (See Exhibit 1 for the organization structure.)

In 2002, a new front office was created with the responsibility for handling visitors and patients, scheduling appointments, facility and records management and public relations. The HRA manager was given responsibility of the new front office. Around the same time, an integrated Hospital Management System was introduced and aimed among other things, to replace written medical records with digital ones. Until then all medical records, particulars of patients along with their payment details were handwritten and recorded in ledgers.

When the new hospital management system was introduced, all doctors and key people were provided desktop computers, with internet connection. According to Dr. Mukherjee, connectivity helps one excel in the profession and speeds up execution. The internet was identified as a good medium to spread the clinic's work and build image. The clinic created its own page on popular social networking sites which aimed to spread the clinic's name. Additionally, public awareness about eye care was built by hosting educational documentaries and other literature in the site. Bless Clinic actively participated in the eye donation campaign as a part of its corporate social responsibility.

Minu had joined Bless Eye Clinic as Trainee Receptionist and she was confirmed as regular employee two months before the clinic shifted. She was a highly motivated employee and took keen interest in using computers. The Excel-based patient scheduling system was implemented on her initiative, which eased the coordination between doctors and other offices to a great extent. She was very comfortable in dealing with people, including doctors, hospital staff, and patients. In 2004, she was promoted and designated as the front office coordinator and was assigned two floor assistants to help her. (See Exhibit 2 for Minu's job description.)

Along with the shifting of the clinic, formal administrative and HR practices were introduced. In addition to streamlining the employee management activities, a structured induction program for new employees was initiated. Grades, corresponding pay scales, and allowances were defined for the nursing and non medical staff. Doctors and senior management personnel pay and terms of appointment were managed directly by the founders.

Suggestion for a formal performance management system was also floated with the aim to introduce pay for performance, but the idea was rejected by the Directors and the Managing Director. According to the ongoing compensation practice, all employees would receive approximately 10% annual increase in their salary. Better performers would be sometimes promoted to higher levels, but in a small clinic, such opportunities were limited.

Accessing Social Networking Sites During Work Hours

With upgradation in technology and availability of internet to most employees, apprehensions were raised about the negative effects of the facility. Sensing that there would be a possibility of misuse, HRA manager had raised the issue with the senior team. His concerns included internet use for personal purposes, accessing social networking sites or playing games during work hours, etc. After discussions, an internet policy was introduced that explained the behaviour to be followed during working hours. The policy was communicated to all employees. Doctors and both managers were exempted from the policy, since their work required social media access.

As per the policy, the use of social networking sites was prohibited during working hours, except for exempted personnel. However, keeping in mind that social networking sites were appreciated and used extensively by people worldwide[2&3], particularly the younger generation, management did not prohibit their employees from using such sites after work hours or during breaks.

Having seen Minu using a social networking site while she was at her desk, Sargi Desai went and met his supervisor Dr. Shah. The discussion went like this: "Though we have put the internet policy to practice, I have seen that it is being breached by Minu. Some steps would have to be taken, after I have witnessed Minu online on her Facebook account." After some discussions, they decided to give her the benefit of doubt, since the breach occurred during the staggered lunch hours. Dr. Shah asked Sargi Desai to keep a close eye on the usage of social media across the firm. Dr. Shah suggested that, if required specific sites could be blocked in the organization's network. After sometime, it occurred to Sargi Desai that Minu was a friend in his Facebook profile. He immediately logged on to Facebook and on seeing her online he called her to his cabin.

The conversation was short: "I just saw that you are online on Facebook. We have a policy that prohibits using internet for personal reasons during office hours. It affects performance." She replied that one of her family members must be using the account since they have access to her account. She assured that she accesses

---

[2] Arun Prabhudesai, published on (June 24, 2011). Interesting Facebook India Statistics [Numbers, Growth, Brands]. Track.in- India Business Blog retrieved on June 9, 2012 from http://trak.in/tags/business/2011/06/24/facebook-india-statistics/

[3] Employees addicted to social networking sites, published on (2008, December 15). HC online. Retrieved on June 9, 2012 from http://www.hcamag.com/news/domestic/employees-addicted-to-social-networking-sites/115125/

Facebook only during breaks or after working hours. Desai advised, "May be you need to change your personal page password so that they do not use your account," to which Minu replied, "I cannot say no to my family members and prevent them from accessing my account. Everybody at home keeps in touch with the larger family through facebook. If you want, I can change the privacy settings and block non family members."

After the discussion, Sargi Desai decided to keep her under observation and informed Dr. Shah. In the days that followed, he noticed that she had stopped using social networking sites from her office computer. But the same errors continued with her work. Sometimes he observed Minu glued to her smartphone, happily typing something. That was not unusual, because many customers used SMS to communicate with the clinic regarding appointments and other needs. Minu was specifically given ₹500 per month as mobile allowance, while she used her own number for the clinic's work.

The clinic had introduced the practice of observing every third Saturday afternoon of the month as training day for all employees, other than doctors. The following Saturday, the topic "Employee Attitude" was taken up for learning. Sargi Desai designed a role play that linked employee behavior with the impact on patients. Minu was purposefully asked to perform the part of a patient and another employee played part of an office staff who misguided patients due to constant engagement with the phone.

After the training Sargi Desai reported to Dr. Shah, "She should have received the message. Minu herself commented during discussions that patients require full attention and such behavior is unacceptable. I concluded the session by talking about our company policy." Dr. Shah replied, "Minu may not be the only person violating the rule. Hence, I do not advice singling her out. We need to ensure that the policy is being followed consistently amongst all staff. Junior Consultant Dr. Bhatt told me that most employees are on social media sites the entire day, mostly through mobile devices."

Several thoughts crossed Sargi Desai's mind about the possible solutions to stop this problem from further worsening. Should he issue a warning letter to Minu? Or should he directly fire her for consistent poor performance that has been noticed lately? Or even worse, should he ban mobile phones in the clinic like many organizations do? Would these steps set a right example for other employees in the organization?

Exhibit 1

Current Organization Chart

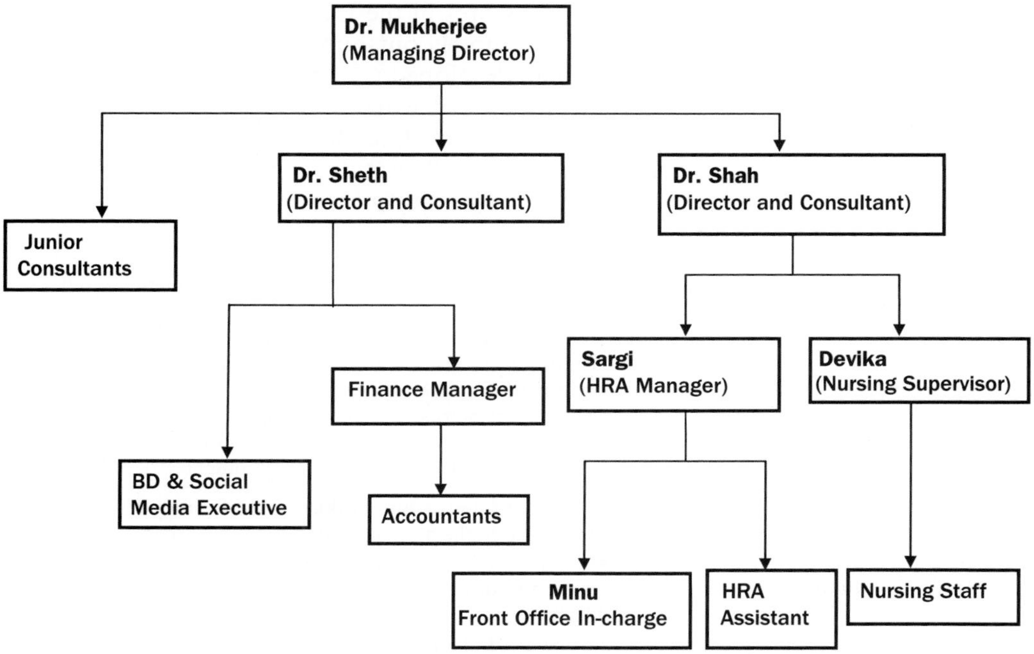

Exhibit 2

Minu's Job Description as Front Office Coordinator

- Attending to and guiding patients who visit the clinic.
- Recording patients' details.
- Registering new cases.
- Providing Registration ID-card to patients.
- Maintaining old case sheets and patient data.
- Giving appointments to patients of cataract, cornea, glaucoma, pediatric doctors for OPD, Pre-Operative and following up as and when required.
- Providing information to patients, solving their grievances and queries.
- Keeping a check on the smooth functioning of floor assistants so that doctors can carry out their work without any hindrance.
- Manage the floor assistants who are accountable to front office in charge.
- Maintaining the flow of communication that flows from the front office to other doctors and employees of the clinic.
- Providing the list of patients for the suceeding day to doctors as per their patients.

This job description was given to Minu when she was assigned role as front office coordinator. In her opinion, she does much more than all this.

BRANDED WITH ALLEGATIONS: LABOR RIGHTS VIOLATION IN THE SUPPLY CHAIN*

On 25 August 2010, Gurgaon in the state of Haryana once again witnessed factory worker unrest.[4] The movement of needles, scissors, and sewing machines came to halt at a garment manufacturing factory. Workers had protested claiming they were made to work 16 hours a day and even denied minimum wages.[5] The working conditions were also poor. Subsequently workers went on a strike that lasted for some time. Viva Global, the company, manufactured garments for Marks & Spencer (M&S) and other international brands. In 2009–10, Viva Global had a turnover of ₹100 million, and employed about around 500 workers. It produced close to 80,000 pieces a month for M&S Girls' Limited and Kidswear ranges and contributed to 1% of M&S's output from India. M&S sourced garments from over 800 garment factories around the world, including 92 in India.

M&S was one of UK's renowned garment retailers, employing 75,000 people in over 600 stores in the UK and 300 stores in other countries.[6] The manufacturing process was mostly outsourced to local vendors in many countries, mostly low wage ones. It had developed *Global Sourcing Principles* to ensure better quality and to have decent and ethical work practices across the supply chain. In January 2007 M&S introduced *Plan A*[7] (see Box 1) and aimed to become the world's most sustainable retailer by 2015.[8] *Plan A* depicted how M&S did business and extended its social and environmental commitments.

---

[4] Mehta, G.S. (August 28, 2010). 'Unfair labor practices' cost textile co deal. *The Economic Times.* Retrieved September 5, 2010 from http://economictimes.indiatimes.com/news/news-by-industry/cons-products/garments-/-textiles/Unfair-labour-practices-cost-textile-co-deal/articleshow/6448690.cms

[5] The minimum wage is the minimum amount a worker should legally be paid, as opposed to wages that are determined by the forces of supply and demand in a free market. In India minimum wages is legalised under the *Minimum Wages Act, 1948 (for more information see* www.paycheck.in*).*

[6] http://corporate.marksandspencer.com/aboutus/company_overview.Retrieved September 21, 2010.

[7] http://plana.marksandspencer.com/media/pdf/planA-2010.pdf. Retrieved September 12, 2010.

[8] http://corporate.marksandspencer.com/home. Retrieved September 20, 2010.

---

* Prepared by Professor Biju Varkkey and Mrinmoy Majumder, Academic Associate, on the basis of articles published in the national and international media. The sources are acknowledged in the case.
  Cases of the Indian Institute of Management, Ahmedabad, are prepared as a basis for class discussion. Cases are not designed to present illustrations of either correct or incorrect handling of administrative problems.

  © 2010 by the Indian Institute of Management, Ahmedabad.

Box 1: Plan A

Summary

- **Climate change:** *Remain committed to make M&S UK and Irish operations carbon neutral by 2012 and reduce our energy use 35% per square foot by 2015.*
- **Waste:** *Send no operational and construction waste to landfill and increase clothes recycling from 2 million items a year to 20 million.*
- **Natural resources:** *Ensure vulnerable raw materials come from sources that don't contribute to deforestation.*
- **Fair partnership:** *Helping M&S clothing suppliers to pay a fair living wage starting in Bangladesh, India, and Sri Lanka.*
- **Health and wellbeing:** *Promote active lifestyles for M&S customers and employees.*

On 8 August 2010, *The Observer,* London (a UK newspaper, published on Sundays), reported that garment workers in India, especially in Gurgaon, were paid below the standard minimum level of wages and decent work practices[9] were not being followed. The sweatshop conditions in the global supply chain had been often discussed by national and international media. The report argued that such practices were prevalent in a few Indian factories that supplied to brands like Gap, Next, and M&S. The report alleged violation of Ethical Trading Initiatives (ETI) and Indian labor laws.

Allegations by *The Observer*

Apart from violation of minimum wages laws, there were also complaints about faulty overtime payment, excessive overtime work, (though overtime wages were paid, workers were often forced to work), and even seven days of work in a week. The manufacturing unit was housed in a shabby three-storied building. Workers were threatened and even fired if they complained or refused to work. One factory worker, a father of two, was quoted as saying that workers were unwilling to work at the factory, but to bear family expenses like the school fees of their children and house rent, they had to. Another worker at the same factory said they could not feed their children on a meager salary of ₹5,000 per month. Some workers added that they had to work from 9am to 10pm for a basic pay of ₹4,600 a month, with overtime paid at single rate, in violation of the legal overtime rate of twice the normal wages under Section 59, Factories Act, 1948.

The Chief Operating Officer of Viva Global told *The Observer* reporter that the company had been working closely with M&S to rectify issues raised in the past. According to him, the company had never dismissed the complaints of its workers, and there was continuous propaganda by the union and some workers to tarnish the company's image. While he knew that some workers put in eight hours of work in his factory, and then another eight in another company, he denied knowledge of any worker putting in 16 hours in one shift and was quoted by *The Observer, "We love our employees. They are the source of our existence and their concerns of any nature are our priorities"*.

---

[9] Chamberlain, G. (2010, August 8). Gap, Next and M&S in new sweatshop scandal. *The Observer.* Retrieved September 19, 2010 from http://www.guardian.co.uk/world/2010/aug/08/gap-next-marks-spencer-sweatshops.

M&S Comments on the Allegations

An M&S representative told *The Observer* that *"Viva Global is a factory we have had issues with as it has fallen short of the high standards we require and we are in the process of working closely with it (and the union) to do what we can to address them."* He also said *"We also believe it is important to do this to improve conditions for the workers and put right any wrongs that we have uncovered"*. Globally, in July 2010, the Chairman of M&S had promised to put the ethical policy at the heart of its business model.

After *The Observer* Report

As days passed, the workers' discontent gained momentum and they found support from a local trade union. Meanwhile, talks for a tripartite agreement between the management, the District Labor Commissioner's office and the union were progressing. The situation became much more intense when the Garment and Allied Workers Union (GAWU) alleged that protesting factory workers had been beaten, and one worker had been abducted on August 25.[10]

The union leader was quoted as saying, "about 100 have been dismissed and another 200 are on an indefinite agitation outside the factory." The president of GAWU went on a hunger strike outside the factory, following the abduction. Police found the missing worker in a badly bruised condition after a day. Following this incident, workers of Viva Global went on strike. A representative of workers stated that they had been beaten up by the labor contractor firm that had been hired to supply temporary workers[11].

The Mazdoor Ekta Manch, Gurgaon,[12] accused the employer of not paying the minimum wage and not providing basic sanitation facilities at the factory premises. The Chairman of the Apparel Export Promotion Council (AEPC), the body of apparel exporters in India (it provided assistance to Indian exporters as well as importers/international buyers), told the media that the council had been taking steps to align the industry and stake holders with ethical trade practices through its Common Compliance Code (CCC).[13] A senior AEPC official mentioned that labor unrest was not new to India and China, and the garment factory incident was a case of industrial dispute, "at times, the demands of laborers are unjustified. But such problems do crop up when employing unorganized labor".[14]

The factory owner again claimed that the company had never dismissed any worker's complaint. He agreed that because of the allegations made by some union members and NGOs, M&S had canceled orders worth ₹30 million. At that time M&S denied to reporters that it had canceled orders following the allegations, and insisted that it was working with the factory to resolve issues. An M&S India representative also rejected allegations about the non-payment of minimum wages, or any violence against workers as reported.[15] A top executive of M&S blamed the

---

[10] According to *The Economic Times* report (Mehta, G.S. 2010, August 28. Unfair labor practices' cost textile co deal) 60 workers were beaten. Retrieved September 5, 2010 from http://economictimes. indiatimes.com/news/news-by-industry/cons-products/garments-/-textiles/Unfair-labour-practices-cost-textile-co-deal/articleshow/6448690.cms

[11] After M&S, workers turn up heat on firm (2010, September 6). *The Telegraph*. Retrieved September 20, 2010 from http://www.telegraphindia.com/1100906/jsp/frontpage/story_12901545.jsp

[12] Mazdoor Ekta Manch (MEM) is a platform of workers in Gurgaon. MEM's mission is to build the power of workers and their families, and secure their dignity and rights where they work and live (http://www.sld-india.org/msmission.htm.Retrieved September 12, 2010).

[13] CCC developed by AEPC, spells the frame work for creating a safe and healthy work culture in the unit premises. Trade unions and campaigners have developed 'model codes' that have been used as a benchmark for developing acceptable practices. The code concentrates on five key areas within ILO Conventions:-forced and bonded labour, freedom of association, the right to collective bargaining, no discrimination, health and safety. (http://www.aepcindia.com/files/AEPC-Common-Compliance-Code. pdf.Retrieved September 20, 2010).

[14] Mehta, G.S. (2010, August 28). Unfair labor practices' cost textile co deal. *The Economic Times*. Retrieved September 5, 2010 from http://economictimes.indiatimes.com/news/news-by-industry/cons-products/garments-/-textiles/Unfair-labour-practices-cost-textile-co-deal/articleshow/6448690.cms

[15] Menon, S. (2010, September 4). Marks & Spencer denies labour law abuse in Gurgaon supply factory. *Business Standard*. Retrieved September 5, 2010 from http://www.business-standard.com/india/news/marksspencer-denies-labour-law-abuse-in-gurgaon-supply-factory/406963/

union and revealed that M&S had received a petition signed by 80 workers, stating that union members were intimidating them and forcing them not to work. He also rejected the charge of low wages, saying that the legal monthly minimum wage for unskilled workers was ₹4,215 and at the unit, unskilled workers earned ₹4,600 on average, excluding annual bonus and other benefits. Wages had never been an issue and the company was known as one of the best paying in the region.

At the same time, M&S admitted that their regular audit showed that issues related to working conditions, such as holidays, overtime, air quality and drinking water existed, and M&S had been working closely with the company to resolve them. There were multiple visits every week by the local M&S team to inspect the premises. Based on a recommendation from M&S, a senior HR Manager was hired to develop a better relationship with workers. Reported improvements included the installation of 11 air coolers and 2 desert water coolers.

M&S had been working with Viva Global for five years, and it was in 2009–10 that problems surfaced. M&S had a large team in Delhi to check the ground realities at the suppliers' end, to ensure that the strictest ethical standards were followed. *The Times of India* on 5 September 2010 reported that M&S had stopped placing any further orders with Viva Global since May 2010. An M&S representative was quoted as saying that it had stopped doing business with the company for commercial reasons, but remained in contact with them, attempting to resolve the dispute.[16]

Questions:

1. Analyze the role played by different actors in the situation? Why should a firm like M&S be worried about such incidents?
2. Evaluate the concept of decent work and its implementation across the supply chain?

APPRAISAL BLUES*

"It's going to be a tough day," murmured Raj Melhotra, Vice President, Human Resources, and Chief Officer for Ethics (COE) of Central Telecommunication Company (CTC) to himself as he logged into the company intranet on Monday morning. It was quite unusual for his boss, the Chief Executive Officer (CEO) of CTC to have telephoned him at home, that too on a Sunday, and talked shop. Raj had been traveling the whole week and had returned only the day before. He was relaxing at home with his family when the call came. The CEO had ended the call with, "Don't spoil your evening for it. But we need to discuss this in detail tomorrow itself. I'll give you a buzz around ten in the morning." The call was regarding an email written by one of the managers, addressed to the COE, with a copy marked to the CEO. It concerned Pratosh, an Associate Vice President and member of the India management team of CTC.

CTC was a joint venture between a large diversified Indian group and an international telecom company, formed when the mobile telephone market opened up for private investment. The four-year-old mobile telecommunication company had licenses to operate in three mobile telecom circles in India. It obtained through open bidding licenses to operate in three mobile telecom circles in India and within one year launched commercial operations in the first circle. Over the next few months the remaining two circles also became operational.

---

[16] Marks & Spencer drops Gurgaon factory (2010, September 5). *The Times of India*. Retrieved September 18, 2010 from http://timesofindia.indiatimes.com/business/india-business/Marks-Spencer-drops-Gurgaon factory/articleshow/6501370.cms

---

* Prepared by Prof. Biju Varkkey, Indian Institute of Management, Ahmedabad on the basis of case lead obtained from a business magazine. Identity of the organization and people involved has been masked. Cases of the Indian Institute of Management, Ahmedabad, are prepared as a basis for class discussion. Cases are not designed to present illustrations of either correct or incorrect handling of administrative problems.
© 2002 by the Indian Institute of Management, Ahmedabad.

In addition to funds and technology, the foreign partner deputed few key personnel to CTC, including the current CEO. The Indian partner handled the day-to-day management of the company. At present, CTC had market leadership in two circles and expected to generate profits within a few years. Direct employment (all circles) was around 600 and female employees accounted for less than 10 percent of this number. Though there was no legal mandate, CTC was committed to increase the number of female employees. Compensation across levels was linked with performance, both of the division and the individual. A balanced scorecard measured the divisional performance. Individual performance was assessed through a system of participative performance enabler (PPE). PPE was similar to the performance management system followed in other organizations. Goal setting, year-end rating of performance and feedback were its critical components. Though there was provision for an in-course review of performance it was considered optional. Supervisors were expected to discuss performance issues with subordinates whenever it was necessary and make modifications to the PPE. Annual performance rating and forced classification into five categories happened during April and May. At that time supervisors had to discuss performance ratings and proposed classifications with each subordinate individually and obtain their consent before forwarding it to HR for further processing. Goals for the year ahead were also agreed upon at that time. The forced classification not only determined the annual increment and bonus, but also impacted career advancement.

Before Raj left station, he had scrolled through a mail from Pratosh (see Exhibit I). Pratosh was considered as one of the bright stars of CTC. A telecommunication engineer with an MBA degree, he had been identified by the CEO to head the customer service division and headhunted for the position. He joined CTC one year after it went commercial, as Senior Manager for customer service and reported to Vice President-Marketing. One year later he was promoted as Associate Vice President with independent responsibility for customer service. He was responsible for customer service across all three circles, with seven managers as direct reportees.

Pratosh was known within the company for his drive for achievement as also for his intolerance of poor performers. His abrasive style was a concern and the CEO, VP Marketing, and Raj had informally discussed it with him. At the same time he was among the most preferred bosses to work with, since he took interest in developing subordinates by exposing them to challenging assignments that gave them visibility with the top management.

The mail referred to by the CEO came from Madhavi, Manager, Relationship Management Services, and one of Pratosh's direct reportees (see Exhibit II). A hotel management professional, she had worked in the front office of a five-star hotel before joining CTC as Assistant Manager. She was among the initial group of CTC employees who joined during the start-up phase. She worked in business development for one year and moved to customer service after promotion as manager. By then Pratosh had joined CTC and started the independent customer service department. A special cell to manage high-worth customers like corporate houses was carved out and he was on the lookout for a person to be in charge. Madhavi was chosen for the assignment and her case was strongly supported by the VP, Marketing. She managed a six-member team and was responsible for single window services to high-worth customers.

High-worth customers were demanding and much sought after by competition. CTC had contracted a reputed agency to conduct frequent customer satisfaction surveys and the results were regularly discussed across levels. Wherever possible, PPEs were to include customer satisfaction as a key deliverable.

In her first year with CTC, Madhavi was rated a top performer and got promoted as manager. Next year, Pratosh too rated her in the top bracket, but the qualitative recommendations were not as glowing as it was in the previous year. During the PPE discussions, Pratosh insisted on inclusion of customer retention as a specific goal for Madhavi. In the past, retention had been clubbed with customer satisfaction scores. During the year under review, though overall customer satisfaction scores for her cell remained at an acceptable level, customer retention in Pratosh's opinion was a cause for concern. Two major corporate customers had switched accounts. Another had almost switched, but was persuaded against it after considerable effort. Further, the market was predicted to become more competitive, with more mobile telecom operators expected to start operations. Customer base growth was not happening as expected. Signs of a price war were imminent.

Decision Situation

As Raj finished reading through Madhavi's mail, the intercom rang. The call was from the CEO and the message was short: "Raj, can you come over? We need to talk about Madhavi's complaint."

Exhibit I

SUB: Appraisal Discussions
Date: Monday, May 23 (Time: 6:30pm)
From: Pratosh (Prad@ctc.company)
To: Raj Melhotra (RajM@ctc.company)

Raj

Completed appraisal discussions with five direct reportees. Should be able to send the compilation with classification this week. (OK OK, hard copies, signed, sealed. Why are you guys making life so difficult?)

Incidentally, discussions with Madhavi could not be completed. That female did not agree with my rating. Will talk again on Wednesday.

Thanks.

PS: Boss, I am off to Thailand with family. Leaving on Wednesday night, will be back after a week.

Exhibit II

SUB: Attn: Chief Officer for Ethics
Date: Wednesday, May 25 (Time: 4:30pm)
From: Madhavi (Madhavi@ctc.company)
To: Raj Melhotra (RajM@ctc.company)
CC: CEO (CEO@ctc.company)

Dear Sir:

I had a scheduled meeting with Mr. Pratosh, my reporting officer, on Monday, 23 May for discussing my performance for last year. To my surprise, he had given me a lower rating, something that I did not agree with. When I voiced my objection, he started accusing me about my behavior in office and work. When I remained firm, he raised his voice and pointed to the door, ordering me to get out. As I was walking out, he came behind me, yelling, and slammed the door after me.

Today morning his secretary called me up and asked me to meet him at 11:45am to continue discussions. I refused, since I was yet to recover from the earlier experience. Moreover, I wanted the discussions to happen in front of another responsible person so that the earlier behavior was not repeated. Soon he barged into my office and leaning on the desk said in a loud voice, "Who do you think you are? If I am your boss, you will be out in two days." Then he made an obscene gesture with his finger and left the room.

I am surprised that a senior professional, whom I had held in high esteem, could speak like that. I believe that this company insists that people respect each other and every person has an equal right to speak and be listened to. I wonder whether he would have dared to speak and behave like that with a man.

I am not writing this as a general note about my experience, but as a formal complaint against a male manager's behaviour with a female employee. Since the incident happened in my office, there are no witnesses. However, I sincerely believe that you will take necessary action and not allow such an incident to pass.

Thank You.

GLOSSARY

4/5ths rule Federal agency rule that a minority selection rate less than 80% (4/5ths) of that for the group with the highest rate is evidence of adverse impact.

401(k) plan A defined contribution plan based on section 401(k) of the Internal Revenue Code.

action learning A training technique by which management trainees are allowed to work full-time analyzing and solving problems in other departments.

adaptability screening A process that aims to assess the assignees' (and spouses') probable success in handling a foreign transfer.

adverse impact The overall impact of employer practices that result in significantly higher percentages of members of minorities and other protected groups being rejected for employment, placement, or promotion.

affirmative action Steps that are taken for the purpose of eliminating the present effects of past discrimination.

Age Discrimination in Employment Act of 1967 (ADEA) The act prohibiting arbitrary age discrimination and specifically protecting individuals over 40 years old.

agency shop A form of union security in which employees who do not belong to the union must still pay union dues on the assumption that union efforts benefit all workers.

alternation ranking method Ranking employees from best to worst on a particular trait, choosing highest, then lowest, until all are ranked.

alternative dispute resolution or ADR program Grievance procedure that provides for binding arbitration as the last step.

alternative staffing The use of nontraditional recruitment sources.

Americans with Disabilities Act (ADA) The act requiring employers to make reasonable accommodations for disabled employees; it prohibits discrimination against disabled persons.

annual bonus Plans that are designed to motivate short-term performance of managers and that are tied to company profitability.

applicant tracking systems Online systems that help employers attract, gather, screen, compile, and manage applicants.

application form The form that provides information on education, prior work record, and skills.

appraisal interview An interview in which the supervisor and subordinate review the appraisal and make plans to remedy deficiencies and reinforce strengths.

apprenticeship training A structured process by which people become skilled workers through a combination of classroom instruction and on-the-job training.

arbitration The most definitive type of third-party intervention, in which the arbitrator usually has the power to determine and dictate the settlement terms.

authority The right to make decisions, direct others' work, and give orders.

authorization cards In order to petition for a union election, the union must show that at least 30% of employees may be interested in being unionized. Employees indicate this interest by signing authorization cards.

bargaining unit The group of employees the union will be authorized to represent.

behavior modeling A training technique in which trainees are first shown good management techniques in a film, are asked to play roles in a simulated situation, and are then given feedback and praise by their supervisor.

behavior modification Using contingent rewards or punishment to change behavior.

behavior-based safety Identifying the worker behaviors that contribute to accidents and then training workers to avoid these behaviors.

behavioral interview A series of job-related questions that focus on how the candidate reacted to actual situations in the past.

behaviorally anchored rating scale (BARS) An appraisal method that aims at combining the benefits of narrative critical incidents and quantified ratings by anchoring a quantified scale with specific narrative examples of good and poor performance.

benchmark job A job that is used to anchor the employer's pay scale and around which other jobs are arranged in order of relative worth.

benefits Indirect financial and nonfinancial payments employees receive for continuing their employment with the company.

bias The tendency to allow individual differences such as age, race, and sex to affect the appraisal ratings employees receive.

bona fide occupational qualification (BFOQ) Requirement that an employee be of a certain religion, sex, or national origin where that is reasonably necessary to the organization's normal operation. Specified by the 1964 Civil Rights Act.

boycott The combined refusal by employees and other interested parties to buy or use the employer's products.

broadbanding Consolidating salary grades and ranges into just a few wide levels or "bands," each of which contains a relatively wide range of jobs and salary levels.

burnout The total depletion of physical and mental resources caused by excessive striving to reach an unrealistic work-related goal.

business process reengineering Redesigning business processes, usually by combining steps, so that small multifunction process teams using information technology do the jobs formerly done by a sequence of departments.

candidate-order (or contrast) error An error of judgment on the part of the interviewer due to interviewing one or more very good or very bad candidates just before the interview in question.

career The occupational positions a person has had over many years.

career development The lifelong series of activities that contribute to a person's career exploration, establishment, success, and fulfillment.

career management The process for enabling employees to better understand and develop their career skills and interests, and to use these skills and interests more effectively.

career planning The deliberate process through which someone becomes aware of personal skills, interests, knowledge, motivations, and other characteristics and establishes action plans to attain specific goals.

case study method A development method in which the manager is presented with a written description of an organizational problem to diagnose and solve.

cash balance plans Plans under which the employer contributes a percentage of employees' current pay to employees' pension plans every year, and employees earn interest on this amount.

central tendency A tendency to rate all employees the same way, such as rating them all average.

citation Summons informing employers and employees of the regulations and standards that have been violated in the workplace.

Civil Rights Act of 1991 (CRA 1991) The act that places the burden of proof back on employers and permits compensatory and punitive damages.

classes Grouping jobs based on a set of rules for each group or class, such as amount of independent judgment, skill, physical effort, and so forth, required. Classes usually contain similar jobs.

closed shop A form of union security in which the company can hire only union members. This was outlawed in 1947 but still exists in some industries (such as printing).

cloud (the) Refers to placing software programs and services on vendors' remote servers, from which they can then deliver these programs and services seamlessly to employees' digital devices.

coaching Educating, instructing, and training subordinates.

Co-determination An employee representation system in which workers elect their own representatives to the supervisory (management) board of the employer and have the legal right to a viice in setting company policies on matters such as company organizatio, hiring, and performance appraisal.

collective bargaining The process through which representatives of management and the union meet to negotiate a labor agreement.

college recruiting Sending an employer's representatives to college campuses to prescreen applicants and create an applicant pool from the graduating class.

compa ratio Equals an employee's pay rate divided by the pay range midpoint for his or her pay grade.

comparable worth The concept by which women who are usually paid less than men can claim that men in comparable rather than in strictly equal jobs are paid more.

compensable factor A fundamental, compensable element of a job, such as skills, effort, responsibility, and working conditions.

competency model A graphic model that consolidates, usually in one diagram, a precise overview of the competencies (the knowledge, skills, and behaviors) someone would need to do a job well.

Competency-based job analysis Describing the job in terms of measurable, observable, behavioral competencies (knowledge, skills, and/or behaviors) that an employee doing that job must exhibit to do the job well.

competency-based pay Where the company pays for the employee's range, depth, and types of skills and knowledge, rather than for the job title he or she holds.

competitive advantage Any factors that allow an organization to differentiate its product or service from those of its competitors to increase market share.

competitive strategy A strategy that identifies how to build and strengthen the business's long-term competitive position in the marketplace.

compressed workweek Schedule in which employee works fewer but longer days each week.

construct validity A test that is construct valid is one that demonstrates that a selection procedure measures a construct and that construct is important for successful job performance.

content validity A test that is content valid is one that contains a fair sample of the tasks and skills actually needed for the job in question.

controlled experimentation Formal methods for testing the effectiveness of a training program, preferably with before-and-after tests and a control group.

corporate campaign An organized effort by the union that exerts pressure on the corporation by pressuring the company's other unions, shareholders, directors, customers, creditors, and government agencies, often directly.

corporate-level strategy Type of strategy that identifies the portfolio of businesses that, in total, comprise the company and the ways in which these businesses relate to each other.

criterion validity A type of validity based on showing that scores on the test (predictors) are related to job performance (criterion).

critical incident method Keeping a record of uncommonly good or undesirable examples of an employee's work-related behavior and reviewing it with the employee at predetermined times.

cross training Training employees to do different tasks or jobs than their own; doing so facilitates flexibility and job rotation.

Davis-Bacon Act A 1931 law that sets wage rates for laborers employed by contractors working for the federal government.

decertification Legal process for employees to terminate a union's right to represent them.

deferred profit-sharing plan A plan in which a certain amount of profits is credited to each employee's account, payable at retirement, termination, or death.

diary/log Daily listings made by workers of every activity in which they engage along with the time each activity takes.

digital dashboard Presents the manager with desktop graphs and charts, and so a computerized picture of where the company stands on all those metrics from the HR scorecard process.

direct financial payments Pay in the form of wages, salaries, incentives, commissions, and bonuses.

discrimination Taking specific actions toward or against a person based on the person's group.

dismissal Involuntary termination of an employee's employment with the firm.

disparate rejection rates A test for adverse impact in which it can be demonstrated that there is a discrepancy between rates of rejection of members of a protected group and of others.

distributive justice Refers to a system of distributing rewards and discipline in which the actual results or outcomes of are evenhanded and fair.

diversity The variety or multiplicity of demographic features that characterize a company's workforce, particularly in terms of race, sex, culture, national origin, handicap, age, and religion.

downsizing The process of reducing, usually dramatically, the number of people employed by a firm.

early retirement window A type of offering by which employees are encouraged to retire early, the incentive being liberal pension benefits plus perhaps a cash payment.

earnings-at-risk pay plan Plan that puts some portion of employees' normal pay at risk if they don't meet their goals, in return for possibly obtaining a much larger bonus if they exceed their goals.

economic strike A strike that results from a failure to agree on the terms of a contract that involves wages, benefits, and other conditions of employment.

Electronic Communications Privacy Act (ECPA) The ECPA is a federal law intended to help restrict interception and monitoring of oral and wire communications.

electronic performance monitoring (EPM) Having supervisors electronically monitor the amount of computerized data an employee is processing per day, and thereby his or her performance.

electronic performance support systems (EPSS) Sets of computerized tools and displays that automate training, documentation, and phone support; integrate this automation into applications; and provide support that's faster, cheaper, and more effective than traditional methods.

employee assistance program (EAP) A formal employer program for providing employees with counseling and/or treatment programs for problems such as alcoholism, gambling, or stress.

employee compensation All forms of pay or rewards going to employees and arising from their employment.

employee engagement The extent to which an organization's employees are psychologically involved in, connected to, and committed to getting their jobs done.

employee orientation A procedure for providing new employees with basic background information about the firm.

employee recruiting Finding and/or attracting applicants for the employer's open positions.

employee relations The activity that involves establishing and maintaining the positive employee–employer relationships that contribute to satisfactory productivity, motivation, morale, and discipline, and to maintaining a positive, productive, and cohesive work environment.

Employee Retirement Income Security Act (ERISA) The 1974 law that provides government protection of pensions for all employees with company pension plans. It also regulates vesting rights (employees who leave before retirement may claim compensation from the pension plan).

employee stock ownership plan (ESOP) A corporation contributes shares of its own stock to a trust in which additional contributions are made annually. The trust distributes the stock to employees on retirement or separation from service.

Equal Employment Opportunity Commission (EEOC) The commission, created by Title VII, empowered to investigate job discrimination complaints and sue on behalf of complainants.

Equal Pay Act of 1963 The act requiring equal pay for equal work, regardless of sex.

ethics The study of standards of conduct and moral judgment; also the standards of right conduct.

ethnocentric The notion that home-country attitudes, management style, knowledge, evaluation criteria, and managers are superior to anything the host country has to offer.

ethnocentrism The tendency to view members of other social groups less favorably than members of one's own group.

executive coach An outside consultant who questions the executive's associates in order to identify the executive's strengths and weaknesses, and then counsels the executive so he or she can capitalize on those strengths and overcome the weaknesses.

exit interviews Interviews with employees who are leaving the firm, conducted for obtaining information about the job or related matters, to give the employer insight about the company.

expatriates (expats) Noncitizens of the countries in which employees are working.

expectancy chart A graph showing the relationship between test scores and job performance for a group of people.

expectancy A person's expectation that his or her effort will lead to performance.

fact finder A neutral party who studies the issues in a dispute and makes a public recommendation for a reasonable settlement.

fair day's work Output standards devised based on careful, scientific analysis.

Fair Labor Standards Act This 1938 act provides for minimum wages, maximum hours, overtime pay, and child labor protection. The law, amended many times, covers most employees.

fair treatment Reflects concrete actions, such as "employees are treated with respect," and "employees are treated fairly."

family-friendly (or work–life) benefits Benefits such as child care and fitness facilities that make it easier for employees to balance their work and family responsibilities.

Federal Violence Against Women Act of 1994 The act that provides that a person who commits a crime of violence motivated by gender shall be liable to the party injured.

financial incentives Financial rewards paid to workers whose production exceeds some predetermined standard.

flexible benefits plan/cafeteria benefits plan Individualized plans allowed by employers to accommodate employee preferences for benefits.

flextime A work schedule in which employees' workdays are built around a core of midday hours, and employees determine, within limits, what other hours they will work.

forced distribution method Similar to grading on a curve; predetermined percentages of ratees are placed in various performance categories.

foreign service premiums Financial payments over and above regular base pay, typically ranging between 10% and 30% of base pay.

functional strategy A strategy that identifies the broad activities that each department will pursue in order to help the business accomplish its competitive goals.

gainsharing plan An incentive plan that engages employees in a common effort to achieve productivity objectives and share the gains.

gender-role stereotypes The tendency to associate women with certain (frequently nonmanagerial) jobs.

geocentric The belief that the firm's whole management staff must be scoured on a global basis, on the assumption that the best manager of a specific position anywhere may be in any of the countries in which the firm operates.

golden parachute A payment companies make in connection with a change in ownership or control of a company.

good faith bargaining Both parties are making every reasonable effort to arrive at agreement; proposals are being matched with counterproposals.

good-faith effort strategy An affirmative action strategy that emphasizes identifying and eliminating the obstacles to hiring and promoting women and minorities, and increasing the minority or female applicant flow.

grade definition Written descriptions of the level of, say, responsibility and knowledge required by jobs in each grade. Similar jobs can then be combined into grades or classes.

grades A job classification system like the class system, although grades often contain dissimilar jobs, such as secretaries, mechanics, and firefighters. Grade descriptions are written based on compensable factors listed in classification systems.

graphic rating scale A scale that lists a number of traits and a range of performance for each. The employee is then rated by identifying the score that best describes his or her level of performance for each trait.

grievance procedure Formal process for addressing any factor involving wages, hours, or conditions of employment that is used as a complaint against the employer.

group life insurance Provides lower rates for the employer or employee and includes all employees, including new employees, regardless of health or physical condition.

halo effect In performance appraisal, the problem that occurs when a supervisor's rating of a subordinate on one trait biases the rating of that person on other traits.

hardship allowances Payments that compensate expatriates for exceptionally hard living and working conditions at certain locations.

health maintenance organization (HMO) A prepaid health-care system that generally provides routine round-the-clock medical services as well as preventive medicine in a clinic-type arrangement for employees, who pay a nominal fee in addition to the fixed annual fee the employer pays.

high-performance work system (HPWS) A set of human resource management policies and practices that promote organizational effectiveness.

home-country nationals Citizens of the country in which the multinational company has its headquarters.

HR audit An analysis by which an organization measures where it currently stands and determines what it has to accomplish to improve its HR functions.

HR scorecard A process for assigning financial and nonfinancial goals or metrics to the human resource management–related chain of activities required for achieving the company's strategic aims and for monitoring results.

human resource management (HRM) The process of acquiring, training, appraising, and compensating employees, and of attending to their labor relations, health and safety, and fairness concerns.

human resource metrics The quantitative gauge of a human resource management activity, such as employee turnover, hours of training per employee, or qualified applicants per position.

illegal bargaining items Items in collective bargaining that are forbidden by law; for example, a clause agreeing to hire "union members exclusively" would be illegal in a right-to-work state.

impasse Collective bargaining situation that occurs when the parties are not able to move further toward settlement, usually because one party is demanding more than the other will offer.

in-house development center A company-based method for exposing prospective managers to realistic exercises to develop improved management skills.

indirect financial payments Pay in the form of financial benefits such as insurance.

injunction A court order compelling a party or parties either to resume or to desist from a certain action.

inside games Union efforts to convince employees to impede or to disrupt production—for example, by slowing the work pace.

instrumentality The perceived relationship between successful performance and obtaining the reward.

insubordination Willful disregard or disobedience of the boss's authority or legitimate orders; criticizing the boss in public.

interest arbitration Arbitration enacted when labor agreements do not yet exist or when one or both parties are seeking to change the agreement.

interest inventory A personal development and selection device that compares the person's current interests with those of others now in various occupations so as to determine the preferred occupation for the individual.

international human resource management (IHRM) The human resource management concepts and techniques employers use to manage the human resource challenges of their international operations.

intrinsic motivation Motivation that derives from the pleasure someone gets from doing the job or task.

job aid A set of instructions, diagrams, or similar methods available at the job site to guide the worker.

job analysis The procedure for determining the duties and skill requirements of a job and the kind of person who should be hired for it.

job classification (or job grading) A method for categorizing jobs into groups.

job descriptions A list of a job's duties, responsibilities, reporting relationships, working conditions, and supervisory responsibilities—one product of a job analysis.

job enlargement Assigning workers additional same-level activities.

job enrichment Redesigning jobs in a way that increases the opportunities for the worker to experience feelings of responsibility, achievement, growth, and recognition.

job evaluation A systematic comparison done in order to determine the worth of one job relative to another.

job hazard analysis A systematic approach to identifying and eliminating workplace hazards before they occur.

job instruction training (JIT) Listing each job's basic tasks, along with key points, in order to provide step-by-step training for employees.

job posting Publicizing an open job to employees (often by literally posting it on bulletin boards) and listing its attributes, like qualifications, supervisor, working schedule, and pay rate.

job requirements matrix A more complete description of what the worker does and how and why he or she does it; it clarifies each task's purpose and each duty's required knowledge, skills, abilities, and other characteristics.

job rotation A management training technique that involves moving a trainee from department to department to broaden his or her experience and identify strong and weak points.

job sharing Allows two or more people to share a single full-time job.

job specifications A list of a job's "human requirements," that is, the requisite education, skills, personality, and so on—another product of a job analysis.

job-related interview A series of job-related questions that focus on relevant past job-related behaviors.

Landrum-Griffin Act of 1959 Also known as the *Labor Management Reporting and Disclosure Act*, this law aimed at protecting union members from possible wrongdoing on the part of their unions.

layoff An employer sending employees home due to a lack of work; this is typically a temporary situation.

lifelong learning Provides employees with continuing learning experiences over their tenure with the firm, with the aims of ensuring they have the opportunity to learn the skills they need to do their jobs and to expand their occupational horizons.

line authority The authority exerted by an HR manager by directing the activities of the people in his or her own department and in service areas (like the plant cafeteria).

line manager A manager who is authorized to direct the work of subordinates and is responsible for accomplishing the organization's tasks.

locals Citizens of the countries in which employees are working; also called *host-country nationals.*

lockout A refusal by the employer to provide opportunities to work.

management assessment center A simulation in which management candidates are asked to perform realistic tasks in hypothetical situations and are scored on their performance. It usually also involves testing and the use of management games.

management development Any attempt to improve current or future management performance by imparting knowledge, changing attitudes, or increasing skills.

management game A development technique in which teams of managers compete by making computerized decisions regarding realistic but simulated situations.

management process The five basic functions of planning, organizing, staffing, leading, and controlling.

manager The person responsible for accomplishing the organization's goals, and who does so by managing (planning, organizing, staffing, leading, and controlling) the efforts of the organization's people.

managing To perform five basic functions: planning, organizing, staffing, leading, and controlling.

managing diversity Maximizing diversity's potential benefits while minimizing its potential barriers.

mandatory bargaining items Items in collective bargaining that a party must bargain over if they are introduced by the other party—for example, pay.

market-competitive pay plan Pay plan where pay rates are equitable both internally (based on each job's relative value) and externally (in other words when compared with what other employers are paying).

mass interview A panel interviews several candidates simultaneously.

mediation Intervention in which a neutral third party tries to assist the principals in reaching agreement.

mentoring Advising, counseling, and guiding.

merit pay (merit raise) Any salary increase awarded to an employee based on his or her individual performance.

miniature job training and evaluation Training candidates to perform several of the job's tasks, and then evaluating the candidates' performance prior to hire.

mission statement Summarizes the answer to the question, "What business are we in?"

"mixed-motive" case A discrimination allegation case in which the employer argues that the employment action taken was motivated not by discrimination, but by some nondiscriminatory reason such as ineffective performance.

mobility premiums Typically, lump-sum payments to reward employees for moving from one assignment to another.

national emergency strikes Strikes that might "imperil the national health and safety."

National Labor Relations (or Wagner) Act This law banned certain types of unfair practices and provided for secret-ballot elections and majority rule for determining whether a firm's employees want to unionize.

National Labor Relations Board (NLRB) The agency created by the Wagner Act to investigate unfair labor practice charges and to provide for secret-ballot elections and majority rule in determining whether or not a firm's employees want a union.

negligent hiring Hiring workers with questionable backgrounds without proper safeguards.

negligent training A situation where an employer fails to train adequately, and the employee subsequently harms a third party.

Norris-LaGuardia Act of 1932 This law marked the beginning of the era of strong encouragement of unions and guaranteed to each employee the right to bargain collectively "free from interference, restraint, or coercion."

occupational illness Any abnormal condition or disorder caused by exposure to environmental factors associated with employment.

Occupational Safety and Health Act of 1970 The law passed by Congress in 1970 "to assure so far as possible every working man and woman in the nation safe and healthful working conditions and to preserve our human resources."

Occupational Safety and Health Administration (OSHA) The agency created within the Department of Labor to set safety and health standards for almost all workers in the United States.

Office of Federal Contract Compliance Programs (OFCCP) This office is responsible for implementing the executive orders and ensuring compliance of federal contractors.

on-demand recruiting services (ODRS) Services that provide short-term specialized recruiting to support specific projects without the expense of retaining traditional search firms.

on-the-job training Training a person to learn a job while working on it.

operational safety reviews Reviews conducted by agencies to ascertain whether units under their jurisdiction are complying with all the applicable safety laws, regulations, orders, and rules.

organization People with formally assigned roles who work together to achieve the organization's goals.

organization chart A chart that shows the organization-wide distribution of work, with titles of each position and interconnecting lines that show who reports to and communicates with whom.

organizational climate The perceptions a company's employees share about the firm's psychological environment, for instance, in terms of things like concern for employees' well-being, supervisory behavior, flexibility, appreciation, ethics, empowerment, political behaviors, and rewards.

organizational culture The characteristic values, traditions, and behaviors a company's employees share.

organizational development A special approach to organizational change in which employees themselves formulate and implement the change that's required.

organization-wide incentive plan Incentive plan in which all or most employees can participate.

outplacement counseling A formal process by which a terminated person is trained and counseled in the techniques of self-appraisal and securing a new position.

paired comparison method Ranking employees by making a chart of all possible pairs of the employees for each trait and indicating which is the better employee of the pair.

panel interview An interview in which a group of interviewers questions the applicant.

pay (or rate) ranges A series of steps or levels within a pay grade, usually based upon years of service.

pay (or wage) grade A pay grade is comprised of jobs of approximately equal difficulty.

Pension Benefits Guarantee Corporation (PBGC) Established under ERISA to ensure that pensions meet vesting obligations; also insures pensions should a plan terminate without sufficient funds to meet its vested obligations.

pension plans Plans that provide a fixed sum when employees reach a predetermined retirement age or when they can no longer work due to disability.

performance analysis Verifying that there is a performance deficiency and determining whether that deficiency should be corrected through training or through some other means (such as transferring the employee).

performance appraisal Evaluating an employee's current and/or past performance relative to his or her performance standards.

performance appraisal process A three-step appraisal process involving (1) setting work standards, (2) assessing the employee's actual performance relative to those standards, and (3) providing feedback to the employee with the aim of helping him or her to eliminate performance deficiencies or to continue to perform above par.

performance management The *continuous* process of identifying, measuring, and developing the performance of individuals and teams and *aligning* their performance with the organization's *goals*.

personnel replacement charts Company records showing present performance and promotability of inside candidates for the most important positions.

picketing Having employees carry signs announcing their concerns near the employer's place of business.

piecework A system of pay based on the number of items processed by each individual worker in a unit of time, such as items per hour or items per day.

point method The job evaluation method in which a number of compensable factors are identified and then the degree to which each of these factors is present on the job is determined.

polycentric A conscious belief that only the host-country managers can ever really understand the culture and behavior of the host-country market.

portability Instituting policies that enable employees to easily take their accumulated pension funds when they leave an employer.

position analysis questionnaire (PAQ) A questionnaire used to collect quantifiable data concerning the duties and responsibilities of various jobs.

position replacement card A card prepared for each position in a company to show possible replacement candidates and their qualifications.

preferential shop Union members get preference in hiring, but the employer can still hire nonunion members.

Pregnancy Discrimination Act An amendment to Title VII of the Civil Rights Act that prohibits sex discrimination based on "pregnancy, childbirth, or related medical conditions."

problem-solving teams Teams that identify and research work processes and develop solutions to work-related problems.

procedural justice Refers to just procedures in the allocation of rewards or discipline, in terms of the actual procedures being evenhanded and fair.

process chart A workflow chart that shows the flow of inputs to and outputs from a particular job.

productivity The ratio of outputs (goods and services) divided by the inputs (resources such as labor and capital).

profit-sharing plan A plan whereby employees share in the company's profits.

programmed learning A systematic method for teaching job skills, involving presenting questions or facts, allowing the person to respond, and giving the learner immediate feedback on the accuracy of his or her answers.

promotion Advancement to a position of increased responsibility.

protected class Persons such as minorities and women protected by equal opportunity laws, including Title VII.

qualified individuals Under ADA, those who can carry out the essential functions of the job.

quality circle A special type of formal problem-solving team, usually composed of 6 to 12 specially trained employees who meet once a week to solve problems affecting their work area.

ranking method The simplest method of job evaluation that involves ranking each job relative to all other jobs, usually based on overall difficulty.

ratio analysis A forecasting technique for determining future staff needs by using ratios between, for example, sales volume and number of employees needed.

reality shock Results of a period that may occur at the initial career entry when the new employee's high job expectations confront the reality of a boring or otherwise unattractive work situation.

recruiting yield pyramid The historical arithmetic relationships between recruitment leads and invitees, invitees and interviews, interviews and offers made, and offers made and offers accepted.

reliability The consistency of scores obtained by the same person when retested with the identical tests or with alternate forms of the same test.

restricted policy Another test for adverse impact, involving demonstration that an employer's hiring practices exclude a protected group, whether intentionally or not.

reverse discrimination Claim that due to affirmative action quota systems, white males are discriminated against.

right to work A term used to describe state statutory or constitutional provisions banning the requirement of union membership as a condition of employment.

rights arbitration Arbitration that interprets existing contract terms, for instance, when an employee questions the employer's right to have taken some disciplinary action.

role-playing A training technique in which trainees act out parts in a realistic management situation.

safety awareness program Program that enables trained supervisors to orient new workers arriving at a job site regarding common safety hazards and simple prevention methods.

salary survey A survey aimed at determining prevailing wage rates. A good salary survey provides specific wage rates for specific jobs. Formal written questionnaire surveys are the most comprehensive, but telephone surveys and newspaper ads are also sources of information.

savings and thrift plan Plan in which employees contribute a portion of their earnings to a fund; the employer usually matches this contribution in whole or in part.

Scanlon plan An incentive plan developed in 1937 by Joseph Scanlon and designed to encourage cooperation, involvement, and sharing of benefits.

scatter plot A graphical method used to help identify the relationship between two variables.

scientific management movement Management approach based on improving work methods through observation and analysis.

self-managing/self-directed work team A small (usually 8 to 10 members) group of carefully selected, trained, and empowered employees who basically run themselves with little or no outside supervision, usually for the purpose of accomplishing a specific task or mission.

severance pay A one-time payment some employers provide when terminating an employee.

sexual harassment Harassment on the basis of sex that has the purpose or effect of substantially interfering with a person's work performance or creating an intimidating, hostile, or offensive work environment.

sick leave Provides pay to an employee when he or she is out of work because of illness.

situational interview A series of job-related questions that focus on how the candidate would behave in a given situation.

situational test A test that requires examinees to respond to situations representative of the job.

social responsibility Refers to the extent to which companies should and do channel resources toward improving one or more segments of society other than the firm's owners or stockholders.

Social Security Federal program that provides three types of benefits: retirement income at the age of 62 and thereafter, survivor's or death benefits payable to the employee's dependents regardless of age at time of death, and disability benefits payable to disabled employees and their dependents. These benefits are payable only if the employee is insured under the Social Security Act.

staff authority Staff authority gives the manager the right (authority) to advise other managers or employees.

staff manager A manager who assists and advises line managers.

standard hour plan A plan by which a worker is paid a basic hourly rate but is paid an extra percentage of his or her rate for production exceeding the standard per hour or per day. Similar to piecework payment but based on a percent premium.

Standard Occupational Classification (SOC) Classifies all workers into one of 23 major groups of jobs that are subdivided into minor groups of jobs and detailed occupations.

stereotyping Ascribing specific behavioral traits to individuals based on their apparent membership in a group.

stock option The right to purchase a stated number of shares of a company stock at today's price at some time in the future.

straight piecework An incentive plan in which a person is paid a sum for each item he or she makes or sells, with a strict proportionality between results and rewards.

strategic human resource management Formulating and executing human resource policies and practices that produce the employee competencies and behaviors the company needs to achieve its strategic aims.

strategic management The process of identifying and executing the organization's strategic plan by matching the company's capabilities with the demands of its environment.

strategic plan The company's plan for how it will match its internal strengths and weaknesses with external opportunities and threats in order to maintain a competitive advantage.

strategy A course of action the company can pursue to achieve its strategic aims.

strategy map A strategic planning tool that shows the "big picture" of how each department's performance contributes to achieving the company's overall strategic goals.

strategy-based metrics Metrics that specifically focus on measuring the activities that contribute to achieving a company's strategic aims.

stress interview An interview in which the applicant is made uncomfortable by a series of often rude questions. This technique helps identify hypersensitive applicants and those with low or high stress tolerance.

strictness/leniency The problem that occurs when a supervisor has a tendency to rate all subordinates either high or low.

strike A withdrawal of labor.

structured (or directive) interview An interview following a set sequence of questions.

structured sequential interview An interview in which the applicant is interviewed sequentially by several persons; each rates the applicant on a standard form.

structured situational interview A series of job-relevant questions with predetermined answers that interviewers ask of all applicants for the job.

succession planning The ongoing process of systematically identifying, assessing, and developing organizational leadership to enhance performance.

suggestion teams Temporary teams whose members work on specific analytical assignments, such as how to cut costs or raise productivity.

supplemental pay benefits Benefits for time not worked such as unemployment insurance, vacation and holiday pay, and sick pay.

supplemental unemployment benefits Provide for a "guaranteed annual income" in certain industries where employers must shut down to change machinery or due to reduced work. These benefits are paid by the company and supplement unemployment benefits.

sympathy strike A strike that takes place when one union strikes in support of the strike of another.

Taft-Hartley Act of 1947 Also known as the *Labor Management Relations Act*, this law prohibited unfair union labor practices and enumerated the rights of employees as union members. It also enumerated the rights of employers.

talent management The goal-oriented and integrated process of planning, recruiting, developing, managing, and compensating employees.

task analysis A detailed study of a job to identify the specific skills required.

task statement Written item that shows *what* the worker does on one particular job task; *how* the worker does it; the *knowledge, skills, and aptitudes required* to do it; and the *purpose of the task*.

team (or group) incentive plan A plan in which a production standard is set for a specific work group, and its members are paid incentives if the group exceeds the production standard.

terminate at will In the absence of a contract, either the employer or the employee can terminate at will the employment relationship.

termination interview The interview in which an employee is informed of the fact that he or she has been dismissed.

test validity The accuracy with which a test, interview, and so on measures what it purports to measure or fulfills the function it was designed to fill.

third-country nationals Citizens of a country other than the parent or the host country.

Title VII of the 1964 Civil Rights Act The section of the act that says an employer cannot discriminate on the basis of race, color, religion, sex, or national origin with respect to employment.

tokenism When a company appoints a small group of women or minorities to high-profile positions, rather than more aggressively seeking full representation for that group.

training The process of teaching new or current employees the basic skills they need to perform their jobs.

transfer Reassignments to similar positions in other parts of the firm.

trend analysis Study of a firm's past employment needs over a period of years to predict future needs.

unclear standards An appraisal that is too open to interpretation.

unemployment insurance (or compensation) Provides benefits if a person is unable to work through some fault other than his or her own.

unfair labor practice strike A strike aimed at protesting illegal conduct by the employer.

Uniform Guidelines Guidelines issued by federal agencies charged with ensuring compliance with equal employment federal legislation explaining recommended employer procedures in detail.

union salting A union organizing tactic by which workers who are in fact employed full-time by a union as undercover organizers are hired by unwitting employers.

union shop A form of union security in which the company can hire nonunion people, but they must join the union after a prescribed period of time and pay dues. (If they do not, they can be fired.)

unsafe conditions The mechanical and physical conditions that cause accidents.

unstructured (or nondirective) interview An unstructured conversational-style interview in which the interviewer pursues points of interest as they come up in response to questions.

unstructured sequential interview An interview in which each interviewer forms an independent opinion after asking different questions.

valence The perceived value a person attaches to the reward.

variable pay Any plan that ties pay to productivity or profitability, usually as one-time lump payments.

video-based simulation A situational test in which examinees respond to video simulations of realistic job situations.

virtual classroom Teaching method that uses special collaboration software to enable multiple remote learners, using their PCs or laptops, to participate in live audio and visual discussions, communicate via written text, and learn via content such as PowerPoint slides.

virtual teams Groups of geographically dispersed coworkers who interact using a combination of telecommunications and information technologies to accomplish an organizational task.

vision statement A general statement of the firm's intended direction; it shows, in broad terms, "what we want to become."

Vocational Rehabilitation Act of 1973 The act requiring certain federal contractors to take affirmative action for disabled persons.

voluntary (or permissible) bargaining items Items in collective bargaining over which bargaining is neither illegal nor mandatory—neither party can be compelled against its wishes to negotiate over those items.

wage curve Shows the relationship between the value of the job and the average wage paid for this job.

Walsh-Healey Public Contract Act A 1936 law that requires minimum wage and working conditions for employees working on any government contract amounting to more than $10,000.

Web 2.0 learning Training that uses online technologies such as social networks, virtual worlds (such as Second Life), and systems that blend synchronous and asynchronous delivery with blogs, chat rooms, bookmark sharing, and tools such as 3-D simulations.

wildcat strike An unauthorized strike occurring during the term of a contract.

work samples Actual job tasks used in testing applicants' performance.

work sampling technique A testing method based on measuring performance on actual basic job tasks.

work sharing Refers to a temporary reduction in work hours by a group of employees during economic downturns as a way to prevent layoffs.

workers' compensation Provides income and medical benefits to work-related accident victims or their dependents regardless of fault.

workflow analysis A detailed study of the flow of work from job to job in a work process.

workforce (or employment or personnel) planning The process of deciding what positions the firm will have to fill, and how to fill them.

works councils Formal, employee-elected groups of worker representatives.

NAME/ORGANIZATION INDEX

SUBJECT INDEX